Intermediate Accounting

Volume 1

Intermediate Accounting

VOLUME 1

Thomas H. Beechy
Schulich School of Business
York University

Joan E. D. Conrod
Faculty of Management
Dalhousie University

Morton Nelson
Wilfrid Laurier University
Consulting Editor

McGraw-Hill Ryerson Limited

Toronto • Montreal • New York• Burr Ridge • Bangkok • Bogotá
Caracas • Lisbon • London • Madrid • Mexico City • Milan
New Delhi • Seoul • Singapore • Sydney • Taipei

McGraw-Hill
Ryerson Limited

A Subsidiary of The **McGraw·Hill** Companies

Intermediate Accounting, Volume 1

ISBN: 0-07-560378-0

5 6 7 8 9 10 GTC 0 9 8 7 6 5 4 3 2 1

Printed and bound in Canada

Senior Sponsoring Editor: Jennifer Dewey
Developmental Editor: Bonnie Moran
Senior Supervising Editor: Kelly Dickson
Production Editors: Erin Moore and Shirley Corriveau
Production Coordinator: Brad Madill
Cover Design: Citrus Media
Cover Images: © Photodisc
Interior Design and Formatting: FiWired.Com
Art Director: Dianna Little
Printer: Transcontinental Printing

Canadian Cataloguing in Publication Data

Beechy, Thomas H., 1937-
          Intermediate accounting

Includes index.
ISBN 0-07-560378-0 (v. 1)

1. Accounting. I. Conrod, Joan E. D. (Joan Elizabeth Davison),
1956- . II. Title.

HF6535.B466 1999   657'.044 C99-930564-6

The authors gratefully acknowledge the permissions granted by the CICA, CGA-Canada, Atlantic School of CAs, Ontario Institute of CAs, CGAA, and CMA Canada to reprint selected material and cases.

About the Authors

Thomas H. Beechy

Thomas H. Beechy is a Professor of Accounting at the Schulich School of Business, York University. For many years, he was also the Associate Dean of the school. He currently holds the additional titles of Executive Director of International Relations, Assistant Dean-Special Projects, and BBA Program Director. Professor Beechy holds degrees from George Washington University (BA), Northwestern University (MBA), and Washington University (DBA). He has been active in research and publication for almost 40 years, having published six books, including *Canadian Advanced Financial Accounting*, and numerous articles in major accounting journals. Professor Beechy has been a leader in Canadian accounting education, emphasizing the importance of case analysis in developing students' professional judgement and accounting skills. He has been an active researcher and advocate in both business and non-profit financial reporting, and has been particularly active in international accounting circles.

Joan E. D. Conrod

Joan E. D. Conrod is a professor of accounting in the Faculty of Management at Dalhousie University. In recognition of her excellent teaching, she was chosen as the 1996 Distinguished Teacher by the Atlantic Association of Universities, and also received the 1996 Award for Teaching Excellence from the Dalhousie Alumni Association. Joan is an active member of the University community, having served as Vice-Chair of Senate, Secretary to the Academic Priorities and Budget Committee; chair of Senate's Financial Planning Committee, as well as a member of the Board of Governors and numerous other university committees. Joan is actively involved in professional accounting education. She has taught financial and managerial accounting courses to CA students across Canada, but particularly in Atlantic Canada, for eighteen years. Her other publications include a financial accounting casebook, *Financial Accounting 3* for CGA-Canada, and a variety of case material and other publications.

Contents — Volume 1

Preface

What is intermediate accounting all about? There is a vast body of knowledge that must be mastered before you can account for the activities of an enterprise. Intermediate accounting is the nitty-gritty course where it all happens. Although a few topics are covered in greater depth in advanced accounting courses, virtually *every* important topic is included in intermediate. Therefore, a mastery of the content of intermediate accounting is crucial for anyone who hopes to either use or prepare accounting information.

Accounting in general involves a blend of technical know-how and professional judgement. So that's what *Intermediate Accounting* appropriately dwells on: technical knowledge and professional judgement, covering the range of corporate reporting topics.

In selecting material to include in this book, we have taken a fresh look at the realities of Canadian business practice. Some topics that have been included in other books for decades are omitted because they are no longer important, while others have been included because of their relevance to today's environment. Here's what this book reflects:

Technical Knowledge. Accountants have to be able to account for things! There is a base level of expertise that must become part of every accountant's body of knowledge — how to defer a cost, capitalize a lease, account for a pension, or prepare a cash flow statement. Accounting is very quantitative, and it takes lots of practice. Some of the transactions that we must account for are very complex. Their accounting treatment is equally complex. An affinity for numbers is important!

Professional Judgement. Judgement, it is often said, is the hallmark of a profession. There are often different ways to account for the same transaction. Professional accountants have to become good at sizing up the circumstances and establishing the appropriate accounting policy for those circumstances. Even once an accounting policy has been established, there are often many estimates that must be made before the numbers can actually be recorded. Accounting estimates also require the exercise of professional judgement. Professional judgement is not acquired overnight. It is nurtured and slowly grows over a lifetime. In this book, we begin the development process by explicitly examining the real variables that companies consider when evaluating their options, and the criteria accountants use to make choices.

Non-GAAP Situations. For a variety of reasons businesses often have to follow generally accepted accounting principles. However, companies can and do prepare reports based on accounting policies that are tailored for their unique circumstances and the specific decisions that are to be made based on the financial statements. Therefore, accountants cannot wear GAAP like a pair of blinders. Accountants have to be aware of accounting alternatives, and the circumstances under which such policies are needed. This book provides practice in this area.

A Canadian Agenda. Issues that receive the most attention in this book are those that are relevant in a Canadian context. Many times, the topics covered in other intermediate texts are determined by U.S. standards and priorities because those books are adaptations of U.S. texts. However, there are some significant differences between Canadian and U.S. businesses and business environments that dictate a different emphasis and coverage. We hope you appreciate the redirected emphasis!

An International View. Of course, following a Canadian agenda does not mean that we're blind to what is happening in the rest of the world. This book informs you about major developments around the world, and other acceptable accounting practices. In particular, most chapters explain the differences between Canadian practice and the policies recommended by International Accounting Standards.

A Lively Writing Style. We've consistently heard from students who used this manuscript in pre-publication form that this material is fresh and easy to read. Difficult? Sometimes. Boring? Never!

Key Features

Chapter Table of Contents. Each chapter begins with a topical table of contents, serving as a road map through the chapter.

Introduction. Each chapter has an introduction that supplements its table of contents. The introduction explains the objectives of the chapter in narrative form.

Concept Reviews. Throughout each chapter, there are periodic pauses for the student to stop and think through the answers to basic questions covering the previously explained material. This helps comprehension and focus! If you have trouble finding the correct response to the concept review questions, the answers can be found in the Study Guide and on the book's Web site.

Summary of Key Points. At the end of each chapter, a summary of key points lists the key ideas explained in the chapter. This is meant to reinforce the chapter material.

International Perspective. Most chapters include a review of international accounting policies, and differences that are found both internationally and in different countries. While the U.S. position is very important to us here in Canada, and is discussed when appropriate, there are many other countries around the world worth keeping an eye on! Discussions of international issues are highlighted by a special icon in the page margin.

Integration of Cash Flow Material Throughout the Text. In intermediate accounting, the cash flow chapter is often found at the end of the text, and instructors may use the opportunity to integrate and review by doing endless cash flow statements. The only problem is that students have a hard time dealing with *both* the cash flow statement and the complex transactions, turning the experience into a nightmare! As well, deferring the cash flow statement to the end of the course leaves the impression that it is not a "real" financial statement — just an "add-on." But the cash flow statement *is* one of the major financial statements. To some users, it may well be the most important. As a result of our classroom experiences, we decided to move the cash flow chapter up to the beginning of the course, to make sure that students learn how to do a basic cash flow statement. Following this chapter, though, the cash flow implications of various complex transactions are reviewed in each relevant chapter. There is cash flow problem material in most chapters of the book. For those instructors who like to use cash flow material at the end, there's still lots of complex and integrative material, which can be covered in a block at the end of the course.

Cases. Over 50 cases are included in the book. The cases typically are not single-subject, paragraph-long "think pieces" but rather are meant to portray circumstances evocative of real life. Students have to put themselves into the situation and grapple with the facts and real users and uses, to arrive at appropriate accounting policies for the circumstances. A blend of professional judgement and technical skills is needed to respond to a case. Case coverage is not limited to "one chapter" bites, but integrates material learned to date. For those trying to build a base of professionalism, the use of cases consistently over the term is highly recommended! Cases can be assigned for class debriefing, class presentations, or as written assignments.

Questions, Exercises, and Problems. There is an extensive range of assignment material at the end of each chapter. The exercises and problems give students the opportunity to learn by doing. We have selected a few exercises and problems from each chapter and have put their solutions in the Study Guide and on the book's Web site; students can practice on their own. These selected exercises and problems are highlighted by an icon in the margin. Also included in the text and marked with an icon in the margin are Excel templates for selected problems and exercises (SPATs).

Integrative Problems. From time to time in the book, there are integrative problems that formally deal with accounting topics covered in five or six chapters. These problems are meant to be a great pre-test review!

Ethics Material. Ethics material has been incorporated into the case material. Essentially, when an accountant makes a recommendation on a contentious choice of accounting policy, ethics are tested. We decided against putting in smaller ethics "vignettes," as it is always painfully obvious that the accountant is meant to take the high path and demonstrate good ethics. We feel that our students learn more true-to-life ethics decisions when they have to make a tough judgement call and recommend an accounting policy that is "good" for one group but "bad" for another. Ethical overtones are highlighted in the case solutions, to help instructors draw them out in discussion and evaluation.

The Accounting Cycle. The basic debit and credit of the accounting world is hardly a topic for an intermediate accounting course. It represents the baby steps, and we're trying to learn how to run, or at least jog. Well, baby steps come first, don't they? For many students, this material was covered in a high school course or an introductory accounting course. Others, who avoided the course in high school and who took a conceptually-oriented introductory course in college or university, may need grounding in this area. Therefore, we decided to include the accounting cycle as an Appendix to Volume 1, to allow maximum flexibility to instructors. Some courses may formally devote time to this Appendix, and others may use it as a reference only.

Annual Report Supplement. When a student completes an intermediate accounting course, he or she should be able to understand a corporate annual report. To provide practice, we have selected a series of annual reports to accompany this text. We also have provided a series of questions relating to each annual report, arranged by chapter. These questions will highlight current reporting issues and choices. We've made the annual report a supplement to the book so it can be updated regularly to reflect new reporting issues. The annual reports and the related questions are also available on the book's Web site. Use of a real live annual report is a good way to integrate much of the intermediate material, and always increases the interest level in our classrooms.

Topical Highlights of the Text

Chapters 1 and 2. The book starts with a review of the GAAP (and non-GAAP) world, and establishes the common reporting motivations of companies and financial statement users, as well as the basic concepts of accounting. This is fundamental material underlying professional judgement.

Chapters 3 and 4. These chapters review the income statement, balance sheet, retained earnings statement and disclosure notes. Real-life examples show the degree of diversity that exists, and how little information some companies actually provide in their financial statements. The chapters highlight the judgement issues that are obvious from the statements and disclosures.

Chapter 5. The cash flow statement chapter has been moved to the front of the book, to accompany the review of the other required financial statements. This should allow students to focus on learning the mechanics of the cash flow statement and the areas of judgement concerning formatting and display. The cash flow material reflects the recently released *CICA Handbook* section governing cash flow statements. More CFS problems are included throughout the rest of the text in order to allow integration of more complex topics. Instructors who like to do the cash flow statement at the end of the course as review may use these problems to accomplish their objectives.

Chapters 6 and 7. Are there any more judgemental areas than revenue and expense recognition? These two chapters look at the financial statement effects of early versus late revenue and expense recognition. There is extensive discussion about how accrual and deferrals actually work, and the circumstances under which each is appropriate. The expense chapter, in addition to dealing with basic cost deferral issues, also examines two of the most significant accounting expense policy choices: amortization and inventory costing. While the mechanics of these areas are discussed in later chapters, students get to look at the policy issues together, as a group. This is a heavy dose of reality, as firms generally choose consistent families of accounting policies according to their reporting objectives.

Chapter 8. Issues relating to current monetary balances — cash, receivables and payables — are gathered and reviewed together. Important new topics include foreign currency translation of current monetary balances (which is a must, in this age of globalization) and the various forms of securitization.

Chapter 9. Inventory issues are dealt with in this chapter. Since policy issues were covered in Chapter 7, this chapter looks at the mechanics of inventory costing, lower-of-cost-or-market write-downs, and inventory estimation methods.

Chapters 10 and 11. Capital assets, both tangible and intangible, fall under one section of the *CICA Handbook*, and accounting for these assets follows a common pattern. These chapters systematically look at acquisition, amortization, and disposal.

Chapter 12. This chapter is an overview of accounting for investments. Policy issues surrounding choice of the cost method, equity method, and consolidation are explored, along with some of the numeric intricacies of these methods. There's an Appendix on consolidation for those who wish to tackle it.

Chapters 13 and 14. These chapters deal with straightforward debt and shareholders' equity issues. The debt chapter looks at accounting for bonds, and includes the standard run through the interest calculations. The financial instruments rules of the *CICA Handbook*, as they relate to straightforward debt, are reviewed. The equity chapter deals with dividends, issuance, and retirements.

Chapter 15. We saved all the surprises for this chapter! The world has changed . . . you'll never look at a convertible bond the same way again. Students are led through the basic debt-to-equity arguments from an accounting theory perspective. Then, the text reviews the characteristics of modern financial instruments that put legal form at odds with the substance for many financial instruments. Convertible debt, convertible at either the investor's or the company's option, is then reviewed, as are the various types of preferred shares. The financial instrument rules are carefully reviewed and evaluated. The chapter concludes with an overview of accounting for stock options but does not cover the largely ineffective U.S. rules.

Chapters 16 and 17. Accounting for future income tax has been split into two chapters, to acknowledge that many instructors choose to spend two blocks of time on this very challenging area. These chapters explore the liability method inherent in the new *CICA Handbook* recommendations, which are mandatory beginning in 2000. The first chapter deals with interperiod and intraperiod allocation of the tax effects of temporary differences (previously known as timing differences). The entire focus of Chapter 17 is on accounting for the tax effects of losses — carrybacks and carryforwards—always difficult material for students.

Chapter 18. The leases material has been split into two chapters, again reflecting the complexity of trying to deal with both sides of the transaction in a single chapter. Chapter 18 deals only with lessees. Since almost every company under the sun leases something as a lessee, this is a very important chapter. We've tried to demonstrate lease contracts, and explain leasing arrangements, that are true to Canadian practice.

Chapter 19. This chapter covers the lessor material. This chapter is more specialized than the lessee chapter, as there are relatively fewer lessors out there. The chapter again looks at lease accounting from a real-world perspective. Some instructors may wish to omit this chapter, since it deals largely with a highly "specialized" industry of asset-based financing.

Chapter 20. The pensions (and other post-retirement benefits) material begins with a review of actuarial techniques and estimation methods. This material is included, not because accountants should act as actuaries, but so that accountants and financial statement users can understand what lies behind the reported figures. Once the scope of methodologies and estimates has been established, the chapter moves on to accounting for post-retirement costs and obligations. The new AcSB pronouncements are reflected in this material.

Chapter 21. Earnings per share coverage includes the explanation of basic, adjusted, fully diluted, and pro-forma EPS. All EPS problems are based on the way that financial statements reflect financial instruments in the wake of Chapter 15, which allows students time to get more familiar with new, common financial statement elements.

Chapter 22. Accounting policy changes and error corrections require *restatement* of one or more prior years' financial statements. Restatement to reflect different accounting policies may also be undertaken by financial statement users, therefore this material leads directly into the next chapter.

Chapter 23. The text ends with a thorough coverage of financial statement analysis. Although ratios do account for the bulk of this chapter, there is a broader emphasis on making sure that the numbers are valid for the intended use, and that different comparative numbers don't simply represent different accounting policies rather than different economic positions. To illustrate the importance of accounting policy choices in financial statement analysis, we have included an extensive case illustration of the impact of changing accounting policy. This case is based on a real Canadian company, and the numbers are all real! Along with the dozens of cash flow problems in the text and the intermittent integrative problems, Chapters 22 and 23 allow review and integration of the body of knowledge that represents *Intermediate Accounting*.

Accuracy

The text has been extensively reviewed and class-tested prior to publication. Many people have also intensively proofread the book. Nevertheless, it is inevitable that a few errors remain, undetected by the many pairs of eyes that have reviewed the material (including the hundreds of students who participated in the class-testing). As well, every problem, exercise, case, and question has been solved independently by at least two individuals in addition to the authors.

We have made every effort to ensure that this text is as error-free as we can make it. If you find errors, please e-mail the authors at **jconrod@dal.ca** or **tbeechy@ssb.yorku.ca**. There are thousands of calculations in this text — it's a daunting task to bring them to the degree of accuracy we'd like to be famous for. Your help will be greatly appreciated.

Supplementary materials

Supplements include:

- Annual Reports with Assignment Material
- Solutions Transparencies
- PowerPoint Teaching Transparencies
- Computerized Test Generator
- Printed Test Bank
- Spreadsheet Application Software for Specific Problems
- Study Guide with Check Figures
- Support for the book is also provided on the McGraw-Hill Ryerson Web site at **www.mcgrawhill.ca/college/beechy/**.

Acknowledgments

The text would not have been possible without the contributions of a great many people. We recognize and appreciate all of their efforts.

Our thanks and gratitude are extended to the outstanding anonymous faculty reviewers who provided criticism and constructive suggestions on the manuscript as it has developed over the last several years. It hasn't been possible to incorporate all the (sometimes conflicting!) suggestions, but the quality of this book has improved thanks to the people who reviewed it: Michael Lee, Humber College; Darrell Herauf, Carleton University; Charles Tax, University of Manitoba; Kevin Berry, University of New Brunswick; and Larry Knechtel, Grant MacEwan Community College.

We've been very fortunate in having intrepid colleagues who have been willing to class-test the manuscript in their classes before it even reached the "preliminary edition" stage. We extend our sincerest thanks to the students and faculty at Dalhousie University, Niagara College, Nipissing College, and York University's Schulich School of Business. These class tests have produced some invaluable insights into the need for improvements in various areas, and also have confirmed the strengths of our work. We've tried to be receptive to the class-testers' excellent and thoughtful feedback.

To numerous other colleagues and users whose constructive comments and suggestions have led to improvements, our thanks. We also appreciate the permissions granted by the following organizations for permission to use their problem and case material:

- The Canadian Institute of Chartered Accountants
- The Certified General Accountants' Association of Canada
- The Society of Management Accountants
- The Ontario Institute of Chartered Accountants
- The Atlantic School of Chartered Accountancy
- The American Institute of Certified Public Accountants

This entire project was made possible only through the foresight of Rod Bannister, who negotiated the potentially bumpy terrain and smoothed the way for the project's initiation. Rod supported our concept of a new approach to an intermediate accounting textbook from the beginning; it is unlikely that we would have been able to bring this book to fruition without his energetic and creative support.

We are indebted to Victor Leung for performing an extremely valuable service as the first person to carefully review the initial manuscript and point out areas for improvement.

Debbie Oickle has been a wonderful resource person in preparing the solutions manual. Its hundreds of pages of careful formatting are to her credit. Thanks also to Alan Mak, Arthur Anderson Consulting, for preparing the Glossary.

We are grateful to the people at McGraw-Hill Ryerson who guided this manuscript through its development process. In particular, we are extremely grateful for the strong and continuous support of Joseph Gladstone who held our hands throughout the development of the manuscript and made sure that everything went smoothly in our relationship with the publisher. Once the manuscript was in final form, Jennifer Dewey, Jennifer Burnell, Kelly Dickson, and copy editor Erin Moore shepherded it smoothly through the complexities of the production process.

On a personal level, we would like to thank our friends and family members for their support and encouragement throughout the lengthy process of bringing this book to fruition, especially: in Halifax — Peter Conrod and Warren and Carmita Fetterly; and in Toronto — Calvin Luong and Brian McBurney.

Last, but certainly not least, we wish to express our thanks to the authors of the previous version of *Intermediate Accounting* that this book replaces in Canada. Parts of this book, particularly some of the vast body of problem material, are from the U.S. *Intermediate Accounting* book written by Thomas Dyckman, Roland Dukes, and Charles Davis. Our previous Canadian co-author, Mort Nelson, has also left an abiding legacy with us. This solid base has made a project of this scope "doable" and we thank all who made a contribution.

Thomas H. Beechy
Schulich School of Business
York University
Toronto

Joan E. D. Conrod
Faculty of Management
Dalhousie University
Halifax

The Environment of Accounting

INTRODUCTION

The purpose of financial accounting is to communicate information, and information is useful only if it can be used to make decisions. It is possible, therefore, to characterize accounting as being a *behavioural* discipline; every financial reporting choice that an accountant makes has the potential power to influence someone's or some group's behaviour.

This chapter will discuss the environment of financial accounting, including various forms of organization and the factors that influence and constrain financial reporting. In particular, we will discuss the question of what constitutes generally accepted accounting principles (GAAP), and how GAAP differs from tailored accounting policies. GAAP is not a specifically prescribed set of rules; instead, it is a rather loosely defined set of alternative approaches to measuring and reporting economic activities.

Accounting is full of choices. To present an organization's financial results, it is necessary to make many choices from among possible accounting policies. It is also necessary to make a continuing series of estimates that affect every single amount reported on the financial statements. There is no one right answer in accounting; the "answer" depends on a series of accounting **policy** choices, accounting **measurements**, and accounting **estimates**. Ultimately, management is responsible for these choices, but it is the accountant who must advise management on the range of acceptable options and feasible measurements and estimates, and who must give effect to management's choices through preparation of the financial statements.

A primary factor that affects management's choice of accounting policies, measurements, and estimates is the financial reporting objectives of the reporting enterprise. This chapter will discuss the most common financial reporting objectives for businesses. The rest of the book will regularly refer to these various possible objectives when discussing the criteria that affect management's choices in dealing with specific accounting issues. Therefore, the discussion of reporting objectives in this chapter should not be glossed over lightly.

In this book, we will continually emphasize the nature of the choice process. We will point out the options available and stress the factors that affect those choices. We also will emphasize the variations in reported results that arise as the result of different choices. This chapter discusses reporting objectives; in Chapter 2, we will discuss additional criteria used to make accounting choices, as well as the nature of professional judgement.

THE DIFFERENCE BETWEEN ACCOUNTING AND BOOKKEEPING

Before proceeding with a discussion of the environment of accounting, it is important to make a distinction between accounting and bookkeeping. Bookkeeping is a *recording* process, much of which has been automated in recent decades through the widespread use of computers, even in quite small organizations. The role of the bookkeeper certainly has declined as computers have taken over most of the routine processing of financial data. But it is the *accountant* who is responsible for telling the computer what to do. The responsibility is not for the programming, of course, but is for deciding how to classify and record transactions, how to disclose those transactions in the financial statements, how to measure the value of assets and liabilities and of their related revenues and expenses, and what additional disclosures are appropriate. An accountant must never lose sight of the fact that financial statements are the end product of a large number of accounting *policy decisions* and *measurement estimates* by management (often with the advice of accountants), many of which are based on expectations about future events. Accounting involves many subjective choices.

THE REALM OF FINANCIAL ACCOUNTING

Financial accounting is concerned with the way an organization communicates financial information about the economic activities of the overall enterprise to its stakeholders. Stakeholders can be both internal and external. The primary internal stakeholder is management, while the primary external stakeholder depends on the nature of the organization. For a large, public corporation, the primary external stakeholder group may be the shareholders, while for a small private corporation in which the shareholder is also management, the only *external* stakeholder may be Revenue Canada, which needs to assess income taxes.

Financial accounting is the realm of accounting that is concerned primarily with producing financial statements that report on the economic well-being of an organization and on the flow of its resources. Financial accounting applies to all types of organizations, including

- Businesses
  - Proprietorships
  - Partnerships
  - Corporations
- Non-profit organizations
  - Charitable
    - Incorporated
    - Unincorporated
  - Non-charitable
    - Incorporated
    - Unincorporated
- Governments
  - Senior governments (federal, provincial, and territorial)
  - Municipal governments (and school boards)

Not all organizations are business enterprises. Many are non-profit organizations, which may or may not be charitable organizations. Charitable organizations are those that Revenue Canada has ruled are engaged in charitable activities and that therefore are authorized to issue tax receipts to donors. The donors can use the tax receipts to reduce their income taxes, via a tax credit. There are at least 80,000 charitable organizations in Canada, roughly half of which are churches or religious charities. The number of non-charitable non-profit organizations is unknown, but it must be in the hundreds of thousands. Just think of all of the student organizations (clubs, volunteer organizations, student governments, etc.) in any college or university. Some are very small, but others may be quite large and have control of substantial amounts of money. Political parties are non-profit organizations, as are labour unions and industry trade associations.

Non-profit organizations may or may not be incorporated. If a non-profit organization is incorporated, it is a corporation without share capital. There are no shareholders in a non-profit corporation. A non-profit corporation may have *capital* on its balance sheet, but that capital is not the result of the issuance of shares. Instead, capital is the result of donations or accumulated operating surpluses.

The third type of organization is *governments*. Governments at all levels must prepare financial statements, but the rules guiding the preparation of governmental statements vary considerably from those guiding businesses. Indeed, there is a completely separate standard setting body, the Public Sector Accounting and Auditing Board, that strives to improve the financial reporting of governments. Furthermore, there is a difference in financial reporting for senior governments (the federal, provincial, and territorial governments) and for municipalities. Municipal accounting varies according to the laws of the various provinces.

Organizations of every type prepare financial statements. Small organizations (particularly non-profit organizations) may use a very simplified statement that serves as both an operating statement and a cash flow statement. Proprietorships may prepare an income statement but no balance sheet because the business assets are co-mingled with the owner's assets; Revenue Canada does not require proprietorships and partnerships to present a balance sheet because the income is taxed directly to the proprietor or partners; only corporations are separate legal entities and are taxed as such.

For all organizations, the financial accounting system produces reports both at a point in time (point statement) and for a period of time (flow statements). The point statement is usually known as the balance sheet, regardless of the type of organization, while flow statements vary depending on the type of organization. All types of organization normally prepare three flow statements:

1. statement of operations
2. statement of changes in capital
3. cash flow statement

Other flow statements may be prepared as the nature of the industry or organizational segment requires. For example

- mutual funds and investment companies normally prepare a statement of changes in net assets and a statement of changes in the investment portfolio;
- many non-profit organizations prepare a statement of changes in fund balances; and
- governments may prepare a statement of changes in capital assets (especially when capital assets are not included on the balance sheet).

The statement of operations for a business is known as the *Income Statement*. In business corporations, the statement of changes in capital is known as the *Statement of Changes in Retained Earnings*; but in proprietorships and partnerships, owners' equity is not subdivided into contributed capital and retained earnings, and therefore the statement is called simply the *statement of changes in capital*. In many corporate businesses, the first two flow statements are combined into a single statement, known in corporations as a *statement of income and retained earnings*. Proprietorships and partnerships may prepare a combined *statement of income and capital*.

Non-profit organizations prepare financial statements that bear a somewhat superficial resemblance to those of a business, both point statements and flow statements. Unlike business organizations, however, non-profits are not seeking a profit and their flow statements often differ sharply from those of businesses. The operating statement usually focuses on the flow of resources rather than on the measurement of net income. The difference in focus is the result of the needs of the users, who usually are the financial supporters of the organization (e.g., members, donors, government ministries) and who want to know what the organization has done with the money with which the managers were entrusted.

In this book, we focus exclusively on business organizations. Within the business group, we focus primarily on corporations. Indeed, several chapters are applicable only to corporations (for example, the chapters on shareholders' equity and on accounting for income taxes). Non-profit and governmental reporting is generally covered in advanced accounting texts, even though both non-business types of organizations are pervasive in our society and economy.[1]

Management accounting is concerned with preparing and analyzing information for the exclusive use of management for decision-making, planning, employee motivation, and internal performance evaluation. The level of detail is much greater, and the basis of accountability may differ from that presented in the organization's financial statements. Management accounting deals primarily with segments of an organization and management's specific decision-making needs. The users of management accounting information are known with certainty, and thus the information can be tailored to suit the specific need. In financial accounting, however, there often are multiple users. The various users often have conflicting objectives, and the financial statements must be prepared on a basis that optimizes the trade-offs between the various users' needs.

Because financial accounting is concerned with reporting on the overall organization, it sometimes is referred to as *macro* accounting to differentiate this type of accounting from management accounting, which is concerned primarily with subsets of an organization and its activities (i.e., *micro* accounting). This is a misuse of the term, however. Macro accounting is the system that accumulates and reports information on the *economy*, such as the Gross National Product system of accounts, the flow of funds accounts, and the balance of payments accounts.

CONCEPT REVIEW

1. What is the essential difference between a bookkeeper and an accountant?
2. What is the general realm of financial accounting? How does financial accounting differ from management accounting?
3. What are *non-business* organizations?
4. Describe the difference between *point* statements and *flow* statements. Give examples of each.

PUBLIC VS. PRIVATE CORPORATIONS

A public corporation is one that issues securities (either debt or equity, or both) to the public. The securities can then be traded on the open market, usually through an *organized exchange* such as the Montreal Exchange or the Toronto Stock Exchange. Public corporations must be *registered* with the securities commissions in each province in which their securities are traded and must comply with the reporting requirements of the securities commissions.

A private corporation is one that does not issue securities to the public. This does not mean that a private corporation has no external sources of capital, however.

---

[1] For example, Statistics Canada data show that approximately one in six employed persons is working for a non-profit organization, plus another 7% that are working for some level of government or governmental body. Together, about 25% of the Canadian workforce is employed by non-business organizations.

Some of Canada's largest corporations are private corporations (e.g., McCain Foods Ltd., with annual revenues in excess of $4 billion), but they obtain capital through private placements of debt or equity instruments. As their securities are not publicly traded, they are beyond the reach of the provincial securities acts and securities regulators. The suppliers of capital to a private corporation are assumed to be either insiders or sophisticated investors who do not need the special protection given to members of the general public who may buy shares on the open market.

A type of private corporation with special accounting implications is a Canadian corporation that is a wholly-owned subsidiary of a foreign parent corporation. For example, General Motors of Canada Ltd. and Ford Motor Company of Canada Ltd., two of the three largest corporations in Canada, are wholly owned by their U.S. parent company and thus are private corporations.

Accounting Implications

The ownership of a corporation has important accounting ramifications. Public corporations must be audited and their reporting generally must conform to generally accepted accounting principles (GAAP). As the remainder of this textbook will repeatedly point out, however, GAAP is not terribly limiting because there is a great deal of reporting flexibility permitted within GAAP.

All corporations are governed by the business corporations act in the province in which they are incorporated or by the *Canadian Business Corporations Act* (CBCA) for federally incorporated corporations. The business corporations acts usually state that an audit is required for corporations that are above a specified size threshold (e.g., in the CBCA, $10 million in gross revenue *or* $5 million in total assets). However, exemptions from the audit requirement are readily available if all the shareholders agree to waive the audit. Effectively, therefore, there is no audit requirement for private corporations.

Wholly-owned subsidiaries of foreign parents are likely to be audited, because the parent is likely to be a public company in its home country (most commonly, the United States). But private corporations, whether domestically-owned or foreign-owned, are not required to issue their financial statements to the public. Since the primary user of the statements will be the foreign parent (and will be consolidated with the parent's statements), the subsidiary is likely to use the parent's home country GAAP instead of Canadian GAAP.

Control Blocks

Even when a Canadian corporation is public, it most likely will be controlled by a small number of shareholders who have the majority of the voting shares. A small number of related or affiliated shareholders who hold a majority of the voting shares is called a control block. It is common Canadian practice for a public corporation to issue two or more classes of shares, one with multiple votes and another with little or no voting rights. Shares that have limited voting power are called restricted shares. Restricted shares are used as a means of raising public capital without losing the power of the control block.

In the *Financial Post*'s annual listing of Canada's 500 largest corporations, known as the *FP500*, approximately half of the companies are public. Of the public companies, however, well over half have control blocks. Only 22% of the companies in the *FP500* list are "widely-held" public companies. This 22% actually overstates the importance of widely-held public companies in Canada, because the list does not include a large number of private companies for which no data is available. For example, Bata Shoes is the world's largest shoe company and has annual revenues of about $4 billion, but the company never appears on lists of the largest Canadian corporations.

The implication of the existence of control blocks for Canadian financial reporting is that the accounting approach is unlikely to be dominated by a concern for the public shareholder, as is often the case in the U.S. Instead, the reporting objectives of the controlling shareholder may well take precedence over those of the public investor.

1. What is the difference between a public corporation and a private corporation? Which type is dominant in the Canadian economy?
2. How can private corporations obtain capital from outside investors without becoming public companies?
3. What is a *control block*?

WHAT IS GAAP?

Generally accepted accounting principles (GAAP) represent the body of accounting practices that has been built up over a long period of time through use. GAAP is sometimes viewed as being synonymous with the accounting standards issued by national standard-setters, which in Canada are the italicized recommendations contained in the *CICA Handbook*. But in fact, GAAP is much broader. The *CICA Handbook* contains only a rather small part of accounting practice, and many of the recommendations are non-specific and allow for a great deal of judgement. The bulk of the more specific recommendations in the *CICA Handbook* relate to

- certain types of liabilities (e.g., pensions, leases, and corporate income taxes);
- some general categories of assets (e.g., research and development costs; capital assets; long-term investments);
- limited aspects of financial statement format and presentation (e.g., the cash flow statement; certain types of disclosure in the income statement and balance sheet);
- problem areas that are important mainly for large corporations (e.g., business combinations; foreign operations); and
- a few disclosures that are required for public companies only (e.g., interim statements; segmented reporting; earnings per share).

A vast amount of accounting practice is not included in the *CICA Handbook*, including most areas of revenue and expense recognition and many accounting practices followed by the so-called *specialized industries* such as real property development, financial services (e.g., insurance, banking, and investment dealers and funds), resource companies (forest products, mining, oil and gas), and agriculture. In Canada, the specialized industries account for a majority of the economic activity of the country.

If the recommendations of the *CICA Handbook* constitute only a part of GAAP, then where does the rest of it come from? Generally acceptable accounting principles are those which have been used in the past and have found general acceptance. That is, over time, preparers (i.e., managers) have devised measurement and reporting approaches that the users accepted as being reasonable, and that auditors have accepted as well. Much of the early development of the *CICA Handbook* was an effort to codify existing practice rather than to *change* existing practice. Indeed, it has been very difficult for the Accounting Standards Board to issue an accounting recommendation unless it already was acceptable to most of the companies that would be affected. To issue an unpopular standard is to risk having the standard ignored, thereby damaging the credibility of the *CICA Handbook* as an authoritative source of accounting standards.

The *CICA Handbook* contains a description of GAAP, part of which reads as follows:

> [GAAP] encompasses not only specific rules, practices and procedures relating to particular circumstances but also broad principles and conventions of general application. ... Specifically, generally accepted accounting principles comprise the Accounting Recommendations in the

Handbook and, when a matter is not covered by a Recommendation, other accounting principles that either:

(a) *are generally accepted by virtue of their use in similar circumstances by a significant number of entities in Canada;* or
(b) are consistent with the Recommendations in the *Handbook* and are developed through the exercise of professional judgement ...

[CICA 1000.59 –.60, italics added]

GAAP is essentially historically-oriented: past practice is the basis for present and future practice. However, past practice was developed in simpler times and does not always provide a suitable guide for current business practices. Indeed, past accounting practice, when applied to modern methods of doing business, can yield quite inappropriate reported results. One class of examples is cited in Chapter 15, Complex Debt and Equity Instruments, where the historically-practiced method of classifying debt and equity securities on the basis of their legal *form* led to financial reporting that was inconsistent with the *substance* of the securities.

Due to the inability of past accounting practice to provide a clear basis for innovative new business methods, GAAP is constantly evolving. From time to time, the CICA's Accounting Standards Board (AcSB) issues new recommendations to deal with recently-developed areas of business practice. These recommendations are always, as a matter of practical necessity, issued *after* companies have already experimented with reporting for at least a couple of years (and usually much more). The *CICA Handbook* recommendations, therefore, usually (but not always) restrict existing accounting practices rather than prescribe new accounting practices. Accounting standard setters normally are followers in developing accounting practice, not leaders. Practicing accountants, therefore, must exercise *professional judgement* in developing accounting treatments for innovative business practices. The criteria by which professional judgement is developed and exercised is the subject of the next chapter.

Additional aspects of GAAP that originate from the CICA, in addition to the *CICA Handbook*, are the **Accounting Guidelines** issued from time to time by the AcSB's Steering Committee and the **Abstracts of Issues Discussed** by the Emerging Issues Committee (EIC). Although both of these sources are issued by the CICA and are included in the binder that includes the *CICA Handbook*, they constitute only expert opinion and do not have the same force as do the recommendations in the *CICA Handbook* itself. For example, the "Introduction to Accounting Guidelines" states that:

> Guidelines express opinions of the Board and do not have the authority of Recommendations issued by the Board.

Both the *Accounting Guidelines* and the *EIC Abstracts of Issues* deal with issues that have arisen in recent years and on which accountants and preparers (i.e., managers) have requested guidance. Neither has gone through the extensive procedures required for introducing new recommendations into the *CICA Handbook*, however, and therefore remain as opinions. The "Introduction to Accounting Guidelines" states quite clearly:

> In issuing Guidelines, the Board recognizes that there is no substitute for the exercise of professional judgment in the determination of what constitutes fair presentation or good practice in a particular case.

Printed sources (other than the CICA) that describe various components of GAAP include the research publications of Canadian professional accounting bodies, specifically the Certified General Accountants Association of Canada, the Society of Management Accountants of Canada, and the Canadian Academic Accounting

Association (which is comprised mainly of post-secondary teachers of accounting). Where there is no specific guidance provided in the Canadian accounting literature, accountants may refer to pronouncements issued by the U.S.'s Financial Accounting Standards Board or by the International Accounting Standards Committee.

Much of GAAP is simply passed down from generation to generation, through training (including textbooks) and through professional interactions among accountants. Relatively little is "officially" set out in authoritative accounting pronouncements.

The Accounting Standard-Setting Process in Canada

Accounting standards in Canada are set by the CICA's Accounting Standards Board (AcSB), which is a committee comprised mainly of practicing chartered accountants (CAs) who serve on a volunteer basis. The recommendations of the AcSB are incorporated into the *CICA Handbook*. The group began life as the Accounting Research Committee (ARC); its name was changed to the Accounting Standards Committee (AcSC) in 1982 and to the Accounting Standards Board in 1991. Older publications may carry the then-current name or initials of the committee, but these earlier designations are synonymous with the current designation of AcSB.

The Accounting Standards Board is a creation of the CICA's Board of Directors. There is no direct legal authority for the AcSB to set standards for Canadian companies. However, in the mid-1970s, the regulations in support of the *Canadian Business Corporations Act* (CBCA) were modified to define compliance with GAAP to mean (or include) compliance with the recommendations of the *CICA Handbook*. Provincial corporations acts (or the regulations thereto) were similarly modified to be consistent with the CBCA regulations, and the regulations of the various provincial securities acts followed suit. As a result, the *CICA Handbook* has achieved quasi-legal status.

The AcSB consists of 13 voting and 2 nonvoting members who serve three-year terms. The nonvoting members are the CICA's (1) Accounting Standards Director and (2) Senior Vice-President, Studies and Standards. The 13 voting members serve on a voluntary basis, and at least two-thirds (i.e., nine) of the voting members must be Chartered Accountants. The CICA's Board of Directors chooses at least eight of the voting members (including the chairperson), while five other groups are invited to appoint one member each:

- Canadian Council of Financial Analysts
- Financial Executives Institute of Canada
- Canadian Academic Accounting Association
- Certified General Accountants' Association of Canada
- Society of Management Accountants of Canada

Any vacancies left unfilled by these five groups are filled by the CICA.

The work of the AcSB is supported by a small full-time professional staff (11, at time of writing) that does the research and writing in support of the Board's standard-setting activities. The process of setting standards generally goes through the following steps:

1. *Write a project proposal.* The proposal defines the project's terms of reference and justifies the need for the standard, identifying the scope of the problem and the affected preparer and user groups.

2. *Appoint a task force.* The task force, consisting of six or seven individuals, is established to develop material for AcSB members. The task force normally will include people who have specialist knowledge of the topic under consideration but who are not members of the AcSB; these non-members usually are invited to attend the AcSB discussions on that topic when it is being debated. These spe-

cialist task force members serve only for the duration of their particular topic and do not vote.

3. *Develop an issues paper* (optional step). Issues papers are developed for more complex topics. The issues papers help the AcSB understand the views of interested parties on major issues before it starts to formulate its position on a particular subject.

4. *Create a statement of principles.* The principles, usually developed by the task force (with the support of the CICA research staff), outline the basic response to the accounting issues raised. The principles must be approved by two-thirds of the AcSB before an exposure draft can be developed.

5. *Review with associates.* Input is sought on a private and confidential basis from associates at key stages in the project's development. This may be at the statement of principles stage, or may follow the release of the exposure draft, or both. Associates provide an outside reaction to the proposed standard.

6. *Develop an exposure draft.* An exposure draft is a *CICA Handbook* section in draft form. After approval by at least two-thirds of the AcSB, the exposure draft is made publicly available by placing it on the CICA's Web site, with a notice inserted in *CA Magazine.* All interested parties are invited to respond to the committee in writing within the exposure period (three to five months, usually).

7. *Make revisions.* The responses to the exposure draft are summarized by the research staff for consideration by the task force and AcSB.

8. *Issue a re-exposure draft* (if deemed necessary). Sometimes, the comments received on the exposure draft are so wide-ranging that the AcSB decides to significantly revise the exposure draft and re-issue it for further response.

9. *Issue the final* CICA Handbook *section.* After the AcSB considers the comments received regarding the exposure draft (or re-exposure draft, if one has been issued), the proposed new or revised *CICA Handbook* section is rewritten in final form. Approval by two-thirds of the AcSB is required before a new or revised section can be issued.

The process usually is lengthy, requiring at least two years to bring new *CICA Handbook* recommendations to fruition. The length of the process is often criticized because it is impossible for the AcSB to respond quickly to emerging issues. It is for this reason that the CICA established the **Emerging Issues Committee (EIC)**, which can issue opinions on new accounting issues that provide guidance to practicing accountants. As noted above, however, the conclusions of EIC discussions are only opinions, not accounting standards.

Some observers of the Canadian standard-setting scene point to the relatively more rapid response time of the Financial Accounting Standards Board (FASB) in the U.S., which issues *Statements of Financial Accounting Standards (SFAS)* by approval of a full-time, paid Board of seven members that is supported by a full-time professional staff of about 30. However, there are significant virtues to slowness of the AcSB procedure:

• the slowness, which allows more time for alternative accounting and reporting treatments to be tested in practice before the field of "acceptable" practices is narrowed;

• it prevents the proverbial "knee-jerk" reaction to issues that turn out to be temporary and of limited concern;

• the members of the AcSB are all engaged in their regular full-time employment elsewhere, so that they maintain an outside perspective; and

• the AcSB requires a two-thirds vote for approval of new recommendations, which helps to ensure that the recommendations have a reasonably wide base of support.

The FASB, perhaps in the interests of keeping themselves busy, issued 134 statements of financial accounting standards between 1972 and the end of 1998, many of which deal with issues of very limited scope (such as accounting for railway track structures, and the plant abandonments by regulated enterprises) or are amendments of earlier standards. In contrast, the issues addressed by the AcSB tend to be issues of wide concern and general applicability rather than issues that are applicable only to specific industries.

Revenue Canada

Revenue Canada is an agency of the federal government established to interpret and enforce the nation's federal tax laws. To do so, Revenue Canada has adopted procedures and reporting requirements whose purpose is to collect money and, at times, to attain specific social or economic objectives considered important by Parliament, such as encouraging investment in research and development.

The general aim of the *Income Tax Act* is to collect revenue. In general, the Act provides for taxation when cash is flowing, so that revenues are usually taxed when they have been substantively realized and costs are deducted from taxable revenue when they are incurred. Taxation principles tend to emphasize cash flows because those flows normally can be measured quite clearly. The computation of taxable income abhors estimates and discourages inter-period allocations, both of which are dear to the hearts of Canadian accountants. There are exceptions to the cash flow emphasis in assessing taxable income, of course. For example, the taxation of revenue often is affected by the revenue recognition policy used by the business, which may differ significantly from the revenue cash flow.

Expenses may be recognized for tax purposes in a way that is quite different from their accounting treatment. This is particularly true for costs that are subject to a defer-and-amortize approach for accounting purposes, such as development costs, pension costs, long-term leases, and goodwill. Capital assets are subject to Capital Cost Allowance for tax purposes, which is completely unrelated to depreciation or amortization expense for financial reporting purposes.

Revenue Canada does not require a corporation (or the owners of proprietorships and partnerships) to use the same reporting principles for tax as for accounting, or vice versa. However, corporations must attach their annual financial statements to the tax return. In addition, one of the basic parts of the corporate income tax form is a required reconciliation of reported pre-tax accounting income to reported taxable income. The corporation must make it clear just what accounting differences caused any discrepancy between the net earnings reported to its shareholders and the taxable income reported to Revenue Canada. This is the principle of *exception reporting* as applied to the taxable income calculation.

Since a corporate tax return must include the corporation's financial statements and a reconciliation of income, there is a tendency for companies to at least consider adopting the same accounting treatment for both tax and financial reporting purposes. The influence of tax considerations is particularly strong in private corporations if there are few (if any) external users.

When corporations adopt the same accounting practices for financial reporting as for tax reporting, this is known as *book-tax conformity*. Many accountants believe that disclosure of variations between tax and book reporting on the tax return acts as a "red flag" for Revenue Canada and invites a tax audit. Two tax experts also observe:

> Firms also adopt book-tax conformity to increase the probability that the courts will uphold the method chosen as appropriate for tax purposes. According to a 1992 decision … the accounting method used in the financial statements will generally prevail unless another method results in a "truer picture of a taxpayer's revenue, which more fairly and accurately portrays income, and which matches revenue and expenditure" [2]

---

[2] Alan MacNaughton and Amin Mawani, "Tax Minimization Versus Good Tax Planning," *CA Magazine* (January – February 1997), p. 41.

Therefore, although there is no requirement in Canada (unlike some other countries, such as Germany and Japan) that tax reporting be identical to financial reporting, tax treatment of items may have an impact on financial reporting. The impact is most likely to be observed for revenue; Revenue Canada generally takes a dim view of a corporation's recognizing revenue in the income statement while deferring revenue recognition for tax purposes.

Influence of Accounting Standards of Other Countries

The accounting standards of other countries can have a profound impact through two forms of accounting imperialism. Historically, accounting has tended to follow both (1) political influence and (2) capital flows. Throughout the British Commonwealth, for example, there is a strong influence from U.K. accounting. Similarly, the former colonies of France tend to use accounting principles that found their origin in the French system of accounting. These groups of similar accounting practices among politically-related (or formerly related) countries are called *families* of accounting standards.

Political connections are a historical influence, but capital-exporting nations have often been able to export their accounting principles along with their capital and override previously existing political accounting heritage. Canada is part of the British Commonwealth and Canadian accounting has its roots in England and Scotland. However, the dominance of U.S. investors (both corporate and individual) as providers of capital for Canadian enterprises soon resulted in Canadian accounting veering away from the U.K. model and becoming part of the U.S. family of accounting practice. While there are significant differences in accounting between the U.S. and Canada, the accounting practices of the two countries are more similar than any other two industrialized countries in the world.

Given the relative dominance of U.S. capital in Canada, it should be no surprise that there is continual pressure to *harmonize* Canadian accounting with that of the U.S. The pressure is due to several factors, including the following:

- Uniform U.S.-Canada accounting standards would simplify life for the large number of U.S. subsidiaries that are operating in Canada.

- Canadian-owned corporations that raise capital in the U.S. would be relieved of the obligation to report under two different sets of accounting standards.

- Securities commissions in the two countries could share the regulatory burden (and reduce their costs) because approval of a public company's financial statement in one country could automatically be transferred to the other country.

- International audit firms could transfer staff between the two countries without the need for local retraining.

The idea behind accounting harmonization is that two or more countries work together to eliminate differences in their accounting approaches when there is no underlying economic or environmental reason to use different approaches. Historically, however, the harmonization process between the U.S. and Canada took the form of the AcSB's deciding whether or not to adopt U.S. accounting standards.

In recent years, there has been stronger cooperation. Not only have the AcSB and the FASB cooperated in establishing standards on issues such as segment disclosures, but a larger group has been working together to formulate a common approach to several contentious issues. The participants in this larger group (known as G4+1) are the standards setters of Canada, U.S., U.K., Australia, and New Zealand, with the active participation of the International Accounting Standards Committee (IASC).

Why doesn't Canada simply adopt the U.S. standards? The reasons are legal, professional, economic, and organizational:

- The U.S. tends to have very procedural, rule-oriented accounting standards. This is due primarily to two circumstances: (1) the much larger number of professional accountants in the U.S., combined with a weaker professional control mechanism, and (2) a tendency for U.S. citizens to resort to lawsuits to settle their differences. The Canadian accounting profession is smaller and more closely knit, and the ethical control mechanism is stronger. As well, Canadian society is less litigious, which permits a greater reliance on professional judgement.

- The U.S. has a proportionately larger mercantile (i.e., retailing and wholesaling) industry and a far larger manufacturing segment. Canadian enterprise, in contrast, is much more oriented towards the resource industries and the service sectors (including financial services). There is little room for professional judgement in U.S. standards, which leaves little scope for adapting accounting standards to differing economic circumstances that exist in special industries.

- The U.S. has a large portion of economic activity carried on by public corporations, probably a higher proportion than any other nation. Canadian enterprise, in contrast, is dominated by private or closely-controlled corporations that need not respond to the expectations of the public securities markets.

- Debt financing is much more common in Canadian business practice than it is in the U.S. The banks and other financial institutions (such as pension funds and insurance companies) are much more important sources of financing compared to the public stock market, which shifts the power structure of users.

There are relatively few Canadian companies that are registered public companies in the U.S. Until recently, those companies have had to include a financial statement note in which they convert their earnings under Canadian GAAP to earnings under U.S. GAAP. Under a recent mutual recognition agreement between the U.S. Securities and Exchange Commission (SEC) and the Ontario Securities Commission (OSC), cross-registered corporations in each jurisdiction may file their financial statements in the host country using home-country GAAP, without adjustment. Nevertheless, there continues to be pressure on the AcSB to adopt FASB standards for the benefit of the small number of cross-registered Canadian corporations, regardless of the cost and inconvenience caused to the vast majority of Canadian corporations that are not SEC registrants.

Standard setting is a costly business, and the costs have been borne exclusively by the members of the CICA (through their dues). Some accountants have suggested that the CICA should abandon the standard-setting process and leave it to the FASB to set standards for both countries. In 1998, the CICA issued a special task force report that argued strongly that the CICA should continue to set standards for Canada, but that the standards be harmonized as much as possible with those of the FASB and the International Accounting Standards Committee.[3]

International Accounting Standards

The International Accounting Standards Committee (IASC) was established in 1973. The IASC consists of representatives from professional accountancy bodies from a wide number of countries (122 bodies from 91 countries, in 1998). The business of the IASC is conducted by a much smaller group, a Board made up of representatives from 13 countries. There are several member countries who are virtually permanent members of the Board: Canada, U.S., U.K., Australia, Germany, France, and Japan.

The members of IASC are representatives of public accountants' groups; essentially, the IASC is comprised of auditors. There is no representation by nations themselves, or by their governments. Nor do the members even represent the standard-setting bodies in the various countries. For example, the United States is represented by the American Institute of Certified Public Accountants (AICPA), not by the FASB. The Canadian member is the CICA, but not the AcSB part of the CICA, although there certainly is a close correspondence.

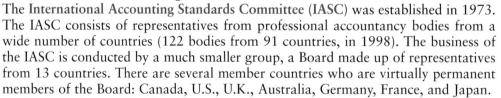

3 Canadian Institute of Chartered Accountants, *Task Force on Standard Setting: Final Report* (Toronto: CICA, 1998).

The objective of the IASC is to promote the world-wide harmonization of accounting principles. The IASC issues International Accounting Standards (IAS) on its own accord, which have no legal status of their own. The Committee encourages developing countries that have no indigenous accounting profession to adopt the IAS as their accounting standards, and encourages developed countries to modify their standards to be in accordance with the IAS.

The IASC has been increasingly successful in its goal of global harmonization. A strong impetus to harmonization has come from securities regulators in many countries, who can see a significant improvement in enforcement standards and a reduction in enforcement costs if similar standards are adopted world-wide. A strong motivator has been the International Organization of Securities Commissions (known as IOSCO). In 1995, IOSCO urged the IASC to improve its core standards to reduce the number of permitted alternative accounting treatments and to achieve better harmonization with major developed countries' indigenous standards. As a part of this "core standards" project, the IASC has cooperated with other standard-setting bodies around the world (primarily English-speaking countries) on many projects.

IASC standards are not just hypothetical. Many public companies list their securities on several exchanges, and not just on the exchanges in their home country. The vast majority of stock exchanges in the world accept financial statements from foreign registrants that are prepared in accordance with IASC standards. Some exchanges also permit foreign registrants to report in by using their home country standards or U.S. standards. For example, the Tokyo Stock Exchange (the world's second largest) permits foreign companies to report in their choice of

- Japanese GAAP,
- U.S. GAAP,
- the company's home country GAAP, or
- IASC standards.

Some exchanges also permit domestic companies to report by using IASC standards. The German and French exchanges, for example, permit domestic companies to report their consolidated results by using IASC standards; unconsolidated statements must be prepared in accordance with local law, however.

Glaring exceptions to the wide acceptance of IASC standards for financial reporting are the exchanges of the U.S. and Canada, which are the only major exchanges that force registrants from outside the country to conform to GAAP in the exchange's country. Many people in the U.S., of course, believe that they have the best accounting standards in the world because they spend the most money at it. The U.S. Securities and Exchange Commission (SEC), however, has clearly indicated their displeasure with some U.S. standards by accepting selected IASC standards in place of FASB standards. Specific examples include acceptance of IASC standards (for foreign registrants) on cash flow reporting, business combinations, and goodwill. Even the FASB, therefore, has been forced to pay attention to what the IASC is doing.

The AcSB board has been very active in attempting to reduce the differences between Canadian standards and international standards. Several standards issued by the AcSB in the late 1990s are identical or nearly identical to their IASC counterparts, such as the standards on segment disclosures, post-retirement benefits, cash flow statements, and financial instruments. The IASC has also issued other special reports in conjunction with the IASC, including lease accounting and financial instrument measurement.

International accounting standards are also used for reporting within a growing list of countries, either without modification (e.g., Croatia, Pakistan, Latvia, Trinidad & Tobago) or with some local modification (e.g., Bangladesh, Colombia, Poland, Thailand). Malaysia uses IAS, but with national standards developed for topics not covered by IAS. China's emerging accounting standards are being based largely on IAS.

There can be little doubt that Canadian standards will continue to become increasingly similar to IASC standards. There also can be little doubt that the world-wide importance of the IASC standards will continue to increase. Throughout this book, we will examine international standards relating to each issue that we discuss. No manager or accountant should venture into the real world without being aware of what's happening on the international financial reporting scene.

TAILORED ACCOUNTING POLICIES

The preceding pages described GAAP, the standard-setting process, and the influence of external standards. The general thrust of the *CICA Handbook* is accounting policy for public companies. A few of the *CICA Handbook* sections pertain exclusively to public companies. However, the audit reporting requirements draw in private companies as well. The beginning of the "Financial Statement Concepts" section of the *CICA Handbook* states that the purpose of the section

> ... is to describe the concepts underlying the development and use of accounting principles in general purpose financial statements (hereafter referred to as financial statements). Such financial statements are designed to meet the common information needs of external users of financial information about an entity.   [*CICA* 1000.01, italics added]

The potential for limited applicability of the *CICA Handbook* recommendations is recognized in the "Introduction to Accounting Recommendations":

> ... no rule of general application can be phrased to suit all circumstances or combination of circumstances that may arise, nor is there any substitute for the <u>exercise of professional judgment</u> in the determination of what constitutes fair presentation or good practice in a particular case.
>
> Recommendations are intended to apply to all types of profit oriented enterprises ... No Recommendation is intended to override the requirements of a governing statute.   [*CICA Handbook*, p. 9]

In public companies, GAAP is used *except* in regulated enterprises. The AcSB's "governing statute" clause comes into effect for regulated industries, and the accounting policies may deviate in some respects from GAAP due to the statute (or related regulations) pertaining to the regulated enterprise. Such accounting policies are known as **Regulated Accounting Policies**, or **RAP**. RAP is different for each regulated industry. Regulated industries include banks, telephone companies, mutual funds, insurance companies, and public utilities in most provinces.

Private companies are not bound by GAAP, unless an external user (such as a major lender) requires that GAAP be used. While many private companies do use GAAP, many others deviate from GAAP in one or more respects. The deviation is usually in order to make the statements more useful for specific users or to coincide with the income tax treatment of specific items.

When non-GAAP accounting policies are used, the company is said to be using **tailored accounting policies (TAP)** and to be reporting on a **disclosed basis of accounting (DBA)**. The *CICA Handbook* recommends that:

> A clear and concise description of the significant accounting policies of an enterprise should be included as an integral part of the financial statements.   [*CICA* 1505.04]

The description of TAP will normally be included in the accounting policy note to the financial statements, and the auditor's opinion (if any) will refer to the fact that the financial statements have been prepared in accordance with the accounting principles described in the accounting policy note (instead of containing the auditor's usual reference to GAAP).

The CICA Handbook suggests that a disclosed basis of accounting is appropriate for meeting contractual requirements:

> Generally accepted accounting principles is the term used to describe the basis on which financial statements are normally prepared. There are special circumstances where a different basis of accounting may be appropriate, for example, in financial statements prepared in accordance with regulatory legislation or contractual requirements.   [*CICA* 1000.59]

If the contractual requirements are those of a public company, then statements prepared on the basis of TAP are *special purpose* statements rather than the *general purpose* statements that the *CICA Handbook* recommendations apply to. In private corporations, partnerships, or proprietorships, the only external users may be for contractual requirements (e.g., lenders or shareholders). In such cases, the TAP statements are the only externally issued statements and there is no need to issue general purpose statements.

In 1996, the CICA's Auditing Standards Board (AuSB) began deliberations on recommendations to clarify the role of the auditor in engagements for companies in which TAP are used. While the AuSB's proposed recommendations are for the guidance of auditors, the proposals clarify the circumstances in which a company may issue *audited* financial statements that are not in compliance with GAAP. An overview of the proposed recommendations is given in Exhibit 1-1 on page 16.

CONCEPT REVIEW

1. Are all Canadian *generally accepted accounting principles* found in the *CICA Handbook*? Explain.
2. What group establishes the recommendations that are found in the *CICA Handbook*?
3. Do the EIC Abstracts have the same authority as the italicized recommendations in the *CICA Handbook*?
4. Why does Canadian GAAP differ from GAAP in the U.S. and other countries?
5. Are International Accounting Standards used anywhere in the world?
6. What is meant by *accounting harmonization*?
7. Why would a company use *tailored accounting policies* instead of GAAP?

OBJECTIVES OF FINANCIAL REPORTING

What is the purpose of financial statements? The purpose is to communicate information to one or more groups or types of users. To be useful to the users, the financial statements must convey information that is useful for their decision purposes. These decision purposes may vary widely, and the information that is suitable for one purpose may not be suitable for another purpose.

An apt analogy is the nature of information presented in management accounting. Readers who have had a course in management accounting will recognize that when accountants provide managers with a measure of the *cost of a product*, the measurement will depend on the type of decision that the manager is about to make. A cost measure that is based on average, fully-allocated costs may be relevant for deciding whether long-range production of the product is feasible or for setting a general selling price, but it is inappropriate for deciding on whether to make or buy the

EXHIBIT 1-1
Proposed Guidelines for Auditors for Non-GAAP Financial Statements

In October 1997, the Auditing Standards Board (AuSB) issued an exposure draft (ED) on the *Auditor's Report on Financial Statements Prepared Using a Basis of Accounting Other Than Generally Accepted Accounting Principles*. This ED strives to clarify the situations in which it is acceptable for an auditor to give an opinion on TAP-based financial statements. The ED cites the circumstances under which non-GAAP statements may be issued (and accepted by the auditor) as follows:

> Generally accepted accounting principles is the basis of accounting normally used for financial statements prepared to meet the common information needs of external users. When intended users have special information needs, financial statements prepared in accordance with generally accepted accounting principles may not meet those needs. In these special circumstances, financial statements may be prepared using a basis of accounting other than generally accepted accounting principles. (ED .04)

The exposure draft cites specific examples in which TAP-based financial statements are appropriate. These examples are

- on a non-consolidated basis (for other than general release by a public company);
- in accordance with the specific terms of a purchase or sale agreement where the specified users are the parties to the transaction;
- under the terms of a shareholders'/partners' agreement where the specified users are the shareholders/partners; and
- on a basis prescribed for a specified user such as a marketing board or other regulatory agency, a lender or funder, to meet its special information needs. (ED .08)

As long as the auditor is satisfied that the basis of accounting used in preparing the financial statements is appropriate for the special information needs of the intended users, the auditor may issue an unqualified opinion addressed to the specific users.

These proposals, if accepted by the AuSB and incorporated into the *CICA Handbook*, will help to alleviate the confusion that now surrounds auditors' positions in relation to TAP-based statements.

product (when *avoidable cost* would be appropriate) or on deciding whether to accept an offer to produce the same product for private branding (when *incremental cost* would be appropriate).

Financial statements often have direct economic impacts for either the enterprise or its stakeholders, or both. For example

- reported earnings may be used as the basis for employee profit-sharing and/or management bonuses;
- accounting methods may increase or decrease a corporation's income tax liability;
- the reported level of accounts receivable and inventories affects the level of financing provided by a bank through an operating line of credit;
- reported earnings and reported net asset value affect the permitted return in regulated industries, such as telephone companies, cable companies, and pipelines;
- various reported numbers in the financial statements may trigger a default on loan requirements, known as *covenants*; and

- in partnerships, co-operatives, and mutual insurance companies, the reported financial results affect the financial rewards of the partners, members, and policyholders.

In addition, many of the decisions that users must make are *evaluative* decisions that may not have immediate economic impacts, but that do affect the users' perceptions of the reporting enterprise and affect their relations with (or stake in) the enterprise:

- lenders evaluate the cash flow potential of a borrower in order to assess the ability of the borrower to service the loan (that is, to pay the interest and principal as they come due);

- income tax authorities evaluate the financial statements to see whether the information that a corporation is reporting to its owners is compatible with (but not necessarily the same as) the information it is reporting to Revenue Canada;

- individual donors, charitable foundations, and government ministries assess a non-profit agency's use of donated funds;

- employees evaluate an employer's ability to pay higher compensation (or the validity of employer requests for reductions in compensation);

- shareholders assess management's ability to conduct the affairs of the enterprise;

- security analysts evaluate public companies' performance and issue recommendations to buy, hold, or sell shares; and

- regulators evaluate a regulated enterprise to see if the enterprise's earnings are reasonable.

The *CICA Handbook* contains the following statement regarding the objectives of financial statements:

> The objective of financial statements is to communicate information that is useful to investors, members, contributors, creditors and other users in making their resource allocation decisions and/or assessing management stewardship.   [*CICA* 1000.15]

As a generic statement of objectives, the AcSB's statement is satisfactory. However, by lumping all users together into a single group (and all decisions into a single category), the definition provides no guidance for accountants to use in exercising their professional judgement. Therefore, we must look beyond the AcSB's definition. The following sections discuss some of the more common objectives of financial reporting.

Bear in mind that, as we discussed in previous sections, relatively few Canadian enterprises are widely-held, public companies. To be able to recommend suitable accounting policies, a professional accountant must be able to discern the financial reporting objectives that affect each individual enterprise. Otherwise, there is no basis for choosing one accounting policy instead of another. The managers of a reporting enterprise must choose accounting policies if they are using TAP, *but they also must make choices that are appropriate to their reporting environment if they are reporting within the GAAP framework*.

Assessing and Predicting Cash Flows

A financial reporting objective that has received much attention in both the professional and academic accounting literature is that of *cash flow prediction*:

> Investors and creditors of profit oriented enterprises are interested, for the purpose of making resource allocation decisions, in predicting the ability of the entity to earn income and generate cash flows in the future to meet its obligations and to generate a return on investment.   [*CICA* 1000.12]

Bankers and creditors need to assess a business's ability to generate enough cash through its normal operations to be able to pay interest and to repay the principal.

The shareholders of public companies may also be interested in cash flow prediction because, in theory, share value is derived from the present value of the perpetual stream of future dividend payments. To the extent that earnings are retained (instead of being paid out as dividends), the reinvested earnings increase the asset base and should generate increased cash flow (and increased dividends) in the future.

There is a subtle difference between the assessment of current cash flows and the prediction of future cash flows. In assessing current cash flows, the financial statement user wants to know the cash inflows and outflows of the enterprise in the current period. Normally, the user places particular emphasis on the cash flow from operations to assess the entity's ability to generate cash. The availability of other sources of financing is also important, as is the disposition of those funds: *How much cash is the company generating or raising externally, and what is the company doing with that money?*

Improvements in the presentation of the cash flow statement have helped this objective in recent years, although much remains hidden from view. In particular, details of cash flow from operations are buried in very broad summary figures, and it is not easy to discern anything beyond gross cash flow from operations. As we will see in later chapters, accounting policy decisions can affect the amount reported as cash flow from operations, and companies have been known to select accounting policies that have the effect of increasing the *apparent* cash flow from operations.

Cash flow *prediction* from historically-oriented financial statements involves taking the current cash flow and extrapolating it into future years. Assumptions must be made in order to do this, and accounting can help this process by measuring and/or disclosing the company's commitments to future cash flows (for example, forthcoming lease and loan payments).

As all accountants are fully aware, the measurement of operating cash flow differs from the measurement of earnings. In the long run, however, they are the same. Revenues and expenses arise from cash flows, but differ from the actual cash flows to the extent that accountants engage in the processes of *accrual accounting* and *interperiod allocation* in order to estimate earnings. Financial analysts and bankers, too, are aware of the difference. But creditors and analysts who are attempting to assess and predict future cash flows tend to prefer earnings measures that are supported by operating cash flows. For this reason, analysts often use the reported *cash flow from operations* to calculate *cash flow per share* for public companies. They compare the operating cash flow per share with the earnings per share, and conclude that if there is a high degree of correspondence between the two measures, the company has high quality earnings. If there is a wide disparity between the two, then the company is said to have low quality earnings. Sometimes, a company will report positive earnings but negative cash flow from operations; this phenomenon is not viewed kindly by analysts.

What impact does an objective of cash flow prediction have on financial reporting? The consequences of adopting cash flow prediction as a primary reporting objective include the following:

- *Accounting policies are chosen that tend to reduce interperiod allocations.* For example, revenue is recognized when cash is received. Similarly, costs that could be deferred and amortized (e.g., start-up costs) will be expensed instead, so that the impact on earnings (as an expense) will coincide with the cash flow.

- *Full disclosure of future cash flow commitments is given in the notes.* There is a great deal of leeway permitted in disclosing future commitments of various kinds. Under a cash flow reporting objective, the choice is to provide liberal disclosure of future cash flows, and particularly to signal forthcoming changes in cash flows (positive or negative).

When cash flow assessment and prediction is the primary objective, financial reporting policies are chosen that provide the clearest indication of the cash flows underlying reported earnings. Accrual accounting and interperiod allocation are still used, but their use is restricted to those instances in which there is little or no choice, such as amortization of capital assets for profit-oriented enterprises. Non-profit organizations, on the other hand, may use no interperiod allocations, even for capital assets, because cash flow assessment may be the overriding objective of financial reporting.

Income Tax Minimization

A very common objective, particularly for private companies, is that of *income tax minimization*. Since there is a time value of money, why pay taxes this year if they can be delayed until next year? The cash saved by reducing the income tax bill can be invested to earn a return, or can be used to service debt or pay dividends. A company has a lot of better things to do with its money than pay income taxes, if the payment is not necessary.

Note that we are not talking about *cheating* on the income tax. There is flexibility in the timing of reporting certain revenues and expenses on the corporate tax return. To some extent, a company can affect the amount of tax that it pays through its selection of accounting policies. The use of legitimate options for reducing a company's current taxable income is known as *tax minimization* or *tax avoidance*. In contrast, deliberate mis-statement on the tax return is *tax evasion*, which is fraud.

If a company wishes to minimize the amount of taxes that it pays, it will adopt accounting policies that tend to

- delay the recognition of revenue to the extent permitted by the *Income Tax Act*, particularly for long earnings cycles, and
- speed up the payment of expenses that can legitimately be deducted for tax purposes.

A common example of legitimate minimization of *personal* income taxes is the rush of Canadians at the end of February each year to invest in RRSPs. By investing up to the permitted level within 60 days following the taxation year, individuals reduce their income tax bill. The motivation is so strong that customers borrow from their banks in order to make the investment. The same principle applies to businesses' motivation to speed up expense payment to reduce their income tax.

Why wouldn't every company attempt to reduce its income tax bill? The reason is that if the company adopts accounting policies that reduce taxable income, those policies will also reduce reported net income:

> This might be a problem for managers whose compensation is tied to book income. A lower book income may also lead to a poorer performance evaluation and hence reduced promotion possibilities for managers. Furthermore, many executive compensation packages include significant amounts of stock options. Anything that lowers the firm's stock price will lower the value of those options. Many managers believe that a firm's stock price is determined more by its book income than by its cash flows.[4]

As a result of the impact on reported earnings, income tax minimization is more likely to be an objective for private corporations and, to a lesser extent, for public corporations that have a strong family control block. The owner-managers of these types of corporations have independent sources of information about the company, and their bankers usually are kept closely informed about the activities of the corporation. A tax minimization objective is in the best interests of bankers and creditors, but they must recognize that reported earnings under a tax minimization objective will *look* poorer, but the cash flow will actually be better. In contrast, public corporations are likely to place less emphasis on tax minimization because their managers

---

[4] Alan MacNaughton and Amin Mawani, "Tax Minimization versus Good Tax Planning,"
     CA Magazine (January – February 1997), p. 40.

are more concerned about external stakeholder perceptions of the company's earnings ability.

Some aspects of taxation are independent of their accounting treatment. For example, the *Income Tax Act* provides for Capital Cost Allowance for capital assets; accounting depreciation is irrelevant to determining taxable income. Similarly, the tax deduction for an employer's liability for an employee pension plan is linked to the cash flow, and does not depend on the accounting treatment. For these types of expenses, adopting an *income tax minimization* objective will have no accounting choice implications.

Contract Compliance

Financial statements often are the basis that external users use for assessing whether an enterprise has complied with contract provisions. The most common type of financial statement contracting is for debt, particularly with bank loans and with issues of bonds (both publicly issued and privately placed). Debt contracts or agreements usually have provisions that require companies to maintain a certain level of performance, such as

- a maximum debt-to-equity ratio
- a maximum percentage of dividend pay-out
- a minimum times-interest-earned ratio
- a minimum level of shareholders' equity

These provisions are known as maintenance tests or covenants. If a company fails to meet the covenants, the lender (or trustee, in the case of publicly-issued bonds) has the right to call the loan and force immediate repayment. Since the debtor seldom will be able to satisfy the call for repayment, the company is forced into reorganization or receivership.

Shareholders' agreements in private corporations also usually contain provisions that affect the valuation of shares if a shareholder decides to sell her or his shares. Sales of shares in a private corporation can be made only through private contracting with a third party, or by selling the shares back to the corporation. Often, shareholders' agreements include a requirement that shares offered for sale must first be offered to the other existing shareholders, who have the *right of first refusal*. If existing shareholders do not agree to buy the shares, then the selling shareholder can approach other interested investors. Since there is no public market for the shares of private corporations, there is no easily identifiable market price. The market price is normally determined on the basis of the financial statements. In theory, the value of shares is a function of future earnings (and cash flow) and of the fair value of the corporation's net assets. In practice, most shareholders' agreements stipulate that the price is based on historical earnings and on net asset book values.[5]

Accounting policy choices and accounting estimates can have a significant effect on the ratios used in debt agreements and for share valuation in shareholders' agreements. GAAP provides quite a bit of flexibility in accounting policy choice, and accounting policy choices can have a substantial impact on financial statement ratios. Therefore, some debt agreements (particularly in private placements) stipulate the accounting policies that will be used in calculating the ratios in order to restrict management's ability to select policies that will enhance the ratios.[6]

Similarly, the share valuation components of shareholders' agreements often contain specific provisions concerning the valuation of net assets. These provisions are not constrained by GAAP, and therefore may be more suitable to the needs of the shareholders for a fair valuation of their shares than would a GAAP-based valuation.

---

[5] Jeffrey Kantor, *Valuation of Unlisted Shares* (CCH Canadian Limited, 1988), p. 224.

[6] For example, see Daniel B. Thornton and Murray J. Bryant, *GAAP vs. TAP in Lending Agreements: Canadian Evidence* (Toronto: Canadian Academic Accounting Association, 1986). Professors Thornton and Bryant studied the use of tailored accounting policies for leases in lending agreements.

Stewardship

A question commonly asked by business investors, by taxpayers, and by donors to charitable organizations is: "What did they do with my money?" A *steward* is a person who is responsible for managing an enterprise on behalf of someone else. The word originally applied to the person who managed large household estates on behalf of the owners. Stewardship reporting, therefore, focuses on showing the financial statement reader just how the resources entrusted to management's care were managed. Transparency is important; full disclosure should exist, not obscured by a large number of allocations and imputations that obscure the operating results for the year.

The stewardship objective is most clearly dominant in reporting for non-profit organizations, where donors and members need to see how managers used the resources at their disposal for the period. In profit-oriented enterprises, the objective of stewardship is reflected in full disclosure, revealing in the notes to the financial statements much information on the company's financial position, disclosure which often is well in excess of the recommendations of the *CICA Handbook*. The role of stewardship is especially clear in the case of mutual fund reporting, where the investment activity of the organization is fully documented in order to satisfy investors' natural inquisitiveness about the nature of the fund's investments and the level of investment activity during the year.

Performance Evaluation

Financial statement readers often use the statements to evaluate management performance. The common use of bonus schemes based on reported earnings as means of compensating senior executives attests to the wide-spread use of financial statements for this purpose.

Performance evaluation is a concern not only of external users, but may also be a concern of managers themselves. Managers are users of financial statements in order to (1) evaluate their own performance and (2) evaluate the performance of the managers of subsidiaries and other related companies in a corporate family of companies.

In order to be useful for performance evaluation, financial statements should reflect the basis on which management decisions are made, at least to the extent possible. For example, suppose that a cruise line builds and introduces a new ship. There are substantial costs involved in staffing and training a new staff. The costs are incurred because a properly trained staff is essential to successful operation of the ship. If performance evaluation is a reporting objective, these costs are deferred and amortized in order to be matched against the revenue that they are intended to enhance. If cash flow prediction were the dominant objective instead, then the costs would be expensed when incurred.

Managers are fully aware of the performance evaluation objective of financial statements, and the managers of widely-held public companies are apt to be quite sensitive to the earnings impacts of accounting policy choices. Therefore, managers have strong motivations to select accounting policies that will enhance their apparent performance. The issue of management motivations in financial accounting policy selection is an important one, and is the subject of the next section.

MANAGEMENT MOTIVATIONS

While the needs of external financial statement users are vital to developing appropriate financial reporting objectives *for each specific enterprise*, managers have motivations of their own that influence their selection of accounting policies and their accounting estimates. These motivations often conflict with users' objectives and may dominate the accounting choice process if the users lack the power to enforce the dominance of their objectives. This section will briefly discuss the most common management motivations.

Income Maximization or Minimization

The maximization of net income is one of the most common motivations of managers. This motive stems from three powerful concerns:

1. to make it easier to comply with debt covenants, and to provide a margin of safety between the covenant requirements and the reported numbers (to keep lenders from getting edgy);
2. to positively influence users' judgement in evaluating the performance of management (to help them keep their jobs and to enhance their public standing); and
3. to enhance managers' compensation, in the many corporations wherein management compensation is tied either to net income or to stock price performance (or both).

These concerns are particularly relevant for the managers of public companies, because ownership is dispersed and there is a general concern on the part of the shareholders and the Board of Directors about the share price. Managers believe, not without reason, that share prices are affected by reported earnings. There is ample evidence to show that investors in an efficient public market are able to "see through" accounting manipulations that are intended to maximize earnings. However, this ability has shown only to be short-run. In the long run, the information that is necessary to make adjustments for accounting policy differences often disappears from view, and there is no evidence that shareholders are able to "see through" complex earnings maximization objectives.

As well, the wide distribution of shares of a widely-held public company makes it infeasible for the managers to point out that their "true" performance may be better than that indicated by earnings numbers that are prepared with the objective (for example) of minimizing income taxes.

Sometimes, a corporation will elect to *maximize a loss* in one year as part of an ongoing strategy to *maximize earnings*. The philosophy is that if there is going to be an operating loss anyway, they might as well take advantage of the opportunity to load as many losses into that year as possible (known as "taking a big bath" or a "big hit"). It is not at all unusual to see a corporation (in a bad year) announcing changes to accounting estimates that increase the total loss, including substantial write-downs of investments and capital assets. If a company writes down its capital assets (tangible or intangible), there remains less amortization to charge in future years, thereby enhancing *future* earnings. Another ploy is to make a substantial provision (charged to expense) for restructuring costs or for the costs of discontinued operations. If these costs turn out to have been over-estimated (justified by the principle of *conservatism*), the company will recognize a *gain* in future periods.

Instead of *maximizing* reported earnings, management may wish to *minimize* reported earnings as an ongoing endeavour. In addition to the possible objective of minimizing income taxes, management may strive to reduce earnings for any of the following reasons:

- to avoid public embarrassment by reducing a high level of reported earnings;
- to avoid attracting competitors into a very lucrative business;
- to discourage hostile takeover bids;
- to avoid the scrutiny of regulators or politicians; or
- to discourage large wage claims (or to justify initiatives for wage reductions and cutbacks).

Accounting policies that serve to maximize earnings include early revenue recognition and delayed expense recognition (including a defer-and-amortize approach to the widest possible array of costs). Accounting policies for minimizing earnings are just the opposite: delay revenue recognition and expense every cost in sight as soon as possible.

Income Smoothing

Canadian managers seem to be fond of showing a smooth record of earnings, free of disturbing peaks and valleys. Widely fluctuating earnings are an indication of business risk, and managers often do not want investors or creditors to perceive the company as being risky.

Income can be smoothed by taking advantage of the many opportunities available (within GAAP) for spreading both revenues and costs over several periods. The defer-and-amortize approach beloved by many managers and supported by the *CICA Handbook* is a reflection of wide acceptance of the income smoothing motivation.

Accounting estimates also provide a great opportunity for income smoothing. By edging various accounting estimates up or down within the feasible range, management often can significantly affect the net income amount. Remember that net income is a residual which is only a small proportion of the overall level of activity of the business. It doesn't take much change in the amount of accruals, the estimate of bad debts, or the write-down of inventory to smooth this residual. The impact of accounting estimates is invisible to the external user. There is no need for management to disclose the vast majority of accounting estimates; their impact is simply impounded in the numbers to which they relate.

Minimum Compliance

Minimum compliance refers to the motivation of managers to reveal the least amount of information that is possible within the recommendations of the *CICA Handbook* and still receive a clean audit opinion (assuming that a clean opinion is needed in the circumstances).

Minimum compliance may be a motivation for managers in a public company because management does not wish to give outsiders any more information about the company than is absolutely necessary. Managers may wish to maintain confidentiality about their business activities in order to keep competitors in the dark.

Minimum compliance is usually equated with *minimum cost* of providing accounting information. However, the buyers and sellers of public companies' shares may value a company's shares at a lower level if they feel that the company is being less than forthcoming about its operations and financial position. Minimum compliance may save accounting and auditing costs, but may bear a cost in reduced share prices.

In a private company, management and the shareholders have access to whatever information they need, and the general financial statements may be of no more use than to accompany the tax return. The information needs of bankers and other lenders may be served by special purpose reports, even when the lenders do require an audited financial statement. In these circumstances, the company is likely also to use accounting policies that coincide (to the extent possible) with the policies used for income tax purposes. Depreciation on fixed assets, for example, will be calculated on the same basis as for Capital Cost Allowance for tax purposes; inventory costs will be calculated on the same basis for accounting and tax purposes; costs that are deductible immediately for income tax purposes will be expensed immediately on the income statement; and so forth.

Expanded Disclosure

The opposite to minimum compliance may be called expanded disclosure. Management may wish to disclose a great deal of information that they are not required to disclose under GAAP. The motivation for expanded disclosure may be simply to indicate that the company and its management are "good citizens" who have nothing to hide and wish to provide the most informative financial statements possible. Sometimes, expanded disclosure is motivated by the expected concerns of specific stakeholders.

For example, a company that might be accused of polluting the environment may choose to disclose its environmental record and its efforts to curb pollution and/or clean up an already-polluted environment. By providing additional disclosure, management may hope to forestall criticism of the company's pollution control efforts.

In other situations, the company may be complying voluntarily with the disclosure expectations of current or expected future stakeholders outside of Canada. For instance, a company that expects to do significant business (or raise significant capital) in Europe may provide supplemental disclosure on its employment record and employment benefits, as well as on environmental and ethical aspects of its business. Such disclosure is expected of responsible companies in Europe, even though these types of disclosures are not a normal part of Canadian reporting practice.

Finally, a company may provide expanded voluntary disclosures in order to reassure the capital markets that the company is a good investment. Although financial projections (e.g., of management's forecast of future earnings) are not provided in annual financial statements, information on product demand may be provided in the notes or in management's discussion and analysis; examples include information such as the value of current contracts for a service company or the order backlog for a manufacturer.

OBJECTIVES VS. MOTIVATIONS

Users' objectives and managers' motivations often conflict. Being aware of users' objectives, it is not uncommon for managers to attempt to put the best picture on the corporation's operations and financial position. The resolution of this conflict depends on general concepts of fair presentation and often presents an ethical dilemma for management, for the company's accountants, and for auditors (if any). Prioritizing conflicting objectives is part of the exercise of professional judgement that is discussed further in Chapter 2.

CONCEPT REVIEW

1. Why is it important to establish the financial reporting objectives for a company?
2. Give an example of how the reporting objectives of a public company may differ from those of a private corporation.
3. How might a *shareholders' agreement* influence a company's financial reporting objectives?
4. Why might the objectives of financial statement users conflict with the motivations of managers?

SUMMARY OF KEY POINTS

1. Financial accounting is concerned with the preparation of financial statements that report on the financial position and results of operations for an entity as a whole.

2. Financial accounting encompasses all types of organizations (profit-seeking, non-profit, and governmental) and all types of ownership (proprietorships, partnerships, share corporations).

3. A corporation that issues securities (debt or equity) to the general public is a public corporation that must abide by the regulations of the securities commissions in the jurisdiction(s) in which its securities are traded.

4. Public corporations generally must comply with generally accepted accounting principles in their financial reporting.

5. The vast majority of corporations in Canada are private corporations. About half of the corporations listed in the *FP500* are private. Many large private corporations are wholly-owned subsidiaries of non-Canadian parents; the others are

family-owned. Of large public Canadian corporations, most have a control block that is in individual or family hands.

6. Private corporations do not need to have an audit, provided that all of the shareholders have access to financial information and agree unanimously to waive the audit. Private corporations, even if they are audited, may choose to use some accounting policies that are not a part of GAAP.

7. Private corporations that use other than generally accepted accounting principles may prepare their financial statements on a disclosed basis of accounting.

8. Generally accepted accounting principles are those that have found general acceptance in practice. The AcSB recommendations contained in the *CICA Handbook* are a part of GAAP, but are only a relatively small part.

9. *CICA Handbook* recommendations are issued by the CICA's Accounting Standards Board (AcSB) after following a process of public exposure of the proposed new or revised recommendations and after being approved by a two-thirds vote of the Board.

10. The *Income Tax Act* and the regulations and policies of Revenue Canada are not a part of GAAP. However, income taxation does have an impact on the accounting policies used by corporations because the accounting policies may affect the amount of tax paid. A copy of a corporation's financial statements (unconsolidated) must be appended to its tax return, and all differences between taxable income and accounting income must be reconciled in a supporting schedule to the tax return, the T2(S1).

11. Accounting standards in the U.S. have an impact on those in Canada. However, the different professional, legal, and economic environment in Canada makes U.S. accounting standards not directly applicable to Canadian enterprise.

12. The CICA has been an active participant in the International Accounting Standards Committee (IASC), which strives to establish world-wide compatibility of accounting standards.

13. International accounting standards are widely accepted on international stock exchanges for the financial reporting of foreign companies. Canada and the U.S. do not accept international standards on their exchanges, however, and therefore are exceptions to general world-wide practice.

14. It is impossible to impose a single, dominant objective on financial reporting. The objectives of financial reporting must be determined with reference to the organization's environment and its stakeholders, and with regard to the users' decisions that the financial statements are intended to facilitate.

15. A financial reporting objective that is often appropriate for lenders, creditors, and shareholders is cash flow prediction. Financial stakeholders need to be able to predict a corporation's ability to generate cash flow from operations to service debt or to pay dividends. Under a cash flow objective, revenues and expenses are recognized in a way that corresponds (on an accrual basis) with cash flow.

16. Another very common objective is that of income tax minimization, especially for private corporations. Public corporations are less likely to have this as a primary objective, however, because they may be more concerned about the perceptions of other users of the statements than about saving taxes in the short run. An income tax minimization objective leads to delayed revenue recognition and faster expense recognition.

17. Financial statement readers often use the statements to assess the corporation's adherence to contract requirements, such as those in loan agreements and shareholders' agreements.

18. A major objective is that of performance evaluation. Statements that are prepared to facilitate the evaluation of management's performance will use reporting policies that coincide as closely as possible to the basis for management's operating decisions.

19. Managers are the preparers of financial statements. Managers often have motivations that stem from their desire to influence the decisions of external users, particularly those of public companies. Managers may be tempted to adopt accounting policies and make accounting estimates that tend to maximize reported earnings, minimize earnings, smooth earnings, or show compliance with contract provisions such as loan covenants.

20. Minimum compliance may be a reporting objective of managers. Minimum compliance may be intended to reduce accounting costs and to conceal information from competitors. Private companies, in particular, may have few external users and may be interested in reducing their accounting costs by preparing statements that are largely in accordance with taxation principles.

21. The motivations of preparers often conflict with the financial reporting objectives that are appropriate for external users in a particular situation. Accountants must use their professional judgement to try to reconcile such conflicts ethically and to avoid issuing financial statements that contain biased measurements.

QUESTIONS

1-1   What is financial accounting?

1-2   Describe the difference between point statements and flow statements, giving an example of each.

1-3   Describe three types of organizations for which financial statements must be prepared.

1-4   Explain the distinction between financial and management accounting.

1-5   What is the difference between public and private companies? What are the accounting implications of this difference?

1-6   What is a control block? What are the accounting policy implications?

1-7   Define generally accepted accounting principles, including their source.

1-8   What body sets standards in Canada? What organizations have given authority to these standards?

1-9   Who appoints the AcSB committee members? Why are a variety of organizations included?

1-10 Briefly explain the steps followed by the AcSB to develop an accounting standard.

1-11 What factors make the AcSB an effective standard-setting body?

1-12 What is the role of the Emerging Issues Committee?

1-13 Name the two major factors that influence the spread of accounting policies from one country to another. What force is most noticeable in Canada?

1-14 Why should Canadian standards be similar to those found in the U.S.? What are the arguments against this phenomenon?

1-15 What is the IASC? Describe the status of IASC standards.

1-16 Explain the importance of IASC standards to stock exchanges around the world.

1-17 What are TAP? RAP? Explain.

1-18 What is a disclosed basis of accounting? Explain.

1-19 What are the objectives of general purpose financial statements? What common specific objectives may a set of financial statements be tailored to serve?

1-20 How can financial statements have an economic impact on an organization?

1-21 If a set of financial statements were meant to portray the cash flows of an organization, what kinds of accounting policies would likely be chosen?

1-22 What accounting policies would best serve the reporting objective of tax minimization?

1-23 What is a covenant? What kinds of accounting policies would be common among companies with severe restrictive covenants?

1-24 Describe how the motivations of managers are different than those of shareholders. What accounting policies might be commonly found if managers receive bonuses based on net income?

1-25 What is income smoothing? What is a "big bath"?

1-26 What would characterize a set of financial statements designed to provide minimum compliance?

CASE 1-1

John Plowit

You, CA, a sole practitioner, are sitting in your office when your most important agricultural client, John Plowit, walks in. Mr Plowit runs a large dairy farm.

"I'm sorry to barge in like this, but I've just been to see my banker. He suggested that I ask you to explain to me some matters that affect my statements. You will recall that I needed to renew my loans this year. The new bank manager wants some changes made to my statements before he will process my loan application.

The banker wants me to switch from a cash basis of accounting to an accrual basis. The cash basis provides me with the information I need to evaluate my performance for the year — after all, what I make in a year is the cash left in the bank once the harvest is sold.

And I only use these statements for my banker and to pay tax! I know the tax department will accept either the cash or accrual basis.

Also, the bank wants me to value all my cattle at their market value. Why do they want me to group all my cattle together when they aren't the same? Some are used for breeding and some just for milk. Personally, I don't see the sense in valuing them at market when most of them won't be sold or replaced for a very long time.

I realize that I must provide the type of information that the bank manager wants, but I am very interested in understanding why. After all, I'm the one who has to pay for all of this!"

Required:

Respond to Mr. Plowit.

[CICA, adapted]

CASE 1-2

Chan & Baaz

Sandy Chan and Philip Baaz have operated an import and sales partnership for 15 years. They import a variety of food products into Canada and distribute them through small grocery specialty stores and some chains in southern Ontario. At times, they have made up to $150,000 per year (profits and losses are split evenly); however, the lingering recession has hurt their business, and profits were $80,000 last year. Philip Baaz, in his late 50s and financially secure, has decided to retire. Tired of Canadian winters, he has retired to Mexico and left the partnership in Sandy Chan's hands.

Sandy Chan is in his mid-40s, and through a series of personal tribulations, is nowhere near as financially secure as his partner. He does not have the resources to buy out Baaz personally, and there is no cash in the partnership at the moment. Assets consist of receivables and inventory. A significant downsizing would be required to buy out Baaz with a payment from the partnership right now. Baaz, however, is in no hurry for his money. The partners have agreed that for the rest of this year, Chan will operate the business alone, and profits will be split evenly. At year-end, Baaz will leave the partnership and take back a five-year note payable for the book value of the balance in his partnership account, which would include his share of current year profits. While Baaz would not have helped generate this year's profits, this allocation was agreed to be fair due to his past contributions.

At the end of the year, you have arrived to prepare the financial statements for the year. You are a professional accountant. The partnership has been your client for 15 years (since the partnership was formed), and you are on excellent terms with the partners and their staff. You have met with the bookkeeper and obtained the following information:

- The partnership has always established an allowance for doubtful accounts based on specific identification of problem accounts, since Chan and Baaz had personal contact with their customers. This year, the allowance has been based on a percentage of sales — at a rate that is double the historical trend. The bookkeeper has assured you that most receivables are current, but "there's a recession on and we expect some problems to crop up."
- During the year, a sizeable amount of inventory acquired during the last two years was written off. The bookkeeper explained that the product was not perishable, and it was still in the warehouse. The product was very slow moving, and Chan had given up trying to sell it.
- A personal computer and laser printer were acquired for office use late in the year. Consistent with prior policy, a full year's amortization was booked in the year of acquisition. Previous office equipment has been amortized using the straight-line method, but the computer is being amortized on a 40% declining balance scheme "because of the risk of technological obsolescence."

You have a meeting scheduled with Chan this afternoon to discuss accounting policies and operating results; Baaz is still in Mexico.

Required:

Write a brief report on which to base your discussion with Chan. Describe how Chan and Baaz have different reporting objectives. Outline the issues and alternatives, then write an analysis of each issue and your recommendation.

[CGA-Canada, adapted]

EXERCISES

E1-1 *Chapter Overview:* Indicate whether each of the following statements is true or false.

1. External decision makers lack direct access to the information generated by the internal operations of a company.
2. The presence of restrictive bond covenants, specifying minimum times-interest-earned ratios, means that an organization will have a tendency to pick discretionary accounting policies that minimize income. (Note: Times-interest-earned is calculated as income before interest and taxes, divided by interest.)
3. The primary objective of financial accounting is to report on stewardship.
4. All generally accepted accounting principles are the result of a designated rule-making body.
5. Company earnings goals are often tailored to a smooth pattern of earnings growth.
6. Accounting imperialism manifests itself in Canada through the prevalence of U.K.

accounting practices, reflecting Canada's roots in the British Commonwealth.

7. The standard-setting process followed by the AcSB allows for due process input by the user and preparer communities before a standard is promulgated.
8. The EIC provides technical guidance to the AcSB on matters of limited importance and scope.
9. GAAP includes practices that have evolved and gained acceptance over time.
10. IASC standards must be followed by countries who do not develop their own standards in order to facilitate access to international capital markets.

E1-2 *Chapter Overview:* Indicate whether each statement is true or false.

1. Financial accounting focuses primarily on the needs of shareholders.
2. GAAP must be followed for financial accounting reports.
3. The presence of a control block can have an impact on a company's choice of accounting policies.
4. Canada and the U.S. have similar legal, economic, and financing structures, so that similar accounting standards are most appropriate for the two countries.
5. Entities whose financial reports are meant to address cash flow objectives are primarily concerned with maximizing cash flows.
6. A company that wishes to report smooth earnings is attempting to appear less risky to financial statement users.
7. Performance evaluation is well served by accounting policies that delay revenue recognition and recognize expenses close to the time that they are incurred.
8. The Accounting Standards Board's due process, used to establish new accounting standards in Canada, is slow and therefore inefficient.
9. IASC standards have no legal status on their own.
10. A company may use a DBA for financial reporting.

E1-3 *Accounting Policy Choices:* Entities may have a variety of corporate reporting objectives specific to their circumstances, such as

　　a. Assessing and predicting cash flows
　　b. Income tax minimization
　　c. Contract compliance (in this case, debt covenants that specify minimum levels of shareholders' equity)
　　d. Performance evaluation of managers

For each of the accounting policies listed below, indicate which of the objectives of corporate reporting is best served. Each policy may serve more than one objective.

1. Capitalize and amortize costs.
2. Provide full disclosure of five-year cash flow for loan repayments.
3. Defer expenses to match them against revenue generated from the activity.
4. Recognize revenue as cash is collected.
5. Defer revenue as long as possible.
6. Recognize revenues as effort is spent.
7. Recognize expenses close to the time that they are paid for.

E1-4 *Effect of Accounting Policies:* A company has two debt covenants in place:

　　a. Maximum debt-to-equity ratio
　　　•Current and long-term liabilities, excluding future (deferred) income taxes, are divided by total shareholders' equity
　　b. Minimum times-interest-earned ratio
　　　•Income before interest and taxes is divided by total interest expense

For each of the accounting policy choices listed below, indicate which ratio(s), if any, would be affected, and whether the policy would increase or decrease the ratio.

1. Depreciation method is straight-line, rather than declining balance.
2. Costs that could either be deferred and written off or expensed immediately are expensed immediately.
3. Interest expense could be measured using straight-line amortization for the debt discount; alternatively, the effective interest rate method could be used. The straight-line method results in lower interest expense in the early years, and is the chosen policy.
4. An issue of preferred shares that has the characteristics of debt (guaranteed cash flows to the investor), is reclassified as debt, from the equity section.
5. Warranty expense is accrued as sales are made, rather than expensing it as warranty claims are paid.
6. Revenue is recorded as goods are delivered, rather than when cash is later collected.

E1-5 *Acronyms:* The language of accounting is littered with acronyms, abbreviations for common organizations or phrases. These are listed on the left in the section that follows. To the right are commonly used abbreviations. Match the phrase or organization with its abbreviation.

Phrase or Organization		Abbreviation	
1.	International Accounting Standards Committee	A.	AcSB
2.	Tailored Accounting Principles	B.	GAAP
3.	Emerging Issues Committee	C.	CICA
4.	Ontario Securities Commission	D.	SFAS
5.	Accounting Standards Board	E.	SEC
6.	Financial Accounting Standards Board	F.	CBCA
7.	Canadian Institute of Chartered Accountants	G.	DBA
8.	Securities and Exchange Commission	H.	EIC
9.	*Canada Business Corporations Act*	I.	IASC
10.	Disclosed Basis of Accounting	J.	FASB
11.	Generally Accepted Accounting Principles	K.	OSC
12.	Statement of Financial Accounting Standards	L.	TAP

E1-6 *Standard Setting Process:* The accounting profession has a long history of developing accounting standards that are part of generally accepted accounting principles (GAAP). Listed below are some stages in the due process that creates accounting standards. Indicate the order of the steps, and match each step with a description of the activity.

Order	Description	Step	Activity
		1. Re-exposure draft	A. A group of experts
		2. Statement of principles	B. Preliminary response to issues raised
		3. Revisions	C. Circulated to accountants and interested users
		4. Project proposal	D. Identify accounting problems
		5. Exposure draft	E. Modifications re-circulated for feed-back
		6. *CICA Handbook* section	F. Comments from specific individuals
		7. Appoint task force	G. Final product
		8. Review with associates	H. Identify issues
		9. Issues paper	I. Changes based on written feedback

P1-1 *Neutrality and Standard Setting:* A speaker at a recent conference stated: "Many groups, including governments, financial institutions, investors, and corporations in various industries, argue that their interests are affected by present and proposed accounting pronouncements. The sometimes contradictory interests of these groups are recognized by the accounting profession in the standard-setting process. However, accounting is neutral and is not influenced by the self-interest of any one group."

Required:

Write a report that discusses the issues raised.

[CICA, adapted]

P1-2 *Accounting Principles:* At the completion of the annual audit of the financial statements of Alt Corporation, the president of the company asked about the meaning of the phrase generally accepted accounting principles, which appears in the audit report accompanying the financial statements.

You have been asked to respond in writing to the president's question. You have decided to respond by considering the following:

a. What is the meaning of the term accounting principles as used in audit reports? (excluding what "generally accepted" means)
b. How does one determine whether an accounting principle is generally accepted?
c. Diversity in accounting practice will, and should, always exist among companies despite efforts to improve comparability. Discuss arguments that support this statement.

[AICPA, adapted]

P1-3 *Canadian versus U.S. Standards:* There are many similarities, but also some significant differences, between Canadian and U.S. standards. Explain the factors that support common standards, and the factors that support differences between accounting standards of the two countries.

P1-4 *International Harmonization of Accounting Standards:* What would Canada gain from achieving a greater harmonization (less diversity) in world-wide accounting standards? Write a brief essay to support your opinion. Include a description of the IASC in your response.

P1-5 *Accounting Policy Disagreement:* You have been hired as the assistant in the finance department of a medium-sized publicly-traded firm. Realizing the importance of accounting to your new duties, you have recently completed an introductory course in financial accounting. In this course, you learned that research costs are expensed during the period they are incurred. You also recall, however, that accountants believe in matching the costs of a given activity with the revenues resulting from that activity.

Recently, your firm has developed an important breakthrough in electronic copying equipment. The research cost has been considerable. If this cost were capitalized this year and written off against expected future revenues from the new machine that will eventually be developed, this year's earnings per share would increase by 10% rather than show a modest decline.

Your superior clearly favours capitalization because the firm's CEO wants to continue a 20-quarter record of increasing earnings per share figures. She has asked your opinion based on your recent exposure to accounting standards. A meeting with your superior is set for tomorrow morning.

In the meantime, you have researched your firm's past practice in this area and you have reread the accounting standard, Section 3450 of the *CICA Handbook*. Although your firm has not previously experienced the level of research expenses associated with the present project, past practice in your firm has been to expense these costs. Your reading of the accounting standard confirms what you recall from class — namely, that these expenditures should be expensed.

Unfortunately, your superior is anxious to take the alternative position and has been known to be intolerant of views differing from her own. How would you handle the meeting the next day?

P1-6 *Non-GAAP Situations:* A manager of a medium-sized, private company recently complained, "I'm confused! I always thought that companies had to comply with GAAP. Now I hear that there are many companies who don't use GAAP, and other circumstances where GAAP is not really appropriate."

Required:

Explain the status of GAAP to this manager. Be sure to distinguish between general purpose and special purpose financial statements.

P1-7 *Objectives of Financial Reporting:* The *CICA Handbook* sets out the objectives of general purpose financial statements, but companies and their managers have objectives that relate to their specific circumstances. Explain these objectives, and how they impact on the choice of accounting policy.

P1-8 *Policy Choice:* Marcon Properties Ltd. is a diversified company that owns approximately 60 retail properties, which they have operated as discount department stores. These stores are small, stand-alone properties that Marcon owns outright, although most properties are heavily mortgaged. In 20X1, the company decided, due to increasing losses from retail operations, that all discount department stores should be closed and properties converted to rental units. This process was successfully started in 20X1, with 22 of 60 properties signed to long-term rental agreements with tenants. It is now the end of 20X1, and all retail operations have ceased. There are 38 properties currently sitting vacant. Marcon believes that it can successfully lease the remaining properties over the next 9 to 23 months.

An accounting policy issue has come up, in relation to the vacant properties, for the 20X1 fiscal year, namely, whether the properties should be depreciated during the period that they sit vacant prior to rental. Those in favour of recording depreciation point out that the properties continue to deteriorate during the period in which they are idle, and that depreciation is meant to allow for obsolescence, not just wear and tear. Those that favour suspension of depreciation point out that depreciation should be matched with the rental revenue that the properties will generate in the future.

Marcon is reporting a positive net income in 20X1, generated from a variety of other activities.

Required:

Explain which accounting policy you would expect to be adopted in the following independent circumstances. Note that in some circumstances, the company will be indifferent as to the policy chosen.

1. Marcon has a team of senior managers that is compensated with a cash bonus based on a percentage of annual net income. Senior managers will pick the policy.

2. Marcon is financed 60% through debt and 40% through equity, and has debt covenants that specify minimum debt-to-equity and return on assets (net income divided by total assets.)

3. Marcon is managed by its major shareholders, who wish to minimize income tax payments.

4. Marcon is a public company and wants to show a smooth earnings trend.

5. Marcon has a team of senior managers that is compensated with a cash bonus based on a percentage of annual income. Assume for this part only that the company will report a loss in 20X1 from other sources, and managers will not receive any bonus this year.

6. Marcon's controlling shareholders are not directly involved in the business and they wish to use the financial statements as a method to evaluate the stewardship and performance of managers.

Criteria for Accounting Choices

INTRODUCTION

This chapter discusses the criteria that accountants use to develop financial statements that external decision-makers can use with reasonable levels of reliability and confidence. Accounting is often a matter of making choices among possible accounting policies and accounting estimates. What criteria should be used to measure the various alternatives, and thus come up with the most appropriate choice?

As we discussed in the last chapter, establishing users and user needs is integral to the choice of accounting policies on a situation by situation basis. After all, accounting information is used by particular individuals to make decisions. If the information can't be used to support decisions, it is worthless. Furthermore, policy should not be chosen to manipulate or misrepresent a particular situation because such information is biased and misleading. Deliberately presenting misleading information in the financial statements is highly unethical, to say the least, and may be tantamount to fraud. Accountants have a vested interest in maintaining the credibility of financial statements, despite some considerable temptation for short-term gain in certain situations!

Accounting standard setters have an even more difficult task than those in charge of picking accounting policies for a particular company. Standard setters must establish accounting policy that is acceptable for a wide variety of situations, and a wide variety of companies. Where do they start? The standard-setting process was reviewed in Chapter 1, and its reliance on due process, which allows many diverse views to be heard, was noted. But again, where do standard setters turn after listening to all the arguments? Clearly, it can't be a majority rule situation, or lobbyists would dominate.

This chapter looks at the financial statement concepts and principles that guide accounting choices. These concepts and principles underlie the exercise of professional judgement. An accountant cannot exercise professional judgement without recognizing the existence of several types of underlying principles; it is these sets of principles that provide the criteria that distinguish professional judgement from the exercise of uninformed opinion or bias.

SORTING OUT ACCOUNTING "PRINCIPLES"

The generally accepted body of accounting principles is a rather motley collection. If one were to ask someone in business to give examples of accounting principles, they would likely come up with a list that includes concepts such as historical cost, consistency, matching, going concern, and objectivity. The general body of accounting "principles," however, actually consists of three different types of concepts: underlying assumptions, measurement conventions, and qualitative criteria. They may be distinguished as follows:

- Underlying assumptions (or postulates) are the basic foundation upon which our generally accepted accounting rests. The accounting principle (or *concept*) of going concern is an *underlying assumption*.

- Measurement methods (or measurement conventions) are the various ways in which financial position and the results of operations can be reported. These are the *accounting choices* that management of every organization must make. The accounting principles of historical cost and matching are examples of *measurement conventions*, both of which are based on the underlying assumption of going concern.

- Qualitative criteria (or qualitative characteristics) are the criteria which, *in conjunction with the organization's reporting objectives*, are used to evaluate the possible measurement options and choose the most appropriate accounting policies *for the given situation*. The principles of consistency and objectivity are examples of *qualitative criteria*.

Measurement conventions (or *methods*) are *how* transactions and events are measured and reported; qualitative criteria (or characteristics) are *why* they are measured that way, provided that the underlying assumptions are valid in the particular situation. For example, historical cost is a widely used (but not universally used) measurement method in which in many (but not all) situations, assets are reported at their acquisition cost. One of the primary reasons that *historical cost* (a measurement method) is so commonly used is that it is perceived as being more *objective* (a qualitative criterion) than possible alternative measurement methods. But the use of *historical cost* depends on the reporting enterprise's *continuity* as a going concern (an underlying assumption).

To understand the accounting choice process, it is necessary to clearly differentiate between underlying assumptions, measurement methods and qualitative characteristics. Otherwise, one becomes hopelessly entangled in fuzzy conceptualization that fails to recognize implicit assumptions. *Historical cost* is not a fundamental concept of financial accounting, but *objectivity* is. Without a high degree of objectivity, accounting reports would have no credibility and accounting would not serve its most basic societal mission of conveying information. But there are many situations in which historical cost is not the appropriate measurement method, situations in which market value is both highly objective and more *relevant* (which is another qualitative criterion).

To construct financial statements for a particular enterprise, it is necessary first to establish the facts of the business and its operating and economic environment, then to determine the objectives of financial reporting, and finally to develop the statements by using situation-appropriate accounting policies to measure the elements of the financial statements. This process can be illustrated by the pyramid shown in Exhibit 2-1. The financial statements themselves are the apex of the process; the foundation is the objectives, facts and constraints for the reporting enterprise. The objectives, facts, and constraints were introduced in Chapter 1; this chapter will focus on the three levels of principles that build upon the objectives, facts, and constraints.

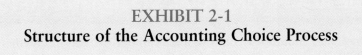

EXHIBIT 2-1
Structure of the Accounting Choice Process

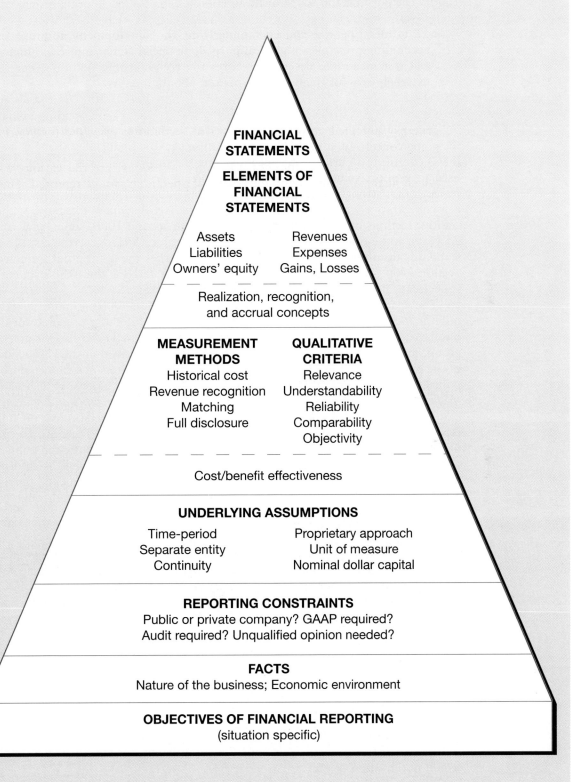

FINANCIAL STATEMENTS

ELEMENTS OF FINANCIAL STATEMENTS

Assets	Revenues
Liabilities	Expenses
Owners' equity	Gains, Losses

Realization, recognition, and accrual concepts

MEASUREMENT METHODS	**QUALITATIVE CRITERIA**
Historical cost	Relevance
Revenue recognition	Understandability
Matching	Reliability
Full disclosure	Comparability
	Objectivity

Cost/benefit effectiveness

UNDERLYING ASSUMPTIONS

Time-period	Proprietary approach
Separate entity	Unit of measure
Continuity	Nominal dollar capital

REPORTING CONSTRAINTS
Public or private company? GAAP required?
Audit required? Unqualified opinion needed?

FACTS
Nature of the business; Economic environment

OBJECTIVES OF FINANCIAL REPORTING
(situation specific)

THE ACSB'S FINANCIAL STATEMENT CONCEPTS

The *CICA Handbook* contains a section on "Financial Statement Concepts" (Section 1000). The purpose and scope of this section is

> ... to describe the concepts underlying the development and use of accounting principles in general purpose financial statements. Such financial statements are designed to meet the common information needs of external users for financial information about an entity.
>
> [*CICA* 1000.01 (italics added)]

Section 1000 is sometimes characterized as the AcSB's *conceptual framework*, but these words are not used in the section. The AcSB's financial statement concepts (FSC) constitute an attempt to put in writing the theoretical basis that the AcSB has used to support solutions to financial reporting problems. The AcSB's conceptual framework is strongly reflected in the tone of its published standards. The framework is a comparatively recent addition (1991) to the *CICA Handbook*; most of the substantive sections of the *CICA Handbook* predate Section 1000, some by as much as 25 years, while other sections have been issued after 1991. Nevertheless, the earlier standards do often reflect the thinking that underlies the conceptual framework in Section 1000. Therefore, to understand the logic underlying the AcSB's standards, it is necessary first to understand the logic behind the FSCs.

The financial statement concepts contained in Section 1000 pertain to general purpose financial statements. *General purpose* statements are those prepared for distribution to a wide, undefined public. Thus, statements prepared for a *specific* use, or user group, may well have attributes different than those described in the FSCs. Since one of the primary purposes of the FSCs is to help standard setters determine appropriate policies for wide application, their focus on generalities is appropriate. *But it also means that there are exceptions to the applicability of the concepts and conclusions!*

The *CICA Handbook* section begins by establishing a perspective on financial reporting and the limitations of information that can be reported therein. The process of financial reporting includes more than just financial statements; for public companies, it includes other information in the annual report as well as information included in prospectuses. The FSCs relate only to the statements themselves. Remember, too, that an enterprise can communicate financial results through various media. For example, press releases and statements made in interviews result in fast, widespread dissemination of information.

The financial statements themselves are limited to financial information about transactions and events. The information is based on *past* transactions, not future events, although many estimates are required about future transactions and events. As well, the basic business environment itself is acknowledged:

> In the Canadian economic environment, the production of goods and services are, to a significant extent, carried out by investor-owned business entities in the private sector and to a lesser extent by government-owned business entities. Debt and equity markets and financial institutions act as exchange mechanisms for investment resources used by these enterprises.
>
> [*CICA* 1000.07]

 The nature of the environment has a profound effect on the entire conceptual framework. If the business environment were different, the choices made in the FSC would not be appropriate:

> In a country like India, for example, private investors play a much less important part in the economy than they do in [North America]; government

and other public agencies play a larger part. The financial reporting needs of the public sector are more important there, and the objectives of financial reporting in those countries should reflect those needs.[1]

Remember, too, that if the environment changes, we must expect the FSCs to change as well, and that what is generally applicable for the business community as a whole may not be appropriate for one firm in its own unique environment.

The FSC defines the elements of financial statements (e.g., assets, liabilities, revenues, expenses) and describes basic recognition and measurement criteria. Only some of the underlying assumptions (e.g., financial capital maintenance, going concern) and a few of the qualitative criteria are discussed in Section 1000. Section 1000 cannot be described as a comprehensive theoretical framework, nor was it intended to be one. The AcSB's stated objective for the section is more modest:

> The Committee expects this Section to be used by preparers of financial statements and accounting practitioners in exercising their professional judgement as to the application of generally accepted accounting principles and in establishing accounting policies in areas in which accounting principles are developing.
>
> [*CICA* 1000.02]

The remaining sections of this chapter discuss the conceptual bases of accounting and the criteria by which accounting choices are made *in a particular situation.* Chapter 1 described the reality of the corporate sector in Canada: less than a quarter of the 800 largest Canadian corporations are widely-held public companies. Therefore, we do not confine ourselves to reporting by public companies only; to do so would be to ignore the structural reality of the Canadian economy. References will be made to the AcSB's financial statement concepts when appropriate, but the discussion is not restricted to those concepts that are included in Section 1000 of the *CICA Handbook.*

PROFESSIONAL JUDGEMENT IN ACCOUNTING

The process of making (or recommending) choices in accounting is the process of exercising **professional judgement**. Professional judgement is pervasive in accounting, and the *CICA Handbook* is full of references to the exercise of professional judgement. Indeed, one of the differentiating characteristics of most AcSB accounting standards, in contrast to their FASB cousins south of the border, is that they place a great deal of reliance on professional judgement in preference to stipulating rigid rules. As well, the need for judgement is pervasive in those many aspects of accounting that are not dealt with in the *CICA Handbook.* As we discuss various specific accounting topics throughout this textbook, we will emphasize their judgemental aspects.

In any specific situation, an accountant exercises judgement by taking into account several factors:

- the users of the financial statements, and their *specific* information needs;
- the motivations of managers;
- the organization's operations, e.g., the type of ownership, the sources of financing, the nature of its operating or earnings cycle, etc.; and
- its reporting constraints, if any, e.g., audit requirements, reporting to securities regulators, constraints imposed by foreign owners, etc.

---

[1]   David Solomons, "The FASB's Conceptual Framework: An Evaluation," *Journal of Accountancy* (June 1986), p. 118.

Alternative measurement methods, both accounting *policies* and accounting *estimates*, are considered in light of the foregoing factors, and a selection of appropriate policies is made with reference to the qualitative criteria, after making sure that the underlying assumptions are valid.

We will return to a discussion of professional judgement and the way that accounting policy choices are made at the end of this chapter. But first, we must examine the three types of accounting principles: (1) underlying assumptions, (2) qualitative criteria, and (3) measurement conventions.

CONCEPT REVIEW

1. What is the difference between the accounting principles known as *measurement methods* and those known as *qualitative criteria*?
2. What are *general purpose financial statements*?
3. What factors must a professional accountant take into account in order to exercise *professional judgement*?

UNDERLYING ASSUMPTIONS

Six basic assumptions significantly affect the recording, measuring, and reporting of accounting information.[2] They are:

1. **Time-period assumption** — that meaningful information can be assembled and reported for a time period that is less than the enterprise's life span.
2. **Separate entity assumption** — that the enterprise can be accounted for and reported independent of its owners and other stakeholders.
3. **Continuity assumption** — that the enterprise will continue in operation for the foreseeable future.
4. **Proprietary assumption** — that the results of the enterprise's operations should be reported from the viewpoint of its owners.
5. **Unit of measure assumption** — that the results of the enterprise's operations can meaningfully be measured in monetary terms.
6. **Nominal dollar capital maintenance assumption** — that the enterprise has generated a profit if its revenues are higher than the historical cost of the resources used.

An accountant must be aware of the existence of these underlying assumptions in order to be aware that there are times when the assumptions are not valid. If any of these assumptions is not valid, then the basis of accounting (or even the possibility of accounting) is called into serious question. To prepare financial statements on the "normal" basis when not all of these assumptions are valid is to prepare useless or highly misleading statements.

Time-Period Assumption

The operating results of any business enterprise cannot be known with certainty until the company has completed its life span and ceased doing business. In the meantime, external decision-makers require timely accounting information to satisfy their analytical needs. To meet their needs, the time-period assumption requires that changes

---

[2]   An early, and still very relevant, study of the underlying assumptions of accounting was published by the American Institute of Certified Public Accountants as their *Research Study No. 1*: Maurice Moonitz, *The Basic Postulates of Accounting* (NY: AICPA, 1961).

in a business's financial position be reported over a series of shorter time periods.

Although the reporting period varies, one year is the standard. Some companies use a calendar year, and others use a fiscal year-end that coincides with the low point in business activity over a 12-month period. Some businesses (e.g. retail; movie chains) report on a 52-week basis (53 weeks every few years) because their activity cycle is weekly. In addition, companies also report summarized financial information on an interim basis, usually quarterly for public reporting or monthly for internal purposes.

The time-period assumption recognizes both that decision-makers need timely financial information and that recognition of accruals and deferrals is necessary for reporting information that reasonably represents the operations of the enterprise. *Accruals* and *deferrals* distinguish **accrual-basis accounting**.

Accruals are the accounting recognition of assets and liabilities that have not yet been *realized* as a cash flow; **deferrals** refer to the delayed recognition of costs and receipts that have been realized through cash flows but have not yet contributed to the earnings process as expenses and revenues. If a demand for periodic reports did not exist during the life span of a business, accruals and deferrals would not be necessary. A company's financial statements are always dated to reflect either a precise date (balance sheet) or a particular period of time covered (income statement, retained earnings statement, and cash flow statement).

The traditional one year time-period assumption may not be appropriate for limited-life enterprises that will last longer than one year. While financial statements may be prepared at the end of a year (for income tax purposes, for example), the statements will be meaningless if both the revenue generation and expense incurring activities are in mid-stream, with no obvious resolution.

For example, the statements of junior mining companies that are still in the process of exploring or developing their sites do little more than convey the amount expended (and capitalized) to date; the attempted measurement of annual operating results in the income statement is of little predictive or evaluative use; the value of the company and its earnings ability will not be known until the exploration and development process is completed.

Separate Entity Assumption

Accounting deals with specific, identifiable business entities, each considered an accounting unit separate and apart from its owners and from other entities. A corporation is an entity that is legally quite distinct from its owners, even if the corporation is a private family corporation or has a single shareholder. No matter how closely the corporation and its owners are intertwined, they are legally separate.

For taxation purposes as well, a corporation is considered to be distinct from its owners. This it true even though many of the financial interactions between a private corporation and its shareholder(s) are strongly affected by tax considerations. Both the legal and tax views of a corporation as a distinct entity are easily translated into accounting terms; a corporation is accounted for as an entity distinct from its owners.

Partnerships and sole proprietorships do not share the legal and tax status of separate entities; in law and in taxation, they are viewed as an extension of their owners. Partners and proprietors are fully liable for the debts of the business, and the personal assets of the owners cannot legally be isolated from the business. Indeed, partners and proprietors often attempt to isolate their personal assets by transferring the legal title to their houses and cars to their spouses, children, or other relatives while retaining "constructive enjoyment" of the assets. This attempt is not always successful; bankruptcy courts may rule that such transfers are invalid and seize the transferred assets to settle debts of the business. Similarly, the profits of partnerships and proprietorships are taxed directly to the owners, as personal earnings. For accounting purposes, however, there must be an underlying assumption that a non-corporate business is distinct from its owners; otherwise, accounting for the business would be impossible.

Under the separate entity assumption, all accounting records and reports are developed from the viewpoint of a single entity, whether it is a proprietorship, a partnership, or a corporation. The assumption is that an individual's transactions are distinguishable from those of the business he or she might own. For example, the personal residence of a business owner is not considered an asset of the business even though the residence and the business are owned by the same person.

There are instances in which the separate entity assumption is not valid. Some proprietors mix their business and personal affairs to such an extent that any attempt to account for the operations of the business as a separate entity is meaningless.

Even when accounting for private corporations, the accountant must be aware of the relationship between the corporation and its owner(s), and must take care to portray this relationship realistically. For example, loans by a controlling shareholder to the corporation are, in substance, equity infusions. Bankers routinely insist that such loans be subordinated (or made secondary) to their own loans and classify the corporation's liability to its owner as equity when they perform their analysis of the company. The accountant must strive to disclose the nature of the shareholder loan so that any external user is able to understand that there is a special relationship between the creditor and the debtor.

Continuity Assumption

The continuity assumption is also known as the going-concern assumption. Under the continuity assumption, the business entity is expected not to liquidate but to continue operations for the foreseeable future. That is, it will stay in business for a period of time sufficient to carry out contemplated operations, contracts, and commitments. Note that this is not an assumption of perpetual life, but rather that the business will continue in operation long enough to recover (or use up) its assets and repay its outstanding liabilities.

This non-liquidation assumption provides a conceptual basis for many of the measurement methods used in accounting. For example, the historical cost concept assumes that the business's fixed assets will be used up over their life-time, which gives rise to the process of interperiod allocation, due to the underlying continuity assumption.

Similarly, the continuity assumption underlies the classifications used in accounting. Assets and liabilities, for example, are classified as either current or long-term on the basis of this assumption. If continuity is not assumed, the distinction between current and long-term loses its significance; all assets and liabilities become current.

If the continuity of a business enterprise is in doubt, then many commonly-used measurement methods are not appropriate. Two instances in which the continuity assumption is not valid are (1) when a business is a limited-life venture, or (2) when a business is in financial difficulty and is expected to be shut down and liquidated.

As an example of the first instance, consider a summer carnival or fair that is organized by an entrepreneur in a resort area. The fair is a one-time event, even if it may be repeated in future years. The future repetition is a separate business decision and a separate venture, and not a continuation of a going concern. In such a situation, the principle of interperiod allocation is rendered nonsensical. There will not be more than one period, and therefore the concept of interperiod allocation of revenues and expenses becomes irrelevant; what matters is the short-term cash flows from revenue and expenditure.

In the second instance, the business may be intended to continue but is unable to do so due to continuing losses. The owners, creditors, and bankruptcy trustees decide that the only remedy is to terminate the business. In a liquidation scenario, the historical cost of the assets is irrelevant and useless; conventional accounting, based on the continuity assumption, is not appropriate. Such circumstances call instead for the use of liquidation accounting, which values assets and liabilities at estimated net realizable amounts (liquidation values).

Proprietary Assumption

One of the fundamental assumptions of Canadian (and U.S.) business accounting is the proprietary assumption (or proprietary concept). The proprietary concept is one of three possible assumptions that can be used in accounting:

- The proprietary concept: an organization's financial condition and results of operations are reported from the point of view of the owners, or proprietors in an economic sense. Net income is calculated by regarding all other claims on the assets as liabilities and all payments other than those to the owners as being expenses. An important aspect of the proprietary concept is that the dominant construct is the *residual*, both owners' equity in the balance sheet and net income in the income statement.

- The entity concept: the owners are just one of many participants in the enterprise. The net value added by the enterprise (that is, the revenue minus the purchases of goods and services from third parties) is distributed to the various *factors of production* (in economic terms), consisting of providers of capital (both interest on debt and dividends on equity), labour (i.e., wages and salaries and benefits), and government (in taxes and fees for services), with any residual representing reinvestment in the enterprise. The owners constitute just one group among many.

- The fund concept: the basic accounting function is to trace the flow of funds in the organization. Net income is not a relevant concept; instead, the net fund surplus or fund deficiency (usually measured on the accrual basis) is the "bottom line."

The proprietary concept is applied to accounting for all types of *business* organizations; it has nothing to do with the *form* of organization, such as proprietorship, partnership, or corporation. *All* businesses are accounted for by using this concept. Since most of GAAP is based on the assumption that the reporting enterprise is a business, the proprietary concept is the assumption that underlies many accounting principles; thus it is known as the *proprietary assumption*.

In Canada (and the U.S.), the entity concept underlies macro-economic accounting; that is, the construction of the national income and GNP accounts. In some other countries, however, the entity concept is either permitted or required for businesses. Some developing countries require corporations to report on the entity basis because this is the only reporting basis that permits public policy-makers to discern whether a guest corporation is contributing to the national economy or is "milking" the economy for the benefit of foreigners. The information conveyed in a value-added report (discussed in the Appendix to Chapter 3) is not visible in a traditional, North American-style income statement.

For example, pick up any published corporate annual report in Canada and try to figure out from the income statement how much the corporation contributed to the economy in the form of wages — it simply cannot be done because there is no separate disclosure of wages! Nor is it possible even to figure out the net economic *value added* by the corporation. Value added is the basis of the Canadian goods and services tax (GST), and therefore the government is in a position to know, at least in gross terms, the net contribution that a business makes to the Canadian economy. However, a business's value added is not public information in Canada, nor is it used by the government for public policy determination.

The fund concept is used in governmental reporting and by many non-profit organizations. There are no owners and no residual interest in the manner that is implicit in the proprietary concept, and therefore the concept of residual interest is irrelevant. The crucial issue in fund accounting is whether expenditures (*not* expenses) were limited to the funds available through revenue. Multi-period interperiod allocations are irrelevant; matching is relevant, but the matching is of outflows to inflows (including *commitments*, unlike business accounting), rather than expenses to revenues.

Unit-of-Measure Assumption

The unit-of-measure assumption means that the results of a business's economic activities can be reported in terms of a standard monetary unit throughout the financial statements. Simply stated, the assumption is that it is possible to meaningfully prepare financial statements for Canadian enterprise because everything of relevance can be measured using the dollar as the unit of measure. Money amounts are thus the language of accounting: the common unit of measure enables dissimilar items such as the cost of a ton of coal and the amount of an account payable to be aggregated into a single total.

Unfortunately, the use of a standard monetary unit for measurement purposes poses a dilemma. If financial statements are to be meaningful, they must include all (or at least most) of the relevant information to enable a user to make informed decisions. The unit-of-measure assumption implies that *if it can't be measured, it can't be reported*. And, by extension, that *if it can't be reported, it can't be used for decision-making by external users*. This assumption means that many important aspects of a modern business's operations cannot be embodied in the financial statements, such as

- the value of customer goodwill,
- the impact of operations on the environment, or
- the value of the intellectual and human capital.

In modern industrial corporations, the environmental impact of the business's operations is very important, not only for society but also for the shareholders and other direct stakeholders. But accounting is unable to incorporate environment impacts into the statements because they do not fit the underlying assumptions of accounting, including the unit-of-measure concept.

Canada is primarily a service-based economy. The value of any successful bank, insurance company, or software company is dependent on the *intellectual capital* of its employees. If key employees leave, they take their intellectual capital with them. The value of this capital to the corporation is crucial, but there is no way (as yet conceived) to put a dollar value to this capital and thus to include it in the financial statements.

Nominal Dollar Capital Maintenance Assumption

The monetary unit of measure is often compared to a ruler, by which the dimensions of a business and its operations are measured. But unlike a ruler, that is always the same length, the relative value of a currency changes over time. The relative value of a currency can be measured in two ways:

1. in relation to the value of other currencies, or
2. in relation to the amount of goods and services that it will buy (its *purchasing power*).

These two relative values are themselves related. As the general purchasing power of a currency declines, its value in relation to currencies that have constant purchasing power also declines. A decline in the general level of purchasing power is a condition of *inflation*. Over time, the relative values of currencies of different nations will adjust to maintain their relative purchasing powers; this is known as maintaining purchasing power parity.

In Canada and the United States, accounting is performed under the assumption that every dollar of revenue and expense has the same value, regardless of whether the dollar was a 1935 dollar, a 1970 dollar, or a 1995 dollar. Dollars of different vintages are accounted for without regard to the fact that some have greater purchasing power than others. Profits and losses are determined by assuming that the value of the dollar does not change over time. Of course, the assumption of an absolutely stable dollar is not correct, but it is used because inflation in Canada has been relatively modest. Over time, however, even modest annual rates of inflation can cause large changes in purchasing power. For example, the purchasing power of the 1995 Canadian dollar was only about one-fourth of the purchasing power of the 1970 dollar.

If the operations of a business result in a profit, this causes an increase in the nominal dollar amount of owners' equity (before dividends). If the company suffers a net loss, the dollar amount of owners' equity will decline and the nominal amount of invested capital will not be maintained. This is called nominal dollar capital maintenance (or maintenance of financial capital); financial measurements are only in nominal dollars, without regard to the purchasing power of the dollars. If a unit of inventory is sold, the profit is measured as the difference between the sales price and the historical cost of the item, in nominal dollars.

Although nominal dollar capital maintenance is often viewed by U.S. and Canadian accountants as being part of the natural order of the universe, such is not the case. Countries that have sustained high rates of inflation have developed a different approach to determining whether a business's capital base has been maintained, enhanced, or eroded.

In countries with high levels of inflation (sometimes at a rate of 100% per year or more), a business is deemed to have earned a profit only if it has generated enough earnings to *maintain the purchasing power of the owners' equity*. Countries that account on this basis include Mexico, Brazil, Argentina, and Israel. Maintaining the purchasing power of the owners' investment is called constant dollar capital maintenance. When an item of inventory is sold, profit is measured as the difference between the sales proceeds and the historical cost of the item after the historical cost is *adjusted for changes in the general price level since its acquisition*.

A third approach to capital maintenance (and thus to measuring net income) is known as productive capacity capital maintenance. Under this approach, a profit is assumed to have been earned only if enough financial capital has been recovered by the end of the year to enable the business to operate at the same level at the end of the year as at the beginning. If a unit of inventory is sold, for example, the profit is measured as the difference between the sale proceeds and *the cost of replacing the item in inventory*. The *replacement cost* is also called the *current cost* of the item, and accounting based on this concept of capital maintenance is widely known as current cost accounting.

Current cost accounting is well developed. Its best known practitioner was the huge Netherlands-based multinational corporation, Philips Electronics. Philips began using current cost accounting for internal reporting in 1936 and for external reporting in 1952. In 1992, however, Philips reverted to the historical cost approach largely under pressure from the Anglo-Saxon dominated international accounting community (and possibly also to improve its apparent profitability by reporting on a nominal dollar basis).

Several Canadian public companies experimented with current cost accounting,[3] and the AcSB issued guidelines (and recommended supplementary reporting on a current cost basis) in 1982. But Canadians lost interest in current cost accounting when the rate of inflation went down (possibly temporarily) in Canada in the late 1980s and 1990s. The AcSB put the final nail in the coffin in 1991 by banning asset revaluations except for *comprehensive revaluations* in extremely limited circumstances.[4] Thus the AcSB has tied Canada's accounting inexorably to historical cost, nominal dollar accounting. If a period of rapid price changes arises again, the Canadian accounting profession will be ill-equipped to cope.[5]

---

3   For more detail, see L. S. Rosen, *Current Value Accounting and Price-Level Restatements* (Toronto: CICA, 1972).

4   Revaluations, including comprehensive revaluation, are discussed in the Appendix to Chapter 15.

5   For a more extensive discussion and illustration of these three basic concepts of capital maintenance, see Thomas H. Beechy, *Accounting for Changing Prices* (Toronto: Allyn and Bacon Inc., 1989).

CONCEPT REVIEW

1. Why may the *separate entity* assumption not be valid for a small corporation with a single shareholder?
2. When might the *continuity assumption* not be valid?
3. Describe the two concepts that are alternatives to the *proprietary concept.*
4. Which underlying assumption is not appropriate in a country that suffers triple-digit annual inflation?

QUALITATIVE CRITERIA

The first widely-distributed effort at defining the qualitative criteria of accounting measurements was published in 1966 by the American Accounting Association (AAA), which is a large association of (primarily) U.S. university and college professors of accounting. The report, *A Statement of Basic Accounting Theory*, did not explicitly use the term *qualitative criteria*, but recommended four basic "standards for accounting information" and five "guidelines for communicating accounting information" that have since come to be known as qualitative criteria.

Successive years saw many similar attempts to create a definitive set of qualitative criteria. Most of the work took place in the U.S. The FASB published a set of criteria, along with an impressive-looking chart that suggests a hierarchy of criteria, in 1980.[6] This criteria set is widely reprinted and reproduced, and seems to be the basis that the AcSB used for the criteria that are briefly described in Section 1000 of the *CICA Handbook*. Although the FASB effort is the most widely known, perhaps the best attempt was part of a CICA Research Study that was also published in 1980, *Corporate Reporting: Its Future Evolution.*[7] The CICA study identified 20 different qualitative criteria, as compared to about a dozen in the FASB statement. However, the real contribution of the CICA study is not in the number of identified criteria, but rather in explicitly recognizing the conflicts that exist between some of the criteria.

The qualitative criteria that were developed in the CICA Research Study are reproduced in Exhibit 2-2. The study categorized the criteria into four groups. The criteria in the first column will often conflict with those in the second. For example, relevance may be difficult to achieve without sacrificing objectivity; conversely, a high level of objectivity may mean reporting measurements that are known to be objective but that are of limited use to the external users (i.e., are not relevant).

The third set of criteria are believed to be compatible with those in both of the first two columns. *Freedom from bias*, for example, is compatible with *relevance* (because biased information is less relevant for the needs of external users) and is also compatible with *objectivity* (because, by definition, an objective measurement is one that is free from bias).

The fourth set of criteria serve as constraints or "brakes" on the criteria in the first three columns. It is a well-accepted principle, for instance, that if a measurement is not *material*, then it is not *relevant*, its *precision* is unimportant, and the impact of any *bias* doesn't matter.

You'll be glad to know that we will not discuss all 20 of the criteria listed in Exhibit 2-2. Certain of the criteria need some additional explanation, however, and we will focus on those that are included in the AcSB's Financial Statement Concepts section. Readers who are interested in a fuller discussion of qualitative criteria are referred to the *Corporate Reporting* research study and to the FASB's Concepts Statement No. 2.

---

6   Financial Accounting Standards Board, *Statement of Financial Accounting Concepts No. 2: Qualitative Characteristics of Accounting Information* (May 1980).

7   Qualitative characteristics are discussed in Chapter 7 of the study. The report was written by Professor Edward Stamp, FCA, but authorship officially is credited to a Study Group. Unfortunately, the report seems to have sunk without a trace in the consciousness of Canadian professional accountants.

EXHIBIT 2-2
Criteria for Assessment of Standards and of Accountability*

Criteria that may be in conflict with those in the other column, or require "trade-offs"		Criteria that are compatible with those in both of the first two columns	Constraints that may apply against any of the criteria in the first three columns
1	**2**	**3**	**4**
Relevance	Objectivity	Representational	Substance over form
Comparability	Verifiability	faithfulness	Materiality
Timeliness	Precision	Freedom from bias	Cost/benefit effectiveness
Clarity		Rationality	Flexibility
Completeness, or		Nonarbitrariness	Data availability
Full disclosure		Uniformity	Consistency
			Conservatism

* Source: Corporate Reporting: Its Future Evolution (CICA: 1980), p. 55.

Relevance

Theoretically, relevance is the most important qualitative characteristic. If accounting information is to be of any use, it must be *relevant* for its intended use. Relevance relates to the objectives of financial reporting. Chapter 1 pointed out that the accounting choices that are made when cash flow prediction is the primary reporting objective are not necessarily the same choices that are made when performance evaluation is the primary objective. The concept refers to the capacity of accounting information to make a difference to the external decision-makers who use financial reports.

Additional qualities that relate to relevance are

1. Timeliness. Accounting information should be reported soon enough for it to be useful for decision-making. Like the news of the world, stale financial information has less impact than fresh information. Lack of timeliness reduces relevance.

2. Predictive value. Accounting information should be helpful to external decision-makers by increasing their ability to make predictions about the outcome of future events. Decision-makers working from accounting information that has little or no predictive value are merely speculating intuitively.

3. Feedback value. Accounting information should be helpful to external decision-makers who are confirming past predictions or making updates, adjustments, or corrections to predictions.

Understandability

Information must be understandable to be useful to users in their decision-making process. Understandability does not mean that all information has to be reduced to the lowest common level or simplified so that the least sophisticated investor should understand it. The assumption is that investors and creditors have a reasonable understanding of business and economic activities, as well as some understanding of accounting. These users are expected to study the information with reasonable diligence. The user groups have been defined to include those who provide advice to investors and creditors; users who lack expertise are assumed to be properly advised.

Reliability

A commonly stated criterion for accounting measurements is that of reliability. Information is reliable if users can depend on it as a sufficiently accurate measure of what it is intended to measure. Reliability is closely related to the general concept of usefulness, but has additional sub-components.

To ensure reliability, accounting information must be free from error and bias and faithfully represent what it claims to represent. It must not mislead or deceive. There are three components to reliability:

1. Representational faithfulness (including substance over form)
2. Verifiability
3. Freedom from bias (or neutrality)

Representational Faithfulness. This attribute is also sometimes called validity.[8] Information must give a faithful picture of the facts and circumstances involved, as a city map should accurately represent the layout of the city that it represents.

In accounting, the balance sheet is considered to be a "statement of financial position," but it represents the financial position of the organization faithfully only if it really does portray all of the assets and liabilities of the business. If our accounting conventions and measurement models do not show all of the assets or liabilities, then the balance sheet does not represent faithfully the financial position of the business.

An important aspect of representational faithfulness is substance over form. Accounting information should represent what it purports to represent and should report the economic substance of transactions, not just their form or surface appearance.

As an example of accountants' efforts to portray substance over form, consider a company that rents, or leases, a computer system. The form of the contract is a rental agreement, which would seem to suggest that payments made by the company should simply be reported as rent expense with no other financial statement impact. However, suppose that the accountant discovers that this company decided to lease the computer instead of buying one outright with money borrowed from a bank. The lease term covers the full expected useful life of the computer, cannot be cancelled by the company, and provides a full return of the cost of the computer, plus a profit margin (in the form of interest) to the lessor. Now it appears as though, *in substance*, the company has acquired property rights over the computer, far more than a simple rental contract would imply. In substance, they own full rights to the use of the asset and are financing it with a lease agreement. Thus, to reflect substance over form, the asset and the obligation should be shown on the balance sheet of the lessee, and the income statement should reflect both depreciation of the computer and interest on the liability.

Verifiability. If knowledgeable and independent observers can apply an accounting measurement and obtain essentially the same result, the measurement is said to be verifiable. This is considered by the AcSB to be a component of reliability, but many accountants and auditors view the essence of *objectivity* as being verifiability. Verification implies that independent *measures using the same measurement methods* would reach substantially the same conclusion. Verifiability of a measurement does not, however, mean that the measurement was necessarily objective or non-arbitrary, but only that its computation can be reproduced or replicated.

Freedom from Bias. Accounting information is biased if the measurements result in consistent overstatements or understatements of the items being measured. Preparers of financial reports should not attempt to induce a predetermined outcome or a particular mode of behaviour (such as to purchase a company's shares).

---

8 In the CICA's 1980 *Corporate Reporting* study, this characteristic is known as isomorphism. *Isomorphism* is a well-established concept in science that indicates a similarity between two different forms or constructs.

The *CICA Handbook* uses the term neutrality to indicate the characteristic of *freedom from bias*. However, the concept of *neutrality* is sometimes taken to mean that reported accounting information should be neutral in its impact and should not influence economic decisions. If accounting information has no impact on economic decisions, then it is essentially useless. But accounting information should not provide the motivation for dysfunctional economic decisions (i.e., those that are contrary to the best economic interests of the enterprise). Management often makes decisions that are influenced by the financial reporting implications of those decisions. For example

> ... the provision of information that is both relevant and objective will tend to eliminate problems of bias. Yet it may creep in if there is a desire on the part of management to influence user decisions in favour of the company. For example, the adoption of accounting practices that help to smooth out fluctuations in periodic income measures will bias users into a belief that the risk attached to the company's operations is less than it really is.[9]

Comparability

The *CICA Handbook* states that "Comparability is a characteristic of the relationship between two pieces of information rather than of a particular piece of information by itself."[*CICA* 1000.22]

There are two aspects of comparability — consistency, which entails using the same accounting policies from year to year within a firm, and uniformity, which means that companies with similar transactions and similar circumstances use the same accounting treatments.

Consistency involves applying accounting concepts and principles from period to period in the same manner. There is a presumption that an accounting principle once used should not be changed. However, if consistency is carried too far, it adversely affects relevance. A change to a preferred accounting principle is permitted, even though this would impair consistency. This apparent conflict is usually resolved by retroactive restatement of financial statements to reflect the new policy and supplemental note disclosure.

Objectivity: The "Missing" Criterion

Objectivity is one of the most-used concepts in accounting, and yet it is not even mentioned in the AcSB's Financial Accounting Concepts section. The reason is that the term *objectivity* often has different implicit meanings for different people. Objectivity can be viewed as being one or a combination of the following characteristics:

- Quantifiability, the ability to attach a number to an event. The impact of some events, like some contingent losses, cannot be measured with any degree of reliability and any attempt to measure them is said not to be objective.

- Verifiability, or the ability of independent accountants to replicate the results of an accounting measurement, discussed previously as a component of *reliability*.

- Freedom from bias, the absence of intentional or unintentional mis-statement or skewing of an accounting measurement. This also is a component of *reliability*.

- Non-arbitrariness, the basing of accounting measurements on observable values.

Because of the wide variety of possible interpretations of *objectivity*, most discussions of qualitative criteria avoid using the word completely.

---

9 *Corporate Reporting: Its Future Evolution* (CICA, 1980), p. 60.

Conservatism

A curious feature of the AcSB's list of qualitative characteristics is that the Board includes conservatism. Most discussions of the qualities of accounting information consider conservatism to be a measurement convention. The AcSB characterizes conservatism as follows:

> When uncertainty exists, estimates of a conservative nature attempt to ensure that assets, revenues and gains are not overstated and, conversely, that liabilities, expenses and losses are not understated. However, conservatism does not encompass the deliberate understatement of assets, revenues and gains or the deliberate overstatement of liabilities, expenses and losses. *[CICA 1000.21]*

Conservatism is a tricky animal. Conservative measurements in one period almost inevitably have offsetting effects in one or more later periods. If assets are "conservatively" measured by deliberately understating assets, then expenses are accordingly reduced when those assets are transferred to the income statement as the assets are used (or amortized). Reducing expenses has the effect of increasing net income, which is not conservative.

Managements have been known to use conservatism as a club to hit auditors with when auditors objected to asset write-downs, even though the obvious result of the write-downs would be to enhance future earnings. In recognition of this problem, the second sentence of the above quotation is an attempt by the AcSB to discourage the deliberate understatement of assets or overstatement of liabilities.

Conservatism originated in the late nineteenth century, when the balance sheet was viewed as the most important statement (and often the only statement given to shareholders). The "conservative" valuation of assets and liabilities made some sense in that environment. But as increased emphasis was placed on the income statement in the mid-twentieth century, conservatism became a tool for manipulation rather than a practice intended to protect investors.

In modern accounting, conservatism might best be characterized as follows:

> "Conservatism" is a reaction to uncertainty and represents in essence merely a counsel of caution. The proper role of conservatism in accounting is to insure that the uncertainties and risks inherent in any given business situation are given adequate consideration.[10]

The Trade-off between Cost and Benefit

The concept of cost/benefit effectiveness holds that any accounting measurement or disclosure should result in greater benefits to the users than it costs to prepare and present. Benefits should exceed the costs.

In standard-setting, this is a very difficult concept to implement, since the benefits of an accounting standard are very vague while the costs of compliance are very real. Furthermore, the costs are borne by the companies while the benefits are enjoyed by the external users. The cost/benefit perceptions of the AcSB and of the preparers of financial statements do not always coincide, with the result that some of the AcSB's recommendations have less than full compliance, even by public companies.

For private companies that are not bound by the GAAP constraint for public companies, the cost/benefit trade-off is a very real one. In particular, if there are no external users of a private company's financial statements (other than Revenue Canada), then there is no benefit to be derived from incurring higher accounting costs. It is for this reason that private companies often adopt simpler measurement

---

[10] Maurice Moonitz, *The Basic Postulates of Accounting* (AICPA, 1961), p. 47.

and reporting conventions. Commonly, such companies will use accounting methods that coincide with their tax treatment. Examples include

- calculating depreciation/amortization expense on the same basis as CCA;
- recognizing revenue on the same basis for accounting as for tax purposes;
- expensing development costs and other costs that could be deferred and amortized for accounting purposes; or
- reporting monetary items that are denominated in a foreign currency at historical exchange rates instead of current rates.

In addition, private companies that are attempting to minimize their preparation costs may choose to report their income taxes on a flow-through basis rather than calculate deferred taxes, or may report pension costs on the basis of their funding formula rather than on the basis recommended by the AcSB.

Other Trade-offs

As was discussed at the beginning of this section, there is often a trade-off between qualitative characteristics, but especially between relevance and reliability. Reliability may have to be reduced to increase the degree of relevance, or vice versa. For example, if financial statements were delayed until all the future events that affect them were to come to pass, they would be far more reliable. Uncollectable accounts, warranty reserves, and useful lives of depreciable assets would not have to be estimated. On the other hand, the timeliness of the financial statements would suffer, and thus the statements would lack relevance. Thus, a degree of reliability is sacrificed to gain relevance. The relative importance of the characteristics changes from situation to situation and calls for the exercise of professional judgement.

The extent of trade-offs is, in itself, subjective. This is particularly apparent in the standard-setting process, where there often is a vigorous debate amongst the participants about what is relevant and what is measurable. The concerns of the auditing profession (and their dominant presence in the Canadian standard-setting process) often shows up in the presence of standards that seem to emphasize verifiability. The historical cost measurement convention often also seems to override what many observers perceive to be the relevance of other highly objective measurements.

CONCEPT REVIEW

1. Why does the criterion of *relevance* relate to financial reporting objectives?
2. Does the criterion of *understandability* mean that anyone should be able to understand the financial statements?
3. What are the three components of *reliability*?
4. What are the four characteristics of *objectivity*?
5. Why must there often be trade-offs between different qualitative criteria?

RECOGNITION AND MEASUREMENT

Elements of Financial Statements

Periodic financial statements are the primary medium used to communicate accounting information about a business enterprise. The building blocks of financial statements are called elements. Elements are the classes of items that financial statements should contain. The FSCs define seven elements, as shown in Exhibit 2-3. The first three elements (assets, liabilities, and equity/net assets) relate directly to the balance sheet; the next four elements (revenues, expenses, gains, and losses) relate directly to

EXHIBIT 2-3
Elements of Financial Statements

Elements	Transaction Characteristics
Balance Sheet (discussed in Chapter 4)	
1. **Assets** are economic resources controlled by an entity as a result of past transactions or events from which future economic benefits may be obtained.	1. To qualify as assets, the resources involved must a. have future economic benefits; b. be under the entity's current control; and c. result from past transactions.
2. **Liabilities** are obligations of an entity arising from past transactions or events, the settlement of which will result in the transfer or use of assets, provision of services, or other yielding of economic benefits in the future.	2. To qualify as liabilities, obligations must a. require future transfer of assets or economic benefits; b. be an unavoidable current obligation; and c. result from past transactions.
3. **Owners' equity/net assets** is the ownership interest in the assets of an entity after deducting its liabilities. While equity in total is a residual, it includes specific categories of items, for example, types of share capital, other contributed capital, and retained earnings.	3. The dollar amounts reported represent the residual interest in the assets after deducting the liabilities. In addition, the equity element is used to report capital transactions.
Income Statement (discussed in Chapter 3)	
4. **Revenues** are increases in economic resources, either by way of (a) inflows or enhancements of assets or (b) reductions of liabilities, resulting from the ordinary activities of an entity, normally from the sale of goods, the rendering of services, or the use by others of entity resources yielding rent, interest, royalties, or dividends.	4. An essential characteristic of a revenue transaction is that it arises from the company's ordinary earning activities, and not from (a) capital transactions, (b) the settlement of monetary liabilities, or (c) the sale of capital assets or investment assets.
5. **Expenses** are decreases in economic resources, either by way of (a) outflows or reductions of assets or (b) incurrences of liabilities, resulting from the ordinary revenue-earning activities of an entity.	5. The essential characteristic of an expense is that it must be incurred in conjunction with the company's revenue generating process. Expenditures that do not qualify as expenses are treated either as assets (future economic benefit to be derived), as losses (no economic benefit), or as distributions to owners.
6. **Gains** are increases in net assets from peripheral or incidental transactions and events affecting an entity and from all other transactions, events, and circumstances affecting an entity that are given accounting recognition except those that result from revenues or equity contributions.	6. The transaction must not be one that meets the characteristics of (a) a revenue-producing transaction or (b) a capital transaction (e.g., capital infusion by the owners).
7. **Losses** are decreases in equity from peripheral or incidental transactions and events affecting an entity and from all other transactions, events, and circumstances affecting an entity that are given accounting recognition except those that result from expenses or distributions of equity.	7. The transaction must not be one that meets the characteristics of (a) an expense transaction or (b) a capital transaction (e.g., dividends or other distributions to owners).

Source: CICA Handbook, "Financial Statement Concepts," Section 1000

the income statement. The definitions of these seven elements are particularly important because they provide the basis for deciding whether or not to recognize the results of a transaction or event in the financial statements.

According to the AcSB, an element should be included in the accounts when

- the item meets the definition of an element;
- the item has an appropriate basis of measurement, and a reasonable estimate can be made of the amount; and
- for assets and liabilities, it is probable that the economic benefits will be received or given up.

Measurability is important. If an item cannot be measured, it cannot be recognized, even if it has a high probability of being realized.

It is entirely possible that an item that meets the first two recognition criteria will not be recognized because of failure of the last criterion — probability. Suppose a company was suing a supplier for $125,000 for damages incurred when faulty materials provided by the supplier were used in a production process. The future economic benefit, or asset, can be measured at $125,000, or a lower amount if the parties are likely to settle. The difficulty arises when assessing the probability of the receipt of the economic benefit, as the lawsuit may not be successful. It may be proven that the company ordered the wrong materials or used them incorrectly. For this reason, such items are disclosed in the notes to the financial statements as contingencies and are not recognized until the result of the court decision is known and the probability of collection assessed.

Assets and liabilities are central to the definitions, since all other definitions are derived from asset and liability definitions. That is, owners' equity equals assets less liabilities. Revenues are defined as increases in assets or decreases in liabilities; expenses are decreases in assets or increases in liabilities. Obviously, the AcSB's definitions place emphasis on the balance sheet and the assets and liabilities that comprise it.

So, what are assets, anyway? According to the AcSB, assets have three essential characteristics:

1. they embody a future benefit, involving a capacity to contribute to future net cash flows;
2. the entity must be able to control access to the benefit; and
3. the asset must be the result of a past transaction or event.

Similarly, consider the three characteristics of liabilities:

1. they embody a duty or a responsibility to others that will involve a future transfer or use of assets, or other economic benefits, or rendering service, at a specific time or after a specific event;
2. the entity has little or no discretion to avoid the obligation; and
3. the liability must be the result of a past transaction or event.

The definitions of both of these two elements (i.e., assets and liabilities) include three components and embody three time frames:

1. An asset must be entitled to a **future** benefit (e.g., through a direct future cash flow or through its use in generating a future cash flow), and a liability must entail a future sacrifice (either a payment of cash or performance of service).
2. The reporting enterprise has a clear **present** right to the asset or obligation for the liability.
3. The asset or liability arose as the result of a **past** transaction or event.

While these three components are *necessary* conditions for recognizing an asset or a liability, they are not *sufficient* conditions. That is, there still are transactions and events that seem to fit the definitions and yet are not recognized as assets and liabilities in the accounts.

For example, suppose that a company signs a three-year contract to hire a special consultant; the contract is non-cancellable. Should the company recognize a liability? The conditions for recognition do seem to be satisfied: (1) the contract will require a cash outflow over the next three years; (2) there is a present obligation that is unavoidable; and (3) the transaction has already occurred. However, such a contract is *not* recognized in business accounting because the consultant has not yet rendered the services for which she was hired. There is a distinction drawn between a recognizable asset or liability on the one hand, and a commitment on the other hand. A commitment, even if irrevocable, does not normally result in recognition of a liability or asset.

From a practical standpoint, a useful way of approaching the question of whether a transaction or event has given rise to a recognizable asset or liability is to ask: "What do I do with the offset?" If the commitment to the consultant were recognized as a liability, there would have to be an offsetting debit. There are only two choices for the debit: an asset or an expense. Clearly, the expense has not been incurred yet, because the service has not been rendered nor has the contract time passed. Therefore, the only choice for an offset is an asset. But what is the asset? It would have to be the future benefit to be derived from the costs that have not yet been incurred. The prospect of recognizing an asset for costs to be incurred in the future for services not yet rendered is a prospect that most accountants would find objectionable. Therefore, the commitment would be viewed as an executory contract — a contract wherein neither party has yet fulfilled the requirements of the contract — and would not be recognized.

The important aspect of these AcSB definitions of assets and liabilities is that they are far from iron-clad. Accountants still must make decisions on whether or not to recognize the future effects of past transactions and events as assets or liabilities.

The AcSB's definitions of the income statement elements — revenues, expenses, gains, and losses — are related to changes in net assets (i.e., total assets minus total liabilities):

- Revenues are increases in net assets, either by way of inflows or enhancements of assets or reductions of liabilities, resulting from the ordinary activities of the enterprise.

- Expenses are decreases in net assets, either by way of outflows or reductions of assets or incurrences of liabilities, resulting from an enterprise's ordinary revenue generating or service delivery activities.

- Gains are increases in net assets from peripheral or incidental transactions.

- Losses are decreases in net assets from peripheral or incidental transactions.

The only difference between revenues and gains and between expenses and losses is the nature of the activity that gave rise to them. Revenues and expenses relate to the ordinary operating activities of the enterprise; gains and losses relate to non-operating activities.

The "ordinary" versus "peripheral" criterion is rather vague. For example, some movie theatre chains regularly report "gains" from the sale of theatre properties in their income statements. But if an enterprise operates hundreds of movie screens, then isn't the purchase and sale of theatre properties an ordinary business activity rather than a peripheral activity? The key is that the business of a theatre chain is not that of buying and selling theatres; such an activity is essential to the health of the company, but it is *incidental* to the primary business activity of exhibiting motion pictures. Revenue should include only the proceeds from the sale of tickets and popcorn and the delivery of other routine services and products, and not from the sale of the capital assets.

Recognition, Realization, and Accrual

Recognition is the process of measuring and including an item in the financial statements. A recognized item is given a title and numerical value. Recognition applies to all financial statement elements in all accounting entities. *Disclosure* (in the notes to the financial statements) is not the same as recognition; when a financial statement element is recognized, it is reported on the face of the financial statements.

Realization is the process of converting an asset, liability, or commitment into a cash flow. A receivable is said to be realized when it is collected; revenues are realized when received; expenses and liabilities are realized when the cash payment occurs.

Once realization has occurred, recognition *must* occur because there has been a cash flow impact that cannot be ignored in the accounts. For example:

- A customer makes a deposit (or pays in advance) for goods yet to be produced and delivered; since the cash has been received (realized), it must be recognized. Since revenue will not yet have been earned, the offsetting credit is to recognize unearned revenue.

- A company pays a retainer to a lawyer who will be acting on the company's behalf in the next fiscal year; the cash outflow triggers recognition of a prepaid expense.

However, recognition often occurs *prior* to realization. For example:

- An accounts receivable is recognized when a service has been performed for a client; realization occurs when the client pays the account. The offset is to recognize revenue.

- A liability for a purchase of inventory is recognized when the goods are received; realization occurs when the creditor is paid. The offset is to recognize inventory as an asset.

- A change in the value of cash held in U.S. dollars is recognized at the balance sheet date; realization occurs only when the U.S. dollars are converted to Canadian dollars. The offset is to a gain or loss account, depending on the direction of the change in value.

- The liability for a purchase of new equipment is recognized; the liability is offset by an increase in an asset account (i.e., equipment).

- Unpaid wages are accrued at the end of a fiscal period; a liability is recogni[zed.] The liability is offset by a debit to an expense account.

When we recognize the effects of transactions and events prior to their real[iza]tion, we are using the accrual concept. The accrual concept says that we recog[nize] assets when we have the right to receive their benefits, and we recognize liabil[ities] when we take on the obligation to deliver cash (or other assets) or services in [the] future. The International Accounting Standards Committee, for example, states t[hat]

> Under the accrual basis of accounting, transactions and other events are recognized when they occur (and not as cash or its equivalent is received or paid) and they are recorded in the accounting records and reported in the financial statements of the periods to which they relate.[11]

Accrual means that assets and liabilities are recognized when the rights and obligations pertaining thereto are established; accrual does *not* refer to the subsequent transfer of amounts from the balance sheet to the income statement, which is a secondary form of recognition. For example:

Accrual
recognition before
realization

---

11 International Accounting Standards Committee, International Accounting Standard IAS 1, *Presentation of Financial Statements* (1997), paragraph 26.

- Inventory is purchased on account. The liability is *accrued* as an account payable, and the asset is recorded as inventory. Both an asset and a related liability are recognized. This is an application of the accrual concept because the transaction is recorded prior to its cash flow impact. When the inventory is sold, its cost is transferred to cost of goods sold, which is recognition of an expense. However, this subsequent expense recognition is not an application of the accrual concept; the liability had already been accrued. The temporary classification of the cost of the inventory as an asset, which then is transferred to an expense, is the result of *matching*, not of accrual.

- Equipment is purchased by giving a 20% cash down payment and giving a promissory note for the remaining 80%. The full cost of the equipment is *recognized* as an asset, including the 80% portion of the cost represented by the liability which is *accrued*. The equipment is recorded as an asset; it is expected to have a four-year useful life. For each of the next four years, 25% of the cost is transferred to the income statement as depreciation, thereby recognizing depreciation expense in each year. The recognition of depreciation is *not* an accrual; it is an *interperiod allocation* (which also is a function of *matching*).

In matching and interperiod allocation, amounts originally recognized as assets are transferred to (or *recognized* as) expense, and amounts recorded as a liability are transferred to the income statement as revenue (or as reduction of expense). Interperiod allocation (e.g., amortization) is *not* part of the accrual concept:

> [Accrual] is a broader concept than the matching concept which simply requires expense to be recognized in the same period as the associated revenue is recognized as income.[12]

Before leaving the concepts of realization and recognition, we must stress that accounting recognition always relates to realized cash flows — past, present, and future. The recognition issue is always one of fitting the actual (or predicted) cash flows into time periods through a complex system of accruals and interperiod allocations. If actual cash flows deviate from those that we presumed in recognizing revenues and expenses, then we must adjust our accounts. *At no time can accounting recognize financial statement elements that are not based on actual or predicted cash flows!*

CONCEPT REVIEW

1. What is the difference between *realization* and accounting *recognition*?
2. What is the difference between *accrual* and *interperiod allocation*?

MEASUREMENT CONVENTIONS

Measurement is the process of determining the *amount* at which an item is recognized in the financial statements. If there is no appropriate basis of measurement, a transaction would fail the second recognition criterion, as previously defined.

Measurement methods encompass not only the process of attaching a number to a construct such as a specific asset or a liability, but also the process of income measurement as it is conventionally practiced in Canadian accounting. The process of income measurement involves not only the initial measurement, but also the disposi-

---

[12] IASC, *Draft Statement of Principles for Presentation of Financial Statements* (1995), paragraph 28.

tion of that measurement as it moves through the financial statements. There are four pervasive measurement conventions:

1. Historical cost
2. Revenue recognition
3. Matching
4. Full disclosure

Historical Cost Convention

There are many alternative measurement bases, including historical cost, price level adjusted historical cost, replacement cost, current sales value, net realizable value, and the sum of the cash flows an item will generate over its life, discounted at an appropriate rate. The FSCs state that, *generally*, historical cost should be used as a measurement base.

Our GAAP model is described as an historical cost model, yet there are many examples in it of other valuation bases — obsolete inventory carried at market value when this amount is less than cost; long-term liabilities with interest rates lower than market rates recorded on the date of issuance at discounted amounts; inventories of agricultural products and precious metals carried at market values; and so on. The implication of the FSCs is that this *ad hoc* basis will continue and that we will continue to see a variety of measurement bases, although historical cost will dominate.

Normally applied in conjunction with asset acquisitions, the historical cost convention specifies that the actual acquisition cost be used for initial accounting recognition purposes. The cost principle assumes that assets are acquired in business transactions conducted at arm's length — that is, transactions between a buyer and a seller are at the fair value prevailing at the time of the transaction.

If an asset is acquired via some means other than cash, the cost of the asset is based on the *value of the consideration given*. Consideration is whatever the buyer gives the seller. For non-cash transactions conducted at arm's length, the cost principle assumes that the fair value of the resources *given up* in a transaction provides reliable evidence for the valuation of the item acquired. This may be the amount of money paid, market value of common shares issued, or the present value of debt assumed in the transaction. If money is paid, there is little controversy over determination of cost. In other situations, judgement is very important. It is often useful to refer to both the market value of the assets or securities given up, if any, and the market value of the assets received. Usually one of these values is more reliable than the other, and provides a basis for valuation.

The cost principle provides guidance primarily at the initial acquisition date. Once acquired, the original cost basis of long-lived assets is then subject to depreciation, depletion, amortization, or write-down in conformity with the *matching* principle, discussed later in this section. Write-ups of appreciated asset values are generally not permitted.

Revenue Recognition Convention

The revenue recognition convention requires the recognition and reporting of revenues when all three of the recognition criteria — definition, measurability, and probability — are met.

Revenue can be defined as inflows of cash or other enhancements of a business's assets, settlements of its liabilities, or a combination of the two. Such inflows must be derived from delivering or producing goods, rendering service, or performing other activities that constitute a company's ongoing business operations over a specific period of time. More generally, revenue is measured as the market value of the resources received or the *fair value* of the product or service given, whichever is the more reliably determinable. This broader definition comes into play in conjunction with non-cash or *barter* transactions (that is, direct exchanges of goods and services).

The revenue recognition convention pertains to accrual-basis accounting and is not relevant to cash-basis accounting. Therefore, completed transactions for the sale of goods or services on credit usually are recognized as revenue for the period in which the sale or service occurs rather than in the period in which the cash is eventually collected. Furthermore, related expenses are matched to these revenues.

Traditionally, four conditions have to be met to satisfy the revenue recognition convention:

1. All significant acts required of the seller have been performed.
2. Consideration is measurable.
3. Collection is reasonably assured.
4. The risks and rewards of ownership have passed to the buyer.

These conditions are applicable to traditional trading activities, wherein a company buys and sells inventory or manufactures items for sale. Many sectors of the Canadian economy do not fit into these traditional modes of business, and multi-period earnings cycles are common. Transactions that do not quite fit into the four conditions above include instalment sales, long-term construction contracts, sales of land with minimal down payments, software development contracts, long-term leases, and sales of franchises that require a certain level of performance on the part of the purchaser as a condition of sale. In these transactions and in others, there are significant uncertainties concerning one or more of the listed criteria. In long earnings cycles, the first condition is particularly troublesome. If *all* significant acts must be performed before revenue can be recognized, there would be no such thing as percentage-of-completion accounting, instalment-basis revenue recognition, loan interest revenue, and so forth. Instead, revenue would be recognized only when all of the effort has been expended and the earnings process is complete.

The AcSB has a somewhat more modest statement of when revenue recognition is appropriate:

> Revenues are generally recognized when performance is achieved and reasonable assurance regarding measurement and collectibility of the consideration exists.   [*CICA* 1000.47]

Note the AcSB's use of the major qualifier "generally," and note that performance is not modified by "all" or "complete." The interpretation of what constitutes *performance* is a major issue in financial reporting for many companies, one that is subject to many different interpretations. As well, *measurability* is an elusive concept in revenue recognition. The issue of revenue recognition is one of the most pervasive and most difficult in the practice of accounting. Chapter 6 is devoted exclusively to a discussion of this important issue.

Matching Convention

Matching refers to the timing of recognition of revenues and expenses in the income statement. Under this concept, all expenses incurred in earning revenue should be recognized in the same period that the revenue is recognized. For example:

- If revenue is carried over (deferred) for recognition in a future period, any related expenses should also be carried over or deferred, since they are incurred in earning that revenue.
- If revenue is recognized in the current period but there are expenditures yet to be incurred in future periods, the expenses are recognized and a liability is created (e.g., the estimated provision for warranty costs).
- If costs are incurred to enhance the general revenue-generating ability of the company in future periods and the future benefits are measurable, the costs are capitalized and amortized.

Matching is widely considered useful for evaluating the ability of a company to generate net income and thus for performance evaluation. After all, if revenue is recognized, then surely all of the expenses related to earning that revenue should also be recognized in the same period. The problem is that most costs are not *directly* related to revenue. Some costs are directly related to revenues, such as inventory costs for goods sold and labour costs in a service contract. But even in those "direct" costs, there is considerable flexibility in measurement. For most types of cost, expenses are only indirectly related to specific revenue-generating activity. These indirect costs are often called *overhead*, and they constitute a majority of the costs of most companies. As a result, most matching is not directly to revenue, but is instead to *time periods*. Examples are the expenditures for administration and for promotional activities. These items are period costs — they are recognized as expenses during the period in which they are incurred. Another type of example is that of investments in long-lived assets. Amortization seldom is allocated on the basis of revenues but instead is usually allocated over an estimated useful life or, in the case of intangible assets, often over an arbitrary number of years.

Adjusting entries may be required at the end of the accounting period to update revenues and expenses in step with recognized sales revenue. Examples include wage expense earned but not paid, estimated uncollectible accounts receivable, estimated warranty expense, and interest expense accrued but not paid.

To illustrate the matching principle, assume a home appliance is sold for cash with a 100% warranty on parts and labour in effect for the first 12 months from date of sale. The revenue from the sale is recognized immediately, as are the directly related costs involved in manufacturing and assembling the unit and the shipping and direct selling expenses incurred. Furthermore, the expenses involved in honouring the warranty should also be recognized in the same period as the sales revenue, even though the actual warranty cost may not be known until the next year. At the end of the year in which the sale occurs, the warranty expense should be estimated, recorded on the books, and recognized for financial statement reporting purposes. In this way, the warranty expense is matched with the revenue to which it is related even though the cash may be expended at a later time. Depreciation on the equipment used in manufacturing the appliance is allocated to the period, but the depreciation is not directly related to (or affected by the amount of) the revenue.

A simple table is helpful in summarizing the accounting disposition of costs and expenses in accordance with the matching principle and the definitions of elements:

Time frame of benefit:	Expenditure should be:
Future verifiable economic benefits	Recorded as an asset
Current economic benefits	Recorded as an expense
No economic benefits	Recorded as a loss

The timing of expense recognition and the measurement of the cost is another matter for professional judgement. There is hardly an expense item in the income statement that is not the subject of several interrelated judgements and estimates. Chapter 7 discusses the issue of expense recognition at some length, and most of the other chapters in this book deal with expense recognition in the context of specific accounting issues, such as inventories, capital assets, leases, pensions, income taxes, and so forth.

Full Disclosure

Full disclosure means that the financial statements should report all *relevant* information bearing on the economic affairs of a business enterprise. The aim of full disclosure is to provide external users with the accounting information they need to make informed investment and credit decisions. Full disclosure requires, among other things, that the accounting policies followed be explained in the notes to the financial statements.

Although the common expression is *full disclosure*, perhaps a more realistic expression is *adequate disclosure*. Obviously, not all information that may be relevant to a financial statement user can be disclosed. Instead, the objective is to disclose enough supplemental information to keep from misleading the users of the statements who are likely to be using the statements to predict cash flows or to evaluate the earnings ability of the company.

A useful guide to deciding what to disclose is as follows:[13]

- Disclose items not in the regular or normal activities of the business.
- Disclose items reflecting changes in expectations.
- Disclose that which a statute or contract requires to be disclosed.
- Disclose new activities or major changes in old ones.

The emphasis in this list is on disclosing what causes changes in expectations for an external reader of the financial statements. Such disclosure will reduce the likelihood of a user being misled by assuming that the company will continue in the future much as it has in the past.

MAKING CHOICES IN ACCOUNTING: THE EXERCISE OF PROFESSIONAL JUDGEMENT

Chapter 1 gave examples of the many accounting choices that are affected by the financial reporting objectives *in any particular situation*. Reporting objectives (and motivations) do vary, and choices of accounting policies and accounting estimates are significantly affected by whether the primary reporting objective is, for example, income tax minimization, cash flow prediction, or net income maximization.

Early in this chapter, we pointed out that the ability to make appropriate choices in accounting is **professional judgement**. Professional judgement permeates the work of a professional accountant, and it involves an ability to build accounting measurements that take into account

- the objectives of financial reporting in each particular situation,
- the facts of the business environment and operations, and
- the organization's reporting constraints (if any).

Choices of accounting policies, accounting estimates, and accounting measurement methods are then based on tests of the validity of the underlying assumptions, followed by an evaluation of the various possible measurement methods with reference to the qualitative characteristics. Throughout the choice process, the accountant must keep the objectives of financial reporting for that organization firmly in mind.

The building blocks for financial statements were illustrated in Exhibit 2-1 in the form of a pyramid. At the base of the pyramid, on which all else is built, are the objectives of financial reporting. There usually are multiple objectives, and the objectives must be prioritized in order to be able to resolve conflicts between them when decisions about specific accounting policies or estimates must be made.

The facts of the organization's operations and its economic environment must be determined in order to understand just what is to be measured.

Next, the reporting constraints must be determined. Is the reporting enterprise a public company, bound by the reporting constraints of the securities commissions? Is it a private company that uses the financial statements only for its owner(s) and for income tax purposes? Is an audit required? If an audit is required (or desired by management), is a "clean" audit opinion necessarily needed? Can the enterprise report on the basis of disclosed (or tailored) accounting policies rather than GAAP?

---

13 Maurice Moonitz, *The Basic Postulates of Accounting* (AICPA, 1961), pp. 48–49.

The underlying assumptions must be tested. In preparing the financial statements for the vast majority of Canadian business organizations, the normal underlying assumptions of continuity, nominal dollar capital maintenance, proprietary approach, etc., are quite valid. But they cannot be taken for granted, and their appropriateness in the specific reporting situation must be evaluated.

Once the objectives have been discerned and prioritized, the facts and constraints have been determined, and the underlying assumptions have been evaluated, only then should the accounting measurement choices be considered. The measurement choices must be consistent with the objectives, facts, and constraints. The measurement choices are further tempered by the qualitative criteria, especially in the realm of recognition. When should revenues be recognized? When should costs incurred or committed be recognized? When costs are recognized, should they be recognized as assets or as expenses? If they are recognized as assets, when should they be transferred to expense (as a secondary recognition)?

The measurement and recognition criteria lead to the financial statement elements, which then are classified in a manner that is appropriate to the industry and consistent with the operational activities of the enterprise. The result is, finally, the financial statements themselves. To be appropriate for the specific reporting situation, the final financial statements must satisfy the specific reporting objectives that are at the foundation of the whole pyramid.

Financial statements are not uniform. They vary considerably by industry and type of company. Although there are *common* forms of balance sheets and income statements, there actually is no *standard* format. The AcSB does not prescribe a format for the balance sheet and income statement; only the disclosure of certain types of assets, liabilities, revenues, and expenses is recommended in the *CICA Handbook*. The balance sheet of a life insurance company looks very different from the balance sheet of a steel company; the income statement of a mutual fund is very different from that of a retailer. The next two chapters will discuss the form and organization of the income statement and the balance sheet, and will point out many of the industry differences that arise in practice.

The cash flow statement does have an AcSB-prescribed format, but the accounting choices that go into measurement of the financial statement elements can have an impact on the way cash flows are reported in the cash flow statement, as we will see in Chapter 5.

CONCEPT REVIEW

1. When should revenue be recognized, in the view of the AcSB?
2. How is the concept of *matching* usually applied to period costs?
3. Are there standardized formats for Canadian balance sheets and income statements?

SUMMARY OF KEY POINTS

1. Accounting "principles" consist of three different sets of concepts: (1) underlying assumptions, (2) measurement methods, and (3) qualitative criteria.

2. **Underlying assumptions** include the basic postulates which make accounting measurements possible (such as the *separate entity assumption*, the *unit of measure concept*, and the *time period assumption*), but they also include underlying measurement assumptions that usually, but not always, are true in a given reporting situation. These measurement assumptions include the *going concern assumption*, the *proprietary assumption*, and the *nominal dollar capital maintenance concept*.

3. **Qualitative criteria** are the criteria which are used in conjunction with an enterprise's financial reporting objectives to determine the most appropriate measurement methods to use in that particular reporting situation.

4. The most important qualitative criterion is that of *relevance*; relevance should be determined with reference to the users of the financial statements and the resultant financial reporting objectives.

5. Some qualitative criteria conflict with each other. For example, the most *relevant* measurement in a particular situation may not be sufficiently *objective* to permit its use.

6. *Objectivity* is a general concept that has several components, including measurability, verifiability, freedom from bias, and reliability.

7. The role of *conservatism* in accounting is to ensure that the uncertainties and risks inherent in measuring the effects of any given business situation are given adequate consideration. Conservatism should not be used as a justification for overstating liabilities or understating assets.

8. Measurement methods are the various ways that the results of transactions and events can be reported in the financial statements. There is a group of widely-used measurement methods that can be called *measurement conventions*, but they are not universally applicable. Measurement conventions include historical cost, the revenue recognition convention, matching, and full disclosure.

9. The elements of financial statements are the seven types of accounts that appear on the balance sheet and income statement: assets, liabilities, owners' equity, revenues, expenses, gains, and losses.

10. Initial accounting recognition occurs when the effects or results of a transaction or event are first measured and assigned to an account or *element*. Subsequent recognition occurs when an amount previously recognized is transferred from one element to another, such as by recognizing an expense that previously had been recognized as an asset.

11. Recognition of an asset or liability requires that three time references be present: a *future* benefit or sacrifice and a *present* right or obligation, arising from a *past* transaction or event.

12. Realization occurs when a cash flow occurs. Realization often occurs after recognition, but can never occur prior to recognition because the cash flow forces recognition if it has not occurred previously.

13. The accrual concept relates to the recognition of receivables when the right to receive cash arises, and to the recognition of liabilities when the obligation is created. Accrual does not refer to subsequent secondary recognition through matching and interperiod allocations.

14. Accounting is full of choices. The choice process includes these elements: (1) financial statements are constructed from (2) the financial statement elements that have been recognized (3) using measurement methods that (4) optimize the qualitative characteristics and that (5) are based on the appropriate underlying assumptions which reflect the organization's (6) reporting constraints and (7) the facts of its business and environment, and that provide information that (8) best satisfies the objectives of financial reporting in any given situation. This series of related decisions is what constitutes *professional judgement in accounting*.

QUESTIONS

2-1 What are the three different building blocks that comprise accounting principles?

2-2 Does the *CICA Handbook's* Section 1000, Financial Statement Concepts, include an explanation of all accounting principles? Explain.

2-3 What topics are covered in the *CICA Handbook's* Section 1000, Financial Statement Concepts?

2-4 Identify and describe the six underlying assumptions included in accounting principles.

2-5   Explain why the time-period assumption causes accruals and deferrals in accounting.

2-6   Does the separate entity assumption follow the tax and legal status of a corporation? A sole proprietorship?

2-7   Relate the continuity assumption to use of historic cost in financial statement measurements.

2-8   How are owners viewed under the proprietary assumption as compared to the entity assumption?

2-9   Financial statements only record goodwill when it has been purchased in a business combination. How does this relate to the unit of measure assumption and the historic cost convention?

2-10   Which assumption or principle discussed in this chapter is most affected by the phenomenon of inflation? Give reasons for your choice.

2-11   List and describe the significant qualitative criteria that are part of accounting principles.

2-12   Explain the trade-offs that can occur between relevance and reliability.

2-13   If the financial statements are to be understandable to users, they must be reduced to a very simple level for the benefit of those who are less sophisticated. Is this true? Explain.

2-14   Describe the characteristics that make information (a) relevant, and (b) reliable.

2-15   Describe how consistency and uniformity promote comparability.

2-16   When a company evaluates an accounting policy with reference to its cost/benefit effectiveness, what benefits are under consideration? What are the costs?

2-17   What are the recognition criteria?

2-18   The definitions of assets and liabilities involve a consideration of the past, present, and future. Explain.

2-19   Why is it said that the definitions of assets and liabilities are central to the financial statement element definitions?

2-20   Explain why executory contracts are not recognized in the financial statements.

2-21   What is the difference between a revenue and a gain?

2-22   Contrast recognition and realization. Why can realization not precede recognition?

2-23   Explain the historical cost convention. Why is it used in the basic financial statements instead of current replacement value?

2-24   What criteria must be met before revenue can be recognized?

2-25   What is the purpose of full, or at least adequate, disclosure?

2-26   Describe the role of professional judgement in the choice of accounting policies. What are the influencing factors?

CASE 2-1

SpaceSat Ltd.

CASES

SpaceSat Ltd. (SSL), a Canadian public company established in 1972, is involved in global telecommunication transmissions. SSL has over $1.4 billion in assets, financed by $900 million in liabilities and $500 million in equity. As a federally regulated monopoly in the public spotlight, the company adheres to high standards of disclosure and accountability. SSL owns satellite and underground (and under-ocean) cable communication networks. Access to these facilities is rented to North American customers, including broadcasters, telephone companies, and banking institutions. SSL also has extensive computer facilities, specializing in the development of technology associated with data transmission. Operating revenue for the most recent fiscal year was $420 million. Net income of $26 million provided a reasonable (but not spectacular) return on equity. Income has been stable.

Recently, concern has arisen regarding SSL's abandoned satellites. When satellites reach the end of their technologically useful life, state-of-the-art replacement satellites are launched; the old satellites are either shot out of orbit and into deep space or shut down and "abandoned" in orbit, where they remain indefinitely. There is a risk of the orbit becoming unstable and the satellite crashing to earth. Because of this risk, and the increasing volume of "space junk," there is talk internationally, and within the Canadian government, of requiring owners to properly dispose of abandoned space equipment. How, no one is quite sure. Alternatives include destruction by explosion, retrieval by a shuttle, creation of a "junk yard" on the moon, and so on. All of these alternatives seem far-fetched and extremely expensive. Technology does not exist to achieve many of these alternatives, and the ultimate method of disposal would necessitate extensive research.

SSL is uncertain as to whether it should record, or even disclose, a liability for its abandoned satellites. Legal liability is not established, and at present there is no feasible disposal method. Satellite abandonment is current industry practice; everyone does it. Furthermore, estimates of disposal cost would be based on significant assumptions. It seems clear that any solution will require large initial expenditures.

SSL's Chief Financial Officer has asked the controller's office to prepare a brief report that examines SSL's reporting alternatives for this situation and provides a recommendation. As assistant controller, you have been assigned the task. You have decided to structure your report around a discussion of the recognition criteria, and whether this item meets these criteria.

Required:

Prepare the report.

[CGA-Canada, adapted]

CASE 2-2

G Limited

G Limited (GL) is a private company, incorporated 20 years ago under federal legislation. GL was audited for the first time in the year ended 31 December 20X1 by an auditor who issued a qualified audit opinion on the basis that GL did not record depreciation. During the current year, the vice-president, Finance, has indicated that the company wishes to have an unqualified (or "clean") opinion for the year ended 31 December 20X2, as he anticipates that the company will become a public company in the near future. They believe that a pattern of smooth earnings will be the most attractive to potential shareholders.

The vice-president, Finance, has provided CA with the following list of contentious accounting issues facing the company:

1. GL has not, in the past, recorded depreciation on its capital assets. The president's feelings about this subject were noted in last year's report to the shareholders as follows: "Our capital assets are increasing in value, not decreasing. In my opinion, the recording of a fictitious expense like depreciation makes our financial statements unreliable and less useful to investors and creditors."

2. During 20X2, GL was sued by a customer who incorporated one of GL's components in manufactured products that were subsequently returned by its customers due to the failure of the GL component. GL refutes this claim. The amount in dispute is $250,000. Correspondence indicates that a settlement of $100,000 would be acceptable to the customer; GL has not agreed to this. Court proceedings will commence early in 20X3. The claim has not been recorded in GL's books.

3. GL incurred expenditures of approximately $400,000 related to refining an existing product, which is now expected to have a significantly longer life and thus increased sales. GL plans to defer this cost and amortize it over a period of 10 years. The product life cycle has rarely been longer than five years in this line, but management are optimistic in this particular case that the product will have a sales life of 10 years.

4. During the year, GL sold a building at a gain of $200,000. The $1.4 million sales price has been included in sales, while the $1.2 million net book value has been included in cost of goods sold.

5. GL issued preferred shares to investors, who also owned common shares, during 20X2. The preferred shares must be redeemed, or bought back, at their $100 stated value per share, in the year 20X12. The dividends are cumulative, which means that if they are not paid in a given year, dividends in arrears must be made up before common dividends are paid. If there are dividends in arrears on the redemption date, these must be paid at that time. GL plans to classify this preferred share issue consistent with its legal form, in the equity section of the balance sheet.

6. GL plans to prepare minimal note disclosures, as has been its practice in the past in order to reduce the time and effort that the accounting staff have to devote to preparation of the annual report.

Required:

Adopt the role of CA and evaluate the list of contentious accounting policies, referring to accounting principles when appropriate.

[CICA, adapted]

EXERCISES

E2-1 *Underlying Assumptions:* Indicate whether each of the following statements is *true* or *false*:

1. The continuity assumption states that a business entity will last forever.
2. Nominal dollar capital maintenance takes inflation into account before profits are recognized.
3. The unit of measure assumption is the justification for ignoring inflation in the financial statements.
4. The time period assumption requires accrual and deferrals.
5. The continuity assumption justifies the use of historical cost in the financial statements.
6. The separate entity assumption equates the tax, legal, and accounting status of companies.
7. The separate entity assumption equates the tax, legal, and accounting status of partnerships.
8. Owners are viewed as central in the proprietary assumption.
9. Nominal dollar capital maintenance requires financial capital to be preserved before profits are recognized.
10. Quantification is a key element of the unit of measure assumption.

E2-2 *Definitions of Assumptions, Qualitative Criteria, and Measurement Conventions:* The following assumptions, qualitative criteria, and measurement conventions are lettered for response purposes:

A. Time period
B. Separate entity
C. Continuity
D. Proprietary
E. Unit of measure
F. Nominal dollar capital maintenance
G. Relevance
H. Reliability

I. Comparability
J. Conservatism
K. Cost/benefit effectiveness
L. Historical cost
M. Revenue recognition
N. Matching
O. Full disclosure

The following list of key phrases is directly related to the preceding list. Match these phrases with the list by entering the appropriate letter to the left.

Key Phrase
_____ 1. Risks and rewards have transferred
_____ 2. Skepticism in the face of uncertainty
_____ 3. Common denominator — the yardstick
_____ 4. Expenses incurred in earning the period's revenues
_____ 5. Preparation cost versus value of benefit to the user
_____ 6. Separate and apart from its owners and other entities
_____ 7. Report all relevant information
_____ 8. Free from error or bias
_____ 9. Cash-equivalent expenditures to acquire
_____ 10. Going-concern basis
_____ 11. Focus on owners in reporting and measurement decisions
_____ 12. Preserve invested capital before recognizing profits
_____ 13. Capable of making a difference to the decision being made
_____ 14. Reporting periods — usually one year
_____ 15. Uniform and consistent

E2-3 *Definitions — Relevance and Reliability:* Relevance and reliability are two important qualitative characteristics of accounting information. Each has three characteristics. Provide a brief definition of each item using the following format:

Characteristic   **Brief Definition**
A. Relevance
   1. Timeliness
   2. Predictive value
   3. Feedback value

B. Reliability
   1. Representational faithfulness
   2. Verifiability
   3. Freedom from bias (or neutrality)

E2-4 *Questions on Principles:* Indicate whether each of the following statements is *true* or *false*.

1. Acknowledging the needs of users and the decisions that will be made based on the financial statements when picking accounting policies means that information cannot be free from bias.

2. Accounting standards require uniformity, which is necessary to achieve comparability.

3. Financial statement readers are well served by conservative financial statements that understate income and assets.

4. Neutrality in accounting means that the information reported is neither biased in favour of a particular party nor designed to achieve a particular outcome.

5. Relevancy is defined as information that is current, or up-to-date.

6. Relevance and reliability are necessary for recognition.

7. Realization is necessary for recognition to occur.

8. All items (resulting from a transaction) must be recognized if they meet the definition of a financial statement element.

9. Reliability is promoted if accounting information is representationally faithful to the underlying economic events.

10. Useful information may lack objectivity.

E2-5 *Realization versus Recognition:* For each of the following transactions, indicate the point at which the transaction is (1) recognized and (2) realized.

a. A customer buys a product on credit, and takes delivery on 1 July. The money is paid on 31 July.

b. A customer orders a custom-built sign, and pays for the sign when the order is placed on 20 February. The sign is delivered on 10 July.

c. Expected warranty claims on products sold are accrued as the sales are made. Cash payments for warranty claims are made in the subsequent fiscal year.

d. Inventory is bought on 1 August, on credit. It is paid for on 12 September.

e. Interest is accrued daily, and collected at the end of each month.

E2-6 *Elements of Financial Statements:* Financial statement elements have specific definitions. To the right, some important aspects of the definitions are listed. Match the aspects with the elements by entering appropriate letters in the blanks. More than one letter can be placed in a blank.

Elements of Financial Statements
A. Revenues
B. Expenses
C. Gains
D. Losses
E. Assets
F. Liabilities
G. Owners' equity/net assets
H. None of the above

Important Aspect of the Definition of the Element
___ 1. Residual interest in the assets after deducting liabilities
___ 2. Constitute the entity's ongoing major or central operation
___ 3. Probable future economic benefits obtained by an entity
___ 4. Using up of assets or incurrence of liabilities
___ 5. Enhancement of assets or settlements of liabilities
___ 6. From peripheral or incidental transactions of the entity
___ 7. Future sacrifices arising from past transactions
___ 8. Increases in net assets from peripheral or incidental activities

E2-7 *Questions on Principles:* For each of the following circumstances, give the letter item(s) indicating the accounting principle involved:

A. Time period	I. Comparability
B. Separate entity	J. Conservatism
C. Continuity	K. Cost/Benefit effectiveness
D. Proprietary	L. Historical cost
E. Unit of measure	M. Revenue recognition
F. Nominal dollar capital maintenance	N. Matching
G. Relevance	O. Full disclosure
H. Reliability	

1. Goodwill is only recorded in the accounts when it arises from the purchase of another entity.

2. A note describing the company's possible liability in a lawsuit is included with the financial statements even though no formal liability exists at the balance sheet date.

3. Owners are considered the primary focus of the financial statements; others that have a significant stake in the profitability of the company, such as lenders or employees, are not given equal status.

4. The personal assets of partners are excluded from the partnership balance sheet, even though pledged as security for partnership loans.

5. A retail store uses estimates rather than a complete physical count of its inventory for purposes of preparing monthly financial statements.

6. Marketable securities are valued at market value, when market value is lower than cost.

7. An entity reports a $50 profit after buying a unit of inventory for $100 and selling it for $150, even though the cost to replace the unit has escalated to $112, due to inflation.

8. An advance deposit on a sale contract is reported as unearned revenue.

9. A company spends $50,000 to promote a new location. The costs are deferred on the balance sheet, and will be expensed over a period of five years.

10. Accounting policies chosen for revenue recognition are the same as those of the entity's major competitors.

11. Capital assets are amortized over their useful lives.

E2-8 *Identification of Accounting Principles:* In the following cases, indicate the principle that applies to each case and state whether it was followed or violated.

Case A   Loran Company used FIFO in 20X2; LIFO in 20X3; and FIFO in 20X4.

Case B   A tract of land was acquired on credit by signing a $55,000, one-year, non-interest-bearing note. The asset account was debited for $55,000. The going rate of interest was 10%.

Case C   Loran Company always issues its annual financial report nine months after the end of the annual reporting period.

Case D   Loran Company recognizes all sales revenues on the cash basis.

Case E   Loran Company records interest expense only on the payment dates.

Case F   Loran Company includes among its financial statement elements an apartment building owned and operated by the owner of the company.

Case G   Loran Company never uses notes or supplemental schedules as a part of its financial reports.

E2-9 *Recognition:* Some of the following items may not be recognized, or recorded in a company's financial statements. Indicate the likely recognition problem.

a. Recording employee morale as an asset.
b. Recording a future liability for employees related to medical benefits to be paid after retirement.
c. Recording a liability (and expense) for cleaning up chemical dumps.
d. Recognizing the goodwill associated with increased market acceptance of a product brand name.
e. Recognizing an expense associated with the granting of a stock option to an employee, valid in 10 years' time, at a price equal to the shares' current market price. Share prices are expected to increase.

P2-1 *Application of Principles:* During an audit of L.R.T. Company, the following situations were found to exist:

a. The company uses the straight-line method of measuring depreciation on manufacturing machinery, even though it knows that a method based on actual usage would provide better matching, more accurate income determination, and thus better information for financial statement users. The straight-line method is significantly cheaper to calculate, because of the level of data needed to implement a usage method.
b. For inventory purposes, L.R.T. switched from FIFO to LIFO to FIFO for the same items during a five-year period.
c. L.R.T. does not provide information about future contracts, called the "order backlog" in its financial statements, even though this disclosure is quite common in the industry.
d. L.R.T. follows a policy of depreciating plant and equipment on the straight-line basis over a period of time that is 50% longer than the most reliable useful life estimate.
e. Interest is reported at the end of each fiscal year as the net amount of interest expense less interest revenue.

Required:
1. Identify and briefly explain the accounting principle that is directly involved in each situation.
2. Indicate what, if anything, the company should do in the future by way of any change in accounting policy.

P2-2 *Application of Principles:* The following list of statements pose conceptual issues:

a. The business entity is considered to be separate and apart from its owners for accounting purposes.
b. A transaction is always recorded in such a way as to reflect its legal form.
c. It is permissible for a company to use straight-line depreciation, even though the rest of the industry uses declining balance, because the company feels that straight-line better reflects the pattern of benefits received from these assets.
d. All details of transactions must be disclosed in the notes to the financial statements.
e. The lower of cost or market method must be used in valuing inventories.

f. The cost principle relates only to the income statement.

g. Revenue should be recognized only when the cash is received.

h. Accruals and deferrals are necessary because of the separate entity assumption.

i. Revenue should be recognized as late as possible and expenses as early as possible.

Required:

1. Indicate whether each statement is correct or incorrect.
2. Identify the principle(s) posed.
3. Provide a brief discussion of its implications.

P2-3 *Application of Principles:* An inspection of the annual financial statements and the accounting records revealed that the George L. Massey Hardware Company had violated some aspect of accounting principles. The following transactions were involved:

a. Merchandise purchased for resale was recorded as a debit to inventory for the invoice price of $40,000 (accounts payable was credited for the same amount); terms were 2/10, n/30. Ten days later, the account was paid at the net amount due, $39,200 ($40,000 less the 2% discount for paying within 10 days).

b. Accounts receivable of $95,000 were reported on the balance sheet; this amount included a $42,000 loan to the company president. The maturity date of the loan was not specified.

c. Usual and ordinary repairs on operational assets were recorded as follows: debit operational assets, $97,500; credit cash, $97,500.

d. The company sustained a $48,000 storm damage loss during the current year (no insurance). The loss was recorded and reported as follows:

   Income statement: Extraordinary item — storm loss $24,000
   Balance sheet (assets): Deferred charge — storm loss $24,000

e. Depreciation expense of $227,000 was recorded as a debit to retained earnings and was deducted directly from retained earnings on the balance sheet.

Required:

1. For each transaction, identify the inappropriate treatment and the principle(s) violated.
2. Give the entry that should have been made or the appropriate reporting.

P2-4 *Conservatism and Consistency:* Prestan Stores, a specialty retailer, has just purchased a new Canadair jet aircraft for its senior officers' travel needs. The treasurer wants to depreciate the plane for financial accounting purposes using an accelerated method because, she argues, the lower income numbers will be more conservative and this, in turn, will generate shareholder confidence in the firm. The controller, however, argues that the firm uses the straight-line method on other assets, so using an accelerated method to depreciate the plane's cost would violate the consistency of the firm's depreciation policy.

Required:

Which, if either, officer's argument is correct? Write a brief memo to the president of Prestan Stores explaining your reasons for the answer given.

P2-5 *Implementation of Principles:* The following summarized transactions were recorded as indicated for the Brown Construction Company during the current year.

a. The Brown Construction Company needed a small structure for temporary storage. A contractor quoted a price of $837,000. The company decided to build the structure itself. The cost was $643,000, and construction required three months. The following entry was made:

Buildings — warehouse	837,000	
Cash		643,000
Revenue — self-construction		194,000

b. Brown owns a plant located on a river that floods every few years. As a result, the company suffers a flood loss regularly. During the current year, the flood was severe, causing an uninsured loss of $175,000, which was the amount spent to repair the flood damage. The following entry was made:

Retained earnings, flood loss	175,000	
Cash		175,000

c. The company originally sold and issued 100,000 common shares. During the current year, 80,000 of these shares were outstanding and 20,000 were repurchased from the shareholders and retired. Near the end of the current year, the board of directors declared and paid a cash dividend of $4 per share. The dividend was recorded as follows:

Retained earnings	400,000	
Cash		320,000
Dividend income ($4 × 20,000)		80,000

d. The Brown Construction Company purchased a machine that had a list price of $90,000. The company paid for the machine in full by issuing 9,000 common shares (market price $8). The purchase was recorded as follows:

Machine	90,000	
Share capital		90,000

e. On 28 December, the company collected $33,000 cash in advance for merchandise to be available and shipped during February of the next accounting year (the accounting period ends 31 December). This transaction was recorded on 28 December as follows:

Cash	33,000	
Sales revenue		33,000

Required:

1. For each transaction, determine which accounting principle was violated (if any).
2. Explain the nature of the violation.
3. In each instance, indicate how the transaction should have been recorded.

P2-6 *Implementation of Principles:* R. H. Hall has drawn up a financial statement on 31 December 20X2, employing valuation procedures as follows:

Cash	$40,000	Includes cash in the bank, $35,000, and customers' cheques that could not be cashed (insufficient funds) but that Hall feels will ultimately be recoverable, $5,000.

Marketable securities	$90,000	Represents the value on 31 December of securities reported at the beginning of 20X2 at a cost of $81,200.
Value of insurance policy	$15,000	The sum of the payments made on a life insurance policy that requires further payments through 20X1. The cash surrender value of the policy at the end of 20X2 is $7,000.
Intangible assets	$36,000	Recorded in 20X2 when a competitor offered to pay Hall this amount if Hall would move and let the competitor take over Hall's space. Hall entered into the lease when the company was formed. It still has five years to run at a "bargain" rental that is 7% of net sales.
Sundry payables	$ 1	Recorded as a result of a lawsuit of $20,000 against Hall for breach of contract; Hall has offered to pay $5,000 in settlement of the lawsuit, but this has been rejected; it is the opinion of Hall's attorney that the lawsuit can be settled by payment of $10,000.

Required:

1. Indicate what change, if any, you would make in reporting each of the preceding items.
2. In each case, discuss the accounting principle involved.

P2-7 *Implementation of Principles:* Analyze each of the following situations and indicate which accounting principle or principles, as described in the chapter, is in evidence.

Case A   The financial statements of Raychem Corporation included the following note: "During the current year, plant assets were written down by $8,000,000. This write-down will reduce future expenses. Depreciation and other expenses in future years will be lower, and as a result this will benefit profits of future years."

Case B   During an audit of the Silvona Company, certain liabilities such as taxes appear to be overstated. Also, some semi-obsolete inventory items seem to be undervalued, and the tendency is to expense rather than capitalize as many items as possible. Management states that "the company has always taken a very conservative view of the business and its future prospects." Management suggests that it does not wish to weaken the company by reporting any more earnings or paying any more dividends than are absolutely necessary because it does not expect business to continue to be good. It points out that the lower valuations for assets and so on do not lose anything for the company but do create reserves for "hard times."

Case C   There was no comment or explanation of the fact that ABC Company changed its inventory method from FIFO to LIFO at the beginning of the current reporting period. A large changeover difference was involved, and there was no retroactive restatement.

Case D   Current assets amounted to $314,000 and current liabilities, $205,000; the balance sheet of Nelta Corp. reported a single amount "Working capital, $109,000."

Case E   In 20X1, the Tryler Corporation switched its inventory method for financial reporting from LIFO to FIFO. Tryler publicly explained, "Our major competitors have consistently used the FIFO method. Therefore, the reported loss for 20X1 and the restated profit for 20X0 are on a comparable basis as to inventory valuation with competitors."

P2-8 *Recognition Criteria:* In each case below, discuss recognition of the element in the financial statements.

Case A   For some time, airlines have been offering frequent-flyer mileage credits to customers. Currently there exists a huge resource of potential trips the public could sign up for at the airlines' expense. Most airlines only allow passengers to use mileage credits for unused capacity — otherwise empty seats. Industry experts estimate that the incremental cost of putting a passenger on a plane is only around $10 — the cost of the meal and a little extra fuel for the additional weight. If the passenger were to use mileage credits to "bump" a full-fare passenger, then there is obviously a significant opportunity cost associated with the trip. The airlines do not recognize a liability for these outstanding claims on their passenger-flying capacity.

Case B   The value of Coca-Cola's trademark has been estimated in excess of $1 billion. Yet even though Coca-Cola reports over $4 billion of goodwill and other intangible assets, none of this reported value is due to the Coca-Cola trademark, which is unrecognized despite its considerable commercial value.

Case C   Waste Disposal Ltd. is being sued to force it to clean up pollution in over 60 sites; this information is reported in the notes to the company's annual report but no amount is accrued in the financial statements. The extent of the future cleanup costs is reported to be "substantial."

The Income Statement and the Retained Earnings Statement

INTRODUCTION

The income statement is the primary source of information for a company's current profit performance. Investors, lenders, analysts, and other financial statement readers use this and other information in predicting the amount, timing, and uncertainty of the firm's future income and cash flows. This predictive value of the income statement is one of the reasons it is so relevant. The income statement also plays an important role in providing feedback: how good were predictions of prior years' earnings?

Another important use of the income statement is for performance evaluation. The primary financial statement for evaluating the performance of managers (both internally and by external stakeholders) is the income statement. Of course, the income statement must be interpreted within the company's economic, industrial, and competitive environment. Nevertheless, profit is considered to be the main indicator of management's performance. Investors look at the return on and risk of their investment. The level of earnings is viewed as the **return,** while the volatility of earnings is viewed as one measure of risk. That is a major reason that management is so often concerned about maximizing and smoothing net income; managers hope that by maximizing net income, they can improve investors' perception of return, while by smoothing net income, they hope to lower investors' perception of **risk.**

Our purpose in this chapter is to develop an understanding of what information the income statement contains, how that information is presented, and how it might be used. Although measurement and recognition issues are critical, this chapter focuses on the display of revenues, expenses, gains, and losses after they have been recorded. Measurement and recognition issues will be discussed broadly in Chapters 6 and 7, and more specific issues will be discussed in each chapter as the book progresses.

NATURE OF INCOME

Change in Retained Earnings

The income statement links a company's beginning and ending balance sheets for a given accounting period. Under the proprietary concept of accounting (discussed in Chapter 2), the income statement explains changes in owners' equity caused by operations and certain other activities during the period. When there is no new investment or disinvestment by owners (or other minor technical changes), the change in owners' equity from the beginning to the end of the period equals net income. Exhibit 3-1 illustrates this point.

The Appendix to this volume contains a review of the mechanics of the accounting process, for those readers who need a refresher.

Economic Income vs. Accounting Income

The term income means different things to different people. For example, an economist defines a *change in wealth*, whether realized or not, as income. Suppose that a company owns a parcel of land for which it paid $10,000 several years ago. A new highway has just been built next to the property, and several individuals have offered to pay $125,000 to $150,000 for the land. The firm has not yet agreed to sell. The economist would say that an increase in wealth has occurred because the land is worth more than historic cost. The wealth increase is called economic income, and it is based on an events approach rather than on completed transactions.

Using the historical cost measurement principle, an accountant usually would not recognize such an increase in wealth as income. Only if the land is sold to another party in an arm's length transaction would the accountant recognize the increase in wealth as income. This is accounting income, based on the transactions approach.

There are three general problems with the transactions approach to reporting income:

1. The transactions approach may result in the exclusion of important information. The transactions approach captures some information, but not all information that may be relevant for a particular user or decision. For example, the relevant market value of the land in the above example is excluded from recognition in the financial statements, but is of considerable interest to a bank that uses the land as collateral for a loan.

2. Not all transactions are treated equally. Some treatments are more subjective than others. Accounting policies determine which transactions are recorded and how their impacts are measured. Management makes choices about the *accounting policies* to be used, which significantly affect the amount of reported net income. As well, most *accounting estimates* are determined by management. Even within given measurement rules, the flexibility provided by accounting estimates significantly affects reported net income. The events approach is often criticized as being subjective, and yet the choices of which transactions to measure and how to measure the results of those transactions (and their subsequent disposition or recognition, such as an asset versus an expense) may also be highly subjective.

3. With the knowledge of which transactions will be measured (and how they will be measured), management can enter into transactions (or avoid transactions) with the primary purpose of affecting the reported results. In the land example cited above, management could decide to sell the land to a related party in order to trigger recognition of a gain, while still retaining substantive control over the land (or buying it back from the related party after a short period of time).

Revenue and expense recognition are key concepts in accounting. The concepts determine when and how revenues, gains, expenses, and losses are recorded.

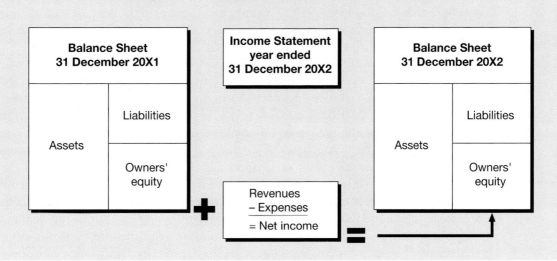

EXHIBIT 3-1
Diagram of Changes in Retained Earnings

Determining the proper treatment for a particular transaction or event is often difficult. Indeed, a large part of the study of accounting addresses measurement and recognition issues as they apply to revenues, gains, expenses, and losses, as well as to assets and liabilities. Chapter 2 discussed the general nature of recognition criteria. Because revenue and expense recognition is such a significant aspect of accounting, Chapter 6 is devoted exclusively to revenue recognition and Chapter 7 discusses expense recognition.

Inclusiveness of the Income Statement

Which items affecting shareholders' equity should be included in the computation of net income and reported in the income statement? That is, what items, if any, should be recorded as direct adjustments to equity and excluded from income? There are two extreme approaches to answering these questions.

Current Operating Performance. At one extreme is the current operating performance approach. Advocates of this approach maintain that only items that are part of the *ordinary recurring operations* of the firm should be included in earnings. Other items such as gains and losses that relate to prior periods or to unusual or non-recurring activities are recorded as direct adjustments to retained earnings. Advocates of this approach believe that users of financial statements attach a particular significance to the figure labelled "net income" and that it should have maximum power for predicting operating income. If users are not able to analyze the income statement and make adjustments for those items that are unrelated to the company's current period operating performance, the predictive power of the income statement will suffer.

All-Inclusive Approach. At the other extreme is the all-inclusive approach, in which all transactions affecting the net increase or decrease in equity during the period are included in the determination of net income, except contributions by or distributions to owners. Advocates of this approach believe that items such as those related to the extraordinary activities and events related to prior years are all part of the earnings history of the firm and that exclusion of such items from the income statement increases the probability that they will be overlooked in a review of the operating

Dividends.

results for a period of years. They also point out the dangers of possible manipulation of the annual earnings figure if preparers of financial statements are permitted to omit certain items in determining net income. Advocates of the all-inclusive approach believe that full disclosure in the income statement of the nature of various transactions enables income statement users to assess fully the importance of each item and its effect on operating results and cash flows.

Current Practice. Accounting standards in Canada generally reflect an approach that is closer to the all-inclusive approach. Virtually all items affecting equity (other than investment by or distributions to owners) are included in net income; the AcSB has largely eliminated the possibility of charging or crediting items directly to retained earnings except for corrections of errors and for restatements due to changes in accounting policies (discussed in Chapter 22). The concerns of advocates of the current operating performance approach are addressed in part by separately identifying and disclosing the various special non-operating items separately on the face of the income statement. For example, income from continuing operations can be measured and reported on the top portion of the statement, with the effects of non-operating items (such as discontinued operations and extraordinary items) separately identified and reported below income from continuing operations. Thus, various subtotals on the income statement have special meaning.

Income as a Predictive Tool

Earnings trends are important analytical tools used by investment analysts and investors in forecasting a company's future earnings. Forecasts of future earnings are one factor often used in making investment decisions. Past trends and performance do not guarantee continuation of such trends and performance in the future, but they are often useful in prediction.

The Royal Bank of Canada reported earnings of $1,169 in 1994 and $1,262 in 1995 (amounts in millions). The increase in 1995 over 1996 was about 8%. Based on this data, and your understanding that the bank operated in a stable environment in 1996, what estimate could you provide for 1996 earnings? Another 8% increase would translate into a prediction of $1,363 ($1,262 × 1.08%), not too far off the bank's reported 1996 earnings of $1,430. The actual increase in 1996 was about 13%. If you predict another 13% increase for 1997, you'd get an estimate of about $1,616; actual 1997 net income was $1,679 (an increase of about 17%). Net income for 1998 rose to $1,824, a further 9% increase. Well, prediction is not really that easy.

Take a look at the income statement for Canadian National Railway Company, shown in Exhibit 3-2. The income statement has columns for three years. Two years are all that is required by accounting standards for full disclosure, but the U.S. Securities and Exchange Commission (SEC) requires all listed public companies to present three-year comparative income statements. CN, a Canadian company that also lists its shares on the New York Stock Exchange, complies with U.S. disclosure standards.

CN reports a loss of $(1,085) in 1995, net income of $805 in 1996 and net income of $402 in 1997. It's hard to see a trend based on bottom-line net income! What will 1998 hold for CN? To answer that question, one would certainly seek forecasts of economic activity in CN's major areas of operation — transportation, industrial products, forest products, mining, etc. These sectors represent major areas of the Canadian economy, and there are lots of sources to consult.

But what about the income statement itself? Three additional subtotals are identified as measures of income (shown in boldface in Exhibit 3-2):

1. Operating (loss) income
2. Income (loss) from continuing operations before income taxes, and
3. Income (loss) from continuing operations.

EXHIBIT 3-2
CANADIAN NATIONAL RAILWAY COMPANY
Consolidated Statement of Income
year ended December 31
(Cdn. $ millions)

	1997	1996 (restated)	1995 (restated)
Revenues			
Industrial products	$ 893	$ 851	$ 838
Forest products	824	787	771
Grain and grain products	692	564	600
Coal, sulphur, and fertilizers	635	618	601
Intermodal	776	677	635
Automotive	435	389	399
Other items	97	109	110
Total revenues	4,352	3,995	3,954
Operating expenses			
Labour and fringe benefits	1,431	1,381	1,477
Material	316	297	318
Fuel	335	314	277
Depreciation and amortization	200	194	231
Operating taxes	186	171	192
Equipment rentals	219	216	194
Net car hire	116	108	117
Purchased services	363	348	354
Casualty and insurance	103	85	52
Other	273	271	302
Special charges	—	381	1,453
Total operating expenses	3,545	3,766	4,967
Operating income (loss)	807	229	(1,013)
Interest expense	(118)	(114)	(198)
Other income	57	27	100
Income (loss) from continuing operations before income taxes	746	142	(1,111)
Income tax (expense) recovery from continuing operations	(325)	694	19
Income (loss) from continuing operations	421	836	(1,092)
Discontinued operations (net of applicable income taxes)	(18)	14	7
Net income (loss)	$ 402	$ 805	$(1,085)

Earnings per share (Note 16)

References to other disclosure notes have been deleted.

These intermediate income measures are meant to provide the reader with information on major causes or sources of income (or loss) and assist the reader in forming estimates of the amount, timing, and uncertainty of future income and cash flows. It seems obvious that discontinued operations will not help in predicting next year, and thus the user is encouraged to back up through the income statement to find a more relevant number. Operating income should be more promising, but it still does not portray a stable relationship with prior years.

One anomaly that might catch your eye is the fact that 1996 shows a huge tax *recovery* of $694, even though operations were modestly profitable and would normally be expected to result in an income tax *expense*. The reason can be traced (in the notes) to a change in accounting policy; CN chose to apply the AcSB's revised income tax accounting rules well in advance of their mandatory effective date of 2000. This accounting change permitted the company to recognize, in 1996, a one-time gain of $768 as the probable *future* tax benefits from *past* operating losses; there is no cash flow associated with this gain, at least not in 1996. If the gain had not been recognized, income tax expense would have been $74. (We'll look at accounting for income taxes in Chapters 16 and 17.)

Going a bit further up CN's income statement, one might notice something called "special charges" which, at $1,453, was fairly instrumental in the 1995 reported loss. In 1996, there was another special charge of $381, but there is no such charge in 1997. Reference to the notes (not reproduced here) indicates that there were a few things in this category, but the biggest item in 1995 was the write-down of one of CN's capital assets, rail properties, by $1,300. Rail properties were written down because their value was impaired: their future cash flow was deemed insufficient to recover their capital cost.

In 1996, the special charge was made for *estimated* workforce reduction costs expected to be incurred in 1997 (but to be paid out over the next seven years). A little detective work has paid off. Will there be more special charges in future years? Or were these one-time events? Information from the company, and from industry experts, will help in this assessment. But, taking out the non-recurring items noted above, earnings from continuing operations would be as follows:

	1997	1996	1995
Income from continuing operations, as reported	$421	$ 836	$(1,092)
Subtract special, non-recurring, income tax gain		(768)	
Add back special, non-recurring, charges		381	$ 1,453
Restated earnings from continuing operations	$421	$ 449	$ 361

With these adjustments for non-recurring items, CN's earnings don't seem to be so unstable after all. The apparent wide swings in net income is due to the non-recurring items which, by their nature, are hard for an outsider to predict.

The *all-inclusive* presentation results in a net income figure, that, of and by itself, may not be ideally suited for prediction. Users of the financial statements must decide which earnings or income figure reported in the income statement best depicts a company's financial growth and offers the most assistance in predicting future earnings. There is no simple answer to this question. The nature of each item must be understood in order to effectively use the information portrayed. And, of course, there is a lot of information that must be compiled to support a prediction — forecasts, public statements about a company's strategy, economic forecasts, and so on. This information is not contained in audited financial statements.

CONCEPT REVIEW

1. Explain the relationship between the income statement and the balance sheet.
2. What is the difference between an *events approach* and a *transactions*

approach to measuring income? Which approach is the dominant one in accounting practice?

3. How is the *all-inclusive approach* to the income statement different from the *current operating performance approach*. Which approach best reflects Canadian practice?

CHOICE IN FORMAT ISSUES

There is a great deal of flexibility in format issues for the income statement, leaving companies leeway to pick policies that suit their individual circumstances and that best serve their user groups and themselves.

Title. The income statement is also known as the *statement of income* (or statement of earnings), *statement of operations, profit and loss statement*, or by other expressions. In this text, we will most often use the term income statement. When a parent company and its subsidiaries are combined for the report, the statement is identified as a **consolidated** income statement.

Fiscal Year-End. A company must choose a fiscal year-end. Normally, companies try to pick a point that represents the low point in their seasonal pattern. This is to ensure that year-end adjustments and the annual report do not have to be prepared during their busy season. However, there are other factors to consider. For example, having the same year-end as other companies in the industry facilitates comparisons. Companies who are part of a corporate group prefer to have the same year-end as their parent to allow consolidation. Some industries are governed by legislation that mandates a certain year-end. For example, the federal Bank Act requires banks to use a 31 October year-end.

Many businesses pick the calendar year as a fiscal year. According to *Financial Reporting in Canada 1997*, a survey of 200 public Canadian companies, two-thirds use a 31 December year-end. The rest are fairly evenly divided among the remaining months.

Reporting Period Length and Composition. Another basic issue to decide is the length of the reporting period. Annual reports are the norm, as companies are expected to use a 12-month period. The 12-month period facilitates preparation of required annual reports to shareholders and securities commissions.

The operating cycle of some companies leads them to end their fiscal period at the end of a *week* instead of the end of a month. Such companies are usually in the retail trade or are suppliers to retail companies. In earlier times, many such businesses were closed on Sundays and therefore the weekend provided a natural time to "take stock" and to close the books. These companies typically define their reporting period as 52 weeks. For example, Loblaw Companies Ltd., a major grocery chain, uses a 52-week reporting period. Every so often, the company must include 53 weeks in the reporting period so as to avoid moving its year-end far from a particular target date. For example, a company may follow the policy of ending its fiscal period on the Saturday closest to 31 January each year.

Companies often also issue financial statements for shorter periods, most often quarterly. Public companies are required by securities commissions to issue quarterly statements to their shareholders. Quarterly statements need not be full sets of statements, but income and cash flow statements are normally required. Quarterly balance sheets are not required, but often are provided by the companies.

Reporting Currency. Companies must also determine the reporting currency used to report to shareholders. Normally, one would assume that a Canadian company, reporting with Canadian GAAP, would report in Canadian dollars. This is the norm, but it is not required. Although Canadian GAAP usually will be followed, any reporting currency can be used. Why would a Canadian company choose to report in, say, U.S. dollars? The primary reason is that most of the company's business is conducted in U.S. dollars. U.S. dollars may be used by companies that have the bulk of their operations in the U.S. (e.g., Cineplex Odeon, Inco, Seagram's) or whose product is priced world-wide in U.S. dollars (e.g. gold mining companies, paper products companies). Another reason may be that a company's major user groups — shareholders and/or lenders — may be in the United States. Since these users perform analyses and comparisons in U.S. dollars, it is obvious that U.S. dollar reports would be more useful to them.

Bear in mind, though, that reporting in U.S. dollars doesn't mean reporting in U.S. GAAP. Canadian-based public companies that report in U.S. dollars still use Canadian GAAP.

Rounding. What degree of rounding is appropriate? Users get bogged down in too many digits, but may lose some trend data if too much rounding occurs. The extent of rounding depends on the size of the company. A company with revenues and assets in the billions will round to the nearest million dollars at least, but many round to the nearest billion. Smaller companies will round to the nearest thousand.

Unrounded figures give an illusion of exactitude that is not appropriate. Reported accounting numbers are the result of many accounting policy decisions and estimates, and the numbers would be quite different under different policies and different, equally valid, estimates and assumptions. Rounding helps to emphasize the approximate nature of the numbers.

Language. What is the language of the user group? Obviously, financial statements are written for that group, in their language. But how are anglophone or francophone users accommodated if they are in the minority? Companies that are incorporated in Quebec or are traded on the Montreal Exchange must publish their statements in French, but many other Canadian public companies publish French versions of their annual reports (and Quebec companies publish English versions). Some present the English and French version together in the same report, but the majority provide a separate French version on request.

Typically, the French version of an anglophone company includes only translation of the disclosure notes and thus must be used in conjunction with the English-language version of the financial statements themselves. Of course, there's no reason for limiting financial statements to English and French — the financial statements can be prepared in any language. Some investors, seeking investment in Germany or Japan, prepare reports that are in the appropriate languages for their target audiences.

The fact that a company translates its financial statements into other languages does not mean that the statements have been adjusted to reflect GAAP in that language's home country. For example, some Canadian companies translate their financial statements into Japanese for the convenience of Japanese investors and business partners, but the statements still reflect Canadian GAAP and not Japanese GAAP. On the other hand, many Japanese companies translate their financial statements into English. Here one must be careful; some of the Japanese companies report in U.S. GAAP (even in Japan), while others use Japanese GAAP in their English-language statements. Users must be careful to ascertain the GAAP choices made by the company.

Comparative Data. Accounting numbers are meaningless unless they can be compared to some other numbers. The most obvious comparison for a company is to look at how they did this year compared to the preceding year. Trends in financial information are much more revealing than information for only one period. In recognition of this fact, paragraph 1500.09 of the *CICA Handbook* recommends that comparative figures be presented *when they are meaningful.* In most situations, comparative statements are meaningful. Presentation of one year's comparative information is the norm, although some companies present two years' comparative results on the income statement to comply with the U.S. SEC regulation requiring this expanded disclosure. As previously mentioned, CN presents two years' comparative information.

Public companies also provide a longer-term comparison of selected numbers, usually on a five-year basis. Five-year comparative numbers usually include operating earnings, net income, earnings per share, and total assets, among others.

Detail. The *CICA Handbook* specifies certain items that have to be separately disclosed on the income statement, as we will see. Other items may be grouped, or separately disclosed. The extent of this grouping is a major policy decision for the company. How much detail should be included on the income statement? Typically, disclosures meet little more than the minimum standards. We'll come back to discuss this policy decision in a few pages, when we review the minimum recommended income statement disclosures.

Display. The manner in which accounting information is displayed in an income statement may influence the reader's interpretation of the information. Positioning of items and other issues of display can confuse or clarify.

Except for extraordinary items and discontinued operations, GAAP does not specify a standard format for organizing and presenting the elements of income on the income statement. Revenue, expense, gain, and loss items are organized in the income statement in two general ways: the **single-step format** and the **multiple-step format.** The question is, "How many subtotals does the entity wish to present?" The single-step format has none, while the multiple-step format can have many.

Single-Step Format. The single-step format uses only two broad section classifications: a revenues and gains section and an expenses and losses section. It is a single-step statement because only one step is involved in computing and displaying income (also labelled as "income from continuing operations"). Exhibit 3-3 shows Petro-Canada's income statement. This is a single-step statement, except for the presentation of income tax expense as a separate category. In a "pure" single-step statement, income tax expense would be listed as just another expense, with no subtotal for earnings before income taxes.

In practice, numerous such variations of the single-step format exist. For example, revenue items, such as interest income or investment income, are sometimes netted against related expenses. Note, however, that even on a single-step income statement, extraordinary items and discontinued operations are shown separately, net of tax, and after appropriately labelled subtotals. The CN income statement (Exhibit 3-2) is primarily single-step, except that it provides a subtotal before income taxes and a separate classification, as required, for discontinued operations.

Multiple-Step Format. The multiple-step format provides several *classifications* and *intermediate subtotal* measures of income. The multiple-step format typically distinguishes among various operations and activities that affect income. A typical multiple-step income statement would contain the following components:

I. Operations section. This section includes the revenues and expenses of the company's primary operations. Revenue, or sales, is followed by cost of sales, and then often a subtotal, called gross profit or gross margin. After that, selling expenses, general and administrative expenses and other operating expenses, however defined, are

EXHIBIT 3-3
PETRO-CANADA
Consolidated Statement of Earnings
(Millions of Cdn. dollars)

For the years ended December 31	1997	1996	1995
Revenue			
Operating	$6,017	$5,514	$4,739
Investment and other income	79	93	81
	6,096	5,607	4,820
Expenses			
Crude oil and product purchases	3,183	2,988	2,405
Producing, refining, and marketing	1,352	1,257	1,198
General and administrative	194	187	308
Exploration	75	60	43
Depreciation, depletion, and amortization	482	440	338
Taxes other than income taxes	68	70	68
Interest	106	109	90
	5,460	5,111	4,450
Earnings before income taxes	636	496	370
Provision for income taxes			
Current	(41)	160	120
Deferred	371	89	54
	330	249	174
Net earnings	$ 306	$ 247	$ 196
Net earnings per share (dollars)	$ 1.13	$ 0.94	$ 0.79

References to disclosure notes have been deleted.

included. The operations section usually ends with a subtotal, computed by deducting the above expenses from revenues or gross margin. The caption found on this subtotal is something along the line of "operating income," or "operating profit."

II. Non-operations section. This subsection includes income and expense items that are routine and ordinary but not components of the company's operations. Examples are interest income or expense, royalty income, dividend income, and equity in the earnings of joint ventures or unconsolidated affiliated companies. This section may also contain, at the company's choice, other revenues, gains, losses, and expenses that they believe are *unusual* in nature and not expected to repeat. Restructuring costs, for example, are frequently found in this section but may be included in operations, too. Display is anything but standardized! Again, this section ends with a subtotal, appropriately labelled.

III. Other possible sections. Occasionally, firms will display non-controlling (minority) interest in earnings or equity in the earnings of investees at this point on the statement. These items are shown separately because they arise from a different source than the operating activities of the company and receive different tax treatment.

Non-controlling (minority) interest in earnings is a deduction from income that results when a company prepares consolidated financial statements combining itself with one or more additional companies that it controls, but in which it does not have a 100% ownership interest. Basically, the controlling company includes all the subsidiary's income, but then deducts the non-controlling or minority portion.

Equity in earnings of investees is a revenue item. It is the pro rata share of earnings of a second company in which the reporting company has an ownership interest that gives it significant influence. These sections end with a subtotal.

IV. Income tax expenses. This subsection presents the portion of combined provincial, federal, and foreign income tax expenses *applicable to the income recognized up to this point in the statement.* If the firm has experienced a loss, income taxes are a credit item that reduce the reported loss. The income tax benefit may include both realized benefits (from a refund of prior years' taxes paid) and unrealized benefits (recognition of future tax benefits that the company will receive from the loss). Accounting for the tax benefits of losses is discussed in Chapter 17.

A subtotal is usually displayed after recognition of income tax expense. If there are no subsequent subsections, this subtotal is labelled "net earnings" or "net income." The word "net" is not used with any subtotal — only with "bottom line" net income.

If there are subsequent subsections, this intermediate amount is labelled so as to reflect these remaining subsections. Discontinued operations and extraordinary items, if any, would also follow.

Many of the above sections are found in a typical multiple-step statement, *but the presentation format of this information is not specified in the CICA Handbook.* Firms can alter the order of listing or grouping of the above items in a wide variety of ways, to emphasize important relationships between revenues and expenses, or important subtotals. For example, a firm that produces and sells both goods and services might show two gross profit figures, one for activities involving the manufacturing and sale of goods and one for its service activities.

A multiple-step income statement as contained in the Cott Corporation annual report, is presented in Exhibit 3-4. In this example, the multiple-step statement presents a number of fairly idiosyncratic subtotals:

- Gross profit
- Earnings before the undernoted
- Earnings (loss) before income taxes
- Earnings (loss) before undernoted

Cott had to present a subtotal before discontinued operations to comply with the recommendations of the *CICA Handbook*. The other subtotals were their choice.

The single-step format has the advantage of simplicity and avoids the need to develop names for intermediate classifications. The multiple-step format is potentially more informative to decision-makers because it highlights important relationships and intermediate subtotals in the report. Advocates of the multiple-step format believe that there are important relationships in revenue and expense data and that the income statement is more useful when these relationships are explicitly shown.

CONCEPT REVIEW

1. How might interest expense on long-term debt be presented differently in a single-step versus a multiple-step income statement?
2. When might a Canadian company choose to prepare its financial statements in U.S. dollars?
3. Why are *comparative* statements usually presented, instead of just the current year's amounts?

EXHIBIT 3-4
COTT CORPORATION
Consolidated Statement of Earnings

(Cdn $ thousands, except per share amounts)

	53 Weeks Ended January 31, 1998	52 Weeks Ended January 25, 1997	52 Weeks Ended January 27, 1996
Sales	$1,481,053	$1, 324,737	$1,280,484
Cost of goods sold	1,246,169	1,104,351	1,120,930
Gross Profit	234,884	220,386	159,554
Selling, general and administrative expenses	116,250	96,341	97,879
Other expense	3,106	276	315
Earnings before the undernoted	115,528	123,769	61,360
Amortization of capital assets	34,116	24,991	17,077
Amortization of goodwill, licences, and trademarks	4,344	2,745	2,044
Amortization of other assets	16,457	17,415	18,143
Interest on long-term debt	37,235	25,357	17,578
Other interest	1,309	732	2,335
Interest income	(4,211)	(2,943)	(774)
Unusual items (Note 12)	30,502	11,454	37,156
	119,752	79,751	93,559
Earnings (loss) before income taxes	(4,224)	44,018	(32,199)
Income taxes (Note 14)			
Current	5,632	5,554	(2,487)
Deferred	(6,900)	7,692	(5,748)
	(1,268)	13,246	(8,235)
Earnings (loss) before the undernoted	(2,956)	30,772	(23,964)
Non-controlling interest	260	(818)	241
Equity in net earnings from long-term investments	1,961	1,388	1,261
Earnings (loss) from continuing operations	(735)	31,342	(22,462)
Earnings (loss) from discontinued operations (Note 15)	(6,971)	2,697	(6,913)
Net earnings (loss) for the year	$ (7,706)	$ 34,039	$ (29,375)
Earnings (loss) per common share from continuing operations			
Basic	$ (0.01)	$ 0.51	$ (0.37)
Fully diluted	$ (0.01)	$ 0.50	$ (0.37)
Net earnings (loss) per common share			
Basic	$ (0.12)	$ 0.56	$ (0.49)
Fully diluted	$ (0.12)	$ 0.55	$ (0.49)

References to disclosure notes have been deleted.

FORMAT ISSUES GOVERNED BY ACCOUNTING STANDARDS

Required Subsections

We have already pointed out that the *CICA Handbook* recommends that there be subtotals in the income statement in certain circumstances. The specific recommendation is as follows:

> The income statement should distinguish the following:
>
> a) Income or loss before discontinued operations and extraordinary items.
>
> b) Results of discontinued operations.
>
> c) Income or loss before extraordinary items.
>
> d) Extraordinary items.
>
> e) Net income or loss for the period.
>
> f) Earnings per share, when and as appropriate.
>
> [CICA 1520.02]

This means that if there are discontinued operations and extraordinary items, there will be a minimum of three subsections to the income statement:

1. Continuing operations
2. Discontinued operations
3. Extraordinary items

The first section includes all of the revenues, expenses, gains, and losses that pertain to those operations except those that management has decided to sell or shut down. The discontinued operations section includes past *and estimated future* revenues, expenses, gains, and losses on those segments of the company's business that management has decided to get out of. The extraordinary items section includes only those few gains and losses that meet the criteria for classification as extraordinary.

We will discuss each of these three parts of the income statement in the following sections of this chapter. First, however, we should comment on the treatment of income tax expense in the income statement, as it affects all three sections.

Intraperiod Tax Allocation

If an item is shown net *of related tax*, it means that the tax consequences of the item have been determined and the reported amount is shown after these tax effects have been adjusted for. Determining this amount is the process of intraperiod tax allocation. *Intra* means that the allocation is within the period and within the income statement and retained earnings statement. Interperiod tax allocation is the allocation of tax expense to different reporting periods, covered in depth in Chapter 16.

To demonstrate *intraperiod* tax allocation, consider the following situation for the Calgary Storage Company. Sales for 20X1 total $1 million and expenses before income taxes total $700,000. During 20X1, the company experiences an extraordinary loss of $200,000 when an earthquake destroys several of the company's uninsured warehouses. Assume that the income tax rate is 40% and that the $200,000 earthquake loss is deductible for income tax purposes. Calgary Storage Company's income statement with and without intraperiod tax allocation is as shown in Exhibit 3-5.

EXHIBIT 3-5
CALGARY STORAGE COMPANY
Income Statement
for the year ended 31 December 20X1

	Without Intraperiod Tax Allocation	With Intraperiod Tax Allocation
Sales	$1,000,000	$1,000,000
Expenses	700,000	700,000
Income from operations	300,000	300,000
Income tax expense:		
On operations ($300,000 × 40%)		120,000
On taxable income ($100,000 × 40%)	40,000	—
Income before extraordinary loss	260,000	180,000
Extraordinary item:		
Loss from earthquake damage:		
Gross amount	(200,000)	(200,000)
Tax reduction	—	80,000
Net extraordinary item	(200,000)	(120,000)
Net income	$ 60,000	$ 60,000

In the column without intraperiod tax allocation, the tax expense is shown at the actual amount that will be paid, or 40% of the $100,000 taxable income (revenues of $1 million less expenses of $700,000 and less the loss of $200,000). In the column with intraperiod tax allocation, the tax effects of the two activities (operations and the earthquake loss) are shown separately. Thus, the income tax expense that would be paid if there were no loss from the earthquake would be 40% of $300,000, or $120,000. The tax effect of the earthquake loss reduces income tax for the period by 40% of the loss, or $80,000. The $80,000 tax savings resulting from the loss is subtracted from the gross loss of $200,000 to arrive at the after-tax amount of $120,000.

In Exhibit 3-5, the tax impact of the extraordinary item is shown directly on the face of the statement for illustrative purposes, but usually only the net amount of $120,000 would be shown. The tax effect is usually disclosed in a note rather than on the face of the income statement, if it is disclosed at all.

Canadian accounting standards require intraperiod tax allocation, as illustrated, for extraordinary items and discontinued operations. Intraperiod tax allocation also applies to *error corrections* and to the *cumulative effect of a retroactive change in accounting policy*, shown on the retained earnings statement. Error correction and accounting policy changes are illustrated in Chapter 22.

Minimum Disclosure of Continuing Operations

Exhibits 3-1, 3-2, and 3-3 illustrate income statements that contain some detail in the expense and revenue categories, but also involve a lot of grouping. For example, Cott groups all selling, general and administrative expenses but shows three categories of amortization expense separately. Management has considerable flexibility in presenting revenue, expense, gain, and loss items in the income statement. What dictates the decision to group an item or disclose it separately? Grouping reduces the length and complexity of the statement, but it may also reduce its predictive value and the information content of the statement. Grouping also hides sensitive information from competitors and other users. It's not an easy decision.

Section 1520 of the *CICA Handbook* specifies the minimum information content of the income statement. The recommended *minimum* information content of the income statement that should be included in arriving at the *income or loss before discontinued operations and extraordinary items* can be summarized as follows:

Recommended disclosures of revenue items include

- revenue
- investment income of various types
- lease income
- revenue from government assistance

Recommended disclosures of expenses include
- depreciation and amortization
- research and development expenses
- interest expenses
- unusual items
- income taxes
- non-controlling interest (or minority interest) in income

The list is probably as interesting for the things it leaves out as for the things it includes. There is no minimum disclosure requirement for major expense categories such as cost of goods sold, or selling, general, and administrative expenses. Many companies follow the minimum disclosure requirements and present extremely aggregated income statements. For example, Petro-Canada (Exhibit 3-3) provides very aggregated categories. CN (Exhibit 3-2), on the other hand, has many more categories on their income statement, including revenue by business sector, and various expense categories. (For all these companies, some of the recommended disclosures are contained in the disclosure notes, which have not been reproduced.)

Section 1520 also contains a list of information that the AcSB considers *desirable*. Major items include

- cost of goods sold
- major operating expenses categories, such as selling and administrative expenses
- rental expense
- certain types of lease income
- the net amount of foreign currency gains or losses included in income
- certain amounts relating to financial assets and financial liabilities that are recognized as income or expense for the period (discussed in Chapters 13 and 15)

Companies whose reporting is constrained by GAAP, such as public companies, are expected to disclose all of the items in the *recommended* list, but disclosure of items in the *desirable* list is strictly optional.

Since there is no requirement that major items of expense be reported, an income statement prepared on the basis of minimum disclosure need not be continuous. Exhibit 3-6 illustrates an income statement that contains only required disclosures. Cara Operations will be best known to readers for Swiss Chalet chicken and Harvey's hamburgers, as well as for a lot of airplane food. After reporting a one-line *gross revenue*, Cara skips everything in between and simply shows *Earnings before the following*. The "following" items are simply all of the disclosures pertaining to this company that are recommended in the *CICA Handbook*.

The Cara statement is an example of a combined statement of income and retained earnings. The "bottom line" of net income isn't at the bottom — it's just below the middle. Also notice that the company doesn't use the usual expression *net income*; instead, *net earnings* is the final income number. Finally, notice that Cara is

EXHIBIT 3-6
CARA OPERATIONS LIMITED
Example of a Non-Continuous Income Statement
Consolidated Statements of Earnings and Retained Earnings
for the years ended March 29, 1998 and March 30, 1997

($ thousands, except earnings per share data)	1998	1997
Gross revenue	$801,202	$712,434
Earnings before the following:	$ 84,743	$ 78,658
Amortization of capital assets	20,685	18,439
Amortization of goodwill	2,041	1,979
Amortization of contracts and trademarks	1,730	2,019
Interest expense, net of interest income of $733 (1997 — $1,381)	5,821	4,795
Earnings before income taxes, equity earnings and discontinued operations	54,466	51,426
Provision for income taxes	(21,925)	(21,488)
Earnings before equity earnings and discontinued operations	32,541	29,938
Equity earnings, net of amortization of $671 (1997 — $524)	2,896	505
Earnings from continuing operations	35,437	30,443
Discontinued operations — net of tax	(410)	(74)
Net earnings for the year	$ 35,027	$ 30,369
Retained earnings — beginning of year	211,217	287,391
Share redemption in excess of book value	(24)	(96,762)
Dividends	(10,824)	(9,781)
Retained earnings — end of year	$235,396	$211,217
Earnings per share from		
continuing operations — Basic	36.1¢	30.1¢
— Fully diluted	35.4¢	30.1¢
Net earnings per share — Basic	35.7¢	30.1¢
— Fully diluted	35.0¢	30.1¢

References to disclosure notes have been removed.

one of those companies that uses a 52 or 53-week year; the fiscal year always ends on a Sunday.

Discontinued Operations

The sale or disposal of a segment of a business has important implications for predicting future income and cash flow. In a troubled economy, rationalization and restructuring of business operations and the sale or windup of business segments are common occurrences.

If the existing business is changed, but the company stays in the same line of business, the company typically reports a loss on restructuring. Cott includes restructuring expense in *Unusual items* on its income statement. The disclosure notes reveal that the company included a non-recurring charge of $27,880,000 "for the restructuring of the North American beverage operations, the U.K. warehousing and distribution operations," and other initiatives. The amount charged against income for restructuring costs includes not just costs actually incurred during the period, but also an estimate of future costs that will arise from the decision to restructure. The total amount charged to income by Cott includes $8,780,000 as an accrued liability for estimated future costs of restructuring.

If the entity leaves the line of business, Section 3475 of the *CICA Handbook* provides explicit reporting guidelines governing the disclosure of a *segment of a business* that is sold, abandoned, or otherwise disposed. Discontinued operations are reported on the statements of both CN and Cott.

The *CICA Handbook* says that two components of income resulting from discontinued operations should be disclosed separately:

1. Results of operations for the discontinued segment up to the *measurement date*, net of tax.
2. Gain or loss (net of tax) from disposal of a segment of a business, including the income or loss from operating the business during any phase out period.

The measurement date is the date on which the company's management adopts a formal plan to sell or wind up the segment. The intent of the disclosure of operating results is to enable users of financial statements to use the income statement for predictive purposes and project the operating results of the company without the division that is to be discontinued.

In practice, it appears that many companies do not actually disclose these two components separately. *Financial Reporting in Canada 1997* reported that of the 26 companies in their sample (of 200 public companies) that reported discontinued operations in 1996, only 10 disclosed the results prior to the measurement date.

The gain or loss on disposal of a segment has two components. First, it includes the actual or estimated gain or loss on operating the segment between the date that management decides to discontinue the operation (the measurement date) and the actual date of disposal, net of tax. This operating gain or loss is considered to be part of the gain or loss on the discontinuance decision, not a regular operating result. Second, the gain or loss on the sale or other disposal of assets, net of tax, is included. If there is expected to be an overall loss on the decision, the loss must be accrued on the measurement date, that is, before the disposal actually takes place. If there is a net gain expected, it may only be recognized when realized. This is an example of conservatism in the choice of accounting practice.

The effects of any discontinued business are displayed on the income statement, net of tax, after income from continuing operations but before extraordinary items.

Companies have considerable latitude in deciding what constitutes a business segment for these disclosures. Normally, a segment would be operationally distinct from other activities of the enterprise. The following are examples of segments that, if discontinued, would require disclosure as a discontinued operation:

- A manufacturer eliminates a significant and distinguishable product line.
- A tobacco and consumer products company sells its interest in an oil and gas joint venture, its only investment in the oil and gas industry.
- A food distributor that normally sells its product directly to restaurants sells its wholesale division, which sold products to retail outlets.

The reporting of discontinued operations is a good example of the use of estimates in financial reporting. Management must estimate, on the measurement date,

- the date on which the segment will be disposed,
- gain or loss on operating the segment between the measurement date and the disposal date, and
- proceeds on the eventual sale.

Estimated future expenses and losses are accrued. The possibility of mis-estimating is significant, as cash flows in a wind-down scenario are hard to accurately predict. Wild estimates sometimes appear!

To illustrate discontinued operations disclosure, assume that Pacific & Eastern, a large consumer products company, decided to sell its Automatic Transmission Diagnostic Centers division on 1 July 20X0. In the first six months of 20X0, the division earned $7 million before tax. The company estimated that (1) the division would operate at a loss of $6 million between 1 July 20X0 and mid-20X1, before tax, and

(2) the division's net assets would be sold in mid-20X1 at a loss of $30. In 20X0, the company's disclosures for discontinued operations, assuming a tax rate of 40% on all income and losses, will be reported in two lines. The first line is for the *actual past* operating profit or loss up to the date that the decision to sell was made ($7.0 income in our example). The second line is for the *estimated future* profits or losses from operations and from sale of assets to the date of disposal ($6.0 loss from future operations plus $30.0 loss on sale). The discontinued operations section of the income statement will appear as follows for 20X0:

Discontinued operations:	
Income (loss) from discontinued operations division, net of tax expense of $2.8	$ 4.2
Loss on disposal of Automatic Transmission Diagnostic Centers division, including anticipated operating losses of $3.6, net of tax of $2.4, and estimated losses on sale of assets, $18.0, net of tax of $12.0	(21.6)
Net loss on discontinued operations	$(17.4)

On 1 August 20X1, the division was actually sold, at a loss of $25 million (before tax). Operating losses of $5 million were incurred between the measurement date and the disposal date. The *difference* between the original estimate and the actual amounts are recognized in income in 20X1; estimates are not adjusted retroactively. That is, there was $1 million *less* lost on operations, and $5 million less lost on the sale of assets. In millions:

	Amount estimated in 20X0	Actual in 20X1	Adjustment necessary in 20X1
Operating loss, 1 July 20X0 to date of disposal, before taxes	$ 6.0 loss	$ 5.0 loss	$ 1.0 gain
Loss on disposal of net assets, before taxes	$30.0 loss	$25.0 loss	$ 5.0 gain
Total	$36.0 loss	$30.0 loss	$ 6.0 gain

Thus, the discontinued operations section shows a net *gain* in 20X1, due to the correction of an estimate

Discontinued operations:	
Income (loss) from discontinued division	$ —
Recovery of loss on disposal of Automatic Transmission Diagnostic Centers division, including recovery of estimated operating losses, $0.6, net of tax of $0.4, and recovery of estimated loss on sale of capital assets, $3.0, net of tax of $2.0	3.6
Net gain on discontinued operations	$ 3.6

The Molson Companies provides an example of a loss from discontinued operations followed by a significant gain. In 1996, Molson recognized a loss of $270.1 million from discontinued operations. There were several components to the loss, but primarily it related to the planned disposal of its Diversey operations, which included a world-wide cleaning and sanitizing business and a chemical specialties business. In 1998, Molson recognized a gain of $51.5 million on the same discontinued operations. The gain had the effect of almost doubling its net income. The gain was the result of "higher-than-expected sale proceeds, combined with the successful outcome of negotiations with respect to claims and prospective claims related to the prior operations of Diversey."

Another example is that of Shaw Communications Inc. Shaw management decided in 1996 to sell its paging division and recorded a charge for discontinued operations. In the following year, however, management changed its mind and reversed the charge. As a result, 1997 earnings were increased by a gain on rescission of discontinued operations of $16,374,000; this gain significantly increased net income from $218,000 to $16,592,000.

It would be unwise to underestimate the difficulty of providing accurate estimates in this area — after all, it's hard to predict how a division slated for disposal or shutdown will perform, and there are no organized markets for "used divisions." As Molson expressed it in 1998:

> While many of the uncertainties relating to the provision have been resolved, there remains a risk that the assumptions and resulting estimates on which the remaining provision is based, may change with the passage of time and availability of additional information and facts. Any further changes to the provision will be recognized as a gain or loss from discontinued operations in the period in which such changes are determined.

On the other hand, it's easy to get cynical about the opportunity presented for over-accrual, since over-accrual creates an opportunity for subsequent recognition of gains.

Full disclosure of a discontinued operation includes the following:

- Identification and description of the business segment discontinued.
- The measurement date and the actual or projected disposal date.
- The actual or expected manner of disposition.
- A description of the assets, by major classification, of the discontinued segment.
- Revenue attributable to the discontinued segment for the reporting period.

CN provides an extensive two-page disclosure note containing information on its discontinued operations, which include AMF Technotransport, CN Exploration, CN Real Estate and the famous CN Tower. Their discontinued operations are shown as one number on the income statement, but the disclosure note provides the breakdown of the results of the discontinued operations before the disposal decision, and the gains and expected losses on sale, which would include estimated operating results until the sale. Gains are *not* recognized until they are realized. CN's disclosure is as follows in millions:

	1997	1996	1995
Net loss from discontinued operations*	$ (6)	$—	$(7)
Provision for loss on disposal of telecommunication business activities, net of income tax recovery of $8 million	(12)		
Gain on disposal of investment in CN France, net of income taxes of $18 million		14	
Gain on disposal of oil and gas assets, net of income taxes of $18 million			25
Gain on disposal of real estate assets, net of income taxes of $25 million			36
Provision for loss on disposal of AMF Technotransport, net of income tax recovery of $33 million			(47)
	(12)	14	14
Discontinued operations, net of applicable income taxes	$(18)	$14	$ 7

* Details for each of the discontinued operations is given in the disclosure note. This is just the total.

Extraordinary Items

Classification of an item as extraordinary is sometimes a tough call. The "attractive" thing about extraordinary items from the perspective of the company is their segregation on the income statement, preceded by a subtotal that clearly encourages users to focus on the "pre-extraordinary item" amount as the continuing amount. It's sort of an official blessing on the one-time nature of the item.

Before Section 3480 of the *CICA Handbook* was issued, there were inconsistencies across firms, and even over time for given firms, in the classification of items as ordinary or extraordinary. Some firms took gains that appeared to be extraordinary and reported them in continuing operations, thereby increasing income from continuing operations! Alternatively, some firms classified all large losses as extraordinary. As a result, these firms reported a higher income before extraordinary items. In 1990, the AcSB provided specific criteria for extraordinary items and their incidence plummeted. In 1989, a survey of 300 public Canadian companies revealed 81 companies with extraordinary items; by 1995, there was only one.

In Section 3480, the *CICA Handbook* identifies extraordinary items as those resulting from transactions or events that have all of the following three characteristics:

1. They are not expected to occur frequently over several years.
2. They do not typify the normal business activities of the entity.
3. They do not depend primarily on decisions or determinations by management or owners.

The following examples are extraordinary items:

- Government expropriation of land and buildings for a highway.
- The destruction of a large portion of a wheat crop by a tornado.
- An explosion in a nuclear reactor resulting in high-level radioactive emissions.

Gains or losses resulting from the risks inherent in an entity's *normal business activities* are not considered extraordinary. The environment in which the firm operates should be considered when determining whether an underlying event or transaction is abnormally and significantly different from the ordinary and typical activities of the business. A firm's environment includes such factors as the characteristics of the industry or industries in which it operates, the geographical location of its operations, and the nature and extent of governmental regulations. An event or transaction may be unusual for one firm, but not for another, because of differences in their respective environments. For example, the following two transactions are similar, but the first is to be treated as extraordinary while the second is not:

- *Extraordinary.* A wheat farmer's crops are destroyed by a hailstorm. Severe damage from hailstorms in the locality where the wheat farmer operates are rare.
- *Ordinary.* An apple grower's crop is damaged by frost. Frost damage is normally experienced every three or four years.

The first situation is considered extraordinary because, given the environment in which the wheat farmer operates, hailstorms are very infrequent. In the second situation, taking into account the environment in which the company operates, the criterion of infrequency of occurrence would not be met. The history of losses by frost damage provides evidence that such damage may reasonably be expected to recur in the foreseeable future.

Section 3480 specifically identifies the following events that should *not* be considered as extraordinary because they are expected during the customary and continuing business activities of a firm:

- Losses and provisions for losses with respect to bad debts and inventories.
- Gains and losses from fluctuations in foreign exchange rates.
- Adjustments with respect to contract prices.
- Gains and losses from write-down or sale of property, plant, equipment, or other investments.
- Income tax reductions on utilization of prior period losses or reversal of previously recorded tax benefits. (Such reductions were once considered extraordinary and were a common example of an extraordinary item.)

A very important criterion for classifying a gain or loss as an extraordinary item is that the gain or loss *does not depend primarily on the decisions of managers or owners*. A transaction would be considered to be outside the control of managers or owners if their decisions would not influence the transaction. For example, consider the following situations:

- A manufacturing concern sells the only land it owns. While this is an infrequent and unusual item, it results from a decision of managers or owners and thus any resulting gain or loss is considered not extraordinary.
- An airplane owned by the company is destroyed by a terrorist act. The item is infrequent, unusual, and not the result of a decision of managers or owners; any gain or loss, net of insurance proceeds, is an extraordinary item.
- A lawsuit is settled out of court. The settlement is clearly an action of management or owners, but the settlement itself is a secondary event and should not dictate classification. The nature of the event causing the lawsuit must dictate whether or not the item is extraordinary.

Probably the largest single extraordinary item ever reported by a Canadian company was the $2.95 *billion* charge taken by BCE Inc. in 1997. The charge was to write down the carrying value of its telecommunications assets to reflect their lower recoverable value in a de-regulated environment. Asset write-downs usually do not qualify as extraordinary items, but the BCE write-down did qualify because the de-regulation was beyond the control of management.

Sometimes, extraordinary items are described as "acts of God or government." It's a useful decision rule to remember — events such as tornadoes, fires, floods, expropriations, and so on, if not frequent, are normally the best examples of extraordinary items. Another decision rule is that extraordinary items are *rare*.

As illustrated in our Calgary Storage Company example (Exhibit 3-5), extraordinary items are reported in the income statement under a separate classification and are net of any income tax effect. If subject to income tax, an extraordinary gain increases income tax and an extraordinary loss reduces income tax. In both cases, the extraordinary gain or loss is adjusted for its tax effects and reported net of tax. Extraordinary items are usually explained in disclosure notes.

Recent examples of extraordinary items found in practice include losses caused by

- plant explosion and fire,
- robbery of an armored car, and
- a provincial government's cancellation of a previously approved mining project, necessitating a write-off of all investment to date plus an estimate of site restoration costs.

Unusual or Infrequent Gains and Losses

Some events or transactions are not extraordinary but should be disclosed separately on the income statement to emphasize their nature as unusual or infrequent. For example, assume a timber company has a material write-down of its pulp and paper inventory and timber resources (a capital asset) due to prevailing low prices in the timber industry. The write-down, an impairment of value, has been determined by management but caused by outside events — low market prices. It is certainly infrequent, since the company reports that it is the first time in the company's 40-year history that such a write-down has been necessary. However, risks associated with price fluctuations in a natural resource market are surely a *typical business risk* in the timber industry. The item is not extraordinary. How should the company report the asset impairment?

The *CICA Handbook* recommends that companies report separately "revenues, expenses, gains, or losses resulting from items that do not have all the characteristics of extraordinary items but result from transactions or events that are not expected to occur frequently over several years, or do not typify normal business activities of the entity" [*CICA* 1520.03(1)]. Such items should *not* be shown net of tax.

A number of companies took liberties with the unusual item category after the extraordinary category was narrowed. These companies would show unusual items, net of tax, at the bottom of the income statement, after some sort of subtotal. Obviously, they were encouraging investors and others to focus on the "pre-unusual item" subtotal when evaluating operations and making predictions about the future. Indeed, the only difference between this renegade disclosure and that given to extraordinary items was the "extraordinary" label. The Ontario Securities Commission stepped in and ended this game for public companies traded in Ontario, announcing that companies that filed on the TSE could not show unusual items net of tax. However, there still is no reason that a company cannot decide to highlight an unusual item by creating a subtotal prior to the unusual item. The unusual item simply cannot be reported net of tax, if it is a public company and bound by GAAP and the OSC.

Classification of an item as "unusual" is quite open to management discretion: Any item deemed "unusual" may be reported in this fashion. Common examples of losses or expenses given separate disclosure include restructuring costs, write-down of capital assets and investments, and severance payments. Common types of gains that are given separate disclosure are gains on disposal of an investment and gains on sale of capital assets. Cott Corporation (Exhibit 3-4) includes two unusual items (in addition to restructuring costs) for 1998: (1) a gain on reduction of investments in joint ventures and (2) an amount the company is obligated to pay the estate of the former CEO.

Not surprisingly, companies tend to highlight losses as being unusual while reporting gains along with other revenue. For example, MacMillan Bloedel reported the following note in its 1997 financial statements:

10. Sale of investments:
During 1997, MacMillan Bloedel sold its transportation business and a log towing and barging division. The assets of the transportation business were sold for net proceeds of $108 million, resulting in a pre-tax gain of $13 million. The log towing and barging division was sold for net proceeds of $33 million, resulting in a pre-tax gain of $31 million.

The total gains of $44 (i.e., $13 + $31) are not reported separately on the face of the income statement. The amount is included in "earnings (loss) from continuing operations," even though these operations obviously are not continuing.[1] On the other hand, the company separately reports a "loss from discontinued operations" of $247 million.

---

[1] The only revenue figure on the income statement is "Sales." The company's inclusion of the gain in continuing operations is evident from the cash flow statement, where the $44 million gain is removed from operating earnings to derive cash flow from operations.

EARNINGS PER SHARE

Public companies are required to report earnings per share. Earnings per share (EPS) is a summary figure that is often quoted by analysts and investors as the primary (and sometimes only) indication of a company's earnings record. Investors find EPS useful because it relates the income of the company to a single common share and automatically adjusts for changes in the number of shares outstanding from year to year. EPS numbers are very widely quoted in the financial press, and historical EPSs for a company often are presented by financial analysts and investment services in graphical form.

The computation of EPS is governed by Section 3500 of the *CICA Handbook*, which is one of only three sections in the *CICA Handbook* that specifically apply only to public companies. Public companies are required to report earnings per share for both (1) income before discontinued operations and extraordinary items, and (2) net income. Refer to the Cott Corporation income statement in Exhibit 3-4, which shows EPS at the bottom of the statement. Companies may also provide the relevant information in a disclosure note cross-referenced to the income statement, as is the case with CN (Exhibit 3-2).

Basic earnings per share is computed by dividing reported income available to the holders of common shares by the weighted average number of common shares outstanding during the year. For computation of EPS on common shares, income must be reduced by any preferred share dividend claims since such dividends are not available to common share owners and have not been subtracted in computing income.

Fully diluted earnings per share shows how earnings per share would change in the event that all common shares promised under the terms of existing option agreements, conversion privileges on bonds or preferred shares, etc., were actually issued. We'll study earnings per share in depth in Chapter 21.

INTERNATIONAL PERSPECTIVE

The financial reporting requirements in virtually every country include an income statement of one form or another. The measurement basis and specific measurement rules vary, but there is always some attempt to measure the results of operations.

In the U.S., the FASB has taken the reporting of income one step further by requiring a statement of comprehensive income. Comprehensive income consists of net income as we know it, plus all changes to shareholders' equity from non-owner sources. Examples are adjustments to retained earnings from changes in accounting policy (that have not been accounted for retroactively) and foreign currency translation adjustments that have not been recognized in income (we'll look briefly at this component in the next chapter). Comprehensive income can be reported either as a continuation of the income statement, as a separate statement, or as a clear and distinct section of a statement of shareholders' equity.

The International Accounting Standards Committee recommends a list of income statement diclosures in IAS 1 that looks a lot like the AcSB recommendations. But the IAS recommends "an analysis of expenses" either by type of expense or by function within the enterprise [para. 77]. The AcSB makes no such recommendation, as we have seen (and can see in Exhibit 3-6).

Income statements in some countries' reporting environments may be even less revealing than those in Canada. Some statements are terse, with very few accounts being reported. In the extreme, an income statement consists of the single net earnings line or of the three lines: earnings before taxes, tax expense, and net earnings. Australian statements usually start with "operating profit before interest, tax, depreciation, and amortization," and then proceed to deduct each of interest, tax, depreciation, and amortization step-by-step. However, total revenue is usually disclosed in a note.

The biggest difficulty a reader has with international financial income statements is understanding what an item means and how it was measured. Although Australia, Canada, the United States, and the United Kingdom identify items as "unusual or infrequent" (these items are called "exceptional" in the United Kingdom, and "abnormal" in Australia) and "extraordinary," the reporting requirements in most countries do not make these distinctions. Moreover, very few countries other than Canada and the United States require separate reporting of discontinued operations, although the practice is beginning to spread, thanks largely to efforts by the IASC.

Some countries have higher disclosure standards, or require disclosure of a longer list of specific items. France, for example, has a fairly detailed list of income statement items, including wages and salaries. Germany also requires disclosure of employment costs and materials costs.

However, the income statements of many European countries may include a wide variety of provisions and reserves that have no counterpart in Canada or the U.S. Germany and Austria have a number of profit reserves that are required by law — an officially sanctioned smoothing technique!

In many countries, the accounting measurement rules are greatly influenced by tax law. For example, an item that is deducted for tax reporting may be required to be expensed in the financial statements. A firm might take a large tax deduction for an item such as bad debt expense, for example, and this same amount would have to be reported on the income statement even though it is an overestimate of the actual expense. Such reporting could mislead the reader who assumes that bad debt expense means the same thing in the foreign financial statement as in a Canadian financial statement.

When reading an income statement generated outside Canada, it is important to remember that even though it may appear very much like a statement prepared under Canadian GAAP, the terms and labels may have quite different meanings. It is important to understand how revenues, expenses, gains, and losses are defined in the environment in which the statement was prepared before trying to interpret the information in the statement.

In most countries, the income statement or statement of operations is prepared on the *proprietary basis of accounting*, which is one of the underlying assumptions that we discussed in Chapter 2. In some countries, however, an alternative approach is sometimes used (e.g., U.K.). Instead of preparing the operating statement from the point of view of the owners (the *proprietary* viewpoint), the statement is prepared with equal consideration to all of the company's stakeholders (the *entity* viewpoint).

Statements prepared on the *entity basis of reporting* are called **value added statements**. While the "bottom line" for the owners in a value added statement is essentially the same as it is under a traditional proprietary-approach income statement, the value added statement reveals much more information that is of interest to other stakeholders and that is very useful for public policy.

Most fundamentally, the value added statement reveals the *value added* to the economy by the enterprise. Canadians will recognize the concept of value added as the basis on which the much-beloved Goods and Services Tax (GST) is levied. A business remits to the government the GST collected on its value added, which is an amount measured by subtracting the cost of goods and services purchased from other companies from the gross revenues. Value added is an amount that is not reported on Canadian income statements and that cannot be derived therefrom.

Information on value added is an essential component of government policy-making in developing countries, and therefore this form of the operating statement is most commonly found in developing countries. Value added statements are explained more fully in the Appendix to this chapter.

CONCEPT REVIEW

1. What are the three basic subsections of an income statement required by Canadian GAAP?

2. Explain what *intraperiod income tax allocation* is.
3. Why is separate disclosure of *discontinued operations* important to users?
4. What are the three criteria that a gain or loss must satisfy before it can be classified as *extraordinary*?

RETAINED EARNINGS STATEMENT

A statement of retained earnings is one of the four basic financial statements, which ties together the income statement and the balance sheet by showing the changes that occurred in retained earnings for the year. The purpose of the retained earnings statement is to report all changes in retained earnings during the accounting period, to reconcile the beginning and ending balances of retained earnings, and to provide a connecting link between the income statement and the balance sheet. The ending balance of retained earnings is reported on the balance sheet as one element of shareholders' equity.

For many companies, the only changes in retained earnings are (1) net income for the year and (2) dividends declared. Because of the simplicity of the retained earnings statement, it often is appended to the income statement. When a company does combine the retained earnings statement with the income statement, the combined statement's title must reveal that fact, such as by titling it the *Statement of Income and Retained Earnings*.

Instead of a retained earnings statement, some companies instead present a statement of shareholders' equity, which shows changes in all shareholders' equity accounts.

The five major components of a statement of retained earnings are:

1. Net income or loss for the period.

2. Dividends.

3. Error corrections.

4. Cumulative effect of retroactive changes in accounting policy.

5. Other changes: capital transactions, appropriations, and restrictions.

Net income and dividends are the most common items. For example, Cott Corporation's retained earnings statement is very straightforward:

COTT CORPORATION
Consolidated Statement of Retained Earnings
(Cdn. $ thousands)

	53 weeks ended January 31, 1998	52 weeks ended January 25, 1997	52 weeks ended January 27, 1996
Retained earnings — beginning of year	$78,171	$45,650	$81,053
Net earnings (loss) for the year	(7,706)	34,039	(29,375)
Dividends	(4,815)	(1,518)	(6,028)
Retained earnings — end of year	$65,650	$78,171	$45,650

Error Corrections

When errors are made, they must be corrected. This sometimes involves restating the financial statements of prior years, and thus changing prior income, which is summarized in retained earnings. Proper disclosure of these changes is accomplished by making an adjustment to opening retained earnings for the cumulative impact of the change to prior income, net of tax. Opening retained earnings *as restated* are presented. Then, the comparative financial statements are adjusted to give effect to the

EXHIBIT 3-7
BAILEY RETAIL COMPANY
Retained Earnings Statement
for the year ended 31 December 20X5

Retained earnings, 1 January 20X5, as previously reported	$378,800
Correction of error (net of income tax of $2,100) [Note 6]	4,900
Retained earnings, 1 January 20X5, as restated	383,700
Net income	81,200
Cash dividends declared and paid during 20X5	(30,000)
Retained earnings, 31 December 20X5 (Note 7)	$434,900

Note 6. Error correction — During the year, the company discovered that a capital expenditure made in 20X2 was incorrectly expensed. This error caused net income of that period to be understated and that of subsequent periods to be overstated. The adjustment of $4,900 (a $7,000 credit less income tax of $2,100) corrects the error.

Note 7. Restrictions — Of the $434,900 ending balance in retained earnings, $280,000 is restricted from dividend availability under the terms of the bond indenture. When the bonds are retired, the restriction will be removed.

error correction. In effect, the transaction is backed out of the current income statement and into the appropriate prior year. A description of the error and its effect on the financial statements must be included in the disclosure notes.

For example, in 1998, Philip Services Corp., a waste disposal and salvage company, corrected accumulated errors in copper trading accounts that required restatement of 1997, 1996 and 1995 reported operating results by a total of almost $93 million.

To illustrate the recording of a retroactive adjustment for an error correction, assume that a machine that cost the Bailey Retail Company $10,000 (with a 10-year estimated useful life and no residual value) was purchased on 1 January 20X2. Further, assume that the total cost was erroneously debited to an expense account in 20X2. The error was discovered 29 December 20X5. A correcting entry would be required in 20X5. Assuming that any income tax effects are recorded separately, the entry is as follows:

29 December 20X5:

Machinery	10,000	
Amortization expense, straight-line (for 20X5)	1,000	
Accumulated amortization (20X2 through 20X5)		4,000
Retained earnings, error correction		7,000

The $7,000 retroactive adjustment corrects the 1 January 20X5, retained earnings balance on a pretax basis. The balance is understated $7,000 before tax:

Understatement of 20X2 income ($10,000 – $1,000)	$9,000
Overstatement of 20X3 and 20X4 income ($1,000 × 2)	(2,000)
Net pretax understatement	$7,000

Assuming that the same error was also made on the income tax return, the entry to record the income tax effect of the error, assuming a 30% income tax rate, would be as follows:

Retained earnings, error correction ($7,000 × 30%)	2,100	
Income tax payable		2,100

Appropriate reporting on the retained earnings statement is illustrated in Exhibit 3-7. Amounts other than the error correction are assumed.

Retroactive Effect of a Change in Accounting Policy

The retroactive effect of a change in accounting policy is also reflected on the retained earnings statement. When an accounting policy is changed, the comparability of the financial statements is compromised unless all comparative numbers, including prior years' net incomes, are restated using the newly adopted principle. This change in prior years' income also changes opening retained earnings as previously reported.

To illustrate the reporting of changes in accounting policy, consider the following example. A company's management decides to change from accelerated to straight-line amortization for its capital assets and has made the change to comply with industry practice. The difference between the accumulated amortization under the accelerated method previously used and the amortization that would have accumulated if the straight-line method had been used in all previous periods is $60,000. That is, amortization expense has been $60,000 more using the accelerated method than would have been recorded using straight-line amortization. Assume an income tax rate of 30%. The cumulative effect of the change in accounting policy, net of applicable income taxes, is $60,000 × 70%, or $42,000. The entry to record the effect of the change in accounting policy is as follows:

Accumulated amortization — machinery	60,000	
Retained earnings — cumulative effect of change in accounting principle		42,000
Future (deferred) income tax		18,000

The tax amount is deferred because the change is made for accounting purposes only — the tax return (and taxes payable) is not changed.

The effect of a retroactive change in accounting policy is shown on the retained earnings statement as follows:

Opening retained earnings, as previously reported (assumed)	$400,000
Effect of change in accounting policy (net of tax)	42,000
Opening retained earnings, as restated	$442,000

Prior financial statements are changed so that only straight-line amortization is shown on the income statements, which obviously would change prior years' net income for all comparative years shown. Appropriate note disclosure would also be prepared.

Accounting policy changes are not always applied with full retroactive restatement. They may also be applied prospectively. Prospective treatment means that the new policy is used for current periods and future periods, but past periods are left as is, with a resulting loss of consistency. This is allowable when specific new accounting standards specifically permit prospective treatment. Prospective treatment is also used as a practical matter when it is simply not possible to reconstruct data for prior periods.

In other circumstances, the company can determine the impact of the change in accounting policy on opening balances in total, but cannot reconstruct the detail needed to restate individual prior years. This will result in an adjustment to opening retained earnings, as illustrated, but no restatement of previous income statements. Again, practicalities force the use of less desirable disclosure of the effect of the new policy on prior years.

It's worth noting that changes in accounting *estimates* are never applied retroactively: the new estimate is used for this year, and future years, but previous income statements are not changed and retained earnings is not touched.

Capital Transactions

The retained earnings statement contains other increases and decreases in equity caused by capital transactions. Most capital transactions are share transactions. Since a corporation is dealing with itself (its owners) in share transactions, gains and losses caused by these transactions are not shown on the income statement because they are not arm's length transactions. Gains normally create contributed capital — separate shareholders' equity accounts — and losses reduce retained earnings. We'll study these more carefully in Chapter 14.

Other Charges

Other charges to retained earnings result from share issue expenses incurred on the issuance of new shares, taxes resulting from a change in control or triggered by dividend payments to shareholders, and adjustments to retained earnings caused by a reorganization.

Appropriations of and Restrictions on Retained Earnings

Appropriations of and restrictions on retained earnings limit the availability of retained earnings to support dividends.

Restrictions result from legal requirements, such as a statutory requirement that retained earnings be restricted for dividend purposes by the cost of any treasury stock held, or contractual agreements, such as a bond agreement (i.e., indenture) requiring that retained earnings of a specified amount be withheld from dividend purposes until the bonds are retired.

Appropriations of retained earnings result from formal decisions by the corporation to set aside, or *appropriate*, a specific amount of retained earnings (temporarily or permanently). The effect of an appropriation is to remove the specified amount of retained earnings from dividend availability. For example, corporations often set up appropriations such as "retained earnings appropriated for future plant expansion." Appropriations are created by the board of directors, and they also can be reduced or eliminated by the board.

The primary purpose of restrictions and appropriations is to inform statement users that a portion of retained earnings is set aside for a specific purpose (usually long term) and that these amounts are therefore not available for dividend declarations.

Exhibit 3-7 illustrates a restriction of $280,000 on the retained earnings of Bailey Retail Company. The unrestricted balance of retained earnings is $154,900 ($434,900 – $280,000 = $154,900). Details regarding restrictions and appropriations are usually reported in a note, as illustrated in Exhibit 3-7.

Prior Period Adjustments

In the past, another category of items, called prior period adjustments were also charged to opening retained earnings, and shown net of tax on the retained earnings statement with full retroactive restatement. These items, such as lawsuits decided in one year but pertaining to events of a prior year, or a tax reassessment related to a prior year, fit established criteria in order to qualify them for exclusion from the income statement. The most stringent requirements were that the items had to be the result of decisions by someone other than owners or managers, and had to relate to specific prior periods.

However, in line with the all-inclusive concept of income, the AcSB decided that these items were, in fact, related to normal operations and should be recorded on the face of the income statement. Thus, the category no longer exists.

This is an example of how the Canadian reporting model is drifting towards an all-inclusive model. We still have not gone as far as U.S. standards, which also require the cumulative effect of a change in accounting principle to be included on the income statement!

On the other hand, most other countries are more permissive about charging items directly to retained earnings. When looking at a non-Canadian set of financial statements, the reader should not ignore the retained earnings statement; sometimes it contains interesting expenses or losses that don't appear on the income statement!

CONCEPT
REVIEW

1. What types of items will appear on the retained earnings statement?
2. Explain the difference between a *restriction* and an *appropriation* of retained earnings.
3. What is the normal approach to accounting for a change in accounting policy?
4. Why aren't gains and losses from capital transactions reported on the income statement?

SUMMARY OF KEY POINTS

1. Accounting income is the result of recording transactions in accordance with established measurement rules. Accounting income suffers from its reliance on *transactions*, which ignore economic events that indicate wealth increases. Accounting income may also be affected by the nature of accounting policies chosen, which determines the quality of earnings.

2. Net income must have some degree of predictive and/or feedback value for users engaged in earnings predictions. Various items on the income statement, as well as outside sources, must be carefully evaluated in the prediction process.

3. Many format issues are not governed by accounting pronouncements, and the company must make choices to create an income statement that is useful to financial statement users. Minimum disclosures are recommended by the *CICA Handbook*; additional note disclosures and format decisions are important for full disclosure.

4. Two general formats for presenting income statement information not specifically regulated by accounting pronouncements are the single-step and the multiple-step formats.

5. The single-step format uses only two broad classifications in its presentation: a revenues and gains section and an expenses and losses section. Total expenses and losses are deducted from total revenues and gains in a single computation to determine the net income (earnings) amount.

6. The multiple-step format income statement presents intermediate subtotals, designed to emphasize important relationships in the various revenue and expense categories.

7. The gains or losses resulting from the sale or abandonment of a business segment, whose activities represent a separate major line of business or class of customer, must be reported, net of income tax effects, as a separate component of income, positioned after income from continuing operations and before extraordinary items. Gains or losses have two components: the operating results from the "decision day," and the gain or loss on sale, which includes the actual asset sale plus operating results after the date of the decision to sell.

8. Extraordinary items result from transactions or events that are infrequent, not normal business activities, and result from the decisions of outsiders. They are required to be reported, net of income tax effects, as a separate component of income, positioned after income from continuing operations.

9. Unusual or infrequent items should be shown separately on the income statement, before tax.

10. Earnings per share amounts relate earnings to common shares outstanding.

11. The statement of retained earnings reports all changes in retained earnings during the period, including net income or loss, dividends declared, and capital transactions.

12. Error corrections that affect the financial statements of prior periods are recorded (net of tax) as a change to opening retained earnings, and comparatives are restated.

13. A change in accounting principle is normally applied retroactively, with the cumulative effect of the change shown as an adjustment to opening retained earnings. Comparative financial statements should be restated. If this treatment is not

possible, only the cumulative effect is shown on the retained earnings statement. In certain circumstances, the change in principle is reflected prospectively. An accounting estimate is changed prospectively.

REVIEW PROBLEM

The following pretax amounts are taken from the adjusted trial balance of Killian Corporation at 31 December 20X5, the end of Killian's fiscal year:

Account	Amount
Sales revenue	$ 1,000,000
Service revenue	200,000
Interest revenue	30,000
Gain on sale of operational asset	100,000
Cost of goods sold	600,000
Selling, general, and administrative expense	150,000
Depreciation expense	50,000
Interest expense	20,000
Loss on sale of long-term investment	10,000
Extraordinary item, loss from earthquake damage	200,000
Cumulative effect of change in accounting policy (gain)	50,000
Estimated loss on sale of business segment	60,000
Loss on operation of discontinued business segment, prior to disposal date	10,000

Other information:
a. The income tax rate is 40% on all items.
b. There were 100,000 common shares outstanding throughout the year. No preferred shares are outstanding.
c. Assume that the capital cost allowance deductible for tax purposes is equal to the depreciation expense shown on the income statement.

Required:
1. Prepare a single-step income statement in good form.
2. Prepare a multiple-step income statement in good form.

REVIEW PROBLEM — SOLUTION

1. Single-step income statement:

KILLIAN CORPORATION
Income Statement
for the year ended 31 December 20X5

Revenues and gains:	
Sales revenue	$1,000,000
Service revenue	200,000
Interest revenue	30,000
Gain on sale of operational asset	100,000
Total revenue and gains	1,330,000
Expenses and losses:	
Cost of goods sold	600,000
Selling, general, and administrative expenses	150,000
Depreciation	50,000
Interest expense	20,000
Loss on sale of long-term investment	10,000
Income tax expense [see computations below]	200,000
Total expenses and losses	1,030,000

Income from continuing operations			300,000
Discontinued operations:			
Loss from discontinued operations, net of tax of $4,000		$ (6,000)	
Loss on disposal of business segment, net of tax of $24,000		(36,000)	(42,000)
Income before extraordinary item			258,000
Extraordinary item:			
Loss from earthquake damage, net of tax benefit of $80,000			(120,000)
Net income			$ 138,000
Earnings per share:			
Income from continuing operations			$ 3.00
Net income			$ 1.38

Computation of income tax expense:		
Total revenues		$1,330,000
Expenses before income taxes:		
Cost of goods sold	$600,000	
Selling, general, and administrative expenses	150,000	
Capital cost allowance (equal to depreciation)	50,000	
Interest expense	20,000	
Loss on sale of long-term investment	10,000	830,000
Taxable income		500,000
Tax rate		40%
Income tax expense		$ 200,000

The discounted operations and extraordinary item are reported net of tax, reflecting intraperiod allocation, and therefore are not included in the computation of income tax expense. The cumulative effect of a change in accounting policy is shown on the retained earnings statement.

2. Multiple-step income statement:

KILLIAN CORPORATION
Income Statement
for the year ended 31 December 20X5

Sales revenue		$1,000,000
Cost of goods sold		600,000
Gross margin		400,000
Operating expenses:		
Selling, general, and administrative expenses	$150,000	
Depreciation expense	50,000	200,000
Income from operations		200,000
Other revenues and gains:		
Service revenue	200,000	
Interest revenue	30,000	
Gain on sale of operational asset	100,000	330,000
Other expenses and losses:		
Interest expense	20,000	
Loss on sale of long-term investment	10,000	30,000
Net other items		300,000

Income from continuing operations before income tax		500,000
Income tax expense		200,000
Income from continuing operations		300,000
Discontinued operations:		
Loss from discontinued operations, net of tax of $4,000	(6,000)	
Loss on disposal of business segment, net of tax of $24,000	(36,000)	(42,000)
Income before extraordinary item		258,000
Extraordinary item:		
Loss from earthquake damage, net of tax effects of $80,000		(120,000)
Net income		$138,000
Earnings per share:		
Income from continuing operations		$ 3.00
Net income		$ 1.38

Alternative arrangements of the information above the *Income from continuing operations* line are allowed for both single- and multiple-step formats. In particular, the other revenues and other expenses are commonly combined into a single category of "other revenues and expenses" instead of being shown in two categories.

The presentation of the items below *Income from continuing operations* should be the same for both single-step and multiple-step statements.

APPENDIX
Value Added Statement

The traditional income statement is prepared from the point of view of the owners of the business. Net income is a residual that is determined by deducting obligations and payments to measure the amount of revenue that makes its way to the shareholders, partners, or proprietor. Chapter 2 described this as the proprietary approach to accounting. The *proprietary approach* is fully in keeping with the view of capitalism that prevails in Canada and the U.S.

The owners of a business obviously are very important stakeholders. However, they are not the only important participants (and beneficiaries) of a business enterprise. Other crucial stakeholders are employees, debt capital providers, and governments. Indeed, most of the economic activity of a business enterprise benefits stakeholders other than the owners.

Value added is the increase in value of goods and services that is the result of an enterprise's efforts. It is measured as the difference between the output value of the company's activities (e.g., its gross revenue) and the input value (i.e., cost of goods and services purchased from other companies). For example

- a manufacturer adds value by buying raw materials and components and turning them into a finished good;
- a wholesaler or retailer adds value by buying goods and distributing them to places where they are needed, thereby adding the value of placement;
- a public accounting firm adds value by using its expertise to prepare and/or audit another company's financial statements.

In general, a company adds value through the use of labour and capital, both debt and equity, to cause some change in the "raw materials" with which it works. The point of a value added statement is

- to identify the amount of value added by the enterprise, and
- to show how the value added was distributed to the various participants (i.e., the *factors of production*, in economic terms).

The information provided by the value added statement is very important for developing countries, but it also is used in developed countries (e.g., the U.K.) where there is a stronger concern for the impact of a company on its various stakeholders, particularly employees. The importance of the statement for developing countries will be discussed shortly, but first we should illustrate the basic nature of the statement.

Basic Illustration

The top portion of Exhibit 3-8 shows a simple income statement. Revenue of $2 million is reduced by expenses of $1.7 million to derive a net income of $300,000. The income statement discloses the amount of interest expense and the amount of income tax, as required by the *CICA Handbook*. The financial statements would also reveal that the general expense categories of "cost of sales" and "general and administrative expenses" include depreciation of $80,000. Dividends declared and paid during the year amounted to $100,000.

Notice that it is not possible to determine the value added by the company. There is no indication of how much of the total expense was incurred simply to buy goods and services from other companies. Nor is there any way to find out how much was paid to employees.

EXHIBIT 3-8
Income Statement Compared to a Value Added Statement

INCOME STATEMENT

Revenue from sales		$2,000,000
Less:		
Cost of goods sold	$950,000	
General and administrative expenses	330,000	
Interest expense	120,000	
Income tax expense	300,000	1,700,000
Net income		$ 300,000
Additional information:		
Depreciation included in expenses		80,000
Dividends paid		100,000

VALUE ADDED STATEMENT

Revenue from sales		$2,000,000
Less goods and services purchased from other enterprises:		
Materials	$200,000	
Services	600,000	
Depreciation	80,000	
		880,000
Value added		**$1,120,000**
Distribution of value added:		
Wages and salaries to employees		$ 400,000
Payments to providers of capital:		
Interest	$120,000	
Dividends	100,000	220,000
Taxes paid to governments		300,000
Reinvested in the enterprise		200,000
Value added		**$1,120,000**

The information that is reported in a value added statement is imbedded in the expense categories reported on an income statement. Because an income statement is prepared from the viewpoint of the owners, the amounts paid to other parties is not generally considered relevant (except for interest and taxes, in Canadian GAAP).

The lower portion of Exhibit 3-8 includes the same data that underlies the income statement, but aggregated and presented in a different way as a value added statement. The top section of the statement shows the amount of value added; the goods and services that were purchased from other companies (including depreciation) are subtracted from gross revenue. The second section of the statement then shows how the value added was distributed to the participants. It clearly indicates how much was paid to employees, to the providers of capital, and to governments. The amount of profit that was not distributed as dividends is shown as capital reinvestment. The sum of dividends plus capital reinvestment is $300,000, which is the same amount shown as net income on the traditional income statement.

Purpose of the Value Added Statement

Why would anyone care whether a statement is an income statement or a value added statement? There are two reasons that many governments care: (1) economic measurement and (2) strategic policy-making.

Economic Measurement. Every country in the world reports economic statistics. These are *macro accounting* measurements that attempt to show the gross national product (GNP) of the country and the components of GNP, such as national income, gross domestic product, and capital investment. In Canada and many other developed nations, these statistics are estimated and derived second-hand or third-hand (or worse) from varied sources. The financial statements of private enterprise are not very helpful for developing economic statistics of any kind.

Developed countries can afford the estimation errors that arise from having private enterprise reporting that is incompatible with the nation's macro accounting needs. Developing countries, on the other hand, are trying to play catch-up. In order to know how they are doing on the economic front, they need reliable statistical information. Therefore, some countries require a financial reporting framework that fits into their macro accounting framework in order to improve the reliability of their statistics.

Strategic Policy-Making. *Every* country, developed and developing, follows a policy of encouraging certain types of investment. In order to know which types of companies and industries to encourage, governments need to know how they contribute to the national economy. For example, it is impossible to say that multinational enterprises (MNE) are bad, while home country-based companies are good, although this is sometimes offered as a simplistic way of viewing private investment. MNEs may contribute enormous amounts of value added to a developing economy by importing its expertise and adding to the host country's export base, while a local company may well send most of its domestically-generated revenue outside the country in the form of purchases of goods or services or as payments into a Swiss bank account!

The information contained in a value added statement therefore can be of prime importance in a developing country, and can also be of value in a developed country. There is no need for the value added statement to be the *only* income-flow statement for an enterprise; in European countries, the value added statement is *supplemental*; the income statement still is the primary reporting mechanism to shareholders.

Value Added Statement in a Developing Country: Example

Exhibit 3-9 shows an example of a realistic value added statement in a developing economy. In practice, a value added statement can be prepared on either a revenue basis or a production basis. A revenue basis statement starts with *revenue*, and treats changes in inventory as part of reinvestment (that is, combined with non-distributed profit). However, in a manufacturing operation, some of the value added is through production activities rather than sales activities, especially value added through labour. Therefore, the alternative is to start the statement with production output, including both sales revenue and the change in inventory; this is known as the production basis of reporting. The example shown in Exhibit 3-8 uses the sales basis.

In Exhibit 3-9, the emphasis is not only on value added, it is on *local value added*. Value added that leaves the country is segregated into the top part of the statement; if the value added (e.g., through salaries, dividends and interest) leaves the country, then it is not contributing to the economic well-being of the company's host country.

The distribution of local value added is explained in the lower part of the statement. This statement shows the purchases of local raw materials and depreciation on

EXHIBIT 3-9
Value Added Statement
(Production Basis)

XYZ PHARMACEUTICAL (BANGLADESH) LTD.
year to December 31, 1987
($ thousands)

Creation of local value added:
Output

Sales Revenue	$431,767	
Change in inventory	15,390	$447,157

Deduct external goods and services
    (paid in foreign currencies):

Import of materials	$215,320	
Royalties/fees to foreigners	13,943	
Salaries to foriegn personnel	900	
Interest on foreign loans	5,887	
Depreciation on imported assets	7,400	
Dividends to foreign shareholders	11,400	254,850

Local value added	$192,307

Distribution of local value added:

Local raw materials purchased	$70,733
Local capital consumption (depreciation)	2,710
Wages/salaries to local employees	52,017
Local finance charges and interest	10,053
Other local expense	28,850
Tax payments	12,800
Profit distibution to local shareholders	4,916
Retained profits	10,188
Local value added	$192,307

locally-obtained capital assets as part of local value added. While this classification is not strictly in accord with the theory of value added, it is useful for policy-making to distinguish between goods and services purchased locally and those purchased from outside the country.

    Value added statements are not used in Canada and the U.S., but Canadian companies operating in developing countries must be aware of local regulations in those countries that may require preparation of a value added statement, either as a primary statement or as a supplemental statement.[2] Therefore, Canadian accountants should be at least aware of the nature of these statements and the uses to which they can be put. Value added statements also demonstrate the application of the entity approach (discussed in Chapter 2) for portraying the operating results of an enterprise.

---

[2] For example, Egypt instituted a uniform set of accounts in 1966 that requires companies to report on what amounts to a value added basis (Dhia D. Al Hashim, "Social Accounting in Egypt," *The Accounting Review*). As another example, Nigeria introduced a recommendation for a voluntary value added statement in 1984, which became mandatory in 1990 (Charles A. Malgwi, "A Comparison of the Emergence of the Value Added Statement in the UK in the 1970s and Nigeria in the 1980s," September 1994).

QUESTIONS

3-1   Briefly explain how the income statement is a connecting link between the beginning and ending balance sheets.

3-2   What is the difference between economic income and accounting income?

3-3   Describe two different approaches to identifying items that are excluded from the income statement. Which approach is dominant in practice today?

3-4   Income statements are prized for their predictive power. Why is this the case?

3-5   Preferences of user groups dictate some policy choices regarding income statement display. Explain two of these areas.

3-6   What factors determine the choice of a fiscal year-end?

3-7   Why might a Canadian company prepare its financial statements in U.S. dollars?

3-8   Briefly explain the two display formats used for income statements. Explain why actual income statements are often a combination of these two formats.

3-9   Explain how cost of goods sold is reported on a single-step income statement and on a multiple-step income statement.

3-10   List the major sections, in their order of appearance, on a typical multiple-step income statement. Are these sections standardized?

3-11   What factors might be taken into consideration when one chooses between the two alternative display formats for the income statement?

3-12   Briefly define intraperiod tax allocation.

3-13   Regis Publishing Corporation computed total income tax expense for 20X5 of $16,640. The following pretax amounts were used: (a) income before extraordinary loss, $60,000; (b) extraordinary loss, $12,000; and (c) correction of a prior year's error, $4,000 (a credit on the retained earnings statement). The average income tax rate on all items was 32%. Compute the intraperiod income tax allocation amounts.

3-14   What is a discontinued operation? How is it reported in the income statement?

3-15   A company has a segment that it decides to sell, effective 1 September, after incurring operating losses of $45,000 to date in the fiscal year. The segment, with net assets of $310,000, was sold for $240,000 on 1 November, after incurring further operating losses of $30,000. Assume a tax rate of 40%. What amounts would be disclosed in the income statement?

3-16   How are gains on the discontinuance of a business segment accounted for differently than losses? Why is this the case?

3-17   List the items that must be disclosed on the income statement in relation to continuing operations. Why would companies choose to disclose more than minimum requirements?

3-18   Define an extraordinary item. How should extraordinary items be reported on (a) a single-step and (b) a multiple-step income statement?

3-19   How are items that are unusual or infrequent reported on the income statement?

3-20   Extraordinary items are sometimes described as "Acts of God or government." Why is this a useful rule of thumb?

3-21   Define earnings per share (EPS). Why is it required as an integral part of the income statement?

3-22   What items are reported on a statement of retained earnings?

3-23   A company has a machine that cost $21,000 when acquired at the beginning of year 1. It had a 10-year useful life and a $1,000 residual value. Toward the end of year five, the company discovered that, in error, the machine had been expensed when acquired. Straight-line depreciation is appropriate. What adjustment to opening retained earnings is appropriate in year five?

3-24 Describe how a change in accounting policy is reflected in the financial statements. Describe two alternate, less desirable approaches and state when each can be used.

3-25 What is meant by appropriations or restrictions on retained earnings? How are such items usually reported?

3-26 What are capital transactions and why are they reported on the retained earnings statement?

3-27 Define value added. What purposes do value added statements serve? Explain.

CASES

CASE 3-1

Delta Ltd.

Delta Ltd. (Delta) is incorporated under the *Canada Business Corporations Act*. At the end of 20X1 the board of directors decided to sell the printing and binding division of the company and concentrate its efforts in its book publishing division. An offer was received for the assets and liabilities of the printing and binding division, and the sale became effective in late January 20X2. The net assets were sold at a gain. Delta's financial year ends on 31 December.

For the past 20 years Delta had been a public company, with preferred shares listed on a Canadian stock exchange. Its bonds were also publicly traded. On receipt of the offer for the assets and liabilities of the printing and binding division, the board began rethinking certain aspects of the status of the company. After several meetings, the board decided that Delta would become a private company, and would therefore call in its bonds for redemption and its preferred shares for cancellation. The necessary legal negotiations were commenced with the provincial securities commissions, the Department of Consumer and Corporate Affairs, the stock exchange, and the holders of the bonds and preferred shares.

The board decided to change the company's status from public to private because the company would gain greater privacy and tax benefits, and it would be easier to reach agreement on the company's future direction. During their discussions on the change in status, some board members argued that the financial disclosure required of private companies is less extensive than that required of public companies. In their opinion, not only is the distribution of the financial statements of a private company (such as Delta would become) restricted to a relatively small group, but the financial information that must be disclosed is less extensive. While readily acknowledging that the change in status would restrict the distribution of Delta's financial statements, other directors maintained that disclosure requirements will not change significantly.

The bonds were redeemed in January 20X2. The preferred shares were bought on the open market in several transactions during January and February and were cancelled in February 20X2. On 7 March 20X2, Delta became a private company. Financing for the redemptions came partially from company resources, and partly from increased borrowing, secured by the personal guarantee of the majority shareholder and a first charge on real estate assets of the company.

During January 20X2, the majority shareholder, Mr. Richards, bought out all the minority holders of Delta's common shares.

It is now April 20X2. The board has engaged you, CA, to help Delta adjust efficiently and effectively to being a private company in the book publishing industry. They want you to prepare a report that includes your recommendations on financial accounting and related matters. You have assembled the information shown in Exhibit 1.

Required:

Prepare the report requested by the board.

Delta, Ltd.
EXHIBIT 1:
INFORMATION ASSEMBLED BY CA

Audited financial statements for the year ended 31 December 20X1 were made available to interested parties in February 20X2. An annual meeting has not yet been scheduled for the calendar year 20X2; the previous annual meeting was held in May 20X1.

1. The legal costs incurred in dealing with the various governmental and stock exchange officials amounted to $70,000.
2. The bonds had to be redeemed at a 2% premium that amounted to $80,000.
3. Some of the preferred shares were bought on the open market in early January 20X2 at a price that was $60,000 more than their recorded book value. The remaining preferred shares, also purchased on the open market, were bought at a price that was $75,000 above their book value.
4. The buyer of the printing and binding division agreed to hire most of Delta's production employees, but not the office staff. Thus, Delta had to offer early retirement or a severance package to these individuals. The cost of this package amounted to $200,000.
5. Other expenses related to the sale of the division amounted to $154,600.
6. The sale of the printing and binding division has reduced Delta's assets to about $3 million, and annual revenues from $15 million to $6 million. This is below the size threshold for mandatory financial statement audit established in legislation.
7. In January 20X2, prior to its sale, the printing and binding division's revenue was $820,000, and cost of goods sold was $430,000. The division incurred other expenses of $170,000.
8. The book publishing division has used the following accounting policies in the years to 31 December 20X1:

   a. Revenue is recognized when books are shipped to book stores. Each store is allowed to return up to 20% of purchases made in the past 12 months. Sales returns are recorded as made.
   b. Inventory is valued at the lower of printing and binding cost or net realizable value.
   c. Depreciation is charged in the accounts on a straight-line basis.
   d. Bonuses to employees and royalties to authors are expensed in the year that they are paid, which is normally the year after the period to which they relate.

[CICA, adapted]

CASE 3-2

Keysource Corporation

Keysource Corporation is a small software development company formed by three MBA graduates in the 1980s. In the early years, they specialized in the design and development of new software products. They had several successful years, and they went public on the strength of their track record. However, they experienced difficulty in replicating early successes.

Software development requires that a large investment be made up front, and the success of the final product is hard to predict. Keysource had several spectacular "losers" in the years following their initial public offering. The company shifted its focus to become a marketer of software products developed by other companies or individuals. For example, an individual might write a new computer game. Keysource would sign an agreement to produce and market the product, with the author receiving royalties.

Keysource pursued a number of other expansion policies as well, the most important of which was to acquire other small software companies that had either good product lists or excellent marketing departments and channels. Thus, the company grew by leaps and bounds, although its financial results continued to be quite volatile.

In 20x4, the company reported results as follows, (in $ thousands)

	20X4	20X3	20X2
Revenues	$121,287	$109,704	$119,519
Net income (loss)	21,145	(57,250)	(4,983)
Assets	90,815	79,334	128,474
Shareholders equity (deficit)	37,485	(8,632)	61,933

The company is well-known for its choice of accounting policies that maximize income. Keysource has always received an unqualified audit report, but has had going-concern disclosures several times over its life. Going-concern disclosures are required when the viability of the company is called into question, which would invalidate the use of historical cost as a valuation basis and several other significant accounting principles. Always, in these circumstances, Keysource has managed to find additional investment to continue operations.

It is now 20X5, and the company is cautiously optimistic about its operating results for the 20X5 year. Three matters have come up that are the subject of dispute between the company and its auditors. The company has asked you, an independent accountant, to provide your opinion as a means to settling the impasse.

1. In 20X0, Keysource obtained a long-term loan from Mr. David Ling, a wealthy Hong Kong industrialist, at a rate of prime plus 6%. To secure the loan, Mr. Ling asked for, and was given, a first charge on the shares of Keysource held personally by the president. No shares could be sold by the president as a result of the conditions of the assignment. The loan had a 20-year term, although the interest rate was to be adjusted every five years. In 20X5, Keysource found another lender, whose interest rate was lower and whose terms were far less onerous. Accordingly, they offered Mr. Ling a payout, which he accepted. However, in return for release of the claim against the president's personal shareholdings, Mr. Ling requested, and received, an additional payment of $200,000.

   The company has requested that this $200,000 payment be recorded as a capital charge, debited directly to retained earnings, because it was related to a share transaction and was not incurred in day-to-day operations. It was related to the personal assets of the shareholder/president, and not company assets. The auditor claims that the $200,000 is a cost of re-financing and should be recorded on the income statement, consistent with the all-inclusive concept of income.

2. In 20X4, Keysource accrued an expense of $2,400,000 in expectation of a settlement of a copyright infringement suit. In 20X5, pursuant to a judgement issued by the Supreme Court of Australia, Keysource paid the plaintiffs $3,658,000, including legal fees. The management of Keysource claim that the amount accrued in 20X4 was in error, and the additional $1,258,000 paid should be treated as an error correction, adjusted to 20X5 opening retained earnings and reflected on the 20X4 comparative financial statements.

3. In September 20X5, Keysource sold an operating unit called "Lansa" to a related party, one of the members of the board of directors. The operating unit was engaged in the business of customizing software for the aircraft industry. The net assets of the operation had a net book value of ($178,000) — that is, liabilities associated with the division exceeded assets by $178,000 — on the date of sale. The proceeds of disposition were $650,000. Proceeds were to be paid through the

forgiveness of a $250,000 account payable from Keysource to the purchaser, plus four, $100,000 instalments due over the next four years. Keysource wished to record the $828,000 gain as "other revenue" in 20X5; the auditors prefer to recognize the gain as proceeds are realized.

Required:

Evaluate the accounting policies, as requested by the Keysource board.

[ASCA, adapted]

EXERCISES

E3-1 *Interpreting the Components of Income:* Excerpts from the Stanley Produce Company comparative income statements for the years 20X2 through 20X4 are as follows:

	20X4	20X3	20X2
	($ millions)		
Income from continuing operations, after tax	$30	$25	$20
Discontinued operations:			
Income from operations of discontinued segment, net of tax	0	10	15
Gain on disposal of discontinued segment, net of tax	50	0	0
Extraordinary items:			
Loss from earthquake damage, net of tax	0	(40)	0
Gain on expropriation of property	0	0	35
Net income (loss)	$80	$ (5)	$70

Required:

1. Stanley Produce has experienced volatile earnings over the three-year period shown. Do you expect this to continue? Why or why not?
2. Net income increased from a loss of $5 million in 20X3 to a profit of $80 million in 20X4. Suppose the company's common share price increased only approximately 20% during the same period. Why might this be the case? Relate the 20% increase in share price to the components of net income.
3. Would you expect net income in 20X5 to be more or less than the amount reported in 20X4? More specifically, assuming no new unusual, non-recurring items, what amount would you estimate net income to be in 20X5?

E3-2 *Accounting Income vs. Economic Income:* On 1 January 20X1, Tyler Trading Company was incorporated by Jim Tyler, who owned all the common shares. His original investment was $100,000. Transactions over the subsequent three years were as follows:

2 January 20X1	Purchased 10 cars for resale at $10,000 each.
30 June 20X1	Sold six cars for total proceeds of $90,000.
31 December 20X1	Remaining four cars have an estimated sales value of $48,000.
15 July 20X2	Bought three cars for resale at $20,000 each.
3 October 20X2	Sold four cars from 20X1 purchase for total proceeds of $50,000.
31 December 20X2	Cars from 20X2 purchase have an estimated sales value of $84,000.
30 November 20X3	Sold all three cars bought in 20X2 for total proceeds of $106,000.

Required:

1. Calculate accounting income, based on transactions, for 20X1, 20X2 and 20X3.
2. Calculate economic income, based on events or changes in value, for 20X1, 20X2 and 20X3.
3. Compare total accounting income with total economic income and explain your findings.
4. In what ways is accounting income superior to economic income? In what ways is economic income superior? Use the accounting principles from Chapter 2 to explain.

E3-3 *Formats of Income Statement, Extraordinary Item:* The following selected items were taken from the adjusted trial balance of Amick Manufacturing Corporation at 31 December 20X5:

Sales revenue	$950,000
Cost of goods sold (including depreciation, $52,000)	575,000
Dividends received on investment in shares	6,500
Interest expense	4,200
Extraordinary item: fire loss (pretax)	48,000
Distribution expenses	135,300
General and administrative expenses	90,000
Restructuring expense	23,000
Cash	136,500
Interest revenue	2,500
Income tax, assuming an average 30% tax rate	?

Required:

1. Prepare a single-step income statement.
2. Prepare a multiple-step income statement.

E3-4 *Formats of Income Statement, Extraordinary Item:* The Sandvik Cement Company's records provided the following information at 31 December 20X5 (the end of the accounting period):

Sales revenue	$95,000
Rental revenue	35,000
Gain on sale of short-term investments	11,000
Distribution expense	18,000
General and administrative expense	12,000
Depreciation expense	6,000
Interest expense	4,000
Income tax expense (30% rate on all items)	?
Earthquake loss on building (pretax)	15,000
Gain on sale of equipment (pretax)	25,000
Loss on flood damage (pretax)	20,000
Loss on sale of warehouse (pretax)	3,000
Cost of goods sold	45,000

Required:

1. Prepare a single-step income statement. State any assumptions made.
2. Prepare a multiple-step income statement.

E3-5 *Formats of Income Statement, Extraordinary Item, Discontinued Operations:* The following items were taken from the adjusted trial balance of the Bigler Manufacturing Corporation on 31 December 20X5. Assume an average 30% income tax on all items (including the divestiture loss). The accounting period ends 31 December. All amounts given are pretax.

Sales revenue	$745,200
Rent revenue	2,400
Interest revenue	900
Gain on sale of operational assets	2,000
Distribution expenses	136,000
General and administrative expenses	110,000
Interest expense	1,500
Depreciation for the period	6,000
Extraordinary item: court-ordered divestiture loss	22,000
Cost of goods sold	330,000
Operating loss of discontinued operation to measurement date	20,000
Operating loss of discontinued operation from measurement date to disposal date	8,000
Loss on sale of assets of discontinued operation	10,000

Required:

1. Prepare a single-step income statement.
2. Prepare a multiple-step income statement.

E3-6 *Minimum Disclosure:* MLP Ltd. wishes to present a single-step income statement that complies with minimum required disclosure requirements of the *CICA Handbook*. Data related to the 20X2 income statement is presented below. They wish items that do not have to be separately disclosed to be added together into two generic categories, "other revenues" and "expenses of operation."

Sales revenue	$1,200,000
Investment revenue, equity method	1,120
Rent revenue	3,000
Royalty revenue	51,000
Cost of goods sold	380,000
Selling expenses	164,400
General and administrative expenses	55,000
Salaries and wages, sales	210,000
Salaries and wages, administration	116,000
Personnel and placement expense	28,000
Travel expenses	43,000
Depreciation expense	61,000
Restructuring expense	150,000
Interest expense	6,600
Income tax expense (tax rate is 35%)	?
Extraordinary gain (pretax)	10,000

Required:

Prepare a single-step income statement, based on the above information, that complies with minimum required disclosure standards of the *CICA Handbook*.

E3-7 *Tax Allocation — Income Statement and Retained Earnings Statement:* The records of Cayuga Corporation for 20x4 provided the following pretax data:

Income Statement — 20X4	
Income before extraordinary items	$ 80,000*
Extraordinary item: Loss from earthquake damage	20,000*
Pretax income	$ 60,000
Statement of Retained Earnings — 20X4	
Beginning balance, previously reported	$170,000
Less: Correction of accounting error	(30,000)*
Corrected balance	140,000
Add: Net income, 20X4	60,000
Less: Dividends declared and paid during 20X4	(40,000)
Ending balance	$160,000

* Subject to a 30% income tax effect.

Required:

Complete the above statements in good form on an after-tax basis (that is, apply intraperiod tax allocation). Assume all income statement items are fully taxable or tax deductible.

E3-8 *Discontinued Operations, Recording and Reporting:* On 1 August 20X5, Fischer Company decided to discontinue the operations of its services division, which qualifies as an identifiable segment. An agreement was formalized to sell this segment for $156,000 cash. The book value of the assets of the services division was $180,000. The disposal date was also 1 August 20X5. The income tax rate is 35%, and the accounting period ends 31 December. On 31 December 20X5, the after-tax income from all operations, including an after-tax operating loss of $20,000 incurred by the services division prior to 1 August 20X5, was $400,000.

Required:

1. Give the entry or entries to record the sale of the services division.
2. Complete the 20X5 income statement, starting with income from continuing operations, after tax.

E3-9 *Classification of Elements on the Income Statement:* Fifteen items are listed to the left below that may or may not affect the income statement. Income statement classifications are listed by letter to the right. Match each transaction with the appropriate letter to indicate the usual classification that should be used.

Answer	Selected Transactions	Income Statement Element Classifications
_____	1. Sales of goods and services	A. Revenues
_____	2. Prepaid insurance premium	B. Expenses
_____	3. Loss on disposal of service trucks	C. Gains (ordinary)
_____	4. Cash dividends received on an investment in African diamond mine	D. Unusual gain
_____	5. Wages liability (unpaid but recorded)	E. Loss (ordinary)
_____	6. Cost of successful oil wells in a foreign country that are taken over (expropriated) by that country's government without compensation	F. Unusual loss
		G. Extraordinary gain
		H. Extraordinary loss
		I. None of the above

_____　7. Cost of goods sold
_____　8. Value of services rendered
_____　9. Gain (unusual but not infrequent)
_____　10. Rent collected in advance
_____　11. Fire loss (infrequent)
_____　12. Loss due to a very rare freeze that destroys the fruit trees
　　　　　in the Annapolis Valley
_____　13. Gain on sale of long-term investments not held for resale
_____　14. Cash dividend declared and paid
_____　15. Loss due to explosion that completely destroys the factory

E3-10 *Income Statement, Retained Earnings Statement, Tax Allocation:* The following pretax amounts were taken from the adjusted trial balance of Avoca Automobile Corporation at 31 December 20X5, the end of the annual accounting period:

Sales revenue	$260,000
Cost of goods sold	88,000
Operating expenses	80,000
Gain on expropriation of property	20,000
Write-down of capital assets to reflect impairment of value	22,000
Retained earnings, balance 1 January 20X5	530,000
Effect of a change in accounting principles, applied	
retroactively (a credit)	50,000
Dividends declared and paid	25,000
Dividends declared and not paid	30,000
Restriction of retained earnings due to loan covenant	
Amount is included in opening balance of $530,000	100,000

Common shares, no-par, shares outstanding, 20,500 shares

Required:

1. Prepare a single-step income statement. Assume an average 30% tax rate on all items. Include EPS disclosures.
2. Prepare a statement of retained earnings. Disclose the restriction in a note.

E3-11 *Error Correction:* It is 31 December 20X5, and Manley Delivery Company is preparing adjusting entries at the end of the accounting year. The company owns two trucks of different types. The following situations confront the company accountant:

a. Truck 1 cost $7,700 on 1 January 20X3. It should be depreciated on a straight-line basis over an estimated useful life of 10 years with a $700 residual value. At 31 December 20X5, the accountant discovered that, in error, the truck was never depreciated.
b. Truck 2 cost $4,550 on 1 January 20X2. In error, the $4,550 expenditure was expensed in 20X2. The truck should be depreciated on a straight-line basis over an estimated useful life of seven years with a $350 residual value.

Required:

1. For each truck, give the required entry to record 20X5 depreciation expense at 31 December 20X5. Show computations.
2. Assume that there was a balance of $50,000 in opening retained earnings on 1 January 20X5. Present the top portion of the 20X5 retained earnings statement. Assume a tax rate of 25%.

E3-12 *Change in Policy, Retained Earnings Statement:* The Hannam Company decided to change from the declining-balance method of depreciation to the straight-line method effective 1 January 20X5. The following information was provided:

Year	Net Income as Reported	Excess of Declining Balance Depreciation over Straight-Line Depreciation
20X1*	$(40,000)	$10,000
20X2	110,000	30,000
20X3	107,000	25,000
20X4	140,000	14,000

* First year of operations.

The company has a 31 December year-end. The tax rate is 40%. No dividends were declared until 20X5; $35,000 of dividends were declared and paid in December of 20X5. Income for 20X5, calculated using the new accounting policy, was $210,000.

Required:

Assuming that the change in policy was implemented retroactively, present the 20X5 retained earnings statement.

E3-13 *Value Added Statement:* The income statement for Alloy Metals Ltd. is presented below.

Revenue	
Sales	$1,550,000
Expenses	
Cost of goods sold, all materials	650,000
Administration, including $50,000 of salaries	120,000
Selling, including $35,000 of wages	55,000
Maintenance, including $21,000 of wages	145,000
Interest expense	29,500
Depreciation expense	95,000
Income tax	200,000
Net income	$ 255,500

Additional information:

1. The balance of selling, administration, and maintenance expenses represent materials (40%) and services (60%) purchased from other entities.
2. Dividends paid were $45,000.

Required:

Prepare a value added statement based on the above information.

P3-1 *Formats of Income Statement, Extraordinary Item:* The following pretax information was taken from the adjusted trial balance of Turkey Hill Foods Corporation at 31 December 20X5, the end of the accounting period:

Sales revenue	$957,000
Sales returns	7,000
Gain on sale of equipment	8,000
Depreciation expense	25,000
Distribution expense	140,000
General and administrative expense	92,300
Rent revenue	18,000
Investment revenue	7,000
Gain on sale of land	6,000
Interest expense	9,000
Gain on expropriation of property	80,000
Loss on sale of long-term investments	10,000
Cost of goods sold	550,000
Loss due to leaky roof	4,000
Earthquake damage loss	30,000

All items listed above are before tax; the tax rate is 30% on all items. There are 40,000 common shares outstanding.

Required:

1. Prepare a single-step income statement. State any assumptions made.

2. Prepare a multiple-step income statement.

3. Calculate the EPS disclosures that would be included on the income statement. Include one EPS figure for net income, and one for income before extraordinary items.

P3-2 *Formats of Income Statement, Extraordinary Item:* The following data was taken from the adjusted trial balance of Montreal Retail Corporation at 31 December 20X6, the end of the accounting period:

Cost of goods sold	$102,000
Accounts payable	121,400
Sales revenue	405,000
Accumulated depreciation	139,500
Sales returns	5,000
Unearned revenue	2,000
Depreciation expense (70% administrative expense, 30% distribution expense)	50,000
Rent revenue	4,000
Interest expense	6,000
Investment revenue	2,500
Distribution expenses (exclusive of depreciation)	105,500
General and administrative expenses (exclusive of depreciation)	46,000
Royalty revenue	6,000
Loss on sale of long-term investments	3,600
Income tax expense	?
Flood loss (extraordinary)	10,000

Assume an average 35% income tax rate on all items, including gains and losses on assets sold and extraordinary items.

Required:

1. Prepare a single-step income statement.
2. Prepare a multiple-step income statement.

P3-3 *Combined Income and Retained Earnings Statement:* The following amounts were taken from the accounting records of Curtis Recyclers Corporation at 31 December 20X5, the end of the annual accounting period:

Sales revenue	$340,000
Service revenue	64,000
Cost of goods sold	170,000
Distribution and administrative expenses	67,000
Depreciation expense	19,000
Investment revenue	6,000
Interest expense	4,000
Loss on sale of long-term investment (pretax)	10,000
Earthquake damage loss	14,000
Cash dividends declared	8,000
Correction of error from prior period, pretax (a debit)	12,000
Balance, retained earnings, 1 January 20X5	80,300

Common shares, 30,000 shares outstanding.
Restriction on retained earnings, $50,000 regarding a bond payable indenture.
Assume an average 35% income tax rate on all items.

Required:

Prepare a combined single-step income and retained earnings statement, including tax allocation and EPS for income before extraordinary items and net income. Show computations. Restrictions to retained earnings should be disclosed in a note. State any necessary assumptions.

P3-4 *Minimum Disclosure:* Review the data given for P3-2, above. Assume that the company wished to publish an income statement that complied with the minimum required disclosures outlined in the *CICA Handbook*.

Required:

1. Draft a single-step income statement that complies with minimum required disclosures. Lump all revenues and expenses that need not be shown separately into "other revenues" and "operating expenses," respectively.
2. Explain why the company might prefer minimal disclosures, referring to material explained in Chapters 1 and 2.

P3-5 *Discontinued Operations:* At its 1 September 20X5 meeting, the board of directors of Hazelton Candy Company approved a plan for disposing of its candy vending division. The vending machine operation has separately identifiable assets and operations and had incurred a loss before tax of $150,000 for the eight-month period ending 1 September 20X5. A tentative agreement has been reached with McAdoo Corporation to buy the vending division for $2,000,000 with delivery of all the assets and operations to McAdoo as of 1 April 20X6. Hazelton will continue operating the division until it is delivered to McAdoo. It is expected that the sale will result in a loss of $250,000 on the net assets of the division.

An operating loss of $30,000 before tax effects was experienced during the last four months of 20X5; an additional pre-tax loss of $50,000 is expected during the time Hazelton will be operating the division in 20X6. Assume an income tax rate of 30%.

Required:

1. Show the discontinued operations section of the 20X5 income statement for Hazelton Candy Company. Assume that the after-tax income from continuing operations in 20X5 is $500,000.

2. Actual operations of the vending machine division for the first three months of 20X6 results in an operating loss before taxes of $40,000, and the sale of the net assets of the division results in an actual pretax loss of $230,000. Show the discontinued operations section of comparative income statements for 20X5 and 20X6 for Hazelton Candy Company. Assume that after-tax income from continuing operations is $600,000 in 20X6.

P3-6 *Disposal of Business Segment:* NSC Ltd. has a 31 May fiscal year-end. NSC disposed of its Information Systems Group (ISG) on 31 January 20X3, during NSC's third quarter. The measurement date was the disposal date. The division was sold for $475,600,000 in cash plus future royalties through 31 May 20X4, which were guaranteed to be $30,000,000. The minimum guaranteed royalties were included in the computation of the 20X3 gain on the sale of the division. Actual royalties received in 20X4 were $35,500,000. Excerpts from comparative income statements found in the 31 May 20X4 financial statements are as follows:

| | Year Ended 31 May | | |
	20X4	20X3	20X2
	($ millions)		
Earnings (loss) from continuing operations	$(29.3)	$(205.5)	$30.1
Discontinued operations:			
Earnings (loss) from operations (net of income taxes of $6.5 in 20X3 [recoveries] and $10.5 in 20X2)	—	(37.7)	32.6
Gain on sale of discontinued operation (net of incomes taxes of $1.2 in 20X4 and $40.5 in 20X3)	4.3	220.0	—
Net income (loss)	$(25.0)	$ (23.2)	$62.7

Required:

1. Determine the net book value of ISG as of the measurement date.
2. Why does NSC report a gain on the sale of the discontinued operation of $4,300,000 in the year ending 31 May 20X4?
3. NSC reports an after-tax loss from discontinued operations of $37,700,000 for the year ending 31 May 20X3. Over what period was the loss accrued?
4. How would the reporting differ if NSC had adopted a formal disposal plan at the beginning of the 20X2 fiscal year?

P3-7 *Discontinued Operations, Unusual Item, Change in Accounting Principle:* In December 20X4, the board of directors of Mead Corporation approved a plan to curtail the development of the company's imaging products division. As a result, the company established a provision before tax totalling $77,000,000 for (a) the loss expected on the disposal of the division's assets and (b) future losses of $29,300,000 expected to be incurred in fulfilling contract obligations over the next four years. The imaging products division had incurred before-tax losses of $50,000,000 in 20X3 and $41,700,000 in 20X4.

In addition, during 20X4, the company retired an issue of bonds early. These bonds had a carrying value of $170,000,000 and were retired at a cost of $159,000,000, resulting in a pretax gain of $11,000,000. The company had never had such a transaction before.

The tax rate on all the above items is Mead Corporation's average income tax rate of 37%.

Assume that earnings from other sources, before income taxes, were $392,500,000 in 20X3 and $168,900,000 in 20X4. This does not include the bond retirement transaction. The average number of common shares outstanding were 65,100,000 shares in 20X3 and 62,200,000 shares in 20X4. Mead Corporation has no preferred shares outstanding.

Required:

1. Prepare the income statements for Mead Corporation for 20X3 and 20X4, beginning with income from continuing operations. Include appropriate earnings per share computations.

2. In 20X5, the imaging products division was operated by Mead as a discontinued business, and it incurred a pretax operating loss of $6,500,000. The original provision for the remaining three years' losses and the disposal of the division is still considered to be a reasonable estimate. Income from continuing operations after tax was $75,600,000 in 20X5, and they had an average of 58,600,000 common shares outstanding during the year. Show the income statements for 20X5 and 20X4, beginning with income from continuing operations. Include appropriate earnings per share computations.

P3-8 *Financial Statement Classification:* Listed below are some financial statement classifications coded with letters and, below them, selected transactions and account titles. For each transaction or account title, enter in the space provided a code letter to indicate the usual classification. Comment on doubtful items.

Code	Financial Statement Classification
	Income Statement
A	Revenue, or ordinary gain
B	Expense, or ordinary loss
C	Unusual gain or loss
D	Extraordinary item
	Statement of Retained Earnings
E	An addition to or deduction from beginning balance
F	Addition to retained earnings
G	Deduction from retained earnings
	Disclosure Notes
H	Note to the financial statements
	Balance Sheet
I	Appropriately classified balance sheet account

Response	Transaction or Account Title
_____	1. Estimated warranties payable.
_____	2. Allowance for doubtful accounts.
_____	3. Gain on sale of operational asset.
_____	4. Hurricane damages in Quebec City.
_____	5. Payment of $30,000 additional income tax assessment on prior year's income.
_____	6. Earthquake damages in Edmonton.

_____ 7. Distribution expenses.

_____ 8. Total amount of cash and credit sales for the period.

_____ 9. Gain on disposal of long-term investments in shares (non-recurring).

_____ 10. Net income for the period.

_____ 11. Insurance gain on casualty (fire) — insurance proceeds exceed the book value of the assets destroyed.

_____ 12. Cash dividends declared and paid.

_____ 13. Rent collected on office space temporarily leased.

_____ 14. Interest paid during the year plus interest accrued on liabilities.

_____ 15. Dividends received on shares held as an investment.

_____ 16. Damages paid as a result of a lawsuit by an individual injured while shopping in the company's store; the litigation lasted three years.

_____ 17. Loss due to expropriation of a plant in a foreign country.

_____ 18. A $100,000 bad debt is to be written off — the receivable had been outstanding for five years. The company estimates bad debts each year and has an allowance for bad debts.

_____ 19. Adjustment due to correction of an error during current year; the error was made two years earlier.

_____ 20. On 31 December of the current year, paid rent expense in advance for the next year.

_____ 21. Cost of goods sold.

_____ 22. Interest collected on 30 November of the current year from a customer on a 90-day note receivable, dated 1 September of the current year.

_____ 23. Year-end bonus of $50,000 paid to employees for performance during the year.

_____ 24. Cumulative effect of a change in accounting policy.

_____ 25. A meteor destroys manufacturing facilities ($5 million book value, no insurance).

P3-9 *Analytical — Discuss Statement Classification:* The following transactions have been encountered in practice. Assume that all amounts are material.

a. A company discovered that in error, a payment to the employee's pension fund was all that was expensed last year, the appropriate calculation of expense was $20,000 higher than the payment.

b. A company suffered a casualty loss (a fire) amounting to $500,000. The company has had three fires in the last 10 years, but this was significantly more than any such loss experienced before by the company.

c. A company paid $175,000 damages assessed by the courts as a result of an injury to a customer on the company premises three years earlier.

d. A company sold a significant operational asset and reported a gain of $70,000.

e. A major supplier of raw materials to a company experienced a prolonged strike. As a result, the company reported a loss of $150,000. This is the first such loss; however, the company has three major suppliers, and strikes are not unusual in the industry.

f. A company owns several large blocks of common shares of other corporations. The shares have been held for a number of years and are viewed as long-term investments. During the past year, 20% of the shares were sold to meet an unusual cash demand. Additional disposals are not anticipated.

g. A timber company wrote down inventory and natural resources (a capital asset) after five years of low pulp and paper prices on world markets. The amount was material, it was the first such write-down in the company's history, and it is not expected to recur.

Required:

1. Write a brief report defining unusual gains and losses, extraordinary gains and losses, and error corrections. Explain how the effects of each should be reported.

2. Classify each of the above transactions. Explain the basis for your decision in each situation.

P3-10 *Change in Accounting Principle, Retained Earnings Statement:* Moncton Developments Ltd. was formed in 20X2. During the year ended 31 December 20X4, the company changed its method of accounting for product development expenses from expensing such items to capitalizing them and amortizing them over the period of expected benefit. The 20X4 statements have been prepared using the old policy. Preliminary statements appear as follows:

MONCTON DEVELOPMENTS LTD.
Statement of Income and Retained Earnings
for the year ended 31 December 20X4

Sales	$2,400,000
Costs and expenses (including product development)	1,482,000
Amortization	70,000
Income before tax	848,000
Tax expense	339,200
Net income	508,800
Retained earnings, opening	690,000
	1,198,800
Dividends ($1 per share)	50,000
Retained earnings, closing	$1,148,800
EPS	$10.18

The following pretax information was gathered:

	20X4	20X3	20X2
Net income, old policy	$508,800	$540,000	$210,000
Product development costs	200,000	150,000	250,000
Amortization, prior to change	70,000	70,000	60,000
Amortization, after change*	118,000	110,000	90,000

* Using new policy

Required:

1. Prepare a revised 20X4 income and retained earnings statement, giving appropriate treatment to the change in accounting policy. All amounts are taxable at 40%. Include note disclosure.

2. If insufficient information is available to treat the accounting policy change as in (1), what other options does the company have? Describe the impact of the alternatives on the financial statements.

P3-11 *Comprehensive Format:* The following trial balance of the Puget Petroleum Corporation at 31 December 20X5, has been prepared and is correct, except that income tax expense has not been allocated.

PUGET PETROLEUM CORPORATION
Trial Balance 31 December 20X5

	Debit	Credit
Cash	$ 636,000	
Accounts receivable (net)	1,695,000	
Inventory	2,185,000	
Property, plant, and equipment (net)	8,660,000	
Accounts payable and accrued liabilities		$ 1,856,000
Income tax payable		399,000
Future (deferred) income tax		285,000
Common shares, 215,000 shares outstanding		5,975,000
Retained earnings, 1 January 20X5		3,350,000
Net sales, regular*		10,750,000
Net sales, plastics division		2,200,000
Cost of sales, regular	5,920,000	
Cost of sales, plastics division	1,650,000	
Selling and administrative expenses, regular	2,600,000	
Selling and administrative expense, plastics division	660,000	
Interest income, regular		65,000
Error correction		200,000
Depreciation adjustment from accounting change	350,000	
Gain on disposal of plastics division		150,000
Income tax expense	874,000	
Totals	$25,230,000	$25,230,000

* Accounts identified as regular include all but plastics division for that account.

Other financial data for the year ended 31 December 20X5:

a. *Income tax expense:*

Tax payments	$475,000
Accrued	399,000
Total charged to income tax expense	$874,000

Tax rate on all types of income: 40%. The $874,000 does not reflect intraperiod income tax allocation which is required for financial statement purposes.

b. The *error correction* involves a revenue item not recorded in 20X3, the year in which it was earned.

c. *Discontinued operations.* On 31 October 20X5, Puget sold its plastics division for $2,950,000, when the carrying amount was $2,800,000. For financial statement reporting, this sale was considered a disposal of a segment of a business. The measurement date and the disposal date were both 31 October 20X5.

d. *Change in depreciation method.* On 1 January 20X5, Puget changed to the declining balance method from the straight-line method of depreciation to conform to industry practice. The pretax cumulative effect of this accounting change was determined to be a charge of $350,000. There was no change in depreciation method for income tax purposes.

Required:

Using the multiple-step format, prepare an income statement for Puget for the year ended 31 December 20X5 (separate disclosure of depreciation and interest expense is not required). Also, prepare a retained earnings statement. All components of income tax expense should be appropriately shown.

[AICPA, adapted]

P3-12 *Comprehensive Format:* In its 20X3 annual report, MBL Limited identified the following accounts and amounts ($ thousands):

	52 weeks ended:	
	25 Jan. 20X3	**26 Jan. 20X2**
Sales	$132,742	$178,318
Selling and promotion expenses	39,089	51,653
Opening retained earnings	?	11,560
Discontinued operations — loss on disposal of real estate division*	2,250	—
Franchise revenue	3,000	3,817
Settlement with ex-senior executive	1,959	—
Loss on closure of selected retail operations	—	1,384
Provision for income taxes (recovery)	(443)	(4,400)
Purchase of common shares — excess of redemption price over original proceeds	—	15
General and administration expenses	15,491	17,246
Discontinued operations — loss from operations of real estate division*	196	13
Cost of goods sold	85,959	122,593

* net of relevant taxes
Common shares outstanding: 9,875

Required:

Prepare a multiple-step format income statement and a retained earnings statement in good form.

P3-13 *Value Added Statement:* The following income statement was prepared to comply with Canadian reporting standards:

YMM MINING LTD.
Income statement
for the year ended 31 December
($ thousands)

	20X4	**20X3**
Sales revenue	$16,200	$15,100
Cost of goods sold	12,900	13,600
Gross profit	3,300	1,500
Selling, general, and administration expenses	2,200	2,100
Interest on long-term debt	400	900
Income taxes	250	—
Net income (loss)	$ 450	$ (1,500)

Additional information:

Depreciation included in cost of goods sold	$ 4,100	$ 4,500
Depreciation included in selling, general, and administration expenses	400	400
Salaries and wages included in cost of goods sold	4,900	3,400
Salaries and wages included in selling, general and administration expenses	900	700
Dividends paid	410	—

Materials included in cost of goods sold and selling, general and administration expenses, $3,100 in 20X4 and $2,800 in 20X3. Cost of services comprises the balance of cost of goods sold and selling, general, and administration expenses.

Required:

1. Prepare a value added statement for YMM Mining Ltd.

2. Explain the additional information provided by the value added statement over a traditional income statement, and the common uses of this statement.

3. In what way is the value added statement reflective of the entity view? How does the traditional income statement reflect the proprietary view?

4. Interpret the value added statement prepared in requirement 1.

Balance Sheet and Disclosure Notes

INTRODUCTION

The **balance sheet** provides economic information about an entity's resources (assets), claims against those resources (liabilities), and the remaining claim accruing to owners (owners' equity). The name "balance sheet" reflects an important aspect of this report; namely, the statement *balances* in conformity with the basic accounting identity:

Assets = Liabilities + Owners' Equity

While the statement is usually called a balance sheet, it may also be called a **statement of financial position**. The balance sheet must be dated at a specific date, such as "31 December 20X2."

Exhibits 4-1 to 4-4 provide four examples of balance sheets. Read through them now and reflect on their similarities and differences.

The first example, Exhibit 4-1, is the Saskatchewan Wheat Pool. This company was created by special legislation of the Saskatchewan government. It has two types of shareholders — farmer members who hold the voting shares (but receive no dividends), and public shareholders who hold non-voting shares (but do receive dividends).

The components of the Saskatchewan Wheat Pool's balance sheet are fairly standard; assets are receivables, inventories, and capital assets. Other assets consist mainly of intangible assets: goodwill and capitalized pre-operating costs. You might notice that the company has no cash; it relies on bank financing to carry it through, and the financing is included as *short-term borrowings* under current liabilities. The company has a bank overdraft as a normal part of its operations. Most elements are summarized — for example, many kinds of inventory are combined into a single aggregate number.

Bombardier, Exhibit 4-2, is active in a number of different industry sectors. They build the famous "Ski-Doo" and other vehicles ("motorized consumer products") but also are involved in transportation, aerospace, defence, financial services, and real estate. There are no subtotals on this balance sheet, which is dominated by finance and other receivables, inventories and capital assets.

The Royal Bank of Canada is one of Canada's largest financial institutions. Exhibit 4-3's balance sheet is peppered with subtotals, and some fairly exotic assets and liabilities. For the most part, however, its assets are cash, investments, and loans to clients. Liabilities are customer deposits. Notice that this $274.4 billion company has only $11.9 billion in shareholders' equity — banks are highly levered, which means they have lots of debt in their financial structures. The financial statements of banks must be prepared in accordance with the *Bank Act*, a piece of federal legislation that governs many aspects of banking. Banks all have to prepare a fairly rigidly defined set of financial statements so that regulators can be effective; GAAP is defined by the *Bank Act* in this industry.

EXHIBIT 4-1
SASKATCHEWAN WHEAT POOL
Consolidated Statement of Financial Position

As at July 31	1998	1997
(in $ thousands)		
Assets		
Current assets		
Short-term investments	$ 17,690	$ 62,568
Accounts receivable	313,358	362,388
Inventories	326,664	327,290
Prepaid expenses	13,512	9,550
	671,224	761,796
Investments	77,158	41,914
Capital assets	646,789	446,503
Other long-term assets	123,279	39,065
	$1,521,450	$1,289,278
Liability and Shareholders' Equity		
Current liabilities		
Short-term borrowings	$ 177,490	$ 79,835
Members' demand loans	84,040	90,260
Accounts payable	295,387	351,483
Long-term debt due within one year	13,251	11,995
Dividends payable	14,969	11,829
	585,137	545,402
Long-term debt	214,877	202,165
Other long-term liabilities	51,113	35,374
Non-controlling interest	4,242	1,680
	855,369	784,621
Shareholders' equity		
Share capital	457,687	297,579
Retained earnings	208,394	207,078
	666,081	504,657
	$1,521,450	$1,289,278

References to disclosure notes have been deleted.

Finally, Exhibit 4-4 shows the balance sheet of Shaw Communications Inc., active in cable TV and the broadcasting business. Notice that capital assets are a major part of their asset structure — all those cable installations! But Shaw's largest single asset is *intangible* — "subscriber base and broadcast licenses," representing 41% of assets ($1,304,904 ÷ $3,201,224). This balance sheet is more conventional in that it provides subtotals for current assets and liabilities.

What policy choices do these very different companies face when preparing a balance sheet? We saw in the previous chapter that income statement preparation is quite judgemental — now it's time to take a long look at the balance sheet.

EXHIBIT 4-2
BOMBARDIER INC.
Consolidated Balance Sheets
as at January 31, 1998 and 1997
(Cdn. $ millions)

Assets	1998	1997
Cash and term deposits	$ 1,227.7	$ 895.7
Accounts receivable	693.2	358.4
Finance receivables and other	2,989.4	1,811.4
Inventories	3,790.9	3,455.2
Fixed assets	1,646.7	1,200.0
Other assets	227.3	229.6
	$10,575.2	$7,950.3
Liabilities		
Short-term borrowings	$ 2,265.6	$1,402.4
Accounts payable and accrued liabilities	2,663.0	2,124.6
Advances and progress billings in excess of related costs	851.6	591.4
Long-term debt	1,548.7	1,354.9
Other liabilities	357.0	264.4
	7,685.9	5,737.7
Shareholders' equity	2,889.3	2,212.6
	$10,575.2	$7,950.3

References to disclosure notes have been deleted.

THE PURPOSE OF THE BALANCE SHEET

The balance sheet *will reflect the unamortized cost of the company's major groups of assets, and the sources used to finance those assets.* If you want to know how Shaw's capital structure is organized, the balance sheet provides this information: long-term debt is 38% of total assets ($1,225,273 ÷ $3,201,224), down from 57% ($1,408,059 ÷ $2,450,648) in the prior year.

The balance sheet can also provide some insight into the *risk profile* of a business and its *financial flexibility*. Are the company's assets old and fully amortized or relatively new? Is the organization in a position to finance new activities with relative ease without incurring excessive debt? These are important questions that the balance sheet helps address. Has the company acquired new businesses? Shaw's assets and share capital obviously grew significantly over the year. The Royal Bank reports significant increases in residential mortgage loans and in personal loans. Business and government loans and something called "assets purchased under reverse purchase agreements" increased by more modest amounts.

While the balance sheet provides some information about actions and strategy over the year, the cash flow statement contains more information about the investment and financing activities of the company; we'll take a look at that statement in Chapter 5.

The balance sheet also reflects *liquidity*, often evaluated with reference to working capital (current assets less current liabilities) or more restrictive measures that

EXHIBIT 4-3
ROYAL BANK OF CANADA
Consolidated Balance Sheet

As at October 31 *(in millions of dollars)*	1998	1997
Assets		
Cash resources		
Cash and deposits with Bank of Canada	$ 834	$ 1,076
Deposits with other banks		
Interest bearing	14,603	19,747
Non-interest bearing	510	569
Cheques and other items in transit	448	—
	16,395	21,392
Securities		
Trading account	28,547	18,740
Investment account	12,093	13,475
Loan substitute	759	822
	41,399	33,037
Loans		
Residential mortgages	57,019	53,316
Personal	22,575	20,764
Credit cards	1,945	2,324
Business and government	63,808	61,221
Assets purchased under reverse repurchase agreements	19,907	18,642
	165,254	156,267
Other		
Customers' liability under acceptances	10,620	10,561
Premises and equipment	1,872	1,696
Other assets	38,859	21,821
	51,351	34,078
	$274,399	$244,774
Liabilities and Shareholders' Equity		
Deposits		
Personal	$ 85,910	$ 86,106
Business and government	76,107	64,368
Bank	17,988	22,755
	180,005	173,229
Other		
Acceptances	10,620	10,561
Obligations related to securities sold short	14,404	11,152
Obligations related to assets sold under repurchase agreements	8,800	9,458
Other liabilities	44,591	25,757
	78,415	56,928
Subordinated debentures	4,087	4,227
Shareholders' equity		
Capital stock		
Preferred	2,144	1,784
Common	2,925	2,907
Retained earnings	6,823	5,699
	11,892	10,390
	$274,399	$244,774

References to disclosure notes have been deleted.

EXHIBIT 4-4
SHAW COMMUNICATIONS INC.
Consolidated Balance Sheets
(*$ thousands*)

	1998	1997
Assets		
Current		
Cash and term deposits	$ 22,047	$ —
Accounts receivable	59,632	45,550
Income taxes recoverable	4,007	—
Prepaids and other	31,152	17,032
	116,838	62,582
Investments and other assets	712,689	156,246
Property, plant and equipment	997,274	879,391
Deferred charges	69,519	57,334
Subscriber base and broadcast licenses	1,304,904	1,294,648
	$3,201,224	$2,450,201
Liabilities and Shareholders' Equity		
Current		
Bank indebtedness	—	$ 20,876
Accounts payable and accrued liabilities	$ 146,501	116,740
Income taxes payable	—	17,536
Unearned subscriber revenue	37,666	35,779
Current portion of long-term debt	121,976	70,192
	306,143	261,123
Long-term debt	1,225,273	1,408,059
Deferred credits	33,304	39,933
Deferred income taxes	220,092	161,012
Minority interest	815	698
	1,785,627	1,870,825
Shareholders' equity		
Share capital	548,077	5,521
Contributed surplus	657,118	362,410
Retained earnings	210,402	211,445
	1,415,597	579,376
	$3,201,224	$2,450,201

References to disclosure notes have been deleted.

exclude non-monetary current assets. Liquidity is evidence of a company's ability to pay short-term debts from its current assets as well as to meet short- and long-term obligations. Creditors are obviously interested in assessing liquidity. Beyond this, equity investors are interested in liquidity because it affects dividend payments. Unions examine liquidity to establish bargaining positions. Employees are concerned with the company's continuing ability to pay wages. Liquidity is a major concern to many financial statement users.

In general, the balance sheet also provides data needed to determine *rates of return*, including return on equity (ROE), return on assets (ROA), the ratio of total debt to owners' equity, and a variety of other ratios. Of course, the income statement has to provide the earnings information used to calculate these ratios. Return figures are very important to financial statement users, both lenders and equity investors. They help determine the company's credit rating and share price. The figures used in ratio calculations will depend on the accounting policies chosen by the company, however, and therefore must be interpreted with caution.

Limitations of the Balance Sheet

A balance sheet based on GAAP has limitations that are the result of several aspects of applying generally accepted accounting principles:

Amounts shown on the balance sheet are the result of the company's reporting policies. Even within the constraints of GAAP, alternative accounting policies are acceptable. Virtually every amount shown on the balance sheet is the result of a company's chosen accounting policies. Different policies will result in different balance sheet amounts. For example, a company's choice of amortization policy (e.g., *straight line* or *declining balance*) will significantly affect the amounts shown for capital assets, and thereby the amounts shown for total assets and for net assets (i.e., owners' equity).

The typical balance sheet also includes many estimated amounts. Not only do accounting *policies* affect the amounts reported on the balance sheet, but also the amounts are significantly affected by accounting *estimates*. For example, the amounts shown for capital assets will be affected not only by the application of a given amortization policy (such as straight line), but also will also be affected by the estimates used in applying the policy, such as each asset's useful life and estimated salvage value. While many accounting policies are disclosed in the notes to the financial statements, accounting estimates seldom are disclosed. Other examples of estimates include the estimated loss from uncollectible receivables and the estimated liability arising from warranties. The impacts of estimates are difficult, if not impossible, to figure out.

Balance sheet values are not current values and are not meant to be current values. The balance sheet reports historical cost, which is not always a relevant attribute. Investors and creditors may be far more interested in market values. In a set of GAAP statements, market values can be disclosed, but generally are not. Companies may choose to prepare non-GAAP statements when market value is significantly different than cost and important decisions have to be based on fair value, not cost. But market value (or fair value) is not a generally accepted practice in Canada except for certain types of financial institutions, and therefore a company that reports market values in its balance sheet may not be able to receive an audit opinion.

The amounts reported for major asset categories such as plant and equipment may be significantly different than cost, given even a modest level of price changes. Individual companies are affected by this problem differently, depending on the date and rate of capital acquisitions and the level of specific price changes for the types of capital assets they use. Uncritical comparisons between companies can therefore be very misleading.

The cost-based balance sheet can be particularly out of synch with market values when a company's assets are primarily intangible. At least capital assets are valued at their fair value on the date of acquisition; the often negligible *cost* of many *internally generated* intangible assets is not even close to their fair value at acquisition. For example, a patent is often recorded only at the legal cost involved in registration. On the other hand, cost may represent fair value if intangibles are purchased. Return figures and ratio comparisons are questionable in these circumstances.

Certain assets and liabilities simply do not appear on the balance sheet. Such assets include intangible assets acquired at no ascertainable cost, such as the abilities and morale of the workforce, customer loyalty, or brand names. Other assets fail recognition criteria at acquisition and must be expensed. For example, the future benefit of research activities is deemed too uncertain to recognize as an asset.

Significant tangible assets do not appear on the balance sheet because they are leased instead of being owned. Only certain types of lease arrangements are recognized on the balance sheet; most are not. An airline, for example, may lease most or all of its aircraft, with the result that none of the planes appear on its balance sheet. Clearly, however, the airline has to have the planes in order to operate — they are necessary capital assets, but are not disclosed.

On the liability side, omitted items include some types of leases, hazardous waste cleanups whose cost cannot be estimated, and unrecorded commitments, such as frequent-flier miles. Difficulties in quantifying most of these items means that they fail the recognition criteria and cannot be recorded.

Numbers are consolidated. A company can be in one business or in a diversified portfolio of operations. The Royal Bank, for example, operates in one industry. On the other hand, Bombardier operates in five major sectors, which are quite different. If users are relying on balance sheet information to portray relationships, those relationships may well be different for each individual sector.

Adding the data together is problematic, as it may mask important information. Bombardier, for example, presents two additional balance sheets (not reproduced here) beside its consolidated balance sheet — one for Bombardier's manufacturing operations, and one for the real estate and financial services sector. Many companies rely on disaggregated, or segmented, information to get around this dilemma; we'll talk about these disclosures later in this chapter.

Consolidated statements also do not tell creditors what assets are available to satisfy their claims. A creditor, whether a trade supplier or a lender, has recourse only to the assets owned by the legal entity to which credit has been extended. Assets held by other corporations within the consolidated accounting entity cannot be claimed. It is not unusual for one corporation in a consolidated group to go bankrupt while other corporations in the group remain solvent. The creditors of the bankrupt corporation are out of luck, if they based their lending decisions only on consolidated statements![1]

FORMATTING CHOICES

Many presentation issues are open to choice by the company. We reviewed some choice issues in the last chapter, such as choice of year-end, reporting currency, language, etc. Some additional issues are unique to the balance sheet.

---

[1] For example, when the Eaton's department store chain went into financial reorganization in 1997, its profitable credit card subsidiary was not included in the reorganization, and Eaton's general creditors had no access to the considerable assets of the subsidiary.

Form of Presentation

The **financing form** follows the classic accounting identity, A = L + OE. That is, assets are totalled, and liabilities and owner's equity are totalled to the same amount, proving the equation. This emphasizes the means used to finance the organization's assets. Funds must be raised from creditors (liabilities) or from owners (owners' equity), often by retaining the organization's earnings. Alternatively, the basic accounting identity can be rearranged to reflect the owners' viewpoint, in the **net assets form**. Thus, A − L = OE. That is, net assets, or assets less liabilities, are totalled on the balance sheet to a number that is equal to owners' equity. According to *Financial Reporting in Canada 1997*, the financing form is the dominant choice, used by 97% of the 200 surveyed public companies. Two versions exist — one lists assets at the top of the statement, followed vertically by liabilities and then equities. This is called the *report format*, which is used by 88% of the surveyed public companies. Alternatively, assets can be listed on the left of the statement and liabilities and equities on the right. This is called the *account format*.

The Saskatchewan Wheat Pool balance sheet in Exhibit 4-1 has a total for assets and another for liabilities and equities, so it is in the financing form. It lists assets, then liabilities, then equities down the statement, so it is in report format. All the other examples are also in financing form and report form.

Classification and Aggregation

To make accounting information as understandable and usable by decision-makers as possible, items are grouped and arranged in the balance sheet according to certain guidelines. Some of these groupings are non-judgemental, as companies have little choice but to comply with generally accepted practice — users have certain expectations, after all. Other display decisions are very subjective.

In U.S. and Canadian practice, assets typically are classified and presented in *decreasing order of liquidity*, or convertibility into cash. Those items nearest to cash, that is, those that can be readily converted to cash at any time without restriction, are ranked first. Assets with the least liquidity, or least likely to be converted to cash, are listed last.

Liabilities are generally classified and presented based on *time to maturity*. Thus, obligations currently due are listed first, and those carrying the most distant maturity dates are listed last.

Owners' equity items are classified and presented in *order of permanence*. Thus, paid-in capital accounts, which typically change the least, should be listed first. Equity accounts used to report accumulated earnings and profit distributions are listed last.

Current Assets and Liabilities. The most common groupings on the balance sheet are current assets and current liabilities; the net amount of current assets minus current liabilities is called **working capital**. Minimum working capital ratios are often stipulated in loan agreements. It's easier for financial statement users to look at working capital when the company provides the current asset and current liability subtotals.

While most companies group current assets and liabilities, not all follow this practice. For example, Bombardier presents an unclassified balance sheet, claiming that each of its major sectors of activity has its own operating cycle to the extent that the aggregated totals lack meaning. The banks are not required to segregate assets as current or non-current according to the provisions of the *Bank Act*.

Current assets include cash and other assets that are reasonably expected to be realized in cash or to be sold or consumed during the normal operating cycle of the business or within one year from the balance sheet date, whichever is longer. The normal operating cycle of a business is the average length of time from the expenditure of cash for inventory, to sale, to accounts receivable, and finally back to cash. This is sometimes called the cash-to-cash cycle. Almost all companies use one year as the time period for classifying items as current or long-term because either the operating cycle is less than one year or the length of the operating cycle may be difficult to measure reliably.

Judgement is required in defining the "normal operating cycle" and elements "reasonably expected to be realized in cash." When there is uncertainty, management may be inclined to classify certain items as current assets in order to produce a positive effect on working capital. For example, an investment in debt or equity securities of another company or the assets of a discontinued division could be classified as a current or non-current asset, depending on the intended holding period and on the likely saleability of the shares or assets. The placement of these assets on a company's balance sheet could be based on the actual intention of management or, alternatively and inappropriately, on management's desire to show its accounts in a better light; this is a problem both for the auditors and for external decision-makers.

Current liabilities are those obligations that are due within one year or one operating cycle, whichever is longer. Current liabilities include the typical range of accounts payable, including accrued amounts, payroll, taxes, and so on. Also included is unearned revenue, which is an obligation to provide service, not cash. The current portion of long-term debt is an important element of current liabilities.

Other Classifications. Other classifications are basically the major asset, liability, and equity items — investments, tangible and intangible capital assets, long-term debt, and so on. Classifications are strongly influenced by the unique characteristics of each industry and each business enterprise. You can readily see by comparing Exhibit 4-2 and Exhibit 4-3 that the balance sheet of a bank reflects different classifications from those of a manufacturing company.

In these classifications, there is some choice, and some accounting policy established by standards and industry norms. "Typical" balance sheet categories are listed in Exhibit 4-5. Later in the chapter, we'll investigate each of these categories individually, looking at their presentation on the balance sheet and note disclosures together.

1. Why may a company's major assets not appear on the balance sheet?
2. What interpretive problems arise from the fact that the financial statements of public companies are consolidated?
3. What is the definition of *current* in current assets and current liabilities?

CONCEPT REVIEW

SPECIFIC BALANCE SHEET ITEMS

Most of this book is spent examining typical financial statement elements; their recognition, valuation, and required disclosures. This chapter provides a review of many of the facets of the balance sheet that you learned in introductory accounting, and it also introduces some additional subtleties that you may not be aware of. This overview of balance sheet items can't replace the detailed study that lies ahead of you. Instead, try to gain an appreciation for the overall nature of typical balance sheet accounts and disclosures.

Assets

In most industries, assets are classified into a minimum of three categories: (1) *current assets*; (2) *capital assets*, tangible and intangible; and (3) *other assets*. Other categories are used only if there are enough items to warrant the use of a separate category instead of including them under the "Other Assets" classification. The major categories and the items included therein are described below. Later chapters discuss each type of asset in more detail.

EXHIBIT 4-5
Typical Balance Sheet Classifications

The classification and presentation order below are representative of current reporting practice and terminology.

A. **ASSETS**
 1. **Current assets**
    a. Cash
    b. Short-term investments
    c. Receivables
    d. Inventories
    e. Prepayments (also called prepaid expenses)
    f. Other current assets

 2. **Non-current assets**
    a. Investments and funds
    b. Tangible capital assets (also called property, plant, and equipment or fixed assets)
    c. Intangible capital assets
    d. Other assets
    e. Long-term deferred charges

B. **LIABILITIES**
 1. **Current liabilities** (including the current portion of long-term liabilities)
 2. **Long-term liabilities** (including shareholders' equity items that have the characteristics of debt)
 3. **(Future) deferred income taxes**
 4. **Other deferred credits**

C. **SHAREHOLDERS' EQUITY**
 1. **Contributed (or paid-in) capital**
    a. Share capital
    b. Debt elements that have the characteristics of equity
    c. Other contributed (or paid-in) capital
 2. **Retained earnings**
 3. **Other equity items** (primarily deferred foreign exchange gains and losses)

Current Assets

Cash. Cash available for operating activities is a current asset. Accounts held for designated purposes (e.g., bond sinking funds) are long-term. Some companies lump **cash equivalents** or term deposits with the cash figure (see the Bombardier and Shaw balance sheets, Exhibit 4-2 and 4-4). Cash equivalents are specifically defined as short-term (usually no longer than three months), interest-bearing investments, providing little risk of market value fluctuations.

Short-Term Investments. Investments in debt securities, such as Canadian government treasury bills (*T-bills*), money market funds, and commercial paper are short-term investments. As noted, some are cash equivalents or term deposits that companies group with the cash account. Others are shown separately as short-term investments. Short-term investments also include corporate equity securities. Any significant amounts of short-term investments in debt or in equity securities should be listed separately among the current assets. Short-term investments are reported at the lower of their cost or current market value. These investments are financial instruments, and, as such, information concerning their terms and conditions, interest rates, credit risk, and market values should be disclosed.

Receivables. Accounts and notes receivable should be reported net of any anticipated reduction because of uncollectible amounts. Any receivables pledged as security for an obligation of the firm should be disclosed. Receivables are also financial instruments and appropriate disclosures are required.

Inventories. Inventories usually are reported at the lower of cost or market (LCM). In addition, the valuation basis and the completion stage should be indicated (e.g., raw materials, work in process, or finished goods). In some sectors of the economy, inventories are valued at market value or net realizable value. Examples include most commodities (e.g., precious metals, copper, many agricultural products) and securities held by investment companies (e.g., mutual funds). Inventories may also be reported at net realizable value when revenue is recognized throughout the earnings process, such as in long-term construction projects.

Prepayments. Prepayments, or prepaid expenses, are cash outlays made in advance of receipt of service. Rent paid 31 May for the month of June is an example. A short-term prepayment should be classified as a current asset, whereas a long-term prepayment should be classified as a non-current asset. Prepaid expenses are current assets because an investment is made by paying cash in advance, thereby reducing cash outlays for the coming reporting period.

Other Current Assets Are there any other assets being held that are expected to produce cash in the current period? If so, they are part of current assets. For example, if the assets of a discontinued division are expected to be sold in the current period, they are appropriately included in current assets.

Non-Current Assets
Assets are non-current if

1. Assets will not be used up in a single operating cycle, or
2. Management plans to retain the assets beyond the current period or operating cycle.

Tangible Capital Assets. *Tangible capital assets* include all property, plant, equipment, and resources that are used in the company's production or service process, either directly or indirectly. It does not include property that is held for resale.

Historically, tangible capital assets have been called **fixed assets** because of their relative permanence, or by the more descriptive term **property, plant, and equipment** (PP&E). A wide variety of terminology is found in practice. They include both (1) items that are amortized, such as buildings, machinery, and fixtures, mineral deposits and timber stands, and (2) items that are not subject to amortization, such as land. Tangible capital assets also include certain leased assets if the lease arrangement is deemed to be a method of financing a permanent acquisition of the facilities.

The balance sheet or the related notes should report additional information on capital assets, including the following:

- Balances of major classes of capital assets.
- Accumulated amortization, by major class of capital assets.
- A description of the methods used in computing amortization for the major classes of capital assets.

Tangible capital assets are usually shown on the balance sheet at their original cash equivalent cost less any accumulated amortization (or depreciation) to date.

Intangible Capital Assets.   Intangible capital assets are long-lived assets that lack physical substance. Examples of intangible assets include brand names, copyrights, franchises, licences, patents, software, subscription lists, and trademarks. These assets usually are reported as a separate element in the balance sheet, although sometimes companies will combine the tangible and intangible capital assets on the balance sheet and provide a breakdown in the notes. The accumulated amount of amortization usually is disclosed in the notes or elsewhere in the financial statements. By convention, amortization is deducted directly from the intangible asset account instead of being recorded in a contra account (i.e., *accumulated amortization*) as is done with tangible capital assets. Intangible assets are shown *net* on the balance sheet and in the notes.

Some important intangible assets are not on company balance sheets at all. This is because intangibles are usually capitalized only when they are purchased as part of the acquisition of another firm or when expenditures such as legal fees are made in regard to them.

Investments and Funds.   The investments and funds classification includes the following investments that are held for the long-term and not as temporary investments:

- Long-term investments in the share capital of another company not intended for sale in the year. Such shares should be recorded at original cost or adjusted cost arising from the application of the equity method, where appropriate.

- Long-term investments in the bonds of another company. Any unamortized premium is added to the investment, and any unamortized discount is subtracted.

- Investments in subsidiaries, including long-term receivables from subsidiaries. If the statements are consolidated, these accounts are eliminated.

- Funds set aside for long-term future use, such as bond sinking funds, expansion funds, share retirement funds, and long-term savings deposits. Funds are shown at the accumulated amount in the fund — contributions plus interest earned to date.

- Investments in tangible capital assets, such as land and buildings, that represent excess capacity and that are not being used in operations. These assets are sometimes left in the tangible asset section, but segregated. Although capital investments are usually shown at their original cost less amortization, they may be recorded at market value if market value is lower than cost and the impairment of value is judged (by management) to be permanent.

The basis of valuation being used for long-term investments should be disclosed. Major classifications of long-term investments should be disclosed separately. Financial instrument disclosures for appropriate items must be satisfied; fair values are of interest here, along with yield rates.

Often, a company will have only one or two types of assets that fit under this category. If there is not a large number of such assets, companies commonly include long-term investments and funds under "Other Assets," as described below.

Long-Term Deferred Charges.   Deferred charges may be the result of the prepayment of long-term expenses. These expenses have *reliably determinable* future economic benefits useful in earning future revenues. On this basis, they are viewed as assets until they are used. The only conceptual difference between a prepaid expense (classified as a current asset) and a deferred charge is the length of time over which the amount is amortized.

Also included under the deferred charges caption are such things as organization costs, machinery rearrangement costs, bond issue costs, and pension costs paid in advance. Deferred charges are sometimes reported as other assets, but should be reported separately. They are items that have economic benefit and qualify for deferral because they will benefit future periods. The nature of these items, their valuation base, and the method and period of amortization must be clearly disclosed.

Other Assets.　The other assets classification is used for assets that are not easily included under alternative asset classifications. Examples include long-term receivables from company officers and employees and assets of discontinued operations, held for eventual sale. Long-term investments, special funds, and long-term deferred charges often are lumped together (though separately listed) under the category of "Other Assets." The nature of, and valuation basis for, these assets should be clearly disclosed. If a reported asset has no future economic benefit, it should be written off and reported in the income statement as a loss.

Liabilities

Current Liabilities.　The current liabilities section of the balance sheet includes all obligations of the company that are due within one year or one operating cycle, whichever period is longer. Commonly found elements include

- Accounts payable for goods and services that enter into the operating cycle of the business (sometimes called *trade payables*).
- Special short-term liabilities (i.e., payables) for non-operating items and services.
- Short-term notes payable.
- Short-term bank debt.
- Current maturities of long-term liabilities (including capital lease obligations).
- Unearned revenue (such as rent collected in advance) that will be earned within the next year or operating cycle, whichever is longer.
- Accrued expenses for payroll, interest, and taxes.
- Future (deferred) income taxes relating to current assets and current liabilities.

Long-Term Liabilities.　A long-term (non-current) liability is an obligation that is due beyond the next operating cycle or during the next reporting year, whichever is longer.

All liabilities not appropriately classified as current liabilities are reported as long-term. Typical long-term liabilities are bonds payable, long-term notes payable, pension liabilities, deferred long-term revenues (advances from customers), and long-term capital lease obligations. Most long-term liabilities are recorded at the exchange value of the assets or services received.

Financial instruments should be classified by substance, not form, and thus the long-term debt classification will include any portion of shares that contain a contractual obligation for a future cash flow to the holders; such a condition makes them debt, in substance. Preferred shares that require the company to redeem them at definite dates and prices are a good example. Such shares have a guaranteed cash flow to the investor, and guaranteed cash flows are the essence of debt!

Note disclosures for long-term debt can be extensive, especially if the debt issue contains unusual features. Disclosure of terms and conditions includes the interest rate, maturity date, sinking fund requirements, redemption and conversion provisions, security, and loan covenants, if applicable. Effective interest rates and fair values should be disclosed. Finally, the aggregate payments (cash flow) required over each of the next five years should be disclosed.

Other Long-term Deferred Credits.　Deferred credits can arise from several sources. One example occurs in pension accounting, when the expense recorded is greater than the payments made to date.　Another example is revenue that has been received (i.e., as a deposit) but that will not become earned revenue within the next year.

Shareholders' Equity

Shareholders' equity is a residual interest, but includes two basic components:

1. Contributed (or paid-in) capital.
2. Retained earnings.

Contributed Capital.   Because of legal requirements, contributed capital is sub-classified to reflect detailed sources. For corporations, the most commonly reported sub-classifications are

a. Share capital.
b. Debt elements that have the characteristics of equity.
c. Other contributed capital.

The breakdown between these two sub-classifications is generally of little significance; they tend to be defined more by legal specifications than by substantive accounting measurement. In some jurisdictions, the amount of share capital is designated as *legal capital* or *stated capital*, but with little or no legal consequences.

Share Capital.   Share capital is the paid-in value or par value of the issued or outstanding preferred and common shares of the corporation. This amount is not available for dividend declarations.

Each share class should be reported at its paid-in amount, or, in the case of par value shares, at par value. Par value shares are only found in a few provincial jurisdictions in Canada, but may be found in other jurisdictions (e.g., in the United States). Details of the terms and conditions of each class of share capital must be reported separately, including the number of shares authorized, issued, outstanding, and subscribed; also disclosed are conversion features, callability, preferences, dividend rates, and any other special features. Changes in share capital accounts during the period must be disclosed, along with outstanding options.

Debt Elements That Have the Characteristics of Equity.   Contributed capital should include financial instruments that have legal characteristics of debt but that, in substance, have terms that give them the essential characteristics of equity. For example, Bombardier's financial statements list "convertible notes" as an item in shareholders' equity. The company's disclosure notes tell us that on the maturity date of these convertible notes, Bombardier has the option to repay the convertible notes with its own voting shares, thus avoiding any cash outflow at maturity. Since this is what they plan to do, the convertible notes don't represent a liability at all — they're share capital with a different name! Such items are classified by substance, and "interest" payments on items that are, in substance, equity, are classified on the retained earnings statement as dividends. Such financial instruments are discussed in Chapter 15.

Other Contributed Capital.   Other contributed capital arises from such transactions as the retirement of shares for less than the original investment made and capital arising from recapitalizations. Details and changes during the period should be disclosed.

Other contributed capital also includes, for corporations that issue par value shares, an account called *contributed capital in excess of par*. If shares are sold for an amount in excess of par value, contributed capital is created. Details and changes during the period should be disclosed.

Retained Earnings.   Retained earnings is essentially a corporation's accumulated net earnings, less dividends paid out, since the company's inception. In many corporations, retained earnings is the largest amount in the owners' equity section. Over a corporation's life, dividends are distributed to the shareholders in amounts that are usually less than the corporation's earnings. This policy establishes a continuing source of internally generated funds. Companies that are in their growth phase normally pay few, if any, dividends to their shareholders; instead, they retain all or most of their earnings for reinvestment and business expansion. Companies that are beyond their growth phase commonly pay out a higher percentage of their earnings in the form of shareholder dividends.

A negative balance in retained earnings is called a deficit and usually arises when a company experiences continuing operating losses.

Other Equity Items. Standard-setters occasionally designate an item to be excluded from income and retained earnings. For example, assume that a company has a subsidiary in Mexico that keeps its records and operates in pesos. The subsidiary runs relatively independently, and manages its own cash flows; the parent company gets royalty and dividend cheques a few times a year but has no other risks in relation to fluctuations in the value of the peso. At year-end, the financial statements of the subsidiary are translated from the peso to the Canadian dollar. Since different exchange rates are used for different financial statement elements according to the accounting rules, an overall exchange gain or loss results to balance the statements. For independent subsidiaries, the cumulative amount of the gain or loss is isolated as a separate component of equity. It will be recognized on the income statement only if the subsidiary is sold or liquidated. Bombardier reports $136.3 million in this category in its detailed statement of shareholders' equity.

In the U.S., investments are often valued at market value, and the cumulative difference between cost and market value is also isolated in equity until realization. We have no similar rules for investments in Canada ... at least, not yet!

Credit Balances That Are neither Liabilities nor Owners' Equity

In theory, all items on the right side of the Canadian balance sheet should be classifiable as either liabilities or as owners' equity. In corporate reporting, however, there are two items that "float" in the area below liabilities but above shareholders' equity:

1. future (deferred) income taxes, and
2. minority interest(s) in subsidiary companies, also known as non-controlling interest.

Both of these items can be seen in Shaw Communication's balance sheet (Exhibit 4-4).

Future Income Taxes. When the amount of taxes legally payable is less than the tax expense recorded on the income statement, a deferred credit results. This deferred credit is called *future income tax liability*, although it is not actually owed by the company to the government. The existence of a future income tax liability is common when expenditures are deductible for tax purposes earlier than they are for financial reporting purposes. For example, capital assets may qualify for fast write-off for tax purposes but may be amortized more slowly for accounting purposes. Taxable income is lower than accounting income in the early years of capital asset ownership; in later years, the situation will be reversed and taxable income will be higher than accounting income.

Historically, in Canada, deferred income taxes have not been included in the long-term debt classification because they have been viewed as an allocation of income tax expense (that is, as a long-term deferred credit) rather than as a monetary liability. Because of their special nature (and often their large amount), the *CICA Handbook* has specifically recommended that these deferred credits *not* be classified under liabilities but rather be given their own classification, below liabilities but above share equity.

However, effective with fiscal years beginning on or after 1 January 2000, companies that are constrained by GAAP must report these credits as a long-term liability. The AcSB uses the term *future income tax liability* instead of deferred taxes, but many companies are continuing to use the older deferred tax terminology in an attempt to avoid having readers think that this is an obligation of the company in the same way as other long-term debt. Many companies will continue to segregate the future tax liability in order to make it clear that these are not liabilities in the same sense as are long-term notes and bonds payable.

Non-Controlling Interest (or Minority Interest). If the reporting enterprise controls a subsidiary, all of the subsidiary's assets and liabilities are added into a consolidated balance sheet for the parent company's reporting purposes, regardless of the actual ~~...~~ary's shares that are owned by the parent. If the parent com- ~~...~~% of the subsidiary's shares, there are outside shareholders ~~...~~e subsidiary's net assets that are included in the parent's bal-

~~...~~consolidated balance sheet balance, it is necessary to include ~~...~~ide of the balance sheet to recognize the proportionate part ~~...~~ets that are *not* owned by the parent. For example, if a com- ~~...~~lling ownership of the voting shares of another company, all ~~...~~ld be consolidated with the parent company and a 20% ~~...~~ reported. This amount is commonly labelled the minority ~~...~~alance sheet), although the *CICA Handbook* uses the more ~~...~~trolling interest (as does the Saskatchewan Wheat Pool,

~~...~~rests are not shown as a liability because the parent company ~~...~~shareholders anything; it is simply a balancing amount and ~~...~~nt. Non-controlling interests are not shown as shareholders' ~~...~~sent outsiders' direct share interest in a subsidiary, and do not ~~...~~e owners of the reporting (i.e., parent) company.

[Handwritten margin note: All the Investee's Assets would be Consolidated to the parent Co's B/S. And the non-Controlling Int is also reported, wouldn't the minority interest be repeated in the B/S?]

Offsetting Assets and Liabilities

Assets and liabilities should not be offset against one another. Offsetting is a procedure by which a liability is subtracted from an asset or vice versa and the resulting net amount is disclosed. Such practice circumvents full disclosure and could permit a business to show a more favourable current ratio than actually exists. Offsetting is permissible only when

- a legal right to offset exists, *and*
- the entity plans to settle the items on a net basis or at least simultaneously.

For instance, it would be permissible to offset a $5,000 overdraft in one bank account against another account reflecting $8,000 on deposit in that same bank, since the bank can legally offset the two deposit accounts. In contrast, it is not acceptable to offset a sinking fund investment account against its related long-term loan, as the company does not have the legal right to offset without creditor acceptance.

CONCEPT REVIEW

1. What is the difference between *tangible* and *intangible* capital assets?
2. In what order are assets normally presented on a Canadian company's balance sheet?
3. What types of credit balances are reported on the balance sheet *between* liabilities and shareholders' equity?

DISCLOSURE NOTES

Disclosure notes are an integral part of the financial statements and must be presented if the statements are to be complete. If the statements are audited, so are the notes. Disclosure notes can adhere to minimal disclosure requirements or be far more extensive; this is a company decision based on their corporate reporting objectives and the needs of user groups. Unlike the purely quantitative financial statements, information in disclosure notes can be provided in qualitative terms. Readers can then make their own assessment of the potential quantitative ramifications of the information presented. Notes sometimes are complex and highly technical.

General Classification of Disclosure Notes

In general, notes can fulfill several functions:[2]

1. *Provide accounting policy information that allows users to evaluate data, including the ability to compare data to other companies and between years.* Section 1505 of the *CICA Handbook*, "Disclosure of Accounting Policies" recommends disclosure of accounting policies used by the firm. Accounting policies include specific accounting principles and the methods of applying these principles. Disclosure should explain important judgements that involve

    *   A selection from existing acceptable alternatives
    *   Principles and methods specific to the industry

    The information may be presented as the first note to the financial statements, or in a separate summary of significant accounting policies. The specific items found in this disclosure note will vary from firm to firm.

    Summaries of significant accounting policies often include descriptions of policies for

    *   Basis of consolidation
    *   Accounting policies for long-term investments
    *   Revenue and expense recognition
    *   Inventory valuation
    *   Property, plant, and equipment (i.e., amortization policy)
    *   Intangible assets (valuation and amortization policies)
    *   Deferred charges
    *   Deferred credits
    *   Income taxes
    *   Foreign exchange

    Changes in policy and significant changes in estimate must also be described in disclosure notes, along with the impact on earnings and net assets, if ascertainable.

2. *Describe recognized items.* Some items that have been recognized in the financial statements should be described, especially those that are unusual in nature and not expected to continue. The notes in this regard contribute to the predictive power of the financial statements. Sometimes, though, even the *nature* of a recognized item is mysterious and must be described. For example, the Royal Bank's "Assets purchased under reverse repurchase agreements" are, the notes tell us, "short-term purchases of securities under agreements to resell." That is, the Bank has purchased, or invested in, a note or other security from a company and the company or a third party has agreed to repurchase, or redeem, the investment at a particular time at a particular price. This is another form of lending.

    Another type of note that describes a recognized item provides *disaggregation.* Some things are added together on the balance sheet to reduce clutter, but more

---

2   This general categorization of notes is adapted from the work of Mary Barth and Christine Murphy, in "Required Financial Statement Disclosures: Purposes, Subject, Number and Trends," *Accounting Horizons* (December 1994), pp. 1–22.

detail has to be provided to comply with accounting standards or to convey important information to users. For example, the Saskatchewan Wheat Pool reports the following breakdown of its aggregated inventory balance sheet amount in the notes:

6. **Inventories**

July 31, in $ thousands	**1998**	**1997**
Grain purchased for sale to the Canadian Wheat Board	$ 24,709	$ 78,847
Non-Board grains	72,964	63,065
Farm supplies	124,750	90,187
Other inventory	104,241	95,191
	$326,664	$327,290

Bombardier, in addition to an inventory breakdown like the one above, provides inventory data for each of its major business sectors.

3. *Describe unrecognized items.* Liabilities such as contingent liabilities that are not probable, or are probable but not measurable, do not qualify for recognition. It is left to the notes to describe the situation, and let the users assess risks for themselves. Other examples of unrecognized items include dividends in arrears, liabilities for environmental cleanups, and so on. For example, Bombardier discloses that

> In connection with the sale of aircraft, the Corporation occasionally provides financial support to its customers in the form of guarantees of financing, lease payments as well as services related to the remarketing of aircraft. The off-balance-sheet risk from these guarantees related to aircraft sold maturing in different periods up to 2014 is [$74.0 million; detail provided but not reproduced in this excerpt]. The net credit risk represents the unrecorded portion of the Corporation's estimated exposure to losses from defaults of third party purchasers to meet their financial obligations under legally binding agreements.

Shaw Communications discloses in its notes that

> The company has various operating lease agreements for building, equipment, furniture, and transportation equipment amounting to $58.3 million.
> The company is not in compliance with the *Environmental Protection Act* (Ontario) and has made no provision for future assessments that may arise as a result.
> • The company has guaranteed a loan of a third party co-packer in the amount of U.S. $9.5 million.
> • The company has sales commitments with various retailers and purchase commitments with various suppliers, at fixed and variable prices with minimum volumes.

4. *Provide information regarding future cash flows.* Financial statements are often used to predict future cash flows; often specific information regarding future cash flows is required by accounting standards or the company deems such disclosure desirable. Companies must disclose principal payments due for the next five years for long-term debt, minimum lease payments for a five-year period, and so on. Bombardier reports, in $ millions:

The repayment requirements on the long-term debt during the next five years are as follows:

1999	$ 87.7
2000	40.2
2001	114.2
2002	132.8
2003	31.3

5. *Provide alternate measurement bases for recognized and unrecognized amounts.* Does the company think that historic cost is irrelevant and market values important? Are they constrained to GAAP for some reason and thus are reporting cost? Not to worry — market value can be disclosed. In fact, companies are required to disclose market values, however defined, for lots of items. For example, Bombardier reports that the fair value of its investment in Eurotunnel share units is $42.1 million in 1998; the carrying value (at cost) of the units is $50.0 million. (Long-term investments have to be written down to market value, if market value is lower than cost, *only* if the impairment in value is deemed to be permanent.)

6. *Provide measures to help investors assess return on investment.* Preferred share dividend rates and effective yields on debt all help investors assess their return on investment.

Specific Disclosure Notes

There are several disclosure requirements that are significant enough to warrant separate discussion, either because they are new or are relatively complex.

Financial Instruments. Financial instruments, including financial assets, financial liabilities, and equity instruments, have special disclosure and presentation requirements. Financial instruments include

- Financial assets: basically cash or contractual rights to receive cash, or equity investments in other firms. Thus, in addition to cash, all types of receivables, loans, and investments in shares are financial assets.
- Financial liabilities: those that establish a contractual obligation to deliver cash, and encompass most liabilities as we know them, except obligations to provide services, like warranty liabilities and unearned revenues. Financial assets and liabilities also include more complicated risk management tools, including swap and option agreements.
- Equity instruments: those that confer a residual interest in net assets of an entity.

The thrust of the financial instruments rules is to classify items in the financial statements according to their substance — for example, a preferred share issue that has a guaranteed payout of principal, including dividends in arrears is *in substance* a liability and should be classified as such. Additionally, there are four disclosure categories that the *CICA Handbook* recommends for specific types of financial instruments:

1. *Terms and conditions.* Complete details regarding the contractual terms for all financial assets, liabilities, and equity instruments should be contained in the disclosure notes. This includes principal amounts, dates of maturity or repricing, interest rates, and any other information that is relevant to predicting future cash flow related to the item. If the financial instrument is complicated, this disclosure can be extensive.

2. *Interest rate.* The effective interest rate should be disclosed for financial assets and liabilities. Thus, if the stated interest rate is different from the market rate, the true return or cost to the company must be clearly disclosed. Also required are maturity or repricing dates.

3. *Credit risk.* Financial assets, both accounts and loans receivable, carry with them credit risk. The maximum credit risk exposure and significant concentrations of credit risk should be disclosed.

4. *Fair value.* The fair value of each class of financial asset and liability should be disclosed, unless fair value is impossible to determine. In these circumstances, data related to fair value should be disclosed in as much detail as possible.

If you compare these disclosures to the general classification of disclosure notes above, you'll find that they are quite similar: information regarding cash flows, alternate valuation, rates of return, and so on. The financial instruments disclosures are interesting in that they extend fair value disclosures to broad classes of balance sheet items. The financial instrument disclosures also apply to items that are currently unrecognized on the financial statements, such as options and swap agreements.

The Royal Bank includes six pages of densely packed notes to comply with the financial instruments disclosures. They include a note on concentration of credit risk, one describing interest rate risk and the terms and conditions of off-balance sheet (i.e., non-recognized) financial instruments, and a note disclosing the fair value of financial instruments. Terms and conditions of recognized financial instruments are incorporated into other notes, as well.

Segmented Information. Consolidated financial information may mask important trends, risks, and opportunities for a diversified company. Therefore, *public companies* are required to disaggregate their reported results by geographical region and by industry.

The AcSB has provided guidelines for reporting segmented information in Section 1701 of the *CICA Handbook*. Every public company must identify its various operating segments — enough segments to explain 75% of its total revenue. Sometimes this is easier said than done. Is an integrated oil company in exploration, refining, and distribution industries, or just in the oil industry? The company must report selected information such as revenues, profits, and assets for each segment. In addition, information about the geographic spread of its operations and customer base must be disclosed.

The company must reconcile the disaggregated data back to the numbers reported on the primary financial statements, to avoid confusion. The segmented information disclosure note can be quite long and complex if the company is involved in a large number of segments.

Can disaggregated information overcome the impression created by publishing primary financial statements that are consolidated? It can be problematic, but users are expected to be diligent in performing financial statement analysis.

Related Party Transactions. When a firm engages in a transaction where one of the parties has the ability to influence the actions and policies of the other, the transaction is termed a **related party transaction**. Such transactions cannot be assumed to be at arm's length because the conditions necessary for a competitive, free-market interaction are not likely to be present. For example, transactions between a firm and its shareholders, management, or members of families of shareholders or management are related party transactions. The following disclosures are recommended for these transactions:

- The nature of the relationship(s) involved.
- A description of the nature and extent of the transaction, including the dollar amounts, and of the measurement basis used.

- Any amounts due to or from related parties as of the balance sheet date, and the terms and manner of settlement planned.

Any contractual arrangements with related parties, as well as any contingencies involving related parties, should be disclosed.

The disclosure of related party transactions is intended to alert financial statement readers to the existence of these relationships, either individual or corporate. The disclosures do not include any measurement of the fair value of transactions (as opposed to the recorded value of the transactions), and therefore there is little opportunity for readers to judge the impact of the non-arm's length transactions on the reporting enterprise's financial statements.

Contingencies. A **contingency** is an event or transaction that will occur only if some other event happens. For example, a civil lawsuit poses a contingent gain for the plaintiff and a contingent loss for the defendant. However, the parties will not know whether they have a gain or a loss until the court reaches a decision. Generally speaking, a contingent loss should be accrued in the financial statements when both of the following conditions are met:

1. It is likely that a future event will confirm that an asset has been impaired or a liability incurred at the date of the financial statements.
2. The amount of the loss can be reasonably estimated.

Few situations meet both conditions and therefore few contingent losses are recognized in the financial statements. If a loss is probable or estimable but not both, or if there is at least a reasonable possibility that a liability may have been incurred, the nature of the contingency must be disclosed in a note along with an estimate of the possible loss or the range of the possible loss if an estimate can be made. Most companies refrain from estimating any expected loss, arguing that no recognition is necessary because

1. The situation does not meet the required reasonable probability level, and
2. It is not possible to estimate the loss.

Companies are particularly reluctant to disclose potential losses arising from litigation because such disclosure might provide the appearance of wrong-doing. The desire not to release information that might be unfavourable to the company coupled with the vagueness of such words as "it is likely that a future event will confirm" allows many contingencies to go unreported. MacMillan Bloedel, for example, briefly describes two lawsuits in a note and then declares that "the outcome of the foregoing proceedings cannot be determined at this time."

Although contingent *gains* are also possible, the accounting profession has adopted a conservative position of nonrecognition, as it has in countless other areas. Contingent gains may be disclosed in notes, and then only if there is a high probability of realization. Many instances of this take-the-loss-but-defer-the-gain approach are found throughout accounting standards.

Subsequent Events. What happens if the company unexpectedly sells a division soon after the end of the fiscal year? It's not an event of the past fiscal year, but shouldn't it be part of the report? Users have probably learned about this significant event through the financial press, or other sources, as news travels fast. But the financial statements must retain their credibility and relevance by reflecting up-to-date information.

Therefore, disclosure is made of significant events that take place after the end of the fiscal year, but before the date that the statements are released. The date of the auditor's report is usually used as a cut-off date. Shaw Communications discloses three subsequent events, including

1. An agreement to sell a number of cable television systems operating in Ontario.

2. An agreement to buy a cable television system in Chilliwack, B.C.

3. The intent to create a new company to hold certain operations of Shaw and of WIC, a newly-acquired interest split with Canwest Global.

Some events that take place *after* the year-end actually reflect economic conditions existing at the year-end; *these events are recognized in the accounts*. For example, if a customer unexpectedly announces bankruptcy after the year-end, the accounts receivable relating to that customer at the year-end would be written down under the reasoning that the customer was actually insolvent at the end of the fiscal year, but this fact did not become known to the company until after the year-end. Such events can be taken into account *in retrospect*, as part of the accounting estimation process that occurs at every financial reporting date.

INTERNATIONAL PERSPECTIVE

In Canada and the U.S., we show the assets first, followed by the liabilities and owners' equity. This is the practice in some other countries, such as Japan, Australia, Sweden, and Switzerland. In most other industrialized counties, however, the order is reversed.

Germany, the U.K., France, Austria, Spain, and the Netherlands all begin the listing of assets with fixed assets; within fixed assets, intangibles are listed first. Liquid short-term assets are at the bottom of the listing. This approach is also the one prescribed by *The Fourth Directive*, the European Union regulation concerning the reporting of individual company financial statements. On the right side, shareholders' equity is the usual starting point, although some countries permit liabilities to be shown first.

The specific items included in the balance sheet also vary from country to country. The predominant practice in the United Kingdom, for example, is not to record goodwill as an asset. Accounting for leased assets and lease obligations also varies greatly across countries. For example, leased assets are not recorded as assets in France or Japan. In Germany, it is legally required that corporations establish "reserves" in their owners' equity based on an allocation of profit.

Finally, the valuation basis used in preparing the balance sheet in many international environments differs from Canadian GAAP. For example, fixed assets such as property, plant, and equipment can be revalued using current prices in Belgium, Finland, and the Netherlands. Mexican companies must report their inventories and fixed assets either at replacement cost or in constant dollars (that is, adjusted for changes in the general price level). Argentina and Brazil also use price level adjustments.

It is very difficult to make comparisons between Canadian balance sheets and those prepared in international settings because the principles underlying their preparation differ greatly between countries. Financial statements, including the notes, must be read with care, and can be adequately interpreted only through knowledge of the reporting framework and economic environment in the company's home country. Balance sheets that look alike on the surface may well hide significant differences beneath the numbers!

THE AUDITOR'S REPORT

When an audit is required (e.g., for public companies), the auditor's report is presented along with the financial statements. The audit report expresses the auditor's professional opinion on the company's financial statement presentation. The auditors do not attest to the "accuracy" of the financial statements; the same audit report would attest to the "fairness" of the financial statements even if the company used a

EXHIBIT 4-6
Petro-Canada's Independent Audit Report

To the shareholders of Petro-Canada: [1]

[2] We have audited the consolidated balance sheet of Petro-Canada as at December 31, 1997 and 1996 and the consolidated statements of earnings, retained earnings and changes in financial position for each of the three years in the period ended December 31, 1997. These financial statements are the responsibility of the Company's management. Our responsibility is to express an opinion on these consolidated financial statements based on our audits.

[3] We conducted our audits in accordance with generally accepted auditing standards. Those standards require that we plan and perform an audit to obtain reasonable assurance whether the financial statements are free of material misstatement. An audit includes examining, on a test basis, evidence supporting the amounts and disclosures in the financial statements. An audit also includes assessing the accounting principles used and significant estimates made by management, as well as evaluating the overall financial statement presentation.

[4] In our opinion, these consolidated financial statements present fairly, in all material respects, the financial position of the corporation as at December 31, 1997 and 1996 and the results of its operations and the changes in its financial position for each of the three years in the period ended December 31, 1997 [5] in accordance with generally accepted accounting principles.

(signed)
Arthur Andersen & Co. [6]
Chartered Accountants
Calgary, Alberta
February 4, 1998 [7]

completely different set of generally acceptable accounting policies that gave significantly different reported results.

The auditors have sole responsibility for all opinions expressed in the auditor's report, while company management has the primary responsibility for the financial statements, including the supporting notes. Compilation and presentation of the accounting information and all supporting text contained in a company's financial statements is company management's concern and responsibility; the auditors, in rendering their opinion, affirm or disaffirm what management has compiled and presented.

Seven required elements in the auditor's report have special significance. They are identified by number in Exhibit 4-6, Petro-Canada's audit report.

1. Salutation. (The auditor is hired, and reports to, shareholders.)
2. Identification of the statements examined.
3. Statement of scope of the examination.
4. Opinion.
5. Reference to fair presentation in conformity with generally accepted accounting principles.
6. Signature of the independent auditor.
7. Date.

When an audit is finished, the auditors are required to draft an opinion paragraph that communicates their professional opinion about the company's financial statements. The auditors can render one of four opinions, although an unqualified opinion is most common.

1. *Unqualified opinion.* An unqualified opinion is given when the auditor concludes that the statements fairly present the results of operations, financial position, and

cash flows in compliance with GAAP and provide reasonable assurance that the financial statements are free of material mis-statement. Petro-Canada's audit report is unqualified.

2. *Qualified opinion.* A qualified opinion is given when the auditor takes limited exception to the client's financial statements in a way that does not invalidate the statements as a whole. A qualified opinion must explain the reasons for the exception and its effect on the financial statements.

3. *Adverse opinion.* An adverse opinion is given when the financial statements do not fairly present the results of operations, financial position, and changes in financial position. An adverse opinion means that the statements, taken as a whole, are not presented in accordance with GAAP. Adverse opinions are rare.

4. *Disclaimer of opinion.* When the auditors have not been able to obtain sufficient evidence, they must state that they are unable to express an opinion (i.e., they issue a disclaimer). The disclaimer must provide the reasons the auditor did not give an opinion.

A major purpose of the auditor's report is to give reasonable assurance to the reader that the financial statements conform to GAAP. However, an audit report does not assure the reader that the numbers in the financial statements are the "right" numbers for the reader's purpose. As the preceding chapters have emphasized (and the following chapters will illustrate), management's selection of "acceptable" accounting practices will strongly colour the resultant financial statements. All that the auditor's report states is that the accounting policies chosen by the company are within the set deemed generally acceptable. Different choices would have given different reported results, and still would have been generally acceptable.

MANAGEMENT'S DISCUSSION AND ANALYSIS

As part of the annual report, companies often include a section entitled Management's Discussion and Analysis (MD&A). This section is required for firms that must comply with the rules of the Ontario, Quebec, and Saskatchewan Securities Commissions. The MD&A provides information about the firm's earnings and financial position for the reporting period, the effects of laws and other environmental aspects, and the effects of economic and business trends on the firm. It is expected to place particular emphasis on the future, but projections are not required, nor do companies provide this level of detail.

The MD&A of the 1997 annual report of Petro-Canada is 22 pages long, and includes a detailed review of the company's operating performance, financial position, Year 2000 systems preparations, management's outlook, 1998 capital budget, environmental factors, and risk management strategies.

MD&A commentaries frequently make general comments about the outlook for the next fiscal year, but specifics usually are harder to find. Most companies are reluctant to discuss future events because positive expectations may not be fulfilled and negative projections are viewed with concern by the investing community. Securities commissions have signalled their concerns that disclosures about future events have been inadequate. In fact, the Ontario Securities Commission is currently studying the area of "Future-Oriented Financial Information" — projections and forecasts — so companies who prefer minimal disclosure may be in for a rude shock in the not-too-distant future.

CONCEPT
REVIEW

1. In general, what functions are served by disclosure notes?
2. Why might financial statement users want to see segmented information? What companies are required to disclose segmented information?

3. Explain what a *related party transaction* is.
4. What two conditions must be fulfilled in order for a contingent liability to be recognized on the balance sheet instead of just being disclosed in a note?
5. What is the purpose of *management's discussion and analysis* (MD&A)? Which companies are required to present an MD&A?

SUMMARY OF KEY POINTS

1. The balance sheet provides information about an entity's assets, liabilities, and equities. The balance sheet, taken together with other financial statements, allows financial statement users to assess financial position, risk profile, financial flexibility, liquidity, and rates of return.

2. The balance sheet reports cost, not fair value, which may reduce its relevance for certain decisions. It also contains many estimates, excludes assets and liabilities that the GAAP model deems unrecognizable, and consolidates financial data from possibly very different industry segments. Financial statement users must proceed with caution.

3. Classification of balance sheet items is governed by accounting standards and industry norms and characteristics, but has room for judgement. Most, but not all, balance sheets classify current assets and current liabilities, to facilitate evaluation of short-term liquidity. Other classifications follow the major asset, liability, and equity groups. Elements are often very summarized on the balance sheet.

4. Disclosure notes provide information regarding accounting principles, describe recognized and unrecognized items, and provide information regarding future cash flows, alternate valuation information, and rates of return.

5. A company should make appropriate disclosures of terms and conditions, interest rates, credit risk, and fair values of its financial instruments.

6. Other important disclosures include segmented information, related party transaction data, subsequent events, and contingencies.

7. The various balance sheet categories have specific display and disclosure requirements in order to meet accounting standards and user's expectations.

REVIEW PROBLEM

The post-closing balance sheet accounts of Ibsen Icons Inc. at 31 December 20X3 are as follows:

Account	Debit	Credit
Cash (overdraft)		$ 3,500
Accounts payable		15,000
Future (deferred) income taxes — long-term		30,000
Common shares		40,000
Preferred shares		24,000
Long-term investment in common shares of Grieg Graphics Inc.	$ 14,000	
Accounts receivable	19,000	
Loan from shareholder, due 1 July 20X9		40,000
Leasehold improvements (net of amortization)	30,000	
Land	120,000	
Furniture and equipment (at cost)	90,000	
Accumulated depreciation, furniture and equipment		30,000
Retained earnings		74,000
Customer deposits received in advance	4,500	

Deferred revenue		6,500
Instalment notes receivable	7,000	
Goodwill	9,000	
Appropriation for restructuring costs		20,000
Prepaid expenses	3,500	
Marketable securities	3,000	
Note payable to bank, due 15 October 20X4		25,000
Allowance for doubtful accounts		2,000
Supplies inventory	14,500	

Required:

Prepare a classified balance sheet in good form, using the financing form and the report format.

REVIEW PROBLEM — SOLUTION

IBSEN ICONS INC.
Balance Sheet
as of 31 December 20X3

ASSETS
Current assets:

Marketable securities		$ 3,000	
Instalment notes receivable		7,000	
Accounts receivable	$19,000		
Less: allowance for doubtful accounts	2,000	17,000	
Supplies inventory		14,500	
Prepaid expenses		3,500	$ 45,000

Capital assets:

Land		120,000	
Furniture and equipment	90,000		
Less: accumulated depreciation	30,000	60,000	
Leasehold improvements		30,000	
Goodwill		9,000	219,000

Investments:

Investment in Grieg Graphics Inc.		14,000
Total assets		$278,000

LIABILITIES AND SHAREHOLDERS' EQUITY
Liabilities:

Current liabilities:

Bank overdraft	$ 3,500	
Note payable to bank, due 15 October 20X4	25,000	
Accounts payable	15,000	
Deferred revenue	6,500	$ 50,000

Long-term liabilities:

Loan from shareholder, due 1 July 20X9	40,000	
Future income tax liability	30,000	70,000
Total liabilities		120,000

Shareholders' equity:		
Contributed capital:		
Common shares	40,000	
Preferred shares	24,000	64,000
Retained earnings:		
Appropriated for restructuring costs	20,000	
Unappropriated	74,000	94,000
Total shareholders' equity		158,000
Total liabilities and shareholders' equity		$278,000

Capital assets could be separated into tangible and intangible categories. Deferred revenue and instalment notes receivable are assumed to be within normal business practice for this company and therefore are classified as current.

QUESTIONS

4-1 What is the primary purpose of a balance sheet?

4-2 Basically, what valuations are reported on the balance sheet?

4-3 Describe the limitations of the balance sheet.

4-4 What is the difference between the net assets and financing form of the balance sheet? The report and account form? What form is the most common in practice?

4-5 Describe the usual order of balance sheet accounts.

4-6 Define current assets, current liabilities, and working capital. Do these subtotals have to be disclosed on the balance sheet?

4-7 List the areas of choice in balance sheet presentation.

4-8 What items are included in the balance sheet category, cash?

4-9 When is an asset non-current?

4-10 What does the "investments and funds" caption cover in a balance sheet?

4-11 What are capital assets? Distinguish between tangible and intangible capital assets.

4-12 Comment on the difficulties associated with evaluating the balance sheet of an entity whose primary assets are intangible.

4-13 Why is the caption "other assets" sometimes necessary? Name two items that might be reported under this classification.

4-14 Explain the term "deferred charge."

4-15 Distinguish between current and non-current liabilities. Under what conditions would a non-current liability amount be reclassified as a current liability?

4-16 What disclosure should accompany a long-term liability? Why is this disclosure important?

4-17 What is the nature of "future (deferred) income tax" such that this item is classified as a liability? Why is the account classification subject to question?

4-18 Explain the term "non-controlling (minority) interest."

4-19 Is it proper to offset current liabilities against current assets? Explain.

4-20 What is owners' equity? What are the main components of owners' equity?

4-21 When is debt reclassified as owners' equity?

4-22 List the primary types of disclosure notes. Give two examples of each type.

4-23 Define financial instruments and identify the four areas of disclosure that are described for financial instruments.

4-24   When is a contingency recognized versus disclosed?

4-25   When is a subsequent event recognized versus disclosed?

4-26   What is the purpose of segmented information?

4-27   Identify some of the differences between balance sheets around the world.

4-28   What is the auditors' report? What are its basic components? Why is it especially important to the statement user?

CASES

CASE 4-1

Autopart Manufacturing Ltd.

Autopart Manufacturing Ltd., incorporated 15 years ago, has grown to be a successful competitor in the cost and quality-conscious autopart manufacturing market. Autopart specializes in relatively standard replacement parts sold under store, or house, brand labels in hardware stores. Since people are now owning cars longer than ever before, now an average of 8.5 years, the auto repair business is a growth sector of the economy.

You've obtained the balance sheet of Autopart Manufacturing Ltd., and have analyzed the basic financial structure of the company. You're thinking of investing in Autopart's common shares, but looking at the balance sheet has reminded you of the definitions of financial statement elements. You've decided to see how well the balance sheet items conform to the definitions. In particular, it's important to explain to yourself exactly why each item is an asset, liability, or equity item. The balance sheet is shown in Exhibit 1, and the notes to the financial statements in Exhibit 2.

Good luck!

EXHIBIT 1
AUTOPART MANUFACTURING LTD.
Consolidated Balance Sheet
31 December 20X1 and 20X0
($ thousands)

	20X1	20X0
Assets		
Current assets		
Cash and short-term investments	$ 9,800	$ 4,390
Accounts receivable	12,464	12,570
Inventories (Note 1)	15,730	14,400
Capital assets		
Property, plant, and equipment (net) (Note 2)	21,529	19,200
Goodwill (Note 3)	5,100	4,750
Licences (Note 4)	1,640	1,490
Other assets		
Deferred contract costs (Note 5)	1,950	2,300
	$68,213	$59,100
Liabilities and shareholders' equity		
Current liabilities:		
Accounts payable and accrued liabilities	$11,384	$15,875
Current portion of long-term debt	450	475
Other	615	655
Long-term liabilities (Note 6)	27,190	10,580
Commitments payable (Note 7)	—	1,900
Prepaid contract (Note 8)	1,650	2,900
Future (deferred) income taxes (Note 9)	950	890
Shareholders' equity (Note 10)	25,974	25,825
	$68,213	$59,100

EXHIBIT 2
Notes to the Financial Statements
as of 31 December
($ thousands)

Note 1. Inventories

	20X1	20X0
Raw materials	$6,700	$6,300
Finished goods	7,700	7,200
Supplies	400	380
Returnable containers	930	520
	$15,730	$14,400

Note 2. Property, Plant, and Equipment (Net)

	Cost	Accumulated Amortization	Net Balance, 31 Dec. 20X1
Land	$ 990	$ —	$ 990
Buildings	5,910	696	5,214
Machinery and equipment			
Owned	11,480	2,600	8,880
Leased	3,720	200	3,520
Furniture and fixtures	2,600	310	2,290
Transportation equipment	1,120	485	635
	$25,820	$4,291	$21,529

Note 3. Goodwill

During the year ended 31 December 20X1, the company acquired 100% of the shares of Benn Mufflers Ltd. for $1,240 in cash. Benn Mufflers Ltd. had tangible assets, at fair value, of $720 on the acquisition date, and goodwill of $520 arose. The amortization period is 40 years. The opening balance in the goodwill account is from a series of similar acquisitions over the past 12 years.

Note 4. Licences

The company manufactures certain autoparts under licence. Licences are acquired for cash at the beginning of the licence period, usually five years.

Note 5. Deferred Contract Costs

The company enters into three-year contracts with retailers, guaranteeing the company a market and specific shelf space for its goods. Payments are made to the retailers to secure these multi-year contracts. The payments are amortized against sales over the term of the related contracts.

Note 6. Long-Term Liabilities

	20X1
Term bank loans, 8%, maturing in 20X9	$17,830
Mortgages, 7 – 10%, maturing 20X3 – 20X6	6,910
Capital leases, 8.5% – 14.3%, maturing 20X3 – 20X9	2,900
	$27,640
Less: current portion	450
	$27,190

Note 7. Commitments Payable

In 20X0, the company set up a provision of $1,900 for potential losses relating to a guarantee provided for Carburettor King Ltd., an associated company. Autoparts had guaranteed a bank loan of Carburettor King, and it appeared in 20X0 that financial difficulties within that company would trigger a payment by Autoparts under the guarantee. In 20X1, Carburettor King was sold and reorganized, and Autoparts was released from their guarantee after a payment of $400,000.

Note 8. Prepaid Contract

Certain customers, in long-term contracts with the company, prepay a portion of the estimated total contract value. This prepayment is taken into income over the life of the contract, in proportion to deliveries.

Note 9. Future (Deferred) Income Taxes

Certain expenses, primarily depreciation, are reported in different periods for income tax and financial statement reporting purposes. The result is a future tax liability.

Note 10. Shareholders' Equity

	20X1
Common shares, unlimited shares authorized, 26,837 shares issued	$14,499
Contributed capital from share retirement	49
Retained earnings	11,426
	$25,974

CASE 4-2

Smith & Stewart

Smith & Stewart (Stewart) is a partnership of lawyers. It was recently formed from a merger of two predecessor partnerships: Becker and Brackman (Becker), and Copp and Copp (Copp). The merged firm has 38 partners, six from Becker and 32 from Copp, and a total of 75 employees. At the date of the merger, Stewart purchased land and an office building for $1.25 million, and fully computerized their new offices. The partners have decided that the financial statements will be audited annually, although neither of the predecessor firms was audited.

The partnership agreement requires an annual valuation of the assets and liabilities of the firm. This valuation is to be used to determine the payment to be made by the partnership to a withdrawing partner and the contribution to be made to the partnership by a newly admitted partner. The partners are unsure of the accounting implications of this requirement.

The partners have been actively engaged in establishing and managing the practice and have paid little attention to accounting policies.

Before the merger, Becker recorded revenue when it invoiced the client. Time reports were used to keep track of the number of hours worked for each client, although this information was not recorded in the accounting system. In general, accounting records were not well maintained.

In contrast, work in progress was recorded for employees of Copp at their regular billing rate, on a client-by-client basis, based on the hours worked, even though the full amount was not always recoverable. At year-end, an adjustment was made to reduce work in progress to the actual salary costs incurred by Copp

The new partnership agreement requires a valuation of the work in progress at (recoverable) billing rates for all employees and partners at the merger date, with this amount to be recorded as goodwill. This amount has not yet been determined.

Stewart has arranged a line of credit with a bank that allows the partnership to borrow up to 75% of the carrying value of receivables and 40% of the carrying value of work in progress as recorded in the monthly financial statements. The bank has also provided mortgage financing of $750,000 on the recently acquired land and building. As well as annual audited financial statements, the bank requires unaudited financial statements monthly.

As of the date of the merger, fixed assets owned by the predecessor firms were transferred to the new partnership.

Each partner receives a monthly "draw" payment, which represents an advance on the partner's share of annual profit.

Your firm has been engaged by Stewart to prepare a report advising the partnership on financial accounting issues. In addition, it has appointed your firm as auditors. The manager in charge of the Stewart engagement has asked you, CA, to prepare a draft report to the client addressing choice of accounting policy.

Required:

Prepare the draft report. [CICA, adapted]

E4-1 *Classification on the Balance Sheet:* A typical balance sheet has the following classifications:

A. Current assets
B. Investments and funds
C. Capital assets (property, plant, and equipment)
D. Intangible assets
E. Other assets
F. Deferred charges

G. Current liabilities
H. Long-term liabilities
I. Share capital (common or preferred)
J. Additional contributed capital
K. Debt elements that have the characteristics of equity
L. Retained earnings

Required:

Use the code letters above to indicate the usual classification for each balance sheet item listed below. If an item is a contra amount (i.e., a deduction) under a caption, place a minus sign before the lettered response. The first item is completed for you as an example.

- C _____ 1. Accumulated depreciation
_____ 2. Bonds payable (due in 10 years)
_____ 3. Accounts payable (trade)
_____ 4. Investment in shares of X Company (long-term)
_____ 5. Plant site (in use)
_____ 6. Restriction or appropriation of retained earnings
_____ 7. Office supplies inventory
_____ 8. Loan to company president (collection not expected for two years)
_____ 9. Accumulated income less accumulated dividends
_____ 10. Unamortized bond discount (on bonds payable; a debit balance)
_____ 11. Bond sinking fund (to retire long-term bonds)
_____ 12. Prepaid insurance
_____ 13. Accounts receivable (trade)

_____ 14. Short-term investment

_____ 15. Allowance for doubtful accounts

_____ 16. Building (in use)

_____ 17. Bonds payable (all interest and principal payments are to be satisfied by issuing common shares)

_____ 18. Interest revenue earned but not collected

_____ 19. Patent

_____ 20. Land, held for investment

_____ 21. Land, idle

E4-2 *Determining Values in the Balance Sheet:* The consolidated balance sheet of Mutron Lock, Inc., is shown below.

MUTRON LOCK, INC.
Consolidated Balance Sheet
as of 31 December 20X5

Assets

Current assets:		
Cash and cash equivalents		$ 10,195
Marketable securities		a
Accounts receivable	$153,682	
Allowance for doubtful accounts	b	147,421
Inventories		201,753
Prepaid expenses		8,902
Total current assets		c
Capital assets:		
Land		12,482
Building (net)		d
Equipment and machinery	195,467	
Accumulated depreciation	(103,675)	91,792
Total capital assets		261,056
Investments		14,873
Other assets		7,926
Total assets		$661,774

Liabilities and Shareholders' Equity

Current liabilities:		
Accounts payable		$ 85,476
Notes payable		e
Income taxes payable		6,421
Current portion of long-term debt		4,893
Accrued expenses		5,654
Total current liabilities		$110,763
Long-term debt		122,004
Future (deferred) income taxes		f
Non-controlling interest		35,136
Total liabilities		g

Shareholders' equity:
Preferred shares, no-par value (authorized
   10,000 shares, issued 2,400 shares for $14,281)   h
Common shares, no-par value (authorized 400,000
   shares, issued 20,000 shares)   i

Total contributed capital	j
Retained earnings	206,471
Total shareholders' equity	$347,668
Total liabilities and shareholders' equity	$ k

Required:

1. For each of the items (a) through (k) in the balance sheet above, calculate the amount that should appear for that item.
2. What kinds of notes would be commonly found for each balance sheet item from the following list?
   i.   Financial instruments disclosure of terms and conditions.
   ii.   Financial instruments disclosure of interest rates, including effective rates.
   iii.   Financial instruments disclosure of credit risk.
   iv.   Financial instruments disclosure of fair value, by class.
   v.   Breakdown of accounts aggregated to arrive at a balance sheet total.
   vi.   Disclosure of accounting policy.
   vii.   Details of changes during the period.

E4-3 *Valuation on the Balance Sheet:* The first list below shows the measurement or valuation approaches commonly used for reporting individual items on the balance sheet. The second list indicates some items from a typical balance sheet of a corporation.

Measurement (valuation) methods:

   A. Amount payable or receivable when due (usually no interest is involved because of the short term)
   B. Lower of cost or market
   C. Original cost when acquired
   D. Market value, or realizable value, at date of the balance sheet
   E. Original cost less accumulated amortization
   F. Amount received on sale or issuance
   G. Face amount of the obligation adjusted for unamortized premium or discount
   H. Accumulated income less accumulated losses and dividends
   I. None of the above (when this response is used, explain the valuation approach usually used)

Valuation   *Balance Sheet Items*

  _B_   1. Land (held as investment)
  _____   2. Merchandise inventory, FIFO
  _____   3. Short-term investments
  _____   4. Accounts receivable (trade)
  _____   5. Long-term investment in bonds of another company held to maturity (purchased at a discount; the discount is a credit balance)

_____ 6. Land used as a plant site (in use)

_____ 7. Plant and equipment (in use)

_____ 8. Patent (in use)

_____ 9. Accounts payable (trade)

_____ 10. Bonds payable (sold at a premium; the premium is a credit balance)

_____ 11. Common shares, no-par

_____ 12. Prepaid expenses

_____ 13. Retained earnings

_____ 14. Land (future plant site; not in use)

_____ 15. Idle plant (awaiting disposal)

_____ 16. Natural resource (in use)

Required:

Use the code letters given in the first list to indicate the usual measurement method (or valuation method) commonly used in the balance sheet for each item in the second list. Comment on any doubtful items. Some code letters may be used more than once or not at all. The first item is completed for you as an example.

E4-4 *Prepare a Classified Balance Sheet; Compare Aggregation Levels:* The ledger of the Alberta Manufacturing Company reflects the following balances, after the books were closed on 31 December 20X5. One adjustment has yet to be made (see below).

Accounts payable	$33,200
Accounts receivable	9,500
Accrued expenses (credit)	800
Bonds payable, 14%	25,000
Share capital, 700 shares	70,000
Cash	10,000
Retained earnings (to be determined)	?
Factory equipment	31,200
Finished goods	13,100
Investments	13,000
Office equipment	9,500
Raw materials	9,600
Reserve for bad debts	500
Reserve for depreciation	9,000
Rent expense paid in advance	3,000
Sinking fund	7,000
Land held for future plant site	14,000
Note receivable	6,600
Work in process	23,300

Other information:

Two-thirds of the depreciation relates to factory equipment and one-third to office equipment. Of the balance in the investments account, $4,000 will be converted to cash in the immediate future; the remainder represents a long-term investment. Rent paid in advance is for the next year. The note receivable is a loan to the company president on 1 October 20X5, and is due in 20X7, when the principal amount ($6,600) plus 9% interest per annum will be paid to the company. No interest has been accrued on the loan in the above trial balance. The sinking fund is being accumulated to retire the bonds at maturity.

Required:

1. Prepare a balance sheet using typical format (financing report format), classifications, and proper terminology. Include all accounts directly on the balance sheet; do not aggregate.

2. Prepare a balance sheet that uses highly aggregated disclosures.

3. Comment on the differences between the two balance sheets. Why might a user prefer one over the other?

E4-5 *Prepare a Balance Sheet:* The following trial balance was prepared by Vantage Electronics Corporation as of 31 December 20X5. The adjusting entries for 20X5 have been made, except for any specifically noted.

Vantage Electronics trial balance, 31 December 20X5:

Cash	$15,000	
Accounts receivable	15,000	
Inventories	17,000	
Equipment	22,400	
Land	6,400	
Building	7,600	
Deferred charges	1,100	
Accounts payable		$ 5,500
Note payable, 10%		8,000
Share capital, no-par, 2,500 shares outstanding		38,500
Retained earnings		32,500
Totals	$84,500	$84,500

Other information: You find that certain errors and omissions are reflected in the above trial balance:

a. The $15,000 balance in accounts receivable represents the entire amount owed to the company; of this amount, $12,400 is from trade customers and 5% of that amount is estimated to be uncollectible. The remaining amount owed to the company represents a long-term advance to its president.

b. Inventories include $1,000 of goods incorrectly valued at double their cost (i.e., reported at $2,000). No correction has been recorded. Office supplies on hand of $500 are also included in the balance of inventories.

c. When the equipment and building were purchased new on 1 January 20X0 (i.e., six years earlier), they had estimated lives of 10 and 25 years, respectively. They have been depreciated using the straight-line method on the assumption of zero residual value, and depreciation has been credited directly to the asset accounts. Depreciation has been recorded for 20X5.

d. The balance in the land account includes a $1,000 payment made as a deposit on the purchase of an adjoining tract. The option to buy it has not yet been exercised and probably will not be exercised during the coming year.

e. The interest-bearing note dated 1 April 20X5, matures 31 March 20X6. Interest on it has not been recorded for 20X5.

Required:

1. Prepare a balance sheet with appropriate captions and subcaptions. Use preferred terminology and the financing report form format. Show the computation of the ending balance in retained earnings.

2. How would your balance sheet be different if the net assets form were used? The account form? Explain, do not illustrate.

E4-6 *Analyzing Data and Reporting on the Balance Sheet:* Akeman Seed Corporation is preparing its balance sheet at 31 December 20X5. The following items are under consideration:

a. Note payable, long-term, $80,000. This note will be paid in instalments. The first instalment, $10,000, will be paid 1 August 20X6.

b. Bonds payable, 12%, $200,000; at 31 December 20X5, unamortized premium amounted to $6,000.

c. Bond sinking fund, $40,000; this fund is being accumulated to retire the bonds at maturity.

d. Rent revenue collected in advance for the first quarter of 20X6, $6,000.

e. After the balance sheet date, but prior to issuance of the 20X5 balance sheet, one-third of the merchandise inventory was destroyed by flood (13 January 20X6); estimated loss, $150,000.

f. Bonds payable, $475,000. At maturity, the company may choose to repay the bond by issuing its common shares to the bond holders. The company plans to exercise this option. Annual interest can also be "paid" in common shares.

g. Redeemable preferred shares, $250,000. At maturity, the company has to repay investors the stated value of the shares plus dividends in arrears, if any.

Required:

Show by illustration, with appropriate captions, how each of these items should be reported on the 31 December 20X5 balance sheet. If amounts are not quantifiable, describe the appropriate reporting that would be followed when numbers are available.

E4-7 *Note Disclosures:* Note disclosures provide the following information:

1. Provide accounting policy information (information to evaluate data and make comparisons).
2. Describe recognized items.
3. Describe unrecognized items.
4. Provide information regarding future cash flows.
5. Provide alternative measurement information.
6. Help assess return on investment.

Typical notes include:

a. Description of income statement item, discontinued operations.
b. Revenue recognition policy.
c. Breakdown of balance sheet total, other assets.
d. Description of contingent loss that is not measurable.
e. Depreciation policy and amounts of accumulated depreciation by asset class.
f. Inventory note — breakdown of inventory into component parts and description of valuation method.
g. Preferred share dividend rate.
h. Description of subsequent event not relating to conditions before balance sheet date.
i. Information on key operating segments of the business.
j. Description of related party transactions.
k. Long-term debt note — interest rates, terms to maturity, five-year cash flow, market value.

l. Details of outstanding stock options (not recorded in the financial statements).
m. Fair value of long-term investments.
n. Consolidation policy.

Required:

For each note (a) to (n) above, indicate the type(s) of disclosure (numbers (1) to (6)) provided. A note may provide more than one type of disclosure.

E4-8 *Contingencies, Subsequent Events:* Zero Growth Ltd. has completed financial statements for the year ended 31 December 20X6. The financial statements have yet to be finalized or issued. The following events and transactions have occured:

1. The office building housing administrative staff burned to the ground on 15 January 20X7.
2. On 15 November 20X6, a customer sued the company for $1,000,000 based on a claim of negligence leading to personal injury; Zero Growth is actively defending the suit and claims it is unfounded. Nothing has yet been recorded in the 20X6 financial statements in relation to this event.
3. On 1 February 20X7, Zero Growth received a $49,700 income tax reassessment for 20X5.
4. On 20 December 20X6, Zero Growth applied for a bank loan to replace an existing line of credit. The loan was granted on 2 January 20X7. Nothing was recorded in the 20X6 financial statements in relation to this event.
5. Zero Growth has reinterpreted a legal agreement entitling it to commission revenue for the sale of a client's products. Zero Growth's interpretation would entitle it to an extra $60,000 over and above amounts recognized in 20X6. The client was billed for this amount in 20X6 but has disagreed with Zero Growth on the contract interpretation. Both parties have consulted their lawyers; resolution of the issue is not expected soon.
6. On 1 March 20X7, Zero Growth issued common shares for cash.

Required:

Discuss the appropriate accounting treatment for the contingencies and subsequent events described.

E4-9 *Financial Instruments:* Financial instruments may require disclosure of

1. Terms and conditions
2. Interest rates
3. Credit risk
4. Fair value

Consider the following balance sheet elements:

a. Accounts receivable
b. Inventory
c. Unearned revenue
d. Bank loan payable
e. Preferred shares
f. Machinery and equipment

g. Loans receivable

h. Bonds payable

i. Long-term investment in the common shares of another company. The investment represents a small fraction of the outstanding shares in the other company.

Required:

1. Which of the above items are financial instruments? Specify whether the item is a financial asset, financial liability, or equity instrument.

2. For the items designated as financial instruments in requirement (1), specify which of the listed disclosures, above, are required.

P4-1 *Classification on the Balance Sheet:* Typical balance sheet classifications along with a code letter for each classification are as follows:

A. Current assets
B. Investments and funds
C. Capital assets, tangible (property plant and equipment)
D. Intangible assets
E. Other assets
F. Deferred charges

G. Current liabilities
H. Long-term liabilities
I. Debt elements that are equity
J. Contributed capital, share capital and other
K. Retained earnings

Typical balance sheet items are as follows:

_____ 1. Cash

_____ 2. Cash set aside to meet long-term purchase commitment

_____ 3. Land (used as plant site)

_____ 4. Accrued salaries

_____ 5. Investment in the common shares of another company (long term; not a controlling interest)

_____ 6. Inventory of damaged goods

_____ 7. Idle plant

_____ 8. Assets of discontinued operations held for resale

_____ 9. Preferred shares that have guaranteed redemption

_____ 10. Goodwill

_____ 11. Natural resource (e.g., a timber tract)

_____ 12. Allowance for doubtful accounts

_____ 13. Investment in bonds of another company

_____ 14. Organization costs

_____ 15. Discount on bonds payable

_____ 16. Service revenue collected in advance

_____ 17. Accrued interest payable

_____ 18. Accumulated amortization on patent

_____ 19. Prepaid rent

_____ 20. Short-term investment (common shares)

_____ 21. Rent revenue collected but not earned

_____ 22. Net amount of accumulated revenues, gains, expenses, losses, and dividends

_____ 23. Trade accounts payable

_____ 24. Current maturity of long-term debt

_____ 25. Long-term debt that is convertible to common shares

_____ 26. Bond issue costs

_____ 27. Special cash fund accumulated to build plant five years hence

_____ 28. Bonds issued — to be repaid within six months out of bond sinking fund

_____ 29. Long-term investment in rental building

_____ 30. Copyright

_____ 31. Accumulated depreciation

_____ 32. Deferred plant rearrangement costs

_____ 33. Franchise

_____ 34. Revenue earned but not collected

_____ 35. Premium on bonds payable (unamortized)

_____ 36. Common shares (no-par)

_____ 37. Petty cash fund

_____ 38. Deficit

_____ 39. Contributed capital on share retirement

_____ 40. Earnings retained in the business

Required:

Enter the appropriate code letter for each item to indicate its usual classification on the balance sheet. When it is a contra item (i.e., a deduction), place a minus sign before the lettered response.

[AICPA, adapted]

P4-2 *Balance Sheet Items — Classification:* The items listed below are taken from the actual balance sheets of the identified companies.

_____ 1. Prepaid income taxes (Sun Microsystems)

_____ 2. Intangibles (D. A. Stuart Ltd.)

_____ 3. Unearned revenue (Dow Jones & Company, Inc.)

_____ 4. Cash and cash equivalents (Noranda, Inc.)

_____ 5. Minority interest in consolidated subsidiary (Alberto-Culver Company)

_____ 6. Equipment under capital leases (Gesco Industries Ltd.)

_____ 7. Deferred subscription costs (New York Times)

_____ 8. Investments in joint ventures (Internetco Ltd.)

_____ 9. Investments in and advances to affiliated companies (W. R. Grace & Co.)

_____ 10. Contributed surplus (Loblaw Ltd.)

_____ 11. Cash surrender value of life insurance policies (Affiliated Publications, Inc.)

_____ 12. Excess of cost over fair value of assets acquired from investees (Seagram Ltd.)

_____ 13. Arena development costs (Northwest Sports Enterprises Ltd., owner of the Vancouver Canucks)

_____ 14. Development costs (M-Corp. Ltd.)

_____ 15. Perpetual 4% consolidated debentures. These bonds have no due date, and thus are permanent but pay interest annually (Canadian Pacific Ltd.)

Required:

Indicate the likely balance sheet classification for the elements listed above, using the following classifications:

A. Current asset
B. Non-current asset (various categories)
C. Current liability
D. Long-term liability and other long-term credits
E. Owners' equity

P4-3 *Setting Up the Balance Sheet:* Below is a typical chart of accounts (in alphabetical order) for Altar Paving Corporation for 20X5.

Accounts payable
Accounts receivable
Accrued expenses
Accumulated amortization, all intangible assets
Accumulated depreciation, all tangible assets
Allowance for decline in value of marketable securities
Allowance for doubtful accounts
Amortization expense
Bad debt expense
Bonds payable
Bond sinking fund
Buildings
Cash
Cash surrender value of life insurance policies
Common shares
Contributed capital from share retirement
Cost of goods sold
Depreciation expense
Discount on bonds payable
Dividends payable
Equipment
Finished goods
Future (deferred) income tax liability
Gain on sale of marketable securities
General and administrative expense
Goodwill
Income tax expense
Income tax payable
Interest payable
Investment in common shares, not intended for resale
Land
Licences
Loss on sale of land
Marketable securities
Miscellaneous expense
Overhead
Patents
Prepaid expense
Purchases
Raw materials
Restricted cash for long-term debt retirement
Retained earnings
Sales revenue

Travel and entertainment expense
Wages expense
Wages payable
Work in process

Required:

Prepare a blank, classified balance sheet in proper form using the financing format. Include all balance sheet accounts — do not summarize.

P4-4 *Prepare Balance Sheet, Analytical Questions:* The following data is from the accounts of Fuere Spice Corporation on 31 December 20X5, the end of the current reporting year.

Cash	$ 16,000
Accounts receivable, trade	37,000
Short-term investment in marketable securities (cost $42,000)	40,000
Inventory of merchandise, FIFO	95,000
Prepaid expense (short-term)	1,000
Bond sinking fund (to pay bonds at maturity)	35,000
Advances to suppliers (short-term)	4,000
Dividends (cash) declared during 20X5	10,000
Rent receivable	2,000
Investment in shares of Life Systems Corporation (long-term, at cost, which approximates market)	22,000
Unamortized discount on bonds payable	2,000
Loans to employees (company president; payment date uncertain)	25,000
Land (building site in use)	30,000
Building	450,000
Equipment	60,000
Franchise (used in operations) (net)	12,000
Deferred equipment rearrangement cost (long-term)	4,000
Total debits	$845,000
Mortgage payable (14%)	$ 50,000
Accounts payable, trade	6,000
Dividends (cash) payable (payable 1 March 20X6)	10,000
Deferred rent revenue	3,000
Future (deferred) income taxes	4,000
Accumulated depreciation, building	210,000
Accumulated depreciation, equipment	20,000
Allowance for doubtful accounts	2,000
Bonds payable (12.5%, maturity 20X13)	100,000
Common shares, no-par (50,000 shares outstanding)	200,000
Preferred shares, no-par (8,000 shares outstanding)	96,000
Retained earnings, 1 January 20X5	56,000
Net income for 20X5	88,000
Total credits	$845,000

Required:

1. Prepare a complete balance sheet. Assume that all amounts are correct, and round to the nearest thousand dollars. Use the account titles as given.

2. Prepare a second balance sheet based on the above information that summarizes accounts. Group smaller items of the same nature.

3. Refer to your response to requirement (1) and respond to the following:
   a. Give the amount of working capital.
   b. By what percent was the building depreciated?
   c. How much of the company is financed by debt, and how much by equity?
   d. What are the important assets of the company?

4. From the perspective of a lender, which balance sheet (from requirement (1) or (2)) would you prefer? Explain your position.

P4-5 *Income Statement and the Balance Sheet; Format, Disclosures:* The adjusted trial balance and other related data for Amana Cement Corporation, at 31 December 20X5, are given below. Although the company uses some obsolete terminology, the amounts are correct.

AMANA CEMENT CORPORATION
Adjusted Trial Balance
31 December 20X5

Debit Balance Accounts

Cash	$ 38,600
Land (used for building site)	29,000
Cost of goods sold	125,500
Short-term securities (shares of Sanders Co.)	42,000
Goodwill (net)	12,000
Merchandise inventory	29,000
Office supplies inventory	2,000
Patent	7,000
Operating expenses	55,000
Income tax expense	17,500
Bond discount (unamortized)	7,500
Prepaid insurance	900
Building (at cost)	150,000
Land (held for speculation)	31,000
Accrued interest receivable	300
Accounts receivable (trade)	22,700
Note receivable, 10% (long-term investment)	20,000
Subscriber lists (net)	9,000
Deferred plant rearrangement costs	6,000
Dividends, paid during 20X5	15,000
Correction of error from prior year — no income tax effect	15,000
	$635,000

Credit Balance Accounts

Reserve for bad debts	$ 1,100
Accounts payable (trade)	15,000
Revenues	245,000
Future (deferred) income tax	7,500
Note payable (short-term)	12,000
Common shares, no-par, authorized 50,000 shares,	
10,000 shares outstanding	115,000
Reserve for depreciation, building	90,000

Retained earnings, 1 January 20X5	37,000
Accrued wages	2,100
Non-controlling interest (balance sheet account)	10,000
Reserve for patent amortization	4,000
Cash advance from customer	3,000
Accrued property taxes	800
Note payable (long-term)	16,000
Rent revenue collected in advance	1,500
Bonds payable, 11% ($25,000 due 1 June 20X6)	75,000
	$635,000

Additional information (no accounting errors are involved):

a. Market value of the short-term marketable securities is $44,000.

b. Merchandise inventory is based on FIFO, lower of cost or market.

c. Goodwill is being amortized (written off) over a 20-year period. The amortization for 20X5 has already been recorded on this and all other intangibles.

d. Operating expenses as given includes depreciation interest expense, and revenues include interest and investment revenues.

e. The "cash advance from customer" was for a special order that will not be completed and shipped until March 20X6; the sales price has not been definitely established because it is to be based on cost (no revenue should be recognized for 20X5).

Required:

1. Prepare a single-step income statement and a separate retained earnings statement. Include EPS disclosures.
2. Prepare a balance sheet. Use preferred terminology, captions, and subcaptions.
3. Indicate the likely note disclosure for balance sheet items.

P4-6 *Income Statement and Balance Sheet — Disclosure:* The adjusted trial balance for Deck Manufacturing Corporation at 31 December 20X5 is given below in no particular order. Debits and credits are not indicated; however, debits equal credits. All amounts are correct.

Work-in-process inventory	$ 29,000
Accrued interest on notes payable	1,000
Accrued interest receivable	1,200
Accrued interest on short-term investments	1,000
Common shares, no-par, authorized 100,000 shares, issued 40,000	150,000
Cash in bank	30,000
Trademarks (amortized cost)	1,400
Land held for speculation	27,000
Supplies inventory	600
Goodwill (amortized cost)	18,000
Raw materials inventory	13,000
Bond sinking fund	10,000
Accrued property taxes	1,400
Accounts receivable (trade)	29,000
Accrued wages	2,100
Mortgage payable (due in three years)	10,000
Building	130,000
Cash equivalent short-term investments	1,900
Organization expenses (amortized cost)	7,800

Deposits (cash collected from customers on sales orders to be delivered next quarter: no revenue yet recognized)	1,000
Long-term investment in bonds of Kaline Corp. (at cost)	50,000
Patents (amortized cost)	14,000
Reserve for depreciation, office equipment	1,600
Reserve for depreciation, building	5,000
Cash on hand for change	400
Preferred shares, $1, no-par, authorized 5,000 shares, issued 600 shares, noncumulative, nonconvertible	68,000
Pre-collected rent income	900
Finished goods inventory	43,000
Notes receivable (short-term)	4,000
Bonds payable, 12% (due in six years)	35,000
Future (deferred) income tax liability	15,000
Accounts payable (trade)	17,000
Reserve for bad debts	1,400
Notes payable (short-term)	7,200
Office equipment	25,000
Land (used as building site)	8,000
Short-term investments (at cost)	15,500
Retained earnings (1 January 20X5)	23,200
Cash dividends, declared and paid during 20X5	20,000
Revenues during 20X5	500,000
Cost of goods sold for 20X5	300,000
Expenses for 20X5 (including interest, depreciation and income tax)	100,000
Income taxes payable	40,000

Required:

1. Prepare a single-step income statement; use preferred terminology. Include EPS disclosure; to compute EPS, deduct $6,000 from net income as an allocation to nonconvertible preferred shares.

2. Prepare a complete balance sheet; use preferred terminology, format, captions, and subcaptions. Indicate likely note disclosure.

3. Assume that between 31 December 20X5, and issuance of the financial statements, a flood damaged the finished goods inventory in an amount estimated to be $20,000. How should this event be reflected in the 20X5 financial statements?

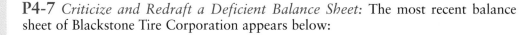

P4-7 *Criticize and Redraft a Deficient Balance Sheet:* The most recent balance sheet of Blackstone Tire Corporation appears below:

BLACKSTONE TIRE CORPORATION
Balance Sheet
for the year ended 31 December 20X5

Assets
Current:

Cash	$23,000	
Short-term investments	10,000	
Accounts receivable	15,000	
Merchandise	31,000	
Supplies	5,000	
Shares of Wilmont Co. (not a controlling interest)	17,000	$101,000

Investments:

Cash surrender value of life insurance			82,500

Tangible:

Building and land ($10,000)	$86,000		
Less: reserve for depreciation	40,000	46,000	
Equipment	$20,000		
Less: reserve for depreciation	15,000	5,000	51,000

Deferred:

Prepaid expenses			5,000
Total			$239,500

Debt and Capital

Current:

Accounts payable		$16,000	
Reserve for future, deferred income tax		17,000	
Customers' accounts receivable with credit balance		100	$ 33,100

Fixed (interest paid at year-end):

Bonds payable, 8.5%, due 20X9		45,000	
Mortgage, 11%		12,000	57,000
Reserve for bad debts			900

Capital:

Preferred shares, authorized and outstanding, 6,000 redeemable shares. Must be repaid in 20X9		50,000	
Common shares, authorized 10,000 shares, no-par		67,000	
Earned surplus		22,500	
Donated capital		9,000	148,500
Total			$239,500

Required:

1. List and explain in writing your criticisms of the above statement.

2. Prepare a complete balance sheet as far as possible; use appropriate format, captions, and terminology.

P4-8 *Balance Sheet Interpretation:* The balance sheet of Karmax Ltd. discloses the following assets:

KARMAX LTD.
Extracts from the Balance Sheet
as at year ended 31 December 20X6
($ thousands)

Assets

Current assets:

Cash	$ 710	
Short-term investments	416	
Accounts receivable	1,011	
Inventory	2,600	
Prepaid expenses	410	
Total current assets		$ 5,147
Tangible capital assets, net		14,755
Intangible capital assets, net		984
Long-term investments		1,077
Total assets		$21,963

The following information has been established in relation to market values (amounts in $ thousands):

	Market value	Source
Short-term investments	$501	Quoted stock market price
Inventory	$4,190	Karmax price list
Tangible capital assets	$20,000 – $25,000	Real estate appraisal
Long-term investment	$3,000	(Note 1)
Intangible capital assets	$10,000	(Note 2)

Note 1

The long-term investment is an investment in the shares of a company owned and operated by the two sons of Karmax's major shareholder. The Karmax investment is 25% of the outstanding shares. The sons' company has never sold shares to a non-family investor. The Karmax shareholder provided this estimate of value.

Note 2

Karmax holds patents on a successful consumer product, licensed to various manufacturers. Significant annual royalties are earned; the recorded balance sheet value consists of legal fees paid during patent infringement cases. The $10 million estimate of market value is based on discounted future cash flow.

Required:

Prepare a brief report that contains:

1. An analysis of the reliability of the various market value estimates as a good predictor of future cash flows.

2. An assessment of the usefulness of the historical cost balance sheet to

   a. A banker making a lending decision.
   b. An investor evaluating return on investment.

P4-9 *Balance Sheet Interpretation:* The following balance sheet reports the financial position of a junior Canadian gold-mining company (amounts in $ thousands):

Assets

Current assets:		
Cash and cash equivalents	$ 4,130	
Accounts receivable, less allowance for doubtful accounts	10,169	
Taxes recoverable	100	
Inventories	10,400	
Prepaid expenses	250	
Investments	915	$25,964
Plant, equipment and mine development costs, net		47,500
Goodwill		1,000
Total assets		$74,464

Liabilities and shareholders' equity
Current liabilities:

Accounts payable and accrued liabilities	$ 3,275	
Royalties payable	280	$ 3,555
Future liability for site restoration costs		1,140
Future (deferred) income taxes payable		915
Non-controlling interest		540
Shareholders' equity:		
Convertible bonds	564	
Share capital	56,000	
Retained earnings	11,500	
Cumulative exchange adjustment	250	
		68,314
Total liabilities and shareholders' equity		$74,464

Required:

1. Explain the meaning of the following accounts:
   a. Mine development costs
   b. Goodwill
   c. Future liability for site restoration costs
   d. Future (deferred) income taxes payable
   e. Non-controlling interest
   f. Convertible bonds
   g. Cumulative exchange adjustment

2. What items on the above balance sheet would mostly likely be estimated? Explain.

3. For what assets would you expect the market value and book value to be the most different? Explain.

4. As a potential shareholder, what additional information would be relevant to any decision to acquire shares in this company? Why is this information not presented with the audited financial statements?

Cash Flow Statement

INTRODUCTION

The balance sheet and income statement are summary presentations of an enterprise's financial activities for a period. The accounting treatments of the cash inflows and outflows are determined under the wide set of principles known as GAAP. Generally speaking, these two statements reflect the goal of *income measurement*. For example, cash paid out to acquire capital assets is not reported directly, but instead is capitalized and amortized. The actual cash flow appears nowhere in the income statement or balance sheet. It might be possible to figure out the amount by which capital assets increased during the year, but it is virtually impossible to find out how much was paid in cash and how much was financed by other means.

The cash flow statement reveals not only the operating cash flow of the company, but also enables the user to reconcile the cash flows to net income. Users can thereby see just how a company can have a cash flow that is different from the reported net income. Most users of financial statements are interested in seeing the cash flows as well as the net income, because in the long run, they base their own projections of cash flow on those of the company. For example, investors are interested in the amount that is available to pay out in dividends, bankers need to know how a company expects to generate cash to pay off its loans, employees need to know the company's "ability to pay" when negotiating wages, salaries and fringe benefits, and so forth.

The cash flows of an enterprise are of prime importance to many users of the financial statements. Indeed, the AcSB has identified cash flow prediction as a principal objective of financial reporting. The starting point of cash flow prediction is the analysis of historical cash flows. Therefore, the objective of the cash flow statement (which has several alternative titles) is to disclose the historical cash flows of the enterprise during the reporting period.

This chapter discusses the preparation and interpretation of the cash flow statement. The topics covered in previous chapters will be used to illustrate the impact of accounting policies on the statement. As we discuss individual categories of assets, liabilities, and shareholders' equity in following chapters, we also will point out the cash flow impact of that topic.

EVOLUTION OF THE CASH FLOW STATEMENT

The cash flow statement has evolved more over the past 20 years than has any other financial statement. The title of cash flow statement is fairly recent. Previously, the generic name for the statement was the statement of changes in financial position, a name that is still widely used. Earlier names included the where-got, where-gone statement, the statement of source and application of funds, and the more general funds flow statement.

The original focus of the statement was on changes in non-current assets, non-current liabilities, and owners' equity. The underlying assumption was that the changes in the current assets and current liabilities were reflected in the income statement through the revenues and expenses. Often, the statement was little more than a listing of the changes in long-term assets, liabilities, and shareholders' equity, with the *net* change in working capital (current assets minus current liabilities) as the balancing amount.

In 1974, the AcSB attempted to get more uniformity in the presentation of the "funds" statement by issuing Section 1540 of the *CICA Handbook*. The focus of the statement was still on changes in long-term assets and equities, but the presentation style actually emphasized changes in the net residual, net working capital (i.e., current assets minus current liabilities). If the components of the accounting equation are re-arranged:

Current liabilities + Long-term liabilities + Owners' equity = Current assets + Long-term assets

Long-term liabilities + Owners' equity – Long-term assets = Current assets – Current liabilities

The statement was often perceived to be an analysis of working capital itself, although that was not the intended purpose. The statement did present a section labelled *funds provided by operations*, and this was widely interpreted as cash flow from operations. However, when "funds" are defined as net working capital, the amount is affected by accounting policies chosen for all of the current assets, including inventories. This led to an anomalous situation when companies that reported a positive funds flow from operations went into receivership; working capital was increasing because inventories were building up and receivable collection periods were lengthening, but actual cash flow was down.

In 1985, the AcSB substantially revised Section 1540 to eliminate the working capital approach and focus instead on cash flows. The overall focus of the statement thereby shifted from the historical approach of analyzing long-term assets, long-term liabilities, and owners' equities to that of analyzing cash flows, regardless of the nature of the flows.

In 1996, the AcSB proposed to further modify Section 1540 to bring it in line with International Accounting Standard (IAS) 7. IAS 7 had been endorsed in 1993 by the International Organization of Securities Commissions and, in 1994, by the U.S. Securities and Exchange Commission as an alternative to existing FASB standards.

The exposure draft was accepted by the AcSB with only minor changes, and was introduced into the *CICA Handbook* in 1998, effective on 1 January 2000. This latest revision is an effort at international harmonization, and increases the emphasis on cash flow as the basic measurement approach for the statement, rather than changes in assets and liabilities. In essence, the new standard is the culmination of a long process of moving from a statement of changes in non-current assets and liabilities to a true cash flow statement — if a transaction doesn't involve cash, then it doesn't go on the cash flow statement!

CASH FLOW REPORTING

Cash vs. Accrual

Under the accrual basis, financial assets and liabilities (that is, receivables and payables) are recorded when the reporting enterprise has a right to receive cash or the obligation to pay cash, rather than later when the cash flows actually occur. It is due to the accrual basis that balance sheets show accounts receivable and payable and accrued revenues and expenses.

Interperiod allocations refer to the revenue and expense recognition policies that a company uses to measure net income. A transaction may give rise to a liability, for example, and recording that liability is an application of the accrual basis. The second decision is when to recognize the cost in net income. The cost that gave rise to the liability could be recorded as an expense immediately, or could be deferred until a later period (such as for prepaid expenses or inventories), or capitalized and amortized (such as long-lived assets that are depreciated or amortized). Interperiod allocation also occurs for revenue, especially when the earnings cycle extends over two or more accounting periods.

It is important to keep in mind the difference between receipts and disbursements and between revenues and expenses:

- Receipts and disbursements are *cash inflows and outflows*. They can be for any purpose, whether to generate operating earnings, change the asset structure increase or decrease liabilities.

- Revenues and expenses relate to receipts and disbursements because without cash flow, there can be no revenue or expense. But revenues and expenses derived from only certain cash flows and relate only to net income determition. For example, receipts from a share issue are not revenues, and payment retire bonds are not expenses. Only a subset of cash flows ever becomes a enue or expense.

- Because of the accrual concept, a cash receipt or disbursement that gives rise revenue or expense may occur in a different period than that in which the revenue or expense is recognized.

On the cash flow statement, the effects of both accruals and interperiod allocations (such as depreciation and amortization) are eliminated, leaving only the cash flows.

As we have seen in previous chapters (and will see in later chapters as well), there are a great many accounting policy choices that the preparers of financial statements must make. The various combinations of choices will affect net income, perhaps very significantly. Cash flow, however, is not affected by accounting policy choices. Actual cash flows may be altered by management to some extent, such as by making discretionary pension funding contributions or by delaying payment of some obligations.

However, as we will see below and in following chapters, accounting policy choices can affect the *way* in which cash flows are reported in the cash flow statement. Indeed, it is quite possible for management to make some accounting choices specifically to affect the reporting of a certain type of transaction on the cash flow statement.

Definition of "Cash"

It might appear that cash is cash; it seems to be an unambiguous term. It is not quite so simple, however. In its purest form, cash is currency, but companies do not keep large amounts of currency on hand except for daily operating purposes in cash registers or petty cash funds. In financial circles, cash is better described as the amount of funds that can be accessed by the company at any time, or **on demand**. In Canada, this is the amount that is held in the company's current account(s) with the bank. The current account is the chequing account, except that unlike personal chequing accounts, deposited cheques are not held for collection and the company's cheques are less likely to be returned NSF ("not sufficient funds") if the account is temporarily overdrawn.

Cash is a non-productive asset, and therefore companies strive to keep their immediately accessible cash balance at a minimum. Instead of carrying large cash balances, companies place their cash in term deposits, guaranteed investment certificates, certificates of deposit, or other money market instruments so that they can earn interest. For purposes of the cash flow statement, therefore, cash includes cash on hand, cash on deposit, and highly liquid short-term investments. These are known as cash equivalents. IAS 7 and Section 1540 recommend that "for an investment to qualify as a cash equivalent it must be readily convertible to a known amount of cash and be subject to an insignificant risk of changes in value" [*CICA* 1540.08]. Three months is suggested as the maximum maturity period. Investments in shares are explicitly excluded.

Corporations often maintain lines of credit with their banks. Lines of credit sometimes may be used as a cash account that can run a negative balance, or overdraft. Overdrafts are included as a component of cash, because they form an integral part of an enterprise's cash management. For example, assume that a company begins the year with a balance of $10,000 in its current account at the bank. By the end of the year, the cash balance is completely used and the company has written $15,000 more cheques than it has cash. The current account will then have an *overdraft* of $15,000. The change in cash for the period is not just the decline in cash from $10,000 to zero, but is the change from a $10,000 asset to a $15,000 liability, a decrease of $25,000.

The components of cash and cash equivalents (including overdrafts) should be disclosed, and the net change that is reported in the cash flow statement should be reconciled to the equivalent items in the balance sheet [*CICA* 1540.48].

Classification of Cash Flows

Once upon a time, the cash flow statement was organized into two sections: (1) sources of cash and (2) uses of cash; the defining characteristic was whether the cash was coming in or going out. This classification was changed when Section 1540 of the *CICA Handbook* was issued in 1985. Since then, the recommended classification is on the basis of the type of cash flow:

- Operating activities are the principal revenue producing activities of the enterprise and the related expenditures. The cash inflow from operations is measured as the cash received from customers or clients, plus ancillary revenue-generating activities such as finance revenue. The cash outflows are those disbursements that are incurred to earn the inflow, such as cash paid for inventories, wages and salaries, and overhead costs.
- Investing activities are those activities that relate to the asset structure of the company, other than current operating assets like inventory and accounts receivable. The acquisition and disposal of tangible and intangible capital assets and investments in other assets that are *not* included in cash equivalents would all be included in this section.
- Financing activities are those that relate to the liabilities (other than operating liabilities, like accounts payable) and owners' equity. Cash flows that increase or decrease the size or composition of the non-operating accounts on the right side of the balance sheet are reported in this section.

Exhibit 5-1 lists some of the transactions that fall into each category.

EXHIBIT 5-1
Examples of Cash Flows by Category

OPERATING CASH FLOWS:

Inflows	Outflows
Receipts from customers	Payments to suppliers
Advance deposits from customers	Wages and salaries to employees
Income tax refunds	Income tax payments
Interest received on customers' notes or accounts	Other tax payments
Dividends and interest received from investments and included in determining net income	Interest paid on bank debt or bonds outstanding and included in determining net income

INVESTING CASH FLOWS:

Inflows	Outflows
Cash received from sale of capital assets	Payments for purchase of capital assets
Cash from sale of debt or equity investments	Cash flows capitalized as intangible assets, such as:
Collection of principal on loans to others	— development costs
Interest and dividends received on investments and not included in determining net income	— start-up costs
	— capitalized interest
	— exploration costs
	Purchase of debt or equity securities of others
	Loans extended to others

FINANCING CASH FLOWS:

Inflows	Outflows
Net proceeds of issuing debt or equity securities	Payment of principal on bonds or bank loans
Principal received from bank loans	Purchase of the entity's own shares
	Interest paid on bank debt or bonds outstanding and not included in determining net income
	Dividends paid to shareholders

Interest income and expense offer a particular classification challenge. Interest income and interest expense that have been included in determining net income should remain as part of operating cash flow, *but separately disclosed* [*CICA* 1540.34]. Interest payments that are *not* included in net income would be classified "according to their nature" [*CICA* 1540.35]. For example, interest that has been capitalized will be reported as part of the investment in the related asset.

Similarly, accountants have had difficulty agreeing on the appropriate classification of dividends in the cash flow statement. In current practice, dividends *received* and reported in net income should be reported as an operating cash flow. Dividends received from controlled or significantly-influenced affiliates are not included in net income and therefore should be reported in the investing activities section.

Dividends *paid* are not included in net income and therefore should not be included in operating cash flow. Instead, dividend payments are separately disclosed as a financing activity (that is, as a payment to providers of capital).

There are three aspects of the cash flow classifications that merit particular attention:

1. For all three categories, the cash flows can be either *positive* or *negative*. If, for example, a company sells off some of its assets during the year, the proceeds (or cash received) from those assets are reported as a source of cash within the investing section of the cash flow statement. Similarly, payments that reduce the amount of long-term debt will appear as a use of cash in the financing section.

2. The positive and negative flows are *not* netted. For example, an issue of new bonds and a retirement of old bonds are disclosed as two separate financing transactions and not offset against each other.

3. The classification is not necessarily determined by the treatment of a transaction on the income statement. For example, a gain on the sale of a capital asset will be reported in the income statement and will be included in net income. For the cash flow statement, however, the transaction will be reported in the *investing* section because it relates to a capital asset.

The income statement reports revenues and expenses. In contrast, the purpose of the cash flow statement is to report cash inflows and outflows within the three categories of activities.

Statement Title

Historically, the most common name for the cash flow statement was *Statement of Changes in Financial Position*. About 60% of Canadian public companies used this title.[1] This name derives from the fact that an alternate name for the balance sheet is *Statement of Financial Position*. Its use also was probably promoted by the fact that until 1998, Section 1540 had the same title.

The intent of the new Section 1540 is to encourage companies to use the simpler and more understandable title of *cash flow statement*, especially since all non-cash transactions have been banished from the statement, as we will demonstrate shortly.

CONCEPT REVIEW

1. What are the three categories of cash flows that should be reported on a company's cash flow statement?
2. Why does *cash from operations* differ from *net income*?
3. What is the definition of *cash*, for purposes of the cash flow statement?
4. How should interest and dividends received and paid be reported in the cash flow statement?

PREPARING THE CASH FLOW STATEMENT

Basic Approach to Preparation

The Balance Sheet, Income Statement, and Retained Earnings Statement are all prepared from the trial balance. Preparation of these statements can be manual or, more commonly, by computerized systems. The classification of the balance of each account is unambiguously pre-specified in the programming, and the statements (other than the cash flow statement) emerge more or less automatically from the system.[2]

However, the cash flow statement is not a statement that is an automatic output from account balances. Instead, it is a statement that is prepared by *analyzing*

---

[1] *Financial Reporting in Canada 1997*, p. 85.

[2] Those readers who need a refresher on the accounting cycle and on preparation of the three statements should consult the Appendix to this volume.

account balances and changes in balances. It is not enough, for example, to know by how much the cash balance has changed over the course of an accounting period; one must analyze the sources of the accounting entries in the cash account. Standard computerized accounting systems normally cannot do that, and therefore the cash flow statement is usually a hand-prepared statement.

If we want to prepare a statement that explains all of the cash flows, it seems logical to start by analyzing the sources of the flows in and out of the cash account(s). The entries to the general ledger cash account are usually summary entries from subsidiary records such as specialized journals or cumulative transaction records. For example, we can see how much cash was received from customers by summarizing the debits to the cash account from the accounts receivable department and/or from the summary posting of the daily cash receipts; we can see how much was paid to employees for wages and salaries by looking at the payroll accounts, etc. The process of describing cash flows by analyzing the cash account(s) is the direct preparation approach. Some large-scale and/or customized computerized accounting systems are capable of the direct preparation approach.

An alternative approach is to describe the cash activities by analyzing the changes in all of the *non-cash* accounts. Since the basic, indisputable characteristic of the balance sheet is that it *balances*, we can determine cash flows by looking at the causes of the changes in all of the other accounts *except* cash and cash equivalents. For example, we can quickly determine how much cash was received from customers by looking at the total sales revenue figure (on the income statement) and adjusting that accrual-basis amount by the change in trade accounts receivable for the period. If the balance in accounts receivable went up, then we received less cash than we recognized in sales for the period; if the accounts receivable balance went down, then we received more cash than we recognized in sales.

This approach of analyzing all of the other accounts in order to discern the cash flows is the indirect preparation approach. The indirect preparation approach is the more commonly used, and is virtually the only method used, when the preparation is manual or when the cash flow statement is prepared from the other financial statements as produced by an off-the-shelf accounting software package such as NuViews® or AccPac®.

In this text, *only* the indirect preparation approach will be illustrated.

There also is both a direct and indirect method for *presenting* the cash flow statement; we will discuss that distinction shortly.

Indirect Preparation Approach: A Simple Example

The data for preparing the cash flow statement for Simple Limited by the indirect preparation approach is shown in Exhibit 5-2. The cash account shows a change from $20 at the beginning of the year to $35 at the end, for a net increase of $15. However, there also is a short-term investment account. Assuming that this account is a *cash equivalent*, it must be included with cash. In that case the net change in the balance of "cash" from the end of 19X1 to the end of 19X2 is a *decrease* of $35:

	Ending	Beginning	Change	
Cash balance	$35	$20	$ 15	increase
Short-term investments	20	70	(50)	decrease
Total	$55	$90		
Net increase (decrease) in cash			$(35)	decrease

The cash flow statement that can be derived from the information in Exhibit 5-2 is shown in Exhibit 5-3. (The letters in the "key" column refer to the explanations just below.) In order to explain the flows that resulted in the net decrease of $35, we analyze all of the changes in the non-cash accounts, starting with information from the statement of income and retained earnings and with the *additional information*, as follows:

EXHIBIT 5-2
SIMPLE LIMITED
Balance Sheets, 31 December

	20X2	20X1
Current assets:		
Cash	$ 35	$ 20
Short-term investments	20	70
Accounts receivable	110	125
Inventory	100	135
	$ 265	$ 350
Fixed assets:		
Plant and equipment	1,100	1,000
Accumulated depreciation	(250)	(300)
	850	700
Total assets	$1,115	$1,050
Current liabilities:		
Bank loan	$ 65	$ 50
Accounts payable	100	125
	165	175
Long-term note payable	300	330
Shareholders' equity:		
Common shares	100	100
Retained earnings	550	445
	650	545
Total liabilities and share equity	$1,115	$1,050

SIMPLE LIMITED
Statement of Income and Retained Earnings
year ended 31 December 20X2

Revenue:		
Sales revenue	$2,000	
Gain on sale of equipment	70	
	2,070	
Operating expenses:		
Cost of goods sold	1,100	
Other expenses	640	
	$1,740	
Net income	330	
Retained earnings, 1 January	445	
Dividends paid on common shares	(225)	
Retained earnings, 31 December	$ 550	

Additional information:
 i. Other operating expenses includes $200 of depreciation expense.
 ii. During the year, Simple sold equipment originally costing $310 for net proceeds of $130.

a. Net income of $330 is the basis for determining cash flow from operations. Therefore, the amount of net income is placed in the Operations section of the cash flow statement.

b. Dividends of $225 were declared (and paid) during the year. This amount is placed in the Financing section. Note that net income and dividends completely explain the change in retained earnings during the year.

c. *Additional information* reveals that Operating Expense includes $200 in depreciation. Since depreciation is an interperiod allocation of previous years' investment cash flows, its impact must be removed from net income. The $200 depreciation is *added back* to net income to eliminate the effect of this interperiod allocation.

d. *Additional information* reveals that equipment that originally cost $310 was sold for $130. The income statement also shows a gain from the sale of equipment amounting to $70. On the cash flow statement, we wish to show the $130 cash received as an investment activity, and we need to eliminate the $70 gain from our operating cash flow. The gain is eliminated for two reasons:

1. The sale of assets is not an operating activity but reflects a change in asset structure; the disposal of assets must be reported as an investing activity.

2. The gain does not measure the actual cash flow during the period, but instead it is the difference between the proceeds of the sale and the net book value of the asset. The net book value is the original expenditure for the asset, reduced by the series of non-cash interperiod allocations through depreciation.

The following entry must have been made when the equipment was sold:

Cash	130	
Accumulated depreciation	250	
Plant and equipment		310
Gain on sale of equipment		70

e. Accounts Receivable decreased by $15 during the year. This means that customers paid more than the amount reported as sales. The $15 is added to net income in the operations section, in order to restate the sales from an accrual to a cash basis.

f. Inventory decreased by $35. Inventory is a component of cost of goods sold. By definition, the beginning of year inventory was acquired in a previous period and not the current period. Therefore, a decrease in inventory indicates that less cash was paid for the goods than were sold during the year.

g. Accounts Payable decreased by $25. This indicates that suppliers received more cash for goods and services than the company accrued during the period. The $25 decrease reduces the amount of cash from operations. The accounts payable adjustment is related to the inventory adjustment, since trade accounts payable relate largely to inventory purchases. This will be further explained later in the chapter.

h. Plant and Equipment increased by $100 during the period. However, this is a net amount. The plant and equipment balance was decreased by the sale, and increased by new investment. To find out how much was invested in new plant and equipment, we must add the $310 historical cost of the equipment sold to the $100 net change in the balance, which gives us $410 as the cash invested in new plant and equipment.

i. Accumulated Depreciation decreased by $50. Since we know that depreciation expense for 20X2 of $200 was added to his account, the net decrease must be attributable to the $250 write-off of accumulated depreciation on the equipment sold. This can be verified by referring to the reconstructed entry for the equipment sale shown in (d), above.

j. The current bank loan increased by $15. This is a loan, and not an overdraft; therefore, the loan will not be included as a component of cash and cash equivalents. The increase in the loan is a source of financing, and will go into the financing section of the cash flow statement.

k. Long-term note payable decreased by $30. This represents a financing activity.

l. Common shares did not change during the period. Therefore, in the absence of any information that shares were purchased and new shares were issued (that is, in off-setting amounts), there will be no impact on the cash flow statement relating to common shares.

The net result of entering all of these amounts in the cash flow statement is that we have explained the net decrease in cash of $35.

Presentation of Operations

In addition to direct versus indirect preparation methods, there also are both direct and indirect *presentation* methods for the Operations section. The differences are:

• *Direct presentation:* The revenues and expenses are adjusted to a cash basis of reporting and shown directly in deriving cash provided by (or used by) operations on the cash flow section.

• *Indirect presentation:* Operations begins with net income, and all interperiod allocations and accruals are reversed out of net income to derive the cash from operations.

In Exhibit 5-3, the indirect method of presentation was used. Operations began with Net Income of $330 and then was adjusted for depreciation, the accounting gain on sale of equipment, and for changes in the balances of the other current assets and current liabilities *except* for those included in the definition of "cash."

Exhibit 5-4 shows the Operations section of Simple Limited's cash flow statement, using the direct approach of presentation. The amounts are obtained as follows:

m. Sales is increased by the $15 decrease in accounts receivable and reported as an inflow of cash, and

n. Cost of goods sold requires two adjustments. The first adjustment is for the decrease in inventory of $35 during the year. Since inventory purchased in the previous year was used this year, the cash flow requirements for buying inventory were $35 less than the expense shown for cost of goods sold. Partially offsetting the decline in inventory is the decrease in accounts payable. The decrease in accounts payable of $25 indicates that more cash was expended to pay creditors (presumably, for inventory purchases and other expense components that comprise cost of goods sold). Therefore, the cash flow for the components of cost of goods sold is higher than the expense by $10.

o. Other operating expenses is decreased by the $200 depreciation.

Other items, such as depreciation and the gain on sale of equipment are not cash flows and simply are left off the statement under the direct presentation approach.

The AcSB permits either the direct or indirect method of reporting cash flows from operations, but enterprises are "encouraged" to report cash flows from operating activities using the direct method [CICA 1540.21]. Regardless of any possible advantages in clarity of using the direct approach, the indirect method of presentation has been by far the more popular approach among accountants. *Financial Reporting in Canada 1997* reports that 99% of the surveyed companies use the indirect method of reporting. Whether companies will follow the AcSB's encouragement in the future remains to be seen.

It can be argued that the direct approach is clearer to financial statement users, because they do not have to understand the reasons for the adjustments that are made

EXHIBIT 5-3
SIMPLE LIMITED
Cash Flow Statement
year ended 31 December 20X2

	Key		
Operating Activities:			
Net income (from income statement)	(a)	$330	
Add (deduct) to reconcile net income to net operating cash flows:			
Depreciation expense	(c)	200	
Gain on sale of equipment	(d)	(70)	
Decrease in accounts receivable	(e)	15	
Decrease in inventory	(f)	35	
Decrease in accounts payable	(g)	(25)	$485
Investing activities:			
Proceeds from sale of equipment	(d)	130	
Purchase of new equipment	(h)	(410)	(280)
Financing activities:			
Increase in current bank loan	(j)	15	
Dividends paid	(b)	(225)	
Reduction of long-term notes payable	(k)	(30)	(240)
Increase (decrease) in cash			(35)
Cash and cash equivalents, 1 January			90
Cash and cash equivalents, 31 December			$ 55

under the indirect approach. Of particular concern is that the indirect method plants in users' minds the idea that depreciation is a source of funds. The addback of depreciation usually is a large positive element in the operations section, and business people have often been heard to remark that they will be using their "depreciation funds" for certain projects.

Of course, this is a mistaken impression, but the indirect presentation method certainly strengthens that impression. In most cash flow statements, as in Exhibit 5-3, the depreciation addback is labelled as an adjustment. But very often, there is no such explanatory label. Exhibit 5-5 shows the operations section of cash flow statement presented by The Molson Companies. What's the second largest item under Operating Activities? It's the amortization of capital assets, which appears to contribute $43.4 million to the company's cash flow!

A common variation on the indirect method of presentation is a two-step approach. First, the net income is adjusted for interperiod allocations, and then it is adjusted for changes in other working capital accounts (usually as a single, summary amount rather than in detail). The operations section of Simple Limited's cash flow statement is illustrated in Exhibit 5-6 by using the two-step approach.

Offsetting Transactions

A basic objective of the cash flow statement is to explain the investing and financing activities of the enterprise. Within each of those two categories, there often are transactions that, overall, have the effect of offsetting each other. For example, if a company refinances its debt by retiring an outstanding bond issue and issuing new bonds,

EXHIBIT 5-4
SIMPLE LIMITED
Cash Flow Statement
year ended 31 December 20X2

Sample of Direct Presentation of Operations

Operating Activities:		
Cash received from customers ($2,000 + $15)	**(m)**	$2,015
Operating expenses:		
Cash paid to suppliers ($1,100 – $35 + $25)	**(n)**	(1,090)
Cash paid for other operating expenses ($640 – 200)	**(o)**	(440)
Cash provided by operations		$ 485

EXHIBIT 5-5
THE MOLSON COMPANIES LIMITED
Consolidated Statement of Changes in Financial Position (excerpt)
year ended March 31, 1998*
(*$ thousands*)

	1998
Operating activities	
Earnings from continuing operations	$ 58,531
Provision for rationalization and other costs	11,946
Amortization of capital assets	43,413
Deferred income taxes	22,010
Other	(25,765)
Cash provided from operations	$110,135

References to disclosure notes have been removed.

* *Comparative column for 1997 is not reproduced here.*

the *net* impact on the balance sheet may be relatively minor. However, these activities do demonstrate the company's ability to renew its capital structure. The flows associated with the refinancing should be disclosed separately and not offset, or netted.

Section 1540 emphasizes that offsetting should not occur. In general, "an enterprise should report separately major classes of gross cash receipts and gross cash payments arising from investing and financing activities" [*CICA* 1540.23]. The two key words are *separately* and *gross*. Both words emphasize that transactions relating to similar items of asset or equity structure should not be netted.

There are some exceptions to the general rule against offsetting, but they are narrowly defined and relate more to financial institutions than to other types of enterprise. In essence, offsetting (or netting) is permitted for

- Cash receipts and payments that are on behalf of customers rather than for the reporting enterprise itself [*CICA* 1540.25(a)]. An example is the cash flows of a

EXHIBIT 5-6
SIMPLE LIMITED
Cash Flow Statement (partial)
year ended 31 December 20X2
Two-Step Presentation of Operating Activities

Operating Activities:	
Net income	$330
Plus (less) items not affecting cash:	
Depreciation	200
Gain on sale of equipment	(70)
	460
Changes in other working capital items:	
Decrease in accounts receivable	15
Decrease in inventory	35
Decrease in accounts payable	(25)
Cash provided by operations	$485

rental agent who collects rents for landlords and passes those rents on to the property owners. The agent may keep a commission, which is the *net* cash flow to the agent.

- Cash receipts and payments for items where the volume of activity is high and the holding period is short (i.e., the *turnover* is quick) [*CICA* 1540.25(b)]. An example is the investing and liquidating of investments by an investment dealer or by a company that is not an investment dealer but that engages in active market transactions. A cereal manufacturer may, for instance, routinely buy and sell a large volume of grain futures on the commodity market.

Section 1540 contains recommendations for netting the cash flows relating to specific types of activities for financial institutions, but those activities fit the two general guidelines.

Non-Cash Transactions

Some transactions have a significant effect on the asset or equity structure of an entity without involving any direct cash flow at all. These non-cash transactions are economically similar to cash transactions. For example, settling a debt by issuing shares directly to the debt holder has the same effect as issuing the shares for cash and using the proceeds to settle the debt. Or, an asset may be acquired without cash by entering into a mortgage or a long-term capital lease; the effect is the same as borrowing money to buy the asset. Common types of non-cash transactions include

- Bond retirement through share issuance
- Conversion of bonds to shares
- Conversion of preferred shares to common shares
- Settlement of debt by transferring non-cash assets
- Bond refunding
- Incurrence of capitalized lease obligations in exchange for leased assets
- Acquisition of shares in another company in exchange for shares of the reporting enterprise
- Distribution of assets other than cash as dividends (e.g., a spin-off of a subsidiary company)

Prior to the revision of Section 1540 in 1998, non-cash transactions such as those listed above were required to be included in the cash flow statement. However, the revised Section 1540 specifically excludes non-cash transactions from the cash flow statement on the grounds that such transactions are not cash flows [*CICA* 1540.46]. For example, the acquisition of a building (an investing activity) that is financed through a capital lease (a financing activity) would not be shown on the face of the cash flow statement because there was no cash involved. Instead, the transaction would be reported in a note to the financial statements.

In one sense, this approach is an additional step away from the old concept of the funds flow statement as a summary of changes in non-current assets and equities. However, the total exclusion of non-cash transactions from the cash flow statement seems to give precedence to form over substance. The purchase of another company (i.e., a *business combination*) through an issue of shares would not be reported in the cash flow statement, while the issuance of shares for cash and the use of the proceeds to buy the company would be reported in the cash flow statement. Also, an acquisition in which part of the consideration is in cash and the remainder is in another asset (or a debt instrument or shares), the cash part of the transaction would be reported in the cash flow statement while the non-cash portion would not.

For example, suppose that a building costing $4,000,000 is acquired by paying $1,000,000 cash and issuing a $3,000,000 long-term note. The cash flow statement would disclose only the $1,000,000 cash paid (as an investing activity), although the entry on the cash flow statement should be referenced to the note that contains the details of the transaction.

OTHER ASPECTS OF CASH FLOW REPORTING

Cash Flow per Share

Financial analysts and other users often compute cash flow per share, which is defined in many different ways. One common measure of cash flow per share is net operating cash flow divided by common shares outstanding. In the United States, FAS No. 95 prohibits disclosure of statistics so labelled in financial statements, except for contractually determined cash flow per share values. The FASB believed that allowing cash flow per share to be disclosed would cause confusion between EPS and cash flow per share. Of course, financial statement users are free to compute any statistic from published information.

The *CICA Handbook* is silent on the issue, which allows Canadian companies to use their judgement in this area. Considerable diversity exists. One example is The Thomson Corporation, a prominent company with widespread publishing interests in North America (including *The Globe and Mail*) and travel interests. In its 1997 annual report, Thomson reported *cash flow per common share provided by operations* of $2.17, up 27% from $1.71 the year before. In contrast, earnings per share *declined* by 4%, from $0.95 to $0.91. However, the cash flow per share is *before changes in working capital and other items* — it isn't really cash flow, it's working capital from operations. In this particular case, the true cash flow amounts are not much different from the working capital flows, $2.00 per share for 1997 and $1.62 for 1996 (a 23% increase instead of 27%). But one must be very careful about interpreting "cash flow per share" amounts; since there is no reporting standard (as there is for earnings per share), reported cash flow per share amounts may not be what they seem to be.

Quality of Earnings

Investment analysts sometimes refer to the earnings quality of a company that they are analyzing. This concept relates the amount of net income to the amount of cash flow from operations. A company is said to have high quality earnings when there is a close correspondence between net income and cash flow from operations, especially if the close relationship between earnings and cash flow persists over several years and move in the same direction.

In contrast, a company that reports earnings that are not closely related to cash flows is said to have low quality earnings. In some companies, cash flows and earnings are actually counter-indicative. That is, a company can have high earnings but a negative cash flow from operations because of soaring receivables or expanding inventories; this situation often makes analysts a bit nervous, especially if it continues for more than one year.

On the other hand, a company can have low earnings (or even a loss) and still have positive cash flows from operations. For example, this can happen when net income includes a large amount of depreciation or amortization of capitalized costs. Banks may be quite willing to lend to such a company on the strength of the cash flow, despite the existence of losses, because they are convinced that there is adequate cash flow to service the loan (that is, to pay the interest and repay the principal).

Effect of Accounting Policy Choices on the Cash Flow Statement

One of the reasons that users like to see the cash flow statement is that "cash doesn't lie." A perception exists among many users that while managers and accountants can adopt accounting policies that can have a significant and substantial effect on the measurement of net income, they have little room to manipulate cash flows.

To a considerable extent, this perception is correct. For example, management of almost every type of enterprise makes accounting policy decisions about revenue recognition, operating expense recognition, depreciation policy (i.e., method, life, and salvage value) or amortization of other long-lived assets. In addition, there are many accounting estimates made by management regarding almost every asset on the balance sheet (such as year-end accruals, bad debt provisions, inventory obsolescence write-downs, and investment write-offs). These estimates are influenced by external events and are not entirely under the control of management, but management is responsible for making those estimates and certainly can influence their amount and timing of recognition.

Accounting policy decisions and management's measurement estimates can significantly affect net income, but they will have no impact on the underlying cash flow. It is true, therefore, that the overall net cash flow for an accounting period is unaffected by accounting policy choices.

However, there is a certain type of accounting policy decision that affects the cash flow statement by affecting the *classification* of items on the statement, and that is whether to expense or capitalize one or more types of cost. If expenditures of a certain category (i.e., start-up costs) are charged to expense, they will be included as a deduction in net income and be included in operating cash flow. On the other hand, if those expenditures are capitalized, they will appear on the cash flow statement as an *investing* activity. In subsequent years, amortization of capitalized costs is deducted in determining net income, but is then added back to net income to derive cash flow from operations. The result is that capitalized costs *never* enter into operating cash flow but will appear only as an investing activity. For example, a retail chain that capitalizes and amortizes its new store start-up costs will show a consistently higher cash flow from operations than one that charges start-up costs to expense, all other things being equal.

Interim Statements

The securities acts require public companies to issue interim financial statements at least quarterly. The importance of the cash flow statement to users is illustrated by the fact that the securities acts require a condensed income statement and statement of change in financial position (i.e., a cash flow statement) as interim financial statements. A balance sheet is not required, although many companies do provide one. The securities acts presume that the flow activities, both earnings and cash, are most important to continuing evaluation of the company. Of course, any significant changes to the asset and equity structure of the company will be revealed in the cash flow statement or, for non-cash transactions, in the notes.

SUMMARY OF DISCLOSURE RECOMMENDATIONS

The *CICA Handbook* recommends the following disclosures relating to the cash flow statement:

- The cash flow statement should report the changes in cash and cash equivalents, net of bank overdrafts, resulting from the activities of the enterprise during the period.
- The components of cash, cash overdrafts, and cash equivalents should be disclosed and should be reconciled with the balance sheet.
- The statement should include only cash flows; non-cash transactions should not be reported on the cash flow statement, but should be disclosed elsewhere in the financial statements as appropriate.
- Cash flows during the period should be classified by *operating, investing* and *financing* activities.
- Reporting enterprises are *encouraged* to report cash flows from operations by the direct method.
- Cash flows from investing and financing activities should not be netted or offset; the *gross* amount of inflows and outflows should be reported.
- Cash flows relating to extraordinary items should be classified according to their nature as operating, investing or financing activities, and should be separately disclosed.
- The gross amounts of cash flows from interest and dividends (both received and paid) should be disclosed separately; interest and dividends that have been included in net income should be separately disclosed as part of operating cash flow.
- Cash flows arising from income tax on operating income should be separately disclosed as an operating activity. *If* income tax cash flows can be specifically identified with investing or financing activities, they should be classified as investing or financing activities.
- The cash flows arising from acquisitions and disposals of subsidiaries or other business units should be presented separately and classified as investing activities. Non-cash exchanges involving such acquisitions or disposals would *not* be reported on the cash flow statement (but would be disclosed in a note). Disposals are not netted against acquisitions.[3]

CONCEPT REVIEW

1. Why is depreciation added in deriving cash flow from operations from a starting point of net operating income? Is depreciation a source of cash?
2. Explain why a gain on the sale of equipment is subtracted in the reconciliation of income and operating cash flows.
3. Why are changes in the balance of accounts receivable disclosed in the cash flow statement under the indirect presentation approach, but not disclosed under the direct presentation approach?
4. If salaries payable increases during the year, why does this imply that salary expense exceeds salary payments?

---

3 This aspect of cash flow reporting is discussed in Chapter 12.

ANALYZING MORE COMPLEX SITUATIONS

Using a Spreadsheet

When preparing the cash flow statement for Simple Limited, we used an informal, ad hoc approach wherein we simply went down the balance sheet and filled in the appropriate amounts in the cash flow statement. In the process, we explained all of the changes in the non-cash accounts, and thus indirectly explained all of the changes in the cash accounts. This approach works because the net change in non-cash accounts must be equal to the change in cash accounts in order for the balance sheet to balance. Furthermore, the transactions we are interested in are those that took place between the cash accounts and the non-cash accounts (as well as non-cash transactions that directly affected the asset/equity structure of the company). For the cash flow statement, we have no interest in the transactions that took place solely within the cash accounts themselves, such as investment in or liquidation of temporary investments.

While the simple approach used in constructing Exhibit 5-3 is completely acceptable, in complex situations it is easy to lose track of what we are doing. Therefore, it is common to use some form of worksheet or spreadsheet to force some discipline on the process and to help assure that we don't overlook any relevant transactions. The spreadsheet approach is useful because it

- provides an organized format for documenting the preparation process,
- facilitates review and evaluation by others,
- provides proofs of accuracy, and
- formally keeps track of the changes in balance sheet accounts and ensures that all accounts are explained.

There are several different analytical methods. The method used is irrelevant; what is important is the cash flow statement that results. In this book, we will use a spreadsheet approach in the main body of the chapter. We will illustrate the approach by considering a somewhat more comprehensive illustration than the example of Simple Limited. The appendix to this chapter presents an alternative analytical approach: the T-account method. The T-account method is useful for understanding the relationships between accounts, but is cumbersome in a realistic setting when there is a large number of accounts.

The comparative balance sheet and the income statement for Accrue Corporation are shown in Exhibit 5-7, along with some important supplementary information. From the balance sheet, we can see that cash increased by $14,000 during the year. (The most recent year is shown in the first numerical column, as is standard practice in Canadian financial statements.) Short-term liquid investments, however, decreased by $24,000. Assuming that short-term liquid investments is a *cash equivalent*, the actual change in cash is really a decrease of $10,000.

	Ending	**Beginning**	**Change**	
Cash balance	$50,000	$36,000	$14,000	increase
Short-term investments	10,000	34,000	(24,000)	decrease
Total	$60,000	$70,000		
Net increase (decrease) in cash			$(10,000)	decrease

The task of the cash flow statement is to explain the transactions that caused this decrease of $10,000 in cash and cash equivalents. On the cash flow statement worksheet, the change in cash is explained by reconciling the change in cash with the changes in all of the other accounts.

EXHIBIT 5-7
ACCRUE CORPORATION
Balance Sheet, 31 December

ASSETS	20X2	20X1
Current assets:		
Cash	$ 50,000	$ 36,000
Short-term liquid investments	10,000	34,000
Accounts receivable	84,000	70,000
Inventories	42,000	30,000
Prepaid expenses	15,000	11,000
	201,000	181,000
Fixed assets:		
Land	50,000	50,000
Plant and equipment	740,000	615,000
Accumulated depreciation	(260,000)	(215,000)
	530,000	450,000
Other assets:		
Deferred development costs	82,000	76,000
Long-term investments	92,000	70,000
	174,000	146,000
Total assets	$905,000	$777,000
EQUITIES		
Current liabilities:		
Bank loan	$ 30,000	$ 10,000
Accounts payable	36,000	45,000
	66,000	55,000
Long-term liabilities:		
Bonds payable	146,000	133,000
Future (deferred) income taxes	27,000	24,000
Total liabilities	239,000	212,000
Shareholders' equity:		
Preferred shares	142,000	120,000
Common shares	230,000	180,000
Retained earnings	294,000	265,000
	666,000	565,000
Total equities	$905,000	$777,000

To set up the worksheet, it is necessary to transfer the accounts and account balances from the balance sheet to a four-column worksheet. Exhibit 5-8 demonstrates the set-up for Accrue Corporation, based on the information in Exhibit 5-7. The 20X1 account balances are entered into the first column, and the 20X2 balances are entered into the last column. In the two intervening columns, we will recreate the transactions that caused the changes in the non-cash accounts. Once all of the changes in the account balances from 20X1 to 20X2 have been explained by reconstructing the entries, we will have all of the data that we need to construct the cash flow statement.

The intent is to identify the cash flows. But instead of debiting and crediting all of the cash flows directly to the cash account, we will classify the "cash" part of the transactions in another section of the worksheet. Below the balance sheet accounts, we create a section of the worksheet in which to record the cash flow effects. Within this lower section, a sub-section is labelled for each of the three types of cash activi-

EXHIBIT 5-7 (cont'd)
ACCRUE CORPORATION
Statement of Income and Retained Earnings
year ended 31 December 20X2

Sales revenue	$960,000	
Gain on sale of equipment	4,000	$964,000
Operating expenses:		
Cost of goods sold	615,000	
Interest expense	18,000	
Provision for income taxes	36,000	
Other operating expenses	231,000	900,000
Net income		64,000
Dividends declared		(35,000)
Retained earnings, 1 January		265,000
Retained earnings, 31 December		$294,000

Additional information:

1. Cost of goods sold includes depreciation of $65,000.
2. Other operating expenses includes amortization of deferred development of $5,000.
3. During 20X2, the corporation issued preferred shares with a market value of $22,000 for 1,000 common shares of THB Corporation. The THB shares are being held as a long-term investment.
4. Old equipment was sold for $9,000; the original cost was $25,000.
5. Bonds with a face value of $20,000 were repurchased at par and retired.
6. Other operating expenses includes a loss of $2,000 from liquidating the short-term investments (for net proceeds of $22,000).

ty: operating, investing and financing. As cash flows are identified by reconciling the individual balance sheet accounts in the upper four-column part of the spreadsheet, the offsetting cash effect is entered into the appropriate lower sub-section of the worksheet.

To facilitate preparation of the cash flow statement under the direct presentation method, we should separately identify the revenues and operating expenses in the operations sub-section of the worksheet. In addition, we must separately disclose interest, dividends, and income taxes that have been included in net income. Therefore, the operations section is further subdivided to specifically identify these components of net income — revenues, interest expense, income tax expense, and other operating expenses. If we also had interest and/or dividend income, we would provide a line or two for each as well as those used in this example.

Worksheet Procedure

Once the beginning and ending account balances have been entered into the worksheet or spreadsheet, we can begin to make the necessary adjustments. Generally speaking, the place to start is with the reconciliation of retained earnings, simply because it is where the net income for the year has been transferred. Starting with net income also focuses our attention on the income statement and on the adjustments that are necessary to remove the effects of interperiod allocations.

Accrue Corporation's statement of income and retained earnings reveals that the change in retained earnings consists of two items: (1) net income, and (2) dividends paid. The net $29,000 increase in the retained earnings balance came about as the result of $64,000 in net income and $35,000 in dividends paid. Therefore, the first reconciling entry on the worksheet is to disaggregate the net income into its separately-reported components:

a. *Cash: operating activities*, revenue   964,000
        Cash: operations, interest expense   18,000
        Cash: operations, income tax expense   36,000
        Cash: operations, other expenses   846,000
        Retained earnings   64,000

The second reconciling entry is to record the dividends declared:

b. Retained earnings   35,000
        Cash: financing activities, dividends declared   35,000

Observe that these entries are recreations of the original entries to (a) transfer net income into the retained earnings account and (b) to record the declaration and payment of dividends. Dividends, for example, are *debited* to the balance sheet account in the upper section of the worksheet and *credited* to cash in the lower section.

The rest of the reconciliations are as follows, considering first the list of items of *additional information* in Exhibit 5-7:

c. Depreciation of $65,000 was expensed during the period. The original entry was as follows:

Depreciation expense (*Operations*)   65,000
        Accumulated depreciation   65,000

This entry is reproduced in the worksheet, with the debit placed under *Operations*.

d. Amortization of deferred development costs amounting to $5,000 was recorded during the year. The entry to record the amortization is recorded on the worksheet.

Amortization of development costs (*Operations*)   5,000
        Deferred development costs   5,000

e. The company entered into an exchange of shares that was worth $22,000. That is, they acquired a long-term investment in another company's shares in exchange for their own preferred shares. No cash changed hands. This is an example of a non-cash transaction. Even though the transaction resulted in a material change in the asset and equity structure of the company, it will be disclosed in a note to the financial statements and will not be reported on the cash flow statement. Therefore, the effect of the increases of $22,000 both on long-term investments and on preferred shares are offset against each other on the worksheet, with no corresponding entry in the lower section:

Long-term investments   22,000
        Preferred shares   22,000

f. Old equipment was sold for $9,000; the original cost was $25,000. Since the income statement shows a gain of $4,000, the net book value at the time of sale must have been $5,000. (The gain is the amount by which the proceeds exceed the net book value; since the gain was $4,000 and the proceeds were $9,000, the net book value must have been $5,000.) Accumulated depreciation on the asset sold must therefore have been $20,000.

Proceeds from sale	$ 9,000	
Net book value of the asset sold:		
Historical cost	$25,000	
Accumulated depreciation	?	5,000
Gain on sale		$4,000

The entry for the sale is as follows:

Cash: sale of *investing activities,* equipment	9,000	
Accumulated depreciation	20,000	
Plant and equipment		25,000
Gain on sale (*Operations*)		4,000

g. Bonds with a face value of $20,000 were repurchased and retired (presumably at face value, since there is no gain or loss on the income statement).

Bonds payable	20,000	
Cash: bonds *financing activities,* retired		20,000

The only other piece of additional information in Exhibit 5-7 is that other operating expenses includes a loss of $2,000 on liquidation of short-term investments. The initial reaction may be to eliminate this by adding it back to Operations and to record $22,000 as an investing activity inflow. However, the catch here is that the loss relates to a component of cash. Since short-term liquid investments is a cash equivalent and included within our definition of cash, the loss really did cause cash and cash equivalents to decrease by $2,000. This amount is appropriately included in net income. Therefore, *there is no adjustment for gains and losses that are incurred within the cash and cash equivalent accounts,* including foreign currency exchange gains and losses.

h. The reconciliation entries that have been described above are those that result from the information provided in Exhibit 5-7. However, there obviously have been other transactions during the year that caused as-yet unexplained changes in the asset and equity accounts. An example is that of bonds payable. The bonds payable account grew from $133,000 to $146,000 during the year, a net increase of $13,000. However, to have a net increase of $13,000 after the $20,000 retirement, the company must have issued $33,000 in new bonds during the year:

Cash: bonds *financing activities,* issued	33,000	
Bonds payable		33,000

Reconciliations such as this one for the bond issuance sometimes are referred to as **hidden entries,** because they become apparent only as the result of reconciling those changes that are known beforehand. Once the known elements are entered, as above, the remaining reconciliation entries are all balancing entries that simply record the change in each account that is required to explain the net change, after taking into consideration the reconciliation entries already made. Starting with the first non-cash account, accounts receivable, they are as follows:

i.
Accounts receivable	14,000	
Cash: operations (*sales*)		14,000

j.
Inventories	12,000	
Cash: operations (*cost of goods sold*)		12,000

k.
Prepaid expenses	4,000	
Cash: operations (*operating expenses*)		4,000

l.
Plant and equipment	150,000	
Cash: *investing activities, purchase of equipment*		150,000

The net increase of $125,000 is explained by the retirement of equipment that originally cost $25,000.

EXHIBIT 5-8
ACCRUE CORPORATION
Cash Flow Statement Worksheet
year ended 31 December 20X2

	31 December 20X1	Key	Reconciliation Debit	Reconciliation Credit	Key	31 December 20X2
Assets:						
Cash	$ 36,000	(z)	$ 14,000			$ 50,000
Short-term liquid investments	34,000			$ 24,000	(z)	10,000
Accounts receivable	70,000	(i)	14,000			84,000
Inventories	30,000	(j)	12,000			42,000
Prepaid expenses	11,000	(k)	4,000			15,000
Land	50,000					50,000
Plant and equipment	615,000	(l)	150,000	25,000	(f)	740,000
Accumulated depreciation	(215,000)	(f)	20,000	65,000	(c)	(260,000)
Deferred development costs	76,000	(m)	11,000	5,000	(d)	82,000
Long-term investments	70,000	(e)	22,000			92,000
Total assets	$777,000					$905,000
Liabilities and shareholders' equity:						
Bank loan	$ 10,000			$ 20,000	(n)	$30,000
Accounts payable	45,000	(o)	9,000			36,000
Bonds payable	133,000	(g)	20,000	33,000	(h)	146,000
Future income taxes	24,000			3,000	(p)	27,000
Preferred shares	120,000			22,000	(e)	142,000
Common shares	180,000			50,000	(q)	230,000
Retained earnings	265,000	(b)	35,000	64,000	(a)	294,000
Total equities	$777,000		$311,000	$311,000		$905,000

Components of the Cash Flow Statement:

	Inflow — dr.	Outflows — cr.	Key	Totals
Operating activities:				
Revenue	(a) $ 964,000			
Gain on sale of equipment		$ 4,000	(f)	
Increase in accounts receivable		14,000	(i)	$946,000
Interest expense		18,000	(a)	(18,000)
Income tax expense		36,000	(a)	
Increase in future income taxes	(p) 3,000			(33,000)
Other operating expenses		846,000	(a)	
Depreciation expense	(c) 65,000			
Amortization of development costs	(d) 5,000			
Increase in inventory		12,000	(j)	
Increase in prepaid expenses		4,000	(k)	
Decrease in accounts payable		9,000	(o)	(801,000)
Investing activities:				
Proceeds from equipment sold	(f) 9,000			
Purchase of plant and equipment		150,000	(l)	
Development costs		11,000	(m)	(152,000)
Financing activities:				
Dividends paid		35,000	(b)	
Bonds retired		20,000	(g)	
Increase in short-term bank loan	(n) 20,000			
Bonds issued	(h) 33,000			
Common shares issued	(q) 50,000			48,000
	1,149,000	1,159,000		
Change in cash and cash equivalents:	(z) 10,000			$(10,000)
	$1,159,000	$1,159,000		

m. Deferred development costs   11,000

     Cash: investing activities, investment in development costs   11,000

Since the net account increase was $6,000 *after* amortization, costs of $11,000 must have been capitalized during the year.

n. *Cash: financing activities*, increase in bank loan   20,000

     Bank loan   20,000

o. Accounts payable   9,000

     Cash: operations (cost of goods sold)   9,000

p. *Cash: operations* (income tax expense)   3,000

     Future income taxes   3,000

The $3,000 increase in the balance sheet account for future income taxes represents the part of income tax expense that was *not* paid in cash. This will be discussed more fully in Chapter 16.

q. *Cash: financing activities,* common shares issued   50,000

     Common shares   50,000

Once we enter all of these reconciliation entries onto the worksheet, we can check for completeness by cross-adding (or cross-footing) each line to verify that the beginning balance plus the reconciliation equals the ending balance. Totalling the inflows and outflows in the lower section of the worksheet reveals that total cash inflows during the year were $249,000; total outflows equalled $259,000.

The final reconciliation is to transfer the change in cash and cash equivalents to the lower section. The $14,000 increase in cash and the $24,000 decrease in short-term investments are reconciled as follows:

r. Cash   14,000

   Change in cash and cash equivalents   10,000

     Short-term liquid investments   24,000

Entering the net change into the lower part of the statement balances the inflows and outflows. Totalling the debit and credit columns in the upper part of the worksheet reveals that they are in balance (at $311,000). The total of the debit and credit columns is meaningless *except* for the important fact that they balance. Any imbalance would indicate a debit-credit imbalance in the reconciliation entries.

The lower section of Exhibit 5-8 now contains all of the information that is necessary for preparing a cash flow statement. It is important to remember that Exhibit 5-8 is *not* a cash flow statement in itself; it is only a working paper. The cash flow statement, using the indirect preparation method, is illustrated in Exhibit 5-9.

The presentation of the cash flow from operations via the indirect method is a bit complicated due to the requirement for separately disclosing cash receipts and payments for interest, cash payments for income taxes, and cash receipts for dividends. The section begins with net income of $64,000, as reported on Accrue Corporation's income statement (Exhibit 5-7). Working from that net figure as the starting point, we must

- remove "non-operating" gains and losses;
- remove the items that should be separately reported, in order to derive the pre-tax operating earnings:
    1. investment income (i.e., interest and dividends received),
    2. income tax expense, and
    3. interest expense;

EXHIBIT 5-9
ACCRUE CORPORATION
Cash Flow Statement (*Indirect approach*)
year ended 31 December 20X2

Operating activities:

Net income (per income statement)	$ 64,000	
Plus (less) non-operating items:		
Gain on sale of equipment	(4,000)	
Interest expense	18,000	
Income tax expense	36,000	
Net operating income, before interest and income tax	114,000	
Plus (less) items not affecting cash:		
Depreciation on plant and equipment	65,000	
Amortization of development costs	5,000	
Operating cash flow before working capital changes	184,000	
Increase/decrease in other working capital items:		
Increase in accounts receivable	(14,000)	
increase in inventory	(12,000)	
Increase in prepaid expenses	(4,000)	
Decrease in accounts payable	(9,000)	
Cash from operations, before interest and taxes	145,000	
Interest paid	(18,000)	
Income taxes paid (net of $3,000 of future taxes)	(33,000)	$ 94,000

Investing activities:		
Acquisition of new plant and equipment	(150,000)	
Investment in development costs	(11,000)	
Proceeds from sale of equipment	9,000	(152,000)

Financing activities:		
Increase in short-term bank loan	20,000	
Issuance of bonds	33,000	
Retirement of bonds	(20,000)	
New common shares issued	50,000	
Dividends paid	$ (35,000)	48,000
Change in cash during 20X2		(10,000)

Reconciliation of cash and cash equivalents:		
Increase in cash		14,000
Decrease in short-term investments		(24,000)
		$ (10,000)

- eliminate the effects of interperiod allocations such as depreciation and amortization; and

- adjust for the changes in working capital amounts other than cash and cash equivalents.

The result of these adjustments is **pre-tax operating cash flow**. For Accrue Corporation, the cash generated from operations before income taxes is $145,000. Then the interest paid ($18,000) and income taxes paid ($33,000: $36,000 expense minus the $3,000 non-cash deferred tax) are deducted. If Accrue Corporation had received any interest or dividend income, these amounts would be added at this stage.

EXHIBIT 5-10
ACCRUE CORPORATION
Cash Flow Statement (Direct approach)
year ended 31 December 20X2

Operating activities:

Cash received from customers	$946,000	
Cash paid to suppliers and employees	(801,000)	
Cash from operations, before interest and taxes	145,000	
Interest paid	(18,000)	
Income taxes paid	(33,000)	$ 94,000

Investing activities:

Acquisition of new plant and equipment	(150,000)	
Investment in development costs	(11,000)	
Proceeds from sale of equipment	9,000	(152,000)

Financing activities:

Increase in short-term bank loan	20,000	
Issuance of bonds	33,000	
Retirement of bonds	(20,000)	
New common shares issued	50,000	
Dividends paid	(35,000)	48,000
Change in cash during 20X2		$(10,000)

Reconciliation of cash and cash equivalents:

Increase in cash		14,000
Decrease in short-term investments		(24,000)
		$(10,000)

Note that the cash flow for income taxes is adjusted for the amount of income tax expense that was credited to future tax liability (i.e., deferred income taxes). If the balance sheet showed any amount for income taxes payable at the beginning and/or end of the year, the income tax line would be adjusted to reflect the cash flow instead of the accrual-basis income tax. Similarly, if there was interest accrued but not paid, the entry for interest would be adjusted accordingly.

Direct Presentation Method

The requirement to separately disclose all interest, dividends and income tax receipts and payments does complicate the operations section if the indirect presentation method is used. The alternative (which is "encouraged" by the AcSB) is to use the direct method.

The cash flow amounts in the final column of the lower part of Exhibit 5-8 are used in the operations section of the cash flow statement. The direct presentation approach is illustrated in Exhibit 5-10. Note that the presentation is much simpler than the indirect approach of Exhibit 5-9 because it is not necessary to remove interest, dividends and taxes from the net income, only to put them back in again later. As well, the direct approach removes the necessity to list the potentially confusing additions and subtractions for the changes in working capital accounts. In order to derive the pre-tax cash flow from operations, we need to show only two lines, one for receipts from customers and another for payments to suppliers and employees. No more detail is needed in the cash flow statement.

After the pre-tax operating cash flow is reported, the interest and income taxes paid are deducted, to obtain the final cash flow from operations. Any dividends received or interest received would be added at that time as well.

Although the direct presentation approach requires some additional worksheet analysis to convert the accrual basis income statement amounts to the cash basis, the public presentation in the cash flow statement is considerably simpler and easier to understand than it is with the indirect presentation approach. The direct approach also avoids the confusion that surrounds the erroneous concept of "depreciation cash flow," as we discussed earlier. Hopefully, companies will move more towards the direct approach in their public financial statements now that the separate disclosure of interest, dividends, and income taxes is required.

Summary of Reconciling Adjustments

To prepare the cash flow statement, it is necessary to convert the accrual basis earnings to the cash basis and to trace other cash flows that caused changes in the asset and equity structure of the reporting enterprise. Basically, there are three types of adjustments that must be made to the accrual-basis accounts:

1. Accruals must be "backed out" of the monetary asset and liability accounts to determine the cash inflows and outflows for operations during the period.
2. The effects of interperiod allocations of costs and revenues must be reversed.
3. Certain transactions, the net effects of which are included in net income, must be reclassified as investing or financing activities.

Common items of all three types that usually are needed to convert from the accrual basis to cash flows include the following:

1. Adjustments must be made for changes in working capital accounts related to operations, such as accounts receivable, inventory, prepaid expenses, interest receivable, accounts payable, interest payable, income taxes payable, short-term payables to suppliers and others.

| | Change in Account Balance During the Year | |
	Increase	Decrease
Current asset	*Subtract* increase from net income	*Add* decrease to net income
Current liability	*Add* increase to net income	*Subtract* decrease from net income

Long-term payables to suppliers for inventory purchases and other operating activities and long-term receivables from customers are included in this type of adjustment.

The following working capital accounts are *excluded* from this category of adjustments because they are included in the definition of "cash":
- Cash
- Short-term investments considered to be cash equivalents
- Bank overdrafts

2. Interperiod allocations include both costs and revenues. Specific examples are as follows:

- Amortization of capital assets, including depreciation of plant, depletion of natural resources, and amortization of intangibles. These are added to net income because they do not cause cash to decrease. Net income is reduced by these expenses and thus understates operating cash flow, and so they must be added back.

- Allocations of costs associated with liability measurement, including deferred income taxes, amortization of bond discount and premium, and estimated liabilities associated with management decisions such as discontinued operations or operational restructuring.

- Write-downs of assets must be added back to net income because they do reflect a cash flow. Examples include write-downs of inventories (to lower of cost or market), investments, and losses from equity-method investments.

- Non-cash revenues, including investment revenue from equity-method investments, are subtracted from income because they do not cause cash to increase. Net income is increased by these revenues and thus overstates operating cash flow. Revenues received but deferred until the following period must be added to net income, and revenues received in a previous period but not recognized in income until the current period are deducted from net income because the cash was not received in the current period.

3. Gains and losses must be eliminated, and the related cash flows reclassified as financing or investing activities, depending on the nature of the transaction that gave rise to the gain or loss. Gains are subtracted from net income, and losses are added back to net income. Examples are gains and losses on disposals of capital assets, investments, and bond retirements. Related cash flows must be properly classified as investing or financing flows.

INTERNATIONAL PERSPECTIVE

Internationally, a trend toward cash flow reporting has developed, similar to the experience of Canada over the 1980s and 1990s. The revisions to Section 1540 brought Canada's recommended approach into line with that recommended by the International Accounting Standards Committee in IAS 7. The AcSB's change to Section 1540 was a move toward international harmonization, but it also was the final step toward a true cash flow statement instead of a broader and less focused reporting on balance sheet changes. Other countries have moved in this direction also, including the U.K., New Zealand, South Africa, Hong Kong, and the United States.

While the trend clearly is toward cash flow reporting, a variety of fund definitions continue to be found in international settings. Many countries have not followed IAS 7, at least not yet. In France, for example, the statement of changes in financial position is not required; when it is provided, it continues to use a working capital approach rather than a true cash approach. Funds flow statements of any kind are rare in Germany.

Despite the absence of a cash flow reporting requirement in most industrialized countries, those companies that are listed on stock exchanges outside of their home country may (except in the U.S. and Canada) report on the basis of international accounting standards. In that case, the companies will have to prepare and present a cash flow statement in accordance with the requirements of IAS 7.

CONCEPT REVIEW

1. What is the effect on the cash flow statement of selling a short-term investment, classified as a cash equivalent, at a $3,000 loss?
2. A company acquires a substantial amount of capital assets by issuing its own common shares to the seller. What is the impact of this transaction on the cash flow statement?
3. A retailer can choose two alternative accounting policies for new store start-up costs: (1) expense immediately or (2) capitalize and amortize. What effect does the decision to capitalize the cash flows for start-up costs have on the cash flow statement, compared to a policy of direct expensing of start-up costs?

SUMMARY OF KEY POINTS

1. The cash flow statement is one of the three major financial statements. It is structured to report cash flows in meaningful categories.

2. The basic objective of the cash flow statement is to reveal the cash inflows and outflows of the reporting period, segregated between cash flows from operating activities, cash flows related to investing activities, and cash flows relating to financing activities. In each category, *cash flows* includes both inflow and outflows.

3. Cash flow information is used to predict future cash flows and to assess liquidity, the ability of a firm to pay dividends and obligations, the ability of a firm to adapt to changes in the business environment, the quality of earnings, and for other purposes.

4. The reporting basis for the cash flow statement is the net cash position. The net cash position includes cash and cash equivalents, and also includes overdraft accounts.

5. *Cash equivalents* includes all short-term liquid investments that are readily convertible into cash and that bear little risk of change in value.

6. The components of cash and cash equivalents should be disclosed and should be reconciled to the balance sheet.

7. Operating flows are related to the main activities of the business and are connected to the earnings process.

8. Investing flows describe long-term asset acquisitions and the proceeds from sale of long-term assets. Interest and dividend income from investments must be disclosed separately. They may be reported either as a component of operations or as an investing activity.

9. Financing flows describe the sources of debt and equity financing and repayments of liabilities and equities, excluding liabilities directly relating to operations such as accounts payable. Interest paid on debt and included in net income is reported as a component of operations, but separate disclosure is required.

10. Dividend payments to shareholders are reported as a financing outflow, and must be disclosed.

11. Cash paid for income taxes should be disclosed as part of the operations section.

12. There are two allowable methods of reporting cash from operations — the direct and the indirect presentation methods. The direct method reports the cash inflows from the main classifications of revenues and cash outflows from the main classifications of expenses. In contrast, the indirect method reports operating activities by showing a reconciliation of net income before extraordinary items and discontinued operations with net cash flow from operating activities. Examples of adjustments are depreciation and changes in operating working capital accounts. The AcSB "encourages" companies to use the direct method.

13. The operating activity sections of both the direct and indirect cash flow statements convert accrual income to cash-basis income, the net cash flow from operations. The indirect method uses a series of add-backs to negate the effects of accruals and interperiod allocations, which can result in a confusing presentation.

14. In the investing and financing sections, gross cash flows are reported. Transactions are not netted against other flows in the same category.

15. Significant non-cash transactions (e.g., acquiring plant assets by issuing a long-term note) are not shown as outflows and inflows on the cash flow statement. However, they should be disclosed elsewhere in the financial statements, normally in a note.

16. There are many approaches to preparing the cash flow statement. The same objectives apply to all — analyze transactions to identify all cash flows, reconciling items, and non-cash transactions.

17. The format-free approach to preparing the cash flow statement emphasizes transaction analysis and uses no particular format. Search for transactions in the following order: income statement, additional information, and comparative balance sheets.

18. The spreadsheet approach is an organized format allowing substantiation of the preparation process and provides many accuracy checks.

19. The net cash flow is not affected by accounting policy choices or by management's accounting estimates. However, the reported cash flow from operations can be increased by capitalizing certain types of costs (e.g., development costs or start-up costs), because the costs are reclassified as investing activities and amortization has no effect on operating cash flows in future periods.

20. Securities legislation requires that a cash flow statement be included as one of public companies' quarterly reports to shareholders, along with interim income statements.

REVIEW PROBLEM

The Phillies Corporation assembled the following information relevant when preparing its 20X7 cash flow statement:

Balance sheet accounts, 31 December

	20X6	20X7
Cash	$ 50,000	$ 62,000
Temporary investments	150,000	—
Accounts receivable, net	60,000	80,000
Inventory	12,000	20,000
Prepaid expenses	6,000	10,000
Equipment, net of accumulated depreciation	300,000	500,000
Goodwill, net of accumulated amortization	90,000	70,000
Total assets	$668,000	$742,000
Accounts payable	$ 40,000	$ 60,000
Salaries payable	60,000	50,000
Interest payable	6,000	9,000
Income tax payable	12,000	22,000
Mortgage payable	120,000	110,000
Bonds payable	200,000	100,000
Premium on bonds payable	8,000	3,000
Common shares	150,000	170,000
Retained earnings	72,000	218,000
Total liabilities and shareholders' equity	$668,000	$742,000

Income statement accounts, year ended 31 December 20X7

Sales	$820,000
Cost of goods sold	380,000
Depreciation expense	100,000
Amortization of goodwill	20,000
Other expenses	46,000
Loss on bond retirement	3,000
Interest expense	22,000
Income tax expense	72,000
Extraordinary gain — excess of insurance proceeds over book value of equipment destroyed by fire, net of $1,000 income tax	9,000
Net income	$186,000

Additional information:
1. Phillies declared $40,000 in dividends in 20X7.
2. Equipment (cost $100,000, accumulated depreciation, $60,000) was destroyed by fire. Proceeds from insurance, $50,000. Applicable income taxes, $1,000 currently payable.
3. Bonds were retired on 1 January 20X7 at $107,000. The net book value of the bonds was $104,000: $100,000 at par value and $4,000 of premium.
4. The temporary investments are short-term money-market certificates.

Required:

Prepare the 20X7 cash flow statement for Phillies Corporation. Use the direct method of presentation for the operating activities section. Use whichever method of preparation you feel most comfortable with (i.e., choose from among the free-form, spreadsheet, or T-account (see appendix) methods). The suggested solution uses a worksheet.

REVIEW PROBLEM — SOLUTION

	31 December 20X6	Key	Reconciliation Debit	Reconciliation Credit	Key	31 December 20X7
Assets						
Cash & cash equivalents	$200,000			$138,000	q	$ 62,000
Accounts receivable, net	60,000	b	$ 20,000			80,000
Inventory	12,000	c	8,000			20,000
Prepaid expenses	6,000	g	4,000			10,000
Equipment, net	300,000	h	60,000	100,000	e	500,000
		n	340,000	100,000	h	
Goodwill, net	90,000			20,000	f	70,000
Total assets	$668,000					$742,000
Liabilities and equity						
Accounts payable	$ 40,000			20,000	d	$ 60,000
Salaries payable	60,000	g	10,000			50,000
Interest payable	6,000			3,000	i	9,000
Income tax payable	12,000			10,000	l	22,000
Mortgage payable	120,000	o	10,000			110,000
Bonds payable	200,000	j	100,000			100,000
Premium on bonds payable	8,000	j	4,000			3,000
		k	1,000			
Common shares	150,000			20,000	p	170,000
Retained earnings	72,000	m	40,000	177,000	a	
				9,000	h	218,000
Total liabilities and equity	$668,000					$742,000

COMPONENTS OF THE CASH FLOW STATEMENT:

		Inflows/ increases	Outflows/ decreases		Totals
Operating activities:					
Total revenues	a	820,000			
Increase in accounts receivable			20,000	b	800,000
Total operating expenses, excluding interest and income taxes			549,000	a	
Increase in accounts payable	c	20,000			
Increase in inventories			8,000	d	
Depreciation expense	e	100,000			
Amortization of goodwill	f	20,000			
Accrued and prepaid expenses			14,000	g	
Loss on bond retirement	j	3,000			(428,000)

Interest expense			22,000	**a**		
Interest accrued, but not paid	**i**	3,000				
Interest expense, premium amortization			1,000	**k**	(20,000)	
Income tax expense			72,000	**a**		
Increase in income tax payable	**l**	10,000			(62,000)	
Investing activities:						
Net insurance proceeds, equipment	**h**	49,000				
Purchase of equipment			340,000	**n**	(291,000)	
Financing activities:						
Retirement of bonds			107,000	**j**		
Dividends paid			40,000	**m**		
Mortgage principal payment			10,000	**o**		
Common shares issued	**p**	20,000			(137,000)	
		1,045,000				
Net decrease in cash and cash equivalents **q**		138,000	—		(138,000)	
		1,183,000	1,183,000			

Other approaches are equally valid — it's the result that matters. The actual cash flow statement is shown at the end of this solution. Explanations for worksheet entries are as follows:

a. Net operating income (i.e., before extraordinary gain), disaggregated to total revenues, operating expenses, interest expense, and income tax expense. The disaggregation is to facilitate the direct presentation approach. The extraordinary item is added directly to retained earnings, in *h*. The worksheet entry in *a* only deals with ordinary income statement items, which net to $177,000. In summary, the income statement is:

Total revenues		$820,000
Total operating expenses, before interest		
and taxes	$549,000	
Interest expense	22,000	
Income tax expense	72,000	
Total expenses		643,000
Net income from continuing operations		177,000
Extraordinary gain, net of tax		9,000
Net income		$186,000

b. Increase in accounts receivable; less cash received from customers than recognized as revenue.

c. Increase in inventories; more cash paid for inventories than recognized as cost of goods sold.

d. Increase in accounts payable; less paid to trade creditors than recognized as expenses.

e. Depreciation expense removed from operating expenses — a non-cash expense.

f. Goodwill amortization removed from operating expenses — another non-cash expense.

g. Prepaid expenses increased, requiring more cash, and salaries payable decrease, also requiring more cash.

h. Adjustment to write off destroyed equipment and to record the insurance proceeds; gain removed from operating earnings, and proceeds recorded as an inflow in the investing activities section. Proceeds of $50,000 are shown net of taxes paid, $1,000, on the cash flow statement ($49,000).

i. Increase in interest payable, indicating that less cash was paid for interest than the amount of interest expense accrued.

j. Entry to record the bond retirement on 1 January 20X7:

Bonds payable	100,000	
Bond premium (1/2 of $8,000 beginning balance)	4,000	
Loss on bond retirement	3,000	
Cash: financing activities, bond repayment (given)		107,000

k. Amortization of bond premium on those bonds *not* retired in 20X7: total reduction in bond premium account was from $8,000 to $3,000; bond retirement accounted for $4,000 of the reduction; remaining $1,000 must be due to amortization, which would have been charged to interest expense.

l. Increase in income taxes payable; less taxes paid than accrued.

m. Dividends declared *and paid* (i.e., there is no dividends payable account, so all must have been paid).

n. "Plug" entry to account for the otherwise unexplained change in the balance of the equipment account; the increase must have been due to the purchase of new equipment.

o. Decrease in mortgage payable implies repayment of mortgage, in the absence of other information.

p. Increase in common shares implies issuance of additional shares, in the absence of evidence to the contrary.

q. Net decrease in cash and cash equivalents:

Increase in cash account	$ 12,000
Decrease in temporary investment (cash equivalent)	(150,000)
Net decrease in cash and cash equivalents	$(138,000)

PHILLIES CORPORATION
Cash Flow Statement
year ended 31 December 20X7

Operating activities:

Cash received from customers	$800,000	
Cash paid for materials and services	(428,000)	
Cash provided by operations, before taxes	372,000	
Interest paid	(20,000)	
Income taxes paid	(62,000)	$290,000

Investing activities:

Insurance proceeds from equipment destroyed by fire	49,000	
New equipment purchased	(340,000)	(291,000)

Financing activities:

Retirement of bonds	(107,000)	
Dividends paid	(40,000)	
Reduction of mortgage principal	(10,000)	
Issuance of common shares	20,000	(137,000)

Net increase (decrease) in cash	$(138,000)

Reconciliation of cash and cash equivalents:

Cash	$ 12,000
Temporary investments	(150,000)
Net change	$(138,000)

APPENDIX
T-Account Method

The main body of the chapter pointed out that the analytical method used to derive the cash flow statement is not important; what matters is the result. This chapter has illustrated two approaches — the ad hoc approach and a spreadsheet approach. Another method that is popular, especially with students who may be struggling with the rigours of a spreadsheet approach, is to reconstruct the balance sheet T-accounts. In essence, the T-account approach puts the spreadsheet data and analysis into individual T-accounts rather than into columnar format.

The T-account method is somewhat more flexible and less formal than the spreadsheet method. The T-account approach is particularly efficient for shorter and less involved problems, or when there is no need to review or retain working papers. However, location of errors and review of the preparation process may be more difficult under the T-account approach.

The T-accounts used in this approach are not actual ledger accounts. Rather, they are workspaces in account format used to accumulate the information necessary to prepare the cash flow statement and to explain all account balance changes. The cash T-account accumulates all changes in cash (and cash equivalents) and is divided into three sections, corresponding to the three cash flow categories.

T-accounts may be set up using both the beginning and ending balances for all accounts, just as we did in the spreadsheet approach used in the chapter. Alternatively, only the net *change* in the account may be used. In the illustration to follow, we will use the beginning and ending balances, and we will illustrate the T-account method using the direct presentation approach to reporting operating cash flow.

T-Account Method: Simple Limited

To illustrate the T-account method, we will use the data for Simple Limited, Exhibit 5-2. The starting point is to sketch a simple T-account for each balance sheet account, including a single T-account for *cash and cash equivalents*. We will assume that Simple's short-term investments are cash equivalents, and therefore we will set up only one T-account for cash plus short-term investments. Leave lots of space in the cash T-account; remember that that's where all the information necessary for preparing the cash flow statement will be accumulated.

The second step is to insert the beginning balance of each account at the top, and the ending balance at the bottom. Don't forget to check your transcribed balances, to make sure that the balance sheet accounts all balance after you set up the T-accounts.

The third step is to make entries directly in the T-accounts to duplicate (in summary form, of course) the entries that were made during the year, including those made to cash. As always, it is essential to *key* the entries, so that we can tell which debits belong with which credits, especially if we get something wrong and have to go back and re-evaluate what we've done. In more complex situations, it also helps to keep a side record of what each entry means, although it's not necessary.

Exhibit 5-11 shows the balance sheet T-accounts for Simple Limited. The beginning and ending balances are shown in bold-face type, to set them apart from the intervening entries. Remember that the beginning and ending balances (or, alternatively, just the net change) is the starting point for the analysis. Bear in mind that all revenues and expenses are summarized in the net income figure, which is part of the retained earnings account. Therefore, we don't need to set up T-accounts for the income statement accounts.

To begin, we should start with the statement of income and retained earnings, and with the additional information. After recording the relevant information from these sources, we then can make entries to explain the remaining changes in the balance sheet account balances.

EXHIBIT 5-11
T-Accounts for Simple Limited

Cash (including Short-Term Investments)

Beginning balance	90		

Operating activities:
Cash received from customers
a. sales revenue	2,000		
f. decrease in accounts receivable	15		

Cash paid for operating costs
		b. CGS and other expenses	1,740
e. depreciation expense	200	h. increase in accounts payable	25
g. decrease in inventory	35		

Investing activities:
c. proceeds from sale of equipment	130	i. purchase of plant and equipment	410

Financing activities:
j. increase in bank loan	15	d. dividends paid	225
		k. reduction in long-term note payable	30

Ending balance	55		

Accounts Receivable

Beginning balance	125		
		f. net customer collections	15
Ending balance	110		

Inventory

Beginning balance	135		
		g. inventory decreased	35
Ending balance	100		

Plant and Equipment

Beginning balance	1,000		
i. assets acquired	410	c. cost of equipment sold	310
Ending balance	1,100		

EXHIBIT 5-11 (cont'd)
T-Accounts for Simple Limited

Accumulated Depreciation

		Beginning balance	**300**
c. accumulated depreciation on assets sold	250	e. depreciation expense	200
		Ending balance	**250**

Bank Loan

		Beginning balance	**50**
		j. additional bank loan	15
		Ending balance	**65**

Accounts Payable

		Beginning balance	**125**
h. payments to suppliers	25		
		Ending balance	**100**

Long-Term Note Payable

		Beginning balance	**330**
k. partial payment on note payable	30		
		Ending balance	**300**

Common Shares

		Beginning balance	**100**
		Ending balance	**100**

Retained Earnings

		Beginning balance	**445**
b. operating expenses	1,740	a. sales revenue	2,000
d. dividends paid	225	c. gain on sale of equipment	70
		Ending balance	**550**

The income statement shows sales revenue of $2,000. Sales and expenses are part of net income and change retained earnings. The total revenues, $2,000, are entended as inflows in the summary cash account and as increases to be retained earnings (a). The gain of sale of equipment is dealt with seperately in (c). Note that the summary cash T-account is organized by category.

The second posting (b) is for cost of goods sold and other expenses, which represents a cash outflow (or will, once we adjust for depreciation and for changes in inventory and accounts payable).

Posting (c) is to record the transaction for the sale of equipment:

Cash — investing activities	130	
Accumulated depreciation	250	
Plant and equipment		310
Retained earnings — gain on sale of equipment		70

The gain does not appear on the cash flow statement.

Posting (d) recognizes the dividends paid. The credit is to the financing activities section of the cash account.

Depreciation expense is eliminated by posting (e), which reduces the expenses (in cash — operating activities) for this non-cash expense.

Postings (f) through (h) adjust the operating cash flow for the changes in working capital accounts. The change in accounts receivable (f) is an adjustment to the amount of cash collected from customers, while the changes in inventory (g) and accounts payable (h) affect the cash paid for operating costs.

The remaining postings reconcile the balance sheet accounts by recognizing either investing (i) or financing activities (j) and (k).

Once all of the accounts have been reconciled, the cash flow statement can be prepared by using the information that has been summarized in the cash T-account. The cash flow statement is shown in Exhibit 5-12, using the direct method of presenting operating cash flows.

EXHIBIT 5-12
SIMPLE LIMITED
Cash Flow Statement
year ended 31 December 20X2

Operating activities		
Cash received from customers	$2,015	
Cash paid for goods and services	1,530	$ 485
Investing activities		
Proceeds from sale of equipment	130	
Purchase of new equipment	(410)	(280)
Financing activities		
Increase in current bank loan	15	
Dividends paid	(225)	
Reduction of long-term note payable	(30)	(240)
Increase (decrease) in cash and cash equivalents		$ (35)
Cash and cash equivalents, 1 January 20X2		90
Cash and cash equivalents, 31 December 20X2		$ 55

SUMMARY OF KEY POINTS

1. The T-account method is an alternative way to analyze information prior to actually preparing the cash flow statement. The T-account method is an analytical approach; it is *not* a method of presentation.

2. A T-account for *cash* (and *cash equivalents*) is used to accumulate all of the information needed to prepare the cash flow statement.

3. The T-account method may be convenient for relatively small companies with limited numbers of accounts and few complex transactions.

4. It is more difficult to find errors when the T-account method is used, because the debits and credits are not as easily footed and checked, compared to a spreadsheet approach.

QUESTIONS

5-1   Compare the purposes of the balance sheet, income statement, and cash flow statement (CFS).

5-2   During the year, a company records $100,000 in cash sales and $160,000 in credit sales, of which $40,000 was collected from customers. Also during the year, $80,000 was collected from last year's credit sales. Use this data to explain the difference between the accrual and cash basis. Which is reflected on the CFS?

5-3   A company pays $80,000 cash for a piece of machinery. On the date of acquisition, is the expenditure an expense? A cash disbursement? Will it become an expense?

5-4   Explain the basic difference between the three activities reported on the CFS: operating, investing, and financing.

5-5   List three major cash inflows and three major cash outflows properly classified under (a) operating activities, (b) investing activities, and (c) financing activities.

5-6   How is cash defined for CFS purposes? Why is disclosure of the definition so important?

5-7   What is the classification problem in assigning interest expense on the CFS?

5-8   Where are dividends paid classified on the CFS?

5-9   Explain the difference between the direct and indirect preparation approaches to compiling data for the CFS.

5-10   Assume that a company reported net income of $5,000, which included sales revenue of $100,000; the balance sheet shows an increase in accounts receivable of $10,000. What will the operations section of the CFS include, assuming that the indirect presentation approach is used?

5-11   During the year, a capital asset with an original cost of $750,000, and accumulated amortization on the date of sale of $560,000 was sold for $216,000. What will appear on the CFS as a result of this transaction? Assume the indirect presentation approach.

5-12   Explain why cash paid during the period for purchases and salaries is not specifically reported on the CFS as a cash outflow if the indirect presentation approach is used for operating activities.

5-13   Explain why a $50,000 increase in inventory during the year must be considered when developing disclosures for operating activities on the CFS.

5-14   Explain why an adjustment must be made for depreciation to compute cash flow from operating activities if the indirect presentation approach is used.

5-15   Foley Corporation's records showed the following: Net income, $60,000; increase in accounts payable, $15,000; decrease in inventory, $20,000. What items would appear in the operations section of the CFS if the indirect presentation approach is used?

5-16   During 20X5, FRM Company recorded a decrease of $12,000 in the unearned revenue account, and a net increase of $50,000 in accounts receivable. Sales were $500,000. How much cash was collected from customers?

5-17   Why would the gain on sale of temporary investments classified as cash equivalents not be reflected on a CFS prepared using the indirect method?

5-18   Explain the difference between the direct and indirect presentation approaches to the operations section of the CFS. Use the following data to illustrate the difference: a company reports $116,000 of net income, which includes sales of $750,000. During the year, accounts receivable increased by $47,000.

5-19   Why might the direct method of disclosing cash flows from operations be preferable to the indirect method? Which one dominates current practice?

5-20   Why does the requirement to separately disclose cash receipts/payments related to investment income, interest expense and tax expense complicate the presentation of operations when the indirect presentation approach is used?

5-21   Describe the two-step method to disclose cash flow from operations using the indirect method.

5-22   Explain offsetting. Is it ever allowable to offset cash flows in the CFS?

5-23   Give three examples of significant non-cash transactions. Are these items included in the CFS?

5-24   Explain three types of reconciling items used to adjust from net income to cash flow from operating activities using the indirect method.

CASES

CASE 5-1

National Jeans Depot Inc.

"Y'know, Joe, every time I look at one of these Cash Flow Statements, it raises more questions than it answers! I've got some money to invest in the stock market right now, and I'm thinking about buying shares in a retail chain of casual clothing stores, called National Jeans Depot Ltd. But look at their Cash Flow Statement! I know you've been studying accounting, so maybe you can explain a few things to me.

First, what major policy decisions does a company have to make in determining groupings and presentation on this statement? I'd like a general answer to that question, so I know what to look for in other companies' financial statements, but I'd also like you to be specific in relation to National Jeans Depot.

Second, what would you conclude about National Jeans Depot as a result of the information in the Cash Flow Statement? In other words, are there any strategic decisions or trends apparent?

Thanks Joe, I knew I could count on you!"

Required:

Adopt the role of Joe and respond to the request.

NATIONAL JEANS DEPOT LTD.
Cash Flow Statement

	Year ended 31 December	
	20X4	**20X3**
Cash provided by (used in) operating activities:		
Net income	$ 620,784	$ 696,753
Add (deduct) items not involving a current cash flow		
Depreciation	315,542	362,281
Future income taxes	86,000	65,000
Net increase in non-cash working capital balances	(3,642,864)	(479,230)
Cash provided by (used in) operating activities	(2,620,538)	644,804
Cash provided by (used in) investing activities:		
Purchase of fixed assets	(1,343,283)	(1,010,601)
Related investment tax credits	404,015	322,008
Purchase of investment	(10,000)	—
Cash (used in) investing activities	(949,268)	(688,593)
Cash provided by (used in) financing activities:		
Increase (reduction) in long-term debt	440,000	(60,000)
Payment of dividends	(196,000)	(212,667)
Cash provided by (used in) financing activities .	244,000	(272,667)
(Decrease) in cash during the year	(3,325,806)	(316,456)
Bank lines of credit at beginning of year	1,861,341	1,544,885
Bank lines of credit at end of year	$ 5,187,147	$ 1,861,341
Changes in non-cash working capital balances comprise the following:		
Cash provided by (used in)		
(Increase) in accounts receivable	$(2,093,157)	$(1,474,328)
(Increase) in income taxes recoverable	(94,854)	—
(Increase) decrease in inventories	(1,165,065)	623,095
(Increase) in prepaid expenses	(158,300)	(21,525)
Increase in accounts payable	76,492	198,696
Increase (decrease) in income taxes payable . .	(207,980)	194,832
Net cash (used)	$(3,642,864)	$ (479,230)

CASE 5-2

Honore Company

Honore Company has competed for many years in product lines that have recently experienced a great increase in global competition. These products have long been dominated by Canadian firms. Honore has no foreign operations and few personnel with experience in international trade. Honore has made few product changes in recent years and is not actively engaged in product innovation or research and development.

The following information is selected from the company's financial statements and notes for the period 20X2 to 20X4 (in $ thousands):

	20X2	20X3	20X4
Net income	$50,000	$30,000	$10,000
Net accounts receivable (ending)	40,000	12,000	6,000
Inventory (ending)	19,000	14,000	7,000
Net cash inflow from operations	15,000	7,000	4,500
Capital expenditures	9,000	7,000	6,000
Proceeds from sale of plant assets	15,000	10,000	18,000
Net gain on sale of plant assets	6,000	8,000	12,000

The company
- Recently negotiated with banks to extend payment terms on short-term loans.
- Has maintained very low levels of accounts payable during this period.
- Has significant investments in corporate bonds (interest revenue on bonds in 20X5 was $3,000).
- Paid no dividends during this period.
- Issued no shares or long-term debt during this period.

You have been asked to provide an interpretation of the CFS in light of Honore's situation.

HONORE COMPANY
Cash Flow Statement
For the year ended 31 December 20X5
($ thousands)

Cash flows from operating activities:		
Net income	$7,000	
Items reconciling net income and net cash inflow from operating activities:		
Accounts receivable decrease	1,000	
Inventory decrease	1,500	
Dividends received (equity investment)	6,000	
Investment revenue (equity investment)	(10,000)	
Gain on sale of plant assets	(6,000)	
Depreciation, amortization	4,000	
Net cash inflow from operating activities		$ 3,500
Cash flows from investing activities:		
Purchase of plant assets	(4,000)	
Proceeds from sale of plant assets	45,000	
Purchase of corporate bonds	(5,000)	
Purchase of corporate shares	(10,000)	
Net cash inflow from investing activities		26,000
Cash flows for financing activities:		
Principal payments on short-term notes to financial institutions	(15,000)	
Retirement of common shares	(6,000)	
Net cash outflow for financing activities		(21,000)
Net cash increase		8,500
Beginning cash balance		12,000
Ending cash balance		$20,500

CASE 5-3

Compuco Ltd.

You, Sandy Fortunado, have just started work with a firm of public accountants. You've been given a partially completed set of financial statements for a client, Compuco Ltd. You have been asked to prepare a cash flow statement for Compuco Ltd., using the balance sheet provided in Exhibit I, the statement of income and retained earnings provided in Exhibit II, and the selected notes provided in Exhibit III. Use indirect disclosure for the operating activities section. (Include separate disclosure of cash paid/received re: interest and tax in the operations section.)

Based on your cash flow statement, you've also been asked to draft some notes on the strategic operating, financing and investing strategies of the company that are apparent from the CFS.

Required:

Respond to the request. [CICA, adapted]

EXHIBIT I
COMPUCO LTD.
Extracts from Consolidated Balance Sheet
as at 31 December
(in $ thousands)

Assets

Current	20X5	20X4
Cash and term deposits	$ 3,265	$ 3,739
Accounts receivable	23,744	18,399
Inventories	26,083	21,561
Income taxes recoverable	145	—
Prepaid expenses	1,402	1,613
	54,639	45,312
Investments (Note 1)	5,960	6,962
Capital assets (Note 2)	37,332	45,700
Future (deferred) income taxes	4,875	2,245
Goodwill	—	12,737
Development costs (Note 3)	4,391	1,911
	$107,197	$114,867

Liabilities

Current	20X5	20X4
Bank overdraft	$ 6,844	$ 6,280
Accounts payable	3,243	4,712
Current portion of long-term debt	1,800	1,200
	11,887	12,192
Long-term debt (Note 4)	14,900	14,500

Shareholders' Equity

	20X5	20X4
Share capital (Note 5)	79,257	62,965
Retained earnings	1,153	25,210
	80,410	88,175
	$107,197	$114,867

EXHIBIT II
COMPUCO LTD.
Extracts from the Consolidated
Statement of Income and Retained Earnings
for the years ended 31 December
(in $ thousands)

	20X5	20X4
Revenue		
Operating	$ 89,821	$68,820
Interest and other	1,310	446
	91,131	69,266
Expenses		
Operating	76,766	62,355
General and administrative	13,039	12,482
Amortization	10,220	11,709
Goodwill write-off	12,737	—
Interest	1,289	1,521
Loss on sale of capital assets	394	—
	114,445	88,067
Loss before equity loss and income taxes	(23,314)	(18,801)
Write-down of investments to market value (Note 1)	(2,518)	—
Loss before income taxes	(25,832)	(18,801)
Income taxes	2,775	5,161
Net loss	(23,057)	(13,640)
Retained earnings, beginning of year	25,210	38,850
	2,153	25,210
Stock dividend	(1,000)	—
Retained earnings, end of year	$ 1,153	$25,210

EXHIBIT III
COMPUCO LTD.
Extracts from Selected Notes
to Financial Statements
for the year ended 31 December
(in $ thousands)

1. Investments

The company's investments at 31 December are as follows:

	20X5	20X4
	($ thousands)	
XYZ Inc.Shares	$5,962	$5,962
Write-down to market value	(2,518)	—
	3,444	5,962
Other investments	2,516	1,000
	$5,960	$6,962

2. Capital assets

Additions to capital assets for the current year amounted to $2.29 million and proceeds from the disposal of capital assets amounted to $250.

3. Development costs

Development costs for a product are amortized once the product is ready for market. The rate depends on the expected life of the product. In 20X5, $206 of amortization was expensed.

4. Long-term debt

	20X5	20X4
	($ thousands)	
Debentures	$12,500	$12,500
Bank term loans, due 31 December 20X12; Principal repayable $150,000 a month (20X4, $100,000 a month)	4,200	3,200
	16,700	15,700
Current maturities	(1,800)	(1,200)
	$14,900	$14,500

Debentures bear interest at 12% per annum and are due in 20X8. Bank term loans bear interest at 8% and the bank advanced $2.2 million during the year.

5. Share capital

On 14 May 20X5, Compuco Ltd. issued 3.8 million shares. Net proceeds amounted to $15.292 million.

On 31 December 20X5, a stock dividend of $1 million was issued.

E5-1 *Cash Flow Analysis of Sales:* The records of HMC Company showed sales revenue of $100,000 on the income statement and a change in the balance of accounts receivable and unearned revenue. To demonstrate the effect of changes on cash, five independent cases are used. Complete the following tabulation for each independent case:

Case	Sales Revenue	Accounts Receivable Increase (Decrease)	Unearned Revenue** Increase (Decrease)	Cash Flow Amount*
A	$100,000	$ 0	$ 0	
B	100,000	10,000	0	
C	100,000	(10,000)	0	
D	100,000	9,000	5,000	
E	100,000	(9,000)	(5,000)	

* Amount of cash collected from customers
** Cash received but unearned

E5-2 *Cash Flow Analysis of Cost of Goods Sold:* The records of Atlas Company showed cost of goods sold on the income statement of $60,000 and a change in the inventory and accounts payable balances. To demonstrate the effect of these changes on cash outflow for cost of goods sold (i.e., payments to suppliers), five independent cases are used. Complete the following tabulation for each case:

Case	Cost of Goods Sold	Inventory Increase (Decrease)	Accounts Payable Increase (Decrease)	Cash Outflow Amount*
A	$60,000	$(1,000)	$ 0	
B	60,000	1,000	2,000	
C	60,000	(6,000)	(2,000)	
D	60,000	6,000	(4,000)	
E	60,000	4,000	4,000	

* This is the amount of cash paid during the current period for past and current purchases.

E5-3 *CFS — Item Analysis:* The records of Easie Company provided the following data:

a. Sales revenue, $190,000; accounts receivable decreased, $10,000.

b. Cost of goods sold, $84,000; inventory decreased, $6,000; accounts payable, no change.

c. Wages expense, $32,000; wages payable decreased, $3,000.

d. Depreciation expense, $8,000.

e. Purchased productive asset for $36,000; paid one-third down and gave a two-year, interest-bearing note for the balance.

f. Borrowed $40,000 cash on a note payable.

g. Sold an old operational asset for $6,000 cash; original cost, $20,000, accumulated depreciation, $18,000.

h.   Paid a $5,000 note payable (principal).

i.   Paid a cash dividend, $8,000.

Required:

For each of the above items give

1.   its CFS activity (operating, investing, financing).

2.   the item that would appear on the CFS (indirect presentation method for operating activities).

3.   the item that would appear on the CFS (direct presentation method for operating activities).

E5-4 *Transaction Analysis, Indirect Method:* You are requested by the controller of a large company to determine the appropriate disclosure of the following transactions in the CFS. Assume all adjusting entries have been recorded.

a.   Accounts receivable increased $50,000 during the year.

b.   Pension expense is $50,000; the balance of accrued pension cost liability increased $12,000.

c.   Future (deferred) income tax (cr. balance, long-term) increased $40,000; income tax payable decreased $10,000.

d.   Interest of $10,000 was capitalizedto a building under construction, now completed and in use. There is no change in interest payable.

e.   The company sold short-term investments (cash equivalents) at a $2,000 gain; proceeds, $8,000.

f.   The company sold short-term investments (not cash equivalents) at a $4,000 loss; proceeds, $4,000.

Required:

Indicate the complete disclosure of each item in the CFS under the indirect method of presentation for operating activities.

E5-5 *Cash Flow Statement Classification:* The main parts of a cash flow statement are shown below with letter identification. Next, several transactions are given. Match the transactions with the CFS statement parts by entering a letter in each blank space. Assume loans and notes receivable are long-term investments not related to operating activities. State other assumptions or explanations if needed.

Cash flow statement:

A.   Cash inflows (outflows) from operating activities (indirect method of presentation)

B.   Cash inflows (outflows) from investing activities

C.   Cash inflows (outflows) from financing activities

D.   Not a cash flow

Transactions:

_____   1.   Acquisition of operational assets; paid cash

_____   2.   Cash dividends declared but not paid

_____   3.   Proceeds from note payable

_____   4.   Sale of operational assets

_____   5.   Issue a loan (loan receivable)

_____   6.   Purchase of a long-term security as an investment

223

_____ 7. Collections on notes receivable (principal only)

_____ 8. Change in inventory

_____ 9. Depreciation expense

_____10. Payment of debt, 60% cash and 40% common shares issued

_____11. Issuance of the company's common shares, for cash

_____12. Sales revenue, cash

_____13. Repurchase and retirement of common shares.

_____14. Payment on notes payable

_____15. Paid cash dividend

E5-6 *Prepare a Cash Flow Statement:* The records of Rangler Paper Company provided the selected data given below for the reporting period ended 31 December 20X5.

Balance sheet data

Paid cash dividend	$ 10,000
Established restricted construction cash fund (a long-term investment) to build a new building at 8% interest	60,000
Increased inventory of merchandise	14,000
Borrowed on a long-term note	25,000
Acquired five acres of land for a future site for the company; paid in full by issuing 3,000 shares of Rangler common shares, no-par, when the quoted market price per share was $15	45,000
Increase in prepaid expenses	3,000
Decrease in accounts receivable	7,000
Payment of bonds payable in full at book value	97,000
Increase in accounts payable	5,000
Cash from disposal of old operational assets (sold at book value)	12,000
Decrease in rent receivable	2,000

Income statement

Sales revenue	$400,000
Rent revenue	10,000
Cost of goods sold	(190,000)
Depreciation expense	(20,000)
Remaining expenses	(97,000)
Net income	$103,000

Required:

Prepare a cash flow statement (in $ thousands). Use the indirect method for operations. Assume a beginning cash balance of $62,000.

E5-7 *Cash Flow Categories — Transaction Analysis:* Denton Corporation's balance sheet accounts as of 31 December 20X4 and 20X5, and information relating to 20X5 activities, are presented below.

	31 December	
	20X5	**20X4**
Assets		
Cash	$ 230,000	$ 100,000
Short-term investments	300,000	—
Accounts receivable	510,000	510,000

Inventory	680,000	600,000
Long-term investments	200,000	300,000
Plant assets	1,700,000	1,000,000
Accumulated depreciation	(450,000)	(450,000)
Goodwill	90,000	100,000
Total assets	$3,260,000	$2,160,000
Liabilities and Shareholders' Equity		
Accounts payable and accrued liabilities	$ 825,000	$ 720,000
Short-term bank debt	325,000	—
Common shares, no-par	1,170,000	950,000
Retained earnings	940,000	490,000
Total liabilities and shareholders' equity	$3,260,000	$2,160,000

Information relating to 20X5 activities:
- Net income for 20X5 was $690,000.
- Cash dividends of $240,000 were declared and paid in 20X5.
- Equipment costing $400,000 and having a carrying amount of $150,000 was sold for $150,000.
- A long-term investment was sold for $135,000. There were no other transactions affecting long-term investments in the year.
- Ten thousand common shares were issued for $22 per share.
- Short-term investments consist of treasury bills maturing on 15 February 20X6.

Required:
Determine the following amounts for Denton for the year 20X5:
1. Net cash from operating activities (indirect method)
2. Net cash from investing activities
3. Net cash from financing activities

[AICPA adapted]

E5-8 *Cash Flow Statement; Indirect Method:* The following data were provided by the accounting records of Smores Company at year-end, 31 December 20X1:

Income Statement

Sales	$140,000
Cost of goods sold	(84,000)
Depreciation expense	(10,000)
Remaining expenses	(36,000)
Loss on sale of operational assets	(2,000)
Gain on sale of investments	6,000
Net income	$ 14,000

Comparative Balance Sheet
31 December

	20X1	20X0
Debits		
Cash	$ 90,000	$ 68,000
Accounts receivable	34,000	24,000
Inventory	28,000	32,000
Long-term investments	—	12,000
Operational assets	196,000	160,000
Total debits	$348,000	$296,000

Credits

Accumulated depreciation	$ 78,000	$ 96,000
Accounts payable	24,000	38,000
Bonds payable	60,000	20,000
Common shares, no-par	130,000	100,000
Retained earnings	56,000	42,000
Total credits	$348,000	$296,000

Analysis of selected accounts and transactions:

a. Sold operational assets for $12,000 cash; cost, $42,000; two-thirds depreciated.
b. Purchased operational assets for cash, $18,000.
c. Purchased operational assets and exchanged unissued bonds payable of $60,000 in payment.
d. Sold the long-term investments for $18,000 cash.
e. Retired bonds payable at maturity date by issuing common shares, $20,000.
f. Sold unissued common shares for cash, $10,000.

Required:

Prepare the cash flow statement. Use the two-step *indirect* method to present the operations section.

E5-9 *Cash Flow Statement; Direct Method:* Repeat E5-8, operations section, using the *direct* method to disclose the operations section.

E5-10 *Prepare a Cash Flow Statement:* The accounting records of Pall-Mall Company provided the following data:

Income Statement for year ended
31 December 20X1

Sales	$300,000
Cost of goods sold	(180,000)
Depreciation expense	(4,000)
Remaining expenses	(64,000)
Net income	$ 52,000

Comparative Balance Sheets
as at 31 December

Debits	20X1	20X0
Cash	$ 34,000	$ —
Accounts receivable	18,000	19,000
Inventory	25,000	20,000
Investment, long-term	—	3,000
Operational assets	93,000	60,000
Total debits	$170,000	$102,000

Credits		
Bank overdraft	$ —	$ 5,000
Accumulated depreciation	14,000	10,000
Accounts payable	12,000	6,000
Short-term bank loan	4,000	3,000
Notes payable, long-term	36,000	20,000
Common shares, no-par	80,000	50,000
Retained earnings	24,000	8,000
Total credits	$170,000	$102,000

Analysis of selected accounts and transactions:

a. Sold the long-term investment at cost, for cash.
b. Declared and paid a cash dividend of $36,000.
c. Purchased operational assets that cost $33,000; gave a $24,000 long-term note payable and paid $9,000 cash.
d. Paid an $8,000 long-term note payable by issuing common shares; market value, $8,000.
e. Sold common shares for cash.

Required:

Prepare the cash flow statement, using the two-step *indirect* method of presentation for the operations section.

E5-11 *Prepare a Cash Flow Statement; Direct Method:* Repeat E5-10, using the *direct* method to disclose the operations section.

E5-12 *CFS, Operations Section:* The data given below were provided from the accounting records of Darby Company. Prepare the operations section of the CFS using the indirect method. Include separate disclosure of cash flows related to investment income, interest expense and tax expense, if any.

Net income (accrual basis) $80,000, including interest expense of $14,000 and tax expense of $54,000
Depreciation expense, $16,000
Increase in interest payable, $2,400
Increase in trade accounts receivable, $3,600
Decrease in merchandise inventory, $5,000
Amortization of patent, $200
Increase in long-term liabilities, $20,000
Sale of common shares for cash, $50,000
Accounts payable increase, $8,000
Increase in future (deferred) income tax liability $4,000

E5-13 *CFS, Operations Section:* The data given below were provided from the accounting records of Sileo Company. Prepare the operations section of the CFS using the *indirect* method. Include separate disclosure of cash flows related to investment income, interest expense and tax expense, if any.

Net loss (accrual basis), $50,000, including interest expense of $20,000 and a tax recovery of ($16,000)
Depreciation expense, $6,000
Decrease in wages payable, $1,000
Decrease in trade accounts receivable, $1,800
Increase in merchandise inventory, $2,300
Amortization of patent, $200
Increase in long-term liabilities, $10,000
Sale of common shares for cash, $25,000
Decrease in interest payable, $1,000
Increase in tax refund receivable, $16,000

E5-14 *CFS, Indirect Method — Individual Transactions:* For each of the following independent transactions for Morrison Corporation, discuss how the transaction would be disclosed and classified in the 20X5 CFS, *indirect* method.

a. On 31 July 20X5, the corporation issued 1,000 common shares in exchange for a $100,000 debenture issued by Morrison Corporation five years ago.

b. On 31 December 20X5, the corporation sold a piece of machinery with an original cost of $239,000, and accumulated depreciation of $164,000, for $110,000. The resulting gain of $35,000 was recorded on the income statement.

c. On 30 June 20X5, Morrison sold short-term investments with a net book value of $46,000, for $52,000. The resulting gain was recorded on the income statement.

d. On 31 October 20X5, the corporation paid a $50,000 income tax reassessment relating to the 20X1 fiscal period.

e. On 31 December 20X5, Morrison Corporation had inventory levels that were $20,000 higher than the previous year.

E5-15 *CFS, Direct Method — Optional Spreadsheet:* Hubley Corp. reported the following on its 20X4 income statement:

HUBLEY CORP.
Income Statement
for the year ended 31 December 20X4

Sales	$208,000
Cost of goods sold	(110,000)
Depreciation expense	(16,000)
Patent amortization	(600)
Remaining expenses	(35,400)
Net income	$ 46,000

HUBLEY CORP.
Balance Sheet
as of 31 December

	20X4	20X3
Cash	$ 43,000	$ 30,000
Investments, short-term	6,000	—
Accounts receivable	42,000	34,000
Inventory	30,000	20,000
Investments, long-term	20,000	—
Property, plant, and equipment (net)	118,000	120,000
Patent (net)	5,400	6,000
Other assets	14,000	14,000
Total	$278,400	$224,000
Accounts payable	44,000	24,000
Accrued expenses payable	17,400	—
Bonds payable	40,000	80,000
Common shares, no-par	89,000	70,000
Retained earnings	88,000	50,000
Total	$278,400	$224,000

Analysis of accounts:

a. Retired bonds, paid $40,000 cash.

b. Bought long-term investment, $20,000 cash.

c. Purchased operational asset, $14,000 cash.

d. Purchased short-term investment, $6,000 cash.

e. Paid cash dividend, $8,000.

f. Issued common shares, 1,000 shares at $19 cash per share.

Required:

Prepare the CFS, *direct* method. The solution to this exercise features an optional spreadsheet. The short-term investment is not considered to be a cash equivalent.

E5-16 *CFS, Direct Method — Optional Spreadsheet:* Shown below are the income statement, comparative balance sheets, and additional information useful in preparing the 20X5 CFS for Sells Company.

**Income Statement
for year ended 31 December 20X5**

Net sales	$300,000
Cost of goods sold	80,000
Gross margin	220,000
Depreciation expense	45,000
Amortization of intangibles	2,000
Other expenses	44,000
Interest expense	3,000
Income tax expense	65,000
Net income	$ 61,000

**Comparative Balance Sheets
as of 31 December**

	20X5	20X4
Cash	$ 32,000	$ 16,000
Accounts receivable	47,000	50,000
Other receivables	2,000	3,000
Inventory	32,000	30,000
Equipment	77,000	80,000
Accumulated depreciation	(5,000)	(6,000)
Intangibles, net	53,000	55,000
Total assets	$238,000	$228,000
Accounts payable	60,000	50,000
Income taxes payable	50,000	70,000
Interest payable	1,000	2,000
Bonds payable	—	32,000
Discount on bonds payable	—	(2,000)
Common shares, no-par	80,000	70,000
Retained earnings	47,000	6,000
Total liabilities and owners' equity	$238,000	$228,000

Additional information:

a. Dividends of $20,000 were declared and paid in 20X5.

b. Equipment costing $66,000 with a book value of $20,000 was sold at book value. New equipment was also purchased; common shares were issued in partial payment.

c. The bonds were retired at net book value; $500 of bond discount had been amortized in 20X5.

Required:

Prepare the 20X5 cash flow statement, *direct* method, for Sells Company. (The solution to this exercise features an optional spreadsheet.)

P5-1 *Prepare Cash Flow Statement, Indirect Method:* Linda Ray, the president of Zabron Electric Corporation, has asked the company controller for a cash flow statement for the reporting year ended 31 December 20X1. The following balance sheet data has been obtained from the accounting records.

a. Cash account balances: 1 January 20X1, $43,000; 31 December 20X1, $18,000.
b. The balance in accounts receivable decreased by $10,000 during the year. Wages payable decreased by $5,000.
c. Inventory increased $9,000, and accounts payable increased $3,000 during the year.
d. Income tax payable increased $4,000 during the year.
e. During December 20X1, the company settled a $10,000 note payable by issuing its own common shares with equivalent value.
f. Cash expenditures during 20X1 included (1) payment of long-term debts, $64,000; (2) purchase of new operational assets, $74,000; (3) payment of a cash dividend, $16,000; and (4) purchase of land as an investment, $25,000.
g. In 20X1, shares were issued for $20,000 cash.
h. In 20X1, Zabron issued a long-term mortgage note, $30,000.
i. Some capital assets were sold; the following entry was made:

Cash	5,000	
Accumulated depreciation	12,000	
Capital assets		15,000
Gain on sale of capital assets		2,000

Income statement data:

Sales revenue	$295,000
Cost of goods sold	(140,000)
Depreciation expense	(14,000)
Patent amortization	(1,000)
Income tax expense	(17,000)
Remaining expenses	(42,000)
Gain on sale of capital assets	2,000
Net income	$ 83,000

Required:

Prepare a cash flow statement in thousands of dollars using the *indirect* method. Interest and tax cash flows need not be disclosed separately.

P5-2 *Cash Flow Statement:* The items from the 31 December 20X2 CFS for Star Limited are given below, in no particular order.

Closing cash	?
Repayment of long-term debt	$297,139
Depreciation	186,176
Decrease in inventories	
	97,760

Capital expenditures	286,292
Proceeds from issuance of common shares	21,056
Decrease in accounts and taxes payable ($15,000 relates to taxes)	90,000
Income before extraordinary items	37,668
Dividends paid	48,020
Proceeds from expropriation of land	90,600
Opening cash	116,714
Decrease in prepaid expenses	660
Increase in future (deferred) income tax liability	32,400
Proceeds from the sale of a long-term investment	280,020
Increase in long-term borrowings	30,245
Depletion	59,540
Increase in accounts receivable	67,090

Required:

1. Using the above information, prepare a CFS in good format, using the two-step *indirect* method. Interest and tax flows need not be disclosed separately.
2. Repeat requirement (1) using the *direct* method. Sales were $1,743,910, cost of goods sold was $1,149,950, other expenses were $316,900, interest expense was $172,316, and income tax expense was $67,076.
3. Based on this statement, what would you conclude about the company's cash flows for 20X2?

P5-3 *Prepare Cash Flow Statement Showing a Net Loss:* At the end of the current reporting year, 31 December 20X2, Felch Construction Company's executives were very concerned about the ending cash balance of $4,000; the beginning cash balance of $34,000 had been considered seriously low the year before.

During 20X2, management had taken numerous actions to attain a better cash position. In view of the decreased cash balance, they asked the chief accountant to prepare a cash flow statement. The following information was developed from the accounting records:

a. Debt:
　1. Borrowing on long-term note, $10,000.
　2. Payments on maturing long-term debt, $110,000.
　3. Settled short-term debt of $50,000 by issuing Felch common shares.

b. Cash payments:
　1. Regular cash dividends, $18,000.
　2. Purchase of new operational assets, $22,000.

c. Cash received:
　1. Sold and issued Felch common shares, $11,000.
　2. Sold old operational assets at their book value, $1,000.
　3. Sold investment (long-term) in shares of Tech Corporation purchased this year and made the following entry:

Cash	90,000	
Loss on sale of investment	30,000	
Investment in Tech Corporation shares		120,000

d. Relevant balance sheet accounts:
　1. Increase in income tax payable, $10,000.
　2. Decrease in inventory, $38,000.
　3. Increase in accounts receivable, $5,000.

e. Income statement data:

Sales	$160,000
Cost of goods sold	(150,000)
Depreciation expense	(58,000)
Amortization of patent	(2,000)
Income tax expense	(14,000)
Remaining expenses	(31,000)
Loss on sale of long-term investment	(30,000)
Net income (loss)	$(125,000)

Required:

Based on the above data, prepare a cash flow statement (in $ thousands). Use the *direct* method.

P5-4 CFS: *Analysis of Cash Flows and Reporting:* Selected transactions from the records of Dover Company are given below. The annual reporting period ends 31 December 20X2. The company uses the indirect method to present cash flows in the operations section and shows cash flows for interest and tax separately in operations. Analyze each transaction and give the following:

1. Classification of the transaction on the CFS (operating, investing, financing, or none of these).
2. How the amount would be reported on the CFS.
    Example:
    Declared and paid a cash dividend, $10,000.
    Response:
    Financing activity. Cash outflow, dividends paid, $10,000.

a. Purchased operational asset (machine) for $40,000; gave a one-year interest-bearing note for $25,000 and paid cash for the difference.

b. Sold long-term investment, at book value. Received cash of $12,000 and a three-year interest-bearing note for $13,000.

c. Net income, $60,000.

d. Inventory increased $20,000 during the year.

e. Declared a cash dividend of $8,000 and set up a short-term dividends payable account for $6,000 (to be paid in 20X3).

f. Repurchased and retired common shares for $17,000.

g. Depreciation expense, $12,000.

h. Paid a loan payable in full, $5,000.

i. Sold an old capital asset for $5,000 cash; original recorded cost, $20,000; accumulated depreciation to date, $16,000.

j. Issued a stock dividend that was debited to retained earnings, $12,000.

k. Sold an investment in land for $35,000; received $10,000 cash and a one-year interest-bearing note for the remainder. The land was originally recorded in the accounts at $13,000; therefore, a $22,000 gain on sale of land was recorded.

l. Received a cash dividend of $6,000 on a long-term investment in the common shares of Harken Corporation.

m. Interest expense, $12,000; interest payable decreased $3,000.

n. Income tax expense, $13,000; income taxes payable decreased $6,000.

P5-5 *CFS, Direct Method:* The balance sheet, income statement, and additional information are given below for Supreme Company.

Comparative Balance Sheets
31 December

Debits:	20X5	20X4
Cash	$ 44,900	$ 40,000
Accounts receivable	52,500	60,000
Merchandise inventory	141,600	180,000
Prepaid insurance	1,200	2,400
Investments, long-term	—	30,000
Land	38,400	10,000
Capital assets	259,000	250,000
Patent (net)	1,400	1,600
	$539,000	$574,000
Credits		
Accumulated depreciation	$ 79,000	$ 65,000
Accounts payable	53,000	50,000
Wages payable	1,500	2,000
Income taxes payable	13,400	9,000
Bonds payable	50,000	100,000
Premium on bonds payable	1,700	5,000
Common shares, no-par	324,000	315,000
Retained earnings	16,400	28,000
	$539,000	$574,000

20X5 Income Statement

Sales revenue	$399,100
Cost of goods sold	(224,400)
Depreciation expense	(14,000)
Patent amortization	(200)
Salary expense	(80,000)
Interest expense	(4,400)
Other expenses	(44,000)
Investment revenue	900
Gain on sale of investments	10,000
Income tax expense	(24,600)
Net income	$ 18,400

Analysis of selected accounts and transactions:
a. Purchased capital asset, cost of $9,000; payment by issuing 600 common shares.
b. Payment at maturity date to retire bonds payable, $50,000.
c. Sold the long-term investments for $40,000.
d. Reassessment for prior years' income taxes; paid during 20X5 and added to 20X5 tax expense, $6,600.
e. Purchased land, $28,400; paid cash.
f. Cash dividends declared and paid, $30,000.

Required:
Prepare the CFS, *direct* method.

P5-6 *CFS, Indirect Method:* The records of Easy Trading Company provided the following information for the year ended 31 December 20X5:

Income Statement
for the year ended 31 December 20X5

Sales revenue	$ 80,000
Cost of goods sold	(36,000)
Depreciation expense	(5,000)
Insurance expense	(1,000)
Interest expense	(2,000)
Salaries and wages expense	(12,000)
Remaining expenses	(13,000)
Loss on sale of operational assets	(2,000)
Income tax expense	(3,000)
Net income	$ 6,000

Balance Sheet
as at 31 December

	20X5	20X4
Cash	$ 31,000	$ 15,000
Accounts receivable	26,500	28,500
Inventory	15,000	10,000
Prepaid insurance	1,400	2,400
Operational assets	81,000	80,000
Accumulated depreciation	(16,000)	(20,000)
Land	81,100	40,100
Total	$220,000	$156,000
Accounts payable	$ 11,000	$ 10,000
Wages payable	1,000	2,000
Interest payable	1,000	—
Notes payable, long-term	46,000	20,000
Common shares, no-par	136,000	100,000
Retained earnings	25,000	24,000
Total	$220,000	$156,000

Analysis of transactions during the year:

a. Sold operational asset for $4,000 cash (cost, $15,000; accumulated depreciation, $9,000).

b. Issued common shares for $5,000 cash.

c. Declared and paid a cash dividend, $5,000.

d. Purchased land, $20,000 cash.

e. Acquired land for $21,000 and issued common shares as payment in full.

f. Acquired operational assets, cost $16,000; issued a $16,000, three-year, interest-bearing note payable.

g. Paid a $10,000 long-term note by issuing common shares to the creditor.

h. Borrowed cash on long-term note, $20,000.

Required:

Prepare the CFS, *indirect* method. Use the two-step method and include separate disclosure within the operations section for cash flows associated with investment income, interest and income taxes, as applicable.

P5-7 *CFS, Direct Method:* Using the data given in P5-6, prepare the operations section of the CFS using the *direct* method.

P5-8 *CFS, Direct and Indirect Method:* The income statement and balance sheet of Kenwood Company and related analysis are given below.

KENWOOD COMPANY
Income Statement
for the year Ended 31 December 20X4

Sales revenue		$1,000,000
Expenses:		
Cost of goods sold	560,000	
Salaries and wages	190,000	
Depreciation	20,000	
Patent amortization	3,000	
Interest expense	16,000	
Miscellaneous expenses	8,000	
Total expenses		797,000
Other:		
Loss on sale of equipment:	(4,000)	
Gain on bond retirement	12,000	8,000
Income before income taxes		$ 211,000
Income tax expense		82,000
Net income		$ 129,000

Analysis of selected accounts and transactions:
a. On 2 February 20X4, Kenwood issued a 10% stock dividend to shareholders of record on 15 January 20X4. This increased common shares, and decreased retained earnings, by $63,000.
b. On 1 March 20X4, Kenwood issued 3,800 common shares for land. The common shares had a current market value of approximately $40,000.
c. On 15 April 20X4, Kenwood repurchased long-term bonds payable with a face value of $50,000 for cash. The gain of $12,000 was correctly reported on the income statement.
d. On 30 June 20X4, Kenwood sold equipment that cost $53,000, with a book value of $23,000, for $19,000 cash.
e. On 30 September 20X4, Kenwood declared and paid a cash dividend.
f. On 10 October 20X4, Kenwood purchased land for $85,000 cash.

KENWOOD COMPANY
Comparative Balance Sheet
as of 31 December 20X4

Assets	20X4	20X3
Current assets:		
Cash	$ 100,000	$ 90,000
Accounts receivable	210,000	140,000
Inventory	260,000	220,000
Total current assets	570,000	450,000
Land	325,000	200,000
Plant and equipment	580,000	633,000
Less: Accumulated depreciation	(90,000)	(100,000)
Patents	30,000	33,000
Total assets	$1,415,000	$1,216,000

Liabilities and Shareholders' Equity	20X4	20X3
Liabilities:		
Current liabilities:		
Accounts payable	$ 260,000	$ 200,000
Salaries and wages payable	200,000	210,000
Income tax payable	140,000	100,000
Total current liabilities	600,000	510,000
Bonds payable (due 15 December 20X14)	130,000	180,000
Total liabilities	730,000	690,000
Shareholders' equity:		
Common shares, no-par; authorized 100,000 shares, issued and outstanding 50,000 and 42,000 shares, respectively	483,000	380,000
Retained earnings	202,000	146,000
Total shareholders' equity	685,000	526,000
Total liabilities and shareholders' equity	$1,415,000	$1,216,000

Required:

1. Prepare the CFS, *indirect* method. Use the two-step method for operations, and include separate disclosure within the operations section for cash flows associated with investment income, interest and income taxes, as applicable.
2. Prepare the CFS, using the *direct* method, to disclose cash flows in the operating activities section.

[AICPA, adapted]

P5-9 *CFS, Indirect Method:* The differences between the Boole Inc. balance sheet accounts of 31 December 20X4 and 20X5, are presented below:

	Increase (decrease)
Assets	
Cash	$ 120,000
Short-term investments (cash equivalents)	300,000
Accounts receivable	—
Inventory	80,000
Long-term investments	(100,000)
Capital assets	700,000
Accumulated depreciation	—
	$1,100,000
Liabilities and Shareholders' Equity	
Accounts payable and accrued liabilities	$ (5,000)
Dividends payable	160,000
Bank overdraft (part of net cash position on CFS)	325,000
Long-term debt	110,000
Common shares, no-par, an additional 10,000 shares	220,000
Retained earnings	290,000
	$1,100,000

Additional information for 20X5:

1. A building costing $600,000 and having a carrying amount of $350,000 was sold for $350,000.
2. Equipment costing $110,000 was acquired through issuance of long-term debt.
3. A long-term investment was sold for $135,000. There were no other transactions affecting long-term investments.

4. Common shares were issued for $22 a share.

5. Net income was $790,000.

Required:

Prepare Boole's cash flow statement in as much detail as possible under the *indirect* method.

[AICPA, adapted]

P5-10 *CFS, Optional Spreadsheet:* The records of Alberta Company provided the following data for the accounting year ended 31 December 20X5:

Comparative Balance Sheets
as at 31 December

Debits:	20X5	20X4
Cash	$ 75,000	$ 30,000
Investment, short-term (cash equivalent)	8,000	10,000
Accounts receivable	86,000	56,000
Inventory	30,000	20,000
Prepaid interest	2,000	—
Land	25,000	60,000
Machinery	90,000	80,000
Other assets	39,000	29,000
Discount on bonds payable	900	1,000
Total debits	$355,900	$286,000
Credits:		
Accumulated depreciation	26,900	20,000
Accounts payable	54,000	39,000
Salaries payable	2,000	5,000
Income taxes payable	8,000	2,000
Bonds payable	55,000	70,000
Common shares, no-par	130,000	100,000
Preferred shares, no-par	30,000	20,000
Retained earnings	50,000	30,000
Total credits	$335,900	$286,000

Income Statement
for the year ended 31 December 20X5

Sales revenue	$180,000
Cost of goods sold	(90,000)
Depreciation expense	(6,900)
Salaries	(33,900)
Interest expense	(6,100)
Remaining expenses	(4,000)
Gain on sale of land	18,000
Income tax expense	(12,100)
Net income	$ 45,000

Analysis of selected accounts and transactions:
a. Issued bonds payable for cash, $5,000.
b. Sold land for $53,000 cash; book value, $35,000.
c. Purchased machinery for cash, $10,000.
d. Sold short-term investments for cash, $2,000.
e. Retired $20,000 bonds payable by issuing common shares; the common shares had a market value of $20,000.

f. Acquired other assets by issuing preferred shares with a market value of $10,000.

g. Statement of retained earnings:

Balance, 1 January 20X5	$30,000
Net income for 20X5	45,000
Cash dividends	(15,000)
Stock dividend issued	(10,000)
Balance, 31 December 20X5	$50,000

Required:

1. Prepare the CFS, *indirect* method. Use the two-step method, and include separate disclosure within the operations section for cash flows associated with investment income, interest and income taxes, as applicable.

2. Prepare the operations section of the CFS using the *direct* method of presentation. (The solution to this problem features an optional spreadsheet.)

P5-11 *Integrative Problem, Chapters 1–5:* Account balances, taken from the ledger of Argot Flooring Ltd. as of 31 December 20X5, appear below.

Accounts payable	$280,000	Inventory, 1 Jan. 20X5**	$344,000
Accounts receivable	632,000	Land	398,000
Accumulated amortization,		General operating	
building equipment	42,000	expenses	338,000
Allowance for		Notes payable	232,000
doubtful accounts	3,000	Notes receivable	120,000
Building and equipment	198,000	Property tax expense	3,200
Cash	?	Purchases	1,218,000
Common shares	204,100	Purchase discounts	8,000
Extraordinary loss	71,000	Purchase returns and	
Dividends declared	80,000	allowances	32,000
Error correction		Retained earnings,	
(credit)	29,400	1 Jan. 20X5	806,400
Future (deferred) income taxes		Revenue	2,632,000
(credit)	116,700	Salaries expense	232,000
Income tax expense*	334,600	Store supplies inventory	12,400
Interest revenue	5,000	Unearned revenue	32,000

* Assume this amount is properly stated after all subsequent adjustments are considered. Tax includes $28,400 of tax reduction caused by the extraordinary loss, and a $12,000 expense related to the error correction.
** Inventory at 31 December is $480,000.

Additional information:
1. Store supplies were counted at 31 December and found to be valued at $5,600.
2. Amortization of building and equipment is over eight years with an expected salvage value of $10,000.
3. Property taxes of $3,200 were paid on 1 October 20X5, and relate to the year 1 October 20X5 to 30 September 20X6.
4. The note payable was issued on 1 November 20X5 and has an annual interest rate of 12%. Interest must be paid each 30 October along with $30,000 of principal.
5. The note receivable has been outstanding all year. Interest at 10% is collected each 1 June. The note is due 1 June 20X11.
6. The allowance for doubtful accounts now has a $3,000 credit balance. Aging of accounts receivable indicates that $76,000 of the accounts are doubtful.

7. Unearned revenue represents an advance payment from a customer; 75% was still unearned at year-end.
8. At year-end, $10,000 (at retail value) of goods were shipped to customers but the sale was not yet recorded. Correctly, the goods were not included in closing inventory. Only the revenue must be recorded.

Required:

1. Explain the meaning of GAAP and compare GAAP to TAP.
2. Identify common objectives of financial reporting.
3. Prepare adjusting journal entries to reflect the additional information provided above.
4. Explain the following and give and example of an adjusting journal entry in (3) caused by each.
   a. time period assumption.
   b. continuity assumption.
   c. accrual concept.
   d. revenue recognition convention.
   e. matching convention.
5. Prepare a multiple step classified income statement, retained earnings statement, and a classified balance sheet based on the adjusted accounts.
6. Assume that accounts have changed (after the entries made in part 3) as follows over the period:

Accounts receivable (net)	$ 41,900	decrease
Interest receivable	no change	
Inventory	136,000	increase
Store supplies inventory	8,000	decrease
Prepaid property tax	no change	
Buildings and equipment	40,000	increase
Accounts payable	75,000	increase
Interest payable	4,640	increase
Notes payable	232,000	increase
Future (deferred) income tax	26,400	increase

   Prepare the operations section of the CFS using the *direct* method of presentation. The extraordinary loss was caused by an involuntary disposition of capital assets and is not part of the operating activities section on the CFS.
7. What criteria must be met before an item can be considered extraordinary?
8. List the major areas of choice that are present in the format of the income statement and balance sheet.
9. List six functions of disclosure notes and give an example of each.

Revenue Recognition

INTRODUCTION

Revenue recognition is probably the single most difficult issue in accounting. A company's reported results will vary considerably depending on when it chooses to recognize revenue. Policies for recognizing revenue are critical, and contentious. The timing of revenue recognition is especially complex because the business activities that generate revenue are also complex. Some examples demonstrate the issues.

In a recent year, a mining company produced 12,000 ounces of gold at a production cost of $1.2 million. Administrative costs for the year were $0.5 million. Even though the gold could have been sold immediately at a market price of $400 per ounce, management elected not to sell, expecting the price of gold to increase in the future. What will the company show as revenue for the period? What will it report as net income? Is the company better or worse off at the end of the year, compared with the beginning of the year?[1]

University textbooks are typically ordered and shipped 8 to 12 weeks before the beginning of a new term, with orders based on anticipated enrolment. Upon receipt of an order, the publisher ships books in time for stocking before the term begins. The accompanying invoice calls for payment in 30 or 60 days, and the bookstore pays the invoice amount in full. Several weeks into the term, a number of copies of the text remain unsold. Most publishers provide retailers with the right to return unsold, damage-free books for about six months after the original shipping date. At what point during this sequence of events should the publisher record revenue and related expenses on its sales?

Corel Corp., a major developer of computer software (e.g., Corel Draw™ and WordPerfect™) recognized revenue when the company shipped the software to dealers, also recognizing that the company accepted unsold software back from dealers — ordinarily a perfectly acceptable way to recognize revenue. But when the company's fortunes turned down and returns escalated, the company was forced to delay revenue recognition until the inventory was sold by the retailers, even though the retailers are at arm's length from Corel.[2]

Thousand Trails, Inc., develops campgrounds and sells usage rights to campers for a total membership fee of several thousand dollars. Members are allowed to use existing campgrounds and campgrounds planned for future development. One of the attractions of membership is the promise of the inter

---

[1] This example is, in fact, a simplification of the situation faced by the Alaska Gold Company, a placer gold-dredging company. Alaska Gold mined gold for three straight years without selling any of its production. In its annual report to shareholders, Alaska Gold reported zero revenues for gold operations for these periods and thus reported sizeable losses each year because of period expenses. This is one of many interesting cases in G. Pfeiffer and R. Bowen, *Financial Accounting: A Casebook* (Englewood Cliffs, N.J.: Prentice-Hall, 1985), pp. 24–29.

[2] John Greenwood, "Gaps in GAAP can lead to different tale on bottom line," *The Financial Post*, February 26, 1998, p. 37.

esting campgrounds that the company claims will be developed in the future, although it has limited, if any, legal obligation in this regard. Membership fees can be paid in full when the contractual arrangement is signed, but the most typical arrangement is for the member to pay a small percentage down and the balance in periodic instalments over a period of up to seven years. Again the question is when revenue and related expenses should be recognized.[3]

These examples demonstrate how even minor departures from ordinary sales transactions can complicate revenue and expense recognition. A relatively small proportion of Canadian business activity fits into straightforward sales activity. Much economic activity in Canada involves long-term earnings processes, including the broad resource and service sectors. The points at which revenue should be recognized are often not obvious.

This chapter covers the conceptual guidelines for determining when revenue should be recognized and then covers several specific accounting applications that have been developed for use in resolving various types of revenue recognition problems. Revenue recognition also affects expense recognition; expense recognition is the subject of Chapter 7.

DEFINITIONS

What is revenue? It's *not* defined on its own as, for example "the value of goods and services delivered during the period." Rather, it occurs when the net assets (assets minus liabilities) of an entity increase because of normal operating activities. The thought process is sequential, and is balance sheet based. For example, assume that an entity sells goods on credit. An account receivable is created. This increases assets, and the entity has revenue based on that increase in assets, barring other complications.

The financial statement concepts in Section 1000 of the *CICA Handbook* formally define revenues as *increases in economic resources*, either through increases to assets or reductions to liabilities. These increases in resources must be the result of delivering or producing goods, rendering services, or performing other activities that constitute the entity's normal business. Expenses are *decreases in economic resources*, either through outflows or the using-up of assets or incurrence of liabilities from delivering or producing goods, rendering services, or carrying out other activities that constitute the entity's normal business. The definitions are derivative definitions in that they are based on the terms *assets* and *liabilities*. Therefore, clear understanding of assets and liabilities is needed in order to understand revenues and expenses.

As we pointed out in Chapter 2, assets are economic resources controlled by an entity as a result of past transactions or events and from which future economic benefits can be obtained. Liabilities are present obligations of an entity arising from past transactions or events, the settlement of which may result in the transfer or use of assets, provision of services or other yielding of economic benefits in the future.[4] Although our attention in this chapter is focused on recognition and measurement of revenue, this discussion cannot be separated from the issues of asset and liability recognition and measurement.

THE EARNINGS PROCESS

At a conceptual level, a firm earns revenue as it engages in activities that increase the value (or *utility*, in economic terms) of an item or service. For example, an automobile parts manufacturer increases the value of sheet metal when it undertakes activi-

---

3 Thousand Trails, Inc., is another case found in Pfeiffer and Bowen, *Financial Accounting: A Casebook*.

4 These definitions are from Section 1000 of the *CICA Handbook*, "Financial Statement Concepts."

ties to cut, shape, and weld the sheet metal into automobile fenders. Transporting completed fenders to a regional wholesale warehouse also adds value because it makes the fenders readily available for purchase and use by automobile repair shops. The earnings process is fully completed when the fenders are sold and delivered to a customer in return for cash or a promise to pay cash: finally, assets actually increase. All of these activities, and many more, are part of the earnings process.

Exhibit 6-1 graphically illustrates the concept of the earnings process in a highly simplified setting. It focuses on the process of earning revenue; costs are not included. A firm undertakes many different activities, over the five periods shown, for the purpose of earning a profit. The top graph depicts the cumulative amount of revenue the firm has earned over time and thus a constant rate of revenue earned as the different activities are performed. The graph also assumes that we know what the total amount of revenue will be when the earnings process is complete. Usually there is considerable uncertainty at the earlier stages of the earnings process (for example, during the design of a new product) as to whether the product will sell, and for what amount. This uncertainty is only removed when a price is agreed to, and the product is delivered to a customer.

The bottom graph in Exhibit 6-1 shows the amount of revenue that could *conceptually* be recognized in each accounting period as activities in the earnings process are completed. Because we assume that a constant rate of revenue is earned at each stage in the earnings process, the amount of revenue is the same for each period. The shaded area in the bottom graph equals the total amount of revenue earned over the completed earnings process, which is represented in the top graph by the height of the cumulative revenue earned at the end of the fifth period.

Do not confuse the conceptual notion that *economic value is added* (i.e., revenue is created) at each stage along the way in the production and sale process, with the *accounting revenue recognition* issue. The issue in accounting is when during that earnings process should revenue be recognized by recording the increase in value on the books?

The earnings process for most companies involves incurring costs to increase the value of an in-process product. Sometimes the process is very long. The design and development process for a new commercial airplane can take 5 to 10 years from initial design efforts to the delivery of the first airplane to a customer. *Economically, revenue is being earned as each of the many activities is completed*, assuming that the activity brings the company closer to having a saleable product. Companies are required to provide periodic reports on earnings even when the earnings process extends over several accounting periods. In these situations, the question of how much revenue (and expense) to recognize and report in each period must be carefully assessed.

FINANCIAL REPORTING OBJECTIVES

Companies do not necessarily pick their accounting policies with "good accounting" as their first objective. As we saw in Chapters 1 and 2, companies bring a variety of motives to the decision, and may wish to maximize or minimize reported net income and net assets, or affect other key financial statement data in support of their specific financial reporting objectives.

Revenue recognition is an area where firms that are anxious to show increasing sales and profits have followed a number of questionable and sometimes even improper accounting procedures. A relatively innocent-looking example occurs when a firm records as a sale goods that have been ordered for a later delivery. Suppose a firm receives an order in December for goods that the customer desires to receive in mid-January. Should the sale be recorded in December or January? Even more problematic would be a transaction in which goods are shipped (and recorded as a revenue) to a customer who regularly purchases such goods in approximately the

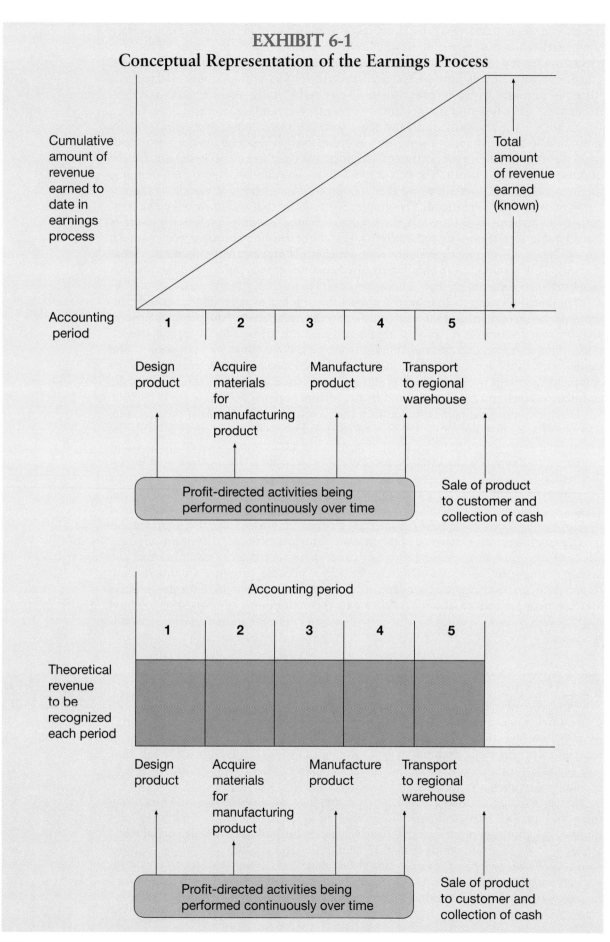

EXHIBIT 6-1
Conceptual Representation of the Earnings Process

amounts shipped, but who has not yet ordered the goods! There have also been cases where the invoices for goods shipped after the fiscal year-end are back-dated to the current fiscal year in order to record them as sales in the earlier period. Yes, this really happens, but it's not acceptable, either ethically or under GAAP. Such actions are deliberate attempts to mislead users, and are tantamount to fraud.

The choice of method used to record revenues is an area where ethical questions are sometimes raised. Thousand Trails, the company mentioned in the introduction to this chapter, used the point-of-sale method to recognize revenue on its membership rights transactions. Most of these transactions were instalment sales and the default rate was high. Since the default rate may be very difficult to estimate with reasonable accuracy, it has been suggested that the instalment sales method would have been a more appropriate choice for revenue recognition. The company and its auditor maintained, however, that the point-of-sale method was appropriate because they felt they could estimate the future default amounts on the instalment receivables with reasonable accuracy. By using the point-of-sale method, Thousand Trails reported rapid growth in sales and profits even though the company had received only a very small portion of the reported revenue in cash. Again, this is appropriate so long as the receivables do eventually convert into estimated amounts of cash. The fact that the company eventually got into severe financial difficulty, in part because of an unexpectedly large number of defaults on the receivables, reinforced concerns about whether the point-of-sale method was appropriate in the first place.

Choice of method and implementation of accounting procedures for revenue recognition must be done with a careful consideration of what is ethical and appropriate for the circumstances.

REVENUE RECOGNITION CRITERIA

When an item is recognized in the financial statements, it is assigned a value and recorded as an element in the appropriate financial statement(s) with an appropriate offset to another element (e.g., cash or accounts payable). Recognized items must meet the definition of a financial statement element, and have a measurement basis and amount. We know that financial statement elements are based on future economic benefits or sacrifices; these must be *probable* for recognition to be appropriate.

In addition to the general recognition criteria, the revenue principle provides that revenue should be recognized in the financial statements when it is

1. earned, and
2. realized or realizable.

Revenues are *earned* when the company has accomplished what it must do to be entitled to receive the associated benefits of the revenue. In a normal sales transaction, this occurs *when the vendor has transferred all the risks and rewards of ownership to the customer* and has no ongoing managerial control over the item. When the earnings process spans more than one accounting period, revenue can sometimes be recognized even though the earnings process is not completed as long as the costs required to complete the earnings process can be reliably estimated.

Revenue is *realized* when cash is received. Revenue is *realizable* when *claims* to cash (for example, financial instruments such as accounts or notes receivable) are received; such financial instruments can be readily converted into cash. This criterion is also met if the product is a commodity, such as gold or wheat, for which there is a public market in which essentially unlimited amounts of the product can be bought or sold at a known or ascertainable market price.

REVENUE MEASUREMENT

The *amount* of revenue to recognize is usually less of an issue than *when* to recognize it, or *how to allocate* it. This is because the sales price is typically part of the implicit or explicit contract between the buyer and the seller. Measurement is one of the recognition criteria, though, and is sometimes a substantive issue. For example, when a sale agreement sets a price, but establishes extended interest-free payment terms, it is clear that part of the purchase price relates to interest. Discounting techniques can be used to separate the principal and interest. For practical reasons, firms do not do this as long as the interest-free period is short, because the amount of interest would be immaterial. Discounting would more clearly be appropriate if the term was longer than a year.

Measurement issues also predominate if the sale transaction is a barter transaction; that is, if the exchange involves only non-monetary goods. For example, an accountant may prepare a tax return for an innkeeper in exchange for a three-day weekend vacation at the innkeeper's facility. At what amount should this transaction be valued? The accountant could keep track of her time, multiply by her charge-out rate, and determine the amount she would have billed the client. Alternatively, she could ascertain the value of the weekend vacation to which she is entitled.

The recommendations in the *CICA Handbook*, found in Section 3830, "Non-monetary transactions," indicate that the transaction should be valued at the fair value of the asset or service given up. However, if the value of the asset or service received is more reliable, it should be used to value the transaction.

For our accountant, this means that she'll look at the value of her time, then look at the value of the weekend trip, and ask which value she's more confident about. Likely she'll use the value of her time, but a comparison of the two values is always informative. If they're close, there's a high degree of comfort with the decision. It's not as easy as it seems: she may have been using otherwise-idle time to do this job, which implies that her time may not have been "worth" the full charge-out rate. She may be able to use the vacation weekend only in shoulder periods, when the room would otherwise have been vacant at the inn — implying that it may not be "worth" the advertised price. Judgement is pivotal to the measurement process.

The non-monetary transaction rules have one more twist. If the barter transaction is not considered to be the culmination (or completion) of the earnings process, then the barter transaction is valued at book value of the resource given up. For example, assume a vendor "sells" a product to a customer, and in return takes a second product, which the vendor plans to sell to yet another company for cash. The first sale is just a step along the "earnings process" path; the vendor has not yet reached the destination. Therefore, the second product should be recorded at the book value of the first product. With no change in net asset value, there is no increase in resources to drive revenue recognition. Only when the second product is sold for cash is revenue recognition appropriate. It also is not appropriate to record a gain on sale if two similar *capital* assets are exchanged. For example, if two real estate development firms swap apartment buildings, the asset acquired is recorded at the book value of the asset given up.

Measurement of consideration may also be a problem if the consideration is contingent on another transaction. For example, a customer may agree to pay a vendor on a sliding scale, based on the amount that the customer, in turn, can sell the product to another firm. If the customer does not have to pay the vendor at all unless the item is resold, the sale is called a consignment sale, and is not recorded by the vendor until re-sale by the customer. However, there are other versions of a sale contract where a base price is agreed to, with further price adjustments based on the terms of eventual re-sale. If these arrangements create uncertainty that is material and unquantifiable, revenue recognition must wait until it is possible to establish the appropriate amount of consideration.

1. What is the difference between the concepts of revenue *creation* and revenue *recognition*?
2. In general, what two criteria must be satisfied before revenue can be recognized in the financial statements?
3. How should revenue be measured in a barter transaction?

APPROACHES TO REVENUE RECOGNITION

Essentially, there are two approaches to revenue recognition. Revenue can be recognized at one **critical event** in the chain of activities, for example, production, delivery, or cash collection. Alternatively, revenue can be recognized on a basis consistent with *effort expended*, a plan that would result in some revenue being recognized with every activity in the chain.

REVENUE RECOGNITION ON A CRITICAL EVENT

What happens if a *critical event* is chosen to trigger revenue recognition? All costs incurred before the critical event *that can be specifically identified as relating to each individual earnings event* are deferred (usually as inventory costs). These expenditures qualify as assets because they will generate resources/sales revenue at the critical event. When revenue is recognized, deferred expenses are expensed, and identifiable costs that *have not yet been incurred* must be accrued as estimated liabilities. *Revenues and expenses are all recognized at the critical event, regardless of when they are incurred.* This is the magic of an accrual-based accounting system.

What events could be chosen as the critical event? Potentially, any activity in the earnings process could be so designated, but the key is that, following the critical event, the remaining aspects of the earnings process should unfold predictably in the normal course of business with no major uncertainties or immeasurables. Once the critical event has occurred, it's all downhill from there! The most commonly-used critical events can be grouped by reference to completion of the earnings cycle:

1. Completion
2. Prior to completion
3. Subsequent to completion

Exhibit 6-2 illustrates revenue recognition associated with specific critical events in the context of production and sale of a manufactured product. Although this figure uses manufactured goods as the reference point, a similar chart could be drawn for other earnings cycles, such as for resource extraction, life insurance, or auditing. Not all possible methods are shown in Exhibit 6-2, even for manufacturing.

For most companies and for most goods and services, revenue is recognized at the time of delivery of the goods or services to the customer. Revenue is considered both earned and realized or realizable when the product or service is delivered.

An earlier critical event — production — may be appropriate if the selling and shipping functions are trivial, such as when the product is a commodity for which there is an organized market (e.g., wheat, copper, gold). A critical event *after* delivery is appropriate when there are measurement problems surrounding the amount of revenue actually generated, collection uncertainties, and/or when it is not possible to accurately estimate all the costs associated with the earnings process, which must be fully accrued at the critical event. In the face of any of these problems, revenue recognition should wait until major uncertainties are resolved.

EXHIBIT 6-2
Alternative Methods of Revenue Recognition

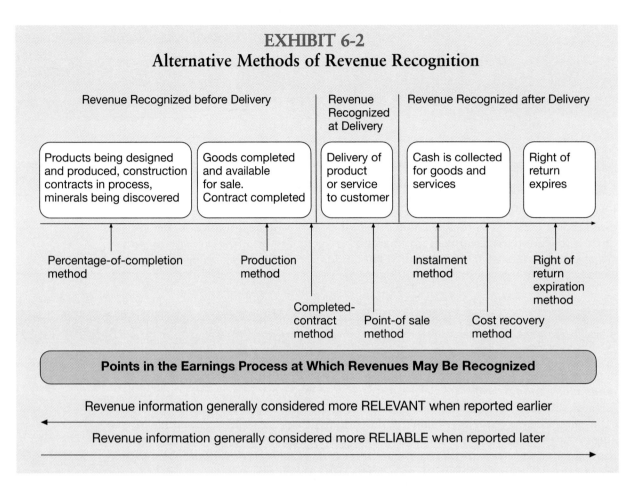

Revenue Recognized before Delivery   Revenue Recognized at Delivery   Revenue Recognized after Delivery

Products being designed and produced, construction contracts in process, minerals being discovered

Goods completed and available for sale. Contract completed

Delivery of product or service to customer

Cash is collected for goods and services

Right of return expires

Percentage-of-completion method

Production method

Instalment method

Right of return expiration method

Completed-contract method

Point-of sale method

Cost recovery method

Points in the Earnings Process at Which Revenues May Be Recognized

Revenue information generally considered more RELEVANT when reported earlier

Revenue information generally considered more RELIABLE when reported later

REVENUE RECOGNIZED AT DELIVERY

The two conditions for revenue recognition, (1) revenue is *realized* or *realizable* and (2) revenue must be *earned*, are usually met at the time goods or services are delivered. Thus, revenue from the sale of products is usually recognized at the date of sale, meaning the date the product is delivered to the customer. Revenue from services rendered is likewise recognized when the services have been performed and accepted by the client.

Some transactions do not result in a one-time delivery of a product or service, but rather in continual "delivery" or fulfilment of a contractual arrangement. For example, revenue from contractual arrangements allowing others to use company assets (such as revenues from rent, interest, lease payments, and royalties) is recognized as time passes or as the asset is used. Revenue is earned with the passage of time and is recognized accordingly.[5]

Separately identifiable costs incurred prior to the critical event are deferred in inventory or other deferred asset accounts. These costs are recognized as expenses at delivery, and thus are recognized at the same time as revenue. All other costs associated with the sale must be recognized in the same period as the revenue; this may include a reasonable estimate of bad debts, and a provision for guarantee or warranty costs. Refer to the sequence of events in Exhibit 6-3, where a company buys inventory, customizes it, and then holds it until sale. It is sold, on account, subject to a four-month warranty. Subsequently, the customer pays, some warranty costs are incurred,

---

[5]   If, however, the contract is a lease and is essentially a noncancellable transfer of all the risks and rights of ownership of the asset, the transaction qualifies as a sale. Such transactions, called capital leases, are considered in Chapter 18.

EXHIBIT 6-3
Critical Events and Impact on Net Assets

Data:

January 15	Inventory purchased, $14,500
January 17	Inventory repackaged and customized, labour and materials cost, $2,250. Now ready for sale.
March 6	Inventory delivered to customer on account. Agreed-upon price, $27,500. Collection is assured; there is a four-month warranty.
April 30	Customer paid.
June 14	Warranty work done, at a cost of $3,900.
July 6	Warranty expired.

Date	Delivery		Pre-delivery: Production		Post-delivery: Warranty Expiration	
Jan. 15	Inventory 14,500		Inventory 14,500		Inventory 14,500	
	Cash, A/P, etc.	14,500	Cash, A/P, etc.	14,500	Cash, A/P, etc.	14,500
Effect on net assets	None		None		None	
Jan. 17	Inventory 2,250		Inventory 2,250		Inventory 2,250	
	Cash, A/P, etc.	2,250	Cash, A/P, etc.	2,250	Cash, A/P, etc.	2,250
			Cost of goods sold 16,750			
			Inventory 10,750			
			Revenue	27,500		
			Warranty expense 3,900			
			Estimated warranty liability	3,900		
Effect on net assets	None		Increase $6,850		None	
March 6	Accounts receivable 27,500		Accounts receivable 27,500		Accounts receivable 27,500	
	Revenue	27,500	Inventory	27,500	Deferred gross margin	10,750
	Cost of goods sold 16,750				Inventory	16,750
	Inventory	16,750				
	Warranty expense 3,900					
	Estimated warranty liability	3,900				
Effect on net assets	Increase $6,850		None		None	
April 30	Cash 27,500		Cash 27,500		Cash 27,500	
	Accounts receivable	27,500	Accounts receivable	27,500	Accounts receivable	27,500
Effect on net assets	None		None		None	
June 14	Estimated warranty liability 3,900		Estimated warranty liability 3,900		Deferred warranty costs 3,900	
	Cash	3,900	Cash	3,900	Cash	3,900
Effect on net assets	None		None		None	
July 6	No entry		No entry		Cost of goods sold 16,750	
					Deferred gross margin 10,750	
					Revenue	27,500
					Warranty expense 3,900	
					Deferred warranty costs	3,900
Effect on net assets	None		None		Increase $6,850	

and, finally, the warranty expires. The first column of Exhibit 6-3 traces the entries appropriate if delivery is considered to be the critical event. Product costs are deferred in the inventory account until delivery. When the item is delivered, the sales price is accrued, inventory is expensed to cost of goods sold, and warranty costs are estimated — with amazing accuracy! Collection is assumed to be certain, and no bad debt accrual is appropriate. Subsequent cash transactions — cash collection and payment of warranty costs — change receivables and payables established at the critical event. *Net assets are increased only at the critical event. Other transactions change the composition but not the total of net assets.* The remaining columns of Exhibit 6-3 will be analyzed in later sections.

For companies that sell services rather than products, revenue recognition policies are analogous to the policies of companies selling tangible goods. Service revenue is usually recognized when performance is complete. Of course, the revenue is really earned by performing a series of acts, but recognition may be considered appropriate only after the final act occurs. This final act is often analogous to delivery of a tangible good, and signifies that the customer accepts the service. For example, a consultant recognizes revenue only when an assignment has been completed. A trucking firm recognizes service revenue only after delivery of freight, even though packing, loading, and transporting preceded delivery. A laundry recognizes revenue when items are picked up by the customer.

Accounting for franchise fee revenue provides an example of the sorts of problems that can be encountered when trying to identify when "delivery" has occurred in a service transaction. Franchisees usually agree to pay a substantial fee to the franchisor. For revenue recognition purposes, it is often difficult to determine when the earnings process is complete and the franchisor's service has been delivered — the point at which the franchisor has "substantially performed" the service required to earn the franchise fee revenue.

One common problem with franchise fee revenue recognition is that of evaluating the collectibility of the initial fee. If the franchisee pays the fee up front, this is less of a concern; if the franchisee plans to pay it over time with profits from the franchise operation, then collection is contingent on profitable operations, and careful assessment of business risk is necessary. A franchisor with no track history, or with franchisees that are financially unsound, may have to delay revenue recognition due to collection concerns.

Another problem is that the franchisor may have significant ongoing obligations to the franchisee. If this is the case, and if the franchisee does not have to pay extra for these services (that is, they are part of the services encompassed by the initial franchise fee) recognition of all or part of the initial franchise fee might be delayed.

To help franchisors (and their auditors) deal with the problems of franchise fee revenue recognition, the CICA issued an *Accounting Guideline* many years ago.[6] The guideline suggests that "substantial performance" has occurred only when:

a. The franchisor has performed substantially all of the initial services required by the franchise agreement or volunteered by the franchisor as a result of normal business practice.

b. The franchisor has no remaining obligation or intent to refund amounts received or forgive unpaid amounts owing.

c. There are no other material unfulfilled conditions affecting completion of the sale.

Thus, "delivery" has occurred only when the franchisor has done what is expected and gets to keep the money.

---

6 "Franchise Fee Revenue," Accounting Guidelines, *CICA Handbook*, July 1984.

REVENUE RECOGNITION BEFORE DELIVERY

Completion of Production

In certain situations, revenue can be recognized at the completion of production but prior to delivery. The key criterion for using this method is that the sale will take place *without any doubt*. The normal criteria for recognizing revenue before sale are

- the sale and collection of proceeds must be assured;
- the product must be marketable immediately at quoted prices that cannot be influenced by the producer;
- units of the product must be interchangeable; and
- there must be no significant costs involved in product sale or distribution.

Essentially, these criteria define a commodity. Examples include agricultural products, precious metals, and other goods that are traded on commodities markets such as orange juice concentrate, crude oil, and pork bellies. Commodities can be sold at any time simply by lifting the telephone and calling a broker; no significant effort is required. When this approach to revenue recognition is used, the increase in net asset value is recorded immediately upon the completion of production, and *involves valuing inventory at market value*.

While commodities that are traded on a public market are the most obvious candidates for pre-delivery revenue recognition, some companies may use this method if their product is in such strong demand that sale is virtually assured. It is a bit dangerous, however, because if demand suddenly falls off, the company is left with a lot of inventory carried at market value but no ready buyers. Substantial effort is then required to sell the product, which means that the earnings process is not complete and the criteria for revenue recognition have not been met.

Refer to the second column of Exhibit 6-3, which demonstrates the sequence of entries that would be appropriate for revenue recognition on the completion of production. When inventory is customized and ready for sale, revenue is recognized in full by increasing the inventory value from its cost of $16,750 (that is, $14,500 plus $2,250) to market value ($27,500), a difference of $10,750. On the income statement, the gross margin will be disaggregated and will be presented as sales of $27,500 and cost of sales of $16,750.[7]

At the same time the inventory is revalued, warranty costs are accrued, to include all costs of the sale in the same accounting period. Note that the overall change in net assets is $6,850, the same that was recorded under the "delivery" alternative. *All that has changed is the point at which the increase in net assets is recognized*. After the critical event (i.e., production), all transactions change the allocation of the net asset balances but do not increase or decrease total net assets.

Completion of production for a service company is the completion of the service, also called specific performance. Is this any different than "delivery"? For many service activities, services are completed and delivered simultaneously (consider haircuts, tooth extractions, music lessons, and so on).

But what if the service is performed and only later accepted by the customer? For example, a consulting report could be written but not presented to the client for a month. Would it make sense to recognize revenue when the work is completed, prior to delivery? As in tangible products, this would be aggressive, as the risks and rewards have not yet passed to the client; there is no assurance that the consultant has fulfilled her or his mandate.

---

[7] Bear in mind that Canadian GAAP requires the amount of *revenue recognized* to be disclosed on the income statement [*CICA* 1520.03(a)].

As a result, revenue recognition at production for service sales is not normally appropriate. In many cases, the lag between production and delivery is likely to be non-existent or very short, and so this isn't much of an issue for most short-term service sales. But long-term service contracts may result in partial recognition of revenue, period by period, as work is performed. This process will be discussed in a later section.

Initiation of Contract

To achieve matching, it is necessary to recognize revenue and the related expenses in the same period. However, GAAP does not approve of the deferral of many types of cost that cannot be specifically identified with a unit of product or service. Promotional expenses, for example, can be deferred to a later period if they relate specifically to that later period, such as the cost of preparing television advertisements which will be aired in the next period, or the cost of publishing a printed catalogue for next year's product line. General advertising and promotional costs cannot be deferred, however, because it is impossible to have reasonable assurance that revenues will arise in the future as the result of this year's promotion.

On rare occasions, a large part of an enterprise's cost is in its promotional activities or in other non-deferrable costs. An example is a company that sells self-improvement home study courses by correspondence. The costs for developing the courses are incurred early, followed by a major TV and print media blitz to sign up customers. The course development costs can be deferred, of course, but the cost of the promotional campaign cannot.

Therefore, such a company may choose to recognize revenue *when it signs up the customer and receives the cash*. The costs of actually delivering the course may be relatively trivial (e.g., printing and mailing costs, and perhaps grading costs that are tightly budgeted and controlled) and are quite predictable; the future costs of delivering the course can be accrued at the time of revenue recognition. Therefore, the *critical event* is perceived to be the sale.

Recognizing revenue at the inception of a contract is usually regarded as *aggressive* accounting policy. Companies that use an aggressive policy and later get into financial difficulty usually find themselves the brunt of aggressive analysts and lawyers. Loewen Group Inc., a very large funeral services company, used early recognition of revenue on the sale of cemetery plots. The sales contracts were usually instalment sales, and the customer paid little or nothing at inception. The revenue for the entire contract was booked in the period that the sale was made, which is industry practice. Getting the sale is the critical event. This practice was used by Loewen for years without raising the concerns of analysts, but once the company got into difficulty (for largely unrelated reasons), it was accused of aggressive accounting.[8]

Another example is that of Livent Inc. Livent sold the rights to the name of its theatres in Vancouver and Toronto to Ford and to AT&T Canada. The sale was for the right to attach the corporate sponsor's name to the theatre for a limited period, usually 10 years. Clearly, the critical event was making the sale. There could be little doubt that Ford and AT&T would come up with the cash, and Livent didn't have to do anything to earn the revenue — just put the name on the theatre and leave it there! Therefore, Livent recognized the full amount of the sales contract at the time of signing, regardless of whether or not the cash was received. Later, analysts (and lawyers) attacked this practice, claiming that the revenue should have been deferred and amortized (the Canadian solution to many accounting problems!).[9]

---

8 "A Deathwatch for Loewen Group," *The Globe and Mail*, 1 August 1998, p. B1.

9 "Fund Companies Write Down Their Investments in Livent," *The Globe and Mail*, 14 August 1998, p. B1.

REVENUE RECOGNITION AFTER DELIVERY

In certain circumstances, revenue recognition must be delayed until after delivery. Typically, this is appropriate when there are uncertainties over the costs associated with the remaining activities in the earnings process, collection, or measurement.

Revenue from the sale of goods should only be recognized when the risks and rewards of ownership pass from the vendor to the customer; substantially all of the elements of the earnings process must be complete before this condition is considered to be met. What if there is a major warranty associated with the sale? This may preclude revenue recognition until the task — the risk — is over. Refer to the third column of entries in Exhibit 6-3. This alternative is appropriate if the cost of the warranty is not estimable at the point of sale, or any point up to its expiration, and is expected to be material.

Notice here that product costs are capitalized in inventory, and even delivery does not cause a change in net assets. Accounts receivable are recognized, inventory is reduced, but the gross margin is deferred; the deferred gross margin account is a contra account to accounts receivable on the balance sheet. Warranty costs actually incurred are deferred. *None of the transactions prior to the critical event — the expiration of the warranty period — triggers a change in net asset value.*

As previously discussed, if the amount of consideration — the sales amount — cannot be ascertained, revenue is recognized when those uncertainties are resolved. In a contract that involves a sliding scale of payment to the vendor based on the price the customer receives on the resale of the item, the critical event would be the resale of the goods for an ascertainable price.

In several industries, such as book publishing and equipment manufacturing, the sales terms allow customers the right to return goods under certain circumstances and over long periods of time. Thus, on delivery, the amount that will ultimately become realizable is not known.

The revenue section of the *CICA Handbook* states the following:

> Revenue would not be recognized when an enterprise is subject to significant and unpredictable amounts of goods being returned, for example, when the market for a returnable good is untested. If an enterprise is exposed to significant and predictable amounts of goods being returned, it may be sufficient to provide therefore.   [*CICA* 3400.18]

This latter point deserves special emphasis; *if the risk can be quantified, then the sale can be recorded on delivery and the contingency accrued.*

No revenue should be recognized if the buyer's obligation to pay the seller is contingent on the resale of the product. If payment is contingent, this is a **consignment**: a marketing arrangement in which the owner of the product (the *consignor*) ships the product to another party (the *consignee*) who acts as a sales agent. The consignee does not purchase the goods, but assumes responsibility only for their care and resale. Upon sale, the consignee remits the proceeds (less specified expenses and commission) to the consignor. Goods on consignment are part of the inventory of the consignor until sold by the consignee. They are not a sale of the consignor when shipped to the consignee, but only when they are sold by the consignee.

Product-financing arrangements include agreements in which a sponsoring company sells a product to another company and in a related transaction agrees to repurchase the product at some future point in time if the customer has been unable to resell the product. This is consignment selling in a different legal form, and it is clear that the risks and rewards of ownership have not passed to the customer.

In these kinds of product-financing agreements, the sponsoring company must record a liability at the time the proceeds are received. It can neither record a sale nor remove the product from its inventory account. Only when the product is sold to an outside party without a related repurchase agreement can the sponsoring company record a sale.

Cash Collection

It is not appropriate to recognize revenue if it is not realized or realizable; accounts receivable must be collectible in order to support an entry that recognizes revenue. If there is no way to quantify collection risk, the critical event becomes cash collection and increases in net asset values are deferred until that time.

However, there is usually some degree of collection risk in every credit sale and delayed revenue recognition is not the norm. Instead, the risk is quantified by estimating an allowance for doubtful accounts, and associated bad debt expense. As long as there is some objective basis for the allowance, such as past history, credit reports, etc., revenue recognition prior to cash collection can be justified.

When the eventual collection of cash is uncertain, companies usually delay revenue recognition until the cash is actually collected. This is common in certain types of retail stores, where credit terms are extended to customers that have very shaky credit records. The company compensates for its high default rate on bad credit by charging high interest to those who do pay and by having a well-organized repossession service.

Recognizing revenue on cash collection does not mean that it is appropriate to recognize revenue *prior* to delivery, if cash is received prior to delivery and there are major costs to be incurred to fulfill the contract with the customer. For example, when a publisher sells a magazine subscription or an airline sells a ticket for future air travel, cash is received before delivery of the product or service. The realizability criterion is met, but significant effort and cost must be incurred before the earnings process is substantially complete; the earnings process is not completed until the product is delivered.

In this case, cash inflow does not result in revenue but in an obligation to produce and deliver the product: a liability. This liability is called deferred revenue or unearned revenue. The revenue is not recognized until the product or service is delivered. The topic under consideration in this section is delayed revenue recognition: when cash is collected *after* delivery.

If revenue is recognized on cash collection, the sequence of entries would be similar to those in the third column of Exhibit 6-3. Cost would be deferred and delivery would only result in recognition of a deferred margin. On cash collection, warranty costs would be accrued, and the cash collection would trigger recognition of the gross margin. Net assets would increase accordingly.

The example in Exhibit 6-3 is relatively straightforward, since the customer has paid in one complete lump sum. However, when cash collection is uncertain, the sale agreement often involves a series of payments for the customer. Then, the company must determine which of two revenue recognition approaches fits its risk profile: the instalment sales method or the cost recovery method.

Instalment Sales Method

Many consumer products are sold on an instalment or deferred payment plan, in which a purchaser makes payments in accordance with a periodic payment plan. If the company has a reasonable basis for estimating an allowance for uncollectible accounts, the company can choose to recognize revenue immediately, at the time of the sale.

However, a company that sells its products on an instalment plan may choose to use the instalment sales method of accounting. Revenue under the instalment sales method is recognized *when cash is collected* rather than at the time of sale. Under this method, revenue (and the related cost of goods sold) are recognized only when *realized*. For instance, the instalment method may be used to account for sales of real estate when the down payment is relatively small and ultimate collection of the sales price is not reasonably assured.

For example, assume that Truro Company makes $80,000 of instalment sales in 20X2. The cost of goods sold is $60,000, and thus the gross margin is $20,000, or 25% of sales. The sale is recorded with a *deferred* gross margin.

Instalment accounts receivable	80,000	
Inventory		60,000
Deferred gross margin		20,000

The deferred gross margin will appear as a liability on the balance sheet, as deferred revenue. Notice that the entry to record the sale does not result in an increase in the company's net assets, because the increase of $20,000 in assets (that is, the increase from $60,000 inventory to $80,000 accounts receivable) is completely offset by the $20,000 increase in the liability.

If $10,000 is subsequently collected, the entries to record the collection and to recognize a proportionate part of the deferred revenue are as follows:

Cash	10,000	
Instalment accounts receivable		10,000
Deferred gross margin ($10,000 × 25%)	2,500	
Cost of goods sold	7,500	
Sales revenue		10,000

It is the last entry that records the increase to net assets that is the sign of revenue recognition. The increase in net assets is accomplished by reducing the amount of the liability for deferred gross margin. Note that the revenue recognition is recorded by disaggregating the realized gross margin of $2,500 into its two components of Sales and Cost of goods sold. This is in accordance with the *CICA Handbook* recommendation that the gross amount of revenue be disclosed on the income statement.

The Cost Recovery Method

The cost recovery method is sometimes called the sunk cost method. A company must recover all the related costs incurred (the sunk costs) before it recognizes any profit. The cost recovery method is used for highly speculative transactions when the ultimate realization of revenue or profit is unpredictable.

The method makes an even match of revenue and expense until all of the deferred cost has been recovered. Only then is any profit recognized. It is common only under extreme uncertainty about collection of the receivables or ultimate recovery of capitalized production start-up costs.

An example is Lockheed Corporation's use of the cost recovery method in the early 1970s when it faced great uncertainty regarding the ultimate profitability of its TriStar Jet Transport program. Lockheed had invested more than $500 million in the initial planning, tooling, and production start-up costs of its widebody aircraft, the L-1011 TriStar. These costs were to be amortized over the production and sale of the first 300 planes, but considerable uncertainty developed concerning how many airplanes might ultimately be sold: the TriStar program might not generate enough sales to recover the development costs. Note 2 to Lockheed's 1973 annual report reported the company's decision to use the cost recovery method for revenue recognition for its TriStar program (italics added):

> All of the development costs and the normal production costs on the TriStar Jet Transport have been included in the inventory except for General and Administrative expenses which are charged to income in the year incurred. G & A expenses amounted to $70 million in 1973 and

$81 million in 1972. Since the cumulative development costs to date have been substantial, it is estimated that 300 aircraft will have to be delivered to make the total program profitable. Since 56 aircraft have been delivered to date (all during 1972 and 1973), the Company does not expect a final determination of recoverability of Inventoried Cost can be made until a later date. *Zero gross profit was recorded on the $730 million of sales in 1973 and $302 million in sales in 1972 (for deliveries in those years) and no gross profit will be recorded on deliveries until uncertainties are reduced.*[10]

The cost recovery method is also justified when there is significant uncertainty regarding the ultimate collectibility of a string of customer payments. Cost recovery accounting is not uncommon in the real estate industry.

For example, assume that the Peninsula Land Sales Company sold undeveloped land during 20X4, with an original cost of $80,000 and a contract sales price of $140,000, to be paid, with interest, over the next five years. Collection is deemed to be highly uncertain. The first $80,000 that is collected is, in essence, credited to the land account; the last $60,000 collected is all profit. If collections cease after $60,000, the adjusted cost basis for the land is $20,000, and it is recorded as an asset at the lower of cost or market.

This revenue recognition method is highly skewed toward later revenue recognition and does a poor job of reflecting performance and cash flows. Its use is justified *only* in the face of significant uncertainties.

CONCEPT REVIEW

1. What is meant by the *critical event* in revenue recognition?
2. What is the net balance sheet effect of revenue recognition?
3. What criteria must ordinarily be satisfied in order for revenue to be recognized on production, prior to sale or delivery?
4. When would revenue recognition be delayed to a point later than production, sale, and delivery?

REVENUE RECOGNITION BY EFFORT EXPENDED

So far, our discussion has examined the *critical event approach* to revenue recognition: identify one event in the earnings process, and recognize revenue and related costs at that event (which could involve multiple events for a single revenue-generating transaction, if the critical event is cash receipt).

An alternative to the critical event approach is to recognize revenue as *effort is expended* along each step in the earnings process. Think about the increase in value resulting from natural causes such as the growth of timberland or the aging of wines and liquors. As the product's value increases, revenue is being earned in an economic sense, and some accountants believe that it should be recognized. Recognition may be important when the natural process is very long, and knowing the change in value is relevant information for decision-making. Could you measure the change in value?

This approach to revenue recognition is not practical in the vast majority of situations: imagine trying to figure out how much a forest grew in a year, or trying to allocate the gross profit associated with a sale of manufactured goods to each activity in the process. Which of the tasks (getting the order, procuring raw materials, man-

---

[10] In 1975, Lockheed reclassified TriStar's initial planning, tooling, and unrecovered production start-up costs as deferred charges and began amortizing them in the amount of approximately $50 million per year. This was done because of "increased uncertainties" regarding the number and timing of future TriStar deliveries. This write-off procedure was a means of spreading the loss over future years. A preferred alternative would have been to write off the entire amount immediately.

ufacturing, shipping, providing after-sales support, etc.) is the most valuable? The allocation problem would be a nightmare!

But accountants can and have solved allocation problems before. The more serious problem is that the revenue principle is not satisfied at any time prior to delivery. Risks and rewards of ownership have not passed to the customer, and the increase in net asset value is not, therefore, reasonably assured. Remember, revenue recognition prior to delivery is aggressive, and rare except in special industries. Notwithstanding this fact, there are a few cases where it is not only acceptable, but even desirable, to take the required leap of faith and recognize revenue as effort is expended.

LONG-TERM CONTRACTS

In some instances the earnings process extends over several accounting periods. Delivery of the final product may occur years after the initiation of the project. Examples are construction of large ships, office buildings, development of space-exploration equipment, and development of large-scale custom software. Contracts for these projects often provide for progress billings at various points in the earnings process.

If the seller waits until the project or contract is completed to recognize revenue, the information on revenue and expense included in the financial statements will be reliable, but it may not be relevant for decision-making because the information is not timely.

For example, the financial reporting objective of performance evaluation is reasonably well served only if the financial statements report on the results of the enterprise's economic activity during the period. Delaying revenue recognition on long-term projects until the project is complete tells the financial statement reader nothing about economic activity (i.e., performance) during the period.

The cash flow reporting objective also is not well served by delaying revenue recognition, because the cash is flowing out (and usually in, as well) as the project is performed, not at the end. Therefore, it often is worthwhile to trade off reliability in order to provide more timely, relevant earnings information. There are two general methods of accounting for revenue on long-term contracts:

1. *Completed-contract method.* Revenues, expenses, and resulting gross profit are recognized only when the contract is completed. As costs are incurred, they are accumulated in an inventory account (*projects in progress*). Progress billings are not recorded as revenues, but are accumulated in a *billings on projects in progress* account that is deducted from the inventory account (i.e., a *contra* account to inventory). At the completion of the contract, all the accounts are closed, and the entire gross profit from the project is recognized.

2. *Percentage-of-completion method.* The percentage-of-completion method recognizes revenue on a long-term project as work progresses so that timely information is provided. Revenues, expenses, and gross profit are recognized each accounting period based on an estimate of the percentage of completion of the project. Project costs and gross profit to date are accumulated in the inventory account (projects in progress). Progress billings are accumulated in a contra inventory account (billings on projects in progress).

The *CICA Handbook* recommends that revenue from long-term contracts should be recognized by whichever method "relates the revenue to the work accomplished":

> Such performance should be regarded as having been achieved when reasonable assurance exists regarding the measurement of the consideration

that will be derived from rendering the service or performing the long-term contract.   [*CICA* 3400.08]

The percentage-of-completion and completed-contract methods are not intended to be free choice alternatives for the same circumstances. Is there a contract that establishes the contract price with a high degree of reliability? Is collection reasonably assured? These conditions would be met by the standard provisions of a long-term contract that involves a creditworthy customer expected to make regular progress payments.

The critical criteria are whether the seller can estimate with reasonable assurance (1) the progress toward completion of the contractual obligation and (2) the costs to complete the project. If these criteria are met, percentage of completion is the method that very clearly *relates the revenue to the work performed*. If the criteria are not met, the completed-contract method should be used. Of course, judgement plays a role in determining whether the criteria are met, and particular reporting objectives usually influence the selection of method.

Measuring Progress toward Completion

Measuring progress toward completion of a long-term project can be accomplished by using either input measures or output measures:

1. *Input measures.* The effort devoted to a project to date is compared with the total effort expected to be required in order to complete the project. Examples are (1) costs incurred to date compared with total estimated costs for the project and (2) labour hours worked compared with total estimated labour hours required to complete the project.

2. *Output measures.* Results to date are compared with total results when the project is completed. Examples are the number of kilometres of highway completed compared with total kilometres to be completed, or progress milestones established in a software development contract.

An expert, such as an engineer or architect, is often hired to assess percentage of completion or achievement of milestones, which is an art, not a science.

The goal is to have a realistic measure of progress made toward completion of the project. Neither input nor output measures are always ideal. Input measures are often used when it is difficult to measure progress using output measures. However, input measures can be misleading when no relatively constant relationship between the input measure and productivity exists. Cost overruns on projects would cause erroneous levels of completion to be estimated. Costs incurred also may be misleading as a measure of progress if costs include one-time, up-front expenditures for quantities of materials and supplies to be used during the construction period.

Despite their shortcomings, input measures are most frequently used because they are the most readily available. Among input measures, the cost-to-cost method is the most common. The cost-to-cost method measures the percentage completed by the ratio of costs incurred to date to the current estimate of the total costs required to complete the project:

$$\text{Percent complete} = \frac{\text{Total costs incurred to date}}{\substack{\text{Most recent estimate of} \\ \text{total costs of project} \\ \text{(past and future)}}}$$

The most recent estimate of total project costs is the sum of the total costs incurred to date plus the estimated costs yet to be incurred to complete the project. Once the percentage completed has been computed, the amount of revenue to recognize in the current period is determined as:

$$\text{Current period's revenue} = (\text{Percent complete} \times \text{Total contract revenue})$$
$$- \text{Revenue previously recognized}$$

Example

There can be dramatic differences between the revenue and income effects of the completed-contract and percentage-of-completion methods. The completed-contract method is the simplest and most straightforward and it is discussed first.

To demonstrate the two methods, assume that the Ace Construction Company has contracted to erect a building for $1.5 million, starting construction on 1 February 20X1, with a planned completion date of 1 August 20X3. Total costs to complete the contract are estimated at $1.35 million, so the estimated gross profit is expected to be $150,000. Progress billings payable within 10 days after billing will be made on a predetermined schedule. Assume that the data shown in the upper portion of Exhibit 6-4 pertain to the three-year construction period. The facts for each of the three years will be ascertained as each year goes by. That is, in 20X1 the contractor does not know the information that is shown in the columns for 20X2 and 20X3.

The total construction costs were originally estimated at $1,350,000, of which $350,000 were incurred in 20X1. In 20X2, another $550,000 in costs were incurred, but the estimated total costs rose by $10,000 in 20X2, to $1,360,000. In 20X3, the total costs rose by another $5,000, and the total cost to complete the project turns out to be $1,365,000. Contract profit therefore drops from the original estimate of $150,000 to an actual amount of $135,000.

As costs are incurred, they are debited to an inventory account called *construction in progress*. This inventory account is a *current* asset even for a multi-year project because the operating cycle of the contractor is the length of the longest project (rather than one year).

Construction companies do not wait until the end of the project to collect their money. Instead, **progress billings** are made throughout the duration of the project. The amount of progress billings is based on the amount of work accomplished to the date of the billing, as verified by an independent facilitator.

Progress billings are debited to *accounts receivable* and credited to *billings on contracts*, which is subtracted from the construction-in-progress inventory on the balance sheet. If the net of the construction-in-progress inventory (inventory less billings on contract) results in a debit balance, it is reported as a current asset. This account balance represents the contractor's net ownership interest in the construction project; it is sometimes referred to as the *contractor's draw*.

If the net amount in the construction-in-progress inventory is a credit balance, it represents the developer's (buyer's) interest in the project and is referred to as the *developer's draw*. A credit balance is reported as a current liability in the contractor's financial statements.

Completed-Contract Method

Under the completed-contract method, there is no recognition of the project *in the income statement* until the project is completed and has been legally accepted by the customer.

The journal entries to record the construction-in-progress inventory, progress billings, and collections of progress billings for each year for Ace Construction are shown in the lower portion of Exhibit 6-4.

At the completion of the contact, income is recognized as the difference between the accumulated credit balance in the billings on contracts account and the debit balance in the construction-in-progress inventory account, assuming that the total price of the contract has been billed. The accumulated amount of billings on contracts is recognized as sales revenue, and the accumulated amount of construction-in-progress inventory on completion of the contract is recognized as cost of goods sold. It is this series of entries that increases net assets:

EXHIBIT 6-4
Example of Completed Contract Accounting

ACE CONSTRUCTION COMPANY
Construction Project Fact Sheet
Three-Year Summary Schedule

Contract Price: $1,500,000

		20X1	20X2	20X3
1.	Estimated total costs for project	$1,350,000	$1,360,000	$1,365,000
2.	Costs incurred during current year	350,000	550,000	465,000
3.	Cumulative costs incurred to date	350,000	900,000	1,365,000
4.	Estimated costs to complete at year-end	1,000,000	460,000	0
5.	Progress billings during year	300,000	575,000	625,000
6.	Cumulative billings to date	300,000	875,000	1,500,000
7.	Collections on billings during year	270,000	555,000	675,000
8.	Cumulative collections to date	270,000	825,000	1,500,000

	20X1		20X2		20X3	
Construction-in-progress inventory	350,000		550,000		465,000	
Cash, payables, etc.		350,000		550,000		465,000
Accounts receivable	300,000		575,000		625,000	
Billings on contracts		300,000		575,000		625,000
Cash	270,000		555,000		675,000	
Accounts receivable		270,000		555,000		675,000

Billings on contracts	1,500,000	
Revenue from long-term contracts		1,500,000
Costs of construction	1,365,000	
Construction-in-progress inventory		1,365,000

On balance sheets during the construction period, the construction-in-progress inventory is reported as total accumulated costs to date less the total progress billings to date.

The completed contract method has the advantage of delaying profit measurement until substantially all of the costs and revenues are known. There may be some remaining costs that are roughly analogous to warranty costs; these can be estimated and accrued. Although the costs and revenues are known with a high degree of assurance, the *timing* of their recognition in the income statement is a matter for some manipulation. Contractors have been known to informally suggest to customers that they may want to delay formal acceptance of the project until after the contractor's year-end, usually in order to delay taxation. Taxation officials are aware of this practice, however, and often reach into the next year and claim tax on the profits generated on projects "closed" during the first two months of the contractor's next fiscal year.

The completed-contract method ranks high on the qualitative characteristic of objectivity because there is so little estimation involved. On the other hand, the method is perceived as lacking in the qualitative attributes of relevance and timeliness because the benefit of the contractor's economic activity during the year is not reflected on the income statement as long as the project is under way. Therefore, the completed-contract method is not very helpful if the dominant reporting objective is performance evaluation. The method is very useful for income tax minimization, however, since there is no taxation until the project is complete (even if there may be dispute about which period it was completed in).

Percentage-of-Completion Method

The objective of the percentage-of-completion method is to provide an estimate of the earnings of the company that will arise as the result of its economic activity (i.e., working on construction projects) during the year. Since the contractor spent a lot of time, effort, and money working on projects in progress, performance evaluation is better served if periodic profit (or loss) is measured on the basis of *effort expended* rather than contracts completed.

Under the percentage-of-completion method, a portion of revenue and expense (and thus income) is recognized as it is earned in each accounting period. The amount of income that is recognized is *added to the construction-in-progress inventory*. By adding the income earned to date to the inventory, the inventory is, in effect, being increased to its net realizable value. Total actual income on the contract will not be known until the project is completed; what is recognized each period is an *estimate* of income that is based on many other estimates, as we discuss shortly.

Using the data shown in the upper portion of Exhibit 6-4, the relative proportion of the total costs that have been incurred to date can be used to determine percentage completed.

	20X1	20X2	20X3
Costs incurred to date	$ 350,000	$ 900,000	$1,365,000
Estimated total costs	1,350,000	1,360,000	1,365,000
Percent completed	26%	66%	100%

The percentage completed is computed by dividing the estimate of *costs incurred to date* by the *estimated total costs*. For example, estimated total costs at the end of 20X1 ($1,350,000) equals costs incurred to date ($350,000) plus estimated costs to complete at the end of 20X1 ($1,000,000). The percentages shown above have been rounded to the nearest full percentage point. The "exact" percentage for 20X2, to be precise, is 66.17647...%. But there is no point in calculating the percentage of completion to more than two digits (or, at the most, three). We are working with estimates here, and it is silly to be "precise" in calculating percentages that are based on approximations.

The next step is to compute the total amount of revenue recognizable *through* each year-end by multiplying the total contract revenue by the percentage completed for each year:

	20X1	20X2	20X3
20X1: $1.5 million × 26%	$390,000	—	—
20X2: $1.5 million × 66%	—	$990,000	—
20X3: $1.5 million × 100%	—	—	$1,500,000
Less: revenue previously recognized	—	(390,000)	(990,000)
Recognized revenue for the year	$390,000	$600,000	$ 510,000

The gross profit to be recognized is the difference between revenue and costs incurred in the period:

	20X1	20X2	20X3	Total
Revenue for the current period	$390,000	$600,000	$ 510,000	$1,500,000
Costs incurred in the current period	350,000	550,000	465,000	1,365,000
Gross profit for the period	$ 40,000	$ 50,000	$ 45,000	$ 135,000

The journal entries to record the costs incurred on the construction, the progress billings, and the collections of progress billings are the same as those for the completed-contract method. An additional entry is needed to record the recognition of revenue and expense each period. The gross profit is debited to the construction-in-progress inventory:

	20X1		20X2		20X3	
Construction-in-progress inventory (B/S)	40,000		50,000		45,000	
Costs of construction (I/S)	350,000		550,000		465,000	
Revenue from long-term contracts (I/S)		390,000		600,000		510,000

The construction-in-progress inventory account is greater under the percentage-of-completion method than under the completed-contract method by the amount of gross margin recognized to date. *This is the increase in net assets that always accompanies revenue recognition.*

Notice that the balance of the construction-in-progress inventory account is *not* reduced each year as the revenue and related costs are recognized in the income statement. On the income statement, the recognized gross profit is disaggregated into revenue less costs of construction. The offset to the inventory account is the billings on contracts account, just as for the completed-contract method.

When the project is completed, the billings on contracts will completely offset the construction-in-progress inventory. A journal entry is needed to remove both accounts from the books of Ace Construction:

Billings on contracts	1,500,000	
Construction-in-progress inventory		1,500,000

Comparison of Results

Exhibit 6-5 compares the financial statement presentations for the completed-contract method and the percentage-of-completion method. Under the completed-contract method, inventory is carried at cost. Under the percentage-of-completion method, inventory is carried at cost plus recognized gross profit.

The difference between year-end inventory amounts under the two methods is the accumulated gross margin recognized under the percentage-of-completion method. Exhibit 6-5 also shows the dramatic difference in gross profit between the two methods on a year-to-year basis. However, *total gross profit over the three years is the same for each method.* This is another of the allocation games of which accountants are so fond.

Accounting for Losses on Long-Term Contracts

When the costs necessary to complete a contract result in losses, two situations are possible:

1. *The loss results in an unprofitable contract.* In this situation, the loss is recognized in full in the year it becomes estimable. For example, assume that, at the end of 20X2, Ace's costs incurred are as shown ($350,000 in 20X1 and $550,000 in

EXHIBIT 6-5
Financial Statement Presentation of
Accounting for Long-Term Construction Contracts

COMPLETED-CONTRACT METHOD

	20X1	20X2	20X3
Balance Sheet:			
Current Assets:			
Accounts Receivable	$ 30,000	$ 50,000	
Inventory:			
Construction in progress	350,000	900,000	
Less: Billings on contracts	300,000	875,000	
Construction in progress in excess of billings	50,000	25,000	
Income Statement:			
Revenue from long-term contracts	$0	$0	$1,500,000
Costs of construction	0	0	1,365,000
Gross profit	0	0	135,000

Note 1: Summary of significant accounting policies.
Long-term construction contracts. revenues and income from long-term construction contracts are recognized under the completed-contract method. Such contracts are generally for a duration in excess of one year. Construction costs and progress billings are accumulated during the periods of construction. Only when the project is completed are revenue, expense, and income recognized on the project.

PERCENTAGE-OF-COMPLETION METHOD

	20X1	20X2	20X3
Balance Sheet:			
Current Assets:			
Accounts Receivable	$ 30,000	$ 50,000	
Inventory:			
Construction in progress	390,000	990,000	
Less: Billings on contracts	300,000	875,000	
Construction in progress in excess of billings	90,000	115,000	
Income Statement:			
Revenue from long-term contracts	$390,000	$600,000	$510,000
Costs of construction	350,000	550,000	465,000
Gross Profit	40,000	50,000	45,000

Note 1: Summary of significant accounting policies.
Long-term construction contracts. Revenues and income from long-term construction contracts are recognized under the percentage-of-completion method. Such contracts are generally for a duration in excess of one year. Construction costs and progress billings are accumulated during the periods of construction. The amount of revenue recognized each year is based on the ratio of the costs incurred to the estimated total costs of completion of the construction contract.

20X2), but the estimate of the costs to complete the contract in 20X3 increases to $625,000 from $465,000, an increase of $160,000.

Since costs incurred through 20X2 total $900,000, the total estimated cost of the contract becomes $1,525,000 (instead of $1,365,000), and there is now an expected loss on the contract of $25,000.

The $25,000 loss would be recognized in 20X2 under both methods of accounting for long-term construction contracts. A simple accrual entry is made for the completed-contract method, and the percentage-of-completion would record a gross loss of $65,000 ($25,000 + $40,000), which records the loss and reverses the profit recorded in prior years.

2. *The contract remains profitable, but there is a current-year loss.* Suppose Ace's costs incurred to the end of 20X2 are as shown, but the estimate to complete the contract has increased to $550,000. Total costs of $900,000 have already been incurred; thus, the total estimated cost of completing the contract has risen to $1,450,000. The contract will still generate a gross margin of $50,000.

Under the completed-contract method, all items are deferred until 20X3, and no entry is needed in 20X2. For the percentage-of-completion method, the 20X2 completion percentage is reworked (now 62%; $900,000 ÷ $1,450,000). This decreases the amount of revenue that will be reported, and results in a reported gross loss in 20X2.

Estimating Costs and Revenues

It is important to understand the extent of the estimates and approximations that underlie the percentage-of-completion method. Obviously, the *cost to complete* is an estimate. It may be wildly off the mark, because large scale projects are often begun before the final design is even completed.

A six-week television series produced by PBS titled "Skyscraper" showed the progress on construction of a Manhattan office building from design to final acceptance. One point made early in the show was that the developer couldn't wait until the building's design was fully developed before beginning construction; there was just too much potential revenue to be lost by waiting another year or so to completely finish all of the details. The old cliché is that "time is money," and nowhere is this adage truer than in real property development. Therefore, estimates of "cost to complete" are informed judgements, but they can change radically over the course of the contract.

As well, the "costs incurred to date" is an estimate! How much of the contractor's overhead is to be included in the costs assigned to the project, and how much is charged as a period cost? What proportion of purchased and/or contracted materials should be included in cost to date? If the contractor has ordered and had delivered 5,000 tons of bricks for exterior sheathing, should the cost of those bricks be included in the cost to date when the bricks are purchased or should the cost be excluded until the bricks are actually used in construction of the building?

Finally, a commonly overlooked estimate is that of the *revenue*. True, any long-term construction contract starts out with a contract price, but the initial price hardly ever ends up being the real revenue figure. Indeed, contractors often bid on jobs at zero profit or even at a loss in order to get the job. The reason is that every construction job involves *change orders*, which is a change in the original design of the building (or of whatever is being constructed). Change orders require additional revenue, and the contractor often bids low on the original contract because he knows that he will make his money on the change orders (which can hardly be submitted to a competitive bidding process!). So, in the course of a construction project

- the estimated cost to complete will change each period;
- the cost incurred in the current period (to be used in the percentage calculation) is an estimate; and
- the estimated total revenue will change from period to period.

It is safe to say that the percentage-of-completion method is an approximation! It represents a trade-off between conflicting qualitative criteria; objectivity is sacrificed for timeliness and relevance.

PROPORTIONAL PERFORMANCE METHOD FOR SERVICE COMPANIES

The proportional performance method is used to recognize service revenue that is earned by more than a single act, when the service extends beyond one accounting period. In fact, recording interest revenue or rental revenue as time passes are really applications of proportional performance methods. Revenue is recognized based on the proportional performance of each act.

The proportional performance method of accounting for service revenue is similar to the percentage-of-completion method and has to meet the same criteria as a long-term construction contract:

- a fixed price contract with reasonable assurance of collection,
- a way to measure extent of performance, and
- an ability to estimate the remaining costs to completion.

Many service contracts are subject to at least as many uncertainties as are construction contracts. In particular, it is not unusual for the revenue to change as the client changes the scope of the assignment or the specifications of the task. Software contracts, for example, can double or triple in price if the client keeps changing his mind about what he wants the software to do.

Proportional measurement takes different forms depending on the type of service transaction:

1. *Similar performance acts.* An equal amount of service revenue is recognized for each such act (for example, processing of monthly mortgage payments by a mortgage banker).

2. *Dissimilar performance acts.* Service revenue is recognized in proportion to the seller's direct costs to perform each act (for example, providing examinations, and grading by a correspondence school). If the direct cost of each act cannot be measured reliably, the total service sales revenue should be prorated to the various acts by the relative sales value method. If sales value cannot be identified with each act, the straight-line method to measure proportional performance can be used.

3. *Similar acts with a fixed period for performance.* Service revenue is allocated and recognized by the straight-line method over the fixed period, unless another allocation method is more appropriate (for example, providing maintenance services on equipment for a fixed periodic fee).

CHOOSING A REVENUE RECOGNITION POLICY

This chapter has illustrated many different ways in which revenue can be recognized. Revenue recognition is the most pervasive and most difficult single accounting policy choice that many companies must face. With such a plentiful supply of alternatives, how can a company choose an appropriate policy?

Although there are many theoretical alternatives, the choice of policy is not a free game. The revenue recognition policy is, first and foremost, a function of the revenue-generating activity of the enterprise. When there is more than one revenue-generating activity, then there *may* be a different policy for each. For example, a retail company that engages in straightforward sales activity for cash or credit will probably recognize sales revenue at the point of delivery, while for interest revenue on its outstanding credit card balances the company will likely recognize interest revenue as time elapses.

A chosen revenue recognition policy must satisfy the general recognition criteria of *measurability* and *probability*. Revenue must be measurable with reasonable assurance, and its eventual realization (in cash) must be highly probable. It is important to bear in mind that the act of revenue recognition *increases the net assets of the company*. The increase may be through an increase in cash, accounts receivable, or inventories, but ultimately the amount must be realizable in cash.

Measurability and probability are essential requirements for revenue recognition, but those are relative terms. There is a trade-off between those two qualitative characteristics and those of relevance and timeliness. The earlier revenue is recognized, the more difficult it is to measure and the less certain it is of eventual realization. But the later revenue is recognized, the less useful it is for predicting cash flows and for evaluating management's performance.

Often, there are several different points in a single revenue-generating activity at which revenue can be recognized. This is especially true if the activity involves a sustained effort to earn the revenue or to collect it. The choice of revenue recognition policies depends very heavily on the financial reporting objectives of the company and on the motivations of its managers. An objective of income tax minimization will lead to a much different revenue recognition policy than will an objective of maximizing net income. Revenue recognition policy is, very often, the supreme test of an accountant's professional judgement.

CONCEPT REVIEW

1. What qualitative characteristics are better served by completed-contract reporting than by percentage-of-completion reporting?
2. Which financial reporting objectives are satisfied more by the percentage-of-completion method than by the completed-contract method?
3. What estimates are required in order to use the percentage-of-completion method?
4. How does the construction-in-progress inventory balance differ between the percentage-of-completion method and the completed-contract method?

RECOGNITION OF GAINS AND LOSSES

Gains and losses are distinguished from revenues and expenses in that they usually result from peripheral or incidental transactions, events, or circumstances. Whether an item is a gain or loss or an ordinary revenue or expense depends in part on the reporting company's primary activities or businesses.

For example, when a company that is primarily involved in manufacturing and marketing products sells some of its land, the transaction is accounted for as a net gain or loss because this is not the primary business of the company. When a real estate sales company sells land, however, the transaction gives rise to revenues and expenses.

A gain or loss may result from purely internal transactions, such as a write-down related to a plant closing. Such gains and losses are also recognized in the period when the transaction occurs and are shown net.

Most gains and losses are recognized when the transaction is completed. Thus, gains and losses from disposal of operational assets, sale of investments, and early extinguishment of debt are recognized only when the final transaction is recorded. However, estimated losses are recognized before their ultimate realization if they both (1) are probable and (2) can reasonably be estimated.

Examples are losses on disposal of a segment of the business, pending litigation, and expropriation of assets. If both conditions are not met, the nature and possible amount of the possible loss must be disclosed in a note to the financial statements. In contrast, gains are almost never recognized before the completion of a transaction that establishes the existence and amount of the gain. A gain should be recognized only when realized, except as explained in the following paragraph. This reflects an appropriate degree of skepticism.

There are circumstances in which gains and losses are recognized when there has been a *change in value* rather than a transaction. This happens when inventory items are reported at market value instead of cost. Examples of such inventory items include

- *Commodities that are carried at market value.* If a company produces commodities that are readily saleable on an open public market or to a marketing board, as described above for *recognition prior to delivery*, the act of revenue recognition means that the inventories are revalued from the cost of production to their market price. If the company holds the inventory from one period to another, changes in market value are recognized as gains or losses for the period. Examples include farm products (e.g., hogs, cattle, wheat, eggs) and many natural resources (e.g., gold, silver, copper, oil).

- *Marketable securities held by a financial institution.* Securities dealers must report their inventory of securities held for sale at market. Investment companies (such as mutual funds) must carry their investment portfolio at market value so that investors can be informed of the net asset value of the company's holdings. Banks must carry the securities held in their trading account at market value. Life insurance companies report their investments on a five-year moving average of market prices. Companies such as these will recognize gains or losses on their investment portfolios. In some industries the *realized* gains and losses are segregated from the *unrealized*, but both realized and unrealized are *recognized*.

It should be noted that changes in the market value of these types of items are referred to as gains and losses even though they are a part of the normal business activities of the enterprise. There is nothing peripheral about gains and losses on securities held by a bank!

Losses may also be recognized when the recoverable value of an asset falls below its historical cost. Common examples are inventory (discussed in Chapter 9), capital assets (discussed in Chapter 11), and long-term investments (discussed in Chapter 12).

REVENUE ON THE CASH FLOW STATEMENT

This chapter discussed the concept that economic revenue grows or is earned over time — sometimes in a brief time span, but often over quite a long period of time. Accounting, on the other hand, tends to recognize revenue at a particular *point* in a more continuous earning cycle. On occasion, revenue recognition also coincides with the cash inflow, but that circumstance is quite rare. Usually, a company recognizes revenue prior to receiving the cash. Cash flow seldom coincides with revenue recognition.

In order to report cash flow from operations, the accruals relating to revenue recognition must be removed. The primary adjustments are

- Any increase in accounts receivable or notes receivable from customers must be deducted from net income (or from revenue); a decrease in receivables would be added.

- Expenses that are recorded in order to achieve matching must similarly be added back to net income (or deducted from total operating expenses, if the direct method is used); examples include warranty provisions and bad debt expense.

- Unearned revenue must be added to revenue; the cash has been received but revenue has not yet been recognized.

Revenue can be recognized only if the cash flow is highly probable. The reporting problem is that revenue recognition and cash flow often do not occur in the same accounting period.

DISCLOSURE

The choice of revenue recognition method can have enormous impact on a company's reported earnings. As we have seen, most methods require some accounting estimates, and some methods require a great deal of estimation.

The *CICA Handbook* contains no explicit requirement for disclosure of revenue recognition policies, except for the general requirement that a company disclose its policies when there is a choice of policy. In practice, less than half of public companies seem to disclose their revenue recognition policies.[11]

A good example of detailed disclosure is that of Western Star Truck Holdings Inc.:

> Revenue from the sale of trucks is recognized when ownership is transferred. Revenue from the sale of manufactured buses is recognized on a percentage of completion method, applied on the basis of defined milestones. Provisions are made for anticipated losses, if any, as soon as they become evident. Unbilled revenue represents revenue that has been recorded under the percentage of completion method but has not yet been invoiced to the customer. Revenue from sales of after-market parts is recognized upon shipment to customers.

Other disclosures are less informative. Cara Operations reports its revenue recognition policies as follows:

> Income on the sale of franchises is recognized when it is considered earned. Revenues from services are recognized as services are rendered.

This note leaves an important question hanging: when does the company consider franchise revenue (e.g., Swiss Chalet; Harveys) as having been earned?

An example of a company that is silent on its revenue recognition policies is The Molson Companies. Molson's has significant business interests in brewing (Molson; Coors; Foster's), sports (Montreal Canadiens; the Molson Centre, Montreal), and retailing (Home Depot; Beaver Lumber). A reader of the financial statements might think that there are significant revenue recognition issues surrounding some of these businesses, but the company presents no information regarding revenue recognition.

CONCEPT REVIEW

1. What basic recognition criteria must be satisfied before a particular revenue recognition policy can be used?
2. What is the relationship between *revenue recognition* and a company's *net asset value*?
3. When there is more than one feasible revenue recognition policy that a company could use for a revenue-generating activity, how is a single policy chosen from the feasible set of policies?
4. When might a company recognize a gain due to an *event* rather than a *transaction*?
5. What adjustments must be made to *revenue* when the cash flow statement is prepared?

---

[11] *Financial Reporting in Canada 1997*, p. 56.

SUMMARY OF KEY POINTS

1. For most companies, the earnings process is continuous. That is, the profit-directed activities of the company continually generate inflows or enhancements of the assets of the company.

2. Revenue recognition policies must be chosen carefully because of their profound effect on key financial results.

3. Before the results of the earnings process are recognized in the accounting records, revenue must meet the recognition criteria of *probability* and *measurability*. Revenue must also be *earned*, and *realized or realizable*.

4. A sale transaction is usually measured at the sales invoice price. When there are long-term, interest-free payment terms, discounting may be appropriate.

5. Barter transactions are typically recognized at the value of the asset or service given in the exchange.

6. Revenue can be recognized at a *critical event* or on the basis of *effort expended*. Critical events can be delivery, prior to delivery (e.g., on production, if there are no uncertainties regarding the sale transaction), or after delivery (if there are significant uncertainties about measurement, collection, or remaining costs). *Delivery* is the normal critical event that triggers revenue recognition.

7. The recognition of revenue results in an increase in net assets, which is recognized at the critical event. Costs incurred prior to the critical event are deferred. When revenue is recognized, deferred costs are expensed, and future costs are accrued.

8. The instalment sales method of revenue recognition delays recognition of gross profit until cash is collected.

9. The cost recovery method is a conservative method in which no profit is recognized until all costs associated with the sale item have been recovered in cash. All subsequent cash collections are profit.

10. Long-term contracts can be accounted for using the percentage-of-completion method, or the completed-contract method. If a long-term, fixed-price contract with a creditworthy customer is accompanied by reasonably reliable estimates of (a) cost to complete and (b) percentage of completion, based either on output or input, percentage-of-completion is appropriate.

11. Under the completed-contract method, revenues and expenses are recognized when the contract obligations are completed. Costs incurred in completing the contract are accrued in an inventory account, and any progress billings are accrued in a contra-inventory account.

12. Long-term contracts are often accounted for on the basis of effort expended. Under the percentage-of-completion method, revenues and expenses are recognized each accounting period based on an estimate of the percentage of completion. Costs incurred in completing the contract and recognized gross profit are accrued in an inventory account.

13. Revenue recognition policies are chosen in accordance with the financial reporting objectives of the enterprise, constrained by the general recognition criteria of probability and measurability. The choice of a revenue recognition policy involves a trade-off between qualitative criteria, such as between verifiability and timeliness.

14. Cash flow from operations must be computed by adjusting revenue (or net income) for changes in accounts and notes receivable, for changes in unearned revenue, and for accrued expenses that do not represent cash expenditures during the period.

REVIEW PROBLEM

Precision Punctual Construction Company has agreed to build a 10-storey office building for Mountain Bank Limited. The contract calls for a contract price of $15,000,000 for the building, with progress payments being made by Mountain as the construction proceeds. The period of construction is estimated to be 30 months. The contract is signed on 1 February 20X5, and construction begins immediately. The building is completed and turned over to Mountain Bank on 1 December 20X7.

Data on cost incurred, estimated costs to complete, progress billings, and progress payments over the period of construction are as follows:

	($ thousands)		
	20X5	**20X6**	**20X7**
Costs incurred this period	$ 1,500	$ 7,875	$ 3,825
Costs incurred to date	1,500	9,375	13,200
Estimated costs to complete at year-end	10,500	3,125	0
Estimated total costs of project	12,000	12,500	13,200
Progress billings this period	1,200	6,000	7,800
Progress payments received this period	825	6,300	7,875

Required:

1. Show the entries to account for this project over the period of construction, assuming that PPC uses
   a. the completed-contract method of recognizing revenue.
   b. the percentage-of-completion method of recognizing revenue
2. Show the relevant balance sheet and income statement items for 20X5, 20X6, and 20X7 for PPC, assuming that the company uses
   a. the completed contract method.
   b. the percentage-of-completion method.

REVIEW PROBLEM — SOLUTION

1 and 2: The entries to record the construction of the building for both the completed-contract method and the percentage-of-completion method are as follows (in $ thousands):

Entries for 20X5:

		Completed-contract method		Percentage-of-completion method	
a.	To record incurrence of construction costs:				
	Construction-in-progress inventory	1,500		1,500	
	Cash, payables, etc.		1,500		1,500
b.	To record progress billings:				
	Accounts receivable	1,200		1,200	
	Billings on contract		1,200		1,200
c.	To record billing collections:				
	Cash	825		825	
	Accounts receivable		825		825
d.	To recognize revenue for percentage of completion:*				
	Construction-in-progress inventory			375	
	Cost of construction			1,500	
	Revenue from long-term contract				1,875

* The percentage of completion is the cost incurred to date divided by total esti-mated project costs, or $1,500 ÷ $12,000 = 12.5%. The total amount of revenue recognizable to this point is $15,000 × 12.5% = $1,875.

Entries for 20X6:

		Completed-contract method		Percentage-of-completion method	
a.	To record incurrence of construction costs:				
	Construction-in-progress inventory	7,875		7,875	
	Cash, payables, etc.		7,875		7,875
b.	To record progress billings:				
	Accounts receivable	6,000		6,000	
	Billings on contract		6,000		6,000
c.	To record billing collections:				
	Cash	6,300		6,300	
	Accounts receivable		6,300		6,300
d.	To recognize revenue for percentage of completion:*				
	Construction-in-progress inventory			1,500	
	Cost of construction			7,875	
	Revenue from long-term contract				9,375

* The percentage of completion is the cost incurred to date divided by total esti-mated project costs, or $9,375 ÷ $12,500 = 75%. The total amount of revenue recognizable to this point is $15,000 × 75% = $11,250. Since $1,875 was recog-nized in 20X5, the amount recognizable in 20X6 is $11,250 – $1,875 = $9,375.

Entries for 20X7:

		Completed-contract method		Percentage-of-completion method	
a.	To record incurrence of construction costs:				
	Construction-in-progress inventory	3,825		3,825	
	Cash, payables, etc.		3,825		3,825
b.	To record progress billings:				
	Accounts receivable	7,800		7,800	
	Billings on contract		7,800		7,800
c.	To record billing collections:				
	Cash	7,875		7,875	
	Accounts receivable		7,875		7,875
d.	To recognize revenue for percentage of completion:*				
	Cost of construction			3,825	
	Revenue from long-term contract				3,750
	Construction-in-progress inventory				75

* The project is completed; any remaining portion of the contract price not previously recognized as revenue should be recognized this period. In prior years, $1,875 + $9,375 = $11,250 was recognized, thus $3,750 (i.e., $15,000 – $11,250) is recognized in 20X7.

e. *To record elimination of contract*
      costs from inventory:
      Billings on contract   15,000
         Construction-in-progress
            inventory   15,000

f. *To recognize revenue for*
      completed contract:
      Billings on contract   15,000
      Cost of earned construction revenue   13,200
            Revenue from long-term contracts   15,000
            Construction-in-progress inventory   13,200

	31 Dec. 20X5		31 Dec. 20X6		31 Dec. 20X7	
	Completed contract	Percentage of completion	Completed contract	Percentage of completion	Completed contract	Percentage of completion
Balance sheet:						
Accounts receivable	$ 375	$ 375	$ 75	$ 75	0	0
Inventory:						
Construction in progress	$1,500	$1,875	$9,375	$11,250	0	0
Less: Billings on contract	(1,200)	(1,200)	(7,200)	(7,200)	0	0
Construction in progress in excess of billings	$ 300	$ 675	$2,175	$ 4,050	0	0
Income statement:						
Revenue from long-term contracts	$ —	$1,875	$ —	$ 9,375	$15,000	$3,750
Cost of construction	$ —	(1,500)	$ —	(7,875)	(13,200)	(3,825)
Gross profit	$ —	$ 375	$ —	$ 1,500	$ 1,800	$ (75)*

* This is an example of a current year loss on a contract that is profitable overall.

QUESTIONS

6-1   Explain the relation between the definition of revenue and the definitions of assets and liabilities.

6-2   When is revenue earned in economic terms? How does this relate to typical accounting revenue recognition?

6-3   What impact do individual corporate reporting objectives have on revenue recognition policies?

6-4   What are the fundamental criteria for recognition of any element in the financial statements? Explain the additional criteria that revenue must meet before being recognized.

6-5   What do the terms "realization" and "earned" mean in the context of revenue recognition?

6-6   Give two typical examples of revenues for which recognition occurs on the basis of the passage of time.

6-7   How is revenue measured in a barter transaction?

6-8   What is meant by revenue recognition at a critical event? Give examples of several critical events.

6-9   Why is revenue typically recognized on delivery?

6-10   Under what circumstances is revenue recognized at a critical event before delivery? After delivery?

6-11   Explain how a net asset increase is triggered by appropriate entries at the point of revenue recognition.

6-12   Why might a franchisor have to delay revenue recognition past the point in time at which the franchisee takes control of their franchise operation?

6-13   What is a consignment? How is revenue recognized on a consignment transaction?

6-14   What conditions must be met in order for revenue to be recognized when a customer has the right to return purchased products? What accounting procedures are used until all conditions are met?

6-15   Describe the instalment sales method of recognizing revenue and when it is appropriately used.

6-16   Describe the cost recovery method of recognizing revenue. When is it appropriate?

6-17   Identify and explain two different approaches for determining the extent of progress toward completion of a construction project.

6-18   Why is the ending inventory of construction in progress different in amount when the percentage-of-completion method is used compared with the completed-contract method? Explain the amount of the difference.

6-19   When a loss is projected on an unprofitable long-term construction contract, in what period(s) is the loss recognized under (a) percentage-of-completion and (b) completed contract methods?

6-20   Under what circumstances do gains and losses reflect changes in value, rather than realized transactions?

CASE 6-1

John and Mike

John and Mike set up a partnership early this year in order to speculate in real estate. They specialize in the acquisition of small, run-down apartment buildings, which they then renovate, rent out to improve occupancy rates, and resell. Mike works at this enterprise full-time, overseeing the renovation and rental process. John continues to work at a full-time salaried job in an unrelated business.

Annual profits are allocated as follows:

1. "Salary" of $50,000 to Mike
2. Interest to both partners of 10% per annum, based on monthly average capital balances
3. Remainder equally.

The partners have agreed on a schedule of monthly drawings, to be charged against each partner's capital accounts. Drawings may not exceed profit allocations.

In their first year, the partners successfully "flipped" three apartment buildings, and owned four more at year-end, awaiting resale. It is now the end of their first year, and accounting policies have yet to be finalized. The following are areas of contention:

1. *Revenue recognition, rental income*

Mike has proposed that revenue be recognized as rent is collected from tenants. John has proposed that rent revenue be recognized on the first day of the month, when it is due, whether collected or not. Typically, most rent is collected within a week, but there are always some problem tenants, especially in newly-bought buildings, which need extensive renovations and often have undesirable tenants.

2. *Depreciation policy, rental buildings*

John reasons that rental buildings are all for resale, and are thus "inventory." As such, he claims that no depreciation should be charged as long as net book value is less than market value. Mike is not convinced that this reasoning is valid, as he thinks depreciation is always incurred and must be recorded.

3. *Revenue recognition, building sale*

Often, there is a time lag between the sale of a building (that is, the date upon which the sale agreement is signed), the date on which title passes, and the date that the partnership receives all the sale proceeds. For example, in a recent sale, the agreement was signed on 1 November, and title passed on 15 December, at which time half of the proceeds were paid. The other half is due on 15 December in three years' time, with accrued interest, since the partnership took back a long-term note as part of the sale financing. John favours revenue recognition when the sale agreement is signed; Mike prefers to wait until the cash is collected.

Both partners have agreed that statements will primarily be used for profit allocation and need not necessarily follow GAAP. They are more concerned about cash flow, and in particular, making sure there is enough cash flow for partner's withdrawals.

Required:

Analyze the issues and present your recommendations to the partnership.

[CGA-Canada, adapted]

CASE 6-2

Tempus Fugit

Tempus Fugit is a large conglomerate of 30 subsidiary companies with plants and branches throughout the world. The company has been in the business of manufacturing and distributing clocks, watches, and other timepieces for over 50 years. Recently, the company experienced a change in management when the original founder retired and sold his controlling interest.

On 1 May 20X5, Smith & Smith, a publicly-traded international consulting firm, was awarded the contract to design and install a computerized management information system in each of Tempus Fugit's subsidiaries. The project was projected to take four years to complete. Michael Smith, the founder and managing partner of Smith & Smith, and his staff, worked exclusively on this project from May to October. Currently, one-half of the company's workforce is working on the job. Smith & Smith obtained this project after submitting a bid on 1 March 20X5, which took most of February to prepare; the bid price was $45,000,000.

It is January 20X6, and annual financial statements for Smith & Smith are being prepared. Michael Smith has come to you, the controller of the company, to discuss how the contract will be reported. He is anxious to present the contract as favourably as possible under the limitations of GAAP. His comments to you are:

"I know this is the first long-term contract that we have entered into, and I have heard that we can recognize revenue based on the percentage of the project that is complete. That percentage should be based on management's best estimates, as are so many things under GAAP. In my opinion, even though we are behind in the installation, we should recognize revenue according to the percentage that we estimated would be done in our contract bid. If we don't, Tempus Fugit's management will be on our backs, wondering what is going on and slowing us down even more. I sure don't need that with all of the problems we are experiencing on this project!"

You ask Smith about the problems that are being experienced on the project. He responds that they are of a highly technical nature. He urges you to complete the financial statements as soon as possible, since Smith & Smith is experiencing a cash flow shortage and Tempus Fugit will not release the first payment on the contract until the year-end statements have been received.

You are aware of the following facts about Smith & Smith and Tempus Fugit:

- Smith & Smith has been in business for five years. This is the first time the company has landed a contract of this magnitude. Previous contracts have all been completed within a one-year time frame.
- The contract provides for Tempus Fugit to pay in four equal annual instalments on receipt of audited statements from Smith & Smith. One-quarter of the project should be completed each year.
- Much of the contract involves design and testing of computer programs, and it is difficult to determine the degree of completion of the project at any time. Few external experts in the area exist, since Smith & Smith is in a new industry and a specialized field. The company has never been too concerned about estimating completion before because all of its contracts have been short-term.
- The auditor has no way of determining the percentage of completion of the project, since the work is so subjective. Because the same audit firm has been engaged by Smith & Smith for the past five years and has found the partners to be reputable, the auditor is generally able to rely on management's best estimates.

After your conversation with Michael Smith, you find yourself in the coffee room with Rachel Harris, the chief programmer on the Tempus Fugit project. You have always had a good relationship with Rachel since you share a common interest in show dogs. Out of curiosity, you ask her how much of the project she believes is done and about the problems the company is experiencing. Her response is:

"You know, the partners bid on this one to get us into the big leagues, and let me tell you, the big leagues are tough! We have never handled a project this large, and it is taking us a lot longer to get some of the basic systems developed than we ever imagined. Although it's hard to tell, I would say we are only about 10% done at this time. We are in the process of hiring more staff and establishing supplier relationships, and all of this takes time. I am still confident that we will complete the project in four years, but I don't think we will catch up to our original estimates until the third year. By then, the staff will be trained and we will be much more effective."

After coffee, you run into Michael Smith again. He asks that you meet him in his office Monday morning, ready to discuss the accounting options available for the project and your recommended accounting treatment. He is rushing out the door to a meeting with the banker, who called with some concerns about the company's cash flow problems.

Required:

Identify and analyze the alternative treatments available to account for the timing of the revenues and expenses that will be recognized in the contract with Tempus Fugit. What are the ethical issues you must consider before making your recommendation to Michael Smith? What should you say during the Monday morning meeting with Smith?

[CGA-Canada, adapted]

CASE 6-3

Kryton Corporation

Kryton Corporation is a property development company, with expertise in larger, multiple-unit apartment buildings. Kryton must comply with GAAP to satisfy bank lenders who provide project and working capital financing. Typically, the company finds a site, arranges for interim and mortgage financing, and then constructs the building through subcontractors. As the building is being built, Kryton looks for an investor to take over ownership of the building; often life insurance companies are interested, as are individuals through limited partnerships. Kryton has a property management division that runs such large apartment buildings.

It is now the end of 20X3, and their latest project, a 255-unit apartment building, has been harder to sell. A deal is finally in place. An agreement has been signed with a group of individual investors, who have formed a limited partnership. When the project is completed, in July 20X5, the building will be sold to the partners, who will pay Kryton as follows:

Cash, provided by first mortgage from Confidential Insurance	$11,000,000
Cash, payments by the partners to Kryton	1,000,000
4% notes receivable to Kryton from the investors, payable in four equal instalments on the anniversary of the turnover date	2,000,000
Five-year, 18% second mortgage provided by Kryton	1,500,000
	$15,500,000

The estimated costs of the project are $12,300,000, of which $6,500,000 have been incurred to the end of 20X3. Kryton intends to record the profit ($3,200,000) in July

20X5, when the building is completed. The assets received in consideration (listed above) would be recorded at that time. Further details on the purchase agreement are below.

Required:
Explain how Kryton should recognize revenue for the project.

KRYTON CORPORATION LTD.
Information on Purchase Agreement

The project differs from previous projects in both the manner of financing and in the number of indemnities and covenants that Kryton must provide. The turnover date, referred to below, is the date that the partnership assumes ownership of the project. It occurs when the project is 90% leased to occupants. Extracts from the offering memorandum:

Kryton second mortgage
The Kryton second mortgage will be in the principal amount of $1.5 million and will bear interest at the rate of 18% after the turnover date.
The mortgage will include the following terms:

1. The mortgage will be without recourse to the partners' personal assets.

2. Payments of principal and accrued interest at the maturity date are required only to the extent that proceeds are available from the refinancing of the first mortgage; the second mortgage is to be renewed for any unpaid balance for a further term, without interest.

3. The partnership will have the right to set off any amount owing by it under the second mortgage agreement against amounts by which Kryton is in default under the cash flow guarantee (see below).

Initial leasing period indemnity
The agreement provides that Kryton will operate the project on behalf of the partnership and will indemnify the partnership for all losses incurred in operating the project during the initial leasing period which ends on the turnover date.

Cash flow guarantee
Kryton has agreed to provide interest-free loans to the partnership for the following purposes:

1. To fund, as required, for a period of 10 years from the turnover date, the amount, if any, by which the total operating expenses of the project (including payments on account of principal and interest due on the first mortgage, but excluding non-cash items such as depreciation and reserves for replacement of equipment and chattels) exceed the aggregate gross income receipts from the project.

2. To fund, during the period commencing on the turnover date and ending on 31 December 20X5, the amount (the "Guaranteed Amount"), if any, by which the actual net cash flow is less than the Kryton-prepared forecast of net cash flow (this forecast is not reproduced here).

Management of the project
Kryton will be appointed manager of the project for a term of 10 years, and will be paid 5% of monthly gross cash receipts. Kryton will be responsible for the ongoing leasing of apartment units comprising the project, maintenance and repairs, collection of rents, payment of all expenses properly incurred in connection with such duties out of revenues received from the project including all amounts payable under the mortgages, the maintenance of fire and liability insurance on the project, the preparation of a cash budget for each year, and the annual remittance of cash surpluses to the partners.

CASE 6-4

Acme Construction Ltd.

Bob Bothwell had started Acme Construction Ltd. early in 20X2 after working for several years as a supervisor for a local construction company. An inheritance from his parents had provided the start-up capital. Bob's wife, Susan, did all of the book-keeping on weekends without pay to help conserve cash.

For the 20X2 and 20X3 year-ends, the firm, where you are employed as a stu-dent-in-accounts, had performed a review of the financial statements and prepared the tax returns for the company. In late December 20X4, Bob Bothwell phoned the partner in charge of the engagement to arrange a meeting in Bob's office on 30 December 20X4.

The partner asked George Cathcart, the senior field auditor on the engagement in 20X2 and 20X3, to represent him at the meeting and asked that you accompany George.

At the meeting, Bob explained that business was booming, and that he was con-sidering privately raising additional equity capital to undertake some very large pro-jects. He wanted to retain control of the company but was willing to relinquish sole ownership instead of increasing his bank loan. However, the preliminary draft state-ments for 20X4 did not look as impressive as he had expected.

He handed George and you a copy of the income statement (Exhibit 1), along with a summary of contracts undertaken (Exhibit 2). He shook his head and said, "I didn't bring the balance sheet because I don't think it is correct. The materials in inventory are worth $200,000 now, not the $150,000 I paid for them. The same thing applies to the temporary investments. My broker assures me that they are worth twice what I paid. I also don't see anything reflected in the financial statements about the lawsuit that I'm involved in. My lawyer says that, when we go to court next week, I'll be sure to win $27,000 from the subcontractor that delayed the curling rink pro-ject."

"My biggest problem is with the income figure," he continued. "I don't seem to get credit for the projects that are in progress, even though my costs are usually in line, and I know I'm making money. Is there any way to improve my net income with-out paying any additional income tax?"

Required:

Prepare a memo to George Cathcart. The memo is to include a revised net income fig-ure for both 20X4 and 20X3 assuming that the company changes its revenue recog-nition policy from completed-contract to percentage-of-completion, but continues to calculate taxes on the completed-contract basis. You should also include your thoughts on the best way to deal with the problems Bob raised. Cathcart will be using your work as a basis for his report to the partner.

[ICAO, adapted]

EXHIBIT 1
ACME CONSTRUCTION LTD.
Income Statement (draft)
for the year ended 31 December

	20X4	20X3
Net revenue from completed contracts	$365,000	$136,000
General and administrative expenses	172,000	100,000
Income before taxes	193,000	36,000
Income taxes	48,250	9,000
Net income for the year	$144,750	$ 27,000

Significant Accounting Policies

Revenue recognition: the company follows the completed contract method of recognizing revenue from construction projects.

EXHIBIT 2
ACME CONSTRUCTION LTD.
Summary of Contracts Undertaken

Started in 20X2

Mainline Apartments

The contract price was $600,000, and costs were estimated at $450,000. The project was one-half completed at the end of 20X2, and costs were on target at $225,000. In 20X3, the project was completed but costs were $14,000 higher than estimated. The customer was billed $600,000 and all but $90,000 was received in 20x3. The balance was collected in 20X4.

Started in 20X3

Harbour View Apartments

The contract price was $940,000 and costs were originally estimated at $800,000. At the end of 20X3, the project was 80% completed, but price declines on materials resulted in costs of only $600,000. Progress billings were sent out for $470,000, of which $310,000 had been received at the year-end.

In 20X4, the project was completed with additional costs of $150,000. The customer paid the full contract price by November 20X4.

Sunnyside Curling Rink

The contract was awarded at $1,425,000 and costs were estimated at $1,250,000. At the end of 20X3, the project was 20% completed, and costs were on target at $250,000. Progress billings had been sent for $200,000 and one half had been received by 31 December 20X3.

The contract was completed in 20X4. Costs were higher than estimated because of a subcontractor that delayed the project. Completed contract income of $148,000 is included in income, and all of the contract price was received from the customer before 31 December 20X4.

Started in 20X4

Victoria Mall

This contract for a three-unit mall was completed in 20X4. The contract price of $450,000 has been billed, but $70,000 has not been received. Total costs of $423,000 were incurred.

DaVinci Apartments

The contract price was $1,825,000 and costs were estimated at $1,500,000 At the end of 20X4, the project was 15% completed and actual costs included in construction in progress were $225,000. Although progress billings were sent out for $150,000, nothing had been received by 31 December 20X4.

Discount Don's Department Store

The contract was awarded in November 20X4, but no construction has started. The cost of preparing the bid was $9,000 and this has been included in general and administrative expenses.

EXERCISES

E6-1 *Revenue Recognition:* Answer each of the following questions.

1. Define revenue.
2. What should be the dollar amount of revenue recognized in the case of (a) product sales and services for cash and (b) product sales and services rendered in exchange for non-cash considerations?
3. How might revenue be recognized when there is a highly speculative transaction involving potential revenue whose amount cannot be reliably estimated?
4. When should revenue be recognized in the case of long-term, low down-payment sales, for which collectibility is uncertain?
5. When should revenue be recognized for long-term construction contracts?

E6-2 *Revenue Recognition:* For each of the following independent items, indicate when revenue should be recognized.

a. Interest on loans made by a financial institution, receivable in annual payments.
b. Interest on loans made by a financial institution, receivable in three years when the customer, who has an excellent credit rating, will make payment.
c. Interest on loans made by a financial institution, where the loans are in default and payment of principal and interest is highly uncertain.
d. Recognition of revenue from the cash sale of airline tickets, where the travel purchased will occur in the next fiscal period.
e. Transportation of freight by a trucking company for a customer; the customer is expected to make payment in accordance with the terms of the invoice in 60 days.
f. Growing, harvesting, and marketing of Christmas trees; the production cycle is 10 years.
g. Building houses in a subdivision, where the project will take two years to complete and each house must be individually sold by the contractor.
h. Building houses in a subdivision, where the project will take two years to complete and the contractor is building the houses under a contract from the local government.
i. Selling undeveloped lots for future retirement homes in a western province, with very low down-payment and long-term contracts.
j. Sale of a two-year parking permit by a Montreal parking garage, with one-half the sale price received on the sale, and the remainder to be received in equal monthly payments over the period of the permit.
k. A fixed-price contract with the government to design and build a prototype of a space arm; the costs to complete the project cannot be reliably estimated.
l. A silver-mining company produces one million ounces of silver but stores the silver in a vault and waits for silver prices to increase.

E6-3 *Revenue Recognition — Four Cases:* The York Lumber Company has been involved in several transactions that require interpretation of the revenue principle. For each of the following 20X5 transactions, write a brief one- or two-paragraph explanation, stating

1. the amount of revenue that you believe should be recognized during 20X5, and

2. an explanation of the basis for revenue recognition.
   a. The value of goods delivered to customers was $500,000, of which two-thirds was collected by the end of 20X5; the balance will be collected in 20X6.
   b. Regular services were rendered on credit amounting to $290,000, of which three-fourths will be collected in 20X6.
   c. An item that had been repossessed from the first purchaser and carried in inventory at $4,000 was sold again for $5,000 in 20X5. A $3,000 cash down-payment was received in 20X5. The balance is to be paid on a quarterly basis during 20X6 and 20X7. Repossession again would not be a surprise.
   d. On 1 January 20X4, the company purchased a $10,000 note as a speculative investment. Because the collectibility of the note was highly speculative, the company was able to acquire it for $1,000 cash. The note specifies 8% simple interest payable each year (disregard interest prior to 20X4). The first collection on the note was $1,500 cash on 31 December 20X5. Further collections continue to be highly speculative.

E6-4 *Revenue Recognition — Three Cases:* Three independent cases are given below for 20X5. The accounting period ends 31 December.

Case A. On 31 December 20X5, Zulu Sales Company sold a special machine (serial no. 1713) for $100,000 and collected $40,000 cash. The remainder plus 10% interest is payable 31 December 20X6. Zulu will deliver the machine on 5 January 20X6. The buyer has an excellent credit rating.

Case B. On 15 November 20X5, Victor Cement Company sold a ton of its product for $500. The cement was delivered on that date. The buyer will pay for the product with two units of its own merchandise that are commonly sold for $250 each. The buyer promised to deliver the merchandise around 31 January 20X6.

Case C. On 2 January 20X5, Remer Publishing Company collected $900 cash for a three-year subscription to a monthly magazine, *Investor's Stock and Bond Advisory*. The March 20X5 issue will be the first one mailed.

Required:
Write a brief report covering the following:
1. The revenue recognition method that should be used.
2. Any entry that should be made on the transaction date.
3. An explanation of the reasoning for your responses to (1) and (2).

E6-5 *Entries for Critical Events:* Mylar Industries imports goods from the People's Republic of China and resells them to domestic Canadian markets. Mylar uses a perpetual inventory system. A typical transaction stream follows:

8 July	Purchased goods for $356,000 (Canadian dollars)
14 August	Goods repackaged and ready for sale. Cost incurred, $59,500
30 August	Goods delivered to customer. Agreed-on price, $612,000
22 November	Customer paid

Required:
1. Prepare journal entries assuming the following critical events:
   a. Delivery to customer
   b. Cash receipt
   c. Preparation of goods for resale
2. Explain the circumstances under which each of these methods would be appropriate.

E6-6 *Entries for Critical Events:* Dominum Corporation is a mining company that mines, produces and markets teledine, a common mineral substance. The mineral is mined and produced in one large batch per year, as the mine is only accessible for a brief period in the summer due to severe weather conditions at the mine site. Transactions in 20X6:

30 August	146,000 tons of ore removed from mine, at a cost of $3,400,000
30 September	Ore refined to 75,000 tons of teledine, at a cost of $416,000
15 October	Teledine delivered to 20 customers, total contract price, $ 8,675,000
25 October	Teledine returned for full credit; ore improperly refined and teledine unusable; customer given full credit for $375,000 and unusable product scrapped. No other returns are anticipated.
30 November	Customers all paid except one that went bankrupt still owing $76,000

Required:

1. Prepare journal entries assuming the following critical events:
   a. 30 September
   b. 15 October
   c. 25 October
   Assume at each of these dates that the company can make appropriate, accurate accruals for future events such as sales returns and bad debts, if needed.
2. Explain the point at which net assets change for each alternative in requirement (1).
3. Explain the circumstances under which revenue recognition at each of these dates would be appropriate.

E6-7 *Critical Event; Financial Statements:* In each case below, several balance sheet accounts are presented. Determine, based on this information, the likely point at which revenue has been recognized.

Case A

Inventory, at market value	$367,300
Accrued selling costs	31,900
Allowance for estimated sales returns	16,400

Case B

Accounts receivable	$2,567,700
Allowance for doubtful accounts	359,100
Inventory, at cost	1,876,400
Warranty liability	341,100

Case C

Inventory, at cost	$ 566,300
Accounts receivable	1,040,000
Allowance for doubtful accounts	119,600
Deferred gross margin	249,700

E6-8 *Unconditional Right of Return:* In 20X5, McLaughlin Novelty Corporation developed a new product, an electric shoe tree. To increase acceptance by retailers, McLaughlin sold the product to retailers with an unconditional right of return, which expires on 1 February 20X6. McLaughlin has no basis for estimating returns on the new product. The following information is available regarding the product:

Sales — 20X5	$180,000	
Cost of goods sold — 20X5	120,000	
Returns — 20X5	12,000	(cost, $8,000)
Returns — January 20X6	15,000	(cost, $10,000)

All sales are on credit. Cash collections related to the sales were $40,000 in 20X5 and $113,000 in 20X6. McLaughlin uses a perpetual inventory system.

Required:

Include the entry made on 1 February 20X6 when the right of return expires. Give journal entries for sales, returns, and collections related to the new product. How much sales revenue should McLaughlin recognize in 20X5?

E6-9 *Instalment Sales Method:* Barr Machinery Corporation had credit sales of $55,000 in 20X5 that required use of the instalment method. Barr's cost of merchandise sold was $44,000. Barr collected cash related to the instalment sales of $25,000 in 20X5 and $30,000 in 20X6. A perpetual inventory system is used.

Required:

1. What circumstances would dictate use of the instalment sales method?
2. Give journal entries related to the instalment sales for 20X5 and 20x6.
3. Give the ending 20X5 balances in the following accounts: instalment accounts receivable, instalment sales revenue, cost of instalment sales, and deferred gross margin on instalment sales.

E6-10 *Cost Recovery Method:* The Trusett Merchandising Company has an inventory of obsolete products that it formerly stocked for sale. Efforts to dispose of this inventory by selling the products at low prices have not been successful. At the end of the prior year (20X4), the company reduced the value to a conservative estimate of net realizable value of $22,000. On 1 March 20X6, Watson Trading Company purchased this entire inventory for $10,000 cash as a speculative investment. Watson hopes to be able to dispose of it in some foreign markets for approximately $30,000. However, prior to purchase, Watson concluded that there was no reliable way to estimate the probable profitability of the venture. Therefore, Watson decided to use the cost recovery method. Subsequent cash sales have been as follows: 20X6, $4,000; 20X7, $5,000; and 20X8, $8,000. Approximately 12% of the inventory remains on hand at the start of 20X9.

Required:

Give the 20X6, 20X7, and 20X8 entries for Watson Trading Company to record revenues and cost of sales.

E6-11 *Completed-Contract and Percentage-of-Completion Methods Compared:* Watson Construction Company contracted to build a plant for $500,000. Construction started in January 20X4 and was completed in November 20X5. Data relating to the contract are summarized below:

	20X4	20X5
Costs incurred during year	$290,000	$120,000
Estimated additional costs to complete	125,000	
Billings during year	270,000	230,000
Cash collections during year	250,000	250,000

Required:

1. Give the journal entries for Watson in parallel columns, assuming (a) the completed contract-method and (b) the percentage-of-completion method. Use costs incurred to date divided by total estimated construction costs to measure percent completed.
2. Complete the following table:

	Completed-contract method	Percentage-of-completion method
Income statement:		
Income:		
20X4	$	$
20X5	$	$
Balance sheet:		
Receivables:		
20X4	$	$
20X5	$	$
Inventory — construction in progress, net of billings:		
20X4	$	$
20X5	$	$

E6-12 *Completed-Contract and Percentage-of-Completion Methods Compared:* Mullen Construction Company contracted to build a municipal warehouse for the city of Moncton for $750,000. The contract specified that the city would pay Mullen each month the progress billings, less 10%, which was to be held as a retention reserve. At the end of the construction, the final payment would include the reserve. Each billing, less the 10% reserve, must be paid 10 days after submission of a billing to the city. Transactions relating to the contract are summarized below:

20X4   Construction costs incurred during the year, $200,000; estimated costs to complete, $400,000;   progress billing, $190,000; and collections per the contract.

20X5   Construction costs incurred during the year, $350,000; estimated costs to complete, $115,000; progress billings, $280,000; and collections per the contract.

20X6   Construction costs incurred during the year, $100,000. The remaining billings were submitted by 1 October and final collections completed on 30 November.

Required:

1. Complete the following table:

Year	Method	Net income recognized	Contract receivables, ending balance	Construction-in-progress inventory, ending balance
20X4	Completed contact	$	$	$
	Percentage of completion*			

(continued)

20X5	Completed contract			
	Percentage of completion*			
20X6	Completed contract			
	Percentage of completion*			

* Use costs incurred to date divided by total estimated construction costs to measure percentage of completion.

2. Explain what causes the ending balance in construction-in-progress to be different for the two methods.
3. Which method would you recommend for this contractor? Why?

E6-13 *Completed-Contract and Percentage-of-Completion Methods Compared:* Pedlar Construction Company contracted to build an apartment building for $2,800,000. Construction began in October 20X4 and was scheduled to be completed in April 20X6. Pedlar has a 31 December year-end. Data related to the contract are summarized below:

	20X4	20X5	20X6
	($ thousands)		
Costs incurred during year	$ 400	$1,500	$ 700
Estimated additional costs to complete	2,200	400	—
Billings during year	350	1,450	1,000
Cash collections during year	325	1,300	1,175

Required:

1. Prepare the journal entries for Pedlar, assuming the completed-contract method.
2. Prepare the journal entries for Pedlar, assuming the percentage-of-completion method. Use costs incurred to date divided by total estimated construction costs to measure percent complete. Round your estimate of revenue to the nearest thousand.

PROBLEMS

P6-1 *Revenue Recognition:* Assume that in 20X5, the Public Utilities Board (PUB) issued a ruling raising the ceiling price on regulated gas, but with a "vintaging" system: gas suppliers could charge $1.42 per thousand cubic feet on "new gas" drilled after 1 January 20X5, and $1.01 on gas (now in inventory) drilled between 1 January 20X3, and 31 December 20X4. The old price had been 52 cents per thousand cubic feet and remained at this for all "old" gas (i.e., pre-20X3 gas). The PUB soon reduced the $1.01 rate to 93 cents but retained the $1.42 rate. As a result of a lawsuit by consumers against the PUB seeking a rollback to the old 52-cent rate, a court of appeal decided that gas suppliers should go ahead and collect the higher prices provided they would agree to refund the money if the final decision went against the PUB.

Required:

1. If you were part of the management of a gas supplier at the time of the court decision, what position would you take with respect to recognition of the extra amounts of revenue from the sale of new gas? Give reasons for whatever position you take.

2. Disregard the answer you gave to (1) above. If the revenue is deferred, explain how the deferral would affect the financial statements until a final court decision is rendered. How would the deferred revenue be recognized if the final court decision is delayed until a new accounting year and then is favourable?

P6-2 *Magazine Subscription Revenue:* At a meeting of the board of directors of Vanguard Publishing Company, where you are the controller, a new director expressed surprise that the company's income statement indicates that an equal proportion of revenue is earned with the publication of each issue of the magazines the company publishes. This director believes that the most important event in the sale of magazines is the collection of cash on the subscriptions and expresses the view that the company's practice smoothes its income. He has suggested that subscription revenue should be recognized as subscriptions are collected.

Required:

Discuss the propriety of timing the recognition of revenue on the basis of

1. Cash collections on subscriptions.
2. Publication of issues, concurrent with delivery to customers.
3. Both events, by recognizing part of the revenue with cash collections of subscriptions and part with delivery of the magazines to subscribers.

[AICPA adapted]

P6-3 *Revenue Recognition:* Scientific Development Company (SDC) conducts research and development on specific projects under contract for clients; SDC also conducts basic research and attempts to market any new products or technologies it develops.

In January 20X4, scientists at SDC began research to develop a new industrial cleaner. During 20X4, $1,560,000 of costs were incurred in this effort. Late in July 20X5, potentially promising results emerged in the form of a substance the company called Blast. Costs incurred through the end of July 20X5 were $840,000. At this point, SDC attempted to sell the formula of and rights to Blast to Pride and Glory Industries Ltd. (P&G), for $10,000,000. P&G, however, was reluctant to sign before further testing was done. It did wish, though, to have the first option to acquire the rights and formulas to Blast if future testing showed the product to be profitable. SDC was very confident that Blast would pass further testing with flying colours. Accordingly, the two companies signed an option agreement that allowed P&G to acquire the formulas and rights to Blast anytime before 31 December 20X6. Testing costs on the product incurred by SDC for the remainder of 20X5 amounted to $1,080,000.

In early 20X6, P&G exercised its option and agreed to purchase the formulas and rights to Blast for $10,000,000. P&G paid $500,000 immediately with the balance payable in five equal annual instalments on 31 December 20X6 to 20X10. The formula was to be completed and delivered within 18 months.

In April 20X7, SDC delivered the formulas and samples of Blast to P&G Industries. Additional costs incurred by SDC during 20X6 amounted to $360,000; in 20X7, $120,000.

Required:

1. When should revenue be recognized by SDC from its work on Blast? Why?
2. Assume that the total costs of $3,960,000 actually incurred by SDC over the years 20X4 to 20X6 were accurately estimated in 20X4. Determine the amount of revenue and expense that should be recognized each year from 20X4 to 20X10, assuming revenue is to be recognized

a. At the time the option is signed.
b. At the time the option is exercised.
c. At the time the formulas are delivered.
d. As cash is collected (use the instalment method).

Note that the $1,560,000 of research costs must be expensed in all alternatives to comply with accounting standards for research costs. Other costs may be deferred if appropriate. Do not attempt to do journal entries; your solution should focus on income statement presentation.

P6-4 *Unconditional Right of Return:* McLaughlin Novelty Corporation developed an unusual product, electric clip-on eyeglass wipers. McLaughlin felt the product would appeal to hikers, joggers, and cyclists who engaged in their sports in rainy climates. Because retail establishments were skeptical about the market appeal of the product, McLaughlin sold the product with a declining unconditional right of return for up to 10 months, with 10% of the right-of-return amount of the purchase expiring each month for 10 months. Thus, after the retailer had the product for one month, only 90% could be returned. After two months, only 80% could be returned, and after 10 months, the right of return was fully expired.

McLaughlin had no basis for estimating the amount of returns. Consistent with the terms McLaughlin offered its customers, all retailers paid cash when purchasing the clip-on eyeglass wipers but received cash refunds if goods were returned. McLaughlin had its first sales of the product in September 20X5. Sales for the remainder of the year, and returns prior to 31 December 20X5, were as follows:

Month of Sale	Units Sold	Sales Price	Monthly Sales	Units Returned
September	10,000	$10	$100,000	2,500
October	12,000	10	120,000	1,000
November	15,000	12	180,000	1,000
December	11,000	12	132,000	0
Totals	48,000		$532,000	4,500

Each unit of product costs McLaughlin $6 to produce.

Required:

1. Show the journal entries to record the four months of sales transactions, including the deferral of gross margin. Prepare one summary entry.

2. Show a summary entry to record the returns in 20X5.

3. Compute the amount that McLaughlin can record as (realized) sales for 20X5. How much is gross margin? Record the revenue recognition entry.

4. For the above transactions, total returns in all of 20X6 were as follows:

Month of Sale	Units Returned
September	1,000
October	2,000
November	2,500
December	4,000

Show the entries to record the returns in 20X6 and to record sales revenue and cost of sales from the 20X5 shipments of this product.

P6-5 *Revenue Recognition:* Fly and Mattox, a professional corporation, contracted to provide, as required, all legal services for Brown Company until the end of 20X5. The contract specified a lump-sum payment of $60,000 on 15 November

20X4. Assume that Fly and Mattox can reliably estimate future direct costs associated with the contract. The following services were performed based on the estimate by Fly and Mattox:

	Direct Costs	Date Completed
Research potential lawsuit	$ 5,000	15 December 20X4
Prepare and file documents	15,000	1 March 20X5
Serve as Brown's counsel during legal proceedings	15,000	15 October 20X5

Required:

1. When should Fly and Mattox recognize revenue in this situation? Explain.
2. Give entries to recognize revenues related to this contract for Fly and Mattox.

P6-6 *Critical Event:* BC Corporation sells large pieces of construction equipment. The company had the following three sales in 20X5:

	Sales Amount	Cost of Goods Sold	Other Information
Byron Foods	$345,700	$210,000	Unlimited right of return until 30 June 20X6. Extent of returns is not estimable.
Addison Roads	$?	$166,800	Price to be determined after Addison has use of the equipment for six months: to be determined based on revenue generated and operating costs. BC believes that the sales price will likely be in the range of $200,000 to $230,000, but has no previous experience with this kind of contract.
Carson Construction	$567,000	$399,000	Collection contingent on Carson's continued operations; company close to bankruptcy. Title to equipment still in BC's name so that assets would not be lost in bankruptcy; Carson paid $50,000 up front as security. Balance to be paid within 12 months.

Required:

1. At what point should BC recognize revenue for each of the above sales transactions?
2. Show how the transactions would be reflected in the 20X5 balance sheet and income statement.

P6-7 *Critical Event:* Manzer Manufacturing had transactions in 20X6 as follows:

30 June	Purchased inventory, $378,000.
17 July	Sale to customer, $271,000, on account. Cost of goods sold, $164,500.
15 September	Customer returns $29,000 of goods for full credit; goods were spoiled and worthless.
30 November	Warranty work of $20,000 was performed.
15 December	Customer paid all outstanding amounts.

All goods were sold with unlimited right of return for 60 days and a one-year warranty.

Required:

1. Prepare 20X6 entries to record the above transactions assuming that the critical event is deemed to be
   a. the date of delivery
   b. the date that the warranty expires
   c. the date that the return privilege expires
   If necessary, assume that total warranty cost can be estimated to be $41,000, and returns, $29,000.
2. Show how the income statement and balance sheet would reflect each of the alternatives in (1).
3. Comment on the relative timing of the increase in net assets.

P6-8 *Instalment Sales:* Baxter Land Corporation made a number of sales in 20X4 and 20X5 that required use of the instalment method. The following information regarding the sales is available:

	20X4	**20X5**	**20X6**
Instalment sales	$200,000	$150,000	$ 0
Cost of instalment sales	160,000	112,500	0
Collections on 20X4 sales	40,000	50,000	60,000
Collections on 20X5 sales		30,000	75,000

Baxter uses a perpetual inventory system.

Required:

1. Give journal entries relating to instalment sales for the years 20X4 to 20X6.
2. What is the year-end balance in instalment accounts receivable (net of any deferred gross margin) for 20X4, 20X5, and 20X6?
3. If the sales qualified for revenue recognition on the date of sale (i.e., delivery), what amounts of gross margin would Baxter report in 20X4, 20X5, and 20X6?

P6-9 *Instalment Sales Method:* Ontario Retail Company sells goods for cash, and on normal credit terms of 30 days. However, on 1 July 20X4, the company sold a used computer for $2,200; the inventory carrying value was $440. The company collected $200 cash and agreed to let the customer make payments on the $2,000 whenever possible during the next 12 months. The company management stated that it had no reliable basis for estimating the probability of default. The following additional data are available: (a) collections on the instalment receivable during 20X4 were $300 and during 20X5 were $200, and (b) on 1 December 20X5, Ontario Retail repossessed the computer (estimated net realizable value, $700).

Required:

1. Give the required entries for 20X4 and 20X5; assume that the instalment method is used.
2. Give the balances in the following accounts that would be reported on the 20X4 and 20X5 income statements and balance sheets: instalment sales revenue and cost of sales, instalment accounts receivable, and inventory of used computers.
3. How much profit would be recognized in 20X4 and 20X5 if the cost recovery method is used?

P6-10 *Cost Recovery Method:* Slatt Department Store has accumulated a stock of obsolete merchandise. Routine efforts have been made to dispose of it at a low price. This merchandise originally cost $60,000 and was marked to sell for $132,000. Management decided to set up a special location in the basement to display and (it was hoped) sell this stock starting in January 20X5. All items will be marked to sell at a cash price that is 30% of the original marked selling price. On 31 December 20X4, the company accountant transferred the purchase cost to a perpetual inventory account called "inventory, obsolete merchandise," at 30% of its purchase cost, which approximates estimated net realizable value. Management knows that a reliable estimate of the probable sales cannot be made. Therefore, the cost recovery method will be used. Subsequent sales were $9,000 in 20X5 and $7,000 in 20X6, and in 20X7 the remaining merchandise was sold for $8,000.

Required:

Give the entries that Slatt should make for 20X4 through 20X7.

P6-11 *Long-Term Construction — Percentage-of-Completion Method:* Thrasher Construction Company contracted to construct a building for $975,000. The contract provided for progress payments. Thrasher's accounting year ends 31 December. Work began under the contract on 1 July 20X5, and was completed on 30 September 20X7. Construction activities are summarized below by year:

20X5   Construction costs incurred during the year, $180,000; estimated costs to complete, $630,000; progress billings during the year, $153,000; and collections, $140,000.

20X6   Construction costs incurred during the year, $450,000; estimated costs to complete, $190,000; progress billing during the year, $382,500; and collections, $380,000.

20X7   Construction costs incurred during the year, $195,000. Because the contract was completed, the remaining balance was billed and later collected in full per the contract.

Required:

1. Give Thrasher's entries assuming that the percentage-of-completion method is used. Assume that percentage of completion is measured by the ratio of costs incurred to date divided by total estimated construction costs.
2. Prepare income statement and balance sheet presentation for this contract by year; assume that the percentage-of-completion method is used.
3. Prepare income statement and balance sheet presentation by year; assume that the completed-contract method is used. For each amount that is different from the corresponding amount in (2), explain why it is different.
4. Which method would you recommend to this contractor? Why?

P6-12 *Long-Term Construction: Methods Compared:* Wallen Corporation contracted to construct an office building for Ragee Company for $1,000,000. Construction began on 15 January 20X4, and was completed on 1 December 20X5. Wallen's accounting year ends 31 December. Transactions by Wallen relating to the contract are summarized below:

	20x4	20x5
Costs incurred to date	$400,000	$ 850,000
Estimated costs to complete	420,000	—
Progress billings to date	410,000	1,000,000
Progress collections to date	375,000	1,000,000

Required:

1. In parallel columns, give the entries on the contractor's books; assume
   a. the completed contract method, and
   b. the percentage-of-completion method.
   Assume that percentage of completion is measured by the ratio of costs incurred to date divided by total estimated construction costs.
2. For each method, prepare the income statement and balance sheet presentation for this contract by year.
3. What is the nature of the item "costs in excess of billings" that would appear on the balance sheet?
4. Which method would you recommend that the contractor use? Why?

P6-13 *Percentage-of-Completion and Completed-Contract Methods:* Banks Construction Company contracted to build an office block for $3,200,000. Construction began in September 20X4 and was scheduled to be completed in May 20X6. Banks has a 31 December year-end. Data related to the contract are summarized below:

	20X4	20X5	20X6
	($ thousands)		
Costs incurred during year	$ 500	$1,800	$ 850
Estimated additional costs to complete	2,500	800	0
Billings during year	450	1,300	1,450
Cash collections during year	400	1,100	1,700

Required:

1. Prepare the journal entries for Banks, assuming the completed-contract method.
2. Prepare the balance sheet and income presentation for this contract by year, assuming the completed-contract method is used.
3. Prepare the journal entries for Banks, assuming the percentage-of-completion method. Use costs incurred to date divided by total estimated construction costs to measure percent complete.
4. Prepare the balance sheet and income presentation for this contract by year, assuming the percentage-of-completion method is used.

Expense Recognition

INTRODUCTION

Cott Corporation is the leading Canadian manufacturer of private-label soft drinks. In 1994, Cott's stock price dropped 66% in the course of a year, falling to $16.88 per share in August 1994, from a high of $49.50 in October of the prior year. There were several reasons for this spectacular drop, but one reason was criticism in the financial press of Cott's financial position, and, in particular, one of their expense accounting policies. Each year, Cott pays retailers millions of dollars to put Cott's drinks on their shelves. These costs are paid by Cott at the beginning of three to five-year contracts with the retailer. Cott defers these costs, a policy that resulted in a balance sheet asset, "prepaid contract costs," of $19.1 million, or 4.7% of assets, in 1994. The prepaid contract costs are amortized over the life of the related contract. Analysts claimed this was aggressive accounting, and that expensing the costs was the norm for other companies. Cott responded by reminding investors that their multi-year contracts were not typical in the industry. They even hired Roman Weil, a University of Chicago accounting professor, to comment on their policy; his conclusion was that Cott's policy complied with generally accepted accounting principles. But what is GAAP in this area?

Common rationales for accounting policy choice were reviewed in Chapters 1 and 2. Essentially, the premise is that accounting policies are chosen by managers to be consistent with the company's financial reporting objectives. For example, a firm may choose policies to reduce income and report lower taxable income (to the extent acceptable by Revenue Canada). Some have hypothesized that large firms prefer lower, but stable, net income, so as to avoid the political pressure and perhaps intervention that comes with what some deem "excess profits." For other companies, there may be positive cash flows resulting from higher net income. These include lower borrowing costs, as lenders observe stronger performance in key ratios and reduce interest rates or restrictive covenants. Perhaps the decision revolves around the personal cash flows of the executive team, who may have compensation packages tied to net income. Companies have to carefully evaluate the impact of those bonuses!

What's the message? Policies must be chosen to recognize expenses, and there are areas where generally accepted accounting principles allow significant latitude. Accountants and financial statement users have to be on their toes in this area. This chapter examines the general area of expense policy; the standards, practices and policies that govern this crucial area of accounting policy choice. Later chapters will discuss expense recognition policies for specific types of expenditures in more detail.

EXPENSE RECOGNITION

Cost, Expenditure, and Expense

Before embarking on an extended discussion of expense recognition, we should firmly establish the terminology:

- When we agree to pay out cash (or other assets) for goods or services received, we have incurred a cost.

- When we actually pay the cash, we have an expenditure.

- When the benefits of the cost have been used and we put that cost (or a portion thereof) on the income statement, we have recognized an expense.

Often, all three occur at the same time, or at least in the same accounting period. For example, when we pay salaries to administrative employees, we incur a *cost* for labour, make an *expenditure*, and recognize the full cost on the income statement as an *expense*. This sort of simultaneous occurrence is common for many of a company's routine transactions.

However, there are many expenditures that result in a cost that is *not* recognized immediately as an expense. A purchase of equipment is an obvious example. Equipment is recorded as an asset, and is only gradually amortized to expense as the equipment is used. Furthermore, the cost assigned to the equipment may be comprised of several expenditures rather than just one; expenditures for shipping, installation, and testing may be included in the cost of the equipment (or they may be expensed separately — this accounting policy choice is discussed in Chapter 10). Even expenditures for labour may not be an expense; for example, factory labour is added to the cost of manufactured inventory.

An expenditure may *follow* recognition of an expense. For example, think of a common year-end adjustment:

Income tax expense	176,000	
Income taxes payable		176,000

This adjustment is made in order to recognize the income tax *expense* for the period, even if the company has not yet made the *expenditure* to pay the tax.

Thus, we must be very careful not to use the word "expense" when we really mean "cost" or "expenditure" — terminology does matter, especially when it comes to other people's understanding of what we are doing.

General Recognition Criteria

In order for an item to be recorded in the financial statements, it must meet the general recognition criteria that were outlined in Chapter 2. Recognized items must

- meet the definition of a financial statement element, and
- have a valid measurement basis and amount.

We know that the financial statement elements are based on future economic benefits or sacrifices; these must be *probable* for recognition to be appropriate.

How do the recognition criteria apply to expenses? Like revenues, expenses are not defined on their own. Their derivative definition rests on reduction of assets or increases in liabilities. That is

> Expenses are decreases in economic resources, either by way of outflows or reductions of assets or incurrences of liabilities, resulting from an entity's ordinary revenue generating or service delivery activities.
>
> [*CICA* 1000.38]

Expenses are costs that are charged against revenue and that are related to the entity's basic business. The business may be the sale of a consumer or industrial product, design or management services, natural resource exploration, or any one of hundreds of other activities that represent core activities. But costs that are charged as expenses are distinct from costs incurred in peripheral activities that may give rise to gains and losses. The costs of peripheral activities are *netted* against the related gain (or loss) when the gain (or loss) is reported in the financial statements.

For example, the business of a land developer is dealing in land. If a land developer sells a parcel of land acquired for $113,500 for proceeds of $249,000, this would give rise to revenue and cost of goods sold on the income statement, and result in recognized gross profit of $135,500. On the other hand, if a manufacturer of automobile parts sold idle land with the same cost and proceeds, a net gain on sale of land would be reported on the income statement as a single net gain of $135,500. The impact on net income and net assets (equity) would be identical, but the reporting is far less informative; this is considered to be an acceptable loss of detail for a peripheral transaction.

Asset or expense? An entity spends some cash (or incurs a liability) to acquire a good or a service. The offset to that expenditure or liability is going to be a debit. Is the debit an *expense* or an *asset*? The definitions tell us that an entity has an asset if there is future economic benefit (that is, a cash flow, either direct or indirect) that will come from the item. If there is no such benefit, then the entry involves a debit to an expense because the item has no intrinsic value or future cash flow. If there is no future benefit that is both probable and measurable, then the item is treated as an expense.

Exhibit 7-1 identifies the impact that these two alternatives will have on the financial statements. In one, the *distribution of assets* is changed; in the other, *net assets and shareholder wealth goes down. The decision about what to debit is not a free choice: if the asset recognition criteria are met, an asset is recorded. If not, an expense is recorded.*

Think about a transaction that involves buying goods for resale in a cash exchange. Cash goes down; what goes up? The goods are for resale, so they can be sold to a customer for at least their cost, the goods clearly represent a future cash flow to the entity and are an asset, *inventory*. Inventory becomes an expense, called cost of goods sold, when it's sold. At this point, inventory is converted into cash, a financial instrument, or some other benefit to the entity. When might goods bought for resale *not* be an asset? If the goods were bought and became unsaleable due to their physical condition or because they were obsolete, then the entity has no future cash flowing from the ownership of the items and the purchase would be reported as an expense. Inventory is only an asset if it can be resold for at least its carrying value. The cost of unsaleable inventory must be written down, a common occurrence.

As this chapter progresses, we'll look critically at the criteria that must be met to establish the probable future benefit that must accompany asset recognition.

In Chapter 6, one of the key themes was that the point of revenue recognition is accompanied by an increase in net assets. When expenses are recognized, net assets go down. When revenues and expenses are recognized simultaneously, one expects that revenues will exceed expenses and the combined impact on net assets will be positive.

Expense recognition is highly dependent on the revenue recognition point chosen by a company. If a company buys an item that will later be sold, its cost is deferred. If the revenue recognition point comes and goes but not all expenses are yet incurred, then they must be accrued. Refer again to the previous chapter, Exhibit 6-1, and observe how and when expenses (versus assets) were created. Remember that deferred costs are assets, and the future sale transaction is the future cash flow that backs up the asset value.

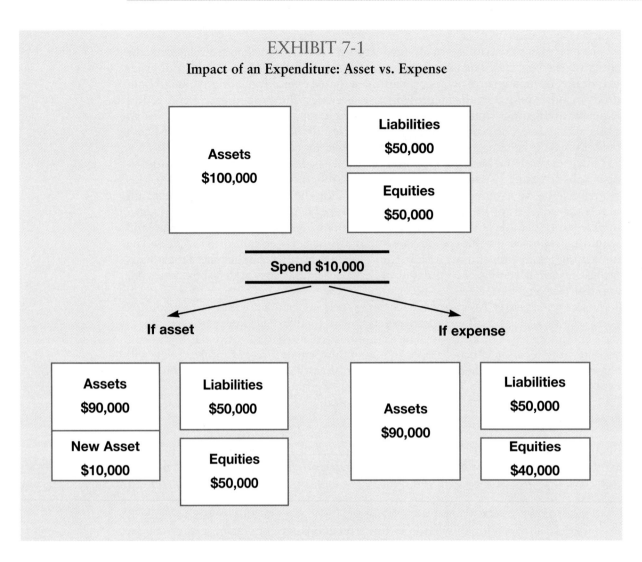

EXHIBIT 7-1

Impact of an Expenditure: Asset vs. Expense

Approaches to Expense Recognition

What have you learned about expense recognition?

1. The debit to offset an outflow of cash (i.e., a credit) is either an expense or an asset. Criteria must be met to justify recognizing an asset.
2. The activity must be central to the core operations of the entity.

Given these two initial requirements, we can identify two general approaches to deciding whether an expenditure results in an asset or an expense.

Definitional Approach. In this approach, expenses are determined in relation to the definition of assets and liabilities that is included in Section 1000 of the *CICA Handbook*. Expenses are created either through the reduction of an asset or the increase in a liability. We'll call this, for lack of a better term, the *definitional approach* to expense recognition. The definitional approach is oriented towards the balance sheet.

Matching Approach. In this approach, expense recognition policy is based on the doctrine of *matching*. The matching principle requires that once revenues are determined in conformity with the revenue principle for any reporting period, the expenses incurred in generating the revenue should be recognized in that period. The essence of the matching principle is that as revenues are earned, expenses are incurred to generate those revenues. These expenses must be recognized and reported as expenses of the period during which the related revenue is recognized. Matching typically involves the primacy of revenue and expense recognition and accurate net income measurement, not an analysis of changes in asset and liability balances.

To illustrate how expense recognition is affected by these two approaches, consider the following two examples of accounting policies and how they are justified under the definitional approach versus the matching approach.

Policy 1. Defer expenditures related to revenue generation activities incurred prior to the revenue recognition point. Expense these items when revenue is recognized.

Definitional: Up to the revenue recognition point, these items have probable future benefit arising from the revenue transaction: the cash flow, etc., that will be provided by the customer. As long as the revenue transaction is probable, the expenditure meets the recognition criteria for an asset. After revenue recognition, the asset is clearly an expense.

Matching: The expenses must be deferred prior to the revenue recognition point so that they can be matched with the associated revenue.

Policy 2. Accrue expenses incurred but not yet substantiated by a transaction if they relate to revenue recognized on the income statement.

Definitional: The entity has incurred an obligation for the expenditures by virtue of the revenue transaction. The element (the liability) exists and must now be recognized.

Matching: The expenses must be accrued at the revenue recognition point to properly match revenues and all expenses of the transactions.

Both lines of reasoning appear to support the same types of policies. So what's the big deal?

Accountants are quite schizophrenic in this regard. Matching has been with us for a long time. It was central in an influential monograph that was sponsored by the American Accounting Association in the 1960s and that dominated accounting thought for decades. Matching involves deferring expenditures as assets on the balance sheet if projected revenues are still on the horizon. Criteria for such deferral were not well developed through this period, and there were problematic cases of assets — cost deferrals — that had, in the end, no associated cash flow. Application of matching sometimes led to recording an expense even though no liability was created or asset used up. For example, an amount debited to expense was credited to an account called "deferred credits." Deferred credits were often not liabilities, at least not in conformity with the definition of liabilities that is presented in the *CICA Handbook*.

Many accountants feel that the balance sheet has to have integrity. That is, only "real" assets and liabilities can be properly included on the balance sheet. Thus, revenues and expenses become derived definitions, and assets and liabilities are tied to cash flows, or future economic benefits. Deferred credits and deferred debits should be increasingly under pressure and should gradually be disappearing from the financial statements. However, the continued devotion of the AcSB to the "defer and amortize" approach to many costs (and revenues) calls into question the real impact that the definitional approach is having. The matching approach still seems to be firmly entrenched.

Where does that leave us? The habit of matching is firmly entrenched, but is inconsistent with the definitional approach. The safest thing to say is that we are, as a profession, in transition! Many of our customs and established accounting policies are firmly rooted in the doctrine of matching. New rules *may* be based on the definitional approach, which is considered theoretically superior by those who subscribe to the balance sheet view of the financial statements. But it's hard to leave matching behind.

We'll point out some of the substantive differences between matching and the definitional approach in the section on "cost deferral" later in the chapter. At this stage, it would be helpful for you to orient your thinking on accounting policy toward the definitional approach.

MEASUREMENT

Recognition is not possible unless there is a reliable amount to record. When is measurement an issue for expenses? Obviously, if the item is one where the cost transaction precedes the revenue recognition point, there's likely an invoice sitting around and measurement isn't much of an issue. The more complicated problem arises when the expense has to be accrued at the revenue recognition point, prior to settlement. Accurate measurement of the liability, and, by inference, the expense, is a major concern.

Consider the issue of environmental liabilities and clean-up costs associated with certain operations. For example, in the mining industry, provincial legislation requires mining companies to restore mine sites to their original condition (minus the extracted resources, of course) after mining operations have ceased. The extent of restoration varies from province to province, and is subject to change — sometimes retroactively — by legislative action. Therefore, mining activities clearly create an obligation for site restoration. The only problem is: how much will the obligation amount to? To answer this question, a mining company would have to estimate the extent and cost of the restoration activities that will happen many years in the future — a highly uncertain amount.

For decades, mining companies responded to this situation by refusing to accrue any cost on the basis that the recognition criteria for measurement failed. That is, without the existence of a definitive estimate, no recognition was appropriate. Over the past 10 years, there has been a steady increase in the number of firms that choose to accrue an estimate. Has their ability to estimate improved? Perhaps, but another plausible explanation is that shareholders and other stakeholder groups now have higher expectations. They want to see indications that the company accepts its responsibilities for site restoration, and intends to honour its obligations. Recording a liability is one way to signal the company's intentions.

The *CICA Handbook*, Section 1508, "Measurement Uncertainty," requires that entities disclose the nature and extent of a measurement uncertainty, in an explanatory note to the financial statements. This encourages firms to record items despite lack of precision in the numbers. It should also help financial statement users understand the "soft spots" in the financial statements themselves.

Another major issue in expense measurement deals with the issue of *interperiod allocation*: what amortization policies are appropriate? How much amortization should be booked in a given period? We will return to this issue as the chapter continues.

EXPENSE CATEGORIES

Expenses are often described in two categories:

1. **Direct expenses** are expenses, such as cost of goods sold, that are associated directly with revenues. These expenses are recognized at the same time as the related

revenues. Direct costs that are incurred prior to the recognition of revenue should be deferred as prepayments until revenue recognition; those incurred after revenue recognition should be accrued. If direct costs can be traced to a product held for resale or to a specific business activity, they can also be called **product costs** or **project costs**. Examples of direct costs in a manufacturing environment include

- Costs of materials and labour for manufacture, or the cost to purchase materials that are used in production during the period.
- Wage costs for employees working directly on producing the product.
- Some direct costs of selling, such as sales commissions and shipping costs.
- Warranty expense on products sold.

Examples of direct costs in a service business include

- Initial direct costs directly associated with negotiating and consummating service transactions. These costs include commissions, legal fees, salespersons' compensation other than commissions, and non-sales employees' compensation that is applicable to negotiating and consummating service transactions.
- Direct costs that have an identifiable causal effect on service sales. Examples include the cost of repair parts and service labour included as part of a service contract.

2. **Indirect expenses** are expenditures such as interest costs and administrative salaries, which are not associated directly with revenues. These costs are recognized as expenses during the period in which cash is spent or liabilities are incurred for goods and services that are used up either simultaneously at acquisition or soon after. These are often called **period costs**.

CONCEPT REVIEW

1. What is the difference between an *expenditure*, an *expense*, and a *cost*?
2. What are the general recognition criteria for financial statement elements?
3. How do we decide whether a cost should be reported as an *asset* or as an *expense*?
4. What is the difference between *direct* expenses and *indirect* expenses?

SPECIFIC EXPENSE POLICIES

So far in this chapter, we've examined expense policy in general terms. Now, we will turn to two specific expenses: cost of goods sold and amortization. These are important areas: first, they represent significant expense categories on many income statements, and, second, there are potentially material differences in expense patterns associated with different policies. Keep in mind though, that the differences in patterns relate to the *timing* of the expense, not its *total amount* over time. All expenses arise from cash flows; it's the pattern of expense recognition over time that's under discussion. In this chapter, we'll look at expense policy for broad categories of expenditure and leave most of the detailed calculations to later chapters.

COST OF GOODS SOLD

Underlying Concepts of Cost Flow

Management must choose a cost allocation procedure for allocating the total cost of goods available for sale during each period between (1) the cost of goods sold and (2) the cost of the ending inventory. If inventory unit acquisition or production costs are constant over time, the choice of an allocation process will not affect the result. However, inventory item costs — both acquisition and manufacturing costs — typically vary, changing up or down in response to prevailing conditions in the economy.

For inventory accounting purposes, this cost variability creates a need for management to select an explicit cost flow method (or *assumption*) for use in allocating the total cost of goods available for sale between expense (cost of goods sold) and assets (ending inventory). The physical movement of goods is nearly always on a first-in, first-out basis, especially if the product is perishable or subject to obsolescence. But the cost flow method used to account for the value of both the inventory used up during the period and the inventory on hand at the end of the period can be quite different from the actual flow of goods. *Inventory accounting policy determines the flow of costs through the accounting system, not the flow of goods physically in and out of a stockroom.* The *CICA Handbook* states that

> The method selected for determining cost should be one which results in the fairest matching of costs against revenues regardless of whether or not the method corresponds to the physical flow of goods.
>
> [*CICA* 3030.09]

Notice the way matching is invoked: this section of the *CICA Handbook* is dated 1973, and pre-dates the work on the definitional approach to expense recognition. It's one of the many inconsistencies in the *CICA Handbook* in this regard.

The central issue in cost flow policy is the order in which the actual unit costs incurred are assigned to the ending inventory and to cost of goods sold. Selection of an inventory flow method determines the cost of goods sold, which is deducted from sales revenue for the period. Four inventory cost flow methods — specific cost identification, average cost, FIFO, and LIFO — are discussed in this section. Which cost flow assumption results in the "fairest" matching? The AcSB does not provide guidance in this regard, but indicates only that the decision depends on the circumstances of the enterprise and industry. As is true of all accounting policy choices, the selection of inventory cost flow assumption depends on the financial reporting objectives of each individual enterprise. The two methods in common use in Canada are FIFO and average cost; you'll understand why as this section progresses.

Each flow assumption has direct impacts on the income statement and the balance sheet. The impacts arise because of the choice that each method implicitly contains for deciding which costs go on the income statement (as cost of goods sold) and which stay on the balance sheet (as inventory). There is no difference in reporting on the cash flow statement, however.

Specific Cost Identification

The specific cost identification method requires that each item stocked be specifically marked so that its unit cost can be identified at any time. It used to be that this was only practical when the items involved were large or expensive. However, information technology — bar codes and scanners, point of sale and stockroom data capture — now allows detailed cost data to be efficiently tracked for thousands of items. Specific cost identification makes it possible to identify at date of sale the specific unit cost of each item sold and each item remaining in inventory. Thus, the specific cost identification method relates the cost flow directly with the specific flow of physical goods. It is the only method to do so.

The specific cost identification method requires careful identification of each item, which can be a practical limitation because of the detailed records that are required. Computerized inventory systems involve significant up-front investment and careful training.

An undesirable feature of the method is the opportunity to manipulate income by arbitrary selection of items at time of sale. Assume that three identical stereo sets are for sale that cost the retailer $800, $850, and $900. When one is sold for $1,250, the reported cost of goods sold and gross profit would depend on the unit arbitrarily selected for sale. Want to maximize earnings? Minimize earnings? There's a huge potential for manipulation here.

Automotive dealers use the specific cost method for two reasons. First, the dealer's specific cost is an important determinant of the sales price. Second, each car is unique, and the serial number links it to a specific invoice cost. Dealers carefully trace each car on the lot, for internal control reasons and because each is individually financed, so it's no big deal to use specific identification to determine cost of sales.

Average Cost

The average cost method assumes that the cost of inventory on hand at the end of a period and the cost of goods sold during a period is representative of all costs incurred during the period. Application depends on the inventory system used; some companies determine inventory only at the end of the period (the periodic system); others maintain continuous, or **perpetual** records. The cost flow policies associated with the perpetual method will be discussed; more detail on both methods is presented in Chapter 9.

With the perpetual method average cost system, a moving weighted-average unit cost is used. This weighted-average unit cost is computed each time there is a purchase, by dividing the sum of the existing inventory cost plus current purchase costs by the number of units in the beginning inventory plus units purchased. The formula is:

(Inventory cost + current purchase cost) ÷ total units on hand
= weighted-average unit cost

For example, assume a company has an opening inventory of 1,000 units with a cost of $9 each. The company then buys 500 more units at $12 each. The weighted average will be:

Weighted average cost = [(1,000 × $9) + (500 × $12)] ÷ 1,500 units
= [$9,000 + $6,000] ÷ 1,500 units
= $15,000 ÷ 1,500 units
= $10 per unit

If 700 units are then sold, the cost of goods sold will be $7,000, and ending inventory (800 units) will be $8,000.

The moving-average method is generally viewed as objective, consistent, and not subject to easy manipulation. It provides a current average cost on an ongoing basis. This may be convenient, but an average is an artificial thing. The $10 average cost used above is not what any unit actually cost to buy.

First-In, First-Out

The first-in, first-out method treats the first goods purchased or manufactured as the first units expensed out on sale or issuance. Goods sold (or issued) are valued at the oldest unit costs, and goods remaining in inventory are valued at the most recent unit cost amounts. There are two common rationalizations for the use of FIFO:

1. FIFO approximates the physical flow of merchandise and materials — generally speaking, items that are purchased first *are* sold first or used first in operations.

2. Under historical cost accounting, costs should be matched to revenue in historical sequence — the costs first incurred should be the first that are matched to revenues.

These two reasons for using FIFO are not mutually exclusive; both make sense.

The application of FIFO requires the company to keep track of unit cost by *inventory layers*. Using the numbers in the example above, there are two layers:

1. the beginning inventory layer of 1,000 units @ $9
2. the purchase during the period of 500 units @ $12

Cost of goods sold will be 700 units at the cost of the first inventory layer, or 700 × $9 = $6,300. The ending inventory of 800 units will be comprised of the remainder of the first layer plus the entire second layer:

$$\text{Ending inventory} = [(\$300 \times \$9) + (500 \times \$12)] = \$8,700$$

FIFO is the most commonly used method in Canada. It produces an inventory value for the balance sheet that reflects the most recent prices paid for the inventory; the inventory value is said to approximate *current replacement cost*, as the most recent costs are on the balance sheet. The flow of costs tends to be consistent with the usual physical flow of goods. While this is explicitly *not* a requirement for choice of a cost flow policy, many people find it intuitively appealing. It is systematic and objective and is not subject to manipulation. FIFO also yields the same results under both periodic and perpetual inventory systems.

A criticism of FIFO is that it does not expense the most current costs; instead, the oldest unit costs are expensed. When costs are rising, reported income under FIFO is higher than under LIFO or average cost. The difference between the cost of goods sold and the cost to replace the inventory is called an inventory profit (or *phantom profit*) because this portion of gross profit must be used to replace inventory the next period if the company is to stay in business.

Criticism of FIFO on the grounds of not expensing an amount sufficient to enable the company to replace its inventory is really an implicit rejection of the nominal dollar capital maintenance assumption. This assumption was discussed in Chapter 2.

When inventory replacement costs are rising, companies that use FIFO report more income than those using other methods, all other factors constant. On the other hand, when prices are falling, FIFO reports lower income than other methods.

Last-In, First-Out

The last-in, first-out method of inventory costing charges the cost of the most recently acquired items to cost of goods sold. As a result, the units remaining in ending inventory are costed at the *oldest* unit costs incurred, and the units included in cost of goods sold are costed at the *newest* unit costs incurred, the exact opposite of the FIFO cost assumption. For example, if the company discussed above sold 700 units and used LIFO for a cost flow policy, cost of goods sold would be [(500 × $12) + (200 × $9)] = $7,800; closing inventory would be $7,200 (e.g., 800 units @ $9).

When LIFO is applied with a perpetual inventory system, sales are costed currently throughout the accounting period as each sale occurs. The most recently acquired units are considered sold, and the oldest kept. As long as prices are rising, this results in higher cost of goods sold, lower profits, and lower inventory costs.

Well, LIFO is the mirror image of FIFO, so the things that FIFO does well, LIFO does not. The balance sheet inventory reported by LIFO will be "old costs," rapidly out of synch with replacement costs if the prices consistently increase (or consistently fall). The LIFO inventory prices can be decades old if the entity rarely changes the nature of its inventories. On the other hand, the most current replacement cost is reported on the income statement, reflecting current sales value and the most current replacement cost in the same period. LIFO cost flow assumptions are often exactly opposite to the actual physical flow of goods. It may also be possible to manipulate profits in a LIFO system if prices have been increasing for a long time and the base level of inventory is carried at very old, low prices. If a company wants to boost earnings, it can delay inventory acquisition, so that the base inventory is expensed. The gross margin generated will be significantly in excess of the norm!

Comparison of Methods

The results of applying the three cost flow assumptions (that is, excluding specific identification) in our example are as follows:

Method	CGS	Ending Inventory
Average cost	$7,000	$8,000
FIFO	6,300	8,700
LIFO	7,800	7,200

The impact that the inventory cost flow assumption has on the financial statements depends on whether prices are going up or down. General price levels have been increasing in the North American economy almost continuously since World War II. However, some products have bucked this trend and have declined in price, in response to supply and demand or changing technology.

In periods of rising prices, FIFO results in higher inventory balances, lower cost of goods sold, and higher profits. For companies with loans secured by current assets, higher inventory balances are appealing. Higher profits are also appealing to a certain subsection of companies — debt-laden or start-up companies trying to improve their financial ratios, for example. LIFO has the opposite effect: lower inventories and lower profits.

Revenue Canada does not allow firms to use LIFO for tax purposes. A firm can use LIFO for external reporting, but would have to use FIFO or average cost for tax purposes. Some do this, but it is an expensive data collection exercise. Canadian LIFO adopters tend to be Canadian subsidiaries of U.S. parent companies, and use LIFO so that all companies in the consolidated group have similar accounting policies (LIFO is acceptable for U.S. tax purposes and is popular in the U.S., especially during periods of rising prices)

Average cost is always in the middle between FIFO and LIFO — the middle inventory value, and the middle cost of goods sold figure. Average cost is allowed for tax purposes, and is likely to result in a lower taxable income than FIFO if prices are rising; one can suggest that this may be a major reason for its widespread use in Canada, although its ease of use in a computer-based inventory system must certainly be another reason.

Other Issues in Inventory Costing

The foregoing sections described the *flow* assumptions that can be used for inventory costs. These are general methodologies, and they reflect different methods of *allocating* the costs of purchased goods and supplies and *matching* the costs to revenue. There are many other issues involved in the measurement of inventory cost and allocation to periods.

In particular, there is an important issue of determining which costs to include in inventory and which to treat as period costs. There is a great deal of flexibility in the matter, and it is not unusual for a company to use three different definitions of inventoriable cost: one for internal decision-making (management accounting), another for income tax purposes, and yet another for external financial reporting. This and other issues relating to inventory costing will be discussed in Chapter 9.

1. What is meant by a *cost flow assumption*?
2. Which inventory cost flow assumptions are most commonly used in Canada?
3. Why is LIFO seldom used in Canada?

CONCEPT REVIEW

ASSET AMORTIZATION

When an expenditure is made, it becomes either an expense (no future benefit that meets the recognition criteria) or an asset (recognition criteria are met). But the asset does not remain on the balance sheet forever, except for land. Some assets are expensed in their entirety at the revenue recognition point — inventory is the best example of this. Some are expensed as they are consumed in the earnings process — supplies, for example. Others are used or consumed in the earnings process over a period of time, and must be amortized, or expensed, gradually.

We typically think of amortization in connection with tangible assets such as plant and equipment, but amortization applies to all capital assets, tangible or intangible, and also to deferred charges and a variety of other financial statement elements. There are a number of alternative patterns that accomplish the amortization process. The various alternatives can have a profound impact on reported income and net assets.

Amortization is the general term for allocating any long-lived asset's cost to the periods of its use or benefit, regardless of the type of asset. Traditionally, however, depreciation is the term used for amortization of tangible capital assets — buildings, furniture, and equipment. The costs of natural resources are subject to depletion. Other capitalized costs have to make do with the general term, but the general term can also be used for tangible capital assets and for natural resources. The *CICA Handbook* uses only the term *amortization*, but the other terms continue in wide use.

Nature of Amortization

In referring to capital assets, the *CICA Handbook* states that

> Amortization should be recognized in a rational and systematic manner appropriate to the nature of the capital asset.   [*CICA* 3060.31]

In the section on research and development costs, the *CICA Handbook* states that amortization

> ... should be charged as an expense on a systematic and rational basis by reference, where possible, to the sale or use of the product or process.
>   [*CICA* 3450.28]

These statements are quite vague. The phrase *rational and systematic* implies only that amortization methods should be regular and pre-determined rather than haphazard and arbitrary, and the methods should be defensible on the grounds that the result follows logically from the asset's use. However, this still leaves a lot of choice among amortization methods.

For financial reporting purposes, capitalized costs can be thought of as long-term expense prepayments. A portion of the cost is assumed to benefit each period of use, and amortization expense is the systematically determined amount recognized for this purpose. That is, as the asset is used to generate revenue, a portion of the cost must be transferred from the asset account to an expense account.

Amortization expense is not recognized for sudden and unexpected factors, such as damage from natural phenomena, sudden changes in demand, or radical misuse of assets that impair their revenue-generating ability. These events trigger a one-time write-down (which is discussed in Chapter 11).

Accounting amortization is not a valuation process. Declines in the market value of an asset that is intended for use (rather than for resale) are not recorded unless the asset suddenly loses its usefulness for generating future revenue. Therefore, the book value (cost less accumulated amortization) of a capital asset does not equal its market value except by sheer accident. Remember, GAAP generally measures historical cost, not market value.

Amortization is not meant to measure the decline in an asset's value in any one period, but it is justified by the sure knowledge that, at the end of an asset's useful life, its residual value, or sales value, will be minor. This decline in utility over an asset's life is caused by two factors: usage and obsolescence. Usage speaks for itself: many assets simply wear out. Others will be in good shape at the end of their "useful lives" but better, more efficient, cheaper technologies exist, and the item is replaced. There are still a lot of very nice typewriters out there!

CAPITAL ASSETS

Amortization (Depreciation) Alternatives

Do you remember the various depreciation methods from your introductory accounting course? Let's briefly describe them before we examine the likely reasons for their popularity, or lack thereof. There's a whole chapter on capital asset amortization later in this text; what you see here is just an overview.

The straight-line (SL) method relates amortization directly and evenly to the passage of time rather than to the asset's use, resulting in a constant amount of amortization recognized per time period. The formula for computing periodic amortization is:

Annual SL amortization = [Acquisition cost – residual value]
÷ Estimated useful life in years

The units of production method associates amortization with units that are produced. It is based on usage rather than the passage of time. Hence, amortization is not recorded when assets are idle. An important precondition for this method is that it must be possible to ascertain both the total lifetime output of a particular asset, and yearly or periodic output. The formula for computing periodic amortization is:

Amortization *rate* per unit of output = [Acquisition cost – Residual value]
÷ Estimated total units of output over the asset's productive life
Annual *amortization* = Amortization rate per unit of output
× Units produced during the year

Another version of units of production is based on usage, or service hours.

Like the straight-line method, the declining balance (DB) method allocates cost as a function of time, but recognizes larger amounts of amortization early in the useful life of assets and lesser amounts later. Thus, it accelerates the recognition of amortization. The formula for computing periodic amortization is:

Annual DB amortization = [Acquisition cost – Accumulated amortization] × DB
rate

The rate is based on the expected useful life of the asset in some fashion. Also popular are the rates established in the federal *Income Tax Act*, which requires the use of a similar amortization method, called *capital cost allowance*, for tax purposes.

The sum-of-the-years-digits (SYD) method also is a time-based method that provides more amortization at the beginning of an asset's life than at the end. The formula for computing periodic amortization is:

Annual SYD amortization = [Acquisition cost – Residual value] × *Fraction*

The fraction has the sum of the years of useful life as a denominator (e.g., the sum of 5 is 15, or 5 + 4 + 3 + 2 + 1). The numerator is the number of years remaining in the useful life at the beginning of the period. The numerator declines with each year of asset use. That is, for an asset with a five-year life, the first year's fraction is 5/15, the second year's, 4/15, etc.

Sinking fund amortization methods are also called *present value* (or *interest*) methods. The cost of a capital asset is presumed to represent the present value of the stream of cash receipts generated by the asset. Each receipt consists of interest (return on investment) and principal (amortization expense or return of investment). The calculation associated with this method is demonstrated in Chapter 11. For now, you should simply understand that this amortization method results in a pattern of *increasing* amortization: less in the early years, more in the later years.

Amortization Methods Used in Practice

A 1997 survey of 200 public Canadian companies reported that straight-line depreciation was the most common amortization method by far, used by 90% of the 101 companies that reported using only one method. Of the companies that used more than one method, 80% used straight-line for at least part of their capital assets. Therefore, straight-line was used by 85% of all companies in the sample. The declining balance method was used by 24% of the companies, and units of production was used by 22%.[1] So, the overwhelming pattern is straight-line, followed distantly by declining balance and units of production. Some companies use different amortization patterns for different assets.

So what explains the adoption patterns? Industry practice is one factor — companies try to use the same policies as their competitors, so that comparisons are valid. Once a method becomes commonly used, it's pretty well entrenched.

Companies are taken with the simplicity of the straight-line method. Why waste time and money on more complicated calculations that will not be comparable with the rest of the industry? Straight-line produces lower amortization amounts in early years compared to the declining balance method, attractive to those who want to look good in the short run. Perhaps the asset was acquired as part of an expansion, financed by debt, which introduced profitability covenants. If so, there are significant incentives to make sure that income is "high enough"! Straight-line also presents a stable expense from period to period. It's easier to predict next year with stable patterns.

Declining balance methods should theoretically be more common for assets that run significant risk of technological obsolescence, like computer equipment. More cost is written off earlier. It's also popular when repair costs are expected to mount up later in an asset's life — a pattern of decreasing amortization expense and increasing repairs expense produces a more-or-less stable total expense pattern.

Some companies prefer the declining balance method because they must use a form of declining balance for many assets for tax reporting. The two are not identical, but differences can be minimized when declining balance is used for accounting purposes, too.

Why is this desirable? If accounting and tax amortization are similar, there are fewer temporary differences that give rise to deferred (future) income taxes. Many companies prefer to minimize this deferred credit. Declining balance amortization is especially popular with small businesses for this reason, as well as because it reduces accounting cost if the same method can be used for both tax and accounting.

Units of production is used in the resource industry, since their businesses revolve around total reserves available for extraction and the physical volume produced each year. While estimation errors are common, the needed data is more available in this industry than in most other industries, and amortization is then geared to swings in production.

The other alternatives? SYD is allowable for U.S. tax reporting, and is more common in the U.S. as a result. Any Canadian adopters are likely Canadian subsidiaries of U.S. parents, whose choice of accounting policy is dictated from head office. Sinking fund amortization, which starts low and ends high, is found in real estate

---

[1] *Financial Reporting in Canada 1997*, p. 201.

companies, whose commercial, office, and apartment building investments carry a lot of debt. They incur high interest costs early in the buildings' lives, and lower costs later; an increasing amortization policy teams up with decreasing interest to approach a stable pattern — at least, in theory! Real estate developers are always very highly levered and typically try to maximize earnings to satisfy lenders' covenants.

In their choice of amortization methods, firms will be motivated by a desire to manage earnings patterns, for whatever reason. Firms may be motivated to maximize or minimize earnings, in both the short or long run. It seems logical to suggest that the impact of amortization expense will be weighed before a policy is adopted.

Firms may also be engaged in earnings management when estimating residual values and useful lives. Let's say that a company adopts a given amortization method and has earnings maximization as an important reporting objective. If short-term income maximization is a goal, you can bet the straight-line amortization will be chosen; the higher, earlier expense produced by declining balance will not be attractive! In any event, amortization will be minimized if residual values are high and useful lives are long.

All amortization methods are profoundly affected by the management's choice of useful lives and residual values. While a company must muster evidence to support its estimates for audit purposes (when there is an audit), there is still considerable room for bias to creep in.

When estimates are changed, they are changed prospectively: the current and future periods are affected, but no retroactive changes are made. Disclosures of useful lives and rates are required to allow the users to assess this area for themselves, but few are expert in estimating appropriate useful lives. As well, many such disclosures are too vague or generalized to be of any real assistance to a user.

In 1987, Cineplex Odeon was in the last stages of a major expansion, total assets having increased 520% in 1986 and 46.5% in 1987. Debt took spectacular jumps, as well: the company was highly levered at the end of 1987. In 1987, the company changed their estimates of the useful lives of buildings and goodwill from 20 years to 40 years, and "other assets" from 10 years to 15 years. Support for the estimate changes was gathered and outlined in the annual report. These estimate changes decreased amortization by about $5 million dollars, or 7% of net income, after tax.

1. What is the basic purpose of amortization?
2. What *estimates* affect the amount of amortization that is expensed each year for an asset?
3. Which amortization method is most widely used by Canadian companies?

CONCEPT REVIEW

DEFERRED COSTS

At the beginning of this chapter, we established that expenditures, as debits to offset cash outflows, were either assets or expenses. To qualify as assets, the recognition criteria for assets must be met; specifically, there must be a *probable* and *measurable* future economic benefit. Future cash flow is key.

Pre-Operating Costs
What would you recommend in this scenario?

Samatron Corporation has been in business for 15 years, and manufactures automobile subassemblies for one of the Big Six auto manufacturers. In June of the current year, Samatron's Board of Directors approved the development of a new division, selling a product unrelated to automobile parts. The new product will be an underwater mobile device capable of deep water recognizance and salvage activities.

Between October and December, the end of the fiscal year, Samatron spent $1.4 million in connection with the new venture. Manufacturing equipment was leased under operating leases, employees were hired and relocated to Kitchener, Ontario, where the facility is located. Money was spent on promotional activities, marketing studies, administrative salaries, and a wide range of other activities. By the end of December, the division was preparing to manufacture some sample goods for promotional activities, but they were, in management's view, still six months away from commercial production. How should Samatron account for the $1.4 million of expenditures to date?

If you agree with the premise that the operation is viable, then there will be future cash flows when the operation goes into commercial production; cash flows that will recoup the pre-operating period expenditures. Clearly, there must be reasonable grounds to assume that this is the most likely scenario, or the board of directors would never have approved the project in the first place.

On the other hand, new businesses are risky things. There is no precedent for the operation, and no guarantee that there will be future profitable operations. If the company defers the expenditures as assets, then it, in some respects, implies a guarantee about the success of future operations. Is this appropriate?

The CICA's Emerging Issues Committee considered appropriate accounting policy in this area, and suggested that an established company can defer (and amortize) expenditures in the pre-operating period to the extent that

- the expenditure is related directly to placing the new business into service,
- the expenditure is incremental in nature (i.e., a cost that would not have been incurred in the absence of the new business), and
- it is probable that the expenditure is recoverable from the future operation of the new business.

[EIC - 27]

Notice especially the last criterion: the asset (deferred pre-operating costs) *must be related to future economic benefits (cash flow in the operating period)*. Matching is not invoked as a criteria, even though deferral of these expenditures, to be later amortized when revenue is reported on the income statement, achieves matching.

What kind of evidence would be appropriate to establish whether the expenditure is recoverable from the future operation of the business? This is obviously the critical issue; in the absence of appropriate evidence, these expenditures must be expensed. At a minimum, one would expect market research and detailed cash flow projection; some orders would be nice, too. In the end, it's always a judgement call.

The EIC opinion applies only to established businesses with a record of profitability; this stable base and successful history is clearly important in establishing a track record. The EIC suggests that the duration of the pre-operating period should be finite, ending when the operation is ready to commence commercial production. Once in commercial operation, the pre-operating expenditures should be amortized; the EIC indicated that this amortization period should not normally exceed five years, although they did not explain the rationale for this arbitrary cut-off. Choice of amortization pattern is left to the discretion of management.

EIC recommendations are non-binding even for public companies. Therefore, the capitalization of pre-operating costs and start-up costs is a common practice, especially among firms that are attempting to maximize their reported net income. The rationale is usually one of matching, rather than one of asset definition.

Other Deferred Charges

Section 3070 of the *CICA Handbook* deals with the disclosure of deferred charges, but recognition concerns are not discussed. In the sense used by the *CICA Handbook* (and in general practice), deferred charges must be distinguished from prepaid expenses. Prepaid expenses are normally included as a part of current assets. Long-term deferred charges are excluded from current assets and reported either as a separate category or under other assets on the balance sheet.

Section 3070 recommends that companies disclose major components separately and report whether the deferred charge is net of accumulated amortization. In addition, the basis of amortization, and the amount, must be disclosed.

These disclosure requirements seem appropriate, and hardly onerous, but they beg the larger question: what expenditures can be deferred? In practice, perhaps the most common deferred charges are those related to obtaining long-term debt: bond discounts, bond issue costs, and up-front fees paid to secure long-term financing. Costs related to long-term debt are discussed in Chapter 13. Other common deferred charges are development costs (dealt with in the next section) and pre-operating expenditures, discussed previously.

Research and Development Costs

Broadly defined, research and development includes the activities undertaken by firms to create new products and processes, or to improve old ones, and to discover new knowledge that may be of value in the future. For many firms, R&D is a very important part of ongoing activities and can be a large and significant expenditure. These expenditures are undertaken because the R&D effort is expected to more than pay for itself in the future by providing the firm with competitive, profitable products and processes.

Prior to the implementation of Section 3450 of the *CICA Handbook* in 1978, the reporting and accounting for R&D costs varied greatly. Because there was no clear guidance on what constituted R&D activities, different firms included the costs of different activities in R&D. R&D costs were sometimes capitalized as intangible assets (and amortized over time); at other times they were expensed immediately.

Due to these variations in accounting for R&D costs, financial statements were not comparable among firms, and firms could potentially manipulate income by expensing or capitalizing R&D costs as needed to obtain the desired amount of income. Section 3450 was issued by the AcSB to provide guidance both in defining research and development costs and in recommending how to report R&D costs.

First, in attempting to distinguish between costs to be included in R&D and similar costs to be excluded from R&D, Section 3450 defines both research and development:

> Research is planned investigation undertaken with the hope of gaining new scientific or technical knowledge and understanding. Such investigation may or may not be directed toward a specific practical aim or application.
>
> Development is the translation of research findings or other knowledge into a plan or design for new or substantially improved materials, devices, products, processes, systems, or services prior to the commencement of commercial productions or use. [*CICA* 3450.02]

Because there is considerable similarity between R&D activities and some other activities, Section 3450 goes on to provide examples of activities to be included and of activities to be excluded from R&D costs:

Activities included in research:
- Laboratory research aimed at discovery of new knowledge.
- Searching for applications of new research findings or other knowledge.
- Conceptual formulation and design of possible product or process alternatives.

Activities included in development:

- Testing in search for, or evaluation of, product or process alternatives.
- Design, construction, and testing of pre-production prototypes and models.
- Design of tools, jigs, molds, and dies involving new technology.

Activities excluded from both research and development:

- Engineering follow-through in an early phase of commercial production.
- Quality control during commercial production, including routine testing of products.
- Troubleshooting in connection with breakdowns during commercial production.
- Routine or periodic alterations to existing products, production lines, manufacturing processes, and other ongoing operations, even though such alterations may represent improvements.
- Adaptation of an existing capability to a particular requirement or customer's needs as part of a continuing commercial activity.
- Routine design of tools, jigs, molds, and dies.

[*CICA* 3450.04–.06]

Section 3450 of the *CICA Handbook* recommends that *research costs* should be charged to expense when incurred. Development costs, however, may be capitalized and amortized if *all* of the following criteria are met:

(a) the product or process is clearly defined and the costs attributable thereto can be identified,

(b) the technical feasibility of the product or process has been established,

(c) the management of the enterprise has indicated its intention to produce and market, or use, the product or process,

(d) the future market for the product or process is clearly defined or, if it is to be used internally rather than sold, its usefulness to the enterprise has been established, and

(e) adequate resources exist, or are expected to be available, to complete the project.

[*CICA* 3450.21]

Development costs that do not meet all of these five criteria should be charged to expense.

These five criteria are often regarded as being clear and relatively unambiguous. But who makes the estimates that are involved?

(a) The first criterion simply says that the costs relating to specific development projects can be separately identified — it is not sufficient just to arbitrarily allocate part of the research budget to a new product development and call it "development cost." Fair enough.

(b) The second criteria says only that the product can be produced. This means that the cost of dead-end projects that are not technically feasible should not be capitalized. But technical feasibility is essentially assessed by *management*.

(c) *Management* must decide whether it intends to market the product or process. There is no external validation or verification needed; it's a management call.

(d) Who is to say that the future market for the product is clearly defined? Clearly, *management* does.

(e) If *management* is intending to go ahead with the development, they most certainly will assert that there are or will be adequate resources to proceed.

These apparently iron-clad criteria are almost completely subject to management determination. If management wishes to capitalize identifiable development costs for products or processes that they are undertaking, it will be a brave auditor who tries to challenge them.

Nevertheless, these criteria do represent an effort by the AcSB to recognize that some development efforts do have future benefit, and that they qualify as assets. Thus, this section of the *CICA Handbook* involves an example of the *definitional* approach to expense recognition.

Research and development programs are undertaken by entities with a clear expectation of future profitable results. Their future benefits establish them as assets. Why do accounting standards try to recommend that most of them be expensed? Typically, research costs fail the recognition criteria of "probability." That is, one cannot be certain that future cash flows will accrue. Unfortunately, for some firms, the expensing of research costs means that an item that some consider the firm's most valuable asset is not shown at all on its balance sheet and that current period expenses are overstated.

If development costs are capitalized, they must also be amortized; amortization is charged over the period of commercial production. But there are many different methods that can be used for amortization. A building or a piece of equipment has an ascertainable life before it ceases to be useful. Management must estimate that useful life in order to amortize the asset, but the reasonableness of management's estimate can be tested by auditors or external users of the financial statements (provided that the useful life is disclosed in the notes to the financial statements). But the probable economic life of development costs is even fuzzier; there is a great deal of discretion given to management in making those estimates of amortization period.

When research expense is material, the financial statements should disclose, either in the income statement or in the notes to the financial statements, the total research and development costs included in expense for each period for which an income statement is presented [*CICA* 3450.34].

Computer Software Costs

One type of research and development cost that has become increasingly important in recent years is that of computer software development. Accounting issues concerning the costs of developing computer software arise in two different contexts:

1. Many companies develop computer software systems for their internal use, either by developing the software with their own staff or by contracting with an outside developer.
2. Other companies develop software as a product, to be sold to outsiders.

There is no specific Canadian accounting standard that applies to computer software costs, and companies in these two contexts tend to approach the issue in somewhat different ways.

The first category of companies, those that develop software for their own use, generally apply the AcSB's criteria as outlined in the previous section. The guidelines are applicable because they quite specifically refer to *internal use* of the product or process being developed. Bear in mind that we are not talking about small software programs that can be stored on a floppy diskette and be easily pirated; instead, we are referring to large-scale systems and program development that is the life blood of many modern corporations.

Think, for example, of the massive systems banks must use (and of the extensive security precautions that must be built in) or of the many inter-related systems that an airline must use to keep its planes in the air and to get its customers into their seats. Banks routinely talk about development costs running as high as $1 billion.

Companies that develop large-scale systems normally will capitalize their software development costs and amortize them over three to five years. The accounting policy is the same whether the software is developed internally or under contract from a consultant or specialist.

When software is developed internally, two questions arise about which costs to capitalize:

1. Should all costs be capitalized, from the very beginning of the project, or should early feasibility and systems development studies be expensed; and

2. Should only direct costs be capitalized, or should indirect and overhead costs also be capitalized?

Obviously, a lot of different measures of cost could be used. The use of different cost bases (and the impact on its financial results) is illustrated by Manitoba Telecom Services in reporting a *change* in *accounting policy* in its annual report:

> Effective January 1, 1995, the Manitoba Telephone System changed its method of accounting for costs associated with developing and implementing non-national software development projects from expensing internal salaries and other related costs incurred on these projects to capitalizing all such costs. This treatment is consistent with existing accounting policies for national software development projects. . . . Increases in property, plant and equipment, decreases in operating expenses and increases in net income amounted to $2.2 million in 1995.

Companies that develop software as a product may have a somewhat different approach. Software product development, like most other types of product development activities, has an initial period of feasibility testing to determine whether a proposed product is technically and financially feasible. Costs incurred during this period may be viewed as research costs rather than as development costs and be written off.

In the Canadian software industry, this approach is often used by *public* companies that wish to report on a basis that is consistent with their U.S. competitors, with whom they also are competing for capital. Since the FASB prohibits capitalization of any research and development costs, it was necessary for the FASB to issue a special standard to permit computer software companies to capitalize the costs.[2] As usual, the FASB standard is very detailed, but the essence is that the costs are accounted for in two phases:

1. All costs incurred to establish the technological feasibility of a computer software product are treated as research and are expensed as incurred.

2. Once the technological feasibility of the software product is established, subsequent costs incurred to obtain product masters are capitalized as an intangible asset.

Under the FASB standard, software development costs are expensed as incurred until all the planning, designing, coding, and testing activities necessary to establish that the product can be produced to meet its design specifications are completed, or until a working model of the software is completed.

Subsequent costs for further coding, testing, debugging, and producing masters of the software product to be duplicated in producing saleable products are capital-

---

2 *SFAS No. 86*, "Accounting for the Costs of Computer Software to be Sold, Leased, or Otherwise Marketed," FASB, Stanford, Conn., August 1985.

EXHIBIT 7-2
Disclosure Example — Deferred Software Development Costs

NEWBRIDGE NETWORKS CORPORATION
year ended April 30, 1998

Notes to Financial Statements:

Note 1: Significant Accounting Policies (excerpt)

Software Development Costs
Certain applications and systems software development costs are capitalized once technical feasibility has been established for the product, the company has identified a market for the product and intends to market the developed product. No other development costs are capitalized. Such capitalized costs are amortized over the expected life of the related product.

Note 10: Software Development Costs

	April 30, 1998	April 30, 1997
Balance, beginning of the year	$ 22,299	$ 18,285
Amount capitalized	15,627	12,457
Amortization	(9,627)	(8,443)
Balance, end of the year	$ 28,299	$ 22,299

ized. In general, the largest portion of software development costs is incurred before a working model is produced, so the amount of computer software costs capitalized is usually a small portion of the total development costs. The capitalization of these costs stops when the product is available for release to customers. Exhibit 7-2 gives an example of the accounting policy disclosure relating to computer software product development.

Costs of producing software from the masters, producing documentation and training materials, and physically packaging the material for distribution are inventoriable production costs. These costs are capitalized as inventory and are recognized as cost of goods sold when sales revenue is recognized.

Exploration and Development Costs

Exploration and development (ED) costs are the costs that oil and gas companies and mining companies incur in exploring and developing their resource properties. *Exploration* is the process of seeking mineral deposits, while *development* is the process of turning a found deposit into a productive mine site or oil field. Much exploration is fruitless; that is the nature of the business. Most development does work out, since development is not undertaken unless there is reasonable assurance of generating enough revenue from the site to recover the development costs. It can take years to develop a mine site or an oil field. How should the costs of exploration and development be accounted for?

The accounting for exploration and development costs varies widely. One extreme is to treat all ED costs as expenses in the period in which they are incurred. This approach results in a net income figure that is closest to the actual cash flows of the company, and therefore may be the most useful for cash flow prediction. As well, immediate expensing has the advantage that once a mine site or oil field enters production, net income reflects the net cash flow generated by the site because revenue is matched to the operating costs without the additional burden of amortized ED costs.

Immediate expensing is an alternative that is most suitable for large mining companies and large oil and gas companies that engage in a more or less constant search for new assets. Since the ED activity is constant, there is no undue strain on profitability as the result of immediate expensing. Expensing obviously is also the least expensive way of accounting.

Most companies in the resource industry do not immediately expense their ED costs, however. The more common approach is to defer and amortize those costs. This is particularly true for "junior" resource companies, which are companies that have only one site or a small number of sites and that do not engage in perpetual, world-wide exploration. There are a lot of junior resource companies in Canada. These companies do not expense their ED costs, because they have no revenue during the development stage and immediate expensing would result in a huge deficit in shareholders' equity. Therefore, they generally capitalize the costs and amortize them once the site or field becomes productive.

Capitalized ED costs consist of two components, (1) structures and (2) other costs. Structures (that is, buildings and equipment) are tangible capital assets that are depreciated once production begins. The other costs are an intangible capital asset that is subject to *depletion*, which is the name traditionally given to amortization of natural resources. The carrying value of the intangible asset is not the *value* of the mineral resources; it is only the *cost* of getting at them.

Depletion is usually calculated on a unit-of-production basis, using the **estimated reserves** as the denominator in the per-unit calculation. The *estimated reserves* is the quantity of minerals or oil and gas that the geologists and engineers estimate can be profitably extracted and processed. The rate of depletion is adjusted for major changes in estimated reserves during a period.

Notice that there are a lot of estimates in the depletion calculation, perhaps even more than are present in depreciation calculations. The degree of estimation is even more pronounced because the depletion should, according to a CICA accounting guideline (i.e., *not a CICA Handbook* recommendation), include "estimated future costs to be incurred in developing proved undeveloped reserves."[3] In other words, the depletion (for oil and gas companies) should be based not only on the costs incurred to date, but also on the *future* costs that will be incurred for further development of the field. That is so that later production will not be burdened by higher amortization than will early production.

When there is only one mine site or oil and gas field, depletion is based simply on the output of that site or field. However, large companies usually operate over a wide geographic area, sometimes world-wide. If big companies don't expense their ED costs immediately, how should they amortize the ED costs? There are two general approaches to depletion:

1. the **full cost method**, in which ED costs for the company's entire sphere of operations are accumulated and amortized on the basis of global production; or

2. the **successful efforts method**, in which the ED costs relating to unsuccessful exploration and development efforts are expensed (once the site has been determined to be unproductive) and the ED costs of successful sites are segregated and amortized by geographic region.

In the *full cost method*, the assumption is that unsuccessful efforts are a part of doing business; not every attempt to find mineral deposits or to find oil and gas reserves is going to be successful. Unless it is extraordinarily lucky, a resource company is not going to hit "pay dirt" every time it tries to find natural resources.

Under the *successful efforts method*, unsuccessful efforts are written off *once they are determined to be unsuccessful*. The costs are capitalized, since the effort may last more than one reporting period, but the accumulated costs relating to that site are

---

3 "Full Cost Accounting in the Oil and Gas Industry," CICA Accounting Guideline (October 1990), para. 34.

EXHIBIT 7-3
Examples of Accounting Policy Disclosure for ED Costs

METALORE RESOURCES LIMITED

1. Summary of Significant Accounting Policies (extracts)

(b) Natural Gas Properties

The company owns and/or controls approximately 40,000 acres of leases in Norfolk County, Ontario, and follows the full cost method of accounting for natural gas properties whereby all acquisition and development costs relating to the properties are capitalized. These costs are depleted by the unit of production method based on estimated proven drilled gas reserves. The natural gas reserves of the company have been determined by A.I. MacKay Petroleum Limited as of January 1, 1988 and updated by management's estimates to March 31, 1998.

The carrying value of the company's natural gas properties is limited to an ultimate recoverable amount which is the aggregate of future net undiscounted revenue from proven reserves based upon year-end prices and costs.

(c) Mining Properties

The company owns and/or controls in excess of 600 contiguous mining claims in the Beardmore area of Ontario. Acquistion and exploration costs are capitalized net of any government grants relating to mining properties. If exploration activities are followed by production, capitalized costs are amortized on the unit of production method based on the estimated reserves in the area. If exploration activities are unsuccessful and the area ia abandoned, all capitalized costs relating to the area are written-off.

PETRO-CANADA

1. Summary of Significant Accounting Policies (extract)

(d) Properties, Plant and Equipment

Investments in exploration and development activities are accounted for on the successful efforts method. Under this method the acquisition cost of unproved acreage is capitalized. Costs of exploratory wells are initially capitalized pending determination of proved reserves and costs of wells which are assigned proved reserves remain capitalized while costs of unsuccessful wells are charged to earnings. All other exploration costs are charged to earnings as incurred. Development costs, including the cost of all wells, are capitalized.

The interest cost of debt attributable to the construction of major new facilities is capitalized during the construction period.

---

charged to the income statement when management gives up the effort. Note that this is a management decision; timing of that decision will determine which accounting period's earnings bear the cost.

The successful efforts method requires management to segregate its ED costs by geographic area. There is a great deal of flexibility in this regard. One company may decide to segregate its successful sites on the basis of geological formation, while another may choose to use national boundaries as the definition of area. Some may view U.S. and Canada as a single area, while others may view Oklahoma as one area, Alberta as another, and the Maritime Provinces' offshore fields as yet another. Management choice is at the core of the successful efforts method.

Since allocation methods are inherently arbitrary, there is no real reason to choose one depletion method over another. The AcSB has stayed clear of this issue.

In practice, junior resource companies usually use full cost, while large public companies usually use successful efforts. An accounting policy disclosure example for each type of company is shown in Exhibit 7-3. Metalore Resources Limited uses the full cost method for its natural gas properties, but successful efforts for its mining properties. Note that there is no mention of the way in which capitalized costs are actually measured.

One hazard of capitalizing ED costs is that the total capitalized amount may exceed the net post-production value of the resources being mined. ED costs are *sunk costs*, of course, and therefore the fact that ED costs have exceeded the value of the resource does not necessarily mean that development should cease. Whether or not development continues depends on the relationship between *future* costs and future revenue. But if amortization of past costs (i.e., depletion), combined with the costs of extracting the resource from the ground, would result in an accounting loss, then the capitalized costs are in excess of their *future benefit* (which is part of the definition of an asset) and should be written down. This process is called the *ceiling test*. Of course, the projected future benefits and future costs consists of a vast array of estimates and assumptions, including the future price of the resource on the open market, and therefore the test is a rather subjective one.

CASH FLOW REPORTING OF CAPITALIZED COSTS

An interesting wrinkle to the issue of capitalizing instead of expensing certain costs is the impact that the capitalization policy has on the reporting of cash flows. In Chapter 5, we pointed out that the cash flow statement is the only one of the primary financial statements that has an AcSB-mandated format. The cash flow statement must include three sections (1) operating activities, (2) investing activities, and (3) financing activities.

It is obvious that the accounting policy decision to capitalize or expense a cost will not affect cash flows. The cost has been incurred and either has been or will be paid in cash. The accounting policy choice is only of whether to put the cost on the balance sheet (as an asset) or on the income statement (as an expense). Consider these differences in cash flow *reporting*, however:

- Costs that are accounted for as expenses are included in the cash flow from *operations*.

- Costs that are capitalized as assets are included in the *investing activities* section of the cash flow statement.

- Amortization on capitalized assets is deducted in determining net income, but is removed from cash flow from operations (either by adding it back in the indirect approach, or leaving it out in the direct approach).

For example, assume that Lorimer Ltd. spends $100,000 on development costs during 20X2, and that net income before deducting the development costs is $300,000. *If* the development costs are capitalized, they will be amortized straight-line over the five years *following* their incurrence (that is, from 20X3 through 20X7).

If Lorimer's management decides to expense the development costs (that is, decides that not all of the criteria in Section 3450 the *CICA Handbook* have been met), the net income for 20X2 is $200,000, and that amount is shown in the cash flow statement as the cash flow from operations (ignoring the many other adjustments that may be made to the net income to convert it to cash flow).

If the 20X2 costs are amortized, however, an interesting thing occurs. Because the costs are not charged as an expense, that $100,000 is shown as an investing activity rather than being included in operations. Cash flow from operations therefore is increased to $300,000. In 20X3, $20,000 of the development costs (i.e., one-fifth) are amortized and are charged against net income. In the operations section, however, amortization is added back to net income, and therefore the effect of the amortization is removed. The result is that *if costs are capitalized, they will **never** affect reported cash flow from operations.*

A company that follows a policy of capitalizing as many expenses as possible will, over time, show a consistently higher cash flow from operations than one that expenses those costs. While this may not fool a sophisticated user of the financial statements, management may choose to follow the capitalize-and-amortize approach consistently in an attempt to improve cash flow per share calculations (made by some analysts) or to increase the company's apparent margin of safety over debt restrictions that are based on operating cash flow.

1. What guidelines should be used to choose an amortization method?
2. Why doesn't depreciation on a capital asset reflect the decline in the asset's market value?
3. What is the difference between *research* costs and *development* costs?
4. When is it appropriate to capitalize development costs?
5. Explain the two general methods for accounting for exploration and development costs.

SUMMARY OF KEY POINTS

1. Entities may have a variety of rationales for their choice of accounting policies. These relate to enhancing cash flows to the entity or its major players and may result in income maximization, minimization, etc.

2. An expenditure may be either an asset or an expense. Items that meet the recognition criteria for assets are capitalized as assets; other expenditures are expensed. Of key importance in establishing an asset is the presence of future economic benefits, essentially cash flow. This is the definitional approach to expense recognition.

3. An expenditure that results in asset recognition simply reorganizes the asset section of the balance sheet but does not affect net assets, assets less liabilities. In contrast, expense recognition reduces net assets.

4. Expense policy has traditionally been described as a matching process, where expenses are matched to revenues recognized on the income statement. Matching results in questionable deferred asset and liability items recognized on the balance sheet; the definitional approach avoids this, which many accountants regard as preferable.

5. Measurement of an expense is usually only an issue when the expense is to be incurred at some future point in time, but must be accrued in the current period. Expenses may be estimated, but the presence of measurement uncertainty seldom is disclosed.

6. Expenses can be described as *direct*, that is, associated directly with revenues, or *indirect*, that is, not directly associated with revenues. Direct costs are more likely to be deferred if incurred prior to revenue recognition, while indirect costs are more likely to be expensed as incurred.

7. An important accounting policy decision is the inventory cost flow assumption, which governs determination of cost of goods sold. Alternatives are specific identification, LIFO, FIFO, and average cost. Only FIFO and average cost are in wide-spread use in Canada.

8. Another major accounting policy decision is the choice of amortization policy for capital assets and deferred charges. Alternatives are straight-line, units of production, declining balance, sum-of-the-years-digits, and, in certain industries,

sinking fund. Straight-line is the prevalent choice in Canada. Amortization amounts are profoundly affected by the amortization method chosen, and also by estimates of residual value and useful life.

9. Pre-operating costs can be deferred, and later amortized, if certain criteria are met. The criteria include an assessment of whether it is probable that expenditures will be recovered from future profitable operations; the asset definition must be met through future cash flow.

10. All research and many development costs must be expensed as incurred.

11. If certain criteria are met, development costs can be deferred and amortized. Again, the criteria are mainly based on management estimates; substantial variation in practice can arise.

12. Companies that develop computer software for their own use usually capitalize the cost and amortize them over three to five years.

13. Companies that develop computer software as their product usually account for the development costs in accordance with general recommendations for research and development costs. Public software companies may follow FASB recommendations, however, so that their financial statements will be comparable to those of their U.S. competitors.

14. Exploration and development (ED) costs are those costs incurred by mining companies and by oil and gas companies for finding and developing their resource sites. ED costs may be expensed as incurred, but usually are capitalized and amortized.

15. Amortization of ED costs is known as depletion. Depletion is usually calculated on a unit of production basis.

16. Resource companies that capitalize their ED costs may use either the full cost method or the successful efforts method of accounting. The full cost method combines the costs of all exploration and development activities for purposes of amortization; the successful efforts method segregates the costs by geographic region, and amortizes the costs of successful regions and writes off the costs of exploration in unsuccessful regions.

17. When costs are capitalized, the impact of those costs are removed from reported operating cash flow. Instead, the expenditures are shown as investing activities, and subsequent amortization is added back to net income in determining operating cash flows. A company that capitalizes costs such as start-up costs and development costs will report a higher cash flow from operations than one that charges those costs to expense when incurred.

REVIEW PROBLEM

Cromax Corp. is a Canadian public company whose shares are listed on the TSE. The following transactions and events occurred in 20X5. For each item, indicate the preferred accounting treatment. Assume all amounts are material.

1. Cromax paid $700,000 to a firm of engineers who undertook a study to determine more energy-efficient policies in Cromax's production facilities.

2. Cromax diverted workers and equipment to help prepare for public celebrations revolving around the G7 Summit in Halifax; the out-of-pocket cost was approximately $127,000; depreciation on equipment was $40,000. Cromax does a great deal of business with governments at all levels, and regards the expenditures as relationship-building that will have future benefit.

3. Cromax has recently signed a four-year contract with a new customer. As part of the terms of the contract, Cromax paid $500,000 up front to the customer to defray expenses the customer will incur as a result of changing suppliers. The contract involves substantial volumes of sales over the next four years between Cromax and the customer.

4. Cromax spent $4.2 million defending itself against an unfair competition lawsuit launched by six smaller firms. The lawsuit has been settled out of court. Of the $4.2 million, $3 million is the settlement, $800,000 is legal fees, and $400,000 is public relations spending to counteract the negative publicity surrounding the dispute. Cromax's future markets are secure as a result of the terms of the settlement.

5. Cromax has just set up a $20-million line of credit with their bank, which allows Cromax to borrow these funds on 24-hours' notice at any time over the next five years. The interest rate will be prime plus 1%. By year-end, Cromax had not borrowed any money under the lending arrangement, but expects to in the next fiscal year as a result of some planned capital expansion. Cromax paid an up-front fee of $125,000 to the bank in order to obtain the agreement. [ASCA, adapted]

REVIEW PROBLEM — SOLUTION

1. Items are recognized if they meet the recognition criteria. This $700,000 payment may be an asset, if it has future benefits that are probable. Can the energy savings be documented? (That is, are they probable?) If sufficient appropriate evidence exists, the expenditure may be deferred, to be amortized on a basis consistent with the projected savings. Otherwise, the item is an expense.

2. An amount of $167,000 can be directly attributed to the activities, which may be an "asset" if it has future benefit. While demonstrating that Cromax is a good corporate citizen may help solidify relationships with governments who are major customers, is there *probable* future cash flow that will validate the asset? It would be difficult to quantify the benefits, and this is most likely an expense of the period.

3. Cromax has future economic benefit associated with the long-term contract with the customer, and, as long as the contract is firm, it is acceptable to defer this payment and amortize it in some fashion over the life of the contract. Note that this is similar to Cott's policy cited at the beginning of the chapter.

4. Should the $4.2 million be recognized as an expense or as an asset, amortized to earnings over some future period of (now secure) profitable operations? All the items are incremental expenditures related to one event and should be accounted for the same way.

   The expenditures can be viewed as an asset if they have future benefits that are probable. Cromax's future operations in this line should be evaluated (cash flow projections) for sufficient appropriate evidence to support the asset value. Analogies can be drawn to pre-operating costs and legal fees spent to defend patents, both of which may be deferred and amortized.

   On the other hand, asset treatment may be inappropriate. Future operations are not enhanced by the expenditures; the status quo has only been preserved. Patents have finite legal lives, but operations in this case might be weakened by the precedent of the lawsuit settlement. Are they better off because of this payment? Would they be even "more" better off (i.e., have higher assets) if the settlement were higher? Under the definitions, in Section 1000, assets are *not* expenses deferred, but rather items with associated future cash flow. An appropriate analogy might be repairing a machine damaged in transportation, or fixing fire damage: the status quo is preserved by subsequent repairs, but no asset is created.

   The arguments for expensing appear stronger; the amount should *not* be capitalized.

5. Cromax has incurred a cost that is analogous to prepaid interest expense. It can be deferred, but should be amortized over the life of the agreement, five years. It does not simply relate to the period of time in which funds are actually borrowed under the facility, as Cromax is benefiting from the flexibility and locked-in interest rate for the entire five years. Deferred financing charges are a common deferred charge in Canada.

QUESTIONS

7-1   Describe the difference in reporting an expired cost related to an entity's basic business, and an expired cost related to a peripheral activity.

7-2   A company spends cash to acquire a service, such as legal fees. Describe the impact on the financial statements if the expenditure is classified as an asset compared to its impact when classified as an expense.

7-3   When does a cash expenditure result in recognition of an asset? An expense?

7-4   Explain when the purchase of a capital asset for cash results in a decline in net assets.

7-5   Describe two alternate ways that net assets can be decreased when expenses are recognized.

7-6   Why is expense recognition dependent on the revenue recognition point?

7-7   Contrast the definitional and matching approaches to explaining expense recognition policies.

7-8   Assume that a company has an expense recognition policy for bad debts that requires bad debt expense to be recognized, and an allowance for doubtful accounts established, as sales occur. The amount is measured as a percentage of sales. This accrual is to take place even though the actual amount of bad debt expense will not be known until specific customers actually default over the following 12 to 24 months. Justify this policy using the definitional approach, and then using the matching approach.

7-9   Give two examples of expenses for which measurement is an issue.

7-10   What is the difference between a direct and an indirect expense?

7-11   Explain four different cost flow assumptions that can be used to measure cost of goods sold. Which alternative will always result in the highest net income when prices are rising?

7-12   What cost flow assumptions used to measure cost of goods sold are most common in Canada? What factors have likely led to these choices of policy?

7-13   Explain five different ways to measure amortization of capital assets.

7-14   What amortization methods are most common in Canada? What factors have likely led to these choices of policy?

7-15   What estimates must be made in order to calculate amortization of a capital asset?

7-16   Under what circumstances can pre-operating costs be deferred and amortized? How do these costs meet the asset definition when they qualify for deferral?

7-17   What is the difference between research and development?

7-18   How must a company account for research? for development?

7-19   Computer software development costs present a particular challenge for policy-makers. What is the basic problem?

7-20   Describe two different approaches to depletion of exploration and development costs incurred by oil and gas companies.

7-21   If a company wished to pick accounting policies that reflect actual cash flows, would you expect the company to use full costing or successful efforts for exploration and development costs?

7-22   Under what circumstances will a cash flow for development expenses appear in the investing activities section of the cash flow statement? Explain.

CASE 7-1

Jaded Jeans

Jaded Jeans Limited operates a nation-wide chain of clothing stores that cater to young men and women. Jaded Jeans has been trying to obtain space in a new downtown shopping development that is extremely popular with young people. The management of Jaded Jeans feels that it is important for Jaded Jeans to have a presence in this development, even if the cost of obtaining a sublease partially offsets the potential profits for this location.

Recently, Jaded Jeans was able to negotiate a sublease with Pencil & Paper Ltd. (PP), an office supply firm that had leased a 2,000 square foot store in the development. To induce PP to sublet, Jaded Jeans agreed to pay $500,000 to PP immediately. Jaded Jeans is to make lease payments directly to the mall owner. None of the $500,000 paid to PP will go to the mall owner; the money will be retained by PP.

Jaded Jeans accounted for the $500,000 payment by charging it directly to expense for the current period. CA, the auditor of Jaded Jeans, objected to Jaded Jeans' treatment of the item and insisted that the payment be capitalized and allocated to the remaining five years of the sublease, preferably by the declining balance method. CA argued that treating the payment as a current expense would result in mismatching revenue and expense.

The vice-president finance (VP), has countered by arguing that although Jaded Jeans made the payment in expectation of large future revenues and profits from the new location, there was no way that the profits could reliably be predicted (if, indeed, they materialized at all). The VP felt that just as the *CICA Handbook*, Section 3450 prescribes that research costs be charged to expense due to the uncertainty of future benefits, so should Jaded Jeans' payment be charged to expense. The VP also stated that this payment could be written off immediately for income tax purposes and wondered why he could not do the same for accounting purposes.

In addition, the VP cited arguments from accounting literature that financial accounting allocations are inherently arbitrary. Since allocations are arbitrary, he argues, they must therefore be useless at best and misleading at worst.

The VP indicated that he had just finished cleaning up his balance sheet last year by writing off the balance of intangibles and he was not anxious to introduce a major intangible amount again. He indicated that bankers and financial analysts "discount" intangibles anyway.

Required:

Discuss the arguments presented and state your conclusion as to the appropriate accounting policy for this expenditure.

[CICA, adapted]

CASE 7-2

Ottawa Orioles

The Ottawa Orioles Ltd. (OOL) operates a professional baseball club. They won the Canadian Baseball League title in October 20X4.

The club's owners are two brothers, wealthy financiers who live in Vancouver. The club is financed about 50/50 through debt and equity. Their goals for the club are to have it break even with its total cash flows (that is, not require infusions of operating capital from the brothers). They also wish to be associated with the glamour and excitement of major league baseball.

The following accounting issues must be addressed for the year ended 30 November 20X4.

1. OOL moved into Big Top, a newly built stadium with a retractable roof, on 1 August 20X4. Seating capacity is 70,000. The new stadium is a great improvement over the 30,000-seat NoWay Park stadium used for the preceding seven years. On 24 July 20X4, OOL signed a 10-year lease with the new stadium's owners. However, OOL's lease on the old premises was not due to expire until 1 January 20X8. OOL therefore paid $3.6 million to terminate its lease.

2. Immediately before the start of the 20X4 baseball season in April, three of the club's top players were signed to long-term contracts. Amounts of the contracts are as follows:

	Term	Salary	
Frank Ferter	3 years	$1,500,000	per year
Hugh G. Blast	5 years	900,000	per year
Bill Board	4 years	1,200,000	per year

The contracts of Ferter and Blast specify that if they suffer a career-ending injury, their contracts will become null and void. Board's contract is guaranteed for the full-term.

On 27 April 20X4, Board was injured, forcing him to retire from playing baseball. As required by his contract, he has since been moved to the front office and is performing public relations and administrative services. Other equivalent PR staff are paid $50,000 – $60,000 per annum.

Ferter has a bonus clause in his contract under which he will be paid $50,000 if he is selected to play for the All Star Team. Although he is favoured to capture this honour in 20X4, the selections will not be announced until after the financial statements will have been issued.

Because of Ferter's exceptional ability and the fact that he is considered a "player who will increase the popularity of the sport in this city for many years to come," management proposes to amortize the total cost of his contract ($4,500,000) over a 10-year period.

3. On 3 October 20X4, the day before the last playoff game, a wind storm caused the roof at Big Top to collapse, resulting in structural damage of $4,500,000 to the stadium. This damage will be paid for by OOL, under the terms of their lease agreement. This unforeseen event forced OOL's last playoff game to be played at NoWay Park. Hence, the club announced that some of the 70,000 tickets sold for Big Top could be used at NoWay Park and that the $35 cost of the remaining tickets could either be refunded or applied towards the cost of tickets for any of OOL's pre-season games next year. Also, the 40,000 fans who could not attend the game at NoWay were given $10 gift certificates that could be used towards purchasing tickets for any future OOL game. The rate and the extent to which these gift certificates will be redeemed is uncertain at 30 November 20X4. What is certain is that the fans who were left seatless were very upset, and talked about a boycott of the 20X5 season.

Required:

Write a report that evaluates the accounting issues raised and includes your recommendations.

[CICA, adapted]

CASE 7-3

Blue River Gold Company

In 20X3, the Blue River Gold Company Ltd. (BRGCL) commenced development activities in northern Alberta. The company is in the process of developing a gold mining property called Castle Mountain, and management is of the opinion that this property contains economically recoverable ore reserves. The recoverability of the amounts spent for resource properties and fixed assets is dependent on the ability of the company to complete development of the property and upon future profitable operation.

Mineral exploration costs (acquisition, exploration and development expenditures) are being capitalized until commercial production is established. These amounts do not necessarily represent present or future values of the ore, just costs incurred to date.

Commercial production is contingent on government approval, which is expected early in 20X4. As a result, construction of mine buildings is in the final planning stage and commercial production is expected to start during the coming fiscal year (20X4).

You have been called to advise the company on the accounting policies it should adopt once it goes into commercial production. As a junior mining company listed on the VSE, the board of directors has indicated that they wish to adopt accounting policies that will "keep them out of trouble with the auditors and regulatory bodies."

Required:

Prepare an appropriate report to the board of directors.

BLUE RIVER GOLD COMPANY LTD.
Schedule of Cash Receipts and Disbursements
to 31 December 20X3

Cash receipts:	
Sale of common shares (Note 1)	$29,433,000
Gold loan (Note 2)	10,714,000
Interest revenue (Note 3)	566,400
	$40,713,400
Cash disbursements:	
Cost of mining properties (Note 4)	18,784,000
Administrative expenses (Note 5)	2,309,000
Acquisition of marketable securities (Note 6)	4,000,000
	$25,093,000
Excess of receipts over expenditures	$15,620,400

Note 1: Common shares were issued on the VSE on 31 January 20X3, for net proceeds of $29,433,000.

Note 2: On 30 November 20X3 BRGCL entered into a loan agreement with a bank consortium to borrow up to 95,000 ounces of gold to finance the development of the Castle Mountain gold mine. The loan will bear interest, payable in gold, at prime rates (7% on 30 November 20X3) plus 2%. The loan is secured by all assets of the company. The lender may elect to be paid cash for any or all principal and interest payments at a fixed conversion rate of $350 per gold ounce. The company has agreed not to incur additional indebtedness and not to create any additional security interests in any of their assets. BRGCL is also restricted from distributing dividends during the term of the loan.

The loan is repayable by delivery of gold in semi-annual instalments, beginning in 20X4 and covering five years. At 31 December 20X3, the loan had been drawn to the amount of $10,714,000, or 30,611 ounces of gold at the conversion price of $350.

BRGCL would like to consider two alternatives to account for this loan.

1. Treat the contract as a deferred sales contract. The loan proceeds, net of the finance charges and interest over the contract term, would be treated as deferred revenue, to be recognized on delivery of gold per the agreement.

2. Treat the contract as a loan. Gold deliveries would be recorded partially as principal repayment, and partially as interest.

Note 3: Interest revenue was earned throughout the year on cash raised through the sale of common shares.

Note 4: Cost of mining properties can be broken down as follows:

Mining properties	
Acquisition costs	$ 2,420,000
Exploration and development expenditures	16,364,000
	$18,784,000

Next year, as construction and mining commence, costs will be incurred for the following capital assets:

Capital Asset	Useful Life
Roads	Indefinite; roads assigned to the province once the mine is depleted
Mine buildings and structures	15 years, no salvage value
Equipment	2 years, minor salvage values

Note 5: Administrative expenses include salaries of executives and the costs of the rented head office facilities located in Vancouver, B.C., as well as other operating costs.

Note 6: In 20X3, BRGCL acquired shares in Brascorp, at a cost of $4,000,000. The current market value of these shares is $2,500,000. BRGCL does not plan to sell these shares until market value recovers.

Note 7: BRGCL has two options for revenue recognition of their gold production:

1. Revenue recognition on production, with inventory carried at net realizable value (sales price).

2. Revenue recognition on delivery to customers, with inventory carried at cost.

Surveys of industry practice show that both alternatives are found in Canadian gold mining companies.

[ASCA, adapted]

CASE 7-4

Good Quality Auto Parts

Good Quality Auto Parts Limited (GQAP) is a medium-sized, privately-owned producer of auto parts which are sold to car manufacturers, repair shops, and retail outlets. In March 20X0, the union negotiated a new three-year contract with the company for the 200 shop-floor employees. At the time, GQAP was in financial difficulty and management felt unable to meet the contract demands of the union. Management also believed that a strike of any length would force the company into bankruptcy.

The company proposed that, in exchange for wage concessions, the company would implement a profit-sharing plan whereby the shop-floor employees would receive 10% of the company's annual after-tax profit as a bonus in each year of the contract. Although the union generally finds this type of contract undesirable, it believed that insisting on the prevailing industry settlement would jeopardize GQAP's survival. As a result, the contract terms were accepted.

The contract specifies that no major changes in accounting policies may be made without the change being approved by GQAP's auditor. Another clause in the contract allows the union to engage a chartered accountant to examine the books of the company and meet with GQAP's management and auditor to discuss any issues. Under the terms of the contract, any controversial accounting issues are to be negotiated by the union and management to arrive at a mutual agreement. If the parties cannot agree, the positions of the parties are to be presented to an independent arbitrator for resolution.

GQAP presented to the union its annual financial statements and the unqualified audit report for the year ended 28 February 20X1, the first year during which the profit-sharing plan was in effect. The union engaged you, CA, to analyze these financial statements and determine whether there are any controversial accounting issues. As a result of your examination, you identified a number of issues that are of concern to you. You met with the controller of the company and obtained the following information:

1. GQAP wrote off $250,000 of inventory manufactured five to eight years previously. There have been no sales from this inventory in over two years. The controller explained that up until this year she had some hope that the inventory could be sold as replacement parts. However, she now believes that the parts cannot be sold.

2. The contracts GQAP has with the large auto manufacturers allow the purchaser to return items for any reason. The company has increased the allowance for returned items by 10% in the year just ended. The controller contends that, because of the weak economy and stiff competition faced by the auto manufacturers with whom GQAP does business, there will likely be a significant increase in the parts returned.

3. In April 20X0, GQAP purchased $500,000 of new manufacturing equipment. To reduce the financial strain of the acquisition, the company negotiated a six-year payment schedule. Management believed that the company would be at a serious competitive disadvantage if it did not emerge from the current downturn with updated equipment. GQAP decided to use accelerated depreciation at a rate of 40% for the new equipment. The controller argued that because of the rapid technological changes occurring in the industry, equipment purchased now is more likely to become technologically, rather than operationally, obsolete. The straight-line depreciation method applied to the existing equipment has not been changed.

4. Six years ago, GQAP purchased a small auto parts manufacturer and merged it into its own operation. At the time of acquisition, $35,000 of goodwill was recorded and was being amortized over 35 years. The company has written off the goodwill

in the year just ended. The controller explained that the poor performance of the auto parts industry, and of GQAP in particular, has made the goodwill worthless.

The union has asked you to prepare a report on the position it should take on the issues identified when discussing them with management.

Required:

Prepare the report.

[CICA, adapted]

CASE 7-5

Penquins in Paradise

"The thing you have to understand is how these stage plays work. You start out with just an idea, but generally no cash. That's where promoters like me come in. We find ways of raising the money necessary to get the play written and the actors trained. If the play is a success, we hope to recover all those costs and a whole lot more, but cash flow is the problem. Since less than half of all plays make money, you cannot get very much money from banks.

Take my current project, *Penguins in Paradise* (PIP). You only have to look at the cash inflows to see how many sources I had to approach to get the cash. As you can see, most of the initial funding comes from the investors in the limited partnership. They put up their money to buy a percentage of the future profits of the play.

The money that the investors put up is not enough to fund all the start-up costs, so you have to be creative. Take reservation fees for example. You know how tough it is to get good seats for a really hot play. Well, PIP sold the right to buy great seats to some dedicated theatregoers this year for next year's performance. These amounts are non-refundable, and the great thing is that the buyers still have to pay full price for the tickets when they buy them.

Consider the sale of movie rights. Lots of good plays get turned into movies. Once the stage play is a success, the movie rights are incredibly expensive. My idea was to sell the movie rights in advance. PIP got a lot less money, but at least we got it up front when we needed it.

The other sources are much the same. We received the government grant by agreeing to have at least 50% Canadian content. We also negotiated a bank loan with an interest rate of 5% a year plus 1% of the gross revenue of the play, instead of the usual 16% annual interest a year. Even my fee for putting the deal together was taken as a percentage of the revenue, so just about everybody has a strong interest in the play's performance."

Required:

Prepare a memo addressing the major financial accounting issues to be established by PIP. Include your recommendations. Do not prepare financial statements.

[CICA, adapted]

SUMMARY OF CASH FLOWS
for the period ended 31 December 20X4
(*$ thousands*)

Cash inflows:	
Investor contributions to limited partnership	$6,000
Bank loan	2,000
Sale of movie rights	500
Government grant	50
Reservation fees	20
	8,570

Cash outflows:	
Salaries and fees	3,500
Costumes and sets	1,000
Miscellaneous costs	1,260
	5,760
Net cash inflows	$2,810

E7-1 *Expense Recognition:* ABC Company recorded a series of recent transactions, in chronological order, as follows:

Date	Entry #			
1 July	1	Inventory	100,000	
		Accounts payable		100,000
	2	Advertising expense	3,500	
		Cash		3,500
	3	Prepaid rent	1,200	
		Cash		1,200
14 July	4	Accounts receivable	65,000	
		Sales		65,000
	5	Warranty expense	16,000	
		Estimated liability for warranty		16,000
	6	Cost of goods sold	35,000	
		Inventory		35,000
27 July	7	Cash	65,000	
		Accounts receivable		65,000
31 July	8	Rent expense	1,200	
		Prepaid rent		1,200
	9	Accounts payable	100,000	
		Cash		100,000
	10	Estimated liability for warranty	5,000	
		Cash		5,000

Required:

1. Explain the effect that each entry has on net assets. What is the revenue recognition point?

2. For each asset recognized above, explain how the asset meets the definition of an asset.

3. For each expense recognized above, explain whether the expense is a direct or indirect expense, and how the expense meets the expense definition.

E7-2 *Expense Recognition:* XYZ Company recorded a series of recent transactions, in chronological order, as follows:

Date	Entry #			
2 June	1	Inventory	165,000	
		Accounts payable		165,000
	2	Prepaid insurance	3,600	
		Cash		3,600
	3	Inventory	56,000	
		Cost of goods sold	60,000	
		Sales		116,000
	4	Warranty expense	9,000	
		Estimated liability for warranty		9,000
	5	Commissions expense	11,600	
		Commissions payable		11,600
20 June	6	Accounts receivable	116,000	
		Inventory		116,000
30 June	7	Cash	116,000	
		Accounts receivable		116,000
	8	Insurance expense	400	
		Prepaid insurance		400
	9	Accounts payable	165,000	
		Cash		165,000
	10	Estimated liability for warranty	3,000	
		Cash		3,000

Required:

1. Explain the effect that each entry has on net assets. What is the revenue recognition point?

2. For each asset recognized above, explain how the asset meets the definition of an asset.

3. For each expense recognized above, explain whether the expense is a direct or indirect expense, and how the expense meets the expense definition.

E7-3 *Expense Recognition:* Kwik-Bild Corporation sells and erects shell houses. These are frame structures completely finished on the outside but unfinished on the inside except for flooring, partition studding, and ceiling joists. Shell houses are sold chiefly to customers who are handy with tools and who will do the interior wiring, plumbing, wall completion and finishing, and other work necessary to make the shell houses liveable dwellings.

Kwik-Bild buys shell houses from a manufacturer in unassembled packages consisting of all lumber, roofing, doors, windows, and similar materials necessary to complete a shell house. Upon commencing operations in a new area, Kwik-Bild buys or leases a site for its local warehouse, field office, and display houses. Sample display houses are erected at a total cost from $13,000 to $17,000 including the cost of the unassembled package. The chief element of cost of the display houses is the unassembled package, since construction is a short, low-cost operation. Old sample display houses have little net salvage value because dismantling and moving costs amount to nearly as much as the salvage value.

A choice must be made between expensing the costs of sample display houses in the period in which the expenditure is made, or capitalizing the cost and spreading it through amortization, over more than one period.   [AICPA, adapted]

Required:

1. Discuss the merits of the two possible accounting policies, referring to the definitions of financial statement elements.
2. Discuss the merits of the two possible accounting policies, referring to matching.

E7-4 *Inventory Cost Flow:* Don Clow, a local businessman, is contemplating investing in a business. He has narrowed his choice to two firms in the same industry, and would like you to take a look at their income statements:

	Company A	Company B
	($ thousands)	
Sales	$210,000	$238,000
Cost of goods sold:		
Opening inventory	7,000	8,000
Purchases	170,000	180,000
	177,000	188,000
Less: Closing inventory	17,000	20,000
Cost of goods sold	160,000	168,000
Gross profit	50,000	70,000
Operating expenses	36,000	35,000
Net income	$ 14,000	$ 35,000

Don has determined that each firm held the same physical amount of inventory at year-end. However, one firm uses the average cost method and one uses FIFO. Prices have been rising over the last year.

Required:

1. Compare the gross profit margins of the two firms. Which firm uses average cost? Redraft both income statements to use average cost.
2. Explain the reasons that a company may prefer either FIFO or average cost as a cost flow assumption.
3. Use of a different cost flow assumption reduces the comparability of financial statements. Why is choice allowed?

E7-5 *Inventory Cost Flow:* First-in, first-out has been used as a cost flow assumption by the Harris Company since it was first organized in 20X0. Results have been as follows (in $ thousands):

	20X0	20X1	20X2	20X3
Reported net income	$ 17,500	$ 30,000	$ 32,500	$ 45,000
Reported ending inventories — FIFO	61,500	102,000	126,000	130,000
Ending inventory — average cost	59,000	75,100	95,000	105,000

Required:

1. Restate net income assuming use of the average cost method.
2. Explain the likely trend in net income if LIFO were to be used.
3. What inventory cost flow policy would you expect this company to adopt if they were trying to
   a. Match the most recent cost of acquisition with sales revenue.
   b. Minimize income tax payments.
   c. Report maximum inventory values on the balance sheet.

E7-6 *Amortization Policy:* You are an accountant in public practice, and have just obtained a new audit client, Magazines Unlimited. This year they began publishing a new magazine, their only product.

The company's cash flow budget anticipates an excess of expenditure over collections in the first four years, followed by year 5 in which collections will exceed expenditures. Subsequent years show a growing net cash inflow.

The president wants your approval for the proposed accounting policy for expenditures related to capital assets. He proposes that all such costs be capitalized, but that amortization not be started until year 5, when there will be reported net income. "After all," he argues, "it is good accounting practice to match income and expenses, and in the first four years, there will be no income." Besides, he doesn't plan to claim CCA (depreciation under the *Income Tax Act*) on the company's return until net income becomes positive; CCA claims are optional under the terms of the *Income Tax Act*.

Required:

Is this policy acceptable? Write a brief memo to the president explaining your position.

E7-7 *Amortization Policy:* Everett MacLaughlin, the president of MacLaughlin Enterprises, is proposing the following amortization policy for the capital assets of the company:

"Since most companies use the rates in the Income Tax Act, we'll do the same. Buildings will be amortized at a rate of 5%, declining balance, equipment at a rate of 20%, automobiles at 30%, still declining balance, and our manufacturing equipment will be written off straight-line, 25% the first year, 50% the second, and 25% in the third year. Those are the tax rules! I know that the manufacturing equipment will last for at least six years, but I prefer the fast write-off to be conservative."

Required:

Is this amortization policy acceptable? Write a brief memo to the president explaining your position.

E7-8 *Amortization Policy:* Five different methods of amortization have been described in the chapter:

1. Straight-line
2. Units of production
3. Declining balance
4. Sum-of-the-years-digits
5. Sinking fund

Required:

Indicate the likely choice of amortization method expected to be chosen if

a. The firm is a real estate property developer and the asset to be amortized is a highly-levered apartment building.

b. The firm has a lot of debt on their balance sheet and is trying to meet minimum net income levels specified in debt covenants.

c. The firm is a mining company and assets to be amortized are mine development costs.

d. The firm wishes to minimize the amount of future (deferred) taxes recognized in the financial statements.

e. The firm wishes to portray stable income patterns over time.

f. The firm wants to be comparable to other firms in its industry who commonly use declining balance. However, usage patterns are level over time.

g. The firm has a parent company who uses SYD.

h. The firm wants to minimize bookkeeping costs by keeping allocation methods simple.

i. The firm expects to use the asset heavily in initial years, and less as it grows older.

j. The firm expects to use the asset sporadically, but the asset will not wear out unless used.

k. Technological obsolescence is a significant factor is estimating the useful life of the asset.

E7-9 *Research and Development Costs:* Airfield Answers Corporation had several expenditures in 20X5:

a. Testing electronic instrument components during their production.

b. Study of the possible uses of a newly-developed fuel.

c. Start-up activities for the production of a newly-developed jet.

d. Construction of a prototype for a new jet model.

e. Design of a new, more efficient wing for an existing airplane.

f. Portion of vice president's salary, in proportion to the time spent managing the research lab.

g. Experimentation to establish the properties of a new plastic just discovered.

h. Current period amortization taken on the company's laboratory research facilities.

Required:

1. Explain the accounting policies required by the *CICA Handbook* for research and development expenditures.

2. Which of the above expenditures are considered research? development? neither?

P7-1 *Policy Choice:* A friend recently complained to you as follows:

"Accounting standard-setters have failed in their attempts to produce credible financial statements that readers can trust. For example, think about inventory issues. A company has free choice between FIFO, LIFO, and average cost. They usually pick the cost flow assumption that produces the highest net income. There's also a choice in amortization methods, between units of production, straight-line, declining balance, and so on. There's too much room to manipulate! Standard-setters should refer to their theory, and pick the right way to do these things. Then they should force companies to get into step. That's the only way to serve financial statement users."

PROBLEMS

Required:

Comment on the issues that your friend has raised.

P7-2 *Expense Recognition:* Simon Steel is a classic example of a "smokestack company." It is in a declining industry that has been heavily beset by foreign competition. Moreover, the industry is regarded as a "dirty" one that is being "cleaned up" by new environmental regulations. Because its profits are already only marginal, Simon is having difficulty financing the costs of complying with those regulations.

However, Simon is required under environmental legislation to install "scrubbers" on its smokestacks, at a price of $3,000,000. If it does not comply with the legislation, it will be forced to shut down, turning hundreds out of work. Because of the company's importance to the local economy, the province is lending Simon the money to install the scrubbers at an interest rate and repayment scheme dependent on the overall profits of the company.

Installation of the scrubbers, which will last for approximately 10 years, will not increase the facility's expected life, efficiency, or capacity.

Required:

1. Present two alternative ways that Simon Steel could recognize the $3,000,000 cost of the scrubbers.

2. Evaluate your two alternatives with reference to the definitions of financial statement elements.

3. Evaluate your two alternatives with reference to matching.

4. Which accounting policy do you believe is more appropriate for the company? Explain.

P7-3 *Expense Recognition:* The general ledger of Airtime, Inc., a corporation engaged in the development and production of television programs for commercial sponsorship, contains the following asset accounts (before amortization) at the end of 20X5:

Account	Balance
"Sealing Wax and Kings"	$75,000
"The Messenger"	36,000
"The Desperado"	19,000
"Shin Bone"	8,000
Studio rearrangement	7,000

An examination of contracts and records revealed the following information:

a. The first two accounts listed above represent the total cost of completed programs that were televised during 20X5. Under the terms of an existing contract, "Sealing Wax and Kings" will be rerun during 20X6 at a fee equal to 60% of the fee for the first televising of the program. The contract for the first run produced $300,000 of revenue. The contract with the sponsor of "The Messenger" provides that, at the sponsor's option, the program can be rerun during the 20X6 season at a fee of 75% of the fee for the first televising of the program. There are no present indications that it will be rerun.

b. The balance in "The Desperado" account is the cost of a new program that has just been completed and is being considered by several companies for commercial sponsorship.

c. The balance in the "Shin Bone" account represents the cost of a partially completed program for a projected series that has been abandoned.

d. The balance of the studio rearrangement account consists of payments made to a firm of engineers that prepared a report about a more efficient utilization of existing studio space and equipment.

Required:

Write a brief report addressed to the chief executive officer of Airtime, Inc., responding to the following:

1. State the general principle (or principles) of accounting that are applicable to recognizing revenue and expense for the first four accounts.
2. How would you report each of the first four accounts in the financial statements of Airtime? Explain.
3. In what way, if at all, does the studio rearrangement account differ from the first four? Explain.

[AICPA, adapted]

P7-4 *Revenue and Expense Recognition:* Pepper Publishing Company (PPC) prepares and publishes a monthly newsletter for an industry in which potential circulation is limited. Because information provided by the newsletter is available only piecemeal from other sources and because no advertising is carried, the subscription price for the newsletter is relatively high. PPC recently engaged in a campaign to increase circulation that involved extensive use of person-to-person long-distance telephone calls to research directors of non-subscriber companies in the industry. The telephone cost of the campaign was $38,000, plus salary payments to persons who made the calls amounting to $51,000.

As a direct result of the campaign, new one-year subscriptions at $175 each generated revenue of $164,500. New three-year subscriptions at $450 each generated revenue of $324,000, and new five-year subscriptions at $625 each generated $157,500. Cancellations are rare, but when they occur, refunds are made on a half-rate basis (e.g., if a subscriber has yet to receive $100 worth of newsletters, $50 is refunded).

Aside from the two direct costs of the campaign cited above, indirect costs, consisting of such items as allocated office space, fringe benefit costs for employees making telephone calls, and supervision, amounted to $21,000.

Required:

1. Identify the specific accounting issues involved in recognizing revenue and expense for PPC.
2. Assume that the campaign was begun and concluded in November of Year 0, new subscriptions begin with the Year 1 January issue of the monthly newsletter, and the company's accounting year ends 31 December. How should costs of the campaign be allocated from years one to five? Show calculations.

P7-5 *Expense Policy:* The president of Aggressive Limited has come to you for advice. Aggressive Limited is a newly established company with great prospects for high growth. Decisions must soon be made concerning accounting policies for external financial reporting. The following information pertains to the company's first year of operations (in $ thousands):

Revenue	$40,000
Purchases	15,000
Closing inventory — FIFO	5,000
Closing inventory — average cost	4,000
Depreciation — straight-line	2,000
Depreciation — declining balance	4,000
Advertising and promotion expense	2,000
Amortization of advertising and promotion over five years	400
Other expenses	5,000

Common shares outstanding (in thousands)	1,000
Income tax rate	40%

Note: For tax purposes, advertising and promotion expenses may be expensed as incurred. Regardless of the depreciation method chosen on the books, CCA on capital assets will be claimed for tax purposes.

Required:

1. Prepare a columnar income statement. In column 1, show net income assuming the use of FIFO, declining balance depreciation and expensing of advertising and promotion. Also calculate earnings per share. In successive columns, show the separate effects of the following on net income and earnings per share: in column 2, average cost, in column 3, straight-line depreciation, and in column 4, amortization of advertising and promotion. In column 5, show all effects of choosing the alternatives presented separately in columns 2 through 4.

2. As president, which accounting policies would you choose? Explain.

P7-6 *Expense Policy:* Two income statements are reproduced below, for two companies, A and B, which are presumed to have had the same volume and kind of business. Despite this similarity, B reported higher earnings than A. Both of them used acceptable accounting methods.

	Company A	**Company B**
Sales	$10,000,000	$10,000,000
Costs and expenses:		
Cost of goods sold	$ 6,400,000	$ 6,000,000
Selling costs	1,500,000	1,500,000
Depreciation	400,000	300,000
Research costs	300,000	20,000
Officers' compensation		
Base salaries	200,000	200,000
Bonuses	200,000	—
Total costs and expenses	$ 9,000,000	$ 8,020,000
Profit before income taxes	$ 1,000,000	$ 1,980,000
Income taxes	520,000	1,029,600
Net Income	$ 480,000	$ 950,400

Other information:

a. B uses a first-in-first-out (FIFO) method of inventory valuation, while A uses average cost.

b. B avoids a $100,000 charge against income by using straight-line depreciation; A uses accelerated depreciation.

c. B classifies its "research" activities as development and amortizes amounts over a 15-year period, while A expenses its costs immediately.

d. A compensates senior executives with cash bonuses, while B provides attractive stock options to executives. Accounting standards for these options dictate that no income statement expense is recognized for them even though they result in cash flow to the executives similar to cash bonuses.

Required:

1. Restate Company B's income statement to use the same policies as Company A, where applicable. Assume that B's cost of goods sold would be identical to Company A's if average cost were used.

2. How can Company B's policy for research costs be "acceptable" when *CICA Handbook* standards require that research costs be expensed?

3. Comment on the lack of comparability between the two statements. Is it desirable?

P7-7 *LIFO versus FIFO:* Witt, a distribution division of Cullen Corporation, holds inventories consisting of tobacco, confectionery, grocery, and paper products. Cullen uses FIFO to value its inventories except for those held by Witt, which are valued on the LIFO basis. Inventories are described in the following portion of Note 5 to Cullen's 20X1 financial statements, dated 30 November 20X1:

Note 5 [in part]: Supplementary Financial Statement Information

Inventories ($000)
Inventories consist of:

	30 Nov. 20X1	1 Dec. 20X0
Raw materials and supplies	$ 62,872	$ 63,524
Work-in-process	4,180	3,938
Finished goods	31,080	56,288
	$ 98,132	$123,750

The cost of Witt's inventories at LIFO was $20,752 and $37,435 at 30 November 20X1 and 1 December 20X0 respectively. On a FIFO basis, the cost of the inventories would have been $34,418 and $60,996, respectively. Cost of sales on a FIFO basis would have been higher by $9,895 in 20X1, and lower by $3,035 in 20X0.

At 30 November 20X1 and 1 December 20X0, Witt's cigarette inventory quantities were less than at the end of the respective previous years, which resulted in liquidations of LIFO inventory quantities carried at lower costs. The effect in 20X1 and 20X0 was to increase pre-tax income by $17,045 and $5,225, respectively.

Required:

Assume that Witt's inventories have been valued on a LIFO basis for the last several years.
1. What would have been the effect on Cullen's pre-tax income for 20X1 if Witt's inventories had always been valued on a FIFO basis?

2. What would have been the effect on Cullen's retained earnings as of 30 November 20X1, if Witt's inventories had always been valued on a FIFO basis? (Use a 34% tax rate.)

3. Suppose Witt had not experienced a liquidation of LIFO layers in either 20X0 or 20X1. What would the effect have been on Cullen's pre-tax income in 20X1? Was the increase in Cullen's pre-tax income a welcome event?

4. Is it desirable to use FIFO for some inventories and LIFO for other inventories? Comment.

P7-8 *Inventory Policy Comparison:* Carlyon and Dennis are North American manufacturers of auto parts. The two firms use different inventory cost flow accounting policies. This problem asks you to determine some of the differences due to the reporting. The two firms report the following selected information for 20X1:

	Carlyon	Dennis
	(in $ thousands)	
Earnings from continuing operations	$ (538)	$ (3,432)
Cost of sales	24,803	71,826
Net earnings per share (continuing operations)	(2.22)	(7.21)
Assets (total)	43,076	174,429
Inventories	3,571	6,215
Total shareholders' equity	6,109	22,690
Comparative units sold: U.S. and Canada	1.661 units	3.114 units
Comparative units sold: World-wide	1.866 units	5.346 units

Carlyon Corporation
Note 1: Summary of Significant Accounting Policies
Inventories are valued at the lower of cost or market. The cost of approximately 41% and 49% of inventories at 31 December 20X1 and 20X0, respectively, is determined on a last-in, first-out (LIFO) basis. The balance of inventory cost is determined on a first-in, first-out (FIFO) basis.

Note 2: Inventories and Cost of Sales
Inventories are summarized by major classification as follows (in $ thousands):

	31 December	
	20X1	20X0
Finished products, including service parts	$1,192	$1,114
Raw materials, finished, production parts, and supplies	873	1,100
Work-in-process	1,476	911
Other	30	25
Total	$3,571	$3,150

Inventories valued on the LIFO basis would have been $239 million and $208 million higher than reported had they been valued on the FIFO basis at 31 December 20X1 and 20X0, respectively (see Note 1). Total manufacturing cost of sales aggregated $24.81 million, and $24.13 million for 20X1 and 20X0, respectively.

Dennis Motor Company
Note 1: Accounting Policies (Inventory Valuation Automotive)
Inventories are stated at the lower of cost or market. The cost of substantially all North American inventories is determined by the last-in, first-out (LIFO) method. The cost of the remaining inventories is determined substantially by the first-in, first-out (FIFO) method.

If FIFO were the only method of inventory accounting used by the company, inventories would have been $1,323,000 and $1,331,000 higher than reported at 31 December 20X1 and 20X0, respectively. The major classes of inventory at 31 December were as follows (in $ thousands):

	20X1	20X0
Finished products	$ 2,979.2	$ 3,628.2
Raw materials and work-in-process	2,800.9	3,025.7
Supplies	435.2	461.5
Total	$ 6,215.3	$ 7,115.4

Required:

1. Are prices rising or falling in the 20X1 supplier markets in which Dennis (and Carlyon) buys? How do you know?

2. Compare Dennis's and Carlyon's inventory levels and comment on the comparison.

3. Is it desirable to have similar companies using different inventory cost flow policies? If not, why do accounting standard-setters not require uniformity?

P7-9 *Expense Recognition Examples:* **Respond to each of the following situations:**

Case A. CSI develops and markets specialized diagnostic equipment for the medical profession. During 20X0, CSI spent $200,000 on a study to help identify the needs of users. As a result of this study, CSI commenced work on a new diagnostic product to be used by the medical profession. Approximately $1 million was spent on creating prototypes, only one of which has turned out to be usable.

CSI's financial statements are prepared in accordance with generally accepted accounting principles. How should CSI account for these costs in its 20X0 financial statements? Support your recommendations.

Case B. The Boring Drilling Company operates in the oil and gas exploration business, and uses successful efforts to account for its exploration and development expenditures. The company commenced drilling a well on Acre 313 in September 20X5. By the end of December 20X5, $1,250,000 of costs had been incurred on this well. Efforts have been unsuccessful and the company is planning to abandon the well in 20X6. However, there are a few more activities to perform (such as cleaning up the site) before the well is formally abandoned.

The controller wants to leave the costs capitalized on the 31 December balance sheet on the basis that the exploration activities were not complete and that a final determination of success had not been made at the end of the year. Is this policy acceptable?

[CGA-Canada, adapted]

Case C. Fox is a new computer software company. In 20X4, the firm incurred the following costs in the process of designing, developing, and producing its first new software package, which it expects to begin marketing in 20X5:

Designing and planning costs	$150,000
Production of product masters	400,000
Cost of developing code	240,000
Testing	60,000
Production of final product	500,000

The costs of designing and planning, code development, and testing were all incurred before the technological feasibility of the product had been established. Fox estimates that total revenues over the four-year life of the product will be $2,000,000, with $800,000 in revenues expected in 20X5.

Calculate the amount of expenditures capitalized versus expensed in 20X4. Assuming 20X5 revenue is on target, how much will be expensed in 20X5?

P7-10 *Research and Development:* In 20X1, Chatham Company purchased a building site for its proposed research and development laboratory at a cost of $95,000 plus legal fees of $4,500. The building was constructed during 20X2 at a cost of $275,000. The building was put into use on 2 January 20X3 and has been used exclusively for research and development activities ever since. The building has an estimated useful life of 40 years and a salvage value of $25,000 at the end of its useful life. The building is being amortized on a declining balance basis at the rate of 4% per year.

Management estimates that about 50% of the projects are development activities which meet the criteria for capitalization of costs. The remaining projects either benefit the current period only or are abandoned before completion. The capitalized development costs are amortized over a 10-year period with a full year of amortization provided in the year the project is completed. A summary of the number of projects and the direct costs incurred in conjunction with the research and development activities for 20X4 appears below.

	Number of Projects	Salaries and Benefits	Materials, Supplies, Other
Completed projects with long-term benefits	20	$185,000	$45,000
Abandoned projects or projects that benefit current period only	15	90,000	35,000
Projects in process results indeterminate	5	25,000	20,000
Total	40	$300,000	$100,000

Required:

1. On the basis of the above information, prepare the capital asset and development costs sections of the balance sheet for Chatham Company at 31 December 20X4.

2. Determine the research and development-related items which will appear on the income statement for Chatham Company for the year ended 31 December 20X4. Assume an appropriate amount of depreciation is included in "other" expenses on the schedule provided.

[CGA-Canada, adapted]

P7-11 *Exploration and Development Costs:*
Resource extraction companies, including those involved in the oil and gas sector, incur a variety of exploration costs prior to the point in time when it is known whether the site is viable or not. Such costs include direct acquisition costs of property, or the mining rights thereto, geological surveys, test drilling, or mining activities and related activities. These expenditures are generally significant for each site, and often for each test drill on a site.

There are two ways to determine depletion for such costs, both acceptable under "generally accepted accounting principles," and both frequently encountered in actual practice. These methods are:

1. *Full Cost Method.* Exploration costs are capitalized on a global basis. For example, if an oil company were carrying out exploration activities in three areas: the Beaufort Sea, Texas, and off the coast of Ireland, the cost of all exploration activities would be included in one pool. A ceiling test is employed annually to ensure costs accumulated by cost centre do not exceed estimated cash flows from proven mineral reserves and the cost of undeveloped properties. Exploration costs are subject to depletion, or amortization, based on successful sites, usually on a units-of-production basis.

The full cost method results in the cost of unsuccessful exploration activities being deferred, and recognized as an expense against the revenue generated by successful sites. Its proponents argue that all exploration activities are not expected to be successful, but are based on probabilities. Exploration of one site or test drill is part of a certain capital commitment to an exploration program. It is this program that represents the cost of exploration that must be expensed with revenue from successful programs. Opponents of full costing point out that this policy results in capitalization of unsuccessful sites and tests. How can a "dry hole" off the Atlantic coast of

Canada be an asset, even backed by a "gusher" in Texas? It may also result in over-capitalization, as the ceiling is difficult to determine.

2. Successful Efforts. Exploration expenditures are deferred on a project basis until the viability of the project is established. If the project is not viable, the costs are immediately expensed. If viable, the capitalized cost is usually grouped with other successful sites and is then subject to depletion, usually on a units-of-production basis. Successful efforts result in less cost deferred, as all unsuccessful projects are written off versus deferred. Depletion charged to subsequent mining revenues is also correspondingly lower. However, over time, both methods result in the same total expense charged to income.

Proponents of successful efforts claim that assets are more representative of future cash flows, therefore less likely to be overstated. Opponents argue that assets are often materially understated, as it is often not possible to locate a viable site without extensive exploration of several areas. Subsequent depletion is also understated, in their view.

Three companies are presently considering the appropriate accounting policy choice in this area. All know that tax rules are different from both successful efforts and full costing, and thus either method may be chosen for external reporting without jeopardizing tax status. All wish to comply with GAAP.

Company 1 is a small, independent oil exploration company. It is financed 60% through equity, and 40% by debt, and there are restrictive debt covenants on debt-to-equity, return on equity, dividends, and executive compensation.

Company 2 is a large, diversified mining company involved in exploration, production, and transportation of a wide range of minerals. The bulk (80%) of its financing is through a wide range of equity instruments.

Company 3 is a small mining company specializing in exploration activities. Successful properties are usually sold to the highest bidder for commercial production. The shares are closely held by a small group of investors who provide the bulk of the financing. Only one of these investors is actively involved in the business. The financial statements are used to measure performance. Cash flow is carefully monitored and is critical to survival.

Required:
After assessing the corporate reporting objectives of each company, evaluate the GAAP alternatives and recommend an accounting policy that would be most appropriate for each.

8

Current Monetary Balances

INTRODUCTION

One objective of financial reporting is to help users assess the amounts, timing, and uncertainty of future cash flows. Current monetary balances — receivables and payables — have the most immediate impact on the cash position, so it's important to get them right! This chapter develops the accounting principles for the recognition, measurement, and reporting of the primary category of liquid resources: cash, accounts receivable, and notes receivable, and the primary short-term claims to cash, the various types of payables. These financial statement elements are all **financial instruments** that represent cash or claims to cash.

The emphasis in this chapter is on *short-term* monetary balances. Long-term balances are discussed at length in Chapter 13.

When valuing receivables and payables, face value is not always the correct value to report. The value of money changes over time; a dollar to be received in the year 2010 does not have same value as a dollar today. There is a time value to money, and therefore monetary balances often must be discounted to their present value, or the implicit interest in a stream of payments must be taken into account. Most students will already be familiar with the principles of compound interest — present value and future value — but, just in case you're out of practice, the Appendix to this chapter contains a brief primer (or refresher) on compound interest calculations. Since there are several different types of notation (or *mnemonics*) for compound interest functions, all readers should consult the Summary of Compound Interest Tables and Formulae, found at the back of each Volume, to acquaint themselves with the notation that is used throughout this book.

DEFINITION OF MONETARY ITEMS

The *CICA Handbook* defines monetary items as follows:

> Monetary financial assets and financial liabilities (also referred to as monetary financial instruments) are financial assets and financial liabilities to be received or paid in fixed or determinable amounts of money.
>
> [*CICA* 3860.05]

There are two key aspects of this definition:

1. the asset or obligation must be settled by means of cash, and
2. the amount of asset, claim, or obligation must be fixed (or determinable) by the nature of the transaction that gave rise to the balance.

Monetary items (i.e., monetary assets or liabilities) include

*   cash and cash equivalents;
*   contractual claims to receive a predetermined amount of cash (or of a cash equivalent); and
*   contractual agreements to pay a predetermined amount of cash (or cash equivalent).

Chapter 5 discussed the definition of cash and cash equivalents; these obviously are monetary assets. Accounts and notes receivable and payable also are monetary items; their amount has been fixed or predetermined by means of a transaction, such as the sale of goods or services, the purchase of goods or services, or the borrowing of a fixed sum of money. In contrast, balances such as inventories and equity investments are not monetary items, even though they eventually will be converted into cash, because their cash value is not fixed in advance. The amount of cash to be obtained from such items will depend on future market conditions.

The definition includes balances that represent assets and obligations to be received or paid in a *determinable* amount of cash. An example of a *determinable* amount is a cash deposit held in foreign currency. The foreign currency deposit represents a claim to a fixed amount of cash, but its value in Canadian dollars is determinable from the exchange rate in effect at the balance sheet date. Similarly, the contracts underlying monetary balances such as accounts receivable, accounts payable, and bank loans payable may be expressed in a foreign currency. Despite the fact that their amount is not fixed in terms of Canadian currency, these balances are monetary items.

ACCOUNTING FOR CASH

Characteristics of Cash and Cash Equivalents

The cash account includes only those items immediately available to pay obligations. Cash includes balances on deposit with financial institutions, coins and currency, petty cash, and certain negotiable instruments accepted by financial institutions for immediate deposit and withdrawal, like cashier's cheques, certified cheques, and money orders.

Cash equivalents are items that can readily be converted to cash. They are limited to temporary investments that are highly liquid and have little risk of price fluctuation — money market instruments — but not equity investments such as preferred share investments. The most common examples of cash equivalents are treasury bills (widely known as T-bills), guaranteed investment certificates (GICs), commercial paper (short-term notes receivable from other companies), and money market funds. Accounting for these temporary investments is covered in Chapter 12. In Chapter 5, you learned that cash is defined as cash plus cash equivalents (and less bank overdrafts) on the cash flow statement. On the balance sheet, cash and cash equivalents are also usually lumped together.

An overdraft is a negative bank account balance and is reported as a separate current liability on the balance sheet, regardless of its inclusion in "cash" on the cash flow statement. Overdrafts occur when the dollar amount of cheques honoured by the bank exceeds the account balance. However, if a depositor overdraws an account but has positive balances in other accounts with that bank, it is appropriate to offset the negative and positive balances as long as

- the bank has the legal right to offset, which is usual, *and*
- the company plans to settle the overdraft in this way — by a transfer from one of the other accounts.

Accounts with different financial institutions may not be offset against each other, since they fail the first condition, above.

A compensating balance is a minimum balance that must be maintained in a depositor's account as support for funds borrowed by the depositor. Technically, compensating balances are long-term, and should not be included in the current cash account because they are not currently available for use. Many companies include these balances in cash and disclose the restrictions in notes to the financial statements. Either disclosure option avoids overstating the firm's liquidity position.

Items properly included in cash generally do not present valuation problems because they are recorded at cash value. That is, they are worth their face value in terms of Canadian dollars. The Canadian dollar value of cash holdings in foreign currency, however, fluctuates with changes in the relevant exchange rate. To get the Canadian dollar equivalent, it is necessary to multiply the amount of foreign currency by the current exchange rate.

For example, assume that DGF Group Ltd. has a U.S. bank account, with U.S. $4,500 on deposit at year-end. The money was received as a result of a cash sale when the exchange rate was U.S. $1.00 = Cdn. $1.34, and was recorded at a Canadian dollar amount of $6,030:

Cash, U.S. dollars [$4,500 × $1.34]	6,030	
Sales		6,030

At the end of the year, the exchange rate is U.S. $1.00 = Cdn. $1.38. The current Canadian dollar equivalency must be established:

Cash, U.S. dollars [$4,500 × ($1.38 – $1.34)]	180	
Exchange gain		180

The cash is included on the balance sheet at the 31 December exchange rate, $1.38, or $6,210. Of course, foreign cash holdings can be converted to the current exchange rate every time it changes, but this is a lot of extra work, and it's usually only important at reporting dates. Only foreign currencies convertible to Canadian dollars without restriction are included in *cash*. Restricted currency balances are reported as *other assets* because they cannot be readily accessed.

Internal Controls for Cash

The need to safeguard cash is crucial. Cash is easy to conceal and transport, carries no mark of ownership, and is universally valued. Cash can be stolen in a lot of creative ways in addition to simply being physically picked up. The accounting system can be used and abused to put cash into the hands of a felon. For example, cheques can be issued to a fictitious company, and cashed by a dishonest employee.

The risk of theft is directly related to the ability of individuals to access the accounting system and obtain custody of cash. Firms address this problem through an internal control system, designed to protect all assets and the integrity of the information system. A sound internal control system for cash increases the likelihood that the reported values for cash and cash equivalents are accurate and may be relied on by financial statement users. There are two internal control issues for cash: (1) ensuring that cash is not stolen, and (2) making sure that cash is wisely managed to maximize returns. You'll learn all about internal controls if you ever study auditing; the important things to remember *vis-à-vis* safeguarding cash are to

- keep cash where it's hard to steal (common sense should tell you this!) and
- make sure that *no one person is in a position to misappropriate cash **and** cover up the theft.*

The most fundamental principle of internal control is that of division of duties — the person who handles the cash must not keep the books. When the bookkeeper handles the cash, it is much too tempting for him or her to set cash aside for personal use and cover up the cash shortage by making a fictitious entry in the books. In a large enterprise, quite a large amount of cash (in personal terms) can go missing before anyone starts to notice. Embezzlement may go undetected for many years, particularly if the enterprise is not audited. Bear in mind that only trusted employees steal from the enterprise; employees who are not trusted are not given the opportunity!

If the functions of cash handling and record keeping are separated, it will be very difficult to embezzle cash unless two people agree together (or *collude*) to take the money. Internal control is built largely on the principle that dishonest collusion is significantly less likely than individual action.

Internal Control and Bank Accounts

The principles of internal control apply just as well to cash held in bank accounts as they do to currency. The record keeper must not have the authority to sign cheques, or at least not the authority to sign cheques without someone else's signature also being required. Few legitimate companies have much real cash lying around; much more money can be stolen by signing cheques and then creating fictitious bookkeeping entries to make the cheques look like they were for legitimate purposes.

Obviously, bank accounts provide one means to physically safeguard cash balances, but they're also integral to proper cash management. For example, advanced electronic fund transfer schemes will transfer funds directly from a customer's bank account to the company's. Cash management is a function of the treasury department of large companies, whose task is to minimize idle cash and maximize returns to shareholders. It's a complex area.

We're mostly interested in the bank account because it provides an absolutely wonderful opportunity to *check the accuracy of the accounting records*. It's the *only* general ledger account that another company completely runs in parallel. If the company has a deposit recorded, so should the bank. If the company has written a cheque, it should also go through the bank account. Now, there are timing problems — it takes a while for cheques and deposits to clear, and banks record some things, like bank charges, before the company … but you get the picture.

By comparing the bank account to the cash general ledger account, the company can make sure that the books are being kept accurately, and that all expenditures and receipts are appropriate. Since cash forms a part of so many transactions, the accuracy of the cash account is usually a good surrogate for the accuracy of other accounts. Of course, it's crucial that the individual who's in charge of cheques and/or deposits is not also in charge of the bank statement reconciliation — it would be too easy to cover something up. You don't get to check your own work; that's division of duties.

Reconciliation of Bank and Book Cash Balances

Banks send monthly statements showing beginning and ending balances and transactions occurring during the month: cheques clearing the account, deposits received, and service charges. Every month, the bank's records and the company's records have to be compared, and the differences reconciled.

Usually, some items listed in the bank statement have not yet been recorded by the firm. These show up on the bank statement as debit and credit memos, and include items such as interest earned, cash collected by the bank from customers, and service charges. The company usually becomes aware of the exact amount of these items only when the company receives its bank statement, and therefore the company cannot record the items when they occur. Instead, the company must record the bank's extra charges and credits as reconciling items.

For a bank, a depositor's cash balance is a liability, the amount the bank owes to the firm. A bank **debit memo** describes a transaction from the bank's point of view — a decrease in their liability to the account holder. Therefore, a debit memo reports the amount and nature of a *decrease* in the firm's cash account. A **credit memo** indicates an *increase* in the cash account. Since this debit-credit memo terminology is derived from the bank's point of view, it seems backwards to the debit and credit convention in the company's cash account, which tends to create a little confusion.

A **bank reconciliation** begins with the two cash balances and lists the differences between those balances and the true ending cash balance. Assume the information in Exhibit 8-1 for West Company. The bank statement reported an ending $38,630 balance, and the cash account reflects an ending $34,870 cash balance. Of course, if they were the same amount, the reconciliation would be over before it even began! These figures are reconciled to $35,630, as shown in Exhibit 8-2. Here are the steps to follow:

1. Compare all deposits made in the bank account with those in the books. If there are differences, determine why. If the bank has processed something that should be on the books, adjust the book balance. If there are errors that the bank has made, or if deposits are in transit, adjust the bank balance. A careful bank reconciliation includes a comparison of the dates of deposits — there should be no delays in getting money to the bank. Deposits in transit from the prior month should clear in the first few days of the next month, and this month's deposits in transit should relate only to the last day or two.

2. Compare all cheques and charges that went through the bank account to the cash disbursements journal. All cheques that the bank paid should be in the cash disbursements journal this month, or have been outstanding last month. If there are errors the bank has made, or cheques that are outstanding, adjust the bank balance. If the bank has processed something that should be on the books, adjust the book balance. Again, one should keep an eye out for irregularities; cheques are usually cashed after only a short delay.

3. Make journal entries for all adjustments to the book balance, and inform the bank of any errors made by the bank, so they can be corrected before the end of next month.

Take a look at the bank reconciliation in Exhibit 8-2 in detail:

I. **Adjustments to the bank balance.** What transactions are recorded in the books but have not yet gone through the bank account because of timing delays? What errors has the bank made? Adjust these things to the bank account.

     A. *Cash on hand.* This is the cash recorded as a debit to the company's cash account, but not deposited at month-end. Cash or cheques are being held — hopefully in a safe — by the company at August 31. This amount is added to the bank balance.

EXHIBIT 8-1
WEST COMPANY
Information for Bank Reconciliation
31 August 20X2

Bank statement

August 1 balance		$32,000
Deposits recorded in August	$77,300	
Cheques cleared in August	(71,240)	
Accounts receivable collected (including $100 interest)	1,100	
NSF cheque, J. Fox, $300 plus $30 fee	(330)	
August service charges	(200)	6,630
August 31 balance		$38,630

Company's cash account

August 1 balance		$29,990
August deposits*	75,300	
August disbursements**	(70,420)	4,880
August 31 balance		$34,870

*Per cash receipts journal
**Per cash disbursements journal

Additional data, end of July:
Deposits in transit, $5,000, and cheques outstanding, $8,000 (these two amounts were taken from the July bank reconciliation).

Additional data, end of August:
Cash on hand (undeposited), $990. This amount will be deposited September 1. A cheque written by West in the amount of $240 for a repair bill in August is included in the cleared cheques. West recorded the cheque for $420, the correct amount, debiting repair expense. The cheque was for the wrong amount. The payee will bill West for the remaining $180 due. The service charges of $200 include a $10 charge to a company named "Weston Company" that was charged to West Company in error.

B. *Deposits in transit.* These are deposits made too late to be reflected in the bank statement. This amount is determined by comparing the firm's record of deposits with the deposits listed in the bank statement or by using a schedule.

Deposits in transit at end of prior period	$ 5,000
Deposits for the current period (per books)	75,300
Total amount that could have been deposited	80,300
Deposits shown in bank statement	(77,300)
Deposits in transit at end of current period	$ 3,000

It's important to pin down the $3,000 deposit — in the schedule, it's an arithmetic result, but it has to be real. Was there a deposit made late in the month that did not clear? Or was some money lost or deposited in the wrong account? This is the time to find it!

EXHIBIT 8-2
WEST COMPANY
Bank Reconciliation
31 August 20X2

Bank statement

Ending bank balance, August 31		$38,630
Additions:		
Cash on hand (undeposited)	$ 990	
Deposits in transit, August 31 ($5,000 + $75,300 − $77,300)	3,000	
Bank error re: service charge	10	
Deductions:		
Cheques outstanding August 31 ($8,000 + $70,240 − $71,240)	(7,000)	(3,000)
Adjusted balance		$35,630

Book balance

Ending book balance, August 1		$34,870
Additions:		
Accounts receivable collected by bank	1,000	
Interest	100	
Error in recording repair repayment	180	
Deductions:		
NSF cheque, J. Fox, $300, plus $30 NSF fee	(330)	
Bank service charges	(190)	760
Adjusted balance		$35,630

C. *Outstanding cheques.* This amount is determined by comparing cheques written with cheques cleared or by using a schedule.

Outstanding cheques at end of prior period	$ 8,000
Cheques written during the current period (per cash payments journal, as corrected: $70,420 − $180 payment overstatement)	70,240
Total cheques that could have cleared	78,240
Cheques cleared shown in bank statement	(71,240)
Outstanding cheques at end of current period	$ 7,000

Again, this amount has to be real — there must be a list of cheques that have not cleared the bank, but are recorded on the books, in the amount of $7,000.

D. *Bank errors.* The bank charged the company $10 too much service charge. They'll have to be informed of the error, and appropriate documentation provided so that the bank will put the $10 back in the account by reversing the charge.

After all appropriate entries are made, the adjusted balance per the bank, is $35,630.

II. Items needed to reconcile the firm's cash ledger account to the correct cash balance. These are amounts the firm did not know about at August 31; none would have been necessary had the bank informed the company of entries in its bank account in enough time for the company to have recorded the entries in its cash receipts or disbursements journals prior to the end of the month. Each of these items now requires an adjusting journal entry to correct the cash balance. *Notice that there are no entries in West's books for anything that is a reconciling item to the bank balance.*

A. *Account receivable collected by bank.* An account receivable for $1,000 plus $100 accrued interest was collected by the bank but was not recorded by West. Customers sometimes do this at the company's request to speed up collection and/or to minimize the risk that the customer's cheque will not clear. Usually, the bank informs the company immediately, but if the item has not been recorded by month-end, it shows up as a reconciling item and is recorded at that time.

Cash	1,100	
Accounts receivable		1,000
Interest revenue		100

B. *Not sufficient funds (NSF) cheque.* A $300 cheque from customer J. Fox, which was not supported by sufficient funds in Fox's chequing account, was returned to West by the bank. West had deposited the cheque, increased cash, and decreased accounts receivable, but the bank was unable to get any money from Fox's account. Again, the company is usually informed immediately, so it can pursue its delinquent customer. However, if there are delays, or the NSF cheque occurs late in the month, it will be recorded now. Note that the company will try to recover the bank fee charged as well as the original receivable.

Accounts receivable, J. Fox	330	
Cash		330

Is this really a bad debt? Fox might be delinquent, but no company will give up after only one try — they'll create a receivable when an NSF cheque is received. The receivable may end up as part of the amount included in the allowance for doubtful accounts — but that's the next section!

C. *Bank service charges.* The bank debited West's account for $190 of bank charges in August for cheque printing, chequing account privileges, and collection of customer cheques. West deducts this amount from the cash account.

Miscellaneous expenses	190	
Cash		190

D. *Error in recording.* West recorded a $240 cheque in the cash disbursements journal as $420, debiting accounts payable and crediting cash for too much. The book balance of cash and accounts payable is now understated by $180 ($420 − $240). West corrects the recording error with the following entry.

Cash	180	
Accounts payable		180

This entry corrects the cash disbursement amount and establishes a payable for the remaining amount due. Correction entries of this kind always either debit or credit the cash account, and the other side of the entry is made to whatever the first cheque was charged to: in this case, accounts payable. It helps to reconstruct the original (incorrect) entry.

Book and bank balances are now reconciled to the same value, $35,630.

But what if they're not? What if it didn't work? Then, the reconciler gets to do it again … and again … until it does work! Everyone's nightmare is that a $10 difference is really a $10,000 error in one direction, and a $10,010 error in the other direction! So the bank reconciliation really is expected to "work." Here are a couple of "tricks" to help find the most common errors:

- If a reconciling item is deducted when it should have been added (or vice versa), the error will be *double* the item. Therefore, try dividing the unreconciled error by 2, then look for an item of that amount.

- Transposition errors are *always* divisible by 9. For example, if $5,012 was written as $5,102, the unreconciled error will be $90. If $5,012 was written as $5,210, the error will be $198, which also is divisible by 9.

Of course, if there is a combination of errors, these tricks won't help much. In practice, after things have been reviewed a few times to make sure there is no possibility of large, counterbalancing errors, small differences are written off to miscellaneous expense.

CONCEPT REVIEW

1. What is the definition of *monetary* assets and liabilities?
2. What is the most basic principle of internal control?
3. Why is it necessary to perform a bank reconciliation each month?

ACCOUNTING FOR RECEIVABLES

Receivables represent claims for money, goods, services, and other non-cash assets from other firms. Receivables may be current or non-current, depending on the expected collection date. **Accounts receivable**, also called **trade receivables**, are amounts owed by customers for goods and services sold in the firm's normal course of business. These receivables are supported by sales invoices or other documents rather than by formal written promises, and they include amounts expected to be collected either during the year following the balance sheet date or within the firm's operating cycle. **Notes receivable** are usually supported by formal promissory notes. **Non-trade receivables** arise from many other sources, such as tax refunds, contracts, investments, finance receivables, instalment notes, sale of assets, and advances to employees. The main accounting issues pertaining to receivables are *recognition and measurement*. Both are affected by collectibility.

Recognition and Measurement of Accounts Receivable

Accounts receivable are recognized only when the criteria for recognition are fulfilled. This echoes the revenue recognition material; you should recall that accounts receivable are recognized when there has been an agreement with a customer, which may be before or after the point at which revenue is recognized, but is usually the revenue recognition point. Accounts receivable are typically valued at the original exchange price between the firm and the outside party. Generally, a 30- to 60-day period is allowed for payment, beyond which the account is considered past due, and interest may begin to accrue.

[handwritten: Unearned rev.]

Individual accounts receivable for customers with *credit balances* (from prepayments or overpayments) are reclassified and reported as *liabilities* on the balance sheet if they are material. Credit balances should not be netted against other accounts receivable in the balance, but netting is a common practice if the amounts are small (i.e., immaterial).

The receivables are meant to be an approximation of the cash that will be collected. Say a company has $2,000,000 in accounts receivable at the end of 20X5. But this may not be the amount of money they'll actually collect. Usually adjustments have to be made at year-end to reduce receivables to *net realizable value*, for things like

- cash discounts,
- sales returns, and
- allowances for uncollectible accounts.

Cash Discounts. Companies frequently offer a cash discount for payment received within a designated period. Cash discounts are used to increase sales, to encourage early payment by the customer, and to increase the likelihood of collection. Sales terms might be 2/10, n/30, which means that the customer is given a 2% cash discount if payment is made within 10 days from sale; otherwise, the full amount net of any returns or allowances is due in 30 days. Theoretically, the sale and the receivable should be recorded at the lowest cash price, or the net amount after deducting the discount. This would be $980 for a $1,000 sale, if the discount for prompt payment is 2%.

In practice, though, sales are usually recorded *gross*, because it is easier to reconcile the balances of individual accounts receivable to the general ledger control account if the receivables are recorded at their gross amount. The subsidiary accounts may be a listing of outstanding invoices (either on paper or in a computer file) rather than a formal "ledger," and it is much easier to simply add up the total (gross) amount of outstanding invoices to reconcile to the control account, instead of figuring out the net amount if the customer takes the discount.

Under the gross method, if a material amount of cash discounts is expected to be taken on outstanding accounts receivable at year-end, and if this amount can be estimated reliably, an adjusting entry is required to decrease net sales and to reduce accounts receivable to the estimated amount collectible. To illustrate, assume that our $2 million of accounts receivable are all on terms of 2/10, n/30, and recorded at gross. Management expects 60% of these accounts to be collected within the discount period. There is no balance in the allowance account. The adjusting entry on 31 December 20X5:

Sales discounts [$2,000,000 × 2% × 60%]		24,000
Allowance for sales discounts		24,000

[handwritten: Contra to sales revenue]

The sales discounts account is a contra account to sales. The allowance account is a contra account to accounts receivable, and reduces accounts receivable to their net cash value. If there had been a $3,000 balance in the allowance account prior to this entry, the entry would have been made for $21,000 ($24,000 − $3,000).

During 20X6, assuming that the estimates were correct, a summary entry records the receipts.

Allowance for sales discounts	24,000	
Cash	1,176,000	
Accounts receivable [$2,000,000 × 60%]		1,200,000

Alternatively, and more commonly, sales discounts can be debited when customers use cash discounts, and the allowance can be adjusted at the end of each reporting period.

Sales Returns and Allowances. Return privileges are frequently part of a comprehensive marketing program required to maintain competitiveness. Sales *returns* occur when merchandise is returned by the customer; sales *allowances* occur when a company gives a price reduction to a customer who is not completely satisfied with purchased merchandise but does not actually return it.

Sales returns and allowances are significant amounts in some industries, including retailing and book publishing. Of course, if returns are material and inestimable, sales revenue cannot be recorded until after the uncertainty is resolved. This issue was discussed in the revenue chapter (Chapter 6). This chapter deals with the more likely case, *estimable returns*, and the problem again is to reduce receivables to their probable cash flow or *net realizable value*, which is net of returns. Sales returns and allowances reduce both net accounts receivable and net sales.

The company must estimate and recognize the returns and allowances expected for the accounts receivable outstanding at the end of 20X5. Assume that total estimated sales returns and allowances relating to the closing receivables balance is $9,000, and there is no balance in the allowance for sales returns account. The company records an adjusting entry on 31 December 20X5:

Sales returns and allowances	9,000	
Allowance for sales returns and allowances		9,000

If there had been a $5,000 credit balance in the allowance account prior to this entry, the entry would have been made for $4,000 ($9,000 – $5,000). Note that the sales returns and allowances account is a *contra account* to sales.

As goods sold in 20X5 are returned in 20X6, they can be charged to the allowance account. It's usually easier, though, to charge the returns directly to a sales returns and allowances account and adjust the balance in the allowance account at the end of each reporting period.

Allowance for Doubtful Accounts. When credit is extended, some amount of uncollectible receivables is generally inevitable. Firms attempt to develop a credit policy that is neither too conservative (leading to excessive lost sales) nor too liberal (leading to excessive uncollectible accounts). Past records of payment and the financial condition and income of customers are key inputs to the credit-granting decision.

If uncollectible receivables are both likely and estimable, an estimate of uncollectible accounts must be recognized, so that accounts receivable are not overstated. This is a form of asset valuation that is a common theme in accounting for assets: at the end of the accounting period, you must ensure that they're not overvalued. Are they representative of probable cash flow? If so, fine. If not, a write-down is made.

Because accounting recognition criteria require companies to anticipate a write-down before actually giving up on a particular account, the write-down is made to an allowance account, called the **allowance for doubtful accounts**. That is, individual accounts are not credited at this point because the company doesn't know which accounts will turn out to be uncollectible — if the company knew which accounts would go bad, they wouldn't have sold to those customers in the first place! Estimated uncollectibles are recorded in *bad debt expense*, an operating expense usually classified as a selling expense.

If uncollectible accounts are likely to arise and are estimable, an adjusting entry is needed at the end of an accounting period. For example, if our company estimates that $120,000 of the $2,000,000 in receivables will not be collected, and the existing balance in the allowance account is $12,000, the adjusting entry is as follows:

Bad debt expense	108,000	
Allowance for doubtful accounts		108,000

Notice that both net income and net assets decline on this entry: this is expense recognition, after all.

Two subsequent events must be considered: (1) the write-off of a specific receivable and (2) collection of an account previously written off. The adjusting entry for bad debt expense creates the allowance for doubtful accounts for future uncollectible accounts. When specific accounts are determined to be uncollectible, they are removed from the accounts receivable and that part of the allowance is no longer needed. The bad debt estimation entry previously recognized the estimated economic effect of future uncollectible accounts. Thus, write-offs of specific accounts do not further reduce total assets unless they exceed the estimate.

For example, the following entry is recorded by a company deciding not to pursue collection of R. Knox's $1,000 account:

| Allowance for doubtful accounts | 1,000 | |
| Accounts receivable, R. Knox | | 1,000 |

This write-off entry affects neither income nor the net amount of accounts receivable outstanding. Instead, it is the culmination of the process that began with the adjusting entry to estimate bad debt expense. The write-off entry changes only the components of net accounts receivable, not the net amount itself (amounts assumed):

	Before Knox Write-Off	**After Knox Write-Off**
Accounts receivable	$2,000,000	$1,999,000
Allowance for doubtful accounts	(120,000)	(119,000)
Net accounts receivable	$1,880,000	$1,880,000

When amounts are received on account after a write-off, the write-off entry is reversed to reinstate the receivable and cash collection is recorded. Assume that R. Knox is able to pay $600 on account some time after the above write-off entry was recorded. These entries are required:

Accounts receivable, R. Knox	600	
Allowance for doubtful accounts		600
Cash	600	
Accounts receivable, R. Knox		600

The net effect of these two entries is to increase cash and *reinstate* the allowance for doubtful accounts to the extent of the cash recovery. The reason for reinstating the allowance is that, since $600 cash was collected, the write-down of $1,000 was excessive; the write-down should have been for only $400. Another way of looking at it is that the only other place to put the credit (to offset the debit to cash) is to a revenue account. But the revenue was already fully recognized when the sale transaction was recorded. Crediting the $600 to a revenue account would be double-counting.

Disclosure. The balance sheet presentation of net accounts receivable provides focus on the realizable cash amount.

| Accounts receivable, net | $1,831,000 |

The net balance is $2,000,000 less the $24,000 allowance for cash discounts, less the $25,000 allowance for sales returns and less the $120,000 allowance for doubtful accounts.

The *CICA Handbook* recommends, in Section 3020, that accounts receivable be segregated between

- ordinary trade accounts
- amounts owing by related parties
- other unusual items of substantial amount

Furthermore, amounts and maturity dates of instalment receivables should be disclosed. Accounts receivable are *financial instruments*, and information on terms and conditions, credit risk and fair values of financial instruments should be disclosed. For most companies, this is trivial. Receivables are stated at their cash equivalencies, which is fair value, the amount of receivables represents the maximum credit risk, and terms and conditions are so standard that separate disclosure is not warranted.

In some cases, concentration of credit risk in certain geographic location or with certain customers might be appropriate.

Calculation of the Allowance for Doubtful Accounts

The previous section illustrated how the allowance is established, in an entry that increased the bad debts expense and increased the allowance. There are two approaches to determining how to get the amount of the entry: the "TO" and the "BY" methods.

Accounts receivables can be examined item by item, or aged, or analyzed statistically, category by category, to determine net realizable value and the size of an appropriate allowance. The allowance is then increased TO this amount, which involves a consideration of the opening balance. This is more formally called the aging method.

Alternatively, traditional pattern of bad debt experience can be correlated to credit sales, to establish a percentage of sales that is normally uncollectible. The allowance is then increased BY this amount, irrespective of the opening balance. This is more formally called the credit sales method.

Exhibit 8-3 presents background information for several examples. The current $500 debit balance in Rally's allowance account does not necessarily indicate that past estimates of bad debt losses were too low, although this is one explanation. Alternatively, it is possible that some receivables originating in 20X2 were written off and the debit balance does not yet reflect the estimate for bad debts based on 20X2 sales.

Aging Method. This method emphasizes the net realizable value of net accounts receivable and uses historical data to estimate the percentage of accounts receivable expected to become uncollectible. Exhibit 8-4 illustrates Rally's aging schedule and the application of the collection loss percentages. The $177,500 receivable balance is divided into four age classifications with a collection loss percentage applied to each age category. Rally's collection loss percentages increase with the age of the accounts. As accounts are collected and removed from each category, the proportion represented by uncollectible accounts increases.

The age categories are based on the extent to which accounts are past due. An account is past due if it is not collected by the end of the period specified in the credit terms. For example, an account arising from a 1 November sale with terms 2/10, n/30, is due 1 December. If the account remains unpaid at 31 December, the aging analysis classifies the account as 30 days past due.

The computation in Exhibit 8-4 yields a required ending balance in the allowance account at 31 December 20X2, of $5,690 (credit). The allowance is increased *to* $5,690. Because the allowance balance is $500 (debit) before adjustment, the entry is for $6,190, yielding an ending $5,690 balance.

Bad debt expense [$5,690 + $500]	6,190	
Allowance for doubtful accounts		6,190

Had the allowance balance been a $500 credit before adjustment, bad debt expense would have been $5,190 ($5,690 − $500). If the allowance is $5,690, net accounts receivable will be shown on the balance sheet at $171,810 ($177,500 − $5,690).

EXHIBIT 8-3
RALLY COMPANY
Information for Bad Debt Estimation Examples

1 January 20X2, balances:
    Accounts receivable (debit) $101,300
    Allowance for doubtful accounts (credit)   3,300
Transactions during 20X2:
    Credit sales   500,000
    Cash sales   700,000
    Collections on accounts receivable   420,000
    Accounts written off as uncollectible during 20X2   3,800

After posting of sales, collections, and write-offs, accounts receivable and the allowance for doubtful accounts appear as follows:

Accounts Receivable			
1 Jan. 20X2 balance	101,300	Collections	420,000
Credit sales	500,000	Write-offs	3,800
31 Dec. 20X2 balance	177,500		.

Allowance for Doubtful Accounts			
Write-offs	3,800	1 Jan. 20X2 balance	3,300
31 Dec. 20X2 balance			
before adjustment	500		

Aging may be more cumbersome than is warranted, and a composite rate, based on the accounts receivable total may be used. Assume that experience leads Rally Company (Exhibit 8-3) to use a single 3% composite rate. Therefore, the required ending allowance credit balance is $5,325 (3% × $177,500). The allowance account currently reflects a $500 debit balance, so the adjusting entry increases the allowance account *to* $5,325 through an entry for $5,825 ($5,325 + $500).

Bad debt expense	5,825	
Allowance for doubtful accounts		5,825

The estimated net realizable value of accounts receivable is $172,175 in this case.

Credit Sales Method. This method emphasizes the matching principle and income statement. The average percentage relationship between actual bad debt losses and net credit sales is estimated on the basis of experience. This percentage is then applied to a period's net credit sales to determine bad debt expense.

Assume that in the past, 1.2% of Rally's credit sales have not been collected. Barring changes in Rally's credit policies or major changes in the economy, Rally expects this rate to continue. Under this method, the following is the required 20X2 adjusting entry, which increases the allowance *by* a percentage of sales.

Bad debt expense [$500,000 × 1.2%]	6,000	
Allowance for doubtful accounts		6,000

EXHIBIT 8-4
RALLY COMPANY
Accounts Receivable Aging Schedule
31 December 20X2

Customer account	Balance 31 Dec. 20X2	Age of account balance			
		Current	1–30 days	31–60 days	Over 60 days
Denk	$ 500	$ 400	$ 100		
Evans	900	900			
Field	1,650		1,350	$ 300	
Harris	90			30	$ 60
King	800	700	60	40	
Zabot	250	250			
Total	$177,500	$110,000	$31,000	$29,500	$7,000
Percent estimated uncollectible		0.2%	1.0%	8.0%	40.0%
Amount estimated uncollectible		$ 220	$ 310	$ 2,360	$2,800

Total amount to include in allowance: $220 + $310 + $2,360 + $2,800 = $5,690

After this entry is posted, the balance in the allowance account is $5,500 ($6,000 from the adjusting entry less the prior $500 debit balance). This method directly computes bad debt expense without regard to the prior balance in the allowance account. Rally would disclose $172,000 ($177,500 − $5,500) of net accounts receivable in the 20X2 balance sheet.

The percentage applied to credit sales should be updated periodically to approximate the rate of actual write-offs.

Which Method to Use?   Either method of estimation is acceptable for financial reporting as long as the resulting allowance is reasonable. Statistical support for the rates used to establish the allowance under either method helps establish this reasonableness. It's also fairly standard to evaluate the allowance with reference to major accounts receivable in various categories, in conjunction with the year-end audit or review.

The credit sales and aging methods may be used together. Each is used to validate the other although only one may be used in the accounts. For interim financial statements, many companies base monthly or quarterly adjusting entries on the credit sales method because of its low cost. At the end of the year, they may age their accounts receivable to check the reasonableness of the allowance balance.

Computerization has reduced costs of implementing the aging method, and increasing cash flow problems prompt companies to monitor the age of their receivables more closely to reduce losses. In addition, the aging method corrects for prior errors in estimating uncollectible accounts because it regularly reevaluates the loss percentages in each age category.

The general condition of the economy, the economic health of specific customers, and the seller's credit policy and collection effort affect the rate of account write-offs. Over time, this rate changes, necessitating adjustment to the percentages applied to credit sales or receivables. If the balance in allowance for doubtful accounts is found to increase each year, the estimate of uncollectibles is decreased to reflect actual experience.

Direct Write-Off of Uncollectible Accounts

Companies in the first year of operation or in a new line of business may have no basis for estimating uncollectibles. In such cases, and when uncollectible accounts are immaterial, receivables must be written off directly as they become uncollectible. The entry for the direct write-off of a $2,000 account receivable from M. Lynx is as follows:

Bad debt expense	2,000	
Accounts receivable, M. Lynx		2,000

No adjusting entry is made at the end of an accounting period under the direct write-off method.

The inability to estimate uncollectible accounts creates several unavoidable problems:

- Receivables are reported at more than their net realizable value, because it is virtually certain that not all receivables are collectible.

- The period of write-off is often after the period of sale, violating the matching principle. If bad debts are material and inestimable, revenue cannot be recognized until the uncertainty is cleared up — usually on collection.

- Direct write-off opens the potential for income manipulation by arbitrary selection of the write-off period.

SPEEDING UP CASH FLOW FROM RECEIVABLES

Credit Card Operations

At one point in time, many retail stores offered credit to customers — in fact, some built a business primarily on offering credit. (Ever heard of People's Credit Jewellers, now usually just called People's?) Now, most retailers prefer to get their money up front, and let the customers owe the credit card company. Retailers are charged a fee, a percentage of the total sale, for the privilege, but prefer this charge because they avoid bad debts, there is no delay in receiving cash, and they hope that customers will spend more when they can charge their purchases. Except for the corner variety store, there aren't many cash-only businesses around these days. Retail customers expect to be able to use credit cards.

Other retailers have expanded their credit-granting operations into their own credit card companies. These operations, usually separate subsidiaries, make money by charging interest on overdue accounts. Their largest expenses are the cost of money and bad debts.

Normally, a merchant accumulates credit card sales in batches, depending on volume. Credit card vouchers are deposited with a bank acting as agent for the credit card company (which may be a subsidiary of a bank). Assume that a merchant accumulates $2,000 in credit card sales. The credit card company deducts a commission of a contracted amount for its services. Assuming that the fee is 6% in this example, the appropriate entry at the time of deposit is as follows:

Cash	1,880	
Credit card fees expense [$2,000 × 6%]	120	
Sales		2,000

Loans Secured by Account Receivable

If a company has a $100,000 account receivable from a creditworthy customer who will not pay for 45 days, how can the company get cash sooner? Well, it would be nice if the customer would pay sooner, and a variety of policies are usually explored

---

EXHIBIT 8-5
MacMILLAN BLOEDEL LIMITED
Sale of Receivables

3. Sale of receivables:

In 1996, MacMillan Bloedel entered into agreements to sell designated pools of trade receivables to two trusts. At December 31, 1997, the two trusts held $226 million (1996 – $219 million) of such receivables. The agreements expire in July 1999.

---

to speed up collection. Then what? The most common course of action is to go to a chartered bank and borrow money using the account receivable as collateral.

This isn't very complicated on the books: a loan is recorded, and interest expense will be recorded as time passes. When the account is collected, the bank is repaid. Assets pledged as collateral are disclosed in the financial statements. Of course, it's less common to make credit arrangements for one receivable at a time: the overall balance of accounts receivable, and usually inventory, too, are used to secure a working capital loan, which is a relatively permanent part of most companies' financial structure.

Sale of Accounts Receivable

Exhibit 8-5 presents a note that appeared in the financial statements of MacMillan Bloedel. The note describes a *sale* of accounts receivable. It is rather unusual for such a sale to be disclosed in the notes to the financial statements, but it is not at all unusual for a company to realize cash for their receivables by selling them to a third party. Receivables can be sold either *without recourse* or *with recourse*. Recourse simply means the right of the third party to come back to the seller of the receivables for payment if the account turns out to be uncollectible. Sales of accounts receivable are also called assignment or factoring.

Without Recourse. Agreements to sell receivables are made on either a notification basis (customers are directed to remit to the new party holding the receivables, usually called the factor) or a non-notification basis (customers continue to remit to the original seller who then, in turn, remits to the factor). Non-recourse arrangements are usually made on a notification basis. Of course, the buyer, or factor, is going to charge more than a bank would for a loan secured by accounts receivable, since the factor takes on the risk that the customer will not pay. This is called a sale of accounts receivable without recourse.

When receivables are sold without recourse, they are removed from the transferor's books — cash is debited, and a financing fee is recognized immediately as a financing expense or loss on sale.

To illustrate factoring without recourse, consider the following case. Largo, Inc. sells $200,000 of accounts receivable without recourse on 15 August 20X2. The buyer is a finance company; the sale is made on a notification basis. The finance company charges a 12% financing fee. In non-recourse transfers, the finance company bears the cost of uncollectible accounts. The entry to record the transfer is:

Largo, Inc.			**Finance Company**		
Cash	176,000*		Accounts receivable	200,000	
Financing fee	24,000**		Deferred financing revenue		24,000
Accounts receivable		200,000	Cash		176,000

* $200,000 – (12% × $200,000)
** 12% × $200,000

It looks pretty straightforward, doesn't it? Accounts receivable can be sold, like any other asset! To simplify this, and the following examples, no consideration was given to the likely sales discounts or returns that are inherent in the receivables balance. In a real situation, the factor would hold back an allowance for this cause, and settle up with the company at the end of the arrangement. It doesn't change the substance of the transaction, though.

With Recourse. It's more common to find that accounts receivable are sold with recourse, because finance companies charge dearly for assuming risk of collection. If receivables are sold with recourse, and the customer does not pay the account receivable, the company bears the risk and will have to pay. Since companies often have ongoing relationships with their customers, they can minimize the risk of nonpayment through timely intervention. Now, the accounting problem is to determine the substance of the agreement in circumstances where risk appears to stay with the selling company. The agreement could be

1. *A sale.* The accounts receivable come off the books of the selling company, and a financing fee is recognized. This is analogous to the example just illustrated.
2. *A loan.* The accounts receivable are left on the books of the selling company, and the amount received from the finance company is recorded as a loan until the customer actually pays.

These are radically different views of the substance of the transaction, and will significantly change financial statement relationships, such as the current ratio. How is the substance of the transaction determined? The CICA's Emerging Issues Committee provides guidance in *EIC-9*, "Transfer of Receivables":

> ...for a transaction involving a transfer of receivables to be recognized as a sale, both of the following conditions should exist:
> i.   the transferor has transferred the significant risks and rewards of ownership of the receivables; and
> ii. reasonable assurance exists regarding the measurement of the consideration derived from the transfer of the receivables.
>
> [*EIC-9*, page 3]

What does all this mean?

- If the transferor retains the right to repurchase the accounts receivable, criterion (1) is not met and the transaction is recorded as a loan.
- If the transferor bears credit risk, interest rate risk, foreign exchange risk, etc., in relation to the agreement, then the first criterion fails. *Some level of reasonable credit risk, if estimable, may be born by the transferor* and have the transaction still meet criterion (1); the reasonableness of the arrangements is a matter of professional judgement. It is unlikely that a sale of receivables has occurred if the total recourse exceeds 10% of the proceeds received.
- If the transferor cannot estimate the ultimate *collectibility* of the receivables, criterion (2) fails.
- If the obligations of the transferor are limited to *estimable payments* under the recourse provisions (payments to the transferee for bad debt losses, cash discounts, returns, and allowances), a sale is properly reported, assuming that the other criteria are met.

In conclusion, the transaction can still be a sale in a recourse situation as long as the bad debt expense (and so on) is relatively low and can be estimated.

Case 1. Recourse Arrangement Recorded as a Sale. Assume that Largo, Inc. sells $200,000 of accounts receivable with recourse on 15 August 20X2, to a finance company on a notification basis. The finance company estimates that uncollectible accounts will amount to $3,000. The financing fee is 6% (less than in the non-recourse example). Both criteria for sale are met, and the arrangement is recorded as a sale. The difference between the book value of receivables transferred and assets received from the factor is recognized immediately as an expense.

```
Cash {$200,000 – $3,000 – [6% × ($200,000 – $3,000)]} 185,180
Bad debt expense                                         3,000
Financing fee* [6% × ($200,000 – $3,000)]              11,820
    Accounts receivable                                          200,000
```

* Also called a loss on sale of receivables.

Again, the impact of expected sales discounts and returns is ignored in this simple example.

This example is different from a sale *without* recourse in that bad debt expense is recognized on the date that the receivables are transferred. It also is different because *there will be final reckoning with the finance company.* If the finance company collects exactly $197,000, then no money will change hands. If the finance company collects less, Largo will have to make up the difference. If the finance company collects more, Largo will get a cheque. If arrangements met the criteria for a sale, collection estimates should have been accurate enough so that the final reckoning is immaterial; otherwise, someone's judgement was at fault when the transaction was classified!

The company selling the accounts receivable has a contingent liability in this scenario — if the customer does not pay, the company will have to. This contingency has been evaluated and deemed to be estimable, and relatively low; otherwise, the transaction would not qualify as a sale. However, *the contingency is still disclosed in the notes to the financial statements.*

Case 2. Recourse Arrangement Recorded as a Loan. In a financing arrangement recorded as a loan, receivables stay on the books, and a loan is recorded. The transferor recognizes the difference between the assets received from the factor and the book value of the receivables as interest *over the term of the loan.* This is in contrast to the sale example, in which the difference was immediately recognized as an expense. Assume the same facts as Case 1, except that Largo retains the option to repurchase the receivables. This means that the transaction is recorded as a loan. Entries to record the loan and estimated uncollectible accounts are:

```
Cash {$200,000 – $3,000 – [6% × ($200,000 – $3,000)]}         185,180
Discount on payable to factor
    [6% × ($200,000 – $3,000)]                        11,820
    Payable to factor                                            197,000

Bad debt expense                                       3,000
    Allowance for doubtful accounts                              3,000
```

The discount account is a contra account to the payable to factor account and represents the total interest to be paid by Largo. This contra account is amortized as interest expense over the loan term. While an interest approach would be appropriate, the discount can also be amortized based on collections. Largo records sales adjustments, like sales discounts and returns, as they occur and reduces the payable as customers remit cash to the finance company. At the end of the arrangement, Largo must pay any outstanding balance on the payable, whether or not customers have remitted on time.

EXHIBIT 8-6
WESTERN STAR TRUCKS HOLDINGS INC.
Factoring Disclosure

6. Factoring Facilities

The Company's factoring facilities represent advances made by factoring companies in respect of assigned invoices for vehicle sales to certain customers. There is no maturity date for these facilities as they revolve on a regular basis. The maximum amount available under these facilities is $157 million (comprised of U.S. $90 million and £10 million) and the amount advanced as at June 30, 1998 is $70,344,000 [1997 — $72,936,000]. The total amount drawn is included in both accounts receivable and accounts payable. The interest rate on the facilities ranges from LIBOR plus 0.8% to LIBOR plus 1.5%. The agreements governing these facilities expire from March 1999 to December 2003.

It's worth noting that the payable to the financing company must be shown as a current liability on the balance sheet, and may not be netted with the related accounts receivable. Netting is only appropriate when there is a legal right to net, *and* intent to net; while intent is present in this case, there is no legal right to net and the balances must be shown as the separate elements they really are.

An example of disclosure of factoring is shown in Exhibit 8-6. The interest rates are expressed in terms of LIBOR, the London Inter-Bank Offering Rate, which is the standard reference point for international finance. LIBOR is sort of the international equivalent of the prime rate in Canada.

NOTES RECEIVABLE AND PAYABLE

A note receivable is a written promise to pay a specified amount at a specified future date (or a series of amounts over a series of payment dates). Notes receivable are a current asset if the term is a year or an operating cycle. Notes payable are a current liability and are the mirror image of receivables. Notes payable are also called short-term commercial paper, issued by large companies with excellent credit ratings, and bought by other companies as temporary investments.

Notes may be non-current assets or liabilities if their term exceeds the cut-off for current classification. Accounting for non-current notes is no different than that explained here; only the classification changes! Remember that classification is as much a function of intent as of term — how long does management mean to hang on?

Notes usually provide

- Extended payment terms.
- More security than sales invoices and other commercial trade documents.
- A formal basis for charging interest.
- Negotiability.

We'll look at notes receivable and payable together in the material that follows.

Most notes represent loans. Notes also arise from normal sales, extension of the payment period of accounts receivable, exchanges of long-term assets, and advances to employees. The borrower is the maker of the note and the lender is the payee (note holder).

Interest Rate

The interest rate stated in a note may not equal the market rate prevailing on obligations involving similar credit rating or risk, although the stated rate is always used to determine the cash interest payments. If the stated and market rates are different, the *market rate is used to value the note and to measure interest revenue or expense.*

The market rate is the rate accepted by two parties with opposing interests engaged in an arm's length transaction. If the value of the consideration given is known, the rate can be determined by equating the present value of the cash flows called for in the note to the market value of the consideration. The rate can be determined with a computer program or calculator that locates the correct rate iteratively — that is, by trial-and-error.

For example, assume that on 30 June 20X5, a firm sells equipment with a cash price of $10,000 and receives in exchange a note that requires a payment of $6,000 on 30 June 20X6, and another $6,000 on 30 June 20X7. The note does not explicitly mention interest, but $2,000 of interest is implicit in the note. The interest rate is computed using the present value of an annuity as follows:[1]

$$\$10,000 = \$6,000 \times (P/A, i, 2)$$
$$\$10,000 \div \$6,000 = 1.66667 = (P/A, i, 2)$$

The value 1.66667 does not appear in the table for the present value of an ordinary annuity, but is almost half-way between the 12% and 14% values; a calculator equipped for present value tells us that $i = 13.066\%$. This rate must at least equal the rate incurred by the debtor on similar financing.

For accounting purposes, the principal amount of a note is measured by the fair market value or cash equivalent value of goods or services provided in exchange for the note, if this value is known, or the present (discounted) value of all cash payments required under the note using the market rate. The principal is also the amount initially subject to interest. The principal represents the sacrifice by the payee, and therefore the present value of the future payments, at the date of the transaction. Any amount paid in excess of the principal is interest. Short-term notes need not be reported at present value, because the difference between present and maturity value is generally not significant.

The face value, or maturity value, is the dollar amount stated in the note. The face value is the amount, excluding interest, payable at the end of the note term, unless the note requires that principal repayments be made according to an instalment schedule. The principal value equals the maturity value if the stated interest rate equals the market interest rate. The total interest over the life of the note equals the total cash receipts less the principal amount.

Notes may be categorized as interest-bearing or non-interest-bearing notes. Interest-bearing notes specify the interest rate to be applied to the face amount in computing interest payments. Non-interest-bearing notes do not state an interest rate but command interest through face values that exceed the principal amount.

Interest-bearing notes in turn can be divided into two categories according to the type of cash payment required: (1) notes whose cash payments are interest only except for final maturity payment and (2) notes whose cash payments include both interest and principal. Actually, there are an unlimited number of principal and repayment options. Payment schedules are not limited to those used in the examples.

A 10%, $4,000, two-year note received by Vancouver Sealines that requires interest to be paid on its face value, is an example of the first type. The annual interest of $400 ($4,000 × 10%) is payable at the end of each year of the note term. The $4,000 face amount is paid at the end of the second year. In total, $800 of interest is required over the term of the note. In notes of this type, the original principal is not decreased by the yearly payment.

---

[1] Refer to the Summary of Compound Interest Tables and Formulae, found at the back of this Volume, for an explanation of the present value and future value notation that is being used in these examples.

Now assume that Vancouver's note is instead a note of the second type, requiring two equal annual amounts payable at the end of each year. These payments each contain interest and principal in the amount necessary to discharge the debt at 10% in two payments. The payment is computed as follows:

$4,000 = Present value of an annuity = Payment × (P/A, 10%, 2)
$4,000 ÷ (P/A, 10%, 2) = Payment
$4,000 ÷ 1.73554 = $2,304.76 = Payment

Payment	Interest Component	Principal Component
1	$400.00 ($4,000 × 10%)	$1,904.76 ($2,304.76 – $400)
2	$209.52 ($4,000 – $1,904.76) × 10%	$2,095.24 ($2,304.76 – $209.52)
	$609.52	$4,000.00

Total interest for the second type of note ($609.52) is less than for the first note because part of the first payment is a principal payment, which reduces the principal on which interest is paid in the second period.

Illustrations

Example 1: Simple Interest Note. On 1 April 20X2, Lionel Company loaned $12,000 cash to Baylor Company and received a three-year, 10% note. Interest is payable each 31 March, and the principal is payable at the end of the third year. The stated and market interest rates are equal. The entry to record the note is as follows:

Lionel			Baylor		
1 April 20X2			*1 April 20X2*		
Notes receivable	12,000		Cash	12,000	
Cash		12,000	Notes payable		12,000

The present value of the principal and interest payments on 1 April 20X2, is $12,000 because the stated and market rates are equal. Cash interest received also equals interest revenue recognized over the terms of the note, as indicated in the remaining entries. The computation for interest assumes months of equal length; in "real life," interest is accrued by days if it is material.

Lionel			Baylor		
31 December 20X2, 20X3, 20X4 — Adjusting entries					
Interest receivable	900*		Interest expense	900	
Interest revenue		900	Interest payable		900
*$12,000 × 10% × 9/12					
31 March 20X3 and 20X4 — Interest payments					
Cash	1,200		Interest payable	900	
Interest receivable		900	Interest expense	300	
Interest revenue		300*	Cash		1,200
*$12,000 × 10% × 3/12					
31 March 20X5 — Payment at maturity					
Cash	13,200		Interest payable	900	
Notes receivable		12,000	Interest expense	300	
Interest receivable		900	Notes payable	12,000	
Interest revenue		300	Cash		13,200

Example 2: Different Market and Stated Rates. Fox Company, which sells specialized machinery and equipment, sold equipment on 1 January 20X3, and received a two-year, $10,000 note with a 3% stated interest rate from its customer, Hound Ltd. Interest is payable each 31 December and the entire principal is payable 31 December 20X4.

The equipment does not have a ready market value. The market rate of interest appropriate for this note is 10%. The present value (and principal) of the note is computed as follows (amounts are rounded to the nearest dollar):

Present value of maturity amount:	
$10,000(P/F, 10%, 2) = $10,000(.82645) =	$8,265
Present value of the nominal interest payments:	
$10,000(3%)(P/A, 10%, 2) = $300(1.73554) =	521
Present value of the note at 10%	$8,786

Typically, if notes are for less than a year, low interest rates are ignored, because the effect of interest on the financial statements of Fox is immaterial. The stated interest would be recorded as interest revenue, and the stated amount of the note would be recorded as the sale. However, when low-interest loans have a term beyond a year, they must be valued with respect to the time value of money.

Notes with stated interest rates below market may be used by companies to increase sales. The Fox Company note, for example, uses a low nominal (stated) interest rate offset by an increased face value. Many buyers of big-ticket items, including automobiles, home appliances, and even houses, are more concerned about the monthly payment than the final maturity payment — the balloon payment, as a large final payment is called. A note with an $8,786 face value and a 10% stated rate achieves the same present value to Fox, but a 3% interest payment on $10,000 ($300) may be more attractive than a 10% payment on $8,786 ($879) for Hound, the customer. Accounting for these arrangements involves appropriate recognition of the principal as the proceeds on sale, and interest as time passes.

As the Fox Company example illustrates, when the stated and market interest rates are different, the face value and principal differ. Notes are recorded at gross (face) value plus a premium or minus a discount amount (the gross method), or at the net principal value (the net method). The two methods are illustrated.

1 January 20X3:

	Gross		Net	
For Fox Company				
Notes receivable	10,000		8,786	
Discount on notes receivable		1,214		—
Sales		8,786		8,786
For Hound Ltd.				
Equipment	8,786		8,786	
Discount on notes payable	1,214		—	
Notes payable		10,000		8,786

Under either method, the net book value of the note is $8,786, the principal value. The discount account is a contra account to notes receivable or payable. The gross method discloses both the note's face value and the implicit interest that is included in the face value of the note. Since the note is disclosed net of its discount on any balance sheet, the two methods are identical in presentation. In the remaining parts of the example, only the gross method will be illustrated, as it is more comparable with accounting for long-term notes payable, as you will see in Chapter 13.

The entries at the end of the fiscal year are as follows:

31 December 20X3:

Fox			**Hound**		
Cash ($10,000 × 3%)	300		Interest expense	878	
Discount on note receivable	578		Discount on note payable		578
Interest revenue ($8,786 × 10%)		878	Cash		300

The balance sheet dated 31 December 20X3, discloses net notes receivable and payable of $9,364 [$10,000 – ($1,214 – $578)]. This amount is also the present value of the note on 1 January 20X4.

$10,300(P/F, 10%, 1) = $10,300(.90909) = $9,364 (rounded)

The market rate of interest is applied to the beginning balance in the net note receivable to compute interest revenue. This approach, called the effective interest method, results in a constant rate of interest throughout the life of the note. Another approach, the straight-line method, amortizes a constant amount of discount each period. The straight-line method produces a varying rate of interest period by period, but it is much simpler and may yield results that are not materially different from the effective interest method. In this example, the straight-line method results in discount amortization of $607 ($1,214 ÷ 2 years) and interest revenue or expense of $907 ($607 + $300) in both years.

Continuing with the effective interest method, the entry at the end of 20X4 is the following:

31 December 20X4

Fox			Hound		
Cash ($10,000 × 3%)	300		Interest expense	936	
Discount on note receivable	636		Discount on note payable		636
Interest revenue ($9,365 × 10%)		936	Cash		300

After the 31 December 20X4 entry, the net notes receivable balance is $10,000, the present value at that date. The discount account balance is now zero (rounded), and the note is paid at this time.

31 December 20X4

Fox			Hound		
Cash	10,000		Notes payable	10,000	
Notes receivable		10,000	Cash		10,000

Example 3: Note Issued for Non-Cash Consideration. Siever Company sold specialized equipment originally costing $20,000 with a net book value of $16,000 on 1 January 20X2 to Bellow. The market value of the equipment was not readily determinable.

Siever received a $5,000 down payment and a $10,000, 4% note payable in four equal annual instalments starting 31 December 20X2. The current market rate on notes of a similar nature and risk is 10%. With the stated rate of 4%, the payment (A) is determined as follows:

$10,000 = A(P/A, 4%, 4) = A × (3.62990)
$10,000 ÷ 3.62990 = $2,755 = P

Therefore, the note's principal (P) equals the present value of four $2,755 payments at 10%, plus the $5,000 down payment.

P = $2,755 × (P/A, 10%, 4) + $5,000 = $2,755 × (3.16987) + $5,000
  = $8,733 + $5,000 = $13,733

The present value of the consideration received is $13,733, which is therefore the agreed-on value of the equipment. The entry to record the sale (gross method) is:

1 January 20X2 (gross method)

Siever		Bellow	
Cash	5,000	Equipment	13,733
Notes receivable	10,000	Discount on note payable	1,267
Accum. depreciation	4,000*	Cash	5,000
Loss on sale	2,267	Notes payable	10,000
Discount on note receivable	1,267**		
Equipment	20,000		

*($20,000 − $16,000)
**($10,000 − $8,733)

The loss on sale equals the net book value of the equipment ($16,000) less the present value of consideration received ($13,733). The discount on the note is its face value minus its present value, $8,733 ($10,000 − $1,267). Interest is accrued on the note receivable at year-end in the typical fashion.

Impairment

Notes receivable will only be an asset if the maker of the note pays on time — both the principal and interest are to be considered in this regard. After all, revenue cannot be recognized, i.e., interest cannot be accrued, unless it is supported by an increase in an asset, the receivable. Therefore, an allowance for doubtful notes receivable must be established when appropriate.

In calculating the extent of such an allowance, two things must be assessed:

1. *The present value of the cash flows expected from the maker of the note over its remaining life.* While some customers will pay nothing, it's quite common to get partial payment, or even complete payment several years late. To assess the fair value of this cash flow, the time value of money must be taken into consideration by calculating the present value of the cash flow.

2. *The fair value of any collateral* that the company can repossess; this collateral has to be valued at its fair market value.

For example, assume that a note receivable was on the books for $4,800, including both principal and interest, and the customer encountered financial difficulties. As a result, the cash flows associated with the note are expected to have a present value of $1,200. A $3,600 loan loss or bad debt expense is recognized, and an allowance for doubtful accounts is established.

A section of the *CICA Handbook*, called "Impaired Loans," governs this area; it contains some technical rules over an area that is vastly complicated by the difficulty in making accurate predictions of cash flows from a party in financial difficulty, and by the need to recognize interest revenue on balances as time passes. There is some room to be pessimistic, take large loan losses, and then watch income bounce back with loan loss recoveries.

Discounting Notes Receivable

Rather than hold a note receivable to maturity, payees may discount the note with a bank or financial institution. Notes can be discounted, or sold, by any holder, as well as by the original payee, at any time before the note's maturity date. Discounting notes receivable may be done with or without recourse, and is very similar to the sale of accounts receivable.

The most common outcome is that the transaction is recorded as a sale — the company records a gain or loss equal to the difference between the proceeds and book value of the note, including accrued interest, and has a contingent liability until the note is paid by the maker. If the note is discounted without recourse, the payee has no contingent liability.

If a note is discounted with recourse, the amount paid by the bank may be recorded as a loan — a liability is recorded and interest expense is recognized over the term of borrowing. The proceeds to the payee are not affected by the reporting alternatives and are based on the total of principal value plus interest to maturity, whether or not the note is interest bearing. The bank charges its discount rate on this total amount for the period between the date of discounting and the date of maturity of the note. The sum of principal and interest is the amount at risk, from the bank's point of view.

A common version of this is an arrangement whereby a retail store's sales are immediately financed by a consumer loan company. It's like discounting a note, but they skip a step — the note is taken out directly with the finance company. Here's how it works: the customer goes to a store and decides on a purchase. The customer fills in a finance company loan application right in the retail store, and credit is granted, or not, usually on the spot. The payment scheme may start immediately, or may be deferred for some time (e.g., "Don't Pay A Cent!"). The store receives the present value of the loan agreement from the finance company, less some kind of financing fee, which is usually built into the discount rate. Since the finance company has approved the credit application, they have no recourse to the retail store, whose relationship with the customer is over as soon as the goods are delivered.

Disclosure

Disclosure of notes receivable and payable must satisfy the requirements of the Financial Instruments section of the *CICA Handbook*. *Terms and conditions* of notes must be disclosed, including maturity dates, amount and timing of future cash flows, collateral, and so on. *Interest rates*, both stated and effective, are also required disclosure.

For notes receivable, *exposure to credit risk* must be disclosed, along with information about significant concentrations of credit risk. *Fair value* for this class of financial asset or financial liability must be disclosed. Fair value would be different than book value if interest rates had shifted from the time that the notes were issued, since fair value would be established through present value techniques using current market interest rates.

CONCEPT REVIEW

1. Which basic accounting concepts underlie the practice of establishing an allowance for doubtful accounts?

2. What is the purpose of an aging schedule?

3. Explain the difference between selling accounts receivable *with recourse* and *without recourse*.

4. What is the basic approach to measuring the carrying value of notes receivable and notes payable?

CURRENT LIABILITIES

Current (short-term) liabilities are amounts payable within one year from the date of the balance sheet or within the normal operating cycle, where this is longer than a year. The time dimension (year vs. operating cycle) that applies to current assets also generally applies to current liabilities. Liabilities that are not due within this current time frame are called long-term, or non-current, liabilities. Long-term liabilities are discussed in Chapter 13.

Most current liabilities are monetary items; they obligate the reporting enterprise to pay a fixed sum of cash in the future, sometimes with interest added and other times as a flat amount. Common monetary current liabilities are

- Accounts payable
- Short-term notes payable
- Cash and property dividends payable
- Advances and returnable deposits
- Monetary accrued liabilities
- Estimated monetary liabilities, including:
  - * Taxes (sales, property, and payroll)
  - * Conditional payments (income taxes and bonuses)
  - * Compensated-absence liabilities (e.g., vacation pay)
- Current loans payable
- Current portion of long-term liabilities

Current liabilities also may include some non-monetary items. Most common non-monetary items are:

- Non-monetary accrued liabilities, such as an airline's obligation to provide free flights under its frequent-flier reward plans, or a manufacturer's obligation to honour warranties on its products.
- Unearned revenues, which are liabilities to provide goods and/or services in the future as the result of cash already received, such as magazine subscription revenue or pre-payment for goods on order.

Special accounting problems related to *monetary* current liabilities are discussed in the following sections. Accounting for *non-monetary* current liabilities is discussed in Chapter 13.

Accounts Payable

Accounts payable — more descriptively, **trade accounts payable** — are obligations arising from the firm's ongoing operations, including the acquisition of merchandise, materials, supplies, and services used in the production and sale of goods or services. Current payables that are not trade accounts (such as income taxes and the current portion of long-term debt) should be reported separately from accounts payable. In determining the amount of the liability, the accountant must adjust for purchase discounts, allowances, and returns, exactly as discussed for accounts receivable. Of course, a company never accrues an allowance for non-payment, since they themselves are the payer!

Cash Dividends Payable

Cash dividends declared but not yet paid are reported as a current liability if they are to be paid within the coming year or operating cycle. Declared dividends are reported as a liability between the date of declaration and payment because declaration gives rise to an enforceable contract.

Liabilities are not recognized for undeclared dividends in arrears on preferred stock or for any other dividends not formally declared by the board of directors. Dividends in arrears on cumulative preferred stock should be disclosed in the notes to the financial statements. These dividends must be paid before any common dividends can be paid.

Monetary Accrued Liabilities

Examples of monetary accrued liabilities include wages and benefits earned by employees, interest earned by creditors but not as yet paid, and the costs of goods and services received but not yet invoiced by the supplier. Monetary accrued liabilities are recorded in the accounts by making adjusting entries at the end of the accounting period. For example, any wages that have not yet been recorded or paid at the end of the accounting period must be recorded by debiting wage expense and crediting accrued wages payable. Recognition of accrued liabilities is consistent with the definition of a liability and the matching principle.

Advances and Returnable Deposits

A company may receive advances or cash deposits from customers as guarantees for payment of future obligations or to guarantee performance on a contract or service. For example, when an order is taken, a company may require an advance payment to cover losses that would be incurred if the order is cancelled. Such advances create liabilities for the company receiving the payment until the underlying earnings process is completed. Advances are recorded by debiting cash and crediting a liability account such as customer deposits.

Deposits may also be made as guarantees in case of non-collection or for possible damage to property. For example, deposits required from customers by gas, water, electricity, and other public utilities are liabilities of such companies to their customers. Employees may also make returnable deposits to ensure the return of keys and other company property, for locker privileges, and for club memberships. Deposits should be reported as current or long-term liabilities depending on the time involved between date of deposit and expected termination of the relationship. If the advances or deposits are interest-bearing, an annual adjusting entry is required to accrue interest expense and to increase the related liability.

Taxes

Provincial and federal laws require businesses to collect certain taxes from customers and employees for remittance to governmental agencies. These taxes include sales taxes, income taxes withheld from employee paycheques, property taxes, and payroll taxes. Similar collections are made on behalf of unions, insurance companies, and employee-sponsored activities. Collections made for third parties increase both cash and current liabilities. The collections represent liabilities that are settled when the funds are remitted to the designated parties. Common examples of such taxes follow:

Sales Taxes. Retail businesses are required to collect sales taxes from customers and remit them to the appropriate government agency. Taxes include the goods and services tax (GST) and, in most provinces, provincial sales taxes (PST), or both together, the harmonized sales tax, (HST). The Emerging Issues Committee of the CICA has indicated that revenues should be recorded net of the GST collected. Purchases of goods and services should be recorded net of any GST recoverable, and the net amount of the GST payable or receivable should be carried as a liability or asset, as appropriate.

Any GST that is not recoverable should be accounted for as a component of the cost of the goods or services to which it relates. If it is paid and is not recoverable in relation to a capital asset, GST is included in the asset's capital cost. If it relates to current costs, it will be included in the determination of net income for the period.

Typical entries, with the 7% GST and assuming a 9% provincial sales tax and $500,000 of sales, are as follows:

1. *At date the tax is assessed (point of sale):*

Cash and accounts receivable	580,000	
Sales revenue		500,000
GST payable ($500,000 × 7%)		35,000
PST payable ($500,000 × 9%)		45,000

Note that in some provinces, the PST is charged on the subtotal of sales plus GST. However, GST is never charged on the subtotal of sales plus PST. It probably goes without saying that companies need to become expert in the rules and regulations that govern sales tax application. Governments have sales tax auditors to encourage compliance.

2. *At date of remittance to taxing authority:*

GST payable*	35,000	
Cash		35,000
PST payable	45,000	
Cash		45,000

*The GST to be remitted to the government will be reduced by the amount of GST paid by the company on purchased goods and services.

Payroll Taxes. Employers act as a collection agent for certain taxes and payments. They withhold appropriate amounts from their employees and send the money off to the appropriate party shortly thereafter; a liability exists in the meantime. Common withholdings include

- *Personal income taxes.* An employee's personal federal and provincial taxes are deducted at source and remitted monthly to the federal government. At the end of the year, the employee receives a record of deductions, and determines, on his or her annual tax return, who owes whom and how much.

- *Canada pension plan (CPP).* Employees have to pay a percentage of their salary to the CPP; employers have to match this amount dollar for dollar.

- *Employment insurance (EI).* Employees have to pay a percentage of their salary to secure EI benefits; the employer must pay 1.4 times the employees' contributions as their share.

- *Union dues.* If stipulated in labour agreements, union dues are deducted at source and remitted to the union monthly.

- *Insurance premiums.* A variety of employee benefits, like group insurance and medical insurance require that employees pay all or a portion of the premiums; these are deducted at source.

- *Pension plan payments.* If employees are required to pay a portion of their salary to secure a pension, these amounts are deducted at source and remitted to the pension plan trustee.

- *Other deductions.* What else does the employee wish to have taken off their paycheque? Examples include certain charitable donations and parking fees. All of these are remitted to the appropriate party after deduction.

Payroll deductions are illustrated in Exhibit 8-7.

Property Taxes. Property taxes paid directly by the company are based on the assessed value of real property, and are used to support city, municipality, and other designated activities. Unpaid taxes constitute a lien on the assessed property. Property taxes are based on the assessed value of the property, which may or may not correspond to market value, and the tax rate per thousand dollars of assessed value.

Property taxes are usually set by the taxing authority part-way through the fiscal year, which means that the company must use last year's tax bill as an estimate to accrue monthly expenses until the final assessment and tax rate are known. Estimates are corrected when the real tax rate is known, but corrections to estimates affect only the current and future periods; retroactive corrections are not made for estimates. Taxes are also paid for a year that reflects the city or municipality fiscal year, which may or may not correspond to the company's; accruals or pre-payments typically result due to these timing problems.

EXHIBIT 8-7
Illustration of Payroll Deductions

Thor Company reported the following information relating to payroll for January 20X5:

Gross Wages		$100,000
Deductions:		
Income taxes	$20,000	
Canada Pension Plan	2,250	
Employment insurance	2,100	
Union dues	1,400	
Charitable contributions	1,600	27,350
Net pay		$ 72,650

To record salaries and employee deductions:

Salary expense	100,000	
Employee income taxes payable		20,000
CPP payable		2,250
EI payable		2,100
Union dues payable		1,400
Charitable contributions payable		1,600
Cash		72,650

To record payroll expenses payable by the employer:

Salary expense	5,190	
CPP payable		2,250
EI payable ($2,100 × 1.4)		2,940

To record remittance of payroll deductions (composite entry):

Employee income taxes payable	20,000	
CPP payable	4,500	
EI payable	5,040	
Union dues payable	1,400	
Charitable contributions payable	1,600	
Cash		32,540

Conditional Payments

Some liabilities are established on the basis of a firm's periodic income. Two examples are bonuses or profit-sharing payments to employees and income taxes based on taxable income. These items can be established at year-end, but the liability must be estimated whenever interim statements are prepared throughout the year — monthly or quarterly. Until paid, they represent current liabilities of the organization.

Income Taxes Payable. Interim reports require a provision for both federal and provincial tax liabilities, so estimates are required. The estimated liability should be reported as a current liability based on the firm's best estimates. After year-end, the tax return is prepared and the estimate is adjusted on the year-end financial statements before the books are finally closed. Periodic instalment payments are required. Some aspects of income taxes are covered in later chapters.

Bonuses. Many companies pay cash bonuses, which depend on earnings. These are estimated at interim periods, but calculated "for real" at the end of the fiscal year. Calculations must be made in accordance with established formula or the authorization of the board of directors. Bonuses can be material — both to the company and to the employee, so it's crucial to ensure that they're properly approved.

Compensated-Absence Liabilities

The Canada Labour Code requires that employees receive paid vacations and holidays. The expense for salaries and wages paid during these absences from work is recognized in the current year. When employees can carry over unused time to future years, GAAP requires that any expense due to compensated absences must be recognized (accrued) in the year in which it is earned, provided that all the following criteria are met (these should look like fairly standard recognition criteria by now):

- The absence from work relates to services already rendered.
- The benefits accumulate (carry over) or *vest*.
- The payment is probable (the absence will occur).
- The amount (i.e., cost) can be reliably estimated.

Implementing the accrual of compensated absences requires an adjusting entry at the end of each fiscal year to accrue all of the compensation cost for the vacation and holiday time that is carried over. An expense and a current liability are recorded. When the vacation or holiday time is taken, the liability account is debited at the time the employee is paid. These entries recognize the cost of the compensated absences as an expense in the period earned rather than when taken.

For example, consider the carryover of vacation time of the Conway Company, which has 500 employees. Each employee is granted three weeks paid vacation time each year. Vacation time, up to a maximum accumulation of four weeks, may be carried over to subsequent years prior to termination of employment. At the end of 20X5, the end of the annual accounting period, personnel records revealed the following information concerning carryover vacation amounts:

Carryovers from 20X5*

Number of Employees	Weeks per Employee	Total Weeks	Salary per week	Total Accrual
10	2	20	$1,500	$30,000
3	1	3	2,000	6,000
				$36,000

* These are carryovers from 20X5 to future years.

Disregarding payroll taxes, which are excluded here to simplify the analysis, the indicated entries are as follows:

31 December 20X5 — adjusting entry to accrue vacation salaries not yet taken or paid

Salary expense	36,000	
Liability for compensated absences		36,000

During 20X6 — vacation time carryover taken and salaries paid (all employees took their carried-over vacation time, except for one person who still carried over two weeks, valued at $1,500 per week)

Liability for compensated absences	33,000	
Cash ($36,000 – $3,000)		33,000

The balance remaining in the liability account is $3,000: 2 weeks @ $1,500 per week.

This illustration assumes that there was no change in the rate of pay from 20X5 to 20X6 (when the carryover was used) for those employees who had the carryover. If there were rate changes, the pay difference would be debited (if an increase) or credited (if a decrease) to salary expense during 20X6. The change is considered a change in estimate. In practice, many firms would simply recalculate the liability at the next year-end and adjust it through salary expense.

This item is only a liability if a company allows employees to carry over vacation entitlements: many do not, and no liability exists. Most banks, for example, require employees to take all their vacation entitlements before the end of each calendar year; it's important to their internal control systems to have someone else go in and do the employee's job regularly, so that the employee can't hide suspicious transactions indefinitely.

Loans as Current Liabilities

Loans are often long-term, but also frequently current liabilities. These amounts are material, and must be carefully classified. Loans are current liabilities if:

1. *Loans are due on demand.* Demand loans are payable on demand, or after a short delay of 7 to 30 business days to arrange alternate financing. These loans are legally current liabilities, and must be classified as such, even though liquidation within the current year is not expected.

2. *Loans are due within the next year.* If the loan has a due date within the next year, it is a current liability, even if the company expects to renegotiate the loan. If debt is partially due within the next year, the current portion must be reclassified. For example:

Current liabilities:	
Current payment on bond issue	$100,000
Long-term liabilities:	
Bonds payable (less current portion: $100,000)	$400,000

3. *Long-term debt is in violation of covenants and thus can be called by the lender at any time.* For example, a company might be in arrears on interest payments, or has exceeded the maximum debt-to-equity ratio on the balance sheet date. They may not yet have had the opportunity to negotiate with the lender; often all that happens in these circumstances is that the lender increases the interest rate. But the lender could call the loan, and thus the current classification is required.

Short-Term Obligations Expected to Be Refinanced

A company may want to reclassify liabilities from current to long-term to improve its reported working capital position. This reclassification is not to be taken lightly — a large reclassification has a material impact on the financial statements. Intent is not adequate proof! On the other hand, it's common to enter into an agreement to restructure debt, prior to actually doing it. A financing agreement may be relied on to support classification of short-term obligations as long-term debt, if it meets the following criteria:

- The agreement must be non-cancellable by all parties and extend beyond one year from the balance sheet date or from the start of the operating cycle, whichever is longer.
- At the balance sheet date and the issue date, the company must not be in violation of the agreement.
- The lender must be financially capable of honouring the agreement.

If a short-term obligation is to be excluded from current liabilities under a financing agreement, note disclosure is required and should include

- A general description of the financing agreement.
- The terms of any new obligation to be incurred.
- The terms of any equity security to be issued.

Disclosure of Monetary Current Liabilities

Need we say it? Current liabilities are *financial instruments*, and must satisfy disclosure requirements for terms and conditions, interest rate risk, and fair value. Disclosure is most likely required for loans and notes payable, as the circumstances surrounding accounts payable renders disclosure trivial.

FOREIGN CURRENCY RECEIVABLES AND PAYABLES

Early in this chapter, we pointed out that if a company has a bank account in a currency other than Canadian dollars, the cash account on the balance sheet must include the *Canadian dollar equivalent* of that foreign currency. Obviously, we cannot simply add Canadian dollars, U.S. dollars, Hong Kong dollars, and Australian dollars all together to derive the total for cash.

The same principle applies to current receivables and payables. If a company has accounts or notes that are receivable or payable in foreign currencies, they must be restated to the current exchange rate at the balance sheet date.

Monetary items that are denominated in a foreign currency always arise from a transaction, of course. The transaction may be sales to a foreign customer, purchases from a foreign supplier, investments in foreign currency financial instruments, or foreign currency loans from a foreign bank (or from a Canadian bank but in a foreign currency). When the transaction occurs, it is recorded at the exchange rate in effect at the date of the transaction. For example, suppose that Trudeau Ltd. sells some of its product to a customer in England for £10,000 when the exchange rate was £1 = $2.20. The sale would be recorded as follows:

Accounts receivable (£10,000)	22,000	
Sales (£10,000 × $2.20)		22,000

The receivable is stated (or *denominated*) in British pounds sterling, and not in dollars. The sale is recorded at the Canadian dollar equivalent of the British sales price. When the British company pays the account, it will pay £10,000, not $22,000. If payment is made before the end of a fiscal period, the cash receipt must be recorded at the current exchange rate. Suppose that the customer pays the £10,000 when the exchange rate is £1 = $2.10. Trudeau will receive only $21,000 in Canadian currency when it converts the cash. The loss is recognized in the current period's income statement.

Cash (£10,000 × $2.10)	21,000	
Foreign exchange loss	1,000	
Accounts receivable		22,000

If the exchange rate had gone up instead of down, Trudeau Ltd. would record a gain instead of a loss.

The difference between the Canadian equivalent of the receivable and of the cash receipt is charged to a *gain or loss* account; this is a normal part of doing business abroad, and the use of the terms *gain* and *loss* for this routine expense is simply an accounting convention. Companies that do business outside Canada in one or more foreign currencies (which is very common) maintain a regular income statement account entitled *foreign exchange gains and losses* (or *foreign currency gains and losses*). The net balance of the account at the end of each accounting period is reported in the income statement.

Assume that at Trudeau's balance sheet date, the receivable is still outstanding. The receivable must be translated to the then-current exchange rate. If the exchange rate at the balance sheet date is £1 = $2.25, the value of the account receivable will be $22,500 (£10,000 × $2.25). The increase of $500 in the Canadian equivalent of the £10,000 balance would be recorded as follows:

Accounts receivable	500	
Foreign exchange gains and losses		500

It is important to understand that changes in the exchange rate following the initial transaction affects only the monetary balance (receivable or payable). The change in exchange rates *does not affect the amount charged or credited to the nonmonetary account*. In the Trudeau Ltd. example above, the sales account is not affected by the subsequent foreign exchange gain or loss.

Similarly, if inventory or capital assets (such as equipment) are purchased in a foreign currency, changes in the exchange rate between the date of purchase and the date of payment will not affect the originally recorded value of the asset. *Historical cost is determined by the exchange rate at the date of the purchase transaction.* Subsequent gains and losses on the outstanding monetary balance are recognized directly and immediately in the income statement, provided that the balance is classified as current.

If a company has long-term monetary balances that are denominated in a foreign currency, exchange gains and losses on those balances are *not* recognized immediately in the income statement. Instead, the unique Canadian practice is to defer this type of foreign currency gains and losses and to amortize them over the period remaining until maturity. Long-term foreign currency receivables are not common, but long-term foreign currency debt is very common in Canadian enterprises. Therefore, a full discussion of this defer-and-amortize procedure can wait until Chapter 13, Liabilities.

CONCEPT REVIEW

1. What are the major categories of current liabilities?
2. Are all current liabilities also monetary liabilities? Explain.
3. How should monetary items that are denominated in a foreign currency be reported at each balance sheet date?

SUMMARY OF KEY POINTS

1. Cash includes only those items immediately available to pay obligations.
2. The bank reconciliation is an internal control mechanism. The reconciliation of the book balance to the correct cash balance provides the data for end-of-month adjusting entries for cash.
3. Doubtful accounts, cash discounts, and sales returns and allowances represent adjustments to the recorded value of sales and receivables, which are necessary to provide an estimate of net realizable value.
4. Accounts receivable can be used as collateral for a loan to speed up the cash cycle. Alternatively, accounts receivable can be sold to a *factor* to obtain immediate cash. The key accounting issue is whether the transfer of accounts receivable is treated as a sale or loan. When the risks and rewards are transferred and the transferor's obligation can be estimated, the transfer is handled as a sale. Otherwise, it is treated as a loan.

5. Long-term notes are recorded at the present value of all cash payments to be received using the appropriate market rate of interest. Interest is based on that market interest rate and the outstanding principal balance at the beginning of the period. Impaired notes are reduced to present value.

6. Current liabilities are obligations that are payable within one year or within the normal operating cycle, whichever is longer.

7. Current liabilities commonly include accounts, notes, accruals, property taxes, cash dividends, taxes, bonuses, and other payables.

8. Debt is a current liability if it is due on demand, if it is the current portion of long-term debt, or if it is long-term debt in default. Current debt that is to be refinanced as long-term may be reclassified as long-term only if certain specific conditions are met.

9. Transactions that are denominated in a foreign currency are recorded at the exchange rate that exists at the transaction date. Monetary balances (i.e., receivables and payables) are restated to the exchange rate that exists on the balance sheet date. Gains and losses on current balances are recognized in income; gains and losses on long-term monetary balances are deferred and amortized over the remaining period to maturity.

REVIEW PROBLEM

At the end of 20X5, three companies ask you to record journal entries in three different areas associated with receivables. The fiscal year of each company ends on 31 December.

1. *Mandalay Company — uncollectible accounts receivable.* Mandalay Company requests that you record journal entries for its bad debt expense and uncollectible accounts receivable in 20X5. Mandalay's 1 January 20X5 balances relevant to accounts receivable are as follows:

Accounts receivable	$400,000 (dr.)
Allowance for doubtful accounts	20,000 (cr.)

During 20X5, $45,000 of accounts receivable is judged to be uncollectible, and no more effort to collect these accounts will be made. Total sales for 20X5 are $1,200,000, of which $200,000 are cash sales; $900,000 was collected on account during 20X5.

a. Assuming that Mandalay uses the credit sales method to estimate bad debt expense and uses 4% of credit sales as its estimate of bad debts, provide the journal entries to record write-offs and bad debt expense for 20X5. Also, provide the 31 December 20X5 balance sheet amounts for net accounts receivable.

b. Assuming that Mandalay uses the aging method to estimate net accounts receivable and uses 9% of accounts receivable as its estimate of uncollectibles, provide the journal entries to record write-offs and bad debt expense for 20X5. Also, provide the 31 December 20X5 balance sheet amounts for net accounts receivable.

2. *Berkshire Company — assigning accounts receivable.* Berkshire Company requests that you record journal entries for the listed events related to accounts receivable it assigned in 20X5:

On 1 January 20X5, Berkshire sells $45,000 of accounts receivable with recourse to a finance company, on a notification basis. Bad debts are estimated to be $2,500. The financing fee is 10%. Criteria for sales are met.

3. *White Mountain Company — accounting for long-term notes (Appendix):* White Mountain Company requests that you record journal entries for a note it received in 20X5. On 1 April 20X5, White Mountain Company sold merchandise for $12,000 and received a $12,000, three-year, 10% note; 10% was also the current market rate of interest at that time. The note calls for three equal annual payments to be made beginning 31 March 20X6. Provide the first three journal entries for this note.

REVIEW PROBLEM — SOLUTION

1. *Mandalay Company*
   a. *Summary entry for write-offs during 20X5:*

Allowance for doubtful accounts	45,000	
Accounts receivable		45,000

   Adjustment on 31 December 20X5:

Bad debt expense ($1,000,000 × 4%)	40,000	
Allowance for doubtful accounts		40,000

   Balance sheet amounts at 31 December 20X5:

Accounts receivable	$455,000 *
Allowance for doubtful accounts	(15,000) †
Net accounts receivable	$440,000

   * $400,000 + $1,000,000 − $900,000 − $45,000
   † $20,000 − $45,000 + $40,000

   b. *Summary entry for write-offs during 20X5:*

Allowance for doubtful accounts	45,000	
Accounts receivable		45,000

   Adjustment on 31 December 20X5:

Bad debt expense	65,950 *	
Allowance for doubtful accounts		65,950

* Calculation of adjustment:		
Ending gross accounts receivable		$455,000
Required allowance balance ($455,000 × 9%)		$ 40,950
Allowance balance before adjustment for 20X5:		
Beginning balance, 1 January 20X5	$(20,000)	
Write-offs during 20X5	45,000	25,000
Increase necessary to adjust balance		$ 65,950

   Balance sheet amounts at 31 December 20X5:

Accounts receivable	$455,000
Allowance for doubtful accounts	(40,950)
Net accounts receivable	$414,050

2. *Berkshire Company*

Cash ($ 45,000 − $2,500 − (10% × $42,500))	38,250	
Bad debt expense	2,500	
Financing Fee (10% × $42,000)	4,250	
Accounts receivable		45,000

3. *White Mountain Company*
The equal annual payment (A) is computed as follows:
   A = $12,000 ÷ (P/A, 10%, 3) = $4,825

a. *1 April 20X5:*

Note receivable	12,000	
Sales revenue		12,000

b. *31 December 20X5:*

Interest receivable ($12,000 × 10% × 9/12)	900	
Interest revenue		900

c. *31 March 20X6:*

Cash	4,825	
Note receivable		3,625
Interest receivable		900
Interest revenue ($12,000 × 10% × 3/12)		300

CHAPTER 8

APPENDIX

Interest — Concepts of Future and Present Value

TIME VALUE OF MONEY

In general business terms, interest is defined as the cost of using money over time. Economists prefer to say that interest represents the time value of money. For example, $100 in hand today will be worth more in one year's time than a second $100 received one year from today. The assumption is that today's dollars can be put to work earning interest. Thus, today's money has a future value equal to its principal (face amount) plus whatever interest can be earned over the period of time, one year in this case. If the interest rate on money invested for one year is 10%, the future value of today's $100 principal at the end of 12 months is $110 ($100 principal + $10 interest).

The $110 is an amount coming in at the end of 12 months, tomorrow's money, scheduled to be received (or paid) at some future date — in this example, one year. Just as today's money has a future value, calculated by adding interest to principal, tomorrow's money has a present value, calculated by subtracting interest. For example, if the interest rate on money invested for one year is 10%, the present value of $110 a year from now is the principal necessary to invest today to obtain $110 in a year. We already know that this required principal is $100, because $100 + ($100 × .10) yields $110 in one year. Suppose, instead, that $100 is to be received in one year. What is its present value? If the interest rate is again 10%, the present value is the principal needed today to yield $100 in one year at 10%. This principal amount is $91, because $91 plus 10% of $91 gives (approximately) $100 in one year ($91 principal + $9 interest).

Accounting involves many applications of the concepts of present and future value. Some of the more prominent applications covered in this book relate to

- Receivables and payables.
- Bonds.
- Leases.
- Pensions.
- Asset valuation.

The purpose of this appendix is to provide the concepts necessary to facilitate measurement of the time value of money. Many students have covered this topic in depth in a business mathematics or finance course; this appendix is simply a review of the relevant basics.

BASIC INTEREST CONCEPTS

Concept of Interest

Interest is the excess of resources (usually cash) received or paid over and above the amount of resources loaned or borrowed at an earlier date. The amount loaned or borrowed is called the principal. The cost of the excess resources to the borrower is called interest expense. The benefit of the excess resources to the lender is called interest revenue.

To illustrate measurement of interest in a simple situation, assume that the Debont Company borrows $10,000 cash and promises to repay $11,200 one period later. The interest on this contract is $1,200, or 12% of the $10,000 principal amount borrowed.

Interest usually is expressed as a rate per year, such as 12%, although interest is often calculated and accumulated for periods of less than one year, such as monthly, quarterly, or semi-annually. This is called compound interest. Thus, a 12% nominal annual interest rate could be compounded 1% monthly, 3% quarterly, or 6% semi-annually. *If an interest rate is specified with no indication of an interest period less than one year, annual compounding should be assumed.* In the case of compound interest, the interest rate and compounding period must be clearly stated.

The effective total interest is a function of the principal amount, the interest rate, and the number of interest periods. If compounding is more than once a year, then the stated nominal interest rate understates the effective interest rate, which includes compounding effects, as we shall see. For example, a credit card agreement might describe its terms as 24%, compounded (at 2%) monthly. This significantly understates the effective interest rate. The effective interest rate of 2% compounded monthly is really about 26.8%.

Business transactions subject to interest must state whether simple or compound interest is to be calculated. Simple interest is the product of the principal amount multiplied by the period's interest rate (a one-year rate is standard). The equation for computing simple interest is

Interest amount = P × (*i*) × (*n*)
where: P = Principal
             i = Interest rate per period
             n = Number of interest periods

When applied to long-term transactions extending over multiple years, simple interest is based on the principal amount outstanding during the year. If there are no changes caused by repayments or additional borrowing, this will equal the principal outstanding at the beginning of each year. Interest is paid periodically (typically yearly or at the end of the contract) and not added to the principal. Thus, interest is paid only on the initial principal and not on interest accumulated but not yet paid. The yearly interest remains the same. Thus, a three-year $10,000 loan at a rate of 10% simple interest incurs $1,000 of interest per year each year, or $3,000 total interest, assuming that no instalment payments are made on the principal.

Compound interest is based on the principal amount outstanding at the beginning of each interest period, to which accumulated interest from previous periods has been added. In compound interest problems, it is assumed that interest is allowed to accumulate rather than being paid (by the borrower) or withdrawn (by the lender). This means that compound interest includes interest on previously computed and recorded interest. When interest periods of less than one year are used, the annual interest rate given must be converted to an equivalent rate for the time period specified for compounding purposes. To demonstrate, we add quarterly compounding to the interest calculation example. The interest rate is now 10% compounded quarterly, or 2.5% (10% ÷ 4) per quarter. The first year's interest calculations are as follows:

Quarter	Beginning Balance	Compound Interest		Ending Balance
1st	$10,000.00	$ 250.00	($10,000.00 × 2.5%)	$10,250.00
2nd	10,250.00	256.25	($10,250.00 × 2.5%)	10,506.25
3rd	10,506.25	262.66	($10,506.25 × 2.5%)	10,768.91
4th	10,768.91	269.22	($10,768.91 × 2.5%)	11,038.13
Total		$1,038.13		

In the above example, quarterly compounding for the first year produces $1,038.13 of interest, $38.13 more than the $1,000 resulting from annual compounding. Quarterly compounding of a 10% stated or nominal interest rate is equivalent to an effective annual interest rate of 10.38% ($1,038.13 ÷ $10,000). The effective interest rate is the true interest rate. Semi-annual, quarterly, monthly, weekly, and daily compounding are all in common use; the more compounding, the more interest. Even continuous compounding is possible.

For whatever reason, business transactions are usually described in contracts by their nominal annual interest rate and the compounding period.

OVERVIEW OF FUTURE VALUE AND PRESENT VALUE

Future value (FV) and present value (PV) *pertain to compound interest calculations.* Future value involves a current amount that is increased in the future as the result of compound interest accumulation. Present value, in contrast, involves a future amount that is decreased to the present as a result of compound interest discounting.

Think of an investment as an example — since many investments have finite starting and ending points, they are good illustrations of present and future values. *Present value in general refers to dollar values at the starting point of an investment, and future value refers to end-point dollar values.* If the dollar amount to be invested at the start is known, the future value of that amount at the end can be projected, provided the interest rate and number of interest compounding periods are also specified. Similarly, if the dollar amount available at the end of an investment period (future value) is known, the amount of money needed at the start of the investment period (present value) can be determined, again if the interest rate and number of interest compounding periods are known.

Present value and future value apply to interest calculations on both single principal amounts and periodic equal payment (annuity) amounts.

Single Principal Amount

Also known as a lump-sum amount, the single principal amount is based on a one-time-only investment amount that earns compound interest from the start to the end of the investment time frame.

Annuity Amount

An annuity is a series of uniform payments (also called rents) occurring at uniform intervals over a specified investment time frame, with all amounts earning compound interest at the same rate. Annuity amounts may take the form of either cash payments into an annuity type of investment or cash withdrawals from an annuity type of investment. An annuity may be an ordinary annuity (or annuity in arrears), where the payments (or receipts) occur at the *end* of each interest compounding period, or an annuity due, with payments (or receipts) occur at the *beginning* of each interest compounding period.

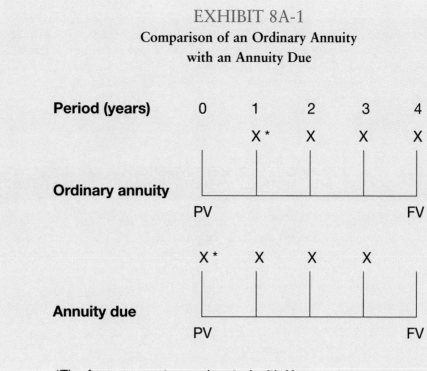

EXHIBIT 8A-1
Comparison of an Ordinary Annuity
with an Annuity Due

*The four payments are denoted with Xs.

The difference between an ordinary annuity and an annuity due is illustrated in Exhibit 8A-1 for a four-year annuity. With an ordinary annuity, *the first payment occurs one period after the present value is established and the last payment coincides with the determination of future value.* For an annuity due, the *first payment coincides with the date the present value is established and the last payment occurs one period before the future value is determined.*

A series of equal payments beginning today — an annuity due — has a greater present value than the same set of payments beginning one year from now — an ordinary annuity. Similarly, a set of payments starting today — an annuity due — discharges a debt with lower payments than the payments required under an ordinary annuity.

Methods to Calculate Present and Future Values
There are four methods used to compute future and present values:

1. Make successive interest calculations.
2. Use a formula.
3. Use tables.
4. Use a financial calculator or personal computer spreadsheet package.

All methods will produce the same results, although rounding will produce minor (immaterial) differences. Most accountants prefer to use a financial calculator or computer spreadsheet, since the result is accurate and the application of the technique is not restricted to the values displayed in the tables. The vast majority of students have possessed calculators from an early age. Most have mathematical calculators with neat things like tangent and cosine functions, but not interest rate functions.

Anyone seriously interested in a career in business, however, should make the small investment necessary for a financial calculator. Besides, it's easier to carry around a calculator than a computer, and for most interest calculations, it's also easier to use!

If you use electronic means, be sure to write down the key variables — interest rate and periods — as you go, to leave a trail. It's also a good idea to check your results for reasonableness; wild answers are produced with the speed of light if you push the wrong buttons!

See the Summary of Compound Interest Tables and Formulae at the back of this Volume.

VALUES OF A SINGLE PAYMENT

Future Value

The *future* value of *present* amount (denoted as F/P) is the future value of a single payment after a specified number of interest periods (n) when increased at a specified compound interest rate (i). For example, the future value of $1 left on deposit for six interest periods at an interest rate of 8% per period (F/P, 8%, 6) is:

$$F/P = (1 + i)^n \qquad\qquad \text{expressed as (F/P, } i, n)$$
$$F/P = (1 + .08)^6$$
$$F/P = 1.587, \text{ or } 1.59 \text{ rounded}$$

The same result can be obtained by using Table I-1, found at the back of this Volume. In the table, first locate the appropriate interest rate column, and then read down the column to the intersecting line representing the number of interest periods involved. The number of interest periods is listed on the left-hand side of the table.

Once the correct future value factor is located, multiply it by the principal amount involved. For example, the future value of $5,000 at 8% for six interest periods is $7,935, or $5,000 × (1.587).

In the tables and formulas, keep an eye on n, the compounding period. It means *periods*, and a period is not necessarily a year. As well, i must correspond to the length of the interest period. For example, 12% compounded annually for five years corresponds to (F/P, 12%, 5), while 12% compounded *quarterly* for five years is (F/P, 3%, 20): i = 12% ÷ 4 quarters per year, and n = 5 years × 4 quarters per year = 20. The results are not the same:

$$\$1 \times (F/P, 12\%, 5) = \$1.762$$
$$\$1 \times (F/P, 3\%, 20) = \$1.806$$

Present Value of 1

The *present* value of a *future* amount (P/F) is the present value of a single payment for a specified number of interest periods (n) at a specific interest rate (i). For example, to find the present value of $5,000 to be received six interest periods from today at 8% (P/F, 8%, 6), use either a financial calculator, the formula to calculate the present value of 1, or Table I-2, found at the back of this Volume. The algebraic formula is as follows:

$$P/F = \frac{1}{(1+i)^n} \qquad\qquad \text{expressed as (P/F, } i, n)$$

$$P/F = \frac{1}{(1+.08)^6} = \frac{1}{1.587}$$

$$P/F = .63017, \text{ or } .63 \text{ rounded}$$

Table I-2 produces the same answer. First locate the 8% interest rate column, and then read down the column to the intersecting line representing the number of interest periods involved, 6, found at the left-hand side of the table.

Then, all that is left is multiplication: the present value of $5,000 at 8% for six interest periods is $3,150.85, or $5,000 × (.63017).

Future Value and Present Value of 1 Compared

Future values and present values of 1 are the same in one respect: they both relate to a single payment. The future value looks forward from present dollars to future dollars. The present value looks back from future dollars to present dollars. Present value and future value, for a given i and n, are reciprocals:

$$F/P = \frac{1}{P/F} \quad and \quad P/F = \frac{1}{F/P}$$

In our example so far, we have determined that:

a. The future value of $1 invested at 8% for six periods is $1.59 (rounded).

b. The present value of $1 discounted at 8% for six periods is $.63.

The reciprocal relationship is as follows:

For (a): 1 ÷ 1.59 = 0.63
For (b): 1 ÷ 0.63 = 1.59

Typical Examples

1. A company buys a machine on 1 January 20X1; the payment terms state that the $40,000 invoice price is not due until the end of 20X2. The going interest rate is 8% compounded annually, but there is no interest added over time; therefore, the conclusion is that part of the $40,000 invoice price is really interest. What is the real cost of the machine? (Interest has to be recorded separately.)

Solution: Cost = $40,000 × (P/F, 8%, 2)
                   = $40,000 × .85734
                   = $34,294
      Interest = $40,000 − $34,294 = <u>$5,706</u>

2. An employee earned $30,000 per year in 20X1, and will retire after another 25 years. If salaries are expected to increase at the rate of 4% per year, how much will the employee be earning after 25 more years? (This information is often needed to calculate pension entitlements.)

Solution: Salary = $30,000 × (F/P, 4%, 25)
                    = $30,000 × 2.666
                    = $79,980

3. A company receives a loan of $32,000 on 1 January 20X2, and will have to repay $41,946 on 31 December 20X5. What is the effective interest rate if interest is compounded annually?

Solution: $32,000 = $41,946 (P/F, i, 4)
         (P/F, i, 4) = $32,000 ÷ $41,946
         (P/F, i, 4) = <u>.76290</u>

The interest rate, i, is found by looking along the 4-year row of Table I-2: the interest rate is 7%.

4. A company wishes to invest $45,811 today so that it will have $100,000 to repay a loan in the future. If interest rates are 10% compounded semi-annually, how long will the investment have to be left in the account?

Solution: $45,811 = $100,000 (P/F, 5%, *n*)
              (P/F, 5%, *n*) = $45,811 ÷ $100,000 = 0.45811

From the 5% interest column of Table I-2, we can find the value of 0.45811, which shows us that the number of semi-annual interest *periods* is 16, which comes to eight years.

In cases 3 and 4, the accuracy of the solution depends on finding the right numerical value in the table. The exact number you are looking for will seldom be there; you must interpolate between the closest two numbers in the table. Since compound interest functions are not linear, the interpolated solution will always be an approximation. The answer? Buy a financial calculator — that will find the exact solution for you very quickly!

VALUES OF AN ANNUITY

Future Value of an Ordinary Annuity

The future value of an ordinary annuity (or annuity *in arrears*) (F/A) is the future value of a series of payments (or receipts) in equal dollar amounts being made over a specified number of equally spaced interest periods (*n*) at a specified interest rate (*i*). Unless otherwise stated, all annuities are assumed to be ordinary annuities, meaning that every payment occurs at the *end* of the interest period. The future value of an ordinary annuity can be determined by compounding each payment separately, and then adding the results, or by adding the interest factors for each number of periods over the entire stream of payments. For example, the future value of an annuity of $1,000 paid at the end of each year for three years, with interest compounding annually at 6% is:

$$\text{Future amount} = \$1,000 \times [(\text{F/P}, 6\%, 2) + (\text{F/P}, 6\%, 1) + 1]$$
$$= \$1,000 \times [1.124 + 1.06 + 1]$$
$$= \$1,000 \times 3.184$$
$$= \underline{\$3,184}$$

The first payment (at the *end* of year 1) accumulates interest for two years, the second payment accumulates interest for one year, and the final payment earns no interest because it is made at the end of the three-year period.

To avoid the necessity of accumulating the individual periodic interest factors, interest tables provide the cumulative compound factor. These are shown in Table I-3, found at the back of this Volume. In Table I-3, the value for three periods at 6% is 3.18360, the same as that derived above. Therefore, the future amount of the stream of $1,000 payments can be determined directly from Table I-3:

$$\text{Future amount} = \$1,000 \times (\text{F/A}, 6\%, 3) = \$1,000 \times 3.1836 = \underline{\$3,183.60}$$

The same F/A factor could be obtained by formula, which is shown at the top of the table.

Present Value of an Ordinary Annuity

The present value of an ordinary annuity (P/A) is today's equivalent dollar amount of a series of payments (or receipts) made over a predetermined time frame. The present value of an ordinary annuity can be determined using a formula or an appropriate

EXHIBIT 8A-2
Comparison of Future Value of an Ordinary Annuity with an Annuity Due

(F/A, 10%, 3) versus (F/AD, 10%, 3)

Future value of an ordinary annuity (F/A) — payment at the *end* of each annuity period (Table I-3, found at the back of this Volume).

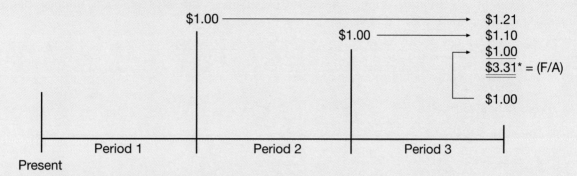

Future value of an annuity due (F/AD) — payment at the *beginning* of each annuity period (Table I-5, found at the back of this Volume).

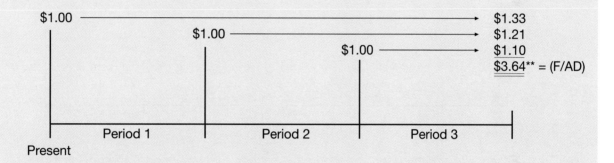

*The first payment is compounded for two periods, the second payment for one period, and the third payment for none because the payment is at the *end* of the period.
**The first payment is compounded for three periods, the second payment for two periods, and the third payment for one period.

table (Table I-4). To find the present value of an ordinary annuity of $5,000 invested at 8% for six interest periods (P/A, 8%, 6) using Table I-4 is $23,114.40, or $5,000 × 4.62288.

The present value of an annuity is also the sum of the present values of the individual payments. For example, the present value (P/A, 8%, 6), which was just determined to be 4.62288, is the sum of the first six entries in the 8% column of Table I-2.

Future Value of an Annuity Due
The best way to understand an annuity due is to compare its cash flows with those of an ordinary annuity. Exhibit 8A-2 shows two time lines that compare the future value of an ordinary annuity (F/A) of 1 with the future value of an annuity due (F/AD) of 1 for the same interest rate and annuity period.

The future value of the ordinary annuity illustrated in Exhibit 8A-2 involves three payments but only two interest periods. The annuity due involves three payments and three interest periods. For each of the three values illustrated in the last column of

EXHIBIT 8A-3

Comparison of Present Value of an Ordinary Annuity
with an Annuity Due

(P/A, 10%, 3) versus (P/AD, 10%, 3)

Present value of an ordinary annuity (P/A) — payment at the *end* of each annuity period (Table I-4, found at the back of this Volume).

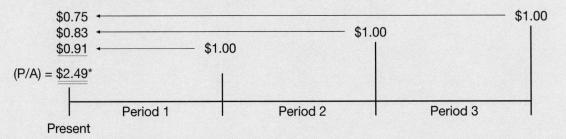

Present value of an annuity due (P/AD) — payment at the *beginning* of each annuity period (Table I-6, found at the back of this Volume).

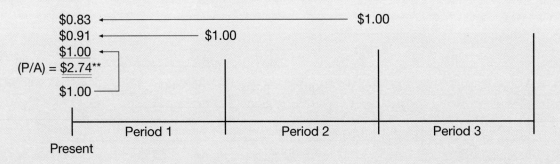

*The first payment is discounted for one period, the second for two periods, and the third for three periods.

**The first payment is not discounted because there is no lapse of time. The second payment is discounted for one period and the third for two periods.

Exhibit 8A-2, F/A × (1 + *i*) = F/AD. This relationship means that if the F/A is known, it can be multiplied by (1 + *i*) to determine the F/AD value for the same *i* and *n*.

$$(F/AD, 10\%, 3) = 3.641 \text{ or}$$
$$(F/A, 10\%, 3)(1 + .10) = 3.31(1.10) = 3.641$$

Table I-5 gives the values for the future value of an annuity due. The algebraic formula is shown at the top of the table.

Present Value of an Annuity Due

Exhibit 8A-3 shows two time lines that compare the present value of an ordinary annuity (P/A) with the present value of an annuity due (P/AD) of 1 for the same interest rate and number of payments.

The present value of the ordinary annuity illustrated in Exhibit 8A-4 involves three payments and three discounting periods. The annuity due involves three payment periods but only two discounting periods. The annuity due is discounted for one less period than the ordinary annuity, so the ordinary annuity amount is less than the corresponding annuity due amount by a factor of $1 \div (1 + i)$; therefore, P/A $\times$ $(1 + i)$ = P/AD. This relationship means that a known P/A value can be multiplied by $(1 + i)$ to yield its corresponding P/AD value. More conveniently, Table I-6, found at the back of this Volume, gives the values for the present value of an annuity due.

Financial calculators give the option of automatically computing an annuity as either an ordinary annuity or an annuity due. They also permit rapid calculation when the unknown quantity in the equation is the amount of the annuity payments, that is, when i is known, n is known, and the desired present value (or future value) is known.

Underlying Assumptions for Annuities

It is important to bear in mind that there are several assumptions underlying the use of annuity calculations:

- the amount of each payment is the same throughout the entire stream of annuity payments;
- the payments are equally spaced (e.g., monthly, quarterly, or annually);
- the interest rate is stable; and
- the periods used for compounding interest coincide with the payment periods (e.g., annual payments *and* annual compounding rather than semi-annual compounding).

If any of these conditions does not exist, then a more labourious calculation is required.

Typical Examples

1. A lease agreement is structured so that it requires a payment of $6,000 every quarter for four years, with the first payment due at the beginning of the first quarter. The interest rate is 8%, compounded quarterly. What is the present value of the payment steam? (This will be capitalized if the lease is a capital lease.)

Solution: Present value = $6,000 $\times$ (P/AD, 2%, 16) = $6,000 $\times$ 13.84926
= $83,096

2. Assume the same lease as in (1), except that payments are due at the end of each quarter.

Solution: Present value = $6,000 $\times$ (P/A, 2%, 16) = $6,000 $\times$ 13.57771
= $81,466

3. A company is required to place $10,000 in a bank account every six months for 10 years; the bank account pays 4% interest, compounded semi-annually. How much will be in the bank account after 10 years if the payments are made at the end of each six-month period?

Solution: Balance = $10,000 $\times$ (F/A, 2%, 20) = $10,000 $\times$ 24.297
= $242,970

4. Repeat example (3), except assume that payments are made at the beginning of each six-month period.

Solution: Balance = $10,000 $\times$ (F/AD, 2%, 20) = $10,000 $\times$ 24.78332
= $247,830

5. A company borrows $56,000 on 1 January 20X1, and is required to make end-of-year payments for eight years. Interest of 8% is compounded annually; what is the payment?

EXHIBIT 8A-4
Cash Flows for Explo Co. Example

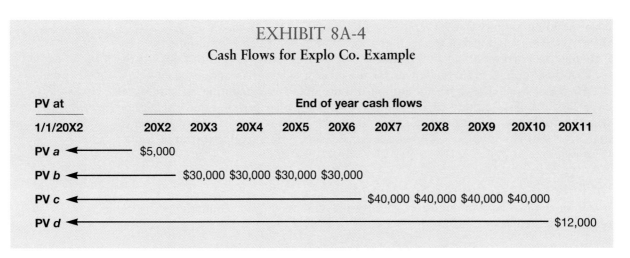

PV at	End of year cash flows									
1/1/20X2	20X2	20X3	20X4	20X5	20X6	20X7	20X8	20X9	20X10	20X11
PV *a* ←	$5,000									
PV *b* ←		$30,000	$30,000	$30,000	$30,000					
PV *c* ←							$40,000	$40,000	$40,000	$40,000
PV *d* ←										$12,000

Solution: The present value (**P**) of the payments must be $56,000 at 8% interest. The annual payments (represented as **A**) is the unknown in the equation:

$$P = \$56{,}000$$
$$\$56{,}000 = A \times (P/A,\ 8\%,\ 8)$$
$$A = \$56{,}000 \div (P/A,\ 8\%,\ 8) = \$56{,}000 \div 5.74664 = \$9{,}745$$

6. A company borrows $100,000 on 1 January 20X1 and is required to make quarterly payments of $6,258 at the beginning of each quarter for five years. What is the interest rate?

Solution: $\$100{,}000 = \$6{,}258 \times (P/AD,\ i,\ 20);$
                   $(P/AD,\ i,\ 20) = \$100{,}000 \div \$6{,}258 = 15.979$

Using Table I-6 along the 20-year line, 2 ½% per quarter, or 10%, compounded quarterly.

Using Multiple Present and Future Values

Some transactions require application of two or more future or present value amounts. These more complex problems require careful analysis. Two cases are given below to illustrate the application of multiple future and present values.

Case A. Deferred Annuity. A deferred annuity occurs in two phases: (1) capital is invested over a period to accumulate maximum interest compounding and principal growth and (2) the principal is paid out in uniform amounts until the total accumulated principal is exhausted. Investment during the accumulation phase may be in the form of either periodic payments or a lump-sum payment at the beginning. During the second phase, while withdrawals are being distributed to the annuitant, the remaining principal continues to earn interest.

To illustrate, assume that on 1 January 20X1, Fox Company invests in a $100,000 deferred annuity for the benefit of an employee, George Golf, who was injured while at work. The terms call for Fox Company to make an immediate $100,000 lump-sum payment, which will earn interest at 11% for four years (the capital accumulation phase of the annuity). Then, beginning on 1 January 20X5, when George Golf retires, the total amount of the annuity will be paid to him in five equal annual instalment payments.

First, the fund grows at 11% for four years. At that time, the fund will equal

$$\$100{,}000(F/P,\ 11\%,\ 4) = \$100{,}000(1.518) = \underline{\$151{,}800}$$

Second, the fund is used in total to pay Golf a five-year annuity beginning 1 January 20X5. The fund is assumed to continue to earn 11% until the last payment is made. The fund will be used up by the payments, so

Annuity × (P/AD, 11%, 5)   = $151,800
Annuity × 4.10245   = $151,800
Annuity = $151,800 ÷ 4.10245 = $ 37,002

Case B. Annuity and Lump Sum. Explo Company is negotiating to purchase four acres of land containing a gravel deposit that is suitable for development. Explo Company has completed a survey that provides the following reliable estimates:

Expected net cash revenues over life of resource:
    End of 20X2 $ 5,000
    End of 20X3 to 20X6 (per year)   30,000
    End of 20X7 to 20X10 (per year)   40,000
    End of 20X11 (last year — resource exhausted)   10,000
Estimated sales value of four acres after exhaustion of gravel,
    net of land restoration costs (end of 20X11)   2,000

What is the maximum amount Explo Company could offer on 1 January 20X2 for the land, assuming that Explo requires a 12% after-tax return on the investment? We will assume that all amounts are measured at year-end and that the above amounts are net of income taxes.

This case requires computation of the present value of the future expected cash inflows. The amount that the company would be willing to pay is the sum of the present values of the net future cash inflows for the various years. The calculation is complex because both single payments and annuities are involved. Because equal but different future cash inflows are expected for years 2 to 5 and years 6 to 9, two annuities must be calculated. Because the cash inflows are assumed to be received at year-end, the annuities are ordinary. The cash flows are depicted graphically in Exhibit 8A-4.

This case is best solved in several steps in which the cash flows are separated into single payments and annuities and each expressed in present value terms. Thus:

1. $5,000 × (P/F, 12%, 1) = $5,000 × .89286 = $ 4,464
2. $30,000 × (P/A, 12%, 4) × (P/F, 12%, 1)
    = $30,000 × 3.03735 × .89286 =   81,358
3. $40,000 × (P/A, 12%, 4) × (P/F, 12%, 5)
    = $40,000 × 3.03735 × .56743 =   68,939
4. ($10,000 + $2,000) × (P/F, 12%, 10) = $12,000 × .32197 =   3,864
                                                                 $158,625

Explo should offer no more than $158,625 for the properties.

Note that the present value of the annuity shown in equation (2) is first calculated as of 31 December 20X2, as $30,000 × (P/A, 12%, 4). It is then discounted for one period using (P/F, 12%, 1). The present value of the annuity shown in equation (3) is first calculated as of 31 December 20X6, as $40,000(P/A, 12%, 4) and is then discounted to 31 December 20X1, using the value for (P/F, 12%, 5). There are several other approaches to manipulating table values to provide this result — all result in the same answer and are perfectly acceptable.

SUMMARY OF KEY POINTS

1. The compounding of interest is a function of the interest rate *per period* and the number of periods.

2. Annual interest rates are usually stated as the *nominal* interest rate, which is the interest rate per period multiplied by the number of periods in a year; the nominal rate understates the *effective* annual interest rate.

3. The factor for determining the present value of a future amount is the reciprocal of the factor for finding the future value of a present amount.

4. A series of *equal* periodic payments is known as an *annuity*.

5. To use an annuity interest factor, the number of payments must correspond with the number of interest periods. If some interest periods have no payment, then an annuity factor cannot be used.

6. When the annuity payments are made at the *end* of each period, the annuity is called an *ordinary annuity* or an *annuity in arrears*.

7. When annuity payments are made at the *beginning* of each period, the annuity is an *annuity due*.

8. Unless specifically stated otherwise, annuities are assumed to be ordinary annuities (i.e., with equal payments at the *end* of each period).

9. The relationship between the factor for an ordinary annuity and the factor for an annuity due is one period's interest.

10. The present or future value of a series of payments cannot be calculated by using an annuity interest factor if the payments are not equal in amount, equally spaced, or correspond to the interest periods. Instead, the present or future value of each payment must be calculated individually. Computer spreadsheet programs can be a big help in such calculations.

QUESTIONS

8-1   Define cash as it is used for accounting purposes. What is a cash equivalent?

8-2   ABC Company has U.S. $160,000 in a U.S. bank account. They received the money from a customer, for a cash sale, when the exchange rate was U.S. $1 = $1.30 Cdn. At year-end, the exchange rate is U.S. $1 = $1.35 Cdn. At what amount is the sale recorded? Cash, on the end-of-year balance sheet?

8-3   Why is internal control over cash so important? What are its major components?

8-4   Briefly explain the basic purposes of a bank reconciliation. Who should perform the reconciliation?

8-5   Define the following terms related to accounting for cash: (a) deposits in transit, (b) cheques outstanding, (c) NSF cheque, and (d) service charge.

8-6   At the end of an accounting period, a company has $4,000,000 recorded in accounts receivable, all for sales. It's likely that the company won't collect all of the $4,000,000, even though all the sales really took place. What are three reasons why collections might not equal $4,000,000?

8-7   Briefly describe the different methods of estimating bad debt expense and the allowance for doubtful accounts for trade receivables.

8-8   It sometimes happens that a receivable that has been written off as uncollectible is subsequently collected. Describe the accounting procedures in such an event.

8-9   Under what circumstances should the direct write-off method for bad debts be used?

8-10   A company has a credit balance of $600 in its allowance for doubtful accounts. The amount of credit sales for the period is $80,000, and the balance in accounts receivable is $15,000. Assume that the bad debt estimates are as follows: (a) related to accounts receivable, 9%, and (b) related to credit sales, 0.5%. What will be the balance of the allowance for doubtful accounts and the bad debt expense, if (a) the credit sales method and (b) the aging method were used?

8-11   Describe several different ways a company could speed cash flow associated with accounts receivable.

8-12   A company with $200,000 in receivables could sell them for $169,000 without recourse, or for $195,000 with recourse. What do the terms "with recourse" and "without recourse" mean? Why is the "without recourse" alternative more expensive? How would each alternative be recognized?

8-13   A company sold accounts receivable of $10,000 for $8,500, with recourse. Estimated obligations due to the with-recourse provision amounted to $700. Give the required entry, assuming that the transaction is recorded as (a) a loan and (b) a sale. What conditions attached to a recourse arrangement would make it likely that the transaction would be recorded as a sale? as a loan?

8-14   Why is a note receivable sometimes preferred to an account receivable?

8-15   How is a note receivable valued if it is (a) a no-interest note and (b) a low-interest note. Assume in all cases that the note had a term of two years. How would your answer change if the note had a term of two months?

8-16   Compute the present value of a $10,000, one-year note payable that specifies no interest, although 10% would be a realistic rate. What is the true amount of the principal and the interest?

8-17   Distinguish between the stated rate of interest and the market rate of interest (yield).

8-18   Assume that $4,000 cash is borrowed on a $4,000, 10%, one-year note payable that is interest-bearing and that another $4,000 cash is borrowed on a $4,400 one-year note that is non-interest-bearing. For each note, give the following: (a) face amount of the note, (b) principal amount, (c) maturity amount, and (d) total interest paid.

8-19   Define a current liability.

8-20   Are dividends on preferred shares a liability? Explain.

8-21   What is a compensated absence? When should the expense related to compensated absences be recognized?

8-22   A company has a short-term bank loan outstanding, due on demand. The loan has been outstanding for several years, and will not be repaid in the coming year. Can it be classified as a long-term loan?

8-23   A company has an account receivable from a U.S. customer, for U.S. $100,000. They also have a payable to another U.S. company, a supplier, in the amount of U.S. $75,000. The payable was incurred when the exchange rate was U.S. $1 = Cdn. $1.40; the receivable, when the rate was $1.35. At year-end, the rate is $1.38. What amount of total exchange gain or loss will the company report for the year? Can the receivable and payable be offset in the financial statements?

CASE 8-1

New Horizon Ltd.

Safe Haven Ltd. was incorporated in 20X3, with common shares owned equally by the three principals: Christine Mullaly, Rick Bui, and John Scaravelli. Previously, these three engineers held positions in the research group of a large public plastics company. Safe Haven was formed to develop, produce, and sell a process that would render various types of packaging "tamperproof," a booming market.

Mullaly, Bui and Scaravelli had been working on this concept for their previous employer. However, when the project was shelved, the three decided to go ahead with it on their own. They agreed to pay their previous employer a royalty of 3% of sales in exchange for the use of research done to date, and left in 20X3 with their employer's blessing and promises of their old jobs back if "things did not work out."

The year 20X3 was spent developing the process to the point where it was technologically and economically viable. By February 20X4, Safe Haven's operations were well under way. A co-ordinated marketing effort and careful recruitment of sales representatives, as well as a little help from their previous employer, resulted in good manufacturer acceptance of the line. Safe Haven dealt mostly with small manufacturers.

Since every application was unique, the machinery and process was customer tailored to each manufacturer's needs. This turned out to be easier than anticipated, although Safe Haven had to provide engineering support for the first month or two of production to iron out any problems that developed.

From the beginning, the firm's accounting and related clerical activities were supervised by John Noble, a recent B. Comm. graduate with a background in accounting. Initially, attention was directed toward controlling cash, establishing cost records, and implementing a cost control system. Orders from customers were accepted after reference to a credit rating service.

It is now the end of 20X4, and various accounting policies have to be established before the 20X4 statements can be prepared. The principals wish to pick policies they will not have to change later, especially if they are successful in their ultimate goal of taking the company public.

They have asked John Noble to evaluate the alternatives for recording bad debt expense: direct write-off, setting up a percentage of sales, or aging the receivables and/or attempting some provision based on percentages or specific identification.

At present, the principals prefer the direct write-off method. It seems to them to be the only one based on objective, real events. They point out that there is no history on which to base a percentage for either percentage of sales or an aging method. Specific identification makes them uncomfortable, as they point out that if a particular firm were not creditworthy, they never should have accepted the sale.

Required:

Adopt the role of John Noble and write a brief report evaluating the alternative policies for calculating bad debt expense.

CASE 8–2

New Design Limited

New Design Limited (NDL) is a jewellery wholesaler that plans to sign an agreement with Canadian Financial Co. in which Canadian will commit to purchase up to $10 million of NDL foreign customer accounts receivable. Under the terms of the agreement, Canadian receives the rights to all collections on the accounts sold, directly from the customer. All these customer accounts are for export sales, and all receivables are denominated in Canadian dollars. Two options are being considered:

Option 1

1. Canadian purchases accounts from NDL within six days of the transaction. Only transactions that are EDC-guaranteed are eligible. EDC is the Canadian federal government's Export Development Corporation, which guarantees collection of accounts receivable with specific foreign countries or companies, as long as there are no legal deficiencies in them. For example, if the customer claimed that they did not receive all the goods, or that the goods received were not those ordered, EDC insurance would not be available. However, if the buyer could simply not pay, EDC insurance would be effective.

2. NDL receives, from Canadian, cash equal to the face value of the receivable, less a financing charge, based on the term of the receivable. There is no bad debt allowance because of the EDC guarantee.

   This agreement would cover approximately $6 million of the total $10 million foreign receivables of NDL; the remainder are not EDC-insured (due to country of origin or identity of specific customer) and would not be eligible. EDC insurance has to be purchased by NDL and is based on country and company risk.

Option 2

All foreign receivables are eligible for this option, which has the following key features:

- NDL is responsible for all bad debts. NDL has been in business for more than 50 years and is able to accurately forecast bad debt losses. Thus, its liability under this recourse provision can be reasonably estimated.

- Accounts are transferred to Canadian at the beginning of each month. This date is called the settlement date.

- Interest on the outstanding amount is determined monthly. The interest rate charged will change regularly based on prime interest rates and risk of the portfolio.

- NDL can be required to repurchase receivables if there are legal deficiencies in them. See the above discussion for an explanation of legal deficiencies.

- NDL may repurchase the receivables on the first settlement date subsequent to transfer of the receivables (i.e., monthly) if NDL and Canadian cannot agree on an interest rate for purposes of calculating the monthly payment (principal less interest) that Canadian pays to NDL. This repurchase option must be exercised within one week of the settlement date.

- NDL has the right to repurchase the receivables when the balances fall to a low level. The repurchase price will be the total forecasted collections less the actual collections to date.

Joe Basinger, the VP finance for NDL, has asked you, the company's independent auditor, how each option would be accounted for. He's aware that some sales of accounts receivable are treated as loans, while others are treated as sales, and he needs to know which treatment is appropriate.

The first option is more expensive for the company and involves a lower dollar value of receivables than the second option. He knows that another alternative is to arrange a loan secured by accounts receivable, and he's wondering if this arrangement would be any different on the balance sheet. He's particularly concerned about the key debt-to-total-assets ratio that is the subject of a loan covenant.

Required:
Respond to the request.

EXERCISES

E8-1 *Define Cash:* Maze Company is preparing its 20X5 financial statements; the accounting period ends 31 December. The following items, related to cash, are under consideration. You have been asked to indicate how each item should be reported on the balance sheet and to explain the basis for your responses.

a. A $900 cheque received from a customer, dated 1 February 20X6, is on hand.

b. A customer's cheque was included in the 20 December deposit. It was returned by the bank stamped NSF. No entry has yet been made by Maze to reflect the return.

c. A $20,000 three-month term deposit. $400 of interest accrued to 31 December has just been recorded by debiting interest receivable and crediting interest revenue. The chief accountant proposes to report the $20,400 as part of cash on the balance sheet.

d. Maze has a $200 petty cash fund. This is cash held in a strong box for miscellaneous disbursements.

e. Postage stamps that cost $30 are in the cash strong box.

f. A money order of $200 payable to Maze Company is in the cash drawer; it is dated 29 December.

g. Three cheques, dated 31 December 20X5, totalling $465, payable to vendors who have sold merchandise to Maze Company on account, were not mailed by 31 December 20X5. They have not been entered as payments in the cheque register and ledger.

h. Maze has two chequing accounts: one with a balance of $76,000, and another with a different bank that has an overdraft of $600. The company plans to show the two balances net, since they could easily pay off the overdraft with available cash.

E8-2 *Bank Reconciliation:* Reconciliation of Crabtree Company's bank account at 31 May was as follows:

Balance from bank statement	$5,250
Deposits in transit	750
Cheques outstanding	(75)
Correct cash balance, 31 May	$5,925

Balance from books	$5,932
Bank service charge	(7)
Correct cash balance, 31 May	$5,925

June transactions

	Bank	Books
Cheques recorded	$5,750	$5,900
Deposits recorded	4,050	4,500
Service charges recorded	6	—
Collection by bank ($1,000 note plus interest)	1,050	—
NSF cheque returned with 30 June statement (will be redeposited; assumed to be good)	25	—
Balances, 30 June	4,569	4,525

Required:

1. Compute deposits in transit and cheques outstanding at 30 June by comparing bank and books for deposits and cheques.

2. Prepare a bank reconciliation for June.

3. Give any journal entries that should be made based on the June bank reconciliation.

E8-3 *Bank Reconciliation:* Jones Company shows the following 30 June bank statement:

Statement Summary:

Balance 1 June	$23,000
Deposits	11,600
Cheques	(12,120)
Interest earned	100
Ending balance, 30 June	$22,580

Deposits and cheques:

Deposits		Cheques			
1 June	$ 2,000	2 June #61	$1,000	17 June #65	$ 400
8 June	3,000	7 June #63	2,000	23 June #60	1,100
17 June	4,500	9 June #66	3,000	27 June #67	2,100
22 June	2,100	14 June #64	1,420	28 June #59	1,100
Total	$11,600				$12,120

Transactions recorded in the cash account in the general ledger:

Balance 1 June	$23,900
Cheques	(13,220)
Deposits	12,300

Deposits and cheques:

Deposits			Cheques		
		60	$1,100	65	$ 400
June 8	$3,000	61	1,000	66	3,000
June 17	4,500	62	900	67	2,100
June 22	2,100	63	2,000	68	1,300
June 30	2,700	64	1,420		

The bank reconciliation at 31 May showed the following items:
Bank balance, $23,000, add deposit outstanding, $2,000,
Deduct cheque #59 outstanding, $1,100,
Book balance, $23,900.

Required:

Prepare the June bank reconciliation and give any entries required.

E8-4 *Receivables and Payables — Corrections:* During the annual audit of Coil Corporation, you encountered the following account with a debit balance of $127,400, entitled "receivables and payables":

Items	Debit	Credit
Due from customers	$156,000	
Payables to creditors for merchandise		$62,000
Note receivable, long-term	80,000	
Expected cumulative losses on bad debts		4,000
Due from employees, current	2,200	
Cash dividends payable		24,000
Note receivable, past due*	22,000	
Accrued wages		4,000
Insurance premiums paid in advance	1,200	
Mortgage payable, long-term		40,000
Balance (debit)		127,400

* Collection probable in two years.

Required:

1. Give the journal entry to eliminate the above account and set up the appropriate accounts to replace it.
2. Show how the various items should be reported on a balance sheet.

E8-5 *Net Accounts Receivable:* At 31 December 20X5, Master Company reported gross accounts receivable of $8,560,000. Investigation showed the following:

a. Terms of 1/10, n/30 were granted to all customers. Accounts receivable were recorded gross, and the discounts taken were recorded when taken by the customers in a discounts account, reported contra to the sales account. Estimated discounts inherent in the closing accounts receivable balance were $45,660. The allowance for sales discounts account was established at $32,900 last year, and has not been adjusted since.

b. Customers are permitted to return 10% of annual sales for full credit, as long as goods are returned in good condition within 60 days of delivery. Based on past years experience, $67,200 of goods might be returned. As returns are received during the year, the sales returns account, a contra account to sales, is increased. An allowance for sales returns exists, at $77,800, unchanged from the previous year-end.

c. The credit balance in the allowance for doubtful accounts of the Master Company was $40,000. The provision (expense) for doubtful accounts is based on a percentage of net credit sales. Total sales revenue for 20X5 amounted to $150 million, of which one-sixth was on credit. Based on the latest available facts, the 20X5 provision needed for doubtful accounts is estimated to be one-fourth of 1% of credit sales.

Required:

1. Prepare year-end adjusting entries with respect to accounts receivable.

2. How would the accounts receivable appear on the balance sheet on 31 December 20X5?

E8-6 *Alternatives for Estimation — Allowance for Doubtful Accounts:* At 31 December 20X5, the end of the annual reporting period, the accounts of Bader Company showed the following:

a. Sales revenue for 20X5, $360,000, of which one-sixth was on credit.

b. Allowance for doubtful accounts, balance 1 January 20X5, $1,800 credit.

c. Accounts receivable, balance 31 December 20X5 (prior to any write-offs of uncollectible accounts during 20X5), $36,100.

d. Uncollectible accounts to be written off, 31 December 20X5, $2,100. These accounts are all in the "past due over 90 days category".

e. Aging schedule at 31 December 20X5, showing the following breakdown of accounts receivable:

Status	Amount
Not past due	$20,000
Past due 1 – 60 days	8,000
Past due over 60 days	6,000
Past due over 90 days	2,100

Required:

1. Give the 20X5 entry to write off the uncollectible accounts.

2. Give the 20X5 adjusting entry to record bad debt expense for each of the following independent assumptions concerning bad debt loss rates:

   a. On credit sales, 1.5%.

   b. On total receivables at year-end, 2.5%.

   c. On aging schedule: not past due, 0.5%; past due 1–60 days, 1%; and past due over 60 days, 8%.

3. Show what would be reported on the 20X5 balance sheet relating to accounts receivable for each assumption.

E8-7 *Accounts Receivable and Bad Debts:* Given below is the history of a sale on credit by Airport Company to J. Doe.

a. 24 December 20X1 — Sold merchandise to J. Doe, $2,000, terms 2/10, n/30.

b. 2 January 20X2 — Doe paid half of the receivable and was allowed the discount.

c. 31 December 20X4 — Because of the disappearance of Doe, Airport Company wrote Doe's account off as uncollectible.

d. 31 December 20X6 — Doe reappeared and paid the debt in full, plus 6% annual interest (not compounded, compute annually).

Required:

Give the entry(s) that Airport Company should make at each of the above dates. Record the receivable initially at its gross amount.

E8-8 *Sale of Accounts Receivable:* On 1 April 20X5, DOS Company transferred $20,000 of accounts receivable to PS2 Finance Company to obtain immediate cash. There was no allowance for doubtful accounts set up on DOS's books in relation to the $20,000.

Required:

1. The financial agreement specified a price of $16,000 on a without-recourse, notification basis. Give the entry(s) that DOS Company should make. The $4,000 reduction from face value represents a $2,000 financing fee and $2,000 of expected bad debts. Explain the basis for your response.

2. The financial agreement specified a price of $17,000 on a with-recourse, notification basis. The $3,000 reduction from face value is related to expected bad debts, $1,300, and a $1,700 financing fee. Give the entry(s) that DOS should make. Criteria for recording the transaction as a sale are not met.

3. Explain the difference to the balance sheet between (1) versus (2).

E8-9 *Sale of Accounts Receivable — Sale or Loan?* The following two cases are independent.

Case A. Appa Apparel manufactures fine sportswear for many national retailers and frequently sells its receivables to financing companies as a means of accelerating cash collections. Appa transferred $100,000 of receivables from retailers to a financing company. The receivables were transferred without recourse on a notification basis. The financing company charged 13% of the receivables total.

Required:

1. Should Appa record the transfer of receivables as a sale or as a loan? Why?

2. Record all entries related to the transfer for Appa.

Case B. Bappa Apparel manufactures fine sportswear for many national retailers and frequently sells its receivables to financing companies as a means of accelerating cash collections. Bappa transferred $100,000 of receivables from retailers to a financing company. The receivables were transferred with recourse on a notification basis. The financing company charged 11%. Bappa has no obligation to the financing company other than to pay the account of a retailer in the event of a default. However, Bappa is unable to estimate the amount of sold accounts that will be uncollectible.

Required:

1. Should Bappa record the transfer of receivables as a sale or as a loan? Why?
2. Record Bappa's entries related to the transfer.
3. How would your answer change if the uncollectible amount could be perfectly estimated on the date of transfer?

E8-10 *Note Receivable:* The following cases are independent. For each case

1. Give all entries related to the transactions. The company uses the gross method to account for accounts and notes receivable.
2. Show the items that will be reported on the 20X5 income statement and balance sheet.

Case A. On 15 April 20X5, Welsch Company sold merchandise to Customer Rodriguez for $18,000, terms 2/10, n/EOM (i.e., end of month). Because of nonpayment by Rodriguez, Welsch received an $18,000, 15%, 12-month note on 1 May 20X5. The annual reporting period ends 31 December. Customer Rodriguez paid the note in full on its maturity date.

Case B. On 1 May 20X5, Darby Company sold merchandise to Customer Domo and received a $26,400 (face amount), one-year, non-interest-bearing note. The going (i.e., market) rate of interest is 10%. The annual reporting period for Darby Company ends on 31 December. Customer Domo paid the note in full on its maturity date.

E8-11 *Note Receivable:* Wilma Company sells large construction equipment. On 1 January 20X5, the company sold Cather Company a machine at a quoted price of $30,000. Wilma collected $10,000 cash and received a note payable for the balance.

Required:

1. Give Wilma's required entries for the two years, assuming an interest-bearing note, face value $20,000. (10% interest, simple interest payable each 31 December.)
2. Assume that the market interest rate is still 10%. Give Wilma's required entries for the two years, assuming a 2% interest-bearing note, face value $20,000. Prepare the entries based on
   a. net basis.
   b. gross basis.
3. Compare the interest revenue and sales revenue under (1) and (2).

E8-12 *Non-interest-bearing and Low-interest Notes:*

a. On 1 January 20X5, a heavy-duty truck was purchased with a list price of $35,500. Payment included $5,500 cash and a two-year, non-interest-bearing note of $30,000 (maturity date, 31 December 20X6). A realistic interest rate for this level of risk is 12%.

b. On 1 January 20X5, a small truck was purchased and payment was made as follows: cash, $5,000, and a two-year, 6%, interest-bearing note of $15,000, maturity date 31 December 20X6. A realistic interest rate for this level of risk is 12%.

Required:

Give all entries for each case from purchase date through maturity date of each note. Disregard depreciation. Round to the nearest dollar. Use the net method to record the note. The accounting period ends on 31 December.

E8-13 *Analysis and Comparison of Notes:* On 1 September 20X5, Dyer Company borrowed cash on a $100,000 note payable due in one year. That is, Dyer agreed to repay $100,000 in one year, plus interest if specified in the loan contract. Assume the going rate of interest was 12% per year for this particular level of risk. The accounting period ends 31 December.

Required:

Complete the following tabulation; round to the nearest dollar:

	Assuming the Note Was	
	Interest-Bearing	Non-interest-Bearing
1. Cash received	$	$
2. Cash paid at maturity date	$	$
3. Total interest paid (cash)	$	$
4. Interest expense in 20X5	$	$
5. Interest expense in 20X6	$	$
6. Amount of liabilities reported on 20X5 balance sheet:		
Note payable (net)	$	$
Interest payable	$	$
7. Principal amount	$	$
8. Face amount	$	$
9. Maturity value	$	$
10. Stated interest rate	%	%
11. Yield or effective interest rate	%	%

E8-14 *Entries to Record Payroll and Related Deductions:* Ryan Company incurred monthly salaries amounting to $120,000. CPP deductions were $3,200 and EI deductions were $3,460. Income taxes withheld were $38,000, and $1,200 was withheld for union dues under the collective agreement.

Required:

Give entries to record

1. salary payment and liabilities for the deductions,
2. employer payroll expenses, and
3. remittance of the taxes and deductions.

E8-15 *Compensated Absences:* Tunacliff Mowers allows each employee to earn 15 fully-paid vacation days each year. Unused vacation time can be carried over to the next year; if not taken during the next year, it is lost. By the end of 20X5, all but 3 of the 30 employees had taken their earned vacation time; these three carried over to 20X6 a total of 20 vacation days, which represented 20X5 salary of $6,000. During 20X6, each of these three used their 20X5 vacation carryover; none of them had received a pay rate change from 20X5 to the time they used their carryover. Total cash wages paid: 20X5, $700,000; 20X6, $740,000.

Required:

1. Give all of the entries for Tunacliff related to vacations during 20X5 and 20X6. Disregard payroll taxes.
2. Compute the total amount of wage expense for 20X5 and 20X6. How would the vacation time carried over from 20X5 affect the 20X5 balance sheet?

E8-16 *Foreign Exchange:* Hare Limited had the following transactions in 20X5:

a. Sold goods on 1 June to a British company for 35,000 pounds sterling with payment to be in four months time.
b. Bought goods from a U.S. supplier on 15 June for U.S. $75,000; payment was due in one month's time.
c. Bought goods from a British supplier on 15 July for 10,000 pounds sterling; settlement was to be in two month's time.
d. Paid the U.S. supplier on 15 July.
e. Paid the British supplier on 15 September.
f. Received payment from the British customer on 1 October 20X6.

Exchange rates:

	Canadian Equivalencies	
	Pounds	**U.S. $**
1 June 20X5	2.10	1.36
15 June 20X5	2.18	1.40
15 July 20X5	2.12	1.46
15 September 20X6	2.19	1.42
1 October 20X6	2.16	1.45

Required:
Prepare journal entries for the above transactions.

E8-17 *Cash Flow Statement:* Selected accounts from the Finch Company balance sheet at 31 December:

FINCH COMPANY
Balance Sheets
31 December 20X5

	20X5	**20X4**
Cash	$172,000	$110,000
Receivables, net	150,000	170,000
Marketable securities	140,000	190,000
Inventory	575,000	498,000
Current liabilities	193,000	186,000
Bank overdraft	130,000	168,000

Other information:

a. Net income for the year was $59,100
b. There was a bad debt expense of $27,500 for the year. The allowance of doubtful accounts was $34,500 at the end of 20X5, and had been $24,600 at the end of 20X4.

c. Marketable securities were short-term interest-bearing securities, considered to be cash equivalents.

Required:

1. Calculate the opening and closing cash figure that would appear on the cash flow statement.

2. Calculate cash from operations for the year based on the information given, using the indirect method of presentation.

[CGA-Canada, adapted]

PROBLEMS

P8-1 *Classification of Balances:* For each of the items listed in below, identify the correct balance sheet classification by using one of the following classifications:

Cash
Short-term cash equivalents
Investments (specify long- or short-term)
Accounts receivable, trade
Contra account to accounts receivable
Other accounts receivable
Accounts payable, trade
Other accounts payable
Other (identify)

The first item is completed for you.

Item	Classification
1. Chequing account	Cash
2. Allowance for sales returns	
3. Accounts receivable — officers (current collection expected)	
4. Accounts payable for merchandise	
5. Savings account	
6. Rare coins kept for long-term speculation	
7. Accounts receivable — customers	
8. Post-dated cheques received	
9. Allowance for doubtful accounts	
10. Expense advances to salespersons	
11. Treasury bills purchased when two months remain in term	
12. Compensating balance for a short-term loan	
13. Short-term loan payable	
14. Sinking fund to retire a bond in five years	
15. Canada Savings Bond (ten-year term; immediately liquid)	
16. Short-term investment in marketable equity securities	
17. Debit balances in supplier accounts	
18. Unpaid salaries	
19. Credit balances in customer accounts	

Required:

Classify the above accounts, as indicated.

P8-2 *Bank Reconciliation:* It is 31 March and Fry Company is ready to prepare its March bank reconciliation. The following information is available:

a. *Company cash account*

1 March balance	$ 28,350 dr.
Cheques	53,000 cr.
Deposits	51,468 dr.

b. *Bank statement, 31 March:*

Balance, 1 March	$30,800
Deposits	51,198
Cheques cleared	(54,118)
NSF cheque (Customer Zinny)	(100)
Collected account receivable on Fry Company's behalf	1,680
Interest on bank balance	36
Bank service charge	(14)
Balance, 31 March	$ 29,482

c. *Additional information:*
   (1) The company overstated one of its cash sales deposits by $20; the bank recorded it correctly.
   (2) The bank cleared a $178 cheque as $187; the error has not been corrected by the bank.
   (3) End of February: deposits in transit, $1,550; cheques outstanding, $4,000.

Required:

1. Based on the data given above, compute the deposits in transit and cheques outstanding at 31 March.
2. Prepare a bank reconciliation as at 31 March.
3. Give all journal entries that should be made based on your bank reconciliation.

P8-3 *Bank Reconciliation:* Ample Company carries its chequing account with Commerce Bank. The company is ready to prepare its 31 December bank reconciliation. The following information is available:

a. *The 30 November bank reconciliation showed the following:*
   (1) cash on hand (held back each day by Ample Company for change), $400 (included in Ample's Cash account);
   (2) deposit in transit, #51, $2,000; and
   (3) cheques outstanding, #121, $1,000; #130, $2,000; and #142, $3,000.

b. *Ample Company cash account for December*

Balance, 1 December	$ 64,000
Deposits: #52 – #55, $186,500; #56, $3,500	190,000
Cheques: #143 – #176, $191,000; #177, $2,500; #178, $3,000; and #179, $1,500	(198,000)
Balance, 31 December (includes $400 cash held for change)	$ 56,000

c. *Bank statement, 31 December*

Balance, 1 December	$ 67,600
Deposits: #51 – #55	188,500
Cheques: #130, $2,000; #142, $3,000; #143 – #176, $191,000	(196,000)
Account receivable collected for Ample Co.	6,720
Cash received from foreign customer: prepayment on order; not yet recorded by Ample Co.	10,000
NSF cheque, Customer Belinda	(200)

United Fund (automatic charitable donation per transfer authorization signed by Ample Co.)		(50)
Bank service charges		(20)
Balance, 31 December		$ 76,550

Required:

1. Identify by number and dollars the 31 December deposits in transit and cheques outstanding.

2. Prepare the 31 December bank reconciliation.

3. Give all journal entries that should be made at 31 December, based on your bank reconciliation.

P8-4 *Cash and Receivables — Multiple Choice:* Choose the correct statement among the alternatives for each question.

1. The following information pertains to Deekers, a men's clothier, at 31 December 20X5:

Bank statement balance	$ 20,000
Chequebook balance	28,000
Deposits in transit	10,000
Outstanding cheques	2,000

   In Deekers' 31 December 20X5 balance sheet, at what amount should cash be reported?
   a. $18,000.
   b. $20,000.
   c. $28,000.
   d. $30,000.

2. When the allowance method of recognizing doubtful accounts is used, the entries to record collection of a small account previously written off would

   a. Increase the allowance for doubtful accounts.
   b. Increase net income.
   c. Decrease the allowance for doubtful accounts.
   d. Have no effect on the allowance for doubtful accounts.

3. Roundtree Company, a manufacturer of natural foods, reported credit sales of $2,300,000 in 20X5. Roundtree also reported the following balances:

	31 Dec. 20X4	31 Dec. 20X5
Accounts receivable	$500,000	$650,000
Allowance for doubtful accounts	(30,000)	(55,000)

   Roundtree wrote off $10,000 of accounts during 20X5.
   Cash collected in 20X5 was
   a. $2,450,000.
   b. $2,175,000.
   c. $2,150,000.
   d. $2,140,000.

4. Brynn Company, a computer servicing company, reported $80,000 of gross cash sales (on which there were $4,000 of actual returns and allowances) and $120,000 of gross credit sales (on which $6,000 of cash discounts were taken) in 20X5. The beginning and ending balances of accounts receivable in 20X5 were $40,000 and $30,000, respectively. Brynn uses the direct write-off method for bad debts and recorded $6,000 of bad debts in 20X5.

How much total cash did Brynn collect in 20X5?
a. $200,000.
b. $194,000.
c. $170,000.
d. $76,000.

[AICPA adapted]

P8-5 *Recognizing Cash Discounts:* The annual reports of the following two companies provided information about cash discounts:

1. K&V Manufacturing:
   Income statement

Sales	$65,438,800
Sales discounts	865,432

   Balance sheet
   Current assets:

Accounts receivable, less allowance of $297,000 for doubtful accounts and sales discounts	$16,938,624

2. GenCo, Inc.:
   Income statement

Sales	$167,435,890
Finance revenue; discounts lost	1,576,320

   Balance sheet

Accounts receivable	$ 61,781,000
Allowance for bad debts	(3,173,000)
Net receivables	$ 58,608,000

Required:

1. Briefly comment on which method (gross versus net) you believe was used to account for cash discounts by these two companies. Assume they offered similar credit and payment terms.
2. How would an allowance for cash discounts be measured?

P8-6 *Estimating Bad Debt Expense:* The accounts of Long Company provided the following 20X5 information at 31 December 20X5 (end of the annual period):

Accounts receivable balance, 1 January 20X5	$ 51,000
Allowance for doubtful accounts balance, 1 January 20X5	3,000
Total sales revenue during 20X5 (on credit)	160,000
Uncollectible account to be written off during 20X5 (ex-customer Slo)	1,000
Cash collected on accounts receivable during 20X5	170,000

Estimates of bad debt losses
   a. Based on credit sales, 1%.
   b. Based on ending balance of accounts receivable, 8%.
   c. Based on aging schedule (excludes SPO's account):

Age	Accounts Receivable	Probability of Noncollection
Less than 30 days	$28,000	2%
31 – 90 days	7,000	10
91 – 120 days	3,000	30
More than 120 days	2,000	60

Required:

1. Give the entry to write off customer Slo's long-overdue account.
2. Give all entries related to accounts receivable and the allowance account for the following three cases:

   Case A — Bad debt expense is based on credit sales.
   Case B — Bad debt expense is based on the ending balance of accounts receivable.
   Case C — Bad debt expense is based on aging.

3. Show how the results of applying each case above should be reported on the 20X5 income statement and balance sheet.
4. Briefly explain and evaluate each of the three methods used in Cases A, B, and C.
5. On 1 August 20X6, customer Slo paid his long-overdue account in full. Give the required entries.

P8-7 *Cash Flow and Doubtful Accounts:* Excerpts from AMI's 20X1 income statement and statement of cash flows and from its 20X1 and 20X0 comparative balance sheets follow:

	20X1	20X0
	($ millions)	
Income statement:		
Revenues	$10,818.4	$10,662.5
Balance sheet:		
Current assets:		
Receivables, less allowance for uncollectibles		
of $124.6 and $134.7, respectively	$ 1,981.7	$ 1,824.2
Statement of cash flows:		
Cash flows from operating activities:		
Net income	$ 1,165.5	$ 1,253.8
Add back non-cash expenses: Bad debts	165.0	121.0

Required:

Answer the following questions assuming that (a) AMI uses the allowance method to estimate bad debts (provision for uncollectibles) and (b) all revenues are credit sales.

1. Are estimated uncollectible accounts increasing or decreasing as a percentage of revenues?
2. How much were net write-offs of accounts receivable during 20X1?
3. How much cash was collected on receivables during 20X1?
4. Why is the provision for uncollectibles added to net income in the operating section of the statement of cash flows, and why was the amount of cash collections from receivables not disclosed in the annual report?

P8-8 *Receivable Financing — Sale or Loan?* The following situations involve transactions that should be classified as either a sale or a loan:

a. Sherman Company pledges $400,000 of accounts receivable as collateral for a loan (notification basis). Interest is charged on the monthly outstanding loan balance, and a 2% finance fee is charged immediately on the accounts assigned.

b. Hopper Company factors $50,000 of accounts receivable on a non-recourse basis. The finance company charges an 8% fee and withholds 10% to cover sales adjustments. The finance company obtains title to the receivables and assumes collection responsibilities.

c. Pineapple Company sells $40,000 of accounts receivable on a recourse basis. Pineapple assumes the cost of all sales adjustments. The receivables are part of a much larger group of receivables. Pineapple's business is stable, and sales adjustments are readily estimable. Pineapple is compelled under the financing agreement to reimburse the finance company for any losses due to default by original customers.

d. Helms Company sells $80,000 of accounts receivable on a recourse basis. At the finance company's option, if it appears that the receivables are not collected as quickly as expected, Helms must repurchase the receivables.

e. Gilbert Company sells on a non-recourse basis a $20,000 note received in a sale.

f. Franklin Company sells on a recourse basis a $10,000 note received in a sale. The only provision of the financing agreement is that Franklin must reimburse the bank in the event of default by the original maker of the note.

g. Puget Company sells on a recourse basis a $30,000 note received in a sale. The bank allows repurchase of discounted notes at face value for a small fee.

h. Bellingham Company sells on a non-recourse basis a $35,000 note received in a sale. The bank can compel Bellingham to repurchase the note if the maker's current ratio falls below 2.3 within five months of the note's due date.

i. Pobedy Company pledges all of its accounts receivable as collateral for a loan. Pobedy must use the proceeds from the accounts receivable to service the loan. Pobedy retains title to the receivables. In the event of default by Pobedy on the loan, the finance company has a claim against any of these receivables for payment of the loan.

Required:

1. For each of the preceding situations, explain whether the financing of the receivables should be recorded as a sale or a loan.

2. Explain the impact that the sale versus loan policy decision will have on the financial statements.

P8-9 *Overview of Notes Payable:* On 1 October 20X5, Reed Travel Company purchased computer equipment. They paid $10,000 cash and signed a two-year note payable, with a face value of $40,000, due on 30 September 20X7. The going rate of interest for this level of risk was 10%. The accounting period ends on 31 December.

Required:

1. Compute the cost of the computer equipment assuming:

   Case A — a 10% interest-bearing note. Interest is due each 30 September.
   Case B — a non-interest-bearing note.
   Case C — a 2% interest-bearing note. Interest is due each 30 September.

2. Give entries for each case from 1 October 20X5, through maturity date (assume that reversing entries were not made). Use the net method to record the note, and disregard amortization on the computer equipment.

3. Complete a tabulation as follows:

	Case A	**Case B**	**Case C**
a. Principal amount			
b. Amount received			
c. Stated interest rate			
d. Effective interest rate			
e. Cash interest paid, total			
f. Principal less amount received			
g. Interest expense, total			
h. Amount of liabilities reported			
on the 20X5 balance sheet			
on the 20X6 balance sheet			
on the 20X7 balance sheet			

P8-10 *Impairment; Change in Present Value:* On 1 January 20X5, Robertson Inc. sold merchandise (cost, $8,000; sales value, $14,000) to Russell, Inc., and received a non-interest-bearing note in return. The note requires $17,636 to be paid in a lump sum on 31 December 20X7.

On 1 January 20X6, Russell requested that the terms of the loan be modified as follows: $7,000 to be paid in five years (at the end of 20X10), balance due in six years (at the end of 20X11). Robertson refused Russell's request.

During 20X6, however, news of Russell's deteriorating financial condition prompted Robertson to reevaluate the collectibility of the note. Consequently, the modified terms requested by Russell were used to estimate the future cash flows to be received, as of 31 December 20X6.

Required:

1. Prepare the entry to record the sale by Robertson, assuming a perpetual inventory system. Also prepare the 31 December 20X5 adjusting entry. Use the net method.

2. Prepare the entry to record the impairment on 31 December 20X6. Compare the book value of the note at 31 December to the present value of the newly acknowledged cash flow stream. Assume that no interest revenue is accrued in 20X6.

3. Prepare the entry to record interest revenue at 31 December 20X7.

P8-11 *Multiple Choice — Liabilities:* Choose the correct statement among the alternatives for each question.

1. Bloy Company pays all salaried employees on a biweekly basis. Overtime pay, however, is paid in the next biweekly period. Bloy accrues salaries expense only at its 31 December year-end. Data relating to salaries earned in December 20X5 are as follows:

   - Last payroll was paid on 26 December 20X5, for the two-week period ended on that day.
   - Overtime pay earned in the two-week period ended 26 December 20X5, was $4,200.
   - Remaining workdays in 20X5 were 29, 30, and 31 of December, on which days there was no overtime.
   - The recurring biweekly salaries total $75,000.

   Assuming a five-day workweek, Bloy should record a liability at 31 December 20X5, for accrued salaries of
   a. $22,500.
   b. $26,700.
   c. $45,000.
   d. $49,200.

2. On 1 September 20X4, Pine Company issued a note payable to National Bank in the amount of $1,800,000, bearing interest at 12%, and payable in three equal annual principal payments of $600,000. On this date, the bank's prime rate was 11%. The first interest and principal payment was made on 1 September 20X5. At 31 December 20X5, Pine should record accrued interest payable of
   a. $44,000.
   b. $48,000.
   c. $66,000.
   d. $72,000.

3. Pam, Inc., has $1,000,000 of notes payable due 15 June 20X6. At the financial statement date of 31 December 20X5, Pam signed an agreement to borrow up to $1,000,000 to refinance the notes payable on a long-term basis. The financing agreement called for borrowings not to exceed 80% of the value of the collateral Pam was providing. At the date of issue of the 31 December 20X5, financial statements, the value of the collateral was $1,200,000 and was not expected to fall below this amount during 20X6. In its 31 December 20X5, balance sheet, Pam should classify notes payable as

	Short-Term Obligations	Long-Term Obligations
a.	$ 0	$1,000,000
b.	$ 40,000	$ 960,000
c.	$ 200,000	$ 800,000
d.	$1,000,000	$ 0

4. A province requires quarterly sales tax returns to be filed with the sales tax department by the 20th day following the end of the calendar quarter. However, the province further requires that sales taxes collected be remitted to the sales tax department by the 20th day of the month following any month such collections exceed $500. These payments can be taken as credits on the quarterly sales tax return.

   Taft Corporation operates a retail hardware store. All items are sold subject to a 6% provincial sales tax, which Taft collects and records as sales revenue. The sales taxes paid by Taft are charged against sales revenue. Taft pays the sales taxes when they are due.

   Following is a monthly summary appearing in Taft's first-quarter 20X5 sales revenue account:

	Debit	Credit
January	$ —	$10,600
February	600	7,420
March	—	9,540
	$600	$27,560

   In its financial statements for the quarter ended 31 March 20x5, Taft's correct sales revenue and sales taxes payable would be:

	Sales Revenue	Sales Taxes Payable
a.	$27,560	$1,560
b.	$26,960	$ 600
c.	$26,000	$1,560
d.	$26,000	$ 960

5. The following information relating to compensated absences was available from Graf Company's accounting records at 31 December 20X5:

   • Employees' rights to vacation pay vest and are attributable to services already rendered. Payment is probable, and Graf's obligation was reasonably estimated at $110,000.
   • Employees' rights to sick pay benefits do not vest but accumulate for possible future use. The rights are attributable to services already rendered, and the total sick pay rights accumulated was reasonably estimated at $50,000.

   What amount is Graf required to report as the liability for compensated absences in its 31 December 20X5 balance sheet?
   a. $160,000.
   b. $110,000.
   c. $ 50,000.
   d. $ 0.

6. Ruhl Company grants all employees two weeks' paid vacation for each full year of employment, up to six weeks. Unused vacation time can be accumulated and carried forward to succeeding years and will be paid at the salaries in effect when vacations are taken or when employment is terminated. There was no employee turnover in 20X5. Additional information relating to the year ended 31 December 20X5, is as follows:

Liability for accumulated vacations at 31 December 20X4	$25,000
Pre-20X5 accrued vacations taken from 1 January 20X5	
to 30 September 20X5, (the authorized period for vacations)	15,000
Vacations earned for work in 20X5 (adjusted to current rates)	20,000

Ruhl granted a 10% salary increase to all employees on 1 October 20X5, its annual salary increase date. For the year ended 31 December 20X5, Ruhl should report vacation pay expense of
- a. $21,000.
- b. $22,500.
- c. $30,000.
- d. $35,000.

P8-12 *Recording and Reporting Transactions:* The following selected transactions of Mattingly Company were completed during the accounting year just ended, 31 December 20X5:

a. Merchandise was purchased on account; a $10,000, one-year, 16% interest-bearing note, dated 1 April 20X5, was given to the creditor. Assume a perpetual inventory system.

b. A customer paid for merchandise on 1 February 20X5, with a two-year, $16,000, 3% note. The going interest rate for this term and risk was 15%. Cost of goods sold was $8,320.

c. A supplier delivered goods, and the price was U.S. $13,580. The Canadian dollar was worth U.S. $0.725 on this day.

d. On July 1, the company borrowed $25,000 in cash from the bank on a demand basis. The interest rate was 15%, to be paid on the anniversary date of the loan.

e. Payroll records showed the following:

Employee					**Employer**	
Gross Wages	Income Tax	EI	CPP	Union Dues	EI	CPP
$50,000	$15,000	$3,100	$2,900	$500	$4,340	$2,900

f. Remittances were income tax, $14,350; EI, $7,250; CPP, $5,720; union dues, $480.

g. The company sold goods to a foreign customer and charged U.S. $23,790. On this day, the Canadian dollar was worth U.S. $0.714. Cost of goods sold was $11,110.

h. Cash dividends declared but not yet paid were $14,000.

i Accrued appropriate interest at 31 December, and adjusted foreign-denominated receivables and payables to the year-end rate, Cdn. $1 = U.S. $0.713.

Required:

1. Give the entry or entries for each of the above transactions and events.

2. Prepare a list (title and amount) of the balance sheet receivables and payables at 31 December 20X5.

P8-13 *Time Value Of Money (Appendix):* Each of the following cases is independent:

a. Julie Able has $25,000 in a fund that earns 10% annual compound interest. If she desires to withdraw it in five equal annual amounts, starting today (i.e., beginning of period), how much would she receive each year?

b. Julie will deposit $250 each semi-annual period starting today (i.e., beginning of period); this savings account will earn 6% compounded each semi-annual period. What will be the balance in Julie's savings account at the end of year 10?

c. Julie purchased a new automobile that cost $14,000. She received a $4,000 trade-in allowance for her old auto and signed a 16% note for $10,000. The note requires eight equal quarterly payments starting at the end of the first quarter from date of purchase. What is the amount of each payment?

d. Julie deposited $2,000 at the end of each year in a savings account for five years at compound interest. The fund had a balance of $12,456 at the date of the last deposit. What rate of interest did she earn?

e. On 1 January, Julie owed a debt of $15,131.14. An agreement was reached that she would pay the debt plus compound interest in 24 monthly instalments of $800, the first payment to be made at the end of January. What rate of annual interest is she paying?

P8-14 *Time Value Of Money (Appendix):* Compute each of the following amounts. Each case is independent. Round to the nearest dollar or percentage.

a. On 1 January 20X4, Marcon Corporation borrowed $120,000 from The Canadian Bank. Repayment is to be in six equal annual instalments, including both principal and interest. Compounding is annual. Calculate the annual payment for
    1. 31 December payment, 10% annual interest $ _____
    2. 31 December payment, 6% annual interest $ _____
    3. 1 January payment, 10% annual interest $ _____
    4. 1 January payment, 6% annual interest $ _____

b. On 1 January 20X3, Marcon Corporation borrowed $40,000 from The Canadian Bank. Repayment is to be made in equal annual instalments, including both principal and interest. Compounding is annual.

    Calculate the implicit interest rate associated with:
    1. 31 December payment of $10,856, 6 payments   _____
    2. 1 January payment of $5,323, 10 payments   _____

    Calculate the number of payments needed for:
    1. 31 December payment of $4,074, 8% rate   _____
    2. 1 January payment of $4,936, 10% rate   _____

    [CGA-Canada, adapted]

P8-15 *Time Value Of Money (Appendix):* It is 1 January 20X4, and Terry Corporation is about to borrow $100,000 from The Canadian Bank. The loan will be repaid in five equal instalments, including both principal and compound interest at 10%; interest is compounded annually. Round calculations to the nearest dollar.

Required:

1. Compute the annual loan payment that would be made if (1) the first payment is made on 1 January 20X4 or (2) the first payment is made on 31 December 20X4.

2. Prepare a debt amortization schedule for each alternative, as follows:

Date	Beginning Principal	Instalment Payment Interest	Instalment Payment Principal	Ending Principal

[CGA-Canada, adapted]

P8-16 *Time Value Of Money (Appendix):* Compute each of the following amounts. Each case is independent. Round to the nearest dollar.

a. On 1 January 20X3, Dardon Corporation signs a contract agreeing to pay $40,000 on 31 December 20X5. What is the present value of the payment, assuming each of the following:

1. Annual compounding, 8% annual interest   _____
2. Semi-annual compounding, 8% annual interest   _____
3. Quarterly compounding, 8% annual interest   _____

b. On 1 January 20x3, Dardon Corporation agrees to pay Servicon Corporation $4,000 per year for five years in exchange for the right to use a patented process. Calculate the present value of the payment stream, assuming the following:

1. Payments each 1 January, 12% annual interest, annual compounding, $
2. Payments each 1 January, 12% annual interest, semi-annual compounding $
3. Payments each 31 December, 12% annual interest, annual compounding $
4. Payments each 31 December, 12% annual interest, semi-annual compounding $

c. On 1 January 20X4, Dardon Corporation agrees to pay Canadian Finance Co., as follows:

31 December 20x4	$ 6,000
31 December 20x5	$ 6,000
31 December 20x6	$ 6,000
31 December 20x7	$ 6,000
31 December 20x8	$106,000

Canadian Finance Co. advances the present value of this payment stream to Dardon Corporation on 1 January 20X4; the present value of the payment stream is the principal amount of the loan, while the rest is interest. Complete the following table:

	Present Value Principal	Present Value Interest
1. 6% annual interest, annual compounding	$_____	$_____
2. 8% annual interest, annual compounding	$_____	$_____
3. 4% annual interest, annual compounding	$_____	$_____
4. 6% annual interest, semi-annual compounding	$_____	$_____
5. 8% annual interest, semi-annual compounding	$_____	$_____

d. On 1 January 20X4, Dardon Corporation agrees to lease a machine, with the following terms required by the lease contract:

31 December 20X4 – 20X8, per year	$40,000
31 December 20X9 – 20X13, per year	$20,000
31 December 20X14	$10,000
31 December 20X15	$ 5,000

What is the present value of the payment stream, assuming

1. 6% annual interest, annual compounding $_____
2. 16% annual interest, annual compounding $_____

[CGA-Canada, adapted]

P8-17 *Time Value Of Money (Appendix):* For each of the independent cases given below, assume that the interest rate is 12% and that compounding is semi-annual.

1. How much will accumulate by the end of eight years if $3,000 is deposited each semi-annual interest period in a savings account (a) at the end of each period and (b) at the start of each period? Verify your answers by calculating the answer to (a) with your answer to (b).

2. What will be the periodic payments each period on a $67,000 debt that is to be paid in semi-annual instalments over a six-year period, assuming compound interest, if payments are made (a) at the beginning of each period and (b) at the end of each period?

3. A special machine is purchased that had a list price of $45,000. Payment in full is $9,000 cash immediately and five equal semi-annual payments of $6,000 each. The first payment will be made at the end of the first semi-annual period from purchase date. How much should be recorded in the accounts as the cost of the machine?

4. A special investment is being contemplated. This investment will produce an estimated end-of-period cash income of $26,000 semi-annually for five years. At the end of its productive life, the investment will have an estimated recovery value of $4,500. Determine a reasonable estimate of the present value of the investment.

P8-18 *Time Value of Money (Appendix):* Compute each of the following amounts. Each situation is independent of the others. Round to the nearest dollar or percent.

1. On 1 January 20X1, $30,000 is deposited in a fund at 16% compound interest. At the end of 20X5, what will the fund balance be, assuming
    a. Annual compounding?
    b. Semi-annual compounding?
    c. Quarterly compounding?

2. On 1 January 20X1, a machine is purchased at an invoice price of $20,000. The full purchase price is to be paid at the end of 20X5. Assuming 12% compound interest, what did the machine cost if compounding is
    a. Annual?
    b. Semi-annual?
    c. Quarterly?

3. If $6,000 is deposited in a fund now and will increase to $12,798 in 13 years, what is the implicit compound interest rate?

4. If the present value of $15,000 is $5,864 at 11% compound annual discount, what is the number of periods?

5. On 1 January 20X1, a company decided to establish a fund by making 10 equal annual deposits of $6,000, starting on 31 December. The fund will be increased by 9% compounded interest. What will be the fund balance at the end of 20X10 (i.e., immediately after the last deposit)?

6. On 1 January 20X1, a company decided to establish a fund by making 10 equal annual deposits of $9,000, starting on 1 January. The fund will be increased by 7% compound interest. What will be the balance in the fund at the end of 20X10?

7. John Day is at retirement and has a large amount of ready cash. He wants to deposit enough cash in a fund to receive back $40,000 each 31 December for the next five years, starting on 31 December of this year. Assuming 10% compound interest, how much cash must Day deposit on 1 January?

8. Ace Company is considering the purchase of a unique asset on 1 January 20X1. The asset will earn $8,000 net cash inflow each 1 January for five years, starting 1 January 20X1. At the end of 20X5, the asset will have no value. Assuming a 14% compound interest rate, what should Ace be willing to pay for this unique asset on 1 January 20X1?

9. In January 20X1, Bigbay Company decided to build a fund to equal $552,026 in seven years by making seven equal annual deposits of $60,000, starting on 31 December 20X1. What is the implicit compound interest rate for this fund? Interpolate if necessary.

10. The present value of several future equal annual cash payments at year-end of $30,000 each is $141,366, assuming 11% compound interest. What is the implicit number of cash payments?

11. Mike Moe will retire 10 years from now and wants to establish a fund now that will pay him $30,000 cash at the end of each of the first five years after retirement. Specific dates are: date of a single deposit by Mike, 1 January 20X1; date of first cash payment from the fund to Moe, 31 December 20X11. The fund will pay 10% compound interest. How much cash must Mike deposit on 1 January 20X1, to provide the five equal annual year-end cash payments from the fund?

CHAPTER 9

Inventories

INTRODUCTION

Inventories are an important asset to most businesses and typically represent the largest current asset of manufacturing and retail firms. In today's competitive economic climate, inventory accounting methods and management practices have become profit-enhancing tools. Better inventory systems can increase profitability; poorly conceived systems can drain profits and put a business at a competitive disadvantage.

Inventory effects on profits are more noticeable when business activity fluctuates. During prosperous times, sales are high and inventory moves quickly from purchase to sale. But when economic conditions decline, sales levels retreat, inventories accumulate and may be sold at a loss. Management must monitor inventory types and levels continuously if profits are to be maintained.

In many companies, inventories are a significant portion not only of current assets but also of total assets. Inventory should be considered a "high-risk" asset. There are lots of examples of fraud perpetrated through inventory schemes — creating fictitious inventory to boost assets, and so on. For example, in March 1998, Philip Services Corp. took a $92.2 million charge for unrecorded copper inventory trading losses, plus $32.9 million for other "errors" in copper inventory, the result of "an elaborate scheme to hide trading losses of $184 million in its copper operations."[1] Many banks insist on audits mainly to pin down the inventory figure for clients with lines of credit that are secured by inventory and receivables.

This chapter covers the various accounting methods used to value and report inventories on the balance sheet and simultaneously measure the cost of goods sold required to determine income. We will begin with a discussion of the types of inventory that may exist (including those of manufacturing companies, resource companies, and service companies) and the types of costs that are included in inventory. Then we review the basic cost flow assumptions, including the popular average cost and first-in, first-out methods. A brief discussion of other costing methods is also included in this chapter, such as standard cost and just-in-time methods.

Most inventories are carried at historical cost, although certain types may be reported at market values. Even inventory carried at historical cost may be written down, however, if its recoverable value falls below its recorded carrying value. Therefore, the application of LCM (lower of cost or market) valuation will be examined.

Finally, the chapter reviews inventory estimation methods. Inventory amounts often must be estimated, particularly for interim statements and as a check on the reasonableness of physical inventory counts — to test for possible "missing" inventory, for example.

---

[1] "Philip Reveals Rogue Trading," *The Globe and Mail*, 6 March 1998, p. B1.

INVENTORY CATEGORIES

Inventories consist of costs that have been incurred in an earnings process that are held as an asset until the earnings process is complete. We typically think of inventories as tangible goods and materials such as raw materials, work in process, finished goods, or merchandise held by retailers. But depending on the nature of the company's business, inventory may include a wider range of costs incurred and held in an inventory account for matching against revenue that will be recognized later.

For example, professional service firms such as a software development company or a law firm may accumulate the costs of fulfilling a particular contract as "inventory" until the contract has been substantially completed and the criteria for revenue recognition have been met. Even in companies that deal with physical goods, "inventory" is likely to consist more of intangible costs such as labour and overhead than of the costs of tangible materials.

The term *inventory*, therefore, must be viewed more broadly than simply the cost of goods purchased for resale. Indeed, mercantile business (i.e., retailing and wholesaling) accounts for only about 15% of the Canadian economy.

Items that may be capital assets to one company may be inventory to another. Machinery and equipment, for example, are considered capital assets by the company that buys them, but before sale they are part of the inventory of the manufacturer who made them. Even a building, during its construction period, is an inventory item for the builder.

The major classifications of inventories depend on the operations of the business. A wholesale or retail trading entity acquires merchandise for resale. A manufacturing entity acquires raw materials and component parts, manufactures finished products, and then sells them. A service company has no raw materials or finished goods but does have work in progress. Inventories are classified as follows:

1. *Merchandise inventory.* Goods on hand purchased by a retailer or a trading company such as an importer or exporter for resale. Generally, goods acquired for resale are not physically altered by the purchaser company; the goods are in finished form when they leave the manufacturer's plant. In some instances, however, parts are acquired and then further assembled into finished products. A bicycle dealer may assemble bicycles from frames, wheels, gears, and so on, prior to selling them at retail, for example.

2. *Production inventory.* The combined inventories of a manufacturing or resource entity, consisting of

   a. *Raw materials inventory.* Tangible goods purchased or obtained in other ways (e.g., by mining) and on hand for direct use in the manufacture or further processing of goods for resale. Parts or subassemblies manufactured before use are sometimes classified as *component parts inventory.*

   b. *Work-in-process inventory.* Goods or natural resources requiring further processing before completion and sale. Work-in-process inventory includes the cost of direct material and direct labour incurred to date, and usually some allocation of overhead costs.

   c. *Finished goods inventory.* Manufactured or fully processed items completed and held for sale. Finished goods inventory cost includes the cost of direct material, direct labour, and allocated manufacturing overhead related to its manufacture.

   d. *Production supplies inventory.* Items on hand, such as lubrication oils for the machinery, cleaning materials, as well as small items that make up an insignificant part of the finished product, such as bolts or glue.

3. *Contracts in progress.* The accumulated costs of performing services required under contract. The costs of performing contract services are charged to a work-in-progress or contracts-in-progress account. The inventory will include the *direct* costs (mostly allocated salaries and wages) of working on the contract, and may include an allocation of overhead or *indirect* costs as well, including amortization on production facilities and depletion of natural resources. Construction companies will also include the costs of raw materials and of equipment purchased for use exclusively on a particular contract.

4. *Miscellaneous inventories.* Items such as office, janitorial, and shipping supplies. Inventories of this type are typically used in the near future and may be recorded as selling or general expense when purchased instead of being accounted for as inventory.

INVENTORY POLICY ISSUES

Since cost of goods sold is often the largest single expense category on the income statement, and inventory is an integral part of current and total assets, it makes sense that accounting policies in this area can cause income and net assets to change materially. In what areas can policies be set? We'll look at

1. Items and costs to include in inventory
2. Cost flow assumptions
3. Application of LCM (lower of cost or market) valuations

ITEMS AND COSTS INCLUDED IN INVENTORY

Items Included in Inventory

All goods owned by the company on the balance sheet date should be included in inventory, regardless of their location. At any time, a business may hold goods that it does not own or own goods that it does not hold. Therefore, care must be taken to identify the goods properly includible in inventory.

Goods purchased and in transit should be included in the purchaser's inventory provided ownership has passed to the purchaser. If the goods are shipped FOB (free on board) destination, ownership passes when the buyer receives the goods from the common carrier, such as a railroad or an independent trucker.

Goods that are out on consignment (that is, goods held by agents) and goods located at branches should be included in inventory. Goods should be *excluded* from inventory if they (1) are held for sale on commission or on consignment (but owned by someone else) or (2) have been received from a vendor but rejected and awaiting return to the vendor for credit.

Some companies enter into repurchase agreements to sell and buy back inventory items at prearranged prices if they are not resold by a certain date. This practice has several advantages. Inventory is, in effect, "parked" outside the company, so the selling company may be able to avoid finance and storage expenses that would be incurred if the inventory stayed in house. This saving is possible because the buyer pays all or most of the retail value of the inventory covered in the repurchase agreement until the goods are reacquired by the seller, again at a prearranged price. However, when a repurchase agreement covers all costs, including holding (financing) costs, the inventory must remain on the seller's books. In effect, repurchase agreements are loans from customers rather than sales because the vendor has an obligation to pay back the customer if the goods are not resold.

Special sales agreements exist for many firms, including those selling items to retailers — sporting goods manufacturers and book publishers provide examples. These agreements permit goods to be returned if not sold. Should such goods be considered sold when delivered to the retailer? Revenue recognition rules suggest that these goods should be considered as sales only if returns can be reasonably estimated or if the return privilege has expired. Otherwise, the items remain in the seller's inventory account.

Although legal ownership is a useful starting point to identify items that should be included in inventory, a strict legal determination is often impractical. In such cases, the sales agreement, industry practices, and other evidence of intent should be considered.

Elements of Inventory Cost

In general, inventory cost is measured by the total cash equivalent outlay made to acquire the goods and to prepare them for sale or, for a service company, to fulfill the requirements of the service contract. These costs include materials purchase cost and incidental costs incurred until the goods are ready for use or for sale to the customer, or until the service contract has been completed.

Freight charges and other incidental costs incurred in connection with the purchase of tangible inventory are additions to inventory cost. When these costs can be attributed to specific goods, they should be added to the cost of such goods. However, in some cases, specific identification is impractical. Therefore, freight costs are often recorded in a special account, such as freight-in, which is reported as an addition to cost of goods sold in the case of a retail company, and to cost of materials used in the case of a manufacturing firm.

Companies in some industries regularly offer cash discounts on purchases to encourage timely payment from buyers (which speeds up cash flow and may save on borrowing costs). Terms of 2/10, n/30, for example, mean that if the invoice is paid within 10 days, a discount of 2% can be taken. Alternatively, the *net* balance, n, is due in 30 days. Most buyers make timely payments and take advantage of cash discounts because the savings are normally quite substantial. In fact, some companies borrow money in order to take advantage of cash discounts. This tactic makes sense because the typical purchase discount terms of 2/10 are equivalent to an annualized effective interest rate of about 43%. Inventory should be recorded at the lowest available cash price, which is 98% of the invoice price. Lost discounts are a cost of financing and should not be included in inventory amounts.[2]

Certain incidental costs, although theoretically a cost of tangible goods purchased, are often not included in inventory valuation but are reported as separate expenses. Examples include insurance costs on goods in transit, material handling expenses, and import brokerage and excise fees. These expenditures are usually not included in determining inventory costs because the cost of allocating them to specific purchased goods is not worth the benefit. They may be included as part of overhead costs, which *may* be allocated to inventories if that is the company's policy.

General and administrative (G&A) expenses are normally treated as period expenses because they relate more directly to accounting periods than to inventory. Distribution and selling costs are also considered to be period operating expenses and are not allocated to inventories.

---

[2] Discounts for prompt payment are very expensive for the vendor. If a 2% discount speeds up customers' payments by 20 days, on average, the cost of the discount is equivalent to an compounded annual interest rate of about 43%! The vendor is better off to not give a discount and to borrow from the bank to finance the receivables (or sell the receivables to a factor). An annoying aspect of discounts is that some large customers will blithely deduct the discount from their payment even if they pay late; the discount is viewed as a price reduction rather than a reward for quick payment.

Variable vs. Fixed Overhead

Manufacturing companies and service firms engaged in long-term contracts often use variable costing (also called direct costing, although there are subtle differences between the two approaches) for internal management planning and control purposes. Under this approach, fixed costs (those that relate to time, such as factory depreciation) and variable costs (those that vary with productive activities, such as direct material and direct labour) are segregated. An important aspect of variable costing is that the cost of goods manufactured is the sum of the variable costs only, which include direct materials, direct labour, and variable manufacturing overhead. All fixed costs, including fixed manufacturing overhead, are treated as period costs and are expensed when incurred rather than being capitalized and carried forward in inventory. Hence, fixed costs are not reported as part of cost of inventory or cost of goods sold.

Valuation of inventories only at variable production costs, although useful for internal management purposes, is not widely followed in practice by public companies. The use of such variable costing methods is more likely in smaller companies and in private companies where the costs of overhead allocations outweigh any potential benefits, and where there is less motivation for management to defer fixed costs in inventory or to show high asset values. Variable costing will report significantly lower values for inventory if fixed costs are material — which may not be desirable for entities with loans secured by inventory, or those with an eye on maximizing net assets.

The *CICA Handbook* recommends that manufacturers' inventories include an allocation of overhead.

> In the case of inventories of work in process and finished goods, cost should include the laid-down cost of material plus the cost of direct labour applied to the product and the *applicable share of overhead expense properly chargeable to production.*   [CICA 3030.06, italics added]

There is a great deal of judgement inherent in this recommendation. The implication is that *some* overhead should be included in inventory, but management could decide that the "applicable" share "properly chargeable" is the variable overhead.

The decision on which elements of overhead to include in inventory and which to treat as period costs will be determined with reference to the enterprise's financial reporting objectives and to the qualitative criteria of materiality, cost-benefit relationship, relevance, and timeliness. Timeliness enters the picture because variable costing eliminates the time-consuming task of allocating overhead.

CONCEPT REVIEW

1. What are the three *policy issues* in inventory valuation?
2. What categories of inventory does a manufacturer have?
3. What are the three elements of cost that should be included in a manufacturer's finished goods inventory cost?

COST FLOW ASSUMPTIONS

Periodic vs. Perpetual Recording Methods

Inventory cost may be measured by use of either a periodic inventory system or a perpetual inventory system. The essential difference between these two systems from an accounting point of view is the *frequency with which the physical flows are assigned a value.*

In a periodic inventory system, the quantity of the ending inventory is established at the end of the accounting period. The unit costs are then applied to derive the ending inventory valuation by using a particular cost flow assumption. Cost of goods sold (or used in production or in a service contract) is determined by subtracting the ending inventory valuation from the cost of goods available for sale.

In a periodic system, purchases are debited to a purchases account, and end-of-period entries are made to close the purchases account, to close out beginning inventory, and to record the ending inventory as an asset (i.e., the ending inventory replaces the beginning inventory in the accounts). Any contra accounts to purchases, such as accounts for purchase returns and allowances or for purchase discounts, are also closed at this time. Under a periodic system, cost of goods sold (also commonly called cost of sales) is computed as a residual amount (beginning inventory plus net purchases less ending inventory) and for all practical purposes cannot be verified independently of an inventory count. The lack of verifiability is one reason that estimation methods may be used as a check; estimation methods are discussed at the end of this chapter.

In a perpetual inventory system, each receipt and each issue of an inventory item is recorded in the inventory records to maintain an up-to-date perpetual inventory balance at all times. The result of the perpetual system is verified at least once a year by physically counting the inventory and matching the count to the accounting records. Thus, the perpetual inventory records provide the units and costs of ending inventory and cost of goods sold at any time. The unit costs applied to each issue or sale are determined by the cost flow assumption used.

Exhibit 9-1 compares these two systems and the typical entries that accompany each. It is important to make a distinction between tracking the *physical flow* of goods and the *costing* of the goods. Many companies maintain an ongoing record of physical flows as quantity information only. A continuous tracking of *physical* flows does not constitute a perpetual inventory system (from an accounting standpoint) unless the costs associated with those flows are simultaneously tracked. A good example is provided by supermarkets that use automated scanners at checkout stations to keep track of physical inventory levels but place accounting values on the physical flows only periodically.

Periodic vs. Perpetual — Illustration

To illustrate the periodic versus the perpetual systems, consider the following data for the Lea Company:

	Units	Unit Cost	Total
Beginning inventory	500	$4.00	$2,000
Purchases	1,000	4.00	4,000
Goods available for sale	1,500		$6,000
Less: Sales	900		
Ending inventory, as calculated	600		
Ending inventory, based on physical count	580		

Note that there should have been 600 units on hand, not 580; 20 must have been damaged and discarded or stolen. The amount by which the physical count falls short of the expected level of inventory is generally (and euphemistically) referred to as shrinkage. However, it also is possible that the sales records are not completely accurate.

EXHIBIT 9-1
Comparison of the Periodic and Perpetual Inventory Systems

Transaction — Routine purchases of various inventory items

Periodic system   All inventory item values are debited to the purchases account regardless of the particular items acquired. That is:

Purchases	xx	
Cash, accounts payable, etc.		xx

Perpetual system   Inventory items are debited to the inventory control account. A subsidiary ledger is kept for control purposes. That is,

Inventory	xx	
Cash, accounts payable, etc.		xx

Transaction — Goods are sold or used

Periodic system   No accounting entries are made.

Perpetual system   Goods are moved from the inventory account and debited to cost of goods sold, or whatever debit is appropriate. Some goods may leave one inventory, raw materials, to move to another inventory, work-in-process, or to an appropriate expense, such as cleaning or maintenance. That is:

Cost of goods sold, etc.	xx	
Inventory.		xx

Transaction — End-of-period accounting entries

Periodic system   Physical count of the ending inventory is taken and dollar values are assigned. This activity is a prerequisite to computing the cost of goods sold (CGS) for the period. Adjusting entries are made to compute the cost of goods sold (CGS) using the following formula: *CGS = Beginning inventory + Purchases – Ending inventory.*

Cost of goods sold	xx	
Inventory (closing, per count)	xx	
Inventory (opening)		xx
Purchases		xx

This process is also frequently accomplished through the closing entries, rather than in an adjusting entry.

Perpetual system   Physical count of inventory is not needed for calculation of cost of goods sold for the period, but such inventory counts are usually made in order to verify the accuracy of the perpetual system and to identify inventory overages and shortages. Shortages are most common. An entry is needed to adjust the inventory account on the books to the actual balance.

Cost of goods sold	xx	
Inventory (actual less accounting balance)		xx

Cost of goods sold is automatically determined from the sum of the daily postings to the cost of goods sold expense account.

Based on the data above, the computation of the cost of goods sold yields the following amounts:

Beginning inventory (carried forward from the prior period):	
500 × $4	$2,000
Merchandise purchases (accumulated in the purchases	
account): 1,000 × $4	4,000
Total goods available for sale during the period	6,000
Less: Ending inventory (quantity determined by a	
physical count): 580 × $4	2,320
Equals: Cost of goods sold (a residual amount)	$3,680

Periodic Recording. At the beginning of the year, the balance of the inventory account will be the $2,000 cost of the 500 units that were on hand. The entries to record the purchases and cost of goods sold under a periodic inventory system are as follows:

To record the purchases

Purchases	4,000	
Accounts payable		4,000

To re-allocate the cost of opening inventory and purchases

Cost of goods sold	3,680	
Inventory (closing, per count)	2,320	
Inventory (opening)		2,000
Purchases		4,000

A slight variation on the second entry above is to explicitly recognize the shrinkage of 20 units as an expense, instead of lumping it in with cost of goods sold.

Cost of goods sold (900 × $4)	3,600	
Inventory shrinkage expense (20 × $4)	80	
Inventory (closing, per count: 580 × $4)	2,320	
Inventory [opening]		2,000
Purchases		4,000

The inventory shrinkage expense will appear as an expense on the income statement.[3]

Under a periodic inventory system, the inventory is counted at least once a year. For interim financial statements, however, the amount of inventory may be estimated. If a perpetual record of only the *physical units* of inventory is maintained, then only the cost of that inventory needs to be estimated. If the company maintains no perpetual inventory count, then both the quantity and unit cost must be estimated. Later in the chapter, we will discuss the two most common methods of inventory estimation.

Perpetual Recording. When a perpetual inventory system is used, detailed perpetual inventory records, in addition to the usual ledger accounts, are maintained for each inventory item, and an inventory control account is maintained in the general ledger. The perpetual inventory record for each item must provide information for recording receipts, issues, and balances on hand, both in units and in dollar amounts. With this information, the physical quantity and the valuation of goods on hand at any time are available from the accounting records. Therefore, a physical inventory count is

---

3   It may be shown as a separate expense line on an income statement prepared for management use. It will not be found on published income statements, however. In public financial statements, management prefers not to indicate that there is any "shrinkage," and the amount is usually buried in the total amount shown for cost of goods sold.

still necessary but only to verify the accuracy of the perpetual inventory records. A physical count is made annually to compare the inventory on hand with the perpetual record and to provide data for any adjusting entries needed (errors and losses, for example).

When a difference is found between the perpetual inventory records and the physical count, the perpetual inventory records are adjusted to the physical count. In such cases, the inventory account is debited or credited as necessary for the correction, and cost of goods sold is increased or decreased. The loss may be accumulated in a separate account such as inventory shortages, to keep track of inventory shrinkage for internal purposes.

In the Lea Company example above, the company began the year with 500 units in inventory, at a cost of $4 per unit. The purchase of 1,000 additional units is recorded as a debit to the inventory account (not to a purchases account).

Inventory (1,000 × $4)	4,000	
Accounts payable		4,000

When goods are sold, two entries are made; one to record the sale and the other to transfer their cost to CGS. Assuming that Lea sells 900 units at a price of $10:

Accounts receivable (900 × $10)	9,000	
Sales revenue		9,000
Cost of goods sold (900 × $4)	3,600	
Inventory		3,600

The company will end the accounting period with an inventory balance of $2,400 (600 × $4). These balances would have been recorded in the year as inventory was bought and sold. At the end of the year, a physical count would reveal only 580 units, and the additional expense would be recorded (it may also be recorded in a separate expense account):

Cost of goods sold	80	
Inventory ($2,320 – $2,400)		80

Thus at the end of the period, both the perpetual and periodic systems report identical inventory ($2,320) and cost of goods sold ($3,680) amounts.

Choosing a Recording Method

The choice of a periodic or perpetual system is not really an accounting policy choice, although modest differences in inventory and cost of goods sold amounts can arise under the average cost assumption and under LIFO, depending on which recording method is used. Instead, the choice of recording method is one of practicality — which method gives the best cost-benefit relationship?

A perpetual inventory system is especially useful when inventory consists of items with high unit values or when it is important to have adequate but not excessive inventory levels. Perpetual inventory systems require detailed accounting records and therefore tend to be more costly to implement and maintain than periodic systems. Computer technology has made perpetual inventory systems more popular today than ever before. Thanks to robotics and computer technology, today there are automated inventory systems that not only account for the inventory but also manage the stocking and handling of inventory goods and materials.

However, even with automated systems, certain aspects of physical inventory management and control are problematic. Theft and pilferage, breakage and other physical damage, mis-orders and mis-fills, and inadequate inventory supervision practices must be dealt with regardless of the type of inventory accounting system used.

The choice of method depends on whether you really need to have *both* quantity information and cost information at your fingertips for control purposes:

- Do you need to know exactly how many units you have at any point in time? If so, then you need to have a perpetual system *for quantities* but not necessarily for costs. Point-of-sale computer terminals that read bar codes are very useful for maintaining quantity flow information, but need not necessarily be tied to the accounting records.
- Do you need to know exactly how many units you have on hand, how old they are, *and how much they cost* on a regular basis (such as weekly or monthly)? The need for frequent interim financial statements will make perpetual tracking of costs more useful.

Bank operating lines of credit (i.e., loans) are often tied to the carrying value of receivables and inventory. If, for example, a company's bank is willing to lend up to 60% of the carrying value of the inventory, it is necessary to know at least monthly (and to report to the bank) the value of the inventory. Then a perpetual system makes sense. Also, full information on quantities and costs may be needed for insurance purposes.

The basic question is whether the additional cost of a perpetual accounting inventory system is worth the cost. If a company doesn't need the full capabilities of a perpetual system, it's likely that the company will use the cheaper, less complicated periodic system.

Remember that a company may have a sophisticated inventory system for quantities and still use the periodic system for its accounting records. For example, a department store may have a point-of-sale perpetual inventory system (using bar codes) to keep track of its merchandise and to facilitate prompt reordering of popular items. This is information that a periodic system could not possibly provide on a timely basis. But the perpetual system may not be integrated into the accounting system. For quarterly reporting, the company may still take a physical inventory or use an estimation method (which will be discussed later in this chapter).

Even with the most sophisticated perpetual system, it still is necessary to take a physical inventory at each fiscal year-end. A physical inventory is necessary to satisfy the auditors (if any), but it also is necessary in order to verify the integrity of the perpetual system. If there is a significant difference between the count revealed by the physical inventory and the quantity of inventory that the perpetual system says should be there, there can only be two reasons: (1) there is a problem with the perpetual system or (2) someone is stealing the merchandise. Prompt investigation and remedial action is required in either case.

Common Cost Flow Assumptions

At date of acquisition, inventory items are recorded at their cash equivalent cost in accordance with the historical cost principle. Subsequently, when an item is sold, net assets decline and expenses increase as a result of the transfer of the item's cost from inventory to cost of goods sold. The cost value assigned to the end-of-period inventory of merchandise and finished goods is an allocation of the total cost of goods available for sale between that portion sold (cost of goods sold) and that portion held as an asset for subsequent sale (ending inventory). This isn't a problem when costs are stable over the period, but when costs change, the allocation issue rears its ugly head: Which item was sold? The central issue is the *order* in which the actual unit costs incurred are assigned to the ending inventory and to cost of goods sold.

Companies have to pick a convention to follow, which does not have to be the same as the physical flow of goods. The alternatives were already examined in Chapter 7:

EXHIBIT 9-2
CHASE CONTAINER CORPORATION
Inventory Data

| | | Units | |
Transaction Date	Purchased	Sold	On Hand
1 January — Inventory @ $1.00			200
9 January — Purchases @ $1.10	300		500
10 January — Sales		400	100
15 January — Purchases @ $1.16	400		500
18 January — Sales		300	200
24 January — Purchase @ $1.26	100		300

The costs to be allocated are the total costs of the goods available for sale:

Beginning inventory	200 × $1.00 =			$ 200
Purchases	300 × $1.10 =	$330		
	400 × $1.16 =	464		
	100 × $1.26 =	126		920
Cost of goods available for sale				$1,120

The $1,120 is allocated between ending inventory and cost of goods sold, using one of the cost flow assumptions described in the next subsections.

- Specific cost identification
- Average cost
- First-in, first-out (FIFO)
- Last-in, first-out (LIFO)

As we will discuss in a later section, LIFO is not a popular method in Canada, due largely to the fact that it is not acceptable for income tax purposes. Specific identification is used mainly for large, unique items, such as custom-built equipment, or in accounting for service contracts. For other types of business, average cost and FIFO are the popular methods.

According to the *CICA Handbook*, the method selected for determining cost should be *one which results in the fairest matching of costs against revenues* [CICA 3030.09]. Since we have discussed this issue before, we won't beat it to death here. If you've forgotten the Chapter 7 material, you should go back and re-read it before you continue. Of all the accounting policies associated with inventory, the cost flow assumption is probably the most important!

The example that follows is a numeric example of the methods applied to both a perpetual and periodic system.

Specific Identification

This method is, in theory, the most straightforward of all the methods. At the end of the year (periodic method) or on each sale (perpetual method) the specific units sold, and their specific cost, is identified to determine inventory and cost of goods sold. In the example in Exhibit 9-2, there are 300 units left in closing inventory. Specific identification under a periodic system reveals that, at the end of January, there are 100 units from the January 9 purchase, 100 units from the January 15 purchase, and 100 units from the January 24 purchase. Ending inventory is then valued at $352, and cost of sales at $768 ($1,120 – $352).

EXHIBIT 9-3
CHASE CONTAINER CORPORATION
Weighted-Average Inventory Cost Method, Periodic Inventory System

	Units	Unit Price	Total Cost
Goods Available:			
1 January — Beginning inventory	200	$1.00	$200
9 January — Purchase	300	1.10	330
15 January — Purchase	400	1.16	464
24 January — Purchase	100	1.26	126
January — Total available	1,000		$1,120
Weighted-average unit cost ($1,120 ÷ 1,000)		1.12	
Ending inventory at weighted-average cost:			
31 January	300	1.12	336
Cost of goods sold at weighted-average cost:			
Sales during January	700*	1.12	784
Total cost allocated			$1,120

*400 units on 10 January plus 300 units on 18 January.

In practice, specific identification may not be so simple for most businesses because it is inconvenient and difficult to establish just which items were sold and what their specific initial cost was. However, it is the method used when each product or service is unique (and substantial), such as for shipbuilding, special-order heavy equipment, custom software, construction contracts, consulting operations, and so forth.

Average Cost

When the average cost method is used in a periodic system, it is called a weighted average system. *A weighted-average unit cost is computed by dividing the sum of the beginning inventory cost plus total current period purchase costs by the number of units in the beginning inventory plus units purchased during the period.* Exhibit 9-3 illustrates application of the weighted-average method under a periodic system using the data given in Exhibit 9-2 for the Chase Container Corporation.

When the average cost method is used in a perpetual inventory system, a moving-average unit cost is used. *The moving average provides a new unit cost after each purchase.* When goods are sold or issued, the moving-average unit cost at the time is used. Application of the moving-average concept in a perpetual inventory system is shown in Exhibit 9-4, based on Exhibit 9-2. For example, on 9 January, the $1.06 moving-average cost is derived by dividing the total cost ($530) by the total units (500). The January ending inventory of 300 units is costed at the latest moving-average unit cost of $1.18 ($354 ÷ 300). The cost of goods sold for the period is the sum of the sales in the total cost column, $766. There's a lot of calculating involved!

First-In, First-Out

The first-in, first-out (FIFO) method treats the first goods purchased or manufactured as the first units costed out on sale or issuance. *Goods sold (or issued) are valued at the oldest unit costs, and goods remaining in inventory are valued at the most recent unit cost amounts.* Exhibit 9-5 demonstrates FIFO for the periodic system. Exhibit 9-6 demonstrates the perpetual system. Using the perpetual system, a sale is costed

EXHIBIT 9-4
CHASE CONTAINER CORPORATION
Moving-Average Inventory Cost, Perpetual Inventory System

Dates	Purchases			Sales			Inventory Balance		
	Units	Unit Cost	Total Cost	Units	Unit Cost	Total Cost	Units	Unit Cost	Total Cost
1 January							200	$1.00	$200
9 January	300	$1.10	$330				500	1.06(a)	530
10 January				400	$1.06	$424	100	1.06	106
15 January	400	1.16	464				500	1.14(b)	570
18 January				300	1.14	342	200	1.14	228
24 January	100	1.26	126				300	1.18(c)	354
Ending inventory									$354
Cost of goods sold						$766			766
Total cost allocated									$1,120

(a) $530 ÷ 500 = $1.06
(b) $570 ÷ 500 = $1.14
(c) $354 ÷ 300 = $1.18

out either currently throughout the period each time there is a withdrawal, or entirely at the end of the period, with the same results. In Exhibit 9-6, issues from inventory on January 10 and 18 (FIFO basis) are costed out as they occur. FIFO produces the same results whether a periodic or perpetual system is used.

Accounting Entries — Illustration

To illustrate the accounting entries typical in a periodic and perpetual system, the data for the FIFO example will be used. The entries are those described in Exhibit 9-1. Both methods begin the period with 200 units in inventory at a cost of $200.

		Periodic		Perpetual	
9 Jan.	Purchases	330		—	
	Inventory	—		330	
	Cash, etc.		330		330
10 Jan.	Cost of goods sold	—		420	
	Inventory		—		420
15 Jan.	Purchases	464		—	
	Inventory	—		464	
	Cash, etc.		464		464
18 Jan.	Cost of goods sold	—		342	
	Inventory		—		342
24 Jan.	Purchases	126		—	
	Inventory	—		126	
	Cash, etc.		126		126
31 Jan.	Cost of goods sold	762		—	
	Inventory (closing)	358		—	
	Inventory (opening)		200		—
	Purchases		920		—

EXHIBIT 9-5
CHASE CONTAINER CORPORATION
FIFO Inventory Costing, Periodic Inventory System

Beginning inventory (200 units at $1)		$ 200
Add purchases during period (computed as in Exhibit 9-2)		920
Cost of goods available for sale		1,120
Deduct ending inventory (300 units per physical inventory count):		
100 units at $1.26 (most recent purchase — 24 January)	$126	
200 units at $1.16 (next most recent purchase — 15 January)	232	
Total ending inventory cost		358
Cost of goods sold		$ 762*

*Can also be calculated as 200 units on hand 1 January at $1 plus 300 units purchased 9 January at $1.10, plus 200 units purchased 15 January at $1.16.

EXHIBIT 9-6
CHASE CONTAINER CORPORATION
FIFO Inventory Costing, Perpetual Inventory System

	Purchases			Sales			Inventory Balance		
Dates	**Units**	**Unit Cost**	**Total Cost**	**Units**	**Unit Cost**	**Total Cost**	**Units**	**Unit Cost**	**Total Cost**
1 January							200	$1.00	$200
9 January	300	$1.10	$330				300	1.10	330
10 January				200	$1.00	$200			
				200	1.10	220	100	1.10	110
15 January	400	1.16	464				100	1.10	110
							400	1.16	464
18 January				100	1.10	110			
				200	1.16	232	200	1.16	232
24 January	100	1.26	126				200	1.16	232
							100	1.26	126
Ending inventory ($232 + $126)									$358
Cost of goods sold					$762				762
Total cost allocated									$1,120

EXHIBIT 9-7
CHASE CONTAINER CORPORATION
LIFO Inventory Costing, Periodic Inventory System

Cost of goods available (see Exhibit 9-2)		$1,120
Deduct ending inventory (300 units per physical inventory count):		
200 units at $1 (oldest costs available, from		
1 January inventory)	$200	
100 units at $1.10 (next oldest costs available; from		
9 January purchase)	110	
Ending inventory		310
Cost of goods sold		$ 810*

*Can also be calculated as 100 units at $1.26 plus 400 units at $1.16 plus 200 units at $1.10

Last-In, First-Out

The last-in, first-out (LIFO) method of inventory costing matches inventory valued at the most recent unit acquisition cost with current sales revenue. The units remaining in ending inventory are costed at the oldest unit costs incurred, and the units included in cost of goods sold are costed at the newest unit costs incurred, the exact opposite of the FIFO cost assumption. Like FIFO, application of LIFO requires the use of inventory cost layers for different unit costs.

When LIFO is used with a periodic system, it's called the unit cost approach. The ending inventory is costed at the oldest unit costs. Cost of goods sold is determined by deducting ending inventory from the cost of goods available for sale. The periodic LIFO system permits the cost of purchases occurring after the last sale to be included in cost of sales, which cannot occur in the perpetual system. This method is illustrated in Exhibit 9-7. For the current example, the LIFO cost of the 18 January sale includes the cost of the 24 January purchase! The ending inventory therefore consists of two layers, one at $1.00 and one at $1.10.

Exhibits 9-6 and 9-8 illustrate the rather tedious nature of the perpetual inventory system under both FIFO and LIFO. Thanks to computers, some degree of relief from the burdensome nature of this work has been made possible, but extensive record-keeping is still required.

Income Tax Factors. Revenue Canada will not accept LIFO for tax purposes. Companies must use either the FIFO or the average cost method when they compute their taxes payable. If a company uses LIFO for financial reporting, it must maintain two different inventory costing systems — one for financial reporting (LIFO) and another for income tax (FIFO or average). Since there is a substantial additional work load to maintaining two different systems, Canadian companies rarely use LIFO. *Financial Reporting in Canada 1997* reported that only about 3% of the sample companies use LIFO for any part of their inventory.

LIFO is most likely to be used by a Canadian subsidiary of a U.S. parent corporation. LIFO is acceptable for computing U.S. income tax, if the same method is also used for U.S. financial reporting. A Canadian subsidiary may then maintain LIFO inventory accounts in order to facilitate the parent's consolidation process. However LIFO still would not be acceptable for the subsidiary's Canadian tax return.

EXHIBIT 9-8
CHASE CONTAINER CORPORATION
LIFO Inventory Costing, Perpetual Inventory System

| | Purchases | | | Sales | | | Inventory Balance | | |
Dates	Units	Unit Cost	Total Cost	Units	Unit Cost	Total Cost	Units	Unit Cost	Total Cost
1 January*							200	$1.00	$200
9 January	300	$1.10	$330				200	1.00	200
							300	1.10	330
10 January				300	$1.10	$330			
				100	1.00	100	100	1.00	100
15 January	400	1.16	464				100	1.00	100
							400	1.16	464
18 January				300	1.16	348	100	1.00	100
							100	1.16	116
24 January	100	1.26	126				100	1.00	100
							100	1.16	116
							100	1.26	126
Ending inventory ($100 + $116 + $126)									$ 342
Cost of goods sold						$778			778
Total cost allocated									$1,120

*Beginning inventory.

Review

Let's review the basics of the cost flow assumption again. This is an accounting policy choice. When prices are rising, as they often are, FIFO will produce higher inventory, lower cost of goods sold, and higher income. It's probably popular with firms that would like to see higher income and net assets in their financial statements. LIFO has the opposite effect: lower inventories, higher cost of goods sold, and lower incomes. It would likely be very popular among those firms trying to minimize income tax payments except for the fact that it can't be used for income tax reporting in Canada. Average cost methods provide inventory and cost of goods sold amounts between the LIFO and FIFO extremes, and is the next best thing to LIFO for income and tax minimization when inventory costs are rising. Canadian practice is about evenly divided between FIFO and average cost. LIFO is very seldom used in Canada, except by Canadian subsidiaries of U.S. companies that mandate its use in order to be consistent with the parent's accounting policies.

The impacts of FIFO versus LIFO are illustrated in Exhibit 9-9.

INTERNATIONAL PERSPECTIVE

Accounting for inventories, called stocks in the U.K. and in some other English-speaking countries, is similar throughout the world, with one exception: the use of LIFO. LIFO is widely used in the United States (largely because it is acceptable for U.S. income tax purposes), but is not generally acceptable in the rest of the world, including Australia, France, the Netherlands, and the United Kingdom.

Germany does permit LIFO, but average cost is the most frequently used method because that is the method used for tax purposes. Belgium permits LIFO, but only if it is used on an item-by-item basis. Italy does not formally permit LIFO, but a pric-

EXHIBIT 9-9				
Comparison of the Effects of FIFO vs. LIFO				
If purchase prices are:	*The impact on ending inventory is:*	*The impact on cost of goods sold is:*	*The impact on net income and retained earnings is:*	
Rising	FIFO > LIFO	FIFO < LIFO	FIFO > LIFO	
Falling	FIFO < LIFO	FIFO > LIFO	FIFO < LIFO	

ing method acceptable for tax purposes is basically a LIFO approach. In Japan, like Canada, LIFO can be used for financial reporting but not for tax reporting.

The International Accounting Standards Committee attempted to eliminate LIFO from its list of acceptable inventory methods, but the U.S. members put pressure on the IASC to include LIFO in its list of acceptable methods, and the IASC retained LIFO as an alternative. However, FIFO remains the benchmark method for international standards, the method identified as the point of reference for firms making a choice from among allowable alternatives.

1. Explain the essential differences in accounting for inventories under the periodic and perpetual inventory systems.
2. If the price to acquire inventory is rising, and the company is pursuing an income maximization reporting strategy over the long term, which inventory cost flow assumption is management most likely to choose?
3. Why is LIFO unlikely to be used by Canadian companies?

CONCEPT REVIEW

SPECIAL ASPECTS

Standard Costs

For manufacturing entities using a standard cost system, the inventories are valued, recorded, and reported for internal purposes on the basis of a standard unit cost. The standard cost, which approximates an ideal or expected cost, prevents the overstatement of inventory values because it excludes from inventory all losses and expenses that are due to inefficiency, waste, and abnormal conditions. Actual historical cost is used only once, on acquisition. Standard cost is used thereafter, which simplifies record-keeping significantly!

Under this method, the differences between actual cost (which includes losses due to inefficiencies, etc.) and standard cost (which excludes losses due to inefficiencies, etc.) are recorded in separate variance accounts. These accounts are usually written off as a current period loss rather than capitalized in inventory. To illustrate, assume that a manufacturing company has just adopted standard cost procedures and that the beginning inventory is zero. During the current period, the company makes two purchases and one issuance and records them as follows:

1. *To record the purchase of 10,000 units of raw material at $1.10 actual cost; standard cost has been established at $1:*

Raw materials (10,000 units × $1)	10,000	
Raw materials purchase price variance		
(10,000 units × $.10)	1,000	
Accounts payable (10,000 units × $1.10)		11,000

2. *To record issuance of 8,000 units of raw material to the factory for processing:*

Work in progress	8,000	
Raw materials (8,000 × $1)		8,000

3. *To record the purchase of 2,000 units of raw materials at $.95:*

Raw materials (2,000 × $1)	2,000	
Raw materials purchase price variance		
(2,000 × $.05)		100
Accounts payable (2,000 × $.95)		1,900

Under standard cost procedures there would be no need to consider inventory cost flow methods (such as LIFO, FIFO, and average) because only one cost — standard cost — appears in the records. In addition, perpetual inventory records can be maintained in units because all issues and inventory valuations are at the same standard cost. Because standard cost represents a departure from the cost principle, it is acceptable for external reporting under GAAP only if results are not materially different than actual costs. However, standard costs can easily be adjusted to actual cost for external reporting by simply pro-rating (i.e., allocating) the variances to inventory and cost of goods sold. Pretty tempting, isn't it? The size of the variances indicates the differences between actual and standard and can be used to assess materiality.

Just-in-Time Inventory Systems

Just-in-time (JIT) inventory systems are a response to the high costs associated with stockpiling inventories of raw materials, parts, supplies, and finished goods. Rather than keeping ample quantities on hand awaiting use, the idea is to reduce inventories to the lowest levels possible and thus save costs. As the name suggests, the ultimate goal is to see goods and materials arrive at the company's receiving dock *just in time* to be moved directly to the plant's production floor for immediate use in the manufacturing or assembly process. Then, taking the concept one step further, finished goods roll off the production floor and move directly to the shipping dock just in time for shipment to the customers. The ideal result is zero inventory levels and zero inventory costs.

In practice, inventories are still not zero under JIT systems, but they are at substantially diminished levels, such as a one-day supply. Minimum inventories are needed. If inventory levels are kept too lean, production can be halted by quite minor irregularities such as a slight interruption in production by a supplier or a traffic jam that delays delivery trucks. A batch of defective parts might be encountered, again causing a work suspension. If a small buffer inventory is not maintained, the JIT system runs the risk of becoming a NQIT (not-quite-in-time) system instead!

Like other inventory systems, the success of a JIT system depends on how well it is conceived and implemented for a particular production setting (or selling situation — JIT techniques apply to merchandise inventories carried by retail outlets as well). Purely from a management standpoint, inventory problems shift from the cost of stockpiling production parts and materials needs — one week's expected needs or one month's or whatever — to coordinating inventory to meet production needs. At the extreme, under a JIT system, some of the inventory may be in-house (today's needs), some of it may be in transit to the plant (tomorrow's needs), some of it may be in the process of being fabricated or otherwise finished by the supplier (the day after tomorrow's needs), and some of it may not have been ordered yet (next week's needs). Extremes aside, minimal inventory levels normally result in reduced need for storage space, materials moving and handling equipment, property and casualty insurance coverage, and materials obsolescence or deterioration.

JIT systems tend to result in simplified inventory accounting procedures, primarily because inventory levels are kept low, but also because raw materials and work-in-process inventories are in many cases combined. At Hewlett-Packard, for example, raw materials are charged to a combined account and then transferred to finished goods upon completion of production.[4]

JIT systems also affect the way companies account for production costs. Conversion costs (labour and direct overhead costs) are charged directly to the cost of goods sold account as a matter of expediency. The working premise is that almost everything being produced is in response to orders from customers. Therefore, all conversion costs are charged to the cost of goods sold account and charge backs are made (finished items not sold or unfinished items still in production as of the end of the accounting period) to finished goods or work-in-process inventories, respectively. In effect, JIT systems work backward in comparison with traditional inventory accounting systems, which put everything into inventory first.

Inventories Carried at Market Value

When revenue is recognized at the point of production, inventory is written up to its net realizable value, prior to sale. This is the increase in net assets that substantiates revenue recognition. Assume that gold is extracted and refined at a cost of $302 per ounce, but has a market value of $350 per ounce on that date. Selling and shipping costs are negligible. If the mining company decided to recognize revenue on production — some do, some don't — then inventory will be valued at $350 per ounce, that is, at market value, not at cost.

Similarly, farm products held for resale may be carried at market value. Farm products can be sold in the open market or, in Canada, to a marketing board that has a fixed price (at any point in time) for that particular product. All it takes to sell the inventory is a phone call, clearly an insubstantial act. Since the earnings process is substantially complete and there is a guaranteed market for the inventory, revenue can be recognized at the point of production and the inventory carried from that point on at its net realizable value.

Revenue recognition at the point of production was discussed in Chapter 6 and will not be repeated here. In the case of either mining or agriculture, there is a speculative element to holding inventories. This risk can be hedged against on the futures markets. Hedging is beyond the scope of this chapter, however.

Special inventory categories often include items for resale that are damaged, shopworn, obsolete, defective, or are trade-ins or repossessions. These inventory items are valued at current replacement cost, defined as the price for which the items can be purchased in their present condition. To illustrate a situation in which the current replacement cost can be determined reliably, assume that Allied Appliance Company has on hand a repossessed TV set that had an original cost of $650 when new. The set, which originally sold for $995, was repossessed when $500 was owed by the customer. Similar used TV sets can be purchased in the wholesale market for $240. The repossessed item should be recorded as follows:

Inventory, repossessed merchandise	240	
Loss on repossession	260	
Accounts receivable		500

Subsequent resale of the TV at a price greater or less than $240 triggers a gain or loss on sale.

When the replacement cost cannot be determined reliably, such items should be valued at their estimated net realizable value (NRV), defined as the estimated sale price less all costs expected to be incurred in preparing the item for sale. Replacement

---

[4] B. Newmann and P. Jaouan, "Kanban, Zips and Cost Accounting: A Case Study," *Journal of Accountancy* (August 1986), pp. 132–141.

cost is preferred over NRV because it is typically a more objective value, established by existing market forces rather than by managerial estimates.

To illustrate accounting for inventory at NRV when replacement cost cannot be determined reliably, assume that Allied suffers fire damage to 100 units of its regular inventory. The item, which originally cost $10 per unit (as reflected in the perpetual inventory records), was marked to sell before the fire for $18 per unit. No established used market exists. The company should value the item for inventory purposes at its NRV. Allied estimates that after cleaning and making repairs, the items would sell for $7 per unit; the estimated cost of the repairs for all the units is $150, and the estimated selling cost is 20% of the new selling price. Given this data, the total inventory valuation for the items is as follows:

Estimated sale price (100 × $7)		$700
Less: Estimated cost to repair	$150	
Estimated selling costs ($700 × 20%)	140	(290)
NRV for inventory		$410

Losses on Purchase Commitments

To lock in prices and ensure sufficient quantities, companies often contract with suppliers to purchase a specified quantity of materials during a future period at an agreed unit cost. Some purchase commitments (contracts) are subject to revision or cancellation before the end of the contract period; others are not. Each case requires different accounting and reporting procedures. A loss must be accrued on a purchase contract when

- the purchase contract is not subject to revision or cancellation, and
- when a loss is likely and material, *and*
- when the loss can be reasonably estimated.

Assume that the Bayshore Company enters into a non-cancellable purchase contract during October 20X2 that states, "During 20X3, 50,000 tanks of compressed chlorine will be purchased at $5 each," a total commitment of $250,000. Suppose that the current replacement cost of the chlorine is $240,000 by year-end. Thus, a $10,000 loss is likely.[5] The loss on the purchase commitment should be recorded at the end of 20X2 as follows:

Estimated loss on purchase commitment		
($250,000 – $240,000)	10,000	
Estimated liability on non-cancellable		
purchase commitment		10,000

The estimated loss is reported on the 20X2 income statement, and the liability is reported on the balance sheet. When the goods are acquired in 20X3, merchandise inventory (or purchases) is debited at the current replacement cost, and the estimated liability account is debited. Assume that the above materials have a replacement cost at date of delivery of $235,000. The purchase entry would be as follows:

Materials inventory (or purchases)	235,000	
Estimated liability on non-cancellable		
purchase commitment	10,000	
Loss on purchase contract	5,000	
Cash		250,000

---

[5] This is known as an *opportunity cost*, because the company missed the opportunity to buy the chlorine at a lower price.

This treatment records the loss in the period when it became likely. Note that inventory is never recorded for more than its replacement cost — so, if the actual historical cost is higher than the replacement cost, historical cost is not used.

If there were a full or partial recovery of the purchase price, the recovery would be recognized (as a loss recovery; gains are not recognized) in the period during which the recovery took place. Thus, if in 20X3 the materials had a replacement cost at date of delivery of $255,000, the purchase entry would be as follows:

Materials inventory (or purchases)	250,000	
Estimated liability on non-cancellable purchase commitments	10,000	
Recovery of loss on purchase commitment		10,000
Cash		250,000

Review the three criteria for accounting recognition of a loss listed above. What if the contract were cancellable? Then the loss is no longer likely, and the amount would not be accrued. What if the loss were not estimable? Recognition criteria are not met, and again no entry can be made. What if commodity prices are going up, not down? Then a loss is not likely and no entry is appropriate. Gains are not recognized. Disclosure of the contracts and terms is appropriate when the contracts are significant, or out of the ordinary, or when an inestimable loss is present.

LOWER OF COST OR MARKET VALUATION

GAAP requires that inventories be valued either at cost or at current market value, whichever is less. While the GAAP model relies on historic cost, it also typically establishes a LCM test of some type for every asset — overstatement of assets is not permitted! Assets should always be substantiated by some kind of future economic benefit. For inventory, it's clear that if you can't sell the asset, the inventory can't really be called an asset.

To illustrate the basic operation of the LCM inventory valuation method, assume that a retailer has an inventory consisting of a single line of office electronics products, all purchased during 20X2 at a cost of $165 per unit, the going wholesale price at the time the merchandise was acquired. Late in the year, stiff competition in the electronics and office products market causes wholesale prices for the retailer's products in inventory to drop substantially, with retail prices following suit. As of the end of the year, manufacturers are quoting wholesale prices of $125 per unit. Assume that none of the retailer's inventory has been sold. The retailer's ending inventory for 20X2 should be valued and reported at $125 per unit, which represents a $40 loss per unit based on the $165 original purchase cost. This $40-per-unit loss must be reported in the retailer's 20X2 financial statements, the period during which the market price decline took place.

Assume that the retailer's inventory is sold in 20X3. For each unit sold, the cost of goods sold is now $125, not $165. Assuming that retail selling prices dropped commensurate with last year's decline in wholesale prices, the lower cost of goods sold provides the retailer with approximately the same gross margin on sales as would have been available in 20X2, when both wholesale and retail prices were higher. The net effect of the LCM application in this instance is to shift the $40-per-unit loss from the period when the inventory was sold to the period in which the replacement cost decreased.

LCM tests are complicated by a couple of policy choices:

1. What is the definition of *market value*?
2. Should the LCM test be applied to individual inventory items, to categories, or to totals? The question of aggregation is not trivial.

Definition of Market Value

The basic difficulty with determining market value is that there are two markets: (1) the supplier market (replacement cost) and (2) the customer market (sales price). Sales price is called net realizable value (NRV) when costs expected to be incurred in preparing the item for sale are deducted. Net realizable value can be taken further, deducting expected costs and also a normal gross profit margin; use of net realizable value less a normal profit margin will preserve normal profits when the item is finally sold. Take a look at Exhibit 9-10 for an example of calculations.

Which one is "market"? If you're looking for a measure of future cash flow, NRV is very attractive, but can be very subjective. Will the sales price hold? Replacement cost is more objective, and chances are that if replacement cost goes down, sales price will, too. It's more onerous to compile, though.

Canadian standard-setters have provided no recommendations as to the meaning of market in the term lower of cost or market. The *CICA Handbook* provides the following comment:

> In view of the lack of precision in meaning, it is desirable that the term "market" not be used in describing the basis of valuation. A term more descriptive of the method of determining market, such as "replacement cost," "net realizable value" or "net realizable value less normal profit margin," would be preferable.   [*CICA* 3030.11]

In the absence of authoritative guidance, Canadian companies are free to choose the definition of market value that is most appropriate in the circumstances — a judgement call. Industry practice undoubtedly plays a role. As seen in Exhibit 9-11, *the majority of Canadian companies use net realizable value as the determination of market value.* However, companies use various methods and it's important to check the disclosure notes to pin down the valuation rule in use.

The net realizable value for raw materials and work in process is more difficult to determine because the costs to complete and ultimate selling prices are more uncertain. Therefore, replacement costs for raw materials, plus manufacturing costs to date for work in process, is often used on the expectation that selling prices tend to move in step with replacement costs. Nevertheless, a write-down may still be required if realizable values have declined despite the absence of a decline in replacement costs.

In the U.S., there is a different approach to the determination of market value. To apply this approach, one must determine three definitions of market value (replacement cost, net realizable value, and net realizable value less a normal profit margin) and then use the *middle* value. Some Canadian firms undoubtedly follow this approach, but it sure requires a lot of data collection!

Extent of Grouping

Application of LCM can follow one of three approaches:

1. Comparison of cost and market separately for each item of inventory.
2. Comparison of cost and market separately for each classification of inventory.
3. Comparison of total cost with total market for the inventory.

Exhibit 9-12 shows the application of each approach. Consistency in application over time is essential. *The individual unit basis produces the most conservative inventory value because units whose market value exceeds cost are not allowed to offset items whose market value is less than cost. This offsetting occurs to some extent in the other approaches.* The more you aggregate, the less you write down. The less you aggregate, the more you write down.

What level of offsetting is appropriate? There is no easy answer to this question. Most people find it uncomfortable to think that a loss in market value say, of the *new*

EXHIBIT 9-10
Net Realizable Value and Net Realizable Value Less a Normal Profit Margin

a.	Inventory item A, at original cost	$ 70
b.	Inventory item A, at estimated current selling price in completed condition	$100
c.	Less: Estimated costs to complete and sell*	– 40
d.	Net realizable value	$ 60
e.	Less: Allowance for normal profit (10% of sales price)	– 10
f.	Net realizable value less normal profit	$ 50

* For goods already completed, as in a retail company, this amount would be the cost to sell.

EXHIBIT 9-11
Methods of Market Value Determination, 1996

Method	Number of companies, 1996
Net realizable value	142
Replacement cost	43
Net realizable value less normal profit margin	3
Estimated net realizable value	4
Sample size (public companies)	200

Source: *Financial Reporting in Canada 1997* (Toronto: CICA, 1997), p. 169.

EXHIBIT 9-12
Application of LCM to Inventory Categories

Inventory Types	Cost	Market	LCM Applied to Individual Items	Classifications	Total
Classification A:					
Item 1	$10,000	$ 9,500	$ 9,500		
Item 2	8,000	9,000	8,000		
	18,000	18,500		$18,000	
Classification B:					
Item 3	21,000	22,000	21,000		
Item 4	32,000	29,000	29,000		
	53,000	51,000		51,000	
Total	$71,000	$69,500			
Inventory valuation under different approaches			$67,500	$69,000	$69,500

car inventory of a car dealer would be avoided because the *used* car inventory has strong resale values. On the other hand, some degree of offsetting, especially within categories, seems appropriate given the nature of the estimates and the fact that sales markets can be hard to predict.

LCM Recording and Reporting

Two methods of recording and reporting the effects of the application of LCM are used in practice:

1. *Direct inventory reduction method.* The inventory holding loss is not separately recorded and reported. Instead, the LCM amount, if it is less than the original cost of the inventory, is recorded and reported each period. Thus, the inventory holding loss is automatically included in cost of goods sold, and ending inventory is reported at LCM. This method is feasible only when LCM is applied to each item of inventory separately.

2. *Inventory allowance method.* The inventory holding loss is separately recorded using a contra inventory account, allowance to reduce inventory to LCM. Thus, the inventory and cost of goods sold amounts are recorded and reported at original cost, while any inventory holding loss is recognized separately. The entry for a loss of $1,000 would be as follows:

Holding loss on inventory	1,000	
Allowance to reduce inventory to LCM		1,000

The major difference between the two methods is the detail in the entries and disclosures on the income statement and balance sheet. The allowance method captures more detail. However, write-downs recognized through the allowance method can reverse in subsequent years, as was true for other allowances, such as the allowance for doubtful accounts and the allowance used to reduce temporary investments to market value. A write-down made directly to inventory is permanent.

CASH FLOW STATEMENT

For retail and wholesale businesses, inventory costs represent expenditures. However, the expenditures do not make their way to the income statement until the inventory is sold. Therefore, the amount of inventory expenditures that are included in cost of goods sold in any accounting period will be different from that amount that was spent to acquire inventory. The cash flow statement must show the amount of inventory *purchased*, not the amount *sold*.

To determine the amount of cash provided by operations, net income must be adjusted by the change in inventory during the period:

- an *increase* in inventory means that the cash flow to purchase inventory was higher than the amount of expense reported as cost of goods sold — the increase must be subtracted from net income in order to reflect higher cash outflow.

- a *decrease* in inventory means that the cash flow to acquire inventory was less than the amount of expense reported in cost of goods sold — the decrease must be added to net income.

A further adjustment must be made for a manufacturing, resource, or service company. The cost of goods sold (or cost of services provided) of such companies almost always includes amortization (e.g., depreciation on facilities or depletion on resources). Any depreciation or amortization that has been charged to inventory, whether to work-in-progress or finished goods, must be added back to net income when determining the cash flow from operations.

DISCLOSURE

According to the inventory section of the *CICA Handbook*, recommended disclosures are as follows:

- the basis for valuation (e.g., historical cost, lower of cost or market, market value) [*CICA* 3030.10];
- major categories of inventory (desirable, not required) [*CICA* 3030.10];
- method of determining cost, *if* the method used for determining cost differs from recent cost of the inventory items [*CICA* 3030.11];
- a definition of market value (desirable, not required), *if* "market" is used in some aspect of inventory valuation [*CICA* 3030.11]; and
- any change in valuation from that used in the prior period, and the effect of a change on net income [*CICA* 3030.13].

Financial Reporting in Canada reports that of the 171 companies (out of a sample of 200) that reported inventories in 1996, all but eight disclosed their bases of valuation. Of the 163 that did disclose their bases of valuation, all used historical cost for at least part of their inventory. About 80% of the companies disclosed the method of cost determination.[6]

MARKET VALUE BASIS

In Chapter 6, we discussed the use of market values for certain types of inventory. Revenue may be recognized when commodities are produced — if a public auction market exists for the commodities and a sale can be completed at any time with minimal effort. Once revenue is recognized, net assets increases. The increase is reflected in the carrying value of the related inventory.

Market value really means net realizable value. Companies that use (or can use) market values include

- Agricultural producers;
- Other commodities, such as oil and certain metals;
- Investment companies, whose activity consists of holding and trading publicly-traded securities; and
- Companies that record revenue on the percentage of completion basis; the recognition of revenue has the effect of increasing the carrying value of the work-in-progress inventory to net realizable value.

The companies that value their inventories at market value are those who use or deal in those inventories as their primary business activity. For example, Franco-Nevada Mining Corporation states in its accounting policies disclosure note that "Gold bullion is valued at the year-end spot price." Open-end investment companies (i.e., mutual funds) are required *by law* to report their securities portfolios at market value.

Companies that produce or deal in commodities may not use market value — market value is an option, not a requirement. If they are bound by fixed-price sales

---

[6] *Financial Reporting in Canada* 1997, p. 168.

contracts, they cannot benefit from an increase in price and therefore cannot recognize revenue based on price changes; historical cost must be used. Similarly, they are protected against price changes if they have hedged the inventory, and historical cost would be the appropriate measure.

Some managers may prefer to use historical cost (or LCM) to value commodity inventories even if they are not bound by fixed price contracts and have not hedged the inventory. While we might be tempted to praise their choice of a "conservative" accounting policy, we must bear in mind that historical cost inventory valuation gives the manager an opportunity to manipulate reported earnings by deciding when to engage in transactions that trigger an accounting gain or loss. Commodity prices (and real economic value) change regardless of whether or not the changes are recognized in the books.

CONCEPT REVIEW

1. Why are cost flow methods irrelevant when *standard costs* are used?
2. When are inventories carried at *market value* instead of cost?
3. What is the definition of *net realizable value*?
4. What does *market* mean in lower of cost or market?
5. What is the difference in reporting holding losses under the direct inventory reduction method and the inventory allowance method?
6. When may inventories be valued at net realizable value, even if it is *higher* than historical cost?

INVENTORY ESTIMATION METHODS

Many large companies rely on the periodic inventory method. Does this mean that they can't prepare monthly or quarterly statements without also taking a physical inventory? Generally, inventory counts are very expensive and therefore may be done only once each fiscal year. So what can be done when statements are needed? The answer is quite simple: inventory can be estimated. In a small business, the owner or inventory manager might be able to provide an accurate estimate. Alternatively, a more formal calculation can be made, using methods such as the gross margin method or the retail inventory method. It's important to understand that these methods *estimate* inventory levels, and thus introduce some unreliability to the financial results, while increasing their timeliness.

Estimation methods are also useful for providing a cross-check on the results of accounting inventory systems. It should be possible to reconcile the estimated inventory (or, more importantly, cost of goods sold) to a physical inventory count or to the accounting records of perpetual inventory. Obviously the reconciliation will not be exact, but there should be a rough similarity between the results of the accounting inventory system (periodic or perpetual) and the estimated inventory. Large discrepancies raise questions of the accuracy of the accounting system, the effectiveness of the system of internal control, or the possibility of theft.

For example, a local manufacturer of fruit juices and soft drinks also distributed Coca-Cola syrup to restaurants and bars. The Coca-Cola syrup was, in fact, the company's biggest single seller and was also the most profitable product. Despite high sales, the company was only marginally profitable. A gross profit analysis revealed that the recorded cost of goods sold was much too high, given the level of sales. A closer examination revealed that the inventory of syrup was too low for the amount that was actually recorded as being sold. It finally was discovered that, due to a supervisory lack of vigilance in reconciling each driver's sales with the inventory loaded onto the truck, it was possible for the company's truck drivers to sell jugs of syrup "on their own account," pocketing the money.

Estimation methods are used primarily in mercantile firms: retailing and wholesaling. They are of more limited usefulness in manufacturing, but still are useful for finished goods inventories. Estimates of inventory cannot be used for audited annual financial statements — a physical count is required.

Gross Margin Method

The **gross margin method** (also known as the *gross profit method*) assumes that a constant gross margin estimated on recent sales can be used to estimate inventory values from current sales. That is, the gross margin rate (gross margin divided by sales), based on recent past performance, is assumed to be reasonably constant in the short run. The gross margin method has two basic characteristics, (1) it requires the development of an estimated gross margin rate for different lines or products and (2) it applies the rate to relevant groups of items.

Is the method accurate? Well, it depends on whether gross margins are really "reasonably constant in the short run" or not! If retail prices are slashed this year to spur consumer demand, or theft has increased, the gross margin method will overstate earnings and inventory, perhaps materially. Similarly, if the product mix changes a lot in the current period, the results will not be accurate.

For example, if a company has traditionally sold about half its volume in a high-profit category, and half in a low-profit category, the historical gross profit margin will reflect this mix. In the current year, if volumes fall off in the high-profit side, the estimation method will produce inaccurate results. It's better to do separate estimates for each different product line. Mis-estimates will be uncovered at the end of the year, when inventory is actually counted — an unpleasant "surprise" for those who relied on the interim statements.

Estimating the ending inventory by the gross margin method requires five steps:

1. Estimate the gross margin rate on the basis of prior years' sales: gross margin rate = (sales – cost of goods sold) ÷ sales.
2. Compute total cost of goods available for sale in the usual manner (beginning inventory plus purchases), based on actual data provided by the accounts.
3. Compute the estimated gross margin amount by multiplying sales by the estimated gross margin rate.
4. Compute cost of goods sold by subtracting the computed gross margin amount from sales.
5. Compute ending inventory by subtracting the computed cost of goods sold from the cost of goods available for sale.

Application of the gross margin method is illustrated in Exhibit 9-13.

The gross margin method is used to:

1. Test the reasonableness of an inventory valuation determined by some other means such as a physical inventory count or from perpetual inventory records. For example, assume the company in Exhibit 9-13 counted inventory, and got a figure of $10,000. The gross margin method provides an approximation of $7,000, which suggests that the physical count may be overvalued and should be examined.
2. Estimate the ending inventory for interim financial reports prepared during the year when it is impractical to count the inventory physically and a perpetual inventory system is not used.
3. Estimate the cost of inventory destroyed by an accident such as fire or storm. Valuation of inventory lost is necessary to account for the accident and to establish a basis for insurance claims and income taxes. This is an example of a case

where it would be helpful to know the markup on cost (i.e., gross profit ÷ cost of goods sold) since cost is used for the insurance claim and to establish the tax deductible loss.

4. Develop budget estimates of cost of goods sold, gross margin, and inventory consistent with a sales revenue budget.

Retail Inventory Method

The retail inventory method is often used by retail stores, especially department stores that sell a wide variety of items. In such situations, perpetual inventory procedures may be impractical, and a complete physical inventory count is usually taken only once annually. The retail inventory method is appropriate when items sold within a department have essentially the same markup rate and articles purchased for resale are priced immediately. Two major advantages of the retail inventory method are its ease of use and reduced record-keeping requirements (compared to perpetual inventory systems).

The retail inventory method uses both retail value and actual cost data to compute a ratio of cost to retail (referred to as the cost ratio), calculates the ending inventory at *retail value*, and converts that retail value to a cost value by applying the computed cost ratio to the ending retail value.

Application of the retail inventory method requires that internal records be kept to provide data on

- sales revenue
- beginning inventory valued at both cost and retail
- purchases during the period valued at both cost and retail
- adjustments to the original retail price, such as additional markups, markup cancellations, markdowns, markdown cancellations, and employee discounts
- other adjustments, such as interdepartmental transfers, returns, breakage, and damaged goods

The retail inventory method differs from the gross margin method in that it uses a computed cost ratio based on the actual relationship between cost and retail for the current period, rather than an historical ratio. The computed cost ratio is often an average across several different kinds of goods sold.

The retail inventory method is illustrated in Exhibit 9-14. The steps are as follows:

1. Determine cost of good available for sale at cost and retail. The total cost of goods available for sale during January 20X3 is determined to be $210,000 at cost and $300,000 at retail, as shown in Exhibit 9-14.

2. Compute the cost ratio (ratio of cost to sales). This is done by dividing the total cost of goods available for sale at cost ($210,000) by the same items at retail ($300,000). In this instance, the cost ratio is ($210,000 ÷ $300,000) = .70, or 70%, as shown in Exhibit 9-14. This is an average cost application of the retail method, because both beginning inventory and purchases are included in determining the cost ratio.

3. Compute closing inventory at retail (goods available for sale at retail, less sales.) This is done by taking the total cost of goods available for sale at retail ($300,000) less the goods that were sold in January ($260,000), resulting in the value of the ending inventory at retail ($40,000), as shown in Exhibit 9-14.

4. Compute ending inventory at cost. This is done by applying the cost ratio (70%), derived in (2), to the ending inventory at retail ($40,000), derived in (3). The result is an ending inventory of $28,000 at cost ($40,000 × 70%).

EXHIBIT 9-13
Gross Margin Method Applied

	Known Data	Following Computations:* Estimated Results
Net sales revenue (base amount)	$10,000	$10,000
Cost of goods sold:		
Beginning inventory	$ 5,000	$ 5,000
Add: Purchases	8,000	8,000
Goods available for sale	13,000	13,000
Less Ending inventory		7,000
Cost of goods sold		6,000
Gross margin		$ 4,000

Steps:
1. Gross margin rate (estimated as percent of sales based on last year's results) = 40%
2. Goods available for sale, above: $13,000
3. Gross margin: $4,000 (i.e., $10,000 × 40%)
4. Cost of goods sold: $6,000, ($10,000 – $4,000)
5. Ending inventory $7,000, ($13,000 – $6,000)

Markups and Markdowns

The data used for Exhibit 9-14 assumed no changes in the sales price of the merchandise as originally set. Frequently, however, the original sales price on merchandise is changed, particularly at the end of the selling season or when replacement costs are changing. The retail inventory method requires that a careful record be kept of all changes to the original sales price because these changes affect the inventory cost computation. To apply the retail inventory method, it is important to distinguish among the following terms:

- **Original sales price.** Sale price first marked on the merchandise.

- **Markup.** The original or initial amount that the merchandise is marked up above cost. It is the difference between the purchase cost and the original sales price, and it may be expressed either as a dollar amount or a percentage of either cost or sales price. Sometimes this markup is called initial markup or markon.

- **Additional markup.** Any increase in the sales price above the original sales price. The original sales price is the base from which additional markup is measured.

- **Additional markup cancellation.** Cancellation of all, or some, of an additional markup. Additional markup less additional markup cancellations is usually called net additional markup.

- **Markdown.** A reduction in the original sales price.

- **Markdown cancellation.** An increase in the sales price (that does not exceed the original sales price) after a reduction in the original sales price markdown.

The definitions are illustrated in Exhibit 9-15. An item that cost $8 is originally marked to sell at $10. This item is subsequently marked up $1 to sell at $11, then marked down to $10, and finally reduced to a sales price of $7.

EXHIBIT 9-14
Retail Inventory Method Illustrated, Average Cost

	At Cost	At Retail
Goods available for sale:		
Beginning inventory (1 January 20X2)	$ 15,000	$ 25,000
Purchases during January 20X2	195,000	275,000
Total goods available for sale	$210,000	300,000
Cost ratio:		
$210,000 ÷ $300,000 = 70%; average, January 20X2		
Deduct January sales at retail		260,000
Ending inventory, 31 January 20X2:		
At retail		$ 40,000
At cost ($40,000 × 70%)	$ 28,000	

EXHIBIT 9-15
Computation of Final Sales Price

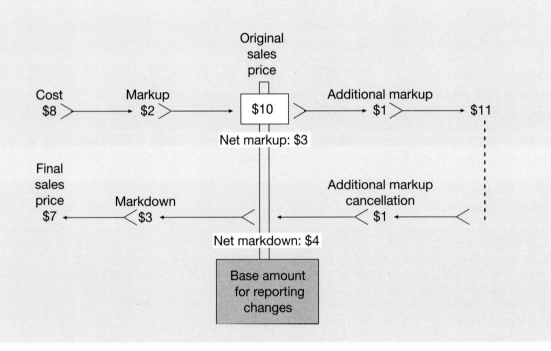

In the application of the retail method, markups and markup cancellations, markdowns and markdown cancellations are all included in the early calculations that determine goods available for sale at cost and at retail. However, in order to provide a conservative cost ratio that will approximate lower of cost or market (LCM), the denominator of the cost ratio *excludes net markdowns*. See the example in Exhibit 9-16.

The retail inventory method can be applied in different ways to estimate the cost of ending inventory under alternative inventory cost flow assumptions such as FIFO and LIFO. In each case, the cost flow assumption will dictate the items to be included in the cost ratio.

EXHIBIT 9-16
Retail Inventory Method Sandia Company

	At Cost	At Retail
Goods available for sale:		
Beginning inventory	$ 550	$ 900
Purchases during period	6,290	8,900
Plus: additional markups during period		225
Less: additional markup calcellations		(25)
		$10,000
Less: markdowns		(600)
Less: markdown cancellations		100
Total goods available for sale	$ 6,840	$ 9,500
Cost ratio:		
$6,840 ÷ ($900 + $8,900 + $225 - $25) = $6,840 ÷ $10,000 = 68.4%		
Deduct:		
Sales		(8,500)
Ending inventory:		
At retail		$ 1,000
At cost, approximating LCM ($1,000 × 68.4%)	$ 684	

Like the gross margin method, the retail inventory method is used only to estimate the amount of the ending inventory and cost of goods sold. A physical inventory count should be taken at least annually as a check on the accuracy of the estimated inventory amounts. This method provides a test of the overall reasonableness of a physical inventory.

The retail inventory method is also useful if the entity counts its inventory and then extends the inventory sheets *at retail*. Remember, retail prices are much easier to determine on the selling floor than cost! The retail value then is converted to cost by applying the retail inventory method without reference to the costs of individual items. This value may be used for external reporting if sufficient evidence is accumulated to support the accuracy of the cost percentages.

Perhaps even more than the gross margin method, though, the retail inventory method is subject to estimation errors. A lot of its accuracy depends on how assiduous the company is at keeping track of markups and markdowns and other data needed to develop an accurate cost ratio.

1. Why would a company use an inventory estimation method?
2. What is the basic difference between the gross profit method and the retail method?
3. Why are markdowns excluded from the cost ratio when the retail method is used?

CONCEPT REVIEW

SUMMARY OF KEY POINTS

1. Inventories are assets consisting of goods owned by the business and held either for future sale or for consumption in manufacture or service provision.

2. Cost at acquisition, including the costs to obtain the inventory, such as freight, is the valuation basis of inventory.

3. Work in process and finished goods inventories of manufacturers should include raw materials, direct labour, and at least the variable portion of manufacturing overhead.

4. All goods owned at the inventory date, including those on consignment, should be counted and valued.

5. Either a periodic or a perpetual inventory system may be used for merchandise inventories and for manufacturers' inventories of raw materials and finished goods, but computer technology now makes it easier and less costly to use a perpetual system, which also provides up-to-date inventory records.

6. Several cost flow assumptions are in current use, including specific identification, average cost, FIFO, and LIFO. LIFO is very rarely used in Canada, except by Canadian subsidiaries of U.S. parent companies that also use that method.

7. Special accounting problems are encountered by firms using standard cost, just-in-time inventory systems, or net realizable value to recognize inventory.

8. Losses on firm purchase commitments, when they can be reasonably estimated and are material, are recognized in the accounts if the loss is likely and can be estimated. Otherwise, such commitments are often disclosed only in the notes.

9. The lower-of-cost-or-market (LCM) method of estimating inventory recognizes declines in market value in the period of decline. The lower-of-cost-or-market method values inventories at market if market is below cost. Market may be interpreted to be net realizable value, net realizable value less a normal profit margin, or replacement cost. Use of net realizable value is most common.

10. Market value may be used as the inventory valuation basis if the inventories are commodities, such as traded securities, precious metals, and agricultural commodities.

11. The gross margin method is used to estimate inventory values when it is difficult or impractical to take a physical count of the goods. The method is most accurate when profit margins are stable.

12. The retail method of estimating inventory applies the ratio of actual cost to sales value to the ending inventory at sales value to estimate the inventory value at lower of cost or market.

13. The cash flow from operations is affected by (1) changes in inventory levels and (2) amortization that has been included in the inventory. Cash flow must be adjusted to reflect the amount of inventory *purchased* rather than sold, and must be adjusted by adding back any amortization.

REVIEW PROBLEM

The inventory data for the Black Eagle Lounge for the beginning of June is shown below. Compute the inventory value at 30 June, using both perpetual inventory and periodic inventory approaches, under each of the following methods:

1. Specific cost identification
2. Average cost
3. FIFO
4. LIFO

```
   1 June — no inventory on hand
   2 June — bought one case of Red Hook Ale @ $10
  13 June — bought one case of Red Hook Ale @ $16
  24 June — sold one case of Red Hook Ale @ $20*
  28 June — bought one case of Red Hook Ale @ $18
  * This case of Red Hook Ale was purchased on 13 June.
```

REVIEW PROBLEM — SOLUTION

At 30 June, there are two cases of ale on hand. The carrying value of the 30 June inventory is shown below under each method:

1. Specific identification:
   Periodic   (1 @ $10) + (1 @ $18) = $28
   Perpetual (1 @ $10) + (1 @ $18) = $28

2. Average cost:
   Periodic   [[(1@$10) + (1@$16) + (1@$18)] ÷ 3] × 2 remaining = $14.67 ×
                  2 = $29.34
   Perpetual (moving average):

Units Bought (Sold)	@ Cost	Total Inventory Cost	Total Inventory Units	Average Cost
1	$ 10	$ 10	1	$ 10.00
1	16	26	2	13.00
(1)	(13)	13	1	13.00
1	8	$ 31	2	15.50

3. FIFO:
   Periodic   (1 @ $16) + (1 @ $18) = $34
   Perpetual (1 @ $16) + (1 @ $18) = $34

4. LIFO:
   Periodic   (1 @ $10) + (1 @ $16) = $26
   Perpetual (1 @ $10) + (1 @ $18) = $28

Comments:

- Under specific identification, *periodic* and *perpetual* always give the same result, because the cost of each specific item sold is identified. Therefore, the same inventory amount is shown for both.
- Average cost yields different results under the periodic and perpetual methods, because the numbers of items and their costs are averaged together differently under a moving average (perpetual) than under a historical tabulation of purchases (periodic).
- FIFO always yields the same result under both periodic and perpetual methods.
- LIFO almost always yields different results under the two methods, unless the purchase cost per unit is constant.

QUESTIONS

9-1   In general, why should accountants and managers be especially concerned with inventories?

9-2   List and briefly explain the usual inventory classifications for a trading entity and a manufacturing entity.

9-3   Explain three areas in which accounting policy must be established for inventories.

9-4   Which of the following items should be included in inventory?
    a. Goods held by our agents for us.
    b. Goods held by us for sale on commission.
    c. Goods held by us but awaiting return to vendor because of damaged condition.

    d. Goods returned to us from buyer, reason unknown to date.

    e. Goods out on consignment.

    f. Goods sold under conditional resale agreements, where we have agreed to repurchase the items that our customer does not resell, and reimburse the customer for carrying costs incurred.

    g. Merchandise at our branch for sale.

    h. Merchandise at conventions for display purposes.

9-5   Which of the following items should be included in determining unit cost for inventory purposes?

    a. Freight-in on purchased goods.

    b. Cash discounts on credit purchases.

    c. Freight on goods purchased.

9-6   What is variable costing? What impact would it have on the inventory account on the balance sheet?

9-7   Explain the principal features of a periodic inventory system.

9-8   Briefly explain the differences between periodic and perpetual inventory systems. Under what circumstances is each generally used?

9-9   Does the adoption of a perpetual inventory system eliminate the need for a physical count or measurement of inventories? Explain.

9-10   What is the primary purpose to be considered in selecting a particular inventory cost flow method? Why is the selection important?

9-11   Explain the specific identification inventory costing method and explain when the method is appropriate.

9-12   Distinguish between a weighted-average and a moving-average in determining inventory unit cost. When is each generally used? Explain.

9-13   Explain the essential features of first-in, first-out (FIFO). Explain the difference in the application of FIFO under a periodic and perpetual inventory system.

9-15   Compare the balance sheet and income statement effects of FIFO with those of LIFO when prices are rising and when prices are falling.

9-16   Can standard cost be used to value an inventory for external reporting? Explain.

9-17   Briefly outline the accounting and reporting of losses on purchase commitments when (a) the purchase contract is subject to revision or cancellation and (b) it is non-cancellable and a loss is probable.

9-18   What types of inventory are most frequently measured at selling price or net realizable value in excess of cost?

9-19   Define replacement cost, net realizable value, and net realizable value less a normal profit margin as approaches used to estimate market values of inventory. Which is GAAP in Canada?

9-20   Why is the LCM rule applied to inventory valuation?

9-21   What is the holding loss (gain) recognized using the LCM, inventory allowance method, for each of the years 20X4 through 20X8?

	Cost	Market
20X3 Ending inventory	$ 0	$ 0
20X4 Ending inventory	12,000	14,000
20X5 Ending inventory	15,000	13,000
20X6 Ending inventory	18,000	17,000
20X7 Ending inventory	20,000	16,000
20X8 Ending inventory	22,000	23,000

9-22   Explain why it is important to decide whether to apply the LCM test to individual inventory items, categories or totals.

9-23   List the required finacial statement disclosures for inventory.

9-24 Approximate the value of ending inventory, assuming the following data:

Cost of goods available for sale	$170,000
Sales	150,000
Gross margin (on sales)	25%

9-25 Explain the gross margin method. What basic assumption is implicit in the gross margin method?

9-26 Explain the approach of the retail method for estimating inventories. What data must be accumulated in order to apply the retail method?

CASE 9-1

Traders International Ltd.

Traders International Ltd. (TIL) has recently been awarded a monopoly to export four different agricultural products grown on a Caribbean island. That is, they are the only enterprise allowed to buy the goods from local farming enterprises and market the products on the international market. TIL is incorporated in the Caribbean island, which has no tax on corporate earnings. TIL is interested in attracting debt or equity investment from multinational companies in the future, as aggressive expansion is planned.

Inventory of the four agricultural products is the major asset of TIL; the products can be stored for several years. TIL acquires the inventory from local farmers for "current market value less 10%." Market value is quite volatile. TIL is expected to earn profits by timing the sale of these products, and selling during periods of high prices. Government equity and private bank loans finance inventory that accumulates when low world prices dominate. Profits of TIL, after bonuses and interest are paid, are distributed to the government, as a shareholder, and finally to the farmers, in relation to their volume with TIL.

It is now the end of the first fiscal year, and you, the accountant, have been asked to comment on issues surrounding the choice of an inventory costing method: FIFO, LIFO, or average cost. Domestic accounting rules allow any of the three.

The company president has asked the following questions:

1. In general, how are "generally accepted accounting principles" chosen?

2. Why would an intelligent and informed reader care about the inventory costing method? It is, after all, just an accounting allocation problem. Cash flow for purchases and inventory carrying costs are not affected by the choice of method.

3. What method do you recommend for TIL?

The president has reminded you that managers' bonuses are a function of reported net income. There continues to be some pressure to create a competitor to TIL, in the hopes that some competition would inspire best operating results.

Required:

Write a report responding to the president's questions.

[CGA-Canada, adapted]

CASE 9-2

Michael Metals Limited

Michael Metals Limited (MML) has been a private company since it was incorporated under federal legislation over 40 years ago. At the present time (September 20X5), ownership is divided among four cousins, each of whom holds 25% of the 100 outstanding common shares of MML. Each shareholder obtained the shares from his or her parents, who formed and operated the company for many years.

The owners have decided to offer the business for sale over a period of years. Laser Investments Limited (LIL), an investment firm holding shares of companies in a number of other businesses, has been given the opportunity to acquire 46.67% of MML immediately and the balance over the next five years. The proposal is as follows:

	Shares	Percentage
Obtain 33.33% by purchasing 50 new shares of MML	50	33.33%
Acquire one-fifth of the shares held by each cousin, reducing their shares from 25 to 20 each	20	13.34
	70	46.67%

The other 80 shares would be acquired at a rate of four per year from each cousin for five years. The purchase price of the 80 shares would be tied to MML's profitability as measured by generally accepted accounting principles (GAAP).

The board of directors of LIL is interested in pursuing the investment in MML. The proposed purchase price of the initial 70 shares is to be partially based on the financial statements for fiscal 20X5 and for future years. The board of directors of LIL has asked its auditors, Bouchard and Co., Chartered Accountants, to assist it in evaluating the proposed purchase. Jules Bouchard, the partner in charge of the engagement, has asked you, CA, to prepare a memo discussing all relevant considerations pertaining to the purchase so that he can discuss the issues with the board of directors.

MML is a scrap metal dealer, primarily dealing in iron and copper. In recent years it has also dealt in lead, brass, aluminum, and other metals. Scrap iron is acquired from a variety of sources (e.g., old automobiles, appliances, and spoilage during manufacturing processes) and is sorted, compacted, and sold to steel mills. Much of the scrap copper is coated electrical wiring, which has to be stripped of the insulation coating and then chopped into pieces. The copper wire pieces are stored in barrels, which are about one metre high. In summary, a limited amount of processing is needed to convert the purchased scrap into saleable products.

Most of the scrap arrives at MML's storage yards on trucks, which are weighed both loaded and empty in order to determine the physical quantities of scrap on the truck. Some of the scrap is kept indoors, but most is kept outdoors in several large piles in different yard locations. MML's property is protected by tall wire fences and monitored by security cameras 24 hours a day.

To be successful in this industry, a scrap dealer has to buy at low prices and store the processed or unprocessed scrap until metal prices are high. Sometimes, quantities of some grades of metal have to be stored for several years. When selling prices are stable, the purchase price has to be sufficiently low that a profit can be made after processing costs have been incurred.

MML tends to operate at its maximum bank line of credit, as it is generally short of cash. MML's maximum line of credit is 70% of its receivables and 50% of its inventory.

Your client arranged for you to have access to all of MML's accounting records and the auditors' working papers. MML's fiscal year-end is 30 June.

From the accounting records and auditors' working papers, you and your staff have assembled the information provided in the following exhibit.

Required:

Prepare the memo.

MICHAEL METALS LIMITED
Information Gathered by CA

1. From audit working paper reviews:

   a. Most of the processing equipment and the buildings are old and almost fully depreciated. The company's land was purchased many years ago. As a result, inventory often represents two-thirds of the balance sheet assets, and receivables are close to one-fifth of assets in most years. Total assets vary between $25 and $32 million from year to year. Accounts receivable turnover can be anywhere between 1.5 and 4.0 times per year. Inventory is $19 million at the end of 20X5.

   b. Perpetual records are limited to estimates of quantity because the quality of the scrap, the amount of insulation on wires, and a variety of other factors affect how much saleable metal will result from a bulk purchase of scrap.

   c. A seller of scrap (to MML) seldom knows how much it weighs. MML usually quotes a price per unit but does not inform the seller of the weight until the delivery truck has been weighed at MML's yard. MML's auditors are suspicious that MML reduces weights before calculating the amount payable.

2. The truck weigh scales produce weigh tickets that can be attached to receivable and payable invoices. However, no numerical ticket sequence exists to account for all tickets that have been printed. Receiving records are handwritten in a looseleaf book.

3. Approximately 15% of sales invoices have to be adjusted for weight discrepancies between what was shipped and what the customer claims to have received. On average, the reductions are approximately 20% of the invoice amount.

4. The perpetual inventory weight records appear to have been adjusted each year, sometimes in material amounts, to whatever the physical inventory count indicated.

5. In recent years, the after-tax profits of MML have ranged between $1.2 and $3 million, after management bonuses.

6. MML maintains two vacation homes, one in Florida and one in Barbados. These homes are usually occupied by suppliers and customers of MML free of charge.

7. Accounts receivable and inventory are pledged as security to MML's bank. In addition, the bank has a general security agreement against all other assets and has limited personal guarantees from the shareholders.

8. Revenue is usually recognized on shipment of the metal. Adjustments for weight discrepancies are made as they become known to MML.

9. MML's management has been considering expansion because one competitor is nearing retirement and wants to sell his company. In recent years, MML has purchased from, and sold to, this competitor. MML has also borrowed inventory from and loaned inventory to this competitor.

10. Some purchases of scrap are acquired on a conditional basis. MML pays the supplier only after it has determined the quality of metal that the scrap yielded when processed.

[CICA, adapted]

EXERCISES

E9-1 *Inventory Cost — Items to Include in Inventory:* On 31 December 20X5, Patco computed an ending inventory valuation of $250,000 based on a periodic inventory system. The accounts for 20X5 have been adjusted and closed. Subsequently, the accountant prepared a schedule that showed that the inventory should be $291,500, not $250,000.

a. Merchandise in store (at 50% above cost)	$250,000
b. Merchandise out on consignment at sales price (including markup of 60% on selling price)	10,000
c. Goods held on consignment from Davis Electronics at sales price (sales commission, 20% of sales price, included)	4,000
d. Goods purchased, in transit (shipped FOB shipping point, estimated freight, not included, $800), invoice price	5,000
e. Goods (office equipment) removed from the warehouse and now used in company marketing office (at cost)	20,000
f. Goods out on approval, sales price, $2,500, cost, $1,000	2,500
Total inventory as corrected	$291,500

Average income tax rate = 40%

Required:

1. Review the items making up the list of inventory. Compute the correct ending inventory amount.

2. The income statement and balance sheet now reflect a closing inventory of $250,000. List the items on the income statement and balance sheet for 20X5 that should be corrected for the above errors; give the amount of the error for each item affected, if possible.

E9-2 *Inventory Cost:* Majestic Stores Inc., a dealer in radio and television sets, buys large quantities of a television model that costs $500. The contract reads that if 200 or more sets are purchased during the year, a rebate of $20 per set will be made. On 15 December, the records showed that 150 sets had been purchased; purchases are recorded at $75,000 (150 × $500). All these units were sold. Fifty more sets were ordered FOB destination. The sets were received on 22 December, and a request for the rebate was made. The rebate cheque was received on 20 January, after Majestic's books were closed. Furthermore, the supplier provides terms of 2/10, n/30. Majestic has a policy of always paying invoices within the discount period. Discounts are recorded as a credit to an interest income account. Further investigation reveals that a total of $1,760 of freight was paid to acquire the sets purchased this year, including $375 on the last order of 50 sets.

Required:

1. Calculate the ending inventory value at 31 December.

2. What entry should be made relative to the rebate on 31 December? Why?

3. What entry would be made on 20 January?

E9-3 *Periodic and Perpetual Inventory — Journal Entries:* The records for Cummings Company at 31 December 20X5 reflected the following:

	Units	Unit Price
Sales during period (for cash)	10,000	$10 (sales price)
Inventory at beginning of period	2,000	6 (cost)
Merchandise purchased during period (for cash)	16,000	6 (cost)
Purchase returns during period (cash refund)	100	6 (cost)
Inventory at end of period	?	6 (cost)
Total expenses (excluding cost of goods sold) = $30,000		

Required:

Give entries for the above transactions, including adjusting entries to correct inventory levels, as needed, at the end of the period. Repeat the entries twice in parallel columns: assume a periodic inventory system for Case A and a perpetual inventory system for Case B.

E9-4 *Perpetual Inventory:* Perforated Pipe Company uses a perpetual inventory system. The items on hand are physically counted on a rotation basis throughout the year so that all items are checked twice each year. After one such count, the following data relating to goods on hand are available:

Product	Perpetual Inventory Units	Physical Count Units	Cost
A	450	390	$12
B	1,500	1,520	5
C	2,000	1,950	4
D	8,000	7,980	2
E	13,000	13,100	6

Required:

Determine the amount of the net inventory overage or shortage and give the adjustment to the perpetual inventory records. Give any entry needed to record the final disposition of any discrepancy.

E9-5 *Inventory Cost Methods:* The inventory records of Acme Appliances showed the following data relative to a food processor in inventory (the transactions occurred in the order given):

Transaction	Units	Unit Cost
1. Inventory	30	$19.00
2. Purchase	45	20.00
3. Sale	50	
4. Purchase	50	20.80
5. Sale	50	
6. Purchase	50	21.60

Required:

Compute the cost of goods sold for the period and the ending inventory, assuming the following (round unit costs to nearest cent):

    a. Weighted average (periodic inventory system)

    b. Moving average (perpetual inventory system)

    c. FIFO

    d. LIFO (periodic inventory system)

    e. LIFO (perpetual inventory system)

E9-6 *Inventory Cost Methods:* The inventory records of Gilman Company provided the following data for one item of merchandise for sale (the six transactions occurred in the order given):

	Units	Unit Cost	Total Amount
Beginning inventory	500	$6.00	$ 3,000
1. Purchases	600	6.10	3,660
2. Sales	(900)		
3. Purchases	600	6.20	3,720
4. Sales	(500)		
5. Purchases	400	6.30	2,520
6. Sales	(300)		$12,900 (for 2,100 units purchased)
Total	400		

Required:

1. Complete the following schedule (round unit costs to nearest cent and total amounts to nearest dollar):

	Valuation	
Costing Method	Ending Inventory	Cost of Goods Sold
a. FIFO	$	$
b. LIFO (periodic inventory system)	$	$
c. Weighted average	$	$
d. LIFO (perpetual inventory system)	$	$

2. Compute the amount of pre-tax income and rank the methods in order of the amount of pre-tax income (highest first), assuming that FIFO pre-tax income is $50,000.

3. Which method is preferable? Explain your choice.

E9-7 *Inventory Cost Methods:* The College Store inventory records showed the following data relative to a particular item sold regularly (transactions occurred in the order given):

Transaction	Units	Unit Cost
1. Inventory	2,000	$5.00
2. Purchases	18,000	5.20
3. Sales (at $13 per unit)	7,000	
4. Purchases	6,000	5.50
5. Sales (at $13.50 per unit)	16,000	
6. Purchases	3,000	6.00

Required:

1. Complete the following schedule (round unit costs to nearest cent and total costs of inventory to the nearest $10):

	Ending Inventory	Cost of Goods Sold	Gross Margin
a. FIFO			
b. Weighted average			
c. Moving average (show computations)			
d. LIFO (periodic inventory system)			
e. LIFO (perpetual inventory system)			

2. Prepare journal entries, including year-end adjusting entries to establish ending inventory, if needed, for the two average calculations (b) and (c) above. Assume that the weighted average method is used with a periodic system and the moving average method with a perpetual system.

3. Explain how your entries in (2) would be different if a standard cost system were used, with the standard cost established at $5.50.

E9-8 *Net Realizable Value of Damaged Goods:* A fire damaged some of the merchandise held for sale by AAA Appliance Company. Seven television sets and six stereo sets were damaged. They were not covered by insurance. The sets will be repaired and sold as used sets. Data are as follows:

	Per Set	
	Television	Stereo
Inventory (at cost)	$400	$250
Estimated cost to repair	50	30
Estimated cost to sell	20	20
Estimated sales price	200	110

Required:

1. Compute net realizable value for each set and for the inventory in total.

2. Give the separate entries to record the damaged merchandise inventory for the television and stereo sets. Assume a perpetual inventory system.

3. Give the entries to record the subsequent repair of the television sets and the stereo sets (credit cash).

4. Give the entries to record sale for cash of two television sets and one stereo set. It will be necessary to record payment of the distribution costs in a separate entry. Credit distribution costs in the entry to record the sale. Assume that actual sales prices equalled the estimated sales prices.

E9-9 *Loss on Purchase Commitment:* During 20X5, Mossback Company signed a contract with Alpha Corporation to "purchase 15,000 sub-assemblies at $30 each during 20X6."

Required:

1. On 31 December 20X5, the end of the annual accounting period, the financial statements are to be prepared. Assume that the cost of the sub-assemblies is dropping and the total estimated current replacement cost is $425,000. Under what additional contractual and economic conditions should disclosure of the contract terms be made only by means of a note in the financial statements? Prepare an appropriate note.

2. What contractual and economic conditions would require accrual of a loss? Give the accrual entry.

3. Assume that the sub-assemblies are received in 20X5 when their replacement cost was $410,000. The contract was paid in full. Give the required entry, assuming the entry in requirement (2) was made, and a periodic inventory system is used.

E9-10 *LCM:* The management of Tarry Hardware Company has collected the following information to do the LCM valuation of inventory items:

- Handyman edgers: 300 on hand; cost, $22 each; replacement cost, $16; estimated sale price, $30; estimated distribution cost, $3 each; and normal profit, 20% of the sales price.
- Handyman hedge clippers: 200 on hand; cost $50 each; replacement cost, $36 each; estimated sales price, $90; estimated distribution cost, $28; and normal profit, 40% of the sales price.

Required:

1. Present alternate values for "market" for each inventory item. Which is to be used for the LCM test?

2. What amount of write-down is required, assuming use of the following definitions of market value:

a. replacement cost

b. net realizable value

c. net realizable value less a normal profit margin.

3. Assume that all the goods are subsequently resold for $17,000. How much gross profit would be recorded after the write-down in (a), (b), and (c)? In retrospect, which do you think portrays reality most accurately?

E9-11 *LCM — Compute the Allowance:* The records of Loren Moving Company showed the following inventory data:

	Cost	Market
Category 1		
Item A	$10,000	$ 9,000
Item B	40,000	35,000
Item C	25,000	33,000
Category 2		
Item D	$18,000	$16,500
Item E	20,000	4,000
Item F	42,000	42,000

Required:

1. Calculate three different amounts that could justifiably be recorded as the allowance to reduce inventory to the lower of cost or market.

2. Which of the above approaches do you prefer? Explain.

E9-12 *Gross Margin and Retail Inventory Methods — Multiple Choice: Choose the best answer for easch question.*

1. Dart Company's accounting records included the following information:

Inventory, 1 January 20X6	$ 500,000
Purchases during 20X6	2,500,000
Sales during 20X6	3,200,000

A physical inventory taken on 31 December 20X6, resulted in an ending inventory of $575,000. Dart's gross margin on sales has remained constant at 25% in recent years. Dart suspects that some inventory may have been taken by a new employee. At 31 December 20X6, the estimated cost of missing inventory is
a. $25,000.
b. $100,000.
c. $175,000.
d. $225,000.

2. Lin Co. sells its merchandise at a gross margin of 30%. The following figures are among those pertaining to Lin's operations for the six months ended 30 June 20X6:

Sales	$200,000
Beginning inventory	50,000
Purchases	130,000

On 30 June 20X6, all of Lin's inventory was destroyed by fire. The estimated cost of this destroyed inventory was
a. $120,000.
b. $70,000.
c. $40,000.
d. $20,000.

3. Dean Company uses the retail inventory method to estimate its inventory for interim statement purposes. Data relating to the computation of the inventory at 31 July 20X7 are as follows:

	Cost	Retail
Beginning inventory, 1 February 20X7	$ 180,000	$ 250,000
Purchases	1,020,000	1,575,000
Markups, net		175,000
Sales		1,725,000
Markdowns, net		125,000

Under the retail method, approximating LCM, Dean's estimated inventory at 31 July 20X7 is
a. $90,000.
b. $96,000.
c. $102,000.
d. $150,000.

4. At 31 December 20X5, the following information was available from Palo Company's accounting records:

	Cost	Retail
Inventory, 1 January 20X5	$ 73,500	$101,500
Purchases	411,600	577,500
Additional markups	—	21,000
Available for sale	$485,100	$700,000

If sales were $553,000 and markdowns totalled $7,000, under the retail method which approximates LCM, Palo Company's estimated inventory at 31 December 20X5 is
a. $97,020.
b. $140,000.
c. $102,900.
d. $98,000.

E9-13 *Gross Margin Method:* You are auditing the records of Coldridge Corporation. A physical inventory has been taken by the company under your observation. However, the valuations have not been completed. The records of the company provide the following data: sales, $315,000 (gross); returned sales, $5,000 (returned to stock); purchases (gross), $155,000; beginning inventory, $100,000; freight-in, $7,000; and purchase returns and allowances, $2,000. The gross margin last period was 35% of net sales; you anticipate that it will be 25% for the year under audit.

Required:

Estimate the cost of the ending inventory using the gross margin method. Show computations.

E9-14 *Retail Inventory Method:* Dan's Clothing Store values its inventory using the retail inventory method at the lower of average cost or market. The following data are available for the month of June 20X5:

	Cost	Selling Price
Inventory, 1 June	$ 53,800	$ 80,000
Markdowns		21,000
Markups		29,000
Markdown cancellations		10,000
Markup cancellations		9,000
Purchases	173,200	223,600
Sales		250,000
Purchase returns and allowances	3,000	3,600
Sales returns and allowances		10,000

Required:

Prepare a schedule to compute the estimated inventory at 30 June, using the retail inventory method to approximate LCM.

[AICPA, adapted]

PROBLEMS

P9-1 *Inventory Issues:* Consider each of the following independent situations. In each, describe the accounting policy decision. Describe the impact that the chosen policy has had on the income statement and balance sheet. If the company's policy is not correct, or if there is an alternate policy that should be considered, explain the alternative.

Case A. Inventory was bought for $675,000 in 20X6 and was recorded at cost. The inventory was bought under the terms of a purchase agreement signed in 20X4; the market value of these goods had been $695,000 at the end of 20X4, $640,000 at the end of 20X5, and was $660,000 on the date of acquisition.

Case B. Inventory at the end of 20X5 (last year) included goods, with a cost of $80,000, plus taxes of $13,500, that was not received until three days after the year-end. The invoice was recorded (purchases and accounts payable) in December, before the goods were received.

Case C. Inventory was received, and recorded at the invoice price of $56,000. The goods had not been sold at year-end. Subsequently, a discount of $5,000 was received on the goods. This discount was recorded as other revenue.

Case D. In the lower-of-cost-or-market valuation at year-end, replacement cost was used as the definition of market value. The evaluation resulted in a write-down of $135,500. The company reports that, although its supplier's prices were lower for certain products at year-end, thus causing the write-down, its prices to its own customers had remained at constant levels.

Case E. Inventories, costing $56,000, with a sales price of $79,000, were with a customer on consignment. These goods were excluded from the physical inventory count, and the $79,000 sale was recorded in the current fiscal year, because in the past this customer has always been able to sell all the goods sent on consignment.

P9-2 *Perpetual Inventory — FIFO:* Walsh Company maintains perpetual inventory records on a FIFO basis for the three main products distributed by the company. A physical inventory is taken at the end of each year in order to check the perpetual inventory records.

The following information relating to one of the products, blenders, for the year 20X5, was taken from the records of the company:

	Units	Unit Cost
Beginning inventory	9,000	$ 8.10
Purchases and sales (in order given):		
Purchase 1	5,000	8.15
Sale 1	10,000	
Purchase 2	16,000	8.20
Sale 2	11,000	
Purchase 3	4,000	8.40
Purchase 4	7,000	8.25
Sale 3	14,000	
Purchase 5	5,000	8.10

Ending inventory (per count), 10,500
Replacement cost (per unit) at year-end, $8.10; sales price was constant all year at $22.00.

Required:

1. Reconstruct the perpetual inventory record for blenders.
2. Give all entries indicated by the above data, assuming that the selling price is $22 per unit. Similar transactions can be summarized into one entry.
3. Prepare the income statement through gross margin for this product.
4. Comment on the need for a LCM write-down of the inventory.

P9-3 *Inventory Cost Methods:* The records of Clayton Company showed the following transactions, in the order given, relating to the major inventory item:

	Units	Unit Cost
1. Inventory	3,000	$ 6.90
2. Purchase	6,000	7.20
3. Sales (at $15)	4,000	
4. Purchase	5,000	7.50
5. Sales (at $15)	9,000	
6. Purchase	11,000	7.66
7. Sales (at $18)	9,000	
8. Purchase	6,000	7.80

Required:

Complete the following schedule for each independent assumption (round unit costs to the nearest cent; show computations):

| | Units and Amounts | | |
| | Ending | Cost of | Gross |
Independent Assumptions	**Inventory**	**Goods Sold**	**Margin**
a. FIFO			
b. LIFO, periodic inventory system			
c. LIFO, perpetual inventory system			
d. Weighted average, periodic inventory system			
e. Moving average, perpetual inventory system			

P9-4 *Inventory Cost — Four Methods:* The records of Johnson Brothers showed the following data about one raw material used in the manufacturing process. The transactions occurred in the order given.

	Units	**Unit Cost**
1. Inventory	4,000	$7.00
2. Purchase 1	3,000	7.70
3. Issue 1	5,000	
4. Purchase 2	8,000	8.00
5. Issue 2	7,000	
6. Purchase 3	3,000	8.40

Required:

1. Compute cost of materials issued (to work in process) and the valuation of raw materials ending inventory for each of the following independent assumptions (round unit costs to the nearest cent for inventory; show computations).

   a. FIFO.

   b. LIFO, periodic inventory system.

   c. Weighted average, periodic inventory system.

   d. Moving average, perpetual inventory system.

2. In parallel columns, give all entries indicated for an average cost system, transaction by transaction. Assume a count of the raw material on hand at the end of the period showed 6,000 units. Remember that goods used are debited to work in process, not cost of goods sold.

   Case A — periodic inventory system; weighted average used.
   Case B — perpetual inventory system; moving average used.

P9-5 *Match Inventory Cost Methods:* Stigler and Sons sells two main products. The records of the company showed the following information relating to one of the products:

	Units	**Unit Cost**
Beginning inventory	500	$3.00
Purchases and sales (in order given):		
Purchase 1	400	3.10
Purchase 2	600	3.15
Sale 1	1,000	
Purchase 3	800	3.25
Sale 2	700	
Sale 3	500	
Purchase 4	700	3.30

In considering a change in inventory policy, the following summary was prepared:

	Illustration			
	(1)	(2)	(3)	(4)
Sales	$16,000	$16,000	$16,000	$16,000
Cost of goods sold	7,110	6,996	6,905	6,930
Gross margin	$ 8,890	$ 9,004	$ 9,095	$ 9,070

Required:

Identify the inventory flow method used for each of the four illustrations, assuming that only the ending inventory was affected. Show computations.

[AICPA, adapted]

P9-6 *Lower of Cost or Market:* Hanlon Company purchased a significant amount of raw materials inventory for a new product it is manufacturing. Hanlon purchased insurance on these raw materials while they were in transit from the supplier.

Hanlon uses the lower-of-cost-or-market rule for these raw materials. The company applies the test to each individual inventory item. The replacement cost of the raw materials is above the net realizable value, and both are below the original cost.

Hanlon uses the average cost inventory method for these raw materials. In the last two years, each purchase has been at a lower price than the previous purchase, and the ending inventory quantity for each period has been higher than the beginning inventory quantity for that period.

Required:

1. What is the theoretically appropriate method that Hanlon should use to account for the insurance costs on the raw materials incurred while they were in transit from the supplier? Why?

2. At what amount should Hanlon's raw materials inventory be reported on the balance sheet? Why?

3. In general, why is the lower-of-cost-or-market rule used to report inventory?

4. What would have been the effect on ending inventory and cost of goods sold had Hanlon used the LIFO inventory method instead of the average cost inventory method for the raw materials? Why?

[AICPA, adapted]

P9-7 *LCM — Three Ways to Apply:* The information shown below relating to the ending inventory was taken from the records of Fast Print Company.

Inventory		Per Unit	
Classification	Quantity	Cost	Market
Paper:			
Stock X	200	$300	$330
Stock Y	60	250	230
Ink:			
Stock D	20	70	65
Stock E	10	55	62
Toner fluid:			
Stock A	8	75	70
Stock B	4	95	80
Stock C	7	100	110

Required:

1. Explain three different ways that the market value listed above could be defined.

2. Determine the valuation of the above inventory at cost and at LCM, assuming application of LCM by (a) individual items, (b) classifications, and (c) total inventory.

3. Give the entry to record the write-down, if any, to reduce ending inventory to LCM. Assume periodic inventory and the allowance method.

4. Of the three applications described in (2) above, which one appears preferable in this situation? Explain.

P9-8 *Gross Margin and Retail Sales Methods:* The records of Diskount Department Store provided the following data for 20X5:

Sales (gross)	$800,000
Sales returns	2,000
Additional markups	9,000
Additional markup cancellations	5,000
Markdowns	7,000
Purchases:	
At retail	850,000
At cost	459,500
Purchase returns:	
At retail	4,000
At cost	2,200
Freight on purchases	7,000
Beginning inventory:	
At retail	80,000
At cost	45,000
Markdown cancellations	3,000

Required:

1. Estimate the valuation of the ending inventory and cost of goods sold using the gross margin method. Last year's gross margin percentage was 51%.

2. Estimate the valuation of the ending inventory and cost of goods sold using the retail sales method, which approximates LCM.

3. Which method is likely to be more accurate? Comment.

P9-9 *Gross Margin Method:* The manager of Seton Book Company, a book retailer, requires an estimate of the inventory cost for a quarterly financial report to the owner on 31 March 20X5. In the past, the gross margin method was used because of the difficulty and expense of taking a physical inventory at interim dates. The company sells both fiction and nonfiction books. Due to their lower turnover rate, nonfiction books are typically marked up to produce a gross profit of 37.5%. Fiction, on the other hand, generates a 28.6% gross profit. The manager has used the average gross profit of 33.333% to estimate interim inventories.

You have been asked by the manager to estimate the book inventory cost as of 31 March 20X5. The following data are available from Seton's accounting records:

	Fiction	Nonfiction	Total
Inventory, 1 January 20X5	$100,000	$ 40,000	$140,000
Purchases	600,000	200,000	800,000
Freight-in	5,000	2,000	7,000
Sales	590,000	160,000	750,000

Required:

Round gross margin ratios to three decimal places.

1. Using the average gross profit margin of 33.333%, compute the estimate of inventory as of 31 March 20X5, based on the gross margin method applied to combined fiction and nonfiction books.
2. Compute the estimate of ending inventory as of 31 March 20X5, based on the gross margin method applied separately to fiction and nonfiction books.
3. Which method is preferable in this situation? Explain.

P9-10 *Retail Inventory Method:* Auditors are examining the accounts of Acton Retail Corporation. They were present when Acton's personnel physically counted the Acton inventory, however, the auditors made their own tests. Acton's records provided the following data for the current year:

	At Retail	At Cost
Inventory, 1 January	$ 300,000	$180,500
Net purchases	1,453,000	955,000
Freight-in		15,000
Additional markups	31,000	
Additional markup cancellations	14,000	
Markdowns	8,000	
Employee discounts	2,000	
Sales	1,300,000	

Inventory at 31 December (per physical count valued at retail) = $475,000

Required:

1. Compute the ending inventory at LCM as an audit test of the overall reasonableness of the physical inventory count. Round the cost ratio to three decimals.
2. Note any discrepancies indicated. What factors should the auditors consider in reconciling any difference in results from the analysis?
3. What accounting treatment (if any) should be accorded the discrepancy?

P9-11 *Inventory Concepts — Recording, Adjusting, Closing, Reporting:* Gamit Company completed the following selected (and summarized) transactions during 20X5:

a. Merchandise inventory on hand 1 January 20X5, $105,000 (at cost, which was the same as LCM).
b. During the year, purchased merchandise for resale at cost of $200,000 on credit, terms 2/10, n/30. Immediately paid 85% of the cash cost.
c. Paid freight on merchandise purchased, $10,000 cash.
d. Paid 40% of the accounts payable within the discount period. The remaining payables were unpaid at the end of 20X5 and were still within the discount period.
e. Merchandise that had a quoted price of $3,000 (terms 2/10, n/30) was returned to a supplier. A cash refund of $2,940 was received because the items were unsatisfactory.
f. During the year, sold merchandise for $370,000, of which 10% was on credit.

g. A television set caught fire and was damaged internally; it was returned by the customer. The set was originally sold for $600, of which $400 cash was refunded. The set originally cost the company $420. Estimates are that the set, when repaired, can be sold for $240. Estimated repair costs are $50, and selling costs are estimated to be $10.

h. Operating expenses (administrative and distribution) paid in cash, $120,000; includes the $10 in (k).

i. Excluded from the purchase given in (b) and from the ending inventory was a shipment for $7,000 (net of discount). This shipment was in transit, FOB shipping point at 31 December 20X5. The invoice had arrived.

j. Paid $50 cash to repair the damaged television set; see (g) above.

k. Sold the damaged television set for $245; selling costs allocated, $10.

l. The ending inventory (as counted) was $110,000 at cost, and $107,000 at market. Assume an average income tax rate of 40%.

Accounting policies followed by the company are:

(1) the annual accounting period ends 31 December,

(2) a periodic inventory system is used,

(3) purchases and accounts payable are recorded net of cash discounts,

(4) freight charges are allocated to merchandise when purchased,

(5) all cash discounts are taken,

(6) used and damaged merchandise is carried in a separate inventory account, and

(7) inventories are reported at LCM and the allowance method is used.

Required:

1. Give the entries for transactions (b) through (k).

2. Give the end-of-period adjusting entries.

3. Prepare a multiple-step income statement for 20X5. Assume that 20,000 common shares are outstanding.

4. Show how the ending inventory should be reported on the balance sheet at 31 December 20X5.

P9-12 *Cash Flow Statement:* Therot Corporation reported the following items in its 20X5 financial statements:

From the balance sheet:	**20X5**	**20X4**
Inventories (net)		
Finished goods	$ 477,226	$ 404,477
Work in progress	197,368	166,193
Materials and supplies	269,974	271,374
	944,568	842,044
Accounts payable	615,904	597,211
Estimated liability on non-cancellable		
purchase commitments	7,943	—
From the income statement:		
Cost of goods sold*	$4,919,316	$4,101,564
Loss on purchase commitment	7,943	—
*Includes loss due to decline in market value		

From the notes:

Inventories are carried at FIFO cost, net of an allowance to reduce finished goods inventory to the lower of cost or market of $64,816 (20X4, $45,719). Market value is defined as net realizable value.

At year-end, the company has outstanding purchase commitments in the amount of $13,299 (20X4, $6,587). The market value of these goods is equal to, or exceeds, the purchase commitment cost except as accrued in the financial statements.

Required:

1. What items would appear on the cash flow statement as a result of the inventory transactions of the year? Assume the use of the indirect method of presentation in the operating activities section.

2. How much did the company pay for inventory during the period?

3. Assume that inventory values as reflected above were standard cost. The income statement reflected unfavourable price variances of $43,110, and favourable usage variances of $19,850. These variances were considered immaterial, so inventory could be reported at standard cost for external reporting. Other facts are unchanged. How much money did the company pay for inventory during the period?

4. Would the LCM write-down have been the same, greater than, or less than that recorded if the company had used (a) average cost or (b) LIFO as a cost flow assumption? Assume that prices have generally been rising in these markets over the last several years.

CHAPTER

10

Capital Assets

INTRODUCTION

Assets are defined as elements that have the capacity to contribute directly or indirectly to future net cash flows of the entity. How do capital assets contribute to cash flows? Most could be sold, but are not held for sale, so that's not it. Instead, capital assets lend themselves indirectly to cash flows from operating activities: they help generate revenue. Capital assets involve risk for an entity: money has been invested in these assets, and they'll only generate a return over time – sometimes lengthy periods of time. Capital assets often constitute the largest single asset category for corporations, and a major source of the business risk that stakeholders assume.

Often there are significant accounting policy choices that have to be made as capital assets are acquired. These policy decisions are affected by accounting standards that govern capital assets, but also by the particular entity's objectives of financial reporting. Organizations may wish to maximize earnings and/or assets, to smooth reported earnings, to aid cash flow prediction, to report on stewardship over resources, and so forth; the specific objectives vary from situation to situation. The most significant policy that must be established is the pattern of amortization, as we'll see in the next chapter.

In this chapter, accounting policy regarding **capitalization** is the substantive issue. That is, what expenditures are to be recorded as assets and then amortized over a period of years? What expenditures are to be immediately expensed? Over time, as capital assets are amortized or sold, the expenditure always eventually flows through the income statement and the two alternatives (capitalize and amortize, or expense immediately) have the same long-run impact on net income. But in the short run the policies chosen can and will have a significant impact on net assets and net income.

Another area of some controversy is the valuation of capital assets obtained in a non-cash trade, or barter transaction. Again, policies will change net assets and net income significantly over the useful life of the assets.

The emphasis in this chapter is on *tangible* capital assets such as buildings, equipment, furniture, vehicles, and so forth. Some attention is given to purchased intangible assets, including purchased goodwill. Other types of intangible capital assets that might be purchased are subscription lists, trademark rights, and franchise rights. Intangible capital assets that are developed internally and for which substantial costs are capitalized (e.g., product development costs; resource industry exploration and development costs) have already been discussed in Chapter 7; that discussion will not be repeated here.

This chapter discusses the valuation of capital assets on acquisition, and accounting for their disposal. The next chapter discusses amortization and revaluation of capital assets.

DEFINITION OF CAPITAL ASSETS

Capital assets can be defined as *the identifiable long-lived assets that have been acquired for use in the revenue-producing activities of the enterprise.* There are five important aspects of this definition:

1. They are *assets* in the general meaning of the term (see Chapter 2), and the enterprise has the rights to their productive use.
2. The assets are *long-lived*, that is, they last more than one year.
3. They have been *acquired* by purchase or donation.
4. They are separately *identifiable*, even if they have been acquired in a basket purchase of several (or many) assets, such as in a business combination.
5. They are used in *generating revenue*, but they are not themselves sold to generate revenue.

It is important to distinguish between capital assets and inventory. A computer is a *capital asset* to the company that buys and uses it, but it is *inventory* to the manufacturer that makes it and to the dealer that sells it. It is not the asset itself that causes it to be classified as a capital asset; it is the intended *use* of the asset that matters. If an asset is held for sale, it is not a capital asset.

Similarly, long-lived assets that were originally acquired for use in generating revenue but that no longer are intended for that purpose cease to be capital assets. Instead, they become investment assets or assets held for sale (and are reported in the long-term *Other Assets* classification on the balance sheet).

There are two general types of capital assets, *tangible* and *intangible*. Tangible capital assets have a physical presence; the word *tangible* means, literally, that the asset can be touched. Tangible assets include land, buildings, equipment, furniture, leasehold improvements, and other such touchable assets. Tangible assets also includes long-life property held to generate revenue through rental, such as office buildings, apartments, cars and trucks, industrial property, furniture, computers, airplanes, etc.

Intangible capital assets are long-lived assets that do *not* have a physical substance, but that nevertheless

*   are separately identifiable,
*   have been acquired, and
*   are used to generate revenue.

Examples include copyrights, patents, subscription lists, mineral rights, oil and gas exploration costs, franchises, computer software, licences, and trademarks. Goodwill is also an intangible asset, but it merits separate discussion because it is not an *identifiable* asset; goodwill arises as a residual in the purchase of other assets.

All tangible and intangible capital assets are amortized, with the one exception of land. Land, since it is assumed to hold its intrinsic value forever, is never amortized.[1] Amortization is a "rational and systematic" allocation of the cost of an asset over its useful life. Amortization is essentially arbitrary, especially for intangible assets where the useful life is not really predictable. Because of the essential arbitrariness of amortization, the AcSB has limited the amortization period (arbitrarily!) to 40 years, unless there is firm evidence to support a longer amortization period. The 40-year maximum period applies to goodwill as well as to separately identifiable intangible assets.

---

[1] Land may lose its value, however, and may then be written down. An example of the loss of value of land arises when land has been heavily polluted. This is called an *impairment of value*, and will be discussed in the next chapter.

VALUATION OF CAPITAL ASSETS

Initial Acquisition

Capital assets are normally recorded at cost, defined as follows:

> Cost is the amount of consideration given up to acquire, construct, develop, or better a capital asset [including] all costs directly attributable to the acquisition, construction, development or betterment of the capital asset including installing it in the location and in the condition necessary for its intended use.   [*CICA* 3060.07]

Cost is usually the *fair value* at the date of purchase. That is, the asset is bought for its fair value as of the date of acquisition. As time passes, the fair value of the asset will change as the price for a comparable asset changes in the market, due to changes in technology and supply and demand forces. Also, the asset itself becomes used; consumed in operations. Historical cost financial statements do not attempt to reflect the current value of capital assets, just the sacrifice made to acquire them.

Many capital assets are not purchased, per se, but are constructed (for tangible assets) or developed (for intangible assets) by the enterprise. The cost of a constructed or developed asset is the sum of the expenditures relating to its construction or development. These costs may not reflect the fair value of the asset, even at the time of its creation. A tangible asset may be constructed at a lower cost than its purchase price, and an intangible asset may be developed for far less than it would cost to buy it from someone else if it were fully developed.

Indeed, developed assets may not be available for purchase at any price; they often are unique, which is what gives them their revenue-generating value. Examples include software development and mine development. The capitalized value for these assets is not, was not, and was never intended to be, fair value at acquisition. Again, this is not the purpose of historical cost financial statements. However, it is difficult to interpret the earnings potential of companies with significant assets of this nature, without detailed knowledge of the assets beyond that provided in the financial statements.

Constructed and developed assets should not be recorded at costs that *exceed* their fair value. For tangible assets, it usually is feasible to compare the capitalized costs with a hypothetical purchase price (for example, what it would have cost to pay a commercial contractor to construct a building). For intangible assets, however, such a comparison may not be feasible. Often, it is impossible to determine whether an intangible asset is worth what was spent to develop it until its development is complete. For example, the costs of developing a mine are capitalized until it is known whether the value of the mineral resources is worth continued development of the mine site.

Post-Acquisition Expenditures

Expenditures related to capital assets subsequent to their acquisition are either capitalized or expensed. Capital expenditures are expenditures expected to yield benefits beyond the current accounting period, that is, have future cash flows, and thus should be added to the capital asset account. The cost of a capital asset is recognized as an expense in current and future periods through depreciation, amortization, or depletion.

Other expenditures, such as ordinary repairs, are expected to yield benefits only in the current accounting period. Therefore, they are recorded in expense accounts and matched against the revenue of the period.

EXHIBIT 10-1 Industry
Common Capitalization Practices

Capital Asset	Capitalize
Buildings, purchased	• purchase price • cost of modifications, if any
Buildings, constructed	• architectural fees • payments to contractors • cost of permits • excavation costs • legal fees, closing costs
Buildings, self-constructed	• direct construction costs • excavation costs • reasonable apportionment of overhead • legal costs, permits, etc. • interest on *specific* construction loans
Machinery and equipment	• invoice cost, net of discounts, whether taken or not • taxes, freight and duty • special platforms, foundations, other required installation costs • costs of building modifications necessary for specific installation
Land	• purchase price • legal fees, closing costs • general land preparation costs, including grading, filling, draining, and surveying • cost of removing structures and other obstructions, if land is acquired for development (proceeds from salvaged materials reduce the costs capitalized) • special assessments for local *government-maintained* improvements, including streets, sidewalks, sewers, and streetlights • property taxes, insurance, and other holding costs incurred on land not in current productive use (may be expensed on grounds of expedience and conservatism) • landscaping and other property enhancements, *if permanent*

Capitalize or Expense?

Accounting practice has developed steadily in this area, and much time and energy has gone into studying the typical kinds of costs that should be capitalized versus expensed in each category. Common practices are summarized in Exhibit 10-1. Read it carefully, and make sure you understand why each capitalized item creates some sort of future enhancement of cash flows. Often, it is because the expenditure is inescapable in order to get the capital asset into operation.

Is there any room for choice or manipulation? You'll find that some firms are quick to disclaim any future benefit associated with a variety of expenditures related to capital assets. For whatever reason, these companies seem to be attempting to minimize current net income and net assets, and enjoy lower future amortization expenses. A company may also prefer to expense rather than capitalize if it has cash flow

EXHIBIT 10-1
Common Capitalization Practices (continued)

Land improvements	• driveways, parking lots, fencing • streets and sidewalks that the company must maintain • landscaping, if not permanent
Patents	• purchase price, transfer and legal fees if bought from another entity • research costs to internally develop a patented item are expensed unless classified development costs (see Chapter 7) • legal and other necessary documentation costs to register the patent, if self-developed • costs of a successful court defence (unsuccessful defences are expensed, along with the now-worthless patent)
Industrial design registrations (i.e., a five-year renewable registration of the shape, pattern, or ornamentation of a manufactured item)	• acquisition and registration cost, as per patents, above • successful defence costs, as per patents, above
Copyrights	• acquisition and registration cost, as per patents, above • successful defence costs, as per patents, above
Trademarks and Trade names	• legal and other necessary documentation costs to register the patent, if self-developed • acquisition cost, as per patents, above • successful defence costs, per patents, above
Franchise rights	• initial franchise fees, not related to annual volumes • legal fees, closing costs
Leasehold improvements (alterations, improvements, or refurbishing of leased space)	• invoice, installation costs
Organization costs	• legal, accounting, promotional, and clerical activities associated with creating a new company
Share issuance costs	• printing share certificates and related items, professional fees, commissions paid for selling capital stock, and the costs of filing with securities commissions

prediction as a primary reporting objective. By including the expenditures in current expenses, a company achieves a net income figure that is closer to the actual cash flows and thereby provides a better basis for predicting cash future flows.

At the other end of the spectrum, some companies are very aggressive in their capitalization policies, seeking higher current income and capital assets, and accepting higher future amortization. For example, a regulated public utility will generally capitalize as many costs as possible because the enterprise's permitted (i.e., regulated) profit is based on its regulated rate of return multiplied by the asset base. The higher the asset base, the larger the profit it is entitled to earn. Another effect of capitalizing rather than expensing is that the expenditures are classified as investing activities in the cash flow statement, and therefore never have an impact on *reported* cash flow from operations.

EXHIBIT 10-2
VITA-LIFE COMPANY
Example of Cost Classification

Vita-Life Company recently acquired several plant assets and began construction on a building. The costs incurred by Vita-Life are classified into the indicated accounts.

Cost Incurred	Equipment	Land	Building under Construction*	Land Improvments	Current Period Expense
Invoice price of equipment	$50,000				
3% cash discount not taken on equipment purchase	(1,500)				$1,500**
4% sales tax on equipment	2,000				
Insurance and freight costs on equipment purchase	600				
Cost of land parcel		$100,000			
Commission and title insurance on land purchase		7,000			
Setup, testing, and practice runs on equipment	2,000				
Cost to train employees on equipment					500
Interest on debt incurred to purchase equipment					1,200
Cost to remove structures from land		30,000			
Proceeds on materials salvaged from structures removed		(2,000)			
Excavation of foundation			$ 3,500		
Surveying and grading		12,000			
Concrete and labour for foundation			26,000		
Property tax paid four months after acquisition of land					550
Asphalt for parking lot				$11,000	
Fencing for property				6,000	
Asset ending account balance	$53,100	$147,000	$29,500	$17,000	

* Reclassified to building account on completion.
** Finance expense.

That's the trade-off. Capitalized costs, in almost all cases, are carried to income through amortization: you can defer, but you can't avoid. The two approaches will provide different income and asset values throughout the life of the asset. As we progress through this chapter discussion, policy choices will be pointed out.

Materiality plays a role in this area, as well. Small capital expenditures are often expensed on the basis that the more correct capitalization and amortization would not produce results different enough to cause investors to make different decisions.

Exhibit 10-2 provides an example of cost classification related to the acquisition of capital assets.

1. What is the difference between *tangible* and *intangible* capital assets?
2. Define a capital *expenditure*.
3. What are the three characteristics of an intangible capital asset?
4. What difference does it make in a company's reported financial results if the company is highly aggressive in its capitalization policies?

DETERMINING THE COST OF CAPITAL ASSETS

Lump-Sum Purchase of Several Assets

Occasionally, several assets are acquired for a single lump-sum price that may be lower than the sum of the individual asset prices, to encourage sale. In other cases, the assets are attached, for example, land and building. This type of acquisition, called a basket purchase, group purchase, or lump-sum purchase, requires allocation of a portion of the single lump-sum price to each asset acquired. The portions of the lump-sum price directly attributable to particular assets in the group are assigned in full to those assets. Land appraisal costs are assigned only to the land account, for example. Allocation of the remaining lump-sum price to each asset is necessary. Under the cost principle, the sum of the individual asset account balances at acquisition is limited to the lump-sum price.

Allocation is based on the best available indicator of the relative values of the several assets involved. Possible indicators include market prices for similar assets, current appraised value, assessed value for property tax purposes, and the present value of estimated future net cash flows, including manufacturing cost savings. The seller's book values generally do not reflect the current value of the assets in the group.

Each asset is valued according to the ratio of its value to the total value of the group; this valuation is called the proportional method. If the value of only the first asset(s) in a group is determinable, the second (or remaining) asset is valued at the cost remaining to be allocated. This less desirable procedure is called the incremental method.

To illustrate the proportional method, assume that $90,000 is the negotiated acquisition price paid for land, a building, and machinery. These assets are appraised individually, as the best available indication of value in this case: land, $30,000; building, $50,000; and machinery, $20,000. The cost apportionment of the single lump-sum price and the entry to record the transaction are as follows:

	Appraised Asset Value	Apportionment of Cost	Apportioned Cost
Land	$ 30,000	30%* × $ 90,000	$27,000
Building	50,000	50% × $ 90,000	45,000
Machinery	20,000	20% × $ 90,000	18,000
Total	$100,000		$90,000

*30% = $30,000 ÷ $100,000

To record the lump-sum purchase

Land	27,000	
Building	45,000	
Machinery	18,000	
Cash		90,000

Assume, instead, that the building was worth $48,000, and the machinery, $17,000, but it was not possible to determine an objective value for the land. In this case, land would be assigned the residual $25,000, using the incremental method.

Capital Assets Purchased with Long-Term Debt

In accordance with the cost principle, the recorded cost of an asset purchased on credit is based on the more objective and reliable choice between the following alternatives:

- The cash equivalent price, or market value.
- The present value of the future cash payments required by the debt agreement discounted at the prevailing (market) interest rate for that type of debt.

If the debt instrument *a note* does not bear interest and the current cash price of the asset can be determined, the excess of the face value of the debt instrument over the cash price is viewed as interest expense. When the debt instrument is issued, the normal procedure is to record its face value as a liability, with the difference between the face value and the cash price of the asset debited to a contra-liability account as *discount on note payable*. The discount is amortized over the term of the debt, thereby increasing interest expense each period . If the cash price is not determinable, the prevailing interest rate is used to determine total interest cost and to compute the asset's present value for recording purposes.

To illustrate the purchase of a capital asset on credit, assume that Cobb Corporation purchases equipment on 1 January 20X2, with a $600 cash down payment and a $1,000, one-year note payable on 31 December 20X2 plus 12% interest. The stated interest rate is equal to the current market rate, so the note's present value equals its face value.

$$P = (\$1,000 + \$120) \times (P/F, 12\%, 1)$$
$$= \$1,120 \times .89286$$
$$= \$1,000$$

The asset is recorded at the sum of the cash down payment plus the present value of the note because the cash equivalent price of the asset is not available. The recorded amount is:

$$\text{Equipment valuation} = \text{Cash down payment} + \text{Present value of note}$$
$$= \$600 + \$1,000 = \$1,600$$

Assume instead that Feller Company acquires a machine on 1 January 20X2, with a non-interest-bearing note that requires $8,615 to be paid on 31 December 20X2, 20X3, and 20X4. The note has no explicit interest, but the prevailing interest rate is 14% on liabilities of similar risk and duration. The face amount of the note is $25,845 ($8,615 × 3). The cash equivalent cost of the machine is unknown, so the asset is recorded at the present value of the three payments discounted at 14%.

$$\text{Recorded cost} = \$8,615 \times (P/A, 14\%, 3)$$
$$= \$8,615 \times 2.32163$$
$$= \$20,000 \text{ (rounded)}$$

Feller's entries to record the asset and the note are as follows:

1 January 20X2

	Gross Method		Net Method	
Equipment	20,000		20,000	
Discount on note payable	5,845		—	
Note payable		25,845*		20,000

* $8,615 × 3.

The discount on note payable is a contra note payable account. It reduces the net note payable balance to the present value of the future cash flows ($20,000). The discount is amortized to interest expense over the life of the liability.

Capital Assets Acquired in Exchange for Equity Securities

When equity securities are issued to acquire capital assets, the assets are recorded at the fair market value of the securities issued, or, if more objectively determinable, at the fair market value of the asset.

The market value of the securities issued provides a reliable fair market value for publicly traded securities if the number of shares in the exchange is below the typical daily trading volume. Assume that Medford Corporation purchases used equipment in 20X5. The equipment is in reasonable condition but is not normally sold before the end of its useful life. Thus, it has no reliable market value. In payment for this equipment, Medford issues 2,000 common shares. Medford's common shares are listed on the Toronto Stock Exchange and currently trade at $10 per share. Medford has 10 million common shares outstanding. Therefore, the proper valuation for the equipment is 2,000 × $10, or $20,000.

Several factors can complicate the situation, however. The effect of a substantial share offering on the market price of the shares is often not known until after issuance. Also, the shares of many companies are not traded with sufficient frequency to establish a daily market price. In other cases, organizers of a newly formed corporation may issue a substantial number of shares for capital assets when there is no established fair value for the shares.

If the market value of the securities (in the volume exchanged) cannot be determined reliably, the market value of the assets acquired is used if it can be determined reliably. In the absence of recent cash sale evidence, an independent appraisal can be used to value the assets. This may be easier said than done: unexplored or unproven mineral deposits, manufacturing rights, patents, chemical formulas, and mining claims are all difficult to value.

If no reliable market value can be determined for either the securities issued or the assets acquired, the board of directors of the corporation establishes a reasonable valuation. The directors have considerable discretion in establishing values, and firms experiencing financial difficulty may be tempted to overstate asset values, overstating owners' equity as well. A disincentive to overvaluation, however, is the increased amortization expense in future years.

Donated Assets

Shareholders and other parties occasionally donate assets and services to corporations. For example shareholders may donate valuable paintings to adorn the corporate boardroom.

The assets cost the company nothing, that is, they are obtained in a **nonreciprocal transfer**, meaning that the company gives nothing in return. Does that mean that the assets need not be recognized? If the balance sheet is to provide a record of assets controlled by the entity, and the income statement is to record the costs of doing business, then it seems logical to include these assets at fair value. But the entity sacrificed no resources to obtain the assets. If the assets are depreciable, they will create an expense in future years, as they are used. Should future years' income be reduced because of a charge created in such a way? Is the return on shareholders' investment understated in such circumstances? It's a thorny issue.

Current practice in Canada is often to record the asset at its fair value, and increase a shareholders' equity contributed capital account (owners' equity). Depreciation based on the market value of the donated asset is matched against future revenue presumably generated by the assets.

However, an additional procedure that sometimes is used is to also amortize the balance of the contributed capital account to retained earnings using the same pattern as the depreciation. The credit may be either directly to retained earnings or to income. If the contributed capital amortization credit is to income, the net effect is to remove the impact of the depreciation from net income. There is no Canadian standard on this issue.

If the donor imposes restrictions on the use of the asset donated, the expected cost of complying with those restrictions should be estimated and deducted from the market value of the asset in determining the valuation to be recorded.

Example   To illustrate accounting by a donee, assume a building (fair market value $400,000), and the land on which it is located (fair market value $100,000) are donated to Stanford Limited. A $5,000 legal and deed transfer cost is borne by Stanford, which records the donation as follows:

Building	400,000	
Land	105,000	
Cash		5,000
Contributed capital — donated assets		500,000

It's interesting to note that this is an area where Canadian and U.S. practices are significantly different: U.S. standards require that the credit for donated assets be *included in income* in the year of donation rather than in contributed capital, a practice never used in Canada.

Government Assistance

Assets sometimes are acquired with monetary assistance from various levels of governments. This may be in the form of a specific government grant, which may require the firm to maintain certain employment levels or pollution control levels. If the conditions of the assistance are not met, the firm may be required to refund the amounts received to the granting agency. Governments may give a money grant to a firm.

Very commonly, government assistance takes the form of an investment tax credit, which reduces the amount of tax otherwise payable based on a set percentage of eligible capital expenditures for a period. For example, assume that a company had a tax bill of $675,000. During the year, they spent $750,000 on new manufacturing machinery, which qualifies for a 10% investment tax credit. The company can reduce its tax bill by $75,000, to $600,000. Taxes payable go down, and are debited, for $75,000. What account is credited?

This question has been very controversial. There are three alternatives.

1. Capital could be credited, consistent with the treatment given to donated assets.
2. Tax expense, or another current income statement account could be credited, reflecting cash flow and the impact on current taxes.
3. The capital asset could be credited, or a related deferred credit established. This would reduce the amount of future depreciation charged: that is, only depreciation on the *firm-financed* portion of the capital asset would be expensed over time. Thus, the income statement will reflect the benefit of the government assistance, but only over the useful life of the asset.

Through lobbying behaviour, some firms have demonstrated their clear preference for the second alternative, which has the happy effect of increasing current earnings. The first alternative is consistent with the treatment given to donated assets. However, the third alternative is very firmly entrenched in Canadian practice.

> Government assistance towards the acquisition of fixed assets should be either:
> (a) deducted from the related fixed assets with any depreciation calculated on the net amount; or

(b) deferred and amortized to income on the same basis as the related depreciable fixed assets are depreciated. [*CICA* 3800.26]

This choice reflects a policy decision on the part of standard-setters to reflect capital assets subject to government assistance, and their related depreciation expense, at the amount that the shareholders have financed. Given that this policy is inconsistent with the choice for donated assets, it is perhaps just as well that donations are relatively rare, and often involve land donations, which do not depreciate.

Example To illustrate accounting for a government grant, assume that machinery costing $100,000 was eligible for assistance of 30%. The machinery has a 10-year life with no salvage value. Because both the net method and deferral method of accounting are acceptable, both sets of journal entries are provided.

	Net Method		Deferral Method	
Record purchase				
Machinery	100,000		100,000	
Cash		100,000		100,000
Record the receipt of the government assistance				
Cash*	30,000		30,000	
Machinery		30,000	—	
Deferred government grant		—		30,000

* Cash is debited if the government assistance is in the form of money. If the assistance were an investment tax credit, taxes payable would be debited.

Record straight-line depreciation expense at the end of years 1 to 10				
Depreciation expense	7,000		10,000	
Accumulated depreciation		7,000		10,000
Deferred government grant	—		3,000	
Depreciation expense		—		3,000

The effect on income is the same under either method. The difference is on the balance sheet where with the deferral method, the gross amount of the fixed asset would appear. The credit may be a contra account to the fixed asset, or shown on the opposite side of the balance sheet. Which method would you choose if you were trying to maximize assets to reassure creditors? The net method always presents the net cost of the long-term asset.

This is another area where Canadian and U.S. accounting practices diverge. In the U.S., practice allows government assistance received in the form of investment tax credits to be included in income in the year in which they arise — that is, alternative (2), above. U.S. standard-setters have tried to switch to alternative (3) a few times, but political action by firms, who obviously appreciate the potential to increase income by the use of this accounting policy, has prevented any change to accounting standards. We'll take another look at the investment tax credit in the Appendix to Chapter 16 — stay tuned!

Before we leave government assistance, perhaps it's worth mentioning that government assistance can be obtained for a wide variety of purposes, not just capital asset acquisition. The purpose of the government assistance governs its accounting. For example, if the assistance is to offset current expenses, then the accounting for the government assistance must reflect that fact, and recognize the assistance on the income statement when the related expenses appear. If the assistance is for future expenses, then assistance should be deferred and recognized when the expenses are recognized.

Finally, government assistance is sometimes in the form of forgivable loans. The loans are forgiven when certain conditions are met, such as maintenance of a stated level of employment or volume levels for specific periods of time. In these circumstances, management must assess the conditions that are attached to the "loan." If the conditions are deemed likely to be met, the "loan" is recorded as assistance, and the conditions and unforgiven balance are disclosed in the notes. Should management's expectations prove to be wrong and the loan becomes repayable in the future, this event should be accounted for in the period that conditions change. But the future is fraught with uncertainties. Therefore, forgivable loans often are classified as loans payable until the conditions have been satisfied, and the conditions are disclosed in the notes.

Self-Constructed Assets

Companies sometimes construct plant assets for their own use. For example, suppose a utility employs its personnel to extend transmission lines and construct pipelines. All costs directly associated with the construction are capitalized to the constructed asset. These costs include incremental material, labour, and overhead costs. Overhead includes general costs not directly related to production, such as utility costs, maintenance on equipment, and supervision.

Under certain conditions, some of the general overhead and interest expense incurred during construction is included in the cost of these assets. Determining the amount of general overhead cost to allocate to a construction project is not well established in practice. One view is that self-constructed assets should bear the incremental overhead cost and the portion of general overhead cost that would be assigned to any regular production displaced by the special project. According to this view, if general overhead is allocated on the basis of labour-hours, and 8% of labour-hours are associated with self-construction, then 8% of total general overhead during construction should be included as a cost of the self-constructed asset.

Many accountants contend that failure to allocate some portion of the general overhead to self-construction projects causes an undervaluation of self-constructed assets. On the other hand, others argue that assets are often self-constructed during slack periods when the production facility and workers would otherwise be idle. Using this line of reasoning, no general overhead should be capitalized because of the income-manipulation potential associated with this "make-work" project.

The amount of overhead to be included in self-constructed assets is quite nebulous. "Overhead" can be interpreted narrowly to include only identifiable and incremental costs, or broadly to include many items of general production costs. Accounting practice in a particular situation will be affected by the financial reporting objectives of the enterprise. The more overhead that is allocated to a self-constructed asset, the greater will be the carrying value of the asset. Companies that want to show high asset values will tend to interpret "overhead" quite broadly and will allocate significant amounts of overhead cost to the project.

The period required for construction of capital assets can be lengthy. There is general agreement that time-related costs, including taxes and insurance during construction, should be capitalized to the asset under construction. Consistent logic supports capitalization of interest during the construction period. After all, if the asset were purchased rather than self-constructed, the purchase price would normally include a cost component to cover the seller's financing expenses. Also, many firms would be unable to construct assets without debt financing.

Interest is usually a period cost, not eligible for capitalization. However, current practice in Canada is to allow cash paid for interest costs on loans specifically related to a construction project to be capitalized, if the company wishes. The interest has to have actually been paid — imputed interest, or opportunity cost, on equity investment is not eligible for capitalization. Furthermore, the loans have to be specifically related to construction. Finally, the company can set its own policy in this regard — they are not forced to capitalize interest.

The *CICA Handbook* provides for interest capitalization but does not contain detailed guidelines to implement the policy. Variety in practice is thus expected. In the U.S., on the other hand, there are excruciatingly detailed rules establishing procedures to be followed. However, Section 3850 of the *CICA Handbook* requires disclosure of interest capitalized, allowing financial statement users to determine the effect of capitalized interest on earnings and assets.

The actual cost of a self-constructed asset does not necessarily equal fair market value at the point of acquisition, as is also the case for some natural resources and intangible assets. Using the higher market value, even if this is a reliable number, would result in recording a gain on construction; no such gain can be recorded. The lower construction cost is ultimately reflected in higher net income through lower depreciation expense in future years.

Consistent with the valuation of other assets, the maximum valuation allowed by GAAP for self-constructed assets is fair market value. If total capitalized cost exceeds the market value of a similar asset of equal capacity and quality, the excess is recognized as a loss. Failure to do so carries forward cost elements that have no future benefit and causes overstated depreciation in future years.

To illustrate the accounting for a self-constructed asset, assume that Kelvin Corporation completes a project with total construction costs as follows:

Material	$200,000
Labour	500,000
Incremental overhead	60,000
Applied general overhead	40,000
Capitalized interest	100,000
Total	$900,000

Kelvin has recorded costs in the equipment under construction account. If the asset's market value at completion equals or exceeds $900,000, the summary entry is:

Equipment	900,000	
Equipment under construction		900,000

If the asset's market value is only $880,000, the entry is:

Equipment	880,000	
Loss on construction of equipment	20,000	
Equipment under construction		900,000

It is important to watch capitalization very carefully — many firms, with a desire to maximize earnings by deferring costs, seize on self-construction as an opportunity to try to defer lots of interesting things! Others wish to capitalize as little as possible. Remember, though, that the higher asset value generated is a base for future depreciation.

1. Why is it necessary to allocate the overall cost of a basket purchase of assets to the individual assets in the basket?

2. At what amount would be recorded a capital asset purchased on credit, if the asset does not have a ready market value?

3. When a government gives a grant to help a company acquire capital assets, how is the grant normally accounted for in Canadian practice?

CONCEPT REVIEW

INTANGIBLE ASSETS

Intangible assets are similar to tangible capital assets in that their cost is capitalized, and they are later subject to systematic and rational amortization. Refer to Exhibit 10-1, and re-read the capitalizable costs for intangibles such as copyrights, trademarks, franchise fees, and the like. Legal fees are a major component of cost, as it can be a long and expensive process to register some of these intangibles. It's interesting to note that legal fees for successful defence of these assets are to be capitalized. These lawsuits clearly establish property rights over the intangible asset. Conversely, unsuccessful lawsuits result in expense recognition and usually mean that any remaining balance in the intangible asset account must be written off — the asset isn't worth anything if it can't be defended!

Goodwill   *Non-amortizable.*

Goodwill is the most common intangible asset. It represents the value associated with favourable characteristics of a firm that result in earnings in excess of those expected from identifiable assets of the firm. Goodwill is *internally generated*, but is only recorded when *purchased*, along with identifiable tangible and intangible assets that constitute an operating unit. Goodwill typically cannot be separated from those identifiable assets. In the absence of a sale, there is no market or arm's length transaction with which to measure the cost of the goodwill a firm creates as it engages in business activities.

Essentially, goodwill represents the expected value of future above-normal financial performance, which is the enhancement of assets or cash flow required of the asset definition. The expectation of enhanced performance arises because intangible, favourable characteristics or factors make it likely that the firm will produce higher than average earnings from its tangible assets. Examples of such favourable factors are[2]

- A superior management team
- Well-established trademarks or brand names
- An outstanding sales organization
- A favourable market position due to weakness in the management of one or more major competitors
- Especially effective advertising
- Exceptionally good labour relations
- A top-flight training program for employees
- An unusually good reputation in the industry for total quality
- Unfavourable developments in the operations of a competitor
- A particularly favourable association with a supplier
- A highly advantageous strategic location
- Favourable government regulations

For accounting purposes, goodwill is the difference between the actual purchase price of an acquired firm or operation and the estimated fair market value of the identifiable net assets acquired. That is, "the excess of the cost of the purchase over the acquiring company's interest in identifiable assets acquired and liabilities assumed should be reflected as goodwill" [*CICA* 1580.44].

Measuring Goodwill. The value of goodwill is computed only indirectly in an acquisition of a firm, in whole or in significant part. The total value of a firm is first deter-

---

2 See G. Catlett and N. Olson, "Accounting for Goodwill," *Accounting Research Study No. 10* (New York: AICPA, 1968), pp. 17–18.

EXHIBIT 10-3
CAFE CORPORATION
Balance Sheet as of 31 December 20X4:
Value as Reported and Fair Market Value

	As Reported	Fair Market Value	Difference
Assets			
Cash	$ 30,000	$ 30,000	
Receivables	90,000	85,000	($ 5,000)
Inventory	60,000	60,000	
Other current assets	33,000	30,000	(3,000)
Plant and equipment (net)	220,000	235,000	15,000
Other assets	85,000	90,000	5,000
Total assets	$518,000		
Liabilities			
Short-term notes payable	$ 85,000	$ 85,000	
Accounts payable	45,000	45,000	
Other current liabilities	30,000	30,000	
Long-term debt	250,000	240,000	(10,000)
Shareholders' equity	108,000		
Total equities	$518,000		
Net assets at fair market value		$130,000	

mined or estimated. Second, the current value of the various identifiable assets, both tangible and separately identifiable intangible, and the current value of the liabilities of the firm are determined. The difference between these two is the current value of the net assets acquired:

Current fair value of net assets acquired	**equals**	Current fair value of tangible and identifiable intangible assets	**less**	Current fair value of liabilities

The value of the goodwill that was purchased is computed as the difference between the total value of the firm, usually measured as the purchase price, less the current fair value of the net assets acquired.

Purchased goodwill	**equals**	Purchase price of firm acquired	**less**	Current fair value of net assets acquired

Example   Assume that Hotel Company is considering the acquisition of the net assets of Cafe Corporation. Hotel Company obtains financial statements and other financial data on Cafe and estimates the fair market value of Cafe's identifiable assets at $530,000 and the fair market value of the liabilities at $400,000. (See Exhibit 10-3.)

The fair market value column in Exhibit 10-3 shows that several assets have an estimated fair market value different from their cost as reported in the published historic cost financial statements.

The total fair market value of Cafe's identifiable net assets is determined to be $130,000 ($530,000 total assets less liabilities of $400,000). Management of Hotel Company, however, must determine the value of Cafe as a going concern. Assume that Hotel negotiates a purchase price with the owners to acquire Cafe as of 31 December 20X4, for $202,000. Goodwill inherent in this price is $72,000, that is, the purchase price of $202,000, less current market value of the identifiable net assets of $130,000. The entry Hotel Company makes to reflect the acquisition of Cafe's operations, at their fair values, is as follows:

Cash	30,000	
Receivables	85,000	
Inventory	60,000	
Other current assets	30,000	
Plant and equipment	235,000	
Other assets	90,000	
Goodwill	72,000	
Short-term notes payable		85,000
Accounts payable		45,000
Other current liabilities		30,000
Long-term debt		240,000
Cash		202,000

Do you *know* that goodwill is present, just because Hotel paid more than the fair value of the net assets? After all, Hotel may have been outbargained by the old owners of Cafe. The $72,000 could be the result of an inflated price. Just because the price is arm's length doesn't mean it can't be stupid. Accountants, however, don't account for stupidity (think of the arguments with clients!) and always make the comfortable assumption that goodwill explains excess purchase price. But beware — the assets acquired are supposed to provide a return consistent with the existence of goodwill, or the goodwill does not, in substance, exist.

In 1988, a major Canadian real property development company, Campeau Corporation, indulged in a spate of acquisitions at inflated prices that resulted in recognition of U.S. $2,862,000,000 of goodwill on the 1988 balance sheet. Unfortunately for Campeau's shareholders, earnings did not follow, the company subsequently initiated bankruptcy proceedings, and goodwill was written off!

Negative Goodwill When the fair market value of the identifiable net assets acquired is greater than the purchase price, the acquiring firm has made what is sometimes called a *bargain purchase*. The amount of goodwill (the difference between the purchase price and fair market value of assets acquired) is negative, that is, **negative goodwill** has been created. Even though it would seem that the seller could benefit from selling the assets individually rather than selling the firm as a whole, such situations do occasionally occur. For example, the seller may not have the time or resources to take on the risks of selling the assets separately.

Any negative goodwill should be allocated to reduce the values assigned to *identifiable non-monetary assets* to the extent that it is eliminated.

Assume now that Hotel Company purchases Cafe Corp. for $91,500, which is $38,500 less than the fair value of the net assets acquired. The negative goodwill of $38,500 could be allocated *proportionally* to reduce the recorded values for plant, equipment, inventory, and other non-monetary assets or, alternatively, it could be assigned to one or more *specific* non-monetary assets. There's a lot of room for income manipulation here: if inventory is reduced, income that is reported in the year that the now-cheap inventory is sold will be artificially high. If capital assets are credited, then future income will be burdened with less amortization, and so on.

Form of Acquisition In the previous example, one company bought the net assets of another company, and goodwill was directly recorded on the purchaser's books. In many acquisition transactions, the acquiring company buys the shares of the target company, which is then left to operate as before, only with new shareholders.

At reporting dates, the two sets of financial statements are combined, or *consolidated*, to produce a report of the economic activity of the combined entity. In consolidation, the assets of the target company are recorded at fair value, and the goodwill inherent in the purchase price is recorded. The nature of goodwill is identical, but the form of the transaction is different. We'll take a brief look at consolidation in Chapter 12.

Organization Costs

Organization costs are expenditures incurred in organizing a business. Costs directly related to the organizing activities, such as expenditures for legal, accounting, promotional, and clerical activities, are capitalizable as organization costs. The rationale for capitalizing organization costs is that they benefit future years' operations. To expense the total amount in the first year of operation would result in a mismatching of expense with revenue.

Because the life of a business is usually indefinite, the length of the period receiving the benefits of these costs usually is indeterminate. Therefore, organization costs are usually amortized over an arbitrarily chosen, short period of time. Forty years is the maximum period, in normal circumstances.

Share Issue Costs

Expenditures associated with issuing capital stock are called share issuance costs. Such costs include printing share certificates and related items, professional fees, commissions paid for selling capital stock, and the costs of filing with securities commissions. Share issuance costs, as opposed to organizational costs, are often accounted for as an offset to the issuance price of the capital stock to which they relate, or as a reduction to retained earnings. Sometimes, though, they appear as an intangible asset, although they aren't used in production or operations and are more technically a deferred charge. Fortunately, they're rarely material in amount.

DISPOSALS OF CAPITAL ASSETS

The disposal of capital assets may be *voluntary*, as a result of a sale, exchange, or abandonment, or *involuntary*, as a result of a *casualty* such as a fire, storm, or by government action, such as expropriation.

If the asset to be disposed of is subject to depreciation, it is depreciated up to the date of disposal in order to update the recorded book value. Applicable property taxes, insurance premium costs, and similar costs are also accrued up to the date of disposal. At the date of disposal, the original cost of the asset and its related accumulated depreciation are removed from the accounts.

The difference between the book value of a plant asset and the amount received on disposal is recorded as a gain or loss. Ideally, the gain or loss is segregated from ordinary income and reported in the income statement as part of income from continuing operations. Occasionally, the gain or loss is an extraordinary item, and thus is shown separately on the income statement, net of tax, after income from continuing operations. Extraordinary item treatment is applied when a company loses a major asset or group of assets through a natural disaster, or is forced to dispose of an asset by outside authority (such as by a government or a court order). Disposals that are not the choice of the company are called involuntary conversions.

To illustrate the disposal of a capital asset, assume that on 1 February 20X1, Brown Company paid $32,000 for office equipment with an estimated service life of five years and an estimated residual value of $2,000. Brown uses straight-line depreciation and sells the asset on 1 July 20X5, for $8,000. The entries for Brown, a calendar-year company, at date of disposal are as follows:

Depreciation expense	3,000*	
Accumulated depreciation — equipment		3,000
* ($32,000 – $2,000) × (1/5) × (6/12)		
Cash	8,000	
Accumulated depreciation — equipment	26,500*	
Equipment		32,000
Gain from disposal of equipment		2,500
* ($32,000 – $2,000) × (53 months used) ÷ (60 months total useful life).		

However, the economic value of Brown Company is unaffected by the disposal. Brown received an asset worth $8,000 (cash) for an asset worth $8,000. Why is a gain recognized? Brown depreciated the equipment faster than it declined in value. The book value ($5,500) is less than market value ($8,000) at date of disposal. If depreciation reflected market value changes, there would be no gain or loss from disposal. *The accounting gain in this example is a correction for excessive depreciation charges recognized before disposal.* In effect, the gain is a *change in estimate.*

If the asset is destroyed in an accident, and was insured, then the entry will mirror the one recorded above. That is, the insurance proceeds will produce a certain amount of cash, and the difference between cash and net book value will determine the gain or loss.

This approach is also used when an asset is abandoned or destroyed without insurance, when there are no proceeds. The loss recognized equals the book value of the asset at disposal. Since the Brown Company asset has no market value, the loss recognized is $5,500.

The costs of dismantling, removing, and disposing of plant assets are treated as reductions of any proceeds obtained from disposal. Therefore, the resulting gain is reduced, or the resulting loss is increased by these costs. If Brown Company incurs $500 in disposal costs, the net cash debit is $8,000 – $500, or $7,500, reducing the gain to $2,000.

When the decision to abandon plant assets is made near the end of a fiscal year, an estimated loss from disposal is recognized in that year if the loss is estimable according to Section 3290, "Contingencies." Gains are not recognized before disposal, however.

Disposal by Donation

Corporations occasionally donate assets to other organizations. Computer manufacturers donate computing equipment to universities, for example. In this event, the donor recognizes a contribution expense equal to the market value of the donated asset, since market value represents the sacrifice made by shareholders. If the assets donated are capital assets, then a gain or loss equal to the difference between book value and market value is recorded on donation. Normally, an expense and a payable are recognized when an unconditional promise to donate the asset is made; recognition need not be delayed until the asset has been physically transferred.

CONCEPT REVIEW

1. How does a company *purchase* goodwill?
2. How does *negative goodwill* arise?
3. What is an *involuntary conversion*?
4. Why would a company dispose of a capital asset at a loss? Is the company in a worse position economically after doing so?
5. How would you interpret the gain on the disposal of a capital asset?

EXCHANGES OF NON-MONETARY ASSETS

Capital assets are often exchanged for other non-monetary assets. Remember that monetary assets are those whose value is fixed in terms of dollars, like cash and receivables. Non-monetary assets, such as inventory and capital assets, *do not have a value fixed in terms of dollars*. Valuation of the acquired asset is the substantive issue in non-monetary asset exchanges. This valuation determines whether a gain or loss is recognized. Non-monetary transactions are

> ... exchanges of non-monetary assets, liabilities or services for other non-monetary assets, liabilities or services with little or no monetary consideration involved. [*CICA* 3830.04]

The rules for exchanges of non-monetary assets are generally quite straight-forward. Use fair market value, and record a gain or loss on the transaction. The only problem is that there are two fair values involved: the fair value of the non-monetary asset given up, and the fair value of the non-monetary asset received. Which one should be used?

A transaction should be valued based on the consideration given up, or the sacrifice that the company has agreed to make to receive the new asset. Therefore, *the fair value of the asset given up should be used to value the transaction*. However, if the fair value of the asset received is more clearly determinable, then it will be more reliable, and should be used. Thus, *both* fair values are consulted in order to properly record the transaction. Finally, if cash is a component of the transaction, then it must be folded into the value assigned to the new asset.

Valuation of non-monetary transactions:

Market value of asset transferred out **or** Market value of asset acquired (if more clearly determinable)	**plus/minus**	cash paid/cash received

Determination and disclosure of gains and losses on exchange is similar to any other capital asset disposal. The gain or loss is the difference between the book value of the asset given up and the market value of the total consideration, as measured above. The gain or loss is reported on the income statement.

The highest value at which any asset received may be recorded is its fair market value at the time of the transfer. Therefore, when cash is paid, the paying enterprise must be careful to check that the sum of the book value of the asset transferred, plus the cash paid, is not greater than the market value of the asset being received. If this is so, the asset must be written down to its market value and a loss recorded on the transaction.

Finally, the non-monetary transaction rules do not mean that there will be perfect symmetry between the seller and the buyer. The rules may result in different values being recorded; only the approach will be similar.

Exchange of Similar Non-Monetary Assets
It often happens that one non-monetary asset is exchanged for a similar asset, and a small (e.g., less than 10%) cash amount is included to even things up. The *CICA Handbook* defines similar assets as

> . . .assets of the same general type, which perform the same function and are employed in the same line of business. [*CICA* 3830.09]

If similar assets are exchanged, should a gain or loss be recognized? Has anything, in fact, changed? Remember that capital assets are meant to generate wealth over a period of years, recapturing their capital cost and providing returns to shareholders through operations. If a firm has an apartment building, and swaps it for a similar apartment building and a little bit of cash, are shareholders really in a different position?

Standard-setters have concluded that exchanges of similar assets do not complete, or *culminate*, an earnings process because the operations of the business are not altered substantively by the exchange. Therefore, gains and losses are not recognized on exchanges of similar assets. The acquired asset is thus recorded at the *book value* of the asset transferred plus any cash paid or minus any cash received.

Valuation of similar non-monetary transactions:

Book value of asset transferred out	**plus** or **minus**	Cash paid
		Cash received

If the cash component is more than 10% of the value of the transaction, then the transaction may be considered to be *monetary*, and *fair values would be used*. The presence of more significant cash amounts changes the complexion of the transaction.

Examples of Non-Monetary Asset Exchanges

The following information for Regina Corporation is used in the examples that follow:

Asset transferred	*Crane*
Original cost	$50,000
Accumulated depreciation, updated to date of exchange	$40,000

1. Dissimilar Assets.

a. *Exchange does not involve cash.* Assume that the crane has a fair value of $12,000 and is exchanged for a used truck whose value is not more clearly determinable; no cash is paid or received. The book value of the crane is $10,000; therefore, a $2,000 gain is recognized and the entry is:

Automotive equipment (truck)	12,000	
Accumulated depreciation — crane	40,000	
Machinery (crane)		50,000
Gain on exchange		2,000

The gain represents the difference between the market value and book value of the crane. If instead we assume the fair value of the crane was $9,000, the truck would be valued at that amount and a $1,000 *loss* would be recognized.

b. *Exchange includes cash paid or received.* Assume that the crane still has a fair value of $12,000 but that Regina also pays $900 to obtain the used truck.

Automotive equipment (truck)	12,900	
Accumulated depreciation — crane	40,000	
Machinery (crane)		50,000
Cash		900
Gain on exchange		2,000

In this case, the truck is valued at $12,900 (the fair value of the crane plus the cash paid), that is, the fair value of the assets given up.

2. Similar Assets.

a. *Exchange does not involve cash.* When similar assets are exchanged and no cash is involved, the asset being received is recorded at the book value of the asset given up. No gain or loss is recorded. Assume that Regina exchanges the crane in the preceding example for another crane. Because both machines perform essentially the same function, there is no culmination of an earnings process. Therefore, the entry for the transaction would be:

Machinery (new crane)	10,000	
Accumulated depreciation (old crane)	40,000	
Machinery (old crane)		50,000

b. *Exchange involves cash paid or received.* The cash paid or received when similar assets are exchanged alters the value at which the asset received is recorded, but still will not result in recording a gain or loss as long as the cash value is less than 10% of the value of the transaction. Assume that the cranes are swapped, but $600 is paid by Regina.

Machinery (new crane)	10,600	
Accumulated depreciation (old crane)	40,000	
Machinery (old crane)		50,000
Cash		600

Assume, instead, that Regina must pay $4,200 in the exchange of the cranes. The old crane has a fair value of $8,000, and the new crane has been appraised at $14,000. The seller agrees to receive the old crane and $4,200. The value of the transaction, based on assets given up, is $12,200, and cash is more than 10%. This time, a gain or loss must be recorded:

Machinery (new crane)	12,200	
Accumulated depreciation (old crane)	40,000	
Loss on asset exchange ($10,000 – $8,000)	2,000	
Machinery (old crane)		50,000
Cash		4,200

The maximum amount at which the asset received may be recorded is its fair value. Therefore, when the asset received has a fair value lower than the book value of the asset given up, it must be recorded at that fair value. For example, assume that, in the previous example, the crane being received by Regina has an estimated fair value of $8,500 and that this value is more clearly determinable. Regardless of other considerations, the maximum value that can be debited to the crane account is $8,500; a larger loss on exchange is created as a result.

Machinery (new crane)	8,500	
Accumulated depreciation (old crane)	40,000	
Loss on asset exchange*	5,700	
Machinery (old crane)		50,000
Cash		4,200
*[10,000 BV + 4,200 cash – 8,500FV]		

Fair Market Value Determination

Where do fair value quotations come from? Sometimes there are quoted cash prices from suppliers of new and used assets. When a quoted cash price is unavailable, a company can invite bids for the asset to be exchanged. The highest bid for the asset in question is used as the market value. However, this approach is not always appreciated by the companies who invest time and energy submitting quotes, only to discover that the asset wasn't really to be sold! A less reliable but commonly used alternative is published information on the average price of specific used assets, such as the *Kelley Blue Book Auto Market Report* for automobiles. Appraisal is another commonly used approach, but appraisals are notoriously subjective.

In the absence of a reasonably determinable market value for either asset, the valuation of the acquired asset is based on the book value of the asset transferred, adjusted for any cash paid or received.

POST-ACQUISITION EXPENDITURES

After acquisition, many costs related to capital assets are incurred. Examples include repairs, maintenance, betterments, and replacements.

Expenditures that increase the original useful life or productivity of an asset (the quantity or quality of service) above the original level estimated at acquisition are capitalized. A capitalized post-acquisition expenditure is depreciated over the number of periods benefited, which can be less than the remaining useful life of the original asset.

The service potential of assets and their estimated useful life at acquisition assume a certain minimum level of maintenance and repair. Costs for maintenance are expensed in the period incurred. Some companies expense all post-acquisition expenditures less than a certain dollar amount (for example, $1,000). This policy is acceptable because the amounts are not material.

Expenditures that result from accident, neglect, intentional abuse, or theft are recognized as losses. For example, if a computer workstation is damaged during installation, the repair cost is recognized as a loss. After repair, the asset is no more valuable than it was before the mishap. Outlays made to restore uninsured assets damaged through *casualty*, or accident, are also recorded as losses. They do not enhance the utility of the asset beyond the value before the casualty. Such losses may or may not be extraordinary.

Significant post-acquisition expenditures fall into four major categories:

1. Maintenance and ordinary repairs.
2. Betterments.
3. Additions.
4. Rearrangements and other adjustments.

Maintenance and Ordinary Repairs

Maintenance expenditures include lubrication, cleaning, adjustment, and painting, incurred on a continuous basis to keep plant assets in usable condition. Ordinary repair costs include outlays for parts, labour, and related supplies that are necessary to keep assets in operating condition but neither add materially to the use value of assets nor prolong their useful life significantly. Ordinary repairs usually involve relatively small expenditures. *Most expenditures made on capital assets are repairs, and expensing is the norm.* Keep this in mind as a rule of thumb — capitalization may look too tempting at times!

Many firms accrue repairs each month, and charge actual repairs to the accrued repair liability account, in order to report smooth monthly expenses. This seems to make some sense, especially in a business where regular repairs and maintenance are all done in a regular slack season. At the end of the year, any remaining balance in the liability account is reversed, so that the repair expense represents the amount actually spent during the year.

Betterments

A betterment is the cost incurred to enhance the service potential of a capital asset. It often involves the replacement of a major component of a capital asset with a significantly improved component. Examples include the replacement of an old shingle roof with a modern fireproof tile roof, installation of a more powerful engine in a ship, and significant improvement of the electrical system in a building.

But, as the name implies, the result should be better than the old — not just more attractive, but better from an asset sense. That is, the asset should be able to deliver enhanced cash flows to the firm, either through more revenue (higher quality output, more service hours per day, or a longer life) or through reduced operating costs. Then, the betterment has status as an asset and capitalization is warranted. Otherwise, the expenditure is a repair. Repairs are the norm, betterments are the exception.

Betterments may be replacements or renewals. A replacement is the substitution of a major component of a plant asset with one of comparable quality. Renewals involve large expenditures, are not recurring in nature, and usually increase the utility or the service life of the asset beyond the original estimate. Major overhauls of equipment and strengthening of a building foundation are examples.

Three different approaches have evolved to account for these expenditures, all causing the book value of the original asset to increase:

1. **Substitution.** This approach removes the cost of the old component and related accumulated depreciation, recognizes a loss equal to the remaining book value, and increases the original asset account in the amount of the expenditure. To illustrate, assume that a shingle roof with an original cost of $20,000 and 80% depreciated is replaced by a fireproof tile roof costing $60,000. The two entries to record the betterment are as follows:

To remove old component accounts

Accumulated depreciation (old roof, $20,000 × 80%)	16,000	
Loss on asset improvement	4,000	
Building (old roof)		20,000

To record cost of new component

Building (new roof)	60,000	
Cash		60,000

This approach works fine in theory. The only problem is that, by the time the building needs a new roof, the portion of the cost of the building that relates to the old roof is virtually impossible to figure out.

2. **Increase Asset Account.** This approach is used when the costs and depreciation amounts of the old component are not known and when the primary effect is to increase efficiency rather than the economic life of the basic asset. The cost of the betterment is simply debited to the original asset account.

One result of this treatment is an overstatement of the basic asset's book value and subsequent depreciation, although this value is usually relatively minor at time of replacement. For example, simply capitalizing the new roof in the previous example means that the building would have two roofs in its capital cost. The net effect is only to *overstate* net book value by $4,000 (the net book value of the old roof).

3. **Reduce Accumulated Depreciation.** This was the traditional approach used when the primary effect was to lengthen the remaining life of the related asset. The expenditure was debited to the relevant accumulated depreciation account on the grounds that some of the useful life is restored. The cost of the unit replaced is not removed from the accounts. The capital assets rules in the *CICA Handbook* require that betterments be added to the cost of capital assets, and as a result this approach has fallen from favour [*CICA* 3060.29].

Sometimes, replacements are required by law to ensure public safety or to meet environmental standards. For example, many localities require removal of asbestos insulation for health reasons. Is asbestos removal and replacement capitalizable, or should it be expensed? A case can be made either way. The useful life of the building is likely to remain unchanged as will the overall productivity of the building. On the other hand, employee safety is increased, and the firm has less exposure to health-related lawsuits.

Additions

Additions are extensions, enlargements, or expansions of an existing asset. An extra wing or room added to a building is an example. Additions represent capital expenditures and are recorded in the capital asset accounts at cost. Related work on the existing structure, such as shoring up the foundation for the addition or cutting an entranceway through an existing wall, is a part of the cost of the addition and is capitalized. If the addition is an integral part of the older asset, its cost (less any estimated residual value) is normally depreciated over the shorter of its own service life or the remaining life of the original asset. If the addition is not an integral part, it is depreciated over its own useful life.

Many firms retrofit production facilities with pollution control equipment to comply with laws and court orders. When the cost of antipollution devices exceeds the cost of the polluting assets, the devices are capitalized separately and depreciated as plant additions.

Rearrangements and Other Adjustments

The costs of reinstallation, rerouting, or rearrangements of factory machinery to increase efficiency are capital expenditures if the benefits of the rearrangement are tangible cash flows that extend beyond the current accounting period. Such costs are capitalized as an other asset, a deferred charge, or a specific plant asset and amortized over the periods benefiting from the rearrangement.

PRESENTATION AND DISCLOSURE

The AcSB recommends disclosure of the cost of each major category of capital assets and the related accumulated amortization [*CICA* 3060.58]. This segregation by major category is important, as the various categories of capital assets are associated with different levels of business risk and may have dissimilar useful lives and amortization policies. Typically, capital assets are shown as one net amount on the balance sheet, or perhaps two net amounts, one for tangible assets and one for intangibles. The required breakdown is usually shown in the notes. For example, Western Star Trucks Holdings Ltd reports, in their 30 June 1998 financial statements, one number for capital assets on the balance sheet: $143,563,000. Detail is provided in a disclosure note, shown in Exhibit 10-4 (comparative figures have been deleted).

The 1997 survey of corporate reporting practices in Canada, *Financial Reporting in Canada*, noted that most (79%) of the surveyed companies disclosed both the cost and the accumulated amortization of tangible capital assets segregated by major category, while some (6%) provided no segregation by type. The rest included segregation of the cost, but not of the accumulated amortization.[3] Western Trucks has segregated both property, plant and equipment and associated amortization.

Conversely, in practice, intangibles are usually disclosed net of amortization, that is, the accumulated amortization is *not* separately disclosed, despite the AcSB's rec-

---

3 *Financial Reporting in Canada 1997* (CICA, 1997), p. 200.

EXHIBIT 10-4
WESTERN STAR TRUCKS HOLDINGS LTD.
Capital Assets Disclosure
30 June 1998
(thousands of Canadian dollars)

4. Capital Assets

	Cost	Accumulated Depreciation	Net Book Value
30 June 1998			
Land	6,764	—	6,764
Buildings and leasehold improvements	44,294	4,615	39,679
Machinery, equipment, and other assets	158,034	60,914	97,120
Total	209,092	65,529	143,563

Included in machinery, equipment, and other assets are $17.8 million of assets under development for which depreciation has not commenced.

Note: Comparative figures have been omitted.

ommendation to do so. Western Trucks does segregate the cost and accumulated amortization of its intangible assets, labelled as *deferred costs* by the company. This is a minority practice. *Financial Reporting in Canada 1997* reported that 115 of their 200 surveyed public companies disclosed at least one intangible capital asset. Of the 115, only 51 disclosed the amount of accumulated amortization.

When a company has purchased goodwill on its books, "the amount attributed to goodwill should be shown separately on the balance sheet" [CICA 1580.61]. *Financial Reporting in Canada 1997* found that most companies (89%) that disclosed the existence of goodwill did report it as a separate balance sheet item. Goodwill was the most common intangible capital asset, and was reported by 57% of the surveyed companies. Only 17% of the companies disclosed other intangibles.

The capital asset note disclosures of Newbridge Networks Corporation is shown in Exhibit 10-5. In note 8, Newbridge discloses the cost and amortization rates for five classes of tangible capital assets, but deducts the accumulated amortization as a single amount, unlike Western Star Trucks. However, Newbridge does disclose both the cost and the accumulated amortization of its two types of intangible assets, goodwill (note 9) and software development costs (note 10).

The *CICA Handbook* recommends that non-monetary transactions be disclosed, so that users of financial statements will understand their impact on the financial statements. To be specific:

> The nature, basis of measurement, amount and related gains and losses of non-monetary transactions, other than exchanges that do not represent the culmination of the earnings process, should be disclosed in the financial statements for the period. [CICA 3830.13]

In practice, however, this is not taken to apply to exchanges of capital assets because "they do not represent the culmination of the earnings process." Only large-scale exchanges are reported in practice, such as when Suncor Inc. transferred ownership of 127 Sunoco service stations in Quebec in exchange for 88 service stations in Ontario previously owned by Ultramar Canada Inc.

EXHIBIT 10-5

NEWBRIDGE NETWORK CORPORATION
Capital Assets Disclosure
(thousands of Canadian dollasr)

8. Property, Plant and Equipment

	Amortization Rate	April 30, 1998	April 30, 1997
Land	-	$ 14,763	$ 5,571
Buildings	2.5%–5%	88,189	72,779
Equipment	10%–50%	705,744	500,602
Furniture and fixtures	20%	45,067	34,485
Leasehold improvements	Lease term	27,797	9,512
		881,560	622,949
Accumulated amortization		(430,825)	(328,010)
		$450,735	$294,939
Capital leases included above		$ 6,606	$ 6,918

	1998	1997	1996
Amortization on property, plant, and equipment	$112,175	$ 73,364	$ 48,662
Amortization on property, plant and equipment under capital leases	$ 2,035	$ 1,523	$ 1,627

9. Goodwill

	April 30, 1998	April 30, 1997
Goodwill	$ 83,817	$133,854
	(11,098)	(8,289)
Accumulated amortization	$ 72,719	$125,565

During the third quarter ended Feburary 1,1998, goodwill of $65,218,000 and accumulated amortization of 8,093,000 (net book value $57,125,000) were written off as part of the restructuring plan in the LAN business (Note 17)

10. Software Development Costs

	April 30, 1998	April 30, 1997
Balance, beginning of the year	$ 22,299	$ 18,285
Amount capitalized	15,627	12,457
Amortization	(9,627)	(8,443)
Balance, end of the year	$ 28,299	$ 22,299

CASH FLOW STATEMENT

Investments in capital assets are shown as *investing activities* on the cash flow statement, provided that the acquisition is for cash. If a capital asset is acquired in a non-cash transaction, the investment may be reported in the notes to the financial statements if the transaction was substantial, but it would not be reported as part of the cash flow statement because no cash was involved. If cash was only part of the consideration to acquire a capital asset, then only the cash portion will be shown.

For self-constructed or self-developed capital assets (e.g., buildings or product development costs), expenditures that otherwise would have been reflected in the operating cash flow end up being shown instead as investing activities. When companies aggressively capitalize expenditures as capital assets, they increase their *reported* cash flow from operations. The actual cash flow doesn't change, of course, but the classification of capitalized expenditures as investing activities changes the *apparent* cash flow from operating activities. Financial statement readers should be careful about comparing operating cash flow across companies. However, there is no way that the financial statement reader can know how much overhead has been capitalized as part of capital assets. A company's accounting policy disclosure may state that capitalized costs include some portion of overhead, but the amount is never disclosed.

Gains and losses on the sale of capital assets are non-cash items, from the viewpoint of operating activities. When an asset is sold for cash, what appears on the cash flow statement is the amount of the proceeds (i.e., the cash actually received) for the asset. The proceeds are shown in the investing activities section as a cash inflow — a *dis*-investment. A gain or loss may be reported on the income statement, but it arises only as the difference between the asset's net book value and the cash received. In effect, the gain or loss is only a balancing item in the journal entry for the sale and does not, in itself, represent a cash flow.

If a capital asset is disposed of through a non-cash transaction or exchange, any reported gain or loss clearly is not a cash item, since no cash was involved in the transaction. Therefore, in all instances of gains and losses reported on the disposal of capital assets, the gain or loss is a non-cash item and would not appear on the cash flow statement (except as an adjustment to net income under the indirect method of reporting operating cash flow).

CONCEPT REVIEW

1. If an asset is acquired in an exchange transaction, how do we determine the amount at which the asset is recorded in the books?
2. When should expenditures made on a capital asset after its acquisition be capitalized instead of expensed?
3. What is the difference between *maintenance* and *betterment*? What accounting treatment is given to expenditures for each?
4. Suppose that a company is very aggressive at capitalizing expenditures related to intangible assets. How will the capitalization of large amounts of expenditures affect the cash flow statement, compared to a company that expenses many of the same types of expenditures?

INTERNATIONAL PERSPECTIVE

Accounting for acquisition costs of tangible capital assets is similar around the world. In general, accounting practice in all countries is to capitalize the initial cost of the asset and any expenses necessary to prepare it for use.

There is substantial variation in practice relating to intangible assets, however. The U.S., Australia, and Germany prohibit the capitalization of any research and development costs, while Spain and Switzerland permit capitalization of all types of

EXHIBIT 10-6
Comparison of International Practice — Intangible Capital Assets

Country	Goodwill		Research & Development			Reorgani-zation Costs	Share Issue Costs
	Acquired	Self-Generated	Basic Research	Applied Research	Develop-ment		
Australia	A	F	F	F	A	R	A
Austria	A	F	F	F	F	A	F
Belgium	A	F	F	A	A	A	A
Canada	R	F	F	F	A	A	A
Denmark	A	F	A	A	A	A	F
France	A	F	F	A	A	-	A
Germany	A	F	F	F	F	A	F
IASC	R	F	F	F	R	R	A
Japan	A	F	F	F	A	F	A
Netherlands	A	F	F	A	A	F	A
Spain	R	F	A	A	A	R	R
Sweden	R	F	F	A	A	A	F
Switzerland	A	F	A	A	A	A	A
U.K.	A	F	F	F	A	F	F
U.S.	R	F	F	F	F	R	R

F = forbidden; A = allowed; R = required

Source: Adapted from *Transnational Accounting: A Reference Matrix* by Dieter Ordelheide and Anne Semler (London: Macmillan Press, 1996).

such costs. The capitalization of other self-generated intangibles, such as patents and trademarks, is *forbidden* in Austria, France, Germany, Sweden, and Switzerland; it is *required* in Spain and by the International Accounting Standards; and it is *allowed* in many other countries. Exhibit 10-6 summarizes intangible asset practices in several countries. The guidelines to determine which costs are to be capitalized are also varied, even among those countries that allow or require the capitalization of internal costs for self-generated intangible assets.

Goodwill is also subject to widely varying practice. Recognition of purchased goodwill is usually permitted, but is required only in Canada, Spain, Sweden, and the U.S. (although only in certain circumstances). Recognition of self-generated goodwill is generally forbidden, as it is in Canada.

SUMMARY OF KEY POINTS

1. Capital assets include tangible property, plant and equipment, and intangible properties that contribute to future net cash flows of the entity by contributing to operating activities.

2. The cost and accumulated amortization of capital assets must be disclosed by major category.

3. Capital assets are recorded at cost, including cost to install the asset and prepare it for use. Specific guidelines exist to aid in classification of expenditure for various asset categories including buildings, self-constructed assets, machinery and equipment, land, land improvements, patents, industrial design registrations, copyrights, trademarks, and other intangibles.

4. Cost less accumulated amortization equals net book value, which is not meant to reflect fair value after acquisition.

5. Major accounting policy decisions for capital assets include amortization method, and determination of cost. Capitalization policy will affect net assets and net income for the length of the asset's life.

6. Assets acquired in a lump sum purchase should be valued using the proportional method, although the incremental method is used when information is not complete.

7. Capital assets purchased on credit are valued at the cash equivalent price, or at the present value of the debt issued. Assets acquired for share capital are valued at the fair value of the share capital issued, unless that value is less reliable than the fair value of the asset received. Donated assets are valued at fair value, and give rise to contributed capital.

8. Government assistance related to the purchase of capital assets is deferred and amortized to income on the same basis as the amortization on the capital asset purchased.

9. Goodwill, the most common intangible asset, is only recognized on the purchase of another entity. It is measured as the excess of purchase price over the fair value of identifiable net assets acquired.

10. When assets are sold or otherwise retired or disposed, the difference between proceeds, if any, and book value is the gain or loss on disposal. The gain or loss is, in substance, a correction of the recorded amortization over the period that the asset was used.

11. When non-monetary assets are exchanged, the transaction is valued at the fair value of the asset given up, unless the fair value of the asset received is more clear. If the assets are similar, then there has been no culmination of the earnings process, and the transaction is valued at the book value of the asset given up and no gain or loss is recognized.

12. Post acquisition expenditures are typically repairs, which are expensed. If the expenditure results in enhanced cash flows for the asset, it is classified as a betterment and is capitalized and amortized over the asset's remaining useful life.

13. On the cash flow statement, cash expenditures to acquire capital assets are reported as *investing activities*. Capital assets acquired in a non-cash exchange are not included on the cash flow statement.

14. When a company capitalizes overhead and other internal costs as capital assets (or as part thereof), the company's reported cash flow from operating activities will appear higher than it would if the expenditures had been expensed.

REVIEW PROBLEM

The following four episodes are independent.
1. *Plant asset cost classification.* Maldive Company completes the construction of a building. The following independent items are the costs and other aspects relevant to the purchase of the lot and construction:

Cash payments to contractor	$100,000
Total sales tax on materials used in construction in addition to payments made to contractor	3,000
Cost of land (building site)	50,000
Gross cost to demolish old building on land	20,000
Proceeds from old building salvage	5,000
Power bill for electricity used in construction	2,000
Interest on loans to finance construction	3,000

What is the final recorded cost (i.e., carrying value) for *each* of the land and building?

2. *Accounting for debt incurred on acquisition.* The Round Wheel Barn Company purchases a tractor by making a down payment of $10,000. In addition, Round Wheel Barn signs a note requiring monthly payments of $2,000, starting one month after purchase and continuing for a total of 20 months. The contract calls for no interest, yet the prevailing interest rate is 24% per annum on similar debts. What is the cost (and initial carrying value) of the asset? What is the interest expense that should be recognized for the month following purchase?

3. *Accounting for exchange of plant asset.* Ocular Company trades an electron microscope for new optical equipment (a similar asset) and receives $30,000 cash as well. The old microscope had an original cost of $200,000 and has accumulated depreciation of $80,000 at the time of the trade. The old microscope has a fair market value of $160,000 at trade-in time. What entry should be made to record the exchange?

4. *Post-acquisition costs.* After one-fourth of the useful life had expired on equipment with an original cost of $100,000 and no salvage value, a major component of the equipment is unexpectedly replaced. The old component was expected to last as long as the equipment itself. Company records indicate that the component originally cost $20,000 and had no expected salvage value. The replacement component cost $30,000 and has no usefulness beyond that of the equipment. What is the entry to record the replacement? Assume straight-line depreciation.

REVIEW PROBLEM — SOLUTION

1. Cost components of the land and building:

Land		Building	
Land cost	$50,000	Cash payments to contractor	$100,000
Demolition	20,000	Sales tax on materials	3,000
Salvage proceeds	(5,000)	Power bill	2,000
		Capitalized loan interest	3,000
Total land cost	$65,000	Total building cost	$108,000

2. The cost of the tractor is the present value of the monthly payment annuity:
   $P = \$10,000 + \$2,000(P/A, 2\%, 20) = \$42,703$
   Interest cost for the first month is the present value times the monthly interest rate:
   $32,703 \times 2\% = \$654$

3. The entry to record the exchange of similar assets is:

Equipment ($160,000 - $30,000)	130,000	
Accumulated depreciation	80,000	
Cash	30,000	
Equipment		200,000
Gain		40,000

4. The new component is a replacement of an old component, and such is a *substitution*. It is not a betterment, because it does not improve or extend the functioning of the asset. The entries to remove the old component and substitute the new are as follows:

Loss on asset replacement	15,000	
Accumulated depreciation ($20,000 ÷ 4)	5,000	
Equipment		20,000
Equipment	30,000	
Cash		30,000

QUESTIONS

10-1   Capital assets are classified as tangible or intangible; distinguish between the two, and give examples.

10-2   Does cost necessarily equal fair value on the date of acquisition for self-constructed assets, and intangibles? Explain.

10-3   Does net book value measure fair market value for a capital asset? Explain.

10-4   What is a capital expenditure? How are capital expenditures accounted for?

10-5   Explain the impact on income and net assets, over an asset's life, of a decision to capitalize or write off certain costs incurred at the time of purchase.

10-6   To determine the cost of a capital asset, how should the following items be treated: (a) invoice price, (b) freight, (c) discounts, (d) title verification costs, (e) installation costs, (f) break-in costs, and (g) cost of a major overhaul before operational use?

10-7   When several operational assets are purchased for a single lump-sum consideration, cost apportionment is usually employed. Explain the alternatives. Why is apportionment necessary?

10-8   A machine was purchased on the following terms: cash, $100,000, plus five annual payments of $5,000 each. How should the acquisition cost of the machine be determined? Explain.

10-9   How is an asset's acquisition cost determined when the consideration given consists of equity securities?

10-10 What is a non-reciprocal transfer? How are assets received in such a transfer valued?

10-11 An investment tax credit is sometimes received when capital assets are purchased. What alternative ways to account for such assistance have been considered in the past? What alternative is now required?

10-12 TRI Ltd. bought a piece of machinery for $67,000, and received 30% of the purchase price in an investment tax credit. If the asset has a five-year life, and no salvage value, how much net depreciation should be recorded each year?

10-13 Some businesses construct plant assets for their own use. What costs should be capitalized for these assets? Explain what to do about (a) general company overhead, (b) costs of construction in excess of the purchase price of an equivalent asset from an outsider, and (c) interest on construction loans.

10-14 What outlays are properly considered part of the cost of an intangible asset?

10-15 Define goodwill and describe how it is calculated.

10-16 What is negative goodwill? How does it arise? How is it treated for accounting purposes?

10-17 What items are properly debited to organization costs? Should organization costs be amortized? Explain.

10-18 What is the nature of a gain or loss on disposal of an operational asset when cash is received?

10-19 How are assets recorded when they are acquired by exchanging another asset? Explain the rules for (a) exchanges of dissimilar assets and (b) exchanges of similar assets.

10-20 What effect does a minor cash payment have on the accounting rules for (a) similar assets and (b) dissimilar assets? What effect does a major cash payment have?

10-21 When are post-acquisition costs capitalized rather than expensed?

10-22 Explain three approaches used when recording a betterment. Which is preferable?

10-23 What items commonly are reported on the CFS in relation to capital assets?

CASE 10-1

Multi-Communications Ltd.

Multi-Communications Ltd. (MCL) is a Canadian-owned public company operating throughout North America. Its core business is communications media, including newspapers, radio, television and cable. The company's year end is 31 December.

You, CA, have recently joined MCL's corporate office as a finance director, reporting to the chief financial officer, Robert Allen. It is October 20X2. Mr Allen has asked you to prepare a report which discusses the accounting issues that might arise when the auditors visit in November.

MCL's growth in 20X2 was achieved through expansion into the United States. MCL acquired a conglomerate, Peters Holdings (PH), which had substantial assets in the communications business, including a number of newspapers, television and cable operations. Since the U.S. side of MCL's operations is now significant, management will begin reporting its financial statements in U.S. dollars in 20X2.

Over the past three months, MCL has sold off 80% of PH's non-communication related businesses. The remaining 20% are also for sale, and are reported as long-term investments in the MCL statements.

To date, the sale of these non-communications assets has generated proceeds of $175 million, while their cost on the date of acquisition was $153 million. The proceeds have been treated as a reduction of the cost of acquiring PH, and no gain on sale has been reported on income statements prepared to date.

Overall, the cost of PH was $498 million, which MCL has reduced by $175 million, to $323 million. The tangible assets acquired have a value in the range of $240 – $280 million, depending on the appraiser's report used (three were obtained). The major variation between the appraiser's reports is the interest rate used in the valuation; interest rates have been volatile.

In MCL's major newspaper markets, newspaper readership has peaked and there is little or no room for expansion. To increase its readership in one major urban market, MCL bought all the assets of a competing newspaper for $10 million in 20X2, which represented $4 million for tangible assets and $6 million for customer lists and goodwill. Later in the year, MCL ceased publication of the competing paper — publicly billed as a merger of the two papers — and liquidated the tangible assets for $3.2 million. MCL has classified the $.8 million loss on sale of these capital assets as an increase in goodwill, bringing the total goodwill from the acquisition to $6.8 million. This is based on the underlying rationale for acquiring the newspaper: to increase their own readership by restricting choice in this particular urban market. While they have not kept the entire customer group, readership in MCL's "merged" newspaper is higher than the single paper circulation before. MCL feels that this enhanced readership clearly justifies the capitalization of goodwill.

MCL estimates the value of its entire intangibles at $250 million. Included as intangibles are newspaper and magazine publication lists, cable subscriber lists, and broadcast licences. Some of these have been acquired through the purchase of existing businesses; others have been generated internally by operations that have been part of MCL for some time.

Amounts paid for acquired intangibles are not hard to determine, but the cost of internally generated intangibles is much more difficult to ascertain. Subscription lists are built through advertising campaigns, cold calls, and product give-aways. MCL estimates that they have expensed $35 million because of such activities over the last 10 years. Independent appraisers have determined the fair value of these internally generated assets to be in the range of $60 to $80 million. Because management feels that accurate portrayal of these assets is crucial to fairly present their financial position, they have included these assets at $60 million on their balance sheet.

Required:

Adopt the role of CA and prepare the report for Mr Allen.

[CICA, adapted]

CASE 10-2

Nova Scotia Timber Resources Ltd.

Nova Scotia Timber Resources Ltd. (NSTR) is a privately held company incorporated under the companies legislation of Nova Scotia. It is owned by a family syndicate based in Bonn, Germany. The syndicate has been actively involved in acquiring timberland in the province of Nova Scotia for the past five years. Early in 20X3, the decision was made to roll the assets into a corporation and harvest timber for the first time. Previously, land acquired had been left idle.

While the immediate objective is to profit from the timber resource, the syndicate's long-term goals include profit on the land itself. Germany has high-density population, and recreational land is scarce. Nova Scotia waterfront properties represent attractive acquisition targets. Regular market value appraisals are obtained on both the land value, and, separately, the timber resource.

The syndicate members have borrowed money to pay for the land in their personal names — the land, not the debt, has been transferred to NSTR, although the land is often collateral for the debt. In addition, though, the syndicate members provided personal guarantees on an operating line of credit for NSTR of up to $4 million with the Chartered Bank of Canada. This loan is also secured by a floating charge on inventory and receivables.

NSTR, in its first year of production, leased a building (for 10 years) which housed sawmill operations, administrative offices, and a warehouse. It also acquired about $1,400,000 of processing equipment, trucks, tools, and other necessary assets. There are many incidental costs associated with these acquisitions: transportation costs, installation costs, (approximately $114,000) and renovations to the leased facility ($178,000).

As trees are harvested, the decision must be made whether to sell the logs to other sawmills or users of timber, or to process the logs in NSTR's own facilities. The quality of logs varies. A five-year contract was signed with a plant in Nova Scotia that used low-quality logs to produce chipboard and panelling. The price agreed on was "fair market value," determined monthly, and minimum delivery quantities were established for each month.

Higher-quality logs, processed internally, become lumber of various dimensions, sold to both building supply companies and independent contractors in the Maritimes and in the Quebec and Ontario markets. Transportation costs make it difficult to compete strongly in the Quebec and Ontario markets. Terms are usually cash payment within 60 days of delivery.

Prices of these finished products are a function of supply and demand at the date of sale. Inventory is stored in NSTR's warehouses, incurring interest and storage costs, if the current market price is deemed unacceptably low by management. They have refused to accept prices below cost, and lumber prices were quite volatile in 20X3.

Management has the responsibility for making these decisions; they also make decisions concerning how much lumber to harvest in any one year, based on their market predictions.

The syndicate has set a policy of reforestation of harvested land, consistent with their long-term goals of land appreciation. The costs to fulfil this policy, while not large in 20X3, are expected to be material in future years.

The company's first year-end has just passed. The syndicate has not indicated how net income is to be computed, nor has Canadian management spent much time considering financial accounting policies. There has been some indication that the syndicate wishes to be able to draw funds, in the form of dividends, to meet debt service charges and principal repayments. In addition, some consideration has been given to awarding senior management a bonus on net income, although details have yet to be worked out.

Syndicate members are very anxious to keep an eye on the market value of the land, as this was a primary financial incentive for the acquisition in the first place.

Required:

Assume the role of an accounting advisor to the company and explain the financial accounting policies and principles the company should adopt.

[ASCA, adapted]

EXERCISES

E10-1 *Asset Cost:* The following cases are independent.

Case A. Bengal Company purchased a $200,000 tract of land for a factory site. Bengal razed an old building on the property and sold the materials it salvaged from the demolition. Bengal incurred additional costs and realized salvage proceeds as follows:

Demolition of old building	$25,000
Legal fees for purchase contract and recording ownership	5,000
Title guarantee insurance	6,000
Routine maintenance (mowing) done on purchase	2,000
Proceeds from sale of salvaged materials	4,000

What balance should Bengal report in the land account?

Case B: Tiger Limited bought a building for $316,000. Before using the building, the following expenditures were made:

Repair and renovation of building	$16,000
Construction of new driveway	3,000
Repair of existing driveways	1,200
Installation of 220-volt electrical wiring	4,000
Deposits with utilities for connections	100
Painting company name on two sides of building	1,800
Installation of wire fence around property	5,000

Required:

What balance would Tiger report in the building account? If any items in the list above are excluded from the building account, indicate the appropriate classification.

E10-2 *Acquisition of Land — Non-Cash Consideration:* Under the cost principle, what amount should be used to record the land acquired in each of the following independent cases? Give reasons in support of your answer.

a. At the middle of the current year, a cheque was given for $40,000 for the land, and the buyer assumed the liability for unpaid taxes in arrears at the end of last year, $1,000, and those assessed for the current year, $900.

b. A company issued 14,000 shares of capital stock with a market value of $6 per share (based on a recent sale of 100 shares) for the land. The land was recently appraised at $80,000 by independent and competent appraisers.

c. A company rejected an offer to purchase the land for $8,000 cash two years ago. Instead, the company issued 1,000 shares of capital stock for the land (market value of the shares, $7.80 per share based on several recent large transactions and normal weekly share trading volume).

d. A company issued 1,000 shares of capital stock for the land. The market value (shares sell daily with an average daily volume of 5,000 shares) was $60 per share at time of purchase of the land. The vendor earlier offered to sell the land for $59,000 cash. Competent appraisers valued the land at $61,000.

E10-3 *Assets Acquired — Note Payable, Discount:* The following situations are independent:

a. Delivery equipment with a list price of $30,000 was purchased; terms were 2/10, n/30. Payment was made within the discount period.

b. Delivery equipment with a list price of $20,000 was purchased; terms were 2/10, n/30. Payment was made after the discount period.

c. Delivery equipment listed at $9,000 was purchased and invoiced at 2/10, n/30. In order to take advantage of the discount, the company borrowed $8,000 of the purchase price by issuing a 60-day, 15% note, which was paid with interest at the maturity date.

d. Vee Corporation acquired equipment on credit. Terms were $7,000 cash down payment plus payments of $5,000 at the end of each of the next two years. The seller's implicit interest rate was 14%. The list price of the equipment was $17,000.

Required:

Give entries in each separate situation for asset acquisition. For (a) to (c), also provide the entry made when cash is paid.

E10-4 *Lump-Sum Purchase:* Freeman Company purchased a tract of land on which a warehouse and an office building were located. The cash purchase price was $140,000 plus $10,000 in fees connected with the purchase. The following data was collected concerning the property:

	Tax Assessment	Vendor's Book Value	Original Cost
Land	$20,000	$10,000	$10,000
Warehouse	40,000	20,000	60,000
Office building	60,000	50,000	80,000

Required:
Give the entry to record the purchase; show computations.

E10-5 *Cost Determination:* The following three cases are unrelated:

Case A. Brushy Machine Shop purchased the following used equipment at a special auction sale for $40,000 cash: a drill press, a lathe, and a heavy-duty air compressor. The equipment was in excellent condition except for the electric motor on the lathe, which will cost $900 to replace with a new motor. Brushy has determined that the selling prices for the used items in local outlets are approximately as follows: drill press, $8,400; lathe, with a good motor, $24,000; and air compressor, $10,500.

Case B. A large company, upon abandoning its operations at a particular site, donated a building and the land on which it was located to another company who was to hire two-thirds of the old company's workforce. The property was reliably appraised at a value of $160,000 (one-fourth related to the land). The recipient company paid transfer costs of $4,000 related to the land.

Case C. The Weipert Widget Company purchased, at a cost of $2,200,000, a factory in an isolated area of Quebec. In consideration for locating in this area, Weipert Widget received a grant from the federal government in the amount of $800,000 for the factory purchase, as well as a grant of $150,000 from the province of Quebec to defray the cost of the necessary land purchase, which cost $175,000.

Required:

Determine the cost of the assets acquired in each case. Explain your reasoning, if choices must be made.

E10-6 *Government Assistance:* On 1 July 20X4, Theriout Corp. acquired a manufacturing plant in Cape Breton for $1,750,000. The plant, employing 50 workers, began operation immediately, and is expected to be in operation for 16 years with no residual value. In connection with the purchase, the following government assistance was received:

a. Theriout received an investment tax credit of 20% of the purchase price. The company has sufficient taxable income from other sources to use the tax credit in 20X4.

b. Theriout received a loan from the provincial government to help buy the capital assets, in the amount of $1,200,000. The loan need not be repaid as long as the plant operates for at least 10 years, and employes an average of 25 people each year. Theriout is optimistic about the prospects for the plant, but is mindful of the high rate of business failure in Cape Breton.

Required:

1. Provide two acceptable ways to record the investment tax credit. Explain the reporting ramifications of the alternatives — that is, what is the difference between the financial statement presentations?

2. Provide the entry to record the loan. Explain your choice of entry.

3. How much net depreciation expense on the manufacturing plant would be recorded in the year ended 31 December 20X4? Provide calculations.

E10-7 *Asset Acquisition:* During the current year, Candle Soap Company began a project to construct its new corporate headquarters. Candle purchased land with an old building for $375,000. The land was valued at $350,000 and the building at $25,000. Candle plans to demolish the building. Additional expenditures on the project include

a. Interest of $93,000 on construction financing paid during construction of the headquarters building.

b. Payment of $9,250 for delinquent real estate taxes assumed by Candle on purchase of the land and building.

c. Liability insurance premium of $6,000 covering the construction period.

d. Cost of $32,500 for razing the existing building.

e. Costs of $68,000 to move into new headquarters.

f. Costs of $875,000 for construction of the building.

Required:

Determine Candle's ending balance in all relevant capital asset accounts given the above information. Also note the total amount of expense, if any, to be recognized.

[AICPA, adapted]

E10-8 *Self-Constructed Asset — Rationale for Accounting Treatment:* Amethyst Company constructed a building and incurred the following costs directly associated with construction:

Materials	$25,000
Labour	40,000
Incremental overhead	15,000
Interest on construction loan	3,500

The building was worth $77,500 (market value) upon completion.

Required:

1. At what value would Amethyst recognize the building?
2. Discuss the rationale for the limitation on the valuation of Amethyst's building in terms of the historical cost principle.

E10-9 *Characteristics of Intangible Assets:* For each of the following independent events, indicate

a. its manner of acquisition (externally bought from another party or internally generated through the actions of the company),
b. whether it should be capitalized, and
c. whether the captialized cost, if any, reflects fair value on the date of acquisition.

	Manner of Acquisition	Capitalized?	Fair Value
1. Purchased a trademark			
2. During ten years of operation, a company's goodwill has increased considerably.			
3. Trademark developed by the company.			
4. Patent developed by the company's research program.			
5. Copyright on material developed by the company over a five-year period.			
6. Purchased $1 million of goodwill when another company's assets were bought.			
7. Purchased a copyright.			
8. Monopoly rights awarded to a public utility company.			
9. Paid legal fees to organize and incorporate a new business.			

E10-10 *Compute Goodwill — Entries:* On 1 January 20X5, the balance sheet of Nance Toaster Company was as follows:

Assets	
Accounts receivable (net of allowance)	$ 60,000
Inventory	90,000
Plant and equipment (net of depreciation)	200,000
Land	30,000
Total	$380,000

Liabilities and owners' equity	
Current liabilities	$ 38,000
Non-current liabilities	80,000
	118,000
Owners' equity	262,000
Total	$380,000

On 1 January 20X5, Major Appliance Corporation purchased all of the assets and assumed all of the liabilities listed on the above balance sheet. They paid $290,000 cash. The assets, on date of purchase, were valued by Major as follows: accounts receivable (net), $50,000; inventory, $85,000; plant and equipment (net), $200,000; and land, $45,000. The liabilities were valued at their carrying amounts.

Required:

1. Compute the amount of goodwill included in the purchase price paid by Major Corporation.

2. Give the entry that Major Corporation should make to record the purchase of Nance Toaster Company.

3. What is the minimum amount of goodwill amortization that Major Corporation can record at the end of 20X5?

E10-11 *Multiple Choice — Acquisition and Exchange:* Choose the correct statement among the alternatives.

1. Deal Company traded a delivery van and $10,000 cash for a newer delivery van owned by East Corporation. The following information relates to the values of the vans on the exchange date:

	Carrying Value	**Fair Value**
Old van	$ 60,000	$ 90,000
New van	80,000	100,000

What amount should Deal report as a gain on exchange of the vans?
   a. $30,000.
   b. $20,000.
   c. $10,000.
   d. $0.

2. Valley Company traded equipment with an original cost of $50,000 and accumulated depreciation of $20,000 for similar productive equipment with a fair value of $30,000. In addition, Valley received $5,000 cash in connection with this exchange. What should be Valley's carrying amount for the equipment received?

   a. $15,000.
   b. $20,000.
   c. $25,000.
   d. $30,000.

3. On 1 July, one of Renee Company's delivery vans was destroyed in an accident. On that date, the van's carrying value was $5,000. On 15 July, Renee received and recorded a $1,400 invoice for a new engine installed in the van earlier in May and another $1,000 invoice for various repairs done at the same time. In August, Renee received $7,000 under its insurance policy on the van, which it plans to use to replace the van. What amount should Renee report as a gain (loss) on disposal of the van in its income statement?

   a. $2,000.
   b. $600.
   c. $0.
   d. $(400).

4. Lamont Company's forest land was expropriated for a provincial park. Compensation for the expropriation exceeded the land's carrying value. Lamont purchased similar, but larger, replacement forest land for an amount greater than the expropriation award. As a result of the expropriation and replacement, what is the net effect of the carrying value of forest land reported in Lamont's balance sheet?

    a. The amount is increased by the excess of the replacement forest land's cost over the expropriated forest land's carrying amount.

    b. The amount is increased by the excess of the replacement forest land's cost over the expropriation award.

    c. The amount is increased by the excess of the expropriation award over the expropriated forest land's carrying amount.

    d. There is no effect, because the expropriated forest land's carrying amount is used as the replacement forest land's carrying amount.

E10-12 *Disposal of Operational Assets — Interpretation of Resulting Gain or Loss:* Renny Company sells a machine on 1 June 20X5, for $139,000. Renny incurred $800 of removal and selling costs on disposal. The machine cost $250,000 when it was purchased on 2 January 20X2. Its estimated residual value and useful life were $40,000 and 10 years, respectively. Renny uses straight-line depreciation and records annual depreciation on 31 December.

Required:

1. Provide the journal entries needed to record the disposal. Record depreciation to the disposal date.

2. How would the gain or loss in (1) be affected if the machine were abandoned (zero market value)?

3. Provide an interpretation of the gain or loss in (1) for someone with little or no background in accounting.

E10-13 *Similar and Dissimilar Assets Exchanged:* Bloem Corporation has some old equipment that cost $70,000; accumulated depreciation is $40,000. This equipment was traded in on a new machine that had a list price of $80,000; however, the new machine could be purchased without a trade-in for $75,000 cash. The difference between the market value of the new asset and the market value of the old asset will be paid in cash.

Required:

Give the entry to record the acquisition of the new machine under each of the following independent cases:

a. The new machine was purchased for cash with no trade-in.
b. The equipment and the machine are dissimilar. The old equipment is traded in, and $50,000 cash is paid.
c. The equipment and the machine are similar. The old equipment is traded in, and $50,000 cash is paid.
d. The equipment and the machine are dissimilar. The old equipment is traded in, and $6,000 cash is paid.
e. The equipment and the machine are similar. The old equipment is traded in, and $3,000 cash is paid.

E10-14 *Assets Exchanged — Five Different Cases:* Seismographics Corporation exchanged old equipment that cost $10,000 (accumulated depreciation, $4,500) for new equipment. The market value of the new equipment was $8,000. The market value of the old equipment could not be reliably estimated.

Required:

Give the entry to record the acquisition of the new equipment under each of the following independent cases:

a. The assets are dissimilar. No cash was involved.

b. The assets are dissimilar. Cash of $3,000 was paid by Seismographics.

c. The assets are similar. No cash was involved.

d. The assets are similar. Cash of $500 was paid by Seismographics.

e. The assets are similar. Cash of $1,600 was paid by Seismographics.

E10-15 *Repairs, Replacements, Betterments, and Renovations:* The plant building of Xon Corporation is old (estimated remaining useful life, 12 years) and needs continuous maintenance and repairs. The company's accounts show that the building originally cost $600,000; accumulated depreciation was $400,000 at the beginning of the current year. During the current year, the following expenditures relating to the plant building were made:

a. Continuing, frequent, and low-cost repairs	$34,000
b. Added a new storage shed attached to the building; estimated useful life, eight years	72,000
c. Removed original roof; original cost, $80,000; replaced it with guaranteed, modern roof	100,000
d. Unusual and infrequent repairs due to damage from flood; repairs did not increase the use value or the economic life of the asset	12,000
e. Complete overhaul of the plumbing system (old costs not known)	25,000

Required:

Give the journal entry to record each of the above items. Explain the basis for your treatment of each item.

PROBLEMS

P10-1 *Acquisition Cost:* An examination of the property, plant, and equipment accounts of James Company on 31 December 20X5, disclosed the following transactions:

a. On 1 January 20X4, a new machine was purchased having a list price of $30,000. The company did not take advantage of a 1% cash discount available upon full payment of the invoice within 10 days. Shipping cost paid by the vendor was $100. Installation cost was $400, including $100 that represented 10% of the monthly salary of the factory superintendent (installation period, two days). A wall was moved two feet at a cost of $800 to make room for the machine.

b. During January 20X4, the first month of operations, the newly purchased machine became inoperative due to a defect in manufacture. The vendor repaired the machine at no cost to James; however, the specially trained operator was idle during the two weeks the machine was inoperative. The operator was paid regular wages ($650) during the period, although the only work performed was to observe the repair by the factory representative.

c. On 1 January 20x4, the company bought plant fixtures with a list price of $4,500; paid $1,500 cash and gave a one-year, non-interest-bearing note payable for the balance. The current interest rate for this type of note was 15%.

d. On 1 July 20X4, a contractor completed construction of a building for the company. The company paid the contractor by transferring $400,000 face value, 20-year, 8% James Company bonds payable. Financial consultants advised that the bonds would sell at 96 (i.e., $384,000).

e. During January 20X5, exchanged the electric motor on the machine in part (a) for a heavier motor and gave up the old motor and $600 cash. The market value of the new motor was $1,250. The parts list showed a $900 cost for the original motor (estimated life, 10 years).

f. On 1 January 20X4, purchased an automatic counter to be attached to a machine in use, cost $700. The estimated useful life of the counter was 7 years, and the estimated life of the machine was 10 years.

Required:

1. Prepare the journal entries to record each of the above transactions as of the date of occurrence. Explain and justify your decisions on questionable items. James Company uses straight-line depreciation.

2. Record depreciation at the end of 20X4. None of the assets is expected to have a residual value except the fixtures (residual value is $500). Estimated useful lives: fixtures, five years; machinery, 10 years; and building, 40 years. Give a separate entry for each asset.

P10-2 *Asset Cost and Related Expenditures:* The following transactions relate to operational assets:

a. Purchased land and buildings for $157,800 cash. The purchaser agreed to pay $1,800 for land property taxes already assessed. The purchaser borrowed $100,000 at 15% interest (principal and interest due in one year) from the bank to help make the cash payment. The property was appraised for taxes as follows: land, $50,000; and building, $100,000.

b. The building was recarpeted and painted at a cost of $20,000. Landscaping, costing $2,200, was completed.

c. Purchased a tract of land for $64,000; assumed taxes already assessed amounting to $360. Paid title fees of $100 and legal fees of $600 in connection with the purchase. Payments were in cash except for the tax balance, which is still owing.

d. The land purchased in (c) above was levelled, and two retaining walls were built to stop erosion that had created two rather large gulleys across the property. Total cash cost of the work was $6,000. The property is being held as a future plant site.

e. Purchased a used machine at a cash cost of $17,000. Subsequent to purchase, the following expenditures were made:

General overhaul prior to use	$2,400
Installation of machine	600
Cost of moving machine	300
Cost of removing two small machines to make way for larger machine purchased	200
Cost of reinforcing floor prior to installation	800
Testing costs prior to operation	120
Cost of tool kit (new) essential to adjustment of machine for various types of work	440

Required:

Prepare journal entries to record the above transactions. Justify your position on doubtful items.

P10-3 *Asset Acquisition — Non-Cash Consideration:* Machinery with a market value of $30,000 is acquired in a non-cash exchange. Below are five independent assumptions (a) to (e) as to the consideration given in the non-cash exchange:

a. Bonds held as a long-term investment, which originally cost $56,000 and had been written down 50% because of a perceived permanent loss of their value.
b. Inventory carried at $19,000 on the most recent balance sheet as part of a perpetual inventory carried at LCM. When originally acquired, the goods had cost $19,800.
c. Similar used machinery with a book value of $12,000 and a market value of $13,400 plus cash of $16,600. When new, the used machinery cost $17,600.
d. Land with a book value of $15,000 and a market value of $30,000.
e. A non-interest-bearing note for $34,500 maturing in one year. Notes of similar risk required 15% interest at the date of the exchange.

Required:

Give the journal entry required for each of the above independent assumptions.

P10-4 *Multiple Choice — Asset Acquisition and Post-Acquisition Costs:* Choose the correct answer for each of the following questions:

1. Discounts available for early payment of liabilities incurred for the purchase of operational assets should be:
    a. Recorded and reported as a contra account to the related liability account.
    b. Given no recognition until taken or until the discount period has expired; if not taken, the discounts should be added to the cost of the asset.
    c. Deducted from the invoice price, whether taken or not.
    d. Capitalized as a part of the cost of the asset, whether taken or not, and subsequently included in depreciation expense.

2. Able Corporation purchased an old building and the land on which it is located. The old building will be demolished at a net cost of $10,000. A new building will be built on the site. The net demolition cost (after salvage proceeds) should be
    a. Depreciated over the remaining life of the new building.
    b. Written off as an extraordinary loss in year of demolition.
    c. Capitalized as part of the cost of the land.
    d. Written off as an expense.

3. Shwee Corporation purchased land by signing a note with the seller calling for $10,000 down, $12,000 one year from purchase, and $8,000 three years from purchase. The note is not interest-bearing, but the going rate for similar land purchase notes is 10%. What value should be recorded in the land account?
    a. $25,019.
    b. $26,920.
    c. $27,000.
    d. $30,000.

4. The cost to train employees to run new robotic technology used in manufacturing should be debited to
    a. Machinery.
    b. Deferred charge.
    c. Manufacturing expense.
    d. Office salaries.

5. At great cost, a special plastic film was applied to all the south- and west-facing windows of a 12-storey office building. This film reduces the radiant energy entering the building and is expected to pay for itself in reduced air-conditioning costs in five years. The useful life of the windows is not affected. The cost of this film should be debited to

   a. Maintenance and repair expense.
   b. Building.
   c. Leasehold improvement.
   d. Other expense.

6. A music system was added to the office building and elevators to create a more pleasant environment. The system consists of new wiring, speakers, and state-of-the-art amplification equipment. The company hopes that employees will be more productive as a result. The cost of the system should be debited to:

   a. Entertainment expense.
   b. Furniture.
   c. Building.
   d. Employee expenses.

7. The parking lot was repaved with a new, longer-life asphalt. The company owns the land and the lot. The new asphalt will increase the life of the present lot significantly over the original expected useful life. The cost of the repaving should be debited to

   a. Land improvements.
   b. Land.
   c. An expense account.
   d. Deferred charge.

P10-5 *Asset Acquisition:* At 31 December 20X4, certain accounts included in the property, plant, and equipment section of Hine Corporation's balance sheet had the following balances:

Land	$ 600,000
Buildings	1,300,000
Leasehold improvements	800,000
Machinery and equipment	1,600,000

During 20X5, the following transactions occurred:

a. Land site number 101 was acquired for $3,000,000. Additionally, to acquire the land, Hine paid a $180,000 commission to a real estate agent. Costs of $30,000 were incurred to clear the land. During the course of clearing the land, timber, and gravel were recovered and sold for $16,000.

b. A second tract of land (site number 102) with a building was acquired for $600,000. The closing statement indicated that the land value was $400,000 and the building value was $200,000. Shortly after acquisition, the building was demolished at a cost of $40,000. A new building was constructed for $300,000 plus the following costs:

Excavation fees	$12,000
Architectural design fees	16,000
Building permit fee	4,000

The building was completed and occupied on 30 September 20X5.

c. A third tract of land (site number 103) was acquired for $1,500,000 and was put on the market for resale.

d. Extensive work was done to a building occupied by Hine under a lease agreement that expires on 31 December 2004. The total cost of the work was $250,000, as follows:

Item	Cost	Useful Life (Years)
Painting of ceilings	$ 10,000	1
Electrical work	90,000	10
Construction of extension to current working area	150,000	25
	$250,000	

The lessor paid half the costs incurred for the extension to the current working area.

e. During December 20X5, $120,000 was spent to improve leased office space.

f. A group of new machines was purchased subject to a royalty agreement, which requires payment of royalties based on units of production for the machines. The invoice price of the machines was $270,000, freight costs were $2,000, unloading costs were $3,000, and royalty payments for 20X5 were $44,000.

Required:

Disregard the related accumulated depreciation accounts.

1. Prepare a detailed analysis of the changes in each of the following balance sheet accounts for 20X5.

   a. Land.
   b. Buildings.
   c. Leasehold improvements.
   d. Machinery and equipment.

2. What items would appear on the CFS in relation to the accounts in part (1)?

3. List the amounts in the items (a) to (f) that were not used to determine the answer to (1) above, and indicate where, or whether, these items should be included in Hine's financial statements.

[AICPA, adapted]

P10-6 *Asset Cost:* This problem consists of three unrelated cases.

Case A. Consolidated Smelting Company agreed in a court settlement to

a. Install pollution control equipment on its smelters at an estimated cost of $18 million.
b. Pay specified medical expenses for children living near its facilities who were suffering from lead poisoning; tentatively estimated cost of $2,000,000 is to be paid as families incur expenses.
c. Pay a penalty of $200,000 over a four-year term in equal $50,000 instalments.

Required:

Discuss whether each of the components of the settlement should be capitalized or immediately expensed. Indicate the amount at which each item should be recognized.

Case B. The invoice price of a machine is $20,000. Various other costs relating to the acquisition and installation of the machine amount to $5,000 and include such things as transportation, electrical wiring, special base, and so forth. The machine has an estimated life of 10 years and no residual value.

The owner of the business suggests that the incidental costs of $5,000 be debited to expense immediately for three reasons: (1) if the machine should be sold, these costs could not be recovered in the sales price; (2) the inclusion of the $5,000 in the machinery account will not necessarily result in a closer approximation of the market price of this asset over the years because of the possibility of changing price levels; and (3) debiting the $5,000 to expense immediately will reduce federal income taxes.

Required:

Discuss each of the points raised by the owner of the business.

Case C. A chartered bank recently acquired ownership of a lot and building located in a historical part of the city. The building was dilapidated and unsuitable for human habitation. The bank planned this acquisition as a site for a new branch. Although a firm of architects recommended demolition, the city council, in whose discretion such activity rests, refused consent to demolish the building in view of its historical and architectural value.

In order to comply with safety requirements and to make the building suitable for use as a branch location, the bank spent $250,000 restoring and altering the old building. It had paid $90,000 for the building and lot and had contemplated spending $200,000 on a new building after demolishing the old structure. Somewhat similar old buildings in less run-down condition could have been bought in the same area for about the same $90,000 price. It is possible, even likely, that some of these that were not so old could have been demolished without governmental intervention, and the bank could have carried out its original plan.

Now that the restoration is finished and the bank is making final plans to open its newest branch in the restored building, the bank has been informed by the Municipal Historical Commission that the building qualifies for and will receive a plaque designating it as a historical site. The designation will be of some value in attracting traffic to the site, as the building will probably be pointed out during tours of the city, and so on. Under present laws, receipt of the designation may well mean that the bank can never demolish the structure and is obligated to preserve it, even if the property is later vacated.

Required:

Explain how the $90,000 original cost, and the $250,000 restoration expenditures should be treated for accounting purposes.

[AICPA adapted]

P10-7 *Donated Assets:* Hermanson Company received a vacant building as a donation. The building has a 20-year estimated useful life (no residual value), which was recognized in the donation agreement at the time that the company was guaranteed occupancy. Transfer costs of $12,000 were paid by the company. The building originally cost $300,000, ten years earlier. The building was recently appraised at $160,000 market value by the city's tax assessor. Anticipating occupancy within the next ten days, the company spent $36,000 for repairs and internal rearrangements, expected to have value for ten years. There are no unresolved contingencies about the building and Hermanson's permanent occupancy.

Required:

1. Give all entries for Hermanson Company related to (a) the donation, (b) the renovation, and (c) any amortization at the end of the first year of occupancy, assuming that Hermanson uses straight-line amortization and that the assets have no residual value.

2. What would appear on the CFS in relation to the transactions recorded in part (1)? Assume that the direct method is used to present cash flow from operations.

3. What objections are raised concerning the accounting policy of capitalizing and depreciating a donated asset? Explain.

P10-8 *Government Assistance:* The Gysbers Company Limited has embarked on a two-year pollution control program that will require the purchase of two smoke stack scrubbers costing a total of $600,000. These scrubbers qualify for an investment tax credit of 20%. In addition, the federal government will lend Gysbers $100,000 for each scrubber installed. Provided that emissions are reduced 95% by the end of 20X8, the loans will be forgiven. The federal funds are received as the expenditures are made. If the emission standards are not met, the loan will have to be repaid. In 20X5, it was impossible to predict the success that the company would have with the scrubbers.

Gysbers will depreciate the devices over 20 years, straight-line (no residual value), and will take a full year's depreciation in the year installed. The purchase and installation schedule is as follows:

		Cost
January 20X5	Device 1	$300,000
January 20X6	Device 2	300,000
Total		$600,000

Required:

1. Prepare journal entries to record the purchase of device 1 and device 2, and the receipt of the federal loans and investment tax credits. The company wishes to record the investment tax credits in a separate deferred credit account, and has enough taxable income in 20X5 and 20X6 to utilize the tax credits.

2. Prepare journal entries to record depreciation and amortization for the year ending 31 December 20X6.

3. Prepare a partial balance sheet showing the relevant information regarding the pollution control devices as at 31 December 20X6.

4. Assume that after testing in early 20X9, it is found that the emissions have been reduced only 85%. After negotiations, it was agreed that 45% of the loans will be refunded to the government in February 20X9. The balance of the loan will be forgiven. Prepare the journal entries to record the repayment and reclassification in 20X9.

P10-9 *Self-Constructed Asset and Interest Capitalization:* Mannheim Company begins construction of a factory facility on 4 January of the current year. Mannheim uses its own employees and subcontractors to complete the facility. The following list provides information relevant to the construction. The facility is completed 27 December of that year.

a. At the beginning of January, Mannheim obtains construction financing: a 10%, $12,000,000 loan with principal payable at the end of construction provides significant financing for the project. Interest on the loan is payable semi-annually. Mannheim pays the interest and principal when due.

b. Mannheim owns the land site (cost, $4,000,000). In January, a subcontractor is employed to raze the building on the site, which was used by Mannheim for a number of years (cost, $800,000; accumulated depreciation, $600,000) for $80,000. Mannheim received $10,000 from salvaged materials.

c. Also in January, subcontractors survey, grade, and prepare the land for construction at a cost of $200,000 and excavate the foundation of the new facility for $1,000,000.

d. In January, a subcontractor poured and finished the foundation for $1,500,000. This work is financed separately through a one-year, 9% loan. Mannheim secured the financing at the beginning of January. The principal and interest were paid on 30 December.

e. The total material cost for construction, excluding other items in this list, is $8,000,000.

f. Payments to subcontractors, excluding others in this list, amount to $2,000,000.

g. Payments to Mannheim employees for work on construction are $9,000,000.

h. General overhead is assigned to all work done for customers on the basis of labour costs. If company-wide rates are used, the share of general overhead applicable to the job would be $7,000,000. The company uses a factory overhead applied account. Of the $7,000,000, $1,250,000 relates to amortization of capital assets.

i. In October, a subcontractor constructed a parking lot and fences for $300,000.

j. Incidental fees and other costs associated with facility construction were $150,000.

k. For purposes of interest capitalization, assume the company records interest to an expense and capitalizes interest once per year as an adjusting entry. Since construction costs were incurred fairly evenly over the year, the company has decided to capitalize one-half of the interest expense related to the general construction loans outstanding during the year (see *a*).

l. The market value of the building upon completion is $25,000,000.

Construction costs are accumulated in Mannheim's *facility under construction* account.

Required:

1. Provide general journal entries to account for all aspects of construction and related events. Your entries should lead to the correct total cost to record for the building. You may record the events in any order you feel is easiest for you.

2. What disclosures would appear on the CFS in relation to the constructed asset? Assume the company uses the indirect method to present cash flows from operations.

P10-10 *Intangible Assets:* Transactions during 20X5, the first year of the newly organized Jenny's Discount Foods Corporation, included the following:

2 Jan.   Paid $8,000 lawyer's fees and other related costs for assistance in obtaining the articles of incorporation, drafting bylaws, and advising on operating in other provinces.

31 Jan.   Paid $2,000 for television commercials advertising the grand opening. This advertising increased customer's awareness of the company name and location.

1 Feb.   Paid $4,000 to the financial institution that assisted in the private placement of $400,000 of the company's no-par value shares. Under the contract, the underwriter charged 1% of the gross proceeds from the stock sale. The stock issuance has already been recorded. The $4,000 must be recorded.

1 May   Acquired a patent from an existing patent holder for $10,200. The patent will not be used in the operations of the corporation but rather will be held as a long-term investment to produce royalty revenue.

1 July   Paid consultants $6,400 for services in securing a trademark enabling the company to market under the now protected name "Jenny's Recipe."

1 Oct.   Obtained a licence from the city to conduct operations in a specific location. The licence, which cost $600, runs for one year and is renewable.

1 Nov.   Acquired another business and paid after analysis $36,000 for its goodwill. Record only the goodwill.

31 Dec.   Paid $5,000 in legal fees in an unsuccessful patent defence related to the patent acquired on 1 May, which, as a result of the lawsuit, now appears to be questionable in its revenue-generating capacity.

Required:

Give the journal entry that Jenny should make for each of the above transactions.

P10-11 *Goodwill Calculation:* During 20X4, the Evergreen Corporation entered into negotiations to buy Pine Company. During December 20X4, a final cash purchase price of $267,000 was agreed on. Evergreen will acquire all assets and liabilities of Pine Company, except for the existing cash balances of Pine.

The 31 December 20X4 balance sheet prepared by Pine Company is shown below in column (a), and the revised market values added later by Evergreen Corporation are shown in column (b).

PINE COMPANY
Balance Sheet
at 31 December 20X4

	(a) Book Values of Pine Co.	(b) Market Values Developed by Evergreen Corp.
Assets		
Cash	$ 20,000	not applicable
Accounts receivable (net)	58,000	$54,000
Inventory	160,000	90,000
Property, plant, and equipment (net)	309,000	285,000
Land	11,000	40,000
Franchise (unamortized balance)	19,000	21,000
Total	$577,000	
Liabilities and shareholders' equity		
Current liabilities	$ 37,000	37,000
Bonds payable	200,000	200,000
Shareholders' equity	340,000	not applicable
Total	$577,000	

Required:

1. Compute the amount of goodwill purchased by Evergreen Corporation.

2. Give the entry for Evergreen Corporation to record the purchase of Pine Company.

3. Give the entry at the end of 20X5 to record the minimum amount of goodwill that can be amortized.

P10-12 *Disposals:* Equipment that cost $18,000 on 1 January 20X1 was sold for $10,000 on 30 June 20X6. It was being depreciated over a 10-year life by the straight-line method, assuming its residual value would be $1,500.

A warehouse that cost $150,000, residual value $15,000, was being depreciated over 20 years by the straight-line method at the beginning of 20X6. When the structure was 15 years old, an additional wing was constructed at a cost of $90,000. The estimated life of the wing considered separately was 15 years, and its residual value was expected to be $10,000.

The accounting period ends 31 December.

Required:

1. Give all required entries to record

   a. Sale of the equipment, including depreciation to the date of sale.

   b. The addition to the warehouse: cash was paid.

   c. Depreciation on the warehouse and its addition after the latter has been in use for one year.

2. Show how the building and attached wing would be reported on a balance sheet prepared immediately after entry 1(c) was recorded.

P10-13 *Multiple Choice — Exchanges of Operational Assets:* Choose the correct answer for each of the following questions.

1. Silo Corporation owns an asset originally costing $75,000, with accumulated depreciation of $38,000. Its current market value is $38,000. Silo traded in this old asset and paid $4,500 for a similar asset. The new asset should be recorded at

   a. $54,000.
   b. $41,500.
   c. $42,500.
   d. $40,500.

2. DDD traded in its old building (cost $350,000, accumulated depreciation $100,000) for a new building whose market value is $180,000, and received $80,000 on the trade. The new building should be recorded on DDD's books at which of the following values?

   a. $170,000.
   b. $180,000.
   c. $100,000.
   d. $270,000.

3. Choose the correct statement concerning operational asset exchanges:

   a. Gains are not allowed on exchanges of similar assets for the corporation receiving cash since the value of the new asset is not objectively determinable.
   b. When there is an exchange of dissimilar assets, the full gain or loss derived from debiting the new asset with its fair market value is recognized.
   c. Gains are allowed on all operational asset exchanges.
   d. Losses are not allowed on non-cash exchanges of similar assets.

   The following information relates to questions (4), (5), and (6), which are independent:

   | Original cost of an operational asset | $10,000 |
   | Accumulated depreciation on the asset | 6,000 |

   XOR Corporation is the owner of the asset.

4. The old asset is traded for a dissimilar new asset with a $12,000 list price. XOR paid $7,000 on the exchange. The new asset's recorded value is

   a. $12,000.
   b. $11,000.
   c. $10,000.
   d. $13,000.

5. The old asset is traded for a similar new asset with a $12,000 fair market value. XOR paid $700 on the exchange. The new asset's recorded value is:

   a. $12,000.
   b. $10,000.
   c. $6,000.
   d. $4,700.

6. The old asset is traded for a similar new asset. XOR received $1,000 on the exchange. The fair market values of the assets are indeterminate, but the new asset has a list price of $14,000. The new asset's recorded value is

   a. $14,000.
   b. $0.
   c. $10,000.
   d. $3,000.

P10-14 *Assets Exchanged — Similar and Dissimilar:* Trader Joe, Inc., has a policy of trading in equipment after one year's use. The following information is available from Trader Joe's records:

1 January 20X2 — Acquired asset A for $12,000 cash.

1 January 20X3 — Exchanged asset A for asset B. Asset B had a market value of $14,000. Paid $1,000 in cash in the exchange.

1 January 20X4 — Exchanged asset B for asset C. Asset C had a market value of $16,000. Paid $1,500 in cash in the exchange.

1 January 20X5 — Exchanged asset C for asset D. Asset D had a market value of $11,000. Received $2,000 in cash in the exchange.

Assume a five-year estimated useful life and no residual value for all assets. Trader Joe uses straight-line depreciation.

Required:

1. Assume that the assets are all similar. Give the journal entries required for each exchange.

2. Assume that the assets are all dissimilar. Give the journal entries required for each exchange.

P10-15 *Assets Exchanged — Similar and Dissimilar:* This problem presents two independent cases — Case A, similar assets, and Case B, dissimilar assets.

Case A. Two similar operational assets were exchanged when the accounts of the two companies involved reflected the following:

	Company M	Company N
Operational asset	$4,000	$4,100
Accumulated depreciation	2,750	2,400

The market value of M's asset was reliably determined to be $1,400; no reliable estimate could be made of N's asset.

Required (round amounts to the nearest dollar):

1. Give the exchange entry for each company, assuming that no cash difference is involved.

2. Give the exchange entry for each company, assuming that a cash difference of $400 was paid by Company M to Company N.

Case B. Two dissimilar operational assets were exchanged when the accounts of the two companies involved reflected the following:

	Company A	Company B
Operational asset	$5,000	$7,000
Accumulated depreciation	3,500	5,250

The market value of A's asset was reliably determined to be $2,250; no reliable estimate could be made for B's asset.

Required:

1. Give the exchange entry for each company, assuming that no cash difference was involved.

2. Give the exchange entry for each company, assuming that a cash difference of $600 was paid by Company A to Company B.

P10-16 *Assets Exchanged — Five Transactions:* In this problem, all items of property refer to operational assets, not inventory, unless specified to the contrary. List prices are not necessarily market values. The following transactions have taken place:

1. Land carried on the books of Company A at $18,000 is exchanged for a computer carried on the books of Corporation B at $25,000 (cost, $35,000; accumulated depreciation, $10,000). Market value of both assets is $30,000. Give the journal entry for both A and B.

2. A truck, which cost Company A $6,000 ($3,000 accumulated depreciation), has a market value of $3,400. It is traded to a dealer, plus a $5,600 cash payment, for a new truck that has a $9,800 list price. Give the journal entry for Company A.

3. A truck that cost Company A $6,000, on which $5,000 depreciation has been accumulated, is traded to a dealer along with $6,300 cash for a new truck. The new truck would have cost $7,000 if only cash had been paid; its list price is $7,500. Give the journal entry for Company A.

4. Land carried on the books of Company A at $90,000 is exchanged for land carried on the books of Corporation B at $78,000. Market value of each tract is $100,000. Give the journal entry for Corporation B.

5. Fixtures that cost Company A $15,000 ($9,000 accumulated depreciation) and are worth $8,000 are traded to Corporation B along with $500 cash. In exchange, A receives fixtures from B carried by B at a cost of $13,000 less $6,000 accumulated depreciation. Give the journal entries for both A and B.

Required:

Give journal entries where specified to record the above transactions.

P10-17 *Replacements and Repairs:* The plant asset records of Reston Company reflected the following at the beginning of the current year:

Plant building (residual value, $30,000; estimated useful life, 20 years)	$150,000
Accumulated depreciation, plant building	90,000
Machinery (residual value, $35,000; estimated useful life, 10 years)	180,000
Accumulated depreciation, machinery	90,000

During the current year ending 31 December the following transactions (summarized) relating to the above accounts were completed:

1. Expenditures for non-recurring, relatively large repairs that tend to increase economic utility but not the economic lives of assets:

Plant building	$45,000
Machinery	15,000

2. Replacement of original electrical wiring system of plant building (original cost, $18,000), $29,000.

3. Additions:

Plant building — added small wing to plant building to accommodate new equipment acquired; wing has useful life of 18 years and no residual value	54,000
Machinery — added special protection devices to 10 machines; devices are attached to the machines and will have to be replaced every five years (no residual value)	10,000

4. Outlays for maintenance parts, labour, and so on to keep assets in normal working condition:

Plant	27,800
Building	16,500
Machinery	14,800

Required:

Give appropriate entries to record transactions (1) through (4). Explain the basis underlying your decisions. Indicate the amortization period, when appropriate.

P10-18 *Cash Flow Statement:* The following items have been extracted from the 20X3 financial statements of MC Ltd:

From the balance sheet

	20X3	20X2
Machinery	$172,600	$145,600
Accumulated amortization, machinery	65,000	58,000
Equipment	350,000	124,000
Accumulated amortization, equipment	71,200	84,600
Buildings	276,800	246,000
Accumulated amortization, buildings	104,600	134,000

From the 20X3 income statement

Loss on disposal of equipment	$ 3,500
Loss on write-off of building components	6,700
Amortization ($25,000 on machinery, $10,400 on equipment, and $9,600 on the building)	45,000

Additional information:

1. Equipment with a market value of $36,500 was donated by a local business to encourage manufacturing activity.

2. Equipment costing $200,000 was purchased. It was eligible for a $30,000 government grant that was credited directly to the equipment account.

3. Equipment with a cost of $58,800 and a net book value of $35,000 was sold at a loss during the year.

4. Machinery with a cost of $38,000 and a net book value of $20,000 was traded for similar equipment that had a market value of $22,000. No cash was exchanged in the transaction.

5. Buildings were renovated during the year. The old roof and electrical work, with a cost of $45,700, and accumulated depreciation of $39,000, were written off and replaced at a cost of $76,500. Further repairs of $12,500 were expensed.

6. Machinery with a fair market value of $45,000 was acquired in exchange for common shares.

7. Additional equipment was acquired for cash.

Required:

Prepare cash flow statement disclosures based on the above information. The company used the indirect method to present cash flows from operations.

CHAPTER

11

Capital Assets: Amortization, Impairment, and Revaluation

INTRODUCTION

You probably have studied amortization methods before, in an introductory course. You will remember that there are several acceptable methods of amortization, but all methods result in the allocation of the cost of an asset — less the expected residual, of course — over the life of the asset. Calculations are relatively straightforward, involving lots of dividing and multiplying. It's really not complicated. The emphasis in this chapter, other than a review of basic calculations, is to remind you that this is a significant area of accounting policy *choice*, since companies are relatively free to choose the amortization method that best suits their financial reporting objectives. We'll also look at some of the theoretical justification for amortization, as it often helps guide policy evaluation.

Another area that is fraught with judgement issues, and choice, is the issue of writing down capital assets when there has been an impairment in value. Lower of cost or market assessments are nothing new — all assets have to be assessed to ensure that their book value does not overstate their future value to the firm. However, this process is very complicated for capital assets, because "market value" is not the correct reference point. The correct alternative is a projection of future cash flows, and it is subjective at best. There's lots of room for the motivations of management to be reflected in the financial statements.

There also are occasions when the assets (and liabilities) of a company may be restated to fair values, thereby establishing a new basis of accounting for those assets. For companies that are bound by the limitations imposed by the *CICA Handbook*, the occasions when revaluation is acceptable are highly restricted.

This chapter will examine the three issues of amortization, write-downs, and revaluation.

DEFINITIONS

A review of terminology is probably the best place to start. Capital assets, both tangible and intangible, produce revenue through use rather than through resale. They can be viewed as quantities of *economic service potential* to be consumed over time in the earning of revenues.

Accounting principles call for *matching* the costs of all types of operational assets against revenue over their useful lives. Amortization allows for the periodic allocation of the cost of capital assets against revenue earned. Amortization is also called depreciation when it is associated with tangible capital assets, and depletion when associated with natural resources. *Amortization* is a broad term that includes both depreciation and depletion.

Depreciation (i.e., on tangible capital assets) is recorded in an accumulated depreciation account, which is a *contra account* that is deducted from the related asset account for balance sheet presentation. Amortization of other assets has generally been recorded as a direct credit to the asset account, particularly for intangible capital assets. However, the use of a contra account is not only feasible for intangible assets, but also is implied by the recommendation in the *CICA Handbook* for separate disclosure of the cost of each category of capital asset and its related accumulated amortization. This disclosure recommendation (and the practice of companies in following — or not following — this recommendation) was discussed in the previous chapter.

The net book value (carrying value) of an asset is its original cost plus any capitalized post-acquisition cost less accumulated amortization to date. Amortizable cost is the total amount of amortization to be recognized over the useful life of the asset, and it equals total capitalized asset cost less estimated residual value. Residual value is the estimated net recoverable amount from disposal or trade-in of the asset at the end of its estimated useful life. It is the portion of an asset's acquisition cost not consumed through use, and it is not matched against revenues through amortization. The minimum net book value is residual value.

NATURE OF AMORTIZATION

What is amortization? Simply put, *it is an allocation of capital cost, expensed over the useful life of the asset.* Amortization applies to all items of limited life that appear on the balance sheet, including long-term deferred charges and credits as well as to both tangible and intangible capital assets. In this chapter, however, we are concerned only with capital assets and not with other types of deferred charges and credits.

Amortization is the general term that applies to the interperiod allocation of the cost of any capital asset. What is amortization *not*? Misconceptions abound. For example:

* Accumulated amortization does not represent cash set aside for replacement of plant assets; nor does amortization recognition imply the creation of reserves for asset replacement.

* Amortization does not measure the decline in market value during the period, and net book value does not equal market value.

Historical cost financial statements track cost, not market value. Depreciation is sometimes used in common parlance to describe a decline in value, for example, "A new car will depreciate by $3,000 as soon as you drive it off the dealer's lot." The accounting meaning of the term is different.

The Conceptual Basis of Amortization

The amount of amortization recognized is not necessarily linked to the decline in an asset's utility or market value over time. However, the *eventual* decline in value justifies periodic recognition of amortization. The decline in utility of capital assets is caused by

- physical factors, mainly usage (wear and tear from operations, action of time and the elements, and deterioration and decay) and
- obsolescence (the result of new technology).

Assets rendered obsolete are often in good condition and still capable of supplying the service originally expected of them, but technological advances may render their operating costs uneconomic. Obsolescence also occurs when facility expansion renders certain assets unusable under new operating conditions or when demand for the product or service supplied by the asset declines.

Technological change does not automatically render older equipment obsolete, however. If the older equipment meets the *present needs* of the company, obsolescence is not a factor. For example, in the computer industry, new computer chips may substantially increase computer speeds and capabilities. The Pentium chip eclipsed the 486 chip, for example, although PCs built around the 486 chip continue to be in widespread use, fully supported by software and maintenance agreements. For many companies, changing to the more expensive computers based on the Pentium chip is not immediately cost-effective.

The Requirement to Recognize Amortization Expense

Do companies have to charge amortization expense for all capital assets? It's now a well-entrenched practice, but such was not always the case. For example, in the early days of the railroads, the nature of obsolescence was not well understood, and there were those who claimed that the assets would last forever if properly maintained. Alas, the steam locomotive is with us no more.

More recently, there have been spirited arguments that some intangibles do not have limited lives and thus should not be amortized. Goodwill associated with a thriving business grows, doesn't it? And why would a subscriber base, the core of a cable TV company, ever lose its value? Surely customers will continue to renew forever!

One by one, these assets have come under the general requirement for rational and systematic amortization. Why? Take a look above again. First, *amortization is an allocation of capital cost, that operations must bear*. Amortization does not reflect a decline in value. Secondly, *amortization may be quite justifiable based on eventual decline in value, often caused by obsolescence*. Who knows what types of products, methods of transportation or sources of entertainment will be popular in the year 2030?

The requirement to recognize depreciation on tangible capital assets has been around a long time in business enterprises. In Canada, goodwill recognized on the acquisition of another entity had to be amortized starting in 1973, and other intangibles, starting in 1991. Thus, today there is a requirement to amortize all capital assets except land, over periods not to exceed 40 years.

The general requirement for periodic amortization is based firmly on the *matching concept* and on the underlying assumption that a primary objective of financial reporting is to match the cost of providing services to the revenue generated. Revenue comes from the use of the assets. In business enterprises, this underlying assumption is usually valid.

Non-profit and public sector organizations have different operational objectives, however: they exist to benefit the general welfare, and their dominant reporting objective usually is that of *stewardship* over the resources placed at their disposal by governments and donors. Revenue is not generated by the assets; instead, the assets are acquired as a result of obtaining the revenue (in the form of government grants and private donations). Nevertheless, the AcSB has decreed that all organizations, for-profit and non-profit, should amortize their capital assets. Not all non-profit organizations follow this practice.

Land is a special case, as it isn't at risk due to obsolescence and it doesn't suffer from wear and tear. If there are other capital assets with this quality, then they don't have to be amortized, but a company had better be able to marshal some impressive proof. The *CICA Handbook* requires that "when the useful life of a capital asset other than land is expected to exceed 40 years, but cannot be estimated and clearly demonstrated, the amortization period should be limited to 40 years." (*CICA* 3060.32)

Forty years is arbitrary, but is supposed to avoid abuse of the amortization system. Well, 40 years is a long time — more than the average person's working life. Clear proof would likely involve projections and expert opinions, such as engineers' studies. There are lots of assets that have long lives: many Canadian cities abound with houses built in the 1800s, for example. Business assets, though, have to be able to *generate income* for their "useful life." For example, heavy water, used as a coolant in CANDU nuclear reactors, has an indefinite life. But would you care to bet that the technology will still be in use after 40 years? It's hard to predict ordinary things; nuclear physics is in a different league! Again, amortization seems appropriate.

CONCEPT REVIEW

1. What are the main causes of the decline in value or usefulness of plant assets over time?

2. Why is amortization expense not necessarily an accurate measure of the decline in value of capital assets?

3. What is the conceptual difference between the amounts reported as accumulated depreciation for capital assets and the allowance for doubtful accounts?

ACCOUNTING POLICY CHOICE

The *CICA Handbook* requires only that the method of amortization chosen be *rational and systematic*. Within those boundaries, firms may pick among the methods as they choose. The choices are:

1. Based on equal allocation to each time period — the straight-line (SL) method.
2. Based on inputs and outputs.
   a. Service-hours (SH) method.
   b. Productive output (PO), or units-of-production, method.
3. Accelerated methods.
   a. Declining balance (DB) methods.
   b. Sum-of-the-years-digits (SYD) method.
4. Sinking fund methods

For tangible capital assets, there also is a choice between *individual depreciation* or *group depreciation*. Large individual items such as buildings are depreciated individually. When a company owns large numbers of similar assets, however, the company may use a **group depreciation method**. Group methods collect many assets together and depreciation them without separately identifying the individual assets in the group; for tax purposes, most assets are grouped into classes and depreciated as a group. The choice between individual versus group methods may be influenced by tax reporting considerations.

The following discussion focuses on individual depreciation/amortization; group methods will be discussed briefly thereafter. Capital cost allowance (CCA) for tax purposes is described in the Appendix to this chapter.

In theory, at least, the amortization method should describe the primary causes of the decline in value. For example, assume that a delivery truck has an estimated useful life of five years or 300,000 kilometers. Amortization based on distance driven might yield a more accurate matching of expense and revenue than amortization based on useful life in years. Based on this reasoning, the methods based on usage appear to be the most logical, unless obsolescence is a major factor, in which case straight-line is appealing.

However, GAAP does not mandate an amortization method based on the pattern of benefits derived from the asset, the pattern of its use, or its decline in usefulness or value. The method simply has to be *rational and systematic*. Why? Lack of one "correct method," really. The amount of revenue or cash produced by the use of one specific capital asset is usually impossible to determine unequivocally. Revenues are not generated by assets used in isolation. Rather, they are produced by a number of assets and people working together. Therefore, it is impossible to associate specific revenues (benefits) to specific assets, and thus impossible to allocate the cost of most operational assets on the basis of benefits or revenues. That is, as an allocation, amortization is *incorrigible* — it cannot be supported or refuted without question.[1] If you can't establish one right way, then all rational and systematic methods are equally acceptable. This does not do wonders for comparability, though.

Fortunately, studies of the stock market have suggested that investors are not fooled by accounting policy choices that do not have any impact on cash flows. That is, investors are smart enough to see the fundamental equivalency between two identical firms, earning identical return but reporting different incomes only because of different amortization policies, at least in the short run. However, that's just one group of users. Most Canadian companies are not traded on large, well-disciplined, stock exchanges.

Policy Choice in Practice

Financial Reporting in Canada 1997 reports the following about choice of amortization policy:

Amortization Policy	Number	Proportion
Straight-line	170	64%
Declining balance	48	18
Units of production	42	16
Sinking fund	5	2
	265	100%

There are two points of interest here: first is the fact that 200 companies report use of 265 methods. This isn't a misprint; many companies use more than one method! For example, it would be commonplace to use straight-line amortization for intangible assets and declining balance methods for tangible assets, and so on. Of the 200 sample companies, 170 use straight-line for at least some of their capital assets.

---

1   The *incorrigibility* of accounting allocations was definitively demonstrated by Professor Arthur L. Thomas (McMaster University) in two research studies published by the American Accounting Association in the series, *Studies in Accounting Research: #3: The Allocation Problem in Financial Accounting Theory* (1969), and *#9: The Allocation Problem: Part Two* (1974). The conclusions of these studies were not greeted warmly by many accountants who preferred to believe in the "truth" of their allocations, but no one has ever been able to demonstrate that allocations are not inherently arbitrary.

The second thing to note is the overwhelming use of the straight-line method; in use 64% of the time. It, and declining balance, represent 82% of the observations. The units of production method is quite common in natural resource companies to measure depletion and amortization on assets used in mining or forestry operations, and the sinking fund method is used mostly for real estate. If these two industry peculiarities were removed, the dominance of the first two amortization methods would be even more remarkable.

Factors Influencing Choice

How do companies pick an accounting amortization policy? There are numerous factors that enter into the equation:

- **Corporate reporting objectives.** On a situation by situation basis, it is important to analyze the various elements that drive reporting objectives. Is there a bonus? Is the entity regulated? Are they held under restrictive loan covenants governing debt-to-equity ratios, profitability, etc? These factors have a powerful impact on the accounting policies chosen.

- **Industry norms.** Comparability is an important qualitative characteristic of financial reporting. Companies' financial statements are used by investors, creditors, and others to assess their performance relative to their competition. Using the same amortization method helps. Amortization methods — such as sinking fund amortization for apartment buildings — become generally accepted within an industry.

- **Parent company preferences.** Is the company a subsidiary of another company (the parent)? If so, its financial statements will be combined, or *consolidated*, at the end of the fiscal year. These consolidated financial statements are more meaningful if all constituents follow the same accounting policies, and thus the parent company often dictates key policies to its subsidiaries. A lot of Canadian companies that are wholly-owned subsidiaries of foreign parents (usually U.S.) do what their parents tell them, which may include accounting methods not widely used by Canadian-owned enterprises.

- **Minimize future (deferred) taxes.** Many smaller firms don't really care what amount of amortization is booked, but are interested in keeping their financial statements simple. Therefore, it seems logical to use an accounting policy that results in amortization that coincides with the required tax treatment (which generally is a form of declining balance amortization, as we'll see in the appendix to this chapter).

- **Accounting information system costs.** Notwithstanding the computer revolution, detailed information about acquisition costs, post-acquisition costs, useful life, residual value, and accumulated amortization must be maintained. Which system is the least complex?

The latitude in adoption of amortization methods and the variety of estimates of useful life and residual value are at odds with the uniformity and consistency objectives of financial reporting. The large dollar amount of amortization expense reported combined with the inherently approximate nature of amortization results in a potentially difficult comparison problem for financial statement users.

Management Estimates Required

All amortization methods require that the preparer make the following estimates:

1. Acquisition cost and capitalized post-acquisition costs
2. Estimated residual value
3. Estimated useful life

The first item, acquisition cost, may not appear to be an estimate. In some cases, the cost of an asset is readily determinable. Acquisition cost is particularly "fuzzy" for intangible assets; many of the acquisition or development costs may have been expensed, and only a portion capitalized. However, acquisition cost often is a bit of an approximation even for tangible capital assets because ancillary acquisition costs such as excise taxes, shipping costs, installation, and start-up training costs either are estimated or ignored. Thus, the measurement of "historical cost" is governed by various policies concerning capitalization (versus expensing), as we discussed in the last chapter.

The second two items quite clearly are estimates. To estimate residual value, allowance is made for the costs of dismantling, restoring, and disposing of the retired asset. Future removal and site restoration costs also reduce residual value and can be material. These include all the costs to dismantle and restore a property, and are particularly important for natural resources. For example, if the estimated realizable value upon retirement of an asset is $2,500 and estimated dismantling and selling costs are $500, the net residual value is $2,000.

Net residual value is *negative* if disposal costs exceed the expected proceeds from sale of the asset. Using the same example, if estimated restoration costs are $3,000, residual value is $500. When negative, residual value increases the asset's amortizable cost but not the recorded value of the asset, because the disposal costs will be incurred in the future and do not enhance the asset's value. At the end of such an asset's life, it might have a negative book value if restoration costs are material, which means that the "asset" should be reclassified as a liability, to reflect the firm's obligation to restore or remove the capital asset. Usually, however, companies exclude restoration costs from the residual value calculation. When the asset is retired, any restoration liability is then separately accrued.

In practice, residual values are often ignored. This is acceptable when assets are held almost until the end of their useful lives and restoration or removal costs are low. By their nature, intangible assets rarely have a residual value.

The useful life (economic life) generally has a greater impact on amortization than estimated residual value. The useful life of an asset must be finite to justify amortization recognition. Therefore, land is not amortized. Estimates of useful life require assumptions about potential obsolescence, severity of use, and maintenance. Inadequate maintenance is a short-run cost-saving strategy that can both result in higher future cost and contribute to a shortening of useful life. As we have already seen, there is a 40-year ceiling on useful life, unless there is strong evidence of a longer useful life.

It can be difficult to estimate the useful life of an intangible asset. A good starting point is the legal life of the intangible (see Exhibit 11-1), along with renewal options. After that, though, it's important to take a hard look at other factors, including

1. Provisions for renewal or extension that may alter a specified limit on useful life.
2. Effects of obsolescence, demand, and other economic factors that may reduce useful life.
3. The service life expectancies of individuals or groups of employees.
4. Expected actions of competitors and others that may restrict present competitive advantages.
5. Indefiniteness of useful life and benefits that cannot be reasonably projected.
6. Whether an intangible asset is a composite of many individual factors with varying effective useful lives.

Amortization is not recognized (that is, useful life does not begin) until the asset is in its intended condition and location and is contributing to revenue. When facilities are temporarily idle, recognition of amortization continues when the method

EXHIBIT 11-1
Legal Life of Certain Intangible Assets

Patent	17 years
Industrial Design Registration	Five years; renewable for a further five years
Trademarks	20 years; renewable for infinite successive periods
Franchise	Unlimited unless specified in contract with franchisor
Copyrights	Life of the author plus 50 years

used is based on the passage of time, reflecting increased obsolescence and the reduced economic usefulness of the asset.

When a company stops using a capital asset, its amortization also should cease. If a capital asset is no longer going to be used, its carrying value should be reduced to the fair market disposal value (or cost) *if* the fair value is less than the cost, and the loss should be recognized in the income statement.

Assets should not be amortized below residual value under any method or system. Although declining balance methods do not use residual value in calculating periodic amortization expense, a determination should, in theory, be made at the end of each accounting period to ensure that book value is at least equal to residual value. Where the residual value of individual assets is relatively small, however, this test often is not performed and the assets are amortized to zero.

CONCEPT REVIEW

1. What is the most popular method of amortization in Canada?
2. Name three factors that influence management's choice of amortization policy.
3. What *estimates* must be made before a capital asset can be amortized?

AMORTIZATION METHODS

Exhibit 11-2 summarizes the amortization formulas for the six generally-used amortization methods. Each of the six amortization methods will be illustrated in the following sections, using the data shown in Exhibit 11-3. Only four of the six methods are in wide-spread use, however. Exhibit 11-4 summarizes the amortization schedules for the four most common methods.

Straight-Line Method
The straight-line (SL) method is based on the assumption that an asset provides equivalent service, or value in use, each year of its life. The SL method relates amortization directly to the passage of time rather than to the asset's use, resulting in a constant amount of amortization recognized per time period. The formula for computing periodic SL amortization, with its application to the asset in Exhibit 11-3, is

Yearly SL amortization
= (Acquisition cost – Residual value) ÷ Estimated useful life in years
= ($6,600 – $600) ÷ 5
= $1,200 per year

EXHIBIT 11-2
Amortization Formulas

Straight-line (SL):
Annual SL amortization = (Acquisition cost – Residual value) ÷ Estimated useful life in years

Service hours:
Amortization rate per service-hour = (Acquisition cost – Residual value) ÷ Estimated service life in hours
Annual service hour amortization = Amortization rate per service hour × Hours of usage

Productive output:
Amortization rate per unit of output = (Acquisition cost – Residual value) ÷ Estimated productive output in units
Annual productive output amortization = Amortization rate per unit of output × Units produced

Declining balance (DB):
Annual DB amortization = (Acquisition cost – Accumulated amortization) × DB rate

Sum-of-the-years-digits (SYD):
Annual SYD amortization = (Acquisition cost – Residual value) × SYD Fraction

Sinking fund
Annual sinking fund amortization = [(Acquisition cost – Residual value) ÷ (F/A, i%, # of periods)] + annual compound interest to date

The SL method is logically appealing as well as rational and systematic. It is especially appropriate when the use of the asset is essentially the same each period, and repairs and maintenance expenditures are constant over the useful life. The method is less appropriate for assets whose decline in service potential or benefits produced relates not to the passage of time but rather to other variables, such as units produced or hours in service.

The SL method is the most popular method in use in Canada, by far. Ease of use partially explains the method's popularity. It is also popular because it provides a stable amortization pattern, and expenses a relatively low amount in its initial year, popular with firms trying to maximize earnings and net assets in the short run.

Methods Based on Inputs and Outputs

Amortization methods that associate periodic amortization with a measurable attribute of capital assets include the service-hours method and productive output method (also called the units-of-production method). The input-output methods are rational and systematic and logically match expense and revenue if the asset's utility is measurable in terms of service time or units of output.

These methods do not relate amortization to the passage of time, as the other individually applied methods do. Hence, amortization expense under these methods is not recorded when assets are idle, and thus are appropriate when obsolescence is not as much of a factor in determining useful life as wear and tear. If obsolescence is a factor, an asset's utility decreases whether used or not, and these methods will not portray this reality.

EXHIBIT 11-3
Data Used to Illustrate Amortization Methods

Acquisition cost, 1 January 20X1	$ 6,600
Residual value	600
Estimated useful life:	
Years	5
Service-hours	20,000
Productive output in units	10,000

Activity	Service Hours	Units Produced
20X1	3,800	1,800
20X2	4,000	2,000
20X3	4,500	2,400
20X4	4,200	1,800
20X5	3,500	2,000

Service-Hours Method. The service-hours (SH) method is based on the assumption that the decrease in useful life of a plant asset is directly related to the amount of time the asset is in use.

Amortization rate per service-hour = (Acquisition cost – Residual value) ÷
            Estimated service life in hours
            = ($6,600 – $600) ÷ 20,000 = $0.30

Yearly SH amortization, 20X1   = Amortization rate per service hour × Hours
            used
            = $0.30 × 3,800 = $1,140

Exhibit 11-4 illustrates the service-hours method for the life of the asset.

Productive Output Method. The productive output (PO) method is similar except that the number of units of output is used to measure asset use. A constant amount of amortizable cost is allocated to each unit of output as a cost of production, so annual amortization amounts fluctuate with changes in the volume of output:

Amortization rate per unit of output = (Acquisition cost – Residual value) ÷
            Estimated productive output in units
            = ($6,600 – $600) ÷ 10,000 = $0.60

Yearly PO amortization, 20X2   = Amortization rate per unit of output × Units
            produced
            = $0.60 × 1,800 = $1,080

Exhibit 11-4 illustrates the PO method over the life of this asset.

The service-hours and productive output methods can produce different results, depending on the ratio of machine-hours to units produced. For the asset under study, 2.11 machine-hours were required to produce one unit in 20X1 (3,800 ÷ 1,800), while in 20X2 that figure was reduced to 2.00 (4,000 ÷ 2,000), indicating a greater efficiency (see Exhibits 11-3 and 11-4). The SH method, therefore, yielded slightly higher amortization per unit of output in 20X1 than in 20X2. If the ratio is constant, the two methods would produce identical results and the firm would choose the one that is easier to implement.

The productive output method is commonly used to measure depletion of natural resources. For example, assume that a company incurs costs of $4,000,000 to lease, explore and develop a mine site that is expected to produce two million tons of coal. Costs of $1,350,000 will be incurred to restore the mine site after production is complete. The depletion per ton is $2.675, [($4,000,000 + $1,350,000) ÷ 2,000,000]. Annual depletion is based on actual production levels. For these companies, mining equipment is often also amortized on a units of production basis.

The major problem in applying the productive output method is obtaining an *accurate* estimate of the productive output, and capturing the annual usage data needed to apply the method. Often, the extra cost of this data is not worth the effort. Remember, too, that if usage is relatively constant, the result will not be materially different from the straight-line method. Another problem arises when the running time of an asset varies without a corresponding effect in the output of service. For example, the increasingly heavy traffic in urban areas causes vehicles to run many more hours per week with no increase in their productive service. Also, for many assets such as buildings, furniture, and office equipment, application of these methods is impracticable because no measure of service or output is available.

Accelerated Amortization Methods

Accelerated amortization methods recognize greater amounts of amortization early in the useful life of capital assets and lesser amounts later. Thus, they accelerate the recognition of amortization.

Accelerated methods are based on the assumption that newer assets produce more benefits per period because they are more productive and require less maintenance and repair. Accelerated methods match more of the acquisition cost against the revenue of these earlier periods when greater benefits are obtained. A smoother pattern of total annual operating expense is often the result, with the sum of annual amortization and maintenance expense more constant than is likely with SL amortization. The accelerated method in wide use today is the declining balance method.

Declining Balance Method. Declining balance (DB) methods are significantly different from other methods in two ways:

1. Residual value is not subtracted from cost when computing amortization. Instead, declining balance amortization stops when the net book value of the asset is equal to residual value.
2. The amortization rate is applied to a declining (net) balance rather than to a constant cost.

How do companies arrive at an amortization rate? There is a formula that can be used to find the rate that will reduce the book value of the asset to its estimated salvage value at the end of its estimated useful life, but the formula is never used in practice! Instead, firms may pick a fairly arbitrary rate, based on their assessment of useful life, on industry norms, or perhaps based on corporate reporting objectives.

Another approach is to use the rates established in the *Income Tax Act*, which requires use of an amortization method called Capital Cost Allowance (CCA). CCA is mostly a declining balance method, but uses straight-line for some kinds of assets. CCA doesn't work exactly the same as declining balance amortization, but, if the same rates are used (and a half-year's depreciation is charged in the year of acquisition), the tax and book amortization are often identical and deferred tax balances are avoided as a result. The CCA system is briefly described in the appendix to this chapter.

Another approach to determining the rate is to use what is called *double-declining balance* amortization (DDB), which uses a rate equal to twice the straight-line rate. For example, the asset in Exhibit 11-3 has a 20% straight-line rate (the reciprocal of the years of life; 1/5 = 20%), and so the DDB rate would be 40%. This is a fairly aggressive amortization rate — 40% of the capital cost would be written off in the first year. If this capital asset is a piece of machinery, its CCA rate would be 20%.

Rates, which must be disclosed, should be reviewed by financial statement users to see if they are aggressive or not!

For our example, assume that the firm has chosen a 40% DB rate.

Annual DB amortization = (Acquisition cost – Accumulated amortization) × DB rate
20X1 DB amortization   = $6,600 × 40% = $2,640
20X2 DB amortization   = ($6,600 – $2,640) × 40% = $1,584

See Exhibit 11-4 for the complete set of calculations. Notice in particular the last line, where amortization expense *stops* when accumulated amortization equals the $6,000 amortizable cost, leaving the $600 residual value intact. Thus, the maximum amortization for 20X5 is $256 ($6,000 – $5,744) rather than $342 (40% of $856).

Sum-of-the-Years-Digits Method. The sum-of-the-years-digits (SYD) method computes annual amortization as follows:

Annual SYD amortization = (Acquisition cost – Residual value) × SYD Fraction

The SYD fraction is calculated with a numerator and a denominator:

- *Numerator.* The number of years remaining in the useful life at the beginning of the period. The first year for the asset in Exhibit 11-3 would have a numerator of 5; the second year, 4; the third year, 3; and so on. The numerator always declines with each year of asset use.

- *Denominator.* The name of the method tells it all: the denominator is the *sum of the years digits*. For our asset, with a five-year life, this is 15, (1 + 2 + 3 + 4 + 5).

Amortization expense in 20X1 in our example:

20X1 SYD amortization = ($6,600 – $600) × (5/15) = $2,000
20X2 SYD amortization = ($6,600 – $600) × (4/15) = $1,600

Hardly any Canadian companies use this method. It's a lot more popular in the U.S., where it may also be used for tax reporting. Canadian adopters almost always are subsidiaries of U.S. parents.

Sinking Fund Amortization

So far, we've seen amortization methods that produce level amounts of annual amortization, decreasing amounts of annual amortization, and amortization that will go up and down based on output or usage. The last amortization method we'll talk about produces a pattern of *increasing* amortization — less in the initial years, and more in later years.

This amortization method has gained a toehold in real estate companies that hold apartment buildings, office buildings, and shopping complexes. These properties are usually highly levered — lots of debt, which translates into lots of interest, especially in the early years. The combination of high interest and straight-line — or especially declining balance — amortization would destroy the profit picture for one of these operations. Highly levered companies are often saddled with debt covenants that specify debt-to-equity ratios, and the like, and thus they have a motive for wishing to maximize income. Subsequently, when interest declines because the mortgage is paid down later in the building's life, there's more "room" for amortization expense.

EXHIBIT 11-4
Illustration of Amortization Calculations — Four Popular Methods

Straight-Line Method

Year	Amortization Expense	Accumulated Amortization	Cost	Net Book Value
1 January 20X1			$6,600	$ 6,600
31 December 20X1	$1,200	$1,200	6,600	5,400
31 December 20X2	1,200	2,400	6,600	4,200
31 December 20X3	1,200	3,600	6,600	3,000
31 December 20X4	1,200	4,800	6,600	1,800
31 December 20X5	1,200	6,000	6,600	600 (residual)
Total	$6,000			

Service-Hours Method

	Service Hours	Amortization Expense	Accumulated Amortization	Cost	Net Book Value
1 January 20X1				$ 6,600	$6,600
31 December 20X1	3,800	(3,800 × $.30) = $1,140	$ 1,140	6,600	5,460
31 December 20X2	4,000	(4,000 × $.30) = 1,200	2,340	6,600	4,260
31 December 20X3	4,500	(4,500 × $.30) = 1,350	3,690	6,600	2,910
31 December 20X4	4,200	(4,200 × $.30) = 1,260	4,950	6,600	1,650
31 December 20X5	3,500	(3,500 × $.30) = 1,050	6,000	6,600	600 (residual)
Total	20,000	$ 6,000			

Productive Output Method

	Units Produced	Amortization Expense	Accumulated Amortization	Cost	Net Book Value
1 January 20X1				$6,600	$6,600
31 December 20X1	1,800	(1,800 × $.60) = $ 1,080	$ 1,080	6,600	5,520
31 December 20X2	2,000	(2,000 × $.60) = 1,200	2,280	6,600	4,320
31 December 20X3	2,400	(2,400 × $.60) = 1,440	3,720	6,600	2,880
31 December 20X4	1,800	(1,800 × $.60) = 1,080	4,800	6,600	1,800
31 December 20X5	2,000	(2,000 × $.60) = 1,200	6,000	6,600	600 (residual)
Total	10,000	$6,000			

Declining Balance Method

	Amortization Expense	Accumulated Amortization	Cost	Net Book Value
1 January 20X1			$6,600	$6,600
31 December 20X1	(40% × $6,600) = $2,640	$2,640	6,600	3,960
31 December 20X2	(40% × $3,960) = 1,584	4,224	6,600	2,376
31 December 20X3	(40% × $2,376) = 950	5,174	6,600	1,426
31 December 20X4	(40% × $1,426) = 570	5,744	6,600	856
31 December 20X5	256*	6,000	6,600	600 (residual)
Total	$6,000			

* Should be 40% of $856, or $342, but limited to $256 so that net book value does not go below residual.

There is probably some energetic theoretical basis for this method, too, but it's primarily popular because of the profit pattern it produces when combined with interest expense. And, of course, it's rational and systematic, and that's all we require!

Any method that provides for increasing amortization is risky in some sense, because it leaves a material amount of cost unamortized until the very end of an asset's life. What if the estimate of useful life were optimistic? A large write-off would result. Also, repair costs can escalate in later years, which, combined with higher amortization expenses, has an unfortunate impact on earnings.

There are several methods of increasing amortization, but the most popular is called sinking fund amortization. It is calculated as though there was a sinking fund being accumulated for asset replacement. Each year, amortization is equal to the increase in the sinking fund, both "principal" and "interest." *All these amounts are purely notional, as no sinking fund exists*; the numbers are just used to provide the amortization expense calculation.

If a $5,500,000 building with no residual value were to be amortized over 20 years, using an interest rate of 8%, the principal portion of the amortization would be equal to $120,187 [$5,500,000 ÷ (F/A, 8%, 20)].

	Principal Payment	Interest @ 8%	Increase in Fund	Balance
1	$120,187	—	$120,187	$120,187
2	120,187	$ 9,615	129,802	249,989
3	120,187	19,999	140,186	390,175
etc. ...				

By the end of the 20th year, the balance in the "fund" will be $5,500,000 amortizable cost. Annual amortization expense is equal to the increase in the "fund" — $120,187 the first year, $129,186 the next, and so on. If you worked the table all the way through you'd discover that the amortization in year 20 was $518,691, which is a hefty increase from the $120,187 booked in the first year!

Although this method has, in the past, been used only by real estate companies, it's interesting to see that in 1998, Shaw Communications Ltd., with operations in television and home cable, reported a $1.3 billion dollar asset (41% of total assets) called "subscriber base and broadcast licences." The amortization method for this identifiable intangible, which was exempt from amortization until 1991, was the sinking fund method, at a rate of 4% and an amortization period of 40 years.

CONCEPT REVIEW

1. When is a company most likely to use an output-based amortization method?
2. What is *double* about double-declining balance amortization?
3. Why might a company want to use an amortization method that coincides with tax-basis capital cost allowance?

ADDITIONAL AMORTIZATION ISSUES

Additional amortization issues include a minimum amortization test, fractional-year amortization, and amortization systems.

Minimum Amortization Test

Capital assets are not held for sale, but sometimes their fair market values are apparent, and recording amortization seems counter-intuitive. For example, assume that you're in the following situation:

Asset	Apartment building
Expected life	An additional 20 years
Original cost	$3,750,000
Net book value	$3,150,000
Residual at the end of 20 years	nominal; structure would have to be dismantled
Market value of similar buildings now, excluding land value	$ 4,350,000

Market values may be responding to increased demand for rental properties, but more likely to interest rate shifts. Why should any amortization be claimed on this property, whose current fair value exceeds its book value by a significant margin? Again, refer to the rationale for amortization at the beginning of the chapter: amortization is an *allocation* of capital cost, and is still appropriate in these circumstances.

However, there's another angle on the game: what if the company announces that they plan to hold the building for only another five years, and then sell it. The amortization formulas mostly start by taking cost and subtracting the residual value, the fair value on the expected sale date. Now, it's quite possible that the fair value five years' hence might still be higher than the existing net book value.

Assume that several appraisals of the real estate market, and this building in particular, conclude that the building could be sold for something in the range of $4,400,000 in five years time, again excluding a land value. If the company used straight-line amortization, the calculation would go as follows:

$$(\$3,150,000 - \$4,400,000) \div 5 = -\$1,250,000 \div 5 = -\$250,000$$

Note that the calculation starts with net book value as an amortizable cost, because the company is in the process of changing the estimate of useful life — we'll take another look at these accounting changes in Chapter 22. The amortization number produced by the formula is negative, but negative amortization is never recorded.

Can the company avoid amortization on these grounds? Remember that the company is not committed to the sale; they can change this estimate when the time comes if they don't like market conditions, or if they really weren't on the level in the first place. The accountant is relatively powerless to prevent the manipulation of "intention." Fortunately, an auditor would not be powerless when it comes to dealing with the amortization issue. In these circumstances, the *CICA Handbook* recommends that:

> The amount of amortization that should be charged to income is the greater of:
> (a) the cost less the salvage value over the life of the asset; and
> (b) the cost less residual value over the useful life of the asset.
> [*CICA* 3060.31]

Salvage value is defined as the asset's fair value *at the end of its life*; scrap value, for our building. Residual value is the asset's fair value when the company is done with it; the $4,400,000 appraisal. Assuming scrap value is negligible, this company would have to do a second calculation, under (a): ($3,150,000 − $0) ÷ 20, or $157,500. This greater amount of amortization would have to be recorded under the requirements of the accounting standard.

This situation is not really common — it's not often that a second-hand asset is worth a lot more than its net book value. But it does sometimes happen, and the rule acts to prevent an end-run around the amortization requirements.

Fractional-Year Amortization

The calculations illustrated in Exhibit 11-4 assume that the company takes a full year of amortization in the year that the asset was acquired. This seems logical in the specific example, because the asset was assumed to have been purchased on 1 January. However, most capital assets are not placed in service at the beginning of a reporting period, nor do disposals occur neatly at the end of a year. Firms adjust for fractional periods in two different ways. Some compute the exact amount of amortization for each fractional period, and others apply an accounting policy convention. A *convention* is a standardized way of doing something.

Exact Calculation Approach. This approach computes the "precise" amount of amortization for each fractional period. For example, assume that an asset costing $20,000 with a residual value of $2,000 and useful life of four years is placed into service on 1 April 20X1. The firm has a calendar-year reporting cycle. The asset in question is used only 9/12 of a year in 20X1. Under SL amortization, the asset's fractional service period is applied to the annual amortization amount, as illustrated:

Amortization expense for 20X1 = ($20,000 – $2,000) × (1/4) × (9/12) = $3,375
Amortization expense for 20X2 through 20X4 = ($20,000 – $2,000) × (1/4) =
$$\$4,500 \text{ per year}$$
Amortization expense for 20X5 = ($20,000 – $2,000) × (1/4) × (3/12) = $1,125

The service-hours and productive output methods automatically adjust for fractions of a year. The number of hours used or units produced in the partial-year period is applied to the amortization rate in the normal manner.

Under accelerated amortization methods, first compute amortization for each whole year of the asset's useful life (without regard to the fiscal year). Then apply the relevant fraction of the fiscal year to the appropriate whole-year amortization amount. This is demonstrated using an (aggressive) 50% DB rate.

Whole Year	DB Amortization
1 April 20X1 to 31 March 20X2	.50($20,000) = $10,000
1 April 20X2 to 31 March 20X3	.50($20,000 – $10,000) = $5,000
1 April 20X3 to 31 March 20X4	.50($20,000 – $15,000) = $2,500
1 April 20X4 to 31 March 20X5	.50($20,000 – $17,500) = $1,250, but $500 max.*

*Limited to $500 so that net book value does not go below residual value

Recognized amortization expense
    20X1 amortization = $10,000 × (9/12) = $7,500
    20X2 amortization = $10,000 × (3/12) + $5,000 × (9/12) = $6,250, etc.

Although this is the "exact" approach, that word should not be interpreted too literally. The "exact" approach usually means that amortization is calculated to the nearest month. Seldom will a company try to figure out depreciation to the exact day — what would be the benefit of doing that? Amortization involves the adoption of one from among many possible policies, applied to amounts that are estimates. There is nothing less "precise" in accounting than amortization, and therefore it makes no sense at all to try to be highly precise about an arbitrary number!

Accounting Policy Conventions. To avoid tedious fractional-year amortization, many firms adopt a policy convention. Examples of conventions in current use are:

1. *Half-year convention.* Under this approach, a half-year's amortization is charged on all assets acquired or disposed of during the year. The implicit assumption is that assets are acquired throughout the year and as a result are, on average, acquired in the middle of the year. Given that amortization is an approximation at best, this assumption is as good as any. This method also has the added convenience that it coincides with the convention used for income tax purposes in the year of acquisition.

2. *Full first-year convention.* A full year's amortization is charged to all assets that exist at the end of the year, including those acquired throughout the year. No amortization is taken on assets disposed of during the year. This is particularly popular in group depreciation methods, which generally are based on the asset account balance at the end of the year.

3. *Final year convention.* Annual amortization is determined solely on the basis of the balance in the capital asset accounts at the beginning of the period. Assets disposed of during a period are depreciated a full period, and assets purchased during a period are not depreciated that period. In a period of high capital expenditures and increasing asset bases, this method tends to lower the amount of depreciation taken each period, thereby enhancing net income.

When a company reports on an interim basis, such as quarterly, these conventions may be applied to the *quarter* instead of to the *year*. For example, the half-year convention becomes the *half-quarter* convention — one-half quarter's amortization is taken on all assets acquired or disposed of during the quarter.

Regardless of the convention chosen, the same policy should be used consistently. The exact approach to fractional-year amortization should be used only if the information advantages justify the added cost.

Amortization Systems

Unique features of certain capital assets, as well as practical considerations, may cause firms to modify the application of standard amortization methods. We call these adaptations amortization systems because they apply amortization computations to *groups* of assets.

1. "Inventory" appraisal systems.
2. Group and composite systems.
3. Retirement and replacement systems.

Amortization systems reduce accounting costs because fewer amortization calculations are required and accumulated amortization records are not maintained on individual assets.

"Inventory" Appraisal System. Under the inventory appraisal system, capital assets are appraised at the end of each accounting period in their present condition through application of a deterioration percentage to the cost of the assets in place or through an outside assessment of replacement cost. This system is especially suitable for firms with numerous low-cost capital assets. The word inventory is not used in the sense of goods available for sale, but rather in the sense of an on-going supply of capital assets, usually of small individual value.

The decline in the total appraisal value during the period is recorded directly in the asset account as amortization expense. Cash received on disposal is recorded as a credit to amortization expense. The book value (appraisal value) of the assets at the end of the period is an estimate of current acquisition cost that takes into account current condition and usefulness.

To illustrate how this system works, assume the following information on the *hand tools* capital asset account of Miller Company, which began operations in 20X1:

Purchases of hand tools in 20X1	$1,900
Appraisal value of tools at the end of 20X1	$1,080
Proceeds from disposal of tools in 20X1	$70

The value of tools on hand decreased $820, but the $70 received on disposal offsets that decline, resulting in $750 of net amortization expense.

Accounting cost savings are evident from the elimination of individual subsidiary accounts, with amortization recorded only for the group. Disposals do not require retrieval of accumulated amortization information, and no gain or loss is recorded when an individual asset is sold or scrapped. Furthermore, the appraisal is made for the entire group rather than for each individual asset.

Although inventory appraisal systems appear to be a departure from the historical cost principle, assets are not written up in value, and the resulting amortization expense must be consistent with results obtained with historical cost-based amortization methods. The method is open to criticism, however, because appraisals can be quite subjective.

Group and Composite Systems. Capital assets are sometimes grouped together for application of an average amortization rate that reflects the characteristics of the group. There are two approaches:

1. **Group amortization** is used for homogeneous assets. For example, a company may group all of its delivery trucks together in a single account, or may account for all of its computers as a group.

2. **Composite amortization** is used for heterogeneous assets that form a working whole. For example, a pipeline pumping station functions as a single unit, but it is comprised of a variety of different components that have different costs, useful lives, and residual values. Individual components must be replaced as they fail or wear out in order to protect the functioning of the pumping station as a whole.

Although there is a difference in the underlying rationale between group accounts and composite accounts, the general approach is similar.

Group accounts work on the principle of statistical averaging. For each individual asset, the estimates of salvage value and useful life are almost certain to be incorrect. For a group of assets as a whole, however, the law of averages can be applied. As long as the estimates are correct *on average*, the amortization will be correct (given the depreciation policy chosen). Not only will the amortization be correct statistically, it also will be consistent from period to period and will always be based on a combination of the assets in use and the undepreciated cost.

Depreciating assets on an individual basis results in the recognition of many gains and losses as the assets are disposed of. These gains and losses can cause variations in reported net income, even though there really is nothing unusual happening. The group method, in contrast, avoids recognition of gains and losses on dispositions of individual assets and concerns itself with amortization of the accumulated capital costs. The concept of group accounts is the same as that used as the basis for income tax deductions for tangible capital assets (i.e., *capital cost allowance*, explained in the Appendix).

Composite accounts work on the principle that it is meaningless to account individually for assets that function together as a cohesive and mutually-dependent group. An assembly line can function only as long as all of its component parts are functioning properly. Even at acquisition, it may be difficult to isolate the cost of each individual part of the assembly line. To amortize each part as though it were an independent asset is to ignore the economic reality of the process. Therefore, the assembly line is accounted for (and amortized) as a single unit.

In a very real sense, group and composite depreciation systems are similar to inventory systems; accountants generally reject the notion of trying to separately identify the cost of each unit of inventory that is sold (or used up, in the case of supplies inventories) in preference for accounting for cost *flows*. The group and composite depreciation system applies the same philosophy to tangible capital assets.

Not only are group and composite systems theoretically sound, they also are easier for accounting purposes. There is no need to maintain detailed cost and amortization records for each asset, and no need to figure out, when an asset is scrapped or sold, exactly which asset it was and what its initial cost and accumulated depreciation were.

When a company is accounting for many similar assets (which easily can run into the thousands of units for assets like desks and personal computers), the record keeping for individual asset accounting is an enormous burden. Group accounts do away with the need to maintain that level of detail and reflect an apt application of the cost/benefit constraint. Of course, the company must still maintain adequate *physical* control over the assets.

Although the original cost for each asset acquired is maintained, only one control account for capital assets and accumulated amortization is used. As with the inventory appraisal method, gains and losses are not recognized on disposal. Instead, the asset control account is credited for the original cost of the item, and the accumulated amortization account is debited for the difference between cash received and the original cost of the item.

For example, assume that in the year 20X8 a company sells a filing system that it had acquired in 20X2 for $10,000. The company received $1,200 from the sale of the asset. The asset is part of a group account that is depreciated at the rate of 10% per year, straight line. When the asset is disposed of, only two pieces of information are needed in order to record the sale: (1) the original cost of the asset, and (2) the proceeds from the sale. The sale is recorded as follows:

Cash	1,200	
Accumulated depreciation — filing systems	8,800	
Capital assets — filing systems		10,000

Notice that the debit to accumulated depreciation is the plug figure for this entry. Notice also that there is no attempt to calculate the book value for the asset, nor any gain or loss.

Effectively, what happens is that the full cost of the asset is removed from both the capital asset account and the accumulated depreciation account, and the disposal proceeds are credited to the accumulated depreciation account.

Accumulated depreciation — filing systems	10,000	
Capital assets — filing systems		10,000
Cash	1,200	
Accumulated depreciation — filing systems		1,200

Some companies simplify this system even further by not attempting to identify the actual cost of the asset retired. Instead, a FIFO approach is often used (just as with inventory).

Exhibit 11-5 presents information and calculations for an example that uses *composite* amortization. Annual amortization expense is the product of an average amortization rate and the balance in the asset control account. The composite amortization rate equals the percentage of total cost depreciated each year.

(Annual group SL amortization ÷ Total group acquisition cost) = Composite rate

Residual value is taken into account because the numerator used in determining the composite rate reflects the SL method. Declining balance amortization methods may also be applied.

EXHIBIT 11-5

Case Data for Composite Amortization Example:
Components of Operating Assembly Acquired Early 20X1

Component	Quantity	Original Cost	Residual Value	Useful Life	Annual SL Amortization
A	10	$50,000	$5,000	15 years	$3,000
B	4	20,000	4,000	10 years	1,600
C	6	7,000	600	8 years	800
D	20	3,000	0	3 years	1,000

Total annual amortization: 10($3,000) + 4($1,600) + 6($800) + 20($1,000) = $61,200
Total asset acquisition cost: 10($50,000) + 4($20,000) + 6($7,000) + 20($3,000) = $682,000
Total amortizable cost: $682,000 – 10($5,000) – 4($4,000) – 6($600) = $612,400
Composite annual amortization rate = $61,200 ÷ $682,000 = 0.0897
Composite group useful life = $612,400 ÷ $61,200 = 10 years
Annual amortization expense = Composite rate × Acquisition cost = (.0897)($682,000) = $61,200

If no changes occur in the makeup of the group during the entire composite life, annual amortization does not change. When assets are added or disposed of before the end of their useful life, the original amortization rate is maintained if the changes are not significant to the overall amortizable cost and useful life composition of the group. Amortization is computed with the old rate and the new balance in the group asset control account, which reflects the addition or deletion of assets. Material changes in the makeup of composite groups may require changes in amortization rates because these assets are heterogeneous.

Retirement and Replacement Systems. These amortization systems are used by public utilities and railroads to reduce record-keeping costs. Such companies typically own large numbers of items dispersed over extensive geographic areas, including rolling stock, track, wire, utility poles, and telephone equipment. The bookkeeping cost to amortize these items individually is prohibitive.

Under both the retirement system and the replacement system, amortization is not recorded for individual assets, no gain or loss is recognized on disposal, and an accumulated amortization account is not used. The total original cost of acquisitions is maintained although often not on an individual asset basis. Residual value is treated as a reduction of amortization expense in the disposal period. Amortization expense under both systems is based on assets *retired* during the period.

The key difference between the two systems is the assumed cost of the retired assets, which can be substantial. *Amortization under the retirement system equals the original cost of the item retired less residual value.* If the cost of acquisition cannot be associated with specific physical units, the oldest remaining cost of the type of asset retired less residual value is used for amortization purposes. This is essentially a FIFO system.

Amortization under the replacement system equals the cost of the most recent acquisition of the type of item retired less residual value. This is essentially a LIFO system. The most recent acquisition is considered the replacement for the item retired.

Retirement and replacement systems can result in amortization amounts that bear no relationship to those of individually applied methods. For example, if no retirements are made, no amortization would be recorded. Furthermore, the asset balances under both systems can be distorted to the point of meaninglessness if there are a large number of early retirements, or a large number of delayed retirements. Only if a firm replaces assets on a regular basis do amortization results approximate those of one of the more traditional methods; neither system meets the requirement of being rational and systematic. Perhaps the most important point is that the only companies who use this approach are very, very large, with tremendous volumes in capital assets and regular replacement. This minimizes the chance that error is material.

1. Why is it pointless to calculate and record amortization to the exact number of days that a capital asset was owned during its year of acquisition?
2. Explain the *half-year convention* for capital asset amortization. Why do companies use a *convention* like the half-year convention for amortizing capital assets?
3. Why are *group* and *composite* systems of amortization useful for large companies?
4. What similarity does group depreciation have to inventory costing systems?

IMPAIRMENT OF CAPITAL ASSETS

Capital assets are subject to the same sort of "lower of cost or market value" assessment as other assets — overvaluation of any asset is a major issue in our GAAP model. Therefore, one has to critically examine capital assets periodically and ask, "Do they still have the ability to generate revenue commensurate with their net book value?" The question is not, "What is market value?" for these assets are not for sale, but instead are these capitalized costs of continuing value to the operation through their ability to increase net assets through profitable operation. Plant assets that lose a significant portion of utility or value suffer an impairment of value.

When is value impaired? What is the extent of the impairment? There are no easy answers to these questions. In practice, accounting for impairment losses has not been uniform. The amount and timing of recognized impairment losses have varied depending on the particular situation.

A very good example of impairment was presented by National Sea Products Limited in 1993. Exhibit 11-6 shows the disclosures in the financial statements of the company regarding restructuring costs (in $ thousands). To give you an idea of the severity of these write-downs, National Sea Products Limited was reporting an accumulated deficit of $109 million at the end of 1993 and was in very precarious financial position — there wasn't much equity left. Capital assets were $60.5 million at the end of 1993; they had been $99.6 million at the end of 1991, before the write-downs started. A major creditor, the Bank of Nova Scotia, was also a major shareholder, as a result of a previous financial crisis. The bank's continued financial support ensured the continuation of the entity.

So, what happened? It became obvious that operations wouldn't support the asset base. The company prepared a plan to restructure, and figured out how much it would cost to lay off workers and to create an efficient operation. They projected the net recoverable amount for capital assets, many of which were production facilities or boats that would never be used again. They factored in the cost to mothball and/or sell capital assets. An allowance was created to reduce the book value of capital assets to the net recoverable amount, which was an estimate of the far-from-certain future. Cash expenses were accrued. The restructuring cost was booked prior to the actual layoffs, asset sales, and write-downs: as long as the restructuring was "likely" and all were comfortable with the estimates, recognition criteria were met.

Note that restructuring has more than one component. It usually involves write-downs of capital assets but also accrual of termination costs and other activities needed to change the operation so that it can produce positive cash flows in the future. Technically, restructuring could include anything from computer upgrades to a new distribution system. We're more concerned in this chapter with the asset write-downs, but restructuring involves quite a bit more. Restructuring is also quite prevalent —

EXHIBIT 11-6
NATIONAL SEA PRODUCTS LIMITED
Excerpts from 1993 Financial Statements

From the income statement:

	1993	**1992**
Restructuring costs and write-down of non-productive assets	$ 48,975	$ 6,500

From the notes:

Restructuring costs and write-down of non-productive assets
Non-productive assets

	1993	**1992**
Expenses	$ 5,465	$ —
Write-down to net recoverable amount	26,837	6,500
Restructuring costs	16,673	—
	$ 48,975	$6,500

The above expenses and write-downs reflect the revaluation of the company's Nova Scotia and Newfoundland harvesting and processing assets and further rationalization of operations. These revaluations resulted from the dramatic reduction in the 1994 fishing quotas and the scientific information available which suggests no increases in quotas in the near future. These assets were idle throughout the year and the expenses are not expected to recur in the future.

restructuring costs or provisions among the 200 survey companies were observed by *Financial Reporting in Canada 1997* 25 times in *each* of 1996 and 1997! Canadian companies seem to be very industrious restructurers.

Another example of a combination of restructuring costs and asset write-downs is shown in Exhibit 11-7. MacMillan Bloedel reported a charge of $201 million in 1997, of which $60 million was "for the write-down of specific investments and capital assets." Note in particular that the write-downs and other restructuring costs were based on a comprehensive review of the company's businesses that was undertaken in the fourth quarter of 1997. At year-end 1997, therefore, very few of the costs recorded as restructuring costs could have actually been incurred. Indeed, the disclosure states that the restructuring will "be substantially complete by the end of 1998," thereby implying that the substantial portion of the costs will be incurred in the future (from the viewpoint of year-end 1997). Restructuring costs and capital asset write-downs involve a great deal of estimating.

The write-down of capital assets is also commonly found as part of the accrual for discontinued operations. Classification of the write-down depends on the extent of the change in operations. If a whole division, or line of operations is to cease, then the correct category is *discontinued operations*. If the line of business is to continue in a more efficient mode, then it is a *restructuring*.

Discontinued operations and asset write-downs are also commonly found in Canadian financial statements. In the note reproduced in Exhibit 11-7, MacMillan Bloedel refers to discontinued operations in addition to the restructuring costs. The company charged $247 million to operations in 1997 for discontinued operations, in addition to the $201 million attributed to restructuring costs. *Financial Reporting in Canada 1997* found 32 of the 200 surveyed companies reported asset write-downs in 1996, while 26 reported discontinued operations.

How did National Sea Products do after the restructuring? In 1995, they reported a $5.5 million profit, modest net assets, and appear to be paying their bills. Of course, operations in 1995 have to bear amortization expense of only $6.5 million on the written-down assets, compared to the normal $10 million in the 1991 era. By 1997, net income had risen to $8.6 million, still with amortization of only $6.8 million.

EXHIBIT 11-7
McMILLAN BLOEDEL LIMITED
Disclosure of Restructuring Costs

13. Restructuring and other unusual charges

	1997	1996	1995
Restructuring costs and asset write-downs	$145	$42	—
Other unusual charges	56	—	—
	$201	$42	$—

During the fourth quarter of 1997, a comprehensive strategic evaluation of each of the Company's businesses was undertaken. As a result, a major reorganization and downsizing of administrative, manufacturing, and distribution operations was initiated. The restructuring is expected to be substantially complete by the end of 1998.

Restructuring costs and asset write-downs recorded in 1997 include $69 million related to severance costs for hourly and salaried employees, $13 million for closure and lease termination costs, and $60 million for the write-down of specific investments and capital assets to estimated realizable value.

Other unusual charges amounting to $56 million are primarily related to a provision for funding a subsidiary company's working capital requirements, including its product warranty claims.

Additional restructuring costs, asset write-downs and other unusual charges relate to specific businesses for which a formal plan of disposal was adopted prior to the 1997 year-end. These costs have been included in the results from discontinued operations and are referred to in Note 14.

The 1996 organization restructuring costs include $17 million related to provisions for employee severance and business relocation costs and $25 million associated with the write-down of a non-core asset.

Were their estimates good? During 1995, the company *brought into income*, or reversed, $6.4 million of restructuring costs previously accrued. That is, it cost them less to restructure than previously expected. National Sea Products reported that "This was the result of several factors, including sale of vessels and other assets at prices higher than expected, disposing of assets earlier than expected and other payments for less than the amounts estimated." Capital assets were written down $1,980,000 less than anticipated, for example. Reversal of restructuring costs was one major cause of reported earnings in 1995.

It seems obvious that if an asset will not generate net assets — eventual cash flow — for the entity, then it should be written down. The *CICA Handbook* recommends that:

> When the net carrying amount of a capital asset, less related accumulated provision for future removal and site restoration costs and future income taxes, exceeds the net recoverable amount, the excess should be charged to income.　　　　　　　　　　　　　　　　　　　[*CICA* 3060.42]

Sometimes asset impairment is as plain as day, such as when a building is destroyed in a fire. In such a case, the asset is written off and the insurance proceeds (if any) reduce the loss (and can even create a reported *gain* if the insurance proceeds are greater than the asset's net book value). In other situations, recognition is highly judgemental. Asset impairment will not be recorded every time losses from operations are encountered. The persistence of such conditions over time is cited as an important factor. Thus, severe losses in one year may trigger a write-down, but might not. Prolonged, smaller losses may trigger a write-down, but might not. There's lots of leeway for judgement in these circumstances!

The *CICA Handbook* suggests several conditions that may indicate that a write-down is appropriate:

(a) an excess of cost over budget for an asset's acquisition, construction or development costs;
(b) an inability to complete a capital asset under development or construction due, for example, to an inability to acquire contiguous property or an inability to obtain financing;
(c) a loss from operation of the capital asset;
(d) a negative cash flow from the capital asset;
(e) significant technological developments;
(f) physical damage;
(g) changes in external economic conditions, including significant changes in foreign currency or interest rates;
(h) a substantial decline in the market for the product;
(i) a change in the law or environment affecting the extent to which the net carrying amount can be recovered;
(j) a decline in the net realizable value of the capital asset below the net carrying amount.

[*CICA* 3060.46]

A capital asset seldom generates revenue on its own, except in the case of rental assets. Therefore, related balance sheet accounts normally are grouped together when assessing the need for a write-down. Net recoverable amount is compared to the assets on a net-of-tax basis, and net-of-accrued-restoration-cost basis.

The write-down of capital assets usually arises out of the risks inherent in an entity's normal business activities. As such, the write-downs would not be considered extraordinary, although they are often shown separately.

When circumstances suggest that an asset's carrying value is not recoverable, the future net cash inflows expected from the asset's *use and disposal* are estimated. That is, the net recoverable amount includes both its estimated cash flow from use and its eventual residual amount. The intentions of the company, and the company's ability to carry them out, must be assessed. For example, a company might be forced to sell assets because they can't afford to run them, or be unable to sell assets and thus be forced to keep maintaining them.

Determining cash flow from use can be quite a challenge, as it requires estimates of future sales volume, often at a time when markets are very unsettled. It seems prudent to (consciously) neither over-estimate nor under-estimate; the most probable set of economic conditions should be used as a base. This is easier said than done, though; predictions are uncertain things! Added to this is a temptation to maximize the write-off so that it only has to be done once, and complete the "big hit." Estimates are occasionally wildly incorrect, either through bias, or because business conditions pan out quite differently than expected.

In any event, cash flows are measured net of direct costs, but also general and administration costs, carrying costs, future removal and site restoration costs, and income taxes. An impairment loss is recognized if the undiscounted sum of the future net cash inflows is less than the carrying value of the asset. The asset then is written down to its net recoverable amount.

The use of the undiscounted sum of cash flows for determining when an impairment has occurred may appear to be inconsistent with the use of fair (or present) value to measure the impairment loss. An asset is impaired when its carrying value is not recoverable using the most liberal definition of recovery — the nominal sum of future cash flows. This definition produces fewer asset impairment losses than would a discounted cash flow definition and is consistent with the need to investigate for impairment losses on an exception basis only.

An interesting aspect of Canadian GAAP is that once a write-down has occurred, the written down amount becomes the new carrying value of the asset. In effect, the old historical cost is segregated between the amount recognized as a loss and the amount that continues to be carried on the balance sheet. Having recognized a loss by writing down the asset, that recognized loss should not be reversed and the asset *should not be written back up if the asset's value recovers.*

> A write down should not be reversed if the net recoverable amount subsequently increases. [*CICA* 3060.43]

Canadian practice is similar to U.S. practice, but both are contrary to general international practice. The Canadian (and U.S.) approach is consistent with the view that losses, once recognized, should not be reversed. The prohibition of such reversals limits the capability of management to manipulate earnings by recognizing losses in some years and gains in others through judicious capital asset write-downs and recoveries. The use of such *hidden reserves* to "control" the reported level of earnings is not uncommon in many other countries.

INTERNATIONAL PERSPECTIVE

International accounting practice is characterized by a variety of approaches to recognizing asset impairments. For example, French firms recognize temporary impairments that may be recovered as a charge to an allowance account instead of reducing current earnings. For other countries, the cause of the impairment affects the recognition and classification of the impairment loss. In Japan, write-downs related to casualties are treated as extraordinary losses, whereas impairments from obsolescence are absorbed through changes in amortization rates. China forbids write-downs in state-owned companies, except by special permission.

The Fourth Directive of the European Union requires write-downs of permanently impaired assets to be recognized in earnings immediately. The directive also requires reversal of write-downs upon recovery. Although such practice is not allowed in Canada, it is consistent with the standards of the International Accounting Standards Committee.

The vast majority of industrialized countries either permit or require written down capital assets to be written back up if their values recover. Japan and Sweden generally *forbid* a restoration of the written down amount, but do allow it in exceptional cases. Austria *allows* a write-up, but doesn't require it; France *requires* restoration, but generally does not permit the restoration to affect income; Australia, U.K., Germany, Netherlands, and Spain all *require* a restoration if the reason for the write-down has ceased to exist, with the write-up credited to income.

International Accounting Standard 16, *Property, Plant, and Equipment*, establishes two different approaches to accounting for asset impairments. The two acceptable approaches depend on the treatment chosen for measuring asset carrying value.

The first, or benchmark, treatment is to carry plant assets at cost less accumulated amortization. Under this treatment, the first part of which is similar to Canadian GAAP, if the recoverable amount of a plant asset declines below carrying value, an expense is recognized in the amount necessary to reduce the carrying value to the asset's recoverable amount. Recoverable amount is the expected future value to be obtained through use and disposal of the asset. However, if circumstances after the write-down imply that the asset's value has been recovered, the write-down is reversed and the carrying value increased to the pre-write-down amount less amortization to the current date.

A subsequent increase in the recoverable amount of an asset . . .should be written back when the circumstances and events that led to the write-down or write-off cease to exist and there is persuasive evidence that the new circumstances and events will persist for the foreseeable future.   [IAS 16, para. 59]

This reversal of the write-down is not allowed under Canadian GAAP.

The second "allowed alternative" treatment, which is markedly different from the more conservative Canadian GAAP, permits revaluation of plant assets above or below carrying value. Thus, when a plant asset becomes impaired, the asset is written down and an expense recognized unless the asset had been revalued above carrying value previously. In this case, the reduction is charged first to the owners' equity account that was credited when the asset was written up.

REVALUATION OF CAPITAL ASSETS

Historical cost has long been the generally accepted basis for reporting capital assets in Canada. On rare occasions, however, a company may restate one or more of its capital assets *upward*, generally by using appraisal values. Sometimes, a company will establish an entirely new basis of accountability, not only for its assets but also for its liabilities. This is known as a **comprehensive revaluation**.

Revaluation of Individual Assets

In the high-inflation period of the 1980s, some companies experimented with writing up their assets, using appraised values, in an attempt to restate their depreciation on a *current cost* basis. This was an instance in which companies (including public companies) decided that the nominal dollar capital maintenance assumption (see Chapter 2) was no longer valid and attempted to move towards a productive capacity capital maintenance basis.

Another situation in which it makes sense to revalue individual assets (or groups of assets) arises primarily in private companies. Bankers grant mortgage loans (and other secured loans) on the basis of assets' *values*; recorded historical costs are irrelevant. Private corporations sometimes end up with a balance sheet in which the total liabilities exceeds the total assets, simply because loans have been granted on the basis of fair values while the balance sheet shows assets at their depreciated historical cost. Consequently, the corporation appears to have negative net worth, which is a condition of *technical insolvency*. Since corporations dislike showing negative net assets, a logical response is to restate the assets to the market values by which the loans are secured, thereby reinstating a positive net worth.

Prior to 1990, there was no specific recommendation in the *CICA Handbook* that historical cost should be used as the carrying value for capital assets. While historical cost clearly was an important aspect of GAAP, it was possible to depart from historical cost and to record appraised values when circumstances warranted, without necessarily deviating from GAAP. Practice recognized that sometimes the trade-off between relevance and objectivity was better served by recording appraisals, as long as they were based on arm's length professional valuations (usually, two or three independent appraisals were solicited).

The permissibility of appraisal revaluations changed when Section 3060 was introduced. The flat statement that "a capital asset should be recorded at cost" [*CICA* 3060.18] effectively limits the ability of companies to revalue (upward) specific assets, regardless of their motivation to do so and regardless of the company's situation-specific financial reporting objectives. The *CICA Handbook's* insistence on historical cost effectively prevents public companies (and any other companies constrained by GAAP) from restating individual assets.

EXHIBIT 11-8
Example of Recorded Asset Revaluations

Carrying value at date of appraisal

Historical cost (20X1)		$100,000
Accumulated depreciation ($100,000 × 4% × 5 years)		20,000
Net book value at date of revaluation (20X5)		$ 80,000

Recording the appraisal

Capital asset — building	150,000	
Accumulated depreciation	20,000	
Shareholders' equity — appraisal increment		170,000

Annual depreciation subsequent to the revaluation

Depreciation expense ($250,000 × 5%)	12,500	
Accumulated depreciation		12,500
Shareholder's equity — appraisal increment	8,500	
Retained earnings ($170,000 × 5%)		8,500

Nevertheless, Section 1625 does contain an explanation of how appraisals should be accounted for, which is a carryforward of an earlier *CICA Handbook* section that dealt specifically with appraisal increments.[2]

When individual assets are restated on the basis of appraisal values, there is no *gain* recorded. Instead, the asset value is written up to the appraised value and the offsetting credit is to a separate component of shareholders' equity. Future amortization of the asset is then based on the new carrying value. As the asset is amortized, an amount equal to the increase in amortization is transferred from the appraisal increment account (in shareholders' equity) to the retained earnings account. When the asset has been fully amortized, the appraisal increment account also will have disappeared from the balance sheet.

For example, suppose that Yvan Ltd. has a building that was purchased for $100,000 (not including the value of the land) in 20X1. Yvan began depreciating the building in 20X1 on a straight-line basis over 25 years. The area in which the building is located increased substantially in value, and in 20X6 the company decides to restate the building. Yvan obtains two independent professional appraisals: $270,000 and $250,000. Yvan chooses to record the lower of the two values. Yvan will continue to use the original estimate of useful life: 25 years from 20X1; 20 years more from 20X6. The revalued asset will be depreciated at a straight-line rate of 5%.

Exhibit 11-8 illustrates the accounting for Yvan Ltd. for this revaluation. The undepreciated book value after four years of depreciation was $80,000. The appraisal requires an increase in the net book value of $170,000. Since a new basis of account is being established for the asset, the accumulated depreciation account is eliminated in the entry to record the revaluation.

The intent of the accounting procedures illustrated in Exhibit 11-8 is to prevent a company from reporting inconsistent amounts in its balance sheet and in its income statement. If a company is going to write up its assets, then the amortization should be based on the written up amount. Some companies would prefer to write up the asset (to improve the balance sheet) but continue to base depreciation on historical cost (to improve income), with "excess" depreciation of the appraisal increment deb-

---

2   Specifically, the recommendations concerning appraised values were intended as a transition provision, "when an enterprise has a capital asset which was recorded at an appraised value prior to the effective date of [section 3060]." [CICA 3060.64]

ited directly to the appraisal increment account in shareholders' equity rather than to the income statement.

Comprehensive Revaluation

While write-ups of individual assets did occur in the past, the more common type of asset revaluation arose when the interests of creditors and owners were rearranged in a *financial reorganization*. In a financial reorganization, the standings of shareholders and unsecured (or inadequately secured) creditors are altered because the company is not able to meet its debt obligations. Financial reorganizations can be voluntary, but they also can be triggered by creditors. A financial reorganization results in a new basis of accountability for the liabilities and share equity. Since the liabilities are restated, the corporation often restated its asset accounts as well.

Another motivation for restatement may arise from corporate takeover activity. When one corporation buys control of another, subsequent consolidated statements of the parent must include the net assets of the new subsidiary (i.e., the *acquired* company) *at their fair values at the date of acquisition.*

The mechanism of consolidated statement preparation requires the controlling shareholder to add the subsidiary's balance sheet to its own each year after buying control, then add on the fair values at the date of acquisition, and then amortize the subsidiary's restated assets. (The principles underlying this process are illustrated in Chapter 12.) The whole process can be greatly simplified if the fair values can be transferred to the books of the subsidiary at the time of the takeover.

More often than not, a takeover results in the new parent company owning 100% of the shares of the acquired company. Since there are no minority shareholders that have an interest in the previous basis of accounting, many companies followed a practice of restating the newly-acquired subsidiary's net assets to accord with the fair values that were established at the date of acquisition. This practice became known as **push down accounting** because the fair values were "pushed down" from the parent's consolidated statements to the subsidiary's books and separate-entity statements.

The activity in push-down accounting (and other general revaluations) then caused the AcSB to look at the issue of *comprehensive revaluation*. In 1992, the AcSB issued Section 1625, "Comprehensive Revaluation of Assets and Liabilities." In this section, the AcSB sharply limits the practice of general revaluation of assets and liabilities. The limitation is expressed as follows:

> The following conditions are required to be satisfied for an enterprise's assets and liabilities to be comprehensively revalued:
> (a) All or virtually all of the equity interests in the enterprise have been acquired, in one or more transactions between non-related parties, by an acquirer who controls the enterprise after the transaction or transactions; or
> (b) The enterprise has been subject to a financial reorganization, and the same party does not control the enterprise both before and after the reorganization;
> and in either situation new costs are reasonably determinable.
>
> *[CICA 1625.04]*

The crucial element in this recommendation is that *there is a change in control*. This statement recognizes the two situations in which revaluations had already become a part of GAAP, (1) push down accounting and (2) financial reorganizations, but attempts to eliminate all other reasons for revaluation.

The accounting for comprehensive revaluations varies, depending on whether the revaluation is the result of financial reorganization or push-down accounting. In a financial reorganization, the net "plug" amount that is needed to balance the restatement of assets and liabilities "should be accounted for as a capital transaction and recorded as share capital, contributed surplus, or a separately identified account within shareholders' equity." [*CICA* 1625.43] In other words, do whatever you want to with it, but just keep it in shareholders' equity. An explanation of push-down accounting can wait for an advanced accounting course, where business combinations are dealt with at some length.

The AcSB rejected revaluation in other situations where revaluation might seem to provide more useful or relevant information for the users of the financial statements. Those situations explicitly considered and rejected by the AcSB are when:

(a) an enterprise issues shares to the public;
(b) an enterprise issues debt based on asset appraisals;
(c) an enterprise results from a spin-off transaction to shareholders;
(d) an enterprise undergoes a change in its operations or line of business; and
(e) transactions in the equity interests when an enterprise is a joint venture.

[*CICA* 1625.17]

Of particular note are the first two. The AcSB refuses to recognize that when a company has an initial public offering (IPO), its financial reporting objectives are likely to change because there is an important new group of stakeholders. For debt-based appraisals, the AcSB seems to believe that it is more important to preserve historical cost than to permit a consistent basis of asset and liability presentation, even for private companies where there are no external stakeholders other than the bank that issued the debt. It remains to be seen whether these prohibitions will be generally accepted in practice, particularly by companies that are not legally constrained by GAAP and that therefore have greater leeway for adopting accounting policies that better serve the financial reporting objectives of their users.

INTERNATIONAL PERSPECTIVE

Canada is clearly out of step with international accounting standards on capital asset valuation. We already have discussed the fact that Canada's refusal to permit the restoration of written down costs is at variance with widespread practice (and with the IASC standards). Canada's refusal to permit revaluations of individual assets also is unusually strict. Austria and Germany also forbid revaluations, while Japan, Spain, and the U.S. permit it only under special circumstances. On the other side are Australia, Belgium, Denmark, France, the Netherlands, Sweden, Switzerland, and the U.K., all of whom permit revaluations of tangible capital assets. If Canada is going to achieve international harmonization of its capital asset accounting standards, we will have to drop our rigid stance against revaluations of individual assets.

DISCLOSURE OF AMORTIZATION

Not surprisingly, the requirement to disclose amortization policy is front and centre in the "Capital Assets" section of the *CICA Handbook*. If you're going to let companies pick a policy, it is crucial that financial statement readers be told about the choice. Thus, "for each major category of capital assets there should be disclosure of. . .the amortization method used, including the amortization period or rate" [*CICA* 3060.58]. Other recommended disclosures relating to capital asset amortization are

- the accumulated amortization of each major category of capital assets [*CICA* 3060.58],
- the amount of amortization charged to income for the period [*CICA* 3060.60],
- the amount of any write-down during the period [*CICA* 3060.61], and
- details about comprehensive revaluations [*CICA* 1625.50 – 1625.52].

EXHIBIT 11-9
NORANDA FOREST INC.
Disclosures in 1997 Relating to Capital Assets

On the 1997 income statement:
Depreciation $ 155
On the balance sheet:
Property, plant, and equipment (net) $1,962
On the cash flow statement (Operating Activities):
Charges not affecting cash:
    Depreciation $ 155

From the notes

1. Accounting Policies — Property, Plant, and Equipment

Property, plant, and equipment are recorded at cost and are depreciated on a straight-line basis. The rates of depreciation are intended to fully depreciate manufacturing and non-manufacturing assets over the following periods which approximate their useful lives:

Buildings	20 – 40 years
Sawmills and panelboard production equipment	10 – 20 years
Pulp and paper mill machinery and production equipment	20 years
Logging machinery and equipment	4 – 10 years

Depletion of timber is determined on an appropriate basis related to log production and included in depreciation.

4. Property, plant and equipment

	Cost	Accumulated Depreciation	Net Book Value 1997	Net Book Value 1996
Papers	$1,457	$ 678	$ 779	$ 587
Building materials	958	398	560	572
Pulp	837	404	433	421
Timber and timberlands	132	45	87	85
Corporate assets and other	89	41	48	47
Construction in progress	55	—	55	194
	$3,528	$1,566	$1,962	$1,906

The amount of amortization charged to income is a recommended disclosure not only in the capital assets section, but also in the income statement section of the *CICA Handbook*. In practice, however, the amount may not be reported directly on the face of the income statement. Amortization may be included in various other components of the income statement, such as in cost of goods sold, cost of goods produced, cost of contracts completed, and general and administrative expense. If the amount of amortization is not shown on the face of the income statement, the disclosure is usually either in a note to the financial statements or in the cash flow statement (i.e., as an add-back to net income in the operating activities section). The amortization disclosures of Noranda Forest Inc. are illustrated in Exhibit 11-9.

The *CICA Handbook* also suggests that it would be desirable to disclose the amount of "future removal and site restoration costs" [CICA 3060.63]. Inco Limited, a large Canadian mining company, devotes about one and one-half pages in

EXHIBIT 11-10
Example of Site Restoration Costs Disclosure — Inco Limited

Note 11. Future removal and site restoration costs (*excerpt*)

The Company incurs substantial removal and site restoration costs on an ongoing basis which willl significantly reduce future removal and site restoration costs that may otherwise be incurred following the closure of any of the Company's sites. This progressive rehabilitation includes tailings management, land reclamation and revegetation programs, decommissioning and demolition of plants and buildings, and waste management activities. Operating costs associated with ongoing enviromental and reclamation programs, including progessive rehabilitation, aggregated $27 million in 1997, $18 million in 1996 and $17 million in 1995. Capital expenditures on environmental projects aggregated $25 million in 1997, $27 million in 1996 and $26 million in 1995.

Although the ultimate amount to be incurred is uncertain, the total liability for the future removal and site restoration costs in respect of the Company's worldwide operations, to be incurred primarily after cessation of operations, is estimated to be approximately $350 million. In recognition of this future liability, the Company, starting in 1995, annually provides $10 million for future removal and site restoration costs. This amount is based upon the estimated remaining lives of the Company's applicable ore reserves and facilities and is in addition to ongoing operating and capital expenditures. The estimate of the total liability for future removal and site restoration costs has been developed from independent environmental studies including an evaluation of, among other factors, currently available information with respect to closure plans and closure alternatives, the anticipated method and extent of site restoration using current costs and existing technology, and compliance with presently enacted laws, regulations and existing industry standards. The total liability for future removal and site restoration costs represents estimated expenditures associated with closure, progressive rehabilitation and post-closure care and maintenance. Potential recoveries of funds from the future sale of assets upon the ultimate closure of operations have not been reflected in the estimate of the total liability or related annual provision.

In view of the uncertainties concerning environmental remediation, the ultimate cost of future removal and site restoration to the Company could differ from the amounts provided. The estimate of the total liability for future removal and site restoration costs is subject to change based on amendments to law and regulations and as new information concerning the Company's operations becomes available. Future changes, if any, to the estimated total liability as a result of amended requirements, law, regulations and operating assumptions may be significant and would be recognized prospectively as a change in estimate, when applicable.

its disclosure notes to discussion of these costs. Part of this note is shown in Exhibit 11-10. Inco's balance sheet shows a liability of $30 million (out of total assets of about $7.8 billion), but the note explains that the total estimated liability is about $350 million, which is being accrued at the rate of $10 million per year — a 35-year amortization schedule. The note also discloses that the current year's expenditures (for 1997) totalled $27 million plus $25 million. Adding this to the liabilty provision yields a total charge to income in 1997 of $62 million. Inco's 1997 income from continuing operations was only $17 million, so it is obvious that the restoration costs are a substantial drain on the company's profitability. The $10 million charge for future costs is arbitrary, however, so the income might have been significantly higher or lower, depending on management's decision on cost accrual.

Inco's note also points out the tentative nature of any estimate of restoration costs, given that rules and regulations are constantly evolving, as is the technology and the projects of future costs. Inco's disclosure is much more complete than that of many other mining companies.

CASH FLOW STATEMENT

Amortization expense is an add-back to the operations section of the cash flow statement, if the common indirect form of presentation is used. It's important to remember that amortization is a little different from other expenses, because amortization is a non-cash expense. Clearly, the company has to pay out cash or other resources to obtain the capital asset, but the timing of the sacrifice (and therefore the timing of amortization) is likely to be a lot different than the timing of the expense recognition.

CONCEPT REVIEW

1. In general, when is it necessary to write down a capital asset? How can we determine the value to which it should be written down?
2. When, under Canadian GAAP, is it permissible to write up capital assets on the basis of appraisals?
3. How do Canada's practices regarding the restoration of write-downs and the revaluation of individual assets differ from the most common international practice?

SUMMARY OF KEY POINTS

1. Amortization is a rational and systematic process of allocating amortizable cost (acquisition cost less residual value) to the periods in which capital assets are used. Amortization expense for a period does not represent the change in market value of assets, nor does it necessarily equal the portion of the asset's utility consumed in the period. Amortization is justified on the basis of eventual decline in value, through physical wear and tear and obsolescence.

2. Several methods of amortization are acceptable under GAAP: the straight-line, service-hours, productive output, accelerated methods, and sinking fund methods. Factors affecting choice include individual corporate reporting objectives, information processing costs, a desire to minimize income tax temporary differences, industry norms, and parent company preferences.

3. Companies should disclose the amortization method chosen for major categories of capital assets, the amortization period or rate, and the amount of amortization charged to income for the period.

4. Three factors contribute to the determination of periodic amortization expense: original acquisition cost and any capitalized post-acquisition costs, estimated residual value, which includes consideration of restoration costs, and, finally, estimated useful life or productivity measured either in service-hours or units of output.

5. For all methods, the estimated residual value is the minimum book value. Except for the declining balance methods, amortizable cost is multiplied by a rate to determine periodic amortization. Declining balance amortization ceases when net book value equals residual value.

6. Fractional-year amortization is necessary when capital asset acquisitions and disposals do not coincide with the fiscal year. Amortization is computed on a whole-year basis, with the appropriate fraction of a period applied to the amortization for the relevant whole year of the asset's life. Some firms apply an accounting convention and do not record non-material fractional amortization.

7. Three amortization systems (appraisal, composite and group, and replacement/retirement) are alternatives to amortization methods applied individually to assets. These systems save accounting costs and are justified under cost-benefit and materiality constraints.

8. An impairment loss is recognized when the sum of undiscounted expected future net cash inflows from use and disposal of an asset is less than the asset's carrying

value. The loss equals the difference between the asset's carrying value and fair value. These losses are difficult to estimate and can be quite subjective.

9. Revaluations of individual assets are no longer permitted within Canadian GAAP; historical cost must be used.

10. Comprehensive revaluation of assets and liabilities can occur, but only if there is a change in control as the result of (a) a financial reorganization or (b) a business combination.

11. Amortization is not a cash flow; the cash flow occurred when the capital asset was acquired. Amortization is added back to net income when cash flow from operations is determined on the cash flow statement.

REVIEW PROBLEM

The following cases are independent.

1. *Partial-year depreciation.* Whitney Corporation purchased equipment on 1 April 20X4 for $34,000. The equipment has a useful life of five years and a residual value of $4,000. What is depreciation for 20X4 and 20X5, using declining balance depreciation at a 40% rate?

2. *Asset impairment.* Rancho Company purchases equipment on 1 April 20X3 for $34,000. The equipment has a useful life of five years, a residual value of $4,000, and is depreciated using the straight-line method and the half-year convention. At the end of 20X5, Rancho suspects that the original investment in the asset will not be realized; the total remaining future cash inflows expected to be produced by the equipment, including the original residual value, is $10,000. The equipment's fair value at 31 December 20X5 is $7,000. Determine whether the asset is impaired and, if so, the impairment loss at 31 December 20X5.

3. *Composite depreciation.* Baja Company uses the composite method of depreciation and has a composite rate of 25%. During 20X5, it sells assets with an original cost of $100,000 (residual value of $20,000) for $80,000 and acquires $60,000 worth of new assets (residual value $10,000). The original group of assets has the following characteristics:

Total cost	$250,000
Total residual value	30,000

Assuming that the new assets conform to the group and that the company does not revise the depreciation rate, calculate depreciation expense for 20X5.

REVIEW PROBLEM — SOLUTION

1. Depreciation for 20X4: $34,000 × 40% × 9/12 = $10,200
   Depreciation for 20X5: $34,000 × 40% × 3/12 = $3,400; [$34,000 - ($10,200 + $3,400)] × 40% × 9/12 = $6,120; total, $9,520

2. Book value of equipment at 31 December 20X5:

Cost	$34,000
Accumulated depreciation, 31 December 20X5:	
($34,000 – $4,000) ÷ 5 × 2.5 years	15,000
Net book value	$19,000

The asset is impaired because the book value ($19,000) is greater than either the sum of future cash flows ($10,000) or the fair value of the asset ($7,000). Since depreciation is not intended to mirror the decline in fair value of a capital asset, the fact that the fair value is less than book value is not, in itself, significant. The key aspect of impairment is that the estimated future net cash flows generated by the asset are less than its book value, indicating that the unamortized cost cannot be recovered either through operations or through resale at fair value.

The asset must be written down to the higher of the two values, which is $10,000. This is a loss of $9,000.

3. Depreciation for 20X5 = ($250,000 − $100,000 + $60,000) × 25% = $52,500

The capital asset account is adjusted for the original cost of the assets sold ($100,000) and acquired ($60,000). The proceeds from the sale ($80,000) are credited to accumulated depreciation. No gain or loss is recognized under group and composite systems.

APPENDIX
Capital Cost Allowance

The *Income Tax Act* does not allow the deduction of accounting amortization expense in the determination of taxable income. Instead of amortization, the taxpayer must either (1) deduct the expenditure from taxable income in the year that it is incurred or (2) use the form of amortization mandated by the *Income Tax Act*. There is not a *choice* between these two treatments; the tax treatment depends on the type of expenditure (that is, on the type of capital asset for accounting purposes).

Just because an expenditure (or group of expenditures) is classified as a capital asset for accounting purposes does not mean that Revenue Canada will view it as a capital asset. Many of the costs that are capitalized for accounting purposes are viewed as expenses for tax purposes. This is particularly true of a large number of expenditures that accountants tend to capitalize as intangible assets, particularly when they are self-developed assets such as development costs.

Expenditures that are considered by the *Income Tax Act* to be capital assets are subject to amortization for tax purposes, but the amortization is completely independent of accounting amortization. Under GAAP, amortization is intended to allocate an asset's historical cost to the accounting periods in which the asset is used. In contrast, tax amortization is geared to the revenue needs of the federal government, which change in response to economic conditions and the fiscal policies of Parliament. For example, tax amortization currently provides an incentive for replacement, modernization, and expansion of manufacturing facilities through accelerated amortization rates.

The Capital Cost Allowance System

Tax amortization is known as *capital cost allowance, or CCA*. Basically, the CCA system is a group depreciation method. CCA requires the grouping of assets into various CCA classes established by the Act. An exception to the group requirement is that buildings that are held for rental (i.e., "income properties") are treated individually; each one is a separate class.

Most classes provide a maximum rate of amortization that approximates double-declining balance amortization, although some classes use the equivalent of straight-line amortization. Classes and rates for some of the more common assets are shown in Exhibit 11-11, with the prescribed maximum rate shown in parentheses for the declining-balance classes.

An important point is that the rates are *maximums*. A taxpaying company does not have to use the maximum rate, and in fact does not need to deduct any CCA at all if the company chooses not to do so. CCA is an optional deduction. Why would a company not want to deduct CCA? If it is not making any taxable income! If a company's taxable income is not sufficient to absorb all of the CCA, the CCA can be "saved" to offset against future earnings. Regardless of whether or not a company takes CCA in a year, however, the CCA cannot be piled up in future years. A maximum of 20% is a maximum of 20%, regardless of whether or not the company has taken CCA in past years.

The basic rules for the capital cost allowance system can be explained for most classes as follows:

1. When assets are purchased, their purchase price (capital cost) is added to the balance (unamortized capital cost, or UCC) of the appropriate asset class.

EXHIBIT 11-11
Sample CCA Rates

Asset Classes Using Declining-Balance CCA

Class 1 (4%)   Buildings or other structures, including component parts acquired after 1987.

Class 3 (5%)   Buildings or other structures, including component parts acquired before 1988.

Class 8 (20%)   Tangible capital property and machinery or equipment not included in another class.

Class 10 (30%)   Automotive equipment and electronic data processing or decoding equipment.

Class 12 (100%)   Jigs, patterns, tools, utensils costing less than $200, linens, computer software.

Class 39 (25%)   Manufacturing and processing equipment acquired after 1987; rate was established at 40% in 1988, decreasing by 5% per year until it reached 25% in 1991.

Asset Classes Using Straight-Line CCA

Class 13   Leasehold improvements (life of lease plus one renewal period; minimum five years, maximum 40 years).

Class 14   Patent, franchise, concession, or licence (life of asset) with a limited life.

EXHIBIT 11-12
Example of Calculating Capital Cost Allowance

20X1 UCC opening balance		0
Additions (4 × $5,000)		$20,000
CCA for 20X1; ($20,000 × 20% × 1/2 year)		(2,000)
20X2 UCC opening balance		$18,000
Additions		5,700
CCA for 20X2; ($18,000 × 20%) + ($5,700 × 20% × 1/2)		(4,170)
20X3 UCC opening balance		$19,530
Additions	$ 6,500	
Proceeds on disposal	(1,200)	
Net additions		5,300
CCA for 20X3; ($19,530 × 20%) + ($5,300 × 20% × 1/2)		(4,436)
20X4 UCC opening balance		$20,394
Proceeds on disposal		(1,100)
CCA for 20X4; [($20,394 – $1,100) × 20%]		(3,859)
20X4 UCC closing balance		$15,435

2. When assets are sold, the lesser of the proceeds or the capital cost is deducted from the balance in that asset's class.

3. Assets are considered to be purchased in the middle of the taxation year (half-year rule).

4. The maximum capital cost allowance deductible for a particular class is the balance of unamortized capital cost (UCC), *after adjusting for the half-year rule in the year of purchase*, multiplied by the CCA rate for that class.

Exhibit 11-12 provides an example of a calculation for capital cost allowance. Iles Machine Shop begins business in January 20X1 and purchases four lathes (class 8) for $5,000 each. A fifth lathe is purchased in 20X2 for $5,700. In 20X3, one of the original lathes is sold for $1,200 and is replaced with another lathe costing $6,500. In 20X4 one of the lathes was sold for $1,100.

When net asset additions take place, *the net addition is subject to the half-year rule* (see 20X2 and 20X3 in Exhibit 11-12). However, when there is a net asset disposal, the entire amount is deducted prior to determining the CCA for the year (see 20X4 in Exhibit 11-12).

The amount deducted on an asset disposal is the lesser of the proceeds and the asset's capital cost. Any proceeds on disposal in excess of the capital cost are treated, for tax purposes, as a capital gain. Any amount in excess of the asset's *unamortized capital cost (UCC)* is considered to be a recapture of CCA (amortization) claimed and reduces the future CCA claimable in that class.

When *all* of the assets in a class are disposed of, any remaining balances are treated as follows:

- A positive UCC balance is deducted as a terminal loss in determining taxable income.
- A negative UCC balance is added to taxable income as *recaptured* CCA.

In effect, this treatment is similar to the gain or loss on disposal of plant assets on the assumption that either too little or too much amortization (i.e., CCA) was taken over the lives of the assets. Any proceeds received in excess of the assets' capital (original) cost are treated as a capital gain for tax purposes.

SUMMARY OF KEY POINTS

1. Accounting amortization has no tax impact; amortization of capital assets for tax purposes is governed by the *Income Tax Act* and Regulations, and is completely independent of accounting amortization.

2. Income tax amortization is called the *capital cost allowance (CCA)* system.

3. The CCA system groups capital assets into *classes* of assets of similar types. Except for certain buildings, assets are not amortized individually.

4. The regulations specify an amortization *rate* to be used for each class of asset; the rate is a maximum — a company can claim less CCA in any year if management so chooses, without losing the maximum deduction in future years.

5. The half-year rule is applied to assets acquired during a taxation year.

6. Gains and losses are not recognized on the disposal of capital assets in a class, unless all of the assets in the class are disposed of. Proceeds on disposal of individual assets are credited to the asset class.

QUESTIONS

11-1   Explain and compare the terms amortization, depletion, and depreciation.

11-2   A company reported $2 million of amortization expense on its income statement. Explain what this means to a friend who has little or no background in accounting. Also explain what it does *not* imply.

11-3   What are the primary causes of amortization? What effect do changes in the current market value of the asset being amortized have on amortization estimates?

11-4   Explain why land need not be amortized, with reference to the causes of amortization.

11-5   Explain the difference in meaning between the balances in the following two accounts: (a) accumulated amortization and (b) allowance to reduce inventory to the lower of cost or market.

11-6　　List the various alternative amortization methods, and explain which are dominant in practice.

11-7　　Why is disclosure of amortization methods and rates so important?

11-8　　List several factors a firm would consider in choosing an amortization method.

11-9　　What items must be estimated before amortization can be calculated? Explain each item.

11-10　List the 40 year maximum amortization period be used as a ceiling for all capital assets? Explain. Under what circumstances would an asset with indefinite life be amortized over a period shorter than 40 years?

11-11　Compare the effect of straight-line and productive output methods of depreciation on the per unit cost of output for a manufacturing company.

11-12　Why is straight-line amortization so popular in practice?

11-13　What are accelerated methods of amortization? Under what circumstances would these methods generally be appropriate?

11-14　Explain why an amortization method that is based on inputs and outputs would be problematic if obsolescence were a significant factor and usage was sporadic.

11-15　How does sinking fund depreciation work? Why is it popular for real estate companies?

11-16　Explain the minimum amortization test, and the circumstances under which it is important. Your response should include an explanation of the difference between residual value and salvage value.

11-17　Explain the accounting policy alternatives that exist with respect to depreciation when a firm's reporting year and the "asset year" do not coincide.

11-18　Explain the inventory appraisal system of depreciation. Under what circumstances is such a system appropriate?

11-19　Compare retirement and replacement depreciation systems. Explain when each of these systems would be appropriate.

11-20　How are the composite and group depreciation systems similar?

11-21　What are some of the advantages of using depreciation systems?

11-22　What is an impairment in the value of a capital asset? How is it measured and reported? When is an asset write-down part of the discontinued operations disclosure?

11-23　What estimates have to be made when recording an impairment of value? What happens when subsequent experience shows that an estimate was wrong?

11-24　What alternatives has the IASC established to account for asset impairment?

11-25　Is it possible to revalue a specific asset to market value, when market value is higher than net book value? Explain.

11-26　What is a comprehensive revaluation, and when can it be recorded?

CASES

CASE 11-1

Provincial Hydro

Provincial Hydro (PH) is an electric utility which generates, supplies, and delivers electric power throughout a small Canadian province. It is incorporated as a Crown corporation, which operates as a cooperative partnership with the relevant municipalities and the provincial government. It is a financially self-sustaining company without share capital, regulated by the provincial government. Its primary customers are the municipal utilities (which serve about 600,000 end users), 40 large industrial companies (direct service), and 100,000 rural retail customers. PH operates various generating stations, including both nuclear and fossil fuel fired plants. As a result, it is very capital intensive. This, in turn, makes PH sensitive to the cost of money.

PH plays a major role in attracting industry to the province by maintaining competitive rates for electricity. It is profoundly affected by various pieces of provincial legislation.

The financial statement results are used to set utility rates, although there are specific rules about which expenses are permissible and at what time. Many accounting policies are chosen based on the rules for rate recovery. Profits of the corporation are to be applied toward the reduction of the cost of power for the municipalities with whom the utility has a cooperative partnership.

Management and the municipalities are very sensitive to political pressures. PH is in the public spotlight, and financial results and policies can generate considerable publicity.

A major component of the cost of electricity is fuel cost, which includes the following components: fuel (quantity and price), interest on funds tied up in inventory, transportation, and overheads.

PH has two mothballed generating stations, which are not producing energy at present but may be used during peak demand periods when needed. The plants, all oil-fired, were mothballed as more efficient generation methods were developed.

PH has chosen to reflect the situation by accelerating the rate of depreciation to "reflect the reduced economic value" of the assets. PH has produced demand forecasts (which are regularly updated) that predict when and how much energy will have to come from the mothballed plants. Based on these probability factors, PH establishes an amortization rate, higher than the original rate, which takes the change of circumstances into account. Depreciation is only charged when the plant is used. Care is taken to avoid premature write-off while the plant may still be useful.

PH uses the CANDU reactor in its nuclear stations. This reactor has relatively low fuel cost but must use "heavy water," H_2O_2 (versus "light water," H_2O, which other reactors use). Heavy water is not consumed in the fissioning process but acts as a moderator of the process. With periodic in-station upgrading to remove impurities, heavy water has an indefinite life.

Heavy water costs, plus interest on inventories of heavy water designated for future use, are capitalized. These capital costs are being written off over 60 years, which is the date PH estimates heavy water will be replaced by new technology. However, the last committed CANDU nuclear unit is due to be retired in 40 years. Management has indicated that nuclear units are regularly upgraded by replacing pressure tubes, which extends their useful life. In addition, the useful life of heavy water does not depend on the life of the station since it can be transferred to another station.

Inventories of fossil fuels are expensed based on an average costs system where the average is calculated monthly on a rolling basis. Average cost was chosen as it seemed the most fair to current and future customers and had a smoothing effect on price fluctuations. Recently, however, with significant declines in fossil fuel prices, there has been considerable public comment as electricity prices did not fall accordingly. Management is beginning to consider the alternatives and their advantages and disadvantages.

Management has reminded you that one-time write-downs are not permissible costs in utility rate-setting formulas, nor is it possible to make retroactive changes to the rate structure.

Required:

PH has asked you, an external adviser, to consider accounting issues raised. They have requested a report incorporating your recommendations.

[ASCA, adapted]

CASE 11-2

May Company

May Company owns a chain of eight small hotels in the Western provinces. The chain specializes in family vacations, promoting "free family breakfasts," reduced rates for children, and a variety of activity packages for special weekends in off-peak seasons and during the busy summer months.

Two hotels, a 75-room unit and a 100-room unit, have had marginal cash flow over the past three years. Management pursued aggressive promotion campaigns to improve business, but the only way to increase occupancy at these locations proved to be deep discounting of room rates, and cash flow has remained unacceptably low. Management concluded that these locations were poor for tourist and holiday business. Both hotels were in line for expensive refurbishing, which was not economically justifiable.

Rather than close the buildings, however, the company investigated the alternative of converting the hotels to residential apartment units. Low residential vacancy rates in the respective towns has convinced management that the plan is feasible. There would be expensive conversion costs up front, basically to install kitchens in each apartment unit. However, thorough marketing, engineering, and construction investigation has provided a level of comfort with the project, which was recently approved by the May Company board of directors. Discussions have been held with lenders, and mortgage financing will be arranged that pays out existing loans secured by these two properties, and provides 80% of the funds needed for renovation. The company will arrange short-term construction loans, which will be replaced by the new mortgage funding when the renovation work is substantially complete. Lenders will require audited financial statements, and pay particular attention to cash flow and the times-interest-earned ratio (net income before tax and interest expense divided by interest expense).

The hotels will be closed at the end of the summer, and will then be vacant for six to eight months while renovations take place. Studies indicate that it will then take 6 to 14 months to rent up the buildings to a target occupancy level, which is around the 80% level.

The company believes that it need not record depreciation expense during the period it takes to convert and rent the buildings. That is, depreciation would cease as soon as the hotels were closed, and recommence when the target rental level is achieved. The company believes that continuation of past depreciation policies during the conversion and rent-up period does not make sense for the following reasons:

- The nature of the business is changing for these two properties, and they are essentially "construction in progress" for the period. New operations will emerge out the other end.

- The properties are currently recorded at amounts lower than their current market values.

- The properties have remaining useful lives as apartment buildings in excess of their current accounting lives estimated for hotels.

The company believes that it makes more sense to match depreciation with revenues achieved at full rent-up so that future periods are not unduly enhanced by charges made to operations in prior years.

Another issue being considered is the method of depreciation to be used for the apartment buildings. The hotel properties are all depreciated using the straight-line method over their useful lives, which are relatively long. The company wonders if this method will be the most appropriate for the apartment buildings.

Required:

Advise the company on appropriate accounting policies with respect to the conversion.

E11-1 *Multiple Choice — Amortization:* Select the best answer for each of the following. Assume a calendar-year reporting period.

1. As generally used in accounting, which of the following is correct about amortization?

    a. It is a process of asset valuation for balance sheet purposes.
    b. It applies only to long-lived intangible assets.
    c. It is used to indicate a decline in market value of a long-lived asset.
    d. It is an accounting process that allocates long-lived asset cost to accounting periods.

2. Property, plant, and equipment should be reported at historic cost less accumulated amortization on a balance sheet dated 31 December 20X5, unless

    a. Some obsolescence is known to have occurred.
    b. An appraisal made during 20X5 disclosed a higher value.
    c. The amount of insurance carried on the property is well in excess of its book value.
    d. Some of the property still on hand was written down in a prior year because of permanent impairment of its value in use.

3. Upon purchase of certain depreciable assets used in its production process, a company expects to be able to replace these assets by adopting a policy of never declaring dividends in amounts larger than net income (after amortization is deducted). If a net income is earned each year, recording amortization will coincidentally result in retention of sufficient assets within the enterprise. If in liquid form, these assets could be used to replace those fully amortized assets if

    a. Prices remain reasonably constant during the life of the property.
    b. Prices rise throughout the life of the property.
    c. The retirement depreciation system is used.
    d. Obsolescence was an unexpected factor in bringing about retirement of the assets replaced.

4. On which of the following assumptions is straight-line amortization based?

    a. The operating efficiency of the asset decreases in later years.
    b. Service value declines as a function of time rather than of use.
    c. Service value declines as a function of obsolescence rather than of time.
    d. Physical wear and tear are more important than economic obsolescence.

5. Accumulated amortization, as used in accounting, represents

    a. Funds set aside to replace assets.
    b. The portion of asset cost written off as an expense since the acquisition date.
    c. Earnings retained in the business that will be used to purchase another operational asset when the related asset becomes fully depreciated.
    d. An expense on the income statement.

6. Corporations A and B purchased identical equipment having an estimated service life of 10 years. Corporation A uses straight-line amortization and B uses declining balance amortization at 20% per year. Assuming that the companies are identical in all other respects, choose the correct statement below.

    a. Corporation B will record more amortization on this asset over the entire 10 years than A.
    b. At the end of the third year, the book value of the asset will be lower for A than for B.

c. Net income will be lower for A in the ninth year than for B.

d. Amortization expense will be higher the first year for A than for B.

[AICPA, adapted]

E11-2 *Amortization Computation:* To demonstrate the computations involved in several methods of amortizing an operational asset, the following information is used:

Acquisition cost	$12,500
Residual value	500
Estimated service life:	
Years	5
Service-hours	10,000
Productive output (units)	24,000

Required:

Give the formula and compute the annual amortization amount using each of the following methods (show computations and round to the nearest dollar):

1. Straight-line amortization.

2. Service-hours method; compute the amortization rate and amount for the first year, assuming 2,200 service-hours of actual operation.

3. Productive output method of amortization; compute the amortization rate and amount for the first year, assuming 4,000 units of output. Is all of the amortization amount (computed in your answer) expensed during the current period?

4. Declining balance method; compute the amortization amount for five years assuming a rate of 50% is used.

E11-3 *Amortization Computation:* Mace Company acquired equipment that cost $18,000, which will be amortized on the assumption that it will last six years and have a $1,200 residual value. Several possible methods of amortization are under consideration.

Required:

1. Prepare a schedule that shows annual amortization expense for the first two years, assuming the following (show computations and round to the nearest dollar):

   a. Declining balance method, using a rate of 30%.

   b. Productive output method. Estimated output is a total of 105,000 units, of which 12,000 will be produced the first year; 18,000 in each of the next two years; 15,000 the fourth year; and 21,000 the fifth and sixth years.

   c. Straight-line method.

   d. Sum-of-the-years-digits.

2. Repeat your calculations for part (1), assuming a useful life of 10 years, a DB rate of 20% that reflects the longer life, but the same number of units of production. The residual value is unchanged. What conclusion can you reach by comparing the results of (1) and (2)?

3. What criteria would you consider important in selecting an amortization method?

E11-4 *Identify Amortization Methods — Amortization Schedules:* Veto Company bought equipment on 1 January 20X5 for $45,000. The expected life is 10 years, and the residual value is $5,000. Based on three acceptable amortization methods, the annual amortization expense and cumulative balance of accumulated amortization at the end of 20X5 and 20X6 are shown below.

| | Case A | | Case B | | Case C | |
| | Annual | Accumulated | Annual | Accumulated | Annual | Accumulated |
Year	Expense	Amount	Expense	Amount	Expense	Amount
20X5	$9,000	$ 9,000	$4,000	$4,000	$7,273	$ 7,273
20X6	7,200	16,200	4,000	8,000	6,545	13,818

Required:

1. Identify the amortization method used in each case.

2. Based on your answer to (1), prepare an amortization schedule for each case for 20X5 through 20X8.

E11-5 *Sinking Fund Amortization:* Brexel Properties Ltd owns apartment buildings in an urban centre. At the beginning of 20X4, Brexel acquired a new building for $14,350,000. The building is expected to last 25 years, and have no salvage value at the end if its life. Brexel uses sinking fund amortization, at a rate of 9%, on similar buildings. Brexel has borrowed $13,500,000 to finance this building, at an interest rate of 10%. Interest is paid at the end of each year, along with a principal payment in the amount of $500,000. Remaining principal is due at the end of the loan term.

Required:

1. Calculate the annual amortization for the first five years.

2. Calculate the amount of interest expense for the first five years.

3. Comment on the expense patterns demonstrated in parts (1) and (2). What factors explain the choice of sinking fund amortization in the real estate industry?

E11-6 *Multiple Choice — Amortization of Intangibles:* Select the best answer for each of the following. Assume a calendar-year reporting period.

1. Goodwill is amortized over

    a. Its useful life if it was acquired externally.
    b. A 40-year period if it was acquired externally.
    c. Its useful life, but not to exceed 40 years, if it was acquired externally.
    d. Its useful life, but not to exceed 40 years, if it was developed internally.

2. On 15 January 20X1, a corporation was granted a patent. On 2 January 20X10, solely to protect its patent, the corporation purchased another patent that was originally issued on 10 January 20X6. Because of its unique processing equipment, the corporation does not believe the competing patent can be used in producing any product. The cost of the competing patent should be

    a. Amortized over a maximum period of 17 years.
    b. Amortized over a maximum period of 13 years.
    c. Amortized over a maximum period of 8 years.
    d. Expensed in 20X10.

3. Chance Company has a lease on land that does not expire for 25 years. With the landowner's permission, Chance erected on the site a building that will last 50 years. Chance should amortize the building's cost

   a. One-fortieth each year.
   b. One-twenty-fifth each year.
   c. In totality as soon as it is completed.
   d. One-fiftieth each year.

4. During 20X4, Starnes Corporation developed a patent. Expenditures related to the patent were: legal fees for patent registration, $7,000; tests to perfect the use of the patent for production processes, $6,000; research costs in the research laboratory, $21,000; and amortization on equipment (that has alternative future uses) used in developing the patent, $4,000. Assuming amortization of the patent costs over the legal life of the patent, the annual patent amortization amount would be

   a. $2,000.
   b. $1,882.
   c. $1,824.
   d. $1,000.
   e. None of the above; explain.

5. A copyright granted to a composer in 20X0 has a legal life of

   a. 17 years.
   b. 28 years.
   c. The life of the composer plus 50 years.
   d. 40 years.

6. Patents and trademarks have definite legal lives and should be amortized over

   a. Their legal life, but not more than 40 years.
   b. Their useful life, but not more than 40 years.
   c. Their legal or useful life, whichever is shorter, but not normally in excess of 40 years.
   d. A period of 40 years.

[AICPA, adapted]

E11-7 *Minimum Amortization Test:* AC Metals bought a piece of manufacturing equipment at the beginning of 20X5.

- The equipment had an original cost of $650,000.
- AC expects to use the equipment for 10 years, and then sell it. The equipment will likely have a five-year useful life remaining at that time.
- Expected residual value at the end of 10 years is $300,000.
- Expected salvage value at the end of 15 years is nil — scrap value only.
- AC Metals uses straight-line amortization on all manufacturing assets.

Required:

1. Explain the difference between the terms residual and salvage values, as used above.

2. How much amortization on the equipment should AC recognize in 20X5? Explain the circumstances that cause this result.

E11-8 *Fractional-Year Amortization:* Jackson Company's records show the following machinery acquisitions and retirements during the first two years of operations:

| Date | Acquisition | | Retirements | |
	Cost of Machinery	Estimated Useful Life(years)	Acquisition Date	Original Cost
1 January 20X5	$50,000	10		
1 April 20X5	40,000	5		
1 December 20X6	20,000	10		
31 December 20X6			20X5*	$ 7,000

* part of machinery acquired on 1 January 20X5

Required:

1. Compute amortization expense for 20X5 and for 20X6 and the balances of the machinery and related accumulated amortization accounts at the end of each year, using straight-line amortization. Machinery is depreciated according to the number of months of ownership in the year of acquisition or retirement. Assume no residual values. There are no sale proceeds upon retirement. Show computations and round to the nearest dollar. Set up separate columns in a schedule for machinery and for accumulated amortization.

2. Compute amortization expense for 20X5 and for 20X6 and the balances of the machinery and related accumulated amortization accounts at the end of each year using straight-line amortization. Machinery is depreciated for one-half year in the year of acquisition. Machinery retired is amortized for one-half year in its year of retirement. Assume no residual values. There are no sale proceeds upon retirement. Show computations and round to the nearest dollar. Set up separate columns in a schedules for machinery and for accumulated amortization.

3. Comment on the differences between (1) and (2).

[AICPA, adapted]

E11-9 *Fractional Year Amortization:* Stoner Co acquired an operational asset at a cost of $10,000. The asset is expected to have a useful life of five years and a residual value of $2,500. The asset was bought on 1 October 20X5 and was sold for $5,400 on 1 May 20X8. Stoner's fiscal year ends on 31 December.

Required:

1. Give entries for acquisition, annual amortization and disposal assuming that amortization is based on the actual months of ownership. Use
   a. straight-line amortization
   b. declining balance amortization using a rate of 30%.

2. Repeat part (1) assuming that the company charges a full year of amortization in the year of acquisition and no amortization in the year of sale.

E11-10 *Inventory Appraisal System:* Mite Engineering Company acquired a large number of small tools at the beginning of operations on 1 January 20X5, for $4,000. During 20X5 and 20X6, Mite disposed of several used tools, receiving cash salvage value of $400 in 20X5 and $500 in 20X6. During 20X6, Mite acquired additional tools at a cost of $1,600. Inventories of tools on hand, valued at current acquisition cost adjusted for the present condition of the tools, indicated a value of $2,800 on 31 December 20X5, and $3,600 on 31 December 20X6. Mite uses the inventory appraisal system of depreciation for small tools.

Required:

How much amortization expense will be recognized on the small tools in 20X5 and 20X6? Show calculations.

E11-11 *Composite Amortization System:* Wilson Company owned the following machines, all acquired on 1 January, 20X5:

Machine	Original Cost	Estimated Residual Value	Estimated Life (years)
A	$ 7,000	None	4
B	0,000	$1,200	8
C	18,000	2,000	0
D	19,000	1,000	12

Required:

1. Prepare a schedule calculating individual straight-line depreciation for each machine that shows the following: cost, residual value, depreciable cost, life in years, and annual depreciation.

2. Compute the composite depreciation rate (based on cost), composite life, and 20X5 depreciation expense if the machines are depreciated using the composite system.

E11-12 *Asset Impairment:* In 20X4, Nytrocks Ltd had manufacturing assets devoted to product RD as follows:

	Cost	Net Book Value
Manufacturing building (exclusive of land)	$2,500,000	$1,780,000
Manufacturing equipment	1,690,000	860,000

Product RD was rendered obsolete by a new product patented by a competitor; Nytrocks ceased production of this product in late 20X4. The manufacturing building was considered to be appropriate for use in the manufacturing operations of product AC, for which markets were growing. However, it was bigger and more elaborate than the base manufacturing needs for this product. An analysis indicated that the base manufacturing needs could be satisfied with a facility that was worth $1,200,000. The manufacturing equipment was specially designed for product RD, and had an appraised value of $200,000. Costs of disposal will be in the range of $40,000.

Required:

1. Provide entries to reflect the asset impairment. In this entry, accumulated depreciation accounts are eliminated and the cost of capital assets is reduced to the net realizable value.

2. Would the loss be extraordinary? Would it be disclosed as part of discontinued operations? Explain.

E11-13 *Asset Revaluation:* Grand Corporation is a privately held corporation. The majority of the shares are held by Ed Grand, and financial statements are prepared primarily to satisfy the needs of the bankers and to keep Mr Grand up-to-date on how well his company is performing. The company has a block of commercial real estate in the downtown core of a small city; this real estate was acquired in 20X1 and has appreciated significantly since then. Mr Grand wished to reflect the current, appraised value of this investment in his financial statements, as the banker continually asks for market value information when assessing loan security.

At the beginning of 20X4, the asset accounts are as follows:

Land	$2,100,000
Buildings, net	810,000

The buildings are being amortized over 30 years, in the amount of $30,000 per year.

Appraisals indicate that land values are in the range of $5,000,000, while the buildings were worth, at the beginning of 20X4, $1,500,000. The estimate of useful life has not changed.

Required:

1. Record the revaluation of assets as of the beginning of 20X4. Note that the accumulated amortization account for the building is eliminated when the building is revalued.

2. How much amortization would be recorded on the 20X4 income statement after the write-up in requirement (1)? Explain.

3. Are the statements reflecting the revaluation in accordance with GAAP? Explain.

4. Assume that appraisals indicated a value of $1,600,000 for land and $700,000 for the buildings. How would the picture change?

E11-14 *Cash Flow Statement:* Idea Ltd reflected the following items in the 20X5 financial statements:

Income statement

Amortization expense, machinery	$200,000
Amortization expense, patent	45,000
Loss on sale of machinery	17,000
Gain on sale of land	20,000

Balance sheet

Decrease in land account	$400,000
Increase in net patent account	10,000
Decrease in net machinery account	356,000

The only entry through the land account was a sale of land. The other accounts may reflect more than one transaction.

Required:

List the items that would appear on the cash flow statement as a result of the above items. Indicate in which section each item would appear. Assume that the indirect method is used for the operating activities section. State any assumptions that you make.

E11-15 *CCA Calculations:* Delton Company purchased several small pieces of equipment in May 20X5 for $200,000, which qualifies as a Class 8 asset for tax depreciation purposes. The equipment has a useful life of six years. Subsequent transactions:

30 September 20X6	Sold equipment bought in 20X5 for $10,000; proceeds, $5,600
1 February 20X7	Sold equipment bought in 20X6 for $20,000; proceeds, $9,900
31 August 20X7	Bought Class 8 equipment for $25,000
16 November 20X8	Bought Class 8 equipment for $18,000

Required:

Calculate CCA and the closing UCC balance for 20X5 to 20X8.

PROBLEMS

P11-1 *Amortization Schedule:* Quick Producers acquired factory equipment on 1 January 20X5, costing $39,000. In view of pending technological developments, it is estimated that the machine will have a resale value upon disposal in four years of $8,000 and that disposal costs will be $500. Quick has a fiscal year end that ends on 31 December. Data relating to the equipment follow:

Estimated service life:

Years	4
Service-hours	20,000

Actual operations:

Calendar Year	Service Hours
20X5	5,700
20X6	5,000
20X7	4,800
20X8	4,400

Required:

Round to the nearest dollar and show computations.

1. Prepare an amortization schedule for the asset, using
   a. Straight-line amortization.
   b. Declining balance amortization, using a 50% rate.
   c. Sum-of-the-years-digits amortization.
   d. Service hours amortization.
2. Express straight-line amortization as a percentage of original cost.
3. Explain whether
   a. the rate of 50% was a good choice for DB amortization.
   b. the 20,000 estimate of total service hours was accurate.

P11-2 *Analysis of Four Amortization Methods — Maximize Income:* On 1 January 20X5, Vello Company, a tool manufacturer, acquired new industrial equipment for $2 million. The new equipment had a useful life of four years, and the residual value was estimated to be $200,000. Vello estimates that the new equipment can produce 14,000 tools in its first year. Production is then estimated to decline by 1,000 units per year over the remaining useful life of the equipment.

The following amortization methods are under consideration:

    a. declining balance (50% rate),
    b. straight-line,
    c. sum-of-the-years-digits, and
    d. units of output.

Required:

Which amortization method would result in maximum income for financial statement reporting for the three-year period ending 31 December 20X7? Prepare a schedule showing the amount of accumulated amortization at 31 December 20X7, under each method selected. Show supporting computations in good form. Ignore present value, income tax, and future (deferred) income tax considerations in your answer.

[AICPA, adapted]

P11-3 *Discussion — Overview of Amortization:* Discuss each of the following situations, as required.

Case A. The manager of a large division of a major corporation has significant input to accounting policy decisions for the division and has authority over all line decisions, including purchasing, maintenance, and capital expenditures. The manager has occupied the position for three years; the average time for promotion to the corporate staff level is five years.

The manager has successfully endorsed capitalizing all post-acquisition costs, including improvements and general maintenance and repair. He has successfully campaigned for a change in amortization methods, and the company has switched from a declining balance method to straight-line.

Divisions are evaluated on rate of return on investment (ROI), the ratio of divisional income to divisional investment.

Required:

Evaluate the manager's choices of accounting policy. Is it good accounting? Does it meet his objectives? Does it meet the objectives of other financial statement users?

Case B. "Earnings Helper," *Forbes*, 12 June 1989, p. 150, discussed the cases of two firms that chose somewhat unusual accounting practices for amortizing assets. Blockbuster Entertainment changed the period of amortization of the videotapes it rents from 9 months to 36 months. In Blockbuster's case, an article in *The Wall Street Journal* critical of its accounting practices was followed by significant declines in the price of its common shares. Cineplex Odeon amortizes its movie theatre seats, carpets, and related equipment over 27 years. In both cases, these firms have adopted accounting practices that are unrepresentative of those chosen by most firms in their respective industries. One effect of these policies is increased income.

Required:

Evaluate the estimates of useful life described above. How is useful life established? What objectives of financial reporting are evident?

Case C. Baker Corporation has certain fully amortized tangible operational assets that are still used in the business.

Required:

Discuss the possible reasons why this could happen, and explain how the fully amortized assets are disclosed in the financial statements.

Case D. Some of the major car rental companies account for the gain or loss on disposal of their used cars as an adjustment to amortization expense in the period of disposal rather than reporting gains or losses on disposal.

Required:

Justify this accounting policy. Would your answer be different if only one company used this policy?

Case E. Megamining Corporation includes the following note in the financial statements:
Depletion of mines is computed on the basis of an overall unit rate applied to the amount of principal products sold from mine production. The corporation makes no representation that the annual amount represents the depletion actually sustained or the decline, if any, in mine values attributable to the year's operations, or that it represents anything other than a general provision for the amortization of the remaining book value of mines.

Required:

Explain the meaning of depletion and the net book value of the mining properties. How does book value compare to market value?

P11-4 *Interpreting Amortization Disclosures:* Portions of the 20X0 financial statements of William's Company, a paint manufacturer, are reproduced below ($ thousands):

Partial Income Statement for the year ended 31 December 20X0

Net sales	$2,266,732
Total expenses	2,079,455
Income before income taxes	187,277
Income taxes	64,611
Net income	$ 122,666

Note 1: Significant Accounting Policies

Property, Plant, and Equipment. Property, plant, and equipment are stated on the basis of cost. Amortization is provided principally by the straight-line method. The major classes of assets and ranges of amortization rates are as follows:

Buildings	2% – 6%
Machinery	4% – 20%
Furniture and fixtures	5% – 20%
Automobiles and trucks	10% – 33%

Note 16: Property, Plant, and Equipment Schedules

	Beginning	Additions	Retirements	Other	Ending
Buildings	$191,540	$11,574	$ 960	($7,185)	$194,969
Machinery	404,156	43,968	16,319	(466)	432,271

Total accumulated amortization and amortization of property, plant and equipment

	Beginning	Additions	Retirements	Other	Ending
Buildings	$ 62,843	$ 7,422	$ 769	($4,951)	$ 64,545
Machinery	211,662	37,085	12,302	(845)	235,600

Required:

1. What method of amortization is used by Williams?
2. What are the average estimated useful lives of buildings owned by Williams?
3. What percentage of the useful life of buildings remains, on average, at the end of the year?
4. What is the book value of machinery retired in the year?
5. Amortization on buildings and machinery was what percentage of (a) total expenses and (b) pretax earnings?

P11-5 *Match Four Amortization Methods with Amortization Expense:* Equipment was acquired for $40,000 that has a six-year estimated life and a residual value of $4,000. The equipment will be amortized by various amounts in this third full year, depending on the amortization method used.

Third-year amortization expense under the four methods listed below (but not in the same order) amounted to (1) $6,000, (2) $5,925, (3) $6,857, and (4) $9,900. The amortization methods used were (a) DB at a 33% rate, (b) productive output, (c) straight-line, and (d) sum-of-the-years-digits amortization.

The productive output method assumed that 800,000 units could be produced; the actual output in the first three years was 200,000 units, 180,000 units, and 220,000 units.

Required:

Analyze the above data, and identify the third year amortization associated with each method. Support each answer with calculations.

P11-6 *Analyze Accounts, Cash Flow Statement:* Selected accounts included under property, plant, and equipment on Abel Company's balance sheet at 31 December 20X5, had the following balances (at original cost):

Land	$220,000
Land improvements	75,000
Buildings (acquired 30 October 20X0)	600,000
Machinery and equipment (acquired 30 April 20X3 and 1 April 20X5)	650,000
Accumulated amortization, building	102,857
Accumulated amortization, machinery and equipment	317,200
Accumulated amortization, land improvements	12,857

- Building and existing land improvements amortization is based on the straight-line method over 35 years.

- Machinery and equipment amortization is based on the declining balance method, using a rate of 20%.

- Residual values are immaterial and are not included in amortization calculations.

- The company claims a full year of amortization in the year of acquisition and none in the year of disposal.

During 20X6, the following transactions occurred:

a. A plant facility consisting of land and building was acquired from Club Company in exchange for 10,000 of Abel's common shares. On the acquisition date, Abel's shares had a closing market price of $32 per share on a national stock exchange. The plant facility was carried on Club's accounts at $95,000 for land and $130,000 for the building at the exchange date. Current appraised values for the land and building, respectively, are $120,000 and $240,000.

b. A tract of land was acquired for $85,000 as a potential future building site.

c. Machinery was purchased at a total cost of $250,000. Additional costs were incurred as follows:

Freight and unloading	$ 5,000
Sales taxes	10,000
Installation	25,000

d. Expenditures totalling $90,000 were made for new parking lots, streets, and sidewalks at the corporation's various plant locations. These items had an estimated useful life of 15 years.

e. A machine that cost $50,000 on 1 April 20X5, was scrapped on 30 June 20X6. DB amortization, at a 20% rate, has been recorded in 20X5.

f. A machine was sold for $25,000 on 1 July 20X6. Original cost of the machine was $37,000 at 1 January 20X3, and it had been amortized from 20X3 to 20X5 using the DB method.

Required:

1. Prepare a detailed analysis of the changes in each balance sheet account for 20X6.

2. Show how the transactions in requirement (1) would be shown in the CFS. The indirect method is used in the operating activities section.

3. List the information items in the problem that were not used to determine the answer to (1) above, showing the relevant amounts and supporting computations for each item. In addition, indicate where, or if, these items should be included in Abel's financial statements.

P11-7 *Multiple Choice — Amortization Systems:* Choose the correct answer for each of the following questions.

1. Information relevant to the assets designated as small equipment for a corporation follows:

Beginning balance	$32,000
Acquisitions this year	6,000
Cash from disposals	200
Ending inventory at appraisal value	$29,000

Assuming that the inventory appraisal system is used, amortization expense for this year for small equipment equals
a. $9,000.
b. $8,800.
c. $6,000.
d. $3,000.

The following information is used for questions 2 and 3:
Mills Corporation began 20X5 with 100 railroad cars each with a $8,000 unit book value. During 20X5, Mills purchased 50 cars for $12,000 each and retired 60 cars. Mills received $120,000 in total from the disposal of the railroad cars. What is the balance in the ledger account for railroad cars on 1 January 20X6, using the

2. Retirement system?

a. $720,000.
b. $920,000.
c. $360,000.
d. $560,000.

3. Replacement system?

a. $720,000.
b. $920,000.
c. $360,000.
d. $560,000.

4. Endo Corporation uses the retirement system of amortization. At the beginning of 20X5, Endo had 200 trucks (cost $16,000 each) in use. During 20X5, Endo sold 50 trucks and received $2,000 each and purchased 80 more at $20,000 each. What is amortization expense for 20X5?

a. $800,000.
b. $700,000.
c. $1,600,000.
d. $1,500,000.

5. Answer question (4), assuming the replacement system.

   a. $1,000,000.
   b. $1,600,000.
   c. $900,000.
   d. $1,500,000.

6. Manara Corporation purchased the following assets 1 January 20X5:

Quantity	Type	Unit Cost	Salvage Value	Estimated Useful Life
10	Truck	$ 6,000	$1,000	5 years
5	Bus	12,000	2,000	8 years

   Under the composite system of amortization, what is the composite rate based on cost?
   a. 13.54%.
   b. 16.25%.
   c. 1.88%.
   d. 6.15%.

7. Without prejudice to your answer to question (6), assume that the composite rate is 20% and that in 20X6, Manara sold two trucks for $4,000 salvage each and replaced them with trucks costing $8,000 each, with $2,000 estimated salvage value each. The new vehicles are considered representative of the group. What is amortization in 20X6?

   a. $16,250.
   b. $24,000.
   c. $24,800.
   d. $20,000.

P11-8 *Composite Amortization System:* Operational assets acquired on 1 January 20X5, by Sculley Company are to be amortized under the composite system. Details regarding each asset are given in the schedule below.

Component	Cost	Estimated Residual Value	Estimated Life (years)
A	$90,000	$10,000	10
B	30,000	0	6
C	76,000	16,000	15
D	12,400	400	8

Required:

1. Calculate the composite life and annual composite amortization rate (based on cost) for the asset components listed above. Give the entry to record amortization after one full year of use. Round the amortization rate to the nearest two decimal places.

2. During 20X6, it was necessary to replace component B, which was sold for $16,000. The replacement component cost $36,000 and will have an estimated residual value of $3,000 at the end of its estimated six-year useful life. Record the disposal and substitution, which was a cash acquisition.

3. Record amortization at the end of 20X6, assuming that the company does not change the composite rate determined in requirement (1).

P11-9 *Accounting for Capital Assets:* Brannen Manufacturing Corporation was incorporated on 3 January 20X4. The corporation's financial statements for its first year's operations were not examined by a public accountant. You have been engaged to examine the financial statements for the year ended 31 December 20X5, and your examination is substantially completed. The corporation's adjusted trial balance appears as follows:

BRANNEN MANUFACTURING CORPORATION
Adjusted Trial Balance
31 December 20X5

	Debit	Credit
Cash	$ 11,000	
Accounts receivable	68,500	
Allowance for doubtful accounts		$ 500
Inventories	38,500	
Prepaid expenses	10,500	
Machinery	75,000	
Equipment	29,000	
Accumulated amortization		12,100
Patents	102,000	
Organization costs	29,000	
Goodwill	24,000	
Licensing agreement 1, net	48,750	
Licensing agreement 2, net	59,000	
Accounts payable		152,400
Unearned revenue		12,500
Share capital		317,000
Retained earnings deficit, opening	17,000	
Sales revenue		661,500
Cost of goods sold	466,000	
Selling and general expenses	173,000	
Amortization expense	0	
Interest expense	4,750	
Totals	$1,156,000	$1,156,000

The following information relates to accounts that may still require adjustment:

a. Patents for Brannen's manufacturing process were acquired 2 January 20X5, for $68,000. An additional $34,000 was spent in late December 20X5 to improve machinery covered by the patents and was debited to the patents account.

b. The balance in the organization costs account properly includes costs incurred during the organization period. Brannen had decided to amortize organization costs over a five-year period beginning 1 January 20X4. No amortization has yet been recorded for 20X4 or 20X5.

c. During the second week of January 20X5, an explosion caused a permanent 60% reduction in the expected revenue-producing value of licensing agreement 1. No entry was made to reflect the explosion in 20X5. The agreement is expected to have an unlimited life at this lower amount.

d. On 1 January 20X5, Brannen bought licensing agreement 2, which has a life expectancy of 10 years. The balance in the licensing agreement 2 account includes the $58,000 purchase price and $2,000 in acquisition costs, but it has been reduced by a credit of $1,000 for the advance collection of 20x6 revenue from the agreement. No amortization on agreement 2 has been recorded.

e. The balance in the goodwill account includes (1) $8,000 paid 30 April 20X5, for an advertising program that management believes will assist in increasing Brannen's sales over a period of three to five years following the disbursement, and (2) legal expenses of $16,000 incurred for Brannen's incorporation on 3 January 20X4. No amortization has ever been recorded on the goodwill.

f. All machinery is being amortized on a straight-line basis, assuming a 10% residual value, over its expected life of 8 years. There were no acquisitions in 20X5 other than that mentioned in (a).

g. Brannen's practice is to provide a full year's amortization in the year of acquisition and no amortization in the year of disposal.

h. Equipment is amortized using the declining balance method, at a rate of 20%, and assuming a residual value of $4,000. Of the accumulated amortization at the end of 20X4, $5,800 relates to equipment. On 1 October 20X5, a piece of equipment had been bought for $9,000, and properly debited to the equipment account.

Required:

1. Prepare journal entries as of 31 December 20X5, as required by the information given above, including correcting entries. If the estimated life is not given, use the maximum. State any assumptions made. Ignore income taxes

2. What items would appear on the cash flow statement as a result of the 20X5 capital asset transactions? Assume that the indirect method is used for the operating activities section.

3. What accounting policy information does the company have to disclose? Be specific.

[AICPA, adapted]

P11-10 *Depreciation and Depletion — Schedule, Entries:* Gaspe Mining Corporation bought mineral-bearing land for $150,000 that engineers estimate will yield 200,000 kilos of economically removable ore. The land will have a value of $30,000 after the ore is removed.

To work the property, Gaspe built structures and sheds on the site that cost $40,000; these will last 10 years, and because their use is confined to mining and it would be expensive to dismantle and move them, they will have no residual value. Machinery that cost $29,000 was installed at the mine, and the added cost for installation was $7,000. This machinery should last 15 years; like that of the structures, the usefulness of the machinery is confined to these mining operations. Dismantling and removal costs when the property has been fully worked will approximately equal the value of the machinery at that time; therefore, Gaspe does not plan to use the structures or the machinery after the minerals have been removed.

In the first year, Gaspe removed only 15,000 kilos of ore; however, production was doubled in the second year. It is expected that all of the removable ore will be extracted within eight years from the start of operations.

Required:

Prepare a schedule showing unit and total depletion and amortization and net book value of the operational assets for the first and second years of operation. Use the units-of-production method of depreciation for all assets.

P11-11 *Amortization, Impairment:* On 1 October 20X5, Flexi-Toys Inc. purchased plastic moulding equipment for $200,000. The equipment has an eight-year useful life and no residual value. The equipment will be amortized using the straight-line method.

On 1 November 20X5, the company bought a delivery vehicle for $18,500, plus $2,300 in freight and taxes. The vehicle is to be amortized using 30% declining balance amortization. It will have a useful life of seven years, and a residual value of $2,000 at that time.

On 1 April 20X6, the company bought a second piece of (more sophisticated) moulding equipment for $450,000. The asset will be kept for 10 years, at which time it is expected to have a residual value of $278,000. The asset has a total useful life of 20 years; at the end of that time, it would have only minor scrap value.

On 1 April 20X7, the firm decided to write down the recorded value of the older moulding equipment, because of the better technology and lower operating costs demonstrated by the newer machine. The total estimated future cash flows from use of the equipment are estimated to be $45,000. Its fair market value was estimated to be $30,000. The remaining useful life has not changed. Depreciation is recorded to the date of write-down.

Flexi-Toys Inc. has a calendar fiscal year, and computes fractional-year amortization using exact calculations.

Required:

1. Compute 20X5 and 20X6 amortization.

2. Compute 20X7 amortization, and prepare the journal entry to record the impairment loss. Note that accumulation amortization on the date of write-down is eliminated in the loss entry, and the equipment is written down to the appropriate value.

3. Prepare cash flow statement disclosures for 20X5 to 20X7. Assume that the indirect method is used for the operating activities section, and that all acquisitions were made for cash.

P11-12 *Comparative Analysis, Amortization:* The amortization policy disclosure notes for the 31 December 20X3 annual reports of Company A, Company B, and Company C are reproduced below, along with summary information from their annual reports. These companies all operate in the same business, mining and smelting operations, which are very capital intensive.

Company A
> *Amortization* — Amortization is calculated on the straight-line method using rates based on the estimated useful lives of the respective assets. The principal rates are 2% for buildings and range from 1% to 4% for power assets, and 3% to 6% for chemical and fabricating assets.

Company B
> *Fixed Assets* — Fixed assets are recorded at their historical cost. Amortization is computed generally by the straight-line method applied to the cost of assets in service at annual rates based on their estimated useful lives, as follows:

Buildings	2.5% – 5 %
Equipment	5% – 7.5%
Mobile equipment	20% – 25%
Mine and quarry	
Processing facilities	4.5% – 5 %
Mobile equipment	4.5% – 20%

Company C
> *Fixed Assets and Amortization* — Fixed assets are recorded at historical cost less investment tax credits realized and include construction in progress. Amortization is provided using the straight-line method applied to the cost of the assets at rates based on their estimated useful life and beginning from the point when production commences.

The following annual amortization rates are in effect:

Buildings	2% – 5%
Equipment	6% – 7%
Automotive and mobile equipment	10% – 20%
Raw material plants and properties	4% – 5%

Financial data (amounts in $ millions)

	Co. A	Co. B	Co. C
Total assets, 31 December 20X3	$ 9,810	$3,218	$2,364
Average owners' equity, 20X3	4,181	1,426	948
Earnings from continuing operations:			
20X3	(104)	66	(36)
20X2	(112)	(38)	(127)
Amortization, 20X3	443	180	122
Gross plant assets, 1 January 20X3	11,015	3,732	3,332
Gross plant assets, 31 December 20X3	11,092	3,618	3,353
Accumulated amortization, 31 December 20X3	5,087	1,769	2,179
Capital expenditures, 20X3	25	17	58

Required:

Discuss the amortization policy of the three firms relative to their financial results. Make an analysis of the relevant summary financial statement information to support your comments.

P11-13 *Integrative Problem, Chapters 6–11:* Hyperium Computers Ltd. is a small producer and marketer of software for personal computers. The company is owned by a group of about 20 shareholders, including two venture capitalists that own preferred shares that must be redeemed in 10 years' time. Bank debt, used to finance inventory and accounts receivable, allows borrowing of up to 40% of the book value of inventory and 70% of the book value of accounts receivable. The company picks many accounting policies to minimize tax payments.

Accounting policy issues facing the company this year are given below.

1. Hyperium began selling products to large discount retailers under the retailer's "house brand" for the first time in 20X5. Agreements with the retailers specify that 80% of products not sold to final customers within six months may be returned to Hyperium for a refund. Data with respect to the sales:

	January–June	**July–December**
Sales at retail	$401,000	$798,600
Cash collected	199,000	362,000
Returns to date (at retail)	76,000	172,500*

*$110,000 relate to sales made in the January–June period.
Hyperium has recorded the sales as cash has been collected. Regardless of the accounting policy chosen, taxable income must include revenue equal to cash collected.

   When should revenue be recognized? Analyze the accounting policy choices and make a recommendation. Evaluate point of sale, cash collection and the end of the return period.

2. Hyperium incurred $657,000 of costs to advertise a new software program this year. The program is expected to sell strongly in the lucrative 10-to-16 year-old age bracket over the next three years.

Should the costs be deferred and amortized or immediately expensed? Provide an analysis and recommendation.

3. Hyperium incurred $340,000 of costs to revise existing software products (goods for resale) so that they utilize the more sophisticated graphics that are available on newer personal computers.

    Should the costs be deferred and amortized or immediately expensed? Provide an analysis and recommendation.

4. Hyperium accrues bad debt expense in the year of sale. An aging of accounts receivable at year-end reveals the following:

	Accounts receivable	Percentage expected to be non-collectable
Current	$613,200	2%
30–60 days	114,900	20
60–90 days	70,700	40
Over 90 days	54,300	60

    The allowance has a debit balance of $47,900 prior to adjustment. Provide the adjusting journal entry to record bad debt expense.

5. Hyperium sold $400,000 of accounts receivable to a finance company the day before the end of the fiscal year. The finance company charged $6,960 in interest. All the receivables were expected to be collected. The cash received was debited to cash, and credited to an account called "suspense."

    Provide the adjusting journal entry to correct the suspense account and record the sale. Indicate the circumstances under which the sale would be recorded as a loan.

6. Hyperium has a U.S. $40,000 account receivable, recorded at Cdn. $54,000. The year-end exchange rate is U.S. $1 = Cdn. $1.41 Hyperium has a U.S. $98,000 account payable recorded at Cdn. $132,900.

    Provide adjusting journal entries.

7. Hyperium uses a FIFO cost flow assumption for inventory. In general, prices of raw materials have increased 10% over the period. While inventories include thousands of items, a data base is available that could be used to reconstruct inventory and cost of sales using LIFO or weighted average.

    The company wishes to understand the financial statement impact of using a different cost flow assumption.

8. Hyperium counted its finished goods inventory and obtained a dollar value, at cost, of $4,413,000. However, they are wondering what level of inventory shrinkage has been experienced. The following data has been provided:

Opening inventory, as counted, at cost	$4,691,400
Closing inventory, as counted, at cost	4,413,000
Purchases, at invoice price	16,924,300
Sales and excise taxes	2,030,900
Freight-in	712,800
Purchase discounts and returns	419,100

    Gross profit margins have been stable at 32%. Net sales during the year were $28,200,000. Note that amounts appropriately exclude inventory and sales related to house brand sales described in requirement (1).

    Provide an estimate of inventory losses due to shrinkage.

9. Hyperium acquired new computer equipment, nine months into the year, part of a regular upgrade program to keep them on the cutting edge of technology. These computers have an expected useful life of five years, although Hyperium has had to upgrade its computers about every two years to stay abreast of technology. Costs associated with the upgrade:

Computer invoice price	$6,450,000
Sales tax	967,500
Delivery charges	57,000
Improvement to wiring necessary to connect computers to network	116,000
Training course for employees to upgrade skills	40,900

The company wishes you to evaluate use of straight-line and declining balance amortization (50%) methods. Your analysis should include calculation of amortization expense for each of the first two fiscal years. Salvage values would be 40% of cost after 24 months and 5% of cost after five years. Be sure to separately calculate the cost of the equipment, and indicate how other (non-capitalized) expenditures should be accounted for.

Required:

Address the accounting policy issues listed above, providing appropriate analysis and entries, as required.

Investments in Debt and Equity Securities

INTRODUCTION

Accounting for investments in the securities of other companies can be very straightforward. Such an investment usually is purchased for cash and thus has a known cost which is recorded as an asset. The investment typically produces an annual cash flow of interest or dividends that can be recorded as investment revenue. On the surface, there would appear to be no particular problems associated with investments.

However, in some cases it gets very complicated. Often, investments in voting securities represent more than just a passive investment undertaken to generate investment income. Long-term investments in voting shares *may* be used to establish an inter-company relationship through which the investor corporation can *control* or *significantly influence* the operating, investing, and financing strategies of the investee corporation. If the investor can control or influence the dividend policy of the investee, dividends received from the investee are not the result of an arm's length transaction. Therefore, it would be misleading to report investment income as the amount of dividends received because the investor can control the amount.

Another complicating aspect of intercorporate investments is that, very often, a corporation carries on its business activities not through only one corporate entity, but through several. Indeed, one corporation may hold a majority of the shares of dozens of other corporations, which are deemed to be **subsidiaries** of the investor corporation, their **parent**. Most subsidiaries are established by the parent company as a means of carrying out part of its operations, and the parent company is the only shareholder; these subsidiaries are said to be **wholly-owned** by their parent. The consolidation process is quite straightforward for wholly-owned subsidiaries that were established by the parent.

However, corporations sometimes buy control of another corporation through a purchase of a *majority of the shares* of an existing company, either through private transactions with controlling shareholders or on the open market. Such purchases are called **business combinations** (popularly known as *mergers*), and the process of consolidating subsidiaries that were acquired through a business combination is considerably more complex than for subsidiaries that were formed (and are 100% owned) by the parent corporation.

In accounting for investments in the securities of other corporations, the accounting problem is two-fold:

1. what is the nature of the investment in the securities of another corporation, and
2. how can the investment be reported to reveal the economic impact of the investment rather than just its legal form?

Inter-company relationships are often complex, and accounting standards require special treatment of investments that confer power on the investor. We'll explore these rules in this chapter, and provide an overview of this complex area. Keep in mind, though, that many accounting programs devote an entire course to this issue, so what you're doing here is only the tip of the proverbial iceberg!

Another complicating factor in the world of accounting for investments is that the market value of the securities might be a lot more important than cost to the people who use the financial statements. However, market valuation of investments is normally permitted in Canada for only a subset of companies, primarily those in the financial sector (e.g., mutual funds, investment companies, and insurance companies); for other types of companies, Canadian GAAP requires that investments be carried at the traditional historic cost. But if you were a lender, holding the investments as collateral on a loan, would you care more about cost or market value? On the other hand, if an investment is held for the long-term, why would market value be important? There is much controversy surrounding whether market value is, in fact, more relevant for "general purpose" financial statements and whether its measurement is reliable enough for recognition.

OVERVIEW OF INTERCORPORATE INVESTMENTS

Investment Objectives
Companies invest in the securities of other enterprises for a variety of reasons:

- *Temporary Investment of Idle Cash.* Companies often have cash on hand that is not needed at present but will be needed in the near future. Rather than allow the idle cash to remain in a low interest bank account, companies find temporary investments where they can earn a higher return. These investments typically have low risk and are easily converted to cash.

- *Long-Term Investments to Generate Earnings.* Similarly, cash on hand can be invested in less liquid securities in order to increase investment income. These investments may be of higher risk and/or a longer term than a temporary investment, and the intent is to leave the investment in place for the medium or long-term.

- *Strategic Alliances.* Another reason firms invest in the securities of other firms, especially in voting shares, is to develop a beneficial inter-company relationship that will increase the profitability of the investing company, both directly and indirectly. Strategic decisions may be made to invest in suppliers, customers, and even competitors.

- *Legal Frameworks.* Companies may choose to establish operations in one large company with numerous branches, or organize activities in a set of smaller companies, all or partially controlled by a central holding company. This may be done for tax reasons, to allow outside shareholders a small stake in particular operations, to satisfy legal requirements in particular jurisdictions, and to limit potential liability claims to particular portions of the enterprise.

Accounting for investments is dictated by how the investment is classified, which in turn is dependent on management's intentions, and also on the substance of the security itself.

Classification and Definition

Investment securities can be marketable securities, with active markets of buyers and sellers, and with readily determinable market prices, or may be privately placed securities, with no public market and therefore no readily determinable market value.

An investment in the *debt securities* of another company can be

- a temporary investment
- a long-term investment.

Investments in debt securities (whether temporary or long-term) are accounted for as passive investments, which means that they are reported as income-earning resources and as *investing activities* in the cash flow statement. There is some difference in the accounting for temporary versus long-term investments in debt securities, as we shall see later, but the difference seldom is major.

An investment in the *shares* of another company can be either a passive investment or a *strategic* investment.

- passive investments:
  - temporary or short-term investments
  - long-term portfolio investments

- strategic investments:
  - an investment that gives the investor *control* over the subsidiary
  - an investment that gives the investor *significant influence* over the affairs of the investee corporation
  - a joint venture

Investments in equity securities are subject to five different types of accounting, depending into which classification (in the list above) they fall. Passive investments are accounted for similarly in most cases, although there can be differences in valuation between short- and long-term, as we will demonstrate shortly. Strategic investments are undertaken not simply to generate revenue (although that may be one objective), but rather to further the strategic objectives of the enterprise. Strategic investments are those that bind the reporting enterprise to one or more other legal corporate entities, and that fact changes the substance of the economic entity and therefore of the financial reporting.

Many securities are financial instruments under the definitions established in Section 3860 of the *CICA Handbook*. A *financial instrument* is any contract that gives rise to both a financial asset of one party and a financial liability or equity instrument of another party. In the context of inter-corporate investments, financial assets are defined as any contractual right to receive cash or another financial asset from another company.

The financial instrument definition specifically *excludes* any investments that are classified as *control* investments, *significant influence* investments, and *joint ventures*, as there are well-established rules for recognition, measurement, and disclosure of these items elsewhere in the *CICA Handbook*. As a result, the financial instrument recommendations apply only to investments in debt securities and to investments in equity securities that are, in substance, financial instruments. Equity instruments that are in substance debt (and therefore are financial instruments) will be examined in Chapter 15.

OVERVIEW OF ACCOUNTING FOR INVESTMENTS

Temporary vs. Long-Term Investments

An investment in debt securities is classified as a temporary investment if *both* of the following conditions are satisfied:

1. the investment matures within the next year (or operating cycle) or is capable of reasonably prompt liquidation (either by sale on the open market or sale to a financial institution), and
2. the investment is *intended* by management to be a temporary use of cash.

If these two conditions are *not* satisfied, the investment is classified as a long-term portfolio investment.

The first characteristic includes short-term money market instruments such as certificates of deposit, treasury bills, and callable loans, as well as marketable equity securities. Indeed, *all* investments that mature or otherwise become payable within the next year (or operating cycle, if longer) are classified as temporary investments, even if management's intent is to renew or *roll over* the investments at maturity. Investments in securities that cannot readily be converted into cash should not be classified as temporary investments. This condition is verifiable by reference to the maturity dates of debt instruments and to the existence of a market for longer-term debt and equity securities.

The second condition is one of management *intent*, and therefore is not subject to critical analysis by an accountant or an auditor.

All investments that are not classified as temporary investments are considered to be *long-term investments*. Long-term investments in *debt* are always considered to be *portfolio investments*, while long-term investments in securities have three possible reporting outcomes, depending on whether the investment is passive or strategic. Passive investments are classified as portfolio investments. Therefore, we can conclude that portfolio investments are those passive investments that have *either* of the following characteristics:

*   investments that do not mature within the next year (or operating cycle) and that cannot be liquidated reasonably promptly, including non-marketable debt and equity instruments, *or*
*   marketable securities that management *intends* to hold for the long term, including both debt and equity instruments and debt instruments that mature more than one year after the balance sheet date.

The classification of investments has two implications for measurement of net income:

1. the treatment of bond acquisition premium and/or discount, and
2. the recognition of loss when an investment's market value falls below its acquisition cost.

Investments in Debt Securities

All debt securities are recorded at their cost on acquisition, which includes any brokers' fees paid. Interest income is accrued as time passes, and *may* include an allocation of any difference — called a *premium* or *discount* — between face value and the price paid on acquisition. Debt securities that are purchased on the open market will, most likely, be purchased at a price that is different from their face or maturity value. If the price is higher than the maturity value it will be because the security has an interest rate that is higher than the market rate of interest; the difference between the purchase price and the maturity value is a premium. Similarly, a debt security will sell at less than its maturity value if its interest rate is less than the market rate of interest for securities of equivalent term and risk; the difference is a discount.

The accounting treatment given to the premium or discount is the one aspect of bond investment that is affected by whether the security is a temporary investment or is to be held for the long-term:

- If an investment in bonds is *temporary*, there is no specific recognition given to the purchase discount or premium. The acquisition cost remains on the books until the investment is sold.

- If a bond is *intended* to be held to maturity, then the purchase discount or premium is amortized to interest revenue over the remaining life of the bond.

There are two difficulties with this temporary versus portfolio classification scheme. One is that the classification relies on management's *intent*, which in turn has an impact on both revenue measurement and balance sheet classification. Revenue measurement is affected because the premium or discount is amortized only *if* the investment is classified as long-term, while asset reporting is affected because temporary investments are classified as current assets instead of as long-term assets.

The second difficulty is that it is a "white-or-black" type of classification rule that has no room for in-between investments. In fact, many investments are made for the long-term, but not necessarily to be held to maturity. What if a company invests in bonds "to maturity" and then, when bond prices rise, decides to sell the bonds to reap the benefit of the capital gain? The accounting rules do not cope well with changes in management's intentions (or, indeed, with changes in management!).

An investment in a debt security is always accounted for as a passive investment on the books of the investor, and is reported as an investment (temporary or portfolio) on the investor's separate-entity balance sheet. However, if the investor *also* has a controlling investment in the shares of the same corporation, the investments in neither the debt instrument nor the share equity will appear on the investor's *consolidated* balance sheet. The investments will be eliminated in the process of consolidation. The consolidation process is illustrated in the Appendix to this chapter.

An investment in a debt security of a *joint venture* is eliminated (in the investor's consolidated statements) only to the extent of the investor's ownership interest, e.g., if the joint venture share is 30%, then 30% of the debt investment is eliminated.

Investments in Equity Securities

Passive investments in equity instruments are accounted for either as temporary investments or as portfolio investments. In either case, the *cost method* of accounting is used (except in certain industries). Under the cost method, the investment is recorded at its acquisition cost and left at that value, unless there is a significant and long-lasting decline in the market value of the investment. Investment revenue is recorded when dividends are declared by the investee. The investment is reported on the balance sheet at its cost. The details of accounting by the cost method are fully illustrated in a later section.

The criteria for classification as a *temporary investment* are the same as those cited above for investments in debt instruments: (1) the investment must be capable of reasonably prompt sale or liquidation within the next year (or operating cycle, if longer) and (2) it must be management's *intent* to hold the equity security as a temporary investment. In order for an equity investment to be readily saleable, it must be a *marketable* security; non-marketable equity securities must be classified as a portfolio investment.

The Nature of Strategic Investments

As we mentioned earlier, there are three different kinds of *strategic investments*:

1. those that give the investor *control* over the investee corporation;
2. those that give the investor *significant influence* over the strategic, financing and operating policies of the investee; and
3. those that give the investor *joint control* (with one or more other investors) over the investee.

The *CICA Handbook* defines "control" as the:

> continuing power to determine ...strategic policies of the other enterprise without the co-operation of others.   [*CICA* 1590.03]

Since strategic policies of the enterprise are typically established by the board of directors, the right to elect a majority of the board of directors would normally constitute control. Of course, percentage share ownership is still a major input to this decision. If a company owns more than 50% of the voting shares of a company, it should have to establish why it does not have control; if it owns 50% or less, it should have to establish why it does have control.

An important phrase in the AcSB's definition of control is "*without the cooperation of others.*" This means that, for control to be deemed to exist, the investor has to be able to withstand hostile takeover attempts. If an opponent can gather enough shares (or the support of enough voting shareholders) to take over control, then control does not exist in fact. Many corporations are "controlled" by a major shareholder who owns the largest single block of shares, but if the exercise of this "control" is contingent on the support (even passive support) of at least some other shareholders, then control does not really exist in an accounting sense.

An investor can control a corporation while holding less than a majority of the corporation's voting shares through any of several methods:

- The investee corporation may have two or more classes of shares that have different voting rights, in which case control can be maintained by holding a majority of the *votes* but not necessarily a majority of voting *shares*. Examples are given in Chapter 14.
- The investor holds convertible securities or stock options that, if control is challenged, can be converted or exercised, thereby giving the controlling investor an absolute majority of the votes.
- A shareholders' agreement gives control to a shareholder who owns less than 50% of the shares (or, to look at the reverse side, restricts the voting power of other investors). This device is common in private corporations, but can exist in public corporations as well.
- An investor with a minority of the shares also is a major source of debt financing, and the debt agreement gives the investor the right to select a majority of the investee's board of directors.

If the investee is controlled by the investor corporation, the investor corporation is called the *parent company* and the investee corporation is known as *a subsidiary*.

Significant influence gives the investor the ability to exert *influence* over the strategic operating, investing and financing policies of the investee corporation even though the investor does not *control* the investee. Significant influence can be exerted through several means, and not just by the equity investment. The *CICA Handbook* cites the following possible indications of significant influence:

The ability to exercise significant influence may be indicated by, for example, representation on the board of directors, participation in policy-making processes, material intercompany transactions, interchange of managerial personnel or provision of technical information.   [*CICA* 3050.04]

Normally, ownership of 20% or more of an investee corporation's shares is deemed to indicate that significant influence exists. But this is a *guideline*, not a rule.

If the investor holds less than 20% of the voting interest in the investee, it is presumed that the investor does not have the ability to exercise significant influence, unless such influence is clearly demonstrated. On the other hand, the holding of 20% or more of the voting interest in the investee does not in itself confirm the ability to exercise significant influence.

[*CICA* 3050.04]

It's important to not put too much weight on the percentage of share ownership, though; a great deal depends on who owns the other shares, as well as on the other non-ownership financial and operating relationships between the investor and the investee corporations. For example, ownership of 30% of an investee corporation may not give the investee significant influence (or *any* influence) if the other 70% is held by a single shareholder who will not tolerate any influence. Conversely, an ownership interest of 15% may give the investor virtually unchallenged influence if ownership of the other 85% is widely dispersed.

It is worth noting that, in the U.S., the 20% to 50% ownership guideline is a firm *rule*; if 20% or more but less than a majority of the shares is owned by an investor, then significant influence is automatically deemed to exist. Therefore, an investor corporation may avoid the presumption of significant influence (and the accounting requirements that significant influence entails) by holding only 19.9%. In Canadian GAAP, however, it is the *substance* that matters, not a fraction of a percentage.

The third type of strategic equity investment is that of a joint venture.

A joint venture is an economic activity resulting from a contractual arrangement whereby two or more venturers jointly control the economic activity.   [*CICA* 3055.03(c)]

Joint ventures are distinct in that they are subject to joint control, regardless of share ownership percentage. That is, the investors *must unanimously agree* on key operating, investing, and financing decisions before they are implemented. This feature of joint control means that majority ownership does not confer control, nor does the right to appoint the majority of the board of directors.

Joint ventures are quite common in mining operations and in oil and gas ventures. The joint venturers all contribute something to exploration activities, and all share in wealth generated, if any. For example, a small mining company may have exploration rights over a property, and agree to explore the property with a larger joint venture partner, who provides management, working capital and capital assets in exchange for a certain percentage of the profits. However, key decisions over when and where to explore, or to put the property into commercial production, etc. are subject to common control of both venturers.

Strategic Equity Investments: Recording vs. Reporting

Strategic investments present a recording and reporting challenge. It is very important to make a distinction between the way that an investor *records* strategic investments in its books and the way that the investment is *reported* in the investor's financial statements. Often, an investor will account for a strategic investment by using the cost method simply because it is the easiest method; this is the investor's *recording* method. When financial statements are prepared, a different reporting method may be more appropriate for the financial reporting objectives of the company. In that case, the accounts relating to the investment are adjusted by means of a worksheet. The financial statement *reporting* for strategic investments in equity securities depends on:

1. the nature of investment — control, significant influence, or joint control; and
2. the reporting circumstances — general purpose or special purpose reporting.

The nature of a strategic equity investment means the investor exerts a significant degree of influence or control over the strategic operating, investing, and financing policies of the investee. Due to this influence or control, the **equity method** may be used for strategic equity investments. Under the equity method

- the original investment is recorded at its acquisition cost;
- the investor's proportionate *share* of the investee's net income (subject to certain adjustments) is recognized on the investor's income statement and as an increase in the investment account; and
- dividends are recorded as a decrease in the investment account rather than as investment revenue.

At any point in time, the equity-method investment account consists of (1) the investment's historical cost, plus (2) the investor's share of the investee's earnings since the investment was made, minus (3) the investor's share of dividends paid by the investee since the shares were purchased. The difference between the investor's share of the investee's net income and the dividends actually received is called **unremitted earnings**.

Strategic equity investments obviously must be recorded on the investor's books and must be reported as an investment in the investor's separate-entity, *non-consolidated* financial statements. However, Canadian (and U.S.) GAAP requires that a corporation's *general purpose* financial statements be **consolidated statements**. The intent is to enable investors (and others) to see the assets, liabilities, revenues and expenses of the entire economic entity consisting of the parent and all of its subsidiaries.

When consolidated statements are prepared, the investment account relating to a controlled subsidiary disappears entirely from the balance sheet. Instead, the subsidiary's assets and liabilities are added to those of the parent and reported together as a single economic entity. If the parent owns less than 100% of the subsidiary's shares, the interest of the non-controlling (i.e., minority) shareholders is shown on the parent's consolidated balance sheet and income statement.

Significantly influenced investments cannot be consolidated because the investor does not *control* the assets and liabilities of the investee. Instead, the equity method generally is used for reporting the investment.

Joint ventures are reported by means of **proportionate consolidation**. The investor's pro-rata share of assets, liabilities, revenues, and expenses is calculated and added to the investor's own financial results. This differs from a regular consolidation, where *all* the subsidiary's assets, etc., are included regardless of the ownership interest, partially offset by the non-controlling interest shown as a separate account on the balance sheet and income statement.

Therefore, the recording and reporting of strategic investments under generally accepted accounting principles can be summarized as follows:

Degree of Influence	Type of Investment	Recording Method	Reporting Method
Some	Significant influence	Equity (may be cost)	Equity
Control	Subsidiary	Cost (may be equity)	Consolidation
Joint control	Joint venture	Cost (may be equity)	Proportionate consolidation

Public companies may prepare non-consolidated (or *separate entity*) statements for specific users, such as for their bankers, as well as consolidated general purpose statements. Indeed, knowledgeable bankers will insist on seeing a corporation's non-consolidated statements because the bank has immediate recourse only to the assets and cash flows of the specific legal entity to which it is making the loan. Business history is full of instances in which a bank has lent money to a parent company only to discover later that all of the cash flow is in an operating subsidiary that is out of reach of the bank (sometimes, in a foreign country). As well, non-consolidated statements are essential for income tax purposes, because every corporation is taxed separately (with some exceptions) and the corporation's financial statements must be attached to the tax return.

Private companies often do not prepare consolidated statements, because they don't really have "general purpose" financial statements; their range of users is limited. The *CICA Handbook* provides an explicit exemption for private companies by stating that non-consolidated financial statements may be prepared when:

> ... the owners of the reporting enterprise have access to all pertinent information concerning the resources and results of operation of the group; and the owners, including those not otherwise entitled to vote, unanimously consent to the preparation of non-consolidated financial statements.
>
> [*CICA* 3050.43]

If non-consolidated financial statements are prepared, *either* the cost or the equity method of reporting may be used, but there should be extensive disclosure of the summary financial position of the non-consolidated subsidiary.

CONCEPT REVIEW

1. Explain the difference between a passive investment and a strategic investment.
2. What are the three types of strategic investments?
3. What two conditions must be satisfied in order for an investment to be classified as a temporary investment?
4. If a bond is purchased at a substantial discount, what difference does it make whether it is classified as a temporary or a long-term investment?
5. Explain the characteristics of a joint venture.
6. Companies often choose to record a strategic investment on the cost basis, even though they report it in their financial statements on the equity basis. Why?

ACCOUNTING BY THE COST METHOD

The cost basis of accounting offers no particular challenges:

- The investment is recorded at its acquisition cost, including transaction costs such as brokerage fees or service charges, but excluding any accrued interest.
- Interest revenue on interest-bearing debt securities is recognized as it accrues, at the nominal rate of interest; dividend income on shares are recognized only when

the issuing corporation has declared the dividends.

- At sale or maturity, any difference between the proceeds received and the recorded cost (plus accrued interest, if any) is recorded as a gain or loss.

Interest-bearing debt securities that are purchased between interest dates are recorded at their market price, *plus* accrued interest since the last interest payment date. Accrued interest is added to the price because, at each interest date, the interest is paid to whomever holds the securities regardless of when they actually purchased them. When the debt securities are purchased, the accrued interest must be recorded separately from the cost of the security itself.

To illustrate the cost-basis accounting for temporary investments, assume that on 1 November 20X1, Able Company purchases:

a. 5,000 shares of Baker Company common shares for $20 per share, and
b. a face amount of $30,000 of Charlie Corporation 8% coupon rate bonds that mature on 31 December 20X7, at 100, for a total of $30,000, plus accrued interest. Interest is paid semi-annually on 30 June and 31 December.

Commissions on the common share purchase are $500; no commission or fees are charged for the bond purchase; and 30% of the purchase price of the common shares (not including the commissions) is borrowed from the selling brokerage firm. Able classifies both investments as temporary investments.

Notice that bond prices are quoted as percentages of the face value of the bond. A quote of 98 implies that a $1,000 face amount bond has a market price of $980. The quoted price does not include accrued interest, which also must be paid to the seller of the bond.

The entries to record the above purchases are as follows:

For the purchase of 5,000 common shares of Baker Company

Temporary investment: Baker Company common shares	100,500	
Cash [(5,000 shares × $20 × 70%) + $500 commissions]		70,500
Payable to broker (5,000 shares × $20 × 30%)		30,000

For the purchase of Charlie Corporation bonds

Temporary investment: Charlie Corporation bonds	30,000	
Accrued interest receivable ($30,000 × 8% × 4/12)	800	
Cash		30,800

When interest is received on 31 December, a portion of it represents the accrued interest recorded at the acquisition date.

To record receipt of interest

Cash ($30,000 × 8% × 6/12)	1,200	
Investment income: Interest		400
Accrued interest receivable		800

When a temporary investment is sold, the difference between the carrying amount and the selling price (net of accrued interest), less commissions and other expenses, is recorded as a gain or loss. Suppose that on 31 March 20X2 Able Company sells one-third of its Charlie Corporation bonds at 105 plus accrued interest, and incurs commissions and other expenses of $350. The *proceeds* from the sale are as follows:

Selling price of bonds ($10,000 × 105%)	$10,500
Plus accrued interest ($10,000 × 8% × 3/12)	200
Less commissions and expenses	(350)
Proceeds from the sale	$10,350

The gain on the sale is

Selling price	$10,500
Less commissions and expenses	(350)
Less carrying value of the investment (at cost)	10,000
Gain	$ 150

The entry to record the sale is as follows:

Cash	10,350	
Interest income		200
Investment in Charlie Corporation bonds		10,000
Gain on sale of investment		150

Gains and losses on disposal are recognized on the income statement as part of income from continuing operations. If securities have been purchased at various times, for different amounts, and then some are subsequently sold, the *average cost* is used to determine gains or losses. The average cost is used to discourage manipulation.

For example, suppose that an investor holds 200 convertible preferred shares, of which 100 were purchased at $50 and 100 at $70. If the investor sells 60 shares at $65, is there a gain or a loss? If management wished to recognize a gain, they would sell the shares purchased at $50; if they wished to report a loss, they would sell the shares purchased at $70. The intent of using the *average cost*, therefore, is to prevent the use of the specific-identification inventory method to "manage" earnings.

Amortization of Premium or Discount

What happens if debt securities are bought for an amount other than face value, for example, at 98 or 104? The investment is recorded at its cost, which is greater or less than the face amount of the debt. If the investment is a *temporary investment*, any difference between the face value and the purchase price is ignored. The carrying value stays at the acquisition cost.

However, if the investment is a portfolio investment, "it would be appropriate to amortize any discount or premium arising on purchase over the period to maturity." [*CICA* 3050.19] If an investor does intend to hold a debt instrument to maturity, then any premium or discount should be amortized in order to bring the carrying value up to face value at maturity. Otherwise, a substantial gain or loss will be recognized at maturity. This is particularly true when the investment is in so-called *zero coupon* bonds that carry little or no interest; such bonds are purchased at a very low price relative to their face value. The implicit interest must then be recognized by amortizing the discount.

General practice is to amortize the acquisition premium or discount on a fixed-term debt instrument over the remaining life of the instrument *if*

1. it is the *intent* of management to hold a marketable financial instrument to maturity, or
2. the instrument is not marketable, and therefore the investor *must* hold it to maturity, or
3. the instrument is intentionally structured with a zero or token interest rate and is intended by the issuer to be sold at a deep discount.

Of course, *materiality* is also a factor. If the amortization has no material impact on the investor's reported financial results (including the impact of any ultimate gain or loss at maturity), then there is no point to amortizing any premium or discount. For companies that invest in debt instruments only as a minor activity, the materiality convention may well result in there being no amortization even if any one of the three conditions listed above exists.

There are two methods of amortization, the *straight-line* and *effective yield* methods. Straight-line is simpler and is much more common in practice and is the only one that will be illustrated in this chapter. However, the effective yield method is used by financial institutions (wherein investment in debt instruments is a major activity) and may be used by other investors when investing in zero coupon instruments. The effective yield method is illustrated (from the issuer's point of view) in Chapter 13.

Example: Purchase at Discount

Wooden Company acquires $100,000 face amount of Olsen Corporation 7% bonds for 98, or $98,000 on 1 January 20X1, and intends to hold the bonds until they mature on 31 December 20X4. The bonds pay interest semi-annually on 30 June and 31 December. Wooden has acquired the bonds at a *discount* of $2,000. Assume that the discount is amortized over the four years using the straight-line method; thus $2,000 ÷ 4, or $500, of the discount is amortized each year, or $250 for each six-month interest period. The entries to record the investment and interest income in 20X1 are as follows:

1 January 20X1 — To record investment in bonds to be held to maturity

Long-term investment in debt securities: Olsen bonds	98,000	
Cash		98,000

30 June 20X1 — To record first receipt of interest and amortization of discount

Cash ($100,000 × 7% × 6/12)	3,500	
Long-term investment in debt securities: Olsen bonds	250	
Investment income: Interest		3,750

31 December 20X1 — To record second receipt of interest and amortization of discount

Cash ($100,000 × 7% × 6/12)	3,500	
Long-term investment in debt securities: Olsen bonds	250	
Investment income: Interest		3,750

At 31 December 20X1, the investment in Olsen bonds is carried at $98,500, which is the amortized cost of the investment. The entry to record receipt of interest payments and amortization of discount is repeated from 20X2 through 20X4. At 31 December 20X4, the investment in Olsen Corporation bonds has increased by $500 per year for four years, and hence the carrying value of the investment on this date is its face amount of $100,000. On this date, Olsen pays the face amount of the bonds to bond holders and retires the debt.

Suppose Wooden paid more than the face of the bonds, say $102,000. The excess over the face amount is a premium. At acquisition, the bonds would be recorded at $102,000, but over the period to their maturity the $2,000 premium would be amortized, reducing the carrying amount (and reducing investment income) each year by the amount of amortization.

Basket Purchases of Securities

A purchase of two or more classes of securities for a single lump sum is a basket purchase. The total purchase price must be allocated to the different types of securities. The general principles are as follows:

- When the market price of each class of security is known, the proportional method of allocation is used, wherein the total cost is allocated in proportion to the market values of the various securities in the basket.

- If the market price is not known for a class of security, the incremental method can be used, wherein the purchase price is allocated first to the securities with known prices, and then the remainder of the lump-sum purchase price is attributed to the class of investment that does not have a market price.

The incremental method is not a lot of help when more than one security in the basket does not have a market price. In this case, recourse had best be made to pricing models offered in finance. Since few accountants are expert at the pricing of financial instruments, valuations may be obtained from independent financial consultants in order to allocate the total purchase price.

Investments Made in a Foreign Currency

It is not unusual for an enterprise to purchase equity or debt instruments that are priced in a foreign currency. The purchase price must be converted into Canadian dollars for recording on the Canadian investor's books and reporting in the investor's financial statements. To record the purchase, the exchange rate on or about the date of purchase is used.

For example, assume that LeBlanc Ltd. purchases 20,000 shares of AllAm Inc., a U.S. corporation. The purchase price is U.S. $65 per share, for a total of U.S. $1,300,000. At the time of the purchase, the U.S. dollar is worth Cdn. $1.35. The purchase would be recorded (in Cdn. dollars) as follows:

Investment in AllAm Inc.	1,755,000	
Cash (U.S. $1,300,000 × Cdn. $1.35)		1,755,000

This entry establishes the cost of the investment to LeBlanc, and will be the carrying value of the investment. Changes in the value of the U.S. dollar in subsequent reporting periods are irrelevant to the cost of an equity investment.

For debt instruments, the issue is a bit more complicated. Debt instruments, by definition, are payable in a given amount of currency. When the debt is stated or *denominated* in a currency other than the investor's reporting currency, the equivalent value of the instrument in the reporting currency changes as the exchange rate changes. Therefore, an investment in foreign currency-denominated bonds must be restated on every balance sheet date to the equivalent amount in Canadian dollars, using the exchange rate at the balance sheet date (known as the spot rate). The change in Canadian dollar equivalents between balance sheet dates is an exchange gain or loss, and is reported as follows:

- for investments in short-term debt instruments or in debt instruments that have no fixed maturity date, the exchange gain or loss for a period is included in the determination of net income for the period;

- for investments in long-term debt instruments that have a fixed maturity date, each year's exchange gain or loss *is deferred and amortized over the remaining life of the instrument.*

The *defer-and-amortize* approach for long-term investments in debt securities is a Canadian specialty — no other country takes this approach. It was initially developed with a view towards smoothing the fluctuations of the substantial U.S.-dollar-denominated *debt* of some large Canadian corporations, but is applied to monetary *investments* as well. The accounting for the defer-and-amortize approach will be illustrated (from the standpoint of the debtor) in Chapter 13.

The defer-and-amortize approach tends to smooth reported exchange gains and losses only if exchange rates move up and down over the life of the debt instrument. If the exchange rate movement tends to be in one direction (e.g., the almost continual climb of the Japanese yen and the Swiss franc), the defer-and-amortize approach actually increases the volatility of earnings because each successive year's gain or loss is amortized over a shorter remaining period to maturity.

> The AcSB has twice issued Exposure Drafts that, among other proposals, would eliminate the defer-and-amortize approach for long-term monetary items. Eliminating this approach would be a step toward international harmonization, since no other country uses the defer-and-amortize approach. The most recent ED was issued in May 1996, but the proposals contained therein have not yet been considered further by the AcSB. It is almost certain that this rather bizarre approach will be abolished at some time in the future, but it seems impossible to predict just when.

DISCLOSURE FOR PASSIVE INVESTMENTS

The disclosure requirements for temporary investments and portfolio investments have, traditionally, been modest. For both temporary and portfolio investments, the *CICA Handbook* has, for decades, recommended disclosure only of the following:

1. the basis of valuation (e.g., cost or market), and
2. the quoted market value of any *marketable securities* that are included in temporary investments or portfolio investments.

More recently, disclosure recommendations have increased appreciably with the addition of Section 3860, "Financial Instruments," in 1996. Effective for fiscal years beginning on or after 1 January 1997, recommended disclosure is expanded to include extensive disclosures for financial assets, by class:

- *Significant terms and conditions*. This disclosure is meant to help financial statement users assess the amount, timing, and uncertainty of cash flows related to the investment.

- *Interest rate risk*. Financial statement readers must be informed of the *effective* interest rate that is embedded in the purchase price, and any maturity dates or contractual repricing dates prior to maturity.

- *Credit risk*. An investor assumes credit risk when lending money to another company, which is what investing in a debt instrument amounts to. What if they don't pay? Collateral is often present to protect the investor. In any event, a company must disclose the maximum credit risk it has accepted, which would be limited to the face value of the investment.

- *Fair value*. Market value information is included in financial statements. While market value is not recognized, it is disclosed. For marketable securities, values are readily determinable. If long-term investments are not marketable, present value could be determined using current market interest rates, as a surrogate for market value.

Disclosure recommendations are not always slavishly followed in practice, even by major corporations. Time will tell just how extensive (and how useful) companies' actual disclosures will be.

CONCEPT REVIEW

1. How is the price of a bond determined if the bond is purchased on the open market between interest dates?
2. Explain the two methods of accounting for a *basket purchase* of securities.
3. Suppose a company buys U.S. bonds, denominated in U.S. dollars, as an investment. How should the bonds be valued on the investor's balance sheet at year-end?

LOWER OF COST OR MARKET

When the value of an investment falls below its acquisition cost, an economic loss has occurred. Accounting practice on recognition of the loss varies, however, depending on whether the investment is classified as temporary or long-term:

- If the investment is temporary, the loss is recognized by applying the *lower-of-cost-or-market (LCM)* rule. However, the LCM rule usually is applied to the temporary investment portfolio as a whole, and therefore the loss may not actually be recognized if the value of other temporary investments has risen enough to offset the loss.

- If the investment is long-term, the loss will be recognized (through a write-down of the investment's carrying value) only if management judges the loss in value to be *other than a temporary decline*. [CICA 3050.20] Management has a great deal of flexibility in deciding when, if ever, to record a decline in market value.

The *CICA Handbook* recommends that companies disclose the market value of marketable securities in a note to the financial statements, but the disclosure is made in the aggregate for the portfolio as a whole, and therefore unrecognized losses on individual investments are not likely to be revealed in the notes.

Lower of Cost or Market for Temporary Investments

The *CICA Handbook* recommends that "When the market value of temporary investments has declined below the carrying value, they should be carried at market." [*CICA* 3010.06] There are two approaches to applying the lower of-cost-or-market (LCM) rule:

1. the allowance method, in which the value of the temporary investments has determined *for the portfolio as a whole* and is compared to the cost of the portfolio; any overall decline in value is recorded in an *allowance* account (or *contra* account, or offset account); or
2. the direct write-down method, wherein the LCM rule is applied to each individual investment and any decline in market value below cost is recorded as a direct write-down of the carrying value of the investment.

Under the allowance method, the allowance can be reduced if market values recover, but in the direct write-off method, the written-down amount becomes the new carrying value and the write-down is not restored if the market improves. The direct write-down method is seldom used for temporary investments, although it is the method that is used for long-term portfolio investments, as will be discussed later in the chapter.

Using the **allowance method**, the investment or portfolio of investments is carried at cost and, should the market value of the portfolio decline to an amount below the cost at the balance sheet date, an allowance is established to reduce the cost value to market. The following example illustrates the application of the allowance method.

Assume that Zero Limited invested temporarily idle cash in three short-term investments as follows:

White common, 500 shares @ $20	$10,000
Blue common, 300 shares @ $25	7,500
Red preferred, 200 shares @ $35	7,000
Total	$24,500

On 31 December 20X1, the quoted market prices were: White common, $17; Blue common, $28; Red preferred, $34. The aggregate cost and aggregate market value for the portfolio of investments:

Stock	Number of Shares	Cost	Market
White common	500	@ $20 = $10,000	@ $17 = $ 8,500
Blue common	300	@ 25 = 7,500	@ 28 = 8,400
Red preferred	200	@ 35 = 7,000	@ 34 = 6,800
Total		$24,500	$23,700

Since total cost, $24,500, is more than total market value, $23,700, a lower-of-cost-or-market (LCM) adjustment of $800 is required. Notice that there has been a $1,500 decline in market value in the White common shares, and a $200 decline in the Red preferred. However, the $900 increase in the Blue common shares is allowed to counter some of the decline, and the required allowance is based on totals.

31 December 20X1 — To record the required allowance

Loss on temporary investments (I/S)	800	
Allowance to reduce temporary investments		
to market (B/S)		800

Reporting for 20X1
  Income statement:

Loss on temporary investments	$ 800

  Balance sheet:
    Current assets:

Temporary investments, at cost	$24,500	
Less: Allowance to reduce to market	800	$23,700

When a temporary investment is sold, any amount in the allowance account is disregarded. After all, the allowance relates to the total portfolio and not to any single part. The allowance account is adjusted only at the balance sheet date.

To illustrate: On 26 January 20X2, Zero sold all of its shares of Blue (for $26 per share) and Red for ($33 per share.) This transaction would be recorded as follows: 26 January, 20X2:

Cash (300 × $26) + (200 × $33)	14,400	
Loss on sale of securities	100	
Temporary investments (300 × $25) + (200 × $35)		14,500

To conclude this example, assume that, on 18 September 20X2, Zero Limited purchased 600 common shares of Black Corporation for $23 per share:

Temporary investments	13,800
Cash	13,800

At the end of 20X2, the quoted market prices were: White shares, $16; and Black shares, $25.50. The aggregate cost and aggregate market value for the portfolio are calculated as follows:

Stock	Number of Shares	Cost	Market
White common	500	@$20 = $10,000	@$16.00 = $ 8,000
Black common	600	@$23 = 13,800	@ 25.50 = 15,300
Total		$23,800	$23,300

The allowance account has a credit balance of $800 carried over from the end of 20X1. However, the market value of the portfolio at the end of 20X2 is only $500 less than cost. Therefore, the following entry must be made to reduce the allowance account by $300:

31 December 20X2 — to adjust allowance

Allowance to reduce temporary investments (B/S)	300	
Loss recovery on temporary investments (I/S)		300

Reporting for 20X2

Income statement

Loss (recovery) on temporary investments	($300)
Loss on sales of securities	100
Net loss (recovery)	($200)

Balance sheet

Current assets

Temporary investments, at cost	$23,800	
Less: Allowance to reduce to market	(500)	$23,300

The allowance method allows the portfolio to be recorded on an ongoing basis at cost. Any erosion of the total market value of the portfolio below cost is accounted for by the use of the allowance account to reduce the net value of the portfolio to a market value. Because the allowance account cannot have a debit balance, the carrying value of the portfolio never increases to an amount greater than its historical cost. There can, however, be recoveries of previous losses due to increases in market values. Such recoveries, or further write-downs, are combined on the income statement with the actual gains and losses on sales during the period.

Notice that the allowance method makes it possible to avoid the need to write down a "loser" whose erosion of market value is offset by the remainder of a "winning" portfolio. Should this bother you? Remember that market values may not be stable. Market values can fluctuate significantly, and thus the use of an allowance, and the netting of unrealized gains and losses is more justifiable when this lack of stability is acknowledged.

This example is based on investments in shares, but could just as easily be based on investments in debt instruments, whose market values also fluctuate. Market values of debt instruments are based on the present value of future cash flows, discounted at risk-adjusted current market interest rates. When market interest rates fluctuate, so does market value. If the credit rating of the borrower changes, the market value of the investment will also fluctuate, as the risk attached to future cash flow is changed, becoming either more likely or less likely. This, again, changes the risk premium appropriately included in the discount rate.

For tax purposes, gains and losses on investments are taxable, or tax deductible, only when realized through a transaction. Thus, no losses on write-down or subsequent reversals of these write-downs, would be taxable. This creates a temporary difference between tax and book measurements of income, and future tax liabilities result. The temporary difference reverses when the investment is sold.

Write-Downs of Portfolio Investments

The lower-of-cost-or-market rule is applied to portfolio investments, but only to a limited extent. There are three characteristics of LCM when applied to long-term portfolio investments that are different from LCM as applied to temporary investments:

1. The market value test is applied individually to each investment rather than to the portfolio as a whole.

2. A write-down is made only "when there has been a loss in value of an investment that is other than a temporary decline." [*CICA* 3050.20]

3. If an investment is written down, the write-down is recorded directly as a reduction in the carrying value of the investment, which then becomes the new carrying value; the allowance method is not used. The write-down cannot be reversed later if the market value increases in years subsequent to the write-down.

The direct write-off method treats each type of investment as a separate account. Therefore, if at the balance sheet date the carrying value of an investment is greater than its market value, and if the loss in value is judged to be a permanent impairment of value, the investment is written down and a loss is recognized. The new carrying value is *not* adjusted if the shares subsequently increase in market value.

The big issue in write-downs of long-term investments is that of the *permanence* of the decline in value. Obviously, this is a question of professional judgement, and is dependent on the facts of each individual situation. The *CICA Handbook* lists several guidelines for determining whether an impairment of value has occurred. A permanent impairment of value may be indicated by conditions such as

(a) a prolonged period during which the quoted market value of the investment is less than its carrying value;
(b) severe losses by the investee in the current period or current and prior periods;
(c) continued losses by the investee for a period of years;
(d) suspension of trading in the securities;
(e) liquidity or going concern problems of the investee; or
(f) the current appraised value of the investee's assets is less than its book value.   [*CICA* 3050.24]

Note that only the first of these situations refers to market value. The others all represent circumstances in which the going concern value of the shares (i.e., what the investment is "buying" for the investor) is impaired. Although these guidelines are offered by the AcSB in order to facilitate the judgemental process, there is a considerable degree of flexibility offered to management. If there is an impairment of value, management may well "manage" the timing (and extent) of the loss recognition to minimize the damage done to its reported results. The AcSB has attempted to strengthen the hand of auditors in dealing with managements who refuse to acknowledge that a permanent decline has occurred by adding the following:

> However, when a condition, indicating that an impairment in value of an investment may have occurred, has persisted for a period of three or four years, there is a general presumption that there has been a loss in value which is other than a temporary decline. This presumption can only be rebutted by persuasive evidence to the contrary.   [*CICA* 3050.24]

In other words, management's flexibility is limited to three or four years after the decline in value first becomes apparent.

To illustrate the direct write-down of portfolio investments, refer to the facts of the Zero Limited example, above, at the end of 20X1, except now we'll assume that investments are all considered to be long-term. Assume also that the impairment in value of White common shares is judged to be permanent, but that the decline in the market value of Red shares is not judged to be a permanent impairment. The only entry that would be made would be to reduce the carrying value of the White shares from cost to market.

Loss on decline in value of long-term investments	1,500	
Investment in White common shares		1,500

The loss would be reported on the income statement. The investment account now has a balance of $8,500, which *cannot* be written back up to original cost if market value subsequently recovers. If and when the investment is sold, the proceeds are compared to the $8,500 balance in the account to determine the gain or loss. Again, for tax purposes, such losses are only deductible when realized, so the 20X1 loss is only tax deductible when the shares are actually sold. This creates a *timing difference* (or *temporary difference*) in the financial statements, and deferred taxes will result.

The market value of the Red shares, lower than cost, will be disclosed in the financial statements, but it is not recognized unless and until deemed permanent or the investment is sold.

Market value is sometimes difficult to ascertain for long-term investments in shares which may, by definition, be non-marketable. For example, if a corporation holds 10% of the common shares of another corporation whose shares are closely held and never traded, how would market value be assessed? Clearly, in these conditions, the financial health of the investee company is a major concern, but a lot is left to judgement.

The scope for financial statement manipulation in LCM write-downs of investments is obvious. First, if there is a portfolio of investments that includes some winners and some losers, there is an obvious incentive to classify all of them as short-term, so that the net balance is all that is considered when evaluating the need for a write-down. If on the other hand, there are only losers, or large losers, then classifying these investments as long-term will provide some scope to delay a potential write-down if the criteria for permanence are not met. Thus, a canny financial statement reader will carefully search for an indication of market value in the notes.

MARKET VALUE METHOD

A different method of accounting for marketable securities, both debt and equity, is the market value method. The market value method is used by companies whose primary business involves investing in the securities of others. Market valuation is required by law for mutual funds (technically known as open-ended investment funds), and is also used by other investment companies, insurance companies, and securities dealers and brokers. Under this method, each individual security investment is revalued at each financial statement date to the current market value of the securities held. The market value method is summarized as follows:

1. At date of acquisition, investments are recorded at cost.
2. After acquisition, each individual investment account balance is adjusted at the end of the accounting year to the current market value of the securities held. The adjusted amount then becomes the new carrying value for subsequent accounting.
3. Interest earned and dividends declared are recognized by the investor as investment revenue.

4. Increases or decreases in the market value of the securities are recognized at the end of each accounting period. One of the following approaches is used:

   a. **Current approach** — the price change during the current period is recognized as investment revenue (or loss) in the current income statement, clearly labelled as the increase or decrease in market value.

   b. **Deferral approach** — the price change during the current period is recorded as a deferred item in owners' equity, labelled *unrealized market gain or loss*. When a security is subsequently sold, the difference between its carrying value in the investment account and its original cost must be removed from its deferred status in the unrealized account and recognized as investment revenue. Any additional difference is recognized as gain or loss on sale of investments.

5. On disposal of the investment, the difference between the carrying value at that date and its sale price is recognized as a gain or loss on disposal.

There are two advantages to using the market value approach:

1. the balance sheet gives a more accurate picture of the *value* of the company's investment holdings, and

2. the use of market values prevents the investor (i.e., management) from manipulating earnings by choosing when to sell investments and thereby trigger accounting recognition of gains and losses.

When investments are carried at cost, managers can increase the level of reported earnings by selling those investments whose market value is well above cost in order to recognize an accounting gain. The proceeds then can be re-invested in securities of similar type and risk (although not usually in *identical* securities; that would be a transparent transaction, known as a **wash transaction**, that would risk not being recognized as a true sale by auditors). Selective sales of investments in order to "manufacture" an accounting gain is referred to as *churning the portfolio*. Market valuation of investments removes the motivation for portfolio churning, especially under the *current approach* of recognizing gains, see 4(a) above, because gains are recognized whether or not they have been realized.

Some managers and accountants object to the market value approach because they claim that it is a departure from the qualitative criteria of *conservatism* and *objectivity*. It departs from conservatism, they claim, because gains are recognized before they are realized. Market valuation departs from objectivity because it uses a subjective market valuation on the balance sheet date that will change the very next day. Cost, in contrast, is a stable and unchanging amount that is evidenced by an actual transaction, which makes it highly objective.

Supporters for carrying investments at market value cite the qualitative characteristics of *relevance* and *freedom from bias* in response. For evaluating the investment performance of management, financial statement readers need to know the market values of investments. Only market values are *relevant* to the decisions of users. *Freedom from bias* is cited because market values are determined in an open market over which the reporting enterprise has no control. Earnings and balance sheet values cannot be influenced by the motivations of managers.

A crucial characteristic that underlies the use of market valuation is that the earnings process has satisfied the requirements for revenue recognition. The events that gave rise to the gains and losses in market value have already occurred, and no significant effort is required to realize those gains and losses. To realize the gains and losses, all management has to do is pick up the telephone and call the company's broker. For a financial statement user, the fact that the investment manager does not pick up the phone to sell an investment is as important as the fact that she or he does sell the investment. For example, suppose that a company buys shares in a gold mining company for $10,000 on 1 May 20X1. After the purchase, rumours of a major discovery of gold deposits circulate in the investment community and the value of the shares quadruples to $40,000 by year-end. The manager decides not to sell the shares.

Now suppose that during the next year, the rumour turns out to be false and the market value declines to $11,000, just slightly above the investment's original cost, whereupon the investment manager decides to sell the shares. The results of this market activity will be reported in the investing corporation's financial statements as follows for the two years under both the cost and market value approaches:

Date	Investment Activity	Market Value	Reported Gain (Loss)	
			Cost Method	Market Value Method
1 May 20X1	buy shares	$ 10,000		
31 Dec. 20X1	hold shares	$ 40,000	nil	$ 30,000
1 October 20X2	sell shares	$ 11,000	$ 1,000	$ (29,000)

Under the cost method, there is no gain or loss reported in 20X1 because the gain has not been realized. When the shares are sold in 20X2, a gain of $1,000 is realized and recognized. Under the market value method, the increase in the market price of $30,000 is reported in 20X1, while the loss in market value of $29,000 is reported in 20X2. The market value method reveals that the manager cost the company (i.e., through an *opportunity cost*) $29,000 through her or his decision not to sell the shares while they were high. The market value approach reports the results of management's *decisions* while the cost approach reports only the results of management's *actions*. But in investing, actions *not* taken are just as important as actions taken.

Presently in Canada, mutual funds are required by law to value their investments at market values so that their investors can evaluate the performance of fund managers. Also, market valuation enables the regular calculation of net asset value per share, a prime indicator of investment performance of mutual funds. Market value recognition is also normally used for those firms whose primary line of business includes investing in the securities of others. Some specialized industries, such as closed-end investment companies, life insurance companies, fire and casualty insurance companies, and brokers and dealers in securities carry equity securities at market with unrealized gains and losses generally recognized as part of the current year's income (or loss). In some industries, notably in insurance, the reported market values are *moving averages*, such as an average of the year-end market values over the most recent five years. Moving averages are used instead of point values in order to *smooth* the reported earnings fluctuations.

In the U.S., the FASB has adopted the market approach for investments in securities *except* for debt securities that are being held to maturity and for situations where there is significant influence or control. All companies that comply with FASB standards are required to carry their investments at market value, as follows:

- marketable securities that are *held for resale* are reported in the balance sheet at market value, and unrealized gains and losses are reported on the income statement;

- other securities *not held for resale* are also reported at market value, but unrealized gains and losses are reported as deferred credits as a separate component of shareholders' equity until the securities are sold.

A similar standard was issued by the IASC in December 1998. IAS 39, *Financial Instruments: Recognition and Measurement*, recommends that all temporary investments, whether in debt or equity instruments, be "remeasured" to fair value at each balance sheet date. Gains and losses on temporary investments shoulds be recognized in income immediately.

In Canada, a 1994 exposure draft would have required a broad range of investments to be carried at market value. However, the responses to this proposal were not favourable, and many respondents worried about the reliability of market value measures in a demonstrably volatile stock market. Many companies were concerned about the impact of this requirement on income and key financial statement ratios.

As a result, disclosure and classification sections of the exposure draft were accepted, but the measurement portions were not brought into the *CICA Handbook*. Thus, there is a major difference between Canadian and U.S. GAAP in this respect.

Why have the FASB and IASC abandoned the historic cost concept? Part of the reason is that the users of financial statement information have indicated that market value is more meaningful to them than cost in most situations, and standard-setters have reacted accordingly. Significant political pressure for the change was present, too; the failure of a string of savings and loan institutions in the U.S. helped this cause along. These financial institution failures, which cost customers, investors, central deposit insurance agencies, and U.S. taxpayers billions of dollars, were a major financial scandal. Subsequently, many thought that the financial statements of these entities, that showed investments at cost, would have reflected financial position more accurately had the investments been valued at market. There was impetus for change.

We can expect to hear more on the issue of market valuation for investments in the coming years, as significant differences between Canadian and international GAAP are often targets for standard-setters!

CONCEPT REVIEW

1. What is an advantage to using the *allowance* method of writing down temporary investments, instead of the *direct write-down* method?

2. Suppose that the value of a company's portfolio investment falls below its cost. Would the carrying value of the investment necessarily be written down? Explain.

3. Why does the use of market value for recording investments make it more difficult for managers to manipulate reported earnings?

EQUITY METHOD

The equity method is used for recording strategic investments in equity securities. It also is used for reporting equity investments in significantly influenced investees, and it may be used for reporting non-consolidated subsidiaries in the parent's special purpose financial statements.

Conceptually, the equity method treats the investee company as if it were condensed into one balance sheet item and one income statement item and then merged into the investor company at the proportion owned by the investor. The equity method is sometimes called the **one-line consolidation method** because it results in the same effect on the investor's earnings and retained earnings as would result from consolidating the financial statements of the investor and investee companies but does so without combining both companies' financial statements.

In its simplest form, the equity method requires that the investment account represent the investor's proportionate share of the book value of the investee and that the investment income represent the investor's proportionate share of the investee's income. Assume, for initial simplicity, that Tanford Computer Company (TCC) makes an initial investment of $100,000 for 40% of the voting shares of Rinceton Software on 1 January 20X1. In 20X1, Rinceton has earnings of $30,000 and pays dividends totalling $10,000. If the investment is accounted for by the equity method, TCC will make the following two entries at the end of 20X1:

To record TCC's share of Rinceton's net income

Investment in Rinceton Software	12,000	
Investment income ($30,000 × 40%)		12,000

To record receipt of dividends from Rinceton

Cash	4,000	
Investment in Rinceton Software ($10,000 × 40%)		4,000

Note that dividends from the investee are not recorded as investment income. Rather, they are viewed as a *dis*-investment, that is, a return *of* the investment to the investor, rather than a return *on* the investment. Under the equity method, the investor company records its proportionate share of the investee earnings as investment income and increases its investment account by this amount. When the investee pays dividends, its net worth is reduced, and thus the investment account of the investor is reduced.

Following the two entries for 20X1, the investment account for Rinceton will reflect the following:

Investment in Rinceton Software, at equity

Original investment	$100,000
Proportionate share of earnings of investee ($30,000 × 40%)	12,000
Dividends received from investee ($10,000 × 40%)	(4,000)
Ending balance	$108,000

The difference between investee earnings and investee dividends is the amount of earnings accruing to the investor that the investee retained, or the unremitted earnings of the investee. Thus, the equity-based investment account is equal to the original investment plus the investor's proportionate share of the investee's *cumulative retained earnings* since the investment was made. In this sense, the equity method represents an extension of accrual accounting to investments in common shares. However, the balance sheet doesn't reflect the cost of the investment anymore. This number isn't market value, either, and is hard to interpret.

When the investee reports extraordinary items, discontinued operations, and cumulative effects of accounting changes, the investor company must separately report its *proportionate share* of these items on its income statement in the same way it would if they were incurred by the investor company (assuming that they remain *material* items on the income statement of the investor, which usually is larger than the investee).

The equity method can get more complicated. It is usually necessary to make certain adjustments to the amount of annual income that is recorded on the investor's books.

1. When an investor company acquires the equity securities of an investee company, it may pay more for the securities than their book value. In that situation, the investor's proportionate share of the investee's net income must be adjusted. The adjustment is to amortize the difference between the investor's original investment and the underlying fair value (at the date of acquisition) of the net assets acquired.

   Every time there is an investment to be accounted for under the equity method, it is necessary to (1) measure the fair value of net assets acquired, (2) compare the proportionate fair value to the price paid, and (3) determine the amount of goodwill, if any.

   The fair value of assets and goodwill are not explicitly recognized under the equity method, but *the investor's share of income must be decreased by appropriate amounts of amortization on both fair values of depreciable assets and goodwill.*

2. If the investor and the investee have transactions with each other during the year, either company, or both companies, will have the profits from these transactions recorded in income. For example, assume that the investor sold inventory to the investee at a profit of $25,000. If the investee subsequently sold these goods to a third party, then the inter-company sales price is validated, or realized, in this subsequent transaction and no particular accounting concerns arise.

   However, if the inventory is still on the investee's balance sheets, then the profit is *unrealized* as far as the investor is concerned. It is not acceptable to recognize an increase in net income if all that's happened is a sale to a "customer" that the vendor can significantly influence. Therefore, the equity method, properly applied, involves *adjustments for unrealized inter-company profits.*

Equity Method Illustrated

On 2 January 20X1, Giant Company purchased 3,600 shares of the 18,000 outstanding common shares of Small Corporation for $300,000 cash. Two Giant Company senior executives were elected to the Small Corporation board of directors. Giant is deemed to be able to exercise significant influence over Small's operating and financial policies, so the equity method of accounting for the investment is appropriate. At the acquisition of the 20% interest in Small, Giant records its investment as follows:

Investment in Small, at equity	300,000	
Cash		300,000

The balance sheet for Small at 2 January 20X1, and estimated market values of its assets and liabilities are as follows:

	Book Value	Market Value	Difference
Cash and receivables	$ 100,000	$ 100,000	$ 0
Inventory (FIFO basis)	400,000	405,000	5,000
Plant and equipment			
(10-year remaining life)	500,000	700,000	200,000
Land	150,000	165,000	15,000
Total assets	$1,150,000	$1,370,000	
Less: liabilities	(150,000)	(150,000)	0
Net assets	$1,000,000	$1,220,000	$220,000

Giant bought 20% of Small's shareholders' equity, which has a book value of $200,000 ($1,000,000 × 20%); $200,000 is the net asset value of the proportion of Small purchased by Giant. Giant paid $300,000 for its 20% interest in Small. The amount above book value that Giant paid, $100,000, is called the purchase price discrepancy. The accounting problem is to determine why Giant paid that much, and then to account for the acquisition price accordingly.

First, each asset and liability is examined to see if book value understates fair market value. To the extent this is true, the $100,000 excess is explained. If there is a remaining unexplained residual, it is attributed to goodwill, on the assumption that intangible assets, which promise future cash flow, explain the purchase price.

The "difference" column shows the specific assets whose market value exceeds book value. Giant acquired a portion (20%) of each of these items, including the amount by which market value exceeds book value.

	Book Value	Market Value	Difference	20% of Difference
Inventory	400,000	405,000	5,000	1,000
Plant & equipment (10-year remaining life)	500,000	700,000	200,000	40,000
Land	150,000	165,000	15,000	3,000
Totals	$1,050,000	$1,270,000	$220,000	$44,000

Thus, $44,000 of the $100,000 purchase price premium over book value that Giant paid can be identified with these specific assets. The remaining difference, $56,000, cannot be specifically identified with any asset and therefore represents goodwill. Goodwill is defined as the excess of the amount invested in acquiring all or a portion of another firm over the fair value of the net identifiable assets acquired. Goodwill can also be computed as follows:

Computation of Goodwill Purchased by Giant Company

Purchase price (of 20% interest)		$ 300,000
Market value of identifiable assets	$1,370,000	
Less: Liabilities of Small	(150,000)	
Total market value of identifiable net assets acquired	$1,220,000	
Market value of 20% of identifiable net assets acquired:($1,220,000 × 20%)		(244,000)
Goodwill		$ 56,000

Giant, then, has acquired a 20% interest in Small at a cost of $300,000, and the items acquired can be represented as follows:

20% of the net book value of Small		$200,000
20% of excess of market value over book value for:		
Inventory (20% × 5,000)		$ 1,000
Plant and equipment (20% × 200,000)	40,000	
Land (20% × 15,000)	3,000	44,000
Goodwill		56,000
Total		$300,000

The equity method requires that Giant record its initial $300,000 investment in Small in one investment account, despite the fact that it has many components. No formal recognition is given to the various component parts of the investment. However, the amount of income recognized annually will be changed as a result of these components.

When Small disposes of any of the above items, either in the normal course of business or by asset sales, Giant must record appropriate adjustments to its investment account, through the annual entry that recognizes investment income.

For example, since Small uses FIFO to cost its inventory, the beginning inventory is treated as sold first during the coming year. Likewise, its plant and equipment is used and depreciated during the coming year. Since the valuation of these items from Giant's investment perspective is different from that recorded by Small, Giant will adjust annual investment income to reflect the using up of the difference between the market value and the book value of these assets.

Assuming that all of Small's beginning inventory is sold during 20X1, Small's cost of goods sold for 20X1 is understated by $1,000 from the single-entity (Giant) perspective. Also, depreciation is understated. If the plant and equipment has a remaining useful life of 10 years and Small uses straight-line depreciation, Giant needs to increase the depreciation expense for Small by $40,000 divided by 10 years, or $4,000 each year for the next 10 years.

Finally, the goodwill must be amortized over a period of 40 years or less. Assuming that Giant amortizes goodwill over the maximum period, the annual charge for goodwill amortization is $56,000 divided by 40, or $1,400 each year for the next 40 years.

No adjustments need be made for the excess of market value over book value for the land. Only if Small disposes of the land would an adjustment need to be made, showing that the cost of 20% of the land from the Giant perspective is understated by $3,000 on Small's books. Giant's proportionate share of any gain (loss) on disposal of the land would be decreased (increased) by $3,000.

Giant's income from its investment in Small requires adjusting entries to reflect the above analysis. Suppose that for the fiscal year ending 31 December 20X1, Small reports the following:

Income before discontinued operations	$ 80,000
Net earnings from discontinued operations	30,000
Net income	$110,000
Cash dividends, paid on December 31	$ 50,000

Furthermore, assume that Small sold goods to Giant for $46,000 during the year, and none have been resold by Giant at year-end. The goods originally cost Small $38,000, and thus Small has recorded an $8,000 increase in income that has not been confirmed by a transaction with an outside party. Since Giant owns 20% of Small, and records only 20% of Small's income, it must eliminate 20% of the gain, or $1,600 of the $8,000 unrealized gain.

Investment income is a combination of Giant's share of a variety of items.

Small's net income before discontinued operations ($80,000 × 20%)	$ 16,000
Cost of goods sold adjustment for the fair value of inventory purchased ($5,000 × 20%)	(1,000)
Additional depreciation on plant and equipment fair value ($40,000 ÷ 10)	(4,000)
Additional amortization of goodwill ($56,000 ÷ 40)	(1,400)
Elimination of unrealized inter-company profit in inventory ($8,000 × 20%)	(1,600)
Net investment income, ordinary income	$ 8,000

The investment revenue for 20X1, after all the adjustments, is $8,000 of ordinary income plus a gain from discontinued operations of $6,000 (i.e., $30,000 × 20%). These two items would be shown separately on the income statement. If no adjustments had been made, Giant would have recorded a total of $22,000 of income ($110,000 × 20%). This result of the equity method is quite common; less income than you might expect is recorded. This is the result because the investor very often pays more than book value for its interest in the investee, and resulting amortizations reduce income. Then, too, inter-company transactions are quite common, and elimination of unrealized portions can also reduce income.

At 31 December Giant would make the following entries to reflect its interest in the earnings of Small:

1. *To recognize investment income based on Giant's proportionate share of income reported by Small*

Investment in Small, at equity	14,000	
Investment income (as above)		8,000
Earnings from discontinued operations ($30,000 × 20%)		6,000

2. *To record the receipt of cash dividends paid by Small*

Cash ($50,000 × 20%)	10,000	
Investment in Small, at equity		10,000

After these entries are posted, the balance in the investment in Small account is $304,000.

Beginning balance (acquisition price)	$300,000
Proportionate share of Small's net income	14,000
Dividends received	(10,000)
Investment account balance, 31 December 20X1	$304,000

The total investment income Giant reports from its investment in Small is $14,000. Since Giant received $10,000 of this in the form of cash dividends, the net increase of its investment is $4,000. This amount is the increase in the investment account from the beginning to the end of the year.

Unrealized Profit Elimination

The example shown above involved an inter-company unrealized profit that had been recorded by the investee. This is called an **upstream** profit, because the transaction went from the bottom of the investment river (the investee) to the top (the investor). Since the investor only picks up their share of the investee's income, they also only pick up a partial, or 20%, elimination of the profit.

Assume instead that the transaction is **downstream**, a sale from the investor to the investee. Again, none of the inventory is sold at year-end. In this case, Giant has recorded, as part of its gross profit, an $8,000 sale that has not been confirmed by a sale to an outside party. No adjustment is made to the investor's sales or gross profit. Instead, investment income is reduced by the full $8,000 inter-company downstream unrealized profit. Thus, the bottom line net income for the investor company will reflect the elimination of the gross profit, but through a reduction of the investment income rather than by a reduction of the investor's reported gross profit.

The rule is that upstream unrealized profits are fractionally eliminated (the investor's share only) but downstream unrealized profits are eliminated in their entirety, because the full amount is in the investor's accounts.

Changing between the Cost and Equity Methods

An investor's ownership level and therefore level of influence over an investee company can change over time. An investor with a small ownership percentage using the cost method might acquire a sufficient number of additional shares or inter-company transactions, etc., to gain significant influence, thereby necessitating a change in accounting to the equity method. Alternatively, an investor currently using the equity method might sell shares, or there might be transactions in the other outstanding shares that deprive the investor of significant influence. For example, control could be acquired by an individual who is not receptive to the ideas of the smaller investor. The investor would be required to change accounting for its investment from the equity method to the cost method.

Changes from the Equity Method *to* the Cost Method. When the ownership influence falls below what is necessary to continue using the equity method, the investor must change to the cost method. At the transfer date, the carrying value of the investment under the equity method is regarded as the cost of the investment. Subsequent dividends received are included in investment income. Comparison of the carrying value and market value should be done to determine if an adjustment is necessary to reflect an impairment in value. There is no further accounting for goodwill or differences between the book value and the fair value of the assets of the investee.

Changes to the Equity Method *from* the Cost Method. When the ownership level in an investee accounted for by the cost method increases to the point where the investor has significant influence, the investment must be accounted for using the equity method. The recorded carrying value at the date of transfer is regarded as the initial cost of the investment, analogous to the purchase price if the investor were to acquire its interest on this date. From this point on, the accounting proceeds exactly as was described earlier for the equity method. The investor must determine the fair value of the net assets owned and determine the amount of goodwill as the difference between the recorded cost and the fair value of the net assets acquired as of the date that significant influence was obtained.

In neither case, whether changing from cost to equity or from equity to cost, is there any restatement of prior results. *This is not considered to be a change in accounting policy.* Instead, it is a consistent application of the criteria under which long-term equity investments are reported, and the change in method is the result of a change in circumstances rather than a discretionary choice by management.

CONSOLIDATION

A parent company is required to *consolidate* its financial statements with those of its subsidiaries when it issues general purpose financial statements. The parent company uses the cost or equity method to account for its investment during the year, but, at the end of the reporting period, must prepare consolidated financial statements for reporting to its shareholders and other financial statement users. Consolidated statement are prepared by combining the sets of financial statements into one, which is intended to portray the activities of the whole enterprise. This is an application of substance over form, as consolidated statements portray the economic entity that exists in substance, rather than relying on the legal form that has been used to organize the activities of an enterprise.

Consolidation of wholly-owned, parent founded subsidiaries is quite straight-forward. However, consolidation of a subsidiary that was acquired in a business combination can be more complex. Consolidation of purchased subsidiaries can follow one of two paths:

1. Pooling — The two companies are combined as though they were always one. Past results are reported on a combined basis and no fair values are recognized as a result of the transaction that brought the two parties together.

2. Purchase — The parent company acquires the subsidiary, and the two companies are combined as of that date. Fair market values of the subsidiary's assets are recognized from this acquisition transaction, including goodwill. Prior results are not combined.

In Canada, the purchase method must be used for any business combination where a purchaser — the controlling party — can be identified. Pooling may only be used in the rare instance where the two groups of shareholders that existed before the business combination emerge with equal power; that is, basically a 50/50 relationship in the combined entity. However, pooling applications are far more common in the U.S., since they have much more permissive criteria. Since purchase accounting is the dominant form of consolidation accounting in Canada, only its application will be discussed here.

It is important to understand that consolidation does not happen on anyone's books; there's a consolidation program in the parent's computer that accepts financial statements from the parent and the subsidiary as inputs, processes certain adjustments, and produces the consolidated financial statements.

Consolidation is mostly an additive process; the financial statements are added together, line by line. Common adjustments include

1. The investment account must be eliminated from the parent company's financial statements, and the corresponding equity accounts must be eliminated from the subsidiary's financial statements.

2. If net assets' book values reflected on the subsidiary's books on the date of acquisition are different from their market values on that date, the difference, called a fair value increment, must be recognized on the consolidated financial statements,

along with any goodwill inherent in the purchase price. This reflects the fact that the parent acquired assets, including intangible assets, at fair value.

3. If fair values (i.e., market values) were recognized, they must be amortized in subsequent years, as must goodwill.

4. Any portion of the subsidiary that is consolidated but is owned by non-controlling, or minority, subsidiary shareholders must be recognized.

5. Inter-company receivables and payables, and revenues and expenses must be eliminated so that the financial statements will only reflect transactions with outsiders.

6. If there are any inter-company unrealized profits at year-end, these must be eliminated so that income is not misstated.

A whole course in consolidations is often offered at the advanced accounting level in many accounting programs. We aren't going to go into that much depth here! The Appendix to this chapter contains a basic consolidation example, along with brief explanations of the elimination entries. This example will give you a taste of the consolidation process. However, it is worthwhile to take a look at the end result for a few minutes, even if you're not covering the Appendix material. Look at Exhibit 12-2 now. What should you notice about these consolidated results that are shown in the final column?

- Consolidated assets are higher than just the parent's alone, and also are different from just the parent and the subsidiary added together. The subsidiary's assets are written up (or down) to reflect their fair values on the date on acquisition. Goodwill inherent in the purchase price is recognized. Goodwill is shown with intangible assets.

- Assets and liabilities of the parent and the subsidiary are added together, and inter-company balances are eliminated.

- Also eliminated are the parent's investment account and investment revenue.

- The portion of the subsidiary that is not owned by the parent is included in consolidated totals, but the outside interests are reflected in consolidated financial statements via a balance sheet account and an income statement account that relate to the non-controlling interests.

- The consolidated income statement contains more expenses, as fair values recognized are amortized, as is goodwill.

- The consolidated income statement reflects eliminations for inter-company unrealized profits.

- Dividends reported are only those dividends paid by the *parent*.

- Equity accounts of the subsidiary that existed on acquisition are eliminated.

Consolidations get considerably more complicated. Many parent companies have more than one subsidiary, and all must be consolidated together, with all inter-company transactions eliminated. This can seem mind-boggling when there are 200 subsidiaries, but it's no big challenge for consolidation computer software as long as all of the inter-company transactions and balances are coded correctly.

Profit eliminations are potentially complex, too, when the impact on future income taxes (deferred taxes) is considered. Then, too, inter-company unrealized profits usually have an impact for multiple years, and appropriate entries must be made. The parent's percentage ownership in the subsidiary can change, either up or down. There are also many subtleties associated with fair value amortizations. We could go on, but we're sure you get the picture.

CASH FLOW STATEMENT

Companies often make short-term investments in highly liquid financial instruments such as certificates of deposit, guaranteed investment certificates, or treasury bills. This type of investment is a temporary use of cash in order to earn some return when the company has a temporary excess of cash. In Chapter 5, we pointed out that such financial instruments are considered to be cash equivalents, and therefore they are included in the definition of cash when the cash flow statement is prepared. Consequently, investments in cash equivalents do not appear in the cash flow statement, but instead are included in the cash balance.

For all other investments in debt and equity securities, the cash flow impacts occur in three ways:

1. there is a cash outflow when an investment is purchased;
2. cash payments are received by the investor (dividends or interest); and
3. cash is received when the investment is sold or is redeemed at maturity.

For any type of investment, the initial cash outflow is reported as an *investing activity* on the cash flow statement in the period that the investment is made. If the investment is partially a cash transaction and partially a non-cash exchange, only the cash portion appears on the cash flow statement.

Similarly, the net cash proceeds that the company receives when it sells or redeems an investment security is reported as a positive (inflow) amount in the investing activities section of the cash flow statement. Any gain or loss on disposal must be removed from net income when computing the operating cash flow, since a gain or loss is merely the difference between the cash proceeds and the investment's carrying value at the time of the sale.

For temporary and portfolio investments, dividends and interest received is reported as revenue on the income statement and should be separately disclosed on the cash flow statement. Investment income can be reported in either the operating section or the investing section, but the presentation should be consistent from period to period.

Portfolio investments might include bonds that were purchased at a substantial premium or discount. If management's intent is to hold the bonds to maturity, the company may well be amortizing the discount or premium. If so, then the amortization must be removed from the reported interest income.

Reporting the periodic cash flows for dividends received on strategic investments presents a somewhat greater challenge. If the investment is being reported on the equity basis, then

- cash received in dividends must be reported on the cash flow statement, along with other dividend income;
- the investor's share of the investee's earnings must be removed from net income when calculating the operating cash flow; and
- adjustments made to amortize goodwill and fair value increments must also be reversed out of net income.

Only the cash actually received for dividends is relevant for the cash flow statement.

If the strategic investment gives the investor *control* over the investee and the parent prepares consolidated statements, the cash flows between the parent and subsidiary are eliminated in consolidation and do not appear on the cash flow statement at all. However, any adjustments made in preparing the consolidated statements to amortize fair value increments and goodwill must be eliminated when preparing the cash flow statement. There really is no difference between these amortizations and others; all amortizations are reversed out when we compute operating cash flows.

DISCLOSURE OF STRATEGIC INVESTMENTS

Disclosures relating to strategic investments are generally more extensive than those recommended for passive or portfolio investments. There are two reasons for the more extensive disclosure.

1. By their nature, strategic investments are intended to extend the reach of the reporting enterprise and to increase the amount of non-arm's length transactions.
2. There are substantial differences between the *income* effects of strategic investments and their *cash flow* effects, as has been described in the preceding section.

The least extensive disclosure relates to controlled subsidiaries. When control exists, normal practice is to consolidate the subsidiaries and the parent, with the result that there is a single reporting entity that includes two or more separate legal entities. When the subsidiaries are consolidated, all inter-company transactions are eliminated and the several enterprises are reported as one.

Some companies list their consolidated subsidiaries in their annual reports, but this is a voluntary disclosure. Most companies do not tell the readers what the subsidiaries are, mainly because the subsidiaries are so thoroughly integrated into the parent's operations that their existence is irrelevant to most statement users.

However, if there are any subsidiaries in which the parent does not own 100%, the amount of the minority interest's equity in those subsidiaries must be shown as a credit amount between liabilities and shareholders' equity on the consolidated balance sheet, and the minority interest's share of the subsidiary's net income must be deducted on the consolidation income statement, if material.

Despite the portrayal of the economic entity via consolidated financial statements, creditors should ask for non-consolidated statements for any companies to which they extend credit or lend money. Creditors can seek repayment only from the individual legal entity (whether the parent or a subsidiary) to which they have extended credit — the consolidated entity is an accounting construct, not a legal reality.

If one company acquired another company during the accounting period — a business combination — the parent company must disclose the transaction and the amounts of the identifiable assets and liabilities that were acquired. The amount and form of consideration given for the purchase must also be disclosed, such as cash, common shares, preferred shares, long-term debt, etc. Only the amount of cash consideration is shown on the face of the cash flow statement, however.

Joint ventures are reported on the basis of proportionate consolidation. The notes to the consolidated statements should disclose summary financial amounts for its interests in joint ventures, such as the total current assets and long-term assets, current liabilities and long-term liabilities, major components of net income, and major categories of cash flow.[1]

The disclosures recommended by the *CICA Handbook* for investments in *significantly influenced* investees are quite extensive. They include disclosure of

- The amount of investment in significantly influenced companies.
- The basis of reporting each investment (i.e., cost or equity).
- The income from investments in significantly influenced investees, reported separately from other investment income.
- The difference between the price paid for the investment and the underlying net book value of the investee's net assets, and the accounting treatment (e.g., amortization policies) for the difference.

---

[1] Detailed disclosures are beyond the scope of this book, as they are dealt with in advanced accounting textbooks. For more detail, see Section 3055 of the *CICA Handbook*.

EXHIBIT 12-1
BCE INC.
Example of Investments Disclosure

Investments in associated and other companies

(Investments accounted for using the equity method, except where otherwise noted)

At December 31 (millions $ Cdn.)	Ownership (%) 1997	1996	1997	1996
Canadian Telecommunications				
Teleglobe Inc.	23.3	22.0	$ 279	$ 273
Maritime Telegraph and Telephone Company, Limited (a)	34.8	35.5	122*	182
Bruncor Inc.	44.9	45.0	147*	170
Telesat Canada (b)	58.7	58.7	92	158
ExpressVu Inc. (c)	90.0	39.5	—	14
Other			88	79
Investments, at cost			108	40
Nortel				
WilTel Communications, LLC	30.0	—	90	—
Telrad Telecommunication and Electronic Industries Ltd.	20.0	—	69	—
FIMACOM			—	25
ICL plc, at cost			129	157
Investments, at cost			104	81
Other			—	4
International Telecommunications				
Cable & Wireless Communications plc	14.2	—	1,138	—
Mercury Communications Limited	—	20.0	—	1,153
Bell Cablemedia plc	—	32.5	—	378
Jones Intercable, Inc.	31.4	31.9	443	417
Other			21	37
Investments, at cost			35	4
Directories			11	14
Corporate				
Investments, at cost			53	49
Total investments in associated and other companies			$2,929	$3,235

* As a result of the discontinued application of regulatory accounting provisions, BCE's investments in Maritime Telegraph and Telephone and Bruncor were reduced by $66 million and $31 million, respectively, representing BCE's share of the extraordinary item of these associated companies.

(a) **Maritime Telegraph and Telephone (MT&T)**
BCE's 34.8% (35.5% in 1996) interest represents 10,254,058 common shares in 1997 and 1996. A Nova Scotia statute provides that no more than 1,000 shares of MT&T may be voted by any one shareholder.

(b) **Telesat Canada**
At December 31, 1997 and December 31, 1996, BCE's voting interest was 26.1%.

(c) **ExpressVu**
During 1997, BCE increased its ownership interest in ExpressVu to 90% for a total cash consideration of $96 million and the transfer of 5.3 million shares that were held by an independent trustee at December 31, 1996 and, as a result, ExpressVu is now consolidated.

In practice, compliance with these recommendations is spotty. Materiality undoubtedly plays a role, since a company may well have investments that confer significant influence but that constitute a small portion of the reporting enterprise's operations.

Financial Reporting in Canada 1997 found that of the 200 surveyed companies, 134 reported the existence of long-term investments other than joint ventures. Only 58 segregated the investments by type. Twenty-two disclosed investment income by type, 61 reported only a single investment income figure, and 51 (38%) made no separate disclosure of investment income at all. As for the final recommended disclosure in the list above, only 11 companies (8%) disclosed both the difference and the accounting treatment; another four disclosed the difference *or* the accounting treatment, but not both.

Exhibit 12-1 shows the investments note of BCE Inc. (slightly edited). Special note should be taken of the three notes at the bottom. Note (a) reports that although BCE owns over 10 million shares (34.8%) of Maritime T&T, the company can vote only 1,000 shares under Nova Scotia law. Note (b) observes that while BCE's share ownership in Telesat Canada is 58.7%, its voting interest is only 26.1%, which explains why Telesat is not consolidated. Note (c) states that BCE increased its ownership in ExpressVu during 1997 from 39.5% to 90.0%, and therefore the investment disappears from the investment account because ExpressVu is now being consolidated. BCE does not report its earnings from these investments as a separate line in its financial statements, nor does it report the difference between purchase price and underlying net asset value for the investments.

1. Why is the equity method sometimes called the *one-line consolidation method*?

2. Explain what is meant by *unrealized profits*. Why should they be eliminated when the investor's financial statements are being prepared?

3. What difference is there between the amounts reported as *income* from equity-reported investments and the *cash flow* from those investments?

CONCEPT REVIEW

INTERNATIONAL PERSPECTIVE

Accounting for investments is an area where there are significant differences between Canadian accounting rules and those of many other countries. Many European companies do not consolidate or include the earnings of unconsolidated subsidiaries on an equity basis in their earnings. Moreover, when the operations of a business segment do not go as well as planned, many countries allow the parent to transfer those operations to an unconsolidated subsidiary. Thus, the income statements and balance sheets of many foreign companies often do not provide the same kind of information as those of Canadian-based companies.

Canadian standards for strategic investments are substantially in line with the recommendations of the International Accounting Standards Committee. The U.S., however, has significantly different standards. Significant influence is rigidly defined in the U.S. as ownership of between 20% and 50% of the outstanding equity of the investee; other factors that shape an investee's influence are ignored.

It is in business combinations that the greatest differences between U.S. and Canadian accounting rules are found. U.S. rules are very permissive of pooling-of-interests accounting, and even a giant company's takeover of a tiny company can be accounted for as a pooling under U.S. standards as long as the deal is structured to satisfy a set of rather easily circumvented rules. Therefore, a company that is buying control over another company will generally choose the accounting method that has the most beneficial impact on the buyer's bottom line and EPS, and will then structure the deal in a way that satisfies the accounting rules.

The U.S. Securities and Exchange Commission regulates public capital markets in the U.S. and prescribes accounting standards for companies whose securities are traded in the U.S. In general, the SEC adopts standards issued by the FASB. However, there are a few reporting issues on which the SEC also accepts International

Accounting Standards as well as FASB standards. Business combinations and consolidations is one such issue. The SEC has expressed considerable displeasure with U.S. standards in this regard. As a result, the FASB is participating in a joint project with the IASC and the standard-setters of Australia, Canada, New Zealand, the U.K., and the U.S. for achieving convergence on the methods of accounting for business combinations. A discussion paper issued in December 1998 recommends that the purchase method be used for *all* business combinations. If the recommendations are adopted by the FASB, it will be the end of pooling of interests accounting. Change seems very likely.

In Japan, consolidated reporting was not generally followed until quite recently. Japan adopted consolidated reporting under pressure from accountancy bodies in other countries, but Japanese consolidated statements don't really mean the same thing as those for countries based in western countries. A great deal of Japanese business is organized through huge "families" of companies, such as Sony and Mitsubishi, that include manufacturers, trading companies, resource companies, primary metals companies, insurance companies, at least one large bank, and so forth.

Japanese consolidated statements don't report on the whole group, however, because there is no parent company. Instead of one parent company controlling a bunch of subsidiaries, as is normal in the U.S., Canada, Australia, and Europe, each company in the group owns a very small percentage of all of the other companies in the group. A majority of the shares of every company is owned within the group, but no company actually "controls" another in the sense that we think of when we prepare financial statements. Japanese consolidated reporting, therefore, does not portray the operations of the economic family the way it does in most other countries.[2]

The European Union (E.U.) has a priority for standardizing the financial reporting among its member countries. In particular, the E.U.'s *Seventh Directive* requires firms to provide consolidated statements that include controlled subsidiaries. Consolidated statements are considered as supplementary statements, however; the unconsolidated, separate-entity statements are the primary statements. The E.U. is also moving toward requiring use of the equity method for investments in which the investor has a significant influence, where significant influence is defined similarly to Canadian GAAP.

A problem in some countries in Europe is that their accounting standards are tied to laws that require a very conservative, stewardship approach that does not permit recognition of fair values. However, these laws usually are written to apply to each individual entity. Rather than re-write the law to permit fair valuation of assets acquired in a business combination, the Ministers of Finance of several countries have simply permitted corporations to report *consolidated* financial statements on the basis of IAS. This route has been taken by Germany, France, Italy, and Belgium. Austria has gone an extra step: public companies listed on the Vienna Stock Exchange are *required* to use either IAS or U.S. standards beginning in 2000. As the countries in the E.U. adopt standards requiring consolidation and the use of the equity method, the financial statements for companies in them will be more comparable to those in Canada.

At the time that this is being written, no country has reporting requirements for temporary investments similar to the U.S. method (i.e., market value) described in this chapter. Some, such as Canada, require an LCM valuation basis, and some allow for writing up the value of assets. The accounting standards in many jurisdictions allow firms to use the cost method for almost all investments.

However, times are changing! The International Accounting Standards Committee now recommends that all financial assets (both debt and equity instruments) be reported at market value *except*

---

2   For more information, see "Shortcomings of Japanese Consolidated Financial Statements" by Howard D. Lowe, *Accounting Horizons*, September 1990.

- the company's receivables,
- fixed-term investments that the investor intends to and is capable of holding to maturity, and
- investments that do not have a quoted market price in an active market and whose fair value cannot reliably be determined.

[IAS 39, para.69]

This standard comes into effect for fiscal years beginning on or after January 2001. Effectively, it means that companies that follow international acounting standards will be required to revalue virtually all investments at market value, including temporary investments, long-term portfolio investments, and strategic investments.

Gains and losses on investments held for trading should be included in income immediately. This includes both temporary investments and non-current portfolio investments. Gains and other losses on other investments that are not held for trading but that nevertheless could be sold (such as strategic investments) can be either

- included in income immediately, or
- included in equity as unrealized gains/losses until the investment is sold or otherwise disposed of (e.g., through a spin-off to shareholders).

IAS 39 is the outcome of a project initated in conjunction with the CICA, and is based largely on a discussion paper issued jointly by the IASC and CICA in 1997.[3] Therefore, we can expect to see an exposure draft issued by the AcSB in the near future that contains similar proposals for Canada.

SUMMARY OF KEY POINTS

1. Companies invest in the securities of other entities for a variety of reasons, including increasing return on idle funds, creating strategic alliances, and the creation of appropriate legal vehicles for business activities.

2. Appropriate accounting for investments is determined by the substance of the investment vehicle, and also the intent of the investor.

3. Securities must be classified as debt or equity investments. In general, debt carries with it the right to receive cash from another enterprise; equity investments involve a residual interest in assets.

4. Investments in debt instruments are classified as temporary investments or as long-term investments according to the nature of the instrument and, for long-term securities, according to management's intent.

5. Temporary investments normally are carried at cost in the financial statements. In certain industries, however, temporary investments are reported at their market value.

6. Some argue that the market value of some kinds of investment is more relevant than cost, and thus market value should be recognized within the financial statements. This is not yet generally accepted in Canada (except in certain industries), but is required in the U.S.

7. Temporary investments are subject to a LCM valuation. For temporary investments, this is done with an allowance for the portfolio of investments. The allowance may be reversed in subsequent years if the market value recovers.

8. If long-term debt instruments are purchased at a premium or discount from face value and are intended (by management) to be held for the long-term, the premium or discount should be amortized to income over the life of the investment.

---

3 IASC/CICA Steering Committee on Financial Instruments, *Accounting for Financial Assets and Financial Liabilities* (1997). *CICA Handbook* section 3860 ("Financial Instruments") and IAS 32 were also based on this discussion paper and are discussed in Chapters 13 and 15.

9. Investments in equity securities are classified as temporary investments or as long term investments, according to management intent. However, investments must be readily marketable in order to be classified as a temporary investment.

10. Long-term investments in equity instruments are classified according to the power of the investor within the corporate governance structure of the investee. If the investor controls the investee, the investment is a subsidiary, and is consolidated. If the investor has power but does not have control without the cooperation of others, there is a significant influence investment that must be accounted for using the equity method. If the investor has no power to control or to significantly influence the investee, the investment is a portfolio investment, which, like short-term investments, is accounted for using the cost method.

11. In the cost method of reporting investments in equity instruments, the investment is recorded at cost and dividends are recognized as income when the dividends are declared. Required disclosure includes significant terms and conditions and fair values.

12. Long-term investments must be written down to a lower market value only when the decline is deemed permanent; this write-down is not reversible.

13. Investments that are acquired in a foreign currency must be reported on the investor's books at their equivalent cost in Canadian dollars, using the exchange rate in effect at the time of the purchase.

14. Investments in debt instruments that are denominated in a foreign currency must be restated to their current equivalent amount in Canadian dollars at each balance sheet date. Exchange gains and losses on temporary investments are recognized in income immediately. Exchange gains and losses arising from investments in long-term debt instruments (denominated in a foreign currency) are deferred and amortized over the remaining life of the instrument.

15. In the equity method, the investment is first recorded at cost, but the balance of the investment account changes to reflect the investor's proportionate share of the investee's adjusted earnings, losses, and dividends. Investment revenue includes the investor's share of profits (or losses), less amortizations of fair values present at acquisition, goodwill amortizations, and elimination of unrealized inter-company profits.

16. Consolidation requires combining the financial statements of the parent and the subsidiary at reporting dates.

17. The dichotomy of the *pooling of interests* and *purchase* approaches to consolidation apply only to subsidiaries that were acquired, not to those that were established by the parent company in the first place and remain wholly-owned.

18. *Pooling* is rarely used in Canada by public companies; when an acquiror can be identified, *purchase* accounting must be used for public reporting.

19. Under purchase accounting, the parent consolidates the *fair values* of identifiable assets and liabilities. Any excess of the purchase price above the fair values of the assets is recorded as *goodwill* and subsequently amortized.

20. When statements are consolidated, all inter-company transactions and any unrealized profits are eliminated. The portion of the subsidiary that is not owned by the parent is reflected in the consolidated statements as a *non-controlling* or *minority* interest.

21. International accounting standards recommend that almost all investments be reported at market value, effective in 2001. Since the IASC recommendations are the result of a joint project with the CICA, we can expect to see similar requirements introduced in Canada in the near future.

REVIEW PROBLEM

Suppose that on 1 January 20X5, Acme Fruit Company has the following temporary and long-term investments:

Security	Original Cost	Net Carrying Value at 1 January 20X5
Temporary investments:		
Apple (2,000 common shares)	$ 20,000	$ 19,000
T-bill (matures 1 July 20X5)	50,000	50,000
Long-term investments:		
Cherry (5,000 common shares)	40,000	40,000

Assume that there are no income taxes. Also assume that Acme Fruit uses the allowance method for LCM valuations of temporary investments. The following transactions and reclassifications occur during the year:

a. On 1 February 20X5, Acme purchases $30,000 of face amount bonds issued by Plum Inc. for $29,500 plus accrued interest. The bonds have a coupon rate of 8%, pay interest semi-annually on 30 June and 31 December, and mature on 31 December 20X9. The investment is classified as long-term. Assume straight-line amortization.

b. Dividends of $0.75 per share are received on the Apple common shares on 30 May.

c. Interest on the Plum bonds is received on 30 June and 31 December.

d. On 1 July, the T-bill matures and is redeemed at its face amount of $54,000. The full amount of proceeds is immediately used to purchase 1,000 common shares of Banana Corporation, and the investment is classified as temporary.

e. On 1 November, the investment in Cherry is reclassified as temporary. The stock has a market price of $11 per share on the reclassification date.

f. At 31 December, the market values of the various investments are determined to be as follows:

Temporary investments:	
Apple common	$ 15,000
Cherry common	57,500
Banana common	53,000
	$125,500
Long-term investments:	
Plum bonds (excluding accrued interest)	$ 31,000

Required:

1. Calculate investment income for 20X5.

2. Show how the above items are reported in the 20X5 financial statements of Acme Fruit Company.

REVIEW PROBLEM — SOLUTION

1. *Investment income*

   Plum bonds:

Interest: $30,000 × 8% × 11/12	$2,200	
Discount amortization: $500 × 11/59	93	$2,293
Apple dividends: 2,000 shares × $0.75		1,500
T-bill: $54,000 − $50,000		4,000
Loss recovery on temporary investments		1,000
Total investment income		$8,793

2. *Partial balance sheet at 31 December 20X5*

Temporary investments (at cost; market value, $125,500)	$114,000
Long-term investments (at amortized cost; market value, $31,000)	$ 29,593

   The schedule of cost and market values is as follows on 31 December 20X5:

	Cost	Market
Apple common	$ 20,000	$ 15,000
Cherry common	40,000	57,500
Banana common	54,000	53,000
Total temporary investments	$114,000	$125,500
Long-term: Plum bonds	$ 29,593	$ 31,000

APPENDIX
Consolidation Illustration

The main body of this chapter explained the general principles underlying consolidation but did not demonstrate a consolidation because of the complexities that quickly arise. This Appendix, however, does provide a simple demonstration of a consolidation following a *business combination* for those readers who are interested in how the numbers fit together. The final section of the Appendix briefly addresses the issue of consolidating foreign subsidiaries.

Basic Illustration

P Co. bought 80% of the voting shares of S Co. one year ago for $4,700,000. The other 20% of S Co. shares are owned by a small group of S Co. top management. P Co. controls S Co. by virtue of its voting control and must consolidate its financial statements at the end of each fiscal period. Refer to the financial statements shown in the first two columns of Exhibit 12-2, which are at the end of the first year of ownership.

During the year, P Co. used the cost method of *recording* the investment, and thus the investment account is still recorded at $4,700,000. P Co. shows $80,000 of other income on its income statement; S Co. had declared $100,000 of dividends, which were paid $80,000 to P Co. and $20,000 to the other shareholders.

As of the date of acquisition, S Co. had *net assets* (that is, assets minus liabilities) of $3,782,000 at book value. By definition, this is equal to shareholders' equity on the date of acquisition. There was $140,000 in the common shares account, and $3,642,000 in retained earnings, to equal $3,782,000. P Co. would determine the fair value of net assets on this date, through appraisal and other examination. Assume that fair values equalled book values except for capital assets with a 10-year life, that were worth $1,000,000 more than book value.

During the year, S Co. had sales of $4,000,000 to P Co. All the goods had been resold to other customers, except goods for which P Co. had paid $300,000, which were still in inventory. These items had cost S Co. $200,000. Finally, P Co. owed $175,000 to S Co. at year-end.

The goodwill on acquisition is calculated as follows:

Purchase price		$4,700,000
Less: Market value acquired		
Book value	$3,782,000	
Market value increment	1,000,000	
Total	$4,782,000	
P Co. share	80%	(3,825,600)
Goodwill		$ 874,400

Notice that 80% of S Co. was purchased and 80% is used in the calculation.

Most of what happens in a consolidation is that the two sets of financial statements are added together. However, entries are needed for a variety of things.

1. *Investment elimination entry.* This is a busy entry, as it eliminates the equity accounts of the subsidiary on the date of acquisition, eliminates the parent's investment account, sets up the non-controlling interest on the date of acquisition, and recognizes fair value differences and goodwill inherent in the purchase price.

Common shares (S Co.)	140,000	
Retained earnings (S Co.)	3,642,000	
Capital assets ($1,000,000 × 80%)	800,000	
Goodwill	874,400	
Investment in S Co.		4,700,000
Non-controlling interest		756,400

The *non-controlling interest* account is a balance sheet account that is typically classified between long-term debt and shareholders equity. It is the portion of the subsidiary's net assets — equity — owned by shareholders other than the parent. This account often is called *minority interest.*

2. *Amortization entry.* Next, accounts created in the investment elimination entry must be amortized to reflect the passage of time, one year in this case. Assuming amortization over 10 years for the capital assets and 30 years for goodwill:

Amortization expense	109,147	
Capital Assets, net ($800,000 ÷ 10)		80,000
Goodwill ($874,400 ÷ 30)		29,147

3. *Dividend entry.* S Co. paid dividends to its shareholders, and these are recorded in its books. Assuming the cost method is used by P Co. for *recording* the investment, the dividend paid to the majority shareholder is recorded as dividend revenue on the parent's income statement, while the dividend paid to the non-controlling shareholders reduces their interest in remaining net assets on the subsidiary. After this elimination, the only dividends left are those paid to the shareholders of P Co.

Dividend revenue	80,000	
Non-controlling interest	20,000	
Dividends declared		100,000

4. *Intercompany balances and transactions elimination entries.* These amounts are eliminated so that all that remains on the consolidated accounts are transactions that the consolidated entity has had with outside parties. Note that the entries do not change net income or net assets; they simply deflate offsetting components.

Sales	4,000,000	
Cost of sales		4,000,000
Accounts payable	175,000	
Accounts receivable		175,000

5. *Intercompany unrealized profit eliminations.* Inventory on the books of the parent is recorded at $300,000, when it has a cost to the consolidated entity of $200,000. The $100,000 overstatement must be eliminated, and, the corresponding overstatement of the subsidiary's net income also has to be corrected.

Cost of sales	100,000	
Inventory		100,000

The debit to cost of sales reduces income. This entry creates a temporary difference between accounting and taxable income, and should result in an adjustment to tax expense and the balance sheet tax future (deferred) income tax account; this tax entry has been omitted in the interests of simplicity.

EXHIBIT 12-2
Consolidation Worksheet

	Elimination P Co.	Consolidated S Co.	Consolidation Entries	P Co. + S Co. Results
Cash	$ 460,000	$ 64,000		$ 524,000
Accounts receivable	2,390,000	790,000	(4) 175,000 cr.	3,005,000
Inventory	4,910,000	1,700,000	(5) 100,000 cr.	6,510,000
Capital assets, net	8,224,000	4,622,000	(1) 800,000 dr.	
			(2) 80,000 cr.	13,566,000
Investment in S Co.	4,700,000	—	(1) 4,700,000 cr.	0
Intangible assets	400,000	—	(1) 874,400 dr.	
			(2) 29,147 cr.	1,245,253
	$21,084,000	$7,176,000		$ 24,850,253
Current liabilities	$ 5,320,000	$1,100,000	(4) 175,000 dr	$ 6,245,000
Long-term debt	8,100,000	1,500,000		9,600,000
Deferred income taxes	1,050,000	640,000		1,690,000
Non-controlling interest	—	—	(1) 756,400 cr.	
			(3) 20,000 dr.	
			(6) 30,800 cr.	767,200
Common shares	2,600,000	140,000	(1) 140,000 dr.	2,600,000
Retained earnings	4,014,000	3,796,000		
			from below	3,948,053
	$21,084,000	$7,176,000		$ 24,850,253
Sales	$16,800,000	$9,300,000	(4) 4,000,000 dr.	$ 22,100,000
Cost of sales	9,900,000	4,216,000	(4) 4,000,000 cr.	
			(5) 100,000 dr.	10,216,000
Operating expenses	5,650,000	4,590,000	(2) 109,147 dr.	10,349,147
Other income	80,000	—	(3) 80,000 dr.	0
Income tax expense	560,000	240,000		800,000
Non-controlling interest	—	—	(6) 30,800 dr.	30,800
Net income	$ 770,000	$ 254,000		$ 704,053
Opening retained earnings	3,454,000	$ 642,000	(1) 3,642,000 dr.	3,454,000
Dividends	210,000	100,000	(3) 100,000 cr.	210,000
Closing retained earnings	$ 4,014,000	$3,796,000	0	$ 3,948,053

6. *Non-controlling interest share of income.* The non-controlling (or *minority*) interest has been allocated its share of equity and subsidiary dividends, but they also have an interest in the earnings of the subsidiary for the current period ($254,000), at least to the extent that these earnings have been confirmed by transactions with outside parties ($254,000 – $100,000). Thus, the non-controlling interest's share in confirmed subsidiary profits is allocated to them by creating an "expense" on the income statement that increases the non-controlling interest item on the balance sheet. This works much the same way as a debit to wages expense increases the wages payable account, if wages have not yet been paid.

Provision for non-controlling interest (I/S)	30,800	
Non-controlling interest (B/S)		30,800
($254,000 – $100,000) × 20% = 30,800		

The final step in the consolidation worksheet is to cross-add each account line, giving effect to the adjustments and eliminations above, as is illustrated in the final column of Exhibit 12-2. The final column provides the amounts that are used to prepare the consolidated financial statements.

Be sure to remember that all of the consolidation entries are *worksheet entries only*. The entries listed above do not get recorded on any company's books.

Foreign Subsidiaries

The procedure that is illustrated above is the same for all subsidiaries. However, an additional complication arises when the subsidiary is in a foreign country. The subsidiary's financial statements will be in a foreign currency, and must be restated to Canadian dollars before consolidation can occur. Because exchange rates change, the net asset value of the subsidiary will be different at each year-end, *even if there has been no change in the assets and liabilities*. Thus, a gain or loss will arise simply from the mechanics of the foreign currency translation and consolidation process. A detailed account of the treatment of this gain or loss is well beyond the scope of this book (again, this is something that is dealt with in advanced accounting courses), but a modest understanding is necessary in order to interpret published financial statements.

The 1997 balance sheet of McMillan Bloedel Limited shows the following in shareholders' equity:

Common shareholders' equity ($ millions):	
Common shares	1,002
Retained earnings	508
Foreign exchange translation adjustment	(87)
	1,423

Where does this negative $87,000,000 item come from? To answer that, we need to understand that the *CICA Handbook* identifies two different types of foreign subsidiaries:

1. Integrated foreign operations, which operate essentially as extensions of the parent in the foreign country and thus are *integrated* with the operations of the parent company.

2. Self-sustaining foreign operations, which operate relatively autonomously, without substantial direct participation or control of the parent company, and thus are *self-sustaining*.

The consolidation treatment of these two types of subsidiaries is different. If the subsidiary is *integrated*, then its transactions are reported as though they all had been transactions of the parent company. Any foreign exchange gains and losses are reported on the income statement either immediately or, for long-term monetary items, by deferring and amortizing them. The treatment is exactly the same as that described in Chapter 8 for foreign currency-denominated receivables and payables.

If the subsidiary is *self-sustaining*, then translation gains and losses do *not* flow into income, but instead are segregated as a separate component of shareholders' equity. The translation gain or loss is viewed as the mechanical result of consolidation rather than as a "true" gain or loss.

The issues involved in translating foreign subsidiaries are more extensive than simply deciding what to do with the translation gain or loss. Indeed, one of the major issues is how to perform the translation itself; another is how to decide whether a subsidiary is integrated or self-sustaining. But, hopefully, this little overview will contribute to your understanding of this item when it is encountered on the balance sheets of companies that have foreign operations.

SUMMARY OF KEY POINTS

1. Goodwill is measured as the amount by which the purchase price (of a purchased subsidiary) exceeds the *fair value of the subsidiary's identifiable assets at the date of acquisition, for the proportion of the the shares purchased by the parent company.*

2. Consolidation is performed on worksheets; there are no entries in either the parent's or the subsidiary's books.

3. When a subsidiary is purchased, the cost of the acquisition is recorded in an investment account on the parent's books.

4. When the subsidiary's financial statements are consolidated with those of the parent, the investment account is eliminated, and instead all of the assets and liabilities of the subsidiary are added to the parent's on the balance sheet. Any offsetting balances between the parent and the subsidiary are eliminated by offsetting one against the other.

5. All of the revenues and expenses of the subsidiary are added to those of the parent on the parent's consolidated income statement. Inter-company transactions are eliminated, to avoid double-counting, and any unrealized profits are eliminated.

6. If the parent does not own all of the subsidiary, the proportion of the subsidiary's net asset book value that is *not* owned by the parent is reported by the parent on its balance sheet as a credit, placed below liabilities but before shareholders' equity.

7. The minority interest's proportionate share of the subsidiary's net income is deducted on the parent's consolidated income statement, to offset the fact that *all* of the subsidiary's revenues and expenses have been combined with the parent's.

8. The account balances of foreign subsidiaries must be translated into Canadian dollars before they can be consolidated. Exchange rate movement causes translation gains and losses, which are accounted for differently depending on whether the subsidiary is *integrated* or *self-sustaining*.

QUESTIONS

12-1 Why do companies invest in the securities of other enterprises?

12-2 Distinguish between debt and equity securities.

12-3 How can a debt investment be classified? An equity investment? How should each catagory be accounted for?

12-4 What investments qualify as financial instruments? What disclosures are required for these investments?

12-5 Are all marketable securities also temporary investments? Define both terms in your response.

12-6 A bond is bought at the beginning of the fiscal year for $98,000. This is a five-year, 6% bond with a $100,000 face value. How much interest income will be recognized in the first year if the investment is temporary? long-term?

12-7 What factors indicate that significant influence may be present between an investor and an investee? How would such an investment be reported?

12-8 What factors indicate that control exists between an investor and an investee? How would such an investment be reported?

12-9 It is often said that an investor with 20% of the voting shares of another company has significant influence, and an investor with 50% has control. Is this always true?

12-10 Why is it particularly important to amortize the discount on an investment in zero-coupon bonds? Under what other circumstances is a premium or discount amortized?

12-11 On 1 August 20X4, Baker Company purchased $50,000 face amount of Sugar Company 6% coupon value bonds for $48,000. The bond pays interest semi-annually on 31 July and 31 January. At the fiscal year-end for Baker, the bonds have a market value of $49,000. Show the journal entries (a) to record the investment, assuming that the bonds are classified as a temporary investment and (b) to record investment income and any other needed adjustments at 31 December.

12-12 On 1 July 20X2, a company bought an investment in IBM shares for U.S. $50,000 when the exchange rate was U.S. $1 = Cdn. $1.32. The company paid cash on the acquisition date. At 31 December, the exchange rate was U.S. $1 = Cdn. $1.38. Prepare journal entries to record the purchase of shares and any adjusting entries at year-end.

12-13 An investor purchased 100 shares of Zenics at $20 per share on 15 March 20X4. At the end of the 20X4 accounting period, 31 December 20X4, the stock was quoted at $19 per share. On 5 June 20X5, the investor sold the stock for $22 per share. Assuming this is a temporary investment, and is the only temporary investment held, show the journal entries to be made at each of the following dates:

    15 March 20X4.
    31 December 20X4.
    5 June 20X5.

12-14 On 31 December 20X1, ABC company owned 10,000 shares of A Company, with a cost of $23 per share and a market value of $24 per share. They also held bonds of Z Company with a cost of $42,000 and a market value of $22,000. What LCM entry would be made, assuming both investments were temporary investments? What if they were long-term?

12-15 Why might a company be tempted to reclassify a temporary investment in common shares as a long-term investment if market value were significantly lower than cost?

12-16 What conditions may indicate that the value of a long-term investment has been impaired?

12-17 When is the market value method used in Canada for accounting for investments? In the U.S.? Why do some prefer the market value method to the cost method?

12-18 Assume that Company R acquired, as a long-term investment, 30% of the outstanding voting common shares of Company S at a cash cost of $100,000. At the date of acquisition, the balance sheet of Company S showed total shareholders' equity of $250,000. The market value of the depreciable assets of Company S was $20,000 greater than their net book value at date of R's acquisition. Compute goodwill purchased, if any.

12-19 Assume the same facts as in 12-18, with the addition that net assets that were undervalued at acquisition have a remaining estimated life of 10 years and goodwill will be amortized over 20 years (assume no residual values and straight-line depreciation). How much investment revenue would Company R report using the equity method if Company S reported $80,000 of net income?

12-20   Investor Ltd. owns 35% of Machines Ltd, and has significant influence. The investment was made five years ago, when Machine's fair values equalled book values; $40,000 of goodwill was inherent in the purchase price. In the current fiscal year, Machines reported $225,000 in income. This includes a $50,000 profit on inventory sold to Investor Ltd, which Investor has not yet resold. How much investment revenue will Investor report? How would your answer change if Investor had reported the sale of inventory to Machines?

12-21   How is cost determined when a company changes its accounting method for a long-term investment from equity to cost?

12-22   What accounts appear in the consolidated financial statements that are not present in either the parent's or the subsidiary's financial statements? Explain each item. What accounts always disappear from the unconsolidated financial statements?

12-23   Explain the difference between the purchase and pooling methods of consolidation.

12-24   Equity income, and consolidated income, is usually lower than one would predict by simply adding the investors income and the pro-rata share of the investee's income. Why does this happen?

12-25   Why does consolidation not capture the substance of economic groups of companies as they exist in Japan?

CASE 12-1

Dornan Ltd.

Dornan Ltd. is a Canadian company that manufactures leather furniture. Sales in 20X3 were $265 million, with strong exports to the U.S. Dornan is the leading Canadian manufacturer of leather furniture, and is ranked fourth in this category in the U.S. market. While Dornan has, in the past, had manufacturing facilities in the U.S., difficulties in quality control and logistics have recently convinced the owner to centralize all operations in Niagara Falls, Canada. The plant employs 250 workers.

Dornan Ltd. is a private company. All shares are held by the president and CEO, Jeff Dornan, who inherited the business from his father. The firm had been founded by Mr. Dornan's grandfather. Dornan himself is a graduate of Harvard Business School and is well regarded in the industry. He focuses on marketing and strategy, and usually leaves operations to his production managers, all of whom receive a bonus based on overall company profits. You, a professional accountant in public practice, review the annual financial statements of the company, prepare the tax returns, and provide advice on a wide range of issues, including financing, tax, personnel and accounting policy. Mr. Dornan has asked you to review accounting policy for the investments Dornan Ltd. has accumulated over the years.

Hyperion
Dornan Ltd. bought 4,000 shares of Hyperion, an aircraft engine manufacturer, two years ago, for $43 per share. Hyperion has 490,000 common shares outstanding, of which 20,000 to 40,000 change hands annually. Mr. Dornan is a personal friend of the president and CEO of this small public company. The investment has been reported as a temporary investment. No dividends have been declared on the shares. Last year, the most recent stock price quoted was $42, and no write-down to LCM was recorded, primarily for materiality reasons. This year, market values have been in the $33 – $35 range. Dornan now reports the investment as long-term, as Mr. Dornan has stated that he would never sell the investment unless market values return to $43. Mr. Dornan is confident that this will be the case sometime in the next five years.

March Ltd.

Mr. Dornan is the sole shareholder of March Ltd., which he incorporated two years ago. The boards of directors for March Ltd. and Dornan Ltd. are almost identical. March is engaged in researching new imitation leather fabrics, and ways of chemically treating real leather to improve its quality. Throughout the last two years, March has spent $216,000 on these activities. All this amount is financed by Dornan Ltd; Mr. Dornan himself has put no money into March Ltd. other than a token investment to create share capital. Dornan Ltd. reports the $216,000 as a long-term investment, a long-term receivable. It has no stated interest rate or term, and will only be repaid when marketable fabrics are developed by March Ltd.

Kusak Ltd.

Dornan Ltd. owns 42% of the outstanding shares of Kusak Ltd. Another 20% of these shares are owned by a small group of friends of the Kusak CEO, all of whom sit on the board of directors. Kusak specializes in waste disposal cleanup, a booming business. However, Kusak is in poor financial condition following rapid expansion and some difficulties with cost control. Dornan Ltd. made a $1,700,000 investment in common shares this past year to ensure the solvency of the organization.

Dornan appoints six members of the 16-person board of directors. All the remaining directors, including Kusak's CEO, are shareholders and are a cohesive, tightly-knit group. Because of this, Dornan's representatives typically feel like "outsiders" in the decision-making process. Dornan's representatives have supported the strategic initiatives of the CEO, which have been intelligent responses to the market challenges facing Kusak. Kusak is reporting modest income this year, but pays no dividends.

Dornan Ltd., in addition to its common share investment, has a $500,000 bond issued by Kusak. The terms of the bond agreement state that if Kusak is unprofitable for two consecutive years, the bond can be converted to common shares amounting to 10% of the then-outstanding common shares.

DML Corp.

Dornan Ltd. owns 19,975 (2%) of the voting common shares of DML Corp., a French furniture manufacturer that Dornan may use to enter the European market sometime in the future. Five years ago, Dornan bought notes and preferred shares in the company. This year, the notes and preferred shares were exchanged for common shares pursuant to an agreement signed when the notes and preferred shares were acquired. On the exchange date, the notes and preferred shares had a book value of $175,000; their market value was indeterminable because the securities were never traded. Common shares, thinly traded over the counter, had sold for $7 – $9 in the preceding 12 months. The exchange was recorded at book value.

At year-end, the most recent trading price was $3 per share, a price that Mr. Dornan attributed to currency woes, and concerns about economic recovery in European markets. He remains convinced that the company is sound and well-managed. Dornan Ltd. has one member on the 18-seat board of directors of DML Ltd. Mr. Dornan himself attends these meetings, and reports that he is well-regarded in debate. Mr. Dornan usually takes a bilingual advisor with him, as proceedings take place in French, a language in which Mr. Dornan is not fluent.

In the past year, DML reported a marginal net income; the company has never declared dividends.

Required:

Provide the requested advice.

CASE 12-2

Air World Inc.

Mr. Bruce Li, financial vice-president of Air World Inc. (AWI), has been requested by the AWI board of directors to prepare a report to the Board on accounting policy issues that may affect the draft AWI consolidated financial statements for 20X1. In particular, he has been asked to focus on the accounting policies of Gerilator Corporation, as well as on some aspects of financial policy relating to the operations of Gerilator. Gerilator is a nation-wide courier company that joined the AWI group of companies on 5 March 20X1, when AWI purchased 57% of outstanding Gerilator shares from Gerilator's founder; the other 43% of the shares remain in the founder's family. Gerilator is unique in that it is the only AWI subsidiary that is not 100%-owned by AWI. AWI paid an amount in excess of book value for the shares; this was partially explained by the understatement of asset values on the balance sheet; for example, computer systems of Gerilator are a major competitive tool but were quickly amortized on Gerilator's books.

Air World Inc.

AWI is a federally-chartered Canadian company headquartered in Hull, Quebec. Both its common and preferred shares are traded on the Montreal Exchange. AWI is engaged in world-wide airline charter activities, operating a fleet of 16 jet aircraft from a base at Montreal's Mirabel Airport.

Like all aircraft operators, scheduled or charter, AWI has a very large debt load. Long-term financing is obtained through private placements of debentures, and short-term financing is obtained through operating lines of credit from two major Canadian banks. All of the lenders are, of course, very concerned about the continuing adequacy of AWI's cash flow for servicing the debt. As an expression of that concern, the debenture agreements and the banks' loan agreements all stipulate certain minimum liquidity and profitability ratios that must be satisfied on the basis of the annual consolidated financial statements; if any of the ratio requirements are not satisfied, the debenture holders and/or banks have the right to demand immediate payment of the full balance owing.

AWI is essentially a holding company; aircraft operation and maintenance are carried out by wholly-owned operating subsidiaries. In Canada, charter aircraft operators are not permitted to sell seats directly to the public; all seats must be sold through tour package wholesalers. Therefore, AWI has a wholly-owned tour subsidiary, Canada World Holidays (CWH), that assembles package tours and sells them through travel agents. AWI sells about 60% of its available seats in blocks to CWH; the other 40% is sold to independent tour operators.

In order to motivate front-line managers, AWI has a bonus system for all managers in each of its operating companies. The bonuses are not based on profitability, but instead are based on a set of performance and efficiency measures tailored to each manager's job responsibilities.

Gerilator Corporation

AWI was eager to make an investment in Gerilator, to preserve a relationship with a customer who provided a large amount of volume. Gerilator has an excellent reputation in the courier industry, which is very competitive. Gerilator has been only barely profitable in recent years. While smaller, letter-size packages are only marginally profitable, larger packages provide a very respectable gross margin, and AWI wished Gerilator to actively pursue such business. Gerilator's founder agrees that this strategy is appropriate, and is enthusiastically developing marketing plans.

The Gerilator board of directors consists of 14 individuals. AWI can appoint eight directors, but to date has put only four members of its own choosing on the board; their other four slots are continuing board members whom AWI found acceptable. One of the AWI board members sits on the three-person executive committee.

Because of its declining profitability, Gerilator has increasingly relied on debt financing for its operations. In particular, the company has relied on term loans from banks for upgrading its truck and van fleet, and the resulting material interest cost has further depressed Gerilator's earnings. These term loans are secured by the truck and van fleet. The AWI board of directors has asked Mr. Li to advise them on the implications of renting all or part of the vehicle fleet, through short-term operating leases.

Following AWI's investment in Gerilator, the Gerilator board approved in principle a major reorganization of Gerilator's operations to more closely coincide with AWI's flight operations. The result should be more efficient combined operations for freight and courier operations (which use the cargo capacity on AWI's charter flights — capacity which would otherwise fly empty). The reorganization, now in the planning stages, will result in a significant cost for revamping facilities, relocating staff, and so forth, but is expected, if accompanied by improved marketing of larger packages, to make Gerilator more profitable. The AWI board has asked Mr. Li to comment on the most appropriate approach to reporting the costs of the reorganization; the costs arise as the result of decisions taken in 20X1, won't be incurred until 20X2, and will benefit operational efficiency in future years.

Required:

Assume that you are Mr. Bruce Li. Draft a concise report to the AWI board of directors.

EXERCISES

E12-1 *Classification of Investments in Securities:* Classify the different securities listed below according to their usual classification as investments:

    A. temporary equity investment;
    B. temporary debt investment;
    C. long-term portfolio debt or equity investment;
    D. significant influence investment;
    E. control investment;
    F. joint venture; and
    G. none of the above.

Typical Securities:

1. Abbot common shares, no-par; acquired on the TSE to use temporarily idle cash.

2. Land acquired for speculation.

3. Government of Canada treasury bills, maturing in six months.

4. Redoubt Corp., common shares; 60% of total shares. All operating, investing, and financing decisions must be agreed to unanimously by three main shareholders.

5. BCE preferred stock, par $100, mandatory redemption within next 12 months.

6. Staufer common shares; able to appoint five of eight members of the board of directors.

7. Frazer bonds, 9%, mature at the end of 10 years; intended to be held for 10 years.

8. Foreign Corporation, common shares; a 30% interest acquired, but difficulties encountered in taking cash out of the foreign country due to government regulations.

9. Certificates of deposit (CDs); mature at end of one year.

10. Savings certificate at Trust Company, mature in one year.

11. Acorn common shares; management plans to hold these shares for the short term, but it's not clear that a buyer can be found quickly.

E12-2 *Temporary Equity Investments:* On 1 November 20X2, Decker Company acquired the following temporary investments in equity securities:

X Corporation — 500 common shares at $60 cash per share.

Y Corporation — 300 preferred shares at $20 cash per share.

The annual reporting period ends 31 December. Decker Company uses the allowance method when appling the LCM rule. On 31 December 20X2, the quoted market prices were as follows:

X Corporation common, $52

Y Corporation preferred, $24

The following information relates to 20X3:

2 March	Received cash dividends per share as follows: X Corporation, $1; and Y Corporation, $0.50.
1 October	Sold 100 shares of Y Corporation preferred at $25 per share.
31 December	Market values were as follows: X common, $46, and Y preferred, $26.

Required:

1. Give the entry for Decker Company to record the purchase of the securities.

2. Give any adjusting entry needed at the end of 20X2.

3. Give the items and amounts that would be reported on the 20X2 income statement and balance sheet.

4. Give all entries required in 20X3.

5. Give the items and amounts that would be reported on the 20X3 income statement and balance sheet.

E12-3 *Temporary Equity Investments:* At 31 December 20X4, the short-term investments of Vista Company were as follows:

Security	Shares	Unit Cost	Unit Market Price
Preferred shares, $.80 dividend, Knight Corp.	600	$ 90	$ 88
Common shares, no-par, Dyer Corp.	200	30	31

The fiscal year ends 31 December, and these securities were all purchased during 20X4. The transactions that follow all relate to the above equity investments and to those additional securities bought and sold during 20X5.

- 2 February — Received the annual cash dividend from Knight Corporation.

- 1 March — Sold 150 Dyer shares at $34 per share.

- 1 May — Sold 400 Knight shares at $89.50 per share.

- 1 June — Received a cash dividend on Dyer shares of $3.50 per share.

- 1 August — Purchased 4,000 common shares of Rote Corporation at $45 per share.

At 31 December 20X5, the quoted market prices were as follows: Knight preferred, $98; Dyer common, $28; and Rote common, $44.50.

Required:

1. Give the entry that Vista Company should make on 31 December 20X4, to record the equity investments at LCM. Use the allowance method.

2. Give the entries for 20X5 through 1 August.
3. Give the entry(s) required at 31 December 20X5.
4. List the items and amounts that should be reported on Vista's 20X5 income statement and balance sheet.

E12-4 *Temporary Investment in Debt Securities:* On 1 September 20X2, New Company purchased 10 bonds of Old Corporation ($1,000, 6%) as a temporary investment at 96 (i.e., $960 per bond) plus accrued interest. The bonds pay annual interest each 1 July. New paid cash, including accrued interest. New's annual reporting period ends 31 December. The bonds mature on 30 June 20X8.

Required:

1. Give the journal entry for New Company to record the purchase of the bonds.
2. Give any adjusting entries required at 31 December 20X2.
3. Give the items and amounts that should be reported on the 20X2 income statement and balance sheet.
4. Give the required entry on 1 July 20X3.
5. On 1 August 20X3, New Company sold four of the bonds at 96.5 plus any accrued interest. Give the required entry(s).
6. How would your answer to (2) change if the investment were considered long-term? Assume amounts are material.

E12-5 *Long-Term Investment in Debt Securities:* The Shepard Hydrant Company purchased $50,000 face amount of Beagle Bugler 9% bonds at a price of 98.5 on 1 January 20X5. That is, the bonds were bought for 98.5% of face value. The bonds mature on 31 December 20X7, and pay interest annually on 31 December. Shepard plans to hold the bonds as a long-term portfolio investment. Assume that Shepard uses the straight-line method of amortizing any premium or discount on investments in bonds. At 31 December 20X5 and 20X6, the bonds are quoted at 98 and 99, respectively.

Required:

1. Show the entry to record the purchase of the bonds.
2. Show the entry(s) to be made on 31 December 20X5.
3. Show the entry(s) to be made on 31 December 20X6.
4. Show the income statement and balance sheet items and amounts related to the above investment that would be reported for 20X5 and 20X6.
5. Show any additional disclosure that would be required for this investment.

E12-6 *Basket Purchase of Securities — Allocation, Entry:* On 1 December 20X4, Voss Company purchased stock in the three different companies listed below for a lump sum of $114,000, including commissions, and will be held as long-term investments.

   N Corporation, common shares, 300 shares.
   O Corporation, preferred shares, 400 shares.
   P Corporation common shares, 500 shares.

At the time of purchase, the shares were quoted on the local over-the-counter stock market at the following prices per share: N common, $100; O preferred, $120; and P common, $84.

Required:

1. Give the entry to record the purchase of these investments. Record each stock in a separate account and show the cost per share.

2. How would your response to (1) change if there was no market value available for the P Corporation common shares?

E12-7 *Long-Term Investments — Entries and Reporting:* During 20X2, Shale Company purchased equity security (shares) in two corporations and debt securities of a third with the intention of holding them as long-term investments. Transactions were in the following order:

a. Purchased 200 of the 100,000 common shares outstanding of Tee Corporation at $31 per share plus a 4% brokerage fee. The fee is part of the share cost.

b. Purchased 300 of 40,000 outstanding preferred shares (nonvoting) of Stone Corporation at $78 per share plus a 3% brokerage fee. The fee is part of the share cost.

c. Purchased an additional 20 common shares of Tee Corporation at $35 per share plus a 4% brokerage fee. The fee is part of the share cost.

d. Purchased $10,000 face amount of Container Corporation, 9% bonds at 96 plus accrued interest. The purchase is made on 1 November; interest is paid semi-annually on 31 January and 31 July. The bond matures on 31 July 20X7.

e. Received $4 per share cash dividend on the Stone Corporation shares (from earnings since acquisition).

f. Interest is accrued at the end of 20X2. Appropriate discount amortization is recorded for 20X2.

Required:

1. Give the entry in the accounts of Shale Company for each transaction.

2. The market value of the shares held at the end of 20X2 were Tee stock, $34, and Stone stock, $75. The Container Corporation bonds were quoted at 98. Give the appropriate adjusting entry, if any, for Shale Company, assuming declines in market value are considered permanent.

3. Show how the income statement and balance sheet for Shale Company would report relevant data concerning these investments for 20X2.

E12-8 *Market Value Method:* Green Corporation bought and held four different short-term investments in 20X2. At 31 December 20X2, the following information was gathered.

Investment	31 December 20X2	
	Cost	Market value
Radcom common shares	$ 45,000	$56,000
Forward preferred shares	110,000	96,000
Halga common shares	58,000	70,000
Hydro bonds	97,000	99,000

Early in 20X3, all investments were sold: the Radcon shares for $60,000, Forward preferred shares for $98,000, Halga common shares for $60,000, and Hydro bonds for $100,000.

Required:

1. What would appear on the income statement in relation to these investments in 20X2 and 20X3 if the cost method is used? Be sure to evaluate the need for a

LCM write-down. Ignore any dividend or investment income that was earned on the shares in 20X2 or 20X3.

2. Repeat part (1), using the market value method to value the investments.

3. Compare your solutions to parts (1) and (2). Why is the cost method generally accepted? Why do some prefer the market value method?

E12-9 *Investments and Foreign Currency:* On 14 June 20X4, Jackson Ltd purchased 40,000 shares of Hardy Ltd. for U.S. $2.15 per share, plus U.S. $2,400 in commissions and fees. The shares were a temporary investment. On this date, the exchange rate was $1 U.S. = Cdn. $1.3423. The account was settled with the broker on 1 August 20X4, when $1 U.S. = Cdn. $1.29.

On 1 July 20X4, Jackson bought a U.S. $100,000 five-year bond at face value, when the exchange rate was $1 U.S. = Cdn. $1.3072. They paid cash on the acquisition date. They plan to hold this bond until maturity.

At 31 December 20X4, the exchange rate was $1 U.S. = Cdn. $1.2821.

Required:

1. Provide journal entries to record the acquisition of the Hardy shares on 14 July, and payment to the broker in August. Brokerage fees are part of the investment cost.

2. Provide the journal entry to record purchase of the bond on 1 July.

3. Explain the adjustment that must be made for the bonds at 31 December 20X9.

E12-10 *Long-Term Equity Investment, Equity Method:* On 1 January 20X4, JR Company purchased 400 of the 1,000 outstanding common shares of RV Corporation for $30,000. The equity method will be used to account for the investment. At that date, the balance sheet of RV showed the following book values:

Assets not subject to depreciation	$40,000*
Assets subject to depreciation (net)	$26,000**
Liabilities	$ 6,000*
Common shares	$50,000
Retained earnings	$10,000

* Book value is the same as market value.
** Market value $30,000; the assets have a 10-year remaining life (straight-line depreciation).

Required:

1. Give the entry by JR Company to record the acquisition.

2. Show the computation of goodwill purchased at acquisition.

3. Assume that at 31 December 20X4 (end of the accounting period), RV Corporation reported a net income of $12,000, and declared dividends of $5,000. Assume goodwill amortization over a 10-year period. Prepare the entries JR Company would record.

4. Repeat requirement (3), assuming that there was an unconfirmed profit on a sale from JR Company to RV Corporation in the amount of $2,000.

E12-11 *Long-Term Equity Investment, Equity Method:* On 1 January 20X2, Case Corporation purchased 3,000 of the 10,000 outstanding common shares of Dow Corporation for $28,000 cash. Case has significant influence, and will be using the equity method to account for this investment.

At the date of acquisition, Dow's net assets were as follows:

	Book Value	Market Value
Assets not subject to depreciation	$25,000*	$28,000
Assets subject to depreciation (net)	30,000	38,000
Liabilities	5,000	5,000
Common shares	40,000	
Retained earnings	10,000	

Required:

1. Show the computation of goodwill purchased at acquisition.

2. At the end of 20X2, Dow reported income of $20,000. In December 20X2, Dow Corporation paid a $1 per share cash dividend. Record appropriate entries to reflect income and dividends in 20X2. Use straight-line amortization of any goodwill and assets over 10 years.

E12-12 *Long-Term Equity Investment, Cost and Equity Methods Compared Entries:* On 3 January 20X4, TA Company purchased 2,000 shares of the 10,000 outstanding shares of common stock of UK Corporation for $14,600 cash with the intention of holding the securities indefinitely. At that date, the balance sheet of UK Corporation reflected the following: nondepreciable assets, $50,000 (book value is the same as market value); depreciable assets (net), $30,000 (market value, $33,000); total liabilities, $20,000 (book value equals market value); and shareholders' equity, $60,000. Assume a 10-year remaining life (straight-line method) on the depreciable assets and amortization of goodwill over 40 years.

Required:

1. Give the entries, if any are required, on TA's books for each item (a) through (e) below assuming that the cost method is appropriate. Assume that the investment is a long-term portfolio investment.

2. Repeat (1) above assuming that the equity method is appropriate.

3. Entries required and other information:

   a. Entry at date of acquisition.
   b. Goodwill purchased — computation only.
   c. Entry on 31 December 20X4 to record $15,000 net income reported by UK.
   d. Entry on 31 December 20X4 to recognize decrease in market value of UK stock, quoted market price, $7 per share.
   e. Entry on 31 March 20X5 for a cash dividend of $1 per share declared and paid by UK.

E12-13 *Consolidation — Explanation:* In 20X1, Pepper Company bought 75% of S Company's common shares, establishing control over the board of directors. Pepper Company used the cost method to account for its investment in S during the year, but prepared consolidated financial statements at the end of the fiscal year, which are shown in summary form:

	P Co.	S Co.	Consolidated
Cash	$ 11,000	$ 12,000	$ 23,000
Accounts receivable	22,000	19,000	37,000
Inventory	14,200	9,200	22,400
Capital assets	83,000	64,300	152,300
Investment in S Co.	74,000	—	—
Intangible assets	—	—	3,725
	$204,200	$104,500	$238,425
Current liabilities	$ 30,000	$ 9,000	$ 35,000
Long-term liabilities	4,000	2,500	6,500
Non-controlling interest	—	—	23,000
Common shares	100,000	60,000	100,000
Retained earnings	70,200	33,000	73,925
	$204,200	$104,500	$238,425
Sales and other revenue	$ 96,000	$ 63,000	$146,750
Cost of Sales	80,500	49,000	120,500
Operating expenses	2,500	4,900	7,500
Non-controlling interest	—	—	2,025
Net income	$ 13,000	$ 9,100	$ 16,725
Opening retained earnings	67,200	26,900	67,200
Dividends	10,000	3,000	10,000
Closing retained earnings	$ 70,200	$ 33,000	$ 73,925

Required:

1. Why does the parent company use the cost method during the year?

2. Identify the accounts on the consolidated balance sheet that do not appear on either of the unconsolidated balance sheets. Explain their meaning.

3. Identify the accounts or amounts that appear on the unconsolidated financial statements that do not appear on the consolidated statements. Explain why they have been eliminated.

4. What is the most likely reason that the unconsolidated accounts receivables and current liabilities do not add to the balance shown on the consolidated balance sheet?

E12-14 *Cash Flow Statement:* For each of the following transactions, identify the item(s) that would appear on the cash flow statement. Identify the appropriate section (i.e., operations, investing, financing) and whether the item is an inflow or an outflow, or an add-back or deduction in operations. Assume that the indirect method of presentation is used in the operations section.

1. ABC Company reported a long-term investment of $46,000, a $50,000, 10-year bond bought at a discount in previous years. The bond pays annual interest of 7%, and $1,000 of discount amortization had been recorded in the current year.

2. The bond reported in (1) was subsequently sold for $52,500 when its book value was $46,500.

3. Common shares were purchased for $36,000, a short-term investment

4. T-bills were purchased for $350,000, a short-term investment that is considered a cash equivalent.

5. The T-bills in (4) were sold for $365,000.

6. The common shares in (3) were sold for $31,000.

7. The company owns 460,000 shares of Therion Co., over which it has significant influence. In the current year, investment revenue of $57,000 was recorded, and cash dividends of $36,000 were received.

PROBLEMS

P12-1 *Classification:* For each situation below, indicate how the investment would be classified, and how it would be accounted for. Assume intent to hold for the long-term, unless told otherwise.

1. Strip bonds (that is, those sold without interest, or "stripped" of interest) are acquired as a temporary investment. Management expects interest rates to fall and the price of the strip bonds to increase significantly over the coming year.

2. Common shares are bought in a small, family-owned business. The investor is the only non-family shareholder. The shares constitute 20% of the voting shares and the investor has one member on an eight-member board of directors, all of the rest of whom are members of the family investor group.

3. A mining property is exchanged for 60% of the voting shares in a company formed to develop the mining property. The remaining 40% of the shares are held by a mining company who will contribute equipment and expertise to physically mine the site. All decisions regarding operations and financing must be agreed to by both shareholders.

4. Common shares are bought in a large public company, whose shares are broadly held and widely traded. The investor owns 14% of the voting shares, is the largest shareholder, and sits on the board of directors.

5. Common shares are bought in a large public company whose shares are broadly held and widely traded. The investor owns 45% of the voting shares, puts eight people on a 20-member board of directors, and generally has its way in operating, investing, and financing policy of the investee.

6. Common shares are bought in a small, family-owned business. The investor is the only non-family shareholder, but sits on the family-controlled board. The investor also allows the company to use patented production processes, for a fee, a right not previously granted to any other company, and provides $5,000,000 in long-term loans to the investee.

7. To invest idle cash, common shares are bought in a large, public company, a tiny fraction of the outstanding common shares. The share price appreciated after sale, but the investor is convinced that significant additional price appreciation is probable. Therefore, the shares were not sold when cash was needed; the company borrowed from the bank instead, using the shares as collateral.

8. The investor owns 80% of the voting common shares of another company, which it plans to sell in the next year. The board of directors has formally approved the planned sale, and determined an appropriate price. To date, there have been no offers, although several parties are interested. In the meantime, the investee is continuing in business as usual.

P12-2 *Investment Classification:* As of 31 December 20X5, Arthur Investments Ltd. holds a number of investments in the securities of other companies:

1. Arthur holds $5,000,000 in bonds of RRM Manufacturing Ltd. These bonds will mature in 20X10. Arthur purchased these bonds at a deep discount — 40% of face value was paid — because RRM was in financial distress. No interest was received this year, and Arthur is in negotiations with RRM concerning the terms

and conditions of future interest and principal payments. Arthur is optimistic that they will receive at least 60% of face value at the end of the day, although the amount and timing of cash flows are very uncertian.

2. Arthur holds 15% of the voting shares of Bellows Manufacturing Ltd. Arthur has two members on the 10-member board of directors, and has extensive inter-company transactions with Bellows.

3. Arthur owns 60% of the outstanding non-voting perferred shares in Carleen Construction, a company with which they have regular inter-company sales. They intend to hold these securities for the long term.

4. Arthur owns 4% of the outstanding common shares of Dorcas Development Corp., a company whose shares are thinly traded on the over-the-counter market. Arthur would like to sell their shares, but no buyer has been found at the price that Arthur is determined to realize.

5. Arthur owns 30% of the common shares of Exxit Research Company. The remaining shares are equally divided among three other investors. Each investor has two representatives on the eight member board of directors. All strategic decisions to date appear to have been suggested and decided by the Arthur representatives on the board of directors; other representatives are quite passive and often do not attend meetings.

6. Arthur owns 60% of the common shares of Formal Marketing Company. The remaining shares are held by Mr. Formal. The six-member board of directors consists of four members appointed by Arthur, and two appointed by Formal. All decisions must be unanimously agreed to by the board members.

Required:

How should Arthur account for each of the above investments? Be specific, and explain your reasoning.

P12-3 *Temporary Equity Investments:* On 31 December 20X2, Raven Company's portfolio of temporary investments in equity securities was as follows (both purchased on 1 September 20X2):

Security	Shares	Unit Cost	Unit Market
Bic Corp., common shares	50	$186	$187
Cross Corp., $2.40 preferred shares	200	40	35

Transactions relating to this portfolio during 20X3 were as follows:

- 25 January — Received a dividend cheque on the Cross shares.
- 15 April — Sold 30 Bic Corporation shares at $151 per share.
- 25 July — Received a $45 dividend cheque on the Bic shares.
- 1 October — Sold the remaining shares of Bic Corporation at $149.50 per share.
- 1 December — Purchased 100 Pilot Corporation common shares at $47 per share plus a $30 brokerage fee. The fee is part of the cost of shares.
- 5 December — Purchased 400 Sanford Corporation common shares at $15 per share.
- 31 December — Management designated the Cross shares as a long-term portfolio investment. A formal transfer between temporary and long-term accounts is recorded in the books at book value.

On 31 December 20X3, the following unit market prices were available: Bic stock, $140; Cross stock, $38; Pilot stock, $51; and Sanford stock, $14. Raven uses the allowance method for LCM valuation.

Required:

1. Give the entries that Raven Company should make on (a) 1 September 20X2, and

(b) 31 December 20X2.

2. Give the investment items and amounts that should be reported on the 20X2 income statement and balance sheet.

3. Give the journal entries for 20X3 related to the temporary investments.

4. Give the investment items and amounts that should be reported on the 20X3 income statement and balance sheet.

5. Comment on a possible motive for reclassification of the Cross shares.

P12-4 *Temporary Debt Investments:* At 31 December 20X4, the portfolio of temporary investments held by Dow Company was as follows:

Security	Par Value	Interest Rate	Interest Payable	Cash Cost*	Date Bought	Maturity Date
X Corp. bonds	$10,000	6%	1 Nov.	$ 9,800	1 Sept. 20X4	1 Nov. 20x9
Y Corp. bonds	20,000	9%	31 Dec.	20,400	31 Dec. 20X4	31 Dec. 20x6

* Excluding any accrued interest.

Dow's annual reporting period ends on 31 December. At 31 December 20X4, the X Corporation bonds were selling at 98.5.

Transactions relating to the portfolio of temporary investments in debt securities during 20X5 were as follows:

- 1 June — Sold the Y Corporation bonds at 103, plus any accrued interest.
- 1 November — Collected interest on the X Corporation bonds.
- 1 December — Purchased $30,000 of Z Corporation bonds at 99.5 plus accrued interest. These bonds pay 8% interest semi-annually each March 1 and September 1. The investment is classified as a temporary investment.
- 31 December — The X Corporation bonds had a quoted market value of 99.5, and the Z bonds were quoted at 99. The X corporation bonds were transferred to the long-term classification because of a change in management intent. A formal entry was made to reflect the reclassification, at book value.

Required:

1. Give the 20X4 entries Dow Company would have prepared to record the purchase of the debt securities and collections of interest, including related adjusting entries.

2. Give all 20X5 entries to reflect transactions in the investments.

3. Show the items that would appear on the 20x5 income statement and balance sheet with respect to the investments.

P12-5 *Cost and Market Value Methods Compared:* Ace Investors Company buys and sells various debt and equity securities. These security investments represent approximately 90% of the firm's total assets. Ace has a policy of classifying all its securities as temporary investments, since it has traditionally sold any individual security when management felt it opportune to do so. Ace uses the market value method because it is more relevant to their primary financial statement users, shareholders, and their bankers.

The following data are taken from their records:

a. 1 January 20X1 — Purchase securities at a cost of $50 million.

b. 31 December — Market value of investment portfolio (in $ millions): 20X1, $56.0; 20X2, $52.0; 20X3, $43. (The $43 value is after the transaction in *d*.)

c. Cash dividends received (in $ millions): 20X1, $4.0; 20X2, $4.2; 20X3, $4.1.

d. 1 December 20X3 — Sold, for $6 million, securities that had an original cost of $5 million and market value at the end of 20X2 of $6.2 million.

Ace's accounting period ends 31 December.

Required:

1. What are the fundamental distinctions between the cost and market value methods for temporary investments?

2. Complete the schedule below using the cost and market value methods.

3. Why might Ace's investors prefer the market value method? Why might some prefer the cost method?

	20X1		20X2		20X3	
		Market		Market		Market
	Cost	Value	Cost	Value	Cost	Value
Items	Method	Method	Method	Method	Method	Method

Balance sheet
Assets:
    Investments

Income statement
Investment income:
    Dividends
    Gain or loss on market value
    Gain on sale

P12-6 *Long-Term Investment in Debt Securities:* On 1 July 20X4, Wyder Door Company acquired the following bonds, which Wyder intended to hold to maturity:

Security	Price	Face Amount Purchased
Flakey Cement 10% bonds, maturity date 1 July 20X9	101.5	$30,000
Green Lawn 8% bonds, maturity date, 31 December 20X6	97.0	20,000

Both bonds pay interest annually on 31 December. Premium and discount can be amortized on a straight-line basis.

Required:

1. Prepare the entry to record the investments. Accrued interest was paid on acquisition dates, as appropriate.

2. Prepare the entries to be made at 31 December 20X4.

3. Show the items and amounts that would be reported in the 20X4 income statement and balance sheet related to these investments.

4. Prepare the entries to be made on 31 December 20X5.

5. Show the items and amounts that would be reported in the 20X5 income statement and balance sheet related to these investments.

P12-7 *Long-Term Investment, Equity Method:* On 1 January 20X1, Parr Company purchased 30% of the 30,000 outstanding common shares of Stub Corporation at $17 per share as a long-term investment (the only long-term equity investment held). Parr had significant influence over Stub at this date. The following data relates to Stub Corporation.

a. At acquisition date, 1 January 20X1

	Value at	
	Book	**Market**
Assets not subject to depreciation	$250,000	$260,000*
Assets subject to depreciation, net		
(10-year remaining life; straight-line)	200,000	220,000
	$450,000	
Liabilities	$ 50,000	50,000
Common shares	300,000	
Retained earnings	100,000	
	$450,000	

* Difference is due to inventory, and this inventory is sold during 20X1.

b. Selected data available at 31 December 20X1 and 20X2

	20X1	20X2
Cash dividends declared and paid by		
Stub Corporation during the year	$ 8,000	$ 5,000
Income reported by Stub:		
Income (loss) before discontinued operations	24,000	(5,000)
Loss on discontinued operations	(2,000)	—
Quoted market price per share, Stub Corporation		
stock (31 December)	$ 20	$18

c. Partial sale

On 2 January 20X3, Parr Company sold 500 of the Stub shares at $18 per share.

Required:

1. Give all of the appropriate entries for Parr Company during 20X1 and 20X2. Use straight-line amortization of goodwill over a 30-year period.

2. Give the entry required on 2 January 20X3.

3. Show what items and amounts based on (1) and (2) will be reported on the 20X1, 20X2, and 20X3 income statements and on the 20X1 and 20X2 balance sheets.

P12-8 *Long-Term Equity Investment, Cost and Equity Methods Compared — Entries and Reporting:* On 1 January 20X5, Redmond Company purchased 3,000 of the 15,000 outstanding common shares of Decca Computer (DC) Corporation for $80,000 cash as a long-term investment. At that date, the balance sheet of DC showed the following book values (summarized):

Assets not subject to depreciation	$140,000*
Assets subject to depreciation (net)	100,000**
Liabilities	40,000
Common shares	150,000
Retained earnings	50,000

* Market value, $150,000; difference relates to land held for sale, which is sold in 20X5.
**Market value, $140,000, estimated remaining life, 10 years. Use straight-line depreciation with no residual value and amortization of goodwill over 20 years.

Additional subsequent data on DC:

	20X5	20X6
Net income	$25,000	$31,000
Cash dividends declared and paid	10,000	12,000
Market value per share	25	26
Extraordinary gain	0	5,000

Required:

1. For Case A, assume that the cost method is appropriate. For Case B, assume the equity method is appropriate. For each case, provide the investor's entries or give the required information for items (a) through (d) in a tabulation similar to the one below.

Entries Required and Other Information	Case A: Cost Method Is Appropriate	Case B: Equity Method Is Appropriate
a. Entry at date of acquisition.		
b. Amount of goodwill purchased.		
c. Entries at 31 Dec. 20X5 to recognize investment revenue and dividends.		
d. Entries at 31 Dec. 20X6 to recognize investment revenue and dividends.		

2. Are any entries need to recognize a LCM write-down at the end of 20X5 or 20X6? Explain.

3. For each case, reconstruct the investment accounts, showing the opening and closing balance and all changes in the account.

4. Explain why the investment account balance is different between the cost and equity methods.

P12-9 *Cash Flow Statement:* The following comparative data is available from the 20X4 balance sheet of Investcorp.:

	20X4	**20X3**
Temporary investments		
Temporary investments — cash equivalents	$ 61,000	$ 493,000
Temporary investments — not cash equivalents	4,950,000	1,216,000
Less: allowance to reduce portfolio to market value	(7,000)	(40,000)
	4,943,000	1,176,000
Long-term investments		
Investment in Tandor Ltd., at equity	971,200	950,000
Investment in Byron bonds, at amortized cost	615,000	609,300

In 20X4, the following transactions took place, and are properly reflected in the balance sheet accounts, above.

1. Dividends of $140,000 were received from Tandor Ltd. No shares of Tandor were bought or sold during the year.

2. Cash equivalents with a cost of $190,000 were sold for $191,500; other cash equivalents were sold at book value.

3. Temporary investments (not cash equivalents) costing $4,000,000 were bought during the year. Other temporary investment were sold at a loss of $18,000.

Other "typical" transactions and entries also occurred in 20X4 that are reflected in the balance sheet accounts. (You may find it helpful to reconstruct the transactions.)

Required:

What items would appear on the 20X4 cash flow statement? Assume the operations section is presented in the indirect format.

P12-10 *Comprehensive:* At 31 December 20X2, Dulles Transport reported the following regarding its investments:

Temporary investments — cash equivalents		$ 40,000
Temporary investments — other	$212,000	
Allowance to reduce temporary investments		
to market value	(15,000)	197,000
Long-term investments		170,000

The cash equivalent temporary investment was a $40,000, 4% (per annum) GIC that had a 30-day term. Other temporary investments were $136,000 invested in the shares of a Canadian public company, AMC Inc., and $76,000 invested in (marketable) 6% bonds with a 10-year term, that have a face value of $80,000.

    The long-term investment is 20,000 common shares in Brodulock Ltd. This investment is a portfolio investment.

Transactions in 20X3:

1. The GIC matured, returning principal plus $132 in interest, of which $79 had been accrued at year-end. A three-month GIC paying 3 3/4% (per annum) was bought for its face value, $50,000. It was sold for $51,250, including accrued interest, after 60 days.

2. The AMC shares held as a short-term investment rendered $4,100 in dividends. Subsequently, half of the investments were sold at a loss of $18,000. Later, a further $2,100 in dividends were received.

3. A further 20,000 common shares of Brodulock Ltd. were bought for $165,000, at which time it was agreed that Dulles had significant influence over Brodulock. At year-end, Brodulock declared dividends of $74,000, of which $29,600 accrued to Dulles. Dulles' share of income for the year was $61,400. Financial analysis at the time of purchase indicated that there were no assets or liabilities whose market value was different from net book value. Dulles' goodwill inherent in the purchase price amounted to $26,000, subject to amortization over 40 years. During the year, Dulles sold goods that cost $25,000 to Brodulock for $35,000. Brodulock has not resold the goods.

4. The bonds held as a temporary investment paid annual interest on 1 September. An amount of $1,600 had been accrued at the end of 20X2.

5. On 1 December 20X3, a $100,000 bond with a 10-year term and an interest rate of 6⅜% was bought as a temporary investment for 101⅞. December 1 was an interest date.

6. At year-end, the market value of the temporary investment portfolio was $4,000 less than cost.

7. At year-end, suitable accruals were recorded on the temporary bond investments.

Required:

Show the amounts that would appear on the 20X3 income statement, balance sheet and cash flow statement as a result of the transactions in investments. The indirect method is used in the operating activities section of the cash flow statement.

P12-11 *Reporting a Subsidiary:* Cohen Corporation is contemplating investing in a supplier company, Abbott Metals Ltd, in order to ensure a reliable source of supply. The controlling shareholder, who owns 147,000 shares, is willing to sell to Cohen for a price of $50 per share. Summarized financial statements and additional information related to Abbott, follow:

ABBOTT METALS
Balance Sheet
at 30 June 20X5

	Book Value	Fair Value
Cash	$ 120,000	$ 120,000
Accounts receivable ($419,000 from Cohen)	849,000	800,000
Inventory	1,310,000	1,800,000
Capital assets	1,492,000	700,000
Mining properties	6,701,000	11,400,000
	$10,472,000	14,820,000
Accounts payable	$ 1,375,000	$1,375,000
Long-term debt	4,990,000	5,219,000
Common shares (250,000 shares)	2,700,000	
Retained earnings	1,407,000	
	$10,472,000	

Required:

Assume Cohen buys 147,000 shares of Abbott at $50 per share. Describe the resulting reporting requirements, and describe the effect on the annual financial statements of Cohen. Include a calculation of goodwill in your response.

P12-12 *Consolidations (Appendix):* At the beginning of the current fiscal year, Poppa Co. bought 90% of the common shares of Son Ltd. for $7,350,000 cash. At that time, the book value of Son's assets reflected fair value except for land, which was undervalued on the books by $1,200,000. Son reported $500,000 of common stock and $5,500,000 of retained earnings on this date. Financial results at the end of the current fiscal year (in thousands):

	Poppa	Son
Cash	$ 1,610	$ 480
Accounts receivable	8,920	1,410
Inventory	12,100	1,400
Capital assets	10,520	1,310
Investment in Son Co.	7,350	0
Mining properties	0	6,050
	$40,500	$10,650
Current liabilities	$ 8,060	$ 1,400
Long-term debt	20,900	3,102
Common shares	8,600	500
Retained earnings	2,940	5,648
	$40,500	$10,650
Sales	$49,700	$12,900
Cost of sales	36,200	8,100
Other expenses	12,925	4,552
Other revenues	665	0
Net income	$ 1,240	$ 248
Opening retained earnings	2,100	5,500
Dividends	400	100
Closing retained earnings	$ 2,940	$ 5,648

During the year, Poppa bought $1,000,000 of goods from Son. Three-quarters had been resold at year-end. Son had recorded a $120,000 gross profit on these sales. Poppa still owed Son $800,000 at year-end. Goodwill should be amortized over 10 years.

Required:

Prepare a consolidated balance sheet, income statement and retained earnings statement for the current fiscal year. Round calculations to the nearest thousand.

P12-13 *Consolidations (Appendix):* P Co. bought 90% of the voting shares of S Co. on 1 January 20X2 for $19,500,000. On that date, S Co. had shareholders' equity of $15,900,000, including $6,000,000 of common shares. On that date, fair values of net assets approximated market values, except land that was undervalued on the books in the amount of $500,000, and depreciable capital assets that were undervalued by $1,400,000. Goodwill is to be amortized over 40 years; amortizable capital assets, 15 years.

During 20X2, P Co. sold goods to S Co in the amount of $600,000. All these goods were resold by S Co. by the end of 20X2. S Co. sold $400,000 of products to P Co.; ¼ had been resold by the end of the year. S Co. had recorded a $220,000 profit on the sale. P Co. still owed S Co. $375,000 at year-end.
Unconsolidated financial statements follow:

Year Ended 31 December 20X2	P Co.	S. Co.
Cash	$ 1,450,000	$ 213,000
Accounts receivable	16,300,000	3,415,000
Inventory	28,900,000	5,900,000
Capital assets	114,300,000	11,100,000
Investment in S Co.	19,500,000	—
Intangible assets	7,916,000	—
	$188,366,000	$ 20,628,000
Current liabilities	$ 39,000,000	$ 2,100,000
Long-term debt	80,000,000	500,000
Future (deferred) income tax	10,195,000	1,400,000
Common shares	17,900,000	6,000,000
Retained earnings	41,271,000	10,628,000
	$188,366,000	$ 20,628,000
Sales	$240,350,000	$ 30,600,000
Cost of sales	170,700,000	18,900,000
Other expenses	42,900,000	10,522,000
Other revenue	405,000	—
Net income	$ 27,155,000	$ 1,178,000
Opening retained earnings	30,316,000	9,900,000
Dividends	16,200,000	450,000
Closing retained earnings	$ 41,271,000	$ 10,628,000

Required:
1. Prepare consolidated financial statements as of 31 December 20X2.
2. Under what circumstances would P Co. not have to consolidate its subsidiary?
3. In what way are the consolidated financial statements superior to unconsolidated statements? Why do some feel consolidated statements are inferior?

APPENDIX

Fundamentals: The Accounting Information Processing System

ACCOUNTS, TRANSACTION RECORDING, AND FINANCIAL STATEMENTS

Financial accounting information is recorded in accounts, which describe specific resources, obligations, and the changes in these items. There are seven major types of accounts, grouped under two headings: permanent accounts (assets, liabilities, and owners' equity accounts) and temporary accounts (revenues, expenses, gains, and losses). Permanent accounts are also called real accounts, and temporary accounts are also called nominal accounts. The permanent accounts are those appearing in the balance sheet. The descriptive term *permanent* means that balances in these accounts are carried over to future accounting periods. *Temporary* accounts are closed out at the end of each fiscal year. Other temporary accounts are used, including cash dividends declared, income summary, and various "holding" accounts that are used for a specific purpose but are not separately disclosed in financial statements.

The accounting identity states the relationship between the balances of the permanent accounts:

Assets = Liabilities + Owners' Equity

The temporary accounts report events related to income-generating activities and appear in the income statement. For example, when rent is paid, the rent expense account describes the reason for the decrease in cash.

Economic events are recorded in an accounting information system (AIS) in such a way as to change at least two accounts. This practice, called the double-entry system, records the change in a resource or obligation and the reason for, or source of, the change. In the rent example above, if only the cash decrease were to be recorded, no record of the transaction's purpose would be maintained.

The double-entry system also ensures that the accounting equation remains in balance. For example, when a company acquires $10,000 worth of equipment by tendering a note payable to the seller for that amount, both assets and liabilities increase by $10,000. The accounting identity remains in balance.

Complementing the double-entry system, the debit-credit convention is used as a recording and balancing procedure. This convention divides accounts into two sides. In North American bookkeeping, the debit (dr.) side is always the left side, and the credit (cr.) side is always the right side.[1] These terms carry no further meaning and can't be interpreted as "increases" or "decreases" since, depending on the account type, a debit or a credit can record an increase or decrease. This is illustrated in the

---

[1] The debit-left and credit-right is reversed in the U.K., where the debits appear on the right and the credits on the left. Why is debit abbreviated as "dr.," when the letter "r" does not appear in the word? It's because the abbreviations *dr.* and *cr.* were originally derived from the words *debtor* and *creditor.*

T accounts summarized in Exhibit A-1. The T account is a form of account used for demonstrating transactions; its skeletal form takes the shape of the letter T. The T account reflects the general format of general ledger accounts, as we will discuss later.

The debit-credit convention helps maintain the accounting identity. For example, increases in assets (debits) are often associated with increases in liabilities (credits). Asset decreases (credits) often are associated with expenses (debits). Salary payments are an example: the dollar amount of the salary expense debit equals the dollar amount of the cash credit.

The debit-credit convention is a convenient way to check for recording errors. When the sums of debits and credits are not equal, an error is evident. (The converse, however, is not true. Equality of total debits and total credits does not imply that no errors have been made.) Without the convention, only increases and decreases in accounts would be recorded. In general, the dollar value of account increases would not equal the dollar value of account decreases for a given group of transactions. For example, paying off a long-term liability results in two decreases to cash and to long-term liabilities. Therefore, inequality of total increases and total decreases could not be used to signal errors.

At the end of a reporting period, after all transactions and events are recorded in accounts, financial statements are prepared. The financial statements report account balances, changes in account balances, and aggregations of account balances, such as net income and total assets. The financial statements include the income statement, the balance sheet, and the statement of cash flows. The income statement reports the portion of the change in net assets (owners' equity) attributed to income-producing activities. The balance sheet reflects the financial position of the entity — the accounting identity. Two other statements, the retained earnings statement and the statement of shareholders' equity, are also commonly reported. The steps leading to these financial statements are discussed in the rest of this chapter.

THE AIS AND THE ACCOUNTING CYCLE

An accounting information system (AIS) is designed to record accurate financial data in a timely and chronological manner, facilitate retrieval of financial data in a form useful to management, and simplify periodic preparation of financial statements for external use. Design of the AIS, to meet the company's information requirements, depends on the firm's size, the nature of its operations, the volume of data, its organizational structure, and government regulation.

The accounting cycle, illustrated in Exhibit A-2, is a series of sequential steps leading to the financial statements. This cycle is repeated each reporting period, normally a year. Exhibit A-2 applies to the preparation of all financial statements except the statement of changes in financial position, which requires additional input. Firms may combine some of these steps or change their order to suit their specific needs. Depending on the information-processing technology used, certain accounting cycle steps can be combined or in some cases omitted. Computerized systems increase the reliability of processing without compromising the relevance of the information. For example, general ledger software is used to perform much of the accounting cycle work in large companies. (Worksheets also facilitate the process and are discussed later in this appendix.) The fundamental nature of the process, however, is the same regardless of the technology used.

The first three steps in the accounting cycle require the most time and effort. The frequency of Step 3, posting, depends on the volume and nature of transactions, and the technology used. For example, firms with many cash transactions post to the cash account daily. Steps 4 through 9 generally occur at the end of the fiscal year. The last step, the posting of reversing entries, is optional and occurs at the beginning of the next accounting period.

EXHIBIT A-1
Debit/Credit Impacts on T Accounts

Permanent Accounts

Assets		=	Liabilities		+	Owners' Equity	
Debit	**Credit**		**Debit**	**Credit**		**Debit**	**Credit**
entries	entries		entries	entries		entries	entries
increase	*decrease*		*decrease*	*increase*		*decrease*	*increase*
assets	assets		liabilities	liabilities		owners' equity	owners' equity

Temporary Accounts

Expenses			Revenues	
Debit	**Credit**		**Debit**	**Credit**
entries	entries		entries	entries
increase	*decrease*		*decrease*	*increase*
expenses	expenses		revenues	revenues

Losses			Gains	
Debit	**Credit**		**Debit**	**Credit**
entries	entries		entries	entries
increase	*decrease*		*decrease*	*increase*
losses	losses		gains	gains

An example of each type of change is illustrated below.

Permanent Accounts

Debit	Credit
Inventory purchased	Cash paid
Wages payable paid	Interest payable accrued
Dividends declared	Common shares issued

Temporary Accounts

Debit	Credit
Sales discount	Sales
Cost of goods sold	Purchases returns
Loss on sale of land	Gain on sale of equipment

THE IMPACT OF COMPUTERIZATION

Few businesses keep manual records. Most use a customized or off-the-shelf computer program that will facilitate most of the steps in the accounting cycle (refer to Exhibit A-2):

- Journalizing transactions, adjustments, closing, and reversing entries.
- Posting entries.
- Preparation of trial balances.
- Preparation of financial statements.

Such programs have many advantages, including speed and accuracy.

EXHIBIT A-2
The Accounting Cycle

STEP 1: Identify Transactions or Events to Be Recorded

Objective: To gather information, generally in the form of source documents, about transactions or events.

STEP 2: Journalize Transactions and Events

Objective: To identify, assess, and record the economic impact of transactions on the firm in a chronological record (a journal), in a form that facilitates transfer to the accounts.

STEP 3: Posting from Journal to Ledger

Objective: To transfer the information from the journal to the ledger, the device that stores the accounts.

STEP 4: Prepare Unadjusted Trial Balance

Objective: To provide a convenient listing to check for debit-credit equality and to provide a starting point for adjusting journal entries.

STEP 5: Journalize and Post Adjusting Journal Entries

Objective: To record accruals, expiration of deferrals, estimations, and other events often not signalled by a new source document.

STEP 6: Prepare Adjusted Trial Balance

Objective: To check for debit-credit equality and to simplify preparation of the financial statements.

STEP 7: Prepare Financial Statements

Objective: To summarize operating results and financial position, and so on, in a form that will be useful to decision-makers.

STEP 8: Journalize and Post Closing Entries

Objective: To close temporary accounts and transfer net income amount to retained earnings.

STEP 9: Prepare Post-Closing Trial Balance

Objective: To check for debit-credit equality after the closing entries.

STEP 10: Journalize and Post Reversing Journal Entries

Objective: To simplify certain subsequent journal entries and reduce accounting costs (this is an optional step).

During Accounting Period

At the End of Accounting Period

At the Beginning of Next Accounting Period

What is left for the accountant to do? First of all, identification and control of transactions and adjustments is crucial. The accountant manages the entire process, ensuring that information entered is accurate and complete. Secondly, many elements in financial reporting require the exercise of professional judgement — choice of accounting policy, composition of the notes to the financial statements, and so on. These tasks require qualified decision-makers.

Regardless of how the steps in the accounting cycle are performed, they accomplish the same task — posting is posting, manual or computerized. The accountant has to understand this process to manage it.

THE ACCOUNTING CYCLE

The annual accounting cycle includes 10 steps, explained in the following section.

STEP 1: IDENTIFY TRANSACTIONS OR EVENTS TO BE RECORDED

The first step will identify transactions and events that cause a change in the firm's resources or obligations and will collect relevant economic data about those transactions. Events that change a firm's resources or obligations are categorized into three types:

1. Exchanges of resources and obligations between the reporting firm and outside parties. These exchanges are either reciprocal transfers or nonreciprocal transfers. In a reciprocal transfer, the firm both transfers and receives resources (e.g., sale of goods). In a nonreciprocal transfer, the firm either transfers or receives current or future resources (e.g., payment of cash dividends or receipt of a donation). All exchanges require a journal entry.

2. Internal events within the firm that affect its resources or obligations but do not involve outside parties. Examples are recognition of amortization and amortization of capital assets and the use of inventory for production. These events also generally require a journal entry. However, other events, such as increases in the value of assets resulting from superior management and similar factors, are not recorded.

3. External economic and environmental events beyond the control of the company. Examples include casualty losses and changes in the market value of assets and liabilities. At the present time, accounting standards allow recording of market value changes for only a few types of assets.

Transactions are defined as all events requiring a journal entry. Transactions are often accompanied by a source document, generally a paper record that describes the exchange, the parties involved, the date, and the dollar amount. Examples are sales invoices, freight bills, and cash register receipts. Certain events, such as the accrual of interest, are not signalled by a separate source document. Recording these transactions requires reference to the underlying contract supporting the original exchange of resources. Source documents are essential for the initial recording of transactions in a journal and are also used for subsequent tracing and verification, for evidence in legal proceedings, and for audits of financial statements.

STEP 2: JOURNALIZE TRANSACTIONS AND EVENTS

This step measures and records the economic effect of transactions in a form that simplifies transfer to the accounts. Accounting principles that guide measurement, recognition, and classification of accounts are applied.

Transactions are recorded chronologically in a journal — an organized medium for recording transactions in debit-credit format. A journal entry is a debit-credit description of a transaction that includes the date, the accounts and amounts involved, and a brief description. A journal entry is a temporary recording, although

EXHIBIT A-3
General Journal

Page J-16

Date 20X5	Accounts and Explanation	Posting Ref.	Amount Debit	Credit
2 Jan.	Equipment	150	15,000	
	Cash	101		5,000
	Notes payable	215		10,000
	Purchased equipment for use in the business. Paid $5,000 cash and gave a $10,000, one-year note with 15% interest payable at maturity.			

journals are retained as part of the audit trail; account balances are not changed until the information is transferred to the ledger accounts in Step 3.

Much of this text is concerned with the appropriate recording of economic events. The journal entry is an important means of illustrating the application of accounting principles, and it is used throughout this text. Accounting systems usually have two types of journals: the **general journal** and **special journals**. Nonrepetitive entries and entries involving infrequently used accounts are recorded in the general journal. Repetitive entries are recorded in special journals. If special journals are not used, all transactions are recorded in the general journal. Special journals are discussed later in this appendix. The general journal is used to illustrate most entries in this text.

The journal entry step is not absolutely essential; transaction data can be recorded directly into the accounts. However, the journal entry step has advantages. A journal is a place to record transactions when access to the ledger accounts is restricted. Transaction processing is more efficient, and less costly, if transactions are grouped in a journal and processed together. By using journals, review and analysis of transactions are much simpler and the accounts consume less storage space. Also, a chronological list of transactions is provided. Transactions can be difficult to reconstruct without a journal because the debits and credits are located in different accounts. Journals are typically part of the paper trail relied on by auditors.

Exhibit A-3 illustrates a portion of a page from a general journal. This entry records the purchase of equipment financed with cash and debt, recorded at the value of the resources used to acquire it. The names of the accounts credited are listed below and to the right of the debited accounts.

Some companies use computerized systems to bypass the traditional journal entry step. Retailers, for example, record relevant information about a transaction by using bar codes printed on many product packages. Optical scanning equipment reads the bar code and transmits the information to a computer, which records the proper amount directly in the relevant ledger accounts. Accounting cost savings can be significant.

STEP 3: POSTING FROM JOURNAL TO LEDGER

Transferring transaction data from the journal to the ledger is called posting. Posting reclassifies the data from the journal's chronological format to an account classification format in the ledger, which is a collection of the formal accounts. Computerized systems store ledger data on tape or disk until it is needed for processing another step in the accounting cycle.

Accounting systems usually have two types of ledgers: the **general ledger** and **subsidiary ledgers**. The general ledger holds the individual accounts, grouped according

EXHIBIT A-4
General Ledger (excerpts)

	Cash					**Acct. 101**
20X5				20x5		
1 Jan.	Balance	18,700		2 Jan.	J-16	5,000

	Equipment					**Acct. 150**
20X5						
1 Jan.	Balance	62,000				
2	J-16	15,000				

	Notes Payable					**Acct. 215**
				20X5		
				2 Jan.	J-16	10,000

to the seven elements of financial statements. Subsidiary ledgers support general ledger accounts that are comprised of many separate individual accounts. For example, a firm with a substantial number of customer accounts receivable will maintain one ledger account per customer, stored in an accounts receivable subsidiary ledger. The individual customer account is called the subsidiary account. The general ledger holds only the control account, the balance of which reflects the sum of all the individual customer account balances. Only the control accounts are used in compiling financial statements.

For example, assume that a firm's accounts receivable consist of two individual accounts with a combined balance of $6,000. The firm's general and subsidiary ledgers might show these balances:

General Ledger

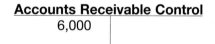

Accounts Receivable Control
6,000

Subsidiary Accounts Receivable Ledger

Graphics Corp.
4,000

Digimax Ltd.
2,000

Exhibit A-4 illustrates a section of a general ledger in T-account form. This ledger depicts three general ledger accounts after posting the journal entry shown in Exhibit A-3. Posting references and page numbers are used in both the journal and the ledger to ensure that an audit trail exists — that is, to indicate where an item in the account ledger came from and to which account the item was posted. Posting references also serve to confirm that an entry was posted. Posting references are provided automatically in a computerized system.

When the $5,000 cash credit from the general journal entry of Exhibit A-3 is posted to the cash ledger account, "101" is listed in the journal to indicate the account number to which the credit is posted. Similarly, in the cash ledger account,

"J-16" indicates the journal page number from which this amount is posted. Cross-referencing is especially important for posting large numbers of transactions, detecting and correcting errors, and maintaining an audit trail.

STEP 4: PREPARE UNADJUSTED TRIAL BALANCE

An unadjusted trial balance is prepared at the end of the reporting period, after all transaction entries are recorded in the journals and posted to the ledger. The unadjusted trial balance is a list of general ledger accounts and their account balances, in the following order: assets, liabilities, owners' equity, revenues, expenses, gains, and losses. For accounts with subsidiary ledgers, only the control account balances are entered into the trial balance, after reconciliation with the subsidiary ledger.

The unadjusted trial balance is the starting point for developing adjusting entries and for the worksheet, if used. Exhibit A-5 illustrates an unadjusted trial balance for Sonora, Ltd., a fictitious retailing company, at the end of the fiscal year. The trial balance reflects Sonora's transaction journal entries recorded during 20X5 and is the basis for the remainder of this accounting cycle illustration.

The unadjusted trial balance is a convenient means for checking that the sum of debit account balances equals the sum of credit account balances. If the sums of debit and credit balances are not equal, the error must be found and corrected. A reexamination of source documents and postings is one way to discover the source of an error. Equality of debits and credits does not, however, imply that the accounts are error-free. An unposted journal entry, an incorrectly classified account, and an erroneous journal entry amount are errors that do not cause inequality of total debits and credits.

As reported in Exhibit A-5, Sonora uses a periodic inventory system. Under this system, merchandise on hand is counted and costed at the end of each accounting period. The resulting inventory amount is used to update the inventory account balance. During the period, however, the inventory account balance remains at the 1 January amount and the cost of goods sold is not readily determinable. The unadjusted trial balance for Sonora reflects the 1 January 20X5 balance.

In a perpetual inventory system, the inventory account balance is constantly updated as merchandise is purchased and sold. Thus, the inventory account balance is correctly stated at the end of the accounting period, and there will be an up-to-date cost of goods sold account before any adjustments are made.

As shown in Exhibit A-5, Sonora's retained earnings account also reflects the 1 January 20X5 balance since no transaction affected this account during 20X5. Income tax expense is not listed in the unadjusted trial balance because the corporate income tax liability for the current year is not known until pre-tax income is computed, although companies that are required to pay quarterly estimated income taxes would have a balance in this account at this point. The loss from discontinued operations does not yet reflect any tax effect.

STEP 5: JOURNALIZE AND POST ADJUSTING JOURNAL ENTRIES

Many changes in a firm's economic resources and obligations occur continuously. For example, interest accrues daily on debts, as does rent expense on an office building. Other resources and obligations, such as employee salaries, originate as service is rendered, with payment to follow at specified dates. The end of the accounting period generally does not coincide with the receipt or payment of cash associated with these types of resource changes.

Accrual-basis accounting requires the recording of these changes at the end of the accounting period so that financial statements are fairly stated. Adjusting journal entries (AJEs) are used to record such resource changes to ensure the accuracy of the financial statements.

Cash-basis accounting, which generally records a journal entry only upon an exchange of cash between firms, does not typically require many adjusting entries. For example, unpaid wages at the end of a fiscal year require an adjusting entry under accrual accounting but not under cash-basis accounting. Cash-basis accounting can

EXHIBIT A-5
Unadjusted Trial Balance Illustrated

SONORA LTD.
Unadjusted Trial Balance
31 December 20X5

Account	Debit	Credit
Cash	$ 67,300	
Accounts receivable	45,000	
Allowance for doubtful accounts		$ 1,000
Notes receivable	8,000	
Inventory (1 January balance, periodic system)	75,000	
Prepaid insurance	600	
Land	8,000	
Building	160,000	
Accumulated amortization, building		90,000
Equipment	91,000	
Accumulated amortization, equipment		27,000
Accounts payable		29,000
Bonds payable, 6%		50,000
Common shares, no-par, 15,000 shares		170,000
Retained earnings		31,500*
Sales revenue		325,200
Interest revenue		500
Rent revenue		1,800
Purchases	130,000	
Freight on purchases	4,000	
Purchase returns		2,000
Selling expenses**	104,000	
General and administrative expenses**	23,600	
Interest expense	2,500	
Loss on discontinued operations	9,000	
Totals	$728,000	$728,000

*   1 January 20X5, balance (no transactions involved retained earnings in 20X5).
**   These broad categories of expenses are used to simplify presentation.

be used if it meets the needs of the financial statements users, which it may if cash flow is the only key variable, or if almost all transactions are immediately cash-based. Cash-basis financial statements are rarely in accordance with generally accepted accounting principles, though, which typically focus on accrual measures of both financial performance and financial position.

AJEs generally record a resource or obligation change and usually involve both a permanent and a temporary account. AJEs are recorded and dated as of the last day of the fiscal period. They are recorded in the general journal and posted to the ledger accounts. Source documents from earlier transactions are the primary information sources for AJEs. AJEs are classified into three categories: *deferrals, accruals*, and *other* AJEs.

Deferrals are for cash flows that occur before expense and revenue recognition. These AJEs are recorded when cash is paid for expenses that apply to more than one accounting period or when cash is received for revenue that applies to more than one accounting period. The portion of the expense or revenue that applies to future periods is deferred as a prepaid expense (asset) or unearned revenue (liability).

The AJE required for a deferral depends on the method used for recording routine operational cash payments and receipts that precede expense and revenue recognition. One method, here called the standard recording method, records an asset upon payment of cash before goods or services are received and records a liability upon receipt of cash before goods or services are provided. For example, if two months' rent is prepaid on 1 July, the standard method debits prepaid rent for that amount. An adjustment later in the year recognizes rent expense and the expiration of prepaid rent.

A second method, here called the expedient recording method, records an expense upon payment of cash before goods or services are received and records a revenue upon receipt of cash before goods or services are provided. In the case of rent paid in advance, the expedient method debits rent expense for two months' rent. This method is expedient because many cash payments and receipts relate to expenses and revenues that apply only to the year in which the cash flow occurs. No AJE is required in this example because rent expense is correctly stated at year-end. If a portion of the expense or revenue applies to a future accounting period, however, an AJE is required.

Accruals are for cash flows that occur after expense and revenue recognition. These AJEs are recorded when cash is to be paid or received in a future accounting period but all or a portion of the future cash flow applies to expenses or revenues of the current period. For example, unpaid wages accrued as wages payable at year-end represent wage costs matched against current-year revenues but not to be paid until next year. If the company is a landlord and rents space to tenants, uncollected rent accrued as rent receivable at year-end represents revenue earned in the current year but to be collected next year. In both cases, the expense or revenue is recognized before the cash flow occurs.

The following types of journal entries are often recorded at the end of the accounting period and are listed here as adjusting journal entries for completeness. These include:

- Reclassifications of permanent accounts.
- Estimation of expenses (bad debt expenses, for example).
- Cost allocations (amortization, for example).
- Recognition of cost of goods sold and inventory losses.
- Correction of errors discovered at year-end.

Cash generally is not involved in AJEs because transactions affecting cash are usually accompanied by source documents. However, corrections of errors involving the cash account discovered at the end of the accounting period are recorded as AJEs. Also, the entry required to adjust the cash balance upon receipt of the end-of-year bank statement, which lists service charges and other items unknown until receipt, is recorded as an AJE.

In the following discussion, Sonora's 31 December 20X5, unadjusted trial balance (Exhibit A-5) and additional information are used to illustrate AJEs.

Deferrals

Deferred Expenses. On 1 November 20X5, Sonora paid a six-month insurance premium of $600 in advance. On that date, the $600 payment is recorded as a debit to prepaid insurance and a credit to cash (the standard method). On the unadjusted trial balance, the full $600 payment is reflected in prepaid insurance. One-third of this payment ($200) is applicable to 20X5. A $200 expense, indicating the partial expiration of the asset, must be recognized. Sonora records insurance expense and other similar expenses in the general and administrative expense account. AJE (a) adjusts prepaid insurance and recognizes the expense:

a. *31 December 20X5*

General and administrative expense	200	
Prepaid insurance		200

The credit to prepaid insurance records the reduction in the asset that took place during the last two months of 20X5 as insurance benefits were received. No source document or transaction signals this entry, although the underlying insurance document was probably consulted. The remaining $400 of prepaid insurance reflects insurance coverage for the first four months of 20X6.

Deferred Revenue.   Sonora leased a small office in its building to a tenant on 1 January 20X5. The lease required an initial payment of $1,800 for 18 months' rent, which is recorded as a debit to cash and a credit to rent revenue (the expedient method). On 31 December 20X5, the unadjusted trial balance reports $1,800 in rent revenue, which is overstated by the $600 (one-third) relating to 20X6. AJE (b) is required to reduce the revenue recognized in 20X5 from $1,800 to $1,200 and to create a liability equal to the amount of rent relating to 20X6 ($600).

b. *31 December 20X5*
      Rent revenue   600
          Rent collected in advance (liability)   600

The result of this adjustment is a liability equal to the resources received for future services.

Accruals

Accrued Expenses.   Sonora has issued, at face value, $50,000 of 6% bonds paying interest yearly each 31 October. For the current accounting period, a two-month interest obligation accrues between 31 October 20X5 and 31 December 20X5. Sonora must recognize the liability and the resulting expense. The amount for the two-month period is $500 ($50,000 × 6% × 2/12). Therefore, on 31 December 20X5, both the interest expense and the associated payable are recognized in AJE (c):

c. *31 December 20X5*
      Interest expense   500
          Interest payable   500

Accrued Revenue.   Sonora's unadjusted trial balance lists $8,000 in notes receivable. The interest rate on these notes is 15% payable each 30 November. As of 31 December 20X5, the maker of the notes is obligated to Sonora for one month's interest of $100 ($8,000 × 15% × 1/12). AJE (d) records the resulting receivable and revenue:

d. *31 December 20X5*
      Interest receivable   100
          Interest revenue   100

Other Adjusting Entries

Amortization Expenses.   Property, plant, and equipment (capital assets) is the balance sheet category used to report many productive assets with a useful life exceeding one year. The cost of these assets is recognized as an expense over their period of use. Amortization or depreciation is a systematic and rational allocation of plant asset cost over a number of accounting periods. Throughout this textbook, the terms depreciation and amortization are used interchangeably. In practice, there is considerable diversity in the terminology used. The amount of amortization expense recognized depends on a number of factors:

• the original expenditure and subsequent capitalized expenditures
• the asset's useful life

- the method chosen for amortization measurement
- the asset's residual value

Amortization is similar to the recognition of an expense on a deferred item such as prepaid insurance in that the cash flow occurs before the expense is recognized. The main differences are the longer life and greater uncertainty of expected benefits of capital assets.

AJE (e) illustrates amortization recorded for Sonora at the end of 20X5 under the straight-line method. Sonora debits two expense accounts because the company uses the building and equipment assets both for selling and for general and administrative functions. Amortization is commonly allocated to several functions, including manufacturing operations. The adjusting entry for amortization is as follows:

e. *31 December 20X5*

Selling expense (amortization)	8,200	
General and administrative expense (amortization)	10,800	
Accumulated amortization, building		10,000
Accumulated amortization, equipment		9,000

				Proportionate Use by Function	
Asset	Cost	Residual Value	Useful Life Years	Selling Function	G & A* Function
Building	$160,000	$10,000	15	46%	54%
Equipment	91,000	1,000	10	40	60

Computation:

Building:					
[($160,000 – $10,000) / 15 yrs.)	= $10,000	x .46 =	$4,600	x .54 =	$ 5,400
Equipment:					
[($91,000 – $1,000) / 10 yrs.]	= 9,000	x .40 =	3,600	x .60 =	5,400
Totals	$19,000		$8,200		$10,800

*General and administrative.

AJE (e) reduces the net book value of the building and equipment accounts. Accumulated amortization is a contra account. A contra account has a balance opposite that of the account to which it relates. Thus, accumulated amortization is subtracted from the gross building and equipment accounts, leaving the net unamortized account balances (net book value). Sonora's balance sheet illustrates this offset. Contra accounts ensure that major assets are reported at original cost.

Many methods of amortization are permitted under GAAP. All entail systematic and rational allocation of capital asset cost to accounting periods. Amortization expense recognized in an accounting period does not generally equal the portion of the asset's value used up in that period. Amortization expense recognition is not an asset valuation process. Furthermore, the net book value of plant assets does not generally equal current value.

Bad Debt Expense. Often, goods and services are sold on credit. Accounts that are never collected result in bad debt expense, which is a risk of doing business on credit terms. Most large firms use a bad debt estimate to reduce income and accounts receivable in the period of sale. This practice prevents overstatement of both income and assets and is required if bad debts are probable and estimable. Recognition of bad debt expense is accomplished with an AJE that debits bad debt expense and credits the allowance for doubtful accounts, a contra account to the accounts receivable account.

Estimates of uncollectible accounts may be based on credit sales for the period or the year-end accounts receivable balance. Assume that Sonora extends credit on

$120,000 of sales during 20X5. Prior experience indicates an expected 1% average bad debt rate on credit sales. Sonora treats bad debt expense as a component of selling expenses and records AJE (f):

f.   *31 December 20X5*
        Selling expense ($120,000 × .01)   1,200
            Allowance for doubtful accounts   1,200

The credit is made to the allowance account, rather than to accounts receivable, because the identities of the uncollectible accounts are not yet known. In addition, the use of the contra account maintains agreement between the balance in accounts receivable control and the total of account balances in the accounts receivable subsidiary ledger.

The $1,200 allowance is the portion of 20X5 credit sales not expected to be collected. Net accounts receivable, the difference between the balance in accounts receivable and the allowance account, is an estimate of the cash ultimately expected to be received from sales on account. Bad debt expense is reported in the income statement, although often not as a separate line item.

Cost of Goods Sold.   The methodology used to determine cost of goods sold (a retailer's largest expense) depends on whether a perpetual or a periodic inventory system is used. In a perpetual system, no AJE is needed to establish cost of goods sold. However, an AJE might be needed to correct errors or to recognize inventory losses due to theft and economic factors. In a periodic system, cost of goods sold is determined either by an AJE or by closing entries, both of which update the inventory account and close inventory-related accounts.

A perpetual inventory system maintains an inventory record for each item stocked. This record contains data on each purchase and issue. An up-to-date balance is maintained in the inventory account. The cost of each item purchased is debited to the inventory account. Suppose an item that sells for $300 is carried in inventory at a cost of $180. A sale of this item requires two entries:

Cash (or accounts receivable)   300
    Sales revenue   300

Cost of goods sold   180
    Inventory   180

In a perpetual inventory system, the ending balance in the inventory account equals the correct ending inventory amount, assuming no errors or inventory losses. The cost of goods sold balance is also up-to-date, reflecting the recorded cost of all items sold during the period. Thus, no AJEs are needed unless the inventory account balance disagrees with the total of individual item costs determined by the annual physical count.

In contrast, a periodic system does not maintain a current balance in inventory or cost of goods sold. Instead, the physical inventory count at the end of the period is used to determine the balances of these two accounts. The purchases account, rather than the inventory account, is debited for all purchases during the period. In this case, the unadjusted trial balance at the end of an accounting period reflects the beginning inventory, and cost of goods sold does not yet exist as an account. An AJE *can* be used to set purchases, purchases returns, and other purchase-related accounts to zero (i.e., close these accounts), to replace the beginning inventory amount with the ending inventory amount in the inventory account; and to recognize cost of goods sold for the period.

To illustrate, Sonora determines its ending inventory to be $90,000. The company uses a periodic system, and computes cost of goods sold and records AJE (g) as follows:

g. *31 December 20X5*

Inventory (ending)	90,000	
Purchase returns	2,000	
Cost of goods sold (see below)	117,000	
Inventory (beginning)		75,000
Purchases		130,000
Freight on purchases		4,000

Cost of Goods Sold Computation —
31 December 20X5

Beginning inventory		$ 75,000
Add (from the current-year accounts):		
Purchases	$130,000	
Freight on purchases	4,000	
Purchase returns	(2,000)	
Net purchases		132,000
Total goods available for sale		$207,000
Less: Ending inventory		
(from physical count)		90,000
Cost of goods sold		$117,000

Two sources of information contribute to entry (g): the unadjusted trial balance from which several account balances are taken, and the physical inventory count indicating $90,000 of inventory on hand. *Alternatively, the accounts related to cost of goods sold may be left in the adjusted trial balance, untouched, and used in detail to create the financial statements. They would then be eliminated in closing entries.* Both approaches are widely used in practice and result in the same reported income and financial position. It's really a question of which method is preferred by a particular accountant or computerized reporting package. The closing entry approach is illustrated below in the discussion of Step 9, closing entries.

Income Tax Expense. The recognition of income tax expense, an accrual item, is often the final AJE. Many firms pay estimated income taxes quarterly, necessitating an AJE at the end of the accounting period to record fourth-quarter taxes due. For simplicity, assume that Sonora pays its income tax once each year after the end of the full accounting period.

A worksheet or partial adjusted trial balance (prior to income tax determination) simplifies the calculation of pretax income. The amounts in parentheses indicate the account balance in the unadjusted trial balance plus or minus the effects of AJEs, denoted by letter.

Assume that Sonora faces an average income tax rate of 40%, that amortization expense equals tax amortization, and that the loss from discontinued operations and all other expenses are fully tax deductible. AJE (h) recognizes the resulting $20,000 ($50,000 × 40%) income tax expense:

h. *31 December 20X5*

Income tax expense	20,000	
Income tax payable		20,000

For simplicity, the entire income tax expense is recorded in one account. Sonora's income statement (Exhibit A-7), however, separates the $3,600 income tax reduction associated with the loss from discontinued operations ($9,000 × 40%) from income

Calculation of Pretax Income
For the Year Ended 31 December 20X5

Revenues:			
Sales revenue	$325,200		
Interest revenue ($500 + $100 (d))	600		
Rent revenue ($1,800 – $600 (b))	1,200	$327,000	
Expenses:			
Cost of goods sold (g)	117,000		
Selling expenses			
($104,000 + $8,200 (e) + $1,200 (f),	113,400		
General and administrative expenses	34,600		
($23,600 + $200 (a) + $10,800 (e))			
Interest expense ($2,500 + $500 (c))	3,000		
Discontinued operations (pretax)	9,000	277,000	
Pre-tax income		$ 50,000	

tax on income before the discontinued operation. This practice is called *intraperiod tax allocation*.

Additional adjusting journal entries are illustrated throughout this text. In all cases, AJEs are posted to the appropriate ledger accounts.

STEP 6: PREPARE ADJUSTED TRIAL BALANCE

At this point in the cycle, the transaction journal entries and the AJEs have been journalized and posted and an adjusted trial balance is prepared. This trial balance lists all the account balances that will appear in the financial statements (with the exception of retained earnings, which does not reflect the current year's net income or dividends). The purpose of the adjusted trial balance is to confirm debit-credit equality, taking all AJEs into consideration. Exhibit A-6 presents the adjusted trial balance for Sonora.

The account balances in the adjusted trial balance reflect the effects of AJEs. For example, the $400 balance in prepaid insurance equals the $600 balance in the unadjusted trial balance less the reduction caused by AJE (a) for this year's coverage. New accounts not appearing in the unadjusted trial balance emerge from the adjustment process. For Sonora, several accounts are created as a result of an AJE: interest receivable, interest payable, rent collected in advance, income tax payable, cost of goods sold, and income tax expense. AJE (g) has the opposite effect: It closes purchases, freight on purchases, and purchase returns. The financial statements now can be prepared from the adjusted trial balance.

STEP 7: PREPARE FINANCIAL STATEMENTS

The financial statements are the culmination of the accounting cycle. Financial statements can be produced for a period of any duration. However, monthly, quarterly, and annual statements are the most common.

The income statement, retained earnings statement, and balance sheet are prepared directly from the adjusted trial balance. The income statement is prepared first because net income must be known before the retained earnings statement can be completed. The temporary account balances are transferred to the income statement, and the permanent account balances (except for retained earnings) are transferred to the balance sheet. Exhibit A-7 illustrates Sonora's 20X5 income and retained earnings statements.

EXHIBIT A-6
Adjusted Trial Balance Illustrated

SONORA LTD.
Adjusted Trial Balance
31 December 20X5

Account	Debit	Credit
Cash	$ 67,300	
Accounts receivable	45,000	
Allowance for doubtful accounts		$ 2,200
Notes receivable	8,000	
Interest receivable	100	
Inventory	90,000	
Prepaid insurance	400	
Land	8,000	
Building	160,000	
Accumulated amortization, building		100,000
Equipment	91,000	
Accumulated amortization, equipment		36,000
Accounts payable		29,000
Interest payable		500
Rent collected in advance		600
Income tax payable		20,000
Bonds payable, 6%		50,000
Common shares, no-par, 15,000 shares		170,000
Retained earnings		31,500
Sales revenue		325,200
Interest revenue		600
Rent revenue		1,200
Cost of goods sold	117,000	
Selling expenses	113,400	
General and administrative expenses	34,600	
Interest expense	3,000	
Income tax expense	20,000	
Loss from discontinued operations	9,000	
Totals	$766,800	$766,800

Total income tax expense ($20,000) in the income statement is allocated as follows: $23,600 on income before discontinued operations and $3,600 tax savings on the loss from discontinued operations.

The retained earnings statement explains the change in retained earnings for the period. If Sonora declared dividends during 20X5, they would be subtracted in the retained earnings statement. A retained earnings statement and a statement of shareholders' equity generally are included in the complete set of financial statements. Sonora chose to report only a retained earnings statement because no changes occurred in the other equity accounts during 20X5.

Exhibit A-8 illustrates the 20X5 balance sheet. The ending retained earnings balance is taken from the retained earnings statement rather than from the adjusted trial balance.

EXHIBIT A-7
Income and Retained Earnings Statements Illustrated

SONORA LTD.
Income Statement
for the year ended 31 December 20X5

Revenues:		
Sales	$325,200	
Interest	600	
Rent	1,200	
Total revenues		$327,000
Expenses:		
Cost of goods sold	117,000	
Selling	113,400	
General and administrative	34,600	
Interest	3,000	
Total expenses before income tax		268,000
Income before tax and discontinued operations		59,000
Income taxes on income before discontinued operations		
($59,000 × 40%)		23,600
Income before discontinued operations		35,400
Loss from discontinued operations	9,000	
Less tax savings ($9,000 × 40%)	3,600	5,400
Net income		$ 30,000

SONORA LTD.
Retained Earnings Statement
for the year ended 31 December 20X5

Retained earnings, 1 January 20X5	$ 31,500
Net income	30,000
Retained earnings, 31 December 20X5	$ 61,500

STEP 8: JOURNALIZE AND POST CLOSING ENTRIES
Closing entries

- reduce to zero (close) the balances of temporary accounts related to earnings measurement and dividends.

- are recorded in the general journal at the end of the accounting period.

- are posted to the ledger accounts.

Permanent accounts are not closed because they carry over to the next accounting period. The retained earnings account is the only permanent account involved in the closing process.

EXHIBIT A-8
Balance Sheet Illustrated

SONORA LTD.
Balance Sheet
at 31 December 20X5

Assets
Current assets:

Cash		$ 67,300
Accounts receivable	$ 45,000	
Allowance for doubtful accounts	(2,200)	42,800
Notes receivable		8,000
Interest receivable		100
Inventory		90,000
Prepaid insurance		400
Total current assets		208,600

Capital assets:

Land			8,000
Building	$160,000		
Accumulated amortization, building	(100,000)	60,000	
Equipment	91,000		
Accumulated amortization, equipment	(36,000)	55,000	
Total capital assets			123,000

Total assets	$331,600

Liabilities
Current liabilities:

Accounts payable	$ 29,000
Interest payable	500
Rent collected in advance	600
Income tax payable	20,000
Total current liabilities	50,100

Long-term liabilities:

Bonds payable, 6%	50,000
Total liabilities	100,100

Shareholders' Equity
Contributed capital:

Common shares, no-par, 15,000 shares issued and outstanding	$170,000	
Retained earnings	61,500	
Total shareholders' equity		231,500
Total liabilities and shareholders' equity		$331,600

Income Statement Accounts

Because net income is measured for a specific interval of time, the balances of the income statement accounts are reduced to zero at the end of each accounting period. Otherwise, these accounts would contain data from previous periods.

While some accountants prefer to close temporary accounts directly to retained earnings, it is quite common to use an account called income summary to accumulate the balances of income statement accounts in the closing entry process. The income summary is a temporary clearing account — an account used on a short-term basis for a specific purpose. The balances in expenses and losses are reduced to zero and transferred to the income summary by crediting each of those accounts and debiting income summary for the total. Revenues and gains are debited to close them, and the income summary account is credited.

This process leaves a net balance in the income summary account equal to net income (credit balance) or net loss (debit balance) for the period. The income summary account is then closed by transferring the net income amount to retained earnings. Sonora makes three closing entries to transfer 20X5 net income to retained earnings:

31 December 20X5

1. *To close the revenue and gain accounts to the income summary*

Sales revenue	325,200	
Interest revenue	600	
Rent revenue	1,200	
Income summary		327,000

2. *To close the expense and loss accounts to the income summary*

Income summary	297,000	
Cost of goods sold		117,000
Selling expenses		113,400
General and administrative expenses		34,600
Interest expense		3,000
Loss from discontinued operations		9,000
Income tax expense		20,000

3. *To close the income summary (i.e., transfer net income to retained earnings)*

Income summary	30,000	
Retained earnings		30,000

After the first two closing entries are recorded and posted, the balance in the income summary equals net income ($30,000):

Income Summary

(2)	297,000		(1)	327,000
			Balance	30,000

The temporary accounts now have zero balances and are ready for the next period's accounting cycle. The third entry closes the income summary account and transfers net income to retained earnings.

Dividends

When cash dividends are declared, firms debit either retained earnings or cash dividends declared, a temporary account. Dividends payable is credited. If cash dividends declared is debited, another closing entry is required:

Retained earnings	amount of dividends
Cash dividends declared	amount of dividends

In this case, the net result of closing entries is to transfer to retained earnings an amount equal to earnings less dividends declared for a period.

Alternative Approach for Inventories

Inventory-related accounts can be adjusted and closed in the closing process as an alternative to the AJE approach illustrated previously in AJE (g). If the closing alternative is used, the following three closing entries replace AJE (g) and the three closing entries illustrated above:

1.	Income summary	389,000	
	Inventory (opening)		75,000
	Purchases		130,000
	Freight on purchases		4,000
	Selling expenses		113,400
	G & A expenses		34,600
	Interest expense		3,000
	Loss from discontinued operations		9,000
	Income tax expense		20,000
2.	Inventory (ending)	90,000	
	Sales revenue	325,200	
	Interest revenue	600	
	Rent revenue	1,200	
	Purchase returns	2,000	
	Income summary		419,000
3.	Income summary	30,000	
	Retained earnings		30,000

Using this approach, inventory-related accounts are included with expenses and revenues for closing entry purposes. The net impact on the income summary account and, in turn, income and retained earnings are identical under both approaches. However, this approach does not isolate cost of goods sold in a separate account.

STEP 9: PREPARE POST-CLOSING TRIAL BALANCE

A post-closing trial balance lists only the balances of the permanent accounts after the closing process is finished. The temporary accounts have balances of zero. This step is taken to check for debit-credit equality after the closing entries are posted. Firms with a large number of accounts find this a valuable checking procedure because the chance of error increases with the number of accounts and postings. The retained earnings account is now stated at the correct ending balance and is the only permanent account with a balance different from the one shown in the adjusted trial balance. Exhibit A-9 illustrates the post-closing trial balance.

STEP 10: JOURNALIZE AND POST REVERSING JOURNAL ENTRIES

Depending on the firm's accounting system and its accounting policies, reversing journal entries (RJEs) may be used to simplify certain journal entries in the next accounting period. RJEs are optional entries that

EXHIBIT A-9
Post-Closing Trial Balance Illustrated

SONOR LTD.
Post-Closing Trial Balance
31 December 20X5

Account	Debit	Credit
Cash	$ 67,300	
Accounts receivable	45,000	
Allowance for doubtful accounts		$ 2,200
Notes receivable	8,000	
Interest receivable	100	
Inventory	90,000	
Prepaid insurance	400	
Land	8,000	
Building	160,000	
Accumulated amortization, building		100,000
Equipment	91,000	
Accumulated amortization, equipment		36,000
Accounts payable		29,000
Interest payable		500
Rent collected in advance		600
Income tax payable		20,000
Bonds payable, 6%		50,000
Common shares, nopar, 15,000 shares		170,000
Retained earnings		61,500
Totals	$469,800	$469,800

- are dated the first day of the next accounting period.
- use the same accounts and amounts as an AJE but with the debits and credits reversed.
- are posted to the ledger.

RJEs are appropriate only for AJEs that

1. defer the recognition of revenue or expense items recorded under the expedient method, or
2. accrue revenue or expense items during the current period (for example, wages expense).

Thus, if a deferral or accrual AJE creates or increases an asset or liability, an RJE is appropriate. RJEs are inappropriate for AJEs that adjust assets and liabilities recorded for cash flows preceding the recognition of revenues and expenses (the standard method) and for some other AJEs, such as reclassifications, error corrections, and estimations.

In the following examples, assume a 31 December year-end.

Deferred Item — Expedient Method. Assume that on 1 November 20X5, $300 is paid in advance for three months' rent:

1 November 20X5 — originating entry

Rent expense	300	
Cash		300

31 December 20X5 — adjusting entry

Prepaid rent	100	
Rent expense		100

	With Reversing Entry	**Without Reversing Entry**
1 January 20X6		
Reversing entry: Rent expense 100		
Prepaid rent 100		
20X6		
Subsequent entry: (No entry needed)	Rent expense 100	
	Prepaid rent 100	

With or without an RJE, rent expense recorded in 20X6 is $100. Use of the RJE, however, saves the cost and effort of reviewing the relevant accounts and source documents to determine the subsequent year's entry. The RJE makes the necessary adjustments to the accounts while the information used in making the AJE is available.

Now consider the standard method applied to the same example.

1 November 20X5 — originating entry

Prepaid rent	300	
Cash		300

31 December 20X5 — adjusting entry

Rent expense	200	
Prepaid rent		200

An RJE is not appropriate when the standard method is used for deferrals because a subsequent entry is required whether or not the AJE is reversed. No purpose is served by reinstating (debiting) prepaid rent $200 because that amount has expired.

Accrued Item. Assume that the last payroll for 20X5 is on 28 December. Wages earned through 28 December are included in this payroll. The next payroll period ends 4 January 20X6, at which time $2,800 of wages will be paid. Wages earned for the three-day period ending 31 December 20X5, are $1,500, which will be paid in 20X6. The following AJE is necessary to accrue these wages:

31 December 20X5 — adjusting entry

Wages expense	1,500	
Wages payable		1,500

	With Reversing Entry	**Without Reversing Entry**
1 January 20X6		
Reversing entry:	Wages payable 1,500	
	Wages expense 1,500	
4 January 20X6		
Subsequent entry:	Wages expense 2,800	Wages expense 1,300
	Cash 2,800	Wages payable 1,500
		Cash 2,800

In this example, the RJE simplifies the subsequent payroll entry, which can now be recorded in a manner identical to all other payrolls. With or without reversing entries, total 20X6 wage expense recognized through 4 January 20X6, is $1,300. RJEs often create abnormal short-term account balances. In the above example, the 1 January 20X6, RJE creates a credit balance in wages expense. The subsequent entry changes the net balance of wages expense to a $1,300 debit.

Some of Sonora's AJEs could be reversed:

- (b) Rent expense (expedient method — deferred item).

- (c) Interest expense (accrual).

- (d) Interest revenue (accrual).

- (h) Income tax expense (accrual).

SUBSIDIARY LEDGERS

Companies typically maintain both *control* and *subsidiary* ledger accounts. Subsidiary ledgers are often kept for accounts payable and accounts receivable, although any ledger account can be supported by a subsidiary ledger if size and complexity warrant.

The sum of all account balances in a subsidiary ledger must equal the related control account balance in the general ledger. To ensure that the control account and its subsidiary ledger are equal, frequent reconciliations are made. All posting must be complete, both to the control account and to the subsidiary ledger, before a reconciliation can be accomplished. Postings are made in total to the control account and to individual accounts in the subsidiary ledger. These postings are described in more depth in the next section.

To illustrate a reconciliation, refer ahead to the accounts receivable subsidiary ledger in Exhibit A-13. A reconciliation for accounts receivable control and the accounts receivable subsidiary ledger based on the information in Exhibit A-13 follows:

Reconciliation of Accounts Receivable Subsidiary Ledger
at 31 January 20X5

Subsidiary ledger balances

		Amount
112.13	Adams Co.	$ 980
112.42	Miller, J. B.	196
112.91	×Y Manufacturing Co.	1,960
Total		$3,136

General ledger balance

Accounts receivable control ($5,000 + $9,360 – $11,224)	$3,136

Subsidiary ledgers contain information that helps the company operate efficiently — individual account receivable and payable balances are essential information. In smaller companies, subsidiary ledgers can be maintained through a simple filing system — for example, a copy of a sales invoice that is not paid can be kept in a special file until the money is received. At any time, the outstanding receivables are equal to the total of the invoices in the file. The same can be done with accounts payable, if all unpaid bills are kept in an accounts payable file. The point is that formal accounting systems are made necessary by size and complexity, but simple methods in simple situations can be just as effective if efficiently operated.

SPECIAL JOURNALS

Both *general journals* and *special journals* are used in many accounting systems. Even when extensive use is made of special journals, a need exists for a general journal to record the adjusting, closing, reversing, and correcting entries and those transactions that do not apply to any of the special journals. A general journal was illustrated in Exhibit A-3.

A special journal is designed to expedite the recording of similar transactions that occur frequently. Each special journal is constructed specifically to simplify the data processing tasks involved in journalizing and posting those types of transactions. Special journals can be custom-designed to meet the particular needs of the business. Commonly used special journals include:

a. *Sales journal* for recording sales of merchandise on credit only.
b. *Purchases journal* for recording purchases of merchandise on credit only.
c. *Cash receipts journal* for recording cash receipts only, including cash sales.
d. *Cash disbursements journal* for recording cash payments only, including cash purchases.
e. *Voucher system*, designed to replace the purchases journal and cash payments journal, composed of:
    i. A *voucher register* for recording vouchers payable only. A voucher payable is prepared for each cash payment regardless of purpose.
    ii. A *cheque register* for recording all cheques written in payment of approved vouchers.

The special journals illustrated in this appendix carry page numbers preceded by letters indicating the journal name. The S in the page number of Exhibit A-4 denotes the sales journal, for example.

Sales Journal. This special journal is designed to record sales on account, which otherwise would be recorded as follows in a general journal:

2 January 20X5

Accounts receivable ($1,000 × 98%)	980	
Sales revenue		980
(Credit sale to Adams Company; invoice price, $1,000; terms 2/10, n/30)		

The sales journal can accommodate any entry that involves a debit to accounts receivable and a credit to sales. However, this is the only entry it can record. If the debit is to cash, or notes receivable, another journal must be used. Exhibit A-10 illustrates a typical sales journal for credit sales for a business with two sales departments. The above entry is shown as the first entry in 20X5. The amount of sale is recorded only once. Each entry in the sales journal records the same information found in the traditional debit-credit format.

Terms 2/10, n/30 mean that if the account is paid within 10 days after date of sale, a 2% cash discount is granted. The cash discount encourages early payment. If the bill is not paid within the 10-day discount period, the full amount is past due at the end of 30 days. Receipt of $1,000 after the 10-day discount period does not increase sales revenue but means that the seller has earned finance revenue of $20 ($1,000 − $980). Hence, it is correct to record *net* sales revenue of $980. However, many companies prefer to record *gross* sales, $1,000 in this example, because it is easier to focus on the amount of the invoice.

The posting of amounts from the sales journal to the general and subsidiary ledgers is simplified. The two phases in posting a sales journal are the following:

1. Daily posting: The amount of each credit sale is posted daily to the appropriate individual account in the accounts receivable subsidiary ledger. Posting is indicated by entering the account number in the posting reference column. For example, the number 112.13 entered in the posting reference column in Exhibit A-10 is the account number assigned to Adams Company and shows that $980 is posted as a debit to Adams Company in the subsidiary ledger. The number 112 is the general number used for accounts receivable (see Exhibit A-14).

2. Monthly posting: At the end of each month, the receivable and sale amount column is totalled. This total is posted to two accounts in the general ledger. In Exhibit A-10, the $9,360 total is posted as a debit to account no. 112 (accounts receivable control) and as a credit to account no. 500 (sales revenue control). The T-accounts shown in Exhibit A-14 illustrate how these postings are reflected in both the general ledger and the subsidiary ledger. The two ledgers show the journal page from which each amount is posted.

Purchases Journal. This special journal is designed to accommodate frequent purchases of merchandise on account. Again, there is only one entry that can go into this journal — a debit to purchases, and a credit to accounts payable. Other entries, including purchases for cash, go elsewhere. Consider the following entry, recorded in general journal format:

3 January 20X5

Purchases ($1,000 × .99)	990	
Accounts payable (PT Mfg. Co.)		990
(terms 1/20, n/30)		

Again note the use of net recording. The invoice is recorded at its net amount, after the 1% discount. Some companies prefer to record purchase invoices gross, and record purchase discounts taken when they record payment. Notice also that the entry assumes a periodic inventory procedure. Under a perpetual inventory system, the debit would always be to the inventory account.

This entry is recorded as the first 20X5 entry in the purchases journal illustrated in Exhibit A-11. The accounting simplifications found in the sales journal are present in the purchases journal as well. Each amount is posted daily as a credit to the account of an individual creditor in the accounts payable subsidiary ledger. At the end of the month, the total of the purchases and payable amount column ($6,760 in Exhibit A-11), is posted to the general ledger as a debit to the purchases account (no. 612) and as a credit to the accounts payable control account (no. 210).

Cash Receipts Journal. A special cash receipts journal is used to accommodate a large volume of cash receipts transactions. This journal can accommodate any entry that involves a debit to cash. Multiple sources of cash (the credits) are accommodated by designing several credit columns for recurring credits, and a miscellaneous accounts column for infrequent credits, as shown in Exhibit A-12. Space is also provided for the names of particular accounts receivable.

During the month, each amount in the accounts receivable column is posted daily as a credit to an individual customer account in the accounts receivable subsidiary ledger. At the end of the month, the individual amounts in the miscellaneous account column are posted as credits to the appropriate general ledger accounts, and the totals for the cash, accounts receivable, and sales revenue columns are posted to the general ledger as indicated by the posting reference. The total of the miscellaneous accounts column is not posted because it consists of changes in different accounts. However, this column is totalled to ascertain overall debit-credit equality.

EXHIBIT A-10
Sales Journal

Date 20X5	Sales Invoice No.	Accounts Receivable (name)	Terms	Post. Ref.	Receivable and Sale Amount	Dept. Sales Dept. A Dept. B
2 Jan.	93	Adams Co.	2/10, n/30	112.13	$ 980	
3	94	Sayre Corp.	2/10, n/30	112.80	490	
11	95	Cope & Day Co.	net	112.27	5,734	
27	96	XY Mfg. Co.	2/10, n/30	112.91	1,960	(Not illustrated: the total
30	97	Miller, J. B.	2/120, n/30	112.42	196	of each column would
31	—	Totals			$9,360	also be posted to a sale
31	—	Posting			(112/500)	subsidiary ledger)

EXHIBIT A-11
Purchases Journal

Date 20X5	Purchase Order No.	Accounts Payable (name)	Terms	Posting Ref.	Purchases and Payable Amount
3 Jan.	41	PT Mfg. Co.	1/20, n/30	210.61	$990
7	42	Able Suppliers, Ltd.	net	210.12	150
xxxxxxx	xxxxxxxx	xxxxxxxxxxxxxxxxxx	xxxxxxxx	xxxxxxxxxxxxxxxxxxxxx	
31	—	Totals	—	—	6,760
31	—	Postings	—	—	(612/210)

Cash Disbursements Journal. Most companies use some form of a cash disbursements journal, which is also sometimes called a cheque register. This journal can accommodate any entry that involves a credit to cash, and has columns for the common debits and a miscellaneous debits column to make it flexible. Exhibit A-13 illustrates a typical cash disbursements journal. Journalizing and posting follow the same procedures explained for the cash receipts journal.

The General Journal. Special journals can be used to record common entries, but there will always be entries that do not fit the format for any special journal and must be recorded in general journal format. Adjusting and reversing entries are prime examples, but unusual operating transactions will also be recorded in this format. The general journal is an essential element of accounting record-keeping.

Voucher Systems. Voucher systems are designed to enhance internal control over cash disbursements. A voucher is a document that describes a liability and lists information about the creditor, a description of the good or service received, authorizing signatures, and other details of the transaction, including invoice number, terms, amount due, and due date. In a voucher system, every transaction requiring payment by cheque begins with an invoice or other document that supplies information for completing a voucher.

Together, the voucher, purchase order, receiving report, and invoice form a packet of information that must be complete before a cash disbursement can be made. All authorizations must be indicated. Verification of amounts and calculations are part of the payment authorization process. Often, several departments, including the internal audit and accounting departments, are required to authorize a large cash payment.

The completed voucher is the basis for an accounting entry in a special journal called the voucher register. The voucher register is not restricted to purchases. Before

EXHIBIT A-12
Cash Receipts Journal

Date 20X5	Explanation	Debit Cash	Account Title	Post. Ref.	Accounts Receivable	Sales Revenue	Misc. Accounts
					Credits		
4 Jan.	Cash sales	$ 11,200		—		$11,200	
7	On acct.	4,490	Sayre Corp.	112.80	$ 4,490		
8	Sale of land	10,000	Land	123			$ 4,000
			Gain on sale of land	510			6,000
10	On acct.	1,000	Adams Co.	112.13	1,000		
19	Cash sales	43,600		—		43,600	
20	On acct.	5,734	Cope & Day Co.	112.27	5,734		
xxxxxxx	xxxxxxx	xxxxxxxx	xxxxxxx	xxxxxxx	xxxxxx	xxxxxxx	xxxxxxxx
31	Totals	$116,224		—	$11,224	$71,000	$34,000
31	Posting	(101)		—	(112)	(500)	(NP)*

*NP — not posted as one total because the individual amounts are posted as indicated in the posting reference column.

EXHIBIT A-13
Cash Disbursements Journal

Date 20X5	Cheque No.	Explanation	Credit Cash	Account Name	Post. Ref.	Accounts Payable	Purchases	Misc. Accounts
					Debits			
2 Jan.	141	Pur. mdse.	$ 3,000		—		$ 3,000	
10	142	On acct.	990	PT Mfg. Co.	210.61	$ 990		
15	143	Jan. rent	660	Rent exp.	1300			$ 660
16	144	Pur. mdse.	1,810		—		1,810	
xxxxxxx	xxxxxxx	xxxxxxx	xxxxxxx	xxxxxxx	xxxxxxx	xxxxxxx	xxxxxxx	xxxxxxx
31		Totals	$98,400		—	$5,820	$90,980	$1,600
31		Posting	(101)		—	(210)	(612)	(NP)

EXHIBIT A-14
General Ledger and Subsidiary Ledger

General Ledger (partial)

Cash   Acct. 101

20X5				20X5		
1 Jan.	Balance	18,700		31 Jan	CP-31	98,400
31	CR-19	116,224				

Accounts Receivable Control   Acct. 112

20X5				20X5		
1 Jan.	Balance	5,000		31 Jan	CP-19	11,224
31	S-23	9,360				

Sales Revenue Control   Acct. 500

				20X5		
				31 Jan	S-23	9,360
				31	CR-19	71,000

Subsidiary Ledger For Accounts Receivable (Acct. No. 112)

Adams Company — Acct No. 112.13

Date 20X5	Post Ref.	Explanation	Debit	Credit	Balance
1 Jan		Balance			1,000
2	S-23		980		1,980
10	CR-19			1,000	980

Cope & Day Company — Acct. No. 112.27

11 Jan	S-23	Balance	5,734		5,734
20	CR-19			5,734	0

Miller, J. B. — Acct. No 112.42

30 Jan	S-23	Balance	196		196

Sayre Corporation—Acct. No. 112.80

1 Jan		Balance			4,000
3	S-23		490		4,490
7	CR-19			4,490	0

XY Manufacturing Company — Acct. No. 112.91

27 Jan	S-23		1,960		1,960

payment is made, the authorized voucher is recorded in the voucher register. Exhibit A-15 illustrates an abbreviated page from a voucher register.

A new account, vouchers payable, is used to record all routine liabilities. This new account replaces accounts payable and other payables used for routine payments. When a voucher is recorded in the voucher payable credit column, it reflects the amount of the liability. The account debited reflects the good or service received. Unlike the voucher register shown in Exhibit A-15, most voucher registers have several debit columns for speedy recording of repetitive cash payments of the same type. The total of the vouchers payable column is posted to the vouchers payable control. The cheque number and date paid do not appear in the voucher register until a cheque is issued and payment is made to the payee. Although a voucher is prepared for each item, one cheque can be issued for the payment of several vouchers to the same creditor.

Unpaid vouchers are placed into a file pending payment and are typically filed by due date. It is important that payments be initiated within cash discount periods to obtain the lowest possible price for merchandise purchases. The unpaid voucher file is the subsidiary ledger in a voucher system.

When a voucher becomes due, it is sent by the accounting department to a person authorized to issue cheques. After a review of the authorization on the voucher is made, a cheque is prepared for the correct amount. The paid voucher is sent back to the accounting department, which enters the cheque number and payment into the voucher register. Information from the voucher is also entered in the cheque register illustrated in Exhibit A-16.

The total of the amount column in the cheque register is posted to the vouchers payable control account (dr.) and to the cash account (cr.). The paid voucher is retained to substantiate cash payments and for audit trail purposes. The voucher register and cheque register replace the purchases and cash payments journals.

WORKSHEETS

A worksheet is a multicolumn work space that provides an organized format for performing several end-of-period accounting cycle steps and for preparing financial statements before posting AJEs. It also provides evidence, or an audit trail, of an organized and structured accounting process that can be more easily reviewed than other methods of analysis.

In manual accounting systems, worksheet input is developed by transferring account name and balance information manually from the general ledger to the worksheet. With most computerized systems, this task is accomplished automatically. Computer spreadsheet and accounting software programs can be used to generate worksheets quickly and with relative ease. Computer spreadsheets also offer important labour and time savings in the planning and mechanical plotting of AJEs on the worksheet. This software is a powerful tool for accomplishing several steps in the accounting cycle.

Use of a worksheet is always optional. The worksheet is not part of the basic accounting records. Worksheets assist with only a portion of the accounting cycle. Formal AJEs are recorded in addition to those entered on the worksheet.

Illustration of the Worksheet Approach

Exhibit A-17 illustrates the completed worksheet for Sonora, Ltd., the company used in this Appendix to present the accounting cycle. The worksheet has a debit and a credit column for each of the following: the unadjusted trial balance, the AJEs, the adjusted trial balance, the income statement, the retained earnings statement, and the balance sheet. The worksheet is prepared in four steps:

Step 1. *Enter the unadjusted trial balance in the first set of columns of the worksheet by inserting the year-end balances of all ledger accounts.*

EXHIBIT A-15
Voucher Register

Voucher Register						
Date 20X5	**Voucher Number**	**Payee**	**Date Paid**	**Cheque No.**	**Voucher Payable Credit**	**Account Debited**
1 Jan	1	Crowell Co.	2 Jan. 20x5	141	$3,000	Purchases
3	2	PT Mfg. Co.	10 Jan. 20x5	142	990	Purchases
9	3	Williams Co.	15 Jan. 20x5	143	660	Rent Expense

EXHIBIT A-16
Cheque Register

Cheque Register				
Date	**Payee**	**Voucher Number**	**Cheque Number**	**Vouchers Payable Dr. and Cash Cr.**
2 Jan. 20X5	Crowell Co.	1	141	$3,000
10	PT Mfg. Co.	2	142	990
15	Williams Co.	3	143	660

⇒ The inventory and retained earnings balances are the beginning-of-year balances because no transactions have affected these accounts. Confirm the debit-credit equality of the totals.

Step 2. *Enter the adjusting entries, including income tax.*

⇒ The lowercase letters refer to the same AJEs discussed in this Appendix for Sonora, Ltd.

⇒ The worksheet AJEs are facilitating entries only and are not formally recorded in the general journal at this point. If a new account is created by an AJE, it is inserted in its normal position. Interest receivable (entry (d)) is one such example. Confirm the debit-credit equality of the totals.

⇒ Determine income tax expense and payable. (Sonora's tax computation was illustrated earlier.) Enter the accounts and the amounts in the AJE columns. Income tax expense (entry (h)) is positioned below the totals of the AJE columns.

Step 3. *Enter the adjusted trial balance by adding or subtracting across the unadjusted trial balance sheet columns and AJE columns, for each account.*

⇒ For example, the adjusted balance of the allowance for doubtful accounts is the sum of its unadjusted balance ($1,000) and the $1,200 increase from AJE (f).

EXHIBIT A-17
Completed Worksheet for Sonora, Ltd.

Account	Unadjusted Trial Balance Debit	Unadjusted Trial Balance Credit	Adjusting Entries Debit	Adjusting Entries Credit	Adjusted Trial Balance Debit	Adjusted Trial Balance Credit	Income Statement Debit	Income Statement Credit	Retained Earnings Statement Debit	Retained Earnings Statement Credit	Balance Sheet Debit	Balance Sheet Credit
Cash	67,300				67,300						67,300	
Notes receivable	8,000				8,000						8,000	
Accounts receivable	45,000				45,000						45,000	
Allowance for doubtful Accounts		1,000		(f) 1,200		2,200						2,200
Interest receivable			(d) 100		100						100	
Inventory (periodic)	75,000		(g) 90,000	(g) 75,000	90,000						90,000	
Prepaid insurance	600			(a) 200	400						400	
Land	8,000				8,000						8,000	
Building	160,000				160,000						160,000	
Accumulated depreciation, building		90,000		(e) 10,000		100,000						100,000
Equipment	91,000				91,000						91,000	
Accumulated depreciation, equipment		27,000		(e) 9,000		36,000						36,000
Accounts payable		29,000				29,000						29,000
Interest payable				(c) 500		500						500
Rent revenue collected in advance				(b) 600		600						600
Bonds payable, 6%		50,000				50,000						50,000
Common shares, no-par, 15,000 shares		170,000				170,000						170,000
Retained earnings		31,500				31,500				31,500		
Sales revenue		325,200				325,200		325,200				
Interest revenue		500		(d) 100		600		600				
Rent revenue		1,800	(b) 600			1,200		1,200				
Purchases	130,000			(g) 130,000								
Freight on purchases	4,000			(g) 4,000								
Purchase returns		2,000	(g) 2,000									
Cost of goods sold			(g) 117,000		117,000		117,000					
Selling expenses	104,000		(e) 8,200 / (f) 1,200		113,400		113,400					
General and administrative expenses	23,600		(a) 200 / (e) 10,800		34,600		34,600					
Interest expense	2,500		(c) 500		3,000		3,000					
Loss on discontinued operations							20,000					
Income tax expense	9,000				9,000		9,000					
							277,000					
							20,000					
							297,000					
	728,000	728,000	230,600	230,600	746,800	746,800		327,000				
Income tax payable			(h) 20,000	(h) 20,000	20,000	20,000						20,000
					766,800	766,800						
Net income to retained earnings							30,000			30,000		
							327,000	327,000				
Retained earnings to balance sheet									61,500			61,500
Totals	728,000	728,000							61,500	61,500	469,800	469,800

⇒ The inventory account now displays ending inventory, purchases and related accounts no longer have balances, and cost of goods sold is present. Confirm the debit-credit equality of the totals.

Step 4. *Extend the adjusted trial balance amounts to the financial statements; complete the worksheet.*

⇒ Each account in the adjusted trial balance is extended to one of the three sets of remaining debit-credit columns. Temporary accounts are sorted to the income statement columns (revenues to the credit column, expenses to the debit column). Permanent accounts are sorted to the balance sheet columns except for the beginning balance in retained earnings, which is extended to the retained earnings columns.

⇒ Total the income statement columns before income tax expense. Pre-tax income is the difference between the debit and credit column totals. A net credit represents income; a net debit represents a loss. For Sonora, pre-tax income is $50,000 ($327,000 – $277,000). Next, determine net income after taxes by extending the income tax expense amount ($20,000) into the debit column and again totalling the columns. Net income is the difference between the columns, equaling $30,000 for Sonora ($327,000 – $297,000).

⇒ Next, add a line description (net income to retained earnings) and enter the $30,000 net income amount as a balancing value in the income statement columns: positive net income is a debit balancing value; negative income is a credit. Then complete this entry by recording $30,000 in the credit column under the retained earnings columns. (Positive net income is a credit entry, and negative income is a debit entry.)

⇒ Total the retained earnings columns and enter a balancing amount (the ending retained earnings balance) in the appropriate column to achieve debit-credit equality. For Sonora, the balancing amount is a $61,500 debit. Add a line description (retained earnings to balance sheet) and enter the balancing amount into the appropriate balance sheet column.

⇒ Total the balance sheet columns and confirm debit-credit equality.

The worksheet is now complete, and the financial statements are prepared directly from the last three sets of worksheet columns. The formal AJEs are then journalized and posted.

SUMMARY OF KEY POINTS

1. The AIS provides information for daily management information needs and for preparation of financial statements.

2. There are seven basic types of accounts. The balance sheet discloses the balances of the permanent accounts, which include assets, liabilities, and owners' equity accounts. The income statement discloses the pre-closing balances of the temporary accounts, which include revenues, gains, expenses, and losses. Debits to assets, expenses, and losses increase those accounts. Credits to liabilities, owners' equity, revenues, and gains increase those accounts.

3. There are 10 steps in the accounting cycle that culminate in the financial statements.

4. The application of accounting principles generally occurs at the journal entry step. Journal entries are the foundation for the financial statements.

5. Companies may use the standard or the expedient method or both to record routine operating cash receipts and payments that precede revenue and expense recognition. The choice of methods affects some AJEs and the use of RJEs.

6. AJEs are required under accrual accounting to complete the measurement and recording of changes in resources and obligations.

7. RJEs are optional entries, dated at the beginning of the accounting period, that reverse certain AJEs from the previous period and are used to facilitate subsequent journal entries.

8. Subsidiary ledgers are used to maintain records on the component elements of ledger control accounts.

9. Special journals are used to record repetitive entries, such as sales, purchases, cash receipts, and cash disbursements. A general journal is used to record entries that do not fit into special journals.

10. A worksheet may be used to organize the adjustment and financial statement preparation phases of the accounting cycle.

REVIEW PROBLEM

Bucknell Company developed its unadjusted trial balance dated 31 December 20X5, which appears below. Bucknell uses the expedient recording method whenever possible, adjusts its accounts once per year, records all appropriate RJEs, and adjusts its periodic inventory-related accounts in an AJE. Ignore income taxes.

BUCKNELL COMPANY
Unadjusted Trial Balance
31 December 20X5

	Debit	Credit
Cash	$ 40,000	
Accounts receivable	60,000	
Allowance for doubtful accounts		$ 6,000
Inventory	90,000	
Equipment	780,000	
Accumulated amortization		100,000
Land	150,000	
Accounts payable		22,000
Notes payable, 8%, due 1 April 20X10		200,000
Common shares, no-par, 60,000 shares		400,000
Retained earnings		50,000
Sale revenue (all on account)		900,000
Subscription revenue		24,000
Purchases	250,000	
Rent expense	60,000	
Interest expense	12,000	
Selling expense	40,000	
Insurance expense	30,000	
Wage expense	110,000	
General and administrative expense	80,000	
Totals	$1,702,000	$1,702,000

Additional information:

a. Ending inventory by physical count is $70,000.
b. The equipment has a total estimated useful life of 14 years and an estimated residual value of $80,000. Bucknell uses straight-line amortization and treats amortization expense as a general and administrative expense.

c. Bad debt expense for 20X5 is estimated to be 1% of sales.
d. The note payable requires interest to be paid semi-annually, every 1 October and 1 April.
e. $5,000 of wages were earned in December but not recorded.
f. The rent expense represents a payment made on 2 January 20X5, for two years' rent (20X5 and 20X6).
g. The insurance expense represents payment made for a one-year policy, paid 30 June 20X5. Coverage began on that date.
h. The subscription revenue represents cash received from several university libraries for an 18-month subscription to a journal published by Bucknell. The subscription period began 1 July 20X5.

Required:

1. Record the required AJEs.
2. Prepare the adjusted trial balance.
3. Prepare the income statement and an unclassified balance sheet for 20X5.
4. Prepare closing entries.
5. Prepare RJEs.

REVIEW PROBLEM — SOLUTION

Requirement 1

a.	Inventory (ending)	70,000	
	Cost of goods sold	270,000	
	Purchases		250,000
	Inventory (beginning)		90,000
b.	General and administrative expense		
	($780,000 − $80,000)/14	50,000	
	Accumulated amortization		50,000
c.	Bad debt expense (.01 × $900,000)	9,000	
	Allowance for doubtful accounts		9,000
d.	Interest expense ($200,000 × .08 × $\frac{3}{12}$)	4,000	
	Interest payable		4,000
e.	Wage expense	5,000	
	Wages payable		5,000
f.	Prepaid rent ($60,000 × $\frac{1}{2}$)	30,000	
	Rent expense		30,000
g.	Prepaid insurance ($30,000 × $\frac{6}{12}$)	15,000	
	Insurance expense		15,000
h.	Subscription revenue ($24,000 × $\frac{12}{18}$)	16,000	
	Unearned subscriptions		16,000

Requirement 2

BUCKNELL COMPANY
Adjusted Trial Balance
31 December 20X5

	Debit	Credit
Cash	$ 40,000	
Accounts receivable	60,000	
Allowance for doubtful accounts		$ 15,000
Prepaid rent	30,000	
Prepaid insurance	15,000	
Inventory	70,000	
Equipment	780,000	
Accumulated amortization		150,000
Land	150,000	
Accounts payable		22,000
Interest payable		4,000
Wages payable		5,000
Unearned subscriptions		16,000
Notes payable, 8%, due 1 April 20X10		200,000
Common shares, no-par, 60,000 shares		400,000
Retained earnings		50,000
Sales revenue		900,000
Subscription revenue		8,000
Cost of goods sold	270,000	
Rent expense	30,000	
Interest expense	16,000	
Selling expense	40,000	
Insurance expense	15,000	
Wage expense	115,000	
Bad debt expense	9,000	
General and administrative expense	130,000	
Totals	$1,770,000	$1,770,000

Requirement 3

BUCKNELL COMPANY
Income Statement
for the year Ended 31 December 20X5

Revenues:		
Sales	$900,000	
Subscription revenue	8,000	
Total revenue		$908,000
Expenses:		
Cost of goods sold	270,000	
Rent expense	30,000	
Interest expense	16,000	
Selling expense	40,000	
Insurance expense	15,000	
Wage expense	115,000	
Bad debt expense	9,000	
General and administrative expense	130,000	
Total expenses		625,000
Net income		$283,000

BUCKNELL COMPANY
Balance Sheet
31 December 20X5

Assets

Cash		$ 40,000
Accounts receivable.	$ 60,000	
Allowance for doubtful accounts	(15,000)	45,000
Prepaid rent.		30,000
Prepaid insurance		15,000
Inventory		70,000
Equipment.	780,000	
Accumulated amortization	(150,000)	630,000
Land		150,000
Total assets		$980,000

Liabilities

Accounts payable	$ 22,000	
Interest payable	4,000	
Wages payable	5,000	
Unearned subscriptions	16,000	
Notes payable, 8%, due 1 April 20X10	200,000	
Total liabilities		$247,000

Owners' Equity

Common shares, no-par, 60,000 shares outstanding	400,000	
Retained earnings	333,000*	
Total owners' equity		733,000
Total liabilities and owners' equity		$980,000

*$50,000 + $283,000.

Requirement 4

Sales revenue	900,000	
Subscription revenue	8,000	
Income summary		908,000
Income summary	625,000	
Cost of goods sold		270,000
Rent expense		30,000
Interest expense		16,000
Selling expense.		40,000
Insurance expense		15,000
Wage expense		115,000
Bad debt expense.		9,000
General and administrative expense		130,000
Income summary	283,000	
Retained earnings		283,000

Requirement 5

Interest payable	4,000	
Interest expense		4,000
Wages payable	5,000	
Wages expense.		5,000
Rent expense	30,000	
Prepaid rent		30,000
Insurance expense	15,000	
Prepaid insurance		15,000
Unearned subscriptions	16,000	
Subscription revenue.		116,000

EXERCISES & PROBLEMS

A-1 *Effect of Transactions:* The following captions are totals or subtotals on the balance sheet for Tyme Corporation:

A. Total current assets.
B. Total plant assets (net of accumulated depreciation).
C. Total current liabilities.
D. Total long-term liabilities.
E. Total contributed capital (or share capital).
F. Total retained earnings (including income effects).

Required:

For each event listed below, indicate which subtotal(s) increased or decreased as a result of the event. Indicate with an X if there has been no subtotal increase or decrease. Consider each event to be unrelated to the others.

Events	*Increase*	*Decrease*
Example: Issued shares for cash		
	A, E	X

1. Wrote off an uncollectible account receivable to the allowance for doubtful accounts.
2. Sold land for cash, received more than the original cost.
3. Declared a cash dividend to be paid in 60 days' time.
4. Increased the allowance for doubtful accounts.
5. Wrote off a fully depreciated machine.
6. Converted long-term convertible bonds into common shares.
7. Paid a previously declared cash dividend.
8. Increased the supplies inventory as part of year-end adjustments; the company uses the expedient method during the year.
9. Reduced the prepaid insurance account as part of year-end adjustments; the company uses the standard method during the year.
10. Recorded depreciation on plant assets.

A-2 *Journalize Transactions:* RCV Company recorded the following transactions in the month of October:

a. Sold merchandise on account, $356,900.
b. Borrowed $100,000 from the bank.
c. Cash sales, $768,000.
d. Paid $136,000 for operating expenses.
e. Bought merchandise on credit, $457,600.
f. Collected $246,000 from customers on account.
g. Bought automotive equipment, $45,100; paid $10,000 in cash and borrowed the rest.
h. Returned $20,000 of the good purchased in (e) because of defects.
i. Paid for $216,000 of the goods bought on credit in (e), plus $167,000 from last month's outstanding bills.
j. Paid dividends to common shareholders, $36,000.
k. Paid wages of $31,000.
l. Paid $16,200 in interest to the bank.

Required:

1. Journalize each of the above transactions in general journal form.

2. Indicate in which special journal each transaction would normally be recorded, assuming that a company keeps purchases, sales, cash receipts, cash disbursements and general journals.

A-3 *Journalize and Post; Unadjusted Trial Balance:* The following selected transactions were completed during 20X5 by Rotan Corporation, a retailer of Scandinavian furniture:

a. Issued 20,000 shares of its own no-par common shares for $12 per share and received cash in full.
b. Borrowed $100,000 cash on a 9%, one-year note, interest payable at maturity on 30 April 20X6.
c. Purchased equipment for use in operating the business at a net cash cost of $164,000; paid in full.
d. Purchased merchandise for resale at a cash cost of $140,000; paid cash. Assume a periodic inventory system; therefore, debit purchases.
e. Purchased merchandise for resale on credit terms 2/10, n/60. The merchandise will cost $9,800 if paid within 10 days; after 10 days, the payment will be $10,000. The company plans to take the discount; therefore, this purchase is recorded net of discount.
f. Sold merchandise for $180,000; collected $165,000 cash, and the balance is due in one month.
g. Paid $40,000 cash for operating expenses.
h. Paid three-fourths of the balance for the merchandise purchased in (e) within five days; the balance remains unpaid and the discount has been lost.
i. Collected 50% of the balance due on the sale in (f); the remaining balance is uncollected.
j. Paid cash for an insurance premium, $600; the premium is for two years' coverage (debit prepaid insurance).
k. Purchased a tract of land for a future building for company operations, $63,000 cash.
l. Paid damages to a customer who was injured on the company premises, $10,000 cash.

Required:

1. Enter transaction in a general journal; use J1 for the first journal page number. Use the letter of the transaction in place of the date.

2. Set up appropriate T-accounts and post the journal entries. Use posting reference numbers in your posting. Assign each T account an appropriate title, and number each account in balance sheet order followed by the income statement accounts; start with Cash, No. 101.

3. Prepare an unadjusted trial balance.

A-4 *Adjusting Entries:* Rivers Corporation manufactures zippers in Quebec. It adjusts and closes its accounts each 31 December. The following situations require adjusting entries at the current year-end:

a. Machine A is to be depreciated for the full year. It cost $90,000, and the estimated useful life is five years, with an estimated residual value of $10,000. Use straight-line depreciation.

b. Credit sales for the current year amounted to $160,000. The estimated bad debt loss rate on credit sales is 0.5%.

c. Property taxes for the current year have not been recorded or paid. A statement for the calendar year was received near the end of December for $4,000; if paid after 1 February in the next year, a 10% penalty is assessed.

d. Office supplies that cost $800 were purchased during the year and debited to office supplies inventory. The inventories of these supplies on hand were $200 at the end of the prior year and $300 at the end of the current year.

e. Rivers rented an office in its building to a tenant for one year, starting on 1 September. Rent for one year amounting to $6,000 was collected at that date. The total amount collected was credited to rent revenue.

f. Rivers recorded a note receivable from a customer dated 1 November of the current year. It is a $12,000, 10% note, due in one year. At the maturity date, Rivers will collect the amount of the note plus interest for one year.

Required:

Prepare adjusting entries in the general journal for each situation. If no entry is required for an item, explain why.

A-5 *Adjusting Entries:* Voss Company, an accounting firm, adjusts and closes its accounts each 31 December.

1. On 31 December 20X5, the maintenance supplies inventory account showed a balance on hand amounting to $700. During 20X6, purchases of maintenance supplies amounted to $2,000. An inventory of maintenance supplies on hand at 31 December 20X6, reflected unused supplies amounting to $1,000. Give the adjusting journal entry that should be made on 31 December 20X6, under the following conditions:

   Case A: Purchases were debited to the maintenance supplies inventory account;
   Case B: Purchases were debited to maintenance supplies expense.

2. On 31 December 20X5, the prepaid insurance account showed a debit balance of $1,800, which was for coverage for the three months, January to March. On 1 April 20X6, the company obtained another policy covering a two-year period from that date. The two-year premium, amounting to $19,200, was paid on

1 April. Give the adjusting journal entry that should be made on 31 December 20X6.

Case A: $19,200 was debited to prepaid insurance;

Case B: $19,200 was debited to insurance expense.

3. On 1 June, the company collected cash, $8,400, which was for rent collected in advance from a tenant for the next 12 months. Give the adjusting journal entry assuming the following at the time of the collection:

Case A: $8,400 was credited to rent revenue;

Case B: $8,400 was credited to rent collected in advance.

Required:

Provide adjusting journal entries.

A-6 *Adjusting Entries:* Pacific Company adjusts and closes its books each 31 December. It is now 31 December 20X5, and the adjusting entries are to be made. You are requested to prepare, in general journal format, the adjusting entry that should be made for each of the following items:

a. Credit sales for the year amounted to $320,000. The estimated loss rate on bad debts is ⅜ of 1%.

b. Unpaid and unrecorded wages incurred at 31 December amounted to $4,800.

c. The company paid a two-year insurance premium in advance on 1 April 20X5, amounting to $9,600, which was debited to prepaid insurance.

d. Machine A, which cost $80,000, is to be depreciated for the full year. The estimated useful life is 10 years, and the residual value, $4,000. Use straight-line depreciation.

e. The company rented a warehouse on 1 June 20X5, for one year. It had to pay the full amount of rent one year in advance on 1 June, amounting to $9,600, which was debited to rent expense.

f. The company received from a customer a 9% note with a face amount of $12,000, in exchange for products purchased. The note was dated 1 September 20X5; the principal plus the interest is payable one year later. Notes receivable was debited, and sales revenue was credited on the date of sale, 1 September 20X5.

g. On 31 December 20X5, the property tax bill was received in the amount of $5,000. This amount applied only to 20X5 and had not been previously recorded or paid. The taxes are due, and will be paid, on 15 January 20X6.

h. On 1 April 20X5, the company signed a $60,000, 10% note payable. On that date, cash was debited and notes payable credited for $60,000. The note is payable on 31 March 20X6, for the face amount plus interest for one year.

i. The company purchased a patent on 1 January 20X5, at a cost of $11,900. On that date, the patent account was debited and cash credited for $11,900. The patent has an estimated useful life of 17 years and no residual value.

j. Pre-tax income has been computed to be $80,000 after all the above adjustments. Assume an average income tax rate of 30%.

A-7 *Adjusting Entries:* The following situations are unrelated:

1. On 1 January, ABC Corporation had a supplies inventory of $4,500. During the year, supplies of $21,900 were bought and recorded in temporary accounts. At the end of the year, inventory of $9,200 was on hand.

2. On 10 December, ABC Corporation received a deposit of $30,000 on a consulting project that was just beginning. This was accounted for as revenue. By the end of the year, the $50,000 job was 40% complete.

3. During the year, ABC Corporation sold 10,000 units of a product that was subject to a warranty. Past history indicates that 3% of units sold require repairs at an average cost of $40 per unit. The sales have been recorded; costs incurred for the warranty to date, totalling $8,700, were debited to warranty liability when paid. No warranty expense has been recognized.

4. The company uses the percent-of-sales method to calculate bad debt expense: 1% of credit sales of $6,250,000 is expected to be uncollectible.

5. In 20X3, a machine was purchased for $174,000. It had a useful life of 12 years and a $24,000 residual value. A full year's depreciation was charged in 20X3 and 20X4. In 20X5, the accountant discovered that she had forgotten to deduct the salvage value when calculating (straight-line) depreciation for these two years. Prepare a journal entry to correct the error (to retained earnings) and record 20X5 depreciation. Ignore income tax.

6. ABC Corporation wrote off a $16,000 bad debt. The allowance method is used.

7. ABC Corporation buys one-year insurance policies each 1 November. The year ends on 31 December. On 1 January 20X5, there was a balance of $9,440 in the prepaid insurance account; a cheque for $12,710 was issued on 1 November 20X5, for new one-year policies and debited to the prepaid insurance account.

Required:
Prepare adjusting journal entries.

A-8 *Adjusting Entries:* The following transactions and events for Stellar Manufacturing Corporation are under consideration for adjusting entries at 31 December 20X5 (the end of the accounting period):

a. Machine A used in the factory cost $450,000; it was purchased on 1 July 20X2. It has an estimated useful life of 12 years and a residual value of $30,000. Straight-line depreciation is used.

b. Sales for 20X5 amounted to $4,000,000, including $600,000 in credit sales. It is estimated, based on the experience of the company, that bad debt losses will be ¼ of 1% of credit sales.

c. At the beginning of 20X5, office supplies inventory amounted to $600. During 20X5, office supplies amounting to $8,800 were purchased; this amount was debited to office supplies expense. An inventory of office supplies at the end of 20X5 showed $400 on the shelves. The 1 January balance of $600 is still reflected in the office supplies inventory account.

d. On 1 July 20X5, the company paid a three-year insurance premium amounting to $2,160; this amount was debited to prepaid insurance.

e. On 1 October 20X5, the company paid rent on some leased office space. The payment of $7,200 cash was for the following six months. At the time of payment, rent expense was debited for the $7,200.

f. On 1 August 20X5, the company borrowed $120,000 from the Royal Bank. The loan was for 12 months at 9% interest payable at maturity date. The loan was properly recorded on 1 August.

g. Finished goods inventory on 1 January 20X5, was $200,000, and on 31 December 20X5, it was $260,000. The perpetual inventory record provided the cost of goods sold amount of $2,400,000.

h. The company owned some property (land) that was rented to B. R. Speir on 1 April 20X5, for 12 months for $8,400. On 1 April, the entire annual rental of $8,400 was credited to rent collected in advance, and cash was debited.

i. On 31 December 20X5, wages earned by employees but not yet paid (or recorded in the accounts) amounted to $18,000. Disregard payroll taxes.

j. On 1 September 20X5, the company loaned $60,000 to an outside party. The loan was at 10% per annum and was due in six months; interest is payable at maturity. Cash was credited for $60,000 and notes receivable debited on 1 September for the same amount.

k. On 1 January 20X5, factory supplies on hand amounted to $200. During 20x5, factory supplies that cost $4,000 were purchased and debited to factory supplies inventory. At the end of 20X5, a physical inventory count revealed that factory supplies on hand amounted to $800.

l. The company purchased a gravel pit on 1 January 20X3, at a cost of $60,000; it was estimated that approximately 60,000 tons of gravel could be removed prior to exhaustion. It was also estimated that the company would take five years to mine this natural resource. Tons of gravel removed and sold were: 20X3 — 3,000; 20X4 7,000; and 20X5 — 5,000. *Hint:* Deplete on an output basis; no residual value. Only 20X5 depletion should be recorded.

m. At the end of 20X5, it was found that postage stamps that cost $120 were on hand (in a "postage" box in the office). When the stamps were purchased, miscellaneous expense was debited and cash was credited.

n. At the end of 20X5, property taxes for 20X5 amounting to $59,000 were assessed on property owned by the company. The taxes are due no later than 1 February 20X6. The taxes have not been recorded on the books because payment has not been made.

o. The company borrowed $120,000 from the bank on 1 December 20X5. The loan is due in 60 days' time, along with interest at 9½% per annum. On 1 December 20X5, cash was debited and loans payable credited for $120,000.

p. On 1 July 20X5, the company paid the city a $1,000 licence fee for the next 12 months. On that date, cash was credited and licence expense debited for $1,000.

q. On 1 March 20X5, the company made a loan to the company president and received a $30,000 note receivable. The loan was due in one year and called for 6% annual interest payable at maturity date.

r. The company owns three cars used by the executives. A six-month maintenance contract on them was signed on 1 October 20X5, whereby a local garage agreed to do "all the required maintenance." The payment was made for the following six months in advance. On 1 October 20X5, cash was credited and maintenance expense was debited for $9,600.

Required:

Give the adjusting entry (or entries) that should be made on 31 December 20X5, for each item. If an adjusting entry is not required, explain why. Assume all amounts are material.

A-9 *Adjusting Entries:* The account balances, taken from the ledger of Paulson Plumbing Ltd. as of 31 December 20X4, appear below in alphabetic order:

Accounts payable	$12,600
Accounts receivable	3,100
Allowance for doubtful accounts	200
Common shares	10,000
Cash	9,650
Dividends	3,300
Interest expense	240
Interest revenue	350
Miscellaneous general expense	12,600
Notes payable	4,000
Notes receivable	2,000
Purchases	82,000
Purchase discounts	2,300
Purchase returns and allowances	1,650

Retained earnings	8,150
Sales	85,000
Sales salaries	8,260
Sales furniture	3,700
Store supplies inventory	600
Tax expense (property)	600
Unearned revenue	2,000

Required:

Record adjusting entries, as needed, for the following facts and events:

1. Store supplies inventory at 31 December 20X4, was $280.

2. Depreciation of sales furniture is to be recorded straight-line over 10 years. The furniture will have no salvage value.

3. Unpaid and unrecorded advertising bills at 31 December 20X4 totalled $395.

4. Property taxes paid (the tax expense of $600, above) in 20X4 were paid on 1 July 20X4 and were related to the period 1 April 20X4 – 31 March 20X5.

5. The note payable had an interest rate of 12% and was borrowed on 1 February 20X4. No interest was paid in 20X4.

6. There was $105 of outstanding accrued interest on the note receivable at 31 December 20X4.

7. Five percent of the outstanding accounts receivable are expected to prove uncollectible.

8. Unearned revenue represented an advance payment from a customer; 75% was still unearned at year-end.

9. Closing merchandise inventory was $16,000. There was no opening inventory. Prepare an adjusting journal entry to record the change in the inventory account and cost of goods sold.

A-10 *Entries and Statements:* Set forth below is the adjusted trial balance of the Hartman Company as of 31 August 20X5:

Cash	$ 5,600	
Accounts receivable	30,000	
Merchandise inventory	100,000	
Prepaid rent	6,000	
Equipment	16,800	
Accumulated depreciation (amortization)		$ 2,400
Accounts payable		40,000
Note payable		20,000
Accrued interest payable		750
Capital stock		50,000
Retained earnings		45,250
	$158,400	$158,400

The following information describes all of Hartman's September transactions and provides all the data required for month-end adjustments:

- Hartman had cash sales of $50,200.
- Hartman had sales on account of $40,000.
- Hartman collected $34,000 in cash from its customers on account.
- Hartman acquired $60,000 of merchandise on account.
- The cost of merchandise sold during September was $50,000.

- Hartman paid its suppliers $38,000 (cash) on account.
- Hartman spent $4,000 for September's advertising.
- During September, Hartman paid $11,000 in cash for wages.
- Miscellaneous expenses of $10,000 were paid in cash.
- $2,000 of wages earned by Hartman's employees in September had not yet been paid.
- Hartman had earlier paid its rent in advance to 31 December 20X5.
- The store equipment had been purchased by Hartman for $16,800 on 1 September 20X4 (one year before the start of the current month). This equipment is expected to last seven years and to have no salvage or residual value at that time.
- The note payable was dated 1 June 20X5 and the principal is due in two equal instalments on 1 June 20X6 and 20X7. Interest on the note is also to be paid on 1 June 20X6 and 20X7. The note bears an interest rate of 15% per year.

Required:

1. Journalize September transactions and adjusting journal entries. Include an adjusting journal entry for cost of goods sold.

2. Prepare an income statement and balance sheet for the month of September.

A-11 *Prepare a Balance Sheet:* Your assistant has prepared the following partial adjusted trial balance data for the Leong Supply Corporation as of 31 December 20X4. The accounts are arranged in alphabetical order; and, unfortunately, the debit and credit balances have been listed in the same column.

Accounts payable	$36,000
Accounts receivable	67,200
Accumulated depreciation — buildings	19,800
Accumulated depreciation — equipment	10,000
Advertising expense	4,800
Bonds payable	40,000
Buildings	72,000
Capital stock	216,000
Cash	24,000
Depreciation expense — buildings	8,000
Depreciation expense — equipment	2,000
Dividends declared	14,400
Dividends payable	2,000
Equipment	54,280
Expired insurance	1,440
Interest earned	660
Interest receivable	300
Inventory (merchandise)	60,600
Land	69,600
Long-term investments	54,600
Mortgage payable	48,000
Notes payable — short-term	15,000
Office expenses	16,080
Premium on bonds payable	2,000
Prepaid insurance	500
Property tax expense	7,980
Retained earnings — 31 December 20X3	9,840
Sales	246,000

Sales returns	1,000	
Selling expenses	49,440	
Supplies on hand	800	
Unearned revenue	1,200	

Required:

Prepare the 31 December 20X4 balance sheet.

A-12 *The Accounting Cycle:* The post-closing trial balance of the general ledger of Wilson Corporation, a retailer of home weight-training machines, at 31 December 20X4, reflects the following:

Acct. No.	Account	Debit	Credit
101	Cash	$ 27,000	
102	Accounts receivable	21,000	
103	Allowance for doubtful accounts		$ 1,000
104	Inventory (perpetual inventory system)*	35,000	
105	Prepaid insurance (20 months remaining at 1 January)	900	
200	Equipment (20-year estimated life, no residual value)	50,000	
201	Accumulated depreciation, equipment		22,500
300	Accounts payable		7,500
301	Wages payable		
302	Income taxes payable (for 20X4)		4,000
400	Common shares, no-par, 80,000 shares		80,000
401	Retained earnings		18,900
500	Sales revenue		
600	Cost of goods sold		
601	Operating expenses		
602	Income tax expense		
700	Income summary		
		$133,900	$133,900

* Ending inventory on 31 December 20X5, by physical count, $45,000.

The following transactions occurred during 20X5 in the order given (use the letter at the left in place of date):

a. Sales revenue of $30,000, of which $10,000 was on credit; cost, provided by perpetual inventory record, $19,500. *Hint:* When the perpetual system is used, make two entries to record a sale: *first*, debit cash or accounts receivable and credit sales revenue; *second*, debit cost of goods sold and credit inventory.
b. Collected $17,000 on accounts receivable.
c. Paid income taxes payable (20X4), $4,000.
d. Purchased merchandise, $40,000, of which $8,000 was on credit.
e. Paid accounts payable, $6,000.
f. Sales revenue of $72,000 (in cash); cost, $46,800.
g. Paid operating expenses, $19,000.
h. On 1 January 20X5, issued 1,000 common shares for $1,000 cash.
i. Purchased merchandise, $100,000, of which $27,000 was on credit.
j. Sales revenue of $98,000, of which $30,000 was on credit; cost, $63,700.
k. Collected cash on accounts receivable, $26,000.
l. Paid accounts payable, $28,000.
m. Paid various operating expenses in cash, $18,000.

Required:

1. Journalize each of the transactions listed above for 20X5; use only a general journal.

2. Set up T-accounts in the general ledger for each of the accounts listed in the above trial balance and enter the account number and 31 December 20X4 balance.

3. Post the journal entries; use posting reference numbers.

4. Prepare an unadjusted trial balance.

5. Journalize the adjusting entries and post them to the ledger. Assume a bad debt rate of ½ of 1% of credit sales for the period at 31 December 20X5; accrued wages were $300. The average income tax rate was 40%. Use straight-line depreciation. Debit expenses to the operating expense account. *Check your work:* Income tax expense is $11,784.

6. Prepare an adjusted trial balance.

7. Prepare the income statement and balance sheet.

8. Journalize and post the closing entries.

9. Prepare a post-closing trial balance.

A-13 *Worksheet, Adjusting and Closing Entries, Statements:* Data Corporation is currently completing the end-of-the-period accounting process. At 31 December 20X5, the following unadjusted trial balance was developed from the general ledger:

Account	Balances (unadjusted) Debit	Balances (unadjusted) Credit
Cash	$ 60,260	
Accounts receivable	38,000	
Allowance for doubtful accounts		$ 2,000
Interest receivable		
Inventory (perpetual inventory system)	105,000	
Sales supplies inventory	900	
Long-term note receivable, 14%	12,000	
Equipment	180,000	
Accumulated depreciation, equipment		64,000
Patent	8,400	
Accounts payable		23,000
Interest payable		
Income taxes payable		
Property taxes payable		
Rent collected in advance		
Mortgage payable, 12%		60,000
Common shares, no-par, 10,000 shares		115,000
Retained earnings		32,440
Sales revenue		700,000
Investment revenue		1,120
Rent revenue		3,000
Cost of goods sold	380,000	
Selling expenses	164,400	
General and administrative expenses	55,000	
Interest expense	6,600	
Income tax expense		
Extraordinary gain (pretax)		10,000
	$1,010,560	$1,010,560

Additional data for adjustments and other purposes:

a. Estimated bad debt loss rate is ¼ of 1% of credit sales. Credit sales for the year amounted to $200,000; classify as a selling expense.

b. Interest on the long-term note receivable was last collected and recorded on 31 August 20X5.

c. Estimated useful life of the equipment is 10 years; residual value, $20,000. Allocate 10% of depreciation expense to general and administrative expense and the balance to selling expense to reflect proportionate use. Use straight-line depreciation.

d. Estimated remaining economic life of the patent is 14 years (from 1 January 20X5) with no residual value. Use straight-line amortization and classify as selling expense (used in sales promotion).

e. Interest on the mortgage payable was last paid and recorded on 30 November 20X5.

f. On 1 June 20X5, the company rented some office space to a tenant for one year and collected $3,000 rent in advance for the year; the entire amount was credited to rent revenue on this date.

g. On 31 December 20X5, the company received a statement for calendar-year 20X5 property taxes amounting to $1,300. The payment is due 15 February 20X6. Classify the adjustment as a selling expense.

h. Sales supplies on hand at 31 December 20X5, amounted to $300; classify as a selling expense.

i. Assume an average 40% corporate income tax rate on all items including the extraordinary gain. *Check your work:* Total income tax expense is $35,132.

Required:

1. Enter the above unadjusted trial balance on a worksheet.

2. Complete the worksheet.

3. Prepare the income statement and balance sheet.

4. Journalize the closing entries.

A-14 *Perform All Accounting Cycle Steps:* Spectrum Enterprises, a calendar-year firm, began operations as a retailer in January 20X5. You are to perform the 10 accounting cycle steps for Spectrum for 20X5. Worksheets, special journals, and subsidiary ledgers are not required. Prepare journal entries in summary (for the year) form. Post to T-accounts. Spectrum uses the expedient recording system and records reversing entries whenever appropriate. Spectrum also uses a periodic inventory system and adjusts inventory in an adjusting entry.

Information about transactions in 20X5:

1. Investors contributed $200,000 in exchange for 10,000 shares of no-par common shares. On the advice of its underwriter, Spectrum offered the shares at $20 per share.

2. Spectrum obtained a 10%, $100,000 bank loan on 1 February. This loan is evidenced by a signed promissory note calling for interest payments every 1 February. The note is due in full on 31 January 20X9.

3. A rental contract for production and office facilities was signed 1 February, which required $10,000 immediate payment covering the first month's rent and a $5,000 deposit refundable in three years or upon termination of the contract, whichever occurs first. Monthly rent is $5,000. As an added incentive to pay rent in advance, Spectrum accepted an offer to maintain rent at $5,000 per month for the first three years if Spectrum paid the 2nd through the 13th (March 20X5 through February 20X6) months' rent immediately. In all, Spectrum paid $70,000 for rent on 1 February. Spectrum intends to occupy the facilities for at least three years.

4. Equipment costing $110,000 was purchased for cash in early February. It has an estimated residual value of $10,000 and a five-year useful life. Spectrum uses the

straight-line method of depreciation and treats depreciation as a separate period expense.

5. Spectrum recognized various cash operating expenses for the year, including the following:

Wages	$60,000
Utilities	40,000
Selling	80,000
General and administrative	100,000

6. Total merchandise purchases for the year amounted to $2,000,000. Ending inventory amounted to $200,000 at cost. Spectrum uses a periodic inventory system.

7. Total payables relating to merchandise purchases and other operating expenses are $40,000 at year-end.

8. All sales are made on credit and totalled $2,500,000 in 20X5; $2,300,000 was collected on account during the year. Spectrum estimates that 1/2 of 1% of total sales will be uncollectible and has written off $3,000 of accounts.

9. Income tax expense is $130,00. All taxes for a fiscal year are payable in April of the following year.

10. Spectrum declared a cash dividend of $117,000, payable in January 20X6.

A-15 *Worksheets:* Following is the unadjusted trial balance for TRM Corporation as of 31 December 20X4:

Account Title	Debit	Credit
Cash	$ 1,335	
Accounts receivable	1,000	
Prepaid insurance	3,400	
Office supplies	365	
Prepaid rent	375	
Office equipment	3,140	
Accum. amortization, OE		$ 855
Delivery equipment	22,185	
Accum. amortization, DE		4,500
Accounts payable		3,845
Rent payable		0
Salaries and wages payable		0
Unearned revenue		1,050
Share capital		14,355
Retained earnings		20,000
Dividends	2,000	
Delivery service revenue		63,085
Rent expense	4,125	
Utilities expense	1,290	
Insurance expense	0	
Office supplies expense	0	
Amortization expense	0	
Salaries expense	30,715	
Delivery wages expense	30,480	
Gas, oil and repairs expense	7,280	
	$107,690	$107,690

Other information:

a. In December 20X3, the company put a one-month deposit down on rental premises. This deposit will be returned when the company vacates. This amount appears as the balance of the prepaid rent account. Rents for January through November were paid each month and debited to the rent expense account. As of the trial balance date, the December rent had not been paid.

b. An examination of insurance policies showed $415 of unexpired insurance.

c. An inventory showed $165 of unused office supplies on hand.

d. Amortization on the office equipment, $450, and on delivery equipment, $3,625.

e. Several stores signed contracts with the delivery service in which they agreed to pay a fixed fee for the delivery of packages. Two of the stores made advance payments on their contracts, and the amounts paid were credited to the unearned revenue account. An examination of their contracts shows $600 of the $1,050 paid was earned by the end of the accounting period.

f. A $55 December power bill and a $90 bill for repairs to delivery equipment were unpaid and unrecorded at year-end.

g. Office salaries, $310, and delivery wages, $160, have accrued but are unpaid and unrecorded.

Required:

1. Prepare adjusting journal entries to reflect the above information.

2. Enter the adjustments into a worksheet, and complete the worksheet columns.

A-16 *Special Journals:* Next to each transaction place the letter of the journal in which that transaction would be recorded. Assume that the company uses special journals whenever appropriate.

Transactions:

1. Collect cash on account.
2. Purchase merchandise on account.
3. Prepare adjusting entries.
4. Pay the insurance bill.
5. Receive cash for services.
6. Prepare closing entries.
7. Record a completed but unpaid voucher.
8. Correct an erroneous journal entry.
9. Sell merchandise on credit.
10. Pay accounts payable.
11. Sell merchandise for cash.
12. Pay the voucher in (7).

Journals:

A. General journal
B. Sales journal
C. Purchases journal
D. Cash receipts journal
E. Cash disbursements journal
F. Voucher register
G. Cheque register

A-17 *Special Journals:* Marigold Corp had transactions in June as follows:

June 1 Received merchandise and an invoice dated 31 May, terms n/60, from Hollingsworth Company, $47,800.

2 Purchased office equipment on account from Dunlap Company, invoice dated 2 June, terms n/10 EOM, $14,625.

3 Sold merchandise on account to Tamara Smith, Invoice No. 902, $22,300. (Terms of all credit sales are 2/10, n/30.)

8 Issued cheque No. 548 to *The Monthly News* for advertising, $275.

10 Issued cheque No. 549 to Hollingsworth Company in payment of its 31 May invoice.

11 Sold unneeded office supplies at cost for cash, $940.

16 Sold merchandise on account to Mary Cortez, invoice No. 903, $9,735.

18 Received payment from Tamara Smith for the sale of 3 June.

20 Received merchandise and an invoice dated 18 June, terms n/60, from Riteway Company, $17,500.

21 Issued a credit memorandum to Mary Cortez for defective merchandise sold on 16 June and returned for credit, $1,835.

24 Received a $1,700 credit memorandum from Riteway Company for defective merchandise received on 20 June and returned for credit.

25 Purchased on account from The Store Depot, merchandise, $22,390, invoice dated 25 June, terms n/10 EOM.

26 Received payment from Mary Cortez for the 16 June sale. She paid the net amount due within the discount period, and deducted 2% from the amount owing.

28 Issued cheque No. 550 to Riteway Company in payment of its 18 June invoice, less the purchase return.

30 Cash sales for the month ended 30 June were $31,230.

Required:

1. Draft special journals as illustrated in the appendix for cash receipts, cash disbursements, sales and purchases. The company also maintains a general journal.

2. Record the transactions in the appropriate journal. Leave columns blank if details (account numbers, for example) are not available. Sales are recorded at the gross amount.

A-18 *Special Journals:* Morra Ltd incurred the following transactions in September:

Sept. 1 Invested $10,000 in the corporation.

2 Purchased $6,000 of automotive equipment for cash.

2 Purchased office equipment by issuing a note payable, $4,760.

5 Purchased inventory priced at $10,320 on account, terms 1/15, n/30.

10 Sold merchandise for $6,210 to a customer on account, terms 2/10, n/30.

12 Received a credit memo from the supplier re: the inventory acquired on 5 September, $1,320 gross, $1,306.80 net.

12 Borrowed $10,000 from the Bank of Nova Scotia at an interest rate of 12%.

13 Paid the supplier for the net purchase of 5 September.

22 Received payment from the customer re: sale on 10 September. This cheque was issued within the discount period.

25 Paid salaries of $1,200.

29 Cash sales for the month of September amounted to $47,250.

Required:

1. Draft special journals as illustrated in this Appendix for cash receipts, cash disbursements, sales, and purchases. The company also maintains a general journal.

2. Record the transactions in the appropriate journal. Leave columns blank if details (account numbers, for example) are not available. Purchases and sales are recorded net.

A-19 *Transactions and Financial Statements:* Multimedia, Inc., a producer of graphics and artwork for movie theatres and other media distributors, provided the following information for 20X5:

Selected Accounts from the Balance Sheet, as of 1 January 20X5

Accounts receivable	$ 10,000
Prepaid insurance	20,000
Supplies	5,000
Equipment (net)	80,000
Accounts payable (suppliers)	40,000*
Unearned rent	13,000
Wages payable	7,000
Common shares (nopar)	27,000
Retained earnings	50,000

* The 31 December 20X5 balance is $50,000.

Income Statement, year ended 31 December 20X5

Sales	$200,000
Insurance expense	(15,000)
Depreciation expense	(10,000)
Supplies expense	(30,000)
Wages expense	(60,000)
Rent revenue	12,000
Net income	$ 97,000

Cash Flow Statement, year ended 31 December 20X5

Operating activities:

Collections from customers	$ 90,000
Insurance payments	(25,000)
Payments to suppliers	(45,000)
Payments to employees	(52,000)
Rental receipts	19,000
Net operating cash flow	$ (13,000)
Cash balance, 1 January 20X5	22,000
Cash balance, 31 December 20X5*	$ 9,000

* No investing or financing cash flows.

Required:

Prepare the 31 December 20X5 balance sheet for Multimedia.

A-20 *Transactions and Financial Statements:* During the first week of January 20X5, Angela Smith began an office design business, Exotic Designs. She kept no formal accounting records; however, her record of cash receipts and disbursements was accurate. The business was an instant success. In fact, it was so successful that she required additional financing to keep up. She approached her bank for a $10,000 loan and was "put on hold" until she brought a balance sheet and an income statement prepared on an accrual basis.

Knowing very little about accounting, she engages you to prepare statements requested by the bank. She supplies you with the following information:

	Receipts	Disbursements
Investment	$30,000	
Equipment		$18,400
Supplies		12,200
Rent payments		9,600
Insurance premium		1,800
Advertising — all ads complete		3,600
Wages of assistant		18,400
Telephone		980
Payments to Angela Smith		19,000
Design revenue received	61,500	
Cash balance		7,520
	$91,500	$91,500

Additional information:

- The equipment has an estimated 10-year life and $400 salvage value.

- Supplies on hand 31 December 20X5 were $1,800.

- Rent payments included $750 per month rental and $600 deposit refundable at termination of the two-year lease.

- Insurance premium was for a two-year policy that expires on 31 December 20X6.

- Wages earned in the last week of December 20X5 to be paid in January 20X6 amounted to $400.

- Design revenue earned but not yet collected amounted to $3,800.

- The organization is set up as a company; the $19,000 withdrawn by Angela is $18,000 salary and $1,000 dividends.

Required:

Prepare the financial statements as requested.

[CGA-Canada, adapted]

A-21 *Transactions and Financial Statements:* Shirt Shack is a retail store operating in a downtown shopping mall. On 1 January 20X5, it reported the following:

SHIRT SHACK
Balance Sheet
as of 1 January 20X5

Cash	$ 4,000
Accounts receivable (net of allowance of $2,000)	28,000
Prepaid rent (rental deposit)	1,000
Inventory	36,000
Leasehold improvements (net)	16,000
Total assets	$85,000
Accounts payable	$32,000
Accrued wages payable	3,500
Accrued interest payable	200
Accrued rent payable	0
Notes payable, 10%	14,800
Common shares	10,000
Retained earnings	24,500
Total liabilities plus equity	$85,000

During 20X5, the company reported the following:

1. Cash paid to employees (salaries and commissions), $67,000. Cash paid to suppliers, $90,000.

2. Cash collected from customers, $220,000.

3. On 31 December 20X5, a physical inventory count revealed that inventory was $42,000.

4. At 31 December 20X5, customers owed Shirt Shack $35,000, and the company owed its suppliers $14,000. Of the accounts receivable, aging analysis indicated that $4,000 was expected to be uncollectible. No accounts were written off in 20X5.

5. Cash paid to landlord, $12,000 ($1,000 per month for 12 months). Shirt Shack is required to pay monthly rent and, at year-end, make an additional payment to bring the total rent expense up to 10% of sales. This payment will be made in January 20X6.

6. Cash paid for miscellaneous operating expenses, $6,000.

7. Cash paid in dividends, $14,500; in interest, $1,680. No interest is owing at 31 December 20X5.

8. Shirt Shack owed employees $500 in wages and $1,000 in commissions at year-end.

9. The leasehold improvements were acquired on 1 January 20X4. They had an expected life of 10 years and were installed in leased premises that had a five-year lease on 1 January 20X4.

Required:

1. Prepare journal entries for all transactions and needed adjustments.

2. Prepare an income statement for the year ended 31 December 20X5. Ignore income taxes. Show all calculations.

Summary of Compound Interest Tables and Formulae

Table	Table Title (and use)	Formula*
I-1	Future value of 1 (F/P) Used to compute the future value of single payments made now.	$F/P = (1 + i)^n$ Also expressed $(F/P, i, n)$
I-2	Present value of 1 (P/F) Used to compute the present value of single payments made in the future.	$P/F = \dfrac{1}{(1 + i)^n}$ Also expressed $(P/F, i, n)$
I-3	Future value of ordinary annuity of 1 (F/A): Used to compute the future value of a series of payments made at the *end* of each interest compounding period.	$F/A = \dfrac{(1 + i)^n - 1}{i}$ Also expressed $(F/A, i, n)$
I-4	Present value of ordinary annuity of 1 (P/A): Used to compute the present value of a series of payments made at the *end* of each interest compounding period.	$P/A = \dfrac{1 - \dfrac{1}{(1 + i)^n}}{i}$ Also expressed $(P/A, i, n)$
I-5	Future value of annuity due of 1 (F/AD): Used to compute the future value of a series of payments made at the *beginning* of each interest compounding period.	$F/AD = \left[\dfrac{(1 + i)^n - 1}{i} \right] \times (1 + i)$ Also expressed $(F/AD, i, n) =$ $(1 + i)(F/A, i, n)$
I-6	Present value of annuity due of 1 (P/AD): Used to compute the present value of a series of payments made at the *beginning* of each interest compounding period.	$P/AD = \left[\dfrac{1 - \dfrac{1}{(1 + i)^n}}{i} \right] \times (1 + i)$ Also expressed $(P/AD, i, n) =$ $(1 + i) (P/A, i, n)$

* In these equations and throughout this text, i is the interest rate per period and n is the number of interest periods.

TABLE I-1: **Future value of $1: (F/P, *i*, *n*)**

n	2%	2.5%	3%	4%	5%	6%	7%	8%	9%	10%
1	1.020	1.025	1.030	1.040	1.050	1.060	1.070	1.080	1.090	1.100
2	1.040	1.051	1.061	1.082	1.103	1.124	1.145	1.166	1.188	1.210
3	1.061	1.077	1.093	1.125	1.158	1.191	1.225	1.260	1.295	1.331
4	1.082	1.104	1.126	1.170	1.216	1.262	1.311	1.360	1.412	1.464
5	1.104	1.131	1.159	1.217	1.276	1.338	1.403	1.469	1.539	1.611
6	1.126	1.160	1.194	1.265	1.340	1.419	1.501	1.587	1.677	1.772
7	1.149	1.189	1.230	1.316	1.407	1.504	1.606	1.714	1.828	1.949
8	1.172	1.218	1.267	1.369	1.477	1.594	1.718	1.851	1.993	2.144
9	1.195	1.249	1.305	1.423	1.551	1.689	1.838	1.999	2.172	2.358
10	1.219	1.280	1.344	1.480	1.629	1.791	1.967	2.159	2.367	2.594
11	1.243	1.312	1.384	1.539	1.710	1.898	2.105	2.332	2.580	2.853
12	1.268	1.345	1.426	1.601	1.796	2.012	2.252	2.518	2.813	3.138
13	1.294	1.379	1.469	1.665	1.886	2.133	2.410	2.720	3.066	3.452
14	1.319	1.413	1.513	1.732	1.980	2.261	2.579	2.937	3.342	3.797
15	1.346	1.448	1.558	1.801	2.079	2.397	2.759	3.172	3.642	4.177
16	1.373	1.485	1.605	1.873	2.183	2.540	2.952	3.426	3.970	4.595
17	1.400	1.522	1.653	1.948	2.292	2.693	3.159	3.700	4.328	5.054
18	1.428	1.560	1.702	2.026	2.407	2.854	3.380	3.996	4.717	5.560
19	1.457	1.599	1.754	2.107	2.527	3.026	3.617	4.316	5.142	6.116
20	1.486	1.639	1.806	2.191	2.653	3.207	3.870	4.661	5.604	6.727
21	1.516	1.680	1.860	2.279	2.786	3.400	4.141	5.034	6.109	7.400
22	1.546	1.722	1.916	2.370	2.925	3.604	4.430	5.437	6.659	8.140
23	1.577	1.765	1.974	2.465	3.072	3.820	4.741	5.871	7.258	8.954
24	1.608	1.809	2.033	2.563	3.225	4.049	5.072	6.341	7.911	9.850
25	1.641	1.854	2.094	2.666	3.386	4.292	5.427	6.848	8.623	10.835
26	1.673	1.900	2.157	2.772	3.556	4.549	5.807	7.396	9.399	11.918
27	1.707	1.948	2.221	2.883	3.733	4.822	6.214	7.988	10.245	13.110
28	1.741	1.996	2.288	2.999	3.920	5.112	6.649	8.627	11.167	14.421
29	1.776	2.046	2.357	3.119	4.116	5.418	7.114	9.317	12.172	15.863
30	1.811	2.098	2.427	3.243	4.322	5.743	7.612	10.063	13.268	17.449
31	1.848	2.150	2.500	3.373	4.538	6.088	8.145	10.868	14.462	19.194
32	1.885	2.204	2.575	3.508	4.765	6.453	8.715	11.737	15.763	21.114
33	1.922	2.259	2.652	3.648	5.003	6.841	9.325	12.676	17.182	23.225
34	1.961	2.315	2.732	3.794	5.253	7.251	9.978	13.690	18.728	25.548
35	2.000	2.373	2.814	3.946	5.516	7.686	10.677	14.785	20.414	28.102
36	2.040	2.433	2.898	4.104	5.792	8.147	11.424	15.968	22.251	30.913
37	2.081	2.493	2.985	4.268	6.081	8.636	12.224	17.246	24.254	34.004
38	2.122	2.556	3.075	4.439	6.385	9.154	13.079	18.625	26.437	37.404
39	2.165	2.620	3.167	4.616	6.705	9.704	13.995	20.115	28.816	41.145
40	2.208	2.685	3.262	4.801	7.040	10.286	14.974	21.725	31.409	45.259
41	2.252	2.752	3.360	4.993	7.392	10.903	16.023	23.462	34.236	49.785
42	2.297	2.821	3.461	5.193	7.762	11.557	17.144	25.339	37.318	54.764
43	2.343	2.892	3.565	5.400	8.150	12.250	18.344	27.367	40.676	60.240
44	2.390	2.964	3.671	5.617	8.557	12.985	19.628	29.556	44.337	66.264
45	2.438	3.038	3.782	5.841	8.985	13.765	21.002	31.920	48.327	72.890
46	2.487	3.114	3.895	6.075	9.434	14.590	22.473	34.474	52.677	80.180
47	2.536	3.192	4.012	6.318	9.906	15.466	24.046	37.232	57.418	88.197
48	2.587	3.271	4.132	6.571	10.401	16.394	25.729	40.211	62.585	97.017
49	2.639	3.353	4.256	6.833	10.921	17.378	27.530	43.427	68.218	106.719
50	2.692	3.437	4.384	7.107	11.467	18.420	29.457	46.902	74.358	117.391

TABLE I-1: **Future value of $1: (F/P, *i*, *n*)**

11%	12%	14%	15%	16%	18%	20%	22%	24%	25%	n
1.110	1.120	1.140	1.150	1.160	1.180	1.200	1.220	1.240	1.250	1
1.232	1.254	1.300	1.322	1.346	1.392	1.440	1.488	1.538	1.562	2
1.368	1.405	1.482	1.521	1.561	1.643	1.728	1.816	1.907	1.953	3
1.518	1.574	1.689	1.749	1.811	1.939	2.074	2.215	2.364	2.441	4
1.685	1.762	1.925	2.011	2.100	2.288	2.488	2.703	2.932	3.052	5
1.870	1.974	2.195	2.313	2.436	2.700	2.986	3.297	3.635	3.815	6
2.076	2.211	2.502	2.660	2.826	3.185	3.583	4.023	4.508	4.768	7
2.305	2.476	2.853	3.059	3.278	3.759	4.300	4.908	5.590	5.960	8
2.558	2.773	3.252	3.518	3.803	4.435	5.160	5.987	6.931	7.451	9
2.839	3.106	3.707	4.046	4.411	5.234	6.192	7.305	8.594	9.313	10
3.152	3.479	4.226	4.652	5.117	6.176	7.430	8.912	10.657	11.642	11
3.498	3.896	4.818	5.350	5.936	7.288	8.916	10.872	13.215	14.552	12
3.883	4.363	5.492	6.153	6.886	8.599	10.699	13.264	16.386	18.190	13
4.310	4.887	6.261	7.076	7.988	10.147	12.839	16.182	20.319	22.737	14
4.785	5.474	7.138	8.137	9.266	11.974	15.407	19.742	25.196	28.422	15
5.311	6.130	8.137	9.358	10.748	14.129	18.488	24.086	31.243	35.527	16
5.895	6.866	9.276	10.761	12.468	16.672	22.186	29.384	38.741	44.409	17
6.544	7.690	10.575	12.375	14.463	19.673	26.623	35.849	48.039	55.511	18
7.263	8.613	12.056	14.232	16.777	23.214	31.948	43.736	59.568	69.389	19
8.062	9.646	13.743	16.367	19.461	27.393	38.338	53.358	73.864	86.736	20
8.949	10.804	15.668	18.822	22.574	32.324	46.005	65.096	91.592	108.420	21
9.934	12.100	17.861	21.645	26.186	38.142	55.206	79.418	113.574	135.525	22
11.026	13.552	20.362	24.891	30.376	45.008	66.247	96.889	140.831	169.407	23
12.239	15.179	23.212	28.625	35.236	53.109	79.497	118.205	174.631	211.758	24
13.585	17.000	26.462	32.919	40.874	62.669	95.396	144.210	216.542	264.698	25
15.080	19.040	30.167	37.857	47.414	73.949	114.475	175.936	268.512	330.872	26
16.739	21.325	34.390	43.535	55.000	87.260	137.371	214.642	332.955	413.590	27
18.580	23.884	39.204	50.066	63.800	102.967	164.845	261.864	412.864	516.988	28
20.624	26.750	44.693	57.575	74.009	121.501	197.814	319.474	511.952	646.235	29
22.892	29.960	50.950	66.212	85.850	143.371	237.376	389.758	634.820	807.794	30
25.410	33.555	58.083	76.144	99.586	169.177	284.852	475.505	787.177	1009.742	31
28.206	37.582	66.215	87.565	115.520	199.629	341.822	580.116	976.099	1262.177	32
31.308	42.092	75.485	100.700	134.003	235.563	410.186	707.741	1210.363	1577.722	33
34.752	47.143	86.053	115.805	155.443	277.964	492.224	863.444	1500.850	1972.152	34
38.575	52.800	98.100	133.176	180.314	327.997	590.668	1053.402	1861.054	2465.190	35
42.818	59.136	111.834	153.152	209.164	387.037	708.802	1285.150	2307.707	3081.488	36
47.528	66.232	127.491	176.125	242.631	456.703	850.562	1567.883	2861.557	3851.860	37
52.756	74.180	145.340	202.543	281.452	538.910	1020.675	1912.818	3548.330	4814.825	38
58.559	83.081	165.687	232.925	326.484	635.914	1224.810	2333.638	4399.930	6018.531	39
65.001	93.051	188.884	267.864	378.721	750.378	1469.772	2847.038	5455.913	7523.164	40
72.151	104.217	215.327	308.043	439.317	885.446	1763.726	3473.386	6765.332	9403.955	41
80.088	116.723	245.473	354.250	509.607	1044.827	2116.471	4237.531	8389.011	11754.944	42
88.897	130.730	279.839	407.387	591.144	1232.896	2539.765	5169.788	10402.374	14693.679	43
98.676	146.418	319.017	468.495	685.727	1454.817	3047.718	6307.141	12898.944	18367.099	44
109.530	163.988	363.679	538.769	795.444	1716.684	3657.262	7694.712	15994.690	22958.874	45
121.579	183.666	414.594	619.585	922.715	2025.687	4388.714	9387.549	19833.416	28698.593	46
134.952	205.706	472.637	712.522	1070.349	2390.311	5266.457	11452.810	24593.436	35873.241	47
149.797	230.391	538.807	819.401	1241.605	2820.567	6319.749	13972.428	30495.860	44841.551	48
166.275	258.038	614.239	942.311	1440.262	3328.269	7583.698	17046.362	37814.867	56051.939	49
184.565	289.002	700.233	1083.657	1670.704	3927.357	9100.438	20796.561	46890.435	70064.923	50

TABLE I-2: **Present value of $1: (P/F, *i*, *n*)**

n	2%	2.5%	3%	4%	5%	6%	7%	8%	9%	10%
1	0.98039	0.97561	0.97087	0.96154	0.95238	0.94340	0.93458	0.92593	0.91743	0.90909
2	0.96117	0.95181	0.94260	0.92456	0.90703	0.89000	0.87344	0.85734	0.84168	0.82645
3	0.94232	0.92860	0.91514	0.88900	0.86384	0.83962	0.81630	0.79383	0.77218	0.75131
4	0.92385	0.90595	0.88849	0.85480	0.82270	0.79209	0.76290	0.73503	0.70843	0.68301
5	0.90573	0.88385	0.86261	0.82193	0.78353	0.74726	0.71299	0.68058	0.64993	0.62092
6	0.88797	0.86230	0.83748	0.79031	0.74622	0.70496	0.66634	0.63017	0.59627	0.56447
7	0.87056	0.84127	0.81309	0.75992	0.71068	0.66506	0.62275	0.58349	0.54703	0.51316
8	0.85349	0.82075	0.78941	0.73069	0.67684	0.62741	0.58201	0.54027	0.50187	0.46651
9	0.83676	0.80073	0.76642	0.70259	0.64461	0.59190	0.54393	0.50025	0.46043	0.42410
10	0.82035	0.78120	0.74409	0.67556	0.61391	0.55839	0.50835	0.46319	0.42241	0.38554
11	0.80426	0.76214	0.72242	0.64958	0.58468	0.52679	0.47509	0.42888	0.38753	0.35049
12	0.78849	0.74356	0.70138	0.62460	0.55684	0.49697	0.44401	0.39711	0.35553	0.31863
13	0.77303	0.72542	0.68095	0.60057	0.53032	0.46884	0.41496	0.36770	0.32618	0.28966
14	0.75788	0.70773	0.66112	0.57748	0.50507	0.44230	0.38782	0.34046	0.29925	0.26333
15	0.74301	0.69047	0.64186	0.55526	0.48102	0.41727	0.36245	0.31524	0.27454	0.23939
16	0.72845	0.67362	0.62317	0.53391	0.45811	0.39365	0.33873	0.29189	0.25187	0.21763
17	0.71416	0.65720	0.60502	0.51337	0.43630	0.37136	0.31657	0.27027	0.23107	0.19784
18	0.70016	0.64117	0.58739	0.49363	0.41552	0.35034	0.29586	0.25025	0.21199	0.17986
19	0.68643	0.62553	0.57029	0.47464	0.39573	0.33051	0.27651	0.23171	0.19449	0.16351
20	0.67297	0.61027	0.55368	0.45639	0.37689	0.31180	0.25842	0.21455	0.17843	0.14864
21	0.65978	0.59539	0.53755	0.43883	0.35894	0.29416	0.24151	0.19866	0.16370	0.13513
22	0.64684	0.58086	0.52189	0.42196	0.34185	0.27751	0.22571	0.18394	0.15018	0.12285
23	0.63416	0.56670	0.50669	0.40573	0.32557	0.26180	0.21095	0.17032	0.13778	0.11168
24	0.62172	0.55288	0.49193	0.39012	0.31007	0.24698	0.19715	0.15770	0.12640	0.10153
25	0.60953	0.53939	0.47761	0.37512	0.29530	0.23300	0.18425	0.14602	0.11597	0.09230
26	0.59758	0.52623	0.46369	0.36069	0.28124	0.21981	0.17220	0.13520	0.10639	0.08391
27	0.58586	0.51340	0.45019	0.34682	0.26785	0.20737	0.16093	0.12519	0.09761	0.07628
28	0.57437	0.50088	0.43708	0.33348	0.25509	0.19563	0.15040	0.11591	0.08955	0.06934
29	0.56311	0.48866	0.42435	0.32065	0.24295	0.18456	0.14056	0.10733	0.08215	0.06304
30	0.55207	0.47674	0.41199	0.30832	0.23138	0.17411	0.13137	0.09938	0.07537	0.05731
31	0.54125	0.46511	0.39999	0.29646	0.22036	0.16425	0.12277	0.09202	0.06915	0.05210
32	0.53063	0.45377	0.38834	0.28506	0.20987	0.15496	0.11474	0.08520	0.06344	0.04736
33	0.52023	0.44270	0.37703	0.27409	0.19987	0.14619	0.10723	0.07889	0.05820	0.04306
34	0.51003	0.43191	0.36604	0.26355	0.19035	0.13791	0.10022	0.07305	0.05339	0.03914
35	0.50003	0.42137	0.35538	0.25342	0.18129	0.13011	0.09366	0.06763	0.04899	0.03558
36	0.49022	0.41109	0.34503	0.24367	0.17266	0.12274	0.08754	0.06262	0.04494	0.03235
37	0.48061	0.40107	0.33498	0.23430	0.16444	0.11579	0.08181	0.05799	0.04123	0.02941
38	0.47119	0.39128	0.32523	0.22529	0.15661	0.10924	0.07646	0.05369	0.03783	0.02673
39	0.46195	0.38174	0.31575	0.21662	0.14915	0.10306	0.07146	0.04971	0.03470	0.02430
40	0.45289	0.37243	0.30656	0.20829	0.14205	0.09722	0.06678	0.04603	0.03184	0.02209
41	0.44401	0.36335	0.29763	0.20028	0.13528	0.09172	0.06241	0.04262	0.02921	0.02009
42	0.43530	0.35448	0.28896	0.19257	0.12884	0.08653	0.05833	0.03946	0.02680	0.01826
43	0.42677	0.34584	0.28054	0.18517	0.12270	0.08163	0.05451	0.03654	0.02458	0.01660
44	0.41840	0.33740	0.27237	0.17805	0.11686	0.07701	0.05095	0.03383	0.02255	0.01509
45	0.41020	0.32917	0.26444	0.17120	0.11130	0.07265	0.04761	0.03133	0.02069	0.01372
46	0.40215	0.32115	0.25674	0.16461	0.10600	0.06854	0.04450	0.02901	0.01898	0.01247
47	0.39427	0.31331	0.24926	0.15828	0.10095	0.06466	0.04159	0.02686	0.01742	0.01134
48	0.38654	0.30567	0.24200	0.15219	0.09614	0.06100	0.03887	0.02487	0.01598	0.01031
49	0.37896	0.29822	0.23495	0.14634	0.09156	0.05755	0.03632	0.02303	0.01466	0.00937
50	0.37153	0.29094	0.22811	0.14071	0.08720	0.05429	0.03395	0.02132	0.01345	0.00852

TABLE I-2: **Present value of $1: (P/F, *i*, *n*)**

11%	12%	14%	15%	16%	18%	20%	22%	24%	25%	n
0.90090	0.89286	0.87719	0.86957	0.86207	0.84746	0.83333	0.81967	0.80645	0.80000	1
0.81162	0.79719	0.76947	0.75614	0.74316	0.71818	0.69444	0.67186	0.65036	0.64000	2
0.73119	0.71178	0.67497	0.65752	0.64066	0.60863	0.57870	0.55071	0.52449	0.51200	3
0.65873	0.63552	0.59208	0.57175	0.55229	0.51579	0.48225	0.45140	0.42297	0.40960	4
0.59345	0.56743	0.51937	0.49718	0.47611	0.43711	0.40188	0.37000	0.34111	0.32768	5
0.53464	0.50663	0.45559	0.43233	0.41044	0.37043	0.33490	0.30328	0.27509	0.26214	6
0.48166	0.45235	0.39964	0.37594	0.35383	0.31393	0.27908	0.24859	0.22184	0.20972	7
0.43393	0.40388	0.35056	0.32690	0.30503	0.26604	0.23257	0.20376	0.17891	0.16777	8
0.39092	0.36061	0.30751	0.28426	0.26295	0.22546	0.19381	0.16702	0.14428	0.13422	9
0.35218	0.32197	0.26974	0.24718	0.22668	0.19106	0.16151	0.13690	0.11635	0.10737	10
0.31728	0.28748	0.23662	0.21494	0.19542	0.16192	0.13459	0.11221	0.09383	0.08590	11
0.28584	0.25668	0.20756	0.18691	0.16846	0.13722	0.11216	0.09198	0.07567	0.06872	12
0.25751	0.22917	0.18207	0.16253	0.14523	0.11629	0.09346	0.07539	0.06103	0.05498	13
0.23199	0.20462	0.15971	0.14133	0.12520	0.09855	0.07789	0.06180	0.04921	0.04398	14
0.20900	0.18270	0.14010	0.12289	0.10793	0.08352	0.06491	0.05065	0.03969	0.03518	15
0.18829	0.16312	0.12289	0.10686	0.09304	0.07078	0.05409	0.04152	0.03201	0.02815	16
0.16963	0.14564	0.10780	0.09293	0.08021	0.05998	0.04507	0.03403	0.02581	0.02252	17
0.15282	0.13004	0.09456	0.08081	0.06914	0.05083	0.03756	0.02789	0.02082	0.01801	18
0.13768	0.11611	0.08295	0.07027	0.05961	0.04308	0.03130	0.02286	0.01679	0.01441	19
0.12403	0.10367	0.07276	0.06110	0.05139	0.03651	0.02608	0.01874	0.01354	0.01153	20
0.11174	0.09256	0.06383	0.05313	0.04430	0.03094	0.02174	0.01536	0.01092	0.00922	21
0.10067	0.08264	0.05599	0.04620	0.03819	0.02622	0.01811	0.01259	0.00880	0.00738	22
0.09069	0.07379	0.04911	0.04017	0.03292	0.02222	0.01509	0.01032	0.00710	0.00590	23
0.08170	0.06588	0.04308	0.03493	0.02838	0.01883	0.01258	0.00846	0.00573	0.00472	24
0.07361	0.05882	0.03779	0.03038	0.02447	0.01596	0.01048	0.00693	0.00462	0.00378	25
0.06631	0.05252	0.03315	0.02642	0.02109	0.01352	0.00874	0.00568	0.00372	0.00302	26
0.05974	0.04689	0.02908	0.02297	0.01818	0.01146	0.00728	0.00466	0.00300	0.00242	27
0.05382	0.04187	0.02551	0.01997	0.01567	0.00971	0.00607	0.00382	0.00242	0.00193	28
0.04849	0.03738	0.02237	0.01737	0.01351	0.00823	0.00506	0.00313	0.00195	0.00155	29
0.04368	0.03338	0.01963	0.01510	0.01165	0.00697	0.00421	0.00257	0.00158	0.00124	30
0.03935	0.02980	0.01722	0.01313	0.01004	0.00591	0.00351	0.00210	0.00127	0.00099	31
0.03545	0.02661	0.01510	0.01142	0.00866	0.00501	0.00293	0.00172	0.00102	0.00079	32
0.03194	0.02376	0.01325	0.00993	0.00746	0.00425	0.00244	0.00141	0.00083	0.00063	33
0.02878	0.02121	0.01162	0.00864	0.00643	0.00360	0.00203	0.00116	0.00067	0.00051	34
0.02592	0.01894	0.01019	0.00751	0.00555	0.00305	0.00169	0.00095	0.00054	0.00041	35
0.02335	0.01691	0.00894	0.00653	0.00478	0.00258	0.00141	0.00078	0.00043	0.00032	36
0.02104	0.01510	0.00784	0.00568	0.00412	0.00219	0.00118	0.00064	0.00035	0.00026	37
0.01896	0.01348	0.00688	0.00494	0.00355	0.00186	0.00098	0.00052	0.00028	0.00021	38
0.01708	0.01204	0.00604	0.00429	0.00306	0.00157	0.00082	0.00043	0.00023	0.00017	39
0.01538	0.01075	0.00529	0.00373	0.00264	0.00133	0.00068	0.00035	0.00018	0.00013	40
0.01386	0.00960	0.00464	0.00325	0.00228	0.00113	0.00057	0.00029	0.00015	0.00011	41
0.01249	0.00857	0.00407	0.00282	0.00196	0.00096	0.00047	0.00024	0.00012	0.00009	42
0.01125	0.00765	0.00357	0.00245	0.00169	0.00081	0.00039	0.00019	0.00010	0.00007	43
0.01013	0.00683	0.00313	0.00213	0.00146	0.00069	0.00033	0.00016	0.00008	0.00005	44
0.00913	0.00610	0.00275	0.00186	0.00126	0.00058	0.00027	0.00013	0.00006	0.00004	45
0.00823	0.00544	0.00241	0.00161	0.00108	0.00049	0.00023	0.00011	0.00005	0.00003	46
0.00741	0.00486	0.00212	0.00140	0.00093	0.00042	0.00019	0.00009	0.00004	0.00003	47
0.00668	0.00434	0.00186	0.00122	0.00081	0.00035	0.00016	0.00007	0.00003	0.00002	48
0.00601	0.00388	0.00163	0.00106	0.00069	0.00030	0.00013	0.00006	0.00003	0.00002	49
0.00542	0.00346	0.00143	0.00092	0.00060	0.00025	0.00011	0.00005	0.00002	0.00001	50

TABLE I-3: **Future value of an ordinary annuity of *n* payments of $1: (F/A, *i*, *n*)**

n	2%	2.5%	3%	4%	5%	6%	7%	8%	9%	10%
1	1.0000	1.0000	1.0000	1.0000	1.0000	1.0000	1.0000	1.0000	1.0000	1.0000
2	2.0200	2.0250	2.0300	2.0400	2.0500	2.0600	2.0700	2.0800	2.0900	2.1000
3	3.0604	3.0756	3.0909	3.1216	3.1525	3.1836	3.2149	3.2464	3.2781	3.3100
4	4.1216	4.1525	4.1836	4.2465	4.3101	4.3746	4.4399	4.5061	4.5731	4.6410
5	5.2040	5.2563	5.3091	5.4163	5.5256	5.6371	5.7507	5.8666	5.9847	6.1051
6	6.3081	6.3877	6.4684	6.6330	6.8019	6.9753	7.1533	7.3359	7.5233	7.7156
7	7.4343	7.5474	7.6625	7.8983	8.1420	8.3938	8.6540	8.9228	9.2004	9.4872
8	8.5830	8.7361	8.8923	9.2142	9.5491	9.8975	10.260	10.637	11.028	11.436
9	9.7546	9.9545	10.159	10.583	11.027	11.491	11.978	12.488	13.021	13.579
10	10.950	11.203	11.464	12.006	12.578	13.181	13.816	14.487	15.193	15.937
11	12.169	12.483	12.808	13.486	14.207	14.972	15.784	16.645	17.560	18.531
12	13.412	13.796	14.192	15.026	15.917	16.870	17.888	18.977	20.141	21.384
13	14.680	15.140	15.618	16.627	17.713	18.882	20.141	21.495	22.953	24.523
14	15.974	16.519	17.086	18.292	19.599	21.015	22.550	24.215	26.019	27.975
15	17.293	17.932	18.599	20.024	21.579	23.276	25.129	27.152	29.361	31.772
16	18.639	19.380	20.157	21.825	23.657	25.673	27.888	30.324	33.003	35.950
17	20.012	20.865	21.762	23.698	25.840	28.213	30.840	33.750	36.974	40.545
18	21.412	22.386	23.414	25.645	28.132	30.906	33.999	37.450	41.301	45.599
19	22.841	23.946	25.117	27.671	30.539	33.760	37.379	41.446	46.018	51.159
20	24.297	25.545	26.870	29.778	33.066	36.786	40.995	45.762	51.160	57.275
21	25.783	27.183	28.676	31.969	35.719	39.993	44.865	50.423	56.765	64.002
22	27.299	28.863	30.537	34.248	38.505	43.392	49.006	55.457	62.873	71.403
23	28.845	30.584	32.453	36.618	41.430	46.996	53.436	60.893	69.532	79.543
24	30.422	32.349	34.426	39.083	44.502	50.816	58.177	66.765	76.790	88.497
25	32.030	34.158	36.459	41.646	47.727	54.865	63.249	73.106	84.701	98.347
26	33.671	36.012	38.553	44.312	51.113	59.156	68.676	79.954	93.324	109.18
27	35.344	37.912	40.710	47.084	54.669	63.706	74.484	87.351	102.72	121.10
28	37.051	39.860	42.931	49.968	58.403	68.528	80.698	95.339	112.97	134.21
29	38.792	41.856	45.219	52.966	62.323	73.640	87.347	103.97	124.14	148.63
30	40.568	43.903	47.575	56.085	66.439	79.058	94.461	113.28	136.31	164.49
31	42.379	46.000	50.003	59.328	70.761	84.802	102.07	123.35	149.58	181.94
32	44.227	48.150	52.503	62.701	75.299	90.890	110.22	134.21	164.04	201.14
33	46.112	50.354	55.078	66.210	80.064	97.343	118.93	145.95	179.80	222.25
34	48.034	52.613	57.730	69.858	85.067	104.18	128.26	158.63	196.98	245.48
35	49.994	54.928	60.462	73.652	90.320	111.43	138.24	172.32	215.71	271.02
36	51.994	57.301	63.276	77.598	95.836	119.12	148.91	187.10	236.12	299.13
37	54.034	59.734	66.174	81.702	101.63	127.27	160.34	203.07	258.38	330.04
38	56.115	62.227	69.159	85.970	107.71	135.90	172.56	220.32	282.63	364.04
39	58.237	64.783	72.234	90.409	114.10	145.06	185.64	238.94	309.07	401.45
40	60.402	67.403	75.401	95.026	120.80	154.76	199.64	259.06	337.88	442.59
41	62.610	70.088	78.663	99.827	127.84	165.05	214.61	280.78	369.29	487.85
42	64.862	72.840	82.023	104.82	135.23	175.95	230.63	304.24	403.53	537.64
43	67.159	75.661	85.484	110.01	142.99	187.51	247.78	329.58	440.85	592.40
44	69.503	78.552	89.048	115.41	151.14	199.76	266.12	356.95	481.52	652.64
45	71.893	81.516	92.720	121.03	159.70	212.74	285.75	386.51	525.86	718.90
46	74.331	84.554	96.501	126.87	168.69	226.51	306.75	418.43	574.19	791.80
47	76.817	87.668	100.40	132.95	178.12	241.10	329.22	452.90	626.86	871.97
48	79.354	90.860	104.41	139.26	188.03	256.56	353.27	490.13	684.28	960.17
49	81.941	94.131	108.54	145.83	198.43	272.96	379.00	530.34	746.87	1057.2
50	84.579	97.484	112.80	152.67	209.35	290.34	406.53	573.77	815.08	1163.9

TABLE I-3: **Future value of an ordinary annuity of *n* payments of $1: (F/A, *i*, *n*)**

11%	12%	14%	15%	16%	18%	20%	22%	24%	25%	n
1.0000	1.0000	1.0000	1.0000	1.0000	1.0000	1.0000	1.0000	1.0000	1.0000	1
2.1100	2.1200	2.1400	2.1500	2.1600	2.1800	2.2000	2.2200	2.2400	2.2500	2
3.3421	3.3744	3.4396	3.4725	3.5056	3.5724	3.6400	3.7084	3.7776	3.8125	3
4.7097	4.7793	4.9211	4.9934	5.0665	5.2154	5.3680	5.5242	5.6842	5.7656	4
6.2278	6.3528	6.6101	6.7424	6.8771	7.1542	7.4416	7.7396	8.0484	8.2070	5
7.9129	8.1152	8.5355	8.7537	8.9775	9.4420	9.9299	10.442	10.980	11.259	6
9.7833	10.089	10.730	11.067	11.414	12.142	12.916	13.740	14.615	15.073	7
11.859	12.300	13.233	13.727	14.240	15.327	16.499	17.762	19.123	19.842	8
14.164	14.776	16.085	16.786	17.519	19.086	20.799	22.670	24.712	25.802	9
16.722	17.549	19.337	20.304	21.321	23.521	25.959	28.657	31.643	33.253	10
19.561	20.655	23.045	24.349	25.733	28.755	32.150	35.962	40.238	42.566	11
22.713	24.133	27.271	29.002	30.850	34.931	39.581	44.874	50.895	54.208	12
26.212	28.029	32.089	34.352	36.786	42.219	48.497	55.746	64.110	68.760	13
30.095	32.393	37.581	40.505	43.672	50.818	59.196	69.010	80.496	86.949	14
34.405	37.280	43.842	47.580	51.660	60.965	72.035	85.192	100.82	109.69	15
39.190	42.753	50.980	55.717	60.925	72.939	87.442	104.93	126.01	138.11	16
44.501	48.884	59.118	65.075	71.673	87.068	105.93	129.02	157.25	173.64	17
50.396	55.750	68.394	75.836	84.141	103.74	128.12	158.40	195.99	218.04	18
56.939	63.440	78.969	88.212	98.603	123.41	154.74	194.25	244.03	273.56	19
64.203	72.052	91.025	102.44	115.38	146.63	186.69	237.99	303.60	342.94	20
72.265	81.699	104.77	118.81	134.84	174.02	225.03	291.35	377.46	429.68	21
81.214	92.503	120.44	137.63	157.41	206.34	271.03	356.44	469.06	538.10	22
91.148	104.60	138.30	159.28	183.60	244.49	326.24	435.86	582.63	673.63	23
102.17	118.16	158.66	184.17	213.98	289.49	392.48	532.75	723.46	843.03	24
114.41	133.33	181.87	212.79	249.21	342.60	471.98	650.96	898.09	1054.8	25
128.00	150.33	208.33	245.71	290.09	405.27	567.38	795.17	1114.6	1319.5	26
143.08	169.37	238.50	283.57	337.50	479.22	681.85	971.10	1383.1	1650.4	27
159.82	190.70	272.89	327.10	392.50	566.48	819.22	1185.7	1716.1	2064.0	28
178.40	214.58	312.09	377.17	456.30	669.45	984.07	1447.6	2129.0	2580.9	29
199.02	241.33	356.79	434.75	530.31	790.95	1181.9	1767.1	2640.9	3227.2	30
221.91	271.29	407.74	500.96	616.16	934.32	1419.3	2156.8	3275.7	4035.0	31
247.32	304.85	465.82	577.10	715.75	1103.5	1704.1	2632.3	4062.9	5044.7	32
275.53	342.43	532.04	664.67	831.27	1303.1	2045.9	3212.5	5039.0	6306.9	33
306.84	384.52	607.52	765.37	965.27	1538.7	2456.1	3920.2	6249.4	7884.6	34
341.59	431.66	693.57	881.17	1120.7	1816.7	2948.3	4783.6	7750.2	9856.8	35
380.16	484.46	791.67	1014.3	1301.0	2144.6	3539.0	5837.0	9611.3	12322	36
422.98	543.60	903.51	1167.5	1510.2	2531.7	4247.8	7122.2	11919	15403	37
470.51	609.83	1031.0	1343.6	1752.8	2988.4	5098.4	8690.1	14781	19255	38
523.27	684.01	1176.3	1546.2	2034.3	3527.3	6119.0	10603	18329	24070	39
581.83	767.09	1342.0	1779.1	2360.8	4163.2	7343.9	12937	22729	30089	40
646.83	860.14	1530.9	2047.0	2739.5	4913.6	8813.6	15784	28185	37612	41
718.98	964.36	1746.2	2355.0	3178.8	5799.0	10577	19257	34950	47016	42
799.07	1081.1	1991.7	2709.2	3688.4	6843.9	12694	23494	43339	58771	43
887.96	1211.8	2271.5	3116.6	4279.5	8076.8	15234	28664	53741	73464	44
986.64	1358.2	2590.6	3585.1	4965.3	9531.6	18281	34971	66640	91831	45
1096.2	1522.2	2954.2	4123.9	5760.7	11248	21939	42666	82635	114790	46
1217.7	1705.9	3368.8	4743.5	6683.4	13274	26327	52054	102468	143489	47
1352.7	1911.6	3841.5	5456.0	7753.8	15664	31594	63506	127062	179362	48
1502.5	2142.0	4380.3	6275.4	8995.4	18485	37913	77479	157558	224204	49
1668.8	2400.0	4994.5	7217.7	10436	21813	45497	94525	195373	280256	50

TABLE I-4: **Present value of an ordinary annuity of *n* payments of $1: (P/A, *i*, *n*)**

n	2%	2.5%	3%	4%	5%	6%	7%	8%	9%	10%
1	0.98039	0.97561	0.97087	0.96154	0.95238	0.94340	0.93458	0.92593	0.91743	0.90909
2	1.94156	1.92742	1.91347	1.88609	1.85941	1.83339	1.80802	1.78326	1.75911	1.73554
3	2.88388	2.85602	2.82861	2.77509	2.72325	2.67301	2.62432	2.57710	2.53129	2.48685
4	3.80773	3.76197	3.71710	3.62990	3.54595	3.46511	3.38721	3.31213	3.23972	3.16987
5	4.71346	4.64583	4.57971	4.45182	4.32948	4.21236	4.10020	3.99271	3.88965	3.79079
6	5.60143	5.50813	5.41719	5.24214	5.07569	4.91732	4.76654	4.62288	4.48592	4.35526
7	6.47199	6.34939	6.23028	6.00205	5.78637	5.58238	5.38929	5.20637	5.03295	4.86842
8	7.32548	7.17014	7.01969	6.73274	6.46321	6.20979	5.97130	5.74664	5.53482	5.33493
9	8.16224	7.97087	7.78611	7.43533	7.10782	6.80169	6.51523	6.24689	5.99525	5.75902
10	8.98259	8.75206	8.53020	8.11090	7.72173	7.36009	7.02358	6.71008	6.41766	6.14457
11	9.78685	9.51421	9.25262	8.76048	8.30641	7.88687	7.49867	7.13896	6.80519	6.49506
12	10.57534	10.25776	9.95400	9.38507	8.86325	8.38384	7.94269	7.53608	7.16073	6.81369
13	11.34837	10.98318	10.63496	9.98565	9.39357	8.85268	8.35765	7.90378	7.48690	7.10336
14	12.10625	11.69091	11.29607	10.56312	9.89864	9.29498	8.74547	8.24424	7.78615	7.36669
15	12.84926	12.38138	11.93794	11.11839	10.37966	9.71225	9.10791	8.55948	8.06069	7.60608
16	13.57771	13.05500	12.56110	11.65230	10.83777	10.10590	9.44665	8.85137	8.31256	7.82371
17	14.29187	13.71220	13.16612	12.16567	11.27407	10.47726	9.76322	9.12164	8.54363	8.02155
18	14.99203	14.35336	13.75351	12.65930	11.68959	10.82760	10.05909	9.37189	8.75563	8.20141
19	15.67846	14.97889	14.32380	13.13394	12.08532	11.15812	10.33560	9.60360	8.95011	8.36492
20	16.35143	15.58916	14.87747	13.59033	12.46221	11.46992	10.59401	9.81815	9.12855	8.51356
21	17.01121	16.18455	15.41502	14.02916	12.82115	11.76408	10.83553	10.01680	9.29224	8.64869
22	17.65805	16.76541	15.93692	14.45112	13.16300	12.04158	11.06124	10.20074	9.44243	8.77154
23	18.29220	17.33211	16.44361	14.85684	13.48857	12.30338	11.27219	10.37106	9.58021	8.88322
24	18.91393	17.88499	16.93554	15.24696	13.79864	12.55036	11.46933	10.52876	9.70661	8.98474
25	19.52346	18.42438	17.41315	15.62208	14.09394	12.78336	11.65358	10.67478	9.82258	9.07704
26	20.12104	18.95061	17.87684	15.98277	14.37519	13.00317	11.82578	10.80998	9.92897	9.16095
27	20.70690	19.46401	18.32703	16.32959	14.64303	13.21053	11.98671	10.93516	10.02658	9.23722
28	21.28127	19.96489	18.76411	16.66306	14.89813	13.40616	12.13711	11.05108	10.11613	9.30657
29	21.84438	20.45355	19.18845	16.98371	15.14107	13.59072	12.27767	11.15841	10.19828	9.36961
30	22.39646	20.93029	19.60044	17.29203	15.37245	13.76483	12.40904	11.25778	10.27365	9.42691
31	22.93770	21.39541	20.00043	17.58849	15.59281	13.92909	12.53181	11.34980	10.34280	9.47901
32	23.46833	21.84918	20.38877	17.87355	15.80268	14.08404	12.64656	11.43500	10.40624	9.52638
33	23.98856	22.29188	20.76579	18.14765	16.00255	14.23023	12.75379	11.51389	10.46444	9.56943
34	24.49859	22.72379	21.13184	18.41120	16.19290	14.36814	12.85401	11.58693	10.51784	9.60857
35	24.99862	23.14516	21.48722	18.66461	16.37419	14.49825	12.94767	11.65457	10.56682	9.64416
36	25.48884	23.55625	21.83225	18.90828	16.54685	14.62099	13.03521	11.71719	10.61176	9.67651
37	25.96945	23.95732	22.16724	19.14258	16.71129	14.73678	13.11702	11.77518	10.65299	9.70592
38	26.44064	24.34860	22.49246	19.36786	16.86789	14.84602	13.19347	11.82887	10.69082	9.73265
39	26.90259	24.73034	22.80822	19.58448	17.01704	14.94907	13.26493	11.87858	10.72552	9.75696
40	27.35548	25.10278	23.11477	19.79277	17.15909	15.04630	13.33171	11.92461	10.75736	9.77905
41	27.79949	25.46612	23.41240	19.99305	17.29437	15.13802	13.39412	11.96723	10.78657	9.79914
42	28.23479	25.82061	23.70136	20.18563	17.42321	15.22454	13.45245	12.00670	10.81337	9.81740
43	28.66156	26.16645	23.98190	20.37079	17.54591	15.30617	13.50696	12.04324	10.83795	9.83400
44	29.07996	26.50385	24.25427	20.54884	17.66277	15.38318	13.55791	12.07707	10.86051	9.84909
45	29.49016	26.83302	24.51871	20.72004	17.77407	15.45583	13.60552	12.10840	10.88120	9.86281
46	29.89231	27.15417	24.77545	20.88465	17.88007	15.52437	13.65002	12.13741	10.90018	9.87528
47	30.28658	27.46748	25.02471	21.04294	17.98102	15.58903	13.69161	12.16427	10.91760	9.88662
48	30.67312	27.77315	25.26671	21.19513	18.07716	15.65003	13.73047	12.18914	10.93358	9.89693
49	31.05208	28.07137	25.50166	21.34147	18.16872	15.70757	13.76680	12.21216	10.94823	9.90630
50	31.42361	28.36231	25.72976	21.48218	18.25593	15.76186	13.80075	12.23348	10.96168	9.91481

TABLE I-4: **Present value of an ordinary annuity of *n* payments of $1: (P/A, *i*, *n*)**

11%	12%	14%	15%	16%	18%	20%	22%	24%	25%	n
0.90090	0.89286	0.87719	0.86957	0.86207	0.84746	0.83333	0.81967	0.80645	0.80000	1
1.71252	1.69005	1.64666	1.62571	1.60523	1.56564	1.52778	1.49153	1.45682	1.44000	2
2.44371	2.40183	2.32163	2.28323	2.24589	2.17427	2.10648	2.04224	1.98130	1.95200	3
3.10245	3.03735	2.91371	2.85498	2.79818	2.69006	2.58873	2.49364	2.40428	2.36160	4
3.69590	3.60478	3.43308	3.35216	3.27429	3.12717	2.99061	2.86364	2.74538	2.68928	5
4.23054	4.11141	3.88867	3.78448	3.68474	3.49760	3.32551	3.16692	3.02047	2.95142	6
4.71220	4.56376	4.28830	4.16042	4.03857	3.81153	3.60459	3.41551	3.24232	3.16114	7
5.14612	4.96764	4.63886	4.48732	4.34359	4.07757	3.83716	3.61927	3.42122	3.32891	8
5.53705	5.32825	4.94637	4.77158	4.60654	4.30302	4.03097	3.78628	3.56550	3.46313	9
5.88923	5.65022	5.21612	5.01877	4.83323	4.49409	4.19247	3.92318	3.68186	3.57050	10
6.20652	5.93770	5.45273	5.23371	5.02864	4.65601	4.32706	4.03540	3.77569	3.65640	11
6.49236	6.19437	5.66029	5.42062	5.19711	4.79322	4.43922	4.12737	3.85136	3.72512	12
6.74987	6.42355	5.84236	5.58315	5.34233	4.90951	4.53268	4.20277	3.91239	3.78010	13
6.98187	6.62817	6.00207	5.72448	5.46753	5.00806	4.61057	4.26456	3.96160	3.82408	14
7.19087	6.81086	6.14217	5.84737	5.57546	5.09158	4.67547	4.31522	4.00129	3.85926	15
7.37916	6.97399	6.26506	5.95423	5.66850	5.16235	4.72956	4.35673	4.03330	3.88741	16
7.54879	7.11963	6.37286	6.04716	5.74870	5.22233	4.77463	4.39077	4.05911	3.90993	17
7.70162	7.24967	6.46742	6.12797	5.81785	5.27316	4.81219	4.41866	4.07993	3.92794	18
7.83929	7.36578	6.55037	6.19823	5.87746	5.31624	4.84350	4.44152	4.09672	3.94235	19
7.96333	7.46944	6.62313	6.25933	5.92884	5.35275	4.86958	4.46027	4.11026	3.95388	20
8.07507	7.56200	6.68696	6.31246	5.97314	5.38368	4.89132	4.47563	4.12117	3.96311	21
8.17574	7.64465	6.74294	6.35866	6.01133	5.40990	4.90943	4.48822	4.12998	3.97049	22
8.26643	7.71843	6.79206	6.39884	6.04425	5.43212	4.92453	4.49854	4.13708	3.97639	23
8.34814	7.78432	6.83514	6.43377	6.07263	5.45095	4.93710	4.50700	4.14281	3.98111	24
8.42174	7.84314	6.87293	6.46415	6.09709	5.46691	4.94759	4.51393	4.14742	3.98489	25
8.48806	7.89566	6.90608	6.49056	6.11818	5.48043	4.95632	4.51962	4.15115	3.98791	26
8.54780	7.94255	6.93515	6.51353	6.13636	5.49189	4.96360	4.52428	4.15415	3.99033	27
8.60162	7.98442	6.96066	6.53351	6.15204	5.50160	4.96967	4.52810	4.15657	3.99226	28
8.65011	8.02181	6.98304	6.55088	6.16555	5.50983	4.97472	4.53123	4.15853	3.99381	29
8.69379	8.05518	7.00266	6.56598	6.17720	5.51681	4.97894	4.53379	4.16010	3.99505	30
8.73315	8.08499	7.01988	6.57911	6.18724	5.52272	4.98245	4.53590	4.16137	3.99604	31
8.76860	8.11159	7.03498	6.59053	6.19590	5.52773	4.98537	4.53762	4.16240	3.99683	32
8.80054	8.13535	7.04823	6.60046	6.20336	5.53197	4.98781	4.53903	4.16322	3.99746	33
8.82932	8.15656	7.05985	6.60910	6.20979	5.53557	4.98984	4.54019	4.16389	3.99797	34
8.85524	8.17550	7.07005	6.61661	6.21534	5.53862	4.99154	4.54114	4.16443	3.99838	35
8.87859	8.19241	7.07899	6.62314	6.22012	5.54120	4.99295	4.54192	4.16486	3.99870	36
8.89963	8.20751	7.08683	6.62881	6.22424	5.54339	4.99412	4.54256	4.16521	3.99896	37
8.91859	8.22099	7.09371	6.63375	6.22779	5.54525	4.99510	4.54308	4.16549	3.99917	38
8.93567	8.23303	7.09975	6.63805	6.23086	5.54682	4.99592	4.54351	4.16572	3.99934	39
8.95105	8.24378	7.10504	6.64178	6.23350	5.54815	4.99660	4.54386	4.16590	3.99947	40
8.96491	8.25337	7.10969	6.64502	6.23577	5.54928	4.99717	4.54415	4.16605	3.99957	41
8.97740	8.26194	7.11376	6.64785	6.23774	5.55024	4.99764	4.54438	4.16617	3.99966	42
8.98865	8.26959	7.11733	6.65030	6.23943	5.55105	4.99803	4.54458	4.16627	3.99973	43
8.99878	8.27642	7.12047	6.65244	6.24089	5.55174	4.99836	4.54473	4.16634	3.99978	44
9.00791	8.28252	7.12322	6.65429	6.24214	5.55232	4.99863	4.54486	4.16641	3.99983	45
9.01614	8.28796	7.12563	6.65591	6.24323	5.55281	4.99886	4.54497	4.16646	3.99986	46
9.02355	8.29282	7.12774	6.65731	6.24416	5.55323	4.99905	4.54506	4.16650	3.99989	47
9.03022	8.29716	7.12960	6.65853	6.24497	5.55359	4.99921	4.54513	4.16653	3.99991	48
9.03624	8.30104	7.13123	6.65959	6.24566	5.55389	4.99934	4.54519	4.16656	3.99993	49
9.04165	8.30450	7.13266	6.66051	6.24626	5.55414	4.99945	4.54524	4.16658	3.99994	50

TABLE I-5: **Future value of an annuity due of *n* payments of $1: (F/AD, *i*, *n*)**

n	2%	2.5%	3%	4%	5%	6%	7%	8%	9%	10%
1	1.0200	1.0250	1.0300	1.0400	1.0500	1.0600	1.0700	1.0800	1.0900	1.1000
2	2.0604	2.0756	2.0909	2.1216	2.1525	2.1836	2.2149	2.2464	2.2781	2.3100
3	3.1216	3.1525	3.1836	3.2465	3.3101	3.3746	3.4399	3.5061	3.5731	3.6410
4	4.2040	4.2563	4.3091	4.4163	4.5256	4.6371	4.7507	4.8666	4.9847	5.1051
5	5.3081	5.3877	5.4684	5.6330	5.8019	5.9753	6.1533	6.3359	6.5233	6.7156
6	6.4343	6.5474	6.6625	6.8983	7.1420	7.3938	7.6540	7.9228	8.2004	8.4872
7	7.5830	7.7361	7.8923	8.2142	8.5491	8.8975	9.2598	9.6366	10.028	10.436
8	8.7546	8.9545	9.1591	9.5828	10.027	10.491	10.978	11.488	12.021	12.579
9	9.9497	10.203	10.464	11.006	11.578	12.181	12.816	13.487	14.193	14.937
10	11.169	11.483	11.808	12.486	13.207	13.972	14.784	15.645	16.560	17.531
11	12.412	12.796	13.192	14.026	14.917	15.870	16.888	17.977	19.141	20.384
12	13.680	14.140	14.618	15.627	16.713	17.882	19.141	20.495	21.953	23.523
13	14.974	15.519	16.086	17.292	18.599	20.015	21.550	23.215	25.019	26.975
14	16.293	16.932	17.599	19.024	20.579	22.276	24.129	26.152	28.361	30.772
15	17.639	18.380	19.157	20.825	22.657	24.673	26.888	29.324	32.003	34.950
16	19.012	19.865	20.762	22.698	24.840	27.213	29.840	32.750	35.974	39.545
17	20.412	21.386	22.414	24.645	27.132	29.906	32.999	36.450	40.301	44.599
18	21.841	22.946	24.117	26.671	29.539	32.760	36.379	40.446	45.018	50.159
19	23.297	24.545	25.870	28.778	32.066	35.786	39.995	44.762	50.160	56.275
20	24.783	26.183	27.676	30.969	34.719	38.993	43.865	49.423	55.765	63.002
21	26.299	27.863	29.537	33.248	37.505	42.392	48.006	54.457	61.873	70.403
22	27.845	29.584	31.453	35.618	40.430	45.996	52.436	59.893	68.532	78.543
23	29.422	31.349	33.426	38.083	43.502	49.816	57.177	65.765	75.790	87.497
24	31.030	33.158	35.459	40.646	46.727	53.865	62.249	72.106	83.701	97.347
25	32.671	35.012	37.553	43.312	50.113	58.156	67.676	78.954	92.324	108.18
26	34.344	36.912	39.710	46.084	53.669	62.706	73.484	86.351	101.72	120.10
27	36.051	38.860	41.931	48.968	57.403	67.528	79.698	94.339	111.97	133.21
28	37.792	40.856	44.219	51.966	61.323	72.640	86.347	102.97	123.14	147.63
29	39.568	42.903	46.575	55.085	65.439	78.058	93.461	112.28	135.31	163.49
30	41.379	45.000	49.003	58.328	69.761	83.802	101.07	122.35	148.58	180.94
31	43.227	47.150	51.503	61.701	74.299	89.890	109.22	133.21	163.04	200.14
32	45.112	49.354	54.078	65.210	79.064	96.343	117.93	144.95	178.80	221.25
33	47.034	51.613	56.730	68.858	84.067	103.18	127.26	157.63	195.98	244.48
34	48.994	53.928	59.462	72.652	89.320	110.43	137.24	171.32	214.71	270.02
35	50.994	56.301	62.276	76.598	94.836	118.12	147.91	186.10	235.12	298.13
36	53.034	58.734	65.174	80.702	100.63	126.27	159.34	202.07	257.38	329.04
37	55.115	61.227	68.159	84.970	106.71	134.90	171.56	219.32	281.63	363.04
38	57.237	63.783	71.234	89.409	113.10	144.06	184.64	237.94	308.07	400.45
39	59.402	66.403	74.401	94.026	119.80	153.76	198.64	258.06	336.88	441.59
40	61.610	69.088	77.663	98.827	126.84	164.05	213.61	279.78	368.29	486.85
41	63.862	71.840	81.023	103.82	134.23	174.95	229.63	303.24	402.53	536.64
42	66.159	74.661	84.484	109.01	141.99	186.51	246.78	328.58	439.85	591.40
43	68.503	77.552	88.048	114.41	150.14	198.76	265.12	355.95	480.52	651.64
44	70.893	80.516	91.720	120.03	158.70	211.74	284.75	385.51	524.86	717.90
45	73.331	83.554	95.501	125.87	167.69	225.51	305.75	417.43	573.19	790.80
46	75.817	86.668	99.397	131.95	177.12	240.10	328.22	451.90	625.86	870.97
47	78.354	89.860	103.41	138.26	187.03	255.56	352.27	489.13	683.28	959.17
48	80.941	93.131	107.54	144.83	197.43	271.96	378.00	529.34	745.87	1056.2
49	83.579	96.484	111.80	151.67	208.35	289.34	405.53	572.77	814.08	1162.9
50	86.271	99.921	116.18	158.77	219.82	307.76	434.99	619.67	888.44	1280.3

TABLE I-5: **Future value of an annuity due of *n* payments of $1: (F/AD, *i*, *n*)**

11%	12%	14%	15%	16%	18%	20%	22%	24%	25%	n
1.1100	1.1200	1.1400	1.1500	1.1600	1.1800	1.2000	1.2200	1.2400	1.2500	1
2.3421	2.3744	2.4396	2.4725	2.5056	2.5724	2.6400	2.7084	2.7776	2.8125	2
3.7097	3.7793	3.9211	3.9934	4.0665	4.2154	4.3680	4.5242	4.6842	4.7656	3
5.2278	5.3528	5.6101	5.7424	5.8771	6.1542	6.4416	6.7396	7.0484	7.2070	4
6.9129	7.1152	7.5355	7.7537	7.9775	8.4420	8.9299	9.4423	9.9801	10.259	5
8.7833	9.0890	9.7305	10.0668	10.414	11.142	11.916	12.740	13.615	14.073	6
10.859	11.2997	12.2328	12.7268	13.240	14.327	15.499	16.762	18.123	18.842	7
13.164	13.7757	15.0853	15.7858	16.519	18.086	19.799	21.670	23.712	24.802	8
15.722	16.5487	18.3373	19.3037	20.321	22.521	24.959	27.657	30.643	32.253	9
18.561	19.6546	22.0445	23.3493	24.733	27.755	31.150	34.962	39.238	41.566	10
21.713	23.1331	26.2707	28.0017	29.850	33.931	38.581	43.874	49.895	53.208	11
25.212	27.0291	31.0887	33.3519	35.786	41.219	47.497	54.746	63.110	67.760	12
29.095	31.3926	36.5811	39.5047	42.672	49.818	58.196	68.010	79.496	85.949	13
33.405	36.2797	42.8424	46.5804	50.660	59.965	71.035	84.192	99.815	108.69	14
38.190	41.7533	49.9804	54.7175	59.925	71.939	86.442	103.93	125.01	137.11	15
43.501	47.8837	58.1176	64.0751	70.673	86.068	104.93	128.02	156.25	172.64	16
49.396	54.7497	67.3941	74.8364	83.141	102.74	127.12	157.40	194.99	217.04	17
55.939	62.4397	77.9692	87.2118	97.603	122.41	153.74	193.25	243.03	272.56	18
63.203	71.0524	90.0249	101.4436	114.38	145.63	185.69	236.99	302.60	341.94	19
71.265	80.6987	103.7684	117.8101	133.84	173.02	224.03	290.35	376.46	428.68	20
80.214	91.5026	119.4360	136.6316	156.41	205.34	270.03	355.44	468.06	537.10	21
90.148	103.60	137.2970	158.2764	182.60	243.49	325.24	434.86	581.63	672.63	22
101.17	117.16	157.6586	183.1678	212.98	288.49	391.48	531.75	722.46	842.03	23
113.41	132.33	180.8708	211.7930	248.21	341.60	470.98	649.96	897.09	1053.8	24
127.00	149.33	207.3327	244.7120	289.09	404.27	566.38	794.17	1113.6	1318.5	25
142.08	168.37	237.4993	282.5688	336.50	478.22	680.85	970.10	1382.1	1649.4	26
158.82	189.70	271.8892	326.1041	391.50	565.48	818.22	1184.7	1715.1	2063.0	27
177.40	213.58	311.0937	376.1697	455.30	668.45	983.07	1446.6	2128.0	2579.9	28
198.02	240.33	355.7868	433.7451	529.31	789.95	1180.9	1766.1	2639.9	3226.2	29
220.91	270.29	406.7370	499.9569	615.16	933.32	1418.3	2155.8	3274.7	4034.0	30
246.32	303.85	464.8202	576.1005	714.75	1102.5	1703.1	2631.3	4061.9	5043.7	31
274.53	341.43	531.0350	663.6655	830.27	1302.1	2044.9	3211.5	5038.0	6305.9	32
305.84	383.52	606.5199	764.3654	964.27	1537.7	2455.1	3919.2	6248.4	7883.6	33
340.59	430.66	692.5727	880.1702	1119.7	1815.7	2947.3	4782.6	7749.2	9855.8	34
379.16	483.46	790.6729	1013.3	1300.0	2143.6	3538.0	5836.0	9610.3	12321	35
421.98	542.60	902.5071	1166.5	1509.2	2530.7	4246.8	7121.2	11918	15402	36
469.51	608.83	1030.0	1342.6	1751.8	2987.4	5097.4	8689.1	14780	19254	37
522.27	683.01	1175.3	1545.2	2033.3	3526.3	6118.0	10602	18328	24069	38
580.83	766.09	1341.0	1778.1	2359.8	4162.2	7342.9	12936	22728	30088	39
645.83	859.14	1529.9	2046.0	2738.5	4912.6	8812.6	15783	28184	37611	40
717.98	963.36	1745.2	2354.0	3177.8	5798.0	10576	19256	34949	47015	41
798.07	1080.1	1990.7	2708.2	3687.4	6842.9	12693	23493	43338	58770	42
886.96	1210.8	2270.5	3115.6	4278.5	8075.8	15233	28663	53740	73463	43
985.64	1357.2	2589.6	3584.1	4964.3	9530.6	18280	34970	66639	91830	44
1095.2	1521.2	2953.2	4122.9	5759.7	11247	21938	42665	82634	114789	45
1216.7	1704.9	3367.8	4742.5	6682.4	13273	26326	52053	102467	143488	46
1351.7	1910.6	3840.5	5455.0	7752.8	15663	31593	63505	127061	179361	47
1501.5	2141.0	4379.3	6274.4	8994.4	18484	37912	77478	157557	224203	48
1667.8	2399.0	4993.5	7216.7	10435	21812	45496	94524	195372	280255	49
1852.3	2688.0	5693.8	8300.4	12105	25739	54597	115321	242262	350320	50

TABLE I-6: Present value of an annuity due of *n* payments of $1: (P/AD, *i*, *n*)

n	2%	2.5%	3%	4%	5%	6%	7%	8%	9%	10%
1	1.00000	1.00000	1.00000	1.00000	1.00000	1.00000	1.00000	1.00000	1.00000	1.00000
2	1.98039	1.97561	1.97087	1.96154	1.95238	1.94340	1.93458	1.92593	1.91743	1.90909
3	2.94156	2.92742	2.91347	2.88609	2.85941	2.83339	2.80802	2.78326	2.75911	2.73554
4	3.88388	3.85602	3.82861	3.77509	3.72325	3.67301	3.62432	3.57710	3.53129	3.48685
5	4.80773	4.76197	4.71710	4.62990	4.54595	4.46511	4.38721	4.31213	4.23972	4.16987
6	5.71346	5.64583	5.57971	5.45182	5.32948	5.21236	5.10020	4.99271	4.88965	4.79079
7	6.60143	6.50813	6.41719	6.24214	6.07569	5.91732	5.76654	5.62288	5.48592	5.35526
8	7.47199	7.34939	7.23028	7.00205	6.78637	6.58238	6.38929	6.20637	6.03295	5.86842
9	8.32548	8.17014	8.01969	7.73274	7.46321	7.20979	6.97130	6.74664	6.53482	6.33493
10	9.16224	8.97087	8.78611	8.43533	8.10782	7.80169	7.51523	7.24689	6.99525	6.75902
11	9.98259	9.75206	9.53020	9.11090	8.72173	8.36009	8.02358	7.71008	7.41766	7.14457
12	10.78685	10.51421	10.25262	9.76048	9.30641	8.88687	8.49867	8.13896	7.80519	7.49506
13	11.57534	11.25776	10.95400	10.38507	9.86325	9.38384	8.94269	8.53608	8.16073	7.81369
14	12.34837	11.98318	11.63496	10.98565	10.39357	9.85268	9.35765	8.90378	8.48690	8.10336
15	13.10625	12.69091	12.29607	11.56312	10.89864	10.29498	9.74547	9.24424	8.78615	8.36669
16	13.84926	13.38138	12.93794	12.11839	11.37966	10.71225	10.10791	9.55948	9.06069	8.60608
17	14.57771	14.05500	13.56110	12.65230	11.83777	11.10590	10.44665	9.85137	9.31256	8.82371
18	15.29187	14.71220	14.16612	13.16567	12.27407	11.47726	10.76322	10.12164	9.54363	9.02155
19	15.99203	15.35336	14.75351	13.65930	12.68959	11.82760	11.05909	10.37189	9.75563	9.20141
20	16.67846	15.97889	15.32380	14.13394	13.08532	12.15812	11.33560	10.60360	9.95011	9.36492
21	17.35143	16.58916	15.87747	14.59033	13.46221	12.46992	11.59401	10.81815	10.12855	9.51356
22	18.01121	17.18455	16.41502	15.02916	13.82115	12.76408	11.83553	11.01680	10.29224	9.64869
23	18.65805	17.76541	16.93692	15.45112	14.16300	13.04158	12.06124	11.20074	10.44243	9.77154
24	19.29220	18.33211	17.44361	15.85684	14.48857	13.30338	12.27219	11.37106	10.58021	9.88322
25	19.91393	18.88499	17.93554	16.24696	14.79864	13.55036	12.46933	11.52876	10.70661	9.98474
26	20.52346	19.42438	18.41315	16.62208	15.09394	13.78336	12.65358	11.67478	10.82258	10.07704
27	21.12104	19.95061	18.87684	16.98277	15.37519	14.00317	12.82578	11.80998	10.92897	10.16095
28	21.70690	20.46401	19.32703	17.32959	15.64303	14.21053	12.98671	11.93516	11.02658	10.23722
29	22.28127	20.96489	19.76411	17.66306	15.89813	14.40616	13.13711	12.05108	11.11613	10.30657
30	22.84438	21.45355	20.18845	17.98371	16.14107	14.59072	13.27767	12.15841	11.19828	10.36961
31	23.39646	21.93029	20.60044	18.29203	16.37245	14.76483	13.40904	12.25778	11.27365	10.42691
32	23.93770	22.39541	21.00043	18.58849	16.59281	14.92909	13.53181	12.34980	11.34280	10.47901
33	24.46833	22.84918	21.38877	18.87355	16.80268	15.08404	13.64656	12.43500	11.40624	10.52638
34	24.98856	23.29188	21.76579	19.14765	17.00255	15.23023	13.75379	12.51389	11.46444	10.56943
35	25.49859	23.72379	22.13184	19.41120	17.19290	15.36814	13.85401	12.58693	11.51784	10.60857
36	25.99862	24.14516	22.48722	19.66461	17.37419	15.49825	13.94767	12.65457	11.56682	10.64416
37	26.48884	24.55625	22.83225	19.90828	17.54685	15.62099	14.03521	12.71719	11.61176	10.67651
38	26.96945	24.95732	23.16724	20.14258	17.71129	15.73678	14.11702	12.77518	11.65299	10.70592
39	27.44064	25.34860	23.49246	20.36786	17.86789	15.84602	14.19347	12.82887	11.69082	10.73265
40	27.90259	25.73034	23.80822	20.58448	18.01704	15.94907	14.26493	12.87858	11.72552	10.75696
41	28.35548	26.10278	24.11477	20.79277	18.15909	16.04630	14.33171	12.92461	11.75736	10.77905
42	28.79949	26.46612	24.41240	20.99305	18.29437	16.13802	14.39412	12.96723	11.78657	10.79914
43	29.23479	26.82061	24.70136	21.18563	18.42321	16.22454	14.45245	13.00670	11.81337	10.81740
44	29.66156	27.16645	24.98190	21.37079	18.54591	16.30617	14.50696	13.04324	11.83795	10.83400
45	30.07996	27.50385	25.25427	21.54884	18.66277	16.38318	14.55791	13.07707	11.86051	10.84909
46	30.49016	27.83302	25.51871	21.72004	18.77407	16.45583	14.60552	13.10840	11.88120	10.86281
47	30.89231	28.15417	25.77545	21.88465	18.88007	16.52437	14.65002	13.13741	11.90018	10.87528
48	31.28658	28.46748	26.02471	22.04294	18.98102	16.58903	14.69161	13.16427	11.91760	10.88662
49	31.67312	28.77315	26.26671	22.19513	19.07716	16.65003	14.73047	13.18914	11.93358	10.89693
50	32.05208	29.07137	26.50166	22.34147	19.16872	16.70757	14.76680	13.21216	11.94823	10.90630

TABLE I-6: **Present value of an annuity due of *n* payments of $1: (P/AD, *i*, *n*)**

11%	12%	14%	15%	16%	18%	20%	22%	24%	25%	n
1.00000	1.00000	1.00000	1.00000	1.00000	1.00000	1.00000	1.00000	1.00000	1.00000	1
1.90090	1.89286	1.87719	1.86957	1.86207	1.84746	1.83333	1.81967	1.80645	1.80000	2
2.71252	2.69005	2.64666	2.62571	2.60523	2.56564	2.52778	2.49153	2.45682	2.44000	3
3.44371	3.40183	3.32163	3.28323	3.24589	3.17427	3.10648	3.04224	2.98130	2.95200	4
4.10245	4.03735	3.91371	3.85498	3.79818	3.69006	3.58873	3.49364	3.40428	3.36160	5
4.69590	4.60478	4.43308	4.35216	4.27429	4.12717	3.99061	3.86364	3.74538	3.68928	6
5.23054	5.11141	4.88867	4.78448	4.68474	4.49760	4.32551	4.16692	4.02047	3.95142	7
5.71220	5.56376	5.28830	5.16042	5.03857	4.81153	4.60459	4.41551	4.24232	4.16114	8
6.14612	5.96764	5.63886	5.48732	5.34359	5.07757	4.83716	4.61927	4.42122	4.32891	9
6.53705	6.32825	5.94637	5.77158	5.60654	5.30302	5.03097	4.78628	4.56550	4.46313	10
6.88923	6.65022	6.21612	6.01877	5.83323	5.49409	5.19247	4.92318	4.68186	4.57050	11
7.20652	6.93770	6.45273	6.23371	6.02864	5.65601	5.32706	5.03540	4.77569	4.65640	12
7.49236	7.19437	6.66029	6.42062	6.19711	5.79322	5.43922	5.12737	4.85136	4.72512	13
7.74987	7.42355	6.84236	6.58315	6.34233	5.90951	5.53268	5.20277	4.91239	4.78010	14
7.98187	7.62817	7.00207	6.72448	6.46753	6.00806	5.61057	5.26456	4.96160	4.82408	15
8.19087	7.81086	7.14217	6.84737	6.57546	6.09158	5.67547	5.31522	5.00129	4.85926	16
8.37916	7.97399	7.26506	6.95423	6.66850	6.16235	5.72956	5.35673	5.03330	4.88741	17
8.54879	8.11963	7.37286	7.04716	6.74870	6.22233	5.77463	5.39077	5.05911	4.90993	18
8.70162	8.24967	7.46742	7.12797	6.81785	6.27316	5.81219	5.41866	5.07993	4.92794	19
8.83929	8.36578	7.55037	7.19823	6.87746	6.31624	5.84350	5.44152	5.09672	4.94235	20
8.96333	8.46944	7.62313	7.25933	6.92884	6.35275	5.86958	5.46027	5.11026	4.95388	21
9.07507	8.56200	7.68696	7.31246	6.97314	6.38368	5.89132	5.47563	5.12117	4.96311	22
9.17574	8.64465	7.74294	7.35866	7.01133	6.40990	5.90943	5.48822	5.12998	4.97049	23
9.26643	8.71843	7.79206	7.39884	7.04425	6.43212	5.92453	5.49854	5.13708	4.97639	24
9.34814	8.78432	7.83514	7.43377	7.07263	6.45095	5.93710	5.50700	5.14281	4.98111	25
9.42174	8.84314	7.87293	7.46415	7.09709	6.46691	5.94759	5.51393	5.14742	4.98489	26
9.48806	8.89566	7.90608	7.49056	7.11818	6.48043	5.95632	5.51962	5.15115	4.98791	27
9.54780	8.94255	7.93515	7.51353	7.13636	6.49189	5.96360	5.52428	5.15415	4.99033	28
9.60162	8.98442	7.96066	7.53351	7.15204	6.50160	5.96967	5.52810	5.15657	4.99226	29
9.65011	9.02181	7.98304	7.55088	7.16555	6.50983	5.97472	5.53123	5.15853	4.99381	30
9.69379	9.05518	8.00266	7.56598	7.17720	6.51681	5.97894	5.53379	5.16010	4.99505	31
9.73315	9.08499	8.01988	7.57911	7.18724	6.52272	5.98245	5.53590	5.16137	4.99604	32
9.76860	9.11159	8.03498	7.59053	7.19590	6.52773	5.98537	5.53762	5.16240	4.99683	33
9.80054	9.13535	8.04823	7.60046	7.20336	6.53197	5.98781	5.53903	5.16322	4.99746	34
9.82932	9.15656	8.05985	7.60910	7.20979	6.53557	5.98984	5.54019	5.16389	4.99797	35
9.85524	9.17550	8.07005	7.61661	7.21534	6.53862	5.99154	5.54114	5.16443	4.99838	36
9.87859	9.19241	8.07899	7.62314	7.22012	6.54120	5.99295	5.54192	5.16486	4.99870	37
9.89963	9.20751	8.08683	7.62881	7.22424	6.54339	5.99412	5.54256	5.16521	4.99896	38
9.91859	9.22099	8.09371	7.63375	7.22779	6.54525	5.99510	5.54308	5.16549	4.99917	39
9.93567	9.23303	8.09975	7.63805	7.23086	6.54682	5.99592	5.54351	5.16572	4.99934	40
9.95105	9.24378	8.10504	7.64178	7.23350	6.54815	5.99660	5.54386	5.16590	4.99947	41
9.96491	9.25337	8.10969	7.64502	7.23577	6.54928	5.99717	5.54415	5.16605	4.99957	42
9.97740	9.26194	8.11376	7.64785	7.23774	6.55024	5.99764	5.54438	5.16617	4.99966	43
9.98865	9.26959	8.11733	7.65030	7.23943	6.55105	5.99803	5.54458	5.16627	4.99973	44
9.99878	9.27642	8.12047	7.65244	7.24089	6.55174	5.99836	5.54473	5.16634	4.99978	45
10.00791	9.28252	8.12322	7.65429	7.24214	6.55232	5.99863	5.54486	5.16641	4.99983	46
10.01614	9.28796	8.12563	7.65591	7.24323	6.55281	5.99886	5.54497	5.16646	4.99986	47
10.02355	9.29282	8.12774	7.65731	7.24416	6.55323	5.99905	5.54506	5.16650	4.99989	48
10.03022	9.29716	8.12960	7.65853	7.24497	6.55359	5.99921	5.54513	5.16653	4.99991	49
10.03624	9.30104	8.13123	7.65959	7.24566	6.55389	5.99934	5.54519	5.16656	4.99993	50

Glossary

Absorption costing: a method of assigning costs to inventory that includes fixed overhead costs in addition to variable overhead costs, direct materials and direct labour costs

Accelerated amortization: a method of allocating the cost of an asset in which annual amortization amounts are larger in an asset's early years and decrease over time

Accounting cycle: a chronological cycle that begins with identification of transactions to be recorded and runs through 10 steps, including financial statement preparation

Accounting income: an increase in the reported wealth of a corporation based on actual transactions completed; a measure of income based on the accounting model

Accounting information system: a system designed to record accurate financial data in a timely and chronological manner, facilitate retrieval of financial data in a form useful to management, and simplify periodic preparation of financial statements

Accounts receivable (trade receivable): cash due to a corporation from their customers because of purchases of goods or services on credit

Accrual: the resulting balance sheet account when cash flows occur after expense or revenue recognition; for example, accrued revenues receivable

Accrual-basis accounting: a basis of accounting that reflects transactions as they occur rather than as cash flows eventually occur

Accumulated amortization (accumulated depreciation): that cumulative amount of the original cost of an asset that has been amortized to date

Accumulated depreciation (accumulated amortization): that cumulative amount of the original cost of an asset that has been amortized to date

Additional markup: any increase in the sales price above the original sales price

Additional markup cancellation: cancellation of all or some of an additional markup

Additions: extensions, enlargements, or expansions of an existing capital asset

Adjusted trial balance: a trial balance prepared after adjusting journal entries; the basis for preparation of financial statements

Adjusting journal entries: entries used to record resource changes that occur continuously and must be recorded to accurately reflect the financial results and position of an entry

Aging method: a method of estimating uncollectible accounts receivable by applying probability estimates of non-collection to specific balances that have been classified by age

Allowance for doubtful accounts: a contra account to accounts receivable that represents the portion of outstanding receivables whose collection is doubtful

Allowance method for LCM: lower-of-cost-or-market evaluation of investments is assessed for the portfolio as a whole and any required write-down is recorded as an allowance, which can be reversed

Amortizable cost: the total amount of amortization to be recognized over the useful life of the asset; generally, cost less residual value

Amortization (depletion, depreciation): the periodic allocation of the cost of capital assets over the useful life of the assets

Annuity due: a payment stream in which the payments (or receipts) occur at the beginning of each interest compounding period

Appropriation of retained earnings: retained earnings not available to support dividend declarations resulting from voluntary actions of the board of directors

Assignment: the sale of accounts receivable, usually to a financial institution; may be with recourse or without recourse to the transferor

Balance sheet (statement of financial position): an accounting statement describing at a specific date the assets, liabilities, and shareholders' equity of an entity

Balloon payment: a large final payment on a note or bond

Bank reconciliation: a schedule that analyses the firm's cash account and the bank's reported cash amount to ensure that transaction recording is complete and accurate; one means of internal control

Barter transaction: an exchange involving non-monetary consideration

Betterment: a cost incurred to enhance the service potential of a capital asset; for example, the replacement of a major component of a capital asset with a significantly improved component

Billings on contract: a contra account to the construction in progress inventory account for long-term construction contracts; represents cumulative billings to the final customer

Business combination: any transaction that results in one entity obtaining control over the net assets of another entity as a going concern

Capital assets: identifiable long-lived assets that have been acquired for use in revenue producing activities of the enterprise

Capital cost allowance (CCA): amortization for tax purposes

Capital expenditures: expenditures expected to yield benefits beyond the current period, to be added to an asset account

Capitalize: to record a transaction such that a balance sheet element, usually an asset, is created

Cash: an asset; the amount of money on hand and in the bank

Cash-basis accounting: a basis of accounting that reflects only cash transactions

Cash discounts: reductions to amounts owed due to early payment

Cash equivalents: one of the components of cash on the cash flow statement; cash on hand, cash on deposit, and highly liquid, short-term (e.g. three-month term) investments

Cash flow statement (statement of changes in financial position): an accounting statement describing the uses and sources of cash flow for a specific period of time

Commodity: any article of commerce; often used to describe homogeneous goods, for example, minerals or agricultural products

Comparability: the relationship between two pieces of information; data that has been prepared using the same accounting policies for a corporation or for different corporations in order that they can be logically compared

Compensating balance: a minimum cash balance that must be maintained as support for funds borrowed

Completed-contract method: used to account for long-term contracts; all revenue and expense are deferred until the contract is completed

Composite amortization: the amortization of a set of related but dissimilar assets using one composite rate

Composite rate: (1) a rate used to estimate uncollectible receivables based on the percentage of historical bad debts and total accounts receivable; (2) the weighted-average amortization rate used for composite group amortization

Compound interest: a method of calculating interest wherein the interest is calculated on both principal of the loan and any previously accrued interest that has not been distributed

Comprehensive revaluation: establishing an entirely new basis of accountability (fair value) for all assets and liabilities on change of ownership

Conservatism: the principle that when two accounting methods are acceptable, the one having the less favourable effect on net income and net assets is preferable

Consideration: the economic resources given to the seller by the buyer in a transaction; for example, "The cash consideration paid was $100,000."

Consignment sale: a sale of goods in which the "customer" pays only if the goods are resold to a final customer

Consistency: using the same accounting policies within a corporation from period to period

Consolidated statements: financial statements that include the accounts of a parent company and all of it's controlled subsidiaries, usually determined through share ownership

Consolidation: combining the financial statements of a parent company and its subsidiary(ies); inter-company transactions are eliminated

Constant dollar capital maintenance: maintaining the purchasing power of the owner's investment in constant dollars after inflation; no income is recognized until capital in constant dollars is preserved

Contingency: an event that will occur only if another event occurs; may be recorded or disclosed depending on nature

Continuity assumption (going-concern assumption): the assumption that the corporation will not be liquidated but will continue to pursue its objectives for the foreseeable future

Contra account: one general ledger account that's always reported on the financial statements with its "main" account; since two accounts will have opposite (debit versus credit) balances, their net amount will result

Contracts (construction) in progress: a balance sheet account associated with long-term construction contracts; the accumulated costs of construction to date (plus profit if percentage of completion is used)

Contributed capital: a section of shareholders' equity reflecting the shareholders' investment in the corporation; includes share capital and other contributed capital

Control: the continuing power to determine the strategic policies of an investee without the cooperation of other shareholders

Control account: a general ledger account that is supported by a subsidiary ledger; the control account holds the grand total and the subsidiary ledger the many accounts that make up the grand total

Control block: a small number of related or affiliated shareholders having a majority of the voting shares of an organization

Cost: the amount of consideration given up to acquire, construct, develop, or better a capital asset

Cost/benefit effectiveness: the benefits derived by external users of the financial statements from certain information should outweigh the costs of preparation

Cost method of accounting for investments: investments are recorded at cost and revenue is recorded as time passes (interest) or as declared (dividends)

Cost recovery method of accounting for revenue (sunk cost method): used normally in high risk transactions; all costs incurred must be recovered before any profit is recognized

Covenants (maintenance tests): provisions used to measure a minimum level of organization performance, usually in debt contracts

Credit memo: a memo issued by a bank that reports an increase in the company's cash account

Credit sales method: a method of estimating uncollectible accounts receivable by establishing the percentage of sales that are historically uncollectible

Critical event: one point in a series of economic activities that is chosen for revenue recognition

Current assets: cash and other assets that are reasonably expected to be realized in cash or to be sold or consumed during the normal operating cycle of the business or within one year of the balance sheet date, whichever is longer

Current cost accounting: an accounting system based on current replacement costs (instead of historical costs)

Current liabilities: obligations expected to be fulfilled within the next year or operating cycle, whichever is longer

DBA (disclosed basis of accounting): a basis of accounting as described in the policy notes to the financial statements; usually not GAAP

Debit memo: a memo issued by a bank that reports a decrease in the company's cash account

Declining balance amortization: a method of accelerated amortization where amortization is calculated as cost less accumulated amortized multiplied by a given rate until net book value declines to residual value

Deferrals: the result of cash flows that occur before expense and revenue recognition

Deficit: a debit balance in retained earnings

Demand loans: loans which are payable on demand

Depletion (amortization): the periodic allocation of the cost of capital assets over the useful life of the assets; depletion refers to amortization of natural resources

Depreciation (amortization): the periodic allocation of the cost of capital assets over the useful life of the assets; depreciation refers to amortization of tangible assets

Direct expenses: expenses directly associated with revenues; for example, cost of good sold

Direct preparation approach: preparing the cash flow statement based on analyzing the increases and decreases in the cash account resulting from operating transactions during the relevant period (versus the indirect approach based on balance sheet accounts)

Direct presentation of operating activities — on the cash flow statement: operations directly states the cash received from customers, cash paid to suppliers, for interest, etc., to arrive at cash flow from operations

Direct write-off: a method of accounting for bad debts whereby bad debt expense is recognized as accounts are written off with no allowance recognized; not normally GAAP

Direct write-off method for LCM: lower-of-cost-or-market evaluation of investments or inventory is assessed on each item individually and any required write-down is directly made to the individual investment or inventory item

Disbursements: cash outflows

Disclosure notes: explanatory notes to the financial statements that include information on accounting policy and description of financial statement elements, recognized and unrecognized

Discontinued operations: when management decides to sell a segment of a business, its operating results to the discontinuance decision (the measurement date) and the gain or loss on disposal is shown in a separate section of the income statement (at the bottom) net after tax

Discount: a difference between the purchase price (or issuance proceeds) and the maturity value of a debt security where the maturity value is higher

Discounting notes receivable: the sale of notes receivable, usually to a financial institution; the purchasing institution discounts the face value of the note by the interest fee being charged

Disposal date: the closing date of the sale of an asset or the date when operations discontinued cease

Division of duties: the principle of internal control that separates critical functions in order to safeguard assets; e.g., the person who writes and records cheques does not do the bank reconciliation

Double-entry system: a method of recording transactions such that the transactions change at least two accounts

Downstream profits: inter-company profits on transactions between a parent company and investee where the parent records the profit

Earnings per share: net income less preferred share entitlement divided by the weighted-average number of common shares outstanding during the accounting period

Earnings quality: the relationship between net income and cash flow; high quality earnings are highly positively correlated with cash flow, low quality earnings are not

Economic income: an increase in the wealth of a corporation; a measure of income based on events rather than transactions

Effective interest rate: the real rate of interest paid or earned on a loan; the discount rate that equates the payment stream to the net proceeds

Elements: the building blocks of financial statements; e.g., assets, liabilities, revenues, expenses

Entity concept: the assumption that the owners are just one of many stakeholders in an entity; others have a claim to net value added and are equally important (versus propriety concept or fund concept)

Equity instrument: any contract that evidences residual interest in the assets of an entity after deducting all of its liabilities

Equity method of accounting for investments: investments are initially recorded at cost but revenue is recorded as the investor's share of earnings, increasing the investment account; dividends received reduce the investment account

Error correction: a correction of a prior year accounting error; adjusted to opening retained earnings net of tax

Events approach: a method of assessing financial performance and position based on economic events rather than completed transactions

Executory contract: one in which neither party has yet fulfilled the contractual obligations; not recognized in the financial statements

Expanded disclosure: the opposite of minimum compliance; an objective of financial reporting to external parties that involves disclosures in excess of those required by the *CICA Handbook*

Expedient recording system: the practice of recording an expense upon payment of cash before goods or services are received and recording a revenue as cash receipt before goods or services are provided

Expenditure: incurrence of a liability or payment of cash (or other asset) to acquire a good or service

Extraordinary items: items shown at the bottom of the income statement after a sub-total net of tax; these items must be not expected to occur too frequently, not typical of normal business activities, and not as a result of a decision of management or owners

Face value (maturity value): the principal value of the note or bond as stated on the instrument itself

Factoring : sale of receivables to a financial institution; may be with recourse or without recourse to the transferor

Fair market value: the value established between a willing buyer and a willing seller in a normal business transaction

Feedback value: the capacity of information to assist decision-makers to confirm and/or correct prior decisions or assumptions

Financial accounting: methods used to report an organization's financial condition and results of operations to internal and external parties

Financial asset: cash or contractual right to receive cash or another financial asset, an equity instrument, or an exchange contract involving financial instruments

Financial instrument: any contract that gives rise to both a financial asset of one party and a financial liability or equity instrument to the other party

Financial liability: a contractual obligation to deliver cash or other financial assets, or an exchange contract involving financial instruments

Financial statements: the report of all financial transactions and events over a specific period of time; includes the income statement, the balance sheet, the retained earnings statement, and the cash flow statement

Financing activities: one of the sections of the cash flow statement; reflects cash from and for transactions that affect long-term assets

Financing form: formatting the balance sheet using the accounting identity A = L + OE

Finished goods inventory: fully processed items completed and held for sale; usually held by a manufacturer

First-in, first-out (FIFO): a method of inventory costing that assigns the oldest cost value of purchases to the first unit sold

Fixed assets: tangible capital assets that benefit operations over multiple periods, usually represented by property, plant, and equipment (PP&E)

Flow statement: a statement related to a specific period of time; flow statements may take several different forms, e.g., statement of operations, statement of changes in capital, and cash flow statement

Forgivable loans: loans that are forgiven when certain conditions have been met, usually granted by a government unit

Freedom from bias (neutrality): when information is not reflective of a particular viewpoint, a predetermined result, or a particular person's opinion

Freight-in: freight costs associated with the purchase and receipt of inventory; distinct from freight-out, or delivery expenses related to sales to customers

Full-cost method: a method in which all costs associated with the exploration for and development of a natural resource, whether successful or not, are capitalized to the natural resource on the balance sheet to be subsequently amortized

Full disclosure: financial statement disclosure of all relevant information about the economic affairs of the corporation

Fully diluted earnings per share: a measure of earnings per common share as if all common shares promised under the terms of existing option agreements and conversion privileges on bonds or preferred shares were actually issued

Fund concept: the assumption that the purpose of accounting is to trace the flow of funds in the corporation (versus propriety concept or entity concept)

Future income tax: arises when there is a difference between the tax basis of a balance sheet item and its accounting basis; measured as the difference multiplied by the appropriate tax rate

Future value: projected future amount of money based on today's amount plus whatever interest, including compounded interest, is accumulated over a specified period of time

GAAP (Generally Accepted Accounting Principles): body of accounting practices built up over time for use in preparing external accounting reports; sources include the *CICA Handbook*, industry practice, and judgement

General journal: a journal with a flexible format in which any transaction can be recorded

General ledger: the ledger holding individual accounts that comprise the elements of financial statements

General purpose financial statements: financial statements prepared to meet common information needs of external parties for financial information about an entity

Going-concern assumption (continuity assumption): the assumption that the corporation will not be liquidated but will continue to pursue its objectives for the foreseeable future

Goodwill: an internally generated intangible capital asset, not usually recognized because no transaction has occurred to establish cost; goodwill is recognized on consolidation when a subsidiary is acquired for a price higher than the fair value of its tangible assets

Gross margin method: a method of estimating inventories based on historical gross profit margins

Group amortization: the amortization of a set of similar assets on average rates designed to be statistically valid

Historical cost convention: all economic transactions are recorded using the cost (historic cost) of the transaction

IASC (International Accounting Standards Committee): an association of professional accounting bodies from around the world whose purpose is to develop and issue international accounting and reporting standards

Impairment: an asset no longer worth its net book value; often triggers a write-down to a lower value

Impairment of value: the loss of a significant portion of the utility or value of a capital asset

Imputed interest: an interest rate that is estimated and assigned based on the internal rate of return if an effective interest rate is not evident or determinable from other factors in a transaction

Income: a generic term indicating revenue from a variety of sources; not to be confused with net income which is revenue minus expenses

Income smoothing: an objective of financial reporting to external parties that emphasizes smooth earning patterns, free from peaks and valleys

Incremental method: in a lump-sum purchase, this method assigns the known value to the one or more known assets' value and the remaining cost is allocated to the final remaining asset

Indirect expenses: expenses associated with a period that are not directly associated with revenue; for example, interest and administrative salaries

Indirect preparation approach: preparing the cash flow statement based on analyzing net income and the changes in related balance sheet accounts (versus a direct approach analysis of the cash account)

Indirect presentation of operating activities — on the cash flow statement: operations is presented as net income plus/minus non-cash expenses or gains and plus/minus changes in working capital to arrive at cash flow from operations

Instalment sales method of accounting: a system that recognizes proportionate revenue at each installment payment date rather than at the time of delivery

Intangible capital assets: those capital assets of an enterprise such as goodwill, trademarks, or trade names, that do not have physical presence

Interest-bearing: notes that have a specified interest rate to be applied to their face value in computing interest payments

Interest expense: the cost of borrowed money

Interest method: a method of recognizing interest income or expense on amounts due to or from a corporation where the interest amount is a constant percentage of the opening net balance; also known as the effective interest method or scientific method

Interest revenue: revenue provided as a return on loaned money

Interim statements: financial statements prepared for less than a full fiscal year, usually monthly or quarterly; usually unaudited

Internal control system: system of organizational design meant to safeguard assets and the integrity of the accounting system

Interperiod tax allocation: allocating the tax paid to appropriate reporting periods based on accounting recoginition of individual revenue and expense items

Intraperiod tax allocation: allocating the income tax expense within the period to various subclassifications on the income statement and retained earnings statement

Inventories: goods held for resale (finished goods) or use in operations (supplies)

Inventory appraisal system: a system under which capital assets are appraised at the end of each accounting period in their present condition; amortization is recorded as the decline in value over the period

Inventory profit (phantom profit): the difference between the cost of goods sold and their replacement cost

Involuntary dispositions: the disposals of assets that are not the companies' decisions

Joint venture: an economic activity — investment — resulting from a contractual arrangement whereby two or more venturers jointly control the economic activity; the joint venture is subject to joint control by the joint venturers

Journal: an organized medium for recording transactions in debit-credit format; also called a book of original entry

Just-in-time (JIT) inventory system: a management system that involves inventories kept at their lowest levels possible; goods and materials arrive just in time for use in the manufacturing or assembly process

Last-in, first-out (LIFO): a method of inventory costing that assigns the most recent cost value of purchases to the first unit sold

Liquidity: a measure of a corporation's cash position relative to its obligations

Long-term investments: all investments in debt or equity securities not classified as short-term

Long-term liabilities: an obligation that does not require payment during the next operating cycle or year, whichever is longer

Lower-of-cost-or-market (LCM): recording an asset (writing it down to) market value if market value is less than cost; required to avoid overstating assets

Lump-sum purchase (basket or group): several assets purchased together for a single lump-sum price

Maintenance of financial capital (nominal dollar capital maintenance): the concept that income results only after preserving financial capital (equity) in dollars; the closing amount of net financial assets must exceed the amount at the start (excluding additional owner transactions) before income is present

Maker: a borrower (as in, the maker of a note payable)

Management accounting: the rules and conventions used by an organization for reporting to internal parties for decision-making, control, planning, and internal performance evaluation

Management's discussion and analysis (MD&A): a section of the annual report that provides an overview of the corporation's operations and financial position noting any special or unusual circumstances that may have affected the financial results

Markdown: a reduction in an original sales price

Markdown cancellation: an increase in a previously reduced sales price that does not exceed the original sales price

Marketable securities: investment securities sold in active markets with readily determinable market prices

Market value method of accounting for investments: investments are valued at market value rather than cost; changes in market value can be included in income of the period or deferred

Markup: the difference between purchase cost and original sales price

Matching: the recognition of expenses in the same time period that the revenues (generated by incurring the expenses) are recognized

Maturity value (face value): the value of a note or bond as stated on the note or bond itself

Measurement conventions (principal measurement methods): ways to report financial positions and the results of operations; accounting choices that determine the way the financial information is reported

Measurement date: the date on which a company's management adopts a formal plan to wind up or sell a segment (re discontinued operations)

Merchandise inventory: goods on hand for resale purchased by a retailer or a trading company

Merger: a combination of two or more companies into a single corporate entity in a business combination

Minimum compliance: an objective of financial reporting to external parties that reveals the least amount of information possible while continuing to comply with recommendations of the *CICA Handbook*

Monetary assets and liabilities: assets or liabilities whose value is fixed in terms of dollars; for example, accounts receivable, accounts payable, bonds payable

Monetary items: financial assets and liabilities to be received or paid in fixed determinable amounts of money

Money market investments: monetary financial assets in the form of short-term interest-bearing securities traded in open markets; for example, T-bills

Moving-average: used with the perpetual inventory system, an inventory costing system that provides a new unit cost after each purchase based on relative costs and quantities

Multiple-step format: presenting an income statement with a number of subtotals that reflect important relationships; for example, gross margin, operating income

Negative goodwill: in a consolidation accounted for as a purchase, when the purchase price is less than fair market value of acquired assets; assigned to non-monetary assets

Net assets form: expressing the balance sheet in the format A − L = OE

Net book value: the original cost of an asset plus any capitalized post-acquisition cost less accumulated amortization to date

Net realizable value (NRV): the amount of funds expected to be received upon the sale or liquidation of an asset net of incremental expenses

Neutrality (freedom from bias): when information is not reflective of a particular viewpoint, a predetermined result, or a particular person's opinion

Nominal accounts (temporary accounts): general ledger accounts closed to retained earnings at the end of an accounting period; usually income statement accounts

Nominal dollar capital maintenance (maintenance of financial capital): the concept that income results only after preserving financial capital (equity) in dollars; the closing amount of net financial assets must exceed the amount at the start (excluding additional owner transactions) before income is present

Non-controlling interest (minority interest): when a company controls a subsidiary but does not own 100% of the voting shares, it still includes 100% of the net assets and net income in the consolidated financial statements; the non-controlling interest in earnings is the portion of the subsidiary's earnings that accrue to the other, minority shareholders; the non-controlling interest in assets — a balance sheet credit — is the portion of net assets that represent the minority shareholders' interest

Non-interest bearing: notes with no stated interest rate; usually with face values higher than the amount borrowed

Non-monetary assets and liabilities: assets or liabilities whose value is not fixed in terms of dollars; for example, warranty liability, capital assets

Non-reciprocal transfer: a transfer, or transaction, in which the firm either (only) transfers resources or receives resources; for example, payment of a cash dividend

Non-trade receivable: cash due to a corporation from transactions other than the sale of goods and services

Note payable (short-term commercial paper): an obligation to repay money or other assets evidenced by a signed contractual agreement or note

Note receivable: an amount due to a corporation because of purchases of goods or services on credit or a loan arrangement which is evidenced by a legal document called a note

NSF cheque: a cheque from a customer deposited by a company returned because of "not sufficient funds" in the customer's account

Objectivity: a combination of quantifiability, verifiability, and freedom from bias

Offsetting — netting: only allowed if the legal right to offset exists and the entity plans to settle on a net basis

On demand: short term; due on request (demand) from the lender after a short delay of 7 to 30 business days

Operating activities: one of the sections of the cash flow statement; may be formatted using the direct or indirect method; reflects cash generated by operations during the period

Ordinary annuity (annuity in arrears): a payment stream in which the payments (or receipts) occur at the end of each interest compounding period

Organization costs: those expenditures made in setting up a business

Overdraft (bank overdraft): a negative bank balance reported as a current liability; part of cash on the cash flow statement

Passive investment: an inter-corporate investment in which the investor cannot significantly influence or control the operations of the investee company

Payee: a note holder; the lender who will receive the principal repayment at maturity

Percentage-of-completion method: used to account for long-term contracts; revenue and expense are recognized as work progresses on a contract

Period costs: expenses recognized as costs in the period in which they were incurred

Periodic inventory system: an inventory record-keeping system that determines the quantity of inventory on hand and related cost of goods sold only at the end of the fiscal period

Permanent accounts (real accounts): general ledger accounts that are not closed to retained earnings at the end of an accounting period; balance sheet accounts

Perpetual inventory system: an inventory record-keeping system that continuously updates the quantity of inventory on hand and cost of goods sold on the basis of transaction records that report units purchased, manufactured, and sold

Point statement: a statement related to an organization at a particular point in time; e.g., the balance sheet

Pooling (as a form of consolidation): a form of consolidation where two or more companies' financial statements are combined as though they were always one; neither company's assets are fair valued at the date of acquisition

Portfolio investment: a long-term non-strategic investment in the shares or bonds of another company

Post-closing trial balance: a trial balance prepared after closing all temporary accounts to retained earnings; reflects balance sheet accounts only

Posting: transferring data from a journal to a ledger

Posting references: cross-referencing codes entered by the posted accounts in a ledger to show the journal in which the account was originally entered

Postulates (underlying assumptions): the basic foundation that underlies generally accepted accounting principles

Predictive value: the capability of information to assist decision-makers in predicting outcomes of events; an attribute of relevance

Premium: a difference between the purchase price (or issuance proceeds) and the maturity value of a debt security where the maturity value is lower

Pre-operating costs: expenditures made in a period that precedes operation, to establish a business; may be deferred in limited circumstances

Prepayments: cash outlays made in advance of receipt of goods or services

Present value: the value today of a future sum calculated by discounting the sum at a specified interest rate; generally a principal amount excluding interest

Principal: the amount loaned or borrowed

Private corporation: an organization that does not issue securities to the public

Privately placed securities: investments in the shares or bonds of other corporations with no public market and therefore no readily determinable market value

Product costs (project costs): direct costs related to products held for resale or some other specific business activity (a project); recognized as expenses when the product is sold

Productive capacity capital maintenance: the concept that income results only after preserving physical capacity (physical assets); if the closing net assets, usually measured in current replacement costs, exceeded opening net assets, then income is present

Productive output (PO) amortization: a method of calculating amortization expense that bases amortization on current production output as related to expected productive output

Professional judgement: the ability of a professional to make appropriate choices based on established criteria and recognizing the facts and circumstances surrounding the specific choices to be made

Project costs (product costs): direct costs related to products held for resale or some other specific business activity (a project)

Proportional method: in a lump-sum purchase, this method assigns each asset a value according to the ratio of its fair value to the value of the group

Proportionate consolidation: combining the financial statements of an investor company and a joint venture enterprise; only the investor's proportionate share of the financial elements of the joint venture are included

Proprietary assumption or concept: the assumption that the financial information of the corporation should be reported from the proprietor's point of view (versus entity concept or funds concept)

Public corporation: an organization that issues securities to the public

Purchase (as a form of consolidation): a form of consolidation where two companies' financial statements are combined; one is identified as the acquirer and one the acquiree; the latter's net assets are recorded at fair value at the date of the acquisition

Purchase price discrepancy: in consolidation under the purchase method, the difference between the purchase price and net book value acquired

Purchasing power parity: over time different values of currencies relative to each other will adjust in the currency markets to reflect relative purchasing power

Push-down accounting: an expression used to describe the revaluation of the net assets of a wholly-owned subsidiary to fair values as reflected in the price the parent company paid to acquire the subsidiary

Qualitative characteristics (qualitative criteria): a set of criteria by which measurement options and accounting policies are evaluated

Quantifiability: the ability to attach a number to an event or transaction

RAP (Regulated Accounting Policies): those accounting policies that are specified in specific statutes or regulations pertaining to specific regulated industries; not GAAP

Raw materials inventory: goods on hand for direct use in manufacturing or further processing of goods for sale

Real accounts (permanent accounts): general ledger accounts that are not closed to retained earnings at the end of an accounting period; balance sheet accounts

Realization: the process of converting an asset, liability, or commitment into a cash flow

Realized revenue: revenue for which cash has been received

Rearrangements: the costs of reinstallation, rerouting, or rearranging factory machinery to increase efficiency

Receipts: cash inflows

Receivables: monetary accounts that will be paid to the corporation in the future; may be accounts, notes, interest, tax, etc.

Reciprocal transfer: a transfer, or transaction, in which the firm both transfers and receives resources; for example, a sale of goods for cash

Recourse: the right of a third party financer to demand reimbursement from the transferor of the receivables if they prove uncollectible

Related party transactions: a transaction in which one of the parties has the ability to influence the actions and policies of the other parties because of a relationship (e.g., common ownership of the two parties)

Relevance: information that is useful or influential for decision-makers; such information is timely and has predictive value and feedback value

Reliability: information that can be depended upon as accurate; reliable information is representationally faithful, verifiable, and free from bias

Replacement cost: the cost to reproduce or replace a given asset; supplier price

Replacement system of amortization: a method of calculating amortization expense commonly used by public utilities; amortization is calculated with reference to current replacement cost of assets retired

Representational faithfulness (validity): the information reported accurately reflects the actual events and transactions

Research and development costs: cost of activities undertaken by firms to create new products and processes, to improve old ones, and to discover new knowledge that may be of value in the future; expensed, except those development expenses that meet specified criteria

Residual value: the estimated net recoverable amount from disposal or trade-in of an asset at the end of its estimated useful life

Restricted shares: shares with limited or no voting rights in an organization

Restrictions to retained earnings: retained earnings not available to support dividend declarations, due to legal contracts

Restructuring: a business reorganization where the entity stays in the same line of business but has streamlined its activities; the costs of restructuring are usually shown as an unusual item on the income statement

Retail inventory method: a method of estimating inventories based on actual mark-ups and mark-downs during the period; the organization calculates its inventory at retail and then converts to the cost price using a cost-to-retail ratio

Retained earnings: a corporation's accumulated net earnings less dividends paid out since inception

Retirement system of amortization: a method of calculating amortization expense commonly used by public utilities; amortization is calculated with reference to original cost of retired assets

Retroactive effect of a change in accounting policy: the income effect of a retroactive change in policy; adjusted to opening retained earnings net of tax

Return: a corporation's level of earnings (as in return on assets or return on investments)

Revenue: the inflow of assets, the reduction of liabilities, or both from transactions involving the corporation's normal business activities

Revenue recognition convention: the recognition and reporting of revenues that have met the recognition criteria; revenues typically must be earned, measurable, and realizable before recognition

Risk: the volatility of earnings

Sales allowances: a reduction in the price of merchandise to a customer who keeps the merchandise, often because of defects

Sales returns: merchandise that was previously recorded as a sale that has been returned by the customer for full credit

Salvage value: an asset's fair value at the end of its life

Segmented information: disclosure note information concerning geographic and business segments of an entity

Separate entity assumption: accounting information reflects the assumption that a corporation and its shareholders and stakeholders are separate economic entities

Service-hours amortization (SA): a method of calculating amortization expense that bases amortization expense on current service hours used as related to total service hours expected

Share issue costs: the expenditures associated with issuing share capital

Short-term commercial paper: short-term notes payable

Short-term investments: investments that are capable of liquidation (in a ready market) that management intends to hold for the short term

Significant influence: ownership interest to the extent that the investor can affect strategic operating, investing, and financing policies of the investee

Simple interest: principal amount multiplied by the period's interest rate; excludes any compounding effect

Single-step format: presenting an income statement with no subtotals; all revenues and all expenses are included in one category each

Sinking fund amortization: a method of allocating costs in which amortization expense is lowest in an asset's early years but increases over time

Special journal: a journal with a non-flexible, pre-determined format in which only specific transactions that fit the format can be recorded

Specific cost identification: a method of inventory costing that identifies the specific invoice cost of the specific units sold; for cost of goods sold

Standard cost: a pre-determined, expected cost per unit; sometimes used for inventory valuation if not materially different than cost

Standard recording system: the practice of recording an asset upon payment of cash before goods or services are received and recording a liability upon cash receipt before goods or services are provided

Stated (nominal) interest rate: annual interest rate as stated by contract; may not represent effective interest rate due to compounding, premium or discount, or up-front fees

Stewardship: an objective of financial reporting to external parties that emphasizes management care or responsibility for assets

Straight-line amortization: an amortization method where the annual expense is equal over the asset's life; the amortizable amount is divided by the asset's useful life

Subsequent events: events that occur after the year-end but before the financial statements are issued; may be recorded or disclosed depending on nature

Subsidiary: an investee company in which the investor company (the parent) controls the investee, usually by holding in excess of 50% of the voting shares

Subsidiary ledger: support ledger for the general ledger accounts; the general ledger has master, or control accounts, and the subsidiary ledger has the many separate individual accounts that comprise the control account

Substance over form: accounting information should represent what it purports to represent, the economic substance of a transaction, not just its legal form

Successful efforts method: a method in which only the costs associated with successful exploration and development activities of a natural resource are capitalized to the balance sheet accounts to be subsequently amortized; the costs of unsuccessful exploration activities are expensed

Sum-of-the-years digits amortization: a method of accelerated amortization where amortization is calculated by multiplying the amortizable cost by a fraction whose denominator is the sum of the years' digits

Sum-of-the-years-digits (SYD) method: a system to amortize the cost of a capital asset in which the allocated cost is greater in the early periods of the asset's life; a fraction with SYD as a base is used in the calculation

Supplies inventory: inventory of items on hand not held for resale but rather to be used in production or maintenance activities

T-accounts: an accounting form in the shape of a "T" used to demonstrate transactions; the left side is used for debits and the right side for credits

Tangible capital asset: those capital assets of an enterprise such as property, plant, and equipment, that have physical characteristics or presence

TAP (Tailored Accounting Policies): those accounting policies used by an organization to reflect individual or unique needs different than GAAP; a disclosed basis of accounting

Temporary accounts (nominal accounts): general ledger accounts closed to retained earnings at the end of an accounting period; usually income statement accounts

Temporary investment: an investment in debt or equity securities that can be liquidated quickly and is intended by management as a short-term use of cash

Time period assumption: the activities of a corporation can be divided into artificial time periods that by definition are shorter than the life span of the corporation

Time value of money: the cost of using money over time (interest)

Timeliness: information delivered within an appropriately short time period so that it has usefulness (relevance) to influence decision-makers

Trade accounts payable: amounts owed to suppliers for goods and services purchased on credit

Trade receivable (accounts receivable): amounts due to a corporation due to purchases of goods or services on credit

Transaction: an event requiring a journal entry

Transactions approach: a method of assessing financial performance and position based on completed transactions rather than events

Trial balance: a listing of all general ledger accounts, done to identify all accounts in the ledger and ensure that they balance

Unadjusted trial balance: a trial balance prepared before adjusting journal entries

Undepreciated capital cost (UCC): net book value for tax purposes; equal to cost less capital cost allowance deducted to date

Underlying assumptions (postulates): the basic foundation that underlies generally accepted accounting principles

Understandability: accounting information can be interpreted as it was intended by persons who possess reasonable business and economic understanding

Uniformity: the use of the same accounting policies in different corporations for similar events/transactions

Unit cost system: a synonym for the LIFO inventory cost flow assumption under the periodic system

Unit of measurement assumption: the assumption that the results of the corporation's operations can be meaningfully reported in terms of a standard monetary unit throughout

Units-of-production method: a system to amortize the cost of a capital asset in which the allocated cost is based on actual production of the asset versus its total production potential; often used for natural resources

Unremitted earnings: the difference between an investor's share of an investee's net income and the dividends actually received

Unusual items: items that are shown as separate items in the continuing operations section income statement but not net of tax; such items are designated as unusual by management and are often infrequent and/or not typical of normal business activities

Upstream profits: inter-company profits on transactions between an investor company and investee where the investee records the profit

Validity (representational faithfulness): the information reported accurately reflects the actual events and transactions

Value added statements: statements that reflect the increase in the value of goods and services as a result of a corporation's efforts; part of the entity concept

Variable cost method (direct costing): a method of assigning costs to inventory that includes variable overhead as well as direct materials and direct labour; fixed overhead costs are excluded and treated as period costs

Verifiability: independent persons using an appropriate measurement method would reach substantially the same results

Voluntary disposition: sale, exchange, or abandonment of capital assets based on decisions of management

Wash transaction: selective sales of investments and repurchase of the same or similar investments in order to manufacture an accounting gain or loss; more generally, any transactions the net results of which are zero, or a "wash"

Weighted average: a method of inventory costing that uses the weighted-average cost for inventory and cost of goods sold; weighted average is a general term that refers to an average cost weighted by the relative size of acquisitions at various prices

Wholly-owned (subsidiary): an investee, all of whose shares are owned by the investor

Working capital: the net amount of current assets minus current liabilities

Work-in-progress inventory: goods requiring further processing before completion and sale

Index

The page on which a Company appears is printed in boldface